The endpapers and page 1 are decorated with "Gyotaku", fish prints in which the fish itself is inked and the paper is pressed against it. Guidance in this Oriental art is to be found on page 383.

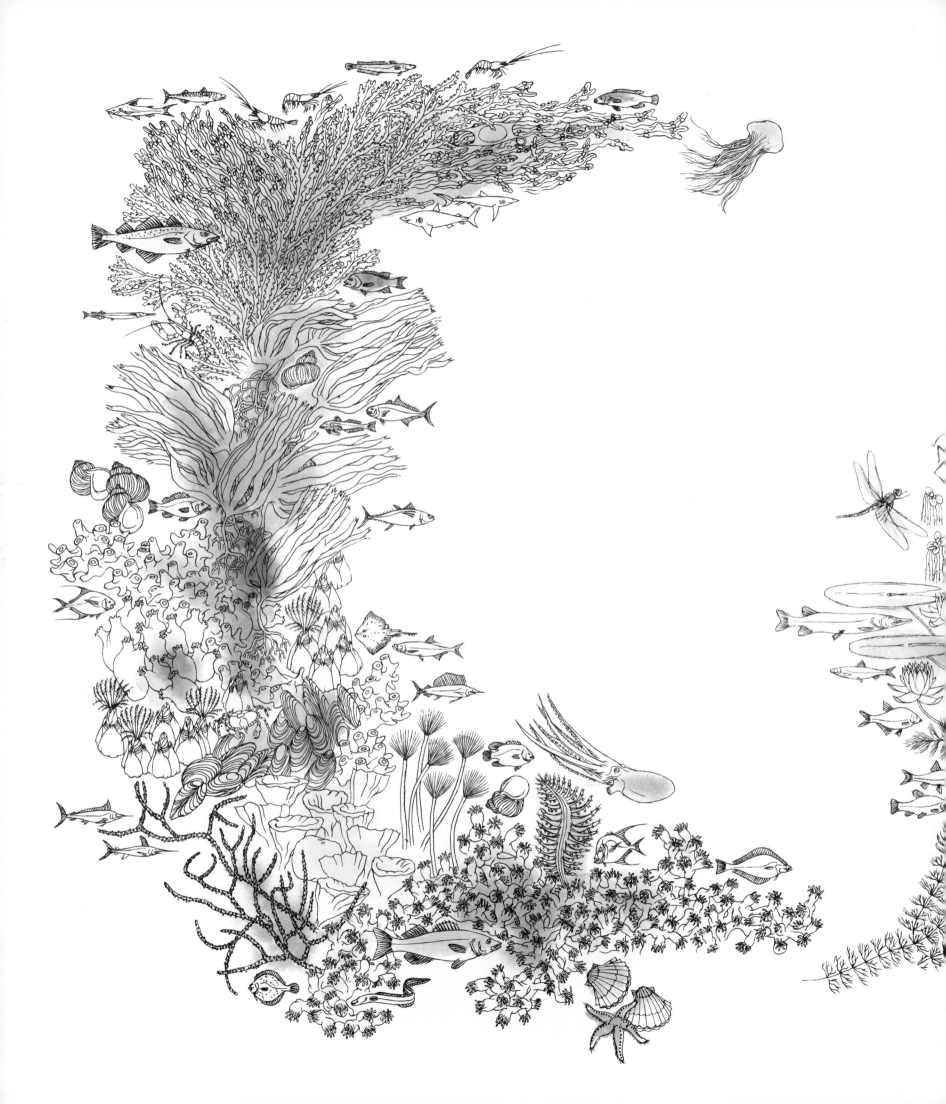

FISHING
THE COMPLETE BOOK

by Tre Tryckare, E. Cagner

DAVID & CHARLES, NEWTON ABBOT

Fishing: The Complete Book is an international book of which two different issues will appear, one for the U.S.A. and one, in twelve different language editions, for Europe and other parts of the world. Each edition will be revised in accordance with local sport fishing conditions. This is a copy of the first British edition.

Fishing: The Complete Book can be regarded as a description and summing up of sportfishing, fishing methods, equipment, etc. in the world today.

It is a product of years of close collaboration with specialists and contributors from the U.S.A., Europe, and many other parts of the world.

DESIGN AND PRODUCTION
Fishing: The Complete Book is created and produced by E. Cagner.
Assistant Editors: Vera Fahlström, Susanne Hjort, Marita Westberg.

ILLUSTRATIONS
Åke Gustavsson has been the principal illustrator of the book and has created most of the artwork.
Fritz Rohde painted the illustrations of fishes in colour.
Yusuke Nagano drew the illustrations of fishes reproduced in black, the main part of the anatomy section and some of the illustrations for other sections in the book.

Other artists, who have been used for a minor part of the illustrations:
Rune Bågmark
Greta Cagner
Bertil Ekman
Tomas Håkansson
Johan Lindström
Keith Linsell

Tre Tryckare wishes to give special thanks to the following experts and collaborators in various countries, who have contributed to the creation of the American and European editions of this book:

Heinz von Bidder, Switzerland
Rudolf Boddeke, Ph.D., Netherlands
Tony Burnand, France
Bernt-Ingemar Dybern, Ph.D., Sweden
Peter Goadby, Australia
Prof. Yoshio Hiyama, Japan
Olof Johansson, Sweden
Ken Kaiko, Japan
Prof. Nick Lyons, U.S.A.
Kenneth Mansfield, England
Prof. Orvar Nybelin, Sweden
Erik Poulsen, Ph.D., Denmark
Ossi Seppovaara, Ph.D., Finland
E. Horsfall Turner, England

First published in Great Britain 1977 by David & Charles Publishers plc Brunel House, Forde Road, Newton Abbot, Devon.

ISBN 0 7153 7523 7

Printed in Spain by Cayfosa, Barcelona
Dep. Leg.: B-16974 - 1987
5th printing

AUTHORS

PETER COLLINS
Match Fishing

BERNT-INGEMAR DYBERN, PH.D.
The Habitat

PETER LANCASTER-BROWN
Fish Descriptions

FRANK T. MOSS
Conservation of Fish and
Their Habitat
Fishing Methods
Equipment
Boats
Appendix

EWERT CAGNER
and
FRANK T. MOSS
Casting and Casting Technique

ERIK POULSEN, PH.D.
Fish Descriptions

C. LAVETT SMITH, PH.D.
The Fish
Fish Recognition
and Description

HUGH STOKER
Boats and Electronic
Equipment

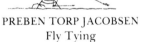

PREBEN TORP JACOBSEN
Fly Tying

TRE TRYCKARE EDITORS
Taxidermy
Japanese Fish Prints

H. F. WALLIS
Coarse Fishing
Reservoir Trout Fishing

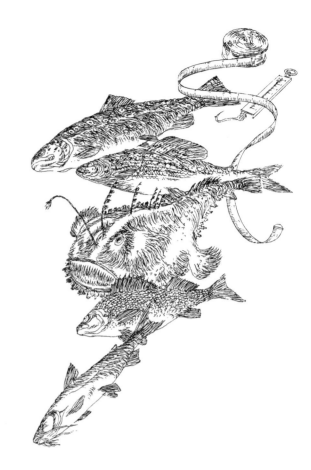

CONTENTS

TODAY'S "COMPLEAT ANGLER"

Any work which seeks to be up-to-date and comprehensive must not only take into account the extraordinary growth of angling to a position where in several countries it has become the largest participant sport, but also the remarkable developments in tackle and techniques. Indeed, it can be said without fear of contradiction that no period has seen so many innovations as the 30 years or so since the war. One has only to think of the hold which fibreglass rods, monofilament lines and fixed-spool reels now have over the market to appreciate how dramatic the changes have been and how much better equipped the modern angler is now than his predecessors.

Izaak Walton's 'Compleat Angler' would today have to be a man of very many parts, one who has absorbed the traditional wisdom as well as keeping pace with the changing situation. But it remains just as true today as in Walton's time that the most consistently successful sport fisherman will be he who knows the nature and habits of his quarry.

This knowledge helps to create a greater appreciation of fish as living creatures and of their need for a clean, unpolluted environment. The compilers of this book believe that every fisherman owes it to himself and to his "brothers of the angle" to devote some time, thought and energy towards the conservation of life in our rivers and seas.

A word of explanation may seem appropriate here of the term "sportfishing", widely used throughout this book – first produced in an American edition.

This is one of those international generic descriptions which can mean many things to many people, often depending upon their particular location. In Britain, for example, where the precise classification of angling terms is specially important, sportfishing has a somewhat vague connotation. For many it would be deemed synonymous with game fishing – that is, the pursuit of salmon species in freshwater – and of the more sporting fish of the sea, like bass and pollack. It might also embrace big-game fishing, though in British waters this is largely confined to shark and tope; tunny were taken in the North Sea until the early 1950s but then apparently disappeared.

So far as this book is concerned, sportfishing has a wider meaning, designed to reflect its international content. It embraces the pursuit of any species regarded as sporting in the locality by normally accepted sporting methods and for pleasure rather than commercial profit – though the sport fisherman might well take his catch home for the table.

To assemble all this knowledge from many parts of the world in one complete volume has been a formidable task, but one we feel has been well worth-while. We hope this book will be read with profit and pleasure by sport fishermen everywhere and that it will help to explain to interested non-fishermen the nature of this passion which afflicts so many of their otherwise well-balanced fellow human beings.

H. F. WALLIS.

. . . an abandoned mill, a silent water wheel,
lily pads resting upon a lake sparkling in the wilderness.
The angler knows deep in his heart that
his secret sanctuary will always be there,
ready to restore his strength
and rekindle his spirit after the trials and frustrations
of his workaday existence.

SPORT FISHING FROM PRE-HISTORY TO THE PRESENT

The earliest anglers caught fish with their bare hands. The first Europeans who emigrated to North America learned from the American Indians the fine art of "guddling," slowly moving the hand under the body of a resting wild fish until the fish could be seized by the gills and yanked from the water. There is no reason to believe that *Homo erectus* and other early hominids were not equally skillful at collecting a fish dinner with their hands or primitive fishing tools.

The antiquity of spear, net, trap, and even hook and line goes far back beyond the dawn of recorded history. A man-made fishing gorge, predecessor of the hook, was found under 7 meters (22 ft) of peat in a French bog in the Somme valley. Its age has been estimated at possibly 30,000 years.

Fishing was highly developed when men first began to record their activities in the earliest forms of literature and art. The concept that angling is something special, that it is a sport as well as a foodgathering activity, seems to be almost as old. Five hundred years before Christ, Confucius wrote: "The master angled, but did not use the net; he shot, but not at birds perching."

Artificial lures are very old. Prehistoric anglers must have found it a relatively easy step from the simple straight gorge to a wooden or bone fish-like object that incorporates the gorge as an angled point or barb on which the fish is impaled when it strikes the fish-like lure. Examples of these primitive hooked or barbed lures have been unearthed from the islands of the South Pacific, Africa, Alaska, Northern Europe, and Asia. "Angle" is archaic English for "hook."

Most modern fishing lures had their ancient counterparts. The present-day trolling spoon and feathered jig lure are designed almost exactly on the pattern of early Polynesian trolling lures. The modern cod jig is a direct descendant of wood, bone, ivory, and metal jigs used by ancient Norsemen voyaging westward from Scandinavia across the stormy Atlantic, living by what they caught on their flax and horsehair lines.

Even that delicate lure, the artificial fly, dates back to the start of the Christian era. Claudius Aelian in his "De Natura Animalium" from the second century A.D. told of Macedonian anglers on the River Astracus fishing with rod and line, using an artificial fly to catch what modern biologists claim was a close relative of the brook trout. The fly that Aelian described in considerable detail appears to be none other than the modern Red Hackle.

In her historic volume "The Book Of St. Albans," printed in England in 1486, Dame Juliana Berners, the Lady Prioress of Sopwell Nunnery, advised in detail how to make the rod, the hook, and the line. There were no tackle shops in fifteenth-century Britain and an angler had to be a jack-of-many-trades. Fishing rods were enormous affairs sometimes used to vault a flooded brook or to beat off surly farm dogs. The best fishing lines were braided of the tail-hair of a white stallion.

Izaak Walton in his "Compleat Angler," said that a three-hair line would handle most trout, but the man

who could fish a single hair without breaking it would have more strikes.

Then, as now, skill was recognized and honoured. The more skillful angler wins his honours by being willing to take greater risks.

But the modern angler has many advantages over his predecessors. He is blessed with tackle and equipment that is lighter, more efficient, more durable, and more versatile than any previously constructed. He has at his command many innovative fishing systems and techniques.

The sophistication of modern anglers is expressed in many forms. Until recent times, salt water fishing was considered to be "coarse" and commercial in intent, and only fresh water angling was "pure". But, during the last quarter of the nineteenth century and the first two decades of the twentieth, several unconnected "pure" forms of salt water angling took shape.

One was the development of ocean shore or surf angling. Another was the beginning of light tackle angling for such oceanic big game as tuna, marlin, swordfish, and sharks. A third form of "pure" salt water angling was the light tackle fishing of such tropical species as tarpon, bonefish, and permit pioneered in Central America and the Florida Keys.

This is, perhaps, the most demanding fishing of all, for it requires that the angler stalk his quarry in open shallow water either by wading afoot or by drifting in a specially constructed shallow-draft boat, approaching within casting range without scaring the wary fish. Developments of tackle and methods are still going on in each of these forms of salt water angling at the present time.

Most of the specialized tackle, equipment, and fishing methods now in use were invented before World War II, but the period from the close of those hostilities to the present time has witnessed tremendous improvements in methods, boats, equipment, and tackle. The most important of these are:

- The development and perfection of the fibreglass fishing rod for just about every style of fishing.
- The design and development of boats specifically intended for popular types of inland and offshore fishing.
- Perfection of star-drag, lever-drag, spinning, baitcasting, and fly casting reels of all calibres.
- The universal use of inexpensive, durable, standardized synthetic fishing lines.
- The development of whole families of artificial lures and fishing techniques that make these lures consistently productive.
- Adaption of modern nautical electronics to provide sensitive, relatively inexpensive depth sounders, radio communications equipment, navigating instruments, and improved safety devices.

The important point in discussing points of view regarding angling sportsmanship is that while there are still divergences of opinion about many types of fishing behaviour, modern anglers have synthesized from a long and honourable history a well-defined code of rules and ethics that can be outlined in the following general terms:

- An angler fishes with tackle consistent with what is accepted as "sporting" for the fish and the aquatic habitat involved.

- He may give away fish, but he does not sell them.
- He voluntarily limits his catch to what he can use and stops fishing entirely if he cannot release excess fish without harming them.
- He observes both the letter and the spirit of the game and property laws where he fishes.
- He uses modern knowledge and equipment not to catch a maximum number of fish, but to increase his understanding and appreciation of the fish he is after.
- He grants to other anglers the privilege of fishing according to their personal codes of behaviour as long as these codes remain within the generally accepted rules of fishing practice and conservation.

What are the qualities that cause modern anglers to call certain species of fish "game"? Some of these qualities are innate in the nature of the wild fish, others are the result of the codes of fishing behaviour and the equipment restrictions that anglers apply to their fishing. Izaak Walton, in his humble simplicity, loved the wary fish over the gross feeder that could be lured with a handful of corn. Now, as then, the important element on river, lake, or sea is challenge.

Wariness, reluctance to be taken in by an artificial lure or dead natural bait, aggressiveness in finally taking the bait, a spirited and courageous fight for freedom after being hooked, power, jumping ability, endurance to test a man's resources to the limit – these are the qualities that endear many species of fish to anglers and earn for the fish the honour, if one can call it that, of being called "game."

The deep sea big game angler finds the ultimate angling experience in the sea's mists and fogs, its silent calms, tempestuous winds, and teeming pyramids of life. To him the ocean is the last frontier in a world fast shrinking into reeking cities, ravaged mountains, filthy rivers, and polluted atmosphere. On the sea in his swift fishing cruiser he is captain of his ship and master of his soul.

Purposefully he seeks the quarry of this special choice, ignoring lesser fish as the deer hunter ignores hares and grouse that scatter before his footsteps. The boat is his tireless trail horse. He owns a boat not because he loves boats beyond other human toys, but because he needs the boat to carry him to the fish. Yet the boat is more than a mere tool. He speaks of himself and his boat as "we."

He begins hungry for fish, but as his experience broadens he becomes more selective of targets and less inclined to go baying off after every chance migrant school. Eventually he finds himself recognizing the fish of the oceans as brother passengers of this space-ship, Earth. This is when he stops regarding fish as prey to be captured and begins to study them because they are so marvellously alive.

At the opposite end of the human fishing spectrum, the trout or salmon purist cares not a fig for boats and strenuous fishing. He sees angling as a ritual, an opportunity for quiet reflection and soul-resting alone or in the company of selected boon companions of like persuasion. He cultivates patience and self-control. He prides himself that his form of angling is contemplative, in tune with nature.

The ocean big game angler may view the purist's preoccupation with tiny flies as intellectual myopia, but the latter recognizes this preoccupation as part of the

slow maturing of understanding which cannot be avoided if one is to know salmon and trout. The purist is invulnerable to the jibes of nonbelievers, secure in the heritage of an ancient and honorable piscatorial art. He scorns the applause of those who are unqualified to judge his achievements. Only the approbation of acknowledged peers can touch his soul.

Between these extremes lies the great army of modern anglers. In recent years, angling on both salt and fresh water has become much less a matter of luck and more a matter of applied science. Not all anglers agree that this is good. Many conservative fishermen claim that the "mechanization" of modern angling is degrading the sport. Others, however, claim this is not necessarily so.

They cite that fact that in many fresh water fishing areas throughout the world, modern fish-and-game laws and fisheries management practices effectively prevent deliberate or accidental over-fishing. They also point out that the rapid rise of efficiency of tackle and implements of angling has been accompanied by a widespread, self-regulating increase in public understanding of fish, their ecology and management, and their role in the life cycles of our inland and oceanic waters.

Few modern laymen understand the world of fish better than the experienced angler. The seasoned fisherman is a pragmatist, always looking for the relationship between cause and effect. He is also a philosopher. He knows that records are made to be broken, but that memory and anticipation make life worth living, which is why he is usually a contented man. Increasingly, he feels that responsibility for protecting endangered species of fish lies in his hands.

We live in what future generations of anglers will no doubt call the Golden Age of angling. We see imaginative fisheries management rejuvenating vast areas, such as some of the North American Great Lakes, and Britain's River Thames, which only a few years ago were considered lost to the inroads of pollution and ecological imbalance. Yet we can easily find other vast areas where wild, natural fish prevail. Millions of nonanglers are becoming aware of the need for preserving wilderness, clean waters, and wildlife as part of the vital balance of life on earth. From these will emerge the anglers of the future.

The earth is full of Thy riches;
So is this great and wide sea,
Wherein are things creeping innumerable,
Both small and great beasts.

PSALM 104:24–26
King James version of the Holy Bible

Habitat is where an organism spends its life-time. The habitats of fishes are thus natural and artificial water bodies all over the world. In these we also find the smaller and bigger plants and animals on which the fishes are dependent in one way or other – and also most of their enemies.

The aquatic habitats vary tremendously. Some are deep, some are shallow; the water may be cold, warm, or intermediate, fresh, brackish, or saline. The bottoms may be rocky or sandy, stony or muddy. The nutrient content may vary and so may the species composition of both the fish stocks and the stocks of other organisms.

Many people now are discovering the fascination of the relationships between fishes and their surroundings. In a natural habitat a fish is always a necessary component of the special environment in which it lives. The ecologist[1] studies how the entirety is built up, and the ethologist[2] studies how the fish behaves within the entirety. Both the ecologist and the ethologist are also concerned with what happens when an entirety breaks up, that is when a habitat and its world of inhabitants changes. This often happens today due to the increasing environment-transforming activities of man.

For example, in many areas, often near large cities, what once were called "useless" marshlands are being filled in and converted to residential and industrial use. Until recently this was thought to be "good use" of these wetlands, producing new lands to be used for commerce and industry.

But ecologists and aquatic biologists recently have been able to demonstrate that these "useless" coastal wetlands are, in most cases, prime nursery grounds for many species of game and forage fish and aquatic life. Without these coastal nursery grounds in which their young can mature, safe from predation during their vulnerable juvenile days, the populations of these game, food and forage fish will wither and ultimately cease to exist.

The advice of the ecologist and the ethologist is also necessary when new fish habitats are created or when non-indigenous species are released into old ones. In the following section we will meet the main types of environment where fishes are to be found.

[1] Ecology (Greek *oikos,* house, *logos,* word, speech) = the study of organism in relation to their environment and to each other.
[2] Ethology (Greek *ethos,* attitude, character, *logos,* word, speech) = the study of the behaviour of organisms.

THE AQUATIC ENVIRONMENT

Water is essential to life and makes up a large proportion of all living flesh (about three-quarters of the body weight of most fishes). It has many functions in the body. Because of its ability to absorb and retain heat, water serves to stabilize the body temperature and thus ensures that the physiological processes operate at the proper speed. As a universal solvent, it carries materials to the various parts of the body. Blood, which distributes oxygen, nutrients, and other substances and carries away waste products, consists mainly of water.

Modern biochemistry has suggested that life probably began in an anaerobic environment (that is, an environment in which free oxygen did not yet exist). Soon afterward a variety of organisms began to develop in water. The oldest discovered fossils of living organisms have come from sea deposit at least 1,000 million years old.

During their biological development many animals and plants have adapted to a life on land, but many others are still restricted to an aquatic life in order to maintain their water balance. Some fishes, it is true, can spend a short time on land. Others can survive dry periods by burying themselves in moist soil. But on the whole fishes belong to the organisms still living in water, where different species have adapted themselves to almost every kind of aquatic environment.

Plants and animals living on the bottoms of rivers, lakes, and seas are known as benthos (from the Greek, *benthos*, "depth of the sea"). The bottoms therefore constitute the *benthic environment*. Hard bottoms are formed by rocks, stones, shells, and corals and contain many sessile plants and animals. Here – among algae, under stones, in caves or crevices – free-moving animals find protection. Soft bottoms are formed by sediments which usually contain varying amounts of organic material. Many animals, including some fishes, burrow into the soft bottom. Mixed bottoms are different combinations of the above two and have a rich variety of organisms.

The free water masses constitute the *pelagic environment* (from the Greek, *pelagos*, "the sea"). The organisms living here are plankton, drifting about with the movements of the water, and nekton, which can move against the current. Most adult fishes are nekton although they may have been plankton as larvae. Organisms drifting on the water's surface are sometimes called seston.

Both the benthic and the pelagic environments can be divided into very important sub-zones – the light upper and the dark lower. Plant life is restricted to the upper zone because plants need light as a source of energy for their photosynthesis. The depth of the light zone varies considerably. In some inland lakes with turbid water it may reach only a few inches below the surface while in the open sea it can penetrate some hundreds of yards down.

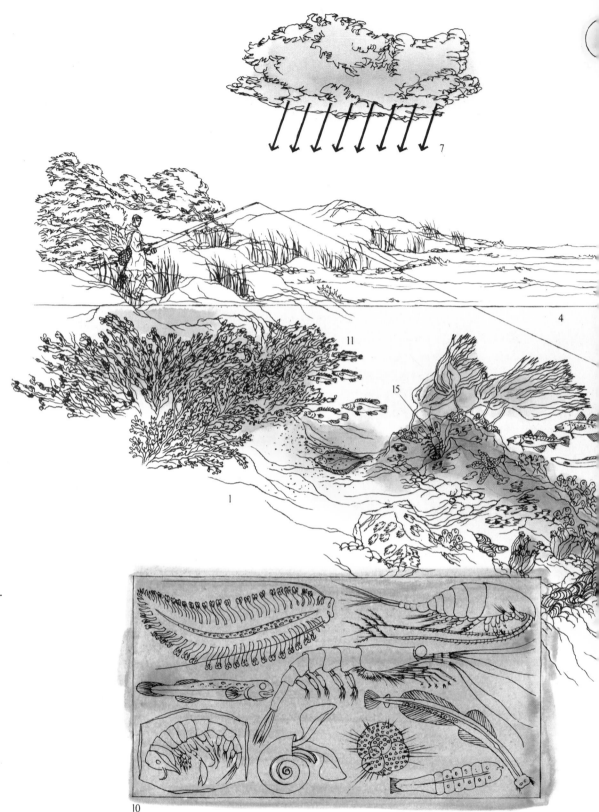

1 Sandy bottom
2 Hard bottom
3 Muddy bottom
4 Upper pelagic zone
5 Lower pelagic zone
6 Evaporation
7 Precipitation
8 Winds
9 Plant plankton or phytoplankton

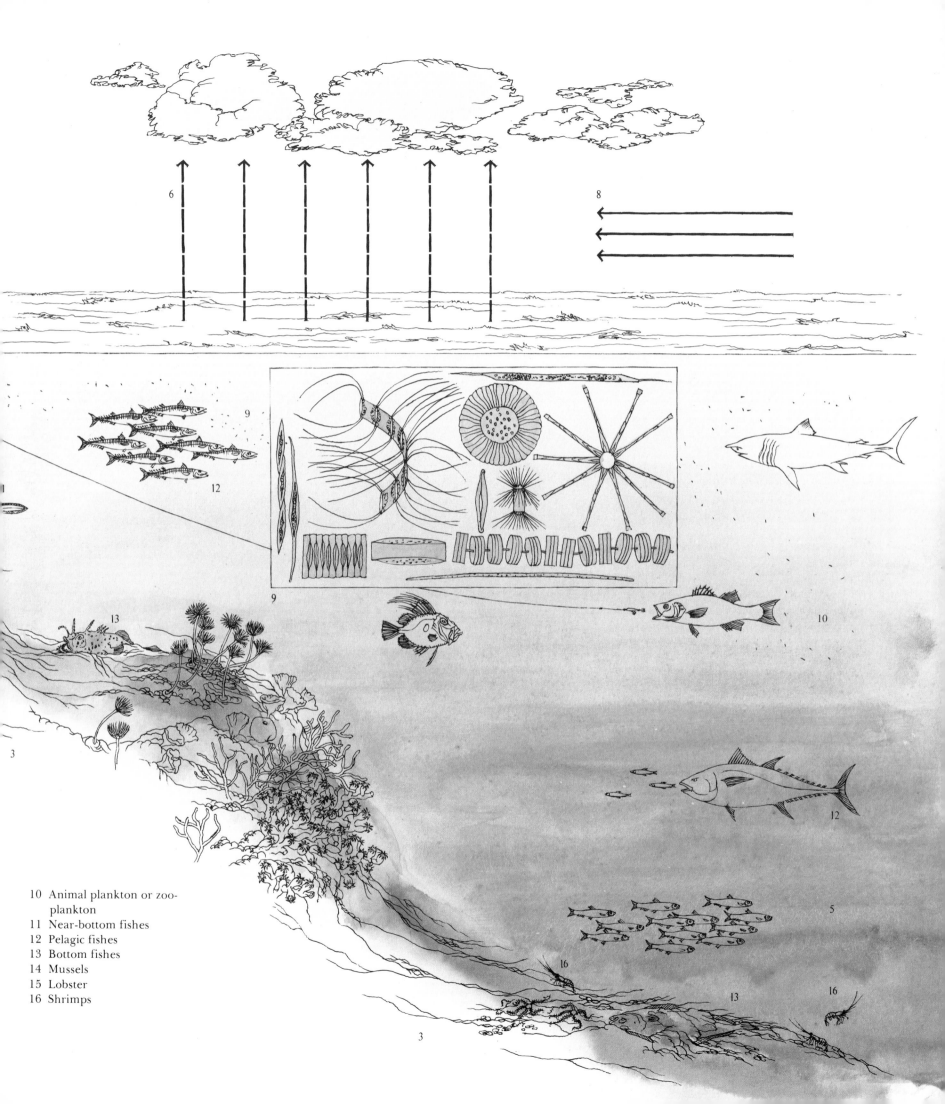

6

8

9

12

9

13

10

12

3

5

16

13

16

3

10 Animal plankton or zooplankton
11 Near-bottom fishes
12 Pelagic fishes
13 Bottom fishes
14 Mussels
15 Lobster
16 Shrimps

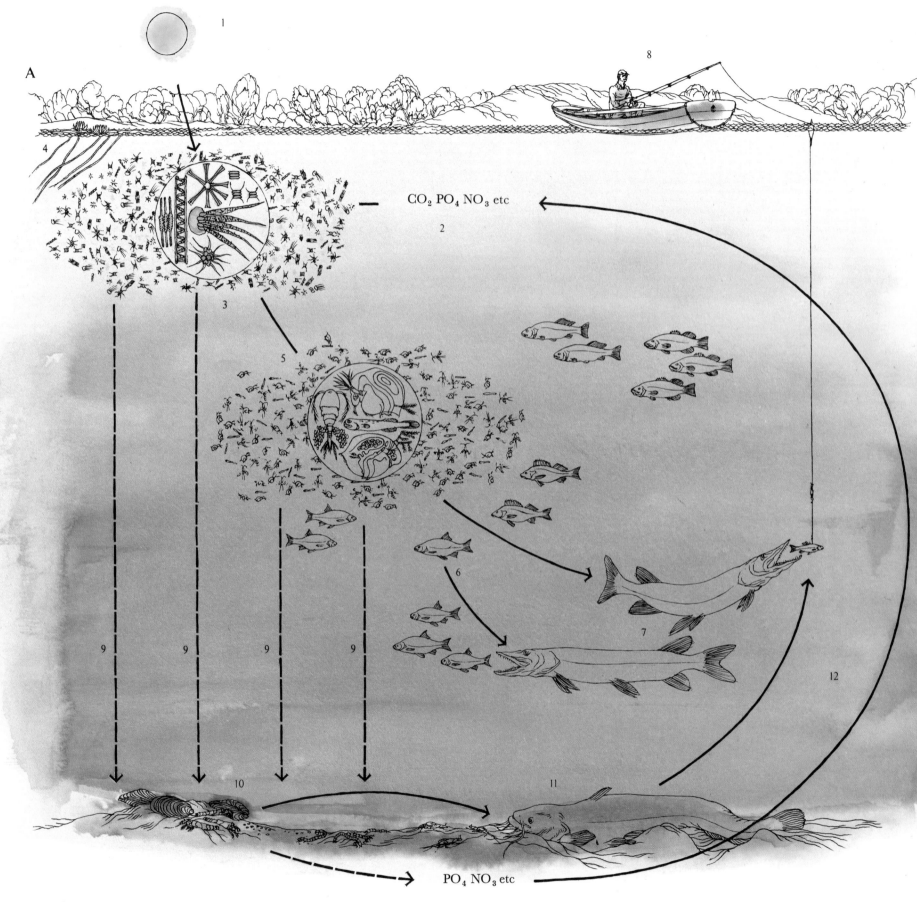

CO_2 PO_4 NO_3 etc

PO_4 NO_3 etc

A

FOOD CHAIN IN A
LAKE

1 Energy from the sun
2 Nutrients
3 Producers (phytoplank-
ton)
4 Producers (bigger plants)

5 Consumers, 1st step
6 Consumers, 2nd step
7 Consumers, 3rd step
8 Consumers, 4th step
9 Organic material

10 Consumer, 1st step
11 Consumer, 2nd step
12 Nutrients recycled

FOOD CHAINS

All the organisms in fresh and salt waters belong to food chains. Plants produce organic material from nutrients dissolved in the water and by photosynthesis (the reaction of carbon dioxide and sunlight to produce organic carbohydrates). The first consumer step occurs when these plants are eaten by small herbivorous plankton animals. Further consumer steps are taken when the small animals are eaten by larger carnivorous animals such as fishes, and when they in their turn are eaten by larger fishes, birds, or aquatic mammals such as seals and man.

Dead organic material, especially from the first steps of the food chain, sinks toward the bottom where it becomes food for an abundant fauna of bottom-living animals. On the way down and when lying on the bottom it is successively broken down by bacteria. In this way new inorganic nutrients are released which, if there are enough vertical movements in the water, may be brought up to the light upper zone where the cycle can start again.

A decrease in the amount of nutrients brought up will inhibit the production of new organic material such as plants, thus limiting the amount of animals the body of water can support. This happens in many waters. An extra supply of nutrients from land or running waters may, however, compensate for this.

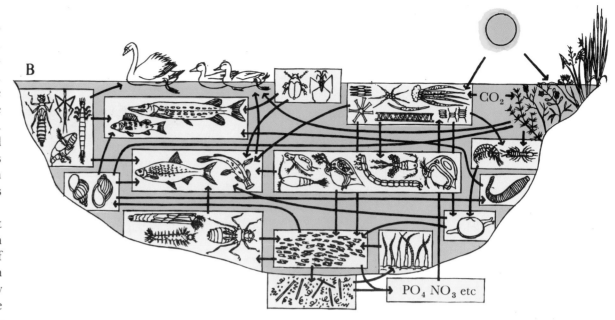

B

B

THE FOOD WEB

Food chains in sea, lake, or running waters do not exist in isolation from each other, but together form complicated food webs. The figure above has been simplified in order to show more clearly the interrelationships between food chains in a food web in a small inland lake.

C

THE ECOLOGICAL PYRAMID

The production of organic materials at the different steps in a food chain can be likened to a pyramid (right) with man and the higher animals at the top and inorganic nutrients at the base. A large part of the organic production of each step is not consumed by the next step. That is to say, not all plants are consumed by animals and not all fishes are consumed by other fishes, birds, seals, man, etc.

As an average only about 10 % of the organisms of one step are consumed by those of the next step. The rest is lost as energy or waste. In fact, as we can see from this pyramid, man uses very little of the productive capacity of the waters.

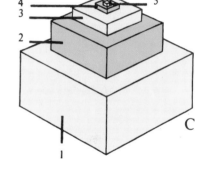

1 Inorganic nutrients
2 Producers (plants)
3 Primary consumers (e.g., zooplankton)
4 Secondary consumers (e.g., fish)
5 Tertiary consumers (e.g., man)

THE SEA

The sea covers about 70 percent of the earth's surface. The topography of the sea bottom varies as greatly as that of the mainland and has many submarine mountain ranges and plains. Shallows around the continents can slope down to deep-sea trenches, sometimes more than 33,000 ft. (c. 10,000 m) deep. Submarine earthquakes and volcanos can alter the seabed, while coastlines are changed by the action of the waves, currents, and sedimentation processes. Many coasts are split by deep fjords, reefs, and archipelagos. Rock pools, lagoons, and, in many warm areas, coral reefs can further complicate coastlines.

The seabed and the free water masses are divided into zones (figure A). The intertidal zone (between the tide marks) is called the eulittoral. Outside this the continental shelf stretches down to 600–900 ft. (c. 200–300 m). The bathyal zone is also called the continental slope and reaches down to 9,000–12,000 ft. (c. 3,000–4,000 m) where it becomes the abyssal zone, the deep sea which covers most of the seabed. The deepest part, which is below 18,000–21,000 ft. (c. 6,000–7,000 m) and includes the deep-sea trenches, is called the hadal zone.

Most commercial fishing is carried out on the continental shelf and in the upper part of the bathyal zone. Most sport fishing is restricted to the innermost part of the shelf, sometimes called the neritic zone. However, big-game fishing is usually carried out in the uppermost epipelagial zone of the open sea.

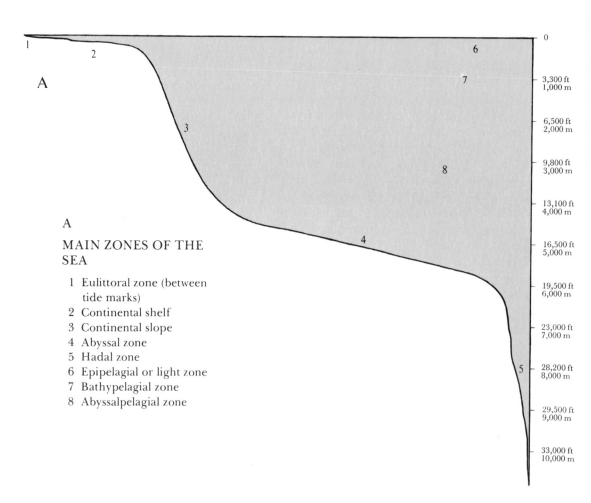

A

MAIN ZONES OF THE SEA

1. Eulittoral zone (between tide marks)
2. Continental shelf
3. Continental slope
4. Abyssal zone
5. Hadal zone
6. Epipelagial or light zone
7. Bathypelagial zone
8. Abyssalpelagial zone

SALINITY

The mean surface salinity of sea water is 3.5 % (35 g of salt per litre of water). Warm areas of the open sea with a high evaporation rate have a fairly high salinity, for example the subtropical high pressure areas and warm parts more or less separated from the water mass, such as the Red Sea, the Mediterranean, and many lagoons.

Low salinity occurs in the Arctic and Antarctic seas where melted ice is a source of fresh water, in areas off the estuaries of big rivers, and in partially enclosed areas which receive a lot of fresh water, such as the Baltic Sea and Hudson Bay.

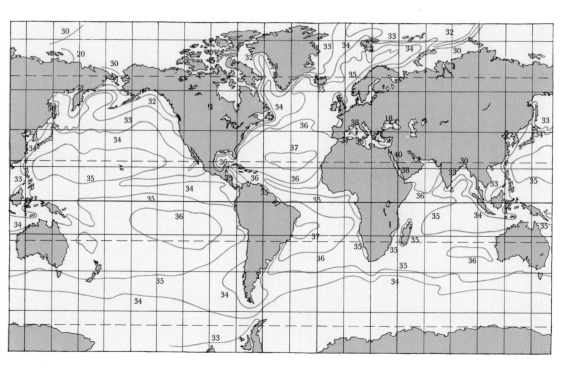

B

SURFACE SALINITIES OF THE SEA

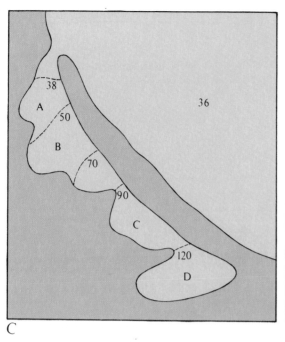

C

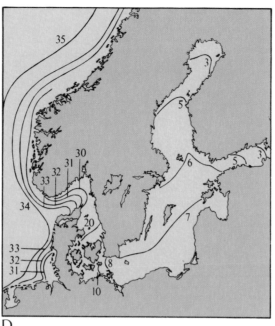

D

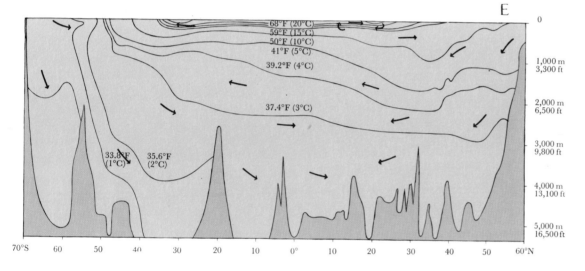

E

High and low salinities occur only in shallow waters or in the surface areas of deeper waters (deep water always having a salinity of about 3.5%), and in these places the fishing is quite good. Generally, the more the salinity diverges from the normal, the fewer are the species of both fishes and other animals found there. However, those fish which do exist in these waters are for the most part excellent sport fishes. For example, fish in brackish water along coastlines usually provide good sport.

TEMPERATURE

Temperature plays a vital role in the production and well-being of all organisms. In warmer waters the growth rate of organisms and the breakdown of dead organic matter are most rapid. Provided that enough nutrients are present the productivity of the sea can be very high.

In the cold seas, water temperature is about equal from the surface to the bottom all the year round. In the temperate areas a fairly thin layer of the upper surface (only some tens of meters in most places) is warmed up during the summer. In the subtropical and still more in the tropical areas the surface layers become much warmer than the deep water and may penetrate down to 600–1,500 ft. (c. 200–500 m).

The deep and bottom layers of the open oceans are always cold and much of the water comes originally from the Arctic or Antarctic seas. The fauna of these cold-water layers consists of cold-resistant forms and is generally sparse.

C

Enclosed waters which do not receive fresh water often have a very high salinity, especially in warm areas with a high evaporation rate. This occurs, for example, in lagoons on the coasts of the Caribbean and the Gulf of Mexico. Very few fishes are found in such waters. This typical lagoon illustrated above shows how the presence of fish species diminishes from the open to the closed end of the lagoon. Salinity is shown in arabic numerals as a percentage.

  A Renewed water from the open sea provides an acceptable salinity for about twenty fish species.

  B Only three fish species can survive here.

C–D No fish species can live in these areas.

D

The Baltic Sea has a heavy supply of fresh water through numerous rivers and a low rate of evaporation. The surface and bottom salinity decreases gradually to zero as one moves northwards. In the brackish coastal waters the marine fishes meet some of the freshwater species. Thus the sport fisherman can catch both marine and freshwater fish from the same spot.

E

The figure above shows a diagrammatic length section through the central Atlantic Ocean with the main iso-

therms for the temperatures in degrees Fahrenheit and centigrade inserted. The Antarctic is on the left and the North Atlantic on the right.

CURRENTS

The main cause of the sea-surface currents is the winds, especially where they blow steadily in the same direction, as in the trade-wind regions and in the belts of prevailing westerlies. Because of the rotation of the earth the currents in the Northern Hemisphere flow clockwise and in the Southern Hemisphere counterclockwise. The great ocean circulation systems are thus formed.

The circulation systems in the deep water of the oceans are based on salinity and temperature differences. Cold polar water sinks and travels toward the tropics while warm equatorial water travels toward the poles. This system also helps to transport nutrients from one part of the ocean to another.

The currents that carry cold water to warm parts and warmer water to colder parts play an important role in the dispersal of fishes and other pelagic organisms. That is why warm water species may be found off the west coast of Scandinavia, for instance.

Vertical movements occur most easily where there are no or only very slight differences in temperature and salinity throughout the depth. This is the case in the cold seas (in Figure A, the arrows show the transport of organic matter). The ascent of nutrients from the deep waters to the sunlit surface layers where the main production occurs is thus made easy and the production of new organic material can be astonishingly high.

This also happens in large areas of the temperate zones during winter. During summer, however, the water is stratified and much of the nutrient substances cannot reach the warm uppermost layers where they are most needed (see Figure B). Production of living material therefore decreases until the stratification is broken up in the autumn. But by then the temperature and sometimes also the light intensity may be so low that a real increase in production has to wait until the following spring.

In the open warm seas the surface water is always stratified because it is much warmer than the deep water. Therefore it is often short of nutrients and production is not high (see Figure C). In non-stratified shallow coastal and coral-reef areas, productivity may be very high due to the combination of nutrients, light, and high temperatures.

As mentioned, surface currents flow slightly clockwise or counterclockwise depending upon which hemisphere they are in. Off the west coast of South America, for instance, the Humboldt current flows north and bears to the left away from the continent. Deep water, rich in nutrients, is then sucked up to the surface (see Figure D). Such *zones of upwelling* occur in many places, for instance on the west coasts of the continents, in the Antarctic, and in the equatorial parts of the oceans where two currents diverge from each other. These upwellings of nutrient-laden water to the light zone produce enormous quantities of phytoplankton and, consequently, an abundant fish life.

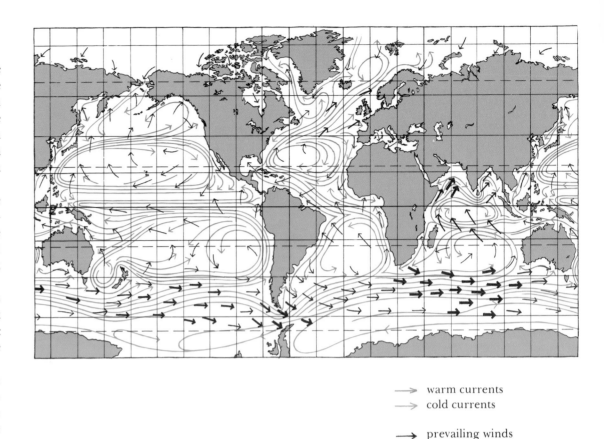

$\longrightarrow$ warm currents
$\longrightarrow$ cold currents

$\longrightarrow$ prevailing winds

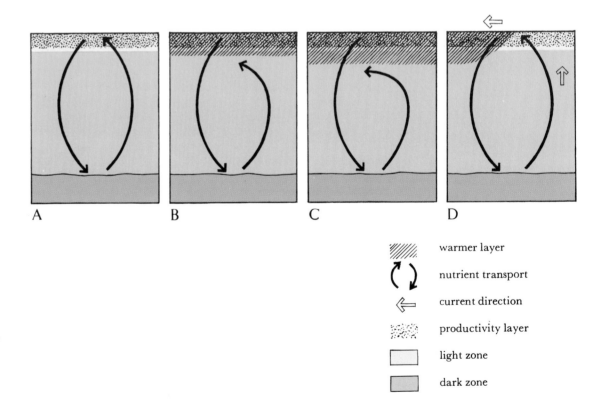

A   B   C   D

▨ warmer layer

⟳ nutrient transport

⇐ current direction

⸛ productivity layer

▢ light zone

▨ dark zone

POLLUTION

The breakdown processes can be hindered through a lack of oxygen. This can happen especially in coastal waters which are more or less cut off from the open sea by such barriers as underwater sills or reefs when there is a heavy supply of organic material from sewage and other waste disposal from cities and industrial complexes. When all the oxygen is used up, toxic hydrogen sulphide (H_2S) develops and the fishes and their food die. In this way several local areas have been denuded of aquatic life.

CORAL REEFS

Most living coral reefs are restricted to the warmer parts of the oceans where there is ample sunlight. They constitute colorful and highly diversified environments for the skin diver and the sport fisherman. They provide food and shelter for a vast variety of organisms and have a flourishing fish life.

In some coastal areas artificial "reefs" are sometimes constructed of stones, concrete blocks, old cars, and the like, in order to increase the yields of commercial or sport fishing. Sunken ships can very often fulfil the same function.

TIDAL ENVIRONMENTS

The tides are diurnal or semidiurnal and vary considerably. The difference between high and low tide can range from near zero to more than c. 30 ft. (c. 10 m). The highest tides generally occur in bays with a narrow inner end where the water is pushed inwards and upwards along the sides of the bay.

The movements of the tides disturb the food substances which flourish in the shallow waters around coasts and therefore fishes generally become most active on a flooding or ebbing tide. Tidal coasts, especially in warm or temperate seas, often contain a rich and varied population of organisms of which most hide under shelters like stones or algae or dig themselves down into the bottom. Others follow the water movements in and out.

A

B

A

The tidal shores may be sandy, muddy or rocky, or partly covered with vegetation like the mangrove shore. The mangrove swamps are important reservoirs of food for many fishes which during high tides dwell among the roots of the trees.

B

A popular pastime is to go out during low tide and collect fishes and other organisms dwelling under stones or in pools. Fishermen often collect their natural bait in this way.

1. Shrimp
2. Mussels
3. Starfish
4. Crab
5. Worm
6. Limpets

1

2

3

4

5

6

B

LAKES

The innumerable lakes in the world have been created in different ways. Some are water-filled volcanic craters or fault valleys. Others were formed in depressions in the landscape, often dammed up by soil or rocky ridges. Some were formed when new land was raised from the sea. Man has created many lakes as reservoirs for domestic and industrial water supplies, for power stations, and for fish cultivation.

Lakes are much more influenced by the surrounding land than is the sea. This means that almost every lake has an individual character, with its own type of food web. Certain main types can, however, be distinguished. *Eutrophic* lakes, rich in nutrients, occur in fertile regions, while *oligotrophic* lakes are found in infertile or cold areas and have a scarcity of nutrient matter. Special factors may cause lakes to be extreme in one way or the other. Where the surrounding land is woody and boggy with a heavy production of humus substances, we find *dystrophic* lakes which are more acid than normal. In calciferous (chalk or limestone) regions the water can have a high alkali content. Both these types of lakes have specialized fish faunas which are usually not abundant. In certain warm areas with a heavy evaporation, salts accumulate in the water and sometimes the salinity is so high that very little life is possible. This is the case in the Dead Sea and the Great Salt Lake.

As a rule, the pollutants from human settlements, industries, agriculture, and forestry have a more direct effect on lakes than on the sea. Organic substances may cause overfertilization or eutrophication which have an undesirable effect on the flora and fauna. Game fishes (such as salmonid species) are particularly likely to be affected. Toxic substances such as the insecticide DDT, polychlorinated biphenyls (PCB) which are much used in the plastic industry, mercury, and many others are found in lakes throughout the world. In some industrialized countries the mercury content in fish is so high that fish caught must not be eaten.

Lakes are relatively young when compared with the sea but all lakes are ultimately destined to disappear. The aging process is often accelerated by man when he discharges waste waters with a high content of organic material into them.

But over the centuries man has also created new lakes or ponds where fish are cultivated for commercial use or, more recently, for sport fishing. In recent years old lakes have been cleared of their original flora and fauna and new species of more valuable fish have been introduced. This has, in many cases, greatly improved the quality of the sport fishing.

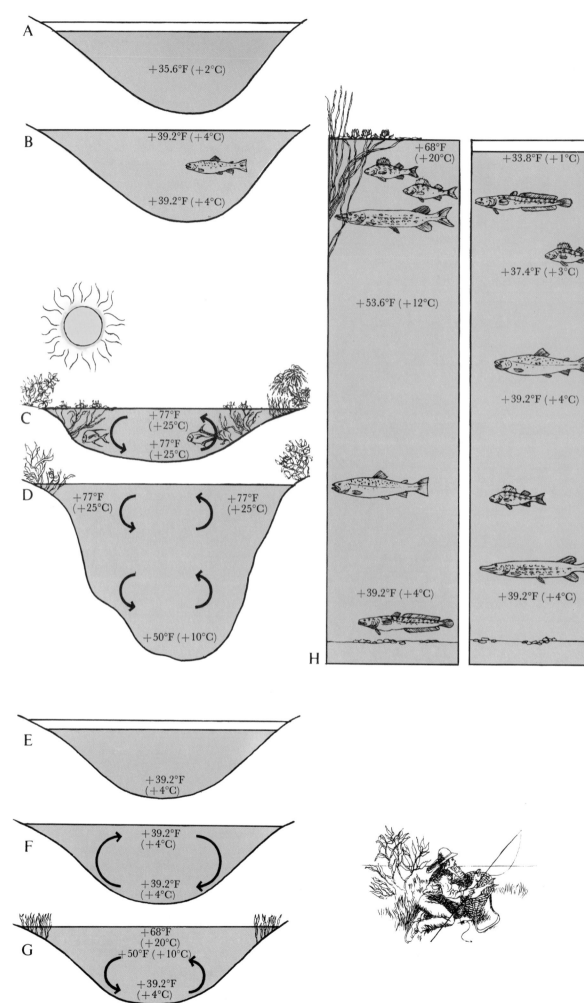

A

Lakes in the *coldest regions*, including the high mountain ranges, are covered by ice during a great part of the year.

B

Even during the summer the temperatures remain low, seldom more than some degrees above freezing point. The organisms living there are scarce and extremely well adapted to cold water. Very few fish species are found.

C

Lakes in *warm regions*, if they are not too deep, are warm all the year from the surface to the bottom. As the food substances can circulate, these lakes may contain a very rich world of organisms with many fishes like the cichlids and cyprinids.

D

If the warm lakes are deep, however, circulation may be difficult, usually because the deeper water is colder. This prevents bottom food substances from being carried up to the sunlit surface zone, thus lowering the production of new organic material. In some cases the deep-water layers may be depleted of oxygen and fishes cannot survive there. Many deep tropical lakes are, therefore, relatively poor in fish production.

E

In *cold-temperate regions* the lakes are usually ice-covered during winter. Fresh water is heaviest at 39°F (4°C) and water at this temperature sinks down to form the bottom layer during the cold period. In some shallow lakes, if the ice prevents the light from penetrating, the plants may die and use up all of the oxygen as they decompose. This can cause "winterkill" of the fishes.

F

During the spring the ice melts and the surface water is gradually warmed. When it reaches 39°F (4°C) the entire body of water becomes homogenous. Winds then cause a vertical circulation to begin, nutrients are brought up to the sunlit layer and the production of new organic material starts.

G

In summer a temperature discontinuity layer (thermocline) is formed in all but the very shallow lakes. This prevents deeper water from reaching the surface. The breakdown processes below the thermocline may cause an oxygen shortage, especially where there is a plentiful supply of organic material from land. "Summerkill" of fishes may then occur.

Since deeper lakes have a plentiful oxygen supply there is no danger of "summerkill". Furthermore, deep lakes are usually situated in less fertile areas with a low supply of nutrients and a correspondingly low production rate. Such lakes tend to be poor in fish species although many of the best game fishes, such as salmonids, are found there.

H

Many freshwater fishes vary the depths at which they live as the temperature of the water changes during the different seasons. The burbot, for instance, spends the summer in the cold bottom water and moves up toward the surface during the winter. The pike and the perch swim around at most depths during winter and then move up to the zone of bottom plants in summer. The lake trout spends the summer in the cold bottom water, but during winter it moves up into the free water masses.

I

The building of dams across river valleys to provide a water supply for electricity generating stations has also created new lakes. Here the original fish fauna of the area is maintained as far as possible and, where possible, new game fishes are introduced. Stocks of migratory species are maintained with the assistance of technical arrangements like salmon ladders and by the introduction of young fish specially reared in hatcheries.

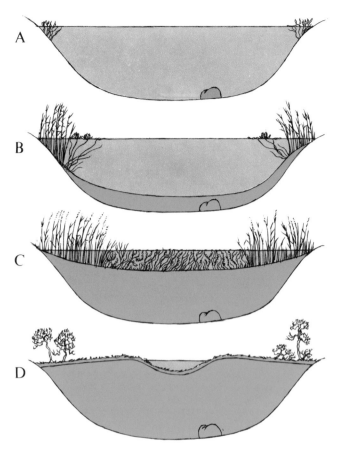

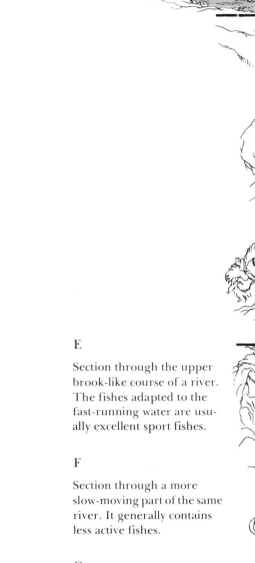

A

A new lake is more or less oligotrophic, i.e., poor in nutrients. If the surrounding land is also oligotrophic the lake may remain in this state for a very long time. Many lakes in North America and northern Europe, created after the withdrawal of the great glaciers, are of this type. They contain salmonids and similar fishes.

B

Where the surroundings are especially fertile the production in the lake will be so great that all the organic material cannot be broken down but accumulates on the bottom. The lake is now aging and grows more shallow as layer piles upon layer on the bottom. Generally such a lake will have a flourishing zone of rooted plants along the shore and a population of perch, pike, and cyprinids.

C

When the lake has become so shallow that (in temperate regions) there is not even space for a thermocline, the shore plants grow outward and may cover most of the surface. The lake now successively changes to a swamp, often a paradise for birds, but with few interesting fishes. Finally it disappears.

D

In forest areas like the *taiga* in Russia and Canada the former sea bottom is rich in humus substances and is often successively overgrown with mosses so that a bog forms.

E

Section through the upper brook-like course of a river. The fishes adapted to the fast-running water are usually excellent sport fishes.

F

Section through a more slow-moving part of the same river. It generally contains less active fishes.

G

Discharged pollutants negatively change the river by, for instance, overfertilization. Toxic substances may even destroy most of the life there.

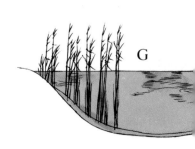

RUNNING WATERS

There are many types of running waters, varying from small, fast mountain brooks to the large rivers which slowly meander through plains toward the sea.

A river changes many times along its course. It may, for example, begin as a small fast-running brook with a stony bottom where the organisms depend wholly on nutrients from the land and where the breakdown of organic matter occurs while the water is running downstream. Most of the animals are adapted to the special environment: smaller ones are flat or have organs to anchor themselves; the fish species are good swimmers and are able to maintain their positions against the current.

In lower parts the river may look rather like a lake, with slow-moving water, muddy bottom deposits, and a rich shore vegetation. Although still dependent on nutrients from the land it has by now an organic production of its own. The animals, including fishes, are often identical with those in lakes in the surrounding area and are adapted to that type of habitat.

The water of many rivers contains a lot of suspended particles which are caused by land erosion. Sometimes the water may become so turbid that most fishes are scared away. River life is also very sensitive to the different pollutants discharged into the water through sewage pipes and from the waste disposal from industrial complexes.

Where a river meets the sea an estuary may be formed. Freshwater and marine fishes may intermingle in the brackish water there.

CONSERVATION OF FISH AND THEIR HABITAT

Until the middle of the present century most people took it for granted that fish and the other living resources of the sea were practically limitless. Hadn't Mediterranean fishermen been harvesting tuna in huge fish traps since the earliest days of the Christian era? Hadn't northern European seafarers been taking cod from the Grand Banks since before Columbus sighted San Salvador?

But as the fish-catching ability of maritime nations grew at an exponential rate following World War II, it became apparent that many species of fish and some sea mammals were in danger of following certain fresh water species into virtual extinction. Inland in the narrow confines of fresh water rivers and lakes it is easy to observe the effects of overfishing, pollution, and the destruction of habitat on vulnerable species. It is also relatively easy for single responsible governments to take action to conserve species and habitats considered important.

The great problem of bringing conservation of species and habitat to endangered creatures of the oceans is the fact that on the high seas, beyond national territorial limits, the fish "belong to everybody", and nobody has power to regulate overfishing or misuse of the marine environment. Furthermore, agreement on what constitutes conservation of marine species has been difficult to achieve.

Chile, Peru, and Ecuador, for example, were the first nations to declare that all fish within 200 nautical miles of their shores belonged to them and foreign fishing boats could fish for these fish only after paying a stiff licence fee. The United States in 1976 legalized its own 200-mile exclusive fisheries zone even while the issue of international control of ocean fishing rights was being debated in a United Nations Law of the Sea convention.

Other countries in Europe are setting up, or have imposed, similar ocean fishing limits. The Icelandic Cod War was evidence of the increasing competition for rich fishing grounds.

The term conservation itself needs careful definition. To some commercial fishing operators it is the act of putting restrictions on certain types of fishing only after the species in question have been brought to the point of zero economic return. To many fishery managers it means extracting the maximum sustainable yield that a species or population can render over a period of time. To some laymen of the so-called preservationist point of view it means preserving all possible fish from any form of commercial exploitation. To the majority of concerned and enlightened sport fishermen it has a meaning somewhere in between these divergent and sometimes contradictory definitions.

The sad plight of the world's whales is a prime example of deliberate overfishing in the face of strenuous scientific disapproval. To restore the endangered whale populations to viable levels would require a heroic type of industrial self-regulation, a brand of conservation that is not frequently encountered these days.

Other aquatic species have been rendered practically non-existent not so much by overfishing as by pollution and degradation of their environment. Salmon and sea trout have gone from many European waters, where they were formerly abundant, and so has the sturgeon. To abate the pollution and restore the damaged habitats requires a type of expensive conservation that governments and taxpayers find difficult to put into action.

Fortunately, we live in a time of awakening awareness of the fragility and finiteness of our Space Ship Earth. We also live in a time in which increasing numbers of people actively seek the lakes, rivers, and seas for contact with nature and relief from social and industrial pressures. Fishing is the fastest-growing individual participation sport in those countries where there are waters into which the growing ranks of anglers can expand. These anglers are increasingly concerned that the relatively good fishing they now enjoy shall not be lost to future generations through lack of effort to achieve a new level of conservation of fish and aquatic habitat in which both living aquatic resources and man's use of the waters can coexist.

Meanwhile, anglers in some parts of the world already are enjoying the benefits of enlightened, modern conservation practices. In the North American Great Lakes, for example, a ten-year programme of fisheries rehabilitation has made a literal fishermen's paradise out of what seemed destined to become a polluted biological wasteland populated only by fish-killing sea lampreys and billions upon billions of stunted, worthless alewives, both uninvited invaders from the sea.

Fish are returning to the River Thames and to the Stockholm area in ever-increasing numbers following extensive anti-pollution measures. What has been done in these cases can be repeated elsewhere. The definition of conservation; "use without abuse", is as valid and clearcut today as it was when it was voiced by Theodore Roosevelt, 26th President of the United States, more than 70 years ago.

THE FISH

*Fisherman: I marvel how the fishes
live in the sea.*
*Master: Why, as men do a-land;
the great ones eat up the
little ones.*

PERICLES

Fish have always held a special fascination for mankind. Perhaps it is because fish belong to a world that is so totally unlike ours. Possibly it is because there are so many kinds of fishes that they seem to be endless variations on an ever-changing theme. Perhaps it is because the fish, with his streamline body, his flashing silver sides, and his brilliant colours, seems so at home and so in harmony with his universe that we are moved to wonder and perhaps to feel a trace of envy.

Somehow we equate fishing with peace and relaxation in a way that goes beyond the mere anticipation of a pleasant meal. Even those who fish for a living seem to reflect an inner serenity as if they had absorbed some of the tranquillity that fishes seem to have. This is even reflected in the language of the fisherman who never uses the word kill to describe his successes.

One can never really think like a fish. After years of study a careful observer can learn his quarry's habits and can anticipate the fish's movements and responses but no mere human can ever know the sensations of vibrations striking a lateral line. Man is insulated from his environment by a waterproof

skin and his warm blood protects him from the vicissitudes of changing temperature. The fish, in contrast, is truly part of his environment, water flows freely through his skin and gills, and his temperature assumes that of his surroundings. When it is cold he eats less and moves slower.

In this section we will consider how man and fish meet the same basic problems of survival, feeding and reproduction, and how they do so in very different ways.

2

THE FISH'S BODY PLAN–SIMILARITY TO MAN

Fishes are vertebrates or backboned animals and their basic body plan is the same as that of the other vertebrates – amphibians, reptiles, birds, and mammals, including man. Life arose in the sea and the ancestors of all modern vertebrates were certainly fish-like creatures, but it is not correct to say that man descended directly from any fish that is still alive today. Because of the fundamental similarity of structure it is easiest to understand the anatomy of the fish by comparing it with our own physical structure. The similarities we observe are inherited from our common ancestor; the differences represent adaptations to vastly different ways of life.

Let us consider first the basic similarities between fish and man and then the special structures that enable fishes to live in water.

The vertebrate body consists of an internal framework of many separate bones moved by surrounding muscles. This skeleton includes the backbone or vertebral column which is a central rod of individual pieces called vertebrae. At the head end of this rod there is a complicated skull that houses the brain and the paired sense organs, the eyes, ears, and olfactory organs. The skull also supports the jaws and the gill mechanism. Immediately behind the skull there is a body cavity containing the digestive tube and related organs, the excretory and reproductive organs, and various glands that control the general body processes. The heart lies in a separate chamber at the front of the body cavity.

A central nerve cord runs from the brain backward through a protected canal along the dorsal side of the vertebral column. Branch nerves emerge between the segments of the vertebral column, some carrying messages from the organs to the brain and others relaying impulses from the brain to the organs.

There are two pairs of limbs, each supported by a series of bones. The shoulder or pectoral appendages correspond to our arms and the pelvic appendages correspond to our legs. In fishes the pectoral girdle is attached to the skull and the pelvic bones lie within the ventral body wall, often attached directly to the pectoral girdle.

The outside of the body is protected by a skin consisting of several layers. The skin is the first line of defense against injury and attack by disease organisms. It also contains pigment cells for camouflage. The outer layer, called the epidermis, also contains cells and glands that secrete the slime which protects the fish. This slime is toxic to bacteria and other disease organisms and to a certain extent it protects the fish against abrasion. Fish culturists are careful never to handle fish with dry hands for this removes the slime and exposes the fish to secondary infection.

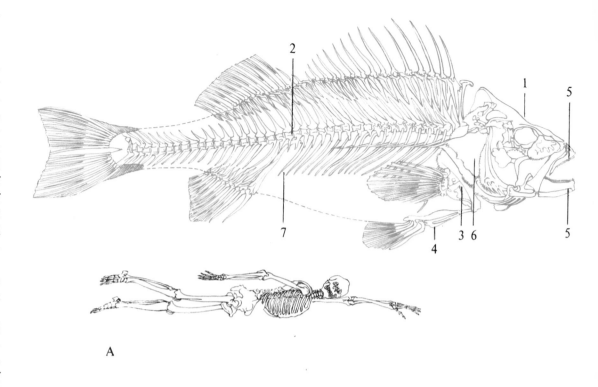

A

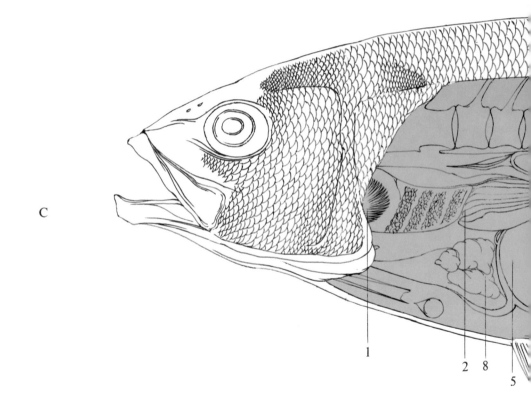

C

A

The vertebrate skeleton consists of a jointed spinal column with a skull (neurocranium) that surrounds and protects the brain. Other bones support the fins (limbs) and protect the internal organs.

1 Skull
2 Spinal column (vertebrae)
3 Pectoral girdle
4 Pelvic girdle
5 Jaws
6 Gill cover
7 Ribs

B

The change from aquatic to land living required modification of the limbs.

1 Pectoral fin of a bony fish.
2 Pectoral fin of an extinct lobe-fin fish (Rhipidistian).
3 Forelimb of a salamander.
4 Forelimb arm of a man.

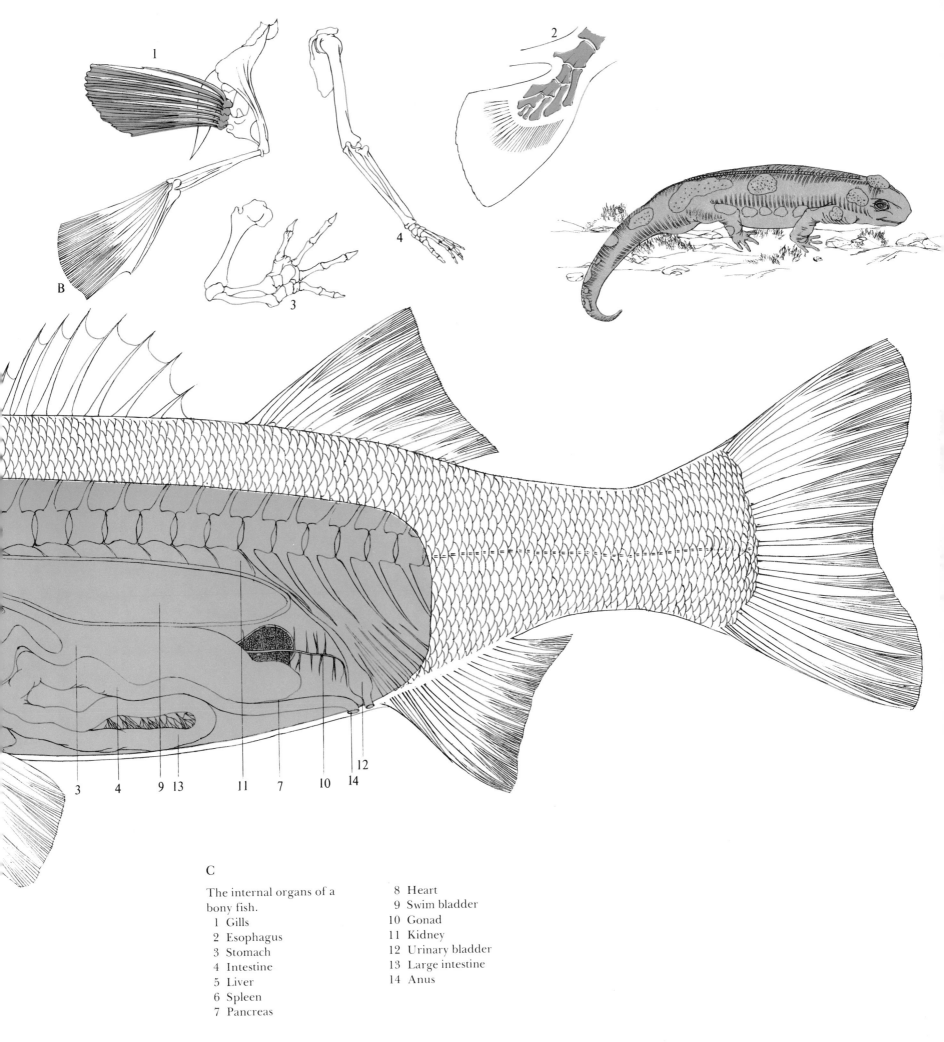

B

C

The internal organs of a
bony fish.
 1 Gills
 2 Esophagus
 3 Stomach
 4 Intestine
 5 Liver
 6 Spleen
 7 Pancreas

 8 Heart
 9 Swim bladder
10 Gonad
11 Kidney
12 Urinary bladder
13 Large intestine
14 Anus

THE AQUATIC ENVIRONMENT

Fishes are wholly adapted for living in water just as man is completely adapted for living on land. Each environment has its special demands and the animals that live there must meet these demands in order to survive. Because water is many times denser than air, fishes must have streamlined bodies so that they can move effectively and their limbs, the pectoral and pelvic fins, are specialized as control surfaces. Because of the buoyancy of water fishes are able to move up and down as well as horizontally and their world is truly three-dimensional whereas man is confined to whatever surface he happens to be on.

MOVEMENT AND MUSCLES

Most of the propulsive force that drives the fish through the water comes from wave-like movements of the body. This is most easily seen in eel-like fish and has come to be called anguilliform (eel-like) movement. This is a very effective way to move because all parts of the body are applying the force at the same time, pushing the water aside and allowing it to close behind the fish with a minimum of disturbance.

The anguilliform movements of the body are produced by segmental body muscles. When the skin of a fish is removed one can see that the trunk muscles are divided into short W-shaped segments. Because these segments operate independently some of the muscles on one side can be relaxed at the same time other muscles on the same side are contracted, thus the body can be bent into a series of S-shaped curves, which would not be possible if the muscles were continuous along the side.

FINS AND BODY SHAPE

In addition to the pectoral and pelvic fins, which are paired fins (one on each side of the body), there is a series of median fins – dorsal fins on the back or dorsal side, anal fins on the ventral or belly side and behind the anus, and the tail or caudal fin at the end of the vertebral column. All fins consist of a membrane supported by long rods called fin rays. The tail fin continues the anguilliform motion of the body and in fast-swimming fishes like the tunas most of the force is applied by the tail while the rest of the body flexes very little. The other fins act as stabilizers and control surfaces. When the fish is at rest or hovering the fins can be used for propulsion and maneuvering but during high-speed swimming they are used mainly for steering.

While all fishes are streamlined, there is a great deal of variation in body shape and in the shape of the fins according to where and how the fish lives. Fishes that live in midwater tend to be either spindle-shaped or flattened from side to side. Fishes that live close to the surface are usually long and

A The fish's body shape is correlated with its way of life. Sluggish bottom-dwelling fishes like the sea bass (1) have robust, heavy bodies but swift-moving openwater species, for example the mackerel (2) and tuna (3), are streamlined and torpedo-shaped. The snake-like body of the eel (4) enables it to move effectively in mud and small crevices.

B Sequential contraction of the W-shaped body muscle segments (1) causes wave-like curves (2) that push the fish through the water, aided by sweeps of the tail fin (3). Other fins are used for steering (4) and braking (5) as well as propulsion. Sometimes the pectoral fins propel the fish with oar-like strokes (6).

C The dorsal and anal fin rays are controlled by pairs of muscles that raise, lower, and incline them.
1 Fin spine
2 Fin support (pterygiophore)
3 Erector muscle
4 Depressor muscle
5 Inclinator muscle

slender. Fishes that live near the bottom tend to have heavy shorter bodies and some are flattened top to bottom. The flatfishes – flounder, plaice, sole, and similar fish are actually flattened from side to side but they rest on their side rather than swimming upright. In these fishes both eyes are on the uppermost side.

Fishes that live in labyrinthine habitats such as coral reefs come in a variety of shapes depending on how they live. Some are short and deep bodied, some are elongate and eel-like, and some are rather ordinary in shape.

The fins also reflect the way of life. Fast-swimming fishes tend to have deeply forked tail fins, long sickle-shaped pectoral fins, and low dorsal and anal fins. Sometimes the dorsal fin folds into a groove so that it can be retracted during rapid swimming. Fishes that are more sluggish have rounded or only shallowly forked tails, rounded pectorals, and higher dorsal and anal fins. The dorsal and anal fins sometimes have elongate thread-like rays that may serve as camouflage or perhaps have some role in courtship.

Fin rays are of two general types – spines and soft rays. Spines are single unbranched solid shafts of bone. Soft rays are composed of short segments and they are usually branched (though not always). They also have left and right halves that can be seen in the dried fin skeleton. True spines are present only in the more advanced fishes and they are nearly always confined to the front of the fin. Typically the first dorsal fin of a perch-like fish will have only spines while the second dorsal consists of one spine followed by soft rays, the anal fin will have one to three spines followed by soft rays and each pelvic fin will has one spine and five soft rays. Neither the tail nor the pectoral fin have spines.

Some lower fishes that lack true spines have hardened rays which often have sawtoothed edges. The dorsal and pectoral fins of catfishes are examples and the dorsal and anal fins of carp and goldfish also have hardened serrated rays at the front of the dorsal and anal fins.

Each spine and ray has sets of muscles that erect the ray, depress it, or move it from side to side. Like our own muscles these are arranged in pairs; as one muscle contracts the opposite one relaxes to permit the bone to move.

Primitive fishes such as the herrings and salmon have their pelvic fins far back – near the anus – and the pectoral fins low on the sides of the body with their bases almost horizontal. Advanced spiny-rayed fishes tend to have the pelvic fins far forward and the pectoral fins higher on the side with their bases vertical rather than horizontal.

A few groups of fishes have extreme specializations of the paired fins. Gobies and sea snails have the pelvic fins joined into sucker-like discs with which they cling to the bottom; gurnards and shads have the lower pectoral rays separate so that they can be used for walking along the bottom.

D

Cross section of fishes.
1 Robust
2 Terete
3 Compressed
4 Depressed

E

Fins may also be modified for special purposes.
1 The filamentous fins of the young African pompano serve for camouflage.
2 The pelvic fins of gobies and clingfishes (3) work like suckers to enable the fish to grip the bottom.

4 The gurnard uses separated lower rays of its pectoral fin to walk along the bottom.

BREATHING

Another special feature of living in water is that the oxygen the animal breathes must be extracted from the water. This, of course, is done by the gills, which are one of the most complicated mechanisms of the fish's anatomy. Fish gills typically consist of four pairs of bony arches in the throat region. At the back of each of these arches there are two rows of filaments and on the surface of each filament there are tiny blade-like lamellae. Blood is pumped by the heart through these lamellae where oxygen is absorbed through the extremely thin walls of the lamellae while carbon dioxide is released at the same time. From the gills blood is circulated through the body and finally returned to the heart.

Water is taken in through the mouth and pumped past the gills, then expelled through gill openings. Thin flaps of tissue just behind the jaw and a membrane at the edge of the gill cover act as valves to prevent backward flow. By successively opening and closing the mouth, expanding and contracting the cheek area and opening and closing the gill cover the fish actually pumps water across the gills.

Fishes are much less insulated from their environment than are terrestrial organisms. In fact, it is this insulation that makes terrestrial life possible. For fishes both the skin and especially the gills are permeable to water, and a variety of other substances freely pass in and out of the body. (The outer layer of the skin is a thin layer only a few cells thick; scales and other protective bony plates are part of the deeper dermal layer and thus are not really the first line of defense.)

This intimacy with the environment leads to some particular problems such as maintaining water balance. It also makes fishes extremely sensitive to chemicals in the water whether from natural sources or pollution by human agencies.

Because of the lack of insulation and because water is an extremely good conductor of heat, the fish's body temperature is nearly always just about the same as that of the surrounding water. The only known exceptions are tunas and some sharks that have the blood supply to some of the body muscles so arranged that heat is retained in order that those muscles can operate at a higher temperature during periods of prolonged high-speed swimming.

The permeability of the skin and gills allows water to pass into or out of the body depending on the environment. In salt water the fish lose water because the flow by osmosis is outward. Saltwater fishes overcome this loss by drinking water and excreting excess salt through the gills. With freshwater fish the problem is reversed: they constantly absorb water and so they must excrete a copious, dilute urine to rid themselves of the excess. This is reflected in the structure of the kidneys which must extract large amounts of water in addition to the nitrogenous wastes that the kidneys normally remove from the blood.

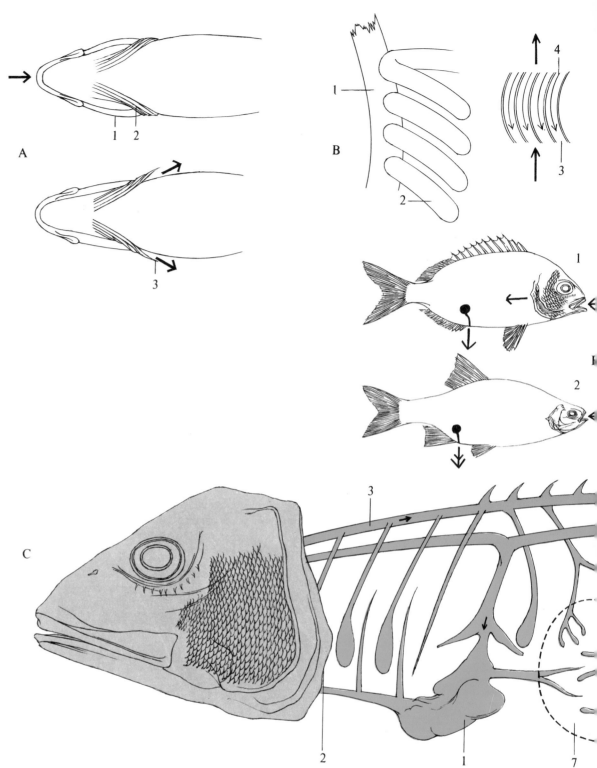

A
Outward movements of the cheeks (1) and gill covers (2) draw water into the mouth cavity. After this the cheeks are drawn in and the gill covers move outward to pump water across the gills and out through the gill slits (3).

B
Each gill arch (1) supports rows of filaments (2). On the filaments there are thin blade-like lamellae (3). As water flows past the lamellae, blood is pumped through thin-walled capillaries (4) in the opposite direction, thus ensuring maximum exchange of oxygen and carbon dioxide.

C
Blood is pumped from the heart (1) through the gills (2) to the dorsal aorta (3), then to arteries which distribute it to capillaries in all parts of the body. Returning blood flows through veins (4) back to the heart. Blood from the tail region passes through the kidney (5) where wastes are removed. Blood from the intestines (6) passes into the liver (7) before returning to the heart.

In fishes the kidneys are the reddish material lying just beneath the backbone and covered by the lining of the body cavity. They are not well encapsulated organs like the mammalian kidneys and are often mistaken for blood clots. The kidneys also manufacture blood cells and the anterior part of the kidney, called the head kidney, has lost its excretory function and serves only as a blood-cell manufacturing organ. Blood cells are also produced by the spleen but fishes have no bone marrow which is where some mammalian blood cells are produced.

CIRCULATORY SYSTEM

The fish heart is usually called a two-chambered heart to distinguish it from the four-chambered, two-circuit arrangement in mammals. Actually there are four chambers in the fish heart but they are in a series, so that the heart is essentially an S-shaped tube with chambers separated by valves that force the blood to flow in only one direction. Blood from the liver and the rest of the body enters the sinus venosus, is forced into the atrium, then into the ventricle which is the most powerful of the chambers. Finally it passes through the elastic-walled bulbus arteriosus into the ventral aorta.

Soon after leaving the heart the blood enters the gills, passing through a capillary network to receive oxygen and give up carbon dioxide. As a result of this the blood pressure in the rest of the body is rather low and this is one of the reasons that fish are not capable of long periods of intense activity.

D

A few fish, such as tunas and the porbeagle shark, have heat-exchanging *rete mirabile* that enable them to maintain a body temperature above that of the surrounding water.

E

Saltwater fish (1) tend to lose water by osmosis. They drink seawater and secrete excess salt through their gills. Freshwater fish (2) get rid of excess water by secreting copious dilute urine.

EYES

The aquatic environment makes special demands on the sense organs. Even in the clearest waters it is not possible to see great distances and fish eyes are essentially nearsighted. They also see a much wider field view than mammalian eyes. What little focusing is done is achieved by moving the lens back and forth rather than changing its curvature as is the case with human eyes. Fishes that are nocturnal often have very large eyes that enable them to see quite effectively in dim light, but species that live in murky environments such as muddy rivers often have quite small eyes and rely on senses other than sight. Some cave fishes have lost their sight altogether and have vestigial eyes or none at all.

SMELL AND TASTE

Chemical senses – smell and taste – are important to all fishes and are the primary senses of many, particularly those that live where there is not enough light for vision to be effective. The sense of smell is centered in the olfactory organs contained in a pair of sacs near the front of the snout. Usually there are two openings to each sac. Water is pumped in through one and out through the other, passing over the olfactory organ in the process. Some fishes, however, have only a single nostril on each side. Unlike our own nasal system, which also conveys air to the lungs, there is no internal opening to the throat. In some fishes the anterior nostrils are extended as short tubes, projecting from the snout, and in some eels both nostrils, front and back, are tubular.

Taste buds are not confined to the tongue as ours are but are found in various parts of the mouth and outside the mouth on other parts of the body as well. Both taste and smell are responses to minute amounts of chemicals and the distinction is made on the basis of which receptors respond to the stimulus.

HEARING

Hearing in fishes is quite different from that of land animals. Experiments have shown that fish are able to detect sounds from 50 to about 5,000 Hz (cycles per second), although this of course varies with the species. (For comparison, a human being normally has sensory awareness of sounds from about 16 to about 20,000 Hz and can distinguish sounds clearly in a range of about 1,000–4,000 Hz. The ability of fish to distinguish between sounds also varies widely from species to species. The goldfish, for example, which has a chain of small bones connecting the swim bladder with the middle ear, is able to distinguish between tones that are only 3.5 to 5 percent different. Other fish without the connection are not able to discriminate between such similar tones.

Fish lack both middle and outer ears. They have no eardrum, no ear ossicles, and no cochlea, and at present no one is sure exactly how they discriminate between sounds of different frequencies. The inner ear consists of three fluid-filled semicircular canals, which help the fish to detect motion, and larger sacs that contain calcarious otoliths (ear stones) that rest

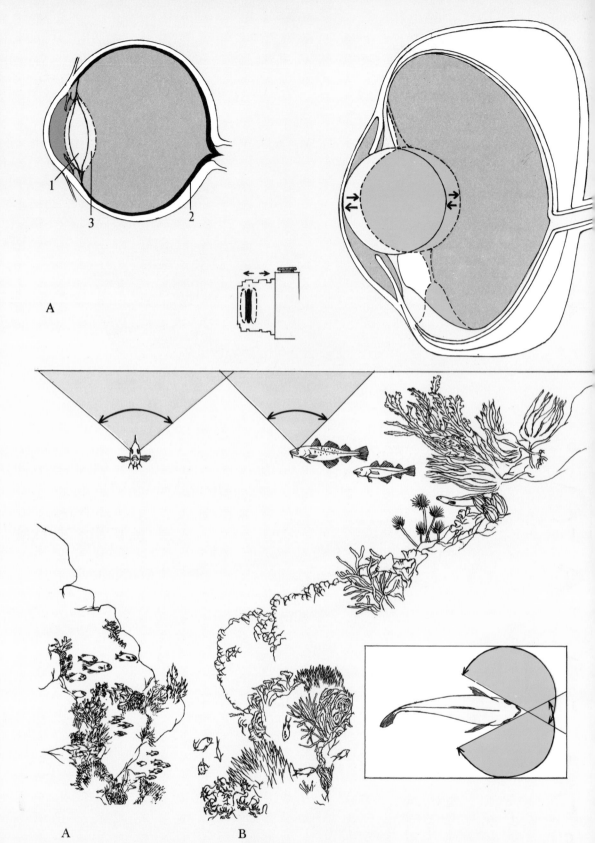

A

In the vertebrate eye light is focused by a lens (1) upon a light-sensitive membrane, the retina (2). In mammals focusing is achieved by changing the shape (3) of the lens but in fish, as in a camera, the lens moves back and forth to produce a sharp image.

B

Fishes that live in clear water and are active at night have large eyes (1) that gather light like a "fast" camera lens. Those that live in murky habitats have smaller eyes (2) and depend on other senses. Some cave fishes have lost their eyes altogether (3).

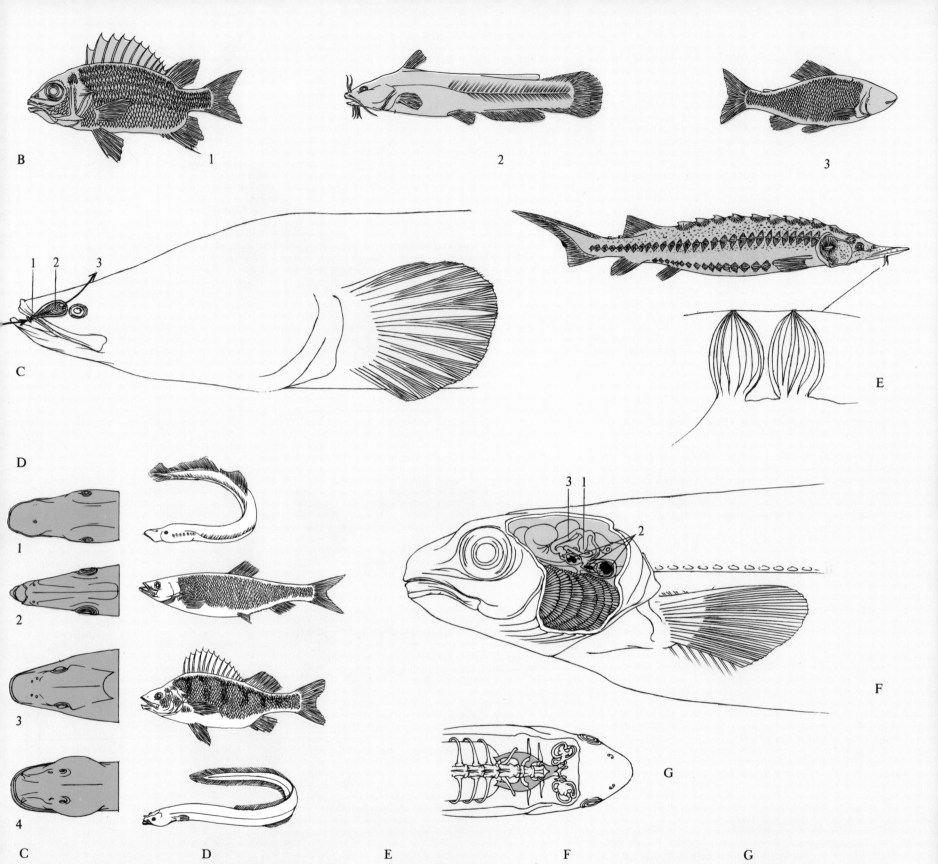

B

1

2

3

C

1 2 3

D

1

2

3

4

E

3 1

2

F

G

C

Unlike man, in fish there is no connection between the nostrils (1) and the throat. The nasal sacs are used only for the detection of odors in the water. Water is drawn in, passed over the sensitive olfactory epithelium (2), then pumped out again (3).

D

Lampreys (1) have only one nasal opening but all higher fishes have a pair of nasal sacs (2,3), each with one or two openings. Some eels (4) have elaborate tubular nostrils.

E

In many fishes taste buds are found outside the mouth as well as inside and sometimes also on the surface of the body.

F

The inner ears (1) of fish like those of man detect gravity and motion as well as sound. Stone-like otoliths (2) rest on sensory structures. As the fish tips the otolith stimulates different cells so that the fish can tell how it is oriented. There the semicircular canals (3) detect motion whichever way the fish moves.

G

The Ostariophysial fishes – catfishes, carps, characins, gymnotids, and their relatives – have a chain of small bones connecting the swim bladder with the ear. The "Weberian apparatus" enables them to detect sound vibrations in the water.

on sensory hairs and enable the fish to detect the direction of the force of gravity and thus to know what its position is with respect to gravity. These otoliths increase in size as the fish grows; when the fish stops growing during the winter months a mark is formed in the otolith. Thus these marks can be used to determine the age of the fish. They are often used for fish that have no scales or whose scales do not show clear annual marks. Of course, the fish must be killed in order to examine the otoliths.

LATERAL LINE SYSTEM

Fishes have a sixth sense in the lateral line system, a series of canals on the head and body running just beneath the surface with openings to the exterior at frequent intervals. In the bottom of the canal there are sensory spots with special structures called cupulae that respond to movement of the fluid within the canal. The function of the lateral line is to detect water movements, particularly low-frequency vibrations from a nearby source. Many fishes also have additional structures similar to the lateral line sense organs that are arranged in rows or pits on the surface of the skin but not within a roofed-over canal. Both the lateral line and the inner ear are considered parts of the hearing apparatus. Some fishes have lateral lines only on the head; others have several extra lateral line canals on the body.

SWIM BLADDERS

Even though fishes are only slightly heavier than water, they would gradually sink to the bottom unless they kept swimming were it not for the presence of the swim bladder, a gas-filled chamber in the dorsal part of the body cavity. The swim bladder is derived from the gut and is thought to represent a primitive lung that has lost its respiratory function and now serves to regulate the fish's buoyancy. A few fishes, however, still use the swim bladder for breathing atmospheric air, and many bottom-dwelling fishes have reduced swim bladders or have lost them entirely. In some deep-sea fishes the swim bladder is filled with fat rather than gas but this also serves to regulate buoyancy.

There may be an open tube, the pneumatic duct, connecting the swim bladder with the esophagus or this duct may be completely lacking. Fishes that have a pneumatic duct are physostomes; those without it are physoclists. Physostomes can gulp atmospheric air and they can also expel it through the esophagus. This enables them to move up and down in the water column rapidly without damage. Physoclists can also control the amount of gas in the swim bladder by secreting or absorbing it through special glands in the wall of the swim bladder. This, however, is a slower process and when physoclistous fish are hooked at considerable depth and brought to

A The lateral-line septem is a network of canals on the head and body, open to the outside through a series of pores (1). Vibrations and water movements are detected by hair-like cupulae (2) which cause impulses to be sent to the brain via the lateral-line nerve (3).
4 Scales
5 Lateral-line canal

B The swim bladder serves to regulate the fish's buoyancy so that it can hover in midwater without constantly swimming. In physostomous fishes (1) a pneumatic duct (2) connects the swim bladder with the gut. In physoclists (3) the duct is closed or absent. On some fishes the swim bladder serves as a lung; such swim bladders (4) are divided into

chambers to increase their surface. In some other fish the swim bladder is vibrated by special sonic muscles (5) so that it functions as a sound-producing organ.

Gas is secreted into the swim bladder by a special gas gland (6). In fishes that have no pneumatic duct, excess gas is absorbed into the bloodstream through a spot called the oval (7). A special

38

the surface rapidly the sudden expansion of the swim bladder will often force the stomach out through the mouth.

Sometimes the swim bladder serves as a sound-producing mechanism. Special muscles in the body wall or in the wall of the swim bladder vibrate rapidly to produce sounds. The swim bladder also aids in receiving sounds; it may be connected to the inner ear by a chain of bones, as in the carps, catfishes, and their allies, or by horn-like extensions of the swim bladder itself, as in sardines and certain squirrel fishes.

Sounds play an important role in many fishes in courtship, schooling, and in locating their prey. Most fish sounds occur as short pulses of sound, and it has been suggested that the pattern of these pulses can be detected and interpreted by other fishes as a kind of language.

THE FISH'S FOOD SUPPLY

Throughout its life most of a fish's activity is directed toward obtaining a more or less constant supply of food. Fishes exhibit a wide variety of food habits including some extreme specializations. Most fish are carnivorous, and although some feed on plant material there are relatively few groups of fishes that are strictly herbivorous. Usually fish are opportunistic feeders and their diet will be dominated by whatever kind of food that they can use is most available to them. Thus a fish that is a predator on other fishes may feed on one species during part of the year and on different species during the rest of the year. How and what a fish eats is largely limited by its anatomical specializations for feeding. These specializations include body form and color; the placement of the fins; size, shape, and location of the mouth; shape of the jaws, teeth, and gill rakes; and structure of the digestive tract and affiliated organs.

Herrings that feed on phytoplankton (and zooplankton) sometimes have fine elongated gill rakes that strain the plankton from the water as it passes over the gills. Gill rakes are slender bones attached to the front of the gill arches. Such fish have only to swim about with their mouths open to get their food. Often they have special sensory structures such as elaborate lateral lines on the head to enable them to detect and locate swarms of plankton.

Some fishes that feed on zooplankton do not use the straining technique; rather they chase down individual organisms – usually locating the prey visually and out-maneuvering it as it drifts past with the currents.

In order to feed effectively near the surface some species have their mouths directed upward so that the gape is near the level of the top of the head. Some freshwater fishes that feed on insects at the surface have this arrangement. Conversely many fishes that are bottom feeders, such as sturgeons, catfishes, and suckers, have the mouth on the un-

cover regulates how much of the oval will be exposed and how much gas absorbed.

Bass are surface insect feeders with upward-pointing mouths. Shape of mouth indicates:
1 Sunfish
2 Smallmouth bass
3 Largemouth bass

Halfbeak is a surface feeder, has a mouth that opens upward.

E Paddlefish's upper jaw is designed to root in the bottom for food.

F Filter feeders like herring have gill rakers that strain plankton from the water. Lateral lines on the head help to locate plankton.

G Sturgeon is a bottom feeder with the mouth placed underneath.

H Predators like the pike and houndfish have forward pointing mouths with long, sharp teeth.

I Anglerfish lies in wait to engulf fish in its upward-pointed mouth.

derside of the head, sometimes well behind the tip of the snout.

Size of the mouth, too, is correlated with food habits. Predacious carnivores tend to have larger mouths than species that feed on minute zooplankton.

Midwater piscivores usually feed by seizing their prey in a quick rush. Sometimes they come from a distance, but sometimes the predator gets close to the prey using whatever camouflage it has to avoid detection until it is too late for the prey to do anything about it. Bottom-living predators tend to stalk their prey until they are close enough to make a short rush and "inhale" their prey by suddenly drawing a large amount of water into the mouth bringing the helpless prey along with it. This latter technique is used by the tube-snouted fishes, sticklebacks, sea horses, and relatives, whose tiny mouths are at the end of elongated tubular faces. This configuration apparently allows them to aspirate their prey from a considerable distance and with great accuracy.

Bottom-dwelling fishes have a wide variety of mouth adaptations. Some have the jaw at the end of a beak so that they can reach into openings for small food particles. Surmullets have a pair of finger-like chin barbels that are used to detect and stir up sand-dwelling invertebrates. Some sand dwellers have a screen of fleshy tentacles over the mouth to act as a screen that keeps sand from entering the mouth when the fish is breathing.

TEETH

The teeth also reflect the food habits. Piscivorous species usually have slender, sharp, needle-like teeth that are effective for holding slippery prey. Plankton feeders have fine rugged teeth and those that eat shellfish have heavy molar-like teeth. There are many variations and combinations. Porgies, for example, have chisel-like teeth at the front of the jaws and blunt molariform teeth on the sides of the jaws. Sometimes the teeth are in one or two rows; often they are in patches like short bristled brushes. Fish teeth do not fit into sockets as ours do, rather they are attached directly to the surface of the supporting bones.

The arrangement of the teeth is much more complex in fishes than it is in man. Instead of a single series of teeth in each jaw there is an inner and an outer series of teeth in the upper jaw. The outer teeth are attached to the movable premaxillary bones. The inner teeth are on the prevomer in front and the adjacent palatine bones on each side. A few fish have a row of teeth down the middle of the palate and others have patches of teeth on the tongue.

In addition to the teeth at the front of the mouth, most fishes have pharyngeal teeth farther back in the throat. The upper pharyngeals are attached to the uppermost bones of the gill arches. The lower

A

Fish teeth.
1 Blade-like cutting teeth (shark and barracuda)
2 Cardiform teeth for grasping soft bodied animals (catfish)
3 Molariform teeth for crushing shelled animals (porgies)

pharyngeals are the remnants of a fifth pair of gill arches. Pharyngeal teeth are the only teeth in the carps and minnows. Like the jaw teeth they vary in form and structure according to the habits and relationships of the particular species.

Herbivorous fishes sometimes have saw-edged teeth that are useful for cutting pieces of larger plants. Those species that feed on fine filamentous algae often have very fine brush-like teeth flexibly attached to the jawbones. Freshwater fishes that feed on diatoms often have cartilaginous ridges at the edge of the jaws with which they scrape these microscopic plants from the surface of rocks. All plant-eating fishes have some type of grinding mechanism by means of which they crush the cellulose walls of the plant cells. Sometimes this is done by the pharyngeal teeth; sometimes it is done by a muscular esophageal gizzard or an especially muscular stomach.

THE DIGESTIVE TRACT

The digestive tract is divided into an esophagus and stomach (foregut), small intestine (midgut), and large intestines (hindgut), with associated liver, gall bladder, and pancreas. The pancreas is rather more diffuse than in mammals and is spread through the membranes that support the digestive tube. The fish's stomach varies from a simple curved tube to a deep blind pouch. There are a number of unrelated fishes that have no functional stomach at all. This seems to be a specialization but its significance is not clear. The midgut is not as specialized as that of mammals and mostly it is just a tube. At or near the point where the midgut joins the stomach, however, there are sometimes blind tubes numbering from one to several hundred, called pyloric caeca. They provide additional surface for the digestive processes.

The hind gut is also a straight tube, although the sharks, rays, sturgeons, and other lower fish have an auger-like spiral valve that increases the wall surface of this region of the gut.

There is a general correlation between length of the intestinal tract and food habits. Herbivorous fish tend to have a straight stomach, few or no pyloric caeca, and a long digestive tract – often several times the length of the body. Carnivores, on the other hand, tend to have short guts, a deep stomach pouch, and many pyloric caeca. There is also a tendency for the lining of the body cavity to be black in herbivores and silvery in carnivores. There are many exceptions to all of these generalizations.

Feeding is a complicated operation. The food items must be located and recognized, captured, swallowed, digested, absorbed, and the inedible parts eliminated in the feces. All of these operations have to be coordinated for it would do a carnivorous species no good at all to eat plant material that it could not digest.

4 Chisel-like teeth for cutting (sheepshead)
5 Beak-like teeth for scraping plants (parrotfish)
6 Needle-like teeth for grasping fish prey

DEFENSE MECHANISMS

At the same time the fish is finding and capturing its food it has to avoid becoming prey for something else. The most usual cause of death among fishes is predation, although this may be facilitated by disease, parasitism, injury, or degenerative changes of ageing. Few fish ever die of old age alone. Most predators are other fishes although birds, mammals, and reptiles feed on fishes in inland waters and larger invertebrates such as squids, anemones, and jellyfish are predators in the sea. For commercial and sport fish species the most important predator is man. Both structure and behavior must be correlated for a defense mechanism to be effective.

The most important defense mechanisms are the ability to outrun or outmaneuver predators, camouflage and hiding, invulnerability because of size, armor, spines which may be venomous, or unpalatability. With defense, as with feeding, the first requirement is that the fish must recognize potential danger in order to avoid it. The same sensory systems that enable the fish to detect food must also serve to warn it of danger. Because of the effectiveness of the lateral line system, fishes are quick to respond to motion in the water, either vibrations from land or movements in the water.

Fishes that are normally fast swimmers are quick to use this ability to escape predators. Slower swimmers on the other hand flee to shelter rather than attempting to outrun their attackers. Extremes of fleeing behavior are the flying fishes and marine mudfish which leave the water to avoid predators.

Fishes that do not outrun their attackers depend on hiding or camouflage to protect them from predators. The danger of being eaten is of course greatest when the fishes are resting and therefore not as alert as they are when they are actively searching for food. There are many kinds of camouflage. Fishes of the open sea tend to be dark blue above and lighter below. This is called countershading, and is almost universal in animals that live in exposed environments. The dark back matches the open sea, the lighter color of the underpart reflects more light to eliminate the shadow effect so as to render the fish inconspicuous. This is demonstrated dramatically when we watch a school of fish. They are almost invisible except when they turn, momentarily exposing the light parts. Fishes that live in near shore and freshwater environments are generally greenish or olive above rather than blue but the countershading effect is the same.

Bottom-dwelling fishes usually are colored to match their resting sites. Those that live on rocks are brownish or gray or black according to their background. Many bottom fish have fleshy skin tabs that give them the appearance of an algae-covered rock. Patterns of spots, bars, and stripes are common among fishes, these too, although seemingly conspicuous when the fish is out of water, blend in with the fish's natural environment.

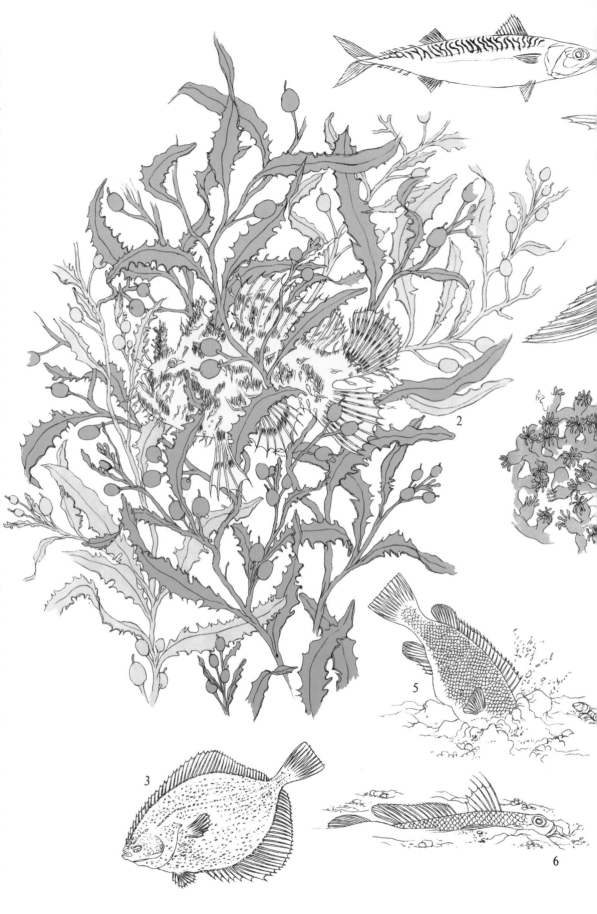

Throughout their life fish must avoid predators. Some are able to escape, like the flying fish (1), others avoid detection by camouflaging or confusing color patterns or body shapes, for example the sargassumfish (2), the flounders (3), the stonefish (4), the wrasse and the sanddwelling goby (5,6), and the blackbanded ponny-fish (7).

The sharply defined round pupil of the eye is the most difficult feature to conceal. Sometimes color patterns of dark bars or radiating lines conceal the outline of the pupil and some species have leafy appendages on the eyeball, for example, scorpionfish (8) and blenny (9). Sometimes there will be a "false eye" at the back of the fish that may confuse would-be predators, like the butterfly fish (10).

Fish that live on sand are usually hyaline or whitish in color. Many fishes, especially some of the flatfishes, have the ability to change color to match their background. This is done by redistributing pigment granules in pigment cells called melanophores. Where the granules are dispersed throughout the cells the skin appears dark – whenever the granules are concentrated near the center of the cell the skin appears pale. Other cells with red or yellow pigments and silvery granules do not have the ability to expand and contract as effectively.

One of the most difficult parts of the body to conceal is the eye. In order to be an effective light-receiving organ the retina must be dark and the edge of the pupil must be sharply defined. Since distinct lines are rare in nature the eye is always conspicuous. Many fishes have bars or lines through the eye to conceal the pupil and it is thought that distinct spots near the tail serve to confuse predators so that they aim for the wrong end of the fish, which increases the chance of escape.

SCALES

The scales and superficial head bones form a protective armor that makes fish invulnerable to attack. There are many different kinds of scales, ranging from thin bony plates deeply embedded in the skin to heavy rugged plates. The placoid scales of sharks and rays are formed like miniature teeth indeed, teeth are evolved from placoid scales. These scales have a central point attached to a tiny base plate that is embedded in the skin. There is even a central pulp cavity like that of mammalian teeth.

Primitive bony fishes have thick diamond-shaped scales called ganoid scales or a modified type called the cosmoid scale. These are distinguished by the nature and material of the different layers of the scale. Modern bony fishes have their scales made up of fibrous layers in which there are bony ridges called circuli. As the scale grows more circuli are added at the edge of the scale so that they form rings around a central area called the focus. In order that the scale remain somewhat flexible there are radial gaps in the circuli, these form lines called radii. Usually the scales overlap like shingles on a roof. Some fishes have minute teeth on the exposed part of the scale; such a scale is called a ctenoid scale and fishes with ctenoid scales like perch and basses are rough to the touch. Scales that lack such teeth are called cycloid and fish with cycloid scales are smooth to the touch. If the fish stops growing for any long period some of the circuli will be incomplete; when growth resumes the first circulus will appear to cross the incomplete segment. If this distinctive mark is correlated with a yearly event such as cessation of growth during the winter months it can be used to tell the fish's age. Such marks are called annuli. They have to be used with caution, however, because other events such as spawning, an injury or disease,

Heavy armor-like scales are excellent protection for many fishes.

A *Types of fish scales.*
  1 Puffer fish
  2 Box fish
  3 Annual growth rings
4 Perch-like fishes
5 Pike, muskellunge
B *Specialized scales of a shark are actually "skin teeth" called denticles. Scale points are aligned toward the tail.*
C *Weaver fish has a sharp spine*

projecting from the upper rear corner of the gillcover, an effective means of defense.
All fish slime is slightly toxic and serves to prevent infection. Some fishes have extra-powerful poison cells as-

or unfavorable water conditions that inhibit growth can all cause false checks. This is why it takes considerable experience to be able to determine a fish's age accurately.

Some fish have extremely modified scales. The trunk fishes of tropical waters have the scales fused into a bony case so that only the eyes, mouth, gill opening, tail, and fins can move. The porcupine fish has long points on its scales and is capable of inflating its body with air or water until it is nearly spherical with the spines radiating in all directions.

For some ways of life the presence of scales would be a disadvantage and numerous fishes have secondarily lost their scales either partially or completely. Fishes like the cod that live in close contact with the bottom tend to have smaller scales than those that swim in midwater, and burrowing fish such as eels tend to lack scales, but this is by no means a universal rule.

SPINY FINS

Spiny fins are also a deterrent to predators, particularly if there is a poison associated with them as is often the case. All fish slime is mildly toxic and in fishes such as the scorpion fishes there are special poison cells in the skin covering the fin spines. The tropical Indo-Pacific stonefish has sac-like venom glands at the base of grooved dorsal spines. This venom causes excruciating pain and, not infrequently, death, especially if the spine enters a blood vessel. The spine of the sting ray is a particularly vicious weapon. It is a modified dorsal fin spine located well back on the tail where it can be driven into any attacker that seizes or steps on the ray's body. The spine is saw toothed along both sides and also has a groove lined with poison-producing cells.

Poison glands are sometimes associated with spines on the superficial bones of the head, and the weaver fishes have venom sacs connected to hollow spines on the gill covers.

ELECTRIC ORGANS

Electric organs are defensive weapons for the torpedo rays, the African electric catfish, the electric stargazers, and the so-called electric eel of South America, which is not a true eel but is a gymnotid related to the catfishes and carps. These organs are modified muscles in all except the sternarchids, weak electric fishes from South America, whose electric organs are derived from nerves. The electric organs of the torpedo ray are modified gill muscles. In the stargazers it is the eye muscles that have given rise to the electric organs and in the electric catfish the organs are modified pectoral muscles and in all other electricity-producing fishes it is the body or tail muscles that have become specialized. The strength of the shock may range from very weak in elephant

sociated with fin spines or spines on the opercle, for example:

D *Dorsal spines of scorpion fish are hollow and can inject poison from glands under the skin into any predator seizing the fish.*

E *Sting ray carries a barbed erectile spine on its tail. Poison in a wound from the spine can cause serious pain and infection.*

fish and gymnotids to 5 volts in stargazers, 60 volts in rays, 300 volts in catfish, and more than 500 for larger electric eels.

In addition to serving as a defensive weapon electrical discharges are used by torpedo rays and catfish to stun prey. Fishes with weak electric fields use the electricity mostly for locating prey and navigation in murky waters. Disturbances to the electric fields are detected by specialized receptor organs derived from the lateral line. It has been found that many fishes have receptors but no electricity-producing organs.

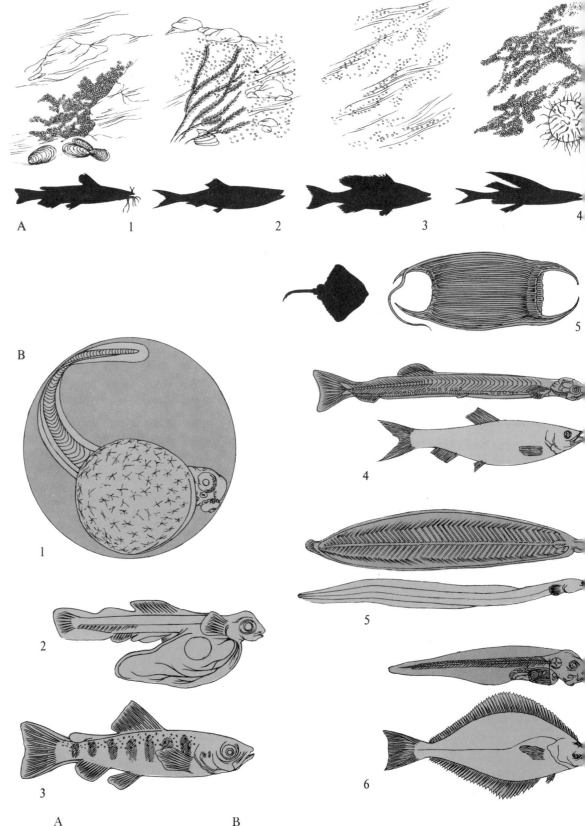

LIFE HISTORY

Fish eggs vary in size from less than .04 in (1 mm) in diameter to more than .8 in (2 cm). Perhaps the largest eggs of all are those of the living coelacanths which are known to be at least 2.8 in (70 mm) in diameter. The eggs of bony fishes are either demersal, that is, heavier than water so that they sink, or pelagic, light enough so that they are carried around by the ocean currents. Some fish eggs have sticky surfaces, others are non-adhesive so that they do not stick together or to other objects. Some eggs have special structures for flotation or attachment, and in some fishes that are live bearers there is no outside membrane. Fish eggs range from perfectly clear to completely opaque. It is believed that transparent eggs allow light radiation to pass through without damage to the egg or developing embryo. It also renders the eggs invisible to predators. Some sharks and skates lay eggs that are enclosed in horny capsules.

While the young fish is still in the egg capsule it is called an embryo; after hatching it is known as a larva. Most fish hatch before the yolk is completely consumed, and the first larval stage is then called a yolk-sac larva. Shortly before the yolk-sac disappears the young fish must begin to feed upon tiny organisms. The change is one of the most difficult periods in the fish's life.

From the time the yolk disappears until the fin rays are fully formed the fish is larva. Many fishes have extremely specialized larvae that suit them for a particular way of life. The larval stage is sometimes followed by a transitional period called the pre-juvenile stage during which the fish develops pigment and scales. When it finally assumes the shape of the adult it becomes a juvenile until it reaches adulthood as indicated by sexual maturity.

REPRODUCTION

All fishes reproduce sexually but there is considerable variety in the means by which the sexes get together. The testes are solid whitish organs usually located in the dorsal part of the body cavity between

A

Types of fish eggs.
1 Demersal, adhesive (catfish)
2 Demersal, non-adhesive (lake herring)
3 Pelagic (sea bass)
4 Eggs with filaments (flying fish)
5 Eggs in horny case (skate)

B

Baby fish.
1 Embryo ready to hatch
2 Newly hatched trout with yolk sac
3 Juvenile salmon with parr marks
4 Herring larvae
5 Leptocephalus larvae of eel
6 Flounder larvae before eye migrates

the swim bladder and the digestive tube. The sperm ducts join to form a common sperm duct that exists together with the urethra in a fleshy area immediately behind the anus. When the fish are near the time of spawning the testes become enlarged and whitish due to the presence of tailed sperm in suspension.

The external form of the female reproductive tract is similar to the testes but the ovaries are usually hollow organs. Eggs are produced in folds lining the cavity and shortly before spawning they are released into the cavity. They then travel into the common oviduct and finally exit to the outside through the area between the anus and the urinary orifice. Some fish have a well defined ovipore, others have a plug of tissue at the end of the oviduct that ruptures when the eggs are ready to be released. Sturgeons and some other lower fishes have ovaries that are not completely enclosed in membrane as we have described. In these fishes the eggs are released directly into the body cavity, then they enter the oviduct which carries them to the outside.

Fertilization usually takes place externally but fishes that bear their young alive have internal fertilization. In these species the male has some way of transferring sperm to the female. In sharks and rays this is done by a modification of the pelvic fins, but in the guppy and related species it is a specialization of the anal fin that serves this purpose. Scorpion fishes and some blennies have a fleshy penis-like modification of the urogenital area. One group of freshwater fishes even has a sperm transfer structure derived from the pelvic and pectoral fin support. Some live-bearing fishes are truly viviparous in that the young receive nourishment from the mother; others are oviparous which means that the eggs are retained by the mother until they hatch. A few fishes are normally hermaphroditic and each individual produces both eggs and sperms. Some species are male and female at the same time but it is more common for the sexes to succeed one another. Such fish are usually protogynous – female first.

Courtship ranges from mass spawnings in large schools to elaborate pairing and courting rituals. Some species such as the salmon make long migrations to the spawning grounds, others may merely move into shallower or deeper water. Similarly there is a wide range in color differences between the sexes. In some the males and female are so similar that they are identical to the human eye, others are so different that they have been classified in different genera. Similarly, while most fishes broadcast their eggs and give them no further attention, others give elaborate parental care. Several unrelated groups of fishes – catfishes, cardinal fishes, cichlids, jawfishes – practice oral brooding, the parents carrying the eggs in the mouths until they hatch. All of these specializations serve to ensure that there will be an adequate number of young to replace those that are lost through predation, disease, or plain old age.

C

Fish courtship.
1 The male largemouth bass scoops out a nest. Then he entices females to deposit eggs in it.
2 Salmons migrate upstream to spawn in gravel redds, a nest in the gravel that is dug by the female. After spawning the female covers the nest.

3 Male sticklebacks build an elaborate nest of plant parts. Then courtship takes place in an elaborate ritual.

D

Fishes that bear their young alive must have some mechanism for transferring sperm to the female's reproductive tract.
1 The modified anal fin (gonopodium) of the guppy
2 Claspers – specialization of the pelvic fin of sharks, skates, and rays
3 Fleshy "penis" of scorpion fish

FISH ASSOCIATIONS

Fish are found in nearly all natural bodies of water from torrential mountain streams to the deepest parts of the ocean. Each aquatic environment has its characteristic inhabitants depending on the habitats it offers and the part of the world in which it is located. There is no one species of fish that occurs everywhere, and this means that each species has its own geographic range within which it is restricted to certain habitats. The fisherman who is familiar with the local fauna and recognizes the habitat requirements will have the best chance of finding the species he prefers, and locating them is the first step toward catching them.

The most important factor is salinity. Most fishes are restricted to either fresh water or salt water. A few such as the salmon and the eels go back and forth during their lifetime and some spend their lives in brackish water, but most fish remain in either fresh or salt water.

Ocean fish are very much limited by temperature to a particular span of latitude – Arctic, Antarctic, north or south, temperate or tropical. Different groups of species inhabit different oceans although some particular species occur on both sides of the Atlantic and Pacific Oceans. The fishes of the Swedish coasts are in general different from those of the American and Canadian Atlantic coasts. It is not always easy to see what barriers there are in the sea, but ocean currents, temperatures, and, for shore fishes, vast stretches of open ocean prevent the fishes from intermingling.

The same principles apply to inland fishes that live in lakes and streams but here the barriers are easier to recognize. Both land masses and salt water as well as temperature limit the distribution of freshwater fish. Each continent therefore has its own distinctive fish fauna. There are, however, a number of similar species that occur in North America and Europe. The pike, *Esox lucius*, occurs in both Europe and America, the perches and rainbow smelts are only slightly different, and the walleye and zander are distinct but closely related species.

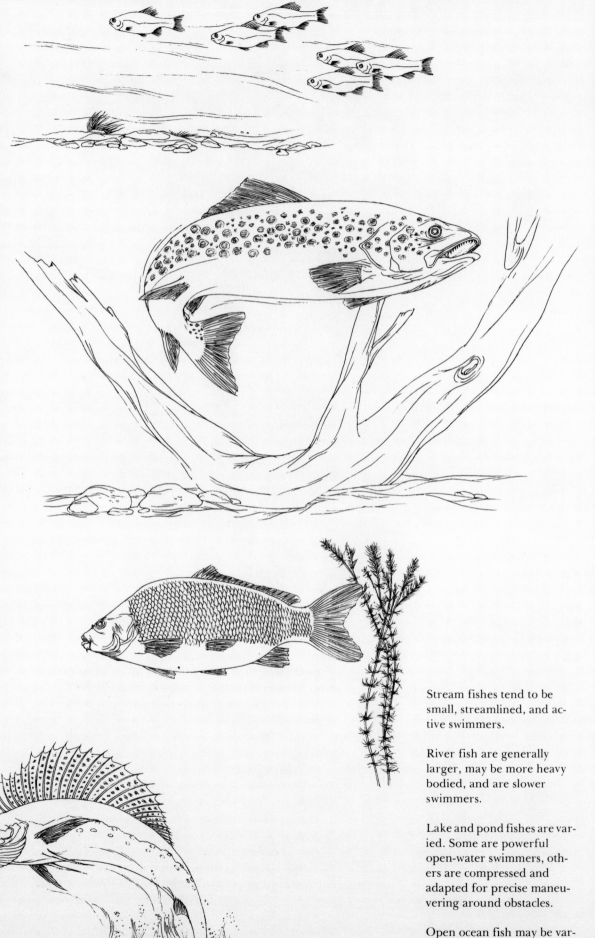

Stream fishes tend to be small, streamlined, and active swimmers.

River fish are generally larger, may be more heavy bodied, and are slower swimmers.

Lake and pond fishes are varied. Some are powerful open-water swimmers, others are compressed and adapted for precise maneuvering around obstacles.

Open ocean fish may be varied in shape but they tend to be silvery or blue in color.

FISH RECOGNITION AND DESCRIPTION

Recognizing different kinds of fishes is very much like recognizing people. For our friends and those we see every day, one quick glimpse is enough, yet how difficult it is to be sure that someone we don't know very well or haven't seen for a long time is really the person we think he is. And how very difficult it is to describe an individual to someone who has never seen that person.

Fortunately, the features that distinguish the different species of fishes are nowhere nearly as subtle as those that we use for recognizing people, and with patience and attention to small details, most fishes can be identified with great confidence. Problems, when they arise, generally stem from one of four sources: first of all, closely related species are very similar and their distinguishing features are often subtle and difficult to describe. Secondly, individuals vary. Some species change drastically during their life history so that the adults are quite different from the young. Sometimes males are quite unlike females. Many species have more than one colour phase or assume different shapes in different environments. Like people, each individual fish is unique, and some individuals may be so different as to cast doubt on their identification. Thirdly, fishes that are adapted to a particular mode of life often tend to bear a superficial resemblance to the species with which they share their habitat. Usually such resemblances won't cause difficulty if one looks carefully but at a quick glance, it can be confusing.

Finally, there are many fishes that are simply not known well enough. It is far more common than one might think for fishermen to capture species that are unknown to science. Large species that are difficult to preserve as museum specimens are especially troublesome because scientists have not been able to examine such specimens enough to evaluate the variation among individuals. Wide ranging species that look somewhat different in various parts of their range are similarly troublesome. And there are some species that are truly rare and haven't been studied thoroughly. Paradoxically, many very common species have gone unstudied simply because no one has bothered with them.

To the thinking fisherman, knowing what he has caught can be almost as satisfying as the actual catching. The fisherman who takes pains to identify his catch will find that he has learned far more than just its name. A fish without a name is just a lump of meat, but a fish with a name has personality.

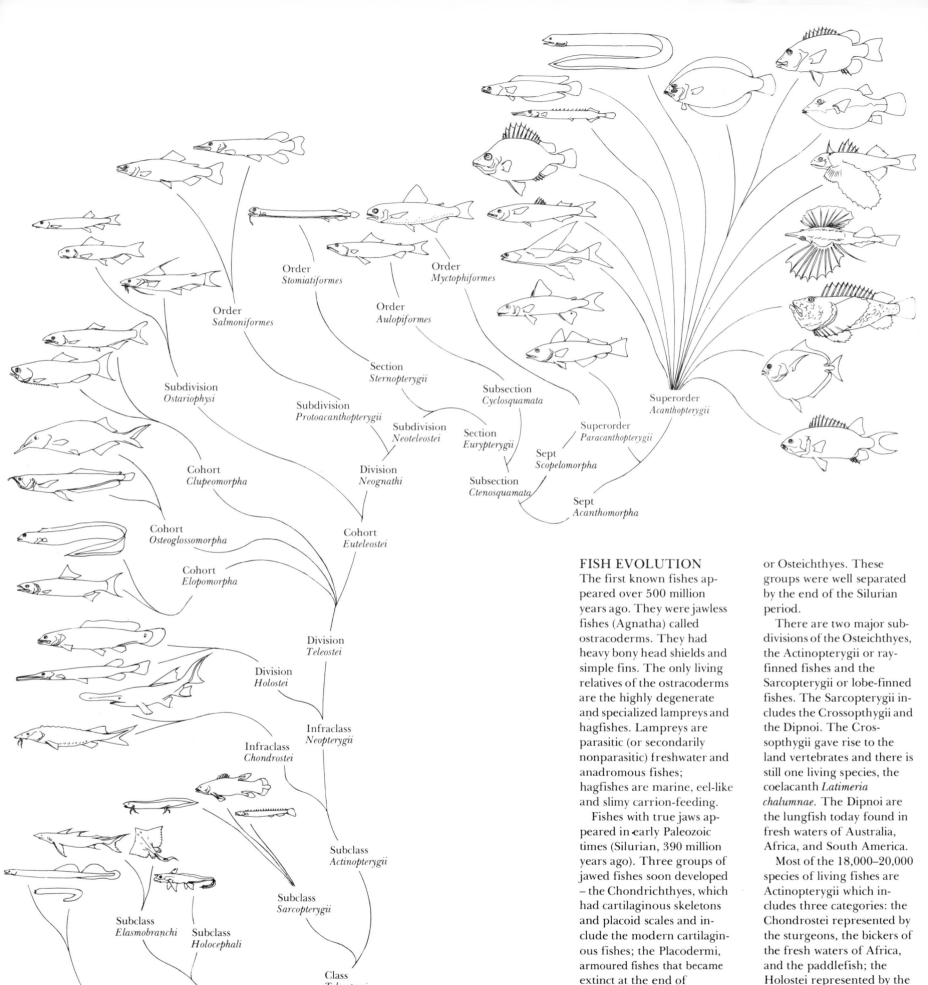

Order
Stomiatiformes

Order
Myctophiformes

Order
Salmoniformes

Order
Aulopiformes

Subdivision
Ostariophysi

Section
Sternoptergii

Subsection
Cyclosquamata

Superorder
Acanthopterygii

Subdivision
Protoacanthopterygii

Subdivision
Neoteleostei

Section
Eurypterygii

Superorder
Paracanthopterygii

Cohort
Clupeomorpha

Division
Neognathi

Sept
Scopelomorpha

Cohort
Osteoglossomorpha

Subsection
Ctenosquamata

Cohort
Euteleostei

Sept
Acanthomorpha

Cohort
Elopomorpha

Division
Teleostei

Division
Holostei

Infraclass
Neopterygii

Infraclass
Chondrostei

Subclass
Actinopterygii

Subclass
Sarcopterygii

Subclass
Elasmobranchi

Subclass
Holocephali

Class
Teleostomi

Superclass
Cyclostomata

Class
Elasmobranchiomorphi

Superclass
Gnathostomata

50   Subphylum
Vertebrata

FISH EVOLUTION

The first known fishes appeared over 500 million years ago. They were jawless fishes (Agnatha) called ostracoderms. They had heavy bony head shields and simple fins. The only living relatives of the ostracoderms are the highly degenerate and specialized lampreys and hagfishes. Lampreys are parasitic (or secondarily nonparasitic) freshwater and anadromous fishes; hagfishes are marine, eel-like and slimy carrion-feeding.

Fishes with true jaws appeared in early Paleozoic times (Silurian, 390 million years ago). Three groups of jawed fishes soon developed – the Chondrichthyes, which had cartilaginous skeletons and placoid scales and include the modern cartilaginous fishes; the Placodermi, armoured fishes that became extinct at the end of Paleozoic times; and Acanthodii – which probably shared a common ancestor with the modern bony fishes or Osteichthyes. These groups were well separated by the end of the Silurian period.

There are two major subdivisions of the Osteichthyes, the Actinopterygii or ray-finned fishes and the Sarcopterygii or lobe-finned fishes. The Sarcopterygii includes the Crossopthygii and the Dipnoi. The Crossopthygii gave rise to the land vertebrates and there is still one living species, the coelacanth *Latimeria chalumnae*. The Dipnoi are the lungfish today found in fresh waters of Australia, Africa, and South America.

Most of the 18,000–20,000 species of living fishes are Actinopterygii which includes three categories: the Chondrostei represented by the sturgeons, the bickers of the fresh waters of Africa, and the paddlefish; the Holostei represented by the North American freshwater gars and bowfin; and Teleostei which includes all of the rest of the fishes.

SCIENTIFIC NAMES

The names applied to fishes and other animals vary widely from country to country according to the language spoken and local custom. For this reason zoologists have devised an international system of naming animals under which each species is assigned a single Latin name that applies wherever that species occurs.

The scientific name consists of two words. The first is the name of the genus (plural, genera) and it is always written with a capital letter. It is like a person's family name and it indicates relationship. For example, the brown trout, rainbow trout and the Atlantic salmon all belong to the genus *Salmo* and are more similar to each other than to the charrs, which belong to the genus *Salvelinus*.

The second word is the name of the species (plural, species) and, like a person's given name it is used for one kind of animal within the genus. Note, however, that the same species name can be used for animals that belong to different genera. The specific name, which is sometimes called the trivial name, is usually a Latin adjective and must follow the rules of Latin grammar. The word itself may come from other languages or it can be coined as a new word, but in scientific nomenclature it must be treated as a Latin word.

Sometimes a species is divided into geographically separated, distinct but intergrading populations, called subspecies. Such populations can be designated by a third word which is the subspecies name. Names consisting of three word names are called trinomials and they are used just like ordinary binomial scientific names. In formal writing the scientific name (genus, species, and subspecies) is set in italic type. The name of the author, the scientist who first published a description of the species, is sometimes added but this is merely for clarity and the author's name is not part of the scientific name.

In order to serve as international language, scientific nomenclature must be as stable as possible. That is, once a name is established it should not be changed unless it is absolutely necessary. Nevertheless, this ideal stability has not been achieved and scientific names do change to the dismay of scientists and laymen alike. These changes fall into a number of categories.

First of all there are minor corrections that result from the rules of grammar. Since Latin adjectives must agree in gender with the word they modify, and it sometimes is difficult to determine the gender of a generic name, we not infrequently find changes like *Chromis cyanea* being replaced by *Chromis cyaneus*. This is a permissible correction but pure spelling errors are *not* corrected. If the original author used *crysolucas* for a name that should have been spelled *chrysoleucas*, the original, incorrect, spelling must be retained. The intent, of course, is to avoid confusion and in the long run this will be achieved best by strict application of the rules.

The author's name should not be confused with the situation in which a species is named in honor of someone. For example, the longbill spearfish is *Tetrapturus pfluegeri* (Robins and de Sylva). The species was named by C.R. Robins and D. de Sylva for Al Pflueger, a well-known Miami taxidermist. Here,

pfluegeri is part of the scientific name, and because it is a species name, it is italicized and not capitalized. Placing the authors' names in parentheses is a way of indicating that in the original description the species was considered to have belonged to some other genus. For example, the striped bonito, *Sarda sarda* (Bloch), was first described by Bloch as *Scomber sarda* (Bloch).

Another kind of change comes as a result of increased knowledge of distribution. Since there can be only one valid scientific name for a species, the general rule is that the name that was first applied to that species should be used; i.e., the oldest name stands. This is called the law of priority. Not infrequently a species is discovered and named from say, North America, and many years later it is discovered that the same species occurs in Europe where it had already been named. In such cases the older name, the European one, must be used for both the American and European population. Occasionally it is discovered that a generic name had already been used for another animal and here, too, the law of priority applies; that generic name can be used only for the animal to which it was applied first. A new name must be found for the genus that was described later.

Sometimes the person who first describes a new animal fails to recognize color phases, sex differences, or life history stages and describes a single species more than once in the same article. In this case the first person to recognize that these different names apply to the same species can choose which of the original names is to be used. This is the rule that has caused a problem with the name of the striped bass. Two American authors recognized in 1882 that *Morone* and *Roccus*, which were both proposed by Mitchill in 1814 were in fact, different names for the same genus of fishes. They selected *Roccus* but recently it was discovered that their action had been preceded by Bleeker, who in 1876 had recognized the identity but had chosen *Morone*. Thus, we have had to make the change from *Roccus* to *Morone* to the disgust of many fishermen who had come to know and like the name *Roccus*.

The third kind of change comes about when new research provides us with a better understanding of relationships, similarities, and differences. Often we find that what had been thought to be a single species is actually a complex of two or more very similar species, all but one of which will then have to have new names.

Sometimes we discover that species belonging to two different genera are so similar that it is best to put them all into the same genus, in which case, of course, the oldest name must be used.

There are other complications that arise, and most of these can be resolved by use of a set of rules called the International Code of Zoological Nomenclature. Sometimes, however, strict application of the rules causes more problems than it solves, so, under very unusual circumstances, a petition can be submitted to the International Commission on Zoological Nomenclature to set aside the rules in a particular case. The International Commission also revises the rules from time to time when there is a real need.

It must be understood that the International Commission deals only with the technicalities of ap-

plying names; they do not pass judgment on the validity of genera or species or on any other biological problem.

Many of the details of zoological scientific nomenclature seem trivial and complicated but in the final analysis scientific names are the basic language by which all information about the animals will be communicated.

THE DERIVATION OF SCIENTIFIC NAMES

Although scientific names are commonly called Latin names, they do not actually have to originate from the Latin language. In fact, as long as they are written in the Latin alphabet they can be treated as Latin words e.g., generic names as nouns; species names as modifier nouns, adjectives or possessives. Scientific names can be derived from almost any language. They can even be composed of arbitrary combinations of letters. In practice, however, most zoologists proposing names for what they believe to be a newly discovered species usually follow certain conventions.

Most frequently they will choose descriptive names that emphasize some outstanding feature of the animal such as:

SIZE

brevi- (Latin) short
macro- (Greek) large
mega- (Greek) great
micro- (Greek) small
longi- (Latin) long

SHAPE

attenuatus (Latin) weakened or reduced
belone (Greek) needlelike, sharp pointed
curvi- (Latin) curved
gibbosus (Latin) humped or bent
gracilis (Latin) slender
pachy- (Greek) thick
nema- (Greek) thread
platy- (Greek) broad, flat
symmetricus- (Greek) symmetrical
teres- (Latin) round or smooth

COLOR

alba (Latin) white
argenteus (Latin) silvery
atra (Latin) black
auratus (Latin) gold
brunneus (Latin) dark brown
caeruleus (*coeruleus*) (Latin) dark blue
chloro (Greek) green
chrysos (Greek) gold
fasciata (Latin) bundled, hence banded
glaucus (Greek) silvery
griseus (Latin) gray
leucas (Greek) white
lineatus (Latin) marked with lines
maculatus (Latin) spotted
mela, melano (Greek) black
niger (Latin) dark, black
ocellatus (Latin) with small eyes
punctatus (Latin) spotted as with punctures
ruber- (Latin) red

PARTS OF THE BODY

anal- (Latin) anus
caudi- (Latin) tail
cephalus (Greek) head
chir- (Greek) hand (fin)
gnathus- (Greek) jaw
gramma- (Greek) line
lepido- (Greek) scale
-nasus (Latin) nose
-odont (Greek) tooth
-ops (Greek) eye, aspect
pinnis- (Latin) wing
pteros- (Greek) wing
-rhynchus (Greek) beak, snout
-rostris (Latin) bill, snout
-stethus (Greek) breast
-stomus (Greek) mouth
-urus (Greek) tail
-ventris (Latin) belly

Sometimes, scientific names will denote a characteristic feature or quality of appearance such as:
acanth- (Greek) spine
call- (Greek) beatiful
elegans (Latin) elegant
ornatum (Latin) ornately decorated
osseus (Latin) bony
regalis (Latin) royal

These terms are often combined to form a com-
pound descriptive phrase such as *brevirostris* (short nose). Other common combinations used for fish are: *microcephalus* (small head), *macrophthalmus* (big eye), *biguttatus* (two spots), *albigutta* (white spots), and *altivelis* (high tail or fin). Two other endings, -oides and -iformis meaning respectively "like" and "of the form" are commonly used to indicate similarity of appearance. The ending -ifer means "bearing." Thus, *furcifer* (carries a fork) refers to the "deeply forked tail of . . . ."

Sometimes scientific names indicate the animal's geographic origin or its habitats:
americanus – of America
pacificus – of the Pacific
surinamensis – of Surinam
fluviatilis (Latin) of rivers
fontinalis (Latin) of springs
lacustris (Latin) of lakes
pelagicus (Greek) of the open sea
subterraneus (Latin) below ground

Names can also indicate the animal's habits:
saltatrix (Latin) dancing girl
petromyzon (Greek) stone sucker
volitans (Latin) flying
limnicola (Latin) mud-loving

Scientific names can be used to honor a person, such as the one who discovered the species, but not the describer of the species. By convention, one does not name a species after oneself. Friends, relatives, colleagues, teachers, early explorers, and political figures are often honored in this way.

Such names are formed by adding:

- i or *ii* to the name of a man
-orum to the name of men, or a man and a woman together
-ae to the name of a woman
-arum to the names of women

Many fish names come from ancient fish names that were used in classical times, or are derived from local common names:
Scomber (Latin) (from Greek *Skombros*) mackerel
Esox (Latin) pike
Perca (Greek) perch
Salmo (Latin) salmon
Clupea (Latin) some small river fish
Alosa (Latin) shad
Platessa (Latin) plaice
Nameycush American Indian for lake trout

While most names are straightforward, a few scientists have demonstrated a real talent for creating whimsical names and otherwise imaginative names like *Diogenichthys* for a genus of lanternfishes or *Satan* for a genus of catfish that lives underground. *Decapterus tabl*, for the redtail scad, gets its trivial name from the anagram for Tropical Atlantic Biological Laboratory under whose aegis this fish was discovered and described.

Such colorful names make our scientific nomenclature richer and easier to master. These names often reveal a lot about the describers themselves, thus humanizing what is otherwise a routine subject.

INTRODUCTION TO FISH DESCRIPTIONS

One of the problems of fishermen and students of fishes is to be able to differentiate among the many species of fish which, at last count, were estimated to exceed 21,000 in number. Unfortunately the illustration of a fish is not always sufficient in itself. Many species have similar appearances, and within a single species physical characteristics and general coloration may be variable. In some instances, such as among the grouper and wrasse families, an individual fish is able to change color rapidly in order to adapt to a new background or emotional situation.

As an international guide to sport fishes the following descriptions lay no claim to being exhaustive. Their purpose is primarily to provide anglers everywhere, as well as others interested in fishes, with sufficient basic characteristics to assist in the accurate identification of the various well-known species that have been selected, and to provide brief essential background information. Technical language has been avoided wherever possible. Some of the fishes selected are not strictly sport fishes, but nevertheless are well represented in sport catches. A number of species are included because they are useful as bait. Others have been chosen because of special characteristics that give them broad general interest.

The selection of species has been guided by the following factors:
General sporting and/or food qualities of fish.
Frequency of occurrence in sporting catches.
Need for careful identification between species with similar appearances.
Need for key species that may be used as a guide to closely related forms.
The need to describe fish that have unusual or especially attractive characteristics.

A plan for the presentation of each species was developed that appears to be the most concise and readable way to present the necessary information to sport fishermen and interested lay readers. It does not strictly follow the usual arrangement of facts used by fisheries biologists and zoologists. Information in the descriptions is set out in the following order:
Common name: The international name with the widest accepted usage, or; for localized species, the local name considered to be most widely used.
Scientific name: The genus and trivial Latin names now generally accepted. In recent years there has been considerable changing of scientific names. Only one scientific name can be correct at a given time. The utmost care has been used to assign the correct scientific name to each species, reflecting present scientific acceptance.
Other common names: Additional international and local names in common usage.
Habitat: The following symbols are used:
"F" for fresh water
"B" for brackish water
"S" for salt water
"Anadromous" means that the species spends its adult life at sea, but ascends freshwater rivers to breed, the young returning to the sea when sufficiently developed.
Features: General body shape and appearance. Fins, number and kind, spines and soft rays, etc., as by the

following established practice:

The count of *spines* is given in Roman numerals;
example: 10 spines is written X.

The count of *soft rays* is in Arabic numerals;
example: 6 soft rays is written 6.

A comma is used to denote the separate spine and soft ray counts in a single fin;
example: a fin with 5 spines and 11 soft rays is written V,11.

A dash between two sets of fin-ray counts denotes a separation into two fins, as in dorsal fins;
example: a pair of dorsal fins with 9 spines followed by a break and a second dorsal with 14 soft rays would be written as IX-14.

Coloration: The dorsal area or back of the fish, the flanks or sides, and the belly or ventral parts of the fish, spots, blotches, bars, stripes, or other special markings. The presence of the lateral line and the scale count along the lateral line, where appropriate.

Size: Average and maximum length and/or weight ranges, given in imperial system followed by metric.

Distribution: Known national and international occurrences, special local notes where applicable.

General: Additional brief information. Some fishes are dealt with more fully than others. This is because of their important sport, commercial, or table interest, or because their biology and behavior merit additional description.

For easy reference, each fish, its illustration and description, have been given the same number. An alphabetical list of all the fishes in the book can be found in the appendix with references to fish and illustration number, and to the page on which it is to be found.

It must be emphasized that a great deal remains to be learned about fishes. Fishermen are much more numerous than fishery biologists. Sport fishermen are now invading every ocean and waterway and can provide useful observations about species that are relatively unknown to science. But to be useful to biologists, information must be in a standard form that meets the requirements of scientific procedures. Familiarity with the ways that observations of fish are made and recorded will prepare sport fishermen to help biologists when the opportunities arise. These fish descriptions are designed to train sport fishermen in some of the basic information-recording methods in a manner that will increase their knowledge of fish and enjoyment of this book.

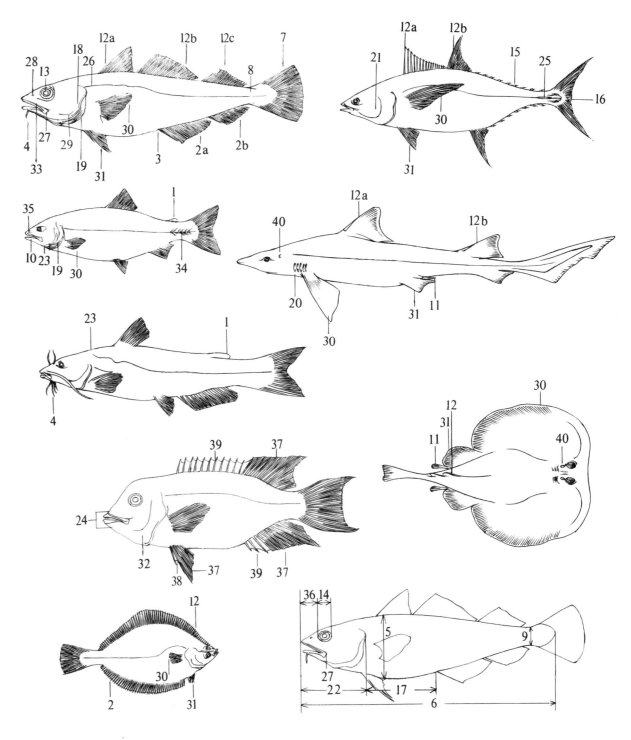

EXTERNAL FEATURES OF THE FISH

1 Adipose fin
2 Anal fin
a 1st anal fin
b 2nd anal fin
3 Anus, vent
4 Barbel, feeler
5 Body depth
6 Body length, standard length
7 Caudal fin
8 Caudal peduncle
9 Depth of the caudal peduncle
10 Chin
11 Clasper
12 Dorsal fin

a 1st dorsal fin
b 2nd dorsal fin
c 3rd dorsal fin
13 Eye
14 Diameter of eye
15 Finlets
16 Fork
17 Trunk length
18 Gill cover
19 Gill membranes
20 Gill slits
21 Head
22 Head length
23 Isthmus
24 Jaws
25 Keel (on sides of tail stalk)
26 Lateral line
27 Maxillary
28 Nostrils

29 Operculum
30 Pectoral fin
31 Pelvic or ventral fin
32 Preopercle
33 Premaxillary
34 Scutes
35 Snout
36 Snout length
37 Soft rays
38 Spine
39 Spiny rays, spines
40 Spiracle

THE ARRANGEMENT OF THE SPECIES ACCOUNTS

To be faced with more than six hundred fishes all at once is discouraging to the extreme, but fortunately, living organisms have evolved in such a way that they can be arranged into distinctive groupings, members of which are immediately recognizable by one or more special features or by a particular combination of characteristics.

The fishes treated here could, of course, have been arranged in alphabetical order or perhaps according to some numbering system, but this would have meant that related species would have been scattered and comparisons would have been difficult or impossible to make. The herrings, for example, would have been dispersed from "A" for anchovy to "W" for wolf herring.

The grouping used here is specially designed for, and therefore unique to, this book. Some groups include only a single family; others include two or more orders, each of which includes a number of families. The chief criteria used for limiting the groups are:
1. The fishes must be related.
2. They must look similar so that they can be assigned to the group unequivocally.
3. The groups must be small enough to be useful.

None of these objectives has been totally achieved simply because the fishes do not conform to our concepts of ready recognition.

(See Table of Contents for page numbers)

1 LAMPREYS, HAGFISH

The only living jawless fishes are the lampreys and the hagfishes. They are eel-shaped with no paired fins and no jaws. Lampreys have seven pairs of gill openings; hagfishes have five to fourteen or only one. Both are highly specialized relics of the most primitive group of fishes.

2 SHARKS, RAYS, SKATES

This group includes the sharks, skates, and rays. The species have cartilage skeletons and toothlike scales. There are five (very rarely 6 or 7) pairs of external gill openings, which are not always obvious in rays. The tail is strongly upturned and the fin rays are numerous and close-set. Sharks are torpedo-shaped with gill slits above the level of the pectoral fin. The rays and skates are flattened, round, or diamond-shaped with the gill slits below the level of the pectoral fin. This group also includes the chimaeras, specialized cartilaginous fishes with a single gill opening.

3 COELACANTH, STURGEONS, PADDLEFISH, GARS, BOWFIN

Several distinct primitive species are placed together here because even though they are very different from one another, they are still more divergent as a group from the rest of the living fishes. This group includes the sturgeons which are recognizable by their upturned tail and sharklike fins, as well as by the bony plates along the body. Also in this group are the heavily armored gars and the distinctive North American bowfin. The paddlefishes, which are merely specialized sturgeons, belong in this same group, along with the coelacanth, the African bichirs and the lungfishes.

4 BONY-TONGUE FISHES: ARAPAIMA, MOONEYE, LEACH

Bony tongues and featherbacks. Although the mooneye and goldeye superficially look like herrings, they are actually members of a widespread group of fishes that also includes the South American Aruana and Arapaima, the African leaches, the Indo-Australian Scleropages, and the featherbacks which have a huge anal fin and a tiny dorsal.

In spite of their external differences, their relationship is clearly indicated by skull and gut structure.

5 BONEFISH, TARPON, EELS

The bonefish, tarpons, and ladyfishes are highly prized for their wariness and fighting qualities and it comes as a surprise to find out that they are related to eels. Nevertheless, the distinctive larval form called the leptocephalus as well as other anatomical peculiarities indicate their close affinity.

6 HERRINGS, SARDINE, SHAD

The shads, herrings, and their allies are characterized by their bright silvery scales, schooling habits, and lack of an adipose dorsal fin. Their relatives, the anchovies and the wolf herring, are allied with them by more fundamental anatomical characteristics such as the structure of the lateral line system.

7 SALMONFISHES, SALMON, TROUT, SMELT, WHITEFISH

The salmons, charrs, whitefishes, grayling, and smelts are all streamlined fishes with well-developed adipose dorsal fins. They are freshwater or anadromus fishes. The silver smelts are marine fishes.

8 PIKES

This is a small group of arrow-shaped predaceous freshwater fishes with the snout prolonged and flattened and the jaws like a duck's bill. The soft-rayed dorsal and anal fins are far back on the body.

9 CATFISHES, CARPFISHES, MINNOWS

Members of this seemingly diverse group are united by the possession of a Webrian apparatus, a chain of bones connecting the swim bladder with the ear. Externally, the fishes belonging to this group are diverse, ranging from the naked catfishes and the electric eel to the minnows, carps and characins.

10 CODFISHES, ANGLERFISH, SARGASSUMFISH

Cods, anglers and their relatives are included in this diverse group of soft-rayed fishes whose relationship is established by certain modifications of the jaw muscles and the skeleton.

11 FLYING FISHES, HALF-BEAKS, GARS, NEEDLE-FISH, KILLIFISH

This group includes the killifishes and the live-bearing tooth carps of the aquarist's tanks as well as halfbeaks, needlefishes, flying fishes and silversides, or whitebait. Some members have spiny dorsal fins; others do not.

12 JOHN DORY, OARFISH, STICKLEBACKS

Several small groups of primitive spiny-ray fishes are considered together here. The berycoid fishes, the opah and the oarfishes the sticklebacks, seahorses and allies, and the dories all represent

separate orders without the typical features of more advanced perchlike fishes.

13 SCULPINS, REDFISHES, GURNARDS, FLATHEADS

The fishes included here have a peculiar bony brace connecting the bones that surround the eye with the preopercle. For this reason, they are sometimes called the mail-cheeked fishes. Often the head is heavily armored or equipped with sharp spines. Mail-cheeked fishes have some codlike features and many perchlike characteristics.

14 SNOOKS, NILE PERCH, BARRAMUNDI

A small distinctive family of spiny-rayed fishes with a dark lateral line, well separated dorsal fins and a characteristic head shape.

15 GROUPERS, SEA BASSES, FLAGTAIL

The basses are a diverse group with typical perciform features such as thoracic pelvic fins, each consisting of 1 spine and 5 rays, heavy rough scales, a well-developed spiny dorsal fin and the pectoral fin bases well up on the side of the body and nearly vertical.

16 PERCHES, ZANDERS

Freshwater fishes of the Northern Hemisphere with one or two anal spines and a deep notch or separation between the spiny and soft parts of the dorsal fin. In addition to the larger species listed here, there are more than 100 species of tiny, often colorful perches called darters in North American waters.

17 FRESHWATER BASSES, SUNFISHES, CRAPPIES

Native only to North America (and with one exception, confined to the region east of the Rocky Mountains), the family Centrarchidae includes the sunfishes and the largemouth, spotted, and smallmouth basses also sunfishes and crappies. They are exceptional sport fishes and have been widely introduced outside of their natural range.

18 PORGIES, SEA BREAMS

Porgies (Sparidae) are a distinct family of deep-bodied fishes with incisorlike and often molariform crushing teeth in the jaws.

19 TILEFISH

Several distinctive small families of fishes are considered here. Although each is a compact group in its own right, there is no strong evidence of affinity between them or with other spinyrayed families.

20 JACKS, POMFRETS, POMPANOS

Jacks and the related bluefish, cobia, dolphins, and remoras (each of which are assigned to separate families) are powerful and maneuverable fishes adapted for predaceous habits.

21 SNAPPERS

The true snappers, Lutjanidae, are bottom-dwelling predators of warm seas with a characteristic shape and frequently with fanglike, caninelike teeth at the front of the jaws. The triple tail, Labotidae, is a circumtropical species often found drifting at the surface. The Indo-Pacific families Nemipteridae and Lethrinidae are quite similar and can be confused with the true snappers. The family Arripidae of the Southern Hemisphere appears to be related to this group.

22 GRUNTS

A group of colorful tropical shore fishes with a few species that enter river mouths.

23 CROAKERS, WEAKFISHES, DRUMS, KINGFISHES

The family Sciaenidae is characterized by having the lateral line extending to the tip of the middle rays of the tail fin. These are marine fishes of coasts and estuaries. There is one species in the freshwaters of North America. Some species are adapted for feeding on molluscs and invertebrates; others, such as the sea trout, are predaceous. Fishes in this group are wellknown sound producers.

24 SURFPERCH, LUDERICK, SWEEP

These are compressed, deepbodied fishes with small mouths.

25 CICHLIDS, TILAPIA

The freshwater cichlids, including the Tilapia and Tucunare are easily recognized by their interrupted lateral line. The damselfishes are similarly shaped marine counterparts. Whether the resemblance indicates a close relationship or not is uncertain.

26 MULLETS, BARRACUDAS

Elongated marine fishes with well-separated dorsal fins. Mullets feed on plants and detritus; barracudas are well-known predators.

27 WRASSES, WEEVERS, WOLFFISHES, BLENNIES, SANDEELS

Here again we have grouped together a number of distinctive families that are not particularly closely related.

28 MACKERELS, BONITOS, TUNAS, MARLINS

These open water, efficient and streamlined fishes such as the mackerels and the billfishes (Scombridae) have one or more finlets behind the dorsal and anal fins. Related families are the Stromateidae (butterfishes) and the Trichiuridae (cutlass fish).

29 PLAICE, FLOUNDERS, SOLES, TURBOTS

Distinctive fishes with both eyes on the same side of the body.

30 TOADFISHES, TRUNKFISHES, TRIGGERFISHES

These highly specialized fishes are characterized by a reduced number of vertebrae and reduction or loss of the pelvic fins. This group includes the triggerfishes and filefishes, the puffers and their allies, as well as the very distinctive ocean sunfish.

1 LAMPREYS, HAGFISH

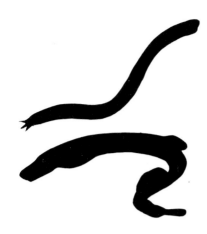

1 LAMPERN; RIVER LAMP-REY F, S, B, (anadromous)
Lampetra fluviatilis

Features: Eel-like body, thickened forward and tapering toward the tail. Oval-shaped sucker-mouth with numerous conical teeth in a characteristic concentric pattern, 7 pairs of gill slits behind the eye. Soft, cartilaginous skeleton. Two dorsal fins which are often connected during the breeding season; the second dorsal fin is separated from the tail by a notch. Coloration: dorsally bronze brown, paling on flanks with greenish hues, but coloration very variable, and fish newly arrived from the sea are golden; belly whitish.
Size: Up to 20 in (50 cm).
Distribution: Western Europe along coasts and in rivers and lakes.
General: The lampern spawns in freshwater rivers and has similar biology and feeding habits to the sea lamprey.

In some areas it is an important commercial species caught by traps or nets. In countries surrounding the Baltic it is much esteemed as a valuable Epicurean table fish and may be eaten cured, smoked, stewed, or fried.

2 SEA LAMPREY S, F
Petromyzon marinus

Features: Eel-like body, cylindrical in front section, compressed behind. Oval shaped sucker-mouth with numerous conical teeth in concentric series; 7 pairs of gill slits starting just behind the eye. Soft, cartilaginous skeleton. Two dorsal fins; a notch between second dorsal and small tail fin; no anal fin. Coloration: dorsally and flanks bluish brown or olive brown to yellow grey and mottled with blackish, confluent patches; belly whitish. General coloration brighter at spawning time with yellowish hues.
Size: Up to 36 in (90 cm).
Distribution: North Atlantic, ranging from southwest Greenland to northern Florida, in west; northern Norway, Iceland, to southern Spain and into the Mediterranean as far east as the Adriatic Sea, in east; including English Channel, North Sea, and Baltic; landlocked in North American Great Lakes.

General: The sea lamprey spawns in the freshwater region of rivers. It matures at sea, but returns to freshwater rivers to breed. The North American Great Lakes population does not go to sea. Predatory on many species of food and game fish. No sport or commercial value to speak of.

3 HAGFISH S
Myxine glutinosa
Other common names: Borer, sucker, slimefish.

Features: One continuous fin fold on the back and around the tail, eyes not visible externally. Eel-like shape, lack of paired fins and jaws, scaleless skin and a completely cartilaginous skeleton. The mouth is lipless and flanked by a pair of barbels while two additional pairs of barbels surround the single nostril at the tip of the snout. Mouth is star-shaped in outline when closed. Evertible tongue studded with rows of horny, rasp-like teeth and a series of mucous sacs on either side of the abdomen. Single gill pore on each side, just forward of the origin of the ventral finfold. Coloration: variable with bottom, greyish brown to a reddish brown above, variously suffused, mottled with dark or pale grey, brown, or bluish; whitish or pale grey below.
Size: Recorded at almost 36 in (90 cm) but generally half that size.
Distribution: Arctic seas and both coasts of the North Atlantic; Murmansk Coast and northern Norway south regularly to the Irish Sea; northern part of Davis Strait south to Cape Fear in North Carolina on the North American coast. Found also in the Southern Hemisphere in similar or the same forms.
General: Found on the bottom in soft mud in fairly cool temperatures. Scavenger rather than a true parasite. Bores into the body cavities of dead fish, eating out intestines first and then the meat, leaving nothing but a bag of skin and bones. Damages haddock, hake and cod plus other species commercially valuable. Pours out slime from its mucous sacs in quantity out of all proportion to the size of the fish. No commercial or sporting value; considerable nuisance to the commercial fisheries.

2 SHARKS, RAYS, SKATES

4 SIX-GILLED SHARK S
Hexanchus griseus
Other common names: Griset, brown shark, Mediterranean shark.

Features: This big, long and slender shark is characterized by having six gill slits on each side. Round, blunt snout; large eyes. The mouth is large, the teeth in the lower jaw are pointed and serrate, those in the upper jaw have strong spines. The single dorsal fin is placed far backwards over the interval between the ventral fins and the small anal fin. The upper lobe of the tail fin is very long and deeply notched. The pectoral fins are large and broad. Coloration: back and sides dark brownish or almost black, belly paler; a lighter stripe along the sides continues right to the end of the tail fin.
Size: Attains a length of 16 ft (5 m), but one fish of 26 ft (7–8 m) is recorded.
Distribution: Atlantic Ocean from Scotland into the Tropics. Mediterranean Sea and the West Indies. Australasia.
General: This deep-water shark is rather common between 100 and 550 fathoms (200–1000 m). The food is mainly fish and crustaceans. It is oviparous with up to 50–100 young in a litter.

5 SEVEN-GILLED SHARK S
Heptranchias perlo
Other common name: Perlon.

Features: Slender body. Long, pointed snout; seven long gill slits on each side. Mouth with large teeth. The single dorsal fin is placed far backwards over the anal fin. Upper lobe of tail fin long, lower short. Coloration: back and sides brown to grey, belly with lighter colours, the back may, mostly in smaller individuals, have many small, black spots.
Size: Reaches a length of 10 ft (3–4 m); larger individuals are reported.
Distribution: Mediterranean and adjacent parts of the Atlantic. Other species of seven-gilled sharks are known from the Indian and Pacific Oceans.
General: This large shark with its big teeth is

reported to be dangerous to man. Its food consists mainly of larger fish.

6 FRILLED SHARK S
Chlamydoselachus anguineus
Other common name: Frill shark

Features: Very slender, eel-like body. Rounded head with large mouth; the teeth are placed in transverse rows of 5 teeth, each tooth with 3 sharp points. Six gill slits; their edges form collar-like flaps, the foremost of them are united under the throat. The ventral fins, the dorsal and the anal fin are placed far back, the two latter just in front of the large tail fin; the upper lobe of the tail fin is pointed and not notched. Coloration: dark brown to greyish, with paler belly; a dark streak along the side.
Size: Up to 6 ft ($1^3/_4$–2 m).
Distribution: Northeastern Atlantic from Norway to Madeira, reported also from Japan; is possibly cosmopolitan.
General: Caught in depths of 100–600 fathoms (100–1100 m). The main food is fish.

7 BLACK-TIPPED SHARK S
Carcharhinus limbatus
Other common names: Small blacktip, lesser blacktipped shark, spinner. (The last name is more often applied to the large blacktipped shark).

Features: Dorsal fin begins above or slightly forward of the anal fin. The upper teeth are erect; the lowers have slightly outward-pointing tips. All have finely serrated edges. Several other sharks share the black-tipped fin characteristic, including the rather similar large blacktip shark, *C. maculipinnis*. *C. limbatus* can be distinguished by the lack of a dermal ridge along the centre of the back. The first dorsal is medium sized, sloping moderately backward. The pectorals are of moderate size. The pelvic fins are small, as are the second dorsal and anal fins. The upper lobe of the tail is much larger than the lower. There are five short, curved gill slits.
Coloration: Black tips on the pectoral, dorsal, and anal fins, and the lower lobe of the tail, are particularly noticeable in younger fish, but retained throughout life. Body is dark grey, grey-bronze, or ash-blue above, pure white with possible yellowish tinge below. A band of the dark upper body colour extends along each side.
Size: 5–6 ft (150–180 cm), 70 lb (32 kg) on the average. Some fish larger.
Distribution: Throughout the tropical Atlantic from Madeira to the Cape Verde Islands and from southern Brazil to Cape Cod. Common in the Bahamas, southern Florida, and the Gulf of Mexico. Also reported in Indo-Pacific waters from Baja California to Peru, and possibly in the Indian Ocean.
General: An active, swift shark, usually found in schools. It frequently jumps clear of the water, sometimes with a spinning motion. Feeds on small fish and will strike readily at prepared baits or some artificial lures. Not highly regarded as food, but a game fighter on sporting tackle.

8 BULL SHARK S, F
Carcharhinus leucas

Other common names: Ground shark, cub shark, nigrone, fresh water shark, tiburon.

Features: The snout is broadly rounded and very short. Dorsal profile of the moderately stout body is more convex than the ventral profile. Back has no dermal ridge. First dorsal is much larger than the second and has a broadly rounded apex. Anal fin is placed considerably closer to the pelvic fins than to the tail. Skin is rough to the touch when stroked from tail to head. The small eye is circular with a width less than one-fifth of the distance between the inner corners of the nostrils. Broadly triangular upper teeth with both edges coarsely serrated from tip to base. Lower teeth have narrow triangular cusps on broad bases, and stand almost erect at the front of the jaw and only partially oblique at the corners. Lower lobe of the tail is less than half as long as the upper, which has a slightly convex leading margin and rounded tip. Base and free rear corner of anal fin are about as long as those of the second dorsal. Pelvic fins have nearly straight leading edges and slightly concave trailing margins. Pectoral fins measure nearly as long as the length of the head from tip to point of pectoral origin, and are half as broad as long.
Coloration: Shades from dark grey on the back to white on the belly, but individuals may vary as to exact shading, depending on environmental conditions. No conspicuous fin markings.
Size: Up to 10 ft (300 cm), 440 lb (200 kg).
Distribution: Primarily in western Atlantic from southern Brazil north to Cape Hatteras and occasionally to New York. A landlocked subspecies occurs in fresh water lakes and rivers of Guatemala and Nicaragua. Reported, but not confirmed, from Algeria and tropical West Africa. Indo Pacific.
General: An abundant shallow water shark frequenting harbours, bays, and estuaries. Normally considered to be a sluggish scavenger, but takes bait readily. Slow, but powerful fighter on sporting tackle. Reputed to be dangerous to man in salt and fresh water. Edible if one is hungry enough.

9 SANDBAR SHARK S, B
Carcharhinus milberti

Features: Body is rather stout with a strongly arched dorsal profile. There is a low dermal ridge extending rearward down the centreline of the back behind the first dorsal, but not quite to the second dorsal. The first dorsal is large and placed far forward with its origin about over the middle of the base of the pectoral fin. The second dorsal has a free rear margin about as long as its base. The head is about one-quarter of the total length or slightly less, with a broad, oval snout that sharpens to a rounded point at the forward tip. The eye is small and circular. The five gill slits are practically straight and evenly spaced. Upper teeth are broad, triangular, with edge serrated from base to tip. The second dorsal originates over the origin of the anal fin, is considerably lower than the first with a slightly concave rear margin. Tail is slightly more than one-quarter of

total length, the tip narrowly rounded. The upper lobe is more than twice as long as the lower.
Coloration: Varies from brown through grey-brown to slate grey above with the belly shading to white. No conspicuous marks on the fins. May show a flush of bright blue when fresh-caught.
Size: Averages about 7 ft (210 cm), 130 lb (60 kg).
Distribution: Temperate to tropical Atlantic waters including western Atlantic from northeastern U.S.A. through Caribbean and Gulf of Mexico to Brazil; eastern Atlantic from Iberian Peninsula, Mediterranean, the Canary and Cape Verde Islands.
General: Commercially valuable; liver yields oil and vitamins, skin is sought for leather and was once used as a substitute for sandpaper.
Plentiful in many coastal areas, it is relatively harmless to man and locally popular with sport fishermen who fish for it in the 10–30 fathom (5–15 metres) depth range. Edible, but not popular as seafood.

10 SILKY SHARK S
Carcharhinus falciformis

Other common names: Sickle shark, silky, dusky, cazon de playa, wharf shark, sandbar shark.

Features: Long snout, elongate body with the first dorsal fin placed halfway between the pelvic and pectoral fin vertical lines. Pectoral fins quite long in adults with inner and outer margins curved. A dermal ridge is apparent on dorsal midline between the dorsal fins. Second dorsal and anal fins are only half as high as they are long. The large eye has a diameter of one-third the distance between the nostrils. Snout is broadly rounded at the tip. Pelagic in habits. Coloration: Black, dark grey, or grey-brown above, shading to white below. Tips of pectoral fins are shaded with black or dusky colour, especially in smaller sharks. Fin shading disappears with maturity. Skin is quite smooth.
Size: Up to 10 ft (300 cm), 440 lb (200 kg).
Distribution: Warmest parts of the Atlantic and tropical eastern Pacific.
General: Usually found offshore, but some are taken on reefs and near shore. Eats squid, crabs, and other slow, small fish. Sometimes runs in schools of one sex only. Young born alive, up to 2 ft (60 cm) long. Little commercial or sport value, not prized as food.

11 DUSKY SHARK S
Carcharhinus obscurus

Other common name: Dusky ground shark.

Features: Moderate to large body. Broadly rounded snout; broad, deep head and large mouth; upper teeth triangular-shaped and broader than lower ones. Five gill slits, first two over base of long pectoral fin. Two dorsal fins; first triangular, second small and above small anal fin; tail fin, upper lobe long and notched. Coloration: dorsally greyish brown or leaden; flanks paler; belly white or greyish white.
Size: Up to 140 in (350 cm), 400 lb (180 kg).
Distribution: Western Atlantic from Georges Bank off Massachusetts and south to Brazil.

General: An offshore species of relatively little sporting interest.

12 SPINNER SHARK S
Carcharhinus maculipinnis

Other common names: Blacktip, greater blacktip, spinner.

Features: Among the smooth-backed sharks, *C. maculipinnis* most closely resembles the related lesser blacktip, *C. limbatus* (which see). Distinguishing characteristics include smaller eyes, relatively longer upper labial furrows and gill slits, the more slender free rear tip of the second dorsal fin, and the smooth edges of the lower teeth, which are serrated in *limbatus*. The body is moderately slender, tapering forward and to the rear. Midline of the back is smoothly round with no trace of a dermal ridge. The close-packed and evenly overlapping dermal denticles almost completely conceal the skin. Their slightly raised tips cause the body to feel rough when stroked from tail toward head. The head is less than one-quarter of the body length and slightly flattened. Snout is ovate, thin-lipped, with a narrowly rounded point. The circular eyes are noticeably small. The upper teeth have narrow, triangular cusps with finely serrated edges. Tips of teeth are smooth-edged. Cusps of lower teeth are more slender than those of the uppers, on very broad bases, smooth edges. Origin of first dorsal fin lies slightly behind the inner corner of the pectoral fin. Its tip is narrowly rounded. The second dorsal originates over the anal fin and has a free rear tip about as long as the fin base, and quite slender. Upper lobe of the tail is much larger than the lower, is slender with a narrow, rounded tip. Coloration: Light to dark grey above, white below, a faint dark band along the sides from tail toward pelvic fin. Tip of lower caudal, second dorsal, and under surfaces of the pectorals marked with black. Tip of the first dorsal touched with black.
Size: Up to 8 ft (240 cm), 330 lb (150 kg).
Distribution: Cuba, Puerto Rico, and both coasts of Florida with little other range reported. Indo Pacific.
General: A predacious shark, feeding on small fishes, squids, etc, possibly dangerous to man. No commercial value, but occasionally taken by accident or design by sportsmen. Flesh is indifferent as food. Skin was once actively sought as a substitute for sandpaper in carpentry.

13 GREY WHALER SHARK S, B, F
Carcharhinus menisorra

Features: Moderately robust body. Snout flat and acute; upper teeth broadly serrated and notched, lower teeth narrower with a smooth base. Five gill slits, fourth is longest, and the fifth is above the pectoral fin base. First dorsal fin much larger than second. Coloration: dorsal area and flanks grey; pectoral fin tips are blackish.
Size: Up to 7 ft (2.10 m).
Distribution: Indo-Pacific seas.
General: One of a related group of "whaler" sharks (but not to be confused with the plankton-eating whale shark *Rhincodon*

typus) which is described under various names such as bronze whaler, black whaler, tufi whaler, white-cheeked whaler, etc. The whaler-sharks of the Indo-Pacific are certainly very similar to the dangerous bull shark (*Carcharhinus leucas*) an inshore species which penetrates far into fresh water and is well known from its presence in Lake Nicaragua.
All whaler sharks are dangerous to man. Several are schooling species and enter estuaries and often travel upstream into the freshwater reaches. Whaler sharks are now much sought after as sport fish in Australian waters where local specialised fishing methods have been evolved. As sport fish they are strong fighters. A few of the smaller or immature fish occasionally make high leaps after taking a hook, and many of the larger ones make fast runs when they feel the bite of the hook for the first time. As table fish they are reasonably palatable, and many reach Australian markets and restaurants under the commercial name flake.

14 TIGER SHARK S, B
Galeocerdo cuvieri

Features: Large, wedge-shaped body. Blunt, square head; snout broadly rounded; characteristic coarsely serrated, notched (cockscomb-shaped) teeth; eye with well-developed nictating membrane. Five gill slits with last two over pectoral fin base. Two dorsal fins, first medium large, second very small and above similar small anal fin; keeled tail stalk; tail fin, long upper lobe with a deep notch. Coloration: dorsally and flanks mottled dark blue or blue and light grey with dark spots, which fuse to bars, but pattern variable according to locale, age, and sex; young are more strongly marked; belly white.
Size: Range up to 18 ft (6 m) 2,500 lb (1,100 kg).
Distribution: Worldwide in temperate and tropical seas.
General: Extremely dangerous to man. One of the largest sharks. Ovoviviparous. Normally an open-sea fish, but a voracious scavenger and often seen foraging inshore in harbours and rivers. It is frequently caught as a sport fish in Australian waters, and landing a tiger shark has been known to take several hours. Edible but not usually eaten, but flesh and liver are often utilized in shark fishing for ground baiting (chumming).

15 BLUE SHARK S
Prionace glauca

Other common name: Blue whaler.

Features: Long, slender, but thickset about mid-length. Long pointed snout with rounded tip; teeth large and sharp-pointed, some with serrated edges; eyes with nictating membrane. Five short gill slits in front of very long and characteristic saberlike pectoral fins. Two dorsal fins, first of moderate size and about midway, second about half the height of first and above the anal fin; tail fin large with upper lobe twice as long as lower and notched. Coloration: dorsally uniform dark blue; flanks shading to a clear bright blue; belly white; tips of pectoral and anal fins dusky. Body colours

58

fade rapidly after death. No spiracle.

Size: Very variable and according to locale. In North Atlantic waters largest up to 13 ft (4 m), 400 lb (180 kg), but larger in Southern Hemisphere.

Distribution: Worldwide in warm temperate seas.

General: Dangerous to man. A deep-sea pelagic shark with a good turn of speed and sometimes found in schools. A popular sport fish in some locales. Viviparous and up to fifty young per litter. Its qualities as a table fish are variable, but the flesh is considered edible in some parts of the world.

16 SMOOTH DOGFISH s
Mustelus canis
Other common names: Smooth hound, Sweet William, common hound.

Features: Body slender, flattened below. Snout tapering but blunt; oval eye; five gill slits. Two dorsal fins; tail fin with upper lobe prolonged and a large deep notch toward the tip; lower lobe very small; one anal fin about half the length of the second dorsal. Coloration: dorsally olive to slaty grey or brown; flanks lighter; belly greyish white. Capable of adapting overall colour to suit background habitat. Occasional black spots on subforms. Rough skin (see also Index for related forms).

Size: Up to 5 1/4 ft (1.6 m).

Distribution: Atlantic in subtropical to temperate waters and found worldwide in several closely related forms.

General: A bottom-living, nocturnal predator found over sandy or muddy bottoms from *c.* 15 ft (5 m) downward along continental shelf regions. A migratory summer species in colder seas. Viviparous. Rated a nuisance by anglers in most areas. Edible, but not popular as food.

17 LEMON SHARK s, b, f
Negaprion brevirostris

Features: Long and slender. Snout short and broadly rounded. Two dorsal fins, first medium-sized, second slightly smaller and similar in shape to first; tail fin has longer upper lobe with a right-angled notch; anal fin slightly smaller than second dorsal. Coloration: dorsally yellowish brown and belly paler.

Size: Up to 11 ft (330 cm), 330 lb (150 kg).

Distribution: Western Atlantic, from North Carolina south to Brazil.

General: A marine shark which often enters brackish and freshwater regions of rivers. Many lemon sharks are used in research work, for they survive extremely well in captivity. A species dangerous to man. Edible.

18 BRONZE WHALER SHARK s, b
Eulamia ahena
Other common names: New Zealand whaler, whaler shark, toiki (Maori).

Features: Shape of the teeth distinguishes this whaler shark from similar species "down under". Teeth of the upper jaw are broad-based, triangular, serrated, with a shallow notch on one edge. In the lower jaw the edge serrations are finer and the teeth

are narrower and smaller. The body is fairly stout; the caudal peduncle is compressed laterally. The high dorsal fin is set behind the base of the pectoral fin. The head is broad with a bluntly pointed snout. Pectoral fins are large. The slender upper lobe of the tail has no D-shaped notch, and is much longer than the lower lobe. Coloration: A bright lustre over golden brown on the sides, shading to darker above and to white below. The black whaler, by contrast, is grey to almost black above with no hints of bronze.

Size: Reported up to 12 ft (360 cm), and 700 lb (320 kg), but a 9 ft (270 cm) average is more often found.

Distribution: Primarily Australia and New Zealand.

General: A relatively slow shark that enters bays, estuaries, and harbours, scavenging extensively. A dangerous man-eater occasionally sought for sport.

19 LEOPARD SHARK s
Triakis semifasciata
Other common name: Cat shark.

Features: Distinctive barred colour pattern provides easy identification. The body is rather heavy forward with a slightly hump-backed profile. The first and second dorsal fins are of equal size, upper lobe of the tail is much larger than the lower and bent backward at an angle almost parallel with the axis of the body. Coloration: The body is light to medium grey with 12 or more dark bands crossing the back and dark spots along the sides.

Size: Maximum about 5 ft (150 cm), 65 lb (30 kg).

Distribution: Eastern Pacific coasts, most common along central and southern California. Reported from Oregon to Lower California.

General: The flesh is reported good to eat, and the shark is frequently taken by sport fishermen, primarily while bait-fishing. At least one substantiated attack on a skin diver, so it must be considered dangerous to man in the water.

20 WHITE-TIPPED SHARK s
Carcharhinus longimanus
Other common names: White-finned shark, whitetip.

Features: Distinguished by the broadly rounded top of the first dorsal fin, the convex trailing edge of the lower lobe of the tail, the very short nose before the nostrils, and by the fact that the lower precaudal pit lies almost over the rear tip of the anal fin. The body is moderately stout with body depth about one-quarter of length. Moderately flattened caudal peduncle with well-marked upper precaudal pit that is sub-rectangular in shape. The lower pit is less strongly defined. The dermal denticles overlap very little and are so flat that the skin feels smooth. Head about one fifth of body length with thick-tipped, broad, rounded snout. Upper teeth are serrated, triangular; lowers are erect with a broad base, tips with fine cusps. The eye is circular. First dorsal quite large, second dorsal about one-third as long as the first at the base. Base of anal equals length of base of second dorsal. Pelvic fins equal in length to

the anal fin, measured along the leading edge. Coloration: Varies from light brown or grey to slate blue above, and dirty white below. Pelvic fins and lower surfaces of the pectorals have grey spots. Tips of the dorsal fins are light grey or off-white with similar spots, giving the popular common name to this shark.

Size: Recorded up to 13 ft (390 cm) and about 660 lb (300 kg), but larger specimens probably exist.

Distribution: Tropical and subtropical Atlantic and eastern Pacific waters. Also reported from the Mediterranean. Usually found well out to sea.

General: Travels singly or in schools. Is well-armed and may be dangerous to man. Often causes damage to tuna in seines or traps, but not considered a sport species. No commercial value.

21 TOPE s
Galeorhinus galeus
Other common names: Sweet William, vaal-haai (South Africa), soupfin shark.

Features: Slender body. Long pointed snout; slightly flattened forehead; oval eye with nictating membrane. Two dorsal fins; first positioned well back behind pectoral fin; second dorsal fin below anal fin; tail fin typically sharklike; upper part much broader than the lower; large notch on lower edge of upper lobe; large pectoral fin. Coloration: dorsally dull grey or light brown with lighter flanks; belly paler. Lateral line is straight. Skin is very rough and of typical shark texture.

Size: Up to 80 in (2 m); female larger than male.

Distribution: Worldwide in tropical to temperate seas, but represented locally by species or subspecies fish almost identical in features.

General: A bottom-living shark found singly or in small schools, often near coasts. An ovoviviparous species, and female gives birth up to 50 offspring per litter. Food generally is any kind of fish, but also includes a wide range of bottom fauna.

The tope is a very popular sport fish in European waters where several national clubs have developed tope fishing into a specialized sport-fishing cult. Most are caught in offshore waters by boat fishing, but progressively more are taken by beach casting as techniques are further developed. This European interest is due to the sparsity of other large sport fish in northwest European offshore waters.

In Europe it has no commercial interest, and it is not usually considered a table fish, although the flesh is quite edible. In South Africa and North America, particularly in the Pacific Coast region, the liver was formerly much in demand as a rich source of vitamin A. As a result the species was almost exterminated along the Pacific Coast during the period of World War II, but the switch to other sources for vitamin A has now resulted in a population increase.

22 SOUPFIN SHARK s
Galeorhinus zyopterus
Other common names: School shark, sand shark.

Features: Body of this clean-looking shark is

rather slender, tapering smoothly to head and tail. Its deepest point is immediately under the first dorsal fin. Upper profile of the forward part is almost a flat line, with a slight concave tendency where the head joins the trunk. The nose is pointed. The second dorsal and anal fins are exactly opposite and are mirror images of each other. The closely similar brown smoothhound shark has an anal fin that is distinctly smaller than the second dorsal. First dorsal is fairly large and almost a perfect equilateral triangle with a sharply pointed tip. The upper lobe of the caudal fin is much larger than the lower and deeply indented. There are no side keels to the caudal peduncle. The teeth are small and similar in both jaws. They have points that are slightly recurved with small cusps at the base of each tooth. Coloration: Grey-brown on the upper surface shading to pale grey and white below. Some specimens show a bluish sheen on the back. Leading edges of the various fins are shaded with black.

Size: Up to about 7 ft (210 cm) and 110 lb (50 kg).

Distribution: Worldwide in tropical and temperate waters.

General: Widely used commercially for food, skin, and liver oil. Fins form stock of legendary Chinese sharkfin soup. Primarily a fish-eater of deep waters. Slow-swimming and not considered much of a game fish, although it is occasionally taken when bait fishing for other species on the bottom.

23 SMOOTH HOUND s
Mustelus mustelus
Other common names: European dogfish, Sweet William.

Features: Small shark with an elongate and flattened head, two large dorsal fins that are widely separated but of approximately equal size. The ventral surface is flat, the teeth blunt and rather small pavement-like, with entire free border, rounded, lacking accessory points. The origin of the first dorsal fin is noticeably forward of the posterior border of the pectoral fin. The dermal denticles on the shoulders are rather long, pointed and ridged only about fifty per cent of the way; their tips are smooth. Coloration: a dull grey back, shading on the sides to a lighter grey and to white or creamy coloured below.

Size: Reported variously at maximum of 48 in (122 cm) and 72 in (180 cm) with the young born at about 12 in (30 cm).

Distribution: Coasts of the British Isles and Southern Europe mainly, occasionally in America with recent reports of specimens taken off the coast of New Jersey in the United States.

General: Rather sluggish sharks living mainly on the bottom but occasionally found in mid-water; not important commercially; not sporting though it will take baits.

24 GREAT HAMMERHEAD S

Sphyrna mokarran

Other common names: Hammerhead, shovelhead, shovelnose, mango-pare (Maori).

Features: The very broad, flattened, hammershaped head with eyes at the outer extremities is a major identification. Profile of the leading edge of the head is nearly straight when viewed from above. The dorsal fin is not as erect as in the closely related common hammerhead and scalloped hammerhead. The triangular teeth have regularly serrated edges and broad bases. Pelvic fins are slightly concave along the trailing edges. The second dorsal fin has a short, free lower corner, as does the dorsal. The body is laterally compressed to a moderate degree with a slightly humped profile forward of the dorsal fin. No mid-dorsal ridge, nor side keels on the caudal peduncle, which is higher than it is wide in cross section. The upper precaudal pit shows as a broad, triangular depression, but there is no corresponding lower pit. Gill openings extend toward the ventral area with the first four slits nearly straight, but the fifth slightly concave toward the rear. The eye is slightly wider than high. The pectoral fins are smaller than in other hammerhead species. Coloration: Immature specimens are grey-brown above and a lighter shade of the same colour below, with darker tips of the caudal fins and the dorsals. In full-grown individuals the body colour is dark olive-brown above shading to pale olive below. No definite fin shadings.

Size: Up to 18 ft (5 1/2 m) and about 1,100 lb (500 kg) with smaller specimens the rule.

Distribution: Tropical and subtropical seas throughout the world.

General: A large, powerful, ocean-roving shark, sought by sportsmen where available. Should be considered dangerous to men in the water. The hide has commercial value as does the liver for oil, but the flesh is ranked poor table fare.

25 COMMON HAMMERHEAD SHARK S

Sphyrna zygaena

Other common names: Smooth hammerhead, strizzle-nose.

Features: Head strongly compressed and expanded sideways, with the eyes at the outer edges of the characteristic hammer-like expansions (eyes have nictating membrane); snout smoothly rounded and convex without an indention in the midline; teeth triangular and pointed, uppers larger than lowers. Five gill slits, the fifth over base of pectoral fin. Two dorsal fins, first with high profile, second very small and directly above small anal fin; tail fin, upper lobe long and sometimes up to one third of the total length of the body and notched. Coloration: dorsally olive, brownish grey, or slate grey; flanks paler; belly greyish white.

Size: Up to 13 ft (4 m).

Distribution: Worldwide in temperate and tropical seas.

General: One of several migratory species of shark (including the bonnethead shark). The different species are identified by the shape of the front (leading) edge of the head, which may be rounded, straight, or indented.

Generally a species found in deep water, but occasionally it approaches close inshore. Food consists of fish, squid, crabs, other small sharks, stingrays, and possibly seals in some locales. Ovoviviparous, but little is known about its breeding habits. One female was found to contain 37 embryos.

The precise function of the hammerhead is not fully understood. One idea is that since the nostrils are positioned at the end of each lobe, the wide spread may be helpful in locating the precise direction of a prey – in effect, providing the fish with a unique kind of stereo–olfactory organ.

26 BONNETHEAD SHARK S

Sphyrna tiburo

Other common name: Shovelhead.

Features: Slender body not much compressed. Head depressed, semicircular in front and kidney-shaped (reniform); mouth small and crescentic; small, very oblique teeth. Two dorsal fins, first high with rounded tip, second small; tail fin crescentic with upper lobe longer and notched; anal fin small but larger than second dorsal. Coloration: uniform grey-brown; belly paler.

Size: Up to 6 ft (180 cm), 100 lb (45 kg).

Distribution: Worldwide in warmer seas.

General: A small shark belonging to the hammerhead group. Food consists of small fish and crustaceans. A slow-moving creature not infrequently encountered by sport fishermen in shallow waters, it requires only light tackle. Not dangerous to man. Undistinguished as a table fish.

27 MAKO SHARK S

Isurus oxyrhynchus

Other common names: Blue pointer, sharp-nosed mackerel shark.

Features: Long, slender body. Pointed, bullet-shaped snout; jaws have long, narrow, and curved teeth which are a characteristic recognition feature. Five long gill slits in front of pectoral fins. Two dorsal fins, first large, second very small and directly above anal fin; tail stalk with keels either side; tail fin crescentic (mackerel-like) with longer notched upper lobe; one small anal fin. Coloration: Dorsally bluish grey or cobalt blue; flanks greyish; belly white. In all waters the mako shark is often confused with the porbeagle shark (see below for characteristic differences).

Size: Up to 12 ft 2 in (3.6 m), 1,061 lb (482 kg). Larger specimens probably exist.

Distribution: Worldwide with a preference for warmer seas; some of the Indo-Pacific makos are almost indistinguishable from the Atlantic mako, but others have a more rotund appearance.

General: Included among sharks dangerous to man.

The mako shark represents the best sport fish among the sharks, and, when hooked, is renowned as a powerful and tenacious fighter. It will often leap clear of the water, displaying many of the characteristics associated with marlin and swordfish. Jumps as high as 20–30 ft (6–9 m) have been recorded. The flesh has a taste and texture similar to that of swordfish.

28 PORBEAGLE SHARK S

Lamna nasus

Other common names: Blue dog, beaumaris shark, mackerel shark

Features: Stout, robust body, heavy in forward parts. Conical snout; large eye with no nictating membrane. Five long gill slits in front of pectoral fins. Two dorsal fins, first triangular and large, second small and above single anal fin; tail stalk has strong lateral keels; tail fin crescentic with larger, notched upper lobe. Coloration: dorsally dark bluish grey to bluish black; flanks paler; belly white. The porbeagle is often confused with the mako shark. Some of the differences can be seen in the body form and the shape of snout, but the teeth are the surest guide: the porbeagle's teeth are pointed with base (or lateral) cusps either side, while the mako's teeth are long, narrow, and pointed with no cusps.

Size: Maximum 8 ft (2.4 m), 465 lb (210 kg).

Distribution: Worldwide.

General: A dangerous species to man.

An ovoviviparous species and up to four large-sized young each time. Food generally consists of herring, cod, whiting, mackerel, squid, and dogfish.

The porbeagle is a first-class sport fish, and like the mako shark it may often make spectacular leaps when hooked. It is sometimes caught commercially for its liver and skin; the flesh is rated of only moderate table quality.

29 WHITE SHARK S

Carcharodon carcharias

Other common names: Maneater shark, white pointer, white death, great white shark.

Features: Deep, fusiform body. Conical snout; moderate-sized eye. Teeth triangular with serrated edges, and a highly characteristic recognition feature; teeth in lower jaw narrower than those in upper jaw. Five very long gill slits. Two dorsal fins, first approximately triangular with a semirounded apex, second dorsal very small; keel-like extensions on tail stalk; tail crescentic with notched upper lobe which is only slightly larger than lower; single, very small anal fin. Coloration: dorsally slaty grey, leaden grey, or black; flanks shading to a dirty white, belly light grey; pectoral fins have black tips; pelvic fins darker along front edges. Some large specimens have a gold or coppery dorsal coloration, others are leaden white.

Size: Up to 40 ft (12 m) and 9,500 lb (4,300 kg); larger specimens reported.

Distribution: Worldwide, but it appears to favour the Southern Hemisphere more than the Northern. A common species in the Great Australian Bight where the largest specimens are caught by sport fishermen.

General: Probably the most dangerous shark to man, and often referred to as the man-eater. It will devour any living or dead object that appears to be food. In Shark Bay, Western Australia, large white sharks have been caught which contained seagulls, wallabies, whole sheep, horse-flesh, and even a bulldog; plus nonanimate objects ranging from empty bottles, broken glass and cuckoo clocks to crushed kerosene and biscuit tins.

The white shark is the heaviest fish ever to be caught on rod and line by a sport fisherman. This largest ever fish was caught on a seal liver bait in South Australian waters in 1959 and weighed 2,664 lb (1,208 kg). The flesh of the white shark is edible but is not usually eaten.

30 BASKING SHARK S

Cetorhinus maximus

Other common name: Bone shark.

Features: Elongate, deep body. Pointed snout; teeth very small. Five very long gill slits almost meeting on underside of throat. Two dorsal fins, first large and triangular, second small; heavy keel-like extensions either side of tail stalk: tail fin crescentic, upper lobe larger and notched near rear edge; anal fin equal in size to second dorsal fin. Coloration: dorsally greyish brown to slaty grey; flanks paler; belly white.

Size: Up to 50 ft (15 m).

Distribution: North and south Atlantic and Indo-Pacific temperate seas.

General: Not normally dangerous to man. A schooling species; sometimes 50–60 fish are seen together. Sluggish in habit and often seen swimming near the surface, hence the name "basking" shark. A plankton eater which feeds by filtering tiny organisms from seawater through its gill system in the manner of balleen whales. Does not respond to baits presented by anglers.

31 WHALE SHARK S

Rhincodon typus

Other common names: Basking shark, chagrin, tiburon ballenas, tint reva, East Indian basking shark.

Features: Enormously large with a very robust body and a broad and blunt head. The caudal fin is well bent up with a notch at the base above and a keel on each side of the caudal peduncle. There are two dorsal fins. The mouth is large with many small and conical recurved teeth. The eye is small with no nictating membrane. The gill slits are very large. The entire gill apparatus forms a sieve of innumerable minute meshes through which water is forced when the mouth is closed. Plankton food is thus retained and swallowed. The head is strongly flattened above and there appears to be no distinct snout, the mouth being at the anterior margin of the head. There is a spiracle about as large as the eye, a short distance behind and above the eye. The teeth are similar in the two jaws, in about three hundred and ten rows, with ten to fifteen rows functional all along the dental band. Width of mouth nearly as great as breadth of head. Coloration: dark grey to a reddish or greenish brown on back and sides, including the upper surface of the pectorals. The whale shark is spotted with roundish white or a yellowish series of spots, smallest on the head where they are dense, largest on the hinder portion where they are less frequent. Variable number of narrow white or yellowish transverse stripes. Belly and lower parts are a whitish or white yellow.

Size: Largest of the fish-like vertebrates, reaching 60 ft (18 m) or perhaps more. A

40 ft (12 m) whale shark weighed about 27,500 lb (12,500 kg).

Distribution: Pelagic in tropical and temperate belts of all oceans.

General: Sometimes gathers in schools, basks at the surface. Sluggish enough to be rammed by steamers. Gulps of small animals to feed. Commercially fished off the northwest coast of India but elsewhere of no commercial importance. Harmless to man except by accidental contact.

32 NURSE SHARK s
Ginglymostoma cirratum

Features: The body is moderately stout with a short, broadly rounded snout. Easily recognized by the long feeler or barbel at each nostril, which reaches back as far as the mouth, and by the two dorsal fins of almost equal size, placed far back on the trunk. Very small eyes and five short gill slits, the last two of which are spaced quite close together over the leading edge of the pectoral fin. The transverse mouth is nearly straight with pronounced labial furrows on both jaws at the corners. The teeth are similar in both jaws, have a high, pointed centre cusp flanked by up to 3 smaller cusps on each side. There are 15–18 teeth on each side of the upper jaw and 14–16 on each side of the lower. Pelvic fins located directly under the first dorsal, to rear of shark's midpoint. The pectoral fins are short and broad with rounded outer corner and straight distal edge. Second dorsal starts ahead of the anal fin. The spiracle is small. Coloration: Dirty yellow or pale brown above, shading to a paler hue of the same below. Young fish are marked with small dark spots and cross bars that are usually lost at maturity.

Size: Is mature at 5 ft (150 cm), but grows larger. One 8 1/2 ft (255 cm) specimen weighed 375 lb (170 kg).

Distribution: Eastern and western shores of tropical and sub-tropical Atlantic, being common in the Caribbean, the Gulf of Mexico, and locally from Florida to Brazil. Reported off West Africa and also in the eastern Pacific from Baja California to Ecuador.

General: A rather sluggish, shallow-water shark frequenting reefs and mangrove channels where it is found in groups or singly. Can inflict a painful bite, but is not considered a direct threat to man. Often taken by anglers using bait for other fish, and is considered acceptable as food in some areas. The fins in particular are said to be good eating.

33 GREY NURSE SHARK s
Odontaspis taurus
Other common name: Sand tiger shark

Features: Moderately stout body. Head slightly flattened; short, pointed snout; teeth long and thin, canine-like and smooth-edged with base cusps, and similar in both jaws; no nictating eye membrane. Five gill slits forward of rounded pectoral fins. Two dorsal fins of almost equal size; tail fin heavy, upper lobe longer with a deep notch; anal fin slightly larger than second dorsal fin; pectoral fins about size of first dorsal fin. Coloration: greyish brown; flanks paler; belly greyish white or white;

dorsal region and upper flanks marked with scattered, round, golden yellow spots. In young fish the spots are very marked.

Size: Up to 10 ft (3 m) in Atlantic waters but larger in the Indo-Pacific region.

Distribution: Worldwide in temperate and tropical seas.

General: Probably a dangerous species to man, although in Australian waters it is often confused with the more dangerous grey whaler-shark (*Charcharhinus menisorra*) (which see). A migratory species in some locales. Viviparous. Often described as a sloppily built shark, and this is an apt and very characteristic recognition feature. Not a notable sport fish, although frequently caught in Australian waters.

34 THRESHER SHARK s
Alopias vulpinus
Other common names: Fox shark, sea fox, swiveltail, swingletail.

Features: Moderately stout body, heaviest in front of dorsal fin. Five short gill slits immediately preceding sickle-shaped pectoral fin. Teeth small and triangular-shaped; eyes with nictating membrane. Two dorsal fins, first of moderate height, second very small; no keels on tail stalk; tail fin (a highly characteristic feature) has extremely long upper lobe and may be as long as the head and body together; lower lobe small and equal to size of pelvic fins. Coloration: dorsally dark blue, grey, brown, or black; flanks paler, shading to white on belly; underside of the snout and the pectoral fins dark.

Size: Up to 20 ft (6 m), 1,000 lb (450 kg).

Distribution: Worldwide.

General: The species is not considered dangerous to man.

The prolonged tail fin is highly functional for catching small fish and is utilized for beating, or threshing, the surrounding water to terrify its quarry and herd them into a compact formation. The shark then uses the tail to stun individual fish.

Threshers are ovoviviparous, and females give birth to 2–4 young each time. At birth the young fish has a tail lobe disproportionately longer than the adult fish.

Generally the thresher shark is a solitary swimmer residing near the surface region. It is an excellent sport fish. The flesh is of good table quality.

35 BIGEYE THRESHER SHARK s
Alopias superciliosus
Other common names: Fox shark, swingletail, longtail shark, fish shark, sea fox, pez zorro, pesca pavone, mango-ripi (Maori).

Features: Differs from the closely related common thresher shark in that it possesses a larger eye and longer snout. The body is relatively stout, tapering bluntly at front and rear. Upper lobe of the caudal fin is high, narrow, arched, and is more than half of the total length of the fish. Broad pectoral fins. In the bigeye, the tip of the first dorsal fin is to the rear of the base of the pelvic fins, but in the common thresher (which see), the dorsal tip does not quite reach a vertical line upward from the pectoral fin base. The bigeye's anal fin is well behind the second dorsal, but is under

the second dorsal in the common thresher. Bigeye pectoral fins are less curved and longer than those of the common thresher. Bigeye teeth number 10–11 on each side of the jaw, whereas common thresher teeth number about 20. The bigeye's eye is circular or slightly higher than broad. The teeth are similar in both jaws. Coloration: Dark grey above and only slightly paler below. Trailing edges of the pectorals, pelvics, anal fin, and first dorsal shaded with dusky colour.

Size: Up to 18 ft (540 cm), 880 lb (400 kg).

Distribution: Tropical and sub-tropical Atlantic and Pacific waters.

General: Thought to occupy deeper waters than its close relative, the common thresher. Feeds on hake, squid, lancetfish, mackerel, and the like. Flesh has less urea content than many sharks and is considered quite good. A rare but exciting sport fishing catch.

36 SPINY DOGFISH s
Squalus acanthias
Other common names: Greyfish; spurdog; picked dogfish

Features: Slender body, rounded. Head flattened and blunt snout; teeth have tips bent sideways; oval eyes. Two dorsal fins each preceded by a heavy spine; first dorsal spine is shorter than the margin of the fin; second dorsal spine is as long or almost as long as second dorsal fin margin; tail fin with large upper lobe and no notch; no anal fin (a characteristic distinguishing feature); large almost triangular pectoral fins. Coloration: dorsally dark or slaty grey with brownish hues; flanks lighter; belly white; the flanks have irregular white spots which may be absent in older fish; a few similar spots near dorsal fins.

Size: Female largest and up to 4 ft (120 cm), 30 lb (14 kg), male up to 3 ft (90 cm), 22 lb (10 kg).

Distribution: North Pacific; Mediterranean; Black Sea; North Atlantic, with a range extending in west from southern Greenland to West Indies, and in east from Scandinavia to Morocco, including English Channel, North Sea, and western Baltic.

General: A migratory bottom-living species found in schools ranging from shallow inshore waters to depths up to 3,000 ft (900 m). The spiny dogfish is a voracious feeder eating a wide variety of fish which includes herring, menhaden, mackerel, cod, and pollack; also shrimps, crabs, polychaete worms, and jellyfish. It is ovoviviparous with a long gestation period of 18–22 months. In Europe it is fast developing as a recognized sport fish. In North America, however, it is regarded primarily as a pest.

37 VELVET BELLY s
Etmopterus spinax.

Features: The small body is elongate, rounded and soft, with weak skeleton. Blunt snout, large eyes. Each of the two dorsal fins start with a strong spine; second dorsal fin the largest. Tail fin with long, narrow, slightly notched upper lobe, lower lobe broad; no anal fin. Coloration: overall dark-brownish or almost black with distinct black blotches or stripes over and behind the ventral fins. The underside possesses

densely placed, small, greenish-shining luminous organs.

Size: Rarely over 20 in (50 cm), mean 12–16 in (30–40 cm).

Distribution: North-East Atlantic from Iceland and northern Norway to West Africa.

General: Very common along the continental shelf between 100–400 fathoms (200–700 m). The young, 6–10 in a litter, are born in spring or early summer with a size of about 5 inches (12–14 cm). The food consists of shrimps and other crustaceans, squids and mussels. This small shark has no commercial value, and is of only little interest to the sport fishery.

38 LARGE-SPOTTED DOGFISH s
Scyliorhinus stellaris
Other common names: Greater spotted dogfish, catfish

Features: Slender, elongate body. Rounded snout; nostrils wide apart; oval eyes without nictitating membrane, but with thick fold of skin on lower margins; five gill slits. Two dorsal fins very similar in size and appearance; tail fin has upper lobe more developed than the lower; single anal fin. Coloration: variable, but often dorsally reddish brown or greyish; flanks lighter shade; belly off-white; dorsal region, flanks, and fins are marked with circular brown spots with lighter centres and many smaller black spots. Very rough skin.

Size: Up to 60 in (150 cm), 21 lb (9.5 kg).

Distribution: Mediterranean; eastern Atlantic from Norway south, including North Sea and English Channel.

General: The large-spotted dogfish is a less common species than the lesser-spotted dogfish (*S. caniculus* which see) of similar appearance but smaller size.

The large-spotted dogfish is a small scavenger and bottom-living nocturnal shark found over rocky ground in waters 65–200 ft (20–60 m) deep. Commercial interest is limited to the very rough skin which was once widely used under the trade name "rubskin" for polishing hard wood and other material. Although commercial fishermen rate it only a nuisance, it is nevertheless of interest to sport fishermen in western European waters where large marine game fish are scarce. The species is not usually included as a table fish, but the flesh is quite palatable.

39 LESSER SPOTTED DOGFISH s
Scyliorhinus caniculus
Other common names: Dogfish, rough hound, rough dog, robin huss, sandy dog.

Features: Slender, elongate body. Rounded snout, nostrils wide apart and connected to mouth by a flap (shape of which distinguishes it from *S. stellaris* (which see). Five gill slits. Two dorsal fins; tail fin similar to *S. stellaris*; one anal fin. Coloration: dorsally brown or reddish grey; flanks yellowish grey; belly white; dorsal regions, flanks, and fins are covered with small brown and larger black spots and occasionally with white spots; belly pale.

Size: Average range 16–30 in (40–75 cm), 11 lb (5 kg).

Distribution: Eastern Atlantic from Norway

south to Senegal; English Channel; North Sea; Mediterranean.

General: Found over mud or sand in depths ranging 10–1,300 ft (3–400 m); a nocturnal and bottom predatory species which feeds on a variety of small fishes.

The lesser spotted dogfish is rated a nuisance species by many sport fishermen. As a commercial species it is of variable quality. In some areas it is considered quite palatable. When skinned and headed, it is known in Britain as "rock salmon" or "rock eel", and in France as "saumonette".

40 BLACK-MOUTHED DOGFISH S
Galeus melastomus

Features: Slender body, pointed head and large eyes. Mouth with small, sharp teeth. Small dorsal fins, the first placed behind the ventral fins. Long tail fin with low, notched, long upper lobe and broad lower lobe; the upper lobe with longitudinal rows of serrate teeth along dorsal margin. Coloration: the back and sides are light-brown with large, broken light rings. Belly grey or white. Fins brown or reddish-brown, dorsal fins with dark blotches. The inside of the mouth is black.

Size: Up to 30 in (70–80 cm).

Distribution: Northeast Atlantic from west-coast of Norway to northwest Africa. Western Mediterranean.

General: Lives mainly at the bottom in a depth of 100–400 fathoms (200–700 m). The eggs are laid in horny cases about 2–3 inch (6 cm) long. The food consists of fish and crustaceans. This shark is hardly of any value for commercial or sport fishing.

41 DARKIE CHARLIE S
Dalatias licha

Features: Slender, rounded body. Mouth with thick lips; teeth in lower jaw triangular, serrate. Short, rather flattened head with short, rounded snout; large eyes, rather large spiracles; small gill openings. Tail with lateral ridges. Fins large and broad; tail fin rather short, upper lobe notched; first dorsal fin placed forwardly on middle of back. Coloration: uniform grey-brown or brown to dark-purple, with darker spots; tail fin with black tip. The lips are whitish.

Size: Up to 6 ft (1³/₄ m).

Distribution: East Atlantic from west of the British Isles to the Canary Islands, Mediterranean. Also reported from the West-Atlantic (Georges Bank, New England).

General: Lives in deeper water, 200–400 fathoms (350–650 m). Feeds mainly on fish. Rather common in some places; often caught in deeper trawl hauls, but of no commercial value.

42 GREENLAND SHARK S
Somniosus microcephalus.
Other common name: Gurry Shark.

Features: Large, stout body; small eyes and rather small gill slits. Small dorsal fins without spines; upper lobe of tail fin notched, lower lobe broad; no anal fin. Skin rough with numerous spined denticles. Coloration: dull dark-brownish to red-brownish, somewhat variable, in cases grey with darker bands.

Size: Mean 10–15 ft (3–4 m). Can reach 20–25 ft (6–8 m).

Distribution: North-Atlantic from northern Greenland and Svalbard and south to off Nova Scotia and Scotland.

General: Lives in deeper water, 100–300 fathoms (200–600 m) on a muddy bottom and with a temperature of about 1°C. It is a slow swimmer, with sluggy movements and weak sight; its sense of smell is well developed. The food is larger fish, seals, birds, squids and crabs; it is also a carrion-eater and often takes refuse from whaling and fishery plants. It is of importance to the fishery due to its skin (leather) and the rich content of liver oil (A-vitamin).

43 BRAMBLE SHARK S
Echinorhinus brucus
Other common names: Spiny shark, spinous shark.

Features: Two small dorsal fins situated close together without dorsal fin spines. Both dorsals close to the caudal fin; the first dorsal above the middle of the pelvics. The teeth have several cusps, but so oblique so as to form an almost continuous cutting edge. There are large rounded bucklers, with one or more sharp spines, loosely mounted on the skin. Large gill openings, the last extending well under the throat. Head flattened above, snout ovate and tapering from the eyes, the eyes opposite the front of the mouth and approximately circular. The dorsal fins are brush-shaped with broadly rounded corners, second dorsal smaller than the first. Pelvics much larger than dorsals with rounded apices and tapering rear corners. Pectoral fins are brush-shaped with weakly convex outer margins, broadly rounded corners and a notably broad base. The caudal is very broadly scythe-shaped with a tapering tip, the lower inferior corner rounded. Coloration: dark grey or brown with reflections of silver and yellow, coppery-yellow, or even violet. Pale brown to grey or white below.

Size: Grows to at least 108 in (270 cm) and 330 lb (150 kg) but usually far smaller.

Distribution: Eastern Atlantic, including the Mediterranean, from tropical West Africa to Iceland and the North Sea; apparently accidental in the western Atlantic, also reported from South Africa, California, Hawaii, Japan, and Australia-New Zealand.

General: Caught fairly frequently by hook and line in European waters. Food consists of sharks, fishes and crabs; little is known of its biology or further diet. No commercial value and of only local sport fishing importance.

44 ATLANTIC MANTA S
Manta birostris
Other common names: Manta, sea devil, devilfish, blanketfish.

Features: Shaped like a huge bat. Two horn-like arms or appendages project forward from the head on either side of the wide, slit-like mouth that is located at the forward edge of the head, not underneath as in most rays. These cephalic fins point forward as the manta swims and assist in directing food (usually shrimp, mullet, plankton) into the huge mouth. The large eyes are placed on the sides of the wide head. The body disc is

roughly twice as wide as it is long, with outer edges tapering to a distinct tip. The tail is at least as long as the body. There is a small, rounded dorsal fin on the base of the tail, and a serrated spine usually can be found behind the dorsal fin. The skin of the back, pelvic fin, and tail is rough and marked with small bumps. This roughness extends to the underside. Teeth are minute, but numerous, arranged in 12 to 18 rows with as many as 4,500 counted in a specimen 11 1/2 ft (3 1/2 m) long. The gill openings are quite long. Coloration: Upper side may vary from olive or reddish brown to slate-blue or black. Lower surface is white shading to grey along the margins of the body disc, and along the rear portion of the tail.

Size: Is mature at about 14 ft (420 cm) and 2,200 lb (1,000 kg), but much larger specimens have been recorded.

Distribution: Both sides of the Atlantic in tropical and warm-temperate waters. Mantas of tropical and sub-tropical Pacific and Indian Ocean waters may be identical, but very few specimens have been taken to substantiate this suspicion.

General: Swims at or just under the surface, often splashing the "wingtips" clear or leaping with startling effect. Feeds on plankton and very small fish in the manner of the plankton-eating whales. Sometimes taken by harpoon for food or sport. Flesh of small specimens is said to be good, that of larger ones is sometimes used to make fish meal or to feed animals. Is not directly dangerous to man, but can overturn a small boat with a flip of the immense flippers or swimming fins.

45 SPOTTED EAGLE RAY S
Aetobatus narinari
Other common name: Spotted duck-billed ray.

Features: Body similar to that of the cownose ray, with long, pointed wings. The snout is, however, rather long and bluntly pointed. The tail is long, thin, and whiplike with a strong spine near its base. The teeth in both jaws form crushing plates. Coloration: above – greenish brown to chestnut with numerous whitish or lighter colour spots. By these spots the eagle ray can be distinguished from the cow-nose ray; the underside is white.

Size: Max. 10 ft (3 m), 650 pounds (300 kg); normal size much smaller.

Distribution: Warm and warm-temperate seas; common off the east coast of North America. Indo Pacific.

General: Lives mainly in rather shallow water, where it feeds almost exclusively on mussels. It is known to jump right out of the water. When caught it emits barking or growling sounds. Some commercial importance.

46 EAGLE RAY S
Myliobatis aquila
Other common name: Bat ray.

Features: The flat body is very broad with well-pointed wings. The head is set off as a rounded projection from the trunk. The eyes are placed laterally on the head. The flat teeth form crushing plates. The long, very slender, whiplike tail has close to its base a long, sharp spine, and just in front

of this a small fin. Coloration: above – dark olive green; below – grey to white.

Size: Up to 6¹/₂ ft (2 m), 400–500 pounds (180–225 kg).

Distribution: East Atlantic from the British Isles to South Africa, Mediterranean; a rare guest in the North Sea.

General: Its home waters are the warmer seas from Spain and southward. Although the eagle ray is a fast swimmer, often moving in the free water, its main food is bottom animals, mussels and crabs; especially on mussel beds and oyster banks it can be highly noxious.

47 COWNOSE RAY S, occasionally B
Rhinoptera bonasus
Other common names: Cowfish, spotted eagle ray, bullnose ray.

Features: The very long tail has one or more poisonous spines with saw-edges. The body shape, viewed from above, is a flat, broad disc. The wings (pectoral fins) are interrupted just back of the short head, with the forward part forming a separate twin-lobed fin that extends forward from the lower side ahead of the mouth and nostrils. Head is high-domed with the eyes and spiracles on the sides instead of on top. The tail carries a small dorsal fin ahead of the spines, which are quite long. Large, flat, grinding teeth form a mosaic with 7–9 series of teeth in each jaw. Front of the head has an indented outline and the short sub-rostral fin (previously described) that extends forward from the lower side of the head. Outer pectoral fin corners are pointed and the "wings" have a concave rear margin. Pelvic fins are small, extend only a little way behind the large pectorals. Coloration: Brown above, yellow-white to white below. Some specimens are marked with faint dark radiating lines above and below.

Size: Up to 85 in (216 cm) and 110 lb (50 kg), but generally smaller.

Distribution: Western Atlantic coast from southern New England (U.S.A.) to Brazil.

General: Finds food (crustaceans, shellfish, shrimp, etc) in mud and sand on the bottom. Occasionally swims in large schools or colonies. Bears young alive, 2–6 at a time. Young measure 12 in (30 cm) wide at birth. Matures at about 24 in (60 cm) width. Edible, but not actively sought for food except in a few localities. No great attraction to sport fishermen.

48 COMMON STINGRAY S, B
Trygon pastinaca

Features: Disklike body, much depressed, with rounded angles to wings; snout angle obtuse; tail slender and whiplike; tail *c.* 1 1/2 times as long as body, with a single, large-toothed spine about 1/3 distance along tail. Smooth-skinned, but older fish may have a central row of bony knobs along the midline of body. Dorsal and anal fins lacking. Coloration: dorsally grey, brown, reddish, or olive-green, sometimes with white spots; undersurface white or creamy-white with dark edges.

Size: Up to 96 in (250 cm).

Distribution: Mediterranean; Black Sea; eastern Atlantic, from northern Norway south to Madeira, including English Channel, North Sea, and western Baltic. Related species worldwide.

General: One of more than 100 species of the family *Trygonidae* (or *Dasyatidae*), some of which also live in fresh water. Sting rays are found in calm, shallow waters seldom deeper than 400 ft (120 m) and usually much less. They frequent brackish, shallow-water estuaries where sometimes they may be seen partly immersed on a bottom of sand and mud. Like all stingrays, the common stingray is ovoviviparous, and females give birth to 6–9 offspring in the summer. A carnivorous species which feeds on any living bottom creature.

To many anglers the stingray is not a sport fish but they are frequently hooked accidentally. When attacked or provoked, the stingray lashes out with its tail. At the base of the tail spine is located a poison sac. When the tail spine makes contact, poison is injected. The effects of the poison are immediate, and inflammation quickly spreads around the wound. Preliminary treatment should not be delayed while qualified medical assistance is being sought.

The flesh is considered of poor table quality.

49 ATLANTIC STINGRAY s
Dasyatis sabina
Other common names: Stingray, stingaree, devilfish, pigeon stingray, clam-cracker, chucho, raya aguila.

Features: All stingrays with whip tails are similar and almost circular in outline, with thin outer edges and the pectoral fins fused into the head and body. The eyes and spiracles of the Atlantic stingray are located on the upper side of the body. The mouth, with many small teeth in close bands around the jaws, is located in the forward part of the underside, but some distance back from the sharply pointed snout. The long, tapered tail is armed with one or more serrated, venomous spines on the upper surface, not far back from the body. A row of short spines or thorny bumps extends down the middle of the back and partway onto the tail. There is also a definite skinfold along the upper and lower tail surfaces. Edges of the snout are slightly indented on either side. Distance from eyes to snout is considerably greater than the distance between the dorsal gill openings, or spiracles. Coloration: Upper surface light to medium brown with touches of yellow and light shadings along the body margin. Lower surface is off-white or dirty white.
Size: About 6 ft (180 cm) long, 100 lb (45 kg) at maturity. Some specimens are larger.
Distribution: Primarily a tropical species common around Florida and the Gulf of Mexico, reported as far south as Uruguay on the western South Atlantic shore. Some stray as far north as Cape Cod.
General: Food consists primarily of amphipod crustaceans, some shellfish, marine worms, and occasional small bottom-dwelling fish. No known commercial value, and not considered a sport fish, although occasionally harpooned for sport or for animal food. The tail spine is brought into action when the tail springs erect as it will when the stingray is stepped on by a wader. The wounds caused by the spine are extremely painful and often become badly infected. The poison from the spine can cause shock and serious reactions in some individuals.

50 MARBLED ELECTRIC RAY s
Torpedo marmorata
Other common names: Numbfish, crampfish.

Features: Body shaped as an almost circular disc with a stout, round tail. Eyes small and protruding. Large ventral fins; two small dorsal fins placed backwards on the tail. The comparatively large tail fin has a straight hind margin. Two electric organs are in the anterior part of the body, one on each side of the head. The denticles are so small and so imbedded into the skin that this appears quite smooth. Coloration: above – red brown and marbled with numerous lighter spots; below – whitish or light reddish with darker spots.
Size: Max. 5 ft (1.5 m), 70 pounds (30 kg); normally only 1½–2 ft (40–60 cm).
Distribution: East Atlantic, British Isles to North Africa; Mediterranean and Indian Ocean; a rare guest in the North Sea and Skagerak.
General: The electric organs work as in *T. nobiliana*. Food – fish, mussels, crustaceans. No commercial value. Not a sport fish.

51 ELECTRIC RAY s
Torpedo nobiliana
Other common name: Electric skate.

Features: Disk-shaped, depressed body which contains two large electric organs. Two dorsal fins, first high with rounded corners, second about half as large as first and of similar shape; tail fin moderately large and shaped like an equilateral triangle with broadly rounded corners; pelvic fins with broadly convex outer margins. Coloration: dorsally dark chocolate-brown or nearly black, uniform or slightly spotted; undersurface white and edged with light brown. Skin completely smooth without scales.
Size: Up to 72 in (180 cm), 110 lb (50 kg).
Distribution: Both sides of North Atlantic, south to South Africa; Mediterranean.
General: The electric organs are positioned in the front part of the body opposite the eyes and mouth. Anything touching the ray under water receives an electric shock of some intensity, but it is not usually dangerous to humans. The mouth is very large, and comparatively big fish are swallowed whole after being stunned. The electric ray is ovoviviparous and may give birth to up to 35 offspring per litter. No sport or commercial value.

52 LONG-NOSE SKATE s
Raja oxyrinchus
Other common name: Sharp-nosed skate.

Features: Body ray-shaped. The snout is very long, narrow and pointed. The anterior margins of the disc have a decided concavity off the eyes. Larger thornlike denticles are only present dorsally along the tail. Coloration: above – brown with scattered lighter spots, below – whitish to grey with many small, black spots.
Size: Max. 5 ft (1.5 m), but usually much smaller.
Distribution: East Atlantic from northern Norway to west Africa; western part of the Mediterranean.
General: Lives in deeper water, 40–300 fathoms (100–1000 m), where it feeds on redfish, other fishes from deeper water and prawns. As most other rays and skates it is landed commercially, but not especially fished for and it is only of little interest to the sport fishery.

53 CLEARNOSE SKATE s
Raja eglanteria

Features: Disk-shaped, with depressed body. Prickles comparatively small and very sharp, most numerous on anterior part of the pectoral fins, over the head, on the snout, on the middle dorsal area, and on the tail between rows of large prickles; very sharp, enlarged spines round the eyes and spiracles, on the middle of the snout, in a median row along the back, and in two rows along each side of the tail. There is also a large spine between the tail fin and the middle of each shoulder. Coloration: generally brown with bands, bars, lines, blotches, and spots of darker colour in the middle of the pectoral fins; a characteristic translucent space on each side of the snout.
Size: Up to about 24 in (60 cm).
Distribution: Western Atlantic, ranging Cape Cod south to Florida.
General: Little food or sporting value.

54 COMMON SKATE s
Raja batis
Other common names: Blue skate, grey skate.

Features: Disk-shaped, with depressed body; slightly concave front edge to wings. Prominent snout. Prickles along dorsal area, but in females restricted to front part; immature fish are smooth. Adult fish have a central row of tail spines and occasionally two lateral rows. Coloration: dorsally, upper surface, greenish, greyish or brownish with lighter spots and black dots; two eye spots surrounded by lighter halos; belly region bluish-grey or grey with black dots.
Size: Males up to 80 in (200 cm), females 96 in (240 cm).
Distribution: Mediterranean; north-east Atlantic, from Iceland and Norway south to northern Spain, including English Channel, North Sea, and western Baltic.
General: Found on a sandy or muddy bottom in depths ranging 100–2,000 ft (30–600 m), but younger fish may be found in shallower water.

Food chiefly comprised of other bottom species: crustaceans, including full-sized lobsters, and fish. An important commercial species. As a sport fish its capture entails a weight-lifting operation, for both skates and rays may exert their wings to create suction on the bottom. An excellent table fish, but best flavour is experienced if the wing-flesh is left to hang for a day or so to allow the faint ammoniacal smell to disappear. Many other skate species have a similar general appearance (see Index).

55 THORNY SKATE s
Raja radiata
Other common names: Starry skate, Atlantic prickly skate.

Features: Disk-shaped, depressed body with rounded wings. Upper surface with rows of large and conspicuous "thorns" on each shoulder, tail, and generally scattered over the upper surface. Two small dorsal fins very similar in size and shape, sometimes joined at the base: tail membrane short. Claspers of mature males conspicuously large. Coloration: dorsally and upper surface brown, sometimes with darker spots and occasionally with white spots near each eye and on either side of pectorals; undersurface white.
Size: Up to 40 in (100 cm).
Distribution: Both sides of North Atlantic. Related Indo-Pacific forms.
General: Not usually an inshore species, and mostly found in depths of 65–3,000 ft (20–900 m) on both hard and soft bottoms. One of the most abundant of all the skate species. An important commercial table fish in Europe, but in North America its use is confined to the production of fish meal.

56 SHAGREEN RAY s
Raja fullonica
Other common name: Fullers ray.

Features: Disk-shaped body with angled wings. Head and snout pointed. Upper surface rough with two characteristic rows of spines along the tail except between the dorsal fins; occasionally spines are found at sides of head, wings, and around the eyes. Underside smooth except for leading edge of disk and base of tail. Two small dorsal fins of equal size. Coloration: dorsally and upper surface uniform grey or brown with small, darker dots; undersurface and belly white.
Size: Up to 43 in (110 cm).
Distribution: Eastern Atlantic, from Iceland south to Biscay and occasionally into the Mediterranean.
General: Found over sandy bottoms in depths ranging 115–1,800 ft (35–550 m), sometimes deeper. A commercially important species caught by trawling and longline. An excellent table fish.

57 CUCKOO RAY s
Raja naevus

Features: Typical ray shape. The snout is short and rather blunt. The anterior margins of the disc are slightly concave, the wings are broadly rounded. The denticles of the skin are fairly small; the larger of them are placed in irregular rows dorsally from behind the eyes to the first of the two dorsal fins near the end of the tail. Coloration: characteristic of this species are two black and white (or yellow) marbled spots on the upper side of the wings; the lower surface is greyish.
Size: This small ray reaches a length of 2½ ft (75 cm); the mean size is, however, much smaller.
Distribution: East Atlantic from southern North Sea to Africa; Mediterranean.
General: Prefers shallow and a little deeper coastal waters. The egg capsules have long, curving horns. Due to the small size the

species has no commercial or sporting importance.

58 THORNBACK RAY S
Raja clavata
Other common name: Roker.

Features: Disk-shaped, depressed body with angled wings. Snout only slightly elongate. Males have claspers which reach halfway along the tail. Dorsal surface has prickles or thorns scattered over it; in females, spines are also present over belly area; female and young fish have a central row of spines along body and tail; males only spines along tail. Coloration: dorsally yellowish, greyish, or brownish with lighter or darker spots; pattern more distinct in young fish, especially the darker spots; belly white with a darkish fringe. Rough skin on both upper and lower surfaces.
Size: Up to 32 in (80 cm), 40 lb (18 kg).
Distribution: Mediterranean; Black Sea; eastern Atlantic, from northern Norway south to Madeira, including English Channel, North Sea, and western Baltic.
General: The common name is derived from the thorns, prickles, or spines found along the back. A fairly common species outside the Mediterranean area. Found on sand or muddy ground from the very shallowest water to depths up to 1,650 ft (500 m). Food consists of molluscs, worms, and fish. Breeding occurs inshore and the stranded egg capsules, known as "mermaids purses", are a common feature along beaches. Mature fish may give a mild electric shock if lifted by the tail. Commercially important and a good table fish.

59 BLONDE RAY S
Raja brachyura
Other common names: Blonde, roker.

Features: Comparatively broad disc with rather pointed wings; the anterior margins are slightly concave. The snout is short and broad, terminating in a small, blunt tip. Coloration: above – light red brown with numerous small, black spots and a few larger whitish patches; below – white.
Size: The females reach a length of 3½ ft (110 cm) with a width of 2½ ft (75 cm); the males are much smaller.
Distribution: East Atlantic from the British Isles to Madeira; Mediterranean.
General: The blonde ray prefers a sandy bottom. In the English Channel it is one of the most common rays in depths from 25–60 fathoms (45–110 m). Due to its tasty flesh it is of considerable value to the local fisheries and it is also sought by sport fishermen.

60 BLACK-BELLIED SKATE
S
Raja nidrosiensis

Features: The body has the typical ray shape. The snout is narrow and pointed. Coloration: This species is easily distinguished from other rays and skates by its uniformly grey brown to dark brown underside.
Size: Known to attain a length of 6½ ft (2 m).
Distribution: Northern Atlantic from Nor-

way to Iceland and Ireland. It used to be caught in northern Kattegat.
General: This skate is nowhere common, and hardly anything is known about its biology.

61 ARCTIC SKATE S
Raja hyperborea

Features: Common ray shape. The snout is narrow and pointed. The species is easily distinguished from other skates by its uniformly grey brown to dark brown underside.
Size: Known maximum 6½ ft (2 m).
Distribution: North Atlantic from northern Norway to Iceland and Ireland; once caught in the northern Kattegat.
General: This skate is nowhere common, and hardly anything is known as to its biology.

62 WHITE SKATE S
Raja alba
Other common names: Bordered skate, Burton skate.

Features: Common ray shape. Narrow and much pointed snout. Long, slender tail with three longitudinal rows of rather long spines. Coloration: above – fawny to reddish grey, below – white.
Size: Maximum 3–4 ft (1 m).
Distribution: Atlantic from Ireland to southern Africa, Mediterranean.
General: Occurs mainly in coastal and moderate deep waters.

63 SHARPNOSE SKATE S
Raja lintea

Features: Common ray shape. Rather long, pointed snout. Anterior margins of disc a little concave or almost straight. A series of strong spines dorsally from behind the eyes to near the end of the tail, also longitudinal rows of spines on each side of the tail. Coloration: above – light greyish to brownish, below – white.
Size: Generally 3–4 ft (1–1¼ m), maximum 6 ft (2 m).
Distribution: North Atlantic; west of Greenland, Iceland, Faroes, northern North Sea and Skagerak.
General: Inhabits deeper water, 70–250 fathoms (150–500 m). Feeds on bottom fish, crabs, prawns, and squids.

64 UNDULATE RAY S
Raja undulata
Other common name: Painted ray.

Features: Ray-shaped. Anterior margins concave. Snout blunt. Posterior margins broadly rounded. Upper side with numerous smaller spines. Coloration: above – yellow brown to greyish brown with characteristic irregular small and narrow dark bands and numerous small white spots; white underside.
Size: Maximum 4 ft (120 cm).
Distribution: Northeast Atlantic from southern North Sea to northern Africa; Mediterranean.
General: Mainly inhabits inshore waters.

65 SANDY RAY S
Raja circularis

Features: Ray-shaped. Anterior margins undulated. Wings broadly rounded. The short and broad snout terminates with a small, round knob. Tail comparatively long. Coloration: above – light to reddish brown with a few whitish spots ringed with black; below – white.
Size: The larger individuals reach about 4 ft (120 cm).
Distribution: Off the Atlantic coasts of Europe, including parts of the North Sea; also in the Mediterranean.
General: This deeper-water ray occurs mainly in depths of 30–100 fathoms (60–200 m).

66 SANDY SKATE S
Raja fyllae

Features: Common ray shape, but characterized by the short, rounded wings and the rather long tail. The broad snout ends in a small, round projection. In the adults the anterior margins of the disc are much undulated. The upper side has irregular rows of spines along the back and on the tail and large patches of smaller spines on the wings; the lower side is smooth. Coloration: above – brown with darker round spots; below – whitish.
Size: 1¼–1¾ ft (40–55 cm), rarely 2 ft (60 cm).
Distribution: Northern Atlantic from west of Greenland to Svalbard, and south to Portugal.
General: Found between 200–600 fathoms (400–1000 m). Feeds on small bottomfish and crustaceans.

67 PAINTED RAY S
Raja microcellata
Other common names: Owl ray, small-eyed ray.

Features: Ray-shaped. Snout pointed in males, more blunt in females. Anterior margins undulated. A distinct row of spines along the back and two more laterally on the tail. Coloration: above – greyish to olive with characteristic larger whitish spots and short bands; below – white.
Size: Maximum length 3 ft (90 cm).
Distribution: Northeast Atlantic from Ireland to Morocco.
General: Common in shallow water.

68 SPOTTED RAY S
Raja montagui
Other common name: Homelyn ray.

Features: Ray-shaped. Anterior margins slightly undulated. The snout ends in a rounded point. Upper surface with patches of small spines and a longitudinal row of longer spines along back and tail. Coloration: above – brownish with smaller and larger dark spots.
Size: Maximum 2½ ft (75 cm).
Distribution: Northeast Atlantic off the west coast of Europe from the Shetlands to Morocco; also in the Mediterranean.
General: Lives in coastal areas in shallow and a little deeper waters. Hardly any commercial or sporting value.

69 ATLANTIC GUITARFISH
S
Rhinobatus lentiginosus
Other common names: Spotted guitarfish, fiddler ray.

Features: The shape of the body of the guitarfish species is a cross between a shark and a ray, but such characteristics as the placing of nostrils and gill slits on the underside and the fusion of the large pectoral fins with the head clearly show that these species are close to the rays.

The anterior part of the trunk and the head are flattened, the middle part of the body with the tail is rounded. Rather long snout with blunt tip. The head and the fused pectoral fins form together a triangular plate. The teeth are shaped as crushing plates. Two smaller dorsal fins (placed on the tail), rather large tail fin and broad ventral fins. Coloration: above – uniform grey to light brown with numerous small white spots; below – lighter.
Size: Max. 3–4 ft (1–1.4 m); generally only half as large.
Distribution: Western North Atlantic from Gulf of Mexico to off North Carolina.
General: A typical bottomfish which seeks its food (molluscs, crabs) in or on the muddy bottom. No commercial value and not sought by sport fishermen.

Other guitarfish species are found: Shovelnose guitarfish (*Rh. productus*) in the eastern Pacific; others in the Indian Ocean and in the southern Atlantic.

70 SHOVELNOSE GUITARFISH S
Rhinobatus productus
Other common name: Shovelnosed shark.

Features: The body is depressed with head and forepart flattened. The head is produced into a flat, rather long shovel-shaped snout with rounded tip. The trunk passes gradually into the long, strong tail which bears the two dorsal fins (without spines). The caudal fin has no lower lobe. The 5 gill openings are on the ventral surface of the body. The spiracle has two folds. Along the dorsal mid-line is a series of rather large spines, and similar spines are present on the shoulders and around the eyes. The skin is almost smooth with only minute denticles (shagreen). The females have on the tip of the snout a small, fingerlike flap. The male claspers are slender and pointed. Coloration: above dull greyish without any spots, below white.
Size: The maximum length is c. 2 ft (60 cm).
Distribution: East Pacific from San Francisco to San Diego.
General: This guitarfish lives in the surf area and in sloughs and is most common off southern California. Surf fishermen and other anglers catch it often on hook and line while fishing for more valuable fish. Its importance to the commercial and sport fisheries is only small.

71 COMMON SAWFISH F, B, S
Pristis pectinatus

Features: Large, flattened body. Snout is drawn out into a long, flattened blade (the rostrum) with c. 25 or more teeth on either side; the blade measures between 1/4 to 1/3 the total body length; skin furrow below the eye; the mouth is on the underside; five pairs of gill openings on the underside. Two dorsal fins; tail fin; large pectoral fins not joined to the sides of the head (as in rays and guitarfishes). Coloration: uniform greyish or greyish green.

Size: Average up to *c.* 18 ft (5 1/2 m); maximum weights over 5,000 lb (2,270 kg) have been recorded.

Distribution: Cosmopolitan in warm seas and the brackish and freshwater reaches of rivers.

General: Sawfish are common in the brackish and freshwater reaches of many rivers.

The teeth on either side of the spatulate rostrum blade are not true teeth but similar to dermal denticles–the skin-teeth characteristic of sharks and rays. The rostrum itself is made of cartilage like the rest of the sawfish skeleton, and the teeth are embedded in deep sockets.

Sawfish appear to spend most of their time on muddy bottoms, using their "saws" for grubbing about in the mud in search of molluscs, crustaceans, and sea urchins. The true jaw teeth have small, blunt crowns set in rows to form a crushing/grinding pavement in order to deal with shellfish. However, they can also utilize their saws with more deadly effect in a similar manner to the billfishes. When they sight a school of mullet or herring, they thrash the water with the saw to kill and stun as many as possible before the school escapes. The sawfish then devours its catch at leisure.

The female is ovoviviparous, and hatching occurs within the body just immediately before the young leave. Up to twenty-five offspring have been found in large fish.

Usually the sawfish is very sluggish and not considered dangerous to man. The flesh is quite edible and is consumed in many parts of the world. In Queensland, Australia, it is a popular and well-known market fish. As angling fish they fight a hard battle and earn a high sport-fish rating in many parts of the world.

72 MONKFISH S
Squatina squatina
Other common names: Angel shark, angel ray, fiddle fish.

Features: Flattened body. Head wide and rounded: nostrils with small, branched barbels; eyes small; five gill slits. Two small dorsal fins set well back toward tail; tail fin concave with lower lobe larger; no anal fin; pectoral fins characteristically very large and fleshy; pelvic fins large, but smaller than pectorals. Coloration: dorsally and flanks grey, greenish-grey or brownish with irregular darker mottlings and sometimes white spots; belly white.
Size: Up to 80 in (2 m), 88 lb (40 kg).
Distribution: Eastern Atlantic, from Scandinavia south to Canaries, including W. Baltic, North Sea, and English Channel; Mediterranean. Related Atlantic and Indo-Pacific forms.
General: A bottom-living shark having an appearance halfway between that of a shark and a ray. Found at depths between 15–350 ft (5–100 m) over sand or gravel and lives partially buried in the bottom. An ovoviviparous fish which gives birth to nine

to sixteen young during the summer months in northern European waters and during the winter months in its Mediterranean distribution. Food consists of fish, molluscs, and crustaceans. Occasionally caught by bottom fishermen, it is not usually included among recognised sport fish.

73 RABBITFISH S
Chimaera monstrosa
Other common name: Common chimaera.

Features: The chimaeras (several species) have a cartilaginous skeleton and the mouth on the underside like sharks and rays, but a gill cover is developed covering the gill slits. The rabbitfish has a broad, stout head with a blunt snout. The thick body tapers into a long, thin and fragile tail. Large eyes. The small mouth is placed far back on the underside of the head. Two dorsal fins, the first short and high, in front of it a big poisonous spine; the second is long and low. The tail has above and below a low brim of fins. The pectoral and ventral fins are broad and winglike. The males have on the top of the head a club-shaped spiny organ. The skin has no scales. Lateral line present with branches on the head. Coloration: head, back, and sides brown to grey marbled with dark brown. The belly is whitish to blue grey; green eyes.
Size: Max. 4 ft (1.2 m); the fragile tail is, as a rule, broken in the individuals caught. Females are larger than males.
Distribution: East Atlantic off the coasts of

Europe and Africa; western Mediterranean, also Skagerak and northern Kattegat.
General: The rabbitfish lives in deeper water, 40–300 fathoms (100–700 m). It feeds on crustaceans, mussels, and small fish. In spite of its high abundance it has no commercial importance, nor is it of interest to the sport fishery.

73A RATFISH S
Hydrolagus colliei
Other common name: Chimaera

Features: The head and anterior part of the body are stout. The tail is slender, but not nearly as long and thin as in the rabbitfish. The males have on the head a club-shaped organ similar to that in the rabbitfish. The mouth is provided with several broad crushing plates. Two dorsal fins, the first high and short, its foremost ray is stout, but not an actual spine; the second dorsal fin is long and low, lowest near the middle; tail fin long and pointed; large pectoral and ventral fins. Coloration: back and sides red brown with a golden sheen and with many whitish spots; the belly is lighter, greyish to silvery; fins light blue; the eyes are black with a yellow rim.
Size: Up to 3 ft (1 m).
Distribution: Eastern Pacific from California to Alaska.
General: Little is known about its biology. It appears to live mainly in more shallow waters than the rabbitfish.

3 COELACANTH, STURGEONS, PADDLEFISH, GARS, BOWFIN

74 COELACANTH S
Latimeria chalumnae
Other common names: "Old Fourlegs", the East London Fish, fossil fish.

Features: Very heavy-bodied. Large head. Two dorsal fins, the second is lobed; tail fin double; single lobed anal fin; pectoral fin lobed. Coloration: overall brown, steel blue, or dark blue. The scales are bony-plated and covered with dermal (toothlike) denticles; the body scales have a heavy mucus coating. Many unusual external and internal features (see below).
Size: Up to 5 ft (150 cm), 172 lb (78 kg).
Distribution: Southern Indian Ocean, ranging the Mozambique Channel and the coasts of Natal and Madagascar; probably also elsewhere in the general area.
General: The coelacanth is one of the most unusual fishes known to science. Apart from the evidence provided by the fossil record – which shows that coelacanths flourished millions of years ago – no one had seen the remains of a living coelacanth until 1938. In that year a strange-looking fish was landed from a trawler at the port of East London in South Africa. This fish had been trawled from an area which shelves very rapidly into deep water and was undoubtedly a stray specimen from a nearby deepwater habitat.

The name "Old Fourlegs" was dubbed by the famous South African fish expert J.L.B. Smith who had been alerted to the new find by Miss Courtenay-Latimer, curator of the East London Museum. Smith immediately noted the unusual pectoral and pelvic fins which resembled stalked flippers or paddles, halfway between the normal fins and the walking limbs of primitive land animals.

The characteristic double tail of the coelacanth is not found in any modern fishes and shows a direct link with the Rhipidistian fishes of some 320 million

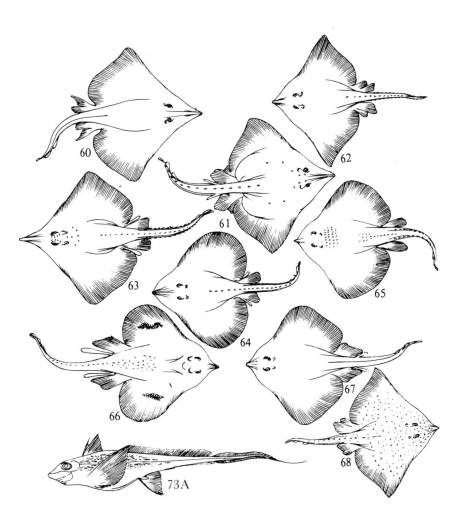

years ago which supposedly were the ancestors of land animals. Although a bony fish, the backbone of the coelacanth is made up almost entirely of a large, tough cartilaginous rod termed the notochord. During the course of evolution the notochord came before the more familiar "solid" backbone. Another unusual feature is that the rays of the fish are made up of hollow cartilage. The name *coelacanth* actually means "hollow spine". The heart is one of the simplest of its kind ever examined, and it is almost exactly what the anatomists had predicted a primitive heart would be like.

The coelacanth appears to spend much of its life in depths ranging between 500 – 1,300 ft (150 – 400 m). After the first capture several attempts were made to catch others, and substantial rewards were offered to native fishermen, but the next was not found until 1952. Since then, however, many other coelacanths have been captured, but all were dead or died soon after reaching the surface.

The most spectacular coelacanth find occurred with the capture of a live fish on 22 March 1972 in the Comoro Islands. This fish was caught by a local native fisherman named Madi Youssouf Kaar while fishing from a dugout canoe. His equipment consisted of a long cotton handline, stained black with tree-bark juice, attached to a nylon trace with a tuna-baited hook, loaded with a stone sinker. In the history of fishing perhaps no other line fisherman has made such a valuable haul with such primitive gear. When the 40-in (1-m), 22-lb (10-kg) fish was hauled to the surface, Madi Youssouf Kaar had no doubts about its identity, for his long-practised eye recognized it at once as the most desirable prize he could wrest from the sea, and exactly the fish he had sought since the announcement offering a reward of £8,000 for a dead coelacanth and £10,000 for a live specimen. The capture coincided with the presence of a Franco-British-American expedition which had come to the Comoro Islands to find a coelacanth, and within a short time the living fish was in the hands of the scientists and was kept under observation for about four hours before it finally died owing to the shock incurred by the radical change of habitat.

The reward of £10,000 was duly paid to Madi Youssouf Kaar, and it was said to be the equivalent of over one hundred years' expected income, certainly a world record for a single night's line fishing.

In earlier times the coelacanth may not have been such a rare fish as it appears to have been in more recent times. Some have identified it with a fish long known in Madagascar in former times, called *Kombessa*. Locally this fish was rated as a poor table fish unless salted and dried.

The elements of the coelacanth's scientific name *Latimeria chalumnae* were chosen to honour Miss Courtenay-Latimer who reported the find and to remember the Chalumna River near the spot where the East London trawler first hauled aboard the historic 1938 specimen.

75 LAKE STURGEON F
Acipenser fulvescens
Other common names: Rock sturgeon, stone sturgeon, rubbernose sturgeon.

Features: Much like the common seagoing Atlantic sturgeon except for the gill rakers, which number 27–39 as against 17–27 for the seagoing variety. Lake sturgeon has one row of plates anterior to anal fin. Atlantic sturgeon has two or three rows of plates between vent and anal fin. Coloration: variable with size and age, young fish usually dorsally buff or reddish with dark blotches of slate grey or black across flanks, and with rough bony skins; large fish are usually dark grey, dark green, or black and have a smooth skin.
Size: Up to 100 lb (45 kg); in former times large fish *c.* 7 ft (200 cm), 300 lb (135 kg) were not unusual but are now very rare.
Distribution: North America, from Hudson Bay, St. Lawrence River, western parts of the Great Lakes, and Winnipeg, south to northwestern states of U.S. and Mississippi Valley.
General: Owing to the sturgeon's slow growth, the fisheries are now carefully regulated. Nowadays it is taken by pound nets, mesh gill nets, or baited hooks. What fish are caught command a very high market price.

76 WHITE STURGEON F, B, S
(anadromous)
Acipenser transmontanus
Other common names: Pacific sturgeon, Oregon sturgeon, Columbia River sturgeon, Sacramento sturgeon.

Features: Young fish have a sharp snout which becomes blunted and shorter in adults. Coloration: greyish and tinged with olive. Apart from differences in coloration it may be distinguished from the green sturgeon (see below) by the number of bucklers (bony plates). The white sturgeon has 38 to 48 in the lateral row as against 23 to 30 for the green sturgeon.
Size: Over 12 ft (370 cm) and up to 1,000 lb (450 kg).
Distribution: Pacific Coast of North America from Alaska south to Monterey, California.
General: Ascends the Pacific Coast rivers in spring to spawn, but some fish probably remain in fresh water throughout the year. A recognized sport fish locally, and prized as food.

77 COMMON ATLANTIC STURGEON F, S (anadromous)
Acipenser sturio
Other common names: Common sturgeon, sea sturgeon, American sturgeon.

Features: Elongate, cylindrical body. Snout is tapered in the young, but long and broad in adults; mouth well back and two pairs of round, pointed barbels on underside. Dorsal fin 38 to 46; tail fin has upper lobe prolonged; anal fin 26 to 28. Coloration: dorsally yellowish to dusky brown or green; flanks paling to silvery grey; belly white. The body is scaleless; and in place of scales are five rows of large plates or bucklers with sharp points.
Size: Average 3–6 ft (1–2 m); large fish *c.* 20 ft (6 m), 880 lb (400 kg) at an age of 80–100

years. Fish age is hard to estimate.
Distribution: Baltic and North Sea and across Atlantic to Newfoundland, New England and south to South Carolina; Mediterranean and Black Sea. A landlocked variety is confined to Lake Ladoga in the Soviet Union.
General: A bottom-living fish which migrates to the sea. It is a slow mover and has poor vision, using the sensitive chin barbels to locate its prey by touch. In fresh water it feeds on insect larvae, worms, crayfish, snails, and small fish; at sea it takes bivalves, molluscs, shrimps and other crustaceans.

In April–May they ascend rivers to spawn. Hatching occurs in 3–7 days, and during the first year they reach a length of 8 in (20 cm). The young sturgeons migrate to sea after 1–2 years where they spend the next 7–14 years. Males mature at 7–9 years, females 8–14 years. Tagging has shown that sturgeons undertake long migratory journeys at sea. In modern times their numbers have diminished considerably.

Sturgeons have been fished primarily for their flesh, oil, and caviar (roe). Nowadays this sturgeon species has practically no interest as a sport fish.

78 GREEN STURGEON S, B, F
Acipenser acutirostris
Other common names: Smaller Pacific sturgeon, brackish-water sturgeon.

Features: Young fish have a sharp snout which becomes blunted in adults. The bucklers are rough with a strongly hooked spine. Dorsal fin 35; anal fin 27 or 28. Coloration: dorsally and flanks olive green; belly shows an olive stripe on the median line and two others on each side above ventral plates.
Size: Up to 7 ft (210 cm), 350 lb (160 kg).
Distribution: Pacific coasts of North America, from San Francisco to Vancouver.
General: A species which remains much of its time in salt or brackish water. An excellent sport fish, but its flesh is considered rank, and it represents the only species of sturgeon rated as nonedible.

79 PADDLEFISH F
Polyodon spatula
Other common names: Spoonbill, spoonbill cat, duckbill cat, spadefish, shovelnose cat, boneless cat.

Features: Distantly related to the sturgeons, its snout is greatly extended into a broad thin, flat spatula-like protrusion which is somewhat flexible and about half as long as the fish's body from the mouth to the tail. Skin smooth and scaleless except on the upper caudal lobe. Skeleton cartilaginous, the vertebral column is a white, flexible, tubelike notochord. Large flap on the gill cover, terminating in a long point, extends rearward to about the middle of the body. The vertebral column reaching out to the point of the upper lobe of the tail. Body robust and thickset. Very small eye. Single large dorsal fin which is set far back; equally large anal even more posterior. Coloration: Blue grey or dull grey or even olive grey, depending on the waters, with dark spots sometimes found on the long opercular flap. Shades to light grey below. Pointed gill

covers are greatly elongated and extend far back on the sides.
Size: Reported historically at 200 lb (91 kg) but fish of one third to one fourth that weight are more the rule.
Distribution: Mississippi Valley and south in the larger streams of the United States, also reported in the Great Lakes and various waters in the nearby Canadian area. Thrives in large impoundments.
General: Flesh is excellent and the eggs, when processed, make good caviar. Inhabits mainly mud-bottomed waterways. Commercial fishing once important but has declined.

80 ALLIGATOR GAR F, B, S
Lepisosteus spatula
Other common names: Mississippi alligator gar, devilfish, jackfish, garjack.

Features: Long body with a broad, flat alligatorlike snout (the jaws are twice as long as the head); large teeth in upper jaw in two rows on each side. Dorsal and anal fins set far back near rounded tail. Coloration: dorsally greenish or brown, paling on flanks; belly whitish; tail fin has black spots. Covered with a tough armour of heavy ganoid scales which do not overlap in the usual fishlike manner.
Size: Often over 10 ft (3 m), 300 lb (136 kg).
Distribution: Mississippi River and lower tributaries of the Gulf of Mexico and Central America to Panama.
General: The largest of the gars. The alligator gar lives mainly in still waters and for long periods remains motionless among the water plants, giving the appearance of a floating log (in much the same way as the alligator). It moves silently and seizes its prey with a sudden slash of the snout. Food consists of both live and dead fish.

Spawning occurs in March–May in shallow water, and hatching takes place a few days later. The hatched young attach themselves to water plants, and after the yolk sac is exhausted, begin to feed on mosquito larvae. The alligator gar represents one of the fastest growing of all freshwater fishes. Young males reach 20 in (50 cm) in one year. Males mature at 3–4 years, females at 6 years. Growth continues for upwards of 13–14 years, and the females generally live longer than the males.

Although gars provide excellent sport, they are usually disliked by some fishermen, who believe that they deplete the water of other more interesting sport fish. They are not classed as table fish.

81 SPOTTED GAR F, occasionally B and S
Lepisosteus oculatus
Other common names: Shortnose gar, billfish, gar pike.

Features: A long, cylindrical body and a large, beak-like and heavily toothed mouth. One posterior dorsal, rounded tail, and extremely hard, armour-like, interlocking, ganoid scales in a diamond-shape. Possesses an air bladder which enables the fish to inhale air at the water's surface. 54 to 58 scales in the lateral line. Coloration: olive green on the back, greyish green on the sides, pale grey on the belly, with large and round black spots on the top of the head and both jaws as well as the dorsal, anal and caudal fins.

Size: Maximum of 36 in (90 cm) but generally smaller.

Distribution: Central North America from Lake Erie southward through the Mississippi drainage to the Gulf of Mexico and westward up the Missouri River in the United States. Found in a few waterways in Ontario, Canada.

General: Almost no value as a commercial or as a sporting species. Such baitfish as perch and minnows form a large portion of its diet. Prefers shallow, weedy bays. Edible but not esteemed.

82 FLORIDA GAR   F, B, occasionally S
Lepisosteus platyrhynchus
Other common names: Long-nosed gar, gar pike, common gar pike, manjuari, spotted gar, shortnose gar.

Features: Body is long and cylindrical with a long, strongly-toothed mouth, single dorsal far back on the body, rounded tail, diamond-shaped, hard, interlocking scales. Distinguished from the spotted gar by the following characteristic: measure the distance from the rear edge of the bony opercle to the front of the eye. If this is under two-thirds of the length of the snout, it is a Florida gar. If more than two-thirds, it is a spotted gar. Coloration: Olive-grey or brown on the back shading to lighter below. Darker round spots on top of the head. Irregular spots on sides and fins.
Size: Up to 36 in (90 cm) and 22 lb (10 kg).
Distribution: Southeastern U.S.A. in fresh water and some brackish tributaries to the sea.
General: Lazy and rather gregarious in habits. Feeds on smaller fish. No real commercial or sport fishing value.

83 BOWFIN   F
Amia calva
Other common names: Mudfish, lawyer, dogfish, blackfish.

Features: Robust body and almost cylindrical in cross section. Large head and mouth, latter equipped with strong, sharp teeth; lower jaws have a hard, bony plate (a gular plate, which is found only in the bowfin among freshwater species); prominent nostril barbels. Long single dorsal fin *c.* 48, tail fin rounded; anal fin 10 to 12. Coloration: dorsally dark green to olive green; flanks with irregular dark blotches or bars; large fish often dorsally brownish green, shading on flanks and belly to cream or yellow; males have a prominent black spot with a yellow border on the upper part of the root of the tail fin; in females the yellow border and often the spot itself may be absent. Lateral line with scale count *c.* 67.
Size: Average up to 2–3 lb (1–1 1/2 kg); large fish up to 10–11 lb (4 1/2–5 kg).
Distribution: North America in shallow waters of warm, weedy bays, inlets, and lagoons.
General: Spawning occurs in spring when the male clears out a circular-shaped nest among the weeds. When the eggs are laid, the male takes guard, and even after the young are hatched, he remains close by for several weeks. The bowfin is the sole representative of a family of primitive fishes

common in fossils in North America and Europe. When continental drift separated the two continents, the bowfin became extinct in Europe. It is able to make direct use of atmospheric oxygen by gulping air at the surface. The bowfin is a very predatory species considered by many sport fishermen to be among the hardest fighters that take a hook. The flesh is soft and not very palatable.

4 BONY-TONGUE FISHES: ARAPAIMA, MOONEYE, LEACH

84 ARUANA   F
Osteoglossum bicirrhosum
Other common name: Arawana.

Features: Slender, somewhat compressed body. Large, upwards opening mouth with strong teeth; the lower lip bears two stout feelers. Eyes large. Body covered with big scales. One high and long dorsal fin along the posterior half of the body and a similarly large anal fin. The ventral fins are placed just behind and below the pectoral fins, their first rays are elongated. Large tail fin with rounded hind margin. Coloration: The adults are brilliantly coloured; back and sides are green with yellow sheen; the lower part of the head is reddish; fins yellow with green to red bands and spots; the scales have red spots.
Size: Maximum 3 ft (90 cm), but usually much smaller.
Distribution: Rivers in the northern, tropical South America.
General: The aruana is a voracious fish which seeks its prey (small fish, insects) on the surface of the rivers.

85 PIRARUCU   F
Arapaima gigas
Other common name: Arapaima

Features: This species and the following four (86–91) are freshwater fish; all rather slender with the dorsal and anal fins placed far back on the body; they are further characterized by a cover of short spines or denticles on the tongue.
The pirarucu is the largest known freshwater fish. The body is rather elongate but also stout; head rather small with very large upwards gaping mouth, comparatively small teeth. The backwards placed dorsal and anal fins are low; the smaller ventral fins are placed only slightly forward of the anal fin; the pectoral and the caudal fins are large. The body is covered by very large, brilliantly coloured scales. Coloration: all over clear red, blue, and grey, the belly lighter, fins reddish.

Size: The species reaches a length of 18–19 ft (6 m) with a weight of 450 pounds (200 kg).
Distribution: Lives in the large rivers of tropical South America (Amazon, also rivers in Guiana).
General: The fish is of importance to the local fisheries, and its flesh is said to be very tasty. With its size it is naturally much sought by sport fishermen.

86 MOONEYE   F
Hiodon tergisus
Other common names: White-eyed mooneye, white shad, toothed herring, river whitefish, laquaiche argentée.

Features: Similar to the goldeye (*Hiodon alosoides* see below). Characteristically the dorsal fin originates forward of the anal fin. Dorsal fin 11 or 12; tail fin forked; anal fin 28. Coloration: overall silvery appearance; dorsally olive or pale green; flanks paling to silver; belly silver. Lateral line scale count *c.* 55.
Size: Average up to 10–12 in (25–30 cm), maximum over 15 in (38 cm), 4.4 lb (2 kg).
Distribution: North America, ranging Mississippi basin, Great Lakes, St. Lawrence River, Manitoba.
General: A common species in larger streams and lakes. Its food consists chiefly of insects, molluscs, worms, plankton, and small fishes. It attracts little angling interest.

87 BELLIE   F
Heterotus niloticus
Other common name: Fantang.

Features: An elongate, compressed fish. Low head with blunt snout; upper jaw overreaching lower jaw. Lateral line a little upwards curved over the pectoral fins. The dorsal and anal fins begin well back of the middle of the trunk and continue right to the base of the very small tail fin which has a convex hind margin. The small ventral fins are placed almost midway between the pectoral fins and the anal fin. All fins have only soft rays. The scales are hard and large. Coloration: very variable, a mixture of several bright colours, mainly found on the large scales.
Size: Up to 30 in (75 cm).
Distribution: West and central Africa.
General: The bellie lives in the rivers. The adults build a large nest of plant debris for the eggs and larvae and watch over them until the young are able to fend for themselves.

88 GOLDEYE   F
Hiodon alosoides
Other common names: Gold-eyed mooneye, northern mooneye, toothed herring, wap, naccaysh, Winnipeg goldeye, laquaiche aux yeux d'or.

Features: Deep, laterally compressed herringlike body, but with rounded belly. Distinct humped shape above forehead; small head; small mouth with strong, sharp teeth on tongue; eyes large and yellow or golden in colour. Dorsal fin 9; tail fin forked; anal fin 32. Coloration: dorsally bluish or greenish; flanks paling to silver. Lateral line scale count *c.* 56.

Size: Average up to 10–12 in (25–30 cm), maximum over 15 in (38 cm).

Distribution: North America, ranging northwestern Canada, Hudson Bay south into the Ohio River basin to Tennessee.

General: An attractive fish found in lakes and rivers. Spawning occurs in spring. Young fish move downstream in late summer. Food consists of insects, fish, mollusks, and crayfish. The goldeye is a popular sport fish which may be caught by baited hook, spinner, or fly. Moderate food value.

89 LEACH F
Mormyrops deliciosus

Features: Elongate, little compressed body. Blunt snout with the mouth not protruding; large teeth; very small scales, about 90 along the lateral line. One long dorsal fin with 20–27 rays is placed far back on the body, much nearer the tail than the head; also the anal fin is long, 40–50 rays, and placed far back. Forked tail fin with rounded lobes. Rather big pectoral and small ventral fins. Coloration: very variable in accordance with the habitat; back and sides dark grey with a sheen of bronze.

Size: 2–3 ft (60–90 cm), 24–30 lb (10–14 kg); maximum 5 ft (150 cm), 40 lb (18 kg).

Distribution: Southern and western Africa, Zambesi River, Congo River.

General: The species prefers slow-flowing streams, also lakes and ponds. The food is small fish, prawns, and insects. The leach is a good gamefish for light gear. It moves and feeds mainly at night; in daytime it remains sheltered at the bottom and in vegetation.

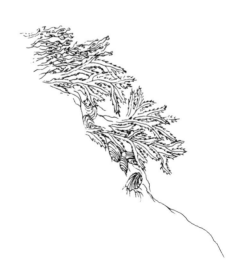

5 BONEFISH, TARPON, EELS

90 BONEFISH S, B
Albula vulpes
Other common names: Grubber, banana fish.

Features: Subcylindrical, spindle-shaped body, flattened below. Lower jaw shorter than upper jaw; jaws with minute villiform teeth; blunt, conical, foxlike snout. Dorsal fin 18 to 20; tail fin large and deeply forked; anal fin 8 or 9; ventral fins 9. Coloration: dorsally silver olive; flanks and belly silver; whole body is overshot with bluish and olive tints with faint longitudinal marks along scale rows above the lateral line. The snout and fins yellowish. Lateral line scale count 70 to 73. Large silvery scales; head scaleless.

Size: Average 15–20 in (38–50 cm), maximum over 40 in (100 cm), 17 lb (7 1/2 kg).

Distribution: Worldwide in tropical and subtropical waters.

General: Frequents harbours, coastal, and estuary waters, and prefers sandy or muddy areas where it may school in fair numbers. Characteristically it feeds by nosing into the soft bottom sediments to root out clams, snails, and other invertebrates. The young in the postlarval stage are transparent and resemble the eel leptocephalus. Renowned for their outstanding speed in the water. Even the smaller fish put up tremendous resistance. As the popular name implies, the fish is bony; although an unpopular table fish for this reason, the flesh is tasty and of good quality.

91 TARPON S, B, F
Megalops atlanticus
Other common name: Silver king.

Features: Oblong, compressed body. Flattened forehead; large undershot mouth and projecting lower jaw. Dorsal fin 12 to 16 (last ray is very long and filamentous); tail fin deeply forked; anal fin 19 to 23 soft rays. Coloration: dorsally greenish or

bluish-silver paling to silver on flanks and belly; fish from brackish water usually more yellowish. Lateral line scale count 41 to 48. Scales large and heavy.

Size: Average range 24–36 in (60–90 cm), maximum 100 in (250 cm).

Distribution: Tropical, subtropical, and occasionally temperate Atlantic waters. A small population in eastern Pacific near Pacific exit of Panama Canal is due to movement of some tarpon through the canal to Pacific waters.

General: Tarpon are found in inshore and offshore waters, sometimes in brackish and fresh water, and are capable of existing in oxygen-depleted water due to their ability to take in air directly from the atmosphere with their lunglike air bladders. The tarpon was probably the first marine species to be declared a game fish, and is still one of the most popular of the larger marine sport fish. When hooked, the tarpon has great endurance and offers a tremendous fight with spectacular leaps. Not recognized as an edible table fish.

92 LADYFISH S
Elops saurus
Other common names: Ten pounder, Springer, Cape salmon, Skipjack.

Features: Slender, elongate body. Mouth very large and at tip of snout; adipose eyelid. Dorsal fin 21–26 (last ray characteristically *not* filamentous which readily serves to identify it from the bonefish (*Albula vulpes*); tail fin very deeply forked; tail lobes long and slender; anal fin 15 or 16. Coloration: dorsally silvery, bluish, or greenish; flanks and belly silvery. Lateral line scale count 103–120.

Size: Up to 3 ft (1 m); maximum size reputed up to c. 15 lb (7 kg) in South African waters.

Distribution: Cosmopolitan in temperate and warmer seas.

General: In North America it is usually known under the name ten pounder, although it seldom appears to reach this weight here; in South Africa it is known as springer due to its proneness to leap when hooked. A schooling species, strikes furiously at lures, but can also be caught on bait. The flesh is very bony and is not rated very highly for the table.

93 MACHETE S, B, occasionally F
Elops affinis
Other common names: Chiro, John Mariggle, bonyfish, bonefish, big-eyed herring, Lisa, Lisa Francesca, ladyfish, matajuelo real, leack or mondi (West Africa), wildevis or cape salmon (Knysna), skipjack, mlakwe, springer.

Features: Carnivorous, scaly, powerful, large-mouthed fishes of warm water. Minute teeth on all the normal bones of the mouth and with a bony plate below the jaws; ten to sixteen rays in the pelvic fin. The depth goes into the length between five and six times. Adipose eyelids are present; pectorals are low down; there are 16 to 17 gill rakers. Herring-like in the arrangement of its fins; single dorsal originating about midway along the back; no adipose fin; ventrals about midway between snout and the fork of the tail; caudal forked. Scales

small. Dorsal fin, 20 to 25; anal, 13 to 17. There are 100 to 120 scales along the lateral line; 12 rows above and 17 below at the shoulder. Coloration: silvery all over with a blue hue to the back, the lower parts of the sides and the lower surface yellowish. The caudal and dorsal fins are dusky yellowish and silvery; the pectoral and ventral fins are yellowish speckled and dusky.

Size: Attains 36 in (90 cm).

Distribution: Found in most warm seas with positive reports off South Africa, the Lower California coast of Mexico in the Pacific, the tropical Atlantic from the West Indies north to Long Island, New York. Also reported off Brazil.

General: Body is bony, fish edible, but not particularly good. Good game fish that jumps repeatedly and may often be caught in tidal rivers. Very well known and pursued in certain areas, virtually ignored in others. Closely related to *E. saurus*.

94 OX-EYE TARPON S (B)
Megalops cyprinoides
Other common name: Ox-eye herring.

Features: Body compressed, high. Head large with big upwards turned mouth and large eyes. Small teeth. Lower jaw projects strongly beyond upper jaw, the latter is broad and reaches to below the posterior rim of the eye; eyes with adipose eyelids. The single dorsal fin is high with a strongly concave upper margin, its last ray is very much elongated. Tail fin deeply forked with large, pointed lobes. The margin of the long anal fin is concave. Large scales. Coloration: back and upper sides olive, lower sides whitish to silvery; the fins are mainly yellow.

Size: About 1¼–1½ ft (40–45 cm).

Distribution: Tropical part of the Indian Ocean; Ceylon – East Indies.

General: The species lives in shallow coastal waters, often also in estuaries. It is much sought by sport fishermen.

95 MORAY EEL S
Muraena helena

Features: Long, elongate, snakelike body. Conical head; short snout; jaws ending back behind eyes; very sharp teeth. Dorsal and anal fins long and ribbonlike meeting at a rounded point; pectoral fins absent. Coloration: dorsally brown to blackish brown with mottling or marbling of yellow or whitish spots; a black spot surrounds the gill openings. No scales; the skin is almost like smooth hide.

Size: Average up 40 in (1 m), maximum 5 ft (1.5 m), 26½ lb (12 kg).

Distribution: Mediterranean and eastern Atlantic, rarely farther north than English Channel. Related forms have a worldwide distribution in warm-temperate to tropical waters.

General: There are more than 100 species of the family *Muraenidae*. Although there are marked differences in coloration, all have similar features and habits to *Muraena helena*; recognition of individual species is not easy.

Moray eels are usually found over rocky ground in deep water where they hide away in deep cracks or crevices from where they can stalk a prey; generally a nocturnal fish, and scent plays an important role in locating food. In the Mediterranean they may often utilize ancient Greek amphora as suitable hideaways. Food consists of fish, crustaceans and cephalopods.

All moray eels may be considered dangerous species, and are best given a wide berth by skin divers and sport fishermen. A bite is very painful and results in severe skin lacerations which frequently turn septic. Not considered a sport species, although frequently sought by pleasure divers.

96 CONGER EEL S, possibly B and F

Conger oceanicus
Other common names: Sea eel, conger, eel pout.

Features: A large, voracious ocean eel having no scales on the body skin, no pelvic fins, and soft-rayed pectoral, dorsal, and anal fins. The backbone forms a straight line from head to tail. The gill openings are very small. Dorsal and anal fins join at the tail to form a single fin with no separations. Body is fairly stout. Tail tip is rounded and soft. Gape of mouth extends to middle or rear of the eyes. Long, pointed snout with slightly undershot lower jaw. In common eels the upper jaw is longer. Conger eyes are large and oval compared to small, round eyes of common eel. Coloration: Blue-grey or grey-brown above, often varying to reddish or black. Pale sides and dirty white below.
Size: Averages up to 9ft (2.10 m) and 22 lb (10 kg), with some specimens considerably larger.
Distribution: Continental shelves of western and eastern Atlantic in temperate and cold waters.
General: Feeds on fish and crustaceans and rated good seafood in some areas. Rather low commercial value, although locally valuable in some European markets. Avidly sought by some European anglers, but not attractive to Americans.

97 GREEN MORAY S

Gymnothorax funebris
Other common names: Moray eel, moray, eel, green eel.

Features: Distinguished from all the other eels by small and round gill openings and the absence of pectoral fins. The body and fins are covered by a thick leathery skin. The occipital region is elevated through the development of the strong muscles which move the lower jaw; the jaws usually narrow and armed with knife-like teeth. A single fin runs over the back, around the tail and forward on the body without being separated into distinct portions recognizable on other fishes. The green moray has an elongate, snake-like form with a single pair of gill openings; large pointed teeth, the posterior vomerine teeth in a double row. The snout is long and pointed. The mouth is relatively large, the gape reaching far behind the eye. Coloration: Often bright green, sometimes brownish or slaty grey, sometimes slightly mottled, also described as blue-grey with a yellow, algae coating. The fins are darker than the body.

Size: Reported at maximum of 6 ft (180 cm) or possibly larger; usually far smaller.
Distribution: Reefs of Bermuda and the West Indies; Florida to Brazil. Also recorded from the Cape Verde Islands.
General: Dangerous when provoked; has been known to inflict severe wounds on divers. Little if any evidence of unprovoked attacks. Known to eat small octopuses. Slow swimmer, generally remaining in caves or crevices on the bottom; rarely found in open water. Not much food or sporting value.

98 EUROPEAN EEL F, B, S

(catadromous)
Anguilla anguilla

98 AMERICAN EEL F, B, S

(catadromous)
Anguilla rostrata
Other common names: Common eel, freshwater eel, silver eel (mature phase), Atlantic eel.

Features: Very elongate body, cylindrical in front section, compressed behind, and tapering to a rounded point. Prominent lower jaw and slightly projecting; gills are enclosed in a pouch forward of pectoral fin. Long dorsal fin 245 to 275; anal fin 205 to 235; pair of pectoral fins behind head. Coloration: variable with habitat and age, in immature phase dorsally black to olive brown; flanks tinged with yellow; belly yellowish white. With approaching maturity dorsally grey or blue green; flanks and belly silvery.
Size: Males 12–20 in (30–50 cm), females 16–39 in (40–100 cm), maximum *c.* 7 3/4 lb (3 1/2 kg). Occasional large specimens considerably heavier.
Distribution: Europe (range extending to the Mediterranean shores of North Africa); the Americas. *Note:* The European and American eels may be synonymous species.
General: The natural history of the eel is one of the most remarkable stories on record. Eel larvae were not associated with the adult fish until the later years of the 19th century. Until then they had been classified as a small fish under the name of *Leptocephalus brevirostris*. Even today the larval eel is always referred to as a *leptocephalus* (which literally means small-headed).

In late summer and autumn the adult eels of Europe and the Mediterranean countries make their way down the rivers to travel 3,000 miles (4,800 km) or more to the Sargasso Sea to spawn. They never return, but the larvae, or *leptocephali*, hatching from their eggs make the return journey. When they reach the coasts of Europe, by then three years old, they undergo a metamorphosis and change into elvers, just under 3 in (7 cm) long. They ascend the rivers to feed and grow before later setting off in their turn into the western Atlantic on their own breeding migration.

During their penetration of the inland waterways, little can hinder their progress. They squirm and wriggle up damp vertical walls of dams and skirt impossible obstacles by land if the ground is wet. In upstream waters the limit of penetration is terminated when the elvers fully develop and lose their ability to climb difficult surfaces.

The males generally tend to remain in

the lower reaches of the river, while the females migrate inland to lakes, ponds, and ditches. Eel growth depends upon available food supply. The males move down to the sea at 4–8 years, the better fed ones going first. The females remain until 7–12 years old. Eels prevented from reaching the sea will grow quite large and may live for over 30 years.

Prior to migration all feeding stops, and they go through significant body changes. Their heads become more pointed, and their colour changes from olive-brown to grey or blue green and silvery white on the flanks and belly. The eyes grow larger, and the pectoral fin develops, becoming pointed and black. Every autumn approximately one tenth of the total eel population begins its migration to the sea.

The American eel makes a similar migration and spawns in an area in the western Atlantic which overlaps the breeding area of the European eel. Its *leptocephali* return to the eastern coasts of North America, taking only a year on the journey.

The larvae of the American and European varieties are outwardly so alike that it is difficult to tell them apart. However, mature eels from each region show differences in numbers of vertebrae. The American eel has between 103 and 111 vertebrae compared with the 110 to 119 vertebrae of the European fish. Some have suggested that the difference is due to environmental conditions in the early larval stages. It is known that the ambient temperature of water can induce changes in the number of vertebrae – even in larvae from the same parent. The American eel population has only a short distance to travel to its spawning ground, and is nowhere near as advanced into breeding condition when it enters the sea as is the European population, which has a longer distance to travel. One suggestion put forward is that the eels found in Europe are recruited from larvae hatching from eggs laid exclusively by American eels, but this idea has not yet been confirmed.

Other species: The Indian and Pacific oceans have their own species of eel. All pass through the *leptocephalus* elver-eel stages, but little is known about their deepwater breeding grounds. It is believed that eels populating the east coast of Africa breed round Madagascar. Three species enter rivers on the East African coast, although only one (*A. mossambica*) is known south of Mozambique. The largest eel is *A. nebulosa labiata*, which is common in the Zambesi River and the region north of it. This species attains a normal length of 60 in (150 cm) and weighs up to 30 lb (13 1/2 kg).

A suggested breeding ground for the Pacific eel lies near the Solomon Islands. Eels invade Japan, parts of China, Australia, New Zealand, Indonesian waters, and several small Pacific islands. The three species which occur in Australasia are generally heavier fish than the American/European variety (see also Index).

Global distribution: Although eels are widely distributed, being found in and around many continents in the sea, coastal waters, estuaries, rivers, lakes, canals, reservoirs, clay pits, ponds, and drains, they are notably absent from the Arctic and Antarctic regions; from the Pacific coast of the

Americas; the Atlantic coast of South America; the west coast of Africa *c.* 20° N to the Cape of Good Hope; and the west coast of Australia.

Eel fisheries are important commercially in many countries, particularly in Europe where the eel is much esteemed as a delicious table fish. Small "bootlace" eels can be a nuisance to anglers, but large specimens, generally caught at night on worms or small fish deadbaits, put up a powerful fight.

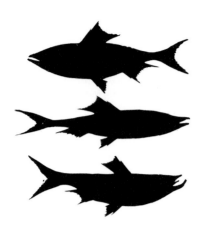

99 NORTHERN ANCHOVY S

Engraulis mordax

Other common names: California anchovy, bait anchovy, anchovy, whitebait.

Features: Of the dwarf-herring family, *Engraulidae*, with the snout projecting beyond a very wide mouth. The vertebrae are numerous, the bones feeble. As a family, anchovies have bodies that are fairly elongate and compressed, snouts rounded, overlapping the large mouth with a long maxilla. Teeth are small or absent, tongue free only at the tip, no lateral line, eyes completely covered by skin. The head length is longer than the depth of the body; anal fin 'shorter than the head. Dorsal fin, about 14 to 16; anal, 19 to 21. There are thirty eight to forty two series of scales. Coloration: A blue to blue-green on the back and above area shading to silvery on the sides and beneath.

Size: Attains about 10 in (25 cm) at maximum but usually about half this length.

Distribution: Along the North American Pacific coast from Lower California north through California to British Columbia.

General: Important commercially when used as pickled and salted fillets as accessories to other dishes; also used as chum for tuna. Used as a live bait for many species of gamefish by anglers; a marine forage fish of considerable importance in the life chain of many marine fishes.

100 MENHADEN, ATLANTIC S

Brevoortia tyrannus

Other common names: Mossbunker, bunker, pogy, menhaden, bonyfish, whitefish, bugfish, fatback, old wife, chebog, hardhead, yellowtail shad.

Features: Elliptical, elongate, compressed body with thickness varying from one-third to one-half of body depth. The head and mouth are large with the cheek not as long as it is deep. Toothless, with densely set, long, slender gill rakers that form a feeding filter. The scales are rather deep with fluted vertical edges. The low dorsal fin is placed fairly well back. The anal fin is small. Dorsal fin 19; anal fin 20; caudal fin moderately forked. Coloration: Dark above, ranging from blue-green to blue-brown. A massed school shows red-brown under the surface. Silvery sides and belly with a brassy or yellowish-tan luster. Prominent black spot behind the gill opening on each side, and a number of smaller dark spots in irregular rows further back. Lateral line scale count 60–80.

Size: 12–20 in (30–50 cm), up to 1.1 lb (1/2 kg).

Distribution: Atlantic coastal waters from Nova Scotia to Florida and Gulf of Mexico, thence south as far as Argentina in closely related subrace forms.

General: One of the most important industrial fishes, caught by purse seines and fish traps. Found in huge schools, and preyed on by many larger fish. Not taken by rod and reel except when accidentally snagged in a dense school. Too bony and oily for good table fare, but excellent bait alive, dead, or as ground fish meal.

101 HICKORY SHAD F, S

(anadromous)

Alosa mediocris

Other common names: Hickory jack, fall herring, tailor herring, Mattowaca, tailor shad, freshwater tailor.

Features: Deep-bodied, laterally compressed. A rather long head; lower jaw projects considerably. Dorsal fin 15; tail fin forked; anal fin 21. Coloration: dorsally and on upper flanks greyish green; lower flanks silvery.

Size: Average up to 2–3 lb (1–1 1/2 kg). Smaller than the American shad.

Distribution: Atlantic coast from Cape Cod south to Florida.

102 ALEWIFE S, F (anadromous)

Alosa pseudoharengus

Other common names: Ellwife, branch herring, gaspereau, sawbelly, wall-eyed herring, big-eyed herring, grey herring, white herring, blear-eyed herring, spring herring, glut herring, golden shad, seth green shad, skipjack, bang, kyak or kiack, mulhaden, "crazy fish".

Features: Deep, laterally compressed body; the belly is compressed to a knife-edge thinness. Dorsal fin 14 to 18; tail fin deeply forked; anal fin 16 to 20. Coloration: dorsally greyish green or bluish; flanks and belly silvery; there is a single black spot on each flank above the eye level and just behind the gill cover. When freshly caught, the flanks have a brilliant iridescent sheen.

Size: Average up to 10–12 in (25–30 cm), maximum 14 in (36 cm).

Distribution: North America, ranging Newfoundland, Nova Scotia to South Carolina; the Great Lakes; occasionally landlocked in fresh water.

General: Primarily a marine species which ascends freshwater streams in spring, but it is now landlocked in many inland lakes. Spawning occurs in May–July when it ascends coastal streams. Excellent live bait for larger fish, but only indifferent table fare.

103 ALLIS SHAD F, S

(anadromous)

Alosa alosa

Other common names: Scotch herring, alewife.

Features: Very similar to twaite shad (see below) except for size and gill-raker differences; usually only a single large spot behind gill cover, but occasionally absent. Lateral line scale count 70 to 80.

Size: Up to *c.* 24 in (60 cm), 8 lb (3 1/2 kg).

Distribution: From Norway to the Mediterranean, but not as far eastward as the twaite shad; less common in the Baltic and the Mediterranean.

General: The biology is similar to the twaite shad except that during the spring migration upriver it travels much further inland, sometimes to a distance of 500 miles (800 km).

104 AMERICAN SHAD F, S

(anadromous)

Alosa sapidissima

Other common names: Shad, alosa, north river shad, Potomac shad, Connecticut River shad, Delaware shad, Susquehanna shad, Atlantic shad.

Features: Deep, laterally compressed body. Lower jaw fits into a notch in upper jaw. Dorsal fin 15 to 19; tail fin forked; anal fin 18 to 24. Coloration: dorsally and upper flanks dark bluish; lower flanks and belly silvery white; a golden tinge over much of the body; one row of dark spots on flanks beginning just behind upper part of gill cover. Scales are large and loosely attached.

Size: Up to 30 in (75 cm), 8 1/4 lb (3 3/4 kg).

Distribution: Native to Atlantic coast of North America. Spawning in many rivers from northern Florida to Canada. Introduced into the Sacramento River, California, in 1871 and is now firmly established along the Pacific coast to Alaska.

General: A seagoing fish which travels inland to spawn during the spring. It moves about in vast schools. Shad populations fluctuate from decade to decade. It is important as a sport and a commercial species. As a table fish it may be eaten fresh or salted, and the roe is in particular demand.

105 SKIPJACK HERRING F, S

Alosa chrysochloris

Other common names: Blue herring, nailrod, government shad.

Features: Deep, laterally compressed body. Single dorsal fin *c.* 16; tail fin forked; anal fin *c.* 19. Coloration: dorsally a brilliant blue or greenish; flanks silvery with golden reflections; 1–9 marks or spots which readily distinguish the skipjack herring from the alewife (*Alosa pseudoharengus*) a closely related species (see above) which has only one.

Size: Up to 15 in (38 cm).

Distribution: North America, Mississippi Valley from Minnesota downstream into the Gulf of Mexico.

General: The common name "skipjack" alludes to its habit of leaping in the air when in pursuit of schools of minnow. In spite of its small size, it is an excellent sport fish. It is very bony, although edible, not usually recognized as a table fish.

106 TWAITE SHAD F, S

(anadromous)

Alosa fallax

Other common names: Scotch herring, alewife.

Features: Deep, laterally compressed body. Lower jaw slightly projecting; upper jaw notched. Dorsal fin 18 to 21; tail fin forked; anal fin 20 to 26. Coloration: dorsally deep blue or greenish; flanks paler with a touch of pink or blue; belly white; flanks show a succession of 6 to 7 dark blotches beginning behind gill cover. No lateral line. Lateral line scale count 60 to 70. The twaite shad is very similar to the allis shad (see above); the only sure way to distinguish between them is to count the gill rakers on the first gill arch; the twaite shad has 40 to 60, the allis 90 to 120.

Size: Up to *c.* 20 in (50 cm), 4 lb (1 3/4 kg).

Distribution: From Iceland, northern Norway, Baltic, south to the Mediterranean. Many live the entire life span in fresh or brackish water; several landlocked populations.

General: During the spring migration upriver, the sea fish travel only short distances. After the young hatch, they grow rapidly and soon move downstream. Males reach maturity at 2–3 years; females 4–5 years, so that spawning males are smaller fish than spawning females.

Shad are basically plankton feeders, and their large gill rakers are used to good advantage to filter out the smallest plankton. They also consume copepods, crustaceans, and small fish. Nowadays they are only rarely encountered by sport fishermen, but they are still caught commercially in some parts by net. They provide an excellent table fish and are often smoked.

107 BLUEBACK HERRING S, B, F

Alosa aestivalis

Other common names: Shad herring, glut herring.

Features: Rather high and compressed body. Short and high head. Small eyes. Lower jaw projecting beyond upper jaw, the latter is very broad. Small teeth. Dorsal fin with concave margin. Tail fin deeply forked; anal fin low, its margin straight. A large, triangular scale at base of ventral fins. Coloration: back bluish, sides and belly silvery; the scales in several rows on back and upper sides have small, dark markings; a larger black spot behind the gill cover.

Size: Maximum 15 in (38 cm), 13 ounces (360 g); usual size below 12 in (30 cm) and 1/2 pound (230 g).

Distribution: Western North Atlantic from Nova Scotia to Florida.

General: Anadromous; enters the rivers for spawning. Food consists of small pelagic crustaceans and fish fry.

108 THREADFIN SHAD F, occasionally B and F

Dorosoma petenense

Other common names: Shad, hickory shad, mud shad, gizzard shad, lake shad, sawbelly, alose à gésier.

Features: Characterized by a forked tail, a single and short, soft-rayed dorsal fin in the middle of the back and the absence of both an adipose fin and a visible lateral line. Deep bodied and strongly compressed laterally with a small mouth lacking teeth. The body narrows to almost a knife-like thickness on the belly which is in turn covered with strong and specialized scales (scutes) projecting along its margin, which is almost saw-toothed in appearance. Greatly elongated last ray of the dorsal fin. The anal base is quite long, but the rays are short or close-cropped. Anal fin, 20 to 23. Coloration: bright and gleaming, a deep blue green or a blue on the back, silvery along the sides. A large black spot is on the shoulder just back of the gill covers. In many fish there is a distinct to pronounced yellow cast of hue to the back and caudal fin.
Size: Seldom over 8 in (20 cm).
Distribution: A wide range starting in British Honduras to the south and along the United States Gulf Coast into Texas, Florida, and northward along the Mississippi drainage to Tennessee, Arkansas and Oklahoma. Introduced into Arizona and California plus many other places not yet reported.
General: Important forage fish for various game species. Used as a bait, wherein it has limited commercial value. No gamefish value. Flesh not esteemed.

109 GIZZARD SHAD F, B

Dorosoma cepedianum

Other common names: Herring shad, threadfin shad.

Features: A typical member of the herring family with single, soft-rayed dorsal fin, forked tail, no adipose fin, no visible lateral line. The elongated last ray of the dorsal fin gives it the common name of "threadfin shad." A long anal fin and belly scales that are saw-toothed in edge profile. Juveniles have small teeth which disappear in adults. Mature fish feed mainly on vegetable matter. The mouth is small and is located in the lower part of the head. Coloration: Silver-blue on top shading to brass or reddish on the sides, white belly. Juveniles have a dark spot on shoulder that fades on maturity.
Size: Up to 15 in (38 cm), 3 1/2 lb (1.6 kg).
Distribution: Eastern and central North America in rivers and some lakes, from Minnesota to the Gulf of Mexico, and along the U.S. East Coast. A few fish in eastern Mexico.
General: An important forage fish for larger game, especially striped bass, largemouth bass, and lake trout. No commercial or food value, nor especially attractive to anglers.

110 PACIFIC SARDINE S

Sardinops sagax

Other common name: Sardina.

Features: Body elongate, a little compressed; front of head flattened; blunt snout. Upper jaw broad. No teeth. The hind margins of the scales are weakly serrate; about 50 scales along the side. Keeled belly scales not very sharp. Dorsal and ventral fins placed midway on body. Forked tail fin, rather long pectoral fins. The two last rays in the anal fin longer than the preceding ones. Coloration: back and upper sides blue, lower sides and belly silvery. A longitudinal line of black spots behind the gill cover, most distinct in the young.
Size: About 8–12 in (20–30 cm).
Distribution: Eastern Pacific from California to Chile.
General: A shoaling fish from the shallow coastal waters, feeding on plankton. Of considerable importance to the fishery, also as bait for tuna fishing.

111 WOLF HERRING S

Chirocentrus dorab

Other common names: Silkfish, parang (Malay).

Features: This large fish has a herringlike shape of body. The eyes are rather large. Big mouth with pointed teeth up to 0.2–0.3 in (5–8 cm) long. One dorsal fin at about the middle of the back; forked tail fin with pointed lobes; rather short ventral fins are inserted midway on the lower contour of the body. All fins have only soft rays, branched right from their bases. Coloration: the back is greyish, sides and belly silvery.
Size: The wolf herring grows to a length of 11–12 ft (300–325 cm); weight ca 220 lb (100 kg).
Distribution: Western Pacific and East Indian seas.
General: A very voracious fish hunting in the open sea.

112 SPANISH SARDINE S

Sardinella anchovia

Other common name: False sardine.

Features: Slender, much compressed body. Mouth upwards turned. Large eyes. Few and small teeth, none in the upper jaw. The single dorsal fin is rather high anteriorly; along its base is a sheath of narrow scales; anal fin low, its two last rays are twice as long as the preceding ones, a sheath of scales along the base. Ventral fins off the dorsal fin, at their base is a sheath of small plates. Coloration: above bluish to blackish, sides and belly silvery.
Size: Maximum 6½ in (16 cm), but most only 4–5 in (10–12 cm).
Distribution: Western North Atlantic from Massachusetts to Florida.
General: A shoaling fish from more shallow waters. Feeds on planktonic creatures. Is of some importance to the fishing industry.

113 ANCHOVY S (B)

Engraulis encrasicholus

Features: Slender, rounded body. The snout reaches well beyond the big mouth. Ventral fins placed well forward of the dorsal fin. Big scales. Coloration: back and upper sides dark blue green, lower sides and belly silvery; running longitudinally between the two colours is a narrow bright blue and black band.
Size: Up to 6 in (15 cm).
Distribution: European coastal waters from the southern North Sea and into the Mediterranean and Black Seas. In some years shoals penetrate from the North Sea through the Belts right into the western part of the Baltic.
General: A pelagic fish from shallow waters, also egg and larvae are pelagic. Considerable commercial importance, especially for the canning industry.

114 PILCHARD SARDINE S

Sardina pilchardus

Other common name: Sardine.

Features: Slender, compressed body. Underlip slightly projecting beyond upper lip. Gill cover with radiated striation. Large eyes. Very large scales, only about 30 along the lateral line.. Dorsal fin on middle of back. Ventral fins placed off the posterior part of dorsal fin. Keeled scales only weakly sharpened. Coloration: uniformly bluish with weak greenish or reddish sheen; belly lighter; fins grey, blue, or brown.
Size: Max. 10 in (25 cm), mostly only 7–8 in (19–20 cm).
Distribution: Coastal East Atlantic from the British Isles to Morocco; Mediterranean and Black Seas. A rare guest in the North Sea.
General: A pelagic species feeding on small crustaceans, fish eggs, and fish larvae. Has considerable commercial importance, especially for the canning industry.

115 SPRAT S (B)

Sprattus sprattus

Other common name: Garvock (in Scotland).

Features: The sprat is shaped very much like a small herring; it can, however, be distinguished by the following characteristics: smaller eyes, much sharper keeled scales on edge of belly between ventral and anal fins, ventral fin placed under the first ray of dorsal fin, body deeper between pectoral and ventral fins, and its larger scales. Coloration: as in the herring but mostly more greenish and less bluish.
Size; Maximum length 6½ in (16–17 cm), generally 4–5 in (10–13 cm).
Distribution: Coastal and near-coastal waters of Europe, including the Baltic, Mediterranean and Black Seas.
General: A pelagical shoaling fish, living in shallow waters from the coast down to some 60 fathoms (100 m). Spawning in spring and early summer, eggs and larvae are pelagic. Highly important for the commercial fishery, especially used in the canning industry; hardly of interest to the sport fisherman.

116 HERRING S

Clupea harengus

Features: Slender, compressed body. Rather large eyes; lower lip projecting slightly beyond upper lip; gill cover smooth. The keeled scales along the edge of the belly between ventral fin and anal fin moderately sharp. One dorsal fin at the middle of the body; tail fin large, forked, ventral fins placed off the anterior third of the dorsal fin. Lateral line indistinct. Scales only loosely fitted. Coloration: uniformly bluish, to slightly greenish, silvery; darkest above; belly much lighter. Fins brown, grey, or yellow.
Size: Can reach 1¼ ft (40 cm) or 1 pound (454 g) in the species from the northern Atlantic. In southern and eastern waters the size is much smaller, in the Baltic 8–10 in (20–26 cm) is the general length.
Distribution: North Atlantic coastal and near coastal regions, from north of Norway to Brittany and from western Greenland to New England; Iceland, Faroes, North Sea, Belts, and most of the Baltic.
General: The herring lives pelagically right from the shallow, coastal waters out to a depth of 150 fathoms (300 m), but during its wide migrations it may pass over still deeper water. It is a typical shoaling fish, moving through the free water masses in huge and often dense shoals. The food consists of planktonic animals: copepods, euphaucians, shrimps, prawns and smaller fish and larvae of fish. In its turn it is a very important food item for larger pelagic fishes: sharks, tunas, mackerel, cod and salmon.

Several races of herring occur, differing from one another in minor morphological features: numbers of vertebrae and fin rays, but mainly in distribution, spawning places and seasons for spawning, to the effect that spawning can take place in almost any month. However, each race has its own spawning area and spawning season.

The eggs are deposited on the sea bottom attached to stones, shells and plants or just stick together in large lumps. The larvae hatch after 1–3 weeks according to the height of the water temperature. The larvae are 6–7 mm long and thin, thread-shaped; through the following weeks they become more compressed and with 4–5 cm the scales appear, and the young acquire the shape and coloration of the adult herring. The growth varies very much from region to region. A two-year-old herring from the Baltic is only 4.5 in (12 cm) long, from Iceland as much as 8 in (20 cm). In the smaller seas (Baltic, Kattegat) the herring reach a size of only *c.* 10 in (26 cm), in the larger open seas (Faroes, Iceland) as much as 14–15 in (35–40 cm).

The herring is – especially in northwest Europe – one of the most important commercial fishes. It is fished over most areas and through almost the whole year. Off western Greenland and Labrador the herring is only rare and hardly fished commercially. Only south of the Grand Banks of Newfoundland it is numerous enough to sustain a commercial fishery. Many kinds of gear are used: purse seines, driftnets, poundnets and trawls. In the open seas special highly developed scouting gear is used: Asdic and echosounder for finding the shoals. Most herring are used for human consumption, fresh or preserved (salted, smoked or canned), but large amounts (mostly of young herring) are used for the production of oil or meal. Fishing for herring has been carried out for many centuries. The fisheries in the Sounds and Belts, Skagerak and the North Sea have been renowned since the twelfth century. In those times, the export of herring salted in barrels was of the highest importance for the economy of the surrounding countries. For centuries the stocks of herring sustained these heavy fisheries, but during our generation the stocks have – at last – become overfished, due partly to the very efficient midwater-trawls used, partly to the huge quantities fished for industrial purposes. The stocks have been sadly diminished, and now international measures are taken for reducing the fisheries, and thus preserving the stocks of this highly important food-item.

117 PEARLSIDE S
Maurolicus mulleri

Features: The small body is much compressed; head and forepart are rather deep, the tail part less deep. Large mouth and big eyes. The dorsal and anal fins are placed back on the body, behind the dorsal fin is a long, low adipose fin; the tail fin is slightly forked; pectoral and ventral fins are rather long but narrow. Coloration: overall bright silvery with weak reddish hues; the back is darker, brownish. On both sides of the ventral edge of the body are series of smaller and larger luminous organs.
Size: Length *c.* 2 3/4–3 in (7 cm).
Distribution: Oceanic along the European and African coasts from northern Norway to western Africa; also Mediterranean Sea.
General: Lives pelagically in depths of 50–100 fathoms (100–200 m); during night the fish moves higher up in the water. Now and then it enters the more shallow, coastal water and it is then often found among the dense shoals of small herring. It is of no value for the commercial or sport fisheries.

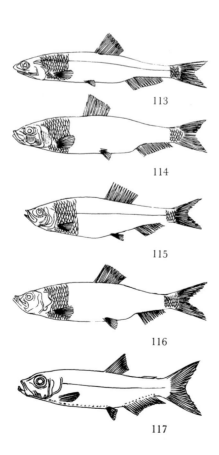

113

114

115

116

117

7 SALMONFISHES: SALMON, TROUT, SMELT, WHITEFISH

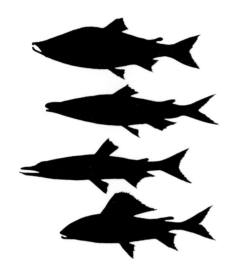

118 RAINBOW TROUT F, S
Salmo gairdneri
Other common names: Trutta shasta, McCloud River rainbow, hatchery rainbow, shasta rainbow, steelhead trout (sea run).

Features: The description "rainbow" trout is often applied to several migratory and nonmigratory populations. The native North American rainbow resembles the brown trout but has a characteristic reddish-purplish band on either flank and a slightly smaller head. It is also black-spotted on the dorsal regions, flanks, and tail; the tail spots are arranged in radiating lines from the base of the fin. *Note:* The name "rainbow" is derived from the aforementioned vivid red, or reddish-purple, broad band which begins immediately behind the eye and extends as a band along the flanks to the tail fin. It is prominent only in mature fish and is especially vivid on breeding males. Dorsal fin 11; adipose fin, tail fin square-cut, anal fin 11. Lateral line scale count *c.* 145 (range varies 120 to 150).
Size: Up to 30 in (75 cm), 20 lb (9 kg). Average North American stream fish 10–14 in (25–35 cm). In central European mountain rivers 8–10 in (20–25 cm), 4–9 oz (120–250 g). Large, above average, specimens common in South America and New Zealand.
Distribution: Native to the west coast of North America, its readiness to adapt elsewhere has led to its introduction almost throughout the world. It had spread to the rest of North America by 1870 and Europe by 1880. Transplanted rainbows appear to thrive exceptionally well in New Zealand and Chile.
General: The rainbow trout does not migrate to the sea as does its sea-run sub-race relative, the steelhead trout (see below), but some *will* migrate if the fish stock contains genetic elements of the steelhead trout. The rainbow is widely used for stocking angling waters, although its tendency to adopt seagoing habits makes it a difficult

fish to confine. However, in the waters of far inland rivers and isolated lakes and reservoirs, the problem does not arise.

Principal food consists of damselflies and their larvae, water beetles, mayflies, caddis-fly larvae, freshwater shrimp and fish such as small chub and minnow.

The value of rainbow trout as a sport fish relates to several factors: its excellence as a food fish, its rapid growth (*c.* 6–7 lb (3 kg) in 3 years), its eagerness to rise to the fly, and, when hooked, its fighting qualities. Another contributory factor is its ability to adapt to higher water temperatures and less aerated waters in comparison with the brown trout (*S. trutta*). It appears to thrive alongside brown trout without either species suffering interference; however, it may be that they prefer separate, but closely related, sections of water.

Males breed at two years, the females at three years. Spawning – usually in running water – is from October–November to February–April, depending on the locality and temperature. Eggs hatch at *c.* 40 days. It is believed that almost 95 percent of the hatched fry are lost during the first 3–4 months. Chief predators appear to be the eel, water shrew, mink, the common rat, and to a lesser extent other large trout, the otter and the heron.

During the winter months trout in frozen lakes depend on trapped oxygen which has been produced by plants. In long periods of heavy snow coverage, when the sunlight is cut off, plants are unable to supply this requirement, and the trout population (and other fish) dies off.

119 STEELHEAD TROUT F, S
(anadromous)
Variety of *Salmo gairdneri*
Other common names: Coast rainbow trout, silver trout, Kamloops trout, truite arc–en–ciel, Nijimasu (Japan).

Features: Similar to rainbow except that flanks are characteristically more silvery.
Size: Similar to rainbow.
Distribution: A coastal and a migratory sea-going fish native to the west coast of North America.
General: The steelhead spawns in the upper reaches of freshwater streams, but many die of exhaustion before reaching the upper spawning grounds. Very highly regarded as a sport fish wherever it occurs. (See also rainbow trout above.)

120 BROWN TROUT
Salmo trutta fario
Other common names: European brown trout, European lake trout, Loch Leven trout, German brown trout, Von Behr's trout, sea-run brown trout. Some biologists recognize various subspecies.

Features: Brown trout resemble salmon in shape and appearance, but can be distinguished by the angle of the jaw which reaches to well *behind* the eye and the fact that the adipose fin is tinged with orange. Dorsal fin 12 to 14; adipose fin; tail fin concave; anal fin 10 to 12. Coloration: variable according to habitat and locale, but dorsally usually greenish-brown, paling on the flanks; belly yellowish, dorsal regions, flanks, and gill covers marked with numerous red and

black spots; spots are surrounded by pale rings. Lateral line scale count 120 to 130. Scales are very small and embedded.
Size: Variable according to locale and environment. Average small-stream fish 6–8 in (15–20 cm); river fish up to 20 in (50 cm), 2–3 lb (1–1 1/2 kg). Largest fish recorded 3 ft 9 in (1.10 m), 40 lb (19 kg).
Distribution: Native to the whole of Europe and parts of North Africa in coastal areas bordering the Mediterranean, and also in western Asia. Successfully introduced into North America in 1883. Also successfully introduced into Australia, South Africa, Kenya, South America and the Indian subcontinent (Kashmir and the Nilgiri Hills).
General: Except for isolated sea-run populations (called locally "sea trout"), the brown trout prefers streams, rivers, and some lakes with cool, clear waters of high oxygen content. It is intolerant of the higher temperatures to which the rainbow trout readily adapts. The young eat large numbers of the larvae and adult stages of aquatic winged insects and also terrestrial insects and small animal life that falls into the water. Adults feed chiefly on fishes, crustaceans, and larger aquatic insect life.

The brown trout has no smolt stage but passes directly to mature coloration from the parr stage. A migratory form, known locally as European lake trout, resides in deep, cool, glacial lakes, but moves into rivers and streams for spawning. Lake-resident brown trout often grow to quite large size and become predatory on younger and smaller trout, their own progeny included. These fish should not be confused with the lake trout of North America. *Salvelinus namaycush.*

Sea-run brown trout have features similar to those of fresh water brown trout, but the coloration is usually dark grey-green to grey-brown on the dorsal region, becoming lighter on the flanks with red markings and a silver belly. In some fish the belly may be light grey, light yellow-brown, or light red-yellow; adipose fin light in colour with red markings. Male fish develop a salmon-like elongated, hookshaped lower jaw. This migratory form is native to Iceland and northern Europe from Norway to Spain. It has been introduced into Chile, Argentina, and New Zealand. There is no native strain of sea-run brown trout in North America, but in many rivers of the northeastern United States, Canada, and Newfoundland, some introduced brown trout have developed a semi-migratory habit of swimming down to river mouths and estuaries.

The widespread introduction of the brown trout, and its propagation via hatcheries, have provided fishermen in many areas with a fish of extremely high sporting qualities and excellent table value.

121 SEA TROUT F, S
(anadromous)
Salmo trutta trutta

The general biology of the sea trout is similar to that of its near relative, the Atlantic salmon, except that it tends to be less migratory.

Features: Physically similar to brown trout of river and lake habitats. Dorsal fin 12 to 14; adipose fin; tail fin slightly concave or square-cut; anal fin 10 to 12. Dorsally darkish grey green to grey brown with blackish spots. During spawning migration it changes coloration and becomes dorsally dark red brown with lighter flanks, red markings and silver belly, but sometimes this may be greyish, yellow brown to red yellow; adipose fin light with red markings; male also develops characteristic elongated, hook-shaped lower jaw.

Sea trout is sometimes difficult to distinguish from salmon in appearance. The head, however, is generally more blunt, the tail stalk broader, and the tail fin often almost square-cut. Below the adipose fin and the lateral line there are 13 to 16 scales (on average *c.* 16), counting backwards including the lateral line. Lateral line scale count 120 to 130. Refer also to recognition features on Atlantic salmon.

Size: Average adult fish up to 3 ft 4 in (1 m), 33 lb (15 kg); large fish 4 ft 7 in (1.4 m), 110 lb (50 kg).

Distribution: The migratory form is native to Iceland and north-west Europe (from the northernmost coasts south to Spain) where rivers flow into the Atlantic, North Sea, Baltic, and White Sea. It has now been successfully introduced in Chile, the Argentine, and New Zealand. There is no native strain of migratory sea trout in North America, but in many rivers of the northeastern United States, Canada, and Newfoundland, some introduced brown trout ('brownies') have developed a semimigratory habit of swimming down to estuary mouths; however, these cannot strictly be included among true sea-going trout.

General: Sea trout, much like salmon, develop through a parr and smolt stage. The parr becomes smolt in 2–3 or 4–5 years, depending on locality. The 4–5-years fish are usually confined to the northern regions. Young trout parr may be distinguished from salmon parr in the following ways:

a) The large blue-grey spots are less distinct.

b) There are a number of white-ringed red spots along the flanks.

c) The adipose fin has an orange tint.

After descending to the sea, some young trout only remain there for a few months (*c.* 3–6) before returning. Others remain at sea for periods up to 5 years. Again much like the salmon, once at sea, they gain weight rapidly, but unlike salmon they feed vigorously in fresh water and spend less time in brackish tidal-waters. Re-entry time into the rivers varies according to the locale, but it usually occurs from mid-summer to early autumn. Spawning takes place in winter and some time later than the salmon. The eggs hatch in spring, and during its spawning migration the trout develops its mating coloration. Most individuals spawn several

times, and one 19-year-old fish has been authenticated.

Sea trout has wide appeal to many sport fishermen. Many indeed consider it superior sport to the freshwater variety. As a table fish it rates in importance alongside salmon.

122 HUCHEN F
Salmo hucho

Features: Similar to the Atlantic salmon but with a more elongate and rounded body. Large head and deeply cleft mouth; characteristic, large eye. Dorsal fin 12 to 14; adipose fin; tail fin forked; anal fin 11 to 14. Coloration: dorsally greenish brown; flanks silvery with a coppery sheen; belly white; juveniles more silvery with transverse dark stripes. Lateral line scale count 180 to 220. Small scales.

Size: Up to 28 in (70 cm), 7 lb (3 kg) at 5 years; 60 in (150 cm) and over 110 lb (50 kg) at about 15 years, but records of large fish are difficult to substantiate.

Distribution: Once fairly extensive in eastern Europe, but now confined to the Danube, its northern tributaries, and a few lakes connected with this system. Introduced elsewhere.

General: An important eastern European, nonmigratory, freshwater game fish but declining in numbers. Spawning occurs in March–April in the lower reaches of the Danube and its tributaries. Growth is rapid; young may reach *c.* 6 in (15 cm) in one year; maturity is reached at 5 years. Both young and adults feed on small fish such as minnow, gudgeon, and nase. Pollution and over-fishing have been blamed for its great decline. It is now rigorously protected by local game fishing regulations in several countries. A table fish of the highest quality.

123 GOLDEN TROUT F
Salmo aguabonita
Other common names: Golden trout of Volcano Creek, Volcano Creek trout, Roosevelt trout. (For other "golden" trout see below.)

Features: A trout species noted for its beautiful yellow golden colour and red markings; closely related to the rainbow trout. Coloration: dorsally olive; flanks golden yellow below lateral line and a wide rosy lateral band crossed by ten black blotches and a midventral red stripe; lower fins reddish; dorsal fin; adipose fin; tail fin; and tail stalk spotted with black. Lateral line scale count 200.

Size: Average up to 12 in (30 cm), 1 lb (1/2 kg), maximum may be considerably more.

Distribution: North America; occurs naturally only in headwaters of Kern River, California, and in the high Sierras, but also introduced elsewhere.

General: It has been described as the most gorgeously coloured trout in the world. The golden trout is one of the strongest fighters for its size, and it is one of the finest local sport fishes in North America.

Another so-called "golden" trout, the Steward white trout (*Salmo whitei*), occurs in the western tributaries of the Kern River. This species is characterized by small dark spots on the dorsal area, upper flanks, dorsal and tail fins, with a brick-red lateral band, and lemon yellow below this on the

lower flanks; the belly is orange or cadmium. The "golden" trout of the south fork of the Kern River, known as the sweet water trout (*Salmo aquabonita aquabonita*), is more richly coloured and has fewer spots than the Stewart white trout; the flanks and belly are yellowish, and the lower fins are characterized by an orange red coloration with white tips.

Another quite different "golden" trout (*Salvelinus alpinus aureolus*) is found in Sunapee Lake (New Hampshire); coloration dorsally is greenish; flanks silvery grey with small, yellow spots; belly orange in highly coloured individual fish.

124 OUANANICHE F
Salmo salar ouananiche

Features: This fish is a landlocked form of the Atlantic Salmon. In appearance it resembles very much other landlocked salmon forms, but it is generally smaller than these. The body is rather slender; the tail fin is slightly concave. Coloration: back, upper sides, dorsal and tail fins are rather densely covered with small, round, dark spots. The belly is lighter.

Size: Up to 20 lb (9 kg), but mostly smaller.

Distribution: Canada, mainly the Quebec Province.

General: This form is to a higher degree than the other landlocked forms a surface feeder. It prefers streams to lakes and is known as a fine game fish for light tackle.

125 LESSER SILVER SMELT S
Argentina sphyraena

Features: The eyes are slightly smaller than in the greater silver smelt; fins as in that species. Large scales. Coloration: the body is silvery with a light-bluish or greenish sheen; fins darker, brown to grey.

Size: Reaches a length of only 10–11 in (27 cm).

Distribution: East Atlantic from western Norway to west Africa and through most of the Mediterranean. Rather rare in Skagerak.

General: The species lives near or at the bottom in 20–30 fathoms (35–60 m) feeding on small bottom animals. The live fish has a cucumber smell.

126 CUTTHROAT TROUT F,
B, S (sometimes anadromous)
Salmo clarki
Other common names: Cutthroat, blackspotted trout, red-throated trout, Rocky Mountain brook trout, spotted trout, mountain trout.

Features: A trout species characterized by two very distinct red or pink streaks on underside of jaws. Large mouth. Dorsal fin 10; adipose fin; tail fin concave; anal fin 10. Coloration: variable, but usually dorsally bluish; dorsal area and flanks are profusely spotted; middle flanks usually marked with a broad rosy hue; sea-run fish have a more silvery appearance. Lateral line scale count 160 to 170.

Size: Average inland fish up to 4–6 lb (1 3/4–2 3/4 kg); sea-run fish up to 12 lb (5 1/2 kg).

Distribution: North America; native to mountainous areas ranging from

California north to Alaska. Introduced elsewhere (including Europe) especially to fish farms.

General: A biology similar to the lake trout's; in some rivers it is anadromous. In small streams the fish reach maturity at a stunted size 5–6 in (13–15 cm). The best sport fish, both for size and fighting qualities, are found in cold, fast-flowing streams. There are many related forms and variants throughout North America, and undoubtedly the cutthroat trout is very closely related to the rainbow trout.

The scientific name of the cutthroat trout, *S. clarki*, commemorates Captain William Clark of the famous Lewis and Clark overland expedition.

127 LANDLOCKED SALMON
Salmo salar sebago

Several varieties of landlocked salmon occur in the lakes of northern New England and Canada. These fish ascend tributary streams where they spawn in the autumn. They show differences in features from the sea-run fish: a larger eye, longer fins, larger scales, and a different coloration (often dorsally deep black; flanks bluishgreen to silvery with irregular black spots). One variety was first described from Sebago Lake in Maine, and as a result of intensive fish culture, it has become widely distributed. The natural prey of landlocked salmon are schools of smelt, which they follow upstream in spring and then back into deep water in summer. Landlocked salmon may attain weights up to *c* 25 lb (11 kg) and in some waters form important sport fish populations. They rise to fly or are taken by bait fishing both early in the season and in summer. Another variety, the ouananiche is smaller and more plentiful and has a more northerly distribution.

128 LAKE TROUT F
Salmo trutta lacustris
Other common names: Common lake trout, Great lake trout, grey trout, tongue, mackinaw trout, mountain trout, salmon trout, laker, masamacush, touladi.

Features: Elongate body. Large head; the snout often projects slightly beyond the lower jaw. Dorsal fin 11; adipose fin; tail fin deeply forked; anal fin 11. Coloration: variable according to locale and size of lake habitat, but usually dorsally, flanks, and head covered with irregular, yellowish splotch dots on a background varying from light grey to almost black; the splotch dots sometimes run together to form wormlike markings. Lateral line scale count 185 to 205. Scales are small.

Size: Specimens over 100 lb (45 kg) have been reported, but rod-caught fish rarely exceed 33 lb (15 kg). European fish 15–19 lb (7–8 kg).

Distribution: Native to North America, previously very common in the Great Lakes region. Has been successfully introduced into several Swiss alpine lakes and elsewhere.

General: Found in deep lakes which provide large volumes of well-oxygenated water, and during the summer months the lake trout may be resident in depths exceeding 330 ft (100 m). The lake trout is a ravenous, carnivorous fish feeding principally on fish such as lake whitefish, ciscoes, yellow perch, and smelt.

As a sport fish it is very highly rated; however, it is sometimes rather sluggish and heavy compared with other salmonids and does not leap in the air. The flesh may be white, pink, or red, but irrespective of colour, the flavour is excellent.

129 ATLANTIC SALMON F, S

(anadromous)
Salmo salar
Other common names: Common Atlantic salmon, Kennebee salmon, black salmon (see also landlocked salmon and special nomenclature for young fish below).

Features: Elongate, streamlined body. Large mouth and jaws. Dorsal fin 12 to 14; adipose fin; tail fin concave (forked in young); anal fin 9 or 10. Coloration: dorsally and flanks a silver grey verging on green; dorsal region, flanks, and head covered with black spots. Lateral line scale count 120 to 130. Large, obvious scales. Occasionally there is difficulty in distinguishing the salmon from the trout. One indication is the absence of red on a salmon's adipose fin. Another is to make a scale count between the rear edge of the adipose fin and the lateral line. If the fish is small, a magnifying lens is useful. A salmon has 10 to 13 rows (usually 11), a trout 13 to 16, but hybrids may confuse identification. A quick and practical rule-of-thumb familiar to experienced fishermen is that a salmon can generally be held by the hands round the tail stalk, while a trout slips through.
Size: Mature fish reach *c.* 4 ft (120 cm); exceptional specimens 5 ft (1.5 m), and about 80 lb (36 kg). The largest female fish do not generally exceed 4 ft (120 cm), and about 44 lb (20 kg).
Distribution: North Atlantic, breeding in streams and rivers of Europe and North America in an area extending from Spain to the White Sea and from New England to Labrador; also in southern Greenland and Iceland. In the sea they are found concentrated near Greenland and the White Sea.
General: The Atlantic salmon is regarded by many game and sport anglers as the king of freshwater fish. The large salmon migrate from the sea in the winter or early spring (spring fish) or summer to autumn (summer fish). As they swim upriver, they are in good condition with firm, red flesh and a silvery sheen to their bodies. After spawning, however, the stored body fat diminishes, and the flesh turns pale and watery. The skin along the back becomes thick and spongy with the scales deeply embedded. The body changes colour to a dark reddish tint, and large, black spots margined by white also appear on the body. The "red fish" are males while the females grow even darker and are known as "black fish". The males can be further distinguished by the development of a very characteristic hook on the lower jaw.

The life cycle of the salmon begins in the shallows of a stream where the water is clear and flows with a moderate current and where there is a gravel bottom. The spawning ground is termed a redd. The eggs are laid in a trough formed in the gravel by the female fish moving her tail rapidly to produce a bottom-water turbulence which pushes the loose gravel aside. The spawning period is from September to January but mainly in November and December. The eggs hatch in 5–21 weeks, depending on the temperature of the water. When they are hatched, the fry emerges from the egg as an alevin, equipped with a yolk-sac on which it feeds for 4–8 weeks while it remains among the pebbles of the redd. Then the fry start to move freely about the bottom. At this stage they become known as fingerlings and measure 1–2 in (25–50 mm).

At the end of a year, having grown to 3–4 in (75–100 mm), the fingerlings become parr and by the end of the second year measure between 4–8 in (10–20 cm). By now the body is marked with 10 or 11 dark bands – much like thumbmarks in appearance – referred to as parr marks; also present is a single red spot between each mark.

The rate of development of the young salmon is much dependent on environmental conditions but principally on the temperature and what is termed the latitude factor. Young salmon may remain 1–5 years in fresh water. In the Rhine and the rivers of southern England, the parr may develop into the smolt (seagoing) stage in a year; while in northern Scandinavia, this period may be extended in exceptional cases to 7–8 years. At the stage of going to sea, the scales become covered with guanine, which obliterates the parr marks and transforms the body to the colour of silver.

The smolts remain in the brackish water of the river mouth for a period to acclimatize to salt water and adjust to a new (sea) diet – usually consisting of herring, sand eel, and various crustaceans. On reaching the sea, the salmon feeds from 1–6 years before returning to its native river to spawn. At this stage some refer to the fish as a grilse, but others use the term maiden, and then later, spawner, when it actually reaches the spawning ground. After spawning, many fish, now called kelts, die off due to exhaustion.

Growth is much slower in fresh water than in the sea. After one year at sea, salmon measure 20–26 in (50–65 cm) and weigh 3 1/2–6 1/2 lb (1 1/2–3 kg). Until recently little was known about the movements of salmon in the ocean, but with the introduction of intensive fish tagging, large numbers have been located in Davis Strait off Greenland, and much more is now known about their migratory habits. Fish-tagging experiments have shown that migrating salmon may travel distances of several thousand kilometres, during which time the average distance covered may be 30–60 miles (50–100 km) per 24 hours.

It is generally believed that the sea fish returning to spawn are guided by an innate biochemical ability to recognize their birth and adolescent waters. What is not yet known, however, is why some salmon return to fresh water after only a year at sea while others remain there up to four years or more. There is, nevertheless, a discernible behaviour pattern followed by fish.

Group 1. *Grilse.* Sea time: one complete year and part of a summer.
Group 2. *Small spring fish.* Sea time: two complete years. Normally returning in spring.
Group 2a. *Small summer fish.* Sea time: two complete years and part of a summer.
Group 3. *Large spring fish.* Sea time: three years.
Group 3a. *Large summer fish.* Sea time: three years and part of a summer.
Group 4. *Very large spring fish.* Sea time: four years.
Group 4a. *Very large summer fish.* Sea time: four years and part of a summer.

Groups 2 and 3 combined represent more salmon than the other groups.

None of these groups includes previous spawners, referred to as mended kelts, which have survived the spawning process and then managed to return to the sea and then subsequently have returned for a second spawning.

There are on record some instances of third or even fourth time spawnings.

In addition to the migratory Atlantic salmon, subspecies have evolved in enclosed waters where passage to the sea has become barred. These landlocked stocks often take a dwarf form and receive local names (see nr 124 and 127).

During recent times the Atlantic salmon populations have been greatly reduced. One primary cause was the accidental discovery of their sea-feeding areas in Davis Strait by Greenlanders while codfishing. They developed a local fishery for them in Greenland waters before European large ships were adapted to this fishing, which led to the subsequent commercial exploitation of the Atlantic salmon, on a grand scale. Other primary factors are accumulative freshwater pollution, commercial overfishing in rivers, damming of rivers for mills, blockading rivers for lumbering operations, and the general spread of industry along waterways. The total effect has been to bring about what is sometimes referred to as "the great international salmon disaster". Although many countries have now introduced rigorous conservation methods, they may have come too late. In Norway, however, it is reported that in recent years fishing has slightly improved. In Sweden the use of salmon hatcheries has so improved the remaining stocks that one in four fish caught comes from the hatcheries.

As far as the sport fisherman is concerned, sea salmon may be caught during their migratory passages along shorelines if they can be located. It is generally accepted that salmon do *not* feed in fresh water but during this period live on their fat accumulation. It has often been said that when salmon *do* take flies, lures, and bait in fresh water, they do it simply through curiosity or annoyance.

Much of the art of river fishing is in knowing exactly where the fish lie. Since sand and fine sediments irritate their gills, salmon prefer stony gravelly reaches, and each waterway has its traditional rock-bottomed salmon-lodges.

In 1972, the United States, backed by Canada, put on diplomatic pressure, and Denmark agreed to phase out their salmon industry of the north during the following years, an action that may save the salmon from eventual extinction.

130 GREATER SILVER SMELT
S
Argentina silus

Features: Body slender, rounded. Rather small mouth. The eyes are large with a diameter longer than their distance to the point of the snout. Scales loose-fitting, large, about 50 along the lateral line. The dorsal fin is placed anteriorly on the back; far behind it near the tail is a small adipose fin. Tail fin large, forked; the ventral fins are placed farther back than the dorsal fin. Coloration: back and sides golden yellow, belly silvery.
Size: 1–1¹/₂ ft (30–45 cm).
Distribution: North Atlantic; from New England to Iceland, the British Isles and Norway.
General: The fish is abundant between 270 and 500 fathoms (150–1000 m), where it feeds on small fish and prawns. The flesh is tasty but fat; the live fish smells like cucumber. Not fished commercially, not sought by the sportfisherman.

131 IWANA F
Salvelinus pluvius
Other common names: Gogi, Yugi.

Features: The body is elongate and a little compressed. The snout is broadly rounded. The upper jaw reaches with about 1/3 its length backwards of the posterior margin of the eye. The outer margins of the dorsal and the caudal fins are slightly concave. Small scales, about 200 along the distinct, light-coloured lateral line. Coloration: back and upper sides darkish yellow brown, lower sides white, silvery. The belly is in many individuals yellow to brown, else grey to whitish. The dorsal fin is dark-yellow with a blackish anterior margin; the pectoral fins are white to yellow; the remaining fins grey or brownish.
Size: About 1–1¹/₂ ft (30–45 cm).
Distribution: Rivers and rivulets in Japan.
General: The iwana prefers rapid mountain streams, where it deposits its eggs in the gravel on the bottom. The spawning occurs from September to October. The fish is well esteemed by sport fishermen.

132 DOLLY VARDEN F, B, S
Salvelinus malma spectabilis
Other common names: Bull trout, Oregon char, western char, red-spotted trout, golet, salmon trout.

Features: A large trout (char) notable for its conspicuous red spots. Dorsal fin 11; adipose fin; tail fin well forked (but becomes more square-cut in large individual fish); anal fin 9. Coloration: variable, usually dorsally and upper flanks olivaceous to dark silvery; dorsal area and flanks have round red or orange spots nearly as large as eye; lower fins with a pale and a dark front stripe like those of brook trout; sea-run fish more silvery, and spots are paler or absent. Lateral line scale count 240.
Size: Up to 30 lb (14 kg), 40 in (100 cm) but river fish are generally much smaller.
Distribution: North America; in lakes, rivers,

and estuaries from Oregon, through British Columbia to Alaska; Japan and the nearby Asian mainland.

General: An autumn spawning fish. Its popularity as a sport fish is much dependent on the locale. In some waters it may be regarded as a nuisance fish, since it is very voracious and gorges itself on the fry of other salmonid species occupying the same water. Where it occurs in rapid, cold water streams it rises readily to a fly and here it has a reputation of being a very game species.

133 WINDERMERE CHAR F
Salvelinus willoughbyi
Other common name: Willoughby's char.

Features: Body compressed, rather high. The mouth reaches to off the hind margin of the eyes; fairly large teeth. The scales are small. Large dorsal fin with straight margin, 12 rays. The tail fin is comparatively deeply forked with pointed lobes; the anal fin, 12 rays, is inserted off the most posterior part of the dorsal fin. Coloration: back and upper sides dark green, back often almost blackish, lower sides silvery; belly orange red to bright red; the sides have around the lateral line numerous red spots.
Size: Reaches rarely more than 10 in (25 cm), maximum 15 in (38 cm).
Distribution: The British Isles.
General: Appears to prefer lakes and slow-running streams. Sought by sport fishermen.

134 ARCTIC CHAR S, F
Salvelinus alpinus
Features: Troutlike appearance. Dorsal fin 12 to 15; adipose fin; tail fin concave; anal fin 10 to 13. Coloration: variable, usually dorsally olive green to deep blue, paling to lighter green or blue on flanks (but silvery on searun forms); belly white; yellow-speckled, splotchlike markings along dorsal regions and flanks; leading edge of pectoral, pelvic, and anal fin generally white; the fins and belly – particularly in the male fish – turn bloodred in the spawning season. Scale count *c.* 190 to 240 along lateral line, and *c.* 36 or 37 across body. The scales are small and inconspicuous.
Size: Variable. The seagoing migratory variety reaches 30 in (75 cm), 22 lb (10 kg), many lake populations consist of stunted and dwarf varieties *c.* 4–6 in (10–15 cm).
Distribution: Migratory varieties are widespread in northern Arctic seas and rivers in and around Alaska, Canada, Greenland, Iceland, Scandinavia, and U.S.S.R. The landlocked nonmigratory variety has numerous variants which populate chill, clear-water lakes in the Arctic and more temperate zones; widespread in North America, found locally in the British Isles and Sweden, Norway, Finland, Greenland, and Iceland. Also found in well-oxygenated, deep glacial lakes in the Swiss Alps. World distribution is confined to north of lat. 50° N.
General: Migratory varieties leave the sea and ascend rivers from September to October at about 5–7 years and spawn in late autumn or early winter. The young spend their first summer in fresh or brack-

ish lower river waters. Migratory varieties at sea feed on young cod and similar fish. The landlocked varieties feed on crustaceans and lesser fish. Char are highly prized game and sport fish, and valuable commercial gourmet fish prepared for table use in many forms.

135 BROOK TROUT F
Salvelinus fontinalis
Other common names: Speckled trout, eastern speckled trout, common brook trout, eastern brook trout, squaretail, coaster, Aurora trout, omble de fontaine.

Features: Actually a small char. Recognised by its large jaws, mottled back, and slightly concave tail fin. Dorsal fin 10; adipose fin; anal fin 9. Coloration: very variable, but dorsally often greenish to dark brown, occasionally almost black with heavy, wavy lines extending onto the dorsal and tail fins; flanks show small but well-defined red spots bordered by a bluish halo. The front edges of the pectoral, pelvic, and anal fins are a pronounced milky white and edged by a black margin. Breeding males become particularly colourful with a strong orange to reddish blush along the lower flanks. Breeding males also develop a characteristic upward-curving hook on the lower jaw. Lateral line scale count 230. Scales are small and numerous.
Size: Rarely over 18 in (45 cm), average 12–16 in (30–40 cm). In brooks and small rivers, a 2-lb (1-kg) trout is a good one. In the lakes and large rivers of Canada, especially Labrador, it may reach more than 10 lb (4 kg). In lake habitats where food is scarce, growth is stunted.
Distribution: Native to northeastern America where it inhabits brooks and small rivers. In Canada it flourishes in deep, wide rivers and in lakes. Successfully introduced into other parts of North America. Introduced into the Argentine and Europe (1884) and now established in several European countries, although in some not a widespread species.
General: Considered one of the most beautifully coloured fish of the salmonid species. Thrives in fast water and in oxygen-rich, cool, clear lakes. It crossbreeds with rainbow and brown trout, but does not produce fertile offspring. However, male brook trout and female lake trout produce fertile offspring, known as splake or wendigo (see below). Food consists of insects, worms, and smaller fish. Spawning occurs in late autumn. Excellent sport fish for fly and spinner. A delicious table fish; the flesh may be amber, pink, or red in colour.

136 CHINOOK SALMON F, S
(anadromous)
Oncorhynchus tschawytscha
Other common names: Columbia River salmon, tyee salmon, king salmon, quinnat salmon, tchaviche, tschawytscha.

Features: Largest of the Pacific salmon and the species with the longest anal fin. Dorsal fin 11; adipose fin; tail fin concave; anal fin 16. Coloration: dorsally and head dark or dusky; flanks olivaceous or bluish; belly paling to silvery white; dorsal area and upper flanks marked with small blackish spots

extending over head, dorsal, adipose, and tail fins; spawning male fish is blackish or dirty red. Lateral line scale count 130 to 155.
Size: Average range 10–50 lb (4 1/2–23 kg), maximum over 108 lb (49 kg).
Distribution: North Pacific, ranging from northern China to Alaska and southern California; at sea they may be found in the central north Pacific. Introduced into Great Lakes and into Europe, Australia, and New Zealand.
General: The chinook salmon is abundant in the larger streams and ascends headwaters several hundred miles from the sea. At sea its chief food appears to be anchovies, rock cod, euphausiids, herring, squid, and larval crabs. It enters the rivers several months before spawning which occurs in the spring and autumn, and in prime condition these fish are of high commercial value. The larger fish over 30 lb are often referred to as tyee. Throughout its distribution it is a most highly prized sport and table fish, especially those caught at sea, whose flesh is of a deeper colour.

Tagged chinook salmon have been caught in the open sea 2,400 miles (3,840 km) from their home river mouth, and when released, have subsequently returned to their home-stream hatch-water. The differential migration pattern of the chinook salmon gives an insight into the biochemical mechanism which regulates fish migration, and in British Columbia the group of chinook salmon which spawn in the Columbia River provide an excellent example. Inland, this river divides into two main branches, the Upper Columbia River and the Willamette. In the Upper Columbia River, the chinook salmon is an autumn-run fish while those in the Willamette are spring-run. In one experiment, eggs were collected from the spawning grounds in the Willamette and then hatched in fish traps in the Upper Columbia where they were tagged. On the return from the sea some four or five years later the marked spring-run salmon from the Willamette made straight for the Upper Columbia – the river they knew as immature smolt. They showed no tendency to deflect into the Willamette with other spring-run Willamette-reared salmon. This was in spite of the fact that the autumn-run salmon of the Upper Columbia had not yet arrived, and water conditions were not suitable in spring (and almost certainly the reason why the Upper Columbia has no natural spring-run population). Clearly the chemical message of the home-stream hatch-water becomes firmly ingrained at birth, and unerringly the fish return to it irrespective of their geographical and genetic origins. Chinook salmon have also been introduced into the Great Lakes although not in as large numbers as silver or coho salmon. They appear to be adjusting well to the freshwater environment there and promise to be a valuable addition to the sport and food fisheries there.

137 COHO SALMON F, S
(anadromous)
Oncorhynchus kisutch
Other common names: Kisutch, silver salmon, slowitz, tschaviche, bielaya ryba, hooped salmon.

Features: Similar in appearance to the chinook salmon, but generally smaller. Dorsal fin *c.* 10; adipose fin; tail fin concave; anal fin 13 or 14. Coloration: dorsally bluish green; flanks paling to silvery; head less dark than the chinook; dorsal area and upper flanks show scattered dark specks; spawning males pink or reddish, later changing to black.
Size: Average range 6–12 lb (2 1/2–5 kg), maximum 30 lb (13 1/2 kg) 36 in (90 cm).
Distribution: North Pacific; ranging from Monterey Bay, California, northward to Canada, Alaska, Japan, and China; introduced into Great Lakes, a few Atlantic rivers.
General: The coho migrates upstream after the chinook salmon, although in late summer both species are travelling at the same time. It penetrates far inland. Like all Pacific salmon the coho ceases to feed on entering fresh water. At Puget Sound many are taken by sport fishermen trolling with spoons or baitfish. The coho is very abundant in Alaskan waters. Highly rated as food.

138 CHUM SALMON F, S
(anadromous)
Oncorhynchus keta
Other common names: Dog, dog salmon, hoyko, le-kai salmon, chum, calico salmon.

Features: Similar in appearance to the chinook salmon with only minor differences, but generally of smaller size. Dorsal fin *c.* 10; adipose fin; tail fin concave; anal fin 13 or 14. Coloration: dorsally and flanks off-white or dirty silvery white; flanks with a tracery of gridironlike bars; dark flecks may or may not be present on dorsal area and flanks; spawning male fish brick red to blackish.
Size: Average range 8–16 lb (3 1/2–7 1/4 kg), maximum 30 lb (13 1/2 kg), 36 in (90 cm).
Distribution: North Pacific, ranging from San Francisco to Kamchatka.
General: Migrates inland only a short distance. Very abundant in Alaska. Not frequently caught as a sport fish; unless from fresh sea-run fish, its flesh is not much esteemed.

139 LITTLE REDFISH F,
Oncorhynchus kennerlyi

Other common name: Kokanee.
Features: This small salmonid fish is distinguished by its large scales and a dense row of gill rakers. The dorsal fin has 10–11, the anal 13–14 soft rays. The tail fin is slightly concave. Coloration: back and upper sides blue, mixed with reddish, lower sides and belly silvery with a red sheen. In the spawning time the males have bright red colours.
Size: Maximum 8 in (20 cm).
Distribution: Rivers and lakes in western North America.
General: The little redfish does not emigrate into the sea, but spends its whole life in freshwaters; for spawning it migrates up into the upper reaches of the rivers. Although small it is of some interest to the sport fisheries. It has recently been introduced in some Swedish rivers and lakes. By some scientists the little redfish is only considered a freshwater variety of the sockeye

salmon (*O. nerka*). It feeds on very small animals, algae, diatoms, and bacteria, sifted from the water by means of the very fine filter on the gills.

140 YAMAME S F
Oncorhynchus masou

Other common names: Masu, cherry salmon, Japanese salmon.

Features: Compressed body with rather pointed head. The dorsal contour is almost straight, the ventral deeply curved. Distinct, dark lateral line. At the base of each ventral fin is a large, triangular scale. Small scales, 130–140 along the lateral line. Coloration: Back and upper sides deep blue; lower sides and belly whitish to silvery; the sides have a few darker, brown spots.
Size: Maximum 2 ft (60 cm).
Distribution: Japan, as far south as Kyushu, but most abundant in the northern part of the country.
General: Anadromous; enters the rivers in August–October for spawning. The young stay in the rivers for a year before emigrating to the sea, where they remain 3–4 years before re-entering the freshwaters. The best fishing season is July–August. In Japan the yamame is a highly appreciated table fish.

141 SOCKEYE SALMON F, S
(anadromous)
Oncorhynchus nerka

Other common names: Kokanee, redfish, sawkeye, Sau-qui salmon, Sukkegh salmon, Fraser River salmon, nerka, krasnaya ryba, blueback.

Features: A small salmon with large scales and many fine gill rakers. Dorsal fin *c.* 11; adipose fin; tail fin concave; anal fin *c.* 14. Coloration: dorsally clear blue; flanks silvery; belly white; spawning male fish crimson with a green head.
Size: Average 5–7 lb (2–3 kg), maximum 15 lb (7 kg).
Distribution: North Pacific; Japan, Alaska, Canada, Oregon, and then in decreasing numbers south to northern California.
General: In Alaska the sockeye represents one of the most important and abundant commercial species around which the local salmon canning industry developed. It spawns at great distances inland, in rivers and streams that mostly flow into glacier-fed lakes. The young fish descend to the lakes where they remain 1–2 years before going to sea. The flesh is much redder than other Pacific species and it is of very high table quality.

142 HUMPBACK SALMON F, S
(anadromous)
Oncorhynchus gorbuscha

Other common names: Pink salmon, haddo, holia, gorbuscha, dog salmon.

Features: The smallest of the Pacific salmon and immediately recognized by its small, fine scales. Dorsal fin *c.* 11; adipose fin; tail fin forked; anal fin 15. Coloration: dorsally bluish; flanks silvery; blackish spots occur dorsally and on flanks; large, black, oblong spots on tail fin; spawning males are dirty red or red-blotched and brownish overall with distorted bodies showing a characteristic hump in front of the dorsal fin.
Size: Average 3–5 lb (1 1/2–2 kg), maximum 11 lb (5 kg), 24 in (60 cm).
Distribution: North Pacific, from California to Alaska. Introduced into northeast America, in Maine and Canada.
General: Spawning occurs near coastal regions, and the humpback enters fresh water only shortly before the autumn spawning. All commercial fish are taken at sea before body changes affect the quality of flesh. The flesh is markedly less red than other Pacific species, hence its common name pink salmon. Less sporting value than other salmon.

143 VENDACE F
Coregonus albula

Other common names: Shannon pollan, Lough Erne pollan, Lough Neagh pollan, white fish.

Features: Much like the powan except for a characteristic projecting lower jaw; the lower jaw fits into a shallow groove in the upper. Dorsal fin 11 to 15, adipose fin; tail fin deeply forked; anal fin 13 to 17. Coloration: dorsally green or greenish blue; flanks silvery, belly whitish; dorsal fin, tail fin, and adipose fin are dusky grey; remaining fins are clear. Lateral line scale count 70 to 91.
Size: Variable according to habitat and food supply. Maximum up to 18 in (45 cm), 4.4 lb (2 kg); but average fish much smaller.
Distribution: Europe, ranging from the northwest region of the U.S.S.R. (Upper Volga) throughout the Baltic, south to Bavaria, and westward into the British Isles.
General: A schooling fish living in large, open-water lakes often containing little food. It appears to remain in deep water for most of the time. In the autumn it migrates shoreward to shallow water to spawn – usually during October and November. As a sport fish it is little known in most locales due to its preference for deeper water. As a table fish the flesh is tasty and has excellent qualities.

144 LARGE BOTTOM WHITEFISH S, F
Coregonus pidschian

Features: Elongate, herringlike body. Upper jaw projecting. Coloration: overall pale silvery.
Size: Maximum up to *c.* 20 in (50 cm), but dwarf and subdwarf forms *c.* 12 in (30 cm) predominate.
Distribution: Europe; Asia; North America; from Alaska, Siberia, Finland, Sweden to Alpine regions.
General: Spawns in September–October at temperatures below 4°C. In subarctic rivers, lakes, and the inner Baltic it occurs in migratory and nonmigratory forms. Food is mainly plankton and other small bottom creatures. Its worth as a sport fish is limited by its deepwater habitat, 65–460 ft (20–140 m). As commercial species it is particularly important especially in parts of Siberia.

145 POWAN F
Coregonus lavaretus

Other common names: Lavaret, Loch Lomond powan, Loch Esk powan, freshwater herring.

Features: Very much like a freshwater herring (with an adipose fin), but the species is very variable in appearance. A long-snouted variety is found in the Baltic region. Dorsal fin 12 to 15; adipose fin; tail fin deeply forked; anal fin 12 to 15. Coloration: dorsally bluish or greenish grey; flanks and belly silvery; snout and tip of dorsal fin blackish. During spawning the males and females develop conical nuptial tubercles on the scales above and below the lateral line. Lateral line scale count 80 to 90.
Size: Dwarf forms 4–8 in (10–20 cm); but large fish up to 28 in (70 cm), 22 lb (10 kg).
Distribution: Deep lakes in Europe, nonmigratory in British and Alpine lakes; migratory in Baltic lakes and Sweden, Finland, and northern U.S.S.R.
General: A schooling species of sluggish habits, tolerant to warm water conditions. A migratory Baltic form spawns in September – December. The nonmigratory form from October – January. Its fine white flesh is much esteemed at the table, and in several locales it is smoked and marketed as an epicurean fish. As a sport fish it rises to an artificial fly.

146 HOUTING F, S
Coregonus oxyrhynchus

Features: Elongate, herringlike body. The head is protruded to form a characteristic fleshy, conical-shaped snout with an underslung mouth. Dorsal fin 12 to 17; adipose fin; tail fin forked; anal fin 14 to 18. Coloration: dorsally greyish blue, green, or bluish green; flanks paling to lighter yellowish white or silvery; belly silvery. During spawning the males and females develop conical nuptial tubercles on the scales above and below the lateral line. Lateral line scale count 80 to 100.
Size: Up to 20 in (50 cm).
Distribution: Europe and northern Asian seas; Swedish and Alpine lakes.
General: Probably best known as a North Sea and Baltic migratory fish and is the only marine and estuarine whitefish in the North Sea. During the spawning season (autumn–winter) it formerly ascended the Rhine, Weser, and Elbe, and some rivers in southwest Europe. Food consists of worms and molluscs, which they root out of the seabed using their highly adapted fleshy snouts (see above); in larger fish the snout may be several inches long.

Now on decline due to pollution and loss of spawning grounds, the houting is fading in commercial value and has no sport fishing value, despite its good table qualities.

147 LAKE WHITEFISH F, B
Coregonus clupeaformis

Other common names: Great Lakes whitefish, inland whitefish, whitefish, gizzard fish, Labrador whitefish, Lake Superior whitefish, Otsego whitefish, coregone de lac.

Features: Elongate and deep laterally compressed body. Mouth overhung by the snout; two flaps of skin between nostrils. Dorsal fin 11; adipose fin; tail fin forked; anal fin 11. Coloration: dorsally light olive or greenish brown; flanks silvery; belly white; fins light-coloured. Lateral line straight, and scale count 70–85. Large scales. Its small mouth and the absence of prominent teeth readily distinguish it from the salmon, trout, and smelt.
Size: Up to 24 in (60 cm), 23 lb (10 kg); average sport fish 3 lb (1 1/2 kg). In former times fish up to 20 lb (9 kg) were caught in the Great Lakes, but these larger fish are now extremely rare.
Distribution: Northern North America, including Newfoundland, chiefly in lakes and occasionally in rivers from Minnesota, the Great Lakes region, and New England northward; occasionally also in brackish water.
General: One of the most valuable sport and commercial species of the Great Lakes, but now almost destroyed in this area due to pollution and predation by sea lampreys.

Spawning occurs in November–December over rocky or gravelly ground; hatching occurs during late winter. They are mainly deepwater bottom feeders, and their food consists chiefly of amphipods, molluscs, and insect larvae but occasionally small fishes. As a winter sport fish they are caught through the ice using jigs or minnows. The flesh is white and has an exceptionally fine flavour.

148 ATLANTIC WHITEFISH F, S
Coregonus canadensis

Features: Very similar to the lake whitefish (see above), but can be differentiated by the terminal mouth (neither snout nor lower jaw projecting), smaller scales (lateral line scale count 91 to 100 compared with 70 to 85 on the lake whitefish), and small but well-developed teeth which are also found on the tongue. Dorsal fin 10 to 12; adipose fin; tail fin forked; anal fin 9 to 12. Coloration: dorsally dark blue or dark green; flanks silvery with scattered black pigment; belly lighter; generally darker overall than the lake whitefish.
Size: Up to 20 in (50 cm), 6 1/2 lb (3 kg).
Distribution: North America; a seagoing whitefish which is found inland only in the lakes and rivers of Nova Scotia.
General: A species previously not separately described and was confused with the lake whitefish (*C. clupeaformis*) but now recognized as being distinct.

149 CISCO F
Coregonus artedii

Other common names: Lake herring, Erie herring, grayback, Michigan herring, blueback herring, shore herring, Lake George smelt, blueback, shoaling water herring, freshwater herring, tullibee, hareng de lac.

Features: Laterally compressed. Moderately large mouth *not* overhung by snout (as in many whitefish); jaw slightly projecting; large silvery eyes. Dorsal fin 10; adipose fin; tail fin deeply forked; anal fin 12. Coloration: dorsally dark blue or black to pale grey green; flanks silvery; pectoral, pelvic, and anal fins slightly white with traces of black on the tips. Lateral line scale count 65 to 75.
Size: Average 1/2–1 lb (1/4–1/2 kg), maximum 8 lb (3 1/2 kg).
Distribution: Eastern North America, rang-

ing Great Lakes region and northward to Hudson Bay.

General: It usually seeks out cooler, deeper water in lakes, especially during the summer months. Spawning occurs in shallow water in the winter. It is an important commercial fish and a voracious species in many lakes of its distribution. As a sport fish it is caught by fly and line bait in spring and summer, and by ice fishing methods in winter. An excellent table fish.

150 ROUND WHITEFISH   F

Prosopium cylindraceum

Other common names: Menominee whitefish, frost-fish, pilot fish, bottlefish, shadwaiter, chivey, blackback, Chateaugeay shad, menomini, pointu blanc.

Features: Long and slender, cylindrical and cigar-shaped body which distinguishes it from the related lake whitefish and ciscoes (which are deep-bodied and laterally compressed); small mouth with an upper jaw not reaching the eye. Single flap between nostrils. Dorsal fin 11; adipose fin; tail fin forked; anal fin 12. Coloration: dorsally dark blue-green; flanks and belly silvery. Lateral line scale count 80 to 90.

Size: Average 1 lb (1/2 kg), maximum 3 lb (1 1/2 kg).

Distribution: Eastern North America and Asia, ranging New England, Great Lakes region, and northwest to Alaska and Siberia.

General: A whitefish frequenting shallow water but also found in cold deepwater lakes. Probably more are caught by winter ice fishing than by any other method, although they readily rise to dry flies. An excellent table fish.

151 AMERICAN SMELT   S, F

(anadromous)

Osmerus mordax

Other common names: Smelt, freshwater smelt, icefish, éperlan d'Amérique.

Features: Slender, compressed body. Pointed head; lower jaw slightly projecting. Dorsal fin 9 to 11; small fleshy adipose fin; tail fin deeply forked; anal fin 15 to 18. Coloration: dorsally a translucent greenish shade; flanks silvery with a broad, satin silvery longitudinal band; belly silvery. Lateral line scale count 68 to 75. Scales are large and easily removed.

Size: Up to 10 in (25 cm), 1 lb (1/2 kg).

Distribution: Atlantic coast of North America from Gulf of St. Lawrence to Virginia.

General: The biology of the American smelt (*O. mordax*) is very similar to that of its close European relative *O. eperlanus* (see below). Several varieties have become adapted to living and breeding in landlocked, freshwater lakes.

The smelts have always been important fishes in North America and are excellent table fish. The larger American smelt offers more challenge to local sport fishermen than does its European relative.

152 SMELT   F, S (anadromous)

Osmerus eperlanus

Other common name: Sparling.

Features: Slender, compressed body. Pointed head; large jaws; lower jaw slightly projecting. Dorsal fin 9 to 12; small adipose fin; tail fin deeply forked; anal fin 12 to 16. Coloration: dorsally transparent olive to bottle or greyish green; flanks paler with a broad longitudinal satin silvery band or stripe; belly silvery; flanks and fins flecked with tiny dusky dots. Straight lateral line with a scale count 60 to 66. Scales are large and easily removed. Note: the teeth and the adipose fin immediately distinguish the smelt from a herring and other similar species.

Size: Nonmigratory, landlocked freshwater variety up to 8 in (20 cm), 1/2 lb (1/4 kg), although smaller fish 4–6 in (10–15 cm) much more common. Seagoing variety occasionally reaches 12 in (30 cm).

Distribution: Primarily a marine fish and one single species from northern Siberia westward through the Baltic and North Sea to northern Spain. Closely related species occur in Siberia and North America.

General: The smelt is a member of the salmonlike fishes, and is a highly valued food fish.

153 POND SMELT   B, F

Hypomesus olidus

Other common name: Small-mouth smelt.

Features: A slender, elongate fish. The upper jaw reaches backwards to a little beyond the anterior margin of the eye. The teeth are rather weak, especially those on the upper surface of the mouth, which are very small and without points. The dorsal fin is high; the adipose fin is placed a little more than midway between dorsal fin and tail; the tail fin is deeply forked; anal fin comparatively short. Coloration: above grey to brownish, sides and belly lighter, silvery.

Size: About 1–1 1/4 ft (30–40 cm).

Distribution: Coasts of the northern Pacific from California to Alaska and from Japan to Kamchatka.

General: Abundant in shallow shore waters, in estuaries it is very numerous. The fish is an important market fish in Japan (fresh, frozen, or dried); it is often reared in lakes and ponds.

154 CANDLEFISH   S

Thaleichthys pacificus

Other common names: Eulachon, oolachan, hooligan, smelt, night smelt, pond smelt, surf smelt.

Features: Small and slender with a blind sac for a stomach. No fleshy appendage at the bases of the pelvic fins. Males tend to be smaller and show tubercles on head, fins and scales. Males have larger lateral line scales and their paired fins are longer. Pectoral fins originate ahead of the dorsal fin origin. Long head with pointed snout and a large mouth situated at the tip of the snout. Small hooked teeth. Upper half of each gill arch contains 4–6 gill rakers. Teeth fall out at spawning season. Behind the dorsal fin there is a small adipose fin. The pelvic fins are under the dorsal fin. Lower jaw is somewhat undershot. Body depth is one-fifth of body length. Back is slightly flattened. Dorsal fin, 9; anal fin, 13. Coloration: Blue-brown with stippling of black on the back, shading to silver on the under surface.

Size: Maximum length 12 in (30 cm), up to about 9–10 oz (1/4 kg), usually smaller.

Distribution: Pacific coast from Alaska to northern California.

General: Once widely used by Indians and early settlers for food. Very oily. Dried candlefish were (and sometimes still are) burned in lieu of other sources of light by Indians and early white emigrants. Good when smoked or salted, and considered locally to be excellent table fare. Not taken by angling, but forms top forage for salmon and other fish.

155 EUROPEAN GRAYLING

F, B

Thymallus thymallus

Other common names: Umber, oumer, silver lady, lady of the stream.

Features: Similar to the Arctic grayling in general appearance (see below). Dorsal fin 17 to 24; adipose fin; tail fin forked; anal fin 10 to 15. Coloration: dorsally ranging from greenish brown to bluish green; flanks silvery grey; belly white; a greenish gold sheen or violet bands are present over the whole fish; dark spots on front half of body; zigzag lines extend longitudinally and mark off the boundaries between rows of scales; dorsal fin has several parallel rows of dusky purple "chessboard" markings. Lateral line scale count 74 to 96.

Size: About 12 in (30 cm) and 1/2 lb (250 g); large fish *c.* 24 in (60 cm), 4 1/2–6 1/2 lb (2–3 kg), but occasionally over this limit.

Distribution: Europe and parts of Asia. Found in rivers in much of central Europe. In Scandinavia and northern U.S.S.R. it is also found in lakes; occasionally also in lakes in the British Isles. In Scandinavia it frequents brackish water.

General: The generic name *Thymallus* refers to the distinct wild thymelike scent of the fish when freshly caught. The common name, grayling, supposedly refers to its overall coloration, but the name belies one of the most beautifully marked freshwater sport fishes. Graylings require cool, clear, swift-flowing, well-oxygenated water with a gravel bottom, and often share the same water with trout. They tend to live close to the bottom and glean the larvae and pupae of midges from among the large bottom stones, but they also rise to feed on insect larvae and caddisflies. Food also includes salmon eggs, freshwater shrimp, worms, and small fish.

Spawning occurs after the spring thaw in early March to mid-May, when the female hollows shallow troughs in the gravel of the stream or riverbed. Sometimes during the spawning season the male assumes a dark coloration, and the dorsal fin may become reddish purple with dark spots. Eggs hatch at 3–4 weeks according to temperature. At 2–3 years males are mature, but females take 3–5 years.

The grayling is long renowned as a sport fish and much esteemed as a table fish.

155 A ARCTIC GRAYLING   F

Thymallus arcticus

Other common names: Northern grayling, Bach's grayling, poisson bleu, American grayling.

Features: Slender, graceful, troutlike body with a small mouth and long, very high characteristic dorsal fin which has been compared to a sail or butterfly wing; when depressed, dorsal fin extends almost to adipose fin. Dorsal fin *c.* 24; adipose fin; tail fin forked; anal fin *c.* 11. Coloration: dorsally darkish blue; flanks and belly grey; flanks overshot with blue and purplish marks; dorsal fin marked with cross-rows of blue spots and edged with red. Lateral line scale count 88 to 90.

Size: Up to 18 in (45 cm).

Distribution: North America; northern Canada, Alaska, northern Siberia. A closely related form in Europe (see above).

General: A species which abounds in clear, cold-water lakes and streams throughout its distribution. A first-class sport fish which rises readily to a fly. An excellent table fish.

156 INCONNU   F, occasionally B, seldom S

Stenodus leucichthys

Other common names: Sheefish (Alaska), nelma or white salmon (Siberia), whitefish.

Features: A whitefish with the adipose fin and soft-rayed dorsal typical of the *Salmonidae*; it possesses an axillary process or projection of cartilaginous material at the base of the ventral fins. 70 to 100 scales in lateral line; tail deeply forked. The inconnu is the largest of the whitefishes with a comparatively large mouth for these species; small teeth in both jaws; lower jaw noticeably projects. Herring-like in general appearance, relatively large silver scales on the body, scaleless head, centrally located dorsal fin. Lateral line is very noticeable along mid-line of the sides. Pelvic fins placed low down on body. Rather deep body that is flattened from side to side. Coloration: Resembles the lesser whitefishes in colour with a dark olive to greenish-blue back and silvery sides. Reports differ regarding numerous small black markings with some fish lacking these markings. The dorsal fin is dark, the forked tail fin greyish, the lower fins uniformly pale.

Size: Has been reported at 55 lb (25 kg) but averages only 5–10 lb (2–4 kg).

Distribution: Ranges from about 60 degrees North Latitude north to the Arctic. Found in rivers and brackish estuaries of the arctic drainage on the North American side at least as far as the Mackenzie River delta; on the Asian side for unknown distances along the Siberian Arctic coast. A non-migratory inconnu lives in large inland waters such as Great Bear and Great Slave lakes in the Canadian Northwest Territories.

General: Regarded as a gamefish though largely unknown to anglers. Edible, unimportant commercially, used for food by northern Eskimo groups in certain areas.

157 CHAIN PICKEREL   F
Esox niger

Other common names: Eastern pickerel, pickerel, chain pike, green pike, lake pike, lake pickerel, reticulated pickerel.

Features: Similar to the northern pike in body shape. Dorsal fin 14; tail fin forked; anal fin 13. Coloration: dark green, shading to lighter greens or blue green on flanks; flanks have a dark chainlike or lace-like network of markings (a characteristic recognition feature); belly cream or white; below eye is a prominent dark vertical line. Lateral line scale count *c.* 125. Scaling extends to cheeks and gill covers (unlike pike and muskellunge).
Size: Average up to 1–2 lb (1/2–1 kg); large fish (now rare) up to 10 lb (4 1/2 kg).
Distribution: Eastern North America.
General: A typical member of the pike family and often known simply as pickerel in some locales, not related to the walleye. Very predacious, and apart from fish it includes in its diet frogs, ducklings, and mice. Spawning takes place in spring, and the eggs are laid over plants in marshy shallows. A popular sport fish and ice-fished winter in the New England states. A table fish of fair quality.

158 EUROPEAN PIKE; NORTHERN PIKE   F, B
Esox lucius

Other common names: Common pike, great northern pike, Great Lakes pike, shovelnose pike, lake pickerel, channel pickerel, pickerel, jackfish, jackpike, jack, snake, gade, pickerel shark, tosh, luce.

Features: Long-bodied. Shovel-shaped head; large, broad, and flat snout; large jaws and powerful teeth; lower jaw projects beyond upper jaw; eyes look upward and forward. Dorsal fin 19 to 23; tail fin concave; anal fin 16 to 21; dorsal and anal fins similar in shape and set far back. Coloration: dorsally and flanks olive to dark green with pale yellowish spots; fish that live in brackish water more yellowish, fish in lakes, where weeds are present, greenish. Young fish are strongly marked with light bars and spots; older pike develop a darker coloration. Lateral line scale count 110 to 130.
Size: Females grow faster and larger than the males. Males mature 2–3 years, 10–16 in (25–40 cm), 1 lb (1/2 kg); mature males occasionally 36–40 in (90–100 cm), 11–18 lb (5–8 kg), but average 5 1/2–6 1/2 lb (2 1/2–3 kg). Females mature at 3–5 years, 16–22 in (40–55 cm); large females in continental Europe up to 5 ft (1 1/2 m), *c.* 80 lb (35 kg).

Distribution: Widespread in Northern Hemisphere (except Greece), introduced into Spain; common to boreal temperate zones up to 5,000 ft (1,500 m) altitude. Introduced into southern and south-western United States from north-east American states.
General: Usually referred to as the northern pike in North America. An omnivorous predatory and cannibalistic fish. It can feed on fish, crayfish, young ducks, small mammals, frogs, and birds taken alive from the water. The upper jaw bristles with teeth slanted backward to prevent large prey from slipping out of the mouth, but owing to this characteristic, a pike may occasionally choke to death because of its inability to disgorge oversize prey. Pike in lakes generally adopt particular camouflaged habitats (or haunts) where they lurk for an opportunity to ambush a passing prey. Its tail has great thrusting power and provides the pike with rapid acceleration, which enables it to outspeed a salmon over a short distance.

Spawning occurs in shallow water, March–May, and in extreme northerly latitudes to middle of July. Larvae hatch at 10–15 days. The young feed on planktonic animals, insect larvae, and crustaceans during first year, then mature into predatory and cannibalistic fish.

A highly esteemed sport fish and an important commercial fish in many places but the larger ones are not particularly noted as table fish.

159 REDFIN PICKEREL   F
Esox americanus americanus

Other common names: Mud pickerel, little pickerel, pickerel, brochet vermiculé, grass pickerel, banded pickerel, barred pickerel, jack.

Features: A small member of the pike family, *Esocidae*. The redfin has an elongate body, long head, and jaws of the northern pike. Redfin has a shorter snout in proportion to either the grass pickerel or the northern pike. Scales number approximately 105 along the lateral line. Hybridization is reported among grass pickerels and the redfins. Opercles and cheeks are fully scaled; 11 to 13 throat bones beneath the gill covers. Caudal and anal fins are directly opposite and similar in shape; tail is forked. Coloration: Back is olive green to green, shading to a lighter green on the sides which are marked with 10 to 13 dark, wavy, vertical bands. There is a very conspicuous black and vertical line below the eye; a similar but less obvious black line behind and in front of the eye.
Size: To a maximum of 15 in (37.5 cm) but more generally far smaller.
Distribution: Great Lakes and Mississippi drainage systems generally. South through the United States coastal plains from Maryland to Georgia and the northern and central portions of Florida.
General: Likes swamps and creeks, weed beds, rather than broad and open waterways, prefers a soft bottom. Fights well on rod and reel; sportsmen enjoy fishing for it immensely. Edible but not particularly tasty.

160 GRASS PICKEREL   F
Esox americanus vermiculatus

Other common names: Redfin pickerel, banded pickerel, barred pickerel, brook pickerel, mud pickerel, little pickerel, pickerel, brochet vermiculé, grass pike, jack pickerel, jack, brochet d'Amerique, northern pike.

Features: Smallest of the pike family, characterized by a single dorsal fin located far back on the tail, matching the anal fin directly opposite. The pickerels are scaled on the whole of the gill cover and cheek, the northern pike on the upper half of the gill cover and the whole cheek, the muskellunge on the upper half of the gill cover and the upper half of the cheek. Throat bones beneath the gill covers number 11 to 13. Tail is forked. The scales number approximately 125 in an extreme lengthwise row on the rather subdued lateral line. Coloration: Back is olive green or green, shading to a lighter green on the sides, with 10 to 13 dark, wavy lines or bands, vertically placed, on the sides. A conspicuous black vertical line is present under the eye. A similar but less obvious dark or black line extends horizontally behind and in front of the eye for a short distance.
Size: Maximum of about 12 in (30 cm) but usually smaller.
Distribution: Sluggish streams and weedy bays of the drainage systems of the St. Lawrence River, Lake Ontario, Erie, St. Clair and southern Lake Huron in Canada, plus additional waters in Ontario. Southward to Florida in the United States, in regions east of the Alleghenies. Occurs from Iowa and Missouri to Wisconsin, Michigan, and tributaries of Lake Erie south to the Ohio River and lower Mississippi drainages.
General: Game species on light tackle, edible. Very often confused with young northern pike. Feeds on other fishes, aquatic insects, crayfish, small frogs, etc.

161 MUSKELLUNGE   F
Esox masquinongy

Other common names: Muskalunge, spotted muskallunge, St. Lawrence muskallunge, musky, great pike, northern muskullunge, tiger muskellunge, maskinonge.

Features: Elongate body. Long, pointed head; projecting lower jaw and powerful teeth. Dorsal fin 16 to 21; tail fin forked; anal fin 14 to 18. Both dorsal and anal fins set well back. Coloration: dorsally and flanks dark grey, deep brown to light green, but varies in different waters, more vivid than the northern pike, and the markings are clear-cut; about the head, gill covers, and upper flanks there is a metallic bronze lustre. Note: the general coloration is *dark* on a *light* background, the reverse of the northern pike pattern of *light* on a *dark* background. Unlike the northern pike there are scales only on the upper half of the cheek and gill cover (the pike is fully scaled on the cheek and half scaled on the gill covers). Lateral scale count 150.
Size: Up to 60 in (150 cm), 62 lb (28 kg), but average smaller. A 69.1 lb (31.7 kg) musky was found to be 30 years old.
Distribution: North America, temperate regions of Canada and U.S., chiefly in

Wisconsin, Minnesota, Michigan, New York State, Pennsylvania, Ohio, and West Virginia.
General: Reckoned as the boldest, fiercest and most voracious of all predatory freshwater fishes. Also the largest freshwater sport fish in North America. Wherever found, the muskellunge is a solitary fish and is never seen in large numbers, since it requires a large feeding area. As a consequence it is not found in mountain waters with low fish densities.

The muskellunge spends much of its time in shallow water where it generally inhabits a weed-bed or other water growths while awaiting its prey such as suckers, frogs, small muskrats, waterfowl, and other muskellunges which stray within its territory. The muskellunge represents one of the most popular sport fish in North America due to its ability to leap, its wiliness, its size, and its hard fighting tactics. A table fish of good quality.

162 MILKFISH S, B
Chanos chanos

Other common names: White mullet, salmon herring, bandeng or bandang (East Indies), bangos, Moreton Bay salmon.

Features: A herring-like fish with a compressed, torpedo-shaped body with small, regular grooved scales. The mouth is small with no teeth. The body might be described as spindle-shaped, a flattish head with a large eye, no scales on the head. An adipose or fatty eyelid is present. The pectorals are low; the dorsal not prolonged. Dorsal fin, 14 to 16; anal, 8 to 10; pelvic, 10 to 11. There are 78 to 90 scales along the lateral line. Coloration: Greenish grey above though it has been described as blue to blue-olive on the back and a yellowish olive on the head; sides bright silver; sides of the head a pinkish gold.
Size: Reaches 60 in (150 cm); 50 lb (22.3 kg) but generally far smaller.
Distribution: Tropical and subtropical Indo-Pacific waters.
General: Important food fish, raised in brackish ponds through much of the Indo-Pacific region.

163 CHANNEL CATFISH F
Ictalurus punctatus

Other common names: Channel cat, fiddler, white cat, silver cat, Great Lakes channel catfish, lake catfish, catfish barbue.

Features: Rotund, elongate body. Snout overhangs mouth; 8 barbels or "whiskers" on head. Single dorsal fin I,7, leading spine is serrated; adipose fin; tail fin strongly forked; single anal fin 25 to 30; sharp spine on pectoral fin. Coloration: variable, in Great Lakes form, dorsally and flanks light pigmented, with scattered dark spots extending over flanks, but absent in young and very large adults; inland lakes form, dorsally and flanks dark green, brown, or black, shading on lower flanks and belly to light silvery grey. In young fish up to 12 in (30 cm) the tail and anal fins have a narrow black border.
Size: Average up to 2–4 lb (1–1 3/4 kg), maximum over 55 lb (25 kg).
Distribution: North America, in rivers of the Great Lakes region, the Mississippi Valley and tributaries to the Gulf of Mexico.
General: Found in cooler, deeper waters than most catfish. Spawning occurs in spring during which time adults often ascend rivers. Food usually is aquatic vegetation, insects, crayfish, molluscs, and fish such as minnow and yellow perch. A commercial species and a useful sport fish. The flesh is white and flaky, and the channel catfish is highly regarded as a table fish.

164 BLUE CATFISH F, B,
occasionally S
Ictalurus furcatus

Other common names: Mississippi cat, great fork-tailed cat, chuckle-headed cat, poisson bleu.

Features: Thickset, elongate body; 8 barbels or "whiskers" on head. Dorsal fin I,6; adipose fin; tail fin moderately forked with pointed lobes; anal fin 32 to 35 its margin straight; sharp spine on each pectoral fin. Coloration: dorsally and flanks dull olivaceous, blue, or slaty; lower flanks paling to silvery; belly silvery white.
Size: Average up to 20 lb (9 kg), maximum 60 in (150 cm), 150 lb (70 kg).
Distribution: North America, Ohio to Iowa and Texas and Mexico. Rare in the northern part of its native range.
General: The largest of the Mississippi River catfishes and one of the most numerous species of the lower Mississippi Valley. A deepwater fish and a migratory species during cold weather when it may occasionally enter brackish and salt water. A bottom feeder and nocturnal. An important commercial species usually caught by nets or set lines. It is an exceptionally popular sport fish and highly esteemed as a table fish.

165 BROWN BULLHEAD F
Ictalurus nebulosus

Other common names: Bullhead, common bullhead, mud cat, mud pout, horned pout, marbled catfish, square-tail catfish, small catfish, black catfish, bull pout.

Features: Thickset, semicylindrical body. Eight barbels or "whiskers" on head. Dorsal fin I,6 or 7, the spine is strongly developed and saw-toothed; adipose fin; tail fin square-cut or slightly concave; anal fin 21 or 22; strong saw-toothed spine on pectoral fin. Coloration: dorsally and flanks olive-green to dark brown and mottled with darker patches; belly cream or white.
Size: Average 3/4–1 lb (350–450 g), maximum 18 in (45 cm), 4 lb (1 3/4 kg).
Distribution: North America, originally native to only certain areas but now introduced elsewhere.
General: It shows a preference for warm, quiet, weedy waters, mud-bottomed lakes and ponds, and slow-flowing rivers and is able to tolerate adverse conditions such as high temperatures and low oxygen content better than most native fishes. The brown bullhead is an omnivorous feeder taking insect larvae, crayfish, molluscs, snails, plant material, and occasional fish. It is

166 FLATHEAD CATFISH F
Pylodictus olivaris

Other common names: Mud catfish, mud cat, pieded cat, opelousas cat, granny cat, Russian cat, banshaw, goujon, hoosier, yellow catfish.

Features: Large, stout-bodied. Head extremely depressed, large mouth with lower jaw projecting. Dorsal fin I,5 or 6 (single spine is weakly developed); large adipose fin; tail fin slightly concave; anal fin 12 to 15 (characteristically with fewer rays than other related North American catfishes). Coloration: dorsally and flanks yellowish and mottled extensively with a brown or greenish pattern; belly whitish or pale grey. Lateral line.
Size: Average up to 4–5 lb (1 3/4–2 1/4 kg), maximum 60 in (150 cm), 100 lb (45 kg).
Distribution: North America, from Great Lakes States, and Mississippi Valley to the Gulf States in large streams and rivers.
General: A large catfish of sluggish lowland waters where it is sometimes extremely abundant. Very predacious, popular with anglers, good eating. The flathead is in short supply. Important commercially and caught on set lines and in traps. A highly prized sport fish, and its flesh has the finest table qualities among North American catfishes.

167 STONECAT F
Noturus flavus

Other common names: Little yellow cat, white cat, mongrel bullhead, deepwater bullhead, doogler, catfish, baubotte des rapides, mad tom.

Features: Small-bodied fish; 8 barbels or "whiskers" on head. Upper jaw overhangs lower, thick lips. Body is covered with thick skin which may have a heavy mucus coating. Dorsal fin I,6; adipose fin separated from tail by a slight notch; tail fin rounded and characteristically keel-like; anal fin 16; pectoral fin unserrated with poison gland (see below). Coloration: dorsally and flanks yellowish brown or grey; fins yellowish-edged.
Size: Maximum up to c. 12 in (30 cm).
Distribution: North America, Great Lakes to Montana and south to Texas.
General: A catfish that frequents the rocky bottoms of swift-flowing rivers. Nocturnal in habit. Although the flesh is of excellent table quality, it is not a commercial species nor a welcome sport fish. The unserrated pectoral spine contains a poison gland at its base which can cause a painful wound.

168 GAFF-TOPSAIL CATFISH F, B, S
Felichthys marinus

Features: Elongate body. Head rather short, broad and round, subconic and depressed; 2 chin barbels, and 2 very long ones emerging from sides of mouth and extending to end of pectoral spine. Dorsal fin I,7 (the spine is characteristically very long and filamentous and has the general appearance of a small sail, giving rise to its common name); adipose fin; tail fin deeply forked with upper lobe longer; anal fin 23; pectoral fin I,12. Coloration: dorsally dusky-grey to bluish; flanks and belly silvery. No body scales.
Size: Maximum 24 in (60 cm), 10 lb (4 1/2 kg).
Distribution: Western Atlantic, from New England states south; abundant round Florida and Gulf of Mexico.
General: A coastal species found in estuaries, harbours, channels, bays, and offshore waters. A similar breeding biology to the sea catfish (see below). As a sport fish they are strong, hard fighters and offer considerable resistance. They are taken by still fishing or surf fishing and readily accept baits or lures. The strong dorsal and pectoral spines can inflict dangerous wounds so care must be exercised when handling. Formerly considered nonedible but nowadays reckoned an excellent table fish.

169 SEA CATFISH F, B, S
Arius felis

Other common names: Common sea catfish, Florida cat, sea barbel, Cape barger, salmon-catfish, estuarine catfish.

Features: Rather elongate body, tapering to slender tail, not compressed. Head subconic, depressed and flattish above; 4 barbels, 2 short ones on chin and 2 nearly as long as head, emerging from sides of mouth. Dorsal fin I,6 or 7; adipose fin; tail fin deeply forked with upper lobe longer; anal fin c. 16; pectoral fin I,7 (dorsal and pectoral spines strongly serrated on inner and outer edges and kept erect by a special locking mechanism). Coloration: dorsally steel blue; flanks and belly silvery; lower fins pale. Coloration may be variable locally according to sex and age. The body has no scales, but the head has armoured plates.
Size: Average 1 1/2 lb (3/4 kg); largest fish up to 24 in (60 cm), 4 1/2 lb (2 kg).
Distribution: Atlantic tropical seas.
General: Inhabits both fresh and salt water and frequently found around estuaries. The dorsal and pectoral fin spines are strongly serrated and can inflict dangerous wounds so that care must be exercised when handling. During the breeding period the male carries the fertilized eggs in its mouth up to two to three months before hatching occurs, and during this time the male probably does not feed. Now a recognized sport fish in many locales and considered a reasonably palatable fish.

170 WHITE CATFISH F
Ictalurus catus

Features: Elongate body. Eight barbels or "whiskers" on head. Dorsal fin I,6 or 7; adipose fin; tail fin somewhat forked; anal fin 18 to 23. Coloration: dorsally and upper flanks blue greyish; lower flanks and belly white.
Size: Up to 24 in (60 cm).
Distribution: North America, from the Delaware River to Texas; introduced into California.
General: Found in coastal streams and swamps. A commercial fish of some importance and an excellent table fish.

171 YELLOW BULLHEAD F

Ictalurus natalis
Other common name: Bullhead.

Features: Short, thickset body, more robust than the brown bullhead (see above); 8 barbels or "whiskers" on head, barbels on chin are characteristically white (unpigmented) rather than black or grey as in other bullhead species. Dorsal fin I,6; adipose fin; tail fin rounded; anal fin 24 to 27. Coloration: dorsally and flanks brown to almost black without dark patches or mottlings; lower flanks and belly bright yellow.
Size: Average 1/2–1 lb (1/4–1/2 kg), maximum 5 lb (2 1/4 kg), 16 in (40 cm).
Distribution: North America, from North Dakota, and Great Lakes region, Hudson River south to Gulf of Mexico.
General: A species which spawns in late spring. When the eggs are laid, the nest is guarded by the male fish. After hatching, the fry continue to be guarded until they attain a length of *c.* 1 1/2 in (4 cm). Food consists of insects, molluscs, crayfish, and occasional small fish. As a sport fish it is frequently confused with the brown bullhead (*I. nebulosus*). A delicious table fish with some commercial importance.

172 WALKING CATFISH F

Clarias batrachus

Features: This catfish, and others of the same genus, are distinguished from other catfishes by having an additional respiration organ consisting of a cluster of hollow, blood-containing branches in the upper part of the gill chamber, by means of which they can assimilate oxygen from the air. The body is slender, head broad and rather flattened. Around the mouth are four pairs of longer feelers. The anal fin is very long. Spiny rays are only present in the pectoral fins. Coloration: back and upper sides brownish and olive, lower sides and belly lighter, fins greyish olive.
Size: Reaches a length of 1 1/4 ft (40 cm).
Distribution: Africa and southern Asia.
General: Lives in slow-running rivers, lakes, and ponds. Due to the air respiration the fish is able to move (walk) up on the beach, and to survive for some time, if the habitat dries up.

173 WELS F, B

Silurus glanis
Other common names: Danubian catfish, sheatfish.

Features: Heavy-bodied. A broad, flat head; wide mouth; two very long barbels hang from upper lip, four shorter barbels hang below mouth. Small dorsal fins 3 to 5, well forward; tail fin small and rounded; anal fins 84 to 92, very long and narrow and joins tail fin. Coloration: variable, but dorsally and flanks generally very dark or with lighter olive green mottlings; belly lighter. The skin is slimy and scaleless.
Size: Average mature fish 40 in (100 cm), 22 lb (10 kg); large fish frequently over 100 lb (45 kg). In eastern Europe and western Asia it sometimes grows to over 10 ft (3 m). In the Dnieper River occasional specimens reach *c.* 660 lb (300 kg).
Distribution: Central and eastern Europe (including the extreme south of Sweden and Finland) into Asia as far as the regions surrounding the Caspian Sea. Introduced into other European locales.
General: After the sturgeon it is the largest freshwater fish in Europe.

The wels is found in lakes, large rivers, and in brackish waters, and it prefers sandy or muddy bottoms. During the daylight hours it remains close to the bottom, or hidden away, and only rises to feed at night. The wels is a voracious feeder that eats a wide variety of food, including ducklings and water voles but mostly fish – with a marked preference for eels and burbot.

During the winter it hibernates in deep water. After spawning range (June–August) the male guards the eggs for *c.* three days until they hatch.

The wels's occurrence is not always favoured by fishermen owing to its ability to reduce the stocks of more popular fish. In the Soviet Union and Eastern Europe the wels is a commercial species. The flesh and roe are delicious and valuable.

174 TIGER FISH F

Hydrocyon lineatus
Other common name: River dog.

Features: Elongate body, deep and compressed; belly rounded. Snout rather elongate; mouth large and equipped with elongate teeth with sharp cutting edges. Teeth remain visible when mouth is closed; below these teeth is a series of "replacer" teeth. Dorsal fin II,8; small adipose fin; tail fin deeply forked with long pointed lobes; anal fin III, 11 to 13. Coloration: dorsally grey brown or olive green; flanks and belly silvery white with more or less distinct longitudinal rows of blackish spots. Above lateral line they run confluently along scales forming streaks. Spots are absent in young fish. Dorsal fin and upper lobe of tail fin yellowish or grey, often blackish toward the end; adipose fin dark grey or whitish, on rare occasions with a black spot; pelvic and anal fins, and occasionally the pectorals, are tinged with pink or pale orange; the lower lobe of the tail fin is a bright red, edged with black.
Size: Up to 40 in (100 cm), 80 lb (36 kg), but average fish much smaller.
Distribution: Africa; *H. lineatus* has a northerly distribution while *H. vittalus* is a more southerly species; both fish are very similar in appearance, and in addition there are several other related species and subspecies of "tiger fish" that occur over the same distribution.
General: Tiger fish are voracious, predatory species which inhabit rivers and the lake systems throughout Africa, although they are notably absent from some locales such as Lakes Victoria and Nyasa. Although they are not large, they are nevertheless excellent sport fish and offer a tremendous fight when hooked.

Tiger fish, although edible, are not usually rated as table fish.

175 ASP F, B

Aspius aspius
Other common name: Rapacious carp.

Features: Elongate, slim, and compressed body. Large mouth; projecting lower jaw with a thickened lip which fits into notch on upper jaw; relatively small eye. Dorsal fin III,8; tail fin deeply forked; anal fin III,12 to 14. Coloration: dorsally greenish; flanks have a coppery or silvery sheen; belly lighter; fins are olive grey tinged with red. Lateral line curves downward and has a scale count 65–74. Scales are small.
Size: Average up to 20 in (50 cm), 2 1/4–4 1/2 lb (1–2 kg); large fish 48 in (120 cm), 20 lb (9 kg), specimens up to 40 lb (18 kg) occasionally reported.
Distribution: Elbe and Danube basins, southern Sweden and extending through Eastern Europe to the Caspian Sea.
General: Found in lakes and rivers. A surface-feeding, predatory fish, but in winter living in the deeper part of the water. The population inhabiting the eastern region of its distribution is partly migratory and moves into brackish water to feed. Spawning occurs April–May. Eggs are deposited between stones, and hatching takes place in 10–17 days. The young begin feeding on planktonic animals, then at 2–3 months they develop into predators of juvenile fish.

As a sport fish it is extremely shy and suspicious, but it is a popular angling fish, renowned for its fighting qualities. An excellent table fish, and taken commercially in southeast Europe with nets, traps, and hooks.

176 PARAHYBA F

Brachyplatystoma filamentosa
Other common name: South American catfish.

Features: Slender body with long, depressed head; blunt snout, small eyes. The upper jaw projects over the lower. Some of the barbels around the mouth reach to off the pectoral fins. The first dorsal fin is short and high; the second, adipose, fin is short and high. Large tail fin with long, pointed lobes, one of the rays in the lower lobe is prolonged into a long filament. Coloration: back and upper sides dark grey with blackish patches or bands, lower sides and belly lighter.
Size: A small fish only reaching a length of 7–8 in (18–20 cm).
Distribution: South America from Peru to southern Argentine, Amazon River.
General: The parahyba is a rather sluggish fish preferring slow-flowing streams.

177 DACE F, B

Leuciscus leuciscus

Features: A small, slim fish. Head pointed; small mouth. In general shape and colouring it closely resembles a roach, and it is often confused with a young chub. Dorsal fin III,7; tail fin concave; anal fin III,8. Coloration: variable, dorsally usually bluish green; flanks and belly silvery or yellowish white; dorsal, tail, and anal fins greyish, pectoral and pelvics pale yellow (or greenish), sometimes with a red tinge. Lateral line scale count 48 to 51. Several forms and subspecies may be distinguished in Europe and Asia.
Size: Average up to 8 in (20 cm). Specimens seldom over 1 lb (1/2 kg); but larger fish up to 12 in (30 cm) not infrequent.
Distribution: Throughout Europe north of the Alps and the Pyrenees eastward in northern Asia almost to Sea of Okhotsk.
General: Found in cool waters of rivers and near estuary mouths, occasionally in canals. Food consists of water and flying insects, worms, snails, and plants. Spawning occurs March-May. Maturity is reached at 3–4 years. Valued as a sport fish, when fished for with light tackle; it also rises to a fly. Although a bony fish and not eaten in Western Europe, large numbers are taken by commercial netting and utilized as food fish in the U.S.S.R.

178 DORADO F

Salminus maxillosus

Features: Stout, a compressed, little body with a long tapering posterior part. Large head with protruding snout; rather small eyes. The jaws are large with several rows of teeth, those in the outer rows are larger than those in the inner rows. One high, short dorsal fin is a long, serrate spine; closer to the tail is an adipose fin, also with a spine. The tail fin is broad with slightly concave hind margin; the anal fin is short and high. The foremost ray in the pectoral fin is a strong, serrate spine; this and also the spine in the dorsal fin have poison glands near their bases. The scales are very high, strong and platelike, overlapping one another with their vertical margins; they are placed in a few longitudinal rows, covering most of the body as an armour. Coloration: all over dark brownish with almost black patches.
Size: About 4–6 in (10–15 cm).
Distribution: South America from Colombia to Argentine.
General: Lives in slow-flowing streams with muddy bottoms and rich vegetation. Several nearly related species occur in South America.

179 TAMBAQUY F

Colossoma bidens

Features: This species is a South American catfish nearly related to *Brachyplatystoma filamentosa* and *Salminus maxillosus* and very similar to them in shape of body and fins. The head and the anterior part of the body are large and stout, but the remaining part tapers into a rather slender tail stalk. The dorsal fin is short and high; adipose fin is present. The species is characterized by a comparatively low number of gill rakers. The large plate-like scales build an armour around the body. Coloration: dark greyish to brown with almost blackish patches.
Size: Up to 6–10 in (15–25 cm).
Distribution: South America, south to Patagonia.
General: Like the other South American catfishes, it lives in slow-flowing streams, in lakes and ponds, mostly on a muddy, vegetation-rich bottom.

180 COMMON CARP
181 LEATHER CARP
182 MIRROR CARP
Cyprinus carpio
Other common name: Koi (Japan).

Features: A broad-shaped, laterally compressed body; a humpbacked appearance. Small mouth; one long and one short barbel on either side of mouth. Dorsal fin III or IV,17 to 22; tail fin forked; anal fin II or III,5. Coloration: dorsally olive green, sometimes bluish and bronze; flanks pale golden; belly pale yellowish or pale greenish brown; all fins except the long, concave dorsal have a reddish tinge. Lateral line scale count 35 to 40. The scales are normally large and cover the body, but there are genetic variations in appearance which occur regionally, and often locally in fish from the same parentage. One variety is known as *scaled carp* (or *king carp*), and these fish are covered by small uniform-sized scales; another is the *mirror carp* which has large scales irregularly distributed and of varying sizes, or small scales along the back and large even-sized scales along the lateral line. The *leather carp* is almost a scaleless fish, but possesses a thick, leathery skin. Cultivated breeds of carp tend to be larger-bodied fish than the wild variety.
Size: Wild fish maximum up to *c.* 40 in (100 cm), 65 lb (30 kg). On reaching maturity at *c.* 4 years, 12–16 in (30–40 cm), 1–2 1/4 lb (1/2–2 kg). On average, cultivated fish develop at a faster rate and reach *c.* 4 1/3 lb (2 kg) in 3 years. Size and growth of wild fish vary widely from locale to locale.
Distribution: Native to Asia in a region extending from the Black Sea to Manchuria, but now widespread throughout the world. First introduced into Europe in Roman times and into the United States in 1876.
General: The carp is commercially of great importance in Central and Eastern Europe as a food fish, and carp pond farming, in association with selective breeding, is carried out intensively in many countries. Carp has the ability to survive in limited waters, and consequently is an easy fish to transport over long distances. As a sport fish it is popular, but it is not an easy victim to entice with either bait or nets.

Spawning occurs from May onward when water temperature is sufficiently high. In the wild, carp sheds its spawn at weekly intervals attaching it to plants. Hatching occurs at 3–8 days, and at first the fry feed on their own yolk sac before floating to the surface when their swim bladders begin to function. Carp mature at 3–4 years.

183 GRASS CARP F
Ctenopharyngodon idella

Features: Despite name no true carp. A relative of the Ide, *Leuciscus idus* (which see). Somewhat compressed fusiform body, snubbed snout overhangs small angled mouth. Dorsal fin ray count I,5 to 8; anal ray count I,6 to 9. Tail fin forked and lateral line scale count 32 to 54. Coloration: Dark dusky yellow on the back paling to greyish yellow on the flanks. Pale off-white underneath. Dorsal and anal and pectoral fins are a pale yellowish, ventral and tail fins darker and tinged with reddish purple.
Size: Averaging about 18 in (45 cm) and weigh-

ing about 3 lb (1.5 kg).
Distribution: Eastern Europe, European Russia, and southern Asian lakes, ponds and slower rivers.
General: This fish has been implanted into Denmark with good results. Spawns in spring and feeds on vegetable matter, insects and smaller crustaceans. A good sportfish and edible.

184 PIRANHA F
Serrasalmus nattereri
Other common name: Piratefish.

Features: Short, very high and compressed body. High head with short, rounded snout and vaulted front; large mouth with strong, sharp teeth. First dorsal fin very high, second small, much like an adipose fin; the anal fin is large and long; it as well as the first dorsal fin is placed far back on the body. The tail fin is very large with concave hind margin; pectoral and ventral fins only small. Coloration: back and upper sides are dark green to grey with small lighter spots; lower sides and belly whitish to silvery; the hind margin of the tail fin is black; part of the anal fin is red, the other fins are dark grey.
Size: 10–12 in (25–30 cm).
Distribution: Rivers in the tropical South America, Amazon.
General: A very voracious fish, which lives in shoals attacking their prey (other fish, waterfowls, small mammals), biting and tearing their flesh from the bones.

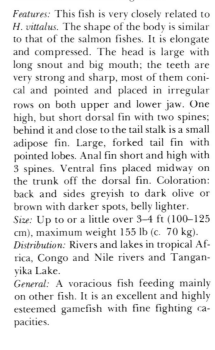

185 BLEAK F
Alburnus alburnus

Features: A small, slender-bodied fish. Dorsal fin III,8 or 9; tail fin forked; anal fin III,16 to 20. Coloration: dorsally blue green; flanks and belly silvery white; fins light grey, with an occasional tinge of orange (usually with males at spawning time). Lateral line curves downward and has a scale count of 48 to 55. Small scales which easily rub off. Occasionally confused with a dace (*L. leuciscus*), but the bleak's anal fin is much longer.
Size: Average 4–6 in (10–15 cm), occasionally up to 8 in (20 cm), 1–2 oz (40 g).
Distribution: Europe except Spain, Italy, and Greece, and some smaller locales.
General: Found in still, open waters in schools especially along lake shores and streams, but it dislikes disturbed waters. Food consists of flies, shrimps, worms, and larvae. At spawning time (April–June) the males develop white tubercles on the head and dorsal area.

The bleak is not usually included as a sport fish, but is useful as baitfish and as a practice fish for young anglers. In some areas it is of great importance to competitive match anglers, and specialised techniques have been developed for catching the greatest possible quantity in a short time.

In Europe there are two similar species: the Danube bleak (*Chalcalburnus chalcoides*) found in the Danube River system and eastward to the Caspian Sea region, and the Italian bleak (*A. albidus*) found around the shores of the Adriatic. Both have features very similar to those of the common bleak.

186 GOLIATH F
Hydrocion goliath
Other common name: Tigerfish.

Features: This fish is very closely related to *H. vittalus*. The shape of the body is similar to that of the salmon fishes. It is elongate and compressed. The head is large with long snout and big mouth; the teeth are very strong and sharp, most of them conical and pointed and placed in irregular rows on both upper and lower jaw. One high, but short dorsal fin with two spines; behind it and close to the tail stalk is a small adipose fin. Large, forked tail fin with pointed lobes. Anal fin short and high with 3 spines. Ventral fins placed midway on the trunk off the dorsal fin. Coloration: back and sides greyish to dark olive or brown with darker spots, belly lighter.
Size: Up to or a little over 3–4 ft (100–125 cm), maximum weight 155 lb (c. 70 kg).
Distribution: Rivers and lakes in tropical Africa, Congo and Nile rivers and Tanganyika Lake.
General: A voracious fish feeding mainly on other fish. It is an excellent and highly esteemed gamefish with fine fighting capacities.

187 BARBEL F
Barbus barbus

Features: Long, cylindrical body; four short barbels or beards on upper lip. Dorsal fin III,7 to 9, leading spine is serrated and ossified; tail fin forked; anal fin III,5. Coloration: dorsally and on upper flanks olive bronze to amber; lower flanks golden or greenish; belly silvery white; fins are green with reddish bases. General overall coloration shows considerable variations. Lateral line scale count 55 to 65. Scales are medium-sized and firmly attached.
Size: Average 12–20 in (30–50 cm), but sometimes up to 40 in (1 m), 20 lb (9 kg). In the Soviet Union barbel in the Dnieper River occasionally up to 35 lb (16 kg).
Distribution: Central Europe from northern France as far as the Black Sea. In the British Isles confined to eastern counties north from a line extending from the Severn to the Thames, to Yorkshire.
General: A bottom-feeder, preferring swift, clear streams and rivers. It is found in small schools and feeds on worms, shrimps, larvae, and occasionally (near spawning time) small fish. Winter is spent in semi-hibernation, but at this period the best sport fishing is obtained. However, in very cold weather the barbel becomes totally inactive.

During spawning, May–June, barbel gather in large schools. Eggs hatch in 10–15 days. Maturity is reached in 4–5 years. The barbel spawn is slightly poisonous, and in old Russia it was a folklore medicine often prescribed as an emetic.

Although the barbel is becoming rarer in some parts of its distribution, it is a popular sport fish and in the past was often affectionately termed "the poor man's salmon" in reference to its craftiness, its speed, and its stubborn fighting qualities. Although most sport fishermen consider it to be a coarse, bony, and tasteless fish, the larger sizes found in continental Europe have some commercial importance; these fish are caught in nets.

There are several species or subspecies in other parts of Europe, including the Italian barbel (*B. plebejus*); the southern barbel (*B. meridionalis*), and the Iberian barbel (*B. comiza*) (see Index).

188 CHUB F
Leuciscus cephalus

Features: Small, slim, cylindrical fish. Head is broad and blunt; mouth is large. Very similar in appearance to and frequently confused with the ide and the dace. Dorsal fin III,8 or 9; tail fin concave; anal fin III,7 to 9. Coloration: variable, dorsally usually dark green or grey; flanks paling to a brassy metallic green or blue; belly silvery. Lateral line scale count 44 to 46. The scales are dark-edged. It may be distinguished from the ide by its broader head (seen from above) and large dark-edged scales, and whereas the ide's anal fin trailing-edge is straight, the chub's is convex. It may be distinguished from the dace by the differences in profile of the dorsal fin trailing-edge, in the dace it is concave.
Size: Average 14 in (35 cm); large older fish

up to 24 in (60 cm), *c.* 6 1/2–9 lb (3–4 kg).
Distribution: Much of northern and Central Europe (except Denmark and northern Scandinavia); Southeast Asia.
General: Often described as one of the greediest of sport fishes, for it tends to feed at all times of the day and is omnivorous, devouring a variety of vegetable and animal matter. It has a marked predilection for young trout, and this makes it an unwelcome species in many trout waters.

The chub is often found near the surface in large schools and prefers river habitats with fast or medium flow, but it is also found in canals and still waters. During the winter it migrates into deeper water. Spawning occurs April–June; the eggs are sticky and adhere to stones, plants, and wood; hatching takes place within a week. A subspecies fish, the Black Sea chub (*L.c. borysthenicus*), more resembles a dace and has a greenish grey dorsal coloration: this species occurs in the waters fringing the Black Sea.

Although an excellent sport fish, taking almost any kind of bait including flies and lures, the chub is so bony that it has little or no value as a table fish.

189 CRUCIAN CARP F
Carassius carassius

Features: Deeper and generally smaller-bodied than the common carp (see above) with no barbels at the mouth, and the tail fin is much less forked. Two divergent forms are recognized with intermediate types. One is found in small ponds, grows very slowly, and develops into large-headed stunted forms (*forma humilis*), the other is found in larger lake waters, where food is more plentiful, and the resulting fish are deeper-bodied (*forma gibelio*). When crossed with common carp, there is also a hybrid form of common/crucian carp with intermediate features. Dorsal fin III or IV,14 to 21; tail fin forked/concave; anal fin III,6 to 8. Coloration: dorsally and flanks olive green or reddish brown; flanks paling to brassy; rounded dark spot near the base of the tail but sometimes very obscure in older fish. Lateral line scale count 32 to 35.
Size: Up to 18 in (45 cm), 7 3/4 lb (3 1/2 kg).
Distribution: Europe.
General: Shows a preference for quiet, reedy waters which are often polluted and quite unsuitable for other less hardy species. A slow-growing fish and often found in a stunted form in waters with limited food supply; the depth of body development has a very close relationship to available food supply. It feeds on insects, larvae, plankton, worms, snails, and plants. During the winter it hibernates in the bottom mud, and its body metabolism undergoes a marked decline until the spring thaw triggers a biochemical response to reactivate it.

The crucian carp is often found in ornamental ponds where it sometimes may be confused with the goldfish; as an ornamental pond fish is readily tamed. In Eastern Europe it is an important food species where it is raised on commercial fish farms or caught in traps. It is also a local sport fish and an important one in areas where poor water conditions inhibit stocking by less hardy species.

190 COMMON BREAM F, B
Abramis brama

Features: Very deep-bodied, compressed, and humpbacked. Small mouth and eye; thick lips. In spawning season males have several white or yellow tubercles on the head and body. Dorsal fin III,9; tail fin deeply forked and lobes unsymmetrical; anal fin III,24 or 30. Coloration: dorsally black, dark olive, or greyish; flanks are bronzed, but silvery in young bream; belly silvery or white; fins are dark grey. Lateral line scale count 51 to 60. Skin is very slimy. A young fish is sometimes difficult to distinguish from the white or silver bream (*Blicca bjoerkna*) (see below).
Size: Average up to 16 in (40 cm), 4 1/2 lb (2 kg), maximum up to 20 lb (9 kg).
Distribution: Much of Europe east to Caspian Sea; absent from some locales (e.g. Iberian peninsula, parts of France, Italy, Yugoslavia, Greece, and northern Scandinavia).
General: The common name "bream" is said to date back to the twelfth century and to derive from an old Germanic word meaning "to glitter." The common bream frequents stagnant or slow-moving waters and brackish waters in the Baltic, but it is also found in fast-moving waters occasionally. It feeds on larvae, molluscs, crustaceans, weeds; and the larger specimens feed on fish.

Spawning occurs in May–June in shallow water amid dense weeds; males occupy defensive territories, and spawning involves much active ritualistic behaviour performed over a period of several weeks. Bream is an important sport fish, though a disappointing fighter. In Europe it is a tasty table species. In many areas bream is important commercially and is caught by seine or stake nets.

191 GUDGEON F, B
Gobio gobio

Features: Small, elongate, cylindrical body similar to, but smaller than, the barbel. Short, heavy head; mouth has two barbels. Dorsal fin III,5 to 7; tail fin forked; anal fin III,6 or 7; Coloration: dorsally and upper flanks olive brown; paling on lower flanks and belly to a silvery yellowish white; dark greenish markings along flanks; tail fin mottled or spotted with black. Lateral line distinct, and scale count 38 to 44.
Size: Up to 8 in (20 cm).
Distribution: Widespread through Europe and northern Asia, but absent from many locales such as Scotland, Spain, Italy, Greece, and northern Scandinavia.
General: A schooling species with a preference for clear, shallow water in lakes and slow-flowing streams, but also occasionally found in brackish water. Spawning occurs in May–June. Mainly a bottom-living fish feeding chiefly on worms, larvae, and crustaceans. In some locales, in spite of its small size, it is included among recognised sport fish; it is also frequently used as a bait fish, particularly for pike. A first class epicurean table fish with an unusual flavour.

192 GALJOEN S
Dichistius capensis
Other common names: Highwater, damba, blackfish, black bream.

Features: Moderately deep, compressed body. Steep profile to forehead (in young more rounded); small mouth with teeth adapted for crushing shellfish. Dorsal fin notched X,18 or 19; tail fin forked; anal fin III,13 or 14. Coloration: variable, but usually almost black overall for fish living in rocky areas to bright silvery for fish from sandy areas; flanks occasionally mottled or with 7–9 dark crossbars of uniform width, especially in young fish. Scales small and rough and covering entire body except snout. A related species, the multi-stripe (*Dichistius multifasciatus*), may be synonymous with *D. capensis*.
Size: Average up to 3 lb (1 1/4 kg), rare above 10 lb (4 1/2 kg), maximum 16 lb (7 1/4 kg).
Distribution: South Africa, from Walfish Bay round the Cape to Natal.
General: A shallow-water fish but rarely enters estuaries. It approaches close inshore at high tide, hence one of the common names "highwater". Food consists mainly of weeds, but it eagerly consumes mussels and crustaceans and most lowly forms of life.. Locally it is a very popular sport fish and has a reputation for fighting hard. As a table fish it is not everywhere esteemed, but flavour and quality are considerably improved by immediate bleeding after capture.

193 NORTHERN SQUAWFISH F
Ptychocheilus oregonensis
Other common names: Squawfish, Columbia River squawfish, chapaul, shepawl, whitefish, chub, bigmouth, yellowbelly, pike.

Features: Large, elongate body. Pike-like mouth. Dorsal fin 9 or 10; tail fin deeply forked; anal fin 8 or 9. Coloration: dorsally muddy greenish, flanks yellowish or silvery; belly yellowish or pale silvery; young fish have a dark spot on tail fin; during the spawning season the fins are often reddish or orange, and the scales show dark specks. Lateral line almost straight, and scale count 67 to 75.
Size: Up to 48 in (120 cm).
Distribution: North America, the Columbia River basin to Montana and Idaho, and north to British Columbia; also elsewhere in the United States.
General: The northern squawfish is one of several North American related schooling species of the carp family which are common in many waters and may reach up to 80 lb (36 kg) (see also Index). Their diet consists of insects and small fish. As sport fish their worth is controversial. Many are caught by ice-fishing methods during the winter. A commercial species and an excellent table fish.

194 MINNOW F, B
Phoxinus phoxinus

Features: Small, cylindrical body. Short, blunt snout. Dorsal fin III,7; tail fin deeply forked; anal fin III,6 or 7. Coloration: very variable, particularly with locality, but dorsally usually very dark olive brown; flanks often mottled olive or pale green with several vertical dark brown or purple stripes extending both across the dorsal area and the flanks; belly silvery, but during the spawning season the male belly develops a bright rosy hue, and the throat turns black; fins and tail are yellowish green. Scale count 80 to 100. Scales are very small.
Size: Average up to 3 1/2 in (9 cm), maximum 4 3/4 in (12 cm), 1/10 lb (50 g).
Distribution: Most of Europe (except parts of Spain, Italy, and Greece); northern Asia.
General: An inhabitant of the upper regions of rivers, brooks, and streams with running water, with preference for a stony or sandy bottom; rarer in lake regions. In the Baltic distribution it is found in large numbers in brackish water. Spawning occurs May–July when, apart from the male changes in coloration, the males (and females to some extent) develop white tubercles on the head, and the pectoral fin is thickened. The minnow is very gregarious and forms large schools and in some waters it may compete with young trout for available food. It is an excellent baitfish which can be transported easily and kept alive for long periods.

195 IDE F, B
Leuciscus idus
Other common name: Orfe

Features: Somewhat similar in appearance to the roach and chub with which it often shares the same water. Body is somewhat thickset and humped behind the head. The snout is rounded, giving a blunt appearance. Dorsal fin III,8 (with high profile); tail fin concave; anal fin III,9 or 10. Coloration: dorsally greenish or grey black; flanks paling to silvery; belly silvery; dorsal fin dark, and all other fins with a reddish or orange tinge. The lateral line scale count 54 to 60. The golden variety, known as the orfe, has an overall pale yellow or golden coloration and is commonly met with in ornamental ponds. The ide can be distinguished from the chub by the straight trailing edge of the anal fin and the lateral line scale count.
Size: 12–16 in (30–40 cm), 2 1/4 lb (1 kg); it may reach 10 lb (4 1/2 kg) or even 20 lb (9 kg) in the eastern parts of the region.
Distribution: Northeast Europe, much of Scandinavia, northern Asia.
General: A migratory species generally found in brackish lagoons, in deep tidal rivers and in lakes. In fresh water they feed in schools on insects and crustaceans, but also smaller fish such as roach and bleak. When feeding on the surface, its dorsal fin often projects above the water in a shark-like fashion.

Spawning occurs in March–April after the ide moves into streams. A recognized sport fish in many countries, and also a commercial species. The flesh is not distinguished, but reasonably palatable and has a yellow coloration.

196 MAHSEER F
Barbus tor

Features: Long, elongate body with dorsal profile usually more convex than belly; occasionally showing great variations in appearance, but these may be subspecies fish. Upper jaw longer than the lower; lips lobed; four barbels under chin. Dorsal fin III,9; tail fin concave, anal fin II or III,5. Coloration: dorsally and upper flanks silvery or greenish brown; lower flanks and belly paling to silver shot with gold; lower fins reddish yellow. Lateral line scale count 25 to 27. Scales are very large, and they approach the size of a human palm.

Size: Maximum length *c.* 5 ft 10 in (1.75 m), 155 lb (70 kg).

Distribution: Asia, found in rivers and mountain streams on both sides of the Himalayas; the wide distribution of numerous related species extends the range into the Philippines to the east, and the Euphrates River to the west.

General: The mahseer is a bottom feeder, preferring clear waters, and it may often be sighted in large schools chasing schools of lesser fry. It is a voracious feeder, accepting almost any kind of food or bait, but its strong, hard mouth demands a vigorous strike to drive home a baited hook or lure. As a freshwater sport fish the mahseer has few peers.

197 CLANWILLIAM OLIFANT'S RIVER YELLOWFISH F
Barbus capensis
Other common name: Geelvis.

Features: Slender and rather compressed body. The head is long and the mouth has thick, protruding lips. One high dorsal fin with concave margin, IV, 9 rays, large, somewhat rounded, anal fin III, 5 rays. Large, pointed pectoral fins; triangular ventral fins are inserted off the dorsal fin; forked tail fin with broad, only little pointed lobes. Several small barbels on the upper jaw. The lateral line is dorsally curved over the pectorals. Rather large, longitudinally striated scales. Coloration: back and upper sides greenish with dark to bluish small spots; lower sides and belly yellow green. Upper fins and tail fin darker, anal fin orange.

Size: *c.* 30 in (75 cm); maximum weight 22 lb (10 kg).

Distribution: Only noted from Olifant's River in western South Africa; closely related species elsewhere in South Africa.

General: A very popular angling fish much sought by game fishermen. The food consists of fish, frogs, and other small animals.

198 ROACH F, B
Rutilus rutilus

Features: Deep-bodied and somewhat humpbacked, but shape may vary according to habitat. Small mouth with a projecting upper lip; eye reddish. Dorsal fin III,9 to 11; tail fin forked; anal fin III,9 to 11. Coloration: variable, dorsally either dark green, brown, blue, or sometimes blue-black; flanks bronze or paling to silver, belly light; lower fins are pink-tinted, but variable and may range from yellowish to darkish tints. Lateral line curves downwards, scale count 42 to 45. Frequently confused with the rudd and the chub (see below).

Size: Occasionally, but rarely, up to 20 in (50 cm); largest generally found in Sweden and

Black Sea areas; may reach only 4–8 in (10–20 cm) in overcrowded waters.

Distribution: Fairly widespread in Europe (except Spain, Italy, Yugoslavia, and Greece), and the northeast parts of U.S.S.R., in the region extending from the Caspian Sea to beyond the Lena River.

General: A very common fish in angling waters, populating streams, rivers, canals, ponds, lakes, reservoirs, and very tolerant to polluted waters. Food consists of aquatic insects, molluscs, algae, and various weeds. Spawning occurs in April–June in shallow water, and hatching takes place 4–10 days; maturity is reached in 2 years by the male and 3 years by the female.

The common roach is an important key fish in angling waters. It provides a basic diet for the larger predatory sport fish such as pike, zander, perch, and eels. In some parts of eastern Europe and Asia it is netted commercially and utilized as an inexpensive food fish. The flesh is white and firm, but it has rather a muddy flavour. In western Europe, however, its role is chiefly that of a sport fish.

199 COMMON SHINER F
Notropis cornutus
Other common names: Redfish shiner, creek shiner, silver shiner, dace, redfin shiner.

Features: Body is deep and laterally compressed with large scales, but no scales on head. Throat contains teeth, but none in mouth. The single short dorsal fin is centrally located. No adipose fin and a deeply forked tail. Mouth, head, and eyes are large. Exposed surfaces of side scales are deeper than long. Snout is rounded and body slab-sided. Lateral line count, 37–40 scales. Dorsal fin, 9; anal fin, 9. Coloration: Olive brown on the back with a dark stripe down the dorsal area. Silvery sides are sometimes slightly mottled with dark spots. Males in spawning season turn red on fins and bodies. No lateral bands on body.

Size: Rarely up to 10 in (25 cm) and 1/2 lb (1/4 kg), but more often about 6 in (15 cm) long.

Distribution: Freshwater in central U.S.A. and southern Canada from Rocky Mountains eastward to the Appalachian range, and south to the Gulf of Mexico coast.

General: Colour changes and variations, plus multiplicity of closely related species, make positive identification often difficult. Good bait for other fish, and excellent fish forage. No real food or sport fishing value.

200 SILVER BREAM F, B
Blicca bjoerkna
Other common name: White bream.

Features: Deep-bodied and moderately humpbacked, strongly compressed. Blunt snout; relatively small head and mouth; thick lips; pharyngeal teeth characteristically in two rows, 5 on inner and 2 or 3 on outer. Dorsal fin III,8 or 9; tail fin forked; anal fin III,21 to 23. Coloration: dorsally olive brown or greyish; flanks pale and overshot with a silvery sheen; belly white; dorsal, tail, and anal fins grey tinted; pelvic fin reddish near base, but the tip is dark. Lateral line scale count 44 to 48. It can be distinguished from the common bronze

bream (*Abramis brama*) by the pharyngeal teeth count (in *A. brama* the teeth are in a single series 5 each side), and by fewer scales along the lateral line (44 to 48 as against 51 to 57); in *A. brama* all the fins are bluish grey, the eye is smaller, and the scales more easily detached.

Size: Average 8–12 in (20–30 cm), large specimens up to 4 1/2 lb (2 kg).

Distribution: North and middle Europe to the Caspian Sea, north to Denmark, Sweden, southern Finland, and White Russia; also found in brackish water in Holland, Germany, and in the Baltic.

General: In continental Europe, the silver bream is among the commonest freshwater fishes. It is found in schools and is typically bottom living, preferring shallow, warm lowland lakes with dense vegetation, and the bream reaches of rivers. It feeds chiefly on worms and crustaceans. Spawning occurs May–July. As an angling fish it rates very low on the scale. Although edible, the flesh is very bony, and because of its small size, its table value is unimportant.

201 BIGMOUTH SHINER F
Notropis dorsalis
Other common names: Butterfish, bream, roach, fathead or blackhead minnow, bluntnose, creek shiner, redfin shiner, silver shiner, bitterhead, chub, gudgeon, windfish.

Features: Large, blunt head and horizontal mouth. Comparatively large scales on body, but no scales on head. Teeth in throat, but lacking in mouth. Single short dorsal fin, no adipose fin, deep tail-fork. Lateral line scale count 36–39. Eye diameter is less than the length of the upper jaw. Upper surface of head is flattened. Coloration: Back light olive to straw-coloured, sides silvery, belly silvery or white. Environment may cause considerable colour change in local populations.

Size: Average 6–10 in (15–25 cm) and up to 1/2 lb (250 g).

Distribution: North-central and northeastern U.S.A., through the Great Lakes region. Closely related species in Europe, Asia, Africa.

General: A fish of small streams and river tributaries, preferring sandy bottom and current. Food is small insect larvae, plankton, diatoms. A common forage species widely used as angling bait, but too small to have other economic value.

202 LAKE CHUB F
Couesius plumbeus
Other common names: Northern chub, lake northern chub, chub, chub minnow, méné de lac, bait chub.

Features: Robust-bodied and chubby with a relatively small head. The mouth is slightly overhung by the snout. The paired fins, most particularly the pectorals, are large, stiff and conspicuous. The tail is deeply forked. The general shape or outline is elongate with the dorsal origin approximately midway between the snout and the tail; the anal origin to the rearward of the hinder portion of the dorsal. Large scales on the body but none on the head, teeth in the throat but none in the mouth. Coloration: Back is black to dark brown shading to silvery on the sides which often display specialized, darkened scales. Breeding males have dashes of red on the forepart of their bodies.

Size: Large specimens attain 6 in (15 cm) at about the optimum.

Distribution: North American streams and lakes from Lake Superior east to the Adirondack region and New Brunswick, and westward to British Columbia in Canada.

General: Leaves the lakes and ascends streams for spawning; sometimes caught by sportsmen fishing with dip nets for smelt while on this journey. Food is principally aquatic insects and plankton. Sometimes used as an early spring bait for lake trout and other sporting species.

203 RUDD F
Scardinius erythrophthalmus

Features: A deep, compressed fish, resembling a roach in general appearance (see above). Mouth moderately large. Dorsal fin III,8 or 9; tail fin concave; anal fin III,10 or 11. Coloration: dorsally brownish olive to green; flanks usually silvery golden; belly paling to white; dorsal and tail fins are brown with a reddish tinge, pectoral, pelvic, and anal fins blood red and grey at base. Lateral line scale count 40 to 45.

The more obvious differences between a rudd and a roach is that the rudd is more heavily built, and the dorsal fin is set well back between the pelvic and anal fins, in the roach it is farther forward. Other differences are that the rudd's fins (including tail fin) are redder; the belly, in the region of the anal fin, is keeled; and the iris of the eye is golden instead of red, as in the roach. Unfortunately, identification is further complicated by hybrid species.

Size: Average up to 16 in (40 cm), 2 1/4 lb (1 kg) at 10 years, maximum *c.* 18 in (45 cm), 4 1/2 lb (2 kg).

Distribution: Widespread throughout Europe (except Spain, Portugal and northern Scandinavia) and across Asia to Lake Baikal and Turkestan.

General: Identification of the rudd is often difficult owing to its readiness to hybridize with roach, bream, and bleak; hybrids are extremely common where the species are resident in the same water.

Rudd are usually found in small schools and feed at the surface but inhabit the midregion in the still or slow-moving, warmer water in ponds and lakes; also found in sluggish rivers. During the winter months they move to the bottom.

Spawning occurs in May–June, sometimes early April in southern Europe. The eggs are attached to plants. Hatching takes place in 3–10 days according to temperature. After the yolk sac is exhausted, the young begin to feed on animal plankton. Growth rate is highly varied and depends on the locality, for they tend to overpopulate many waters.

Among European sport fishermen the rudd is a popular fish and accepts a bait readily. Although often considered of no value as a table fish, its flesh was once esteemed by British anglers, and in Eastern Europe it still has some importance as a food fish. The Greek rudd (*Scardinius graecus*) has a similar but more slender shape.

204 GOLDFISH   F, occasionally B
Carassius auratus
Other common names: Golden carp, crucian carp.

Features: Of the same family as the carp, *Cyprinus carpio*, this member of the minnow family differs by lacking barbels on its jaw; also black bases or spots on the scales; cross hatching. It has a more stocky body and is more varied in body coloration than the carp. It possesses both a dorsal and anal spine; both deeply serrated. The pharyngeal teeth are in a single row of four on each side, not molar-like. Dorsal fin, III to IV, 9 to 15. Anal fin, II to III, 5 to 6. Scales along the lateral line number 28 to 33. Gillrakers, 37 to 43. Coloration: Variable. The back is olive in a wild state, the sides golden and the belly silvery. There is no dark spot before the tail fin; the caudal is forked. The basic body colour must be considered as being from olive green through gold, often with black blotches, to creamy white.
Size: Attaining 12 in (30 cm), 2.2 lb (1 kg) maximum.
Distribution: Natural range from eastern Europe to China but introduced into many other areas including the United States and Canada.
General: Hardy in the outdoors, also a favourite aquarium fish in captivity. Capable of living in small and oxygen-deficient waters such as lawn ponds, etc. Prefers warmer waters, but wild strains are adaptable to changing conditions. Though less hardy than the carp, it is nevertheless a difficult fish to eradicate once it is established. Only moderate food and sport fishing value.

205 LONGNOSE DACE   F
Rhinichthys cataractae
Other common names: Black minnow, blacknose dace, dace, Niagara gudgeon, méné de sable, black shiner.

Features: Long-snouted minnow in which the snout projects far beyond the mouth which is approximately horizontal in outline. Stout-bodied. Tail or caudal is forked; fin outlines typical of the minnow species in general; soft rayed. Coloration: Olive green to brown in streams and grey in the lakes on the back; specialized darkened scales on the sides give the fish a mottled appearance. The fins may be a light olive or

transparent; the ventral sections of the body a milky white.
Size: Attains lengths up to 5 in (12.5 cm).
Distribution: New England to Virginia and Wisconsin in the United States; generally most of the country with the exception of the southeast coastal region. From the upper St. Lawrence River of Quebec through the Great Lakes and northward to Hudson Bay in Ontario and westward to British Columbia in Canada.
General: Found in swiftly flowing streams and occasionally in lakes; caught in traps as a fishing bait but does not live long in a minnow pail. Good baitfish and excellent forage fish for trout.

206 ZAEHRTE   F, B
Vimba vimba

Features: Moderately deep body, breamlike in appearance, but more slender. Head depressed; snout is conical and characteristically projects over lower jaw; lips are fleshy. Dorsal fin III,8; tail fin deeply forked; anal fin III, 18 to 21. Coloration: dorsally and head dark blue grey; flanks normally silvery green; belly white. During spawning the head and dorsal regions become very dark, and the throat and paired fins orange or reddish orange; the males also develop body tubercles. Lateral line scale count 57 to 63.
Size: Average fish up to 12 in (30 cm), maximum *c.* 20 in (50 cm), 2 lb (1 kg). Size variable according to locale.
Distribution: Baltic region and the Elbe, south east Europe in the Danube basin area to the Black, Azov, and Caspian Seas.
General: Six varieties are recognized. Some are migratory forms living in the lower reaches of rivers and then for part of the year in brackish water; also found in lakes. Zaehrte are usually resident over a muddy bottom, and food normally consists of fly larvae, snails, and worms.

The zaehrte is a relatively unimportant sport fish, but important commercially, caught by netting when it travels in schools during its spawning runs. Although extremely bony, the flesh is of good table quality.

207 FATHEAD MINNOW   F
Pimephales promelas
Other common names: Blackhead minnow, fathead, blackhead, bullhead.

Features: Deep, laterally compressed body with large scales on trunk, but none on head. Short, centrally located dorsal fin. Tail is deeply forked and adipose fin is absent. Lateral line is incomplete. Eight short dorsal rays and preceded by a single stout, blunt-tipped half-ray. Coloration: Silver olive with darker-coloured fins. A dark, narrow, vertical bar across the base of the tail. Adults show a dark, horizontal dorsal fin bar. In spawning season the male has copper-gold bands around the body behind the head, plus sharp tubercles on the snout and a thick, soft predorsal pad on the back.
Size: Up to 3 in (7 1/2 cm), insignificant weight.
Distribution: Widespread through southern Canada and the United States from eastern slope of the Rocky Mountains to the eastern

and Gulf states, and eastern Canadian provinces.
General: A valuable food and forage species for many types of larger fish. Important in the life cycles of many fresh water species. Widely raised by hatcheries and commercial fish farms for fish food. No human food or sport fishing value, but frequently taken and used as live or dead bait.

208 TENCH   F, B
Tinca tinca

Features: A deep, thickset, and heavy body. There is a short barbel on either side of mouth; eyes small and red, or orange red. Dorsal fin III,8; tail fin square-cut or slightly concave; anal fin III,6 to 8. Coloration: variable according to locale, usually olive green to dark brown with a bronze lustre on flanks; belly orange yellow; fins are dark pigmented. From 2 years males may be distinguished by a thickened second ray in pelvic fin. Lateral line scale count 95 to 120. The skin is extremely slimy. There is also a cultivated tench with an overall golden coloration.
Size: Up to 16 in (40 cm); a 4 1/2 lb (2 kg) fish generally considered a good size, but in southeast Europe fish up to 28 in (70 cm) and *c.* 18 lb (8 kg) have been recorded in the past.
Distribution: Much of Europe (except Greece and northern Scandinavia), to beyond the Ural Mountains in U.S.S.R.
General: The tench is generally found in quiet, weedy waters and is a shy, lazy fish lurking near a muddy or soft bottom where it may often be detected feeding by the presence of rising bubbles. Food consists of snails, mussels, small crustaceans, shrimps, worms, and the larvae of insects; in the winter the tench is a passive hibernator, and feeding stops. Spawning takes place in May–June, and the eggs are laid in large numbers in clumps and hatch in 3–6 days.

Tench is a popular sport fish and may be caught by floatfishing or ledgering, putting up a determined struggle when hooked. The flesh is soft and has rather a muddy flavour – yet the tench is a tasty table fish widely consumed in continental Europe.

209 WHITE SUCKER   F
Catostomus commersoni
Other common names: Common sucker, common white. sucker, sucker, catostome noir commun, mullet, slender sucker.

Features: The mouth a true suction cup with protrusile lips located on the underside of the head. Dorsal and lower fins soft-rayed, no adipose fin, tail very deeply forked, head completely unscaled but the body scales are large. Teeth absent in the mouth but present in the throat. Elongate and robust body; mouth is overhung by the snout; thick lips with the upper thinner than the lower. Dorsal fin, 10 to 13. There are 55 to 85 scales along the lateral line. Coloration: generally silvery. During the breeding season, the males have many coarse white tubercles on their caudal and anal fins, sometimes extending to the body and other fins also. Fins are large and dusky. Back is dark to blue-black or black, gold, or brassy, shading to silvery on the sides. Juveniles possess three black spots or blotches; behind the head,

below the dorsal and at the base of the caudal; fading after fish reach about three inches.
Size: To about 20 in (50 cm); 6.6 lb (3 kg) at maximum but usually far smaller.
Distribution: From the Mackenzie River across Canada to Labrador, south through the central United States to the Gulf states and Mexico.
General: Caught on light sporting tackle and also in nets, etc. during spawning runs. Edible at times, but soft and bony. Some commercial value in localized areas. Valuable forage fish, also used as live bait for various gamefish such as the pikes.

210 BIGMOUTH BUFFALO   F
Ictiobus cyprinellus
Other common names: Buffalo, buffalofish, common buffalo, lake buffalo, blue buffalo, gourdhead buffalo, red-mouthed buffalo.

Features: A large-scaled sucker easily distinguished from others by its large size and its mouth, which is placed at the front end of the head rather than on the lower surface. The elliptical body profile is more curved above than along the belly. The wide, oblique mouth has its upper lip almost on a level with the eye, and contains no teeth. The dorsal fin starts halfway down the back, extending almost to the tail. Dorsal fin, 27–29; caudal fin moderately forked; anal fin 9; ventral fin 10. Coloration: Varies from copper through olive brown to slate-blue on upper surface, shading to white beneath with no silvery appearance. Lateral line scale count 35–43.
Size: Up to 24 in (60 cm), 22 lb (10 kg), but most specimens smaller.
Distribution: North American mid-continent from southern Canada to Gulf of Mexico in shallow lakes and large rivers.
General: An important fresh water commercial fish with good food qualities, occasionally taken by sport fishermen on doughball and similar baits. Its food is mainly animal plankton.

211 BITTERLING   F
Rhodeus amarus

Features: This small fish is related to the crucian carp and the minnow. The body is compressed and rather high. Small eyes and small mouth. Lateral line only distinct over the pectoral fins. Coloration: back bluish mixed with dark brown, lower sides and belly reddish to yellow, fins brown yellow; each side has from the middle of the body and until the tail a bright blue band.
Size: 2–2 1/2 in (5–6 cm).
Distribution: Central Europe from France to the Caspian Sea, northern Asia Minor.
General: Lives in ponds and small lakes. The species is remarkable by depositing its eggs through a long egg tube unto the gills of live mussels; when the larvae have used up their yolk sacs, they leave the mussels.

212 ELECTRIC EEL   F
Electrophorus electricus

Features: The body is eel-like, but very stout and strong. Rather long head with blunt snout; small eyes. No dorsal fin and no ventral fins; long undulated anal fin and tail fin with rounded margin. Coloration: dark brown all over with a few lighter (yellow) spots; the foremost part of the belly and the underside of the head are yellow to orange. Most of the muscles in the larger part of the body are built as powerful electric organs, which can produce shocks strong enough to kill small fish, frogs, and other smaller animals which then are seized and eaten. Larger animals, even horses and men, can be paralysed by the electric shocks.

Size: The electric eel can grow to a length of 6–7 ft (ca 2 m) with a weight of up to 45 pounds (20 kg).

Distribution: Northeastern South America with most of the Amazon region.

General: The gills are very small and most of the respiration is based on the inner surface of the mouth and throat. The electric organs are not only used against prey and enemies, but their low impulses function as means for orientation; this is the more valuable as the older fish with their very small eyes are almost blind.

213 ANGLERFISH s
Lophius piscatorius
Other common names: Frogfish, angler, monkfish, goosefish.

Features: Body depressed; very flattened appearance from above. Large, grotesque-shaped head much wider than the trunk; mouth very large and gaping; jaws have irregular caninelike teeth; the body is very soft and partially collapses when the fish is removed from the water. Dorsal fins I-I-I-III-10 to 13, the first 3 dorsal spines are stiff, slender, and widely separated and not connected by any membrane; the 1st spine, containing the "lure" or "bait", is located behind the tip of the upper jaw; the 2nd and 3rd spines are depressible; tail fin broom-shaped; anal fin 9 to 11; pectoral fins heavy. Coloration: highly variable but often dorsally brown, greenish brown, or reddish brown with darker mottlings or blotches. Skin is scaleless, smooth, and slippery, but there are some small bony plates and fleshy tabs especially round the lower jaws which extend back along the flanks to the tail stalk.

Size: Average up to 4 ft (120 cm), 50–60 lb (22–27 kg); occasionally maximum *c.* 6 1/2 ft (200 cm).

Distribution: Mediterranean; North and South Atlantic and neighbouring seas, including North Sea and western Baltic.

General: One of the largest of the many species of angler-fishes, monkfishes, or goosefishes (family *Lophiidae*). The North American species *L. americanus* has similar features and is closely related. Although the anglerfish is a predator, it is a relatively slow-moving fish. It derives its name from the method it adopts when catching its prey. The first dorsal spine (the "rod") has a fleshy appendage (the "bait") which the fish manipulates as a lure to attract passing fish, while the angler itself remains hidden on the bottom. When a prey is tempted by the bait and draws closer, the victim is snapped up. Related anglerfish species inhabiting very deep water have luminous lures. Food so attracted includes small dogfish, haddock, herring, menhaden, crabs, etc.

The anglerfish is generally rare in shal-

low waters. To the sport fisherman it usually represents an accidental victim. Although a rather repulsive fish in appearance, the flesh is of good table quality.

214 COD (ATLANTIC) s
Gadus morhua

Features: Elongate, stout body; general potbellied appearance. Large head and jaws; upper jaw projects above lower; single whiskerlike barbel on chin. Three dorsal fins 13 to 16–19 to 24–18 to 21; tail fin slightly concave or square-cut; two anal fins 20 to 24–17 to 22. Coloration: dorsally and flanks grey brown to grey green, with characteristic numerous brownish to reddish spots; belly silvery or greyish white. Lateral line arched in forward part. Small scales.

Size: Average up to 40 in (100 cm), maximum *c.* 68 in (170 cm), 5 lb (2 1/4 kg) up to 25–50 lb (11–23 kg). Specimen fish over 150 lb (70 kg) have been reported from the east coast of North America, and one reputedly 200 lb (90 kg).

Distribution: Several self-contained populations in the North Atlantic; in the west, from coasts of west and east Greenland extending southward to Virginia; in the east, from Spitsbergen southward to northern Spain; North Sea; Baltic. Closely related to the Alaska cod (*G. macrocephalus*) in the North Pacific.

General: The cod is the most important commercial food fish in the North Atlantic and codfishing has been a large industry since the Middle Ages. Cod is also an excellent sport fish, especially in the early winter months, and large specimens are frequently caught close inshore. The flesh is white and firm and has excellent table qualities.

Spawning occurs at different times in its separate populations and locales; subsequent growth is also variable. The young cod (weight up to 4 lb (1 3/4 kg) is often known under a local common name, e.g. codling in British Isles, *småtorsk* in Norway. The cod generally favours a rough, or sand and rock bottom along the continental shelf regions. It is a voracious predatory bottom feeder. Food includes worms, crustaceans, mollusks, and many fish species.

215 ATLANTIC TOMCOD s, b
Microgadus tomcod
Other common names: Frostfish, snig.

Features: Moderately elongate body, only slightly compressed. Upper jaw projects beyond lower; barbel on lower jaw; snout rounded. Dorsal fins 11 to 15-15 to 19-16 to 21; tail fin rounded; anal fins 12 to 21-16 to 20; pelvic fins have long feelerlike appearance. Coloration: dorsally olive brown with green or yellow hues; flanks paler; dorsal area and flanks mottled with dark blotches; belly greyish or yellowish white; anal fins olive at margins. Lateral line well marked. Scales small.

Size: Maximum up to 15 in (38 cm), 2 1/4 lb (1 kg).

Distribution: Western North Atlantic, from southern Labrador to Virginia.

General: Limited to coastal waters and estuaries and sometimes in the freshwater reaches of rivers, but never straying far

---

upstream. Spawning occurs in December–January, often in freshwater reaches; hatching follows in 22–35 days, and the fry remain in brackish water for several months. Food consists of amphipods, hermit crabs, sand shrimp, and small fish such as smelt. Commercially important as a food fish, and usually caught by traps and handlines; also taken as part of the local winter ice fishery.

216 POOR COD s
Gadus minutus

Features: The body and especially its anterior part is more stout than in the Norway pout. The eyes are larger, the diameter being longer than the distance between eyes and point of snout. The upper lip projects well beyond the lower. The feeler on the lower jaw is longer and thicker. Lateral line distinct with an upwards curvature above the pectoral fins. Coloration: back and upper sides yellow to greenish with a weak sheen of copper; belly whitish, silvery. The scales are small.

Size: Up to 10 in (25 cm), generally 6–8 in (15–20 cm).

Distribution: Northeast Atlantic, from Lofoten over the Faroes, round the British Isles and south to Brittany; North Sea, Skagerak and northern Kattegat.

General: The poor cod is nowhere so abundant as the Norway pout; it lives in about the same depth zones, 20–150 fathoms (40–300 m). The food consists of small fish and crustaceans. It has hardly any commercial value.

217 TOMCOD s
Microgadus proximus
Other common name: Piciata.

Features: This species has the usual characteristic of the cod family: only soft fin rays, 3 dorsal and 2 anal fins, tail fin with almost straight hind margin; the thin and weak ventral fins are placed below and a little in front of the larger pectoral fins. A small barbel is present on the point of the lower jaw; the upper jaw is slightly projecting. Eyes rather big. The lateral line is bent strongly upwards below first and second dorsal fins. Coloration: back and upper sides brownish to grey, lower sides and belly whitish to silvery. The snout and the pectoral and the tail fin are dark, the other fins lighter.

Size: Maximum length 12–14 in (30–35 cm).

Distribution: Eastern Pacific from southern California and northwards.

General: Is mostly taken in waters nearer the coast. Its commercial value is only small. The tomcod is now and then caught by sportfishing with hook and line.

218 PACIFIC COD s
Gadus macrocephalus
Other common names: Grayfish, gray cod, tara.

Features: This cod is very similar to the Atlantic cod (*G. morhua*): Three dorsal and two anal fins, tail fin with straight hind margin, a stout barbel on the lower jaw. It is distinguished from it by its head and anterior part of body being higher and stouter, and by the lateral line being abruptly dorsally bent off, the interval between first and second dorsal fins. The mouth is large; the upper jaw reaches the anterior edge of the eye. The small ventral fins are placed well forward of the larger pectoral fins, under the middle of the gill cover. The hind margin of the tail fin is straight. Small scales. Coloration: back and upper sides light brown with irregular, dark patches, lower sides and belly whitish. The lateral line is white.

Size: Up to 2 1/2 ft (75 cm); weight 30–60 pounds (13–25 kg).

Distribution: North Pacific, off the coasts of Oregon, Canada, Alaska, eastern Siberia, Korea, and Japan.

General: The usual depth is 30–250 fathoms (50–450 m). It is often observed in large shoals. The food is smaller fish, squids and crustaceans. Is of considerable importance to the commercial fisheries, especially in northern Japan.

219 NORWAY POUT S
Boreogadus esmarkii

Features: Comparatively slender body. Large eyes; lower jaw a little projecting with a small feeler on its tip. Fins as in the cod, but the first anal fin rather long; unpaired fins with slightly concave margins. Lateral line bent smoothly upwards over the pectoral fins. Coloration: back light brown; sides greyish to bluish, silvery; belly whitish, often with a weak reddish sheen.

Size: This small codfish reaches rarely a length of 10 in (25 cm), generally only 6–8 in (15–20 cm).

Distribution: Northeast Atlantic, from northern Norway to the English Channel, North Sea, Skagerak and northern part of Kattegat.

General: Very abundant in moderately deep water, 10–100 fathoms (20–200 m). Is fished in large quantities for industrial use (meal and oil).

220 GREENLAND COD S
Gadus ogac
Other common names: Fjord cod, uvac.

Features: In body shape and fins the Greenland cod is similar to the common cod, but the body is stouter and the head broader. Small eyes. A well-developed feeler below the mouth. The dark lateral line is strongly upwards bent below the two first dorsal fins. Coloration: bluish-grey, but densely marbled with brown or dark yellow; back darker than sides and belly.

Size: Generally 12–30 in (30–50 cm), rarely 3 ft (60 cm).

Distribution: Coastal and near-coastal waters of Davis Strait and Baffin Bay.

General: It is mostly found from the coasts (also in fjords) and out to 110 fathoms (200 m). It is of some importance to the local fishery.

221 POLAR COD S
Boreogadus saida

Features: .Very slender body. Lower jaw undershot, small barbel. Slender tail stalk. Three dorsal and two anal fins, all about equally long, tail fin forked, ventral fins narrow with elongated rays. Coloration: back and sides brown, belly light bluish to silvery; fins with violet sheen.

Size: Average 8–9 in (20–24 cm), max. 18 in (42–45 cm).

Distribution: All arctic seas: Alaska, Labrador, Greenland, northern Norway, Siberia.

General: Pelagic, near the ice-barrier and in pack-ice. Rather important for the local fisheries.

222 BLUE WHITING S
Micromesistius poutassou
Other common names: Poutassou, Couch's whiting.

Features: Slender body, large eyes, lower jaw undershot. Three dorsal, two anal fins, the first anal very long, forked tail fin. Coloration: back brownish, sides and belly silvery. Inner surfaces of mouth and gill cover black.

Size: Maximum 20 in (50 cm).

Distribution: East Atlantic from northern Norway and Iceland to Morocco; Mediterranean.

General: Mostly pelagic; feeds on crustaceans and fish. Fished for use in the fishing industry (oil and meal).

223 SUKETODARA S
Theragra chalcogramma

Features: This cod species has a very slender body with the lower jaw the longer; pointed snout, rather small barbel, large eyes. Three dorsal and two anal fins, slightly concave tail fin. Coloration: above brownish, below whitish, silvery; two irregular rows of black spots along each side.

Size: Average 20–24 in (50–60 cm).

Distribution: Northwest Pacific, Korea, Japan and north into the Bering Sea.

General: Lives pelagically over rather deep water, c. 100 fathoms (200 m). Important to the local fisheries.

224 PACIFIC HAKE S
Merluccius productus
Other common names: Whitefish, butterfish, mellusa.

Features: A slender fish with thin tail stalk. The snout is blunt, lower jaw a little undershot. Two dorsal and one anal fin, first dorsal short, second very long divided by a notch into a long, low first part and a short, high second part, anal fin similar. Coloration: above light brownish, sides and belly yellow to whitish.

Size: Maximum 3 ft (1 m).

Distribution: East Pacific, from Puget Sound to southern California.

General: Lives mainly pelagically in moderate depths. Only little commercial importance; taken now and then by anglers.

225 MERLUZA S
Merluccius gayi
Other common name: Peje-palo.

Features: Slender, compressed body, thin tail stalk, long, flattened head with lower jaw strongly projecting, large teeth. Two dorsal fins, first 11–12, second 35–40, anal fin 36–38; tail fin emarginate. Small scales. Coloration: back and upper sides dusky, below whitish to silvery. Fins dusky, the pectoral also with black.

Size: Average 16–25 in (40- 60 cm).

Distribution: East Pacific off Peru-Chile. A near relative M. hubbsi lives in the western Atlantic off Argentina.

General: Occurs in coastal waters and is of high importance to the commercial fisheries of Chile, mostly fished for industrial purposes (oil and meal).

226 WHITING S
Merlangius merlangus

Features: Elongate body. Long snout and large mouth; sometimes very small barbel under chin, but often absent in large fish. Three dorsal fins 12 to 15-18 to 25-19 to 22; tail fin square-cut or slightly concave; two anal fins 30 to 35-21 to 23. Coloration: dorsally sandy brown, greyish green, or dark blue with yellowish overtones; flanks silvery; belly white; characteristic dark spot between lateral line and the base of pectoral fin. Lateral line slightly arched and golden bronze.

Size: Average *c.* 16 in (40 cm), maximum 28 in (70 cm). Inshore fish *c.* 12 in (30 cm).

Distribution: Mediterranean; eastern Atlantic, ranging from northern Norway to northern Spain, including English Channel, North Sea, and western Baltic.

General: A species frequenting inshore shallow waters often less than 50 ft (15 m) over sand or muddy bottoms. A schooling fish during the spawning season, January–June. The spawning date is progressively later with an increase in latitude. Food consists of crustaceans (chiefly shrimp) and a variety of small fish. Apart from its interest as a light-tackle sport fish, it is of considerable commercial importance.

227 COALFISH; POLLOCK S
Pollachius virens
Other common names: Saithe, coley, Boston bluefish, blister-back, merlan, colin.

Features: Semifusiform body, slightly deeper than thick. Lower jaw projects beyond upper; very small barbel on lower jaw in young fish which may be absent in older fish. Three dorsal fins 13 or 14-20 to 22-19 to 24; tail fin slightly forked; two anal fins 24 to 28-19 to 23. Coloration: dorsally uniform greenish brown; flanks paling to a yellowish green or smoky grey; belly silvery grey; all the fins are dark except for the pelvic fins which are white with a reddish tinge. Lateral line is white or grey and is almost straight. Small scales.

Size: Average up to 3 ft 4 in (1 m), *c.* 60 lb (27 kg); maximum 47 in (120 cm).

Distribution: North Atlantic, in west from southern Greenland to North Carolina; in east Spitzbergen to northern Spain, including English Channel, North Sea, and western Baltic.

General: The European pollack (*Pollachius pollachius*) is of similar appearance (see below) but may easily be distinguished by the lateral line coloration. The coalfish, or pollock, is generally a deep or midwater, predatory schooling fish, but it may often be found along broken rocky shores, particularly the young fish. Spawning occurs in deep water in the early part of the year.

In all areas the coalfish, or pollock, is an important commercial and sport species and an excellent table fish. It may be caught by bait fishing, casting, jigging, or trolling.

228 POLLACK (EUROPEAN) S
Pollachius pollachius
Other common names: Billet, lythe, black jack.

Features: Fusiform body, slightly deeper than thick. Lower jaw projects beyond upper; no chin barbel. Three dorsal fins 12-19 or 20-17 to 19; tail fin concave; two anal fins 29-17 to 20. Coloration: dorsally variable according to habitat but usually brown or olive; flanks paler, sometimes with dark yellow or orange spots or stripes on upper flanks; all fins are dark except pelvic fins which are pinkish. Lateral line is greenish-brown and appears dark against the paler flanks.

Size: Average up to 32 in (80cm), maximum 48 in (120 cm).

Distribution: Eastern Atlantic, from northern Norway to Spain including Iceland, English Channel, North Sea; also western Mediterranean.

General: In some locales the alternative common name billet is loosely applied to the young of both pollack and coalfish. The young of both species are frequently seen in the same water. As they mature, both species move into deeper waters, but pollack spawn in shallower water than coalfish.

Pollack are predatory inshore bottom-feeders found in the proximity of rocky ground. Food consists of smaller fish, especially schooling fry, but also includes worms, prawns, crabs, squid, etc. They are also excellent sport fish being strong and game fighters; large fish are often encountered close inshore. Successful fishing methods are the same as those used with coalfish. An excellent table fish.

229 HAKE S
Merluccius merluccius (related species *M. capensis*)

Features: Elongate body. Large head; lower jaw more prominent than upper; sharp teeth; no chin barbels. Two dorsal fins 9 or 10-37 to 40; tail fin square-cut; anal fin 36 to 40 (rear sections of second dorsal and anal fins deeper than front sections). Coloration: dorsally grey to blackish grey or brown grey; belly whitish; tail fin rear margin dark; inside of mouth blue black. Lateral line dark. Scales large and easily removed.

Size: Average 20–32 in (50–80 cm), maximum 40–49 in (100–125 cm).

Distribution: Mediterranean; Black Sea; eastern and western Atlantic, from northern Norway south to northwest Africa, including English Channel and North Sea, but rarely in Baltic. Elsewhere in related forms.

General: A schooling fish related to cod and haddock, living near the bottom in depths ranging from 330–3,300 ft (100–1,000 m), but the young and adults, during summer and autumn spawning season, frequent shallow water. The hake is a voracious species with excellent table qualities. In South Africa a related hake species occurs, sometimes referred to as the stockfish, derived from the Dutch *stockvisch* (*M. capensis*) of similar appearance.

230 SILVER HAKE s
Merluccius bilinearis
Other common name: Whiting.

Features: Two dorsal fins 11 to 14–37 to 42; tail fin slightly concave; anal fin 39 to 42 (anal fin almost a mirror image of second dorsal). Coloration: dorsally brownish or dark grey; flanks and belly silvery; inside of mouth dusky blue. Prominent lateral line with double appearance. Lateral line scale count 103 to 130. Scales are small.
Size: Up to 30 in (75 cm), 5 lb (2 1/4 kg).
Distribution: Western Atlantic, along the North American continental shelf from the Gulf of St. Lawrence to South Carolina.
General: The North American representative of the European *M. merluccius*, and found in depths ranging from the very shallowest to over 3,000 ft (900 m). Locally valuable as a food and sport species, good table qualities.

231 RED HAKE s
Urophycis chuss
Other common names: Codling, squirrel hake, thimble-eyed ling, old English hake, chuss, fork-beard, ling, white hake.

Features: Close relative of the cod and haddock, a slender and more soft bodied fish, tapering back from the shoulders to a slim caudal peduncle, small weak tail. Much larger eyes than the cod but smaller chin barbel. Only two dorsal fins, the second much longer than the first; only one anal fin. Large mouth that gapes back below the eyes. Upper jaw projects beyond the lower. First dorsal is triangular, with the third ray prolonged as a filament that is longer than the fin itself is high. Second dorsal runs the whole length of the trunk, equal height from end to end, rounded corners. Anal fin is similar but shorter. Pectorals are rounded when spread, pelvic fins located forward of the pectorals and consist of two very prolonged rays. About 110 oblique rows of scales along the distinct lateral line between the gill opening and the base of the tail fin, scales on both the head and the body. First dorsal fin, 9 to 10; second dorsal, 54 to 57; anal, 48 to 50. Coloration: reddish olive brown on the sides and on the back, darkest above. Lower parts of the sides usually washed with yellow. Belly and lower sides white, grey or light yellow.
Size: Maximum of about 30 in (75 cm); 6.6 lb (3 kg) but generally much smaller.
Distribution: American, in the continental waters from the Gulf of St. Lawrence and the southern part of the Grand Bank of Newfoundland southward to Cape Hatteras.

General: Bites best after dark, less plentiful than its close relative, the white hake, *Urophycis tenuis*. Soft meat with poor keeping qualities but important commercially for human consumption; also used as mink and poultry feeds. No sporting species though readily caught.

232 HADDOCK s
Melanogrammus aeglefinus

Features: Heavy body, laterally compressed. Upper jaws slightly longer than lower; small mouth; barbel on chin. Three dorsal fins 14 to 17–20 to 24–19 to 22; tail fin concave; two anal fins 21 to 25–20 to 24. Coloration: dorsally and upper flanks to lateral line, grey brown to grey green with a violet pinkish sheen; flanks below lateral line, silver grey with coppery sheen; belly and lower side of head white. Characteristic dark blotch "thumbprint of St. Peter" below lateral line and behind base of pectoral fin. Lateral line black.
Size: Average 32 in (80 cm), maximum *c.* 40 in (1 m). Average sport fish range 2–5 lb (1–2 1/4 kg).
Distribution: North Atlantic; in west, from Labrador to North Carolina; in east, from northern Norway and Iceland to northern Spain; North Sea; rarely in Baltic.
General: An important commercial species which reaches the consumer markets in either fresh or smoked forms (the smoked variety is usually marketed under the name finnan haddock or finnan haddie). Found over hard-packed sand, gravel, or mud, on bottoms or in deepwater channels, but occasionally large schools are found in mid-water regions. Food consists of worms, squid, molluscs, sand eels, herring spawn, etc. Spawning occurs January–July depending on area. Lifespan averages up to 10 years, but occasionally older fish up to 15–16 years are encountered.

The haddock is undistinguished as a marine sport fish, but it is an excellent, high quality table fish when it turns up in sport fishermen's catches.

233 MEDITERRANEAN LING (SPANISH LING) s
Molva elongata

Features: Long, slender body, slimmer and more eel-like than *M. molva*; lower jaw longer; forked barbel on chin. Two dorsal fins 10 to 12–76 to 83; anal fin 75 to 78. Coloration: dorsally grey brown; flanks lighter; belly white; no rear blotch on dorsal fin; pelvic fin blue; dorsal tail and anal fins have violet edges.
Size: Average 20–30 in (50–76 cm), maximum 36 in (90 cm).
Distribution: Mediterranean and eastern Atlantic north to southwest Ireland; very rarely in English Channel.
General: Found in depths 660–3,300 ft (200–1,000 m) over muddy ground. Food consists of small fish. An excellent table fish.

234 LING (EUROPEAN) s
Molva molva

Features: Long, moderately compressed, slender body. Upper jaw slightly longer than lower; one barbel on chin. Two dorsal fins 13 to 16–60 to 70; tail fin rounded; anal fin 57–66. Coloration: dorsally brown, olive, or green marbling; flanks lighter with brownish blotches; belly white; a characteristic dark blotch at rear end of both dorsal fins; dorsal and anal fins white-edged. Young fish have yellow olive coloration overshot with a lilac hue. Lateral line arched over pectoral fin.
Size: Average up to 3 ft 4 in (1 m), maximum occasionally 6 ft 8 in (2 m); a 6 ft 8 in (2 m) fish weighs *c.* 88 lb (40 kg).
Distribution: Both sides of North Atlantic, but much less common along North American shores; in the west, south Greenland to Newfoundland; in the east, northern Norway and Iceland to northern Spain, including North Sea and western Baltic.
General: An important commercial species often salted or dried and of good table quality. Found chiefly in depths 1,000–1,300 ft (300–400 m), but immature fish frequent shallow water particularly over broken rocky ground. Spawning occurs March–June, and eggs are buoyant. Young fish mature at two years and then move out to deeper water. Ling is a deepwater species out of range of many sport fishermen, but it is reckoned worth seeking out because of its dogged fighting qualities. It may often be located around offshore wrecks.

235 BLUE LING
Molva byrkelange
Other common names: Trade ling, lesser ling.

Features: Resembles closely the European ling, but is more slender and has only one small feeler on the lower jaw. Coloration: back dark brown, lower sides and belly light brown to grey; margins of fins whitish to grey, but without the distinct black, narrow bands of the European ling.
Size: Maximum length 5 1/2 ft (1 1/2 m).
Distribution: South of Iceland and off the European coasts from northern Norway to Ireland. Rare in the northern North Sea.
General: Lives near the bottom in deeper water, 110–500 fathoms (200–1000 m). Only little commercial value.

236 TUSK; CUSK s
Brosme brosme
Other common names: Torsk, brismak.

Features: Elongate body. Blunt-pointed head, flattened above; upper jaw slightly longer; barbel on lower jaw; several rows of sharp teeth. Long dorsal fin 85 to 105 (notched at junction with tail fin); tail fin small and rounded; anal fin 62 to 75 (notched at junction with tail fin). Coloration: variable and dependent on size and environment; dorsally usually dark reddish, greenish brown to pale yellowish; flanks paler, shading to cream on belly. Young fish have six vertical, yellowish bands on flanks which are absent in adult fish. The dorsal, tail, and anal fins have pale or white margins with a dark submarginal

band. Lateral line is indistinct and arched over pectoral fin. Scales are small and extend over head and body.
Size: Average up to 24 in (60 cm), maximum 40 in (100 cm), 27 lb (12 kg).
Distribution: North Atlantic, both sides.
General: A sedentary deepwater fish of temperate to cool waters found in depths between 330–3,300 ft (100–1,000 m). An important commercial species and a good table fish.

237 GREATER FORKBEARD s
Phycis blennioides
Other common name: Forked hake.

Features: A large feeler on the lower lip. Two dorsal fins, the first short, the second long, both rather high. The two ventral fins, placed anteriorly of the pectoral fins, are long, threadlike; the anal fin is long, but rather low. Coloration: back and upper sides brown, lower sides and belly grey to light blue; fins brown with dark margins.
Size: 1 1/2–2 ft (50–60 cm), rarely up to 3 1/2 ft (110 cm).
Distribution: North Atlantic from Iceland, Faroes, southwestern Norway round the British Isles to Madeira; through the whole of the Mediterranean.
General: Inhabits somewhat deeper water, 80–160 fathoms (150–300 m). Has some commercial importance in the Mediterranean.

238 THREE-BEARD ROCK-LING s
Gaidropsaurus tricirratus

Features: Slender, little compressed body. Upper lip projecting beyond lower; two feelers on upper lip, one on lower. One long dorsal fin, its anterior 1/4 very low, posterior 3/4 high; long and high anal fin; tail fin with broadly rounded hind margin; broad pectoral fins; small, almost threadlike ventral fins inserted below pectoral fins. Lateral line distinct, strongly upwards curved on first half of body. Small scales. Coloration: Light brown with many dark spots.
Size: 1 1/4–2 ft (40–60 cm).
Distribution: East Atlantic from Norway to Gibraltar, Mediterranean, North Sea, and Skagerak.
General: Is found from the shallow coastal waters out to a depth of *c.* 100 fathoms (200 m). Feeds on crustaceans and smaller fish. Only little commercial importance.

239 FOUR-BEARD ROCKLING s
Gaidropsaurus cimbrius

Features: Resembles the threebeard rockling, but is more slender and has four feelers, three above and one below the mouth. First ray in dorsal fin long. Coloration: uniform grey with bluish sheen; posterior parts of dorsal and anal fins black.
Size: 1–1 1/2 ft (30–40 cm).
Distribution: The coastal waters of North Atlantic from Labrador to New England and from Iceland and Lofoten to Brittany. North Sea and further east to middle Baltic.

General: Lives in moderately deep water and on the soft bottom.

240 FIVE-BEARD ROCKLING s
Gaidropsaurus mustela

Features: Rather slender; head with five feelers, four above and one below the mouth. First ray in dorsal fin a little elongated. Coloration: brown with blue grey belly.
Size: 9–11 in (22–28 cm).
Distribution: East Atlantic, from Iceland and Lofoten to Bay of Biscay; North Sea, Skagerak, and Kattegat.
General: Mostly found on the harder bottom, rocks and sand, and in shallow water.

241 OCEAN POUT s
Macrozoarces americanus
Other common names: Eelpout, Congo eel, ling, muttonfish, mother-of-eels, lamper eel, conger eel.

Features: Slender and eel-like with the anal fin continuous with the caudal, the rear portion of the dorsal so low that there seems to be a bare space in outline between it and the caudal. Small but unmistakable ventral fins, separating it from the true eels, situated a little in advance of the pectorals. Blenny-like with the body eight times as long as it is deep (adults) and even longer in young fish. Scales small, slimy like an eel. Anal fin is continuous with the caudal without a trace of a notch. Dorsal fin 95 to 100, then short spiny section, followed by about 17 more short rays. Anal fin, 105 to 124, originates a little in front of the middle length of the fish. Dorsal nearly twice as high as anal; pectoral fins large and rounded. Upper jaw projects slightly beyond the lower. Soft, fleshy upper lip projects still further. Small eyes, gaping mouth, series of blunt conical teeth in both jaws with the largest in front. Coloration: Reddish brown mottled with olive and also some shade of muddy yellow, paler or darker, some tinged with brownish, salmon or orange; a few pure olive green. Colours are variable.
Size: Reaches 42 in (105 cm); 11 lb (5 kg).
Distribution: Atlantic coast of North America generally from Delaware to Labrador.
General: Very close relative of the ocean pout of North Europe, *Zoarces viviparus*. Sweet-meated and once important commercially, but now generally out of favour as food, and disliked by most sport fishermen.

242 LINGCOD s
Ophiodon elongatus
Other common names: Cultus cod, blue cod, buffalo cod, greenling.

Features: Elongate body. Conical head; large mouth; jaws with characteristic hooked canine teeth; lower jaw projecting. Dorsal fin deeply notched XXIV–20; tail fin square-cut; anal fin *c*. 23. Coloration: very variable and dependent on emotional state and environment; usual range from dark greenish blue to greenish brown, occasionally brown or reddish; dorsal area and flanks with numerous dark blotches and mottlings; freshly caught adults usually with characteristic golden spots on flanks.

Single characteristic lateral line (related *Hexagrammos* forms have 5 lateral lines).
Size: Average range 1–5 lb (1/2–2 1/4 kg); large fish *c*. 40 lb (18 kg). Maximum size (not officially confirmed) 60 in (150 cm), 70 lb (32 kg).
Distribution: North American Pacific coast. Abundant north of Point Conception in southern California to Sitka.
General: Lingcod is the most common and important food fish along the North American Pacific coast. It is most abundant in waters shallower than 350 ft (105 m) in areas of dense kelp growth and where tidal currents are influential. Spawning takes place from December to March, and the adhesive eggs are laid in aggregations against rocks. The male guards the eggs until hatching occurs. Lingcod are carnivorous; the young eat shrimp and other crustaceans; the adults eat fish, squid, and octopus.

As a year-round sport fish, lingcod is locally a very important and popular species and is taken from the shore or from boats by trolling, jigging, or baited hooks. It has the reputation of being a vicious striker. Many are also taken by skin divers. The flesh is highly palatable but very variable in colour; it may be white, bluish (sometimes a livid blue), or greenish. The coloured flesh is in no way harmful, and all trace of colour disappears with cooking.

243 SILVERY POUT s
Gadiculus thori

Features: This species is the smallest of the cod species. It is easily recognized by its big head, large eyes, and almost vertically placed mouth; no feeler at mouth. The lateral line continues on the head in the several deep, slimy grooves. Large scales. Coloration: all over silvery with reddish and bluish sheen.
Size: 4–6 in (10–16 cm).
Distribution: Northeast Atlantic, from Iceland and northern Norway, west of the British Isles to Brittany; northern North Sea and Skagerak.
General: Lives in 50–170 fathoms (100–300 m). It is not abundant. A near relative, the Silvery Cod (*Gadiculus argenteus*), is found in the Mediterranean.

244 TADPOLE-FISH s
Raniceps raninus
Other common names: Lesser forkbeard, trifurcated hake.

Features: Tadpole-shaped. Large head, one-third of body length; upper jaw blunt and projecting; cardlike teeth in both jaws; single chin barbel. Dorsal fins 3–63 or 64; tail fin small and rounded; anal fin 57 to 60. Coloration: dorsally and flanks uniform dark brown sometimes overshot with purplish hues; belly paler; fins dark; dorsal, tail, and anal fins have light edges. Lips are characteristically light.
Size: Up to 12 in (30 cm).
Distribution: Northeast Atlantic, ranging Norway (Trondheim) south into western Baltic, English Channel and around Irish coasts.
General: A species more commonly found in Norwegian waters than elsewhere and it prefers shallow water along rocky coasts.

Spawning occurs July–September in water warmer than 50°F (10°C). Food consists of shrimps, crustaceans, and small fish. Insufficient numerically to be of any commercial importance, but the flesh is edible.

245 POUTING s
Gadus luscus
Other common names: Pout whiting, whiting pout, pout bib.

Features: Short, deep-bodied fish. Upper jaw longer than lower; lower jaw has a prominent barbel. Three dorsal fins 11 to 14–20 to 24–18 to 20; tail fin concave; two anal fins 30 to 34–19 to 22. Coloration: dorsally and flanks coppery, paling along flanks, with 4 or 5 darker vertical bands, but presence of these is variable, depending on whether the scales have been abraded; a characteristic dark spot at the base of the pectoral fin. Lateral line has a golden coloration.
Size: Average up to 12 in (30 cm), maximum 18 in (45 cm).
Distribution: European Atlantic coastline, from southern Norway to northern Spain, including English Channel and North Sea; Mediterranean.
General: A schooling species generally found at depths over 100 ft (30 m), but young fish are found in shallow inshore waters usually over a rocky or sandy bottom and show a preference for ground that is a combination of both; also found around offshore wrecks. Food is mainly molluscs and crustaceans, but older fish include fish in their diet. It has little commercial significance nor much interest as a sport fish.

246 BURBOT F, B
Lota lota
Other common names: American burbot, ling, eelpout, freshwater cod, maria, skinling, alekey trout, longtailed cat, mud blower, lake lawyer, methy, loche, lotte, freshwater cusk, gudgeon.

Features: Elongate fish with eel-like body; front half rounded; tail section laterally compressed. Medium-sized mouth with fine teeth; long barbel on lower jaw; distinctive shorter barbel on each nostril. Two dorsal fins 11 to 14–68 to 85; tail fin rounded; anal fin 63 to 85. Coloration: dorsally and flanks dark green with brown mottlings; in some northern locales and inland waters very dark (almost black). Smooth skin and small embedded scales.
Size: Average 16 in (40 cm), *c*. 1 lb (500 g). Specimen fish up to 39 in (1 m), 30–40 lb (14–16 kg), but these are mainly from Siberia, and other subarctic regions in North America.
Distribution: Throughout the cool temperate regions of the Northern Hemisphere, except southwest Europe. However, now much less common in some countries than previously, and very rare in Britain.
General: A member of the codfish family, and its only freshwater representative. A bottom fish found in lakes and in slow-moving rivers with cool, clear water.

The burbot is nocturnal. In certain localities it has become a nuisance fish rather than a sport fish of any value, for the mature burbot develops into a voracious predator and eats large quantities of perch,

roach, and gudgeon. However, in its northern distribution it is regularly included in ice sport-fish catches. Its flesh is esteemed as a table delicacy in Eastern European countries where the eggs are occasionally utilized as "caviar".

247 SARGASSUMFISH s
Histrio histrio
Other common names: Mousefish, fishing frog, frogfish.

Features: Fins, skin appendages, and skin folds are startlingly like the fronds, leaves, and air sacs of the oceanic sargassum weed, in which the sargassumfish is most often found. The small, round body has a head that is flattened sidewise with leaflike appendages on the lower jaw. The forward part of the dorsal fin appears to be a series of separate spines covered with fleshy, rough skin. Posterior portion of the dorsal fin 12 to 14, with the first spine equipped with a bulbous tip and two or more filament-like streamers. Anal fin 7 to 8 and shorter than the second dorsal. Pectoral and ventral fins are stalk-like with fleshy flaps. Caudal fin is fairly short and rounded. Skin is generally smooth, slightly granular. Coloration: Usually pale yellow with dark brown spots, bars, and marblings, and three distinct brown lines radiating from each eye. Belly and sides have whitish spots. Colour of skin changes to match that of weeds in which the fish lives.
Size: Up to about 6 in (15 cm) and 1/4 lb (.1 kg).
Distribution: Tropical Atlantic waters, especially from the West Indies to Bermuda, occasionally drifts into warm-temperate and temperate waters, carried by ocean currents such as the Gulf Stream.
General: Usually solitary and sedentary, but voracious and even cannibalistic. No sport fishing or commercial importance, but quite interesting because of its highly specialized environmental adaptations.

248 ATLANTIC FLYING FISH S

Cypselurus heterurus
Other common names: Flyingfish, single-bearded flyingfish.

Features: Flying fish do not actually fly as do birds, but glide for considerable distances on their large, wing-like pectoral and pelvic fins after a quick, almost horizontal exit from the water. Pectoral fins of this species overlap the anal fin when folded back. The wing-like pelvic fins are about half as long as the pectorals, and are placed well back. The second ray of the pectoral fin is branched, and the fin has a narrow pale edging on the outer margin. Dorsal and anal fins have soft rays. The tail is deeply forked with the lower lobe longer than the upper. The tail is used to propel the fish rapidly into flight in the manner of a "prop-riding" outboard motorboat. The mouth is small and the scales are large and round. Dorsal fin, 12; anal fin, 9. The projecting lower jaw indicates close kinship to halfbeaks, as does the long, slim body. Coloration: Dark bluish-grey on upper sides and back, shading quickly to silver on lower sides and belly. Dorsal fin is medium grey.
Size: Averages 12 in (30 cm), up to 1/2 lb (0.22 kg).
Distribution: Tropical and warm-temperate Atlantic waters with preference for warm "blue water" areas. Primarily a deepwater fish, but often found close to ocean islands where deep water comes close to shore.
General: Glides have been measured at 1,000 ft (455 m) and more at speeds reaching 35 mph (55 km/h). Average glide consumes about 10 seconds. Valued as a seafood delicacy in some regions. There are reports of flying fish being taken on very small flycasting flies. Otherwise, the fish make good marlin and sailfish bait when obtainable.

249 CALIFORNIA FLYING FISH S

Cypselurus californicus

Features: The body is slender, rather compressed with a small head and a rounded snout. Large, round scales. One comparatively small dorsal fin and a similar anal fin both placed near the tail. The pectoral fins are very large, wing-like and placed high up on the body a little behind the upper head; the ventral fins are about half as large, also wing-like, and are placed a little behind the middle of the body. These four wings are the means by which the powerful jumps out of the water can be prolonged into a flight of up to 1500 ft (500 m). The tail fin is deeply forked; its lower lobe is by far the longer and acts in the start of the flight as a propeller, also as a rudder. Coloration: all over grey-bluish, silvery with a greenish sheen. The belly is lighter.
Size: 3/4– 1 3/4 ft (20–50 cm); 1/2 lb (225 g).
Distribution: Pacific, off southern California and Mexico. Related forms in Indo Pacific.
General: The "flying" is as described for *C. heterurus*. Food: small plankton animals. The flesh is very tasty, and the fish can be caught on small, light hooks.

250 HALFBEAK S

Hyporamphus unifasciatus
Other common names: Slender halfbeak, common halfbeak, escribano, pajarito, skipjack, billfish, salt-water gar, sea pike, needlefish, skipper, saury, garfish.

Features: Very slender and elongate body with the dorsal, anal and ventral fins being set extremely far back. No finlets between fins which distinguishes them from the saury pike, *Scomberesox*. The lower jaw is greatly prolonged. The upper jaw is short. Dorsal fin, 14 to 16; anal, 15 to 17; opposite each other and about equal in length and outline. Pelvic fins stand midway between a point below the eye and the base of the caudal. Lateral line is distinct. Teeth are small. Scales are largest on the upper surface of the head. Caudal is forked. Coloration: Translucent bottle green above with silvery tinge. There is a narrow but well defined silver band that extends from the forward part of the caudal to the pectoral fin. In life, the tip of the lower jaw is crimson with a short filament. Three narrow and dark streaks run along the middle of the back. Lining of the belly is black; forward portions of the dorsal and anal fins and the tips of the caudal are dusky.
Size: Seldom longer than 12 in (30 cm).
Distribution: Found in tropical and subtropical Atlantic and Pacific waters.
General: Swift-swimming, feeding mainly on green algae. Not taken deliberately by commercial or sportfishing means to any extent, but widely used as trolling bait.

251 BALAO S

Hemiramphus balao
Other common names: Halfbeak, ballyhoo, common halfbeak, escribano, pajarito, red-tailed balao, piper, hardhead.

Features: A small, long-bodied fish with the lower jaw protruding in the form of a long, slender beak. The ventral fins originate about halfway between the base of the tail and the gill opening, well forward of the origin of the dorsal fin. On some closely allied halfbeak species, particularly the *H. brasiliensis*, the ventral fins may be further back. Dorsal fin, 13 to 16; caudal fin moderately forked; anal fin 15 to 17; scales 52 to 59. Coloration: Silvery green on the back with translucent reflections of gold and blue, paler below. A dark streak runs along the sides from the upper side of the gill opening to the tail. It becomes wider and more diffuse in older specimens.
Size: Averages about 1 ft (30 cm), weighing up to 1 lb (0.45 kg), with some specimens larger.
Distribution: All tropical seas, most often found over reefs in coastal areas.
General: Easily attracted at night by lights. Leaps and skips over the surface when frightened. Congregates in large schools. Important trolling bait for billfish, tuna, sharks, and similar larger game. Flesh is tasty and the balao is popular in the Caribbean as a quality table fish.

252 GARFISH; GARPIKE S

Belone belone
Other common names: Spearfish, hornfish, snipe eel, gore bill, sea needle, old wife, sea pike, longnose, greenbone, longtom.

Features: Very elongate, eel-like body. Long head (more than one quarter total length of body) with beaked mouth; lower jaw projecting, especially characteristic in juveniles. Dorsal fin 17 to 20; tail fin forked; anal fin 20 to 23. Coloration: dorsally blue green or dark blue; flanks paling to silvery; belly silvery yellow; pelvic and anal fins yellowish with darker tips, rest of the fins dusky. Lateral line extends along belly below pectoral fin.
Size: Average 16–32 in (40–80 cm), maximum occasionally up to 36 in (90 cm), *c.* 2 1/4 lb (1 kg).
Distribution: Atlantic, English Channel, North Sea, Baltic, Mediterranean, Black Sea. Related forms in Indo-Pacific seas, and western Atlantic.
General: Known under many names which its rather unusual appearance suggests. A surface-feeding, oceanic fish but frequently found in coastal waters; it has a voracious appetite for white bait, sand eel, and similar small baitfish, and small fry of other species.

253 HOUNDFISH S

Tylosurus crocodilus
Other common names: Hound, agujon, guardfish, aguja de casta, needlefish, sea gar, gar, skipjack.

Features: Elongate fish that is small in diameter, the lower lobe of the caudal fin or tail longer than the upper, the tail forked. Medium to large size dorsal and anal fins are situated far back on the body. Both jaws sharply pointed into a beak or bill. Dorsal and anal fins similar in outline. Dorsal fin, 22 to 24; anal fin, 20 to 22. Scales approximately 350 along the lateral line. Coloration: Silvery sides and belly with a dark green colour above; sides with an indistinct dark silvery band; middle of back with a similar but darker band. The dermal keel on the caudal peduncle is black. All the fins are dusky. The dorsal fin usually mostly black.
Size: Has been reported at 5 ft (1.50 m) but generally far smaller.
Distribution: West Indies and Bermuda, Bahamas, Florida, south to Brazil.
General: Edible but not much used because of the green coloration of the bones. When startled, these fish swim quickly along the water surface, skimming with a sculling motion of the tail. Spectacular surface action when hooked on light tackle.

254 ATLANTIC NEEDLEFISH S, B, F

Strongylura marina
Other common names: Garfish, billfish, agujón, needlefish, saltwater gar, silver gar, green gar, skipjack, sea pike, harvest pike, houndfish, longtom.

Features: Long slender body with both jaws prolonged far in front of the head. No detached finlets. Body is wider than deep, unusual among fish. Head takes up nearly one-third of total length with upper jaw, from the eye forward, being twice as long as the remainder of the head. Both jaws have many sharp, fang-like teeth. Eyes are large. Scales cover body and sides of the head. Dorsal fin, 13–17; anal fin, 17–21. Both are alike in profile with their forward rays being much longer than the rear rays. Rear two-thirds of each can be depressed into a groove in the body with the forward third standing erect. Both fins are located well back with the anal originating a little ahead of the forward end of the dorsal. Pelvic fins are located halfway between a point below the eye and the base of the tail. Tail fin has a slightly concave margin and there is a long, low ridge or keel on each side of the caudal peduncle. Coloration: Green above, shading through silver on the sides to white on the belly. There is a silver-blue stripe along each side that becomes broader and loses colour toward the tail. Dark green snout, and there is a black blotch on the cheek. The fins are without distinct markings for the most part and have a bluish or dusky sheen. The tail is bluish at its root.
Size: Up to 4 ft (120 cm), 10 lb (4 1/2 kg).
Distribution: Western Atlantic and Gulf of Mexico from Maine to Texas, with majority of fish in sub-tropical waters. Often appears in rivers well above tidewater.
General: Spectacular fighter with powerful leaps and skipping runs when hooked on light tackle. Edible, but not favoured as food by most anglers because of the green colour of the bones. This condition, however, has no effect on the flavour or edibility of the flesh. No known commercial value.

255 TIMUCO S (B)

Strongylura timuco
Other common name: Atlantic needlefish.

Features: Body, head, and fins shaped almost as in *S. notata*. Only the scales on the anterior base of the dorsal fin are more numerous and smaller, and the streak along the side of the body is bluish silvery and has nó distinct dark spot at its beginning.
Size: Up to 2 1/2 ft (80 cm).
Distribution: West Atlantic from New England to Brazil.
General: Lives inshore and may ascend into brackish water.

256 AGUJA S (B)
Strongylura stolzmanni
Other common name: Picuda.

Features: The body is rather slender, not deep. The head is flattened above, but the snout is long and thin. Small scales. Lateral line upwards bent over the anal fin. Tail fin deeply concave, its lower lobe the longer; short ventral fins. Coloration: back and upper sides dark green, lower sides and belly lighter, silvery to grey; parts of the margins of the dorsal and anal fins are black.
Size: 8–14 in (20–36 cm).
Distribution: Eastern Pacific, from California to Peru.
General: Occurs mainly in shallow water near the coast, often also in the brackish estuaries. In spite of its small size it is sought by the sport fishery as a good fighting fish for light gear.

257 FLAT NEEDLEFISH S
Strongylura exilis
Other common names: California needlefish, garfish.

Features: Long, slender, round body; anterior part of head depressed; eyes rather large. Both jaws much prolonged into a long, pointed bill. Dorsal and anal fins placed far back only little before the concave tail fin; rounded pectoral fins and very small ventral fins. Coloration: back and upper sides green, lower sides and belly silvery; a bluish band along the sides.
Size: Up to 3 ft (1 m).
Distribution: Along the coast of southern California.
General: Only of little commercial importance, but taken now and then by sport fishing.

258 REDFIN NEEDLEFISH S
Strongylura notata

Features: Elongate and slender body; long head, large eyes; jaws prolonged into a long, pointed bill, lower jaw slightly the longer. Gill rakers vestigial or missing. Fewer and larger scales on the anterior base of the dorsal fin than in *S. timuco*. Dorsal and anal fins far back on the body; tail fin slightly concave. Coloration: pale green, silvery; a dark streak along the sides beginning with a larger blackish spot.
Size: About 12 in (30 cm), may reach 3 ft (90 cm).
Distribution: West Atlantic from Bermuda to West Indian seas.
General: Lives in inshore waters, often in harbours and around piers.

259 PACIFIC SAURY S
Cololabis saira
Other common names: mackerel pike, skipper, samma.

Features: Long, slender body with pointed head and snout. The small mouth is terminal with the lower jaw projecting well beyond the upper; the teeth are rather weak. The short dorsal fin is placed far back on the body; the only slightly longer anal fin is placed only little forward of the dorsal fin; between these fins and the deeply forked caudal fin are an upper and lower series of 5–6 finlets. Pectoral and ventral fins are small, the latter placed midway on the ventral contour. Coloration: back and upper sides dark with bluish and greenish sheen, lower sides and belly silvery.
Size: About 12–18 in (30–45 cm), 1–1 1/2 lb (1/2–3/4 kg).
Distribution: Northern, temperate Pacific off North America and Japan.
General: This cold-water saury is a shoaling fish and one of the more important commercial fish in Japan. It lives in offshore waters, mostly in the surface, but also down to 125 fathoms (225 m).

260 SAURY PIKE S
Scomberesox saurus
Other common names: Needlefish, billfish, skipjack, skipper, Atlantic saury.

Features: Very similar to the garfish (see above) except that the beak is shorter, and it generally appears a more compact fish. Dorsal fin 9 to 12 + 5 or 7 finlets; tail fin concave; anal fin 12 or 14 + 6 or 7 finlets. Readily identified from the garfish by the finlets behind the dorsal and anal fins. Coloration: dorsally dark blue, bluish green, or olive green, shading off to a silvery belly. Scales are small.
Size: Up to 20 in (50 cm), 11 lb (5 kg).
Distribution: Worldwide in temperate and warm seas. Many related forms with a similar worldwide distribution.
General: A deepwater schooling fish that migrates to coastal regions during the summer months and is found near the surface. In young fish the bill is very slow to develop. An excellent sport and a delicious table fish; after cooking the bones do not turn green like those of the garfish. One of its alternative common names "skipper" alludes to its ability to skip or leap several feet when chased by predator fish such as mackerel, bonito, and tuna.

261 BANDED KILLIFISH F
Fundulus diaphanus
Other common names: Freshwater killifish, killifish, topminnow, minnow (Maritime Provinces, Canada), petit barre, pupfish, mummichog.

Features: The upward-oriented small mouth and flat head of this baitfish adapt it to surface feeding. Body is compressed, especially toward the rear. The dorsal fin is placed over the anal, far back on the body. It has a rounded outer edge. The tail is rounded whereas true minnows and shiners always have a forked tail. Softrayed fins; pelvic fins placed far back. No visible lateral line, but lateral line pores on head. Cycloid scales. Coloration: Black alternating with yellow-green on back and upper sides, shading to silvery white below. There may be a violet or rose-coloured band along the middle in some waters. Vertical side bands of dark green number 12–15 and sometimes 20. Pale grey-green fins. First gill arch contains 4–6 gill rakers, compared to 8–12 in the mummichog. Variations due to environmental differences make positive identification of these small fish difficult.
Size: 2–5 in (5–12.5 cm).
Distribution: Eastern Canada, northeastern and central United States from St. Lawrence River through Lake Michigan, south and east to Iowa, Missouri, South Carolina.
General: Prefers fresh water inshore shallows where it spawns in summer. Builds no nest and does not protect the young. Feeds on plankton, small water insects, aquatic vegetation. No commercial value other than as bait for larger fish. Hardy, active, easily kept in bait tanks and cans.

262 STRIPED KILLIFISH F B
Fundulus majalis

Features: The body is small and rather thickset. Flattened head with upwards turned mouth. In shape and colours very similar to the banded killifish. Coloration: very variable; green, yellow, violet, according to the colours in the habitat; the back is darkish, belly much lighter; the male (much smaller than the female) has dark, transverse bands on the sides, the female has a few dark, longitudinal bands.
Size: About 6 in (15 cm).
Distribution: Eastern North America from Canada to Florida.
General: Lives in rivers and brooks, often also in the brackish estuaries.

263 MUMMICHOG F, B, S
Fundulus heteroclitus
Other common names: Common killifish, saltwater minnow.

Features: Stout body, broad in front and compressed behind; very robust, deep tail stalk. Blunt, broad head, depressed above; lower jaw slightly projecting; each jaw has a narrow band of pointed teeth. Dorsal fin 11; tail fin fully rounded; anal fin 10 or 11. Coloration: males, dorsally and flanks dark dull green; flanks with numerous ill-defined silvery bars and irregularly distributed white and yellow spots; belly orange yellow; front edges of pelvic and anal fins yellow; females, dorsally plain olive, paling on flanks with about 15 indistinct crossbars. At spawning time the colouring of the male becomes intensified when the yellow becomes more brilliant. No lateral line. Large scales.
Size: Maximum up to 5–6 in (13–15 cm), 1/4 lb (100 g).
Distribution: Coasts of North America, from the Gulf of St. Lawrence to Texas; also found in fresh- and brackish-water estuaries and tide pools.
General: A member of the killifish family and best known in its role as a live baitfish by trout fishermen. It transports well and is shipped live considerable distances. Because of its hardy qualities, it is frequently utilized as a laboratory research fish.

264 ATLANTIC SILVERSIDE S, B, F
Menidia menidia
Other common names: Green smelt, sand smelt, whitebait, capelin, sperling, shiner, silversides, hardhead, pescado del rey, piexe rey.

Features: This silvery little bait fish lacks an adipose fin (unlike the young smelt), and has a spiny as well as a soft dorsal fin. The anal fin is much longer than that of the smelt. The slender body is six times as long as deep, and is thin with a rounded, not sharp-edged, belly. The short head has a large eye and a small mouth with the gape going hardly as far back as the front of the eye, which is set obliquely. There are large scales on the body and head. First dorsal, III–IV, smaller than the second, starts midway between the nose tip and the base of the tail. Second dorsal 7–10, originates over the center of the anal fin. Anal, I, 22–25, outline falcate. Slender caudal peduncle with moderately forked tail fin. Coloration: Translucent green above, but dusky on top of head, chin, and nose. Speckles of dark brown on upper sides. A silver band with a narrow black line above marks each side from behind the pectoral fin to the tail base. Belly is white.
Size: 4–5 in (10–12 1/2 cm).
Distribution: Present in two almost identical forms or races along the eastern North American coast and coastal rivers and estuaries, from Gulf of St. Lawrence and Nova Scotia to Florida. Most abundant from Gulf of Maine to below Cape Hatteras.
General: Its primary function in the ecology of the sea appears to be forage for predacious fish. Widely used as bait by anglers. Excellent table fare when netted and fried as whitebait.

265 CALIFORNIA GRUNION S
Leuresthes tenuis

Features: A small, slender, somewhat eel-shaped fish. The mouth is turned upwards. Head and eyes rather large; blunt snout. Two dorsal fins, the first with spiny rays; the second, very small, with soft rays. Large, forked tail fin with pointed lobes. No lateral line. Coloration: above greyish-green to bluish, sides and belly lighter, silvery. A bright silvery band with bluish sheen along the sides.
Size: About 7 in (18 cm).
Distribution: Pacific, off the coast of California.
General: This grunion lives in shallow water. It shows highly interesting breeding habits. In March-July the mature individuals run during high tide right up to the sandy beaches, where males and females burrow into the sand and deposit the eggs and seed. When the larvae are hatched, the tidal current carry them out into the sea. The coastwards migrations take place when the tide is high, and they are therefore influenced by the moon phases. The fish is only of minor importance to the commercial fisheries, but is of interest to sport fishermen due to the remarkable spawning migrations.

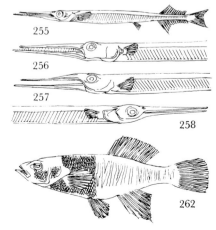

255

256

257

258

262

266 SOLDIERFISH s

Holocentrus spiniferus

Other common names: Scarletfish, squirrelfish.

Features: Short, compressed body. Large head has spines and thorns. Big eyes. The mouth is big and the upper jaw very broad near its end. One spinous and one soft dorsal fin. Tail fin forked. All fins are large. Scales are broad with fine points. Long, pointed ventral fins; the second dorsal and the anal fin are placed far back close to the caudal stalk. Distinct lateral line, only slightly upwards curving. Coloration: all over bright red, each scale has a lighter spot; first dorsal fin red, the other fins yellow to orange.

Size: Reaches a length of 1 1/4 ft (40–41 cm).

Distribution: The tropical mid and west Pacific and around Australia.

General: The soldierfish is common in the coral reefs, especially along the coast of Queensland (Great Barrier Reef).

267 AMERICAN JOHN DORY s

Zenopsis ocellata

Other common names: Ocellated dory, John dory, dory.

Features: Very deep, laterally compressed body, with a rather concave dorsal profile of the head. Obliquely-set large mouth, tail fin very small, armoured body, narrow caudal peduncle. Upper corner of gill cover lies directly under origin of the dorsal fin. The spiny and soft dorsals, together, extend from the nape to the caudal peduncle. Spiny dorsal is shorter than the soft dorsal, but more than twice as tall, with filamentous tips to the spines. Anal fin is almost a mirror image of the soft dorsal fin in size, shape, and location. Pelvic fins are long with ray tips free, and are located forward of the pectorals. The small tail is brush-shaped and the pectoral fins are round and short. Body is covered with naked skin and a series

of bony plates, each bearing a hooked spine or double spine. Two or three plates along the base of the first dorsal fin, four along the base of the second dorsal, two ahead of the pelvic fins, one centered between the pelvics, and six pairs along the belly to the anal fin. Dorsal fin, IX–X, 25–27. First three spiney fin rays are quite long, the rest shorter, declining in height to the rear. Anal fin, III, 24–26, with short, heavy spiny rays. Coloration: Silver overall. Small specimens spotted on each side with 12–24 irregular dark spots. These spots are retained in fish up to 15 in (37 1/2 cm), and fade in larger fish which usually show a single irregular blotch on each side behind the gill.

Size: Up to 24 in (60 cm), 7 lb (3 kg).

Distribution: Outer portion of Atlantic North American continental shelf from off Chesapeake Bay to Sable Island, N.S., and possibly to the Laurentian Channel between the Newfoundland Banks and Nova Scotia. Prefers deep waters.

General: Differentiated from the European John Dory, *Zeus faber,* (see below) by plates at the base of the first spiny dorsal fin, the second soft dorsal fin, and the anal fin; and by anal fin spiny ray count of three. Small commercial value and not usually taken by sport fishermen because of its habitat far from shore.

268 JOHN DORY s

Zeus faber

Features: Short, deep, and strongly compressed body. Large mouth; massive jaw, and lower jaw projecting; mouth is strongly protractile and can be extended well forward during feeding. Dorsal fin IX or X,22–25 (the spiny rays are very prolonged and filamentous); tail fin brush-shaped and rounded; anal fin III or IV,20–23 (spiny rays are very large); very long pelvic fins (twice length of pectorals). Coloration: dorsally and flanks brownish-grey mottling; distinct, characteristic large and round spot on flanks, and a light-coloured ring enclosing the central black area. Lateral line curves over dark spot. Armoured scales along each side of the dorsal and anal fins.

Size: Average range 12–20 in (30–50 cm), 3 1/3 lb (1 1/2 kg) occasional larger fish up to 24 in (60 cm).

Distribution: Worldwide.

General: The John Dory is usually a solitary fish found in depths ranging from *c.* 20–650 ft (6–200 m); food consists of other smaller fish. Being a slow-moving fish, it stalks its prey and when close enough, engulfs the victim with its protrusible, toothless mouth. In many areas it forms a regular part of commercial trawl catches. Although not a distinguished sport fish, it is a highly prized table fish.

269 BOARFISH s

Capros aper

Other common names: Zulu, dory, John Dory, St. Peter's fish.

Features: Resembles the John Dory in having a deep and thin body. The boarfish has been described as being deeper than it is long though this may be modified in some specimens. Large eye, a long, concave snout

with a protruding mouth that forms a short tube. The dorsal spines are strong and long while the anal spines are comparatively short and thin. The pelvic fin has a strong spine and five stout, soft rays that do not extend much further than the second anal spine. The scales are small, rough to the touch, and firmly anchored on the body. First dorsal, IX; second dorsal, 23; anal, III, 23. There are about 51 scales on the lateral line which is wavy or curved. The caudal is rounded. Coloration: pink and pinkish white to brick red from deep water, sometimes with yellow bars, while shallow water fish are often yellow to a straw colour.

Size: Grows to slightly over 6 in (15 cm) at maximum.

Distribution: Tropical and subtropical Atlantic, mostly offshore in deep waters, also reported from British Isles and the Mediterranean.

General: Sometimes taken in immense numbers in offshore trawls but has no commercial value. Occasionally found stranded on shore. Food appears to be mainly crustaceans.

270 OPAH s

Lampris guttatus

Other common name: Moonfish.

Features: The body is much compressed and very high, almost as high as long (excl. the tail). The head is large, about 1/3 the body length. The mouth is rather small with thick lips which can be protruded. No teeth, small eyes. The lateral line is strongly upwards bent over the pectoral fins. The dorsal fin starts midway on the back, the first part is high, it is followed by a long, low brim right to the tail. The anal fin is like the low part of the dorsal fin; the pectoral fins are long, narrow and pointed, the ventral fins are similarly shaped, but smaller. The tail fin is very large, deeply concave with pointed tips. Coloration: back shiny dark blue, sides light blue and silvery, belly reddish. The body is sprinkled all over with white, almost circular, spots; the fins are bright red.

Size: Up to 5–7 ft (150–200 cm), 230 pounds (100–125 kg).

Distribution: Occurs in all tropical and temperate oceans.

General: The opah is a true pelagic fish living from near the surface down to *c.* 220 fathoms (400 m). It feeds on smaller fish, squids, and crustaceans. The flesh is tasty but fat. The fish is caught commercially and also hooked by sport fishermen.

271 DEAL-FISH s

Trachypterus arcticus

Other common name: Vagmaer.

Features: Elongate, much compressed body. Small mouth, large eyes. On top of head a cluster of short finrays; behind these the dorsal fin begins and runs almost to the caudal fin, its first part is low, the second high like a sail. The tail fin is large, fanshaped. No anal fin, small pectorals and pelvics. Coloration: body silvery bluish with 4–5 large, dark blue spots in a line below the dorsal fin. All fins are red.

Size: Up to 10 ft (3 m).

Distribution: Open Atlantic from southern Greenland and Iceland to Argentina and

Southafrica.

General: Lives pelagically over deeper water. It is caught only rarely, more frequently it is found stranded on the shores, mainly round the North-Atlantic.

272 OARFISH s

Regalecus glesne

Other common names: Sea serpent, King-of-the-Herring (European), King-of-The-Salmon (Pacific Northwest Indian), Cock-Of-The-Palace-Under-The-Sea (Japanese).

Features: The extraordinarily long, slender body and bizarre coloration make misidentification difficult. A specimen 11 ft (3 m) long may be only six inches deep. The fish swims with an eel-like motion and feeds on euphausids, small shrimp-like creatures which it collects by straining them from the water with its specialized gill rakers. These number 42 to 58 and form a feeding filter. The name is said to come from the specialized pelvic and caudal fins which are extremely long and thin, with tips enlarged into flattened oar-like blades. The small mouth has no teeth. The eyes are large, as in fish accustomed to living in the darkness of great depths. Coloration: The thin, silvery body is spotted with purple or blue-black spots and short bars. The long, low dorsal fin runs the length of the body and sports a crest of long thin filaments at its forward end. Dorsal, pelvic and caudal fins are bright red. The small, rounded pectoral fins are soft-rayed and semi-transparent.

Size: A specimen 40 ft (12 m) long has been reported, and larger oarfish are probable.

Distribution: The full range of the oarfish is not known, but isolated specimens have been reported from locations as diverse as Japan, Florida, and the Orkney Islands.

General: While little is understood about adult oarfish, probably because they are extremely hard to catch in any sort of a net, oceanographers have captured the eggs and larvae of these fish in plankton nets. Adults are thought to live at depths ranging from 300 to 3,000 ft (90–900 m), where they find some light and adequate food from the ocean's Deep Scattering Layer of shrimplike creatures. Mature adults may occasionally reach the surface in areas of current upwelling, which could explain some stories about "sea serpents" that come to us from the past.

273 NINE-SPINED STICKLE-BACK F, B

Pungitius pungitius

Other common names: Ten-spined stickleback.

Features: Belongs to the stickleback family, *Gasterosteidae*, with a moderately elongate body form, depth about equal to its head length. The head and snout appear more elongate than the body. Two dorsals, the spinous composed of a long series of isolated and alternated spines (spaces between them). The second dorsal and the anal fin are opposite and similar in shape; the pelvics much reduced with a single, long, sharp and stout spine. The snout is relatively blunt in outline. First dorsal fin, VII to XII; second dorsal, 9 to 12; anal, I, 8 to 13. There are 32 scales along the lateral line with three rows above it. Coloration: Variable with the back and sides usually an olive green or green-tinted, darkening almost to a black, occasionally with dark bars on the sides. Underneath and belly is silvery. In the breeding season, the males have a generally brighter coloration.

Size: Grows to 3 in (7.5 cm) but more common at half this length.

Distribution: Europe; also north America and north Asia.

General: Engaging aquarium fish. Tolerates increased salinity so is able to survive very well in brackish waters where it feeds on small crustaceans and fish eggs.

274 THREE-SPINED STICKLEBACK S, B, (F)
Gasterosteus aculeatus

Features: This small fish is characterized by its three spines on the back (two free and one in front of the dorsal fin), spine-shaped ventral fins and by its body being covered by high, narrow, plate-shaped scales. Dorsal and anal fins are placed far back on the body. Coloration: bluish silvery: the belly of the male is reddish in the spawning season.

Size: 3–5 in (8–12 cm).

Distribution: Coasts of northern Europe, America, and Asia.

General: Lives in the very shallow water. Is fished for oil and meal in some places.

275 FIFTEEN-SPINED STICKLEBACK S
Spinachia spinachia

Other common names: Bottlenose, great sea adder, sea stickleback.

Features: Slender fish with long snout; long, thin tail with large tail fin. One large dorsal fin with a series of about 15 short spines in front of it; large anal fin, this and the dorsal fin placed on the middle of the body. Coloration: dark brown and yellow, belly mostly yellow.

Size: 6–8 in (15–20 cm).

Distribution: Coastal waters of northern Europe from Lofoten to Bay of Biscay.

General: Its home is the vegetation belts along the shores. The species is renown for its construction of nests for the eggs and larvae.

276 SEAHORSE S
Hippocampus ramulosus

Other common names: Horsefish, caballito del mar.

Features: The seahorse is specialized with a small mouth at the end of a tube-like snout and with fairly stout bony rings forming a firm covering. The gills are lobed, body elongate, fins small with pelvics absent. *Hippocampus* has a curved neck with the head at about right angles to the body, somewhat like the "knight" in a chess set. The dorsal fin is the largest, pectorals and anal small. There is no caudal fin. Long straight snout may be more than one third of the head length; snout length more than twice the diameter of the eye. Dorsal fin, 18 to 20; pectoral fin, 15 to 18; anal, 4. Coloration: Light to medium brown which is often well sprinkled with small white points offset by a dark outer ring.

Size: Grows to 6 in (15 cm).

Distribution: Vicinity of the English Channel, the Mediterranean and Black Sea; more common on the French Atlantic and Biscay coasts. Related species off the Atlantic and Pacific coasts of the United States, off Africa, and in all warm seas.

General: Spends much time anchored by the tail to marine growth. Does nicely and breeds freely in an aquarium. Swims upright, moving mainly by vibrating the dorsal fin. Sought as food by predators and as a curiosity by man.

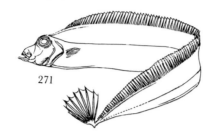

271

274

275

279

280

281

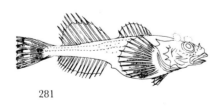

282

13 SCULPINS, REDFISHES, GURNARDS, FLATHEADS

277 SCULPIN S
Cottus scorpius

Other common names: Sculpin, short-spined sea scorpion, short-spined cottus, Greenland bullhead, kanayuk, father-lasher.

Features: Stout body. Wide head flattened from above with fleshy tabs and warty (bony) prominences; snout has 2 small spines; front gill cover has 2 to 4 short spines; large eye (forehead humped above it); characteristically membrane from gill cover stretches to under throat. Dorsal fins VII to XI–14 to 17; tail fin convex or nearly square-cut; anal fin 10 to 14. Coloration: variable but usually dark olive or brown with finely mottled lighter shades; belly white to yellowish; females with distinct orange bellies; males in breeding season overall more coppery; fins dusky, soft dorsal and anal fins have black diagonal stripes. Lateral line is nearly straight with some wartlike prominences. Skin is almost smooth.

Size: Maximum *c.* 25 in (60 cm), 6–7 lb (3 kg). The larger specimens are almost always females.

Distribution: North Atlantic, ranging subarctic and arctic seas on both sides.

General: A common member of the scorpion fishes. In its northern distribution it is found in the littoral zone along shorelines and in rock pools (where it is often recognized by its characteristic "grunt"). It inhabits a variety of bottoms and frequently enters estuaries. Adults generally feed on shrimps, small crustaceans, and fish. Care is required when handling, since the head spines may cause wounds which occasionally turn septic not because of the spines being poisonous, but due to the dirty, unhealthy mudparticles from the harbour clinging to them.

In the arctic waters, where larger individuals are common, the sculpin is of some importance to the local fisheries and used for human consumption. As a sport fish its value is only small. However, it is often taken by anglers from piers and in harbours; many future sport fishermen have started already as boys by angling for this voracious and easy prey.

278 ONI KAJIKA S
Ceratocottus diceraus

Features: This Pacific sculpin has a short, compressed body with a stout, flattened head. Large, protruding eyes. The short and blunt snout bears at the nostrils 2 short spines. Top of head with tubercles. The gill cover has a long, strong spine with secondary small teeth, other smaller spines are also present. A line of small, bony plates or warts runs on each side from gill cover to tail fin. There are two high dorsal fins, the first with 7–8 spines, the second with 13–14 soft rays; the broad, large tail fin has a straight, scalloped hind margin. The anal fin is long, and its posterior part is very high, 12 rays. Pectoral fins are large, fanlike; the ventral fins are narrow with few, long rays. Teeth are present on jaws and farther back in the mouth, they are villiform but rather stout. Coloration: back and sides brownish with reddish or dark blotches; belly light yellow or whitish. The tail fin, the dorsal and pectoral fins have irregular, oblique, dark bands; the anal fin is light with small, dark spots.

Size: On an average *c.* 6–10 in (15–25 cm).

Distribution: Northwestern Pacific as far south as northern Japan.

General: Lives in coastal, shallow waters.

279 PYGMY SCULPIN S
Taurulus lilljeborgi

Features: This small sculpin is characterized by its large spine in front of the gillcover, the rows of spines along the lateral line and on each side of the back. All fins are large. The anal fin has only 8 rays. Coloration: dark or light brownish with distinct darker patches.

Size: 2–2½ in (5–6 cm).

Distribution: European coasts: Iceland, British Isles, southern Norway, Skagerak, and Kattegat.

General: Its home is the soft bottom, 12–15 fathoms (20–30 m). Nowhere common.

280 LONGSPINED BULLHEAD S
Taurulus bubalis

Features: This species can be distinguished from other sculpins by the very long spines on its gillcover. Coloration: yellow and brown with rather distinct darker patches.

Size: 6–7 in (15–18 cm).

Distribution: Northeast Atlantic from Iceland and northern Norway to the Bay of Biscay; Kattegat, Belts, and western Baltic.

General: Occurs in coastal waters. Is less abundant than the sculpin (*Cottus scorpius*).

281 FOUR-HORNED SCULPIN S, B, (F)
Myoxocephalus quadricornis

Features: Large fins, spines on gill cover. Characterized by four yellow, slightly flossy warts on top of head. Coloration: back and sides brown, belly yellow.

Size: About 8 in (20 cm).

Distribution: Along the arctic coasts of Asia and Europe.

General: Survives as a relict from the Glacial Period in the Baltic and in certain lakes in northern Europe and North America.

282 POGGE S

Agonus cataphractus
Other common name: Armed bullhead.

Features: Long, slender body, the foremost part flattened. Head and body are covered with bony plates, thorns and spines on snout, head, and body. The actual tail stalk is thin. Short feelers on snout and on the underside of the head. Coloration: dark brown with yellow patches.
Size: 6–8 in (15–20 cm).
Distribution: East Atlantic from the White Sea to the English Channel; through the North Sea and into the western Baltic.
General: Lives on the soft bottom from the coast and out to 110 fathoms (200 m).

283 CABEZON S

Scorpaenichthys marmoratus
Other common names: Blue cod, bull cod, bullhead, marbled sculpin, crab-eating cabezon.

Features: Stout body. Broad head; large mouth; characteristic long frilly skin flaps at upper rear margins of each eye and on snout; spines over eyes; many teeth. Dorsal fins deeply notched X–15 or 16; tail fin square-cut or rounded; anal fin 12. Coloration: variable, reddish to grey, sometimes green or brown, always mottled; lining of mouth characteristically blue green. The skin is smooth, scaleless, and has a wrinkled appearance.
Size: Average 2–5 lb (1–2 1/2 kg), maximum probably up to 40 in (100 cm), 22 lb (10 kg).
Distribution: Eastern Pacific, ranging from Sitka, Alaska to Abrojos Point, Baja California.
General: One of the many sculpins found along the California coast. The only sculpin along the entire North American seaboard considered to be a genuine game/sport fish. Spawning occurs from November to March.

Cabezons feed heavily on crabs and mollusks of all kinds, but they also include small fish in their diet. As a fairly lively sport fish (especially the larger ones) it is caught on almost any bait or by metal jigs with rod or handlines. They are of only minor commercial importance, and most fish are taken on lines set primarily for rock cod. As a table fish the flesh is esteemed, but since it is often bluish-green in colour, there is little popular demand for it. The roe has been proved highly toxic and should not be eaten.

284 KELP GREENLING S

Hexagrammos decagrammus
Other common name: Rock trout.

Features: Compressed body. Large head and big mouth; small eyes. Two dorsal fins almost united. Tail fin broad with a straight hind margin; long anal fin placed off the second dorsal fin; ventral fins are below the pectoral fins, both fairly large. Distinct, almost straight, lateral line. Coloration: the male is mostly bluish with brown, irregular patches; the female is brown with darker patches.
Size: Maximum 1 1/2 ft (45 cm).
Distribution: North Pacific, coasts of USA.
General: Lives in shallow waters, mostly between rocks and stones, where it feeds on prawns and crabs. Related species occur in the Pacific along the coasts of northern Asia. Only of little commercial importance, but a fine game fish when casting from rocks on the shore.

285 AINAME S

Hexagrammos otakii
Other common names: Aburame, aburako.

Features: A slender fish with a narrow, pointed head. No air bladder. Three lateral lines: one just below the dorsal contour, the other a little farther down the side, and the third in the usual place. One dorsal fin with hardly any incision between the spinous (20 spines) and the soft-rayed part (22). Large tail fin with straight or only slightly concave hind margin; the anal fin is similar to the soft part of the dorsal fin; pectoral and ventral fins are large. Coloration: Brown, red to purple, and black; varies much individually.
Size: The common length is 1–1 1/2 ft (30–45 cm).
Distribution: Coastal areas in the western Pacific: Japan, China, Korea.
General: The fish is common in the Japanese seas from Hokkaido and south to Kyushu. It spawns in late autumn, and the eggs are deposited in large lumps among the seaweed. The ainame is of some importance to the local fisheries.

286 NORWAY HADDOCK S

Sebastes marinus
Other common name: Redfish.

Features: A perchlike fish with a deep, ovate body. Depressed forehead; large mouth; projecting lower jaw with a bony protrusion; very large characteristic eye; cheeks with spines (nonpoisonous). Dorsal fin XIV to XVI, 12 to 16; tail fin variable; anal fin III or IV,7 to 9. Coloration: dorsally and flanks variable between grey, dirty red or orange red; belly paler; diffuse dark spot on gill cover; occasionally several irregular darkish blotches along dorsal area including fin.
Size: Average up to 12–14 in (30–35 cm), maximum *c.* 30 in (75 cm), 15 1/2 lb (7 kg).
Distribution: Atlantic and Arctic seas; in west, from west Greenland south to New England states, in east, from Spitsbergen, east Greenland, and Iceland south to North Sea to *c.* lat. 55° N.
General: The Norway haddock or redfish is a deepwater fish of considerable commercial importance and is now much sought after throughout its wide North Atlantic and Arctic distributions. It is viviparous, the eggs are retained in the ovaries of the female after they hatch until the yolk sac is absorbed. From May to August the fry are released when they measure about 1/4 in (6 mm) and remain at the surface until they reach about 1 in (25 mm) after which they go to the bottom.

As a sport fish it may sometimes be encountered when boat fishing. As a food fish it is much esteemed.

287 LESSER REDFISH S

Sebastes viviparus

Features: Similar to the redfish (*S. marinus*) in shape of body and in colours. Eyes smaller and number of scales lower, ca 75 against 85 along the lateral line. Coloration: the red colour is more mixed with grey and brown, and along the upper sides are vertical darker bands.
Size: 8–12 in (20–30 cm).
Distribution: Both sides of the North Atlantic, from Labrador to New England from the Lofoten Islands to west of the British Isles; also northern North Sea and Skagerrak.
General: Lives in comparatively shallow water, 12–160 fathoms (20–300 cm); often found also in fjords and bays.

288 CHINA ROCKFISH

Sebastodes nebulosus
Other common names: Cifulatano, rock cod, gopher.

Features: A short, thickset sculpin. Large head and big mouth; front depressed between the eyes. Five pairs of short, strong spines on top of head. One dorsal fin with about 12 spines and 13–15 soft rays; large pectoral and ventral fins; the smaller anal fin has 2–3 spines. Tail fin with almost straight hind margin. Coloration: back and sides blackish, speckled with yellow and white, sometimes mixed with blue. A broad yellow band reaches from the second and third spines in the dorsal fin to the base of the tail fin.
Size: Maximum length 12 in (30–32 cm).
Distribution: Eastern Pacific, common from Vancouver Island to southern California.
General: The usual habitat is the rather deep water off the coasts. A valuable commercial fish, highly estimated by the Chinese (hence the common English name).

289 BOCACCIO S

Sebastes paucipinnis
Other common names: Rockfish, merou, jack, salmon grouper, grouper, rock cod.

Features: This relative of the sculpins is basslike or perch-like in appearance, nevertheless has a bony extension of the suborbital bones across the cheek, giving the face a gaunt appearance. Spiny cheeks, but top of the head has no spines, as do the true sculpins. The dorsal fin has a deep notch between the forward spiny portion and the rear soft portion. The space between the eyes is strongly rounded. The large mouth has an undershot jaw and thick lips. The maxilla extends to the rear of the eye. First dorsal, X–XIII; second dorsal, 9. Anal fin, III, 9; Pectoral fin, 15–16. Scales cover the body and the slightly wavy lateral line is uninterrupted. The face appears long in profile, while the tail is square. Coloration: Brownish olive above and red-orange on the sides with a reddish flush throughout. Underbelly is pure white.
Size: Up to 36 in (90 cm), 22 lb (10 kg), but most specimens smaller.
Distribution: Eastern Pacific coast from British Columbia south to Baja California in Mexico.
General: Prefers depths below 40 fathoms (73 m). Commercially important in California where it is plentiful in the southern and central coastal regions. Good on the table, and sought by deep water sport fishermen.

290 BLACK ROCKFISH S

Sebastodes melanops
Other common names: Black rock cod, black snapper, black bass, nero, cherna.

Features: A bony ridge running back over the cheek from under the eye indicates relationship to the sculpins. The long dorsal fin is notched between first and second sections. Top of head is spineless and there is a convex area between the wide-set eyes. The maxilla runs to the rear corner of the eye. Dorsal fin, XIII, 12–12; anal fin III, 7–8. Large pectoral fins with the smaller pelvic fins just below them on the thorax. Scale row count, oblique, from gill opening to start of tail equals 60–70. Coloration: Upper surface black shading to grey mottled sides and silver-white underbelly. Some specimens lightly sprinkled with black specks.
Size: Up to 24 in (60 cm), 6 1/2 lb, 3 kg).
Distribution: From southern California to Alaska in the Pacific, and possibly much further.
General: Found inshore and in deep water. Some commercial value and caught frequently by anglers, usually when after other species. Flesh is good, but its fat content requires refrigeration soon after capture.

291 KELP ROCKFISH S

Sebastes atrovirens

Features: Stout, compressed body, large head; big eyes and mouth, strong teeth; the gill cover has strong spines. The long dorsal fin has spines in its anterior part, the posterior higher part has soft rays. The hind margin of the tail fin is nearly straight. large pectoral and ventral fins. Coloration: back and upper sides reddish and yellow, mixed with brown; lower sides and belly lighter.
Size: About 15–20 in (38–50 cm).
Distribution: Northeastern Pacific off the USA coasts.
General: This rockfish prefers the vegetation belts off the coasts. It is of some importance for the local fisheries, and is taken also by sport fishing with hook and line.

292 ZEBRA FISH S

Pterois volitans

Features: This peculiar fish is related to the redfishes (*Sebastes*). The body is short and stout. Large mouth with numerous teeth. The zebra fish is first of all characterized by the strange development of its fins. The dorsal fin has about 10 long, free spines, almost half as long as the whole body; the spines have furrows by which poison from glands along the base of the fin can flow to the points of the spines. The pectoral fins are large with several partly free, band-formed rays, as long as the whole fish; these featherlike rays account for the scientific name volitans – flying. The anal fin is high with soft rays, tail fin broad with convex hind margin. Coloration: the body is dark brownish or reddish with verti-

cal bright-red and black bands or stripes. The feather-shaped free fin rays have transverse brown, red, and white bands. The posterior part of the dorsal fin, the tail fin and the anal fin are light with many small, black spots.
Size: About 12 in (30 cm).
Distribution: Indian Ocean, tropical part.
General: The home is the more shallow, coastal waters. The poisonous spines are used as defensive and offensive weapons.

293 NORTHERN SEAROBIN s
Prionotus carolinus
Other common names: Common gurnard, common sea robin.

Features: Elongate body. Head encased in rough, bony plates; upper jaw slightly projecting. Dorsal fins X–13; tail fin concave; anal fin I,11; pectoral fins very large and winglike with 3 separated feeler rays; pelvic fins long but smaller than pectorals. Coloration: dorsally reddish brown or grey with c. 5 dark saddlelike blotches; pectoral and pelvic fins yellowish orange; black spot or smudge between fourth and fifth spines of spiny dorsal fin. Distinct lateral line. Small, rough scales.
Size: Up to 14 in (36 cm), 1 3/4 lb (3/4 kg).
Distribution: Western Atlantic, ranging Bay of Fundy to South Carolina.
General: A species usually found close inshore, but also in depths up to 500 ft (150 m), especially during the winter months. Spawning occurs June–August, and the buoyant eggs (with appearance of oil globules) hatch in 2 1/2 days. Food generally consists of small shrimp, amphipods, copepods, and occasional small fish. It has little interest as a sport fish except as bait, although the flesh is tasty.

294 YELLOW GURNARD s
Trigla lucerna
Other common names: Tubfish, tub gurnard, swallow.

Features: Small, elongate body. Snout sharp pointed in profile; head blunt and bony-plated, head has a more humped appearance than the grey gurnard (*Eutrigla gurnardus*); short lobes either side of snout. Two dorsal fins IX or X–15 to 18; tail fin concave; anal fin 14 to 17; a row of small spines along each side of dorsal fins; short spine above pectoral fin; pectoral fin with three separate feeler rays on lower edge. Coloration: dorsally red, reddish yellow, brown, or yellowish with brown or sometimes greenish blotches; flanks are reddish or yellowish; belly paling to pink on white; head dark red; pectoral fin has blue spots and a bluish-black blotch on the underside with lighter blue spots on upper side. Lateral line scale count 70.
Size: Average range 12–24 in (30–60 cm), maximum up to 30 in (75 cm).
Distribution: From Norway south into the Mediterranean and Black Sea, rare in Baltic.
General: A fairly common inshore species from English Channel southward; also ranges from estuary shallows to 650 ft (200 m). A delicious table fish.

295 GREY GURNARD s
Eutrigla gurnardus
Other common names: Hardhead, crooner, croonack-gowdie.

Features: Small, elongate body. Head blunt and bony-plated; lobe projecting either side of snout with 3–4 spines. Two dorsal fins VII to IX–18 or 19; tail fin concave; anal fin 17 to 20. Lateral line spiny. A line of bony spines is present either side of the dorsal fins; a short spine above each pectoral fin; pectoral fin with 3 separated feeler rays. Coloration: variable, but Atlantic form grey or greyish brown, with numerous lighter spots scattered over the dorsal area and flanks; the first dorsal fin has a darkish patch; the Mediterranean form is red or reddish brown, also with darkish patch on first dorsal fin. Prominent straight lateral line, and scale count 72 to 77.
Size: Average c. 12 in (30 cm), maximum up to c. 18 in (45 cm).
Distribution: Eastern Atlantic from Iceland and Scandinavia (including the Baltic) south to Mediterranean and Black Sea. Related grey gurnard forms widespread in Indo-Pacific seas.
General: A very common and abundant species found over sandy, rocky, or muddy bottoms to depths up to 500 ft (150 m), but it may frequent the surface regions particularly at night. Food consists of shrimps and crabs, but it also devours fish. Although a small, very bony fish, it has some commercial value and is a delicious table fish.

296 RED GURNARD s
Aspitrigla cuculus
Other common names: Redfish, cuckoo gurnard, Cape gurnard.

Features: Small, elongate body. Pronounced bony-plated and slightly concave, blunt head; snout has 3–4 spines. Dorsal fins, VIII to X–17 or 18; tail fin concave; anal fin 16 to 18. A row of short spines along each side of the dorsal fins; pectoral fin with 3 separate feeler rays. Coloration: head, dorsal regions, and flanks reddish; belly paler; pectoral fins greyish, pinkish, or yellowish; tail fin has a darker trailing edge. Lateral line scale count 70 to 73. Scales very deep and bony.
Size: Average range 8–12 in (20–30 cm), maximum up to 18 in (45 cm).
Distribution: Eastern and South Atlantic (rare in the western Baltic and North Sea); Mediterranean.
General: A species found in deeper water than other gurnards. A good table fish.

297 TWO-HORNED SCULPIN
Icelus bicornis

Features: This smaller scorpion has bony warts along the lateral line. The eyes are comparatively small. Anal fin short, 15 rays. Coloration: Brownish with large dark patches.
Size: 4–5 in (9–12 cm).
Distribution: Arctic parts of the North Atlantic; also along the coasts of Norway and in the Skagerak.
General: The usual habitat appears to be the shallow, near-coastal waters.

298 PINGEL'S SCORPION s
Triglops pingeli

Features: A slender scorpion with thin tail stalk. Large eyes. Bony, spiny warts along the lateral line and in a row above this line. Long anal fin, 20 rays. Coloration: brownish to grey with distinct dark to black patches.
Size: 5–8 in (12–20 cm).
Distribution: North Atlantic; Greenland, Svalbard to southern Norway; rare in Kattegat.
General: Prefers moderate depths, 8–20 fathoms (15–40 m).

299 HOOK SCULPIN
Artediellus uncinatus

Features: This small scorpion has no bony warts along the lateral line, and no keels on top of head. Gill cover with two thorns, one of them curved. All fins large. Coloration: brown to grey, with black patches or bands, also on the fins.
Size: 2–4 in (5–11 cm).
Distribution: Arctic seas, reaches south to the Norwegian coast and into Skagerak.
General: Its home is the shallow water.

300 THREE-HORNED SCULPIN
Gymnacanthus tricuspis s

Features: This comparatively large scorpion has no warts along the lateral line and no keels on top of head. The gill cover bears a characteristic long, furcate spine. Coloration: brown to grey with greenish sheen, darker spots and bands on body and fins.
Size: 8–11 in (20–28 cm).
Distribution: An arctic fish; Greenland, Svalbard, Novaja Zemlya, northern Norway.
General: Found from the coast and out to a depth of 80 fathoms (150 m).

301 STRIPED SEAROBIN s
Prionotus evolans
Other common names: Northern striped gurnard, brown-winged sea robin.

Features: Moderately elongate body; more rounded profile than *P. carolinus*. Head incased in rough, bony plates. Dorsal fins X–12; tail fin almost square-cut; anal fin I,11; pectoral fin very long and forms almost a wing with 3 narrow, separated feeler rays. Coloration: dorsally and flanks reddish to olive brown; flanks have a distinct darker brown stripe below the lateral line; long winglike pectorals orange brown with pale edges; dark blotch between fourth and fifth spines of spiny dorsal fin. Lateral line well marked. Scales small and rough.
Size: Up to 18 in (45 cm).
Distribution: Western Atlantic, ranging Gulf of Maine to South Carolina.
General: See northern sea robin (*P. carolinus*).

302 SAND FLATHEAD F, B
Platycephalus arenarius

Features: Characteristics very similar to those of the other flathead species but jaws have no canine teeth. Dorsal fin I–VII–13

or 14; tail fin square-cut or slightly rounded; anal fin 14. Coloration: dorsally and flanks brownish; 5–6 longitudinal black stripes on tail fin.
Size: Up to 12 in (30 cm).
Distribution: Indo-Pacific estuaries, inlets, and harbours; in Australia it ranges chiefly along the east coast around Queensland and northern New South Wales.
General: Not a noteworthy sport fish but an excellent table fish.

303 TIGER FLATHEAD s
Neoplatycephalus macrodon

Features: Very similar characteristics to common sand flathead and other flathead species (which see). General distinguishing feature from other flatheads is the presence of large canine teeth in the jaws and on the roof of the mouth.
Size: Up to a maximum of c. 30 in (75 cm), 3 lb (1 1/2 kg).
Distribution: Indo-Pacific seas; in Australia found around New South Wales, Victoria, and Tasmania.
General: A deepwater species usually caught at night; during daylight hours it remains very inactive on the sea floor. It represents an important local commercial (trawling) species and is an excellent table fish of very high quality (see also common sand flathead).

304 RED-SPOTTED FLATHEAD s
Platycephalus coeruleopunctatus
Other common name: Long-nosed flathead.

Features: Slender, elongate, and depressed body. Head long and very depressed; lower jaw projecting; 3 short spines in front of eye, and a spine on the gill cover. Two high dorsal fins I–VII–14; tail fin square-cut; anal fin 13 or 14. Coloration: dorsally and flanks brownish; some blackish markings on tail fin. White and red spots over entire body.
Size: Maximum up to 20 in (50 cm).
Distribution: Indo-Pacific seas.
General: Not a spectacular performer as a sport fish but locally a very popular and delicious table fish with snow-white, tender flesh; best skinned from head downward, prior to cooking.

305 DUSKY FLATHEAD s, B
Platycephalus fuscus
Other common names: Dark brown flathead, sand flathead, black flathead, river flathead, light drab flathead, sea flathead, estuary flathead.

Features: Very similar characteristics to common sand flathead and other flathead species (which see). May be distinguished from other species by its coloration, the wider distance between the eyes, and the broader, flatter, and scaly head. Coloration: dorsally and flanks dark; pelvic and tail fins, and the lower part of pectoral fins are blackish with white margins; dorsal fins are characteristically spotted, and the head dusky with brown spots. Can be distinguished from the marbled flathead, which has similar fin coloration, by the absence of a marbled body coloration.

Size: Average 2–4 lb (1–1 3/4 kg), maximum 40 in (100 cm), 32 lb (14 1/2 kg).
Distribution: Indo-Pacific seas; in Australia found in all states except the Northern Territory.
General: A very numerous species which frequents inshore waters in estuaries, harbours, and inlets; also found in open waters. Many are caught in shallow estuary waters at night by the use of a lantern and a trident spear. An important commercial species and an excellent table fish.

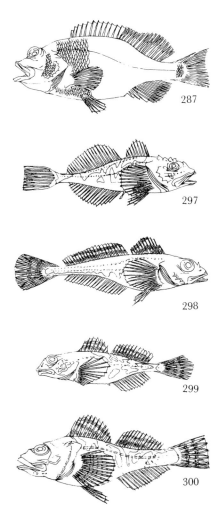

14 SNOOKS, NILE PERCH, BARRAMUNDI

306 SNOOK   B, S
Centropomus undecimalis
Other common name: Robalo.

Features: Body elongate; dorsal line considerably elevated, the ventral (pelvic) outline straight. Head depressed and pikelike, the lower jaw projecting; jaws have bands of crowded, narrow, fingerlike teeth; tongue is smooth; gill covers have sharp, serrated edges. Dorsal fins very deeply notched VIII, 9 or 10; tail fin forked; anal fin III,6 or 7; the spiny rays of dorsal and anal fins move in scaly sheets. Coloration: dorsally bluish green; flanks and belly silvery. Lateral line characteristically broad and dark and extends across tail fin rays to apex of tail fork. Lateral line scale count 69 to 80. Scales ctenoid and varying in size.
Size: Average range up to 5 lb (2 1/4 kg), maximum up to over 50 lb (22 1/2 kg), 50 in (125 cm).
Distribution: Tropical waters on both shores of the Americas; in U.S. distribution chiefly Florida, Texas, and Lower California.
General: A belligerent fish with a temperament much like that of the muskellunge of freshwater habitats. It is usually found close inshore around sandy beaches, flats, and bays, and often near bridges and pilings in tidal brackish waters. Food consists of shrimp, crab, and small fish. Throughout its distribution it is an exceedingly popular light-tackle sport fish. Landing the fish requires some care owing to the sharp-edged gill covers. It is rated an excellent table fish.

307 BLACK SNOOK   S
Centropomus nigrescens
Other common name: Robalo prieto.

Features: Robust body, flanks not compressed. Preorbital (eye) bone faintly serrated. Dorsal fin VIII–I,10; tail fin forked; anal fin III,6 (dorsal spines are not as strongly developed in related species *C. undecimalis* (see above). Coloration: dorsally dusky olive; flanks silvery; dusky shades on gill cover and at base of pectoral fin; pelvic fins mostly black; dorsal fin dusky; characteristic black lateral line. Lateral line scale count 67 to 75.
Size: Up to 30 in (75 cm), maximum *c.* 36 in (90 cm), 22 lb (10 kg).
Distribution: Pacific coasts of tropical America, ranging Baja California south to northern Peru.
General: The black snook is an angling and food fish of some importance throughout its range. As a sport fish it is a tough fighter, particularly on spinning tackle. As a table fish it is best skinned; the flesh is well rated and is best prepared by baking.

308 TARPON SNOOK   S, B, F
Centropomus pectinatus

Features: Moderately elongate and compressed body; angled at front of anal fin. Mouth small, snout pointed; cheek characteristically has *c.* six long, slender, and close-set spines, like the teeth of a comb; gill cover sharply serrated behind. Dorsal fins VIII–I,10; tail fin forked; anal fin III,7. Coloration: dorsally leaden hues; flanks paler; belly white; flank scales have bluish centres which give the overall impression of forming faint lines across the flanks; fins are greenish; lower lobe of tail fin yellow. Lateral line scale count 68.
Size: Average up to 12 in (30 cm), 1 lb (1/2 kg).
Distribution: Gulf of Mexico and West Indies, particularly along the coasts of Cuba, Haiti, and the Dominican Republic.
General: A small species of saltwater snook which enters brackish and freshwater rivers and lakes. Edible.

309 LITTLE SNOOK   S, B, F
Centropomus parallelus
Other common names: Robalo, snook, sergeantfish, brochet de mer, constantino de las aletas prietas, robalito de las aletas prietas, pike.

Features: Long body with a concave head and face profile and a projecting lower jaw. The tail is deeply forked. The ventral surface is nearly straight; the back high; the two dorsal fins distinctly separated; the eye medium to large. The anal fin originates well behind the origin of the soft dorsal fin. The curved, gently wavy lateral line is dark and distinct. The mouth is large; teeth small. There are approximately 79 to 92 scales along the lateral line; 10 to 13 gill rakers. There are usually 11 to 12 gill rakers on the lower limb of the first arch, excluding rudiments. First dorsal fin, about VIII; second dorsal, 10 or more. Anal fin, II or more with the second not extending beyond a vertical line dropped from the caudal base, 6. Pectoral rays are listed as 14 to 16. The relatively large number of lateral scales and the fairly robust body are the chief field characteristics in identifying *parallelus* from other similar snooks.
Size: Reaches a maximum of 20–24 in (50–60 cm) but commonly far smaller.
Distribution: Generally all through the tropical Atlantic areas of the Americas.
General: So easily confused with other species of the snook that all identifications other than scientific are suspect. Popular angling fish, protected in some areas. Edible, though skinning is recommended before baking or broiling.

310 NILE PERCH   F
Lates niloticus
Other common name: Niger perch.

Features: Thickset body with high back. Head concave or depressed, lower jaw projecting, snout rounded. Variations in shape of upper body profile have been noted. Dorsal fin notched, VII or VIII–I to II,10 to 14; tail fin rounded; anal fin III,8 or 9; dorsal and anal fins move in a scaly sheath. Coloration: dorsally and flanks a uniform dull brown or olive, sometimes with a mar-bled effect or crossbands; lower flanks and belly silvery, at times tinged with yellow; young fish up to 10 in (25 cm) usually show brown marblings; fins whitish and dark at the base in the young. Lateral line scale count 60 to 80. Scales are large and thick.
Size: In Nile River maximum over 6 ft (180 cm), and up to 300 lb (140 kg); in Niger and large lakes up to 200 lb (90 kg). Adult females are more than twice the size of the males and average up to 60 lb (27 kg) against 25 lb (11 kg).
Distribution: Nile River system; Niger, Senegal, Congo River systems; Chad Basin. Introduced into Lakes Victoria, Albert, Rudolf, and Abbaya (Congo). Not found in the Zambezi River and other African rivers.
General: The largest freshwater fish in Africa and one of the largest perchlike fishes in the world. The Nile perch has the voracity of a pike, and even very young fish are cannibalistic. Its teeth are quite small, however, and are used only as an aid to grip and hold the prey before swallowing it.

Spawning occurs in relatively still water, in lakes or flooded backwaters. Eggs hatch in 20 hours and then measure only a little over 1/20 in (1 mm). At 1/2 in (13 mm) the body is marked with irregular dark bands, and it begins to assume features of the adult fish. The young feed on plankton and then freshwater prawns. At about 4 in (10 cm) they begin their predatory feeding on small fish and gradually increase the size of their prey as they grow larger; tiger fish and the cichlids form a substantial part of their diet.

In winter the Nile perch is found near the surface and in shallow waters, but in summer it keeps to deeper, cooler stretches.

It is an important local commercial species with excellent table qualities. It is also a recognised sport fish.

311 BARRAMUNDI (see note under *General*); GIANT PERCH   S, B, F
Lates calcarifer
Other common names: Palmer, cock-up.

Features: Large-bodied. Head depressed; sloping, sharply pointed snout; jaws have bands of slender, crowded (villiform) teeth; canine teeth absent. Dorsal fin deeply notched VII or VIII–I,10 to 12; tail fin rounded; anal fin III,9 or 10; exposed serrated bone above base of pectoral fin. Coloration: variable according to local population, dorsally usually olive green, greenish blue, or golden brown (young fish dorsally most frequently olive brown); flanks and belly silvery; fins grey or dark brown, paired fins are paler. Eyes bright pink which glow at night.
Size: Maximum up to 6 ft (1.80 m), 600 lb (270 kg); average sport fish 8 lb (3 1/2 kg).
Distribution: Indo-Pacific seas.
General: The barramundi, or giant perch, is a large primitive fish which inhabits freshwater rivers, brackish estuaries and inshore tropical and subtropical waters throughout its distribution. It is very closely related to the Nile perch (*L. niloticus*). The barramundi is able to survive for long drought periods in isolated rock pools along riverbeds which experience only infrequent seasonal flows. In coastal waters and estuaries very large specimens may frequently be seen lurking just below the

surface beneath jetties and wharfs, but they often prove very elusive fish to entice to a baited hook.

The name barramundi is an Australian aboriginal name. In some areas, particularly in its South China Sea distribution, it is known as the Dawson River salmon. The barramundi is one of the most exciting and prized sport fishes, and, when hooked, offers tremendous fight by using its great weight in attempts to break free. In the South China Sea, and elsewhere, it represents one of the most important commercial species, and the flesh of the saltwater fish is considered a local table delicacy.

15 GROUPERS, SEA BASSES, FLAGTAIL

312 WARSAW GROUPER S
Epinephelus nigritus
Other common name: Black jewfish.

Features: Very large, robust body. Broad head with small eyes; large mouth, lower jaw projecting. Dorsal fin X or XI,14 or 15; tail fin almost square-cut; anal fin III,9. Coloration: dorsally and flanks a uniform brown or bluish black sometimes with a few lighter spots; belly very slightly paler. Lateral line arched.
Size: Up to 80 in (200 cm), 400 lb (180 kg).
Distribution: Western Atlantic, from South Carolina, West Indies to Brazil. Also eastern Pacific.
General: One of the larger groupers. It frequents deeper water than most other grouper species. A good heavyweight sport and table fish.

313 NASSAU GROUPER S
Epinephelus striatus
Other common name: Hamlet.

Features: Large-bodied, compressed seabass. Large head and mouth, lower jaw projecting. Dorsal fin XI or XII,16 or 17; tail fin rounded; anal fin III,8. Coloration: very variable browns, greys, or greens; either plainly marked or with irregular vertical dark bands; a square-shaped black blotch on the upper surface of tail stalk. Lateral line arched. Distinct small black spots around eye.
Size: Average up to 24–36 in (60–90 cm), 10 lb (4 1/2 kg), maximum 48 in (120 cm), *c.* 55 lb (25 kg).
Distribution: Western Atlantic, from the Carolinas south to West Indies and Brazil. Related forms in Indo-Pacific seas.
General: A grouper which passes through at least 8 colour phases during its lifetime, ranging from uniformly dark to paler shadings, which involve stages including coloured bands and mottlings of various kinds, so that each individual fish may appear quite different. It is likely that colour changes have a connection with survival camouflage. Some fish are able to change colour very quickly – sometimes within a few minutes – giving them an almost chameleonlike ability to adapt to different sea-floor backgrounds, especially those in exotic coral-reef habitats.

A hard-fighting sport fish and an important commercial species. The flesh is of high quality, very firm, and lends itself to a wide range of fish cookery.

314 DUSKY PERCH S
Epinephelus guaza
Other common names: Giant rock cod, grouper, merou.

Features: Elongate, medium-large, robust body. Large head and jaws; thick lips; forehead slightly depressed above eyes; lower jaw projecting. Dorsal fin XI,13 to 16, tail fin rounded; anal fin III,8 or 9. Coloration: dorsally green brown or chocolate brown; flanks lighter; belly yellowish; dorsal area, flanks, and head have a lighter green mottling or freckling; on the flanks spots form vertical bands; dorsal fin has an orange margin; other fins dark with paler margins.
Size: Up to 55 in (140 cm), 80 lb (36 kg); average fish much smaller.
Distribution: Eastern Atlantic, from English Channel to South Africa; Mediterranean.
General: Usually a solitary fish found over broken, rocky ground and among reefs in a well-defined territory which it will fiercely defend against all intruders. A good sport and table fish.

315 RED GROUPER S
Epinephelus morio

Features: Stout, perchlike body. Large mouth, lower jaw heavier and projecting. Dorsal fin XI,16 or 17; tail fin concave; anal fin III,8 to 10. Dorsal fin notched between spines. Second dorsal fin spine longer than third. Coloration: variable with several colour phases, but usually dorsally and flanks olive-grey or olive-brown and reddish, paler on lower sides of head and jaws; dark orange spots on head; vertical fins same colour as flanks with white margins; pelvic fins dusky; older fish acquire a more reddish tint. Lateral line present. Small scales. No blotch on caudal peduncle.
Size: Up to 36 in (90 cm), 50 lb (23 kg).
Distribution: Western Atlantic coasts, ranging from Virginia to Rio de Janeiro; occasionally north and south of usual limits.
General: Often found in large numbers in smaller sizes, but larger fish not common in some areas. An important sport fish although not a strong fighter. The flesh has excellent table qualities.

316 QUEENSLAND GROUPER S
Epinephelus lanceolatus
Other common names: Rock cod, brindle bass, garrupa, giant sea perch.

Features: Very large and robust body. Large head and mouth; teeth in bands in both jaws and with caninelike teeth in front; lower jaw projecting. Dorsal fin XI,14 or 15; spines shorter than rays in larger individuals; tail fin rounded; anal fin III,8 to 10. Coloration: dorsally and flanks in adult fish generally dark brown to a dusky grey black; young fish have strong contrasting variegated patterns consisting of blotchings, spots, and bars; dorsal, tail, and anal fins are brownish yellow with black markings; pectoral and pelvic fins lemon yellow blotched with black. Lateral line scale count 58 to 67.
Size: Up to 12 ft (3.7 m) and over 800 lb (360 kg). In Australian waters up to 6 ft (1.8 m), 600 lb (270 kg). But fish 200–300 lb (90–135 kg) more common throughout its geo-

graphical range.
Distribution: Throughout central tropical Indo-Pacific region from Africa to northern Australia and along the length of the Great Barrier Reef south to northern New South Wales. The largest of the true bony fishes. In many areas it is considered a dangerous fish to man. There are numerous authenticated accounts of attacks on bathers and skin divers. A popular sport fish and keenly sought by rod-and-line fishermen and underwater spear fishermen. The smaller fish up to *c.* 30 lb (13 kg) are excellent table fish, but above this limit the flesh is coarse and rank.

317 TIGER GROUPER S
Mycteroperca tigris

Features: Medium-sized, elongate body. Large mouth with large canine teeth; lower jaw projecting. Dorsal fin XI, 16 or 17; tail fin slightly concave with individual membranes continuing beyond, forming "tags" (this feature also sometimes occurs with the dorsal and anal fins); anal fin III,10 to 12. Coloration: variable, but dorsally and flanks usually brownish or greenish white with regular bluish white reticulations over the entire body; some reticulations coalesce to form oblique vertical, pale bars on the dorsal area and on the upper flanks; head and flanks spotted; pectoral fin tips yellow or orange. Juveniles are a bright yellow with a longitudinal black band and diagonal bars showing obscurely along the dorsal area. Lateral line arched, and scale count 80 to 85.
Size: Average up to 30 in (75 cm); large fish 50 lb (22 kg).
Distribution: Western Atlantic, ranging the Carolinas, West Indies, to Brazil.
General: A grouper showing a preference for inshore waters. Valued as a high-class table fish.

318 SCAMP S
Mycteroperca phenax
Other common names: Bacalao, abadejo.

Features: The body is rather elongate with compressed, somewhat pointed head. Big mouth with the teeth placed in narrow belts and with few and rather weak canines. Small scales, long gill rakers. One dorsal fin with XI and 17 rays. The anal fin begins with 3 spines. The longer pectoral fins reach the tips of the short ventral fins. Coloration: back and upper sides grey to light reddish, lower sides and belly greyish with a pale reddish sheen. Most of the fins dusky to black; the tail fin has brown spots and the anal fin a white edge.
Size: About 2 ft (60 cm).
Distribution: West Indian seas and Florida.
General: The scamp is an important food fish especially in the West Indies; it is also an appreciated game fish.

319 MAHATA S
Epinephelus septemfasciatus
Other common name: True bass.

Features: Body much compressed, short and high. Big mouth, rather small eyes. One dorsal fin with a high spinous (11 spines) anterior part and a still higher posterior part with ca 15 soft rays. The tail

stalk is short and high; the tail fin is large with rounded corners and convex hind margin; the anal fin has three spines and a soft-rayed part similar to that of the dorsal fin; the pectoral and ventral fins are large and broad. Coloration: back and upper sides brown to grey with a violet sheen, lower sides, belly paler. Across the sides are 6–7 broad, dark bands which reach up on the dorsal fin; the other fins are dark to black.
Size: The mahata grows to a size of 1 1/4–2 ft (40–60 cm).
Distribution: Western Pacific; common in southern Japanese waters.
General: The species is found both in offshore waters and nearer to the coast. It is of value to the local commercial fisheries.

320 BLACK GROUPER s
Mycteroperca bonaci
Other common names: Marbled rockfish, bonaci acara, aguaji, rockfish.

Features: A medium-sized to large grouper with a moderately compressed body. Pelvic fins almost directly under the bases of the pectorals. Rear edge of tail may be straight, wavy, or slightly convex. Anterior and posterior nostrils about the same size. Dorsal fin XI, 16–18; anal fin III, 11–13; pectoral rays usually 17; gill rakers 15 including rudiments; scale count 98 to 120. Coloration: Rectangular dark patches on back and sides are divided by a reticular pattern of pale lines and bars, and number 8 to 9 generally vertical bars from nose to tail. A dark bar across the nose forward of the eyes.
Size: Mature fish average more than 3 ft (90 cm) and 45 lb (20 kg).
Distribution: Tropical western Atlantic, Caribbean, Bahamas and West Indies.
General: Adult fish prefer deep water to at least 110 fathoms (200 m), but smaller fish are often found in shallower water. Excellent eating and widely sought by sport and commercial fishermen who take the fish with bait or deep-trolled lures.

321 YELLOWMOUTH GROUPER s
Mycteroperca interstitialis
Other common name: Salmon rockfish (Bermuda).

Features: Elongate body. Lower jaw projecting. Dorsal fin XI, 16 to 18; tail fin concave; anal fin III, 11 or 12. Coloration: dorsally light brownish grey; flanks and belly paler; upper flanks covered with close-set, small brown spots; yellow around mouth; some individual fish nearly overall uniform brown; membrane of spiny dorsal fin yellowish.
Size: Average range 4 1/2–6 3/4 lb (2–3 kg).
Distribution: Western Atlantic tropical seas.
General: A reef species found occasionally in Bermuda and the Bahamas. In the West Indies it has some commercial importance due to its good table qualities.

322 YELLOWFIN GROUPER s
Mycteroperca venenosus
Other common names: red rockfish, monkey rockfish.

Features: Medium-sized, laterally compressed body. Dorsal fin XI, 15 or 16; tail fin slightly concave; anal fin III, 11 or 12. Coloration: variable, but dorsally and flanks usually olive green to greyish (but there is also a red form which is dorsally bright scarlet; flanks and head paling to grey); flanks reticulated with red and black, with markings arranged longitudinally; spots on lower flanks reddish, and the same colour is repeated on the upper and lower lobes of the tail fin; pectoral fins with yellow and orange colours; vertical fins with a dark edge; spiny dorsal membrane tips yellow. Lateral line arched, and scale count 120 to 125.
Size: Average range 8–15 lb (3 1/2–7 kg).
Distribution: Western Atlantic, from North Carolina to South America.
General: The yellowfin grouper is an important sport fish and a common species around coral reefs. Good eating, but sometimes said to be poisonous in parts of the West Indies.

323 RED HIND s
Epinephelus guttatus
Other common name: Hind.

Features: Small to medium-sized, compressed body. Large head and mouth; lower jaw projecting. Dorsal fin XI, 15 or 16; tail fin square-cut or slightly rounded; anal fin III, 8. Coloration: variable, but usually dorsally and flanks pale yellowish green or reddish; entire body covered with red spots with dorsal spots darker; flanks sometimes have ill-defined, vertical, olive bands slanting backward; spiny dorsal has a yellowish tint; soft dorsal, anal, and tail fins broadly edged with black or blue black. Lateral line arched. No dark saddles on back.
Size: Up to 18 in (45 cm), maximum 24 in (60 cm).
Distribution: Western Atlantic, Florida, West Indies to Brazil. Related forms in Indo-Pacific seas.
General: A very common species in the West Indies. An excellent table fish. Several related rock-cod forms in Indo-Pacific seas.

324 GAG s
Mycteroperca microlepis
Other common name: Aguaji.

Features: The body is comparatively elongate, compressed. The head is long and pointed. Big mouth, the teeth are small except for 2 larger canines in each jaw. Few gill rakers; the scales are only minute. One dorsal fin, XI and 16–19 rays. The very long anal fin has anteriorly 3 spines. Coloration: Very variable individually and according to the habitat. Back and upper sides brown to grey, lower sides and belly much lighter. Dorsal fin dark olive to blackish; the tail fin is black with a bluish sheen; the pectorals olive, and the ventrals black with whitish spots.
Size: 2–3 ft (60–90 cm), weight up to 50 lb (20–23 kg).
Distribution: Southern part of western Atlantic, north to North Carolina.
General: The gag has its home in shallow, coastal waters and on banks and reefs.

325 ROCK COD s
Epinephelus tauvinus
Other common names: Slimy cod, greasy cod, bullnosed rock cod, estuary rock cod.

Features: Large, perchlike body, robust, oblong, moderately compressed. Large mouth, lower jaw projecting; villiform and canine teeth. Dorsal fin XI, 15 or 16; tail fin rounded; anal fin III, 8. Coloration: olive green with scattered orange red or brown spots and 4 to 6 darker bandlike blotches over the dorsal area; with age the colour becomes uniform brown, and the spots indistinct. Lateral line slightly arched, and scale count 100 to 120. The skin is thick and slimy.
Size: Up to 85 in (215 cm), 500 lb (225 kg).
Distribution: Indo-Pacific warmer seas.
General: One of the larger rock cods found around coral reefs and in estuaries, a carnivorous and voracious species. Owing to its great size it is considered by some to be potentially dangerous to man, and the experience of skin divers tends to support this. As a sport fish it is rather sluggish, and the flesh of the larger ones is coarse, but it ranks among important food fish in several tropical Indo-Pacific areas.

326 ROCK HIND s
Epinephelus adscensionis
Other common name: Ascension Island rock cod.

Features: Medium-sized, robust body. Large head and jaws; lower jaw projecting. Dorsal fin XI, 16 or 17; tail fin rounded; anal fin III, 7 or 8. Coloration: variable, but often dorsally and flanks olive brown with red or orange spots and large, paler irregular ones intermixed; vertical fin bases spotted like rest of fish; dark or black margins on soft dorsal, anal, and tail fins. Lateral line weakly developed and arched.
Size: Average up to 18 in (45 cm), 4 1/5–5 lb (2–2 1/2 kg), maximum 24 in (60 cm), 10 lb (4 1/2 kg).
Distribution: Atlantic, from Florida, West Indies to Brazil, South Africa; Indo-Pacific seas.
General: Found in offshore waters and common around fringing shoreline coral reefs. A valued sport and commercial species and marketed in the West Indies.

327 CABRILLA s
Paralabrax clathratus
Other common names: Kelp bass, sand bass, rock bass, Johnny verde, calico bass.

Features: Member of a large group of basses inhabiting the eastern Pacific, preferring rocks, sand beaches, and kelp beds close to shore. Fairly straight margin on the tail. The pectorals have rounded edges and are large. A deep notch separating the first and second dorsal fins helps to differentiate this fish from the sand bass, *P. nebulifer*, and the spotted bass, *P. maculatofasciatus*. Roof of the mouth has teeth. Space between the eyes has few scales. Large eye and pointed snout. First dorsal fin, X (first two are short, next two are quite long); second dorsal, 13–15. Anal fin III, 7. Coloration: Greenish or brownish grey with blotches of darker colour mottling the back and upper sides. Lower sides and belly are yellowish silver.

Fins have a yellow flush.
Size: Grows to 20 in (50 cm), 11 lb (5 kg), but bulk of the specimens are considerably smaller.
Distribution: Central Californian coast southward to tip of Lower California.
General: Important food fish sought both by sport and commercial fishermen. Responds best to bait fished on bottom.

328 MARBLED GROUPER s
Dermatolepis inermis

Features: Short and deep, much compressed body. The contour of the back elevated. Head with short, little pointed snout; small eyes; small mouth with weak teeth, hardly any of them canine-like. The edge of the preoperculum of the gill cover is only weakly serrate. Slender gill rakers. Small scales. Dorsal fin with XI, 19 rays; long tail fin with rounded hind margin. Anal fin very high with 3 spines anteriorly; long pectoral fins, reaching the anal fin. Coloration: back and upper sides brown with darker patches, lower sides and belly lighter. Head, body, and fins with many small, whitish spots.
Size: About 1 ft (30–32 cm).
Distribution: West Indian seas.
General: This grouper does not appear to be abundant anywhere. It prefers shallower water and a rocky bottom.

329 JEWFISH s
Epinephelus itajara
Other common name: Spotted jewfish.

Features: Very heavy appearance. Broad head slightly depressed between eyes; very large underslung mouth. Dorsal fin XI, 15 or 16 (first spiny section has a very low, even profile); tail fin strongly rounded; anal fin III, 8. Coloration: variable, but usually dorsally and flanks uniform black or brown paling to a creamy white or greenish shade; flanks have c. 4 or 5 dark broken oblique crossbands; head, body, and fins with many black spots. Lateral line arched, and scale count 95 to 135.
Size: Up to 8 ft (2.4 m), 700 lb (315 kg); but average fish considerably smaller. The jewfish is the largest of the groupers.
Distribution: Western Atlantic, tropical and subtropical coastal waters, ranging Florida, West Indies, South America, Indo-Pacific.
General: The common name "jewfish" is a name loosely applied to several unrelated fish with worldwide distributions. A powerful bottom-dwelling fighter and an excellent food fish.

330 CALIFORNIA BLACK SEA BASS s
Stereolepis gigas
Other common names: California jewfish, giant bass.

Features: Stout body with high, short head and blunt snout. The eyes are very small. The first dorsal fin is exceedingly low with 11 spines, the second is high with 10 soft rays. Tail fin slightly concave; short anal fin and small pectoral and ventral fins. Coloration: blackish and brown on back and upper sides, lower sides and belly lighter; the young have many black spots on the back, upper sides, and dorsal fins.

Size: Maximum well over 6–7 ft (180–200 cm) with a weight of 500–600 pounds (220–260 kg).
Distribution: Northeast Pacific, off the coasts of California from San Diego to Point Conception.
General: Lives in coastal waters, where it prefers the more vegetation-rich belts (among the kelp). It is only of little commercial importance, but is often caught in the sport fishery with hook and line and live bait.

331 WHITE BASS F
Morone chrysops
Other common names: Silver bass, white lake bass, striped lake bass, bar blanc, barfish, streaks, sand bass.

Features: Deep, laterally compressed body. Moderate mouth with numerous small teeth; lower jaw slightly projecting. Dorsal fins IX–14 (with spiny rays distinctly separated from soft rays which serve to distinguish it from the sunfishes and crappies); tail fin forked; anal fin III,8 to 12. Coloration: dorsally dark green or grey; flanks paling to silvery with lower flanks golden tinted and usually 7 horizontal dark stripes; belly white. Lateral line scale count 55 to 65.
Size: Average up to 1 lb (1/2 kg); larger fish 3 lb (1 1/2 kg).
Distribution: North America, ranging throughout much of the area with a preference for cold-water lakes and rivers. Introduced elsewhere.
General: A schooling species, and the schools generally consist of fish of equal size. Spawning occurs in spring in shallow water; hatching occurs a few days later. The young fish grow rapidly, attaining a length of 7–9 in (18–23 cm) in their first year. Food consists chiefly of minnows, but plankton, aquatic insects, and crayfish are also eaten in large numbers. An important commercial species, and in the United States in particular, it is a very popular sport fish, and is caught in very large numbers during the period of the spawning runs, and while feeding at the surface in school.

332 STRIPED BASS S, B, F
(anadromous)
Morone saxatilis
Other common names: Striper, rockfish, squid hound.

Features: Stout, slightly compressed, elongate body. Blunt-pointed head; lower jaw projects slightly. Two dorsal fins VIII to X–10 to 13; tail fin slightly forked; anal fin III,7 to 13. Coloration: dorsally olive green to dark blue or black; flanks paling to silver and then white on belly, occasionally flanks have brassy hues; flanks have 7 or 8 (sometimes more) characteristic and prominent horizontal, dark stripes following the line of the scale contours, but the stripes do not extend onto the head. Lateral line visible. Large scales with toothed margins.
Size: Maximum up to 6 ft (1.80 m), 125 lb (56 kg), but average range 8–15 lb (3 1/2–6 3/4 kg).
Distribution: North American Atlantic coasts, from St. Lawrence River south to northern Florida; Gulf of Mexico region of western Florida, Alabama, Mississippi, and Louisiana. Introduced on the Pacific coast

in 1879–82 and has a range extending from central California to southern Oregon. Now established in freshwater lake and river systems in at least 30 of the various states of the United States.
General: The striped bass is a coastal species. Its anadromous characteristics have been studied in great detail. Tagging experiments in the United States have shown that some striped bass move north and east from Chesapeake Bay to the New England states in spring and early summer. In autumn a reverse movement is observed.

In Canada the large striped bass migrates upriver in early June to deposit its eggs. In the United States distribution, spawning takes place in the late April–May period. The eggs have slight negative buoyancy and must be laid in constantly moving water. Hatching occurs in 2–3 days. It is a voracious feeder, and devours a wide variety of small fish and invertebrates.

The striped bass is sometimes a commercial species. In California it is legally a game fish. It is much sought after throughout its distribution and is a very high quality table fish.

333 WHITE PERCH F, B, S
Morone americana
Other common names: Silver perch, sea perch, perch, bass, perche blanche.

Features: Short, deep, laterally compressed body with depressed forehead (similar to white bass). Moderate mouth with numerous small, sharp teeth; jaws of equal length. Dorsal fins deeply notched IX–12 (the thin notched membrane readily distinguishes it from the white bass (*M. chrysops*)); tail fin concave; anal fin III,8 to 10. Coloration: dorsally olivaceous or dark brown; flanks silvery or silvery green; belly silvery white; freshwater, landlocked populations are usually quite dark and much less silvery on the flanks. Lateral line distinct with scale count 50 to 55. Scales are large.
Size: Average up to 10 in (25 cm), 1 lb (1/2 kg), maximum *c.* 20 in (50 cm), 4 3/4 lb (2 1/4 kg); stunted populations predominate in overcrowded, freshwater lakes.
Distribution: In fresh and salt water along the Atlantic coasts of North America, ranging parts of Great Lakes region, the St. Lawrence River, and south to South Carolina.
General: A species equally at home in both fresh and brackish water, but spawning occurs in fresh water during the spring and summer. Although an anadromous species, it is a landlocked, freshwater species in some areas, as for example the Maritime Provinces. Its food is mainly insects and fish, including yellow perch, smelt, elvers, and its own young. A very popular sport and commercial fish. The flesh is sweet tasting.

334 YELLOW BASS F
Morone mississippiensis
Other common names: Gold bass, streaker, black-striped bass, barfish, brassy bass.

Features: Front and rear dorsals not separated but joined by a narrow membrane. No teeth on the base of the tongue. Moderately compressed body, forked tail. Length of the upper and lower jaw approximately

even. The eye is moderately large; the body fairly deep as compared to the length, the arch to the snout from the dorsal distinct. There are 51 to 55 scales, on the lateral line. Dorsal fin, about IX, with I, 9 to 11 on the second dorsal which is really attached. Anal III, about 10. Coloration: a brassy yellow or dark olive green on the upper sides with silvery hues or a yellow gold shading to white below on the belly. Six to seven prominent horizontal, dark bars run along the sides, three of which are above the lateral line. These black stripes are distinct field characteristics.
Size: May reach more than 12 in (30 cm); 2.2 lb (1 kg) but commonly smaller.
Distribution: Lower Mississippi Valley of the United States north to Ohio, Iowa, Missouri.
General: Extremely edible, scrappy panfish pursued by anglers. Found in schools. Likes shallow gravel and/or rocky reefs.

335 BASS (EUROPEAN) S, B
Morone labrax

Features: Long, elongate shape, laterally compressed. Pointed head, lower jaw slightly projecting. Front gill cover serrated and spined on lower edge; main gill cover has two spines. Two dorsal fins VIII or IX–I,12 or 13; tail fin forked; anal fin III,10 or 11. Coloration: dorsally bluish grey or greenish olive; flanks silvery; belly white; diffuse brown spot on gill cover; the eye has a golden circle around the pupil. Head covered with scales.
Size: Maximum up to 3 ft 4 in (1 m), average 16–31 in (40–80 cm); small school bass 3–4 lb (1 1/2–1 3/4 kg).
Distribution: Atlantic; North Sea; Baltic; English Channel; Mediterranean. Found in coastal regions, and a preference for warmer waters.
General: A slow-growing fish; young fish are very gregarious, forming large schools. Although the bass is an extremely spiny fish and requires careful handling, the spines are *not* poisonous. The bass is a highly predatory species and feeds on fish of all kinds, including fish up to the size of medium-sized mackerel. Due to its hard fighting qualities and its excellence as a table fish, it represents one of the finest European marine sport fishes.

336 SEA BASS S
Centropristis striatus
Other common names: Common sea bass, black sea bass, humpback.

Features: Small, but robust, compressed body. Lower jaw slightly projecting. Dorsal fin X,11; tail fin concave/rounded, with upper ray characteristically lengthened in larger fish; anal fin III,7. Coloration: overall dusky brown or black with obscure mottling; flanks with paler longitudinal streaks along scale rows; dorsal fin with several elongate, whitish spots forming oblique light stripes; all other fins dusky mottled; a large blackish spot on the last dorsal spine. Juveniles have a black longitudinal band which later breaks up to form dark cross shades. Lateral line scale count 50 to 60.
Size: Up to 1 ft 6 in (45 cm); large fish average 3–8 lb (1–3.5 kg).

Distribution: Western Atlantic, ranging Massachusetts to the Gulf of Mexico. Most abundant between Connecticut and North Carolina.
General: A species found in shallow and deeper offshore waters and sometimes in estuaries. A very popular local angling fish caught in large numbers offshore from anchored boats. The flesh is of good table quality.

337 WRECKFISH S
Polyprion americanus
Other common names: Atlantic wreckfish, chern, cernier, stonebass, bafaro.

Features: Robust, heavily built, and deep compressed body. Large, pointed head with depressed forehead above eye; also a bony protuberance above eye; mouth large; lower jaw projects markedly; teeth small, sharp, and conical; spines on gill covers. Dorsal fin XI,11 or 12; tail fin heavy, rounded or nearly square-cut; anal fin III,8 or 9. Coloration: dorsally dark brown or greyish; flanks paler; belly yellowish; tail fin edged with white. Young fish have a general mottled appearance. Lateral line well marked, and scale count *c.* 90. Scales small and rough.
Size: Up to 6 ft 8 in (2 m), 220 lb (100 kg).
Distribution: Atlantic, both sides, but more abundant in eastern part; Mediterranean.
General: A deepwater grouper but often encountered in shallower water around sunken wreckage hence its common name. May be either a solitary or schooling species. Usually found between 330–650 ft (100–200 m) but also sometimes up to 3,300 ft (1,000 m). A heavyweight sport fish. An excellent table fish and a commercial species in some locales.

338 HAPUKA S
Polyprion oxygeneious

Features: Robust, elongate body. Large head and mouth with small, pointed teeth, some on tongue; lower jaw larger and projecting. Each gill cover has a short spine. Dorsal fin XI or XII,11 or 12; tail fin square-cut; anal fin III,8–10. Coloration: dorsally drab dark grey; flanks a paler grey; belly silvery white. Lateral line slightly arched.
Size: Up to 55 lb (25 kg).
Distribution: Indo-Pacific temperate seas.
General: A large grouper found round headlands and rocky localities and ranges from shallow to deep water. A voracious species. Its main diet appears to be pilchard, herring, and small flatfishes. An important commercial trawl species and an excellent sport and table fish.

339 CONEY S
Epinephelus fulvus

Features: A moderately compressed sea bass with a small, elongate body. Lower jaw strongly projecting. Dorsal fin IX,15 to 16; tail fin slightly rounded; anal fin III,8 or 9. Coloration: variable, but dorsally and flanks generally yellow, red, orange brown, or cream as a background; dorsal area, flanks, and head covered with small, black, blue, or white spots; two black spots on upper part of tail stalk; two black spots on

tip of lower jaw. Lateral line scale count 89 to 110.
Size: Maximum 16 in (40 cm), 3 1/3 lb (1 1/2 kg).
Distribution: Western Atlantic tropical and subtropical seas, ranging Florida, Bermuda, West Indies, Brazil.
General: A common inshore grouper species found to depths c. 500 ft (150 m). A rather shy sport fish valuable as a commercial table fish in the West Indies.

340 GOLDEN PERCH F

Plectroplites ambiguus

Other common names: Murray perch, perch, yellowbelly, freshwater bream, callop.

Features: Elongate, perchlike. Head characteristically very depressed above the eye, particularly in large fish; lower jaw projecting; teeth very well developed on roof of mouth. Dorsal fin X,10 or 11; tail fin rounded; anal fin III,7 to 9. Coloration: dorsally usually golden yellow to olive green but occasionally bronze, creamy white, or almost black (depending on water habitat); flanks paler; paired fins are yellowish, the others duskier. Lateral line scale count 52 to 63. Scales are small.
Size: Up to about 30 in (75 cm), 60 lb (27 kg); average fish c. 6 lb (2 3/4 kg).
Distribution: Australia, ranging the Murray River system, Queensland, New South Wales, Victoria to South and Central Australia. Introduced into Western Australia and cultivated in dams in Queensland.
General: After the Murray cod, it is the most important Australian freshwater fish, maturing when 2–3 years old, females at c. 11 in (28 cm) males 9 in (23 cm). *P. ambiguus* is a carnivorous species, and it spends much time lying in wait in shady or weedy spots to grab smaller fish as they swim by. Spawning occurs during time of river flooding, and when the temperature exceeds 23.5°C. Between a half million to a million eggs are shed by the female. Like the Murray cod, *P. ambiguus* has disappeared from several areas due to flood control schemes which destroy their natural breeding environment. Apart from their sport-fish interest they are exploited commercially, and they are one of the most delicious table fish of the local freshwater species.

341 HARLEQUIN BASS S

Serranus tigrinus

Features: Body compressed, rather high. Large head with a somewhat pointed snout. Lower jaw projecting beyond upper. Big eyes. The gill cover has several short thorns. Gill rakers short and rather few. Small scales. One dorsal fin, its spinous part is as long as the soft-rayed one, but considerably lower. The tail fin is a little concave; the anal fin is high, it begins with two spiny rays. The pectoral fins are very large, rounded, below them the ventral fins are inserted, they are fairly long and pointed. Coloration: the basic colour is yellow all over: the head, body, and fins have round, black spots and larger indistinct, blackish patches.
Size: About 4 in (10–12 cm).

Distribution: Western warmer Atlantic; Bermudas, Bahamas, Florida to Yucatan.
General: The species prefers shallow water, 1–13 fathoms (2–25 m), it occurs rarely as deep as 20 fathoms (35 m); it is mostly found in vegetation belts, on coral reefs and rocks. The food is mainly crustaceans.

342 ESTUARY PERCH   F, B

Percalates colonorum

Other common name: Bass (Australia).

Features: Elongate, perchlike. Forehead depressed; gill cover serrated. Dorsal fin VIII,I,8 to 11; tail fin forked; anal fin III,7 to 9. Coloration: dorsally olive greenish; flanks paler with a silvery sheen; belly yellowish grey; spiny dorsal fin grey; other fins, except pectorals, green; pectorals and lips sometimes dull orange. Lateral line scale count 48 to 55.
Size: Up to 24 in (60 cm), 11 lb (5 kg); but average fish much smaller.
Distribution: Australasia, ranging southern and eastern Australia from south Queensland to Tasmania. Introduced into western Australia and Fiji.
General: One of Australia's best indigenous sport fishes. Nowadays, because of its diminishing numbers, it cannot be sold commercially. It ranges from estuary mouths to upper reaches, being able to survive in total salt water or pure fresh. As a freshwater table fish it has few peers and was a staple food fish with the early Australian settlers.

343 MURRAY COD   F

Maccullochella peeli

Features: Large, elongate, broad and deepbodied. Large head and mouth; lower jaw larger and projecting. Dorsal fin X,14 or 15; tail fin rounded; anal fin II,19. Coloration: variable, but dorsally and flanks generally greenish brown, with numerous dark green spots; belly whitish. There is a blue to white variant sometimes known locally as the trout cod.
Size: Up to 6 ft (180 cm), 180 lb (80 kg), maximum over 200 lb (90 kg).
Distribution: Australia. Native to the Murray-Darling River system of eastern Australia. Also widespread in lesser tributaries, and has spread to waters in Victoria and South Australia.
General: The fish is actually a species of perch and is the largest and best known sport and commercial freshwater fish in Australia. Food consists of shrimps, mussels, crayfish, frogs, small land creatures, and the western carp gudgeon. This latter is probably the most important source. As a table fish the Murray cod is rated excellent.

344 LUNAR-TAILED   ROCK COD S

Variola louti

Features: Stout, compressed body. Large head with big mouth and strong teeth. Very high tail stalk. One long dorsal fin, the anterior spiny part longer, but lower than the posterior soft-rayed part, in the latter the last rays are the highest; the tail fin is large with a concave, semilunar, hind margin, its two lobes are curved and pointed. Anal fin with two spines, of its soft rays the anterior ones are the highest. Pec-

toral fin broad, rounded, ventral fins long. Coloration: the basic colour is all over red with many smaller whitish spots; the hind margins of the dorsal and anal fins are yellow; the tail fin is blue with a yellow hind margin; pectoral fins red with yellow margin, ventral fins bluish red.
Size: About 30 in (75 cm).
Distribution: Indo-Pacific region.
General: Lives in shallower water on a rocky bottom and among reefs.

345 ROCK FLAGTAIL   B, F, S

Kuhlia rupestris

Other common names: Perch (Tongaland), flagtail, flagfish.

Features: Rather compressed, fairly elongate body with moderate ctenoid scales. Fine teeth arranged in bands on palate and jaws in a moderate-sized mouth. A deep notch between dorsal fins. Fin spines quite strong. Bears resemblance to the sunfishes of North American fresh water. Head depth less than three times body length. Dorsal fin, X, 11; anal fin, III, 9–10. Lateral line scale count 40–43 with 5 rows above and 9 below at the shoulder. Gill rakers number 17–19. Coloration: Silvery, with scales outlined in strong black, but the scale outlines blend into the silver background. Blackish tail with pale yellow trailing edge. Pelvic fins white, anal fin pale yellow. In fresh water most scales have a dusky-coloured spot.
Size: Attains 18 in (45 cm), 2–3 lb (.9–1.3 kg), but most specimens smaller.
Distribution: Throughout central tropical Indo-Pacific, mainly in fresh to brackish coastal waters. Found from Durban northward in South Africa. Reported from fresh water streams in Queensland, Australia.
General: A good food and sporting fish with commercial value linked to availability. Considered gourmet food in some areas.

346 PACIFIC FLAGTAIL S

Kuhlia taeniura

Other common names: Flagfish, ginyugoi.

Features: The much compressed body is elongate, elliptical. The head is high and short with large eyes and short snout. The lower jaw is the longer; small teeth. Lateral line gently curved below first dorsal fin. Scale count 50–53. scales are also present on head below eyes. One dorsal fin IX, 10; anal fin III, 10–11; tail fin concave; pectoral and ventral fins each with one spine. Coloration: back and upper sides brilliant blue, lower sides and belly whitish and silvery; the tail fin has several dark bands.
Size: Maximum length 6–8 in (15–20 cm).
Distribution: Western and central tropical Pacific, Eastindian Seas, east to Hawaii north to Japan.
General: This tropical and sub tropical fish occurs mainly in offshore waters, but can also – especially the young individuals – be common in coastal areas, even in the tidal zone. Where the species is numerous, e.g. around Samoa and Hawaii Islands, it can be – in spite of its small size – of some importance to the local fisheries.

347 COMBER S

Serranus cabrilla

Features: A rather long, elongate, perchlike body. Depressed forehead. Two spines on gill cover. Dorsal fin IX or X,13 to 15; tail fin slightly concave; anal fin III,7 or 8. Coloration: highly variable according to age, season, and habitat, but often reddish yellow to reddish with 7–9 vertical red brown or darker bands, 2–3 horizontal, bluish or bluish green stripes on flanks and head, plus some yellowish stripes; pelvic fin lighter. Deepwater fish have a redder colouration. Lateral line scale count c. 80 to 90.
Size: Average range 6–10 in (15–25 cm), maximum c. 16 in (40 cm).
Distribution: Eastern North Atlantic, ranging north to English Channel; Mediterranean; Red Sea. Related forms in Indo-Pacific seas and Western Atlantic.
General: Usually found on stony bottoms from below c. 70 ft (20 m) ranging into very deep water. A true hermaphrodite species provided with male and female organs from birth. Although an excellent table fish, it is generally of no importance to sport fishermen, but is frequently caught on baits intended for other fish.

348 EASTERN PIKE-PERCH F, B
Stizostedion volgense

Other common names: Pikeperch, sandre (France), snoekbaars (Netherlands), zander (Germany), sandart (Denmark), gös (Sweden).

Features: Pike-like form with elongated head, long body, pointed snout, and large jaws. Upper jaw extends back to or behind the eye. Large, pointed teeth in jaws and a row of curved teeth on either side of the palate. Small, firmly-attached scales that are also present on the gill covers. Lateral line scale count, 80–95. First dorsal fin, XII-XVII. Second dorsal fin, I-II, 19–24. Anal fin, II-III, 11–12. Coloration: Greenish-brown to dark grey on back and sides, shading to white underneath. Young fish bear several dark body bars that fade on maturity. Dorsal fins contain lines of dark spots on the membranes, and dark spots mark the tail.
Size: Up to 44 in (110 cm) and 22 lb (10 kg), but averages around 24 in (60 cm), 6 1/2 lb (3 kg).
Distribution: Rivers and lakes of the Caspian basin and north of the Black Sea, central Europe.
General: Voraciously carnivorous, excellent food value and widely exploited in its range. Some local interest by anglers.

349 ZANDER F
Stizostedion lucioperca

Other common name: European pike perch.

Features: Slender body. Pointed snout, and jaws of about equal length; in large fish the upper jawbone extends well beyond the centre of the eye. Two dorsal fins XIII to XV–I to II,19 to 24; tail fin forked, anal fin II to III,11 or 12. Coloration: dorsally slaty blue or greenish brown; flanks above lateral line marked with vertical bands or stripes similar to perch but sometimes absent in adult fish; belly white or silvery; dorsal and tail fin with rows of black spots. Lateral line scale count 80 to 95. Scales are small and firm.
Size: Average 2–4 1/2 lb (1–2 kg), maximum 48 in (120 cm), 26 lb (12 kg).
Distribution: Native to Eastern Europe, including U.S.S.R., Germany, Sweden, and Finland. Has also been introduced into several other European locales.

General: Found in lakes with well-oxygenated, warm rather than cold water, and in lower reaches of rivers. Spawning occurs in April–June (but earlier in southern distributions) on a sandy or stony bottom. Males mature at 2–4 years at a length of *c.* 14 in (35 cm). Females grow faster, but mature at 3–5 years, *c.* 16 in (40 cm). Young fish live in schools and soon develop the predatory habits of older fish. Owing to their predatory habits, they are not a welcome species in some waters. However, they are excellent sport fish, a valuable commercial species, and are highly prized as a table fish.

350 YELLOW PERCH F
Perca flavescens

Other common names: Perch, lake perch, American perch, ringed perch, raccoon perch, river perch, red perch, striped perch, yellow red, redfin, perchaude.

Features: Deep-bodied, slightly humpbacked and laterally compressed. Concave profile above eyes. Numerous fine teeth. Dorsal fins XIII to XV–II,13 to 15, tail fin slightly forked; anal fin II,7 or 8. Coloration: dorsally green or yellow; flanks paler golden yellow and decorated with 6 to 8 broad, vertical bars which extend to the belly; belly white or silvery white; membrane between spines of first dorsal fin is dark; anal and pelvic fins pale or bright orange; pectoral fins light. Slightly arched lateral line, and scale count 74 to 88.
Size: Average up to 10 in (25 cm), 1 lb (1/2 kg); occasional larger fish up to *c.* 3 lb (1 1/2 kg).
Distribution: North America, throughout much of the area with a preference for cold-water lakes and rivers, but it is essentially a lake fish.
General: It is usually found in schools at depths 20–30 ft (6–9 m). Food consists of plankton, aquatic insects and fishes (small minnows). Spawning occurs April–May, and eggs, in ropelike strands, hatch three weeks later. In larger lakes it forms a principal food for many important game fishes and plays a key role in the food web. Yellow perch is an important commercial species particularly in the Great Lakes. It is easily caught and one of the most popular of smaller sport panfishes. As a table fish it is much esteemed.

351 PERCH (EUROPEAN) F, B
Perca fluviatilis

Features: A slightly humpbacked, laterally compressed body. Large mouth. Two dorsal fins XIII to XVII–I or II,13 to 16; tail fin slightly forked; anal fin II,8 to 10. Coloration: dorsally dark olive; flanks yellowish white and decorated with 5 or 6 vertical, broad, black stripes or bars (but development of this latter feature is very dependent on locale and in some areas may be absent); belly white or silvery white; black spot on rear part of first spiny dorsal; pectoral and anal fins and lower tail fin reddish. Slightly arched lateral line. Lateral line scale count 58 to 68.
Size: Average matured fish *c.* 10 in (25 cm), 1 lb (1/2 kg); large fish maximum 20 in (50 cm), 8 lb (3 1/2 kg).
Distribution: Much of Europe; northern

Asia; northeastern America where it is represented by the related species *P. flavescens* yellow perch (see above).)
General: The perch is the prototype of many perchlike fishes and among the largest order of fishes, the Perciformes.

Found in lakes, ponds, rivers, canals, and brackish lagoon waters among weed beds, preferring clean gravel bottoms and slow-moving water. Generally a sedentary fish living in schools which contain an assortment of sizes and ages.

Spawning occurs March–May, and the sticky eggs are laid in long ribbons, amid dense vegetation, including fallen trees or branches. Hatching occurs after 2–3 weeks. After exhausting the food of the yolk sac, the young graduate to plankton. Males mature at 2–3 years, females usually 4–6 years. Adult food includes many small fish, and perch may sometimes be cannibalistic.

Apart from its value as a sport fish, it is an important commercial species in many European countries. A tasty table fish.

352 WALLEYE F
Stizostedion vitreum

Other common names: Yellow walleye, pike perch, yellow pickerel, yellow pike perch, walleyed pike, glass-eye, white-eye, yellow pike.

Features: Elongate, robust body. Strong, sharp, and conspicuous teeth; large eyes. Dorsal fins XII to XVI–19 to 21; tail fin forked; anal fin II,11 to 14. Coloration: dorsally olive or dark brown; flanks paler; over the entire body and head there are numerous flecks or spots of gold; first dorsal fin is dark smoky with a distinctive black blotch between the second and third spines; lower lobe of the tail fin has a creamy white margin; pelvic fins creamy white.
Size: Average up to 3 lb (1 1/2 kg); large fish up to 5 lb (2 1/4 kg), maximum over 23 lb (10 kg), 40 in (100 cm).
Distribution: Temperate regions of North America.
General: *S. vitreum* is a shallow-water schooling fish inhabiting lakes and large rivers. Spawning occurs in spring over a hard or gravelly bottom shortly after the ice break-up. During hot summers it may seek deeper, cooler water. Food consists mainly of other fishes such as yellow perch, minnows, and suckers, and in deep water, ciscoes.

The walleye pike perch is an important sport and commercial species throughout its distribution. Its flesh is white and tasty, and locally the walleye is a popular restaurant fish.

353 SAUGER F
Stizostedion canadense

Other common names: Sand pike, ground pike, rattlesnake pike, pike perch, pickering, pickerel, jack, horsefish, eastern sauger, dore noir.

Features: Slender, almost cylindrical body. Head and mouth are large; jaws have many strong, sharp teeth. Dorsal fins XI to XV–I,17 to 19; tail fin forked; anal fin II,11 or 12. Coloration: dorsally brown or grey; flanks usually yellow and overlaid with dark, irregularly distributed brown patches or blotches; pelvic and anal fins lightly

sprinkled with dark speckles, but fins tend toward milky white; tail fin shows dark brown vertical bars (but has no lighter lower lobe like that of the walleye). Although the sauger resembles the yellow walleye, it may be distinguished from it by the presence of 2–3 rows of distinct black spots on the membrane of the spiny dorsal fin; no black blotch at end of spiny dorsal fin; in addition the cheek of the sauger is covered with rough scales.
Size: Average up to 1 lb (1/2 kg), maximum seldom above 2 1/4 lb (1 kg).
Distribution: Temperate regions of North America.

354 BLUE PIKE F
Stizostedion vitreum glaucum

Other common names: Blue pickerel, blue walleye, blue pike perch.

Features: In general physical appearance and characteristics much like the walleye (see above). Coloration: dorsally slate blue; flanks paler; pelvic fins are white and contrast with the cream-coloured pelvic fins of the yellow walleye. *Note:* Bluish-coloured yellow walleyes are occasionally found in some lakes, but they are varieties of *S. vitreum* and not *S. vitreum glaucum*.
Size: Average 1/2–1 lb (1/4–1/2 kg), at maturity 12–13 in (30–33 cm).
Distribution: Lake Erie only, now nearly extinct due to sea lampreys, pollution, overfishing.
General: Similar in habit to the yellow walleye except that spawning occurs in May. An excellent sport and table fish.

355 RUFFE F
Gymnocephalus cernua

Features: Much like a small perch with a very concave forehead, but can immediately be separately distinguished by its single continuous dorsal fin, whereas the perch has deeply notched, spaced dorsal fins. Dorsal fin XII to XVI,11 to 15; tail fin concave; anal fin II or III,5 or 6. Coloration: dorsally and flanks green and brown or greyish brown mottlings; belly yellowish white; fins white; pectoral fins tinged with red; dorsal and tail fins have rows of dark spots.
Size: Average 5 in (12–15 cm), maximum up to 10 in (25 cm), 14 oz (400 g).
Distribution: Northern Europe; northern Asia.
General: A bottom-living species frequenting the lower reaches of rivers and muddy, bare-bottom ponds and lakes. It has little sport-fish interest and is often regarded as a nuisance fish in many waters, since it eagerly snatches at the bait before a more valued species can approach it.

356 SPOTTED BASS F
Micropterus punctulatus
Other common names: Kentucky bass, Kentucky spotted bass, spotted black bass, northern spotted bass, Alabama spotted bass, Wichita spotted bass, redeye bass.

Features: Like the smallmouth bass, *Micropterus dolomieui*, the maxillary bone of the upper jaw never extends beyond a point directly under the back of the eye. One dorsal, anterior portion spinous and posterior portion soft-rayed, the two fin sections connected by a broad membrane, forming a shallow notch. Small scales on the bases of the dorsal and anal fins; 15 to 17 oblique scale rows on the cheek, 68 to 80 scales along the lateral line from gill cover to caudal fin. The lateral line curves upward, paralleling the arch of the back. The caudal is moderately emarginate or notched, not forked. Body is robust and fairly deep, laterally compressed, with a large head and mouth, numerous small teeth on the jaws and roof of the mouth. Deepness of body tends to grow more pronounced as the fish grows older. Superficially, the fish appears to be a hybrid between the largemouth and smallmouth bass, but is a distinct, separate species. Coloration: highly variable and can change with transient environmental factors. Lacks the smallmouth's vertical bars; has a similar dark midline to that of the largemouth. Bronze or brassy overcast; evenly spaced rows of small dark spots on the lower sides, so close together that they give the general appearance of stripes. The white or yellowish hue of the belly extends well upward on the sides, contrasting against the spots. There is a dark spot at the base of the tail; another on the rearward end of the gill cover; a third on the tongue. Set of three to five dark bands going rearward from the eye across the cheek; single band radiating forward from the eye to the snout.
Size: Large fish measure 15 in (37.5 cm) and may weigh 2.2 lb (1 kg).
Distribution: Southeastern United States from West Virginia northward to southern Ohio, westward to Kansas and southern Texas, south to western Florida.
General: Important game fish, edible, smallest of the fresh water basses, habitat includes both streams and lakes. Recent transplants to impoundments have been made with varying success.

357 SUWANNEE BASS F
Micropterus notius
Other common names: This species has – as the other, *Micropterus* – many common names of which most are shared by other species of the genus (which see).

Features: The perch-like body is much compressed with a large, high head and big mouth. The lower jaw projects beyond the upper. The teeth in the jaws and far-

ther back in the mouth are small and densely set. The curving of the lateral line follows the dorsal contour. The dorsal fin is by a fairly deep notch divided into two parts, the anterior with IX-X, the posterior with 13–14 rays. Hind margin of tail fin is a little concave with rounded corners; anal fin shorter than dorsal with III, 12–14 rays. Coloration: Very variable according to age and habitat; generally the back is greenish to brownish, sides and belly are lighter. A series of irregularly formed round, dark spots runs along the sides just below the lateral line.
Size: Average length *c*. 12–15 in (30–35 cm).
Distribution: Florida in USA.
General: Lives in smaller rivers, more rare in lakes. Food is surface insects, snails, mussels, worms, and crayfish. This bass is a fine game fish making vigorous leaps when hooked.

358 LARGEMOUTH BLACK BASS F
Micropterus salmoides
Other common names (selection): Black bass, green bass, largemouth black bass, largemouth, Oswego bass, lake bass, marsh bass, moss bass, white bass, grey bass, cow bass, white trout, achigan à grande bouche, achigan noir, etc.

Features: Perchlike and deep-bodied, laterally compressed. Large-mouthed, and mouth extends beyond the eye which distinguishes it from smallmouth bass (see below). Dorsal fin with notched division, IX or X,12 or 13; tail fin concave; anal fin III,10 or 11. Coloration: sometimes variable, dorsally usually greenish-black; flanks dull greenish-silvery; belly pale; dark markings radiate from eye; flanks often marked with a broad, dark lateral band or stripe (especially young fish). Lateral line scale count 65 to 70.
Size: Larger fish are found in southern United States, up to 28 in (70 cm), over 22 lb (10 kg); but generally much smaller averaging *c*. 2.2 lb (1 kg), particularly in northern United States and Canada in areas where the fish has been introduced.
Distribution: Native to North America, from Great Lakes to Florida; introduced into California and into many European countries, and elsewhere in the world where the local water conditions are suitable.
General: (see Smallmouth Black Bass).

359 SMALLMOUTH BLACK BASS F
Micropterus dolomieui
Other common names (selection): Black freshwater bass, black bass, brown bass, dwarf bass, gold bass, hog bass, little bass, minny bass, river bass, swago bass, yellow bass, green trout, mountain trout, speckled hen, achigan noir, achigan petite bouche.

Features: Much like the largemouth bass in general form except in detail. The mouth is still large although relatively smaller than that of the largemouth bass. The smallmouth bass may be distinguished by: (a) The angle of jaw extends only to the eye. (b) Along the lateral line the scale count is 72 to 85, as against 65 to 70 for largemouth bass.

Dorsal fin IX or X,13 to 15; tail fin concave; anal fin III,10 to 12. Coloration: dorsally and flanks dull golden green with a bronze lustre; young fish show dark vertical bands along flanks; belly whitish; large fish become more uniformly greenish. Lateral line scale count 72 to 85.
Size: Average up to 5 lb (2 1/4 kg), maximum up to 10 lb (4 1/2 kg).
Distribution: See largemouth bass, above.
General: There is much confusion over the usage of the name "bass", which internationally and locally has been applied indiscriminately to any number of spiny-finned marine and freshwater species. The largemouth and smallmouth bass are strictly freshwater fishes inhabiting stagnant or slow-moving water. It has been noted that the largemouth bass thrive in either warm or cold water, lakes or streams; the smallmouth bass requires less stagnant and colder water.

Spawning takes place from March to July. After the female spawns, the male takes up guard and later also protects the hatched fry for the first few days. During this period the male is apparently fearless of any water creature and will attack all in defense of its offspring. The fry devour tadpoles, worms, snails, crayfish, and during the first year grow very rapidly.

In North America the largemouth bass is generally admitted to be the most popular of all freshwater sport fishes, and the smallmouth bass runs it a close second. Both are excellent table fishes.

360 REDEYE BASS F
Micropterus coosae
Other common names: Shoal bass, Chipola bass.

Features: A member of the black bass family that is often confused with the smallmouth bass, *M. dolomieui*, and the spotted bass, *M. punctulatus*. Close attention to details is needed for correct identification. The dorsal and anal fins have scales on their membranes at the bases. The dorsal fin outline is not deeply notched and closely resembles that of the smallmouth. The most distinctive identification is the red colour of the eyes and fins. The tail has no spot in mature fish, but the gill cover carries a black spot on the rear tip. The cheek should show oblique scale rows numbering 15–17 as in the smallmouth. The largemouth, by contrast has 9–11. Both the redeye and the smallmouth display 68–80 scales in count from gill cover to tail while the largemouth has 58–65. The anterior part of the dorsal fin in black basses is spiny-rayed, the posterior soft-rayed. The redeye first dorsal count is X, second dorsal about 11. Coloration: Young redeye bass have a distinctive pattern of dark-colored vertical bars. These become less distinct as the fish matures and in old fish may be nearly absent. Fins and eyes are red, as previously mentioned.
Size: Occasionally reaches 4 1/2 lb (2 kg), but the majority of redeyes are much smaller. The fish are mature at 6 in, (15 cm), and average 12–18 in (30–45 cm) in length.
Distribution: Headwaters of the Chattagoochee and Alabama Rivers in Alabama, and the Savannah River in Georgia are the primary range. The fish have spread or been introduced into other rivers of the

southeastern United States, but nowhere can be said to be truly plentiful.
General: Feeding primarily on insects and small, lively bait, they are scrappy fighters on light tackle and excellent on the table.

361 BLUEGILL F
Lepomis macrochirus
Other common names: Bluegill sunfish, blue sunfish, sunfish, bream, blue bream, roach, blue-mouthed sunfish, porgy sunfish, blue joe, copper nosed bream, oreilles bleus, etc.

Features: Deep, oval-shaped, and laterally compressed body. Small mouth barely reaching a point in line with the front of the eye; the gill cover is short and dark, sometimes with a purplish hue. Dorsal fin IX or X,11 or 12; tail fin concave; anal fin III,10 to 12. Coloration: dorsally blue green to olive green; flanks lighter with a series of vertical bars; belly copper red, orange, or yellow; on the last few soft rays of the dorsal fin are a series of oblong blotches together forming a conspicuous round spot; gill cover lobe black. Lateral line scale count 43 to 52.
Size: Average up to 10–12 in (25–30 cm), maximum 14 in (35 cm), 1 1/2 lb (3/4 kg).
Distribution: Native to North America, showing a preference for warm-water lakes and streams. It has been widely introduced elsewhere in the world.
General: The most important member of the true sunfishes (family *Centrarchidae*) and the smallest of the popular panfish; in some regions it may only average 4–7 in (10–18 cm). Often known locally as "bream" or "roach", but the fish has no connection with the European species of these names. It is one of the most prolific of all panfish and is usually found in the warm, weedy waters of protected bays, ponds, and near shorelines in lakes. Spawning occurs in spring; the male guards the eggs and later the hatched fish, but not for long. As a sport fish, in spite of its small size, it shows remarkable fighting qualities and will take almost any kind of bait. An excellent table fish.

362 YELLOW BELLY F.
Lepomis megalotis
Other common names: Redbreast bream, sunfish.

Features: This smaller fish is related to the perches, but can be distinguished from them by the fact that the two dorsal fins, one spinous and one soft-rayed, are united with only a short incision between them. The gill cover is prolonged backwards into an elongate flap, the "earflap", which reaches to above the pectoral fin. The body is oblong or oval. The snout is fairly prominent and the mouth big, oblique; the upper jaw reaches backwards to just behind the anterior margin of the eye. Short gill rakers. One dorsal fin with ten low spines followed by the higher soft-rayed part. Three spines foremost in the anal fin. The hind margin of the tail fin is slightly concave. Coloration: back and upper sides olive, belly orange red; most of the scales are bluish with minute reddish spots; the head has blue narrow bands; the fins are darker.

Size: Most individuals about 8 in (20 cm).
Distribution: Eastern regions of USA, from Louisiana to New England. Not observed west of the Alleghenies.
General: Abundant in rivers and brooks.

363 PUMPKINSEED F
Lepomis gibbosus
Other common names: Common sunfish, eastern sunfish, yellow sunfish, sun bass, sunny, punky, perch, pond perch, robin perch, sand perch, harlequin roach.

Features: Body laterally compressed and rounder in outline than most other sunfishes. Small mouth and teeth. Dorsal fin X,10 to 12; tail fin concave; anal fin III,10 or 11. Coloration: dorsally and flanks greenish olive; flanks spotted and blotched with orange; belly orange yellow (in juvenile fish and mature females there are several vertical bars on the flanks); fins dusky, often with brown spots (in particular the dorsal fin); cheeks and gill covers have streaks or lines of brilliant blue (especially males); gill "ear" flap is dark with a brilliant scarlet spot on the black margin. Lateral line scale count 40 to 47.
Size: Average up to 8–9 in (20–23 cm), 1/2 lb (1/4 kg); many stunted forms in over-crowded waters only attain 4–5 in (10–13 cm).
Distribution: Native to North America but widely introduced elsewhere.
General: One of the commonest and most widely distributed of the sunfishes and found in clear, weedy ponds, lakes, and slow-flowing rivers. Spawning takes place in spring–summer; the male fish (usually the larger) plays a dominant role in constructing the nest by using its tail to sweep a hole in the bottom debris; the male is also very aggressive around spawning time, and after hatching guards the young fish for a short time. The pumpkinseed is occasionally caught by seine nets. Although rather small, it is a good sport fish, especially for young anglers. It has excellent table qualities.

364 WARMOUTH BASS F
Lepomis gulosus
Other common names: Stumpknocker, bigmouth, warmouth, Indian fish, sun trout, wood bass, mud bass, weed bass, red-eye, goggle-eye, goggle-eyed perch, crapet de roche, big-mouthed sunfish, black warmouth, bream, buffalo bass, chub, jugmouth, mud chub, perchmouth bream, sac-a-lait, warmouth perch, warmouth bream.

Features: Deep-bodied and roundish in general outline, the space between the dorsal and ventral margins being approximately half the total length of the fish. Laterally compressed, thin; curves of the upper and lower surfaces roughly similar. Body narrows abruptly, above and below, to the caudal peduncle. The dorsal is long and continuous, lacking the notch characteristic of the basses. Bony projection, known as the "ear flap" at the rear end of the gill cover. Fully scaled with large, moderately ctenoid scales that occur in smaller size on the cheeks and gill covers. Caudal is notched with rounded corners. Teeth on the tongue. The warmouth has a large mouth, a protruding lower jaw; and a red eye. There are three spines on the anal fin. Scales along the lateral line usually number 34 to 49. Coloration: olive brown to a brassy hue with darker blotches or mottling; the young especially showing dark and conspicuous blotches on the sides. Broad and dark vertical bars extend downward almost to the belly and give the fish a mottled appearance. The soft-rayed dorsal and anal fins are usually streaked or spotted. Three or four dark bars radiate from the eye across the cheek and gill cover.
Size: May reach about 12 in (30 cm); 2.2 lb (1 kg) at maximum.
Distribution: Eastern United States from the Great Lakes to Florida and Texas, west to Kansas and the Dakotas; chiefly west or south of the Alleghenies; common in South Carolina. Introduced on the United States West Coast.
General: Small panfish, thriving mainly in the bayous, creeks, muddy rivers and big warm lakes of the South; sought by pan-fishermen. Not a game fish of the first rank, but edible. Nests made singly rather than in colonies in shallow to fairly deep water. Prolific; spawning may occur several times in a season. Feeds mostly in early morning; tolerates muddy waters quite well.

365 WHITE CRAPPIE F
Pomoxis annularis
Other common names: Crappie, pale crappie, timber crappie, bridge perch, bachelor perch, chinquapin perch, speckled perch, strawberry perch.

Features: Shape is more elongate than the black crappie; large mouth equipped with many fine teeth. Dorsal fin V or VI,18; tail fin concave; anal fin VI,18. Coloration: dorsally dark green to black; flanks silvery with dark green or black blotches usually arranged as vertical stripes, often inconspicuous on the larger adults; dorsal, anal, and tail fins bear dark spots or mottlings. Lateral line scale count 36 to 48.
Size: Average 7–10 in (18–25 cm); large fish up to 12 in (30 cm), 1 lb (1/2 kg).
Distribution: North America, but less common in the northern part of its range than the black crappie; also introduced into the Pacific slope area.
General: Often confused with the black crappie whose biology and general habits are similar. Like the black crappie it is an excellent basic, all-seasons sport fish. The flesh is of excellent table quality.

366 REDBREAST SUNFISH F
Lepomis auritus
Other common names: Yellow-breasted sunfish, horned- eared, red sunfish, river sunfish, tobacco box, redbelly, black-eared pondfish, red-tailed bream.

Features: Deep, laterally compressed body and very similar to the pumpkinseed and other sunfishes. Dorsal fin X,11 or 12; tail fin concave; anal fin II,8 to 10. Coloration: dorsally olive; scales on flanks have reddish spots on a bluish background; belly varies from yellow to brilliant orange red; vertical fins orange or yellowish; usually the head has bluish stripes; gill "ear" flap is blue black but has no red colouration (like that of the related pumpkinseed). Lateral line scale count 43 to 48. Several hybrid species with variable features occur.
Size: Average up to 5–7 in (12–18 cm) 1 lb (1/2 kg), but in many areas stunted forms are found.
Distribution: North America, ranging generally from the Great Lakes through to Virginia, Florida, and Texas.
General: Spawning occurs in spring – early summer; the male constructs a shallow nest, and like other sunfishes aggressively guards the eggs and then the hatched fish for a short while. It has a larger mouth than the common sunfish and readily takes a baited hook. A good table fish.

367 ROCK BASS F
Ambloplites rupestris
Other common names: Northern rock bass, redeye, redeye perch, redeye bass, common rock bass, sunfish bass, goggle-eyed bass, sun perch, redeye sunfish, bream, red-eyed bream, goggle-eye, crapet de roche, crapet mondoux, crapet noir, crapet vert.

Features: Elongate, laterally compressed body. Large mouth (larger than most other sunfishes) with lower jaw projecting; the eyes are large and reddish in colour. Dorsal fin XI,10; tail fin concave; anal fin V or VI,10 (anal spine count five or six is characteristic of rock bass, other sunfish have only three spines). Coloration: dorsally and flanks olive-brown or bronze with darker blotches or mottlings; gill cover has a dark blotch; young fish show conspicuous dark blotches on the sides; with the exception of pectoral and pelvic fins all fins are dusky and spotted. Lateral line arched, and scale count 39–43.
Size: Up to 12 in (30 cm), 2 1/4 lb (1 kg).
Distribution: North America, ranging from southern Manitoba eastward to Great Lakes and south through the Mississippi Valley to the Gulf of Mexico. Introduced elsewhere.
General: A schooling sunfish preferring cool, clear water. It is found around patches of vegetation, old stumps, and logs in lakes, ponds, rivers, and creeks. Its general biology and nest building is similar to other sunfishes. Food consists of aquatic insects, crayfish, and small fish. A useful sport fish for very light tackle. Flavour is fair to moderate.

368 BLACK CRAPPIE F
Pomoxis nigromaculatus
Other common names: Calico bass, crappie, Oswego bass, strawberry bass, speckled bass, crapet calicot, lake bass, silver bass, sand perch, spotted perch, sun perch, grass bass, calico bream.

Features: Deep-bodied and laterally compressed. Forehead depressed above the eyes. Dorsal fin VII or VIII,18; tail fin concave; anal fin VI,18. Coloration: dorsally dark green to black; flanks silvery with irregularly arranged dark green or black spots or small blotches; dorsal, anal, and tail fins have dark green speckles.
Size: Average 7–10 in (18–25 cm), 1/2 lb (1/4 kg); large fish up to 12–14 in (30–36 cm), 2 lb (1 kg).
Distribution: North America, ranging throughout much of the region; more common in cold-water lakes and in rivers. Also introduced into the Pacific slope area.

General: A fish of quiet waters of lakes, ponds, and slow-moving streams where there is a good growth of aquatic plants. A very gregarious schooling species; principal food consists of small fishes, crustaceans, and aquatic insects. An excellent basic, all-seasons sport fish which readily takes a hook. The flesh is very sweet and has good flavour.

369 SACRAMENTO PERCH F
Archoplites interruptus

Features: Elongate, laterally compressed body and very similar in appearance to its relative, the rock bass. Dorsal fin XII or XIII,10; tail fin concave; anal fin VI to VIII,10. Coloration: dorsally blackish or brassy; flanks silvery with about 7 irregular and darker vertical bars; gill cover has a dark spot. Lateral line parallels dorsal profile. Scales are saw-toothed along the rear edge.
Size: Up to *c.* 24 in (60 cm), 4 lb (1 3/4 kg).
Distribution: North America. Native to the Sacramento-San Joaquin river system, but introduced elsewhere; very abundant in Lake Clear and Lake Kern, California, and Walker Lake in Nevada.
General: The only western native representative of the bass-sunfish family. Unlike other North American sunfishes it does not build a nest or guard its young, and after spawning, its eggs are much reduced in numbers in waters where catfish have been introduced.

The Sacramento perch is a popular light-tackle sport fish, which may be caught by any methods, but because of its restricted distribution, it is not very widely known. The flesh has excellent table qualities.

370 COUCH'S SEA BREAM S
Pagrus pagrus

Features: Oval body. Very steep profile to forehead with a sharp change in direction above the eye; fanglike teeth in front of jaw. Dorsal fin XII,9 to 11; tail fin forked; anal fin III,8 or 9. Coloration: dorsally rosy or golden; flanks and belly silvery; fins yellow rose; tail fin has a darker rim; there is a small red brown spot at the base of the last ray of the dorsal fin.
Size: Average up to 20 in (50 cm), maximum 30 in (75 cm).
Distribution: Eastern Atlantic, Bay of Biscay south to Senegal; Mediterranean.
General: A shallow-water fish in warmer months, but in winter it migrates to deeper water. A good table fish.

371 RED PORGY S
Pagrus sedecim

Features: Ovalate, deep and compressed body. forehead above eye slightly humped; large eye. Dorsal fin XII,9 to 11; tail fin deeply forked; anal fin III,8. Coloration: pinkish silver overall with indistinct yellow spot on each scale, giving a yellow-striped appearance; yellowish marks on snout, lips, and above eyes; dorsal, tail, and pectoral fins pink. Lateral line distinct and follows approximate curve of dorsal profile.
Size: Up to 20 in (50 cm), 4 1/2 lb (2 kg).
Distribution: Western Atlantic, from New York south to Argentina, but not in West Indies.
General: A species inhabiting moderate depths ranging 30–270 ft (10–80 m). An excellent food fish. Closely related to Couch's sea bream *P. pagrus* (see above).

372 SCUP S
Stenotomus chrysops

Other common names: Porgy, paugy, scuppaug, fair maid.

Features: Ovate-elliptical body much compressed laterally. Blunt-pointed head with slightly depressed forehead above eye. Dorsal fin XII,12; tail stalk extended; tail fin forked/crescentic; anal fin III,11 or 12. Coloration: dorsally dark bluish silver; flanks dull silver and iridescent, dorsal areas and flanks crossed by 12 to 15 indistinct, longitudinal stripes flecked with light blue and with a light blue streak following base of dorsal fin; belly white; head silvery with dusky blotches; fins flecked with blue, but pectorals brownish and pelvics white to bluish. Lateral line curved and slightly irregular. Scales large, and a prominent scaly sheath along the base of the soft dorsal and anal fins.

Size: Up to 18 in (45 cm), 3–4 lb (1 1/4–1 3/4 kg).
Distribution: Western Atlantic, Nova Scotia south to Georgia.
General: A bottom feeder, eating mainly amphipods, worms, sand dollars, and young squid, but occasionally fish fry. An important commercial species in eastern North America. An excellent table fish.

373 PACIFIC PORGY S
Calamus brachysomus
Other common name: Marotilla.

Features: Deep, much compressed body. Dorsal contour strongly convex anteriorly. Rather small mouth; the anterior teeth pointed, the posterior ones molar-like. Short and few gill rakers. The first, spinous, part of the dorsal fin the longer, the soft part much shorter. Tail fin strongly forked with pointed lobes; three spines in front of anal fin. Coloration: back and upper sides dark grey, lower sides and belly silvery; the sides have 6–8 dark, transversal bands, often only weak in older individuals; fins with dark spots.
Size: About 1 ft (30 cm) or less.
Distribution: Coastal waters of the East Pacific from California to Peru.
General: Appears to be a rather rare fish. No commercial importance.

374 TROPICAL BLACK BREAM S, B
Acanthopagrus berda
Other common names: Black bream, pikey bream, river bream, mud bream.

Features: Very similar features to other "silver breams" but with a larger and more projecting snout. Dorsal fin XI or XII,10 to 13; tail fin forked; anal fin III,8 or 9; dorsal and particularly anal spines very strong. Coloration: dorsally and flanks dark grey to black with a tinge of purple; belly lighter grey; long scythelike pectoral fins grey with yellowish tinge; an indistinct black spot at base of pectoral fin. Young have a general olivaceous coloration with dusky longitudinal streaks along the scale rows. Lateral line arched, and characteristically highest point of arch is under sixth or seventh dorsal fin spines which helps distinguish it from the yellowfin and southern breams. Lateral line scale count 46 to 54. Scales medium large.
Size: Average up to 15 in (38 cm), maximum 30 in (75 cm), 15 lb (7 kg).
Distribution: Widespread in tropical Indo-Pacific seas.
General: A coastal and estuarine species frequenting brackish regions in rivers and coastal lagoons. Throughout its distribution it is a popular sport fish and has the reputation of being cunning, wary, and rather furtive. A very game fighter. A first class table fish.

375 SOUTHERN BREAM S, B
Acanthopagrus australis
Other common names: Blue-nosed bream, black bream, bream, silver bream.

Features: Very similar to the other Indo-Pacific "silver breams", but body more symmetrical-elliptical; spine and soft-ray counts on dorsal and anal fins similar to

those of yellowfin bream (see below). Coloration: dorsally and flanks dark brown; in freshly caught fish the dorsal area and flanks are golden-brown or bronze with greenish reflections and with no indications of vertical dusky bands; belly whitish; gill covers have gold and pinkish tints; dorsal fin brown and mottled with purple, blue, and gold with dark margins; pelvic and anal fins brownish; pectoral fin has a black spot at its upper base. Lateral line more gently curvaceous than that of yellowfin bream. Scales large.
Size: Average up to 18 in (45 cm), maximum 22 in (55 cm), 7 lb (3 1/4 kg).
Distribution: Indo-Pacific temperate seas.
General: Large fish over 2 lb (1 kg) known locally as blue-nosed bream. Found in estuaries and rarely encountered along open ocean beaches. Sometimes found in coastal lakes and they may occur as a semilandlocked species. A very popular local sport fish with excellent table qualities.

376 JAPANESE BREAM S
Acanthopagrus latus
Other common name: Yellowfin bream (western Australia).

Features: Very similar general shape and features to other "silver breams" (i.e. tropical black bream (which see) except that there is a characteristic swelling on the forehead above the eye; similar spine and soft-ray counts on anal and dorsal fins. Coloration: dorsally and flanks pale greyish to whitish; dorsal area and upper flanks have crossbars and golden reflections; dorsal fin greyish, pelvic and anal fins whitish, tinged with yellow; characteristic absence of the black mark on base of pectoral fin helps distinguish it from tropical black bream. Lateral line evenly arched with highest part of curve below third or fourth dorsal fin spines. Scales medium large.
Size: Average up to 18 in (45 cm).
Distribution: Widespread in Indo-Pacific area.
General: An important sport and table fish throughout its distribution with similar angling characteristics to other Indo-Pacific bream.

377 JOLTHEAD PORGY S
Calamus bajonado
Other common name: Blue-bone porgy.

Features: Medium-large body, compressed. Large head with convex profile; mouth very low; eye large. Dorsal fin XII,10–12; tail fin deeply forked; anal fin III,10 or 11. Coloration: dorsally and flanks a dull brassy silver with blue green markings; a blue stripe or line below the eye extending forward; a second duller streak above this, and the two meet on the forehead; lower jaw dull purplish; mouth purplish and orange; fins plain but pelvics sometimes slightly dusky, and the tail fin obscurely barred. Lateral line distinct and follows approximate line of dorsal profile.
Size: Up to 24 in (60 cm), 14 lb (6 1/4 kg).
Distribution: Western Atlantic, Rhode Island south to Bermuda, West Indies, and Brazil.
General: A common species found on rocky ground, reefs, and in estuaries. Adult fish feed mainly on sea urchins. Good table fish.

378 GRASS PORGY S
Calamus arctifrons
Other common names: Jolt-head porgy, blue-bone porgy.

Features: High compressed body with large head. Strong teeth. Back elevated. Few and short gill rakers. Long dorsal fin, anteriorly with 12–13 spines; tail fin broad, forked; large, pointed pectoral fins; the anal fin starts with three shorter spines. Coloration: all over yellow with a brassy lustre; below the eye is a narrow, blue band.
Size: This porgy grows to a length of 2 ft (60–65 cm), but the normal size is smaller.
Distribution: Western Atlantic from the Bermudas to the West Indian seas.
General: The species prefers the shallow, vegetation-rich shore waters and a rocky bottom. It feeds mainly on mussels which it tears from the rocks by means of the sharp teeth on the jaws, thereafter crushing them with the strong, molarlike back teeth.

379 BLACK BISKOP S
Cymatoceps nasutus
Other common names: Musselcracker, biskop, blue biskop, poenskop, stompkop, blover or bank blover, witbek steenbras, black steenbras.

Features: Very robust body. The snout, or nose, of the mature adult is very thick and characteristically overhangs the upper lip; four conical teeth in each jaw. Dorsal fin XII,10; tail fin concave; anal fin III,8. Coloration: dorsally and flanks greyish and irregularly mottled with blotchy yellow and brown; fins greyish or blackish, tail margin lighter yellow, pelvic fins dark or rosy. Lateral line scale count 61 to 65.
Size: Average up to 50 lb (22 1/2 kg), attains 120 lb (54 1/2 kg).
Distribution: South Africa, ranging Cape to Natal.
General: Frequents rocky ground to a depth of 250 ft (75 m), but it usually feeds in shallow water; rarely found in estuaries. Food is mainly mollusks and crabs. A well-known premier sport fish and renowned as a dogged fighter. It will take almost any bait. Its table quality is rather poor, particularly so in the large specimens whose flesh is coarse.

380 SHEEPSHEAD S
Archosargus probatocephalus

Features: Robust, angular body, short and deep. Blunt forehead profile but variable according to age, and older fish have more humped appearance. Dorsal fin XI or XII, 11 to 13; tail stalk extended; tail fin forked; anal fin III,10 or 11. Coloration: dorsally and flanks silvery greyish to greenish yellow with about seven broad brown to black bars running vertically across flanks; bars indistinct on older fish. Lateral line curved and indistinct. Large body scales with smaller ones in front of pectorals and pelvics.
Size: Up to 30 in (76 cm), 20 lb (9 kg).
Distribution: Western Atlantic, Bay of Fundy and Cape Cod south to Gulf of Mexico.
General: A common and abundant species throughout its distribution. A bottom species found close inshore in bays, channels, and harbours from 10–270 ft (3–80 m). It feeds mainly on crabs and mollusks.

As a sport fish many are caught from bridges and piers especially around the Texas Gulf coast, and although it is readily attracted to a bait, it often proves elusive to the hook. An excellent high quality table fish.

381 WHITE BISKOP S
Sparodon durbanensis
Other common names: Brusher, mussel cracker, mussel crusher, silver steenbras, steenbras, sand stompkop.

Features: Distinctly blunt-headed; small eye; four curved incisor teeth in each jaw; a pair of teeth in the upper jaw characteristically project over lower lip when the mouth is closed; each jaw has many large round or oval molars forming a pavement. Dorsal fin XI,11 or 12; tail fin concave; anal fin III,10. Coloration: dorsally bluish or greyish; flanks silvery (with faint narrow brown stripes in older juveniles); fins greyish. Young fish are vividly coloured. Lateral line scale count 58 to 61.
Size: Up to 40 in (100 cm), 70 lb (32 kg).
Distribution: South Africa, ranging Cape to Natal.
General: Found in rocky habitats. One of the finest and best known sport fish in South African waters. A splendid fighter which will take almost any bait. It only rarely enters estuary waters and is nowhere abundant. It is sometimes captured in pairs. The table quality of the smaller fish is good, but in larger fish the flesh is coarse.

382 TARWHINE S, B
Rhabdosargus sarba
Other common name: Silver bream.

Features: Ovate, with regular convex dorsal profile. Head blunt and a slightly humped appearance adjacent to eye, but shape is variable with age. Dorsal fin XI,13 to 15; tail fin forked; anal fin III,11 or 12. Coloration: dorsally and flanks silvery and grey with longitudinal golden streaks along scale rows; golden reflections on the snout; belly white; lips silvery; tail fin yellowish or greyish edged with black; pelvic and anal fins dusky silvery or orange tinted. Lateral line gently curved and scale count 55 to 70.
Size: Up to 20 in (50 cm), 5 1/2 lb (2 1/2 kg).
Distribution: South Atlantic and Indo-Pacific seas.
General: A plentiful schooling species in many parts of its distribution. As a sport fish it will accept any variety of bait, but crab is the most successful bait in many areas. When hooked, it is a very game fighter. An excellent table fish often found together with yellowfin bream, and both prefer sandy bottoms and shallow water.

383 YELLOWFIN BREAM S, B
Mylio australis
Other common names: Sea bream, surface bream, black bream, river bream, bream.

Features: Ovate, humped appearance; laterally compressed. Dorsal fin XI,12; tail fin forked; anal fin III,8 to 10. Coloration: variable, but dorsally and flanks usually golden bronze, brown green to silvery; dorsal area and flanks of live fish golden olivaceous, dead fish dull grey; in freshly caught fish the dorsal area is marked with

indistinct, broad vertical bands of brown grey; tail and dorsal fins pinkish with narrow black margins; pelvic and anal fins characteristically canary yellow. Lateral line has a characteristic sharp dip in front part below fourth and fifth dorsal spines. Very similar to the tarwhine (which see) especially the young fish, but may be distinguished by the smaller anal fin soft-ray count.
Size: Average up to 3 lb (1 1/2 kg), maximum 22 in (55 cm), 7 lb (3 1/4 kg).
Distribution: Pacific seas.
General: A plentiful species especially during the summer. It frequents estuaries, bays, coastal rivers, and lagoons as far as the freshwater limit. Fish that live upstream have a darker coloration and are often referred to as river bream. During the spawning season they become paler and more silvery and are then often called sea bream, or surface bream. They represent a popular local sport fish wherever they are found. The white flesh has excellent table qualities.

384 RED SEA BREAM S
Pagellus bogaraveo
Other common names: Red bream, common bream.

Features: Oval, deep-bodied. Forehead slightly depressed; eye very large; short front teeth, curved and pointed; back teeth small and rounded. Dorsal fin XII or XIII,11 to 13; tail fin concave; anal fin III,11 to 13. Coloration: dorsally and flanks silver greyish or rose tinted; large, characteristic diffuse black spot or blotch at start of lateral line above gill cover, but in juveniles this may be absent; fins are reddish. Lateral line scale count 75 to 80.
Size: Average up to 14 in (35 cm), maximum up to 20 in (50 cm).
Distribution: Mediterranean; eastern Atlantic, ranging Scandinavia south to West Africa.
General: The red sea bream is the only common sparid bream visiting northern temperate latitudes during the summer months. A schooling species which is found around offshore reefs and coastlines among weed-covered rocks, but older fish may be encountered to a depth of 1,000 ft (300 m). The larger fish are found chiefly over mud or sand bottoms.

385 BLACK BREAM S
Spondyliosoma cantharus
Other common name: Oldwife.

Features: Elliptical, deep body. Mature males have characteristic humped shoulder and depressed forehead; young fish sometimes have similar depressed forehead and a sharp snout; large front teeth. Dorsal fin XI,12 or 13; tail fin concave; anal fin III,9 to 11. Coloration very variable. Young fish are dorsally grey or yellowish; flanks silvery with numerous longitudinal, light-stippled stripes; fins are occasionally spotted with white, with a broad, dark margin on tail fin. Adult fish are dorsally a shimmering-dark to dark grey; flanks paler with 6–9 vertical crossbars; spawning males are very dark and have an iridescent blue grey band between the eyes. Lateral line distinct.
Size: Average up to 16 in (40 cm), maximum

20 in (50 cm).
Distribution: Eastern Atlantic; from northern Britain and west Norway south to West Africa; Mediterranean. Related Indo-Pacific forms.
General: A fish which frequents weed-covered rocks and reefs but is also found in deep water. In the Mediterranean it is found over sand and sea grass. The black bream has some sport fishing interest locally. Its flesh is edible, but it is not a commercial food fish.

386 JOHN BROWN S
Gymnocrotaphus curvidens
Other common names: Blue-eye John Brown, Jan Bruin (Cape), blauwoog Jan Bruin (Eastern Cape).

Features: Bony fishes of the family *Sparidae*, with well developed fins and a forked tail, the preopercle margin not serrate. Characterized by a groove in the rear upper portion of the premaxilla, into which a part of the maxilla fits, being overlapped by the outer flange of the groove. Has no separate teeth of enlarged size in front of the jaws. Outer teeth are compressed incisiform. The body is plump, depth going into the length a little over two times. The cheek below the eye is not scaly and there are no scales between the eyes or on the preopercle flange. Soft dorsal and anal fins are scaly at the bases, caudal not deeply forked, seven to nine gill rakers. Dorsal fin X, 11 to 12; anal fin III, 9 to 10. There are 64 to 68 scales along the lateral line, eight rows above and 21 rows of scales below the lateral line at the shoulder. Coloration: brownish on the live fish which fades very quickly after death, leaving orange lines along the scale rows.
Size: Up to 14 in (35 cm).
Distribution: Along the African coast from the Cape to Durban, mostly in shallow water in rocky areas.
General: Nowhere abundant; caught by anglers on bait but seldom more than one or two in an area. A shapely fish and excellent eating.

387 BLUE HOTTENTOT S
Pachymetopon grande
Other common names: Das, John Brown, Jan Bruin, fatfish, vetvis, butterfish, bluefish, butter cream, bronze bream, copper bream, damkokker.

Features: Plump, oval body, compressed. Old fish develop a characteristic prominent bulge over the eyes; 22 teeth in outer row in both jaws. Dorsal fin XI,11; tail fin forked; anal fin III,10 or 11. Coloration: dorsally and flanks dark bronze; head iridescent blue and sharply differentiated from body colour; all fins dark or dusky. Lateral line scale count 80 to 85.
Size: Up to 24 in (60 cm), 15 lb (7 kg).
Distribution: South Africa, ranging Cape to Madagascar.
General: A shallow water species found in rocky areas. It feeds mainly on seaweed, but includes also crustaceans. It is very sensitive to cold currents. Blue hottentots are not found in sufficient numbers to be utilized as a commercial species. As a premier sport fish it bites fiercely and fights gamely in spite of its small size. It is, however, a

fastidious feeder and takes only the freshest of redbait or prawn so that often it is a difficult fish to hook. As a table fish it is highly esteemed.

388 WHITE STEENBRAS S, B
Pagellus lithognathus
Other common names: Whitefish (African West Coast), river steenbras, steenbras, varkpek, pignose grunter (Eastern Cape), ngcangolo (native).

Features: The protrusible mouth is characterized by feeble teeth, outer small, sharp canines, two series of small inner molars, thick lips. Scales are relatively large and there are none between the eyes, on the preopercle flange, or on the soft dorsal and anal fins. Gill rakers number 12–14. Dorsal fin XI, 10; anal fin III, 8. Lateral line scale count is 44–51. At the shoulder there are 5 scale rows above the lateral line and 14 rows below. Coloration: Silver with normally seven wide cross bars that become dim in older fish.
Size: Attains 6 ft (180 cm) and 30 lb (14 kg), but normal length runs around 3 ft (90 cm).
Distribution: Coastal salt and brackish water in South Africa.
General: Enters lagoons frequently where it feeds on shallow waters creatures such as crustacea, mollusca, worms, etc, which it blows out of the bottom with a strong jet of water from the mouth. A powerful, vigorous fish much esteemed for food, and prized by anglers for its fighting qualities.

389 PANDORA S
Pagellus erythrinus
Other common name: Spanish bream.

Features: Ovate-elliptical body. Head profile gently concave above eye; pointed snout; large eye. Dorsal fin XII,12 or 13; tail fin forked; anal fin III,12 or 13. Coloration: dorsally rose-red; flanks paler; belly silvery; diffuse black spot at start of lateral line; gill flaps have a red rim; gill cavities and mouth are black. Lateral line scale count 75 to 80.
Size: Average up to 10 in (25 cm), maximum 24 in (60 cm).
Distribution: Eastern Atlantic, from northern Biscay to southern Angola; Mediterranean.
General: A bottom-living fish resident at depths varying between 50–400 ft (15–120 m) and usually found over rocky ground. A commercial and excellent sport fish which readily takes a bait, a good table fish with a delicious flavour.

390 HOTTENTOT S
Pachymetopon blochi
Other common name: Hangberger.

Features: Plump, ovalate body, compressed. Outer row of teeth larger than inner, no molars. Dorsal fin XI,11 or 12; tail fin concave; anal fin III,10. Coloration: dorsally and upper flanks bronzy brown or greyish; paler below. Lateral line scale count 60 to 65.
Size: Up to 18 in (45 cm), 9 lb (4 kg).
Distribution: South West Africa, ranging Table Bay, False Bay; rarely east of Agulhas Bank.
Features: One of the commonest Cape food

fishes. As an angling fish it is not particularly significant, but it is occasionally taken in fair numbers from deep water in rocky areas. Good table qualities.

391 SNAPPER (AUSTRALIAN) s
Chrysophrys auratus

Features: Large, very deep, bony head; body tapers quickly toward tail. A very "humped" and characteristic forehead in mature fish. In large fish the snout is developed into a fleshy nose giving rise to the name "Old Man Snapper" used by fishermen. Dorsal fin XI,9; tail fin deeply concave; anal fin III,11. Coloration: dorsally and flanks a light delicate pink with opalescent blue spots; flanks show iridescent hues. Lateral line arched.
Size: Up to over 48 in (120 cm), 40 lb (18 kg); but average fish *c.* 5 lb (2 kg).
Distribution: Australasian temperate seas.
General: A prolific and valuable species. A member of the bream family (*Sparidae*). Locally, very young fish are referred to as "cockneys"; fish up to *c.* 1 1/2 lb (3/4 kg) are known as red bream or redfish; over 2 lb (1 kg) they become known as "squire"; over 4 1/2 lb (2 kg), generally known as snapper. Fresh from the water they have a golden appearance, hence the usage of the Latin trivial name *auratus*.

The snapper is one of the most popular of all Australasian sport fish, and large numbers are taken each year by commercial and sport fishermen. An excellent, firm, white table fish.

392 GILTHEAD s, B
Sparus auratus

Features: Deep, ovate body. Forehead has a steep, smoothly rounded profile; powerful jaws and upper jaw slightly longer than the lower; thick lips; mouth with strong, conical, and molarlike teeth. Dorsal fin XI,13; tail fin forked; anal fin III,11 or 12. Coloration: variable, but dorsally usually grey or grey blue; flanks paling to silver; belly white, gill-cover margin has a scarlet patch; dark blotch on the head at the beginning of the lateral line. A characteristic feature of a live fish is the greenish-golden band extending between the eyes, but this quickly fades after death.
Size: Average range 14–24 in (35–60 cm), maximum 28 in (70 cm).
Distribution: Eastern Atlantic, ranging from north Biscay to West Africa; Mediterranean.
General: A shallow water species that feeds on mollusks and the larger crustaceans. The flesh has excellent table qualities.

393 RED STEENBRAS s
Dentex rupestris
Other common names: Root steenbras (Cape), yellow steenbras (Natal).

Features: Depth goes into length about three times in this deep-bodied species. A long dorsal which tapers rearward and then abruptly becomes higher between the spinous and soft-rayed area. Lower jaw protrudes in front of upper, tail is lightly forked. Soft-rayed portion of dorsal and anal fins are approximately the same shape in outline and directly opposite each other on top and bottom of back. There are 57 to 63 scales along a pronounced lateral line with 12 rows above and 20 below the lateral line near the shoulder. The soft dorsal and anal have heavy, fleshy, scaly bases. There are four powerful canine teeth in the front of the upper jaw; four to six on the lower, with fine teeth behind them in a band on each jaw. The ridge above the eye becomes more pronounced with age. There are eight to nine short gill rakers. Dorsal fin XI, 10 to 11; anal, III, 8. Coloration: reddish to bronze when taken on the reefs but on soft bottoms reported as varying to a golden yellow. Juveniles have a cross-bar or blotch with a red hue behind the dorsal fin which apparently fades with age.
Size: Recorded at 72 in (180 cm); over 154 lb (70 kg).
Distribution: Found only off South Africa thus far, though a wider range is suspected.
General: Premier game fish among reefs or rocks in deep water but occasionally enters deep estuaries. Powerful fangs with large jaws can inflict serious wounds. Takes baits and live fishes readily. Commercially important, edible, but the liver reputed to be poisonous. Liver oil is rich in vitamins and quite wholesome.

394 DENTEX s
Dentex dentex
Other common name: Toothed sparus.

Features: Oval-shaped body. Massive head with steep convex profile; both jaws have well-developed canine teeth plus numerous smaller teeth of similar shape. Dorsal fin XI to XIII,11 or 12; tail fin forked; anal fin III,7 to 9. Coloration: variable, dorsally usually bluish silver; flanks silvery with 4 or 5 indistinct darker crossbands and dotted with small, blue spots (after death the spots fade quickly); belly silvery-white; pectoral fins rosy; mature specimens over 40 in (100 cm) may be of a uniform dull red. Lateral line distinct, and scale count 60 to 68.
Size: Average up to 28 in (70 cm), maximum over 40 in (100 cm).
Distribution: Eastern Atlantic, Biscay to West Africa; Mediterranean. Several related forms in Indo-Pacific seas.
General: A sea bream found over rocky ground from 30–650 ft (10–200 m). The dentex is an active predatory fish and approaches the shore during the summer, but in winter it migrates to deeper water. An important commercial species. A renowned sport fish much sought after by underwater spear fishermen in Mediterranean. A much esteemed table fish.

19 TILEFISH

395 TILEFISH s
Lopholatilus chamaeleonticeps
Other common names: Atlantic blanquillo.

Features: Characterized by a large fleshy fin on the nape. This fin is forward of the dorsal, close behind the eyes, as high as the dorsal in adult tilefish, higher than long and rounded at the tip. There is another small fleshy flap on the side of the lower jaw close to the angle of the mouth and pointing backward. Large head, strongly convex in dorsal profile. Eye high up, mouth wide, both jaws with outer series of large conical teeth and inner rows of smaller teeth. Trunk is deepest behind the head and thence tapers backward to a flattened caudal peduncle. Anal about half as long as the dorsal, beneath the soft-rayed portion of the dorsal, forward corner rounded but otherwise of a nearly even height. Gill covers and trunk have moderately large scales. Caudal is slightly forked. Dorsal fin, about VII, 15; anal 14 to 15. The lateral line is comparatively indistinct. Coloration: Blue to olive green on the back and also on the upper part of the sides above the lateral line, changing to a yellow or rose-red to golden lower down on the sides, belly is rose hued with a white midline. The head is reddish on the sides and pure white below. The back and sides above pectorals and lateral line are dotted with small yellow spots, particularly conspicuous below the adipose dorsal flap. Dusky dorsal marked with similar but larger yellowish spots; green to green-yellow adipose flap; anal is pink-clouded with a purple hue; pectorals are pale brown with purple reflections at their bases.
Size: Reported rarely to 42 in (105 cm); 55 lb (25 kg) but commonly half this weight and a lesser length.
Distribution: Outer part of the continental shelf and upper part of the continental edge off Nova Scotia and the North and Middle Atlantic United States; southern Florida; Campache Bank in the southern side of Gulf of Mexico. Most generally in the deep waters of the Western Atlantic.
General: A valued and important commercial food fish occasionally caught by anglers in very deep waters. Eats great variety of bottom dwelling invertebrates such as crabs, squid, shrimp, sea urchins and cucumbers.

396 AUSTRALIAN WHITING s
Sillago ciliata
Other common names: Sand whiting, whiting, blue-nose whiting, smelt.

Features: The long, robust, tapering body is covered with small scales that easily rub off. Bands of fine teeth on the vomer, in both jaws, but none on the palatine. Eyes are large and placed high on the head. Tail slightly notched. Although the Australians call it whiting, the fish is actually no cod fish. Depth to body length ratio is about 1–6. First dorsal, X–XI; second dorsal, 16 or more. Lateral line scale count about 70 with about 6 lines of scales above the line and 10 below at the shoulder. Coloration: Dark silver-blue above, shading to silver below with yellow anal and pelvic fins. Rows of black spots between the rays of the soft second dorsal. Lateral line is strongly black. The tail fin is dark with irregular lighter stripes. Mature fish show blue on the head front.
Size: Up to 18 in (45 cm), 2 1/4 lb (1 kg), but usually smaller. Mature at about 11 in (27 1/2 cm).
Distribution: Shallow water coastal fish of the Australia, New Zealand, Tasmania region. Prefers sand flats in estuaries and often invades the surf.
General: Important food fish, delicate, tender white meat with fine flavor. Taken by rod and reel and commercially from ocean beaches in the southern summer. Feeds on worms and small crustaceans, plankton.

397 SPOTTED WHITING s
Sillaginodes punctatus
Other common name: King George whiting.

Features: Long, elongate body, slightly compressed. Horseshoe-shaped mouth with small teeth; soft, conical snout. Dorsal fins IX to XIV–17 to 27; tail fin concave; anal fin II,20 to 22. Coloration: dorsally dark brown; flanks lighter brown or reddish brown; belly silvery; dorsal area and upper flanks conspicuously dark spotted; dorsal fin has larger spots with lighter brown margins. Lateral line scale count 125 to 130. Scales are small.
Size: Up to *c.* 27 in (70 cm), 4 1/2 lb (2 kg); but average fish 1 1/2–2 1/4 lb (3/4–1 kg).
Distribution: Indo-Pacific, ranging the coasts of New South Wales westward to southwestern Western Australia.
General: The largest and most notable of the Australian whiting of which there are about nine species occurring in Australian waters. They are especially plentiful in South Australian waters, but along the entire southern coasts, where they frequent shallow sandy ground (sometimes burying themselves in the sand), they are much sought after as sport fish. Food consists of worms and crustaceans which they dig out with their highly adapted conical snouts. It is a very important commercial species and is one of the finest table fishes in Australian waters.

398 OCEAN WHITEFISH s
Caulolatilus princeps
Other common names: Whitefish, blanquillo, tilefish, sea whitefish.

Features: Body elongate, with a blunt snout and large eyes. Head subconical. Scales small, ctenoid; lateral line present and complete, more or less concurrent with the back outline. The dorsal fin is long and low, continuous, the spinous portion slightly lower than the soft part. Anal fin very long with only a few feeble spines. Caudal is concave. There is no separation notch on the dorsal fin. Large canines are present toward the rear of the jaws. Dorsal fin IX, 24; anal II, 23. Coloration: A light brown on the back and the sides, sometimes of a general yellowish hue, gradually fading to lighter below. The pectorals are blue-grey with a yellowish streak along the center; dorsal and anal fins are yellowish with a blue streak near the edges. All the remaining fins are a yellow hue.
Size: Maximum appears to be about 40 in (100 cm) but generally half this length.
Distribution: California and southward down to Peru along the Pacific Ocean coast.
General: Loves rocky and sandy areas. Fair tasting food fish important in commercial economy; reasonable sport fish but not at all superlative on hook and line. Generally taken on the bottom with bait while angling for other species.

20 JACKS, POMFRETS, POMPANOS

399 ATLANTIC HORSE-EYE JACK s, B
Caranx latus
Other common names: Goggle-eye, yellow jack.

Features: Elongate, deep, and compressed body. Head blunt with a very large characteristic eye. Dorsal fins VIII–I,20 to 22; tail fin deeply forked; anal fin II–I,16 or 17. Coloration: back, flanks, and belly silvery; fins, except pectorals, yellowish; pectoral fin dusky; soft dorsal fin has a black tip. Young fish have vertical, darkish crossbars on flanks. Lateral line arched over pectoral fin; scale count 84 to 92 with the last 35 to 50 as dusky-coloured scutes.
Size: Average up to 24 in (60 cm), maximum 30 in (75 cm), *c.* 8 1/2 lb (3 3/4 kg).
Distribution: Bermudas, New Jersey to Rio de Janeiro.
General: A hard-fighting fish on light tackle, but not considered good table fare.

400 BLUE RUNNER s
Caranx crysos
Other common names: Hardtail, hardtail jack.

Features: Elongate, slender, and compressed body. Short-headed and short-snouted. Dorsal fins VIII–I,23 to 25; tail fin moderately large and deeply forked; anal fin II–I,19 to 21. Coloration: dorsally bluish; flanks more silvery, belly silvery, spiny dorsal and margins of dorsal and tail fins dusky, other fins pale; a black spot on gill cover. Lateral line strongly arched over sicklelike pectoral fins; scale count 86 to 98 including 38 to 52 scutes.
Size: Average up to 20 in (50 cm), 4 lb (1 3/4 kg).
Distribution: Western Atlantic, Cape Hatteras, West Indies to Brazil; eastern Pacific, several related forms.
General: Very abundant schooling species along the North American coast from Texas northward, and a popular hardfighting fish which may often be taken on fly tackle. An excellent food fish and one suitable for broiling whole without skinning. Its flesh is rated of the highest table quality among the Atlantic jacks.

401 CREVALLE JACK s
Caranx hippos
Other common names: Common jack, toro, jack crevalle.

Features: Oblong, compressed body. Very steep, arched profile to head; large mouth; lower jaw projecting slightly. Two dorsal fins VIII–I, 19 to 21; tail fin large and deeply forked, anal fin II–I,15 to 17. Coloration: dorsally bluish green to olivaceous; flanks and belly silvery with golden blotches; a distinct black blotch on gill cover and another on pectoral fin; edge of soft dorsal black; tail fin yellowish. Juveniles have characteristic dark bars (a typical feature of the jacks). Lateral line scutes 25 to 42. Small scales, none on chest area.
Size: Up to 2 1/2 ft (75 cm), 20 lb (9 kg).
Distribution: Warm seas of the Americas.
General: Found in harbours, sheltered bays, and around coastal waters and offshore reefs; juvenile schooling fish frequent brackish river mouths. All jacks possess first class sport fish qualities, and although opinions differ in respect to their table qualities, they represent important commercial food fish whenever they are found in sufficient numbers.

402 GIANT TREVALLY s
Caranx sexfasciatus
Other common names: Turrum, ulua, great trevally.

Features: A powerful, deeply compressed body. Head and dorsal profile strongly convex; forehead high; lower jaw projecting. Dorsal fins VII or VIII–I,19 to 21 (anterior rays falcate); well-formed keels on tail stalk; tail fin deeply forked; anal fin II–I,16 to 18 (anterior rays falcate); long scythe-shaped pectoral fins. Coloration: dorsally dark purplish green or opalescent blue; flanks silvery with a few yellowish spots; belly silvery; small dark spots on gill cover; tail fin yellow with upper tip black. Juveniles with 4–7 broad, dark crossbands. After death general colouration fades to a brownish yellow. Lateral line is well defined and arched above pectoral fin with 28–37 scutes along the posterior straight section.
Size: Up to 110 lb (50 kg), but average fish much smaller.
Distribution: Indo-Pacific tropical seas.
General: The giant trevally is a tremendously tough, hard-fighting fish and is rated very highly in Australasian and Polynesian waters where it is most frequently encountered as a sport fish. The adult fish is common around reefs, and the young school in estuaries and harbours. The flesh has a reddish tint and is rated of fair table quality.

403 KING TREVALLY s
Caranx speciosus
Other common name: Golden trevally.

Features: Ovalate, laterally compressed body. Dorsal fins VII or VIII–I,18–21; tail fin very deeply forked; anal fin II–21. Coloration: dorsally and upper flanks light blue; lower flanks and belly silvery-yellow with iridescent play of colours; the gill cover has a black spot; fins yellowish; younger fish are brighter golden yellow with 10 to 12 narrow, transverse, and darker bands. Lateral line is arched over scythelike pectoral fin and there are 15 to 25 scutes along the posterior straight section.
Size: Average up to 40 in (100 cm).
Distribution: Indo-Pacific seas.
General: A predatory schooling species

common in warm Indo-Pacific waters, particularly around estuaries and reefs. Of some commercial importance. A fine reputation as a sport fish.

404 YELLOW JACK s
Caranx bartholomaei

Features: Small, fusiform body and deeply compressed. Head blunt and short. Dorsal fin deeply notched VIII–I,25 to 28; tail fin deeply forked; anal fin II–I,22 to 25; long, scythelike pectoral fins. Coloration: dorsally iridescent bluish green; flanks and belly silvery; all fins yellow; flanks of young fish have a reticulated gold pattern. Lateral line arched over pectoral fin; scale count 91 to 114 with the last 25 to 36 as weakly developed scutes.
Size: Average up to 15 in (38 cm), maximum 30 in (75 cm), 15 1/2 lb (7 kg).
Distribution: Western Atlantic, from North Carolina, West Indies to Brazil.

405 BAR JACK s
Caranx ruber
Other common names: Skipjack, cibi, mancho, green jack, common jack, hardtail.

Features: Identification requires close attention to details. Body moderately deep and compressed. Posterior straight portion of lateral line has 20 to 23 pointed scutes. The long, tapering head gives the upper profile an almost evenly convex shape. Lower profile from anal fin to mouth is almost straight. Dorsal fin VIII; second dorsal I, 26–30. Anal fin II; second anal I, 23–26. Gill raker count is 31–35 on the lower limb of the first gill arch, 10–14 on the upper limb. Second dorsal and anal fins each has a long sheath of scales along the base. Fins are completely covered with small scales. Coloration: may vary with the local environment. Blue-grey above, shading on the sides to white below. A dark blue or black band or stripe along each upper side from top of gill cover to the tail. Juveniles under 5 in (12.5 cm) have an average of 6 vertical dark bars on the body plus one across the nape. Larger fish develop a dark band across the lower lobe of the tail which contrasts with the relatively unpigmented upper lobe.
Size: Up to 24 in (60 cm), 15 lb (7 kg).
Distribution: Tropical and warm-temperate waters of western Atlantic including West Indies, Caribbean, Gulf of Mexico, Gulf Stream as far north as New Jersey in summer.
General: Primarily an offshore species that strays inshore at times. Swift and aggressive, very good on light sporting tackle. No real commercial value and indifferent as table fare.

406 AMBERJACK s
Seriola dumerili

Features: Semifusiform, elongate body; only moderately compressed. Large mouth with small teeth in bands. Dorsal fins I–VI or VII–I,32 to 34 (leading dorsal spine absent in mature fish); tail fin forked; anal fin II–I,20 to 25 (Smith, South Africa). Coloration: dorsally a brilliant blue; flanks with a broad dull yellow stripe from head to tail. Dark diagonal stripe across the eye. The belly of the amberjack is creamy-white whereas the belly of the yellowtail is silvery white. The amberjack fins are olive blue to dark blue, and the anal fin is margined with white while the tail fin has yellowish tones.

Size: Up to 150 lb (68 kg).

Distribution: Cosmopolitan in warm to temperate seas.

General: Amberjacks are schooling pelagic, species found in open water or round offshore reefs. Rated high among the world's top light-tackle sport fishes. Although the smaller fish are fair table fish, the larger ones are rather coarse.

407 KING AMBERJACK s
Seriola grandis

Other common names: Yellowtail kingfish, kingfish, yellowtail, northern kingfish, haku (Maori), Pacific yellowtail, California yellowtail, amberjack.

Features: Body is elongate and semicircular in cross-section, fully scaled, peduncle slender with low side keels. The head is stout and rounded, the mouth large, the small teeth found in bands in both jaws. There is no adipose eyelid. The lateral line is high up behind the head but reaches the centre of the sides before the beginning or origin of the anal fin. The dorsal fin is very long with the spinous portion containing only a few short rudimentary spines, the soft portion separate with the front rays forming a lobe, the remaining rays short and of approximately equal length. The anal fin is similar in outline to the soft dorsal but far shorter. The tail fin is forked with pointed lobes, a notch present above and below peduncle in front of the tail base. First dorsal fin VII or less; second dorsal 34; anal III, 21. On the first gill arch below the angle, the king amberjack has fifteen to seventeen gill rakers. Coloration: Greyish green dorsal surface and silvery sides with a bright, yellowish to bronze band running from the snout to the tail. The tail is yellow; the fins are yellowish with touch of light green.

Size: To approximately 5 ft (1.5 m); 88 lb (40 kg) but generally far smaller.

Distribution: Widespread off waters of California, the Gulf of California, Canal Zone, Ecuador, Chile, Fiji Islands, Australia and New Zealand.

General: Readily confused with other amberjacks. Little known about life history in the open ocean. Swift and predatory in surface waters; feeds voraciously on smaller fishes. Game for anglers; edible, but not in demand commercially.

408 ALMACO JACK s
Seriola rivoliana

Features: Medium large, elongate, compressed body. Dorsal fin VII–I,28 to 32; tail fin crescentic; anal fin II–I,22 to 24 (second dorsal and anal fins falcate). Coloration: variable, usually dorsally ranging from bluish green to olivaceous or brown; flanks silvery, occasionally with brassy or lavender reflections; front of head brownish; a diagonal dark brown bar on head; young fish more yellowish and with dark bars across flanks which disappear when the fish attains a length of *c.* 7 in (18 cm). Lateral line arched and wavy over pectoral fin.

Size: Up to 50 lb (22 1/2 kg), 48 in (120 cm).

Distribution: Widespread through warm and warm-temperate seas.

General: A deep-sea pelagic fish and rarely seen in shallow waters. A hard-fighting sport fish and of moderate-to-good table quality.

409 BLUNTNOSE JACK (ATLANTIC) s
Hemicaranx amblyrhynchus

Features: Elongate, compressed, and rather deep body. Dorsal fin VIII–I,20 to 22; tail fin deeply forked; anal fin II–I,17 or 18. Coloration: dorsally dark; flanks and belly silvery. Lateral line arched over pectoral fin, and with *c.* 35 lateral scutes along straight section extending into tail stalk.

Size: Up to 24 in (60 cm).

Distribution: Atlantic; western Atlantic range from Cape Hatteras to Brazil, and West Indies; not common along Florida coast. Related forms in Indo-Pacific seas.

General: A wide-ranging schooling species, excellent sport fish, but not esteemed as table fish owing to its rather strong flavour.

410 TREVALLY s
Usacaranx georgianus

Other common names: Silver trevally, white trevally, silver bream, silver fish, skipjack, araara (Maori).

Features: Body compressed and completely scaled, evenly and rather highly arched above but more or less horizontal straight below. Deep head, moderate size mouth, teeth small, lateral line wavy or curved after start of second dorsal. Enlarged scales forming scutes along centre of caudal peduncle, numbering 25 to 29. First dorsal base short, but subsequent spines rather high; second dorsal rather long with last rays more widely spaced than the others and longer than the last few rays. The anal fin is similar in shape but shorter than the soft dorsal with spines separated from the beginning of the fin by a space. The pectoral is roughly scythe-shaped. Caudal is deeply forked. First dorsal, VIII; second dorsal, 24 to 27; anal, III, 23. Coloration: blue green to blue blackish above with the sides a silvery green with a golden flush. Most of the fins have a yellowish hue. There is a dark spot or blotch at the top of the gill plate.

Size: Variously reported at a maximum of about 36 in (90 cm); 11 lb (5 kg) but usually far smaller.

Distribution: Cool Australian waters, New Zealand, and probably sections of the Tasman Sea.

General: Edible, marketed fresh and smoked. Fast-swimming. Should be gutted soon after capture, for flesh spoils easily. Important commercially and as a sporting fish in channels and the surf; takes many different baits.

411 QUEENFISH s
Chorinemus lysan

Other common names: Talang, leatherskin.

Features: The body is stout, compressed and high. Broad and high head with big mouth and rather large eyes. The lateral line is bent a little upwards over the pectoral fins. Elongate scales. The first dorsal fin consists of only 6–7 free spines, the second is long reaching nearly the tail, its anterior part is high, the posterior very low; the anal fin is as the second dorsal, at its beginning are 2 short, stout spines. Coloration: most of the body is silvery; the back is darkest. Above the lateral line are 6–8 dark spots. The fins are yellow.

Size: Up to 20 in (50 cm).

Distribution: The tropical Indo-Pacific region from the east coast of Africa to Tahiti and from the Persian Gulf to Australia.

General: The queenfish inhabits coastal and offshore waters; it is observed often on pearl banks.

412 BANDED RUDDERFISH s
Seriola zonata

Other common names: Amberfish, rudderfish.

Features: Semifusiform, well-compressed body. Dorsal fins VII–I,36 to 39; tail fin forked; anal fin II–I,21. Coloration: dorsally and on the upper flanks bluish; lower flanks and belly lighter with a brassy tinge; on young fish there may be vertical bands present on the flanks which extend to the fins. The lateral line has a conspicuous yellow band. No scutes on lateral line.

Size: Average up to *c.* 24 in (60 cm), 9 lb (4 kg).

Distribution: Western Atlantic coasts from Cape Cod to Cape Hatteras and Bermuda.

General: A representative of the Atlantic carangid (*Caranx*) jacks with many features similar to the amberjacks. Often found associated with floating driftwood or seaweed at sea. No great sport or commercial value.

413 PACIFIC AMBERJACK s
Seriola colburni

Other common names: Amberjack, yellowtail, white salmon.

Features: Has a fairly elongated body though not as deep as a jack. Moderately compressed and fairly deep for an amberjack. Small scales, no tail scutes, teeth feeble, lunar forked caudal fin. A very powerful and streamlined fish with a snubbed or slightly flattened forehead and a distinct lateral line. The soft-rayed portion of the dorsal is high forward, but slopes back to less height after the first few rays. There are 13 to 16 gill rakers on the first gill below the angle. Distinct from *Seriola lalandi*, the Yellowtail of both the Atlantic and Pacific, by having longer first rays of the second dorsal and anal fins. First dorsal fin about VII; second dorsal I, 28 to 31; anal II detached, followed by I, 21. The gill rakers become shorter and more rudimentary with age and growth. Coloration: A dark diagonal band extending through the eye from a position slightly forward of and above the gill opening. Light purple to purple-blue on dorsal surface, sometimes with a grey or bronze hue. Sides are silvery with a touch of yellow. The dorsal and anal fin lobes are reputed to become more elongated as the fish grows.

Size: Specimens over 110 lb (50 kg) have been taken but 33 lb (15 kg) is more a common weight.

Distribution: Reported from the Gulf of Guayaquil in Ecuador through the Pacific coast of Mexico and portion of California in the United States; also the Galapagos.

General: Excellent gamefish for anglers, but food value only fair.

414 BURI s
Seriola quinqueradiata

Other common name: Yellowtail.

Features: Spindle-shaped body. The posterior part of the upper jaw very broad. The first dorsal fin consists of only 5 short, free spines, the second is long, 30–35 soft rays. Very large, deeply forked tail fin with pointed lobes; pectoral and ventral fins of moderate size; anal fin only 2/3 the length of second dorsal. Lateral line much upwards bent over the pectoral fins. Coloration: body above the lateral line dark blue, lower sides and belly silvery to whitish.

Size: The buri attains a length of 3 ft (1 m), or even more, but usually less.

Distribution: Warm-temperate region of the western Pacific; Japan, Korea, Taiwan.

General: Its home is the open sea, but it spawns a little closer to the land, in late spring and early summer. In Japan it is an important food fish known under many local names.

415 YELLOWTAIL s
Seriola lalandi

Other common names: Geelstert, alfkoord, (S. Africa), northern kingfish (Australia).

Features: Semifusiform, elongate body; only moderately compressed. Large mouth with small teeth in bands. Dorsal fins I–VI or VII–I,32 to 34 (leading dorsal spine absent in mature fish); tail fin forked; anal fin II–I,20 to 25. Coloration: dorsally a brilliant blue; flanks with a broad yellow stripe from head to tail; belly silvery white. The pectoral and dorsal fins are bluish grey, and the rest of the fins (and characteristically the tail fin) are yellow.

Size: Up to 150 lb (68 kg).

Distribution: Cosmopolitan in warm to temperate seas, ranging into cooler waters than the amberjack.

General: Yellowtails are schooling pelagic, deep or shallow-water species found in open water or around offshore reefs, and are rated high among the world's top light-tackle sport fishes. Although the smaller fish are fair table fish, the larger ones are rather coarse. In several areas the flesh is considerably improved if the fish is bled immediately after capture.

416 DORADE s
Gnathanodon speciosus

Other common names: Golden trevally, king trevally.

Features: Oblong, compressed body, more convex profile above than below. Large mouth; no visible teeth in jaws, but juveniles have minute teeth which are lost with age. Two dorsal fins VII or VIII–I,18 to 21; tail fin large and deeply forked; anal fin II–I,15 to 17 (soft dorsal and anal fins sickle-shaped (falcate) but length is variable). Coloration: dorsally bluish; flanks silvery yellow or bright golden yellow with 8 to 10 transverse black bands, but they are often absent in older fish; fins yellowish; dusky patch on gill cover. Lateral line arched, beginning below 9th or 10th dorsal ray; 15–25 scutes (but scutes variable in number). Subspecies or variants show minor differences in depth of body, length of soft dorsal and anal fins, and other features.

Size: Up to and sometimes exceeding 40 in (100 cm), 35 lb (16 kg).

Distribution: Indo-Pacific tropical and subtropical seas.

General: Known as king trevally or alternatively as golden trevally in Australasia. Closely related to the Atlantic jacks and crevalles. A species common in coastal waters and estuaries; adults frequent offshore reefs. An excellent hard-fighting sport fish with good table qualities.

417 SCAD S

Trachurus trachurus

Other common names: Maasbanker, saurel (South Africa).

Features: Long, slender body. Prominent, large jaws; lower jaw projecting. Two dorsal fins I,VIII–I,23 to 34; tail fin deeply forked; anal fin II–I,25 to 34. Coloration: dorsally greyish to bluish green; flanks and belly silvery; gill cover has black spot or blotch. Lateral line arched and has a scale count 69 to 79. A complete row of bony scutes extends the length of the lateral line; the rest of the body has very fine scales which easily rub off. Related specimen *T. picturatus* has 91 to 105 lateral line bony scutes. *T. mediterraneus* has 78 to 92 bony scutes.

Size: Average range 8–16 in (20–40 cm), maximum 20 in (50 cm).

Distribution: Mediterranean, Atlantic and bordering seas.

General: A common schooling fish usually found in open waters ranging 30–330 ft (10–100 m). A good sport fish. The dorsal and anal spines are sharp and may inflict painful wounds if fish are not handled carefully. After spawning, young scad (which have overall silvery colouration) often shelter under jellyfishes. Although scad are edible, they are not particularly noteworthy as table fish.

418 MA-AJI S

Trachurus japonicus

Other common name: Japan horse mackerel.

Features: Large head with big eyes, short snout. Lower jaw projecting beyond upper. High, narrow scales along the lateral line, which is upwards curved at the middle of the body. First dorsal fin with 8 spines and separated from the long second (ca 31–33 soft rays) by a short interval. Tail fin large, deeply forked. Large pectoral fins reaching almost to off the anus. Also large ventral fins. Anal fin with two spines and a long soft-rayed part. Coloration: back and upper sides dark blue, lower sides and belly silvery; scales along the lateral line lightly yellow.

Size: Maximum length 2 ft (60 cm).

Distribution: West Pacific, off Japan and Korea.

General: Lives in deeper, offshore waters. In spring it enters more shallow water for spawning. It is of importance to the fisheries, sold fresh or dried.

419 PACIFIC JACK MACKEREL S

Trachurus symmetricus

Other common names: Jurel, jurelcito.

Features: Body rather stout and rounded. Head compressed with a somewhat pointed snout; lower jaw slightly projecting beyond the upper jaw which is rather broad, reaching to the anterior border of the eye. The mouth has many small, pointed teeth. The lateral line is distinct and accentuated by densely placed high and narrow scales; it is bent abruptly upwards below the anterior part of the second dorsal fin. First dorsal fin short, only 6–7 rays, the second is lower and very long; tail fin deeply forked; anal fin similar to second dorsal fin. Coloration: above grey blue, lower sides silvery, gill cover with a dark spot.

Size: 1 3/4–2 ft (50–60 cm).

Distribution: East Pacific from California to Chile.

General: A pelagic shoaling fish. The stock in the southern part of the distribution area is by several authors considered a separate species. (*T. murphyi*).

420 RAINBOW RUNNER S

Elagatis bipinnulatus

Other common names: Hawaiian salmon, runner, prodigal son, rainbow yellowtail, skipjack, shoemaker.

Features: Moderately elongate, streamlined, and fusiform body. Head and mouth small; villiform teeth. Dorsal fin VI–I,24 to 27 + 1 finlet; tail fin large and very deeply forked; anal fin II–I,15 to 17 + 1 finlet. Coloration: dorsally bluish green; flanks have two blue bands or stripes on yellowish background; belly yellowish white or pinkish white; soft dorsal and anal fins olivaceous or yellowish; tail fin yellow. Lateral line gently arched over pectoral fin; no scutes.

Size: Average up to 70 in (180 cm), 30 lb (13 1/2 kg).

Distribution: Worldwide in warm and warm-temperate seas.

General: A pelagic species and rarely seen inshore. A magnificent sport fish with the largest specimens appearing to frequent Hawaiian waters. Older fish grow more heavy bodied. Nowadays frequently used as a first-choice marlin bait and as a chumming fish for sharks and tuna. An excellent table fish with white, firm flesh.

421 AFRICAN POMPANO S

Alectis crinitus

Other common names: Threadfish, cobblerfish, Pacific threadfish, pennantfish.

Features: Medium-large, oval body, much compressed. Steep, humped profile to forehead. Dorsal fin VII–I,18 or 19; tail fin strongly forked; anal fin II–I,15 or 16 (in adult fish first spiny dorsal and anal fins are covered by skin); first rays of dorsal and anal fins filamentous and exceedingly long; particularly in young fish, but becoming shorter with age. Coloration: dorsally silvery bluish or bluish; flanks golden yellow; a dark blotch on dorsal fin and anal fin in front; dark spot on gill cover; juveniles show obscure dark bars on flanks. Lateral line scale count 120 to 140; scales near tail

stalk develop into scutes.

Size: Up to 36 in (90 cm), 33 lb (15 kg).

Distribution: Atlantic, ranging in western Atlantic from Cape Hatteras to Brazil.

General: It has been suggested that the filamentous threadlike dorsal and anal fins allow the juveniles to mimic the medusae and so go protected from predators in the vulnerable period of early life. A food fish of some importance, and a good fighter on light tackle when encountered.

422 PILOTFISH S

Naucrates ductor

Other common names: Leather jack, leatherskin.

Features: Elongate, almost fusiform, compressed. Blunt snout with rounded profile; small mouth with villiform teeth. Dorsal fins III or IV–I,26 to 28 (first spines low and very weakly developed and not connected by membrane except in young fish); fleshy keels on tail stalk; tail fin deeply forked; anal fin II,16 or 17. Coloration: dorsally bluish; flanks and belly paler; flanks characteristically have 5 to 7 dark crossbands which extend onto fins; tail fin dusky with white tips; pectorals and ventrals yellowish but sometimes black. Lateral line is wavy. Small scales.

Size: Up to 24 in (60 cm).

Distribution: Cosmopolitan in all warm seas.

General: The pilotfish can readily be distinguished from the mackerel by the absence of finlets. The very short spines on the first dorsal distinguish it from the bluefish, rudderfish, and the scads; it is also distinguished from other carangids by the lack of scutes on the lateral line.

Young pilotfish are frequently seen sheltering under floating objects such as wreckage, jellyfish, and sargasso weed. Adults seek out the company of sharks, and often several individuals share a single "host". What biological role this has is not certain. It has been suggested that the pilotfish stays with the shark for a share of the prey.

The flesh of the pilotfish is edible but is of very inferior quality.

423 COMMON POMPANO S

Trachinotus carolinus

Other common names: Pompano, moonfish.

Features: Oblong body, rather robust, compressed. Blunt head, mouth nearly horizontal. Dorsal fin VI–I,23 to 27; tail fin deeply forked; anal fin II–I,23 (dorsal and anal fins sickle-shaped). Coloration: dorsally greenish blue; flanks and belly silvery or slightly golden; breast more or less yellowish; top of head bluish; tail stalk and tail with bluish reflections; pectoral and anal fins light orange shaded with blue. Lateral line undulates over pectoral fin.

Size: Up to 18 in (45 cm), 7–8 lb (3 1/2 kg).

Distribution: Western Atlantic, from Cape Hatteras southward to West Indies and Brazil; more plentiful in the Gulf of Mexico area particularly from Florida westward to around the Texas coast.

General: Often referred to as *the* supreme table fish in North America because of its firm flesh and its rich, delicate flavour. Until recent times it was not included

among sport fish mainly due to its reputation of ignoring a baited hook. Pompano are now regularly included among sportfishing catches, and in some locales, where specialized methods have evolved, more fish are now landed with rod and hook than via commercial netting.

Food consists chiefly of crustaceans found in shallow water which are routed out of the bottom sand and mud with the help of the pompanos' highly adapted, blunt snout. One of their favourite crustaceans, the sand flea, has been found to be one of the most effective sport-fishing baits.

424 PACIFIC POMFRET S

Brama japonica

Other common names: Small-scaled pomfret, etchiopia.

Features: Short, high, compressed body; large head and big eyes. The opening of the mouth is turned upwards. Lateral line curved dorsally over the pectoral fin. Large scales. Large and high dorsal and anal fins with fewer rays than in *B. brama*. Tail fin deeply forked with pointed lobes; large pectoral and small ventral fins. Coloration: All over bluish, silvery; back, fins, and head a little darker.

Size: About 12–16 in (30–40 cm); 6–7 lb (3 kg).

Distribution: Northern Pacific between 20° and 60° N. Alaska to Mexico and Kamchatka to northern Japan.

General: A pelagic, migratory species which feeds on squids, shrimps and fish. It has some commercial importance in Japan.

425 COMMON LEATHERJACKET S

Oligoplites saurus

Other common names: Zapatero, skipjack.

Features: Elongate and mackerel-like. Lower jaw projecting; large mouth. Dorsal fin V–10 + c. 9 finlets; tail fin deeply forked; anal fin II–10 + c. 10 finlets (in the dorsal and anal fins the soft rays and finlets merge without a clearcut transition between the two). Coloration: dorsally blue green; flanks paler; belly silvery.

Size: Up to 12 in (30 cm).

Distribution: Both coasts of tropical America, ranging north to New York and California; common in West Indies and Florida.

General: A schooling species and a fish sometimes confused with young mackerel. As a sport fish it is locally very popular and will readily strike at a lure or take baits. It will frequently leap clear of the water, hence its alternative common but very confusing name "skipjack".

426 ATLANTIC PERMIT S

Trachinotus falcatus

Other common names: Round pompano, Indian River permit.

Features: Medium size; oblong, deep, compressed body with a humped appearance. Dorsal fin VI–I,18 to 21; tail fin deeply forked; anal fin II–I,16 to 18; spiny dorsal fin low; first rays of soft dorsal and anal fins falcate. Coloration: dorsally iridescent blue or blue green; flanks and belly silvery sometimes with yellowish tints; fins in adult

fish bluish or blackish with lighter tips; in young fish lobe of dorsal fin black.
Size: Average 12 in (30 cm), 3 lb (1 1/2 kg), maximum up to 40 in (100 cm), 50 lb (22,5 kg).
Distribution: Atlantic; western Atlantic ranging from Cape Cod to Brazil, common southward but occurs northward only in the Gulf Stream. Also known off African coasts. Several closely related forms in Atlantic and Indo-Pacific seas.
General: Not as abundant as the related common pompano but shares the same sandy flats and reefs. A trophy game fish on light tackle. Considered good eating.

427 PALOMETA S
Trachinotus goodei
Other common name: Gaff-topsail pompano.

Features: Medium size, elliptical and oblong, moderately deep, compressed body. Steep profile on forehead; snubsnouted appearance. Dorsal fin VII–I,19 or 20; tail fin large and deeply forked; anal fin II–I,17 or 18; anterior part of soft dorsal and anal fins prolonged in adult fish. Coloration: dorsally bluish-silvery; flanks silvery with four or more narrow dark bars; belly light golden-yellow; in adult fish, lobes of dorsal, tail and anal fins black and in young fish yellow and white. Lateral line distinct, nearly straight, but slightly curved above pectoral fin. Scales are small.
Size: Up to 20 in (50 cm), 3 1/2 lb (1 1/2 kg).
Distribution: Atlantic; western Atlantic, Florida and West Indies to Argentina; also eastern Atlantic.
General: Identity of this species is sometimes difficult. The palometa is the smallest of the western Atlantic pompanos. As table fish it is prized commercially throughout its range, and is an excellent sport fish on light tackle.

428 LEERFISH S
Hypacanthus amius
Other common names: Leavis, garrick.

Features: Long, deep, elongate body, laterally compressed. Medium-sized fish; pointed snout; lower jaw slightly projecting; feeble teeth. Dorsal fins I–VII–I,19–21; tail fin lunate; anal fin II–I,19–21 (soft dorsal and anal fins sickle-shaped). Coloration: dorsally greenish, bluish, or greenish blue; flanks paling to silvery; belly silvery; tail yellowish orange. Lateral line is very undulating but straight near tail. The scales are small with no scutes, and the skin has a characteristic leathery appearance (hence its most used common name leerfish). Juveniles are very different from adults in appearance and colouration: blotched with bright orange and brown markings.
Size: Up to 6 ft (180 cm), 150 lb (70 kg).
Distribution: Mediterranean, eastern Atlantic, ranging from Portugal to South Africa.
General: Rated a fine sport fish (particularly in South African waters) owing to its large size and hard fighting qualities. It is often seen pursuing mullet in estuaries. As a sport fish it may be caught with live or moving bait. The flesh of the larger fish is coarse and rather dry.

429 DOLPHIN (fish) S
Coryphaena hippurus
Other common names: Dorado, dorado de altura, dourade, mahimahi, coryphene.

Features: Body elongate, very compressed laterally. Head massive, male and female show marked differences in frontal profile: male has a very blunt squarish head, while that of the female is more rounded. Both sexes are heavier in frontal part of body, which then tapers to tail. High, long single dorsal fin 55 to 65; tail fin very deeply forked with long lobes; long anal fin 26 to 30. Coloration: dorsally and flanks rich, vivid blue, shot with a brilliant silver and gold iridescence; flanks stippled and mottled with dark and golden spots; belly white to golden; tail fin golden yellow; young fish show a series of crossbands which extend over dorsal fin. Colours quickly fade after death, and preserved specimens are usually dark or greyish. The lateral line forms an angular peak over the sickle-shaped pectoral fin, then extends straight along median line of flank to tail. The scales are very small.
Size: Largest up to 6 ft (185 cm), 70 lb (32 kg); average school fish range 5–12 lb (2 1/2–5 1/2 kg).
Distribution: Worldwide throughout warm seas; also sometimes found in temperate waters.
General: The dolphin fish is sometimes confused with the dolphin (genus *Delphinus*), which is a member of the toothedwhale family. The dolphin is found singly or in large schools. It preys on flying fish. Spawning occurs at sea, and the eggs drift at the surface during incubation. Even small females may produce more than 500,000 eggs.

The dolphin is a magnificent sport fish, and proves a tough, hard fighter when hooked. When encountered in schools, chasing smaller prey, it may hit a lure or bait as soon as it is offered in the water, and when hooked, leaps about in the air like an acrobat. It is also a very excellent table fish.

Another related species is the pompano dolphin (*C. equisetis*). The main difference is in length; the pompano rarely exceeds 30 in (75 cm), with the average fish *c.* 12 in (30 cm). Only by counting the number of rays in the dorsal fin can the smaller member of the two species be readily distinguished; *C. hippurus* has 55 to 65 rays, and *C. equisetis* 48 to 55 rays.

430 POMPANO DOLPHIN S
Coryphaena equisetis
Other common names: Little dolphin, dolphin, small dolphin, dorado, dourade.

Features: Similar to the common dolphin, *hippurus*, with a high forehead, particularly in the males, and a long dorsal fin without spines. Moderately slender and flattened sideways, compressed, elongate and tapering with the very long and high dorsal beginning on the nape. Slightly projecting lower jaw. The anal fin is similar to the dorsal but shorter. Tail is distinctly forked. Small, comb-like teeth in the jaws and on the roof of the mouth. Body is most massive and deepest close behind the head. Large ventral fins; lobes of the caudal are long and slender; moderately long ventrals and

pectorals are situated one below the other. Dorsal fin, 51 to 55; anal, 24 to 26. Coloration: Brilliant in golds, greens and blues when alive but fades rapidly upon death. Sides largely a vivid blue, variously mottled and washed with a golden hue; tail largely a golden yellow. Dorsal fin purplish blue, with paler oblique lines; other fins tinged with blue. Small black spots on lower parts. Scales are minute.
Size: Smaller than the common dolphin. Exact maximum size not known; common proportions under 6.6 lb (3 kg).
Distribution: Open Atlantic and Pacific oceans but rare in the West Indies area. Recently taken in some numbers off the coast of southern California.
General: Sporting fighter for anglers, flesh very good. Sometimes seen when leaping in pursuit of small fish. Offshore, they appear to feed largely on flying fish or, when available, mullet. Found solitary or in schools.

431 ROOSTERFISH S
Nematistius pectoralis
Other common names: Papagallo, pez gallo.

Features: Elongate body. Large head; lower jaw projecting. Pectoral fin long and sickle-shaped. Dorsal fins VIII–I,27 or 28 (both dorsal fins fold into a deep sheath); tail fin deeply forked; anal fin I,17; anterior dorsal spines are characteristically very elongated, supposedly reminiscent of a rooster's comb (hence common name). Coloration: dorsally and gill covers leaden grey blue; flanks golden with overall metallic sheen; an indigo blue crossband on snout, another on forehead, and a third extends from upper part of neck to below gill cover; a broad indigo band extends from first dorsal spine to the anus; a curved band extends from the sixth dorsal spine to base of upper tail fin rays; dorsal spines banded with alternate blue-black and white; lower half of pectoral fins black. Lateral line scale count 119.
Size: Average between 5–20 lb (2 1/3–9 kg), maximum up to 48 in (120 cm), 75 lb (34 kg).
Distribution: Eastern Pacific, ranging from Gulf of California south to Panama.
General: One of the most beautifully coloured game fish found in American waters and widely used as food fish. In Mexico it is known as *papagallo*–meaning papa or boss rooster. Due to the appearance of its very distinctive first dorsal spines, it can easily be identified. When hooked it is a furious fighter and has great stamina. The flesh is excellent.

432 MOONFISH S
Mene maculata
Other common names: Golok kassut (East Indies).

Features: Body very deeply compressed, depth going into the length of the body only slightly more than one time. The fins are low and the belly, through an extension of the pelvic bone, a good deal more prominent than the back. The eye is comparatively large. The caudal or tail fin deeply forked. The dorsal origin is approximately above or slightly behind the origin of the pectorals; the forward portion of the dorsal is high and thereupon descending until it

joins with the tail fin. The anal is abbreviated in height, much like a series of rudimentary finlets all connected. The pelvics are extremely long and flexible. Dorsal fin, III to IV, 40 to 43; anal fin, 30 to 33; ventral fin, I, 5 with the spine small and the rays very long. Coloration: Yellow-hued tail; pinkish silvery tint to body below the pectorals; white-yellowish above to a line extending rearward to the caudal from the eye. Series of irregular dark, blue-black spots on both sides of the lateral line from the rear edge of the gill opening to shortly forward of the caudal; greenish background tint in this area. Fins are dusky to grey.
Size: Not recorded above 12 in (30 cm).
Distribution: Open seas of the East Indies and Japan; widespread in the central tropical Indo-Pacific and reported as reaching Natal.
General: Nowhere abundant, readily dries out in air without being salted; used for food in India. No commercial or sporting value.

433 ATLANTIC BUMPER S
Chloroscombrus chrysurus
Other common names: Bumper, casabe.

Features: Oblong, ovate, compressed; belly-line profile curve more pronounced than dorsal curve. Small mouth with feeble teeth; underslung jaw; large eyes. Dorsal fin deeply notched VIII–I,26 to 29; tail fin deeply forked; anal fin II–I,26 to 28. Coloration: dorsally greenish; flanks and belly silvery or golden; tail stalk dusky above; fins yellowish or dusky. Lateral line strongly curved above falcate pectoral fin. Scales are small.
Size: Up to 8 in (20 cm).
Distribution: Western Atlantic, ranging Maine to Brazil.
General: A common western Atlantic species. Not important commercially. As a sport fish it takes a hook readily. It may be caught by still fishing or trolling. The flesh is thin and dry with large bones and is not much rated as a table fish.

434 BLUEFISH S
Pomatomus saltatrix
Other common names: Elf, skipjack, tailor.

Features: Oblong, stout body, laterally compressed. Heavy jaws; large mouth with very sharp canine teeth; lower jaw large and projecting. Two dorsal fins, first with a low profile, VI to VIII–23 to 27; tail fin large and deeply forked; anal fin II,25 to 27. Coloration: dorsally and flanks bluish green, olive green, or greyish; silvery below; a characteristic black blotch at base of pectoral fin. Lateral line is slightly elevated above pectoral fin. Moderate scaling to body, head, and gill covers. May readily be distinguished from any of the mackerels by the absence of finlets.
Size: Up to 48 in (120 cm), 31 lb (14 kg), usual range 10–15 lb (4 1/2–6 3/4 kg).
Distribution: Worldwide in warm seas; may be found in the open sea, off ocean beaches, and in estuaries.
General: A wide-ranging pelagic species which travels in large schools. Predatory and very voracious; schools of bluefish destroy large schools of anchovies, mackerel,

mullet, herring, menhaden, and alewives. They also feed extensively on small fish, shrimp, and squid.

The bluefish is a favourite hard-biting sport fish and also an important commercial species. The flesh is white and very tender, but should be eaten soon after death.

435 COBIA S
Rachycentron canadum
Other common names: Black kingfish, sergeant fish, ling, crab-eater.

Features: Long, very elongate, cigar-shaped body, cylindrical in cross section; general leathery appearance. Broad, depressed head with large mouth. Long dorsal fin VIII or IX–I,27 to 33 (dorsal spines not connected by membrane and are depressible in a groove); tail crescentic; anal fin I or II,23 to 27. Coloration: dorsally very dark brown; flanks paler with horizontal bands of brown and silver; belly white with orange patch on abdomen between pelvic and anal fins. Scales are minute. Juvenile fish are more brightly coloured than the adults, and the tail is more square-cut.
Size: Up to c. 150 lb (70 kg), but average range 5–30 lb (2–13 1/2 kg).
Distribution: Worldwide in tropical and subtropical seas, and in warm temperate seas during the summer.
General: A very powerful sport fish well known in tropical Atlantic and Indo-Pacific seas. It often frequents shallow coastal waters throughout its range. Food consists of shrimp, squid, a variety of fish, and crabs from which it earns one of its popular common names. As a sport fish the cobia may be caught either by surface trolling or by deepwater lure and bait fishing. An excellent table fish.

436 REMORA S
Remora remora
Other common names: Suckerfish, pilot sucker, white-tailed sucker, swordfish sucker, sucker, pega, pegador, off-shore remora, shark-pilot, pilotfish.

Features: Short body, tapering, round in cross section with a pointed head. Spiny part of the dorsal fin is modified into a flat and oval sucking disc. Lower jaw projects well beyond the upper, many small pointed teeth; soft dorsal fin opposes the anal fin, pectorals set up high on the sides. The oval disc extends from the snout tip to behind the head. The edge of the disc is a free flap, the central part a series of movable transverse ridges. Scales are small and usually not visible. Robustly built. Dorsal fin, 23; anal, 25. Sucking disc longer than the dorsal or anal fin, of 18 lamellae. Coloration: Uniformly dark brown, blackish or sooty, both above and below.
Size: Maximum length about 18 in (45 cm) but usually far smaller.
Distribution: All warm seas. Very common in the West Indies. Reported frequently from New Zealand, Australia, etc.
General: Usually accompanies large sharks, sea turtles, and other large oceanic species. No commercial or sport fishing value.

437 LOOKDOWN S
Selene vomer
Other common names: Moonfish, horsehead.

Features: Very deep, highly compressed body; approximately rhomboidal in appearance. Short head with very steep profile and slightly concave forehead; mouth low; large eye. Dorsal fins VII or VIII–I,22 or 23 (spines in first dorsal are very inconspicuous, and first 3 only are connected by membrane; the first rays of the second dorsal are very long and scythe-shaped and extend over half the total length of the body); tail fin large and deeply forked; anal fin I,18–20 (similar in profile to first dorsal fin but scythe-shaped part slightly shorter; pectorals scythe-shaped; pelvics very small. Coloration: uniformly silver with a more leaden hue dorsally. Some small fish are marked with golden bands. Lateral line straight, then strongly arched over pelvic fins. Body scales minute.
Size: Up to 12 in (30 cm).
Distribution: Atlantic and eastern Pacific, in warm seas.
General: One among several species commonly referred to as moonfishes which have wide distributions in Atlantic and Indo-Pacific seas. Also related to the pompano which locally is sometimes called moonfish. An excellent lightweight sport fish renowned for its good table qualities.

438 GREY SNAPPER S, F
Lutjanus griseus
Other common names: Mangrove snapper, lawyer.

Features: Large, elongate, compressed body. Slightly depressed forehead; large mouth with needlelike (villiform) teeth. Dorsal fin X,14; tail fin large and concave; anal fin III,7 or 8. Coloration: variable, but dorsally and flanks generally grey; some individual fish (especially young) may be dorsally dark green; chest and belly dark red with flank scales having rusty centres forming lines along flanks; a blackish, oblique band along side of head and through the eye (but may often be absent); fins all red with vertical fins darkest. Eye has an iris with a coppery brown and golden pupil rim. Lateral line arched, and scale count 43 to 47.
Size: Up to 36 in (90 cm), 18 lb (8 kg).
Distribution: Western Atlantic, Massachusetts south to Bermuda, Gulf of Mexico, West Indies, Brazil.
General: A species common in shallow inshore waters around mangrove-fringed reefs and shorelines. Known to be a wary sport fish and it bites more readily at night. An excellent table fish.

439 BLACKFIN SNAPPER S
Lutjanus buccanella

Features: Body small to medium size, rather slender and subelliptical, dorsal area moderately elevated. Straight profile from snout to nape and then convex; long pointed snout; villiform teeth in both jaws with 4 strong canines in upper. Dorsal fin X,14; tail fin forked; anal fin III,8. Coloration: crimson; silvery below but flushed with crimson; base of pectoral fin jet black; orange eye; dorsal fin crimson; pectoral fins, base of anal, and pelvic spines are pinkish; last rays of soft dorsal, much of the anal, and pelvics yellow; tail orange yellow. Sometimes overall colour is pale greyish pink with the characteristic black pectoral spot showing very distinctly. Lateral line scale count 63. Scales are rather small.
Size: Average up to c. 12 in (30 cm), 2,2 lb (1 kg).
Distribution: West Indies.
General: A common deepwater species with a vivid appearance. A good table fish. The scientific name *buccanella* is derived from an old name used on the island of Martinique.

440 CUBERA SNAPPER S
Lutjanus cyanopterus
Other common name: Cuban snapper.

Features: Oblong body, compressed, the dorsal area somewhat elevated. Long head, lower jaw projecting. Dorsal fin X,14; tail fin concave; anal fin III,7 or 8. Coloration: dusky grey, paler below; the belly sometimes reddish; membrane of vertical fins greyish-black, especially anal and soft dorsal; pelvic fins blackish at tip; pectorals plain olivaceous; head dusky above, without markings. Lateral line scale count 45 to 47.
Size: Up to 4 ft (120 cm), 100 lb (45 kg).
Distribution: Western Atlantic, Florida and Cuba south to Brazil.
General: a wary species found in shallow waters, formerly fairly common but now rare in some areas. The largest and one of the fiercest fighters among the snappers. Coarse-fleshed and undistinguished as a table fish, particularly the largest specimens.

441 LANE SNAPPER S
Lutjanus synagris
Other common names: Silk snapper, spot snapper, white-water snapper, red-tailed snapper (see also *General* at end of this entry).

Features: Medium-sized, elongate, compressed body. Slightly depressed forehead; large jaws. Dorsal fin X,12 or 13; tail fin concave; anal fin III,8 or 9. Coloration: dorsally and flanks silver pink to rose red; flanks paler with c. 9 horizontal, golden stripes or bands; 3–4 similar bands on head; a characteristic but variable-sized dark blotch (may be dark red) on (or above) lateral line below junction of spiny and soft dorsal rays; anal and pelvic fins golden, dorsal and tail fins reddish, tail fin has a narrow darkish margin. Occasionally flanks show dark vertical or diagonal bars. Lateral line distinct, and scale count 47 to 52.
Size: Average up to 12 in (30 cm), 1 lb (1/2 kg), maximum c. 4 1/2 lb (2 kg).
Distribution: Western Atlantic, Florida, Bermuda, and West Indies to Brazil.
General: A very prolific species often occurring in schools in many parts of its distribution. Ranges from shallow inshore waters to over 1,300 ft (390 m) and it is frequently encountered near coral reefs, and may be found either in clear, turbid, or muddy bottom waters. A sport fish usually taken by bait rather than lure. A good table fish. The Indo-Pacific species, the black-spot seaperch (*L. fulviflamma*), is very similar in features and habits and is probably a close relative. In South Africa this fish is known under the common name Johnny (see Index).

442 DOG SNAPPER S, B
Lutjanus jocu

Features: Medium-sized, elongate body. Depressed forehead; large mouth and teeth; long pointed snout. Dorsal fin X,13 or 14; tail fin concave; anal fin III,8. Coloration: dorsally brown; flanks reddish; scales have a rusty appearance on upper flanks, becoming red on the lower flanks which gives the scale rows the ap-

pearance of distinct lines; head has a characteristic blue stripe broken up into elongate spots in mature fish; there is a broad, whitish bar from the eye to the angle of the mouth, but this may be indistinct or absent in young fish; all fins red, the dorsal and tail fins darker red than the rest. Lateral line arched, and scale count 42 to 46. Scales are medium sized.
Size: Average up to 24 in (60 cm); large fish *c.* 25 lb (11 kg).
Distribution: Western Atlantic; Florida, Bermuda, West Indies to Brazil; occasional young fish to Cape Hatteras via the Gulf Stream drift.
General: A fairly abundant reef species which has the reputation of being easy to hook. The name dog snapper alludes to its very large doglike teeth. A good table fish.

443 RED SNAPPER S
Lutjanus campechanus
Other common names: Pargo colorado, pargo guachinango.

Features: Oblong, deep body, with elevated, compressed dorsal area. Head long, eye red, mouth large; jaws with villiform teeth; gill cover finely serrated. Dorsal fin X,13 or 14; tail fin concave; anal fin III,8. Coloration: deep rose red; belly and throat pale, but general intensity of colour varies according to locality; scales along flanks show as bluish streaks, becoming fainter and disappearing with age; fins brick red; dorsal fin has an orange border with a narrow blackish edge; tail fin has blackish edge; above the lateral line there is a characteristic darkish blotch. Lateral line scale count *c.* 46.
Size: Range 2–3 ft (60–90 cm), 10–35 lb (4 1/2–16 kg).
Distribution: Eastern Atlantic, known from Cape Hatteras to Brazil; most abundant in the Gulf of Mexico.
General: The most important commercial species among the American snappers. It is found in rather deep water over rocky banks. As a commercial species it is now caught on electric-powered reels, as a sport fish many are taken on sporting tackle. Except near spawning time the red snapper readily bites, and when a school is encountered, catches of several hundred kilograms are not uncommon.

444 MAHOGANY SNAPPER S
Lutjanus mahogani
Other common name: Ojanco.

Features: Oblong body. Lower jaw projecting; red eye. Dorsal fin X,11 or 12; tail fin forked; anal fin III,8. Coloration: dorsally and upper flanks deep brown; flanks silvery below; whole body fused with red; narrow bronze or yellowish streaks follow scale rows, more distinct above lateral line; blackish blotch on flanks mostly above lateral line and below first part of soft dorsal rays; dorsal fin edged with blood red; tail fin deep red; anal, pelvic, and pectoral fins scarlet. Lateral line arched and distinct. Scale count 47–50.
Size: Average range up to 10 in (25 cm), maximum *c.* 15 in (38 cm).
Distribution: West Indies ranging north to South Carolina and south to Brazil.
General: A small snapper much utilized as a commercial food fish in the West Indies.

445 MUTTON SNAPPER S
Lutjanus analis
Other common name: Muttonfish.

Features: Large, elongate, compressed body. Deep head and long snout. Dorsal fin IX to XI,13 or 14; tail fin forked and slightly crescentic; anal fin III,7 or 8. Coloration: variable, but dorsally usually greenish brown; flanks yellowish green; tinges of red on chest and belly; irregular blue lines on head; characteristic black spot (more conspicuous in young fish), smaller than the eye, on lateral line below junction of spiny and soft dorsal rays; fins, particularly lower ones, all reddish, the tail fin with a black margin. Lateral line scale count 47 to 51.
Size: Average 10–15 lb (4 1/2–6 3/4 kg), maximum 30 in (75 cm), 25 lb (11 1/4 kg).
Distribution: Western Atlantic, Florida, Bermuda, Gulf of Mexico, and West Indies to Brazil.
General: A reef fish which is more usually found in open waters with a preference for sandy bottoms. A useful sport fish and commercially important. A first-class table fish.

446 SCHOOLMASTER S
Lutjanus apodus

Features: Medium-sized, elongate, compressed body. Long, sharply pointed snout. Dorsal fin X,14; tail fin concave; anal fin III,8. Coloration: dorsally and flanks greenish, red-brown, or greyish with 8 or 9 vertical pale bars (sometimes absent in older fish); fins pale yellow to green; pelvic fins occasionally orange. Lateral line arched, and scale count 40 to 45.
Size: Average up to 8 lb (3 1/2 kg).
Distribution: Western Atlantic; Massachusetts, south to Bermuda, West Indies, and Brazil.
General: An inshore species and one of the most common of the West Indian reef fishes. A cautious sport fish, more easily hooked at night. A prized table fish.

447 RED EMPEROR S
Lutjanus sebae
Other common names: Government bream, king snapper, sea perch, Jock Stewart, scarpee, highlander, fivefinger, scrodie, rock gurnard, pahuiakaroa (Maori).

Features: Body is deep and compressed, head large, mouth large, teeth small and in bands in both jaws. Spines are mostly reduced to low ridges. Pectoral fin is large, ventral fin under and nearly attached to the pectoral fin. Dorsal fin XII, 13; anal III, 5. Lateral line distinct. Fish is fully scaled. Coloration: Variable but commonly orange-brown to brown above, bright orange below. Broad scarlet arrow decorates the sides of immature fish. The bands forming the broad arrow disappear with growth, become red and subsequently a more delicate pink. Deepwater specimens are often bright red with two or three oblique bands along the sides a darker red.
Size: Known to attains weights of 44 lb (20 kg) but this is uncommon.
Distribution: Occurs in Western Australia and along the Great Barrier Reef area, also probably in New Zealand waters. Very common in the Capricorn group of islands toward the lower end of the Great Barrier Reef.
General: Excellent food fish with a fine flavour and texture; takes flesh baits freely. Usually found on rocky grounds and coral reefs where it is often caught by anglers on hand lines.

448 YELLOWTAIL SNAPPER S
Ocyurus chrysurus
Other common name: Yelting.

Features: Medium to large, elongate body. Dorsal fin X,12 to 14; tail fin large and deeply forked with long lobes; anal fin III,8 or 9. Coloration: dorsally olivaceous or violet; flanks and belly silvery; dorsal area and upper flanks have a number of large, irregular, deep yellow blotches; a bright yellow bronze stripe extends from above the snout through the eye to the tail stalk and broadens onto tail fin; below the yellow band are narrow yellow stripes; tail stalk and tail fin a characteristic bright golden yellow. Lateral line arched, and scale count 47 to 52.
Size: Up to 24 in (60 cm), 6 1/2 lb (3 kg).
Distribution: Western Atlantic, Florida to Brazil. Also occasionally in eastern Atlantic.
General: A very abundant shallow water, reef fish found on the bottom. Food appears to be chiefly plankton, but older fish also eat crustaceans and small fish. A very high-quality table fish.

449 TRIPLETAIL S, B
Lobotes surinamensis
Other common names: Dusky tripletail, flasher, jumping cod.

Features: Deep, rectangular-shaped body. Depressed forehead; large mouth and thick lips, lower jaw projecting; serrated cheekbone. Dorsal fin XI or XII,15 or 16 (some of the soft rays extend beyond the base of tail); tail fin rounded; anal fin III,11 or 12 (some of the soft rays extend beyond the base of tail). The soft dorsal and soft anal rays are of similar shape and extension; and give the fish the appearance of having three tails, hence the name tripletail. Coloration: variable, but usually dorsally and flanks brownish or olive brown with some darker (especially on head) and lighter mottled markings, lower flanks lighter; usually a dark bar obliquely upward from eye and another across cheek; there are 3–4 dusky spots along base of soft dorsal and anal fins; pectoral fins yellowish. Arched lateral line, and scale count 42 to 44. Scales small and rough.
Size: Up to 40 in (100 cm), 26 1/2 lb (12 kg).
Distribution: Atlantic and Indo-Pacific seas.
General: A widespread species that occasionally enters estuaries, coastal rivers, and streams. In the North Atlantic the young are often found in sargassum weed. A renowned and popular sport fish and noted for its excellent table qualities.

450 KAHAWAI; AUSTRALIAN SALMON F, B
Arripis trutta
Other common names: See below.

Features: Perchlike fish with a spindle-shaped body. Single dorsal fin IX–XI,15 –17; tail fin deeply forked; anal fin III,8. Coloration: dorsally greenish-grey; upper parts of head marked with irregular black spots and blotches; upper flanks 3 or 4 longitudinal rows of large, rounded golden spots; occasionally lower flanks and head show a golden yellowish tinge; tips of pectoral fins tinged with yellow. Juvenile fish are olive green with a white or silver belly.
Size: Up to 36 in (90 cm), 21 lb (9 1/2 kg); but the average fish is much smaller.
Distribution: Australasian seas.
General: Known universally in New Zealand by its Maori name *kahawai*, but in Australia as the Australian salmon, or sea salmon, although it is not even remotely related to the salmonids. Nevertheless, this very inappropriate name is now firmly entrenched in common usage.

The *kahawai* is often seen in large schools and frequents coastal waters, harbours, and tidal inlets. Spawning occurs in offshore waters during the winter months. The *kahawai* readily takes a bait or lure and is renowned for its ability to leap after taking a hook. The flesh is firm and dry, and in New Zealand it is often smoked or canned. Sometimes important as a local commercial species.

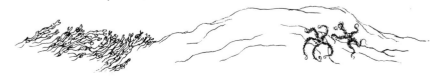

451 BLUE STRIPED GRUNT S

Haemulon sciurus

Other common names: Yellow grunt, boar grunt, grunt, cachicata, ronco amarillo, jallao, ronco, ponce prieto, humpback grunt, open-mouth grunt.

Features: Name derives from its ability to make grunting sounds by rubbing the pharyngeal teeth or moving the complex swim bladder. Body is fairly elongate, large-mouthed, compressed, with a long snout. Dorsal fin, XII, 16–18; anal fin, III, 8–9; pectoral fin, 16–17. Pored lateral line scales, 48–51. Gillrakers, 27–31, usually 29. Naked pectoral fins. Coloration: Easily distinguished from other grunts by the pattern of continuous horizontal blue stripes over a yellow background. Fins are usually translucent or yellow, but may be black with a wide green or yellow rear margin. Juveniles carry a dark mark on the caudal peduncle.
Size: Up to 18 in (45 cm), 2 1/4 lb (1 kg).
Distribution: Bermuda, Florida and Bahamas through West Indies to Brazil.
General: A bottom feeder that readily takes bait. Excellent food value and considerable commercial value locally throughout its range. A favourite of salt water panfishermen, frequently used for live bait when small.

452 TOMTATE S

Haemulon aurolineatum

Other common name: White grunt.

Features: Elongate, small, and slender-bodied. Large eye and a sloping, flattened forehead. Dorsal fin XII to XIV, 14 or 15; tail fin deeply forked; anal fin III, 9. Coloration: dorsally darkish grey; flanks silvery white; a characteristic midlateral, yellow stripe runs from the snout via the eye to a dusky spot at the base of the tail fin; there is a narrower yellow stripe above the lateral line; between the two yellow stripes are several obscure ones of similar colour; mouth is red inside. Lateral line scale count 49 to 52.
Size: Average up to 7 in (18 cm), maximum *c.* 10 in (25 cm).
Distribution: Western Atlantic, Cape Hatteras to Brazil.
General: A common species and a good table fish, but due to its small size its chief sport-fish interest is as a baitfish.

453 FRENCH GRUNT S

Haemulon flavolineatum

Other common names: Yellow grunt, open-mouthed grunt.

Features: Small, elongate compressed body. Mouth and eye very large. Dorsal fin XII, 14 or 15; tail fin forked; anal fin III, 7 or 8. Coloration: flanks have characteristic yellow stripes which run approximately longitudinally above lateral line and obliquely below it; angles of mouth black, and mouth red inside; a black spot on cheek. Lateral line arched over pectoral fin. Lateral line scale count 47 to 50. Scales very large on flanks below lateral line.
Size: Average up to 12 in (30 cm).
Distribution: Western Atlantic coasts, Florida south to Brazil.
General: An abundant species frequenting deeper water than most grunts. Although a good table fish, its small size generally restricts its sport-fish interest to its value as an excellent baitfish.

454 CAESAR GRUNT S

Haemulon carbonarium

Other common names: Black-tail grunt, black grunt.

Features: Elongate and medium-sized. Large eye and flattened forehead. Dorsal fin XII, 15 or 16; tail fin forked; anal fin III, 8. Coloration: dorsally bluish silver or greyish brown; flanks silvery; very characteristic longitudinal yellow or bronze stripes cover whole body; fins are brownish or dark; gill-cover edge has a dark spot; mouth red inside. Lateral line scale count 47 to 56. Scale rows below lateral line approximately parallel the long axis of the body.
Size: Average up to 14 in (35 cm).
Distribution: Western Atlantic tropical seas.
General: A bottom-feeding species with a preference for inshore tidal waters.

455 BROWN SWEETLIPS S

Plectorhynchus nigrus

Other common name: Black sweetlips.

Features: Perchlike with high, compressed body. Small mouth with fleshy lips; jaws with several rows of pointed teeth, no canines. Dorsal fin notched XIII or XIV, 13 to 18; tail fin rounded; anal fin III, 7 or 8. Coloration: back and flanks reddish brown to slaty grey with violet tints; bronze hues on the flanks; sometimes there may be coppery-coloured markings; fins nearly black. In young fish the tail fin and the margins of the dorsal and anal fins are yellowish-white. It may be distinguished from the javelin fish (see below) by the absence of a central groove behind the junction of the two parts of the lower jaw and by the less developed dorsal and anal spines. It may also be distinguished from the golden spotted sweetlips (see below) by a larger number of dorsal fin spines and in adult fish by the absence of a conspicuous spotted body.
Size: Up to 24 in (60 cm), 12 lb (5 1/2 kg).
Distribution: Widespread in Indo-Pacific seas. Related Atlantic forms.
General: One of several common "sweetlips" species widespread in Indo-Pacific shallow coastal waters. A good table fish.

456 SPANISH GRUNT S

Haemulon macrostomum

Other common names: Streaked grunt, striped grunt, grey grunt, sow grunt.

Features: Medium-sized, deeply compressed body. Large mouth and long snout. Jaws end below center of eye. Dorsal fin deeply notched XII, 15 to 17; tail fin forked; anal fin III, 8 or 9. Coloration: dorsally silvery grey; flanks pale silver with scales having pearly centres; flanks have conspicuous dark streaks, with a median-line streak from tip of snout to dorsal fin; dorsal spiny fin brownish green, soft dorsal and anal fins greenish yellow; tail fin dusky. Lateral line scale count 50 to 52.
Size: Average up to 14 in (35 cm), maximum 18 in (45 cm).
Distribution: Western Atlantic coasts, South Carolina south to West Indies and Brazil.
General: A bottom fish, popular with pan fishermen.

457 GOLDEN SPOTTED SWEETLIPS S

Plectorhynchus pictus

Other common names: Black-and-white (South Africa), painted sweetlips.

Features: Perchlike with compressed body. Small mouth with unusually thick lips; narrow bands of pointed teeth, no canines; large pores on chin. Dorsal fin IX or X, 21 to 26 (first spine very short); tail fin rounded in young, square-cut or concave with age; anal fin III, 6 to 8. Coloration and markings very variable and undergo some remarkable changes during growth. Immature fish are yellowish orange with brown or black longitudinal markings. As the fish matures, the 2–3 longitudinal marks diminish in size and break up into spots. Adult fish are generally greyish in appearance with darker spots. In young fish the fins are streamlined, yellow, and blotched with black; fins of adults are greyish.
Size: Up to 26 in (65 cm).
Distribution: Widespread in Indo-Pacific region.
General: One of the numerous closely related, perchlike grunter (sweetlips) species inhabiting the Indo-Pacific seas (see Index). Generally favouring' harbours and estuaries, but the larger fish are found in deeper water. All these related forms are known to be omnivorous feeders and will accept almost any bait. An excellent, tasty table fish.

458 MARGATE S

Haemulon album

Other common name: Margaret.

Features: Medium to large deeply compressed body. Head and snout large; forehead depressed above eye. Dorsal fin XII, 15–17; tail fin forked; anal fin III, 7 or 8. Coloration: dorsally and flanks pearl grey or grey; flanks sometimes with 3 longitudinal bands, one extending from snout through the eye to the tail fin where it ends in a round, dark blotch, two narrow bands above; mouth orange inside; faint dusky spot on cheek. Tail and soft dorsal very dark. Lateral line distinct, and scale count 49–52.
Size: Average 15–20 in (38–50 cm), max-

imum up to 30 in (75 cm).
Distribution: Western Atlantic, chiefly West Indies and Bahamas to Brazil.
General: One of the larger American grunts, a bottom feeder and high-quality table fish.

459 PORKFISH S

Anisotremus virginicus

Other common names: Catalineta, grunt.

Features: A medium size, deep, and small-mouthed grunt with a blunt snout and thick lips. Forked tail and a very blunt forehead, long dorsal in proportion to the general outline of the body of the fish. Dorsal fin, XII, 16 to 17; anal, III, 9 to 10. There are 13 to 15 gill rakers on the lower limb of the first gill-arch; 56 to 63 scales along the lateral line. Coloration: about seven to ten horizontal golden lines on a silvery blue background; stripes may also be light blue or even yellow. There is a wide black band from the nape through the eye and down to the angle of the mouth; head is generally yellowish and silvery. There is another black band from the origin of the dorsal fin to the base of the pectoral fins. The fin colours are yellow mottled with black except the pectorals which are golden. Juveniles have a yellow head with a thin horizontal or longitudinal black stripe running from the eye to the caudal peduncle with a black spot or blotch at the base of the tail and another black stripe on the upper part of the body. The size at which one coloration fades or changes into the other varies widely.
Size: Reaches about 14 in (35 cm) at the maximum; mostly far smaller.
Distribution: West Indies and Florida to Brazil in the Atlantic, introduced and thriving in Bermuda. Fairly common in the Florida Keys area.
General: Highly decorative in any stage, edible but not widely taken because of the small size. Often found in large schools along the range in the United States but apparently not plentiful elsewhere.

460 JAVELIN FISH S, B

Pomadasys hasta

Other common names: Javelin grunter, Port Glasgow, silver grunter.

Features: Perchlike in appearance. Small mouth with narrow bands of pointed teeth, no canine teeth. Dorsal fin XII or XIII, 13 –15; tail fin square-cut or slightly concave; anal fin III, 6–8. Coloration: dorsally and flanks silvery grey; flanks have 4 or 5 interrupted dark grey (longitudinal) lines, 3 or 4 above the lateral line following the scale rows. The flanks also have longitudinal rows of spots. Dorsal fin is very conspicuously spotted with 2 or 3 rows of brown spots which in older fish are reduced to one basal row. Lateral line scale count 45 to 52. Cheeks and gill covers scaly.
Size: Up to *c.* 24 in (60 cm).
Distribution: Indo-Pacific seas, and common in Japanese waters, Southeast Asia, and western Pacific.
General: One of several related Indo-Pacific grunter (javelin fish) species, which may be distinguished from the snapperlike fishes by its weak jaw teeth and its strong pharyngeal teeth. It shows a preference for

shallow waters and is often found in harbours, bays, and rivers. An excellent table fish of good flavour.

461 SAILOR'S CHOICE S
Haemulon parra
Other common names: Ronco blanco, ronco prieto, bastard margaret, grunt.

Features: The sailor's choice is medium sized, somewhat elongate, compressed, with a moderate sized mouth and a long snout. The tail is moderately forked. Dorsal fin, XII, 16 to 18; anal, III, 8 or 9; pectoral, 17. There are 50 to 52 scales along the lateral line; 21 to 24 gill rakers. This grunt is distinguished from others in the family by having scaled pectoral fins. Coloration: dark stripes running along the body vertically, a dark blotch or spot on the shoulder just behind the gill covers, the caudal edged in a dark to black stripe running thickly along the margin, red inside the mouth.
Size: Averages about 10 in (25 cm) when mature but larger specimens are taken.
Distribution: West Indies; southern Florida to Brazil; relatively common around Key West and Cuba. Found along the coast of Central America as well as South America.
General: Not as common as others of the grunt family; found near the bottom in shallow water close to the shore and around camouflage reefs in deeper areas. Takes a bait and offers good sport on light tackle; edible; sold commercially in markets in the West Indies.

462 WHITE GRUNT S
Haemulon plumieri
Features: Elongate, medium-sized, and compressed fish. Slightly depressed forehead; large eye; blunt snout; large mouth. Dorsal fin XII,15 to 17; tail fin forked; anal fin III,8 or 9. Coloration: light bluish, dorsal area with bright blue lines on head, separated by broad, brassy lines, sometimes extending over flanks; flanks have a series of scales, each with a small brown or brassy spot, and these form indistinct narrow lines running upward and backward; body of scales above lateral line bluish, their borders brownish olive; dorsal fin greyish with a narrow edge on spiny part; tail fin plain grey; anal fin grey and tinged with yellow; edge of gill cover yellow; inside of mouth red or deep yellow; lips dusky. Lateral line appears like a brassy band. Lateral line scale count 48 to 52.
Size: Up to 18 in (45 cm), 4 lb (1 3/4 kg), but average is much smaller.
Distribution: Western Atlantic, from Maryland south to Brazil.
General: Found along sandy shores and is by far the most important of all the grunts, and it is common everywhere throughout its distribution. Spawning occurs in August–September when the fish gather in immense shoals; the eggs have a "gritty" feel. After spawning, the fish scatter, but are found together in fair numbers on any suitable ground. As a marine panfish the white grunt is rated as an excellent fish in the South Atlantic states. Also an important commercial species usually caught in fish traps or haul-seine nets.

23 CROAKERS, WEAKFISHES, DRUMS, KINGFISHES

463 SPOTFIN CROAKER S
Roncador stearnsi
Features: Oblong, compressed body, heavy forward, and the back elevated. Head has a steep convex profile; snout rounded and blunt. Dorsal fin notched X–I,21 to 24; tail fin concave; anal fin II,8. Coloration: generally greyish silver with a bluish lustre, some streaks of dark points along the rows of scales; belly and breast areas have two long dusky streaks; a very conspicuous and characteristic jet black spot, as large as the eye, at the base of the pectoral fin; the inside of the gill cavity is black.
Size: Average up to 6 lb (2 3/4 kg), maximum *c.* 12 lb (5 1/2 kg), 36 in (90 cm).
Distribution: Eastern Pacific seas, ranging along the coasts of southern California and northern Mexico.
General: A common species found in depressions or deep gullies just beyond the tide line. The spotfin croaker is one of the gamest of the small croakers and an excellent table fish.

464 ATLANTIC CROAKER S
Micropogon undulatus
Other common names: Hardhead, croaker, golden croaker.
Features: Moderately elongate, elevated, and compressed body. Lower jaw with a row of small barbels each side; teeth in villiform bands; cheekbone is strongly serrated. Dorsal fins X or XI–28 or 29, tail fin slightly concave; anal fin II,7. Coloration: dorsally brassy; flanks and belly paler; flanks with short, irregular and dusky vertical bars crossing the lateral line; many dark brown spots on upper flanks and dorsal area, irregularly placed that do not form continuous streaks along scale rows.
Size: Up to *c.* 4 lb (1 3/4 kg), 15 in (38 cm).
Distribution: Western Atlantic, from Cape Cod to the Gulf of Mexico.
General: A species more common in its southern distribution but does not occur in the West Indies. It generally resides in shallow water over weedy bottoms, and food consists of crustaceans and mollusks. During colder spells the fish retreat to deeper water. The Atlantic croaker will readily take a baited hook, and a wide variety of tackle is used by sport fishermen. It is also an important local commercial species usually caught by seine nets. The flesh has excellent table qualities and is rated equal to that of the channel bass.

465 WEAKFISH S
Cynoscion regalis
Other common names: Common weakfish, squeteague, sea trout.

Features: Body elongate and fusiform, little compressed. Rather pointed head; large mouth; heavy projecting lower jaw. Dorsal fins X–I,26 to 29; tail fin slightly concave; anal fin II,11 or 12. Coloration: dorsally dark olive green; upper and lower flanks burnished with colours ranging from purple through green to golden; above lateral line the flanks have small irregular dark to bronze spots that form irregular lines; belly silvery or white; dorsal fins dusky and tinged with yellow; other fins have a yellowish tint. Lateral line distinct and slightly arched. Body covered with medium-sized scales.
Size: Maximum up to 37 in (93 cm), 20 lb (9 kg); average fish up to *c.* 5 lb (2 1/4 kg).
Distribution: Western Atlantic, from Massachusetts Bay to Florida.
General: The northern representative of the weakfishes. A schooling species which frequents shallow shore water in the summer and is usually found over a sandy bottom. Spawning occurs May–October. Eggs are buoyant and hatch in two days. Food consists mainly of crabs, shrimps, amphipods, worms, and small fish such as herring, menhaden, and mummichogs. The weakfish is an excellent sport fish and a valuable and well-flavoured table fish. The name "weakfish" derives from the fish's easily torn mouth membranes.

466 WHITE SEA BASS S, B
Cynoscion nobilis
Features: Elongate, deep body; a characteristic raised ridge along midline of belly. Lower jaw projecting. Dorsal fin IX–II,20; tail fin concave; anal fin II,10. Coloration: dorsally bluish; middle flanks, lower flanks, and belly silvery; juveniles (up to *c.* 18 in (45 cm) have 4 or 5 fairly broad, dark vertical bars on the flanks. Lateral line.
Size: Up to 83 lb (37 1/2 kg), 66 in (165 cm).
Distribution: North American Pacific coasts, from southern Alaska to California, including the Gulf of California.
General: In spite of its common name, this fish is not a bass but a typical large croaker, equally at home in the shallow surf or in depths to 400 ft (120 m). Its usual range is between 75 to 150 ft (25 to 45 m). Food is chiefly anchovies, sardines, squid, and small mackerel.

An important local commercial species, it is much sought after by shore and boat anglers and skin divers. The flesh is very tasty and is usually cooked as steaks.

467 SPOTTED WEAKFISH S
Cynoscion nebulosus
Other common name: Spotted sea trout.
Features: Elongate body, little compressed. Rather pointed head; large mouth; heavy and projecting lower jaw; teeth very sharp. Dorsal fins X–I,25 to 27; tail fin concave; anal fin II,10. Coloration: dorsally dark silvery grey; flanks silvery; belly paler; upper flanks and soft fins characteristically marked with round, black spots about the size of the fish's eye pupil; tail and dorsal fin

marked in a similar way with smaller spots much like a trout. Whole fish overshot with iridescent hues. Lateral line arched over pectoral fin.
Size: Average up to 5 lb (2 1/4 kg), maximum over 16 lb (7 1/4 kg), 36 in (90 cm).
Distribution: Western Atlantic, from Virginia south through the Gulf of Mexico to Central America.
General: A common southern representative of the weakfishes. Although the fish is frequently referred to as the spotted sea trout, it is not a trout but a typical croaker.

Its sport-angling qualities coupled with its general excellence as a table fish place it among the most important marine sport fish in the eastern United States.

468 TOTUAVA S, B
Cynoscion macdonaldi
Other common name: Sea bass.

Features: Elongate, deep body. Sharp snout; lower jaw protruding; mouth moderate, no enlarged canines on either jaw. Dorsal fins IX–I,24; tail fin rounded; anal fin II,7. Coloration: young fish, dusky silver with coarse black specks along lower part of head and flanks; dorsal area and upper flanks with many irregular blackish spots or blotches showing little or no tendency to form streaks; dorsal fin blackish; tail fin lighter at base; inside of mouth is black. Adult fish, dorsally bluish; flanks and belly dusky silvery, no evident black spots or blotches on body or fins; vertical fins blackish, paired fins dusky.
Size: Maximum up to 200 lb (90 kg).
Distribution: Gulf of California.
General: The largest of the croaker fishes. Enters rivers to feed and spawn in shallow water. This habit allows it to be easily approached, and what was once a very abundant species has been decimated by indiscriminate commercial fishing. Nowadays, with the introduction of a closed season and restricted fishing areas, the totuava has been allowed to rebuild its population. The totuava is a formidable rod-and-line sport fish, and this in conjunction with its large size and excellent table qualities attracts a great number of sport fishermen.

469 CORVINA S
Cynoscion reticulatus
Other common names: Striped corvina, orangemouth corvina.

Features: Body fusiform, deep, and compressed. Head somewhat conical; snout blunt. Dorsal fin notched X–I,28; tail fin almost square-cut; anal fin II,9. Coloration: dorsally and flanks greyish-silver and covered with dark brown streaks and reticulations which obscure the ground colour especially above the lateral line; lateral line a pale streak bordered above and below by darker ones; lower flanks and belly silvery; fins are unspotted; tail fin yellowish orange; inside of mouth deep orange yellow.
Size: Up to 36 in (90 cm).
Distribution: Pacific coasts of tropical America, from the Gulf of California south to Panama, also Salton Sea.
General: A common food and sport fish along the west coast of Mexico, and southern California.

470 ORANGEMOUTH CORVINA S

Cynoscion xanthulus

Other common name: Yellow-finned corvina.

Features: Rather slender body, compressed. Long head, compressed and pointed; large eye; small canine teeth (2 usually present). Dorsal fin IX–I,20; tail fin rounded with middle rays considerably extended; anal fin II,8. Coloration: dorsally and upper flanks bluish or brownish; flanks with numerous scattered dark points; lower flanks and belly silvery; upper fins dark with dusky margins; tail fin yellow; lining of gill cover black; inside of mouth characteristically bright yellow in life. Lateral line scale count 86.

Size: Up to 6 ft (1.80 m), 125 lb (56 kg);

Distribution: Pacific coasts of Mexico.

General: An important member of the weakfishes whose scales are rather smaller than those of closely related species. In Mexico waters it is renowned both as a food and sport fish. In 1950 it was introduced into the Salton Sea, California, and is now its most important sport fish.

471 RED DRUM S, B

Sciaenops ocellatus

Other common names: Redfish, channel bass.

Features: Large, elongate body. Blunt, almost flattish snout; upper jaw projecting. Dorsal fins deeply notched IX or X–26; tail fin square-cut or slightly concave; anal fin I,8. Coloration: overall greyish silver with a reddish or coppery shading overlying lighter background; each scale with a centre of dark points forming rather obscure, irregular undulating brown stripes along scale rows; a very characteristic jet black ocellated spot about as large as the eye at the base of the tail fin; occasionally this may be duplicated; sometimes flanks also have ocelli. Lateral line. Scales large.

Size: Maximum up to 80 lb (36 kg), average *c.* 30 lb (13 1/2 kg); immature fish range 10–15 lb (4 1/2–6 3/4 kg).

Distribution: Western Atlantic, from Gulf of Maine to Gulf of Mexico, but rare north of New Jersey.

General: A bottom-feeding, schooling species and very common along the U.S. Mid-Atlantic and Gulf coasts, and particularly on the Texas coasts where it is one of the most abundant fishes. They frequent shallow water and are easily recognised from the characteristic dark ocellated spot. Food consists of small fish such as young mullet, crustaceans, and molluscs. The red drum is among the most popular marine sport fish in the United States. It also is an important commercial species, and the flesh has excellent table qualities.

472 BLACK DRUM S

Pogonias cromis

Other common name: Sea drum.

Features: Elongate body, laterally compressed. Slightly concave forehead above the eye; chin has a cluster of five spinelike barbels. Dorsal fin deeply notched IX or X–I,20; tail fin square-cut/rounded; anal fin II,6 or 7. Coloration: overall uniform

grey occasionally with a reddish or coppery sheen; juveniles have broad, vertical brownish to black bands on the flanks over a background colour of greyish silver. Lateral line arched and parallels dorsal line.

Size: Maximum up to 150 lb (68 kg); but average fish range 2–8 lb (1–3 1/2 kg).

Distribution: Western Atlantic, ranging both North and South American coastlines, rare north of New Jersey.

General: A rather sluggish inshore schooling fish found over sandy bottoms in the surf near wharfs, bridges, and in channels. Food consists of molluscs including oysters which they crush with their highly adapted teeth. Popular with anglers although indifferent as table fare.

473 FRESHWATER DRUM F

Aplodinotus grunniens

Other common names: Drum, gaspergou, freshwater sheepshead, croaker, thunderpumper.

Features: Humpbacked, laterally compressed body; lower outline almost straight. Mouth overhung by snout (a characteristic feature which distinguishes it from other spiny-rayed fishes in the same distribution). Dorsal fin notched X–30; tail fin rounded; anal fin II,7; pelvic fins terminate with hairlike filaments. Coloration: dorsally dark green; flanks silvery; belly white; fins are dusky except pelvic fins which are white to creamy; pectoral fins are transparent. Lateral line scale count 55.

Size: Average range 1–2 lb (1/2–1 kg), maximum over 10 lb (4 1/2 kg), occasionally but rarely up to 24 lb (11 kg). In pioneer days fish weighing considerably more are well authenticated.

Distribution: North America, ranging Manitoba, Hudson Bay, Great Lakes (except Lake Superior) south to Texas and Mexico.

General: The freshwater representative of the drum fishes, it is capable of producing drumming or grunting noises by using its air bladder. Food consists mainly of snails, mussels, and crayfish, which it crushes and grinds with its specially adapted pharyngeal teeth in the throat. As a sport fish it is rated as a light-tackle species. The flesh is of only moderate quality and not esteemed at the table.

474 SILVER SEA TROUT S

Cynoscion nothus

Other common names: Bastard weakfish, silver weakfish.

Features: Body elongate and fusiform, little compressed. Rather pointed head; large mouth; heavy and projecting lower jaw. Two dorsal fins X–I,26 to 29; tail fin slightly convex; anal fin II,9 or 10. Coloration: dorsally and upper flanks greyish silvery and marked with darker spots to the level of the pectoral fin; flanks below lateral line abruptly silvery; upper fins dusky; lower fins white; snout and lower jaw blackish; mouth whitish inside.

Size: Average up to 3 lb (1 1/2 kg), very small fish more common.

Distribution: Western Atlantic coasts, Gulf of Mexico.

General: An important sport and food fish throughout its range.

475 SPOT S, B

Leiostomus xanthurus

Other common names: Goody, lafayette, roach, chub, chopa blanca, masooka.

Features: Oblong-ovate body, dorsally compressed. Small mouth; upper jaw has a band of feeble teeth, the lower jaw is almost toothless; paved pharyngeal teeth; front of gill cover has a membranaceous border. Dorsal fin deeply notched X–I,31; tail fin concave; anal fin II,12. Coloration: dorsally bluish; lower flanks and belly silvery; *c.* 15 narrow, dark wavy bars extend from dorsal area to below lateral line; a small, round, black or yellow spot on shoulder; fins olivaceous.

Size: Average up to 10 in (25 cm), 1.1 lb (1/2 kg).

Distribution: Western Atlantic, ranging Maine to Texas.

General: A member of the croakers and one of the commonest panfishes along the eastern coast of North America. Found over hard and sandy bottoms. Food consists of worms, molluscs, and crustaceans. Although not particularly renowned for its sporting qualities due to its small size, it is a good table fish.

476 MEAGRE S, B

Argyrosomus regium

Other common and synonymous names: Maigre, cob, kob, kabeljou, omber-visch, jewfish, salmon bass, mulloway.

Features: Long, elongate, compressed body. Medium large mouth and rounded snout. Dorsal fin notched, IX or X–I,27 to 29; tail fin square-cut or rounded; anal fin II,7 or 8. Coloration: dorsally silver grey, silver blue, or brown; flanks lighter with brilliant, golden iridescent reflections; belly silvery or white; fins reddish brown; young fish often with oblique dark stripes above lateral line.

Size: Up to 80 in (200 cm).

Distribution: Worldwide in several related forms in warm or warm temperate seas. In Europe seldom seen north of the English Channel (see also mulloway and kabeljou).

General: A species known under several names. There can be little doubt that the Northern Hemisphere meagre is the cob, or kob, of South African waters and the mulloway of Indo-Pacific seas. However, the South Atlantic and Indo-Pacific regions *may* be populated with distinct subspecies fish involving minor local variations in features and coloration.

The meagre is a carnivorous species which hunts schools of small fish, and in pursuit of small fish it occasionally penetrates into shallow brackish estuaries and for short periods is able to adapt to fresh water as does the synonymous Australasian mulloway. Spawning occurs in warm coastal waters, and the eggs are pelagic. It is an excellent hard-fighting sport fish, and the smaller fish have good table qualities.

477 MULLOWAY S, B, F

Sciaena antarctica

Other common names: See below.

Features: Long, elongate, compressed body. Medium large mouth. Dorsal fin notched IX or X–I,27 to 29; tail fin is markedly rounded but slightly variable; anal fin II,7 or 8. Coloration: variable, dorsally bluish or greenish with brownish shadings which extend over the head; flanks silvery white. Varieties or subspecies fish in southeast Asia show other variations in colour, occasionally with spots and pink tints over dorsal area and upper flanks. The head, gill covers, and body are covered with small scales.

Size: Up to 6 ft (1.80 m), 125 lb (56 kg); specimens 50–60 lb (22 1/2–27 kg) are not uncommon.

Distribution: Indo-Pacific seas in several related forms or varieties.

General: A fish known under several common names throughout its wide distribution. In Australia the recognised common name mulloway is an adopted aboriginal name, but different Australian states have different names: in Western Australia it is called river kingfish; in South Australia, butterfish; in Queensland, jewfish; and in Victoria, kingfish. Sometimes it is simply referred to as croaker fish due to its ability to produce sounds in and out of the water by the movement of its air bladder.

The mulloway frequents inshore and offshore waters and is often encountered in large numbers in harbours, inlets, and estuaries and will ascend rivers into the freshwater region. In the open sea it may be found in deep water near submerged reefs or wrecks. The younger fish form large schools.

The mulloway is a favourite sport fish because of its large size and hard fighting qualities. For table use the smaller fish 3–6 lb (1 1/4–2 3/4 kg) are much preferable. The flesh of the larger fish is coarse, rather soft, and does not keep well.

478 KABELJOU S, B, sometimes F

Sciaena hololepidota

Other common names: Salmon, salmon bass, kob, rietbul (Knysna) boerkabeljou, jewfish (Australian), maigre (Mediterranean).

Features: Elongate, robust body with dorsal fin nearly divided, deeply notched between first and second fins. Small scales rub off easily. The pectoral axil has a fleshy process. Elaborate air bladder. Body depth about 30 per cent of length. First dorsal, X; second dorsal I, 26–28. Anal fin II (weak), 7. Lateral line scale count 50–58, tubules with numerous variable branches; 8 scale rows above and 20 below the line near shoulder. About 10 spiny gill rakers, plus rudimentary rakers. Caudal is rounded in young, changing with age to almost truncated in adult fish. Coloration: Young fish are steel-blue on back, which becomes greenish-brown or dark grey in adult specimens; all are white underneath.

Size: Attains 6 ft (180 cm), 150 lb (70 kg).

Distribution: Eastern Atlantic, Mediterranean, Indian Ocean to Australia and South Africa.

General: Smaller fish up to 24 in (60 cm) are

good eating, but flesh of larger fish is inferior. Likes estuarial habitat, but also found to depths of 200 fathoms (400 m). Good angling fish in cold water, but sluggish in warm.

479 CALIFORNIA CORBINA S
Menticirrhus undulatus
Other common names: Whiting, sea trout.

Features: Long, slender-bodied. Upper jaw projecting; a characteristic single, fleshy barbel on lower jaw. Dorsal fin deeply notched IX–I,27; tail fin concave; anal fin II,8. Coloration: dorsally and flanks a dusky greyish blue with metallic overtones and sometimes several obscure spots. Lateral line.
Size: Up to *c.* 7 lb (3 kg), 20 in (50 cm), but average fish usually less than *c.* 3–4 lb (1 1/4–1 3/4 kg).
Distribution: North American Pacific coast, ranging from Point Conception, California, southward.
General: A species usually encountered over shallow, sandy ground or firm bottom mud in small, loose schools. The larger fish are solitary in habit. During the winter months they move into deeper offshore water. Food consists of sand crabs, clams, and other small crustaceans found along the intertidal zone. Spawning takes place June to September.

Today it is illegal in California to either buy or sell corbina. As sport fish, many are taken in the surf, and the rest chiefly by pier fishermen, but they are often shy fish and difficult to attract to a hook. As a table fish corbina is of the highest quality, and locally the flesh is either broiled or fried.

480 NORTHERN KINGFISH S
Menticirrhus saxatilis
Other common name: Northern king whiting.

Features: Slender body. Blunt, projecting snout. A short barbel on the lower jaw. Two dorsal fins, the first, with spines, high and short, the second soft-rayed, low and long; tail fin a little concave; anal fin short and high. Coloration: above dusky grey with darker bands, lower sides and belly paler, silvery.
Size: 11–12 in (28–30 cm).
Distribution: West Atlantic, Florida to Texas.
General: Lives in shallow water with sandy bottom. A good food fish.

481 PINFISH S, B, occasionally F
Lagodon rhomboides
Other common names: Spanish porgy, bream, sargo, sailor's choice, chopa spina.

Features: Humanlike incisor teeth in the front of the jaws; notched incisor teeth anteriorly and molar teeth posteriorly. Compressed, elliptical fish of small to medium size. Caudal forked. Dorsal fin, XII, 11; anal fin, III, 11. There are 18 to 20 gill rakers and 65 to 70 scales along the lateral line. Coloration: Dark green or a bluish silver above with a silvery lighter tint below; a round dark spot on the shoulder approximately the size of the eye. There are

four to six dark vertical crossbars on the body which vary in intensity, each about the width of the eye. There are numerous longitudinal golden stripes the length of the fish; dorsal spines a purple or silvery blue; membrane a pale yellow. The anal fin is yellow with a light but broad blue margin; pectorals and caudal a pale yellow.
Size: Grows to 14 in (36 cm) at maximum but usually about half that length.
Distribution: Atlantic and Gulf coasts of the United States; Cape Cod to Cuba and south to the Yucatan in Mexico; reported off Bermuda.
General: Abundant on shallow and grassy flats. Tolerant to large changes in the environment. A major part of the diet of many forms of gamefish. Used as live baits by anglers, and popular locally as small panfish.

482 GEELBEK S, occasionally B, rarely F
Atractoscion aequidens
Other common names: Salmon, Cape salmon, salmon bass, teraglin (Australia), silver teraglin.

Features: The rather robust, elongate body has small to moderately-sized scales that are easily shed. Dorsal deeply notched before the soft fin. Tail only slightly forked, emarginated. Small teeth. The elaborate air bladder has many branches. Often confused with the locally common kob or "salmon." First dorsal, X; second dorsal, I, 27–31. Anal fin, II, 9. Forward part of lateral line has many branches, 75–80 tubules; hinder part has 3 branches. Scale rows number 15 and 28 below the lateral line at the shoulder. Short gill rakers number 8–9. Coloration: Blue above shading to silver on the sides and white below; bright yellow inside the mouth, along the lips, and inside the gill covers.
Size: Up to 36 in (90 cm), 20 lb (9 kg), some larger fish recorded up to 40 in (100 cm).
Distribution: Coasts of South Africa, and New South Wales and Queensland in Australia.
General: Primarily an inshore fish, often confused with the mulloway and the true teraglin. Important commercially, the flesh is excellent and easily smoked or cured. Taken mostly by commercial fishermen, but also by a few expert amateurs.

483 BLACK SURFPERCH S
Embiotoca jacksoni
Other common name: Common surf perch.

Features: Elongate, compressed. Lower jaw shorter than upper; fleshy lips. Dorsal fin IX,22; tail fin forked; anal fin III,27. Coloration: male fish dorsally olive brown with diffuse dark blotches or bands extending across the flanks; belly paler; female fish a uniform dark purplish brown. Lateral line scale count *c.* 60.
Size: Up to *c.* 12 in (30 cm), 1.1 lb (1/2 kg).
Distribution: Eastern Pacific, ranging from British Columbia to Baja California.
General: Although during mating the male introduces sperm into the female, the ova are not fertilized until the following spring. The young are hatched within the body where they remain closely packed in a sac-like enlargement of the oviduct (analogous to the uterus) until born. The foetal fishes bear little resemblance to the parents; they are very compressed and have vertical fins extremely elevated. At birth they are 1 1/2–2 1/2 in (4–6 cm) long and they resemble the adults, although still more compressed and reddish in colour.

Black perch are found in bays and generally along the shores of the Pacific. Food consists of small crustaceans and other invertebrates. The black perch readily takes a baited hook and offers stiff resistance; it is now ranked high as a local sport fish. Although they are used extensively for food, the flesh is rather tasteless and bony.

484 KELP PERCH S
Brachyistius frenatus
Other common names: Surfperch, perch.

Features: One of a great numbers of surf fishes of the family, *Embiotocidae*. Rather deep body with no teeth on the roof of the small mouth. The dorsal is comparatively long in outline, and slopes downward ahead of the dorsal origin toward the protruding snout. The tail fin is forked, the pectoral rather long. Both anal and dorsal fins are heavily scaled. A frenum interferes with the rearward groove of the lower lip, the upper jaw is slightly shorter than the lower, the soft-rayed segment of the dorsal fin is slightly lower than the hard-rayed section. The eye is large and prominent. Dorsal fin, about VI in ascending size from the head, 13 to 16; anal fin, 21 to 24. The lateral line is pronounced. Coloration: A

copper brown or brown described as rosy overlaid with an olive hue above and a copperish red below. The fins may be plain or reddish.
Size: To about 8 in (20 cm).
Distribution: The Pacific coasts of the United States and Canada, most common northward in shallow water from Vancouver Island to Lower California.
General: Most often caught along rocky coasts in kelp or weed. Small size makes it of no great commercial importance, but it is a locally very popular sporting panfish.

485 BERMUDA CHUB S
Kyphosus sectatrix
Other common names: Rudderfish, sea chub, butter bream.

Features: Deep, medium-sized, ovate, and compressed body. Small mouth and flattened incisor teeth. Dorsal fin XI,11 to 13 (soft dorsal and anal fins scaly in adult fish); tail fin forked/crescentic; anal fin III,10 to 12. Coloration: dorsally brownish to steel or dark grey; flanks lighter with small lozenge-shaped spots or with horizontal dark and light lines, but the pattern often changes within a short time interval; belly whitish; below the eye there is a diffuse pale streak and a yellowish one above and below; fins all dull grey, but pelvic and anal fins often blackish. Lateral line present, and scale count 51 to 58.
Size: Average up to *c.* 18 in (45 cm).
Distribution: Atlantic, and very closely related *Kyphosus* forms in Atlantic and Indo-Pacific seas.
General: A common perchlike species often found in large schools. Herbivorous, feeding chiefly on seaweed and algae. In spite of its herbivorous feeding habits, however, it may be caught as a sport fish using animal baits.

486 QUEEN ANGELFISH S
Holacanthus ciliaris
Other common name: Isabelita.

Features: Very high, compressed body. The snout is short, the mouth prominent with large, thick lips. The many densely placed teeth are thin and pointed. The species is characterized by the much elongated, pointed hind parts of the dorsal and anal fins, reaching beyond the convex posterior margin of the broad tail fin. The anterior spinous part of the dorsal fin is very low. The basal parts of the fins are covered with scales. Coloration: bright blue, iridescent.
Size: The angelfish reaches rarely a length of 1–1 1/2 ft (30–45 cm); most individuals are much smaller.
Distribution: Tropical region of the western Atlantic; Florida, West Indian seas and northern South America.
General: The home of this pretty fish is the coral reefs, where it moves and hides in the hollows between the coral stocks, feeding on small animals, picking them up among the corals.

487 OPALEYE S

Girella nigricans
Other common names: Green-fish, Catalina perch.

Features: Oblong, ovate, with deep, perch-like body, compressed. Blunt snout; small mouth with no molar teeth; eye large and characteristically tinted an opalescent blue. Single, rather low, dorsal fin XIV,14, scales at base form an imperfect sheath; tail fin slightly concave; anal fin III,12. Coloration: dorsally olive green; flanks paler; fins dusky greenish; younger fish have a large yellowish white blotch on dorsal area on each side of dorsal fin.
Size: Average up to 12 in (30 cm), maximum 25 in (65 cm), 13 1/4 lb (6 kg).
Distribution: Eastern Pacific, in a localised area from Monterey along California coast southward.
General: A herbivorous species and principally a seaweed eater, but crustaceans also provide an important part of its diet. Sometimes found in rock pools and usually just beyond the surf along sandy or rocky shores, and most abundant in depths of about 20 ft (6 m), although range extends from 6–65 ft (2–20 m). A table fish of fair quality and often locally marketed as "perch". As a sport fish the opaleye is a difficult fish to hook owing to its cautious nature and small mouth, but it is a very hard and game fighter.

488 SWEEP F (B, S).

Scorpis aequipinnis
Features: Rather short, much compressed body with a considerably elevated dorsal contour. The lower jaw projects well beyond the shorter upper jaw; the teeth are placed in several bands, those in the outer bands are the largest. The gill cover has serrate edges. One continuous dorsal fin with about 10 spines and 25–30 soft rays; the anal fin has 3 spines and about 25 soft rays. The pectoral and ventral fins are rather small. Coloration: very variable, brown, reddish, and bluish.
Size: Up to 14–15 in (35 cm), 1 lb (0.5 kg).
Distribution: Southern and southwestern Australia, New Zealand.
General: Lives mainly in the lower reaches of the rivers, in estuaries and in shore waters. Related species occur in other Indo-Pacific regions.

489 BUTTERFLY BASS F

Cichla temensis
Other common names: Pavon mariposa (Sp); tucunaré-pinima, tucunaré-brano, tucunaré-tinga (P).

Features: Perchlike, compressed. Similar in appearance to the related peacock bass (*C. ocellaris*) and the North American small-mouth bass (*Micropterus dolomieui*), but it is less stubby and humped than *C. ocellaris*. Dorsal fin notched *c.* XIV–6; tail fin slightly concave; anal fin III,10. Coloration: dorsally dusky olive; flanks shading to bright yellow with three large, characteristic dark blotches along the interrupted lateral line; fins sometimes bright red or orange; a large reddish patch often present on the belly below the pectoral fins; a characteristic eye-like blotch on the tail stalk at the termina-

tion of the lateral line.
Size: Average large fish up to *c.* 24 in (60 cm); but smaller fish predominate.
Distribution: South America.
General: Along with the peacock bass (*C. ocellaris*) it is the only South American cichlid of major interest to sport fishermen. Both fish are often found in the same waters and have similar angling characteristics, but the butterfly bass is not as plentiful as the peacock bass. A table fish of high quality.

490 ATLANTIC SPADEFISH S

Chaetodipterus faber
Other common names: Angelfish, porgee.

Features: Elevated (semiorbicular), compressed body; short tail stalk. Blunt head, mouth small and slightly protractile; jaws with slender, pointed, and movable brush-like teeth. Dorsal fin VIII–I,20 to 23 (spines depressible in a groove); tail fin concave; anal fin III,17 to 19 (dorsal and anal soft rays lobed/falcate; young fish have an elongated filament on the third dorsal spine). Coloration: overall pearly grey or bluish with dark bars; juveniles black overall. Lateral line scale count 46 to 49; scales small and rough (ctenoid).
Size: Average up to 18 in (45 cm), maximum *c.* 36 in (90 cm), 20 lb (9 kg).
Distribution: Western Atlantic in warmer seas, ranging Massachusetts to Brazil.
General: A valuable fish which frequents a wide variety of habitats including old wrecks, wharfs, reefs, and bays. Occasionally a schooling species. Food consists of algae, sponges, polychaete worms, and a variety of planktonic animals.

As a sport fish they are usually taken on very small baited hooks and are powerful fighters. As table fish they are very popular.

491 LUDERICK S, B

Girella tricuspidata
Other common names: Sweep, rock perch, black bream (Australia); blackfish (New Zealand).

Features: Perchlike appearance, small mouth and blunt snout. Dorsal fin XV,12; tail fin slightly concave, anal fin III,12. Coloration: dorsally dark or greenish brown; paling on flanks with *c.* 6 or more dark, vertical stripes. Lateral line lighter coloured and arches over pectoral fin.
Size: Up to 28 in (70 cm), 13 lb (6 kg), but average fish 2–4 lb (1–1 3/4 kg).
Distribution: Indo-Pacific seas.
General: The luderick feeds principally on vegetation and resides in shallow waters where there is an abundance of weed, but it also eats worms, shellfish, and prawns. It is an excellent sport fish and sometimes a commercial species. The palatability of the flesh is variable.

492 WHITE SEAPERCH S

Phanerodon furcatus
Features: This species is closely related to the surfperches (Embiotocidae). The body is oblong, rather much compressed anteriorly, but tapering backwards into a long and slender tail stalk. The mouth is small, but provided with large, conical teeth. The gill rakers are small and short. The dorsal fin is composed of two parts, both the first spinous and the second soft-rayed parts are high. The pectoral fins reach a little farther back than the small ventral fins. The tail fin is strongly forked with the upper lobe being the longer. Coloration: back and upper sides olive, lower sides and belly silvery. The scales are bright and shiny. The posterior edge of the tail fin is dark; the anal fin has a round dark spot, otherwise the fins are yellowish.
Size: Mostly above 1 ft (30 cm).
Distribution: Eastern Pacific from Vancouver Island to San Diego.
General: Its habitat is the coastal waters, even quite shallow water. In some localities the species is very numerous.

493 PESCADA F

Plagioscion squamosissimum
Features: The pescada belongs to the family Sciaenidae. The body is stout, but still elongate and compressed. Blunt snout; the rather large mouth has two rows of teeth in the upper jaw, the teeth in the inner row are the largest. Big scales, especially those along the lateral line. Two dorsal fins, the second very close to the first; the first is spinous and rather short, the second is longer and has only soft rays. The anal fin has anteriorly 1–2 spines followed by 5 soft rays; it is inserted a little behind the triangular pectoral fin. Coloration: Back and upper sides greenish to brown, lower sides and belly lighter. The fins are more dark-coloured than the body.
Size: Up to 10 in (25 cm).
Distribution: South America from Colombia and Guiana to the La Plata River.
General: Its home is the rivers. It is considered to be a marine relict in the Amazon basin.

494 TILAPIA F (B)

Tilapia nilotica
Other common names: Bulti.

Features: High, compressed body. The head depressed between eyes and snout; small mouth. One long dorsal fin with 16–17 spines and 11–12 soft rays. Hind margin of tail fin straight or slightly con-

cave; posterior part of anal fin very high. Pectoral and ventral fins long and pointed. Large scales. Coloration: back brown to green, rather dark; lower sides and belly light. An oval, black spot on the posterior edge of the gill cover. The spinous part of the dorsal fin has a dark line a little below the edge, the soft part has 2–3 curved, dark, longitudinal bands; also the tail and anal fins have similar bands.
Size: Maximum 2 ft (60 cm).
Distribution: North Africa, Israel, and Syria.
General: The eggs are deposited in the bottom and guarded by the parents. When the larvae are hatched, they are kept in the mouth of either male or female; but they can leave this shelter, returning again if threatened. The tilapia is of great importance as a food fish, and therefore it has been introduced in several places.

495 NATAL TILAPIA F, B

Tilapia mossambica
Other common names: Mudfish, large-mouthed kurper.

Features: Elongate, perchlike body. Depressed forehead; teeth in bands and usually notched (the outer ones are bicuspid, and the inner ones are tricuspid). Dorsal fin XV,12; tail fin square-cut; anal fin III,9. Coloration: brownish or olive green; flanks have spots or blotches, and scales have dark centres; a dark blotch on the gill cover; soft dorsal and anal fins are mottled, spotted, or reticulated; flanks of juveniles have dark crossbars. Note: Sometimes it may be confused locally with the imported North American black bass, but it can readily be distinguished by the characteristic interrupted two-section lateral line and the presence of only a single nostril on each side instead of the usual pair of nostrils.
Size: Up to 14 in (35 cm).
Distribution: South and East Africa, ranging from Natal through Rhodesia, Mozambique to Abyssinia. Also widely introduced elsewhere in southern and central Africa, and other tropical areas.
General: One of the mouth breeding (brooding) cichlid species. Well known as a local sport fish which may be caught by traditional bream float-fishing methods. An excellent table fish when eaten fresh.

496 PEACOCK BASS F

Cichla ocellaris
Other common names: Tucunaré-assu, tucunaré-comum (P); pavon cinhado (Sp).

Features: Perchlike in shape, strongly compressed and similar in appearance to the related butterfly bass (*C. temensis*), but the peacock bass has a stubbier and more humped appearance. Dorsal fin is deeply notched XIII to XVI–16; tail fin convex; anal fin III,10. Coloration: very variable and dependent on age; young fish have a grey green ground colour, darker on the dorsal region, which changes to a silver-white shade with increasing age when dorsal area becomes pure leaf green, and the throat and belly often golden; young fish have a longitudinal stripe usually composed of isolated blotches; older fish have vertical bands, but these disappear with age. In all

fish there is a characteristic (eyelike) black blotch (sometimes two) on the upper part of the tail-fin base; with increasing age a reddish or golden margin develops; a similar blotch may sometimes be present below the rear portion of the soft dorsal fin. Fins generally are greenish with dark blotches often joined to form bands; in older fish the lower fins and the lower part of the tail become yellowish, then brick red. Lateral line scale count 83 to 102.
Size: Average large fish up to *c.* 24 in (60 cm), maximum *c.* 32 in (80 cm), 20 lb (9 kg).
Distribution: Native to South America. Introduced elsewhere.
General: One of the two South American cichlids (the other is the butterfly bass) both of which are of considerable interest to sport fishermen. Although fish are known to be *c.* 20 lb (9 kg), 12 lb (5 1/2 kg) is the average range. As a lightweight sport fish it will take almost any moving lure or bait and will often take a fly in a troutlike manner. It is also an excellent high-quality table fish.

497 CORAL FISH s
Abudefduf sordidus

Features: High, compressed, elliptical body. Blunt snout, large eyes. Dorsal fin XIII, 15; anal II, 16. The species differs from *A. saxatilis* by the higher number of soft rays. Tail fin forked. Large scales. Coloration: the body is greyish-brown with purple sheen; *c.* 5 light blue, transverse bands. Foremost part of dorsal fin black, a black spot at base of pectoral fin and another, larger dorsally on the tail stalk.
Size: Up to 8 in (20 cm).
Distribution: Japan, through Indo-Pacific to Red Sea.
General: Lives in shallow, coastal waters. Edible.

498 GARIBALDI s
Hypsypops rubicundus
Other common name: Ocean goldfish.

Features: Body short, very stout and rounded. Large, broad head with small eyes and short, plump snout. Thick lips. Lateral line indistinct; big scales. One dorsal fin with 12 shorter spines and 16 longer soft rays. The tail fin is forked with broad, rounded lobes. The large anal fin has anteriorly two short spines. Pectoral and ventral fins are broad and rounded. Coloration: all over orange red, sides with a few lighter spots. The young have numerous bright blue spots.
Size: 8–14 in (20–35 cm).
Distribution: Coastal waters of southern California.
General: Prefers very shallow water, 3–50 ft. (1–15 m) with rocks and dense vegetation. Its commercial importance is small, but it is now and then taken during sport fishing with hook and line.

499 SERGEANT MAJOR s
Abudefduf saxatilis
Other common names: Cow pilot, nuisance, cock-eye pilot, jaqueta, pintano, morarra raiado, demoiselle, pintanos.
Features: Brilliant and small compressed fish with a tiny terminal mouth; preopercle

and suborbital without serrations. Caudal forked. Body somewhat moon shaped with pronounced ventrals, pectorals and anal as well as a long dorsal fin with relation to the stubby body. Fairly large eye. 16 to 21 gill rakers. Scales along the lateral line number 28 to 30. The maxillary scarcely reaches the anterior margin of the eye in the adult fish. Dorsal fin, XII, 12 to 13; anal, II, 10 to 12. Coloration: Must be judged as variable with relation to ground colour; bluish green to yellow above and below; dusky on upper portions of head; sides with five or six vertical black bands. The pectorals are light green with black axil, the other fins usually the same colour as the body.
Size: Grows to a maximum of about 6 in (15 cm).
Distribution: Atlantic coast of tropical America in general, West Indies and to Brazil. On the Pacific Coast from Lower California to Peru. Common in Bermuda.
General: Panfish of no particular commercial or angling importance but highly decorative in reefs of many tropical and subtropical waters.

500 TARAKIHI s
Nemadactylus macropterus
Other common name: Jackass fish.

Features: Perchlike fish with a compressed body. Depressed forehead. Dorsal fin notched XVII or XVIII,27 to 30; tail fin deeply forked; anal fin III,15 or 16; seventh ray of pectoral fin is greatly lengthened. Coloration: generally silvery overall, with a reddish purple tint over dorsal area; a black band crosses in front of dorsal fin, but does not extend further down either flank than beyond the pectoral fins. It is sometimes locally confused with the red morwong (*Morwong fuscus*), but the tarakihi has a more lengthened seventh ray of the pectoral fin and the characteristic black dorsal band.
Size: Up to 20 lb (9 kg), 40 in (100 cm) but average range 3–4 lb (1 1/2–1 3/4 kg).
Distribution: Southern and central Australasian seas.
General: A deep-water fish which occasionally enters shallow water. Food consists of shrimps, worms, crabs, and sea urchins. Tarakihi is the New Zealand Maori name, pronounced "Teraki". In Australia known as the jackass fish. A good sport fish, frequently taken over rocky areas in snapper waters. An excellent table fish. The flesh has a high oil content and is often smoked.

501 MOKI s
Latridospis ciliaris
Other common name: Bastard trumpeter.

Features: Deep-bodied, compressed. Forehead slightly concave; lips thick and fleshy; teeth in narrow bands in both jaws. Dorsal fins XVII,40; tail fin forked; anal fin III,35. Coloration: dorsally blue grey; flanks silvery grey; belly white; dorsal area has a number of obscure dark blotches. Lateral line slightly arched.
Size: Up to over 30 in (75 cm), 11 lb (5 kg).
Distribution: Indo-Pacific, ranging cool Australasian seas.
General: A fairly abundant species in coastal, rocky waters to depths of about 300 ft (90 m). Food consists of mussels and other

shellfish. An excellent table fish. In New Zealand, only the common name moki is used; in Australia, it is usually called bastard trumpeter.

502 STRIPED TRUMPETER s
Latris lineata
Other common names: Trumpeter, Hobarttown trumpeter.

Features: Long, elongate, perchlike body. Depressed forehead; large mouth with small, sharp teeth. Dorsal fin deeply notched XVIII,35 or 36 (seventh spine longest); tail fin forked; anal fin III,27. Coloration: dorsally and flanks yellowish bronze with 3 whitish longitudinal stripes; belly yellowish white; head same coloration as flanks but no stripes; fins greenish yellow and streaked or blotched with darker markings. All colours quickly fade on death, and the whole fish takes on a drab appearance.
Size: Up to 48 in (120 cm), 60 lb (27 kg).
Distribution: Temperate Australasian waters.
General: Similar in appearance to the smaller silver trumpeter (*Latridopsis forsteri*), but this latter fish has no stripes. In Tasmania, the striped trumpeter occurs in large numbers, and it is better known under the commercial name of Hobarttown trumpeter. During the summer months it is found in inshore and deep waters ranging from 300–900 ft (90–270 m). Food is mainly fish, crab, shrimp, octopus, and squid. It forms both an important sport and commercial species and is an excellent high-quality table fish.

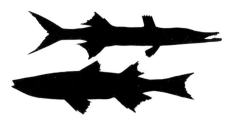

503 GOLDEN GREY MULLET s, B, F
Mugil auratus

Features: Similar to the thin-lipped mullet (see below) except for longer pectoral fins, and there are characteristic golden yellow spots on the gill cover and others on the cheek near the eye. Dorsal fins IV–III,7 to 9; tail fin deeply concave; anal fin III,9.
Size: Average 8–18 in (20–45 cm).
Distribution: Mediterranean; Atlantic (occasionally as far north as the English Channel).
General: A rare species in many locales of its distribution but common in the Mediterranean where it represents an important commercial species.

504 WHITE MULLET s, occasionally B or F
Mugil curema
Other common names: Mullet, blueback mullet, lisa, lisa blanca, macho, machuto, common mullet, silver mullet.

Features: The elongate body lacks a lateral line. Two dorsal fins, a small mouth with minute teeth. The eyes have better vision below than above, the caudal is forked or emarginate. The soft dorsal and anal fins are scaled; the pectoral falling short of the origin of the dorsal. There are usually 38 to 39 scales along the body line. First dorsal fin, IV; second dorsal fin, usually I, 8; anal fin, usually III, 9. Coloration: a blue grey to greenish above, silvery on the lower parts of the sides and below, the fins are sometimes dusky. Young fry are bright silvery in appearance. The eyes are quite small; the head snubbed or blunted in outline.
Size: May reach 30 in (75 cm); 11 lb (5 kg) or even more but generally far smaller.
Distribution: Both coasts of North and South America, Cape Cod to Brazil, Mazatlan to Chile.
General: Important commercially in Florida where it often occurs in large schools. Characteristically, the fish jump and fall back on the surface rigidly. Forage for many gamefish. Snagged with treble hooks, and caught with cast nets or other net fishery. Flesh is sometimes barely edible, other times excellent. Widely used as bait for larger game fish.

505 THIN-LIPPED MULLET S, B, F
Liza ramada
Other common names: Grey mullet, harder.

Features: Ovalate body. Upper jaw remains visible when the triangular-shaped mouth is closed. Dorsal fins IV–8 or 9; tail fin concave; anal fin III,8 or 9. Coloration: dorsally brownish grey or bluish; flanks lighter and with light brown longitudinal stripes; belly silvery white; fins light grey or yellowish, very narrow lips 1/3 eye diameter.
Size: Average 10–20 in (25–50 cm).
Distribution: Mediterranean; North Atlantic, including English Channel.
General: A species of mullet less common in north-western European waters than the closely related thick-lipped form. Fair to good table fare.

506 GREY MULLET S, B, F
Mugil cephalus
Other common names: Mullet, mollet, harder, springer, bully mullet, mangrove mullet, sea mullet, striped mullet, bora (Japan).

Features: Stout, compressed body. Blunt snout and close-set teeth in jaws; eye partially covered by an adipose eyelid. Two dorsal fins IV–I,8; tail fin large and moderately forked; anal fin III,7 or 8. Coloration: dorsally dark bluish or greenish; flanks and belly silvery, scales along flanks have dark centres which give the appearance of a series of dark horizontal stripes. Lateral line not prominent. Scales large and rounded, extending over body and much of the head.
Size: Up to 20 in (50 cm), 8 3/4 lb (4 kg).
Distribution: Worldwide, but is uncommon in some locales.
General: Usually found in dense schools around rocky coasts near freshwater outlets. Males grow to only two-thirds the size of females. In many locales it represents an important commercial species and is sometimes smoked. An excellent sport fish with a reputation for wariness.

In South African waters one of its common names is springer because of its habit of leaping clear of the water. Used in many sport fishing areas as whole or cut bait.

507 THICK-LIPPED MULLET S, B, F
Mugil chelo
Other common names: Warty-lipped mullet, fringe-lipped mullet.

Features: Elongate body. Narrow mouth; a characteristic thickened upper lip with blisterlike papillae (more prominent in older fish). Two dorsal fins IV–9 or 10; tail fin forked; anal fin III,8 or 9. Coloration: dorsally olive or bluish greyish green; flanks lighter with narrow longitudinal stripes or bands; belly silver. No lateral line. Distinguished from thin-lipped mullet (see above) by shape of mouth and by its generally larger size and larger fins.
Size: Average 12–18 in (30–45 cm), maximum over 24 in (60 cm), 5 1/2 lb (2 1/2 kg).
Distribution: Mediterranean; Black Sea, Atlantic, North Sea; occurs only rarely in western Baltic.

General: One of the commoner inshore and estuarine mullets. Food consists chiefly of diatoms and algae, but mollusks and crustaceans are also eaten. An excellent table fish.

508 ATLANTIC THREADFIN S
Polydactylus octonemus

Features: The species is related to the mullets. Strong, stout body. Blunt snout, upper jaw strongly projecting. Two high dorsal fins, the first with spines, the second soft-rayed; deeply forked tail fin. The pectoral fins are characteristic for the threadfin species with the upper part normally shaped, whereas the lower part consists of about 4 long, free, threadlike rays, possibly feeling organs. The numbers of these free rays vary with the species; in the Atlantic threadfin are four on each fin (hence the scientific name *octonemus* (with 8 threads). Coloration: back bluish grey, lower sides and belly yellow to whitish.
Size: 12–14 in (30–35 cm).
Distribution: Atlantic, tropical regions.
General: The species lives in coastal waters, often in the tidal estuaries. Other species of the genus are found in the Pacific.

509 STRIPED BARRACUDA S (B)
Sphyraena obtusata

Features: The body is much elongated and little compressed. Long head with pointed snout; large eyes. The gill cover has no spines. On the tip of the lower jaw is a fleshy wart. The scales are rather large. Two dorsal fins, the first has only 5 spines; one begins just slightly forward of the end of the pectoral fin, the second has one spine and 9 soft rays, it is inserted far back of the first dorsal and right over the anal fin. Forked tail fin. The small ventral fins are placed below and a little backward of the triangular, pointed pectoral fins. Coloration: The back and sides are grey to greenish with 2–3 indistinct, dark, longitudinal bands; the belly is lighter. The pectoral fins are grey, the other fins more or less yellow.
Size: About 16 in (40 cm), up to 25 lb (12 kg).
Distribution: The tropical regions of the Indian Ocean.
General: The striped barracuda lives in rather shallow water, from where it often migrates up into estuaries and lagoons.

510 PICK-HANDLE BARRACUDA S
Sphyraena jello
Other common names: Giant sea pike, asogon.

Features: Elongate strong body. Big mouth with numerous pointed and sharp teeth. Two short dorsal fins, the first with spines, the second soft-rayed; the tail fin is large and forked; the ventral fins are placed below and slightly behind the pointed pectoral fins; the anal fin is as the second dorsal. Coloration: brown to greenish with darker transversal bands.
Size: Maximum 6 1/2 ft. (2 m), weight ca 65 lb (30 kg).
Distribution: Indo-Pacific region.

General: The home of this powerful and voracious fish is the open sea and the deeper coastal waters. It is of some importance to the local fisheries, besides being a first-rate game fish.

511 PACIFIC BARRACUDA S
Sphyraena argentea
Other common name: Scoots

Features: An elongate, very slender fish with long, narrow head and very pointed snout; the lower jaw projects well beyond the upper. Lateral line straight. Large mouth with big, sharp teeth of unequal sizes. Gill rakers short or rudimentary. Two short, widely separated dorsal fins, the first with 5–6 spines, the second with soft rays; tail fin deeply forked with pointed lobes. Pointed pectoral fins; ventral fins placed off first dorsal fin, the anal fin off or slightly behind second dorsal. Coloration: back and sides above the lateral line dark, blackish to grey, with metallic lustre; lower sides and belly silvery. The tail fin has a yellow sheen.
Size: Reaches a length of about 40 in (1 m) with a weight of 20 lb (9 kg).
Distribution: East Pacific, along the west coast of USA. Most abundant off southern California.
General: Occurs mostly in large shoals. It is the most important fish for the California fresh market. Highly appreciated by sport fishermen.

512 GREAT BARRACUDA S
Sphyraena barracuda
Other common names: Sea pike, giant sea pike.

Features: Slender, torpedo-shaped, elongate, and subcylindrical body. Long snout; long mouth reaching back to front edge of eye; lower jaw massive and projecting with sharp-edged, doglike teeth; a small lobe at the end of the lower jaw helps to form a streamlined shape to snout when mouth is closed. Two dorsal fins V–I,7 to 9; tail fin forked; anal fin II,7 to 9. Coloration: dorsally greyish, greenish, or greenish brown; lower flanks and belly silver; adult fish have c. 24 vague and slightly darker crossbars (or bands) on upper flanks, and irregularly spaced, angular black blotches on lower flanks. Lateral line scale count 75 to 90.
Size: Up to 6 ft (180 cm); but average fish much smaller.
Distribution: World-wide in tropical and subtropical waters.
General: The great barracuda is the largest of twenty or so barracuda species that form a worldwide distribution. They are eagerly sought by anglers wherever they are found.

513 AKA-KAMASU S
Sphyraena pinguis

Features: This barracuda is very slender with a long, narrow head, pointed snout; lower jaw projecting strongly beyond upper jaw. Large eyes. The teeth in the upper jaw are short, threadlike, whereas the other teeth are sharp, conical. The two dorsal fins are widely separated and high, the first has 5 spines, the second 9–10 soft rays. The tail fin is large, only little concave. Coloration: back and upper sides

dark grey, belly white.
Size: One of the smaller barracudas, its maximum length is 1–2 ft (30–60 cm).
Distribution: Western Pacific, off Japan and China and farther south.
General: It is of importance to the fisheries, especially in the south of Japan, where it is very common.

514 GUAGUANCHE S
Sphyraena guachancho
Other common name: Southern sennet.

Features: Elongate, slender body, little compressed. Long, low head and pointed snout; lower jaw projecting. Two dorsal fins V–I,8 or 9; tail fin forked (larger than *S. borealis* of similar length); anal fin II,8 or 9. Coloration: dorsally dark olive or dusky blue; flanks lighter with two longitudinal dusky yellow bands; lower flanks and belly silvery; soft dorsal and pelvic fins yellowish. Lateral line scale count 113 to 133.
Size: Up to 18 in (45 cm) 3 1/3 lb (1 1/2 kg).
Distribution: Western Atlantic, West Indies south to Brazil.
General: See great barracuda.

515 NORTHERN SENNET S
Sphyraena borealis
Other common name: Northern barracuda.

Features: Elongate, slender body, little compressed. Long, low head and pointed snout; lower jaw projecting. Two dorsal fins VI–I,8 or 9; tail fin forked; anal fin II,8 or 9. Coloration: dorsally and upper flanks greyish brown; belly silvery; along flanks there is a dark longitudinal stripe which is sometimes broken up into blotches along the lateral line; upper part of head and snout black; dorsal and tail fins dusky; other fins paler. Lateral line gently concave, and scale count 132 to 138.
Size: Up to 18 in (45 cm), 3 1/3 lb (1 1/2 kg).
Distribution: Western Atlantic, from Cape Cod to West Indies and Panama.
General: See great barracuda.

516 EUROPEAN BARRACUDA S
Sphyraena sphyraena
Other common name: Spet.

Features: Long, slender, and semicylindrical body. Snout and mouth long; lower jaw projecting with a small lobe (similar to *S. barracuda* above); numerous pointed teeth. Two dorsal fins V–I,9; tail fin forked; anal fin I,9. Coloration: dorsally and upper flanks a uniform greenish or brownish; lower flanks and belly silvery. Adult fish show c. 25 vague and darker crossbars on flanks. Lateral line, and scale count c. 150.
Size: Up to 20 in (50 cm), maximum 40 in (100 cm), 16 lb (7 1/4 kg).
Distribution: Eastern Atlantic, south from Biscay; Mediterranean.
General: See great barracuda.

517 CALIFORNIA SHEEPHEAD S
Pimelometopon pulchrum
Other common names: California redfish, California fathead.

Features: Large, oblong body. Blunt head and snout, depressed forehead; large "buck" teeth projecting forward. Dorsal fin XI–I,13; tail fin concave; anal fin III,12. Coloration: male fish, purplish black on dorsal, tail, anal fins, head, and rear part of body forward to vent; lower jaw (chin) white; rest of body varying in tint from clear crimson to blackish, with a coppery or purplish lustre. Female fish, dusky rose colour, with black areas ill-defined and sometimes absent. Young fish are orange red overall with seven round, black blotches on fin areas. Lateral line slightly curved.
Size: Average up to 36 in (90 cm), 15 lb (7 kg), maximum over 20 lb (9 kg).
Distribution: Pacific east coasts, California coast from Point Conception to Lower California and Gulf of California.
General: A curious, sex-changing wrasse species and formerly very common along California rocky coasts where it was taken in large numbers in the offshore kelp forests. Nowadays, owing to the disappearance of many kelp areas, the populations are dwindling.

518 ROCK WRASSE S
Halichoeres semicinctus
Other common names: Kelpfish, señorita.

Features: Oblong, somewhat compressed body; rather pointed head, but blunt snout, the front is elevated at the nape. Small mouth with thick lips; 3–4 teeth in each jaw are canine-like; eyes small. Large scales. One dorsal fin with IX, 12 rays, anal fin with 3 spines; tail fin with convex or almost straight margin. Short ventral fins, none of their rays threadlike. Coloration: back and upper sides dark greenish to brown with a lighter, bright sheen; belly lighter. Three to four wavy blue bands below the eyes with bronze colour between them; ventral fins yellow to whitish, the other fins with horizontal reddish streaks.
Size: About 1 ft (30–32 cm).
Distribution: East Pacific from southern California to Mexico.
General: Prefers shallow, coastal waters; abundant in the kelp zone.

519 TAUTOG S, B
Tautoga onitis

Features: Stout, oblong, and compressed body. Blunt head with steep rounded profile. Dorsal fin XVI or XVII,10; tail fin square-cut; anal fin III,7 or 8. Coloration: dorsally blackish or greyish greenish; flanks have irregular dark mottling or blotching especially in small fish, large fish more uniformly blackish; belly slightly paler than flanks. Lateral line is curved, and scale count 69 to 73. Scales medium-sized; membrane of dorsal and anal fins is partially scaled and there is a detached area of small scales adjacent to eye.
Size: Up to 3 ft (90 cm), 22 lb (10 kg), but specimens under 10 lb (4 1/2 kg) much more common.
Distribution: Western Atlantic coasts, from Halifax to South Carolina; most abundant in area from Cape Cod to Delaware Bay.
General: Food is chiefly mussels, gastropods, other molluscs, and crustaceans. Spawning occurs in June, and the eggs float and drift freely on the surface until they are hatched. In Canada the tautog has rapidly developed as a sport fish since the 1950s. Edible, and popular among boat and shore fishermen.

520 HOGFISH S
Lachnolaimus maximus
Other common names: Hog snapper, hog wrasse, capitaine, perro perro.

Features: Fairly stout, deep, and of a large size for the wrasse family, *Labridae*. Three to four anterior spines of the dorsal fin lengthened or extended into filaments. Tips of the soft dorsal, anal, and caudal fins are pointed. Pointed and steep snout with fairly thick lips and a set well-developed and protruding canine teeth. First dorsal, XIII or XIV, 11; anal, III, 10. Scales along the lateral line 39 to 40. The cleft of the mouth on the male is very much wider than in the female. Coloration: Highly variable and not dependable as an identification aid. Usually pinkish or red but also plain greybrown, red-orange, or marbled crimson. Often the top of the head is sharply demarcated in red. A dark spot is present on the body at the base of the posterior rays of the soft dorsal fin. The colour of the males is more vivid than that of the females.
Size: Reaches a length of over 30 in (75 cm); reported at 44 lb (20 kg) but more commonly under 10 lb (4 1/2 kg).
Distribution: Bermuda and the West Indies, to Panama and Key West. Also reported from Brazil.
General: Most common in coral reef areas in the adult phases; sandy and grassy bottoms when younger. Edible, tasty, but reported as poisonous in certain sections of the Caribbean, most probably as a result of specialized feeding habits. Immensely attractive from a visual standpoint; taken frequently by anglers on various baits.

521 CUNNER S
Tautogolabrus adspersus
Other common names: Sea perch, blue perch, bergall, nipper, achigan de mer, tanche vieille.

Features: An elongate perchlike fish with moderately compressed, oblong body. Dorsal fin XVIII,9 or 10; tail fin rounded; anal fin III,9. Coloration: variable, depending on habitat background, but usually mottled brown, reddish, and blue occasionally with some dull olive green; fish from deep water more often reddish; belly white or with a bluish cast; lips yellow; young fish have a distinct black spot in front of soft dorsal fin immediately behind last spine. Lateral line arched above pectoral fin. Large rough scales which extend onto gill covers.
Size: Up to 17 in (43 cm), 3 1/4 lb (1 1/2 kg); usual range up to 12 in (30 cm).
Distribution: Atlantic coasts of North America, from northern Newfoundland and Gulf of St. Lawrence south to Chesapeake Bay.
General: A common bottom-resident, offshore wrasse with a tendency to congregate around wharves, wrecks, and seaweed-covered reefs.

Food consists of molluscs and crustaceans. Not a commercial species. As a light-tackle sport fish it is frequently caught from wharfs in many parts of its distribution. As a table fish it is rated fair.

522 WOLFFISH S
Anarhichas lupus
Other common names: Catfish, sea cat, striped wolffish.

Features: Elongate, compressed body. Head large, heavy, and blunt with a rounded profile; large mouth with doglike teeth in both jaws. Ribbonlike dorsal fin 69 to 79; tail fin small and rounded or square-cut; anal fin 42 to 48. Coloration: very variable, but may be slaty blue or olive green to purplish brown; belly dirty white; usually 10 or more dark vertical bars on forward four-fifths of body which extend across dorsal fin. No lateral line. Body is covered with poorly developed scales.
Size: Average 2 ft (60 cm), maximum up to over 5 ft (150 cm) and 40 lb (18 kg).
Distribution: Both sides of North Atlantic extending into subarctic seas around West Greenland, Spitzbergen, and Iceland. In western Atlantic, from Labrador south to New Jersey; in eastern Atlantic, White Sea south to France.
General: One of several related species of genus *Anarhichas*, all of very similar appearance. They are distinguished by their heavy blennylike bodies and tusklike canine teeth.

A moderately deepwater fish, it feeds on molluscs, whelks, clams, crabs, and sea urchins which can be crushed by its powerful teeth. Wolffish are sometimes caught as sport fish while boat fishing. It is a common commercial species among trawl catches and represents a reasonably acceptable food fish.

523 LESSER CATFISH S
Anarhichas minor
Other common names: Spotted sea cat.

Features: Body, head, jaws, teeth, and fins as in the wolffish (*A. lupus*); only margin of tail fin almost straight. Coloration: uniform brown to yellow with numerous round, often circular, dark brown or blackish spots; belly lighter.
Size: Reaches a length of 2½–5 ft (75–150 cm), 9–17 pound (4–8 kg).
Distribution: Northernmost Atlantic and adjacent arctic waters; North Greenland to Labrador, Iceland, Svalbard, White Sea, and northern Norway.
General: A bottom fish from depths of 55–150 fathoms (100–300 m). It feeds on mussels, crustaceans, and echinoderms.

524 SANDLANCE S
Ammodytes tobianus
Other common name: Sandeel.

Features: Long, slender, eel-like body, slightly compressed. Head long, and snout pointed; lower jaw projecting, jaws without teeth. Long dorsal fin 50–56; tail fin forked; anal fin 25–31. Coloration: variable, dorsally often olive, yellowish green, or bluish; flanks yellowish; belly silver. Lateral line straight. The scales are between diagonal lateral skin folds and are in regular rows forming a distinct chevron pattern.
Size: Up to 8 in (20 cm).
Distribution: Eastern Atlantic; a closely related species, the American sand lance (*A. americanus*), occurs in the western Atlantic; in the eastern north Pacific occurs the Pacific sand lance (*A. hexapterus*).
General: A very common bottom, inshore species. They represent one of the staple sources of food for predatory commercial fishes, and as a consequence are a key species in the food-chain pyramid. For sport fishermen they are a principal source of bait.

525 AMERICAN SAND LANCE S
Ammodytes americanus
Other common names: Sand lance, sand eel, launce, lant, launcefish, Tobias-fish, smelt.

Features: Quite slender with body depth about one-tenth of length, not counting tail. Head is long and nose sharply pointed. Gill openings are wide and lower jaw is undershot. No teeth in jaws or roof of mouth. The long, low dorsal fin originates slightly forward of the tips of the pectoral fins and runs back to the base of the tail. The anal fin starts just behind the mid-point of the dorsal and goes equally far back. The pectorals are low-set and pointed and there are no ventral fins. The small scales lie in cross series between oblique skin folds oriented downward and backward. A low skin ridge occupies either side of the belly. Dorsal fin, 59–67; caudal fin is forked; anal fin 28–36. Coloration: Blue-green, brown, or olive above with silvery sides and belly of dull white. Some specimens exhibit a steel-blue iridescent stripe down each side, others lack this. Colour often depends on environment.
Size: 4–7 in (10–17 1/2 cm), up to 2–3 oz (.27–.32 kg).
Distribution: Atlantic coast of North America in inshore waters, principally from Cape Hatteras north to Nova Scotia, Newfoundland, and Labrador. Related forms reported from Greenland, Iceland, Scandinavia, and the White Sea south to Spain.
General: This prolific small bait fish is important food for many species of larger food and game fish. Sometimes escapes predators by burrowing head-first into soft sand where it also escapes dehydration

when caught in an intertidal zone on the falling tide. Tasty and edible, but rather small for human consumption. Frequently used as live or dead bait for small to medium game fish.

526 SMOOTH SANDEEL S
Gymnammodytes semisquamatus
Other common name: Smooth lance.

Features: Long and slender body. Pointed snout; lower jaw projects well beyond upper jaw. The tail stalk is thin and narrow. The contours of the long dorsal and anal fins are very wavy. Tail fin forked. No ventral fins. Small scales, the anterior part of the body without scales. Coloration: back and upper sides light brown, lower sides and belly blue to silvery; the fins are yellow to greyish.
Size: About 4–6 in (10–15 cm).
Distribution: Western coasts of Europe, from southern Norway, west of the British Isles to Gibraltar; the Mediterranean and Black Seas.
General: Prefers a harder bottom of sand, gravel and shell debris.

527 SANDEEL S
Ammodytes marinus

Features: Very similar to *Ammodytes lancea*, and by several scientists considered only as a variety of this species. It differs from it by a somewhat larger number of vertebrae and by a more slender and elongate body. Coloration: back dark greenish, sides and belly paler.
Size: A little larger than *A. lancea*, 8–10 in (20–25 cm).
Distribution: East Atlantic from north of Norway to the English Channel. North Sea, and through the Danish waters into the Baltic. *General:* Lives on a soft or sandy bottom, where it feeds, as the other sandeels, on all kinds of smaller animals. Also of importance for the fisheries for reduction to meal and oil.

528 GREATER SANDEEL S
Hyperoplus lanceolatus

Features: Long, slender body with narrow head and pointed snout. Lower jaw projects strongly beyond upper jaw. The jaws and lips can be a little protruded. The hind margins of the pectoral fins reach to just below the first ray of the dorsal fin. The margins of the dorsal and anal fins are straight. Coloration: all over bluish to light greenish with a weak sheen of violet; a dark spot on each side of the snout.
Size: Mostly about 8 in (20 cm), rarely up to 1 ft (30–32 cm).
Distribution: Northeast Atlantic, from Iceland and northern Norway to Bay of Biscay. North Sea, Skagerak, Kattegat, Belts, and through the whole Baltic.
General: Very abundant in 10–16 fathoms (20–30 m). Of considerable importance to the fisheries for reduction to meal and oil.

529 BALLAN WRASSE S
Labrus bergylta
Other common names: Sweetlips, sea swine, bergylte, ancient wife.

Features: Long and large-bodied. Heavy head; medium large mouth with thick lips and strong teeth. Dorsal fin XVIII to XXI,9 to 13; tail fin broad and slightly rounded; anal fin III,8 to 12. Coloration: highly variable and dependent on age, habitat, and what has been termed its emotional state; dorsally and on the flanks it may be greenish, bluish, or orange brown and mottled with lighter spots; fins also take on body coloration. Lateral line follows dorsal line. Lateral line scale count 41 to 47. Scales are large.
Size: Average 12–20 in (30–50 cm), 6 lb (2 1/2–2 3/4 kg), but maximum occasionally over 13 lb (6 kg).
Distribution: North Atlantic, from Norway south to Canary Islands, occasionally in the North Sea and western Baltic; Mediterranean.
General: The largest of the European wrasses. Spawning takes place in May–July, and the eggs are laid in a seaweed nest wedged firmly on a reef. Hatching occurs in 21 days. A strong fighter on light tackle.

530 CUCKOO WRASSE S
Labrus mixtus
Other common names: Red wrasse, striped wrasse.

Features: Long, elongate body, laterally compressed. Long head slightly depressed; medium large mouth with front conical teeth well developed; characteristic thick lips. Dorsal fin XVI to XIX,11 to 14; tail fin slightly rounded; anal fin III,9 to 11. Coloration: very variable between individual fish and sexes; females and young fish dorsally brownish red or orange; flanks and belly reddish with blue spots on lines across head; fins are blue-fringed; there are 3 dark blotches on anterior part of dorsal fin; males have a vivid blue head and dorsal area; dorsal area and flanks yellow and orange with vivid, longitudinal, wavy blue lines which extend across gill covers, and distinctive blue spots; during spawning the males develop a white patch on the forehead. In hermaphrodite fish intermediate colorations occur.
Size: Average range 8–14 in (20–35 cm).
Distribution: Eastern Atlantic; occasionally North Sea and western Baltic; Mediterranean.
General: Like all wrasses it frequents the vicinity of rocky shores and weedy ground. Little is at present known about the biology of the cuckoo wrasse. It is usually a nest-building fish, and during the spawning period there is an elaborate courtship display between pairs and aggressive territorial defence by males against other male intruders. Edible.

In Germany it is known as the *Lippfisch* or lip fish. In Norway and Denmark male fish and females have separate common names.

531 CORK-WING S
Crenilabrus melops

Features: In shape similar to the goldsinny, only the body is a little higher, the snout more pointed, and the lateral line rather distinct. Coloration: in the male green with a mixture of blue and red; the female is less strongly coloured, brownish and orange; characteristic for the species is a distinct, dark spot on the sides of the tail stalk close to the tail fin and another bean-shaped, black spot behind the eye.
Size: 4–8 in (10–20 cm).
Distribution: Coasts of western Europe as the goldsinny, but it does not penetrate into the Baltic or eastern Mediterranean.
General: Lives in the vegetation-rich shallow waters.

532 GOLDSINNY S
Ctenolabrus rupestris

Features: A small, rather high and compressed fish; large head with small mouth. Dorsal fin long, the lower anterior part with rather soft spines, the higher posterior part with soft, branched rays. The shorter anal fin has three spines anteriorly. The tail stalk is high and the tail fin broad with a slightly rounded hind margin; pectoral and ventral fins broadly rounded. Large scales. Coloration: back and sides brown mixed with red and orange; the anterior part of the belly is bluish. The goldsinny can easily be distinguished from the other wrasses by its two distinct, black spots, one forward on the dorsal fin, another at the upper margin of the tail stalk.
Size: 3 1/2–4 in (8–10 cm).
Distribution: Coasts of western Europe from southern Norway to Gibraltar; Mediterranean, Black Sea; further North Sea and east into the western Baltic.
General: Its home is the vegetation-rich shallow waters, 1/2–12 fathoms (1–20 m). It feeds mainly on small crustaceans.

533 ROCK COOK S
Centrolabrus exoletus

Features: Shaped similarly to the cork-wing. The lateral line is bent abruptly upwards below the hind part of the dorsal fin. Coloration: The blue is more prominent than in the cork-wing; throat and lower head blue with broad reddish bands; no black spots on body.
Size: Can reach 7 in (18 cm), but mostly smaller.
Distribution: A rather rare species. Norway, British Isles; the belts of vegetation along the shores.

534 SCALE-RAYED WRASSE S
Acantholabrus palloni

Features: This wrasse is very similar to the rock cook, but a little more slender. One long dorsal fin XX-XXII, 8 rays, a shorter anal fin with V, 7–8 rays; broad, short pectoral and small ventral fins. The lateral line is curved gently upwards off the posterior part of the dorsal fin. Rather large scales on body, smaller ones on head and gill cover. Coloration: Variable, a mixture of brown, green, blue, and yellow, darker above, lighter below. The species is distinguished by a black patch on the posterior part of the spinous dorsal fin and another dorso-posteriorly on the tail stalk.
Size: About 6–7 in (16 cm).
Distribution: From southern Norway to the English Channel.
General: Lives in the shallow, coastal waters mostly in the vegetation.

535 RAINBOW WRASSE S
Coris julis

Features: The species belongs to the lipfishes. The body is a little slenderer than in the other lipfishes. The long dorsal fin has comparatively few spines, X-XIII, 13; anal fin III, 11–12; hind margin of tail fin straight or slightly convex. Coloration: The fish has very strong colours, blue, green, brown or yellow with a broad, yellow band along the sides. On the hindmost part of the gill cover is a dark blue spot.
Size: Maximum 10–12 in (25–30 cm).
Distribution: East Atlantic from southern England to the Azores, Mediterranean. Rare in the Belts and North Sea.
General: Lives along the coast on rocky bottoms and feeds on crustaceans and molluscs.

536 BLUE TANG S
Acanthurus coeruleus
Other common names: Surgeonfish, blue doctorfish, doctorfish, tang, blue surgeon, barbero, lancetfish, tangbarbero, saigneur, barberfish.

Features: A small, compressed fish with a small, sharp, erectile spine or blade on either side of the caudal peduncle, a defense weapon that can inflict severe cuts. The close-set, denticulate teeth are adapted to feeding on algae which form the tang's primary diet. Dorsal fin IX, 25–28; anal fin III, 24–26. Lateral line scale count about 160. Coloration: Adults are basically blue with many irregular darker lines on the body. The young, by contrast, are yellow, and may retain this colour into early adulthood. Blue bodies of mature fish have an undertone of brown. Oblique blue and brown stripes on dorsal and anal fins.
Size: Up to 12 in (30 cm), 2 1/4 lb (1 kg).
Distribution: Tropical western Atlantic waters from the Caribbean Sea to Brazil. Frequently found at Bermuda, and occasionally along temperate North American coast as far north as New York.
General: The common names of surgeonfish and lancetfish reflect the tail blades that form the fish's primary defense against predators. Postlarval specimens have poison spines in the pelvic, second dorsal, and anal fins. Poison potential is lost at the time of transformation to the early juvenile stage. Said to be good to eat, but of low sport fishing value.

537 LESSER WEEVER S
Trachinus vipera

Features: The body is not so slender as in the greater weever. Its anterior part with the head is high. The large mouth gapes upward. The fins are as in the greater weever, only the hind margin of the tail-fin is quite straight or slightly convex. Poisonous spines are present on the gill-cover and in the first dorsal fin. Coloration: The body is brownish with minute darker spots; fins greyish to brown; lower head and throat blue.
Size: 4–6 in (10–15 cm).
Distribution: Coasts of western Europe from Skagerak and the British Isles to Gibraltar, also west Africa; Mediterranean.
General: The species is rather rare; it lives in shallow water.

538 GREATER WEEVER s
Trachinus draco

Features: Elongate, tubelike body, laterally compressed. Large head and eyes; small spines above and below the eyes. Two dorsal fins V to VII–29 to 32 (spiny rays are venomous); tail fin concave or almost square-cut; anal fin II,28 to 34. Coloration: dorsally greyish yellow or darker; flanks and belly progressively lighter; flanks marked with characteristic narrow diagonal stripes along scale rows; spiny dorsal fin has a large, black blotch. Venomous spine on gill cover. Lateral line scale count *c*. 83.
Size: Average range 8–16 in (20–40 cm), 2 1/4 lb (1 kg).
Distribution: Mediterranean; eastern Atlantic; English Channel; North Sea; very rarely in western Baltic.
General: One of several closely related species, which inhabit the same waters. All carry poisonous glands connected with the first dorsal fin spines and the spines on the gill covers. Extreme caution must be exercised when handling any of the weever species, for a prick from any of their spines can be extremely painful and may cause serious illness.

Weever fish live on sandy bottoms to a depth of 300 ft (100 m), but some live close inshore, and when partially buried in the sand, may be accidentally stepped on by skin divers or swimmers. They have little interest for sport anglers, but all are recognised table fish.

539 BLUE PARROTFISH s
Scarus coeruleus

Other common names: Clamacore, blue parrot, vieja.

Features: Elongate, robust body with pointed oval forward profile, large scales, especially at the base of the tail. The small mouth contains fused teeth that protrude in the manner of a blunt parrot's bill. Teeth are joined at the plate, but the ends are free. Tail is rounded in young fish, but tips of the lobes may grow longer in adults. Irregular lateral line, the pores are not divergent. Swollen snout in large fish. Head is only slightly longer than deep. Dorsal fin IX, 10; anal fin III, 9. Lateral line scale count, 24–26. Coloration: Bright blue overall, sometimes with a wash of translucent purple. Scales may sometimes have brown bases. Lower lip carries a red bar. Bright blue outer margin on dorsal and anal fins. Colour may vary with habitat, but is always quite bright.
Size: Up to 36 in (90 cm), and 22 lb (10 kg), but most specimens are smaller.
Distribution: Reported from Bermuda, Bahamas, West Indies, western Atlantic coast from Cape Hatteras to Trinidad. Similar and possibly identical fish have been reported in the central tropical Indo-Pacific region, including eastern Africa.
General: Prefers reefs and corals where it finds its food by nipping coral polyps and small vegetation from coral heads and protruberances. Many colour variations, and several closely related species, make identification difficult at times. Meat is said to be edible, although not widely popular. Reported to be poisonous at certain times of

the year, and in certain areas, due to ingestion of poison-containing food. Not much sought by anglers, but greatly admired by skin divers.

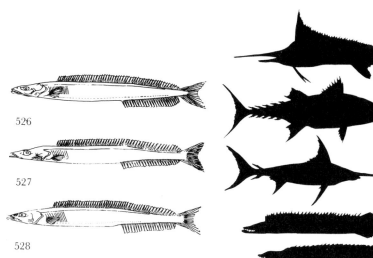

526
527
528
532
533
534

28 MACKERELS, BONITOS, TUNAS, MARLINS

540 CHUB MACKEREL s
Scomber japonicus

Other common names: Japanese chub mackerel, Chub mackerel (G.B.), Pacific mackerel, Cape mackerel.

Features: Elongate, fusiform body. Very similar to the common mackerel, but the head is more pointed and the eye larger. Dorsal fins VIII or X–9 to 13 + 5 or 6 finlets; tail fin deeply forked; anal fin I,9 to 12 + 5 or 6 finlets. Coloration: dorsally dark steel blue with wavy dark lines; flanks and belly silvery or silvery yellow with numerous rounded dusky spots; fins sometimes yellowish in local populations. Lateral line scale count 150 to 170.
Size: Maximum up to 24 in (60 cm), average 14 in (35 cm).
Distribution: Worldwide in warm and warm-temperate seas.
General: One of the most universal of all the schooling mackerel species. In the eastern Atlantic it occurs occasionally north of Biscay; in the western Atlantic it ranges north as far as the Gulf of Maine. In the Mediterranean it is very common and spawns from June to mid-August; in the Pacific, where it is equally common, it spawns March to May. Food consists mainly of anchovies and similar clupeoid fishes, but the young feed on pelagic crustaceans and their larvae.

S. japonicus is very similar to the common mackerel *S. scombrus*, but has a well-developed swim bladder, which is lacking in the common mackerel. As a food fish it is important. As a light-tackle sport fish and table fish some rate it higher than the common mackerel.

541 KINGFISH; KING MACKEREL s
Scomberomorus cavalla

Other common names: Narrow-barred Spanish mackerel, barred Spanish mackerel, katohkel, Natal barracouta, snoek, giant mackerel.

Features: Characterized by an elongate, semi-fusiform, and torpedolike, powerful body. Small head; large mouth furnished with strong teeth. Two dorsal fins XIV to XVII–I,9 – 11 + 9 or 10 finlets; tail fin strongly crescentic; anal fin II,15 – 17 + 9 or 10 finlets. Coloration: dorsally dark blue or dark green; lower flanks and belly silvery; dorsal area and flanks are often mottled with navy-blue crossbars with an iridescent play of colours, but flank coloration may be highly variable according to geographical locale and population. The lateral line is wavy and becomes more prominent with age. Scales are minute and easily rub off.
Size: Up to 150 lb (70 kg) for occasional fish; but average 10–50 lb (4 1/2–23 kg).
Distribution: Worldwide between lat. 35° N and 35° S.
General: A migratory species often found in large schools in certain areas, and during the mating/spawning period it shows much ritualistic jumping. It is probably one of the most internationally confused fishes of the mackerel family, for each geographical locale has its own mackerel nomenclature.

The kingfish is both an important commercial and sport fishing species. As a sport fish it has many of the attributes of the wahoo, but is not as fast in the water. The flesh is of very high quality.

542 MACKEREL (COMMON or ATLANTIC) s
Scomber scombrus

Features: Spindle-shaped, semifusiform, elongate body, slightly compressed laterally. Two dorsal fins XI to XIII–9 to 15 + 4 to 6 finlets; tail fin deeply forked; anal fin I,11 to 13 + 5 or 6 finlets. Coloration: dorsally and upper flanks steely dark blue or bluish green with 20 to 23 dark, wavy bands stopping about the midline; lower flanks and belly silver; the flanks have iridescent flashes; black markings around eyes and black interior to mouth. Black lateral line. Small scales; skin is soft and velvetlike.
Size: Average 10–16 in (25–40 cm), maximum up to 22 in (55 cm) and *c*. 4 1/2 lb (2 kg).
Distribution: Both sides of North Atlantic; Mediterranean; Black Sea, but restricted to continental-shelf regions. In eastern Atlantic, range extends from Scandinavia to North Africa; in western Atlantic, from Labrador to North Carolina.
General: A pelagic schooling fish which in the winter months inhabits moderately deep waters of the open sea; in summer it migrates to inshore continental shelf grounds. Spawning occurs in March–July; eggs are buoyant and hatch in 2–7 days. Early growth is rapid, and yearling fish reach 10–11 in (25–28 cm); then rate slows down; a 4-year-old averages 16 in (40 cm). Mackerel feed on planktonic animals, fish, larvae, worms, small squid, fish eggs, and

young fish fry such as herring.

Throughout its distribution, the mackerel is a very popular angler's fish. It is very important commercially, and methods of catching it vary widely. It may be counted high among the prized staple food fishes, and in Europe is second only to the herring. The flesh is firm with a delicate flavour, but it must be consumed in very fresh condition unless processed.

543 BROAD-BARRED MACKEREL S

Scomberomorus semifasciatus

Other common names: Spanish mackerel, broad-barred Spanish mackerel, southern mackerel, English mackerel, tawatawa (Maori), katonkel (South Africa), barracuda or kuda (Natal), bonita, serra (Portuguese), barracouta, nguru (Kenya), tenggiri (Malaya),

Features: Elongate, cigar-shaped, rather compressed body with minute scales. The large mouth has strongly compressed teeth, about 5 poorly developed gill rakers. Detached finlets on dorsal and anal surfaces of afterbody. A deep notch lies between the fisrt and second dorsal fins. The caudal fin is deeply forked. First dorsal fin, XV–XVII; second dorsal, 14–17 with 9–12 finlets. Anal fin, 14–17, plus 8–12 finlets. The lateral line curves strongly below the finlets. Coloration: Blue-green on the back with wide vertical bands of dark grey on body. In older fish the grey bands tend to break up into less distinct spots. The bands number 12–20 above the lateral line in young specimens. (On the narrow-banded mackerel, the corresponding bands are mainly below the lateral line). Entire body turns dull grey on death.

Size: Up to 6 ft (180 cm) and 100 lb (45 kg), but majority of fish average smaller.

Distribution: Tropical and sub-tropical Pacific and Indian Ocean areas including Australia, South Africa, the Red Sea and Persian·Gulf, East Africa, Malaya, Papua, Fiji, and Philippine Islands. Some reports from China and Japan. Full range not yet established.

General: An excellent sport species with very high food and commercial value. Voracious, aggressive predator, tests light tackle to the limit.

544 CERO MACKEREL S

Scomberomorus regalis

Other common names: King mackerel, kingfish, Spanish mackerel, cavalla, pintada, cero, siering, sier, spotted cero, black-spotted Spanish mackerel.

Features: Easily distinguished from the bonitos by its high second dorsal fin, slender form and spotted sides; and from small tunas by colour, and dorsal outline with long, soft-rayed second dorsal, plus slender body. Pectoral fins are scale-covered. Origin of pelvic fins is a little to the rear of or directly under origin of the first dorsal. Jaws in the large head have conical teeth. Has more numerous and pointed, triangular teeth, longer head, than the true Spanish mackerel, *S. maculatus*. Gill rakers on the first branchial arch number 15–18. First dorsal, XVII–XVIII, triangular; second dorsal, 14–18, concave, originates

slightly ahead of the anal fin, to which it is similar in size and shape. Dorsal and anal finlets, 8–9 on each surface. Coloration: Deep blue on upper half of first dorsal fin. Dark blue-green above shading to silver below. A narrow brown stripe runs from just behind each pectoral fin to caudal peduncle, bisects the lateral line where the line bends down under the second dorsal fin. Rows of oval, yellow orange spots on sides, mostly under the lateral line.

Size: Reported up to 36 in (90 cm), and over 22 lb (10 kg), but most specimens much smaller.

Distribution: Western Atlantic coasts from Brazil to Cape Cod, abundant around Florida and the West Indies.

General: A very popular small game fish and frequently taken by commercial fishermen working inshore. Excellent table fare. Sometimes used as rigged bait for larger game fish.

545 MONTEREY SPANISH MACKEREL S

Scomberomorus concolor

Features: Slender, elongate body; pointed snout with large mouth placed a little obliquely; the upper jaw reaches to just behind the middle of the eye. Teeth comparatively small and only little conical. Few, but long gill rakers. Rather wavy lateral line, curved slightly upwards over the pectoral fin. The first dorsal fin with 17 slender, fragile spines, the second with 16 soft rays, high anteriorly, but very low posteriorly and followed by 9–10 finlets. Forked tail fin, its lower lobe is the longer. Anal fin low I, 16 rays, 7–8 finlets. A single keel on each side of the tail stalk. Air bladder present. Coloration: back and upper sides dark blue, lower sides and belly silvery. The female has 2 series of brown patches on the sides, the males none. The fins have darker colours.

Size: 3–7 ft (1–2 m), 40–60 lb (18–30 kg), mostly only 2 ft (60–70 cm).

Distribution: East Pacific off the coasts of southern California and Mexico.

General: A pelagic fish with its home in the open sea. It is an excellent food fish and much appreciated by game fishermen.

546 SIERRA MACKEREL S

Scomberomorus sierra

Other common name: Sierra.

Features: Much compressed body and head. The snout is pointed, small eyes. Large mouth with upper jaw reaching the hind margin of the eye. large, pointed teeth. Lateral line strongly waved. Small scales. The adults have a strong keel on each side of the tail. First dorsal fin rather low with 14–18 spines, the second is high anteriorly and very low posteriorly, the anal fin is similar; both are followed by about 10 finlets. The tail fin is deeply cleft with long, narrow, pointed lobes. Small ventral fins placed below the much larger pectoral fins. Coloration: back and upper sides dark blue to dark brown, shiny; lower sides and belly silvery to grey; sides with scattered bronze spots.

Size: Up to almost 3 ft (1 m), possibly even more.

Distribution: West Coast of America from

California to Peru.

General: A voracious, pelagic fish, hunting in shoals in the open sea. The species is closely related to *S. maculatus*, and some scientists consider both as one and the same species. It is an important commercial fish, and powerful and agile as it is, it is much estimated by game fishers.

547 SPANISH MACKEREL S

Scomberomorus maculatus

Features: Elongate, semifusiform body, dorsal fins XVI or XVII–I,15 to 18 + 8 or 9 finlets; tail fin strongly crescentic; anal fin II,15 to 17 + 7 to 9 finlets. Coloration: dorsally bluish; flanks and belly silvery; flanks characteristically have numerous dull orange or bronze elliptical spots not arranged regularly in lines; spiny dorsal fin black above and whitish near base; soft dorsal yellowish with black margin; anal fin white. Lateral line undulating.

Size: Up to 36 in (90 cm), 11 lb (5 kg).

Distribution: Warmer Atlantic and Pacific seas.

General: This is the true Spanish mackerel of the Americas. In the Atlantic it ranges north to Cape Hatteras and south to Brazil. Wherever it occurs in schools, it is an important food fish. Spawning in North American waters takes place April–June, and the earliest spawning occurs in its southern distribution. The Spanish mackerel is an excellent light tackle sport fish.

548 TANGUIGUE S

Scomberomorus commersoni

Other common names: Giant mackerel, kingfish.

Features: In shape of body, head and fins very similar to *S. sierra* and *maculatus*. Lateral line very much waved, especially posteriorly. Coloration: back and upper sides dark blue; lower sides and belly light grey to silvery; characteristic for the species are the many irregular, vertical, dark bands across the sides.

Size: The general size is about 2 ft (60–65 cm), but individuals up to 6 ft (180 cm) have been noted.

Distribution: Occurs over the oceans in tropical and near-tropical regions, but is most numerous and best known from Australian seas.

General: This pelagic fish is famous for its high jumps out of the water. It feeds on pelagic fish, among them flying fish which they even may catch during their flight over the surface. It is an important commercial fish and also very highly estimated as a game fish.

549 SPOTTED MACKEREL S

Scomberomorus niphonius

Other common names: Japanese Spanish mackerel, sawara.

Features: A long, slender fish with small head. The teeth on the jaws are curved and sharp. No air bladder. The first dorsal fin, 19 spines, is very long and comparatively low, the second is high anteriorly, but very low posteriorly, 9 finlets. The high anal fin, 16 soft rays, is followed by 8 finlets; the tail fin is deeply forked and its lobes are large with broadly rounded tips; pectoral

fins broad and short, ventral fins small. The somewhat wavy lateral line has many short, transverse branches. Coloration: back and upper sides blue to grey, lower sides and belly white and silvery. The sides below the lateral line have many darker spots.

Size: Reaches about 3 ft (1 m) and 10 pounds (4–5 kg).

Distribution: Western Pacific in Japanese and Chinese waters.

General: The species spawns in late spring in the near-shore waters. It is a highly appreciated food fish and of considerable importance to the commercial fisheries, and also valuable as a game fish.

550 FRIGATE MACKEREL S

Auxis thazard

Other common names: Mackerel, bonito, black skipjack, judeu (Angola), watermelon, leadenall.

Features: The powerful, torpedo-shaped body is covered with minute scales. The dorsal fin is highest well forward and is followed by a number of detached finlets extending along the midline toward the tail. There are also finlets behind the anal fin. Depth of body is about one-quarter of body length. First and second dorsal fins are widely separated. First dorsal, XI; second dorsal, 11–12; finlets, 8. Anal fin, 13; anal finlets, 7. Gill rakers variously described as numbering about 30, or as much as 42–45. One line of sharp, conical teeth on both jaws, none on the palate. Scales form a corselet on the body. Eyes large. Tail slightly forked. Coloration: Dark blue-green back shading to silver on sides and underneath. Variable, irregular lighter markings on rear upper portion of body. The frigate does not have spots below the pectoral fin as does the black skipjack, with which it is sometimes confused.

Size: Up to 30 in (75 cm), 4 1/2–6 lb (2–2 3/4 kg).

Distribution: Tropical to cold-temperate seas, worldwide. There is speculation that the world population may contain several subraces or subspecies.

General: Occurs erratically, being absent in some areas for years, then reappearing in large numbers. Excellent food when available, and considerable localized commercial importance. Puts up a good fight when hooked, but most frequently caught by anglers while fishing for other species.

551 BULLET MACKEREL S

Auxis rochei

Other common names: Frigate mackerel, southern mackerel, English mackerel, tawatawa (Maori), bonito, false albacore, Mexican skipjack.

Features: Despite the common names shared with other members of the mackerel family, the bullet mackerel is a separate species. It has the usual mackerel characteristics of spiny and soft dorsal fins, small finlets on the midline of the dorsal and ventral afterbody, a streamlined form, narrow caudal peduncle, and lunate tail. The skin feels smooth, but is covered with tiny scales on the forebody. Wide space between the two dorsals and about 8 finlets on the dorsal afterbody with 7 below. A fleshy flap, called the interpelvic process, lies between the pelvic fins. An extension of the scaled forward body covering extends rearward along the lateral line. In the frigate mackerel, *Auxis thazard*, this extension is five scale rows wide, or less, under the second dorsal fin. In the bullet mackerel, *Auxis rochei*, it varies from 6 to 28 rows wide at the same point. Gill raker count is 42–45. Large eyes. First dorsal fin, XI; second dorsal, 11–12; anal fin, 13. Coloration: Blue green on upper sides and back with dark, narrow, oblique stripes or bars extending from the back centerline to the lateral line. Lower sides and belly bright silver.

Size: Up to 24 in (60 cm), 11 lb (5 kg), but the majority of fish smaller.

Distribution: Worldwide in tropical and subtropical seas, particularly the Indo-Pacific areas.

General: Strong schooling habits, feeds on small fish, shrimp-like creatures, crustaceans. Excellent bait for large, swift predators. Good on rod and reel when available, but indifferent table fare.

552 WAHOO S
Acanthocybium solanderi

Other common names: Ono, kingfish, queenfish, peto, jack mackerel.

Features: An elongate, semifusiform, mackerel-like body. Long, slender, pointed head; large mouth with teeth close-set. Two dorsal fins XXV to XXVII–12 + 9 or 10 finlets; tail fin crescentic; anal fin II,10 or 11 + 9 finlets. Coloration: dorsally dark steely or metallic blue; flanks bluish grey, paling to silver on belly; dorsal fin blue and second soft dorsal blackish. Young fish show very distinct, narrow, vertical bands on flanks which are visible in adult fish but less prominent and occasionally absent. The vertical bands and brilliant coloration quickly fade after death. Lateral line is arched over pectoral fin and then undulates slightly toward tail. Sometimes the wahoo is confused with Spanish mackerel (*Scomberomorus maculatus*), but may be distinguished by differences in coloration and in fin-ray counts.

Size: Up to c. 160 lb (72 kg), but average fish usually much smaller.

Distribution: Worldwide in tropical and subtropical regions.

General: Not usually a schooling species except during spawning time when small, loosely knit, mixed schools form. Food consists of smaller tuna, puffer fishes, mackerel, flying and lantern fishes. The wahoo is a celebrated sport fish and an important commercial species in many countries. When hooked, it swims at great speed and is able to leap high and reenter the water with hardly a splash. Ernest Hemingway, the celebrated American author and big-game fisherman, called the wahoo the best flavoured of all marine game fishes.

553 SNAKE MACKEREL S
Gempylus serpens

Features: A very elongate fish with long head and big mouth. The lower jaw projects well beyond the upper; strong, sharp teeth, especially two longer in the upper jaw. Small scales. The dorsal fin is long with an incision between the longer spinous part and the short soft-rayed part, between this and the tail c. 6 finlets. The tail fin is deeply forked with pointed lobes; the anal fin is similar to the soft-rayed dorsal, behind it are 6 finlets. Small, pointed pectoral fins, ventral fins missing or rudimentary. Coloration: back bluish grey or brown, below whitish, fins darker.

Size: Maximum 20 in (50 cm).

Distribution: Southern Atlantic, possibly also other oceans.

General: A true pelagic fish, living far from the coasts in deep water.

554 ATLANTIC CUTLASS-FISH S
Trichiurus lepturus

Other common names: Scabbardfish, silver eel, ribbandfish, silverfish, machete, sable, savola, hairtail, silver hairtail.

Features: The ribbon-like body tapers back to a pointed tail with no caudal fins. The long single dorsal fin begins just behind the eyes and tapers (in about 135 rays) to nothing at the tip of the tail. The anal fin is composed of a 100–110 short detatched spines projecting toward the rear. There are four long fang teeth in the upper jaw and two in the lower, which is undershot. Body depth averages about one-fifteenth of body length, of which about one-eighth is the head. The small pectoral fins are overlapped by the rear corners of the gill covers. Ventral fins are absent and the body has no scales. There are four gills with a slit behind the fourth. There is a lateral line. Coloration: Dull silver or bright pewter-colour over all with a yellowish to greenish dorsal fin having a dark or speckled margin.

Size: Up to about 4 ft (120 cm) and 4 1/2 lb (2 kg).

Distribution: All warm and temperate areas, Atlantic Ocean. Closely related species exist in the Pacific and Indian oceans.

General: While little is known about the lives of cutlassfishes, they are valued for food in some areas, notably Japan. A voracious small marine predator that is occasionally caught on shrimp or small fish bait, or artificial lures.

555 SNOEK S
Thyrsites atun

Features: The compressed body is elongate with small scales. Single undulating lateral line. Long snout with large canine teeth in both jaws. Resembles generally the barracuda of southern United States, but not directly related. Deep notch separates the dorsals. First dorsal fin, XVIII to XX; second dorsal, 10–12. Dorsal detached finlets, 5–6. Anal fin, III, 8–10, and 5–6 detached anal finlets. Coloration: Shiny black on back, fins, finlets, and the deeply forked tail, light belly.

Size: Up to 4 1/2 ft (135 cm), 11 lb (5 kg), but average fish are smaller.

Distribution: Widespread in southern hemisphere from South Africa to South America, also in New Zealand and Australian waters.

General: Commercially important where available, but subject to large population changes. Flesh is well flavoured with delicate texture, eaten fresh, smoked, other-

wise preserved. Feeds on krill, shrimps, small fish. A popular sport species that must be handled with care because it can inflict bad wounds with its long, sharp teeth.

556 YELLOWFIN TUNA S
Thunnus albacares

Other common names: Allison tuna, Kihada (Japan), ahi (Hawaii).

Features: Elongate, semifusiform body. Lower jaw projecting. Two dorsal fins XIII or XIV–12 + 8 or 9 finlets; keels on either side of tail stalk; tail fin large and crescentic; anal fin II or III,12 + 8 or 9 finlets; characteristic recognition features are the second dorsal and anal fins which are very long and scythelike, but length and development depend on age; pectorals long and pointed. Coloration: dorsally and upper flanks above the level of the lateral line Prussian blue; flanks below silvery, and across lateral line a golden yellow band extends from behind the eye to the tail stalk; all fins and finlets have a yellowish golden tinge; second dorsal, tail, and anal fins have dusky leading edges particularly near the bases. Lateral line not prominent. Scales are small.

Size: Large fish up to 9 ft (2 3/4 m), 400 lb (180 kg), but in the Atlantic distribution smaller fish 10–100 lb (5–45 kg) more usual.

Distribution: Worldwide in warm seas.

General: An important sport and commercial fish with excellent table qualities.

557 BLUEFIN TUNA S
Thunnus thynnus

Other common names: Horse mackerel, tunny tuna, tunny fish, bluefin, Southern Pacific bluefin, Japanese Central Pacific bluefin.

Features: Stout, semifusiform body, little compressed with greatest depth under the middle of first dorsal fin. Two dorsal fins XIII to XV–I,13 to 15 + 8 – 10 finlets; keels either side of tail stalk; tail large, broad, and crescentic; anal fin II,12 + 8 or 9 finlets. Coloration: dorsally dark blue; flanks paling to greyish or silvery; belly silvery; cheeks silvery; dorsal fins dusky blue grey; anal fin dusky, yellow, or silvery grey; dorsal and anal finlets tinged with yellow, pectoral fin short. There are several minor geographical variations in features and colorations in separate populations. Lateral line. Scales small but large in region of the corselet.

Size: Up to over 1,000 lb (450 kg); reported Mediterranean specimens up to 14 ft (4 1/2 m), 1,800 lb (820 kg); but few exceed 8 ft (2 1/2 m).

Distribution: Believed to be worldwide in cool temperate to subtropical waters. The bluefish tuna may include several local subspecies, and some recognize a separate subspecies *T. thynnus maccoyii* in Indo-Pacific seas.

General: Largest member of the mackerel family. A highly prized commercial fish with excellent table qualities, the flesh especially esteemed in Scandinavian and Mediterranean countries, and in the Far East. The bluefin is an ideal big-game fish renowned for its tremendous strength,

speed, and hard-fighting qualities. A schooling species, and fish of approximately the same size keep together. It has been noted that the size of the fish has a direct bearing on the size of the school. The smaller fish swim in large schools, while large specimens form small schools.

Food consists of crustaceans and schooling fishes such as herring, small mackerel, sprats, whiting, flying fish, sand eels, squid, and cuttlefish.

It is notably absent, or rarely seen, in certain locales, as for example in South African waters. The bluefin tuna are migratory fish, travelling long distances. Their migration is linked with the movements of the fish on which they feed, and on water temperature. Bluefin tuna tagged in the southeast United States have been caught in the Bay of Biscay and off the coast of Norway. One captured fish had travelled 4,500 miles (7,200 km) in 120 days. Another travelled c. 5,000 miles in 50 days on approximately the same route. One migration occurs northward in the Western North Atlantic during July and August. A southern migration occurs off the eastern seaboard of Australia in April and May toward Tasmania and South Australia. A northern migration occurs in the North Sea where it is believed that tuna once followed the herring fleets, but this population is now apparently much reduced in numbers, chiefly owing to commercial overfishing. In the Northern Hemisphere it is known that a cold summer will limit the northward migration from warmer waters, for bluefin tuna cannot tolerate temperatures below 50° to 54°F (10° to 12°C).

The name tunny, or tunny fish, is derived from the Latin *thunnus*, and was first used in England in the fifteenth century. The common name tuna did not come into general use until the beginning of the twentieth century.

558 SKIPJACK TUNA S
Euthynnus pelamis

Other common names: Striped bonito, skipjack, striped tuna, oceanic bonito.

Features: Stout, fusiform body. Dorsal fins XVI–I or II, 12 to 14 + 7 to 9 finlets, keeled tail stalk; tail very broadly crescentic; anal fin II,11 to 16 + 7 or 8 finlets. Coloration: dorsally and upper flanks bluish black with a purple or green metallic sheen; lower flanks show 4 to 6 longitudinal blue to brownish stripes on a lighter background paralleling the line of the belly; belly silvery; anal finlets white; other fins and finlets dark silvery grey. Scaling on front part of body only. Lateral line has a sigmoid (double *S*-curve) sweep.

Size: Average range 20–28 in (50–70 cm), maximum up to 40 in (100 cm), 50 lb (22 1/2 kg); average sport fish 5–15 lb (2 1/4–6 3/4 kg).

Distribution: Worldwide in warmer seas.

General: A gregarious open-water migratory fish of great commercial value, and popular among light-tackle ocean anglers.

559 BIGEYE TUNA S
Thunnus obesus
Other common names: Atlantic bigeye tuna, Pacific bigeye tuna.

Features: Elongate, semifusiform body. Lower jaw projecting; large characteristic eye. Two dorsal fins XIII–13 + 9 finlets; tail fin large and crescentic; keels either side of tail stalk; anal fin II or III,13 + 8 or 9 finlets evenly spaced. Coloration: dorsally dark ashy blue; flanks a leaden hue; tail, tail stalk, and pectoral fins reddish black; first dorsal slightly yellowish; finlets yellow and edged with black. Lateral line indistinct. Scales are small. *Note:* The bigeye tuna has been recognised as a separate species only in more recent years and previously it was included among yellowfin (Allison) tuna. It may be distinguished from the latter species in that the second dorsal and anal fins are blackish and lack any yellowish tinge, whereas in the yellowfin both these fins are a deep yellow. The eye is also larger than that of the yellowfin or bluefin.
Size: Largest 93 in (235 cm), 435 lb (200 kg).
Distribution: Worldwide; two recognised populations, one in the Pacific and one in the Atlantic.
General: An excellent, hard-fighting sport fish, and a commercial species caught extensively by long-line methods. A high-quality table fish.

560 BLACK SKIPJACK S
Euthynnus lineatus
Other common names: Skipjack, bonito; little tuna, false albacore, mackerel tuna, spotted tuna, thunnine.

Features: Body shape is fusiform, tapering from a rounded midsection to a pointed nose and a slender afterbody. Second dorsal is close to the first dorsal with little intervening space. Body depth is about one-fourth length. Strong side keel on each side of the caudal peduncle, with a smaller keel above and below the main keel, totalling three on each side. First dorsal profile is deeply concave. Body lacks scales except on forward upper portions, on the corselet, and down the lateral line, which is relatively straight. The anal fin is based further back than in other bonitos, about under the first dorsal finlet. Gill raker count on limb of first arch is 32–41. No air bladder. First dorsal, XV, concave upper edge, last two-thirds much shorter. Triangular second dorsal, rear edge concave. Anal the same size and shape as second dorsal. Eight small dorsal finlets, 7 anal finlets. Moderate size pectorals. Caudal fin lunate, short, broad. Coloration: Dark blue-grey above, pure white below. Four or five broad black stripes are placed horizontally on the back, extending from the corselet to the caudal peduncle. A few dark spots under the pectoral fin. Black stripes are above the lateral line.
Size: Up to 30 in (75 cm), 11 lb (5 kg).
Distribution: Eastern and central tropical and warm-temperate Pacific waters.
General: Feeds on small surface fishes and squid. Some commercial value. Excellent on rod and reel, although seldom deliberately sought. Considered good to eat in some areas, but not popular in others.

561 ALBACORE S
Thunnus alalunga
Other common names: Long-finned albacore, long-fin tuna, ahipalaha, Spanish mackerel (Western Australia).

Features: Elongate, semifusiform body. Two close-set dorsal fins XIII or XIV–II,12 to 14 + 7 or 8 finlets; keels either side of tail stalk; tail fin broad and crescentic; anal fin (similar to 2nd dorsal) II,12 or 13 + 8 to 10 finlets; pectoral fins very long and narrow (very characteristic recognition feature). Coloration: dorsally and upper flanks metallic steel blue or bluish black; flanks show a sharp transition to silver a little above lateral line; fins dusky or yellowish, but first dorsal and pelvics paler white. Lateral line present. Scales medium.
Size: Up to 4 ft 2 in (1.25 m), 70 lb (32 kg).
Distribution: Worldwide, ranging from very cool to tropical waters.
General: An important commercial species because of its suitability for canning. Also an excellent sport fish.

562 BLACKFIN TUNA S
Thunnus atlanticus
Other common names: Bermuda tuna, albacora, blackfinned albacore, thon.

Features: A small, swift, predacious tuna distinguished by black rather than yellow tail finlets. These small minor fins in tunas and related species occur along the dorsal and ventral midlines of the body between the second dorsal fin and the tail and the anal fin and the tail, respectively. Dorsal finlets number 7–9 and ventral finlets 7–8. Pectoral fin length is .8 to 1.2 times length of head. Gill raker count 20–24 on the first limb, less than any other tuna. Internally, the undivided air bladder is shorter than it is wide. The body is fully scaled. Dorsal fin, XIII to XIV, 7–8; caudal fin is lunate in shape. Coloration: blue-black above, silver below. Pectoral fins are edged with blue. Light bars of colour alternate with light spots on the lower sides. Dorsal finlets are dusky brown, anal finlets dark steel-grey.
Size: Up to 24 lb (11 kg), 30 in (75 cm).
Distribution: Western tropical and warm-temperate Atlantic waters from Brazil north via the Caribbean and Gulf of Mexico to Bermuda and sometimes Cape Hatteras.
General: A primarily surface-feeding fish, eating plankton, squid, small bait fishes. Excellent on light tackle when taken trolling or with live bait. The flesh is tasty and has local commercial importance.

563 LITTLE TUNNY S
Euthynnus alletteratus
Other common names: False albacore, mackerel tuna.

Features: Elongate, robust, fusiform, and slightly compressed body. Dorsal fins XIV to XVI–11 to 13 + 7 or 8 finlets; keeled tail stalk; tail fin crescentic; anal fin 12 to 14 + 7 finlets. Coloration: dorsally blue black or dark green; flanks paler and silvery; upper flanks have wavy mackerel-like markings; usually there are 3 to 6 dark, smudge-like spots behind and below pectoral fin; belly silver. Lateral line arched over short pectoral fin.

Size: Average up to 32 in (80 cm), 20 lb (9 kg); large fish 48 in (120 cm).
Distribution: Worldwide in tropical to temperate waters.
General: A common pelagic schooling species and a hard-fighting sport fish. Frequently used as a baitfish for shark and marlin. Excellent table qualities, although the flesh is darker and stronger in flavour than that of the larger tunas. Commercially important–especially for canning.

564 SLENDER TUNA S
Allothunnus fallai

Features: The body is strong and stout, but a little more slender than in the other tunas. The snout is pointed and the mouth relatively small with small, weak teeth. Many rather thin gill rakers. The whole body is covered with very small scales. No air bladder. The first dorsal fin has 17 spines, only the first 3–4 are high, the following are low and the posterior ones are almost rudimentary; the second dorsal is high and followed by 7 finlets, the similarly shaped anal fin is followed by 6–7 finlets. Tail fin deeply forked with long, pointed lobes. Coloration: above dark bluish, below lighter, silvery.
Size: About 3–3 1/4 ft (ca 1 m), weight 40–65 lb (18–30 kg).
Distribution: Southern Pacific, mainly around New Zealand.
General: A pelagic species which, where abundant, is of some commercial importance; it is an excellent game fish.

565 KAWAKAWA S
Euthynnus affinis
Other common names: Eastern little tuna, black skipjack, suma.

Features: The body is spindle-shaped with big head and blunt snout. The first dorsal fin, with 15–16 spines, is high anteriorly and very low, almost rudimentary, posteriorly; the second dorsal is small followed by 8 finlets; the anal fin is as the second dorsal, and is followed by 7 finlets; the tail fin is deeply forked with narrow, pointed lobes. Pectoral and ventral fins are rather short, but broad. Coloration: back and upper sides dark blue, almost black, lower sides and belly whitish, silvery. Between the pectoral and ventral fins are a few darker spots.
Size: Maximum 3 ft (1 m), 20–22 lb (9–10 kg).
Distribution: Indo-Pacific region, East Indian seas, Philippines, and southern Japan.
General: A voracious fish feeding on smaller pelagic fish. It is of some importance for the local commercial fisheries.

566 DOGTOOTH TUNA S
Gymnosarda nuda
Other common names: Lizard-mouth tuna.

Features: Powerful, torpedo-shaped body, tiny scales, dorsal fin in separate parts, with finlets behind dorsal and anal fins. Deep notch between dorsal fins, caudal fin forked. Anal fin originates to the rear of the origin of the second dorsal. Large mouth with long, curved teeth. A few rows of scales on either side of the lateral line. First dorsal, XIV–XVII; second dorsal, 10; 7–8 dorsal

finlets. Anal fin, 10; anal finlets, 6–7. Coloration: Dark blue or blue-green above and on upper sides, shading to silver on lower sides and belly. Fins are dusky-coloured. Curved lateral line.
Size: Up to 155 lb (70 kg) and 6 ft (180 cm) long, but commonly much smaller.
Distribution: Western Pacific and Indian oceans, Red Sea.
General: A relatively rare tuna of voracious habits that prefers rocky areas not far from a coast. Reported good eating, but of no commercial value other than by accidental local capture, due to its rarity.

567 STRIPED BONITO S
Sarda orientalis
Other common name: Hagatsuwo.

Features: Torpedo-shaped body. Large head, very large mouth, big teeth. First dorsal fin low and long with 19 spines, second short with 15 soft rays followed by 7–8 finlets; tail fin broadly forked; pectoral fins short, pointed, ventral fins small. Lateral line almost straight. Scales are present only round the pectoral fins. The lateral keels on the tail stalk are strong. Coloration: back and upper sides indigo blue with about 6 longitudinal, a little wavy, black bands; lower sides and belly whitish to silvery.
Size: Maximum 2 3/4 ft (80 cm); weight 3–6 1/2 pound (1.4–3 kg).
Distribution: Western Pacific from Japan and further south.
General: It lives, often in large shoals, in the open surface waters well off the coast. The flesh is not very tasty, and its commercial value therefore restricted. However, it is a fine game fish.

568 ATLANTIC BONITO S
Sarda sarda
Other common names: Pelamid, common bonito, bonito, Cape katonkel, belted bonito.

Features: Almost fusiform. Dorsal fins XX to XXIV–I,13 to 16 + 6 to 8 finlets; tail stalk keeled; tail fin broad and crescentic; anal fin I, 11 to 15 + 7 to 10 finlets. Coloration: dorsally and upper flanks bluish green or steely blue, seven or more dark bluish parallel bands run obliquely forward and downward from the dorsal region to just below the lateral line; lower flanks and belly silvery. Lateral line undulating.
Size: Average range 16–24 in (40–60 cm), maximum up to 36 in (90 cm), 11–12 lb (5–5 1/4 kg).
Distribution: Warmer Atlantic seas. In western Atlantic, from Nova Scotia southward. In northeastern Atlantic ranging from Norway southward into the Mediterranean, but rarely in the southern North Sea and English Channel.
General: A fast-swimming school fish with limited commercial value, but good on angling tackle.

569 PLAIN BONITO S

Orcynopsis unicolor
Other common name: Plain pelamis.

Features: Stout, compressed body. Pointed snout; mouth with strong teeth; small eyes. Only scales on the most anterior of the body. Tail stalk with lateral keels. The two dorsal fins are placed close to each other; 8 finlets after the second dorsal fin, 7 after the anal fin. The tail fin deeply forked. Coloration: back steel blue to dark blue, lower sides and belly silvery; no darker bands or spots on body. The first dorsal fin and the pectoral fins have darker margins.
Size: 2–3 1/2 ft (60–100 cm).
Distribution: East Atlantic from the North Sea (here only rare) to Senegal; Mediterranean.
General: Lives in the open ocean.

570 WHITE MARLIN S

Tetrapturus albidus
Other common names: skiligollee (U.S.A.), Spikefish.

Features: Much compressed body, with heavy shoulders. Upper jaw prolonged, forming a slender bill or spear. Two dorsal fins, the first of which is quite prominent. The second is located far back on the body and is called a tail finlet by some. First dorsal has high, ragged, rounded profile tapering into the mid-back. XXXVIII to XLII–6. Second dorsal small and fleshy-looking. Tail fin long, thin, and crescent-shaped with widely separated lobes. Tail stalk has double side keels. Two anal fins II, 12 or 13–6; second anal fin much smaller and similar to second dorsal. Coloration: Dorsally dark blue; flanks lighter in colour, paling to white, frequently with lilac vertical bands; fins usually dark blue-black with black spots on first dorsal fin. Lateral line indistinct. Small spine-like scales are imbedded.
Size: Up to 9 ft (275 cm), 160 lb (73 kg).
Distribution: Atlantic, Mediterranean, Gulf of Mexico, Caribbean, in warm waters.
General: A small marlin common in the West Indies, Madeira, and the Azores. Often seen in concentrations off Venezuela, in the northern Gulf of Mexico, and along the Maryland and southern New Jersey coasts of the U.S.A. Excellent on light tackle. Not generally commercially sold, but the flesh is good, especially when smoked.

571 STRIPED MARLIN S

Tetrapturus audax
Other common names: Red marlin (Japan), striper.

Features: Very compressed body, medium-shouldered fish. Prolonged upper jaw forming a slender bill or spear. Two dorsal fins XXXVII to XLIII–7, first section has a very high profile, particularly first 5 rays; tail stalk has double keels; tail fin large and crescentic; two anal fins II,16 or 11–7; second anal similar to second dorsal; pectoral fins are movable. Coloration: dorsally and flanks to lateral line royal blue or blue with slight bronze and green shadings, flanks characteristically crossed by 10 to 14 vertical lavender or cobalt blue stripes composed of spots on upper flanks; belly paling from bluish silver to white; dark

spots on membrane of dorsal fin. Several variations in coloration have been noted, but these usually refer to immature fish. Lateral line fairly straight. Scales embedded.
Size: Up to 14 ft (4 m), 800 lb (365 kg).
Distribution: Indo-Pacific region in tropical to temperate seas.
General: The striped marlin is a slenderer species than the blue or black marlin, but what it may lack in size, it compensates for in general acrobatic abilities. It is particularly valued in Japan where the flesh is used for sashimi, (raw fish served with a condiment).

572 BLACK MARLIN S

Makaira indica

Features: Much compressed body, very heavy-shouldered. Prolonged upper jaw forming a slender bill or spear. Two dorsal fins XXXVI to XL–7; tail stalk has double keels; tail fin large and crescentic with long symmetrical lobes; two anal fins II,10 or 11–7; second anal similar to second dorsal; pectoral fins are fixed. In young fish up to c. 130 lb (60 kg) they are movable within certain limits, but they do not fold back naturally along the flanks. Coloration: dorsally bluish brown; flanks silvery below lateral line; in the water the flanks and shoulders often show blue stripes, and the flanks generally show vivid light blue patches along the fins. Lateral line straight. Scales embedded. See also key to marlin characteristics.
Size: Probably maximum in excess of 2,500 lb (1,125 kg); fish c. 2,000 lb (9,000 kg) are frequently represented in commercial long-line catches.
Distribution: Indo-Pacific region in tropical to temperate seas.
General: A more pugnacious-looking fish than the blue marlin, and the body is generally heavier and more thickset around the shoulders. The largest fish are females, and judging from both sport and commercial catches, males seldom appear to exceed 500 lb (225 kg). As a sport fish the black marlin gains the highest rating due to the combination of size, great weight, power, and agility. As a table fish it is reasonably good, although the flesh is very dry.

573 BLUE MARLIN S

Makaira nigricans

Features: Very compressed body, heavy-shouldered fish. Prolonged upper jaw forming a slender bill or spear. Two dorsal fins, first large, second far toward tail and very small, XXXVI or XXXVII–6, first section has high profile, second short and low; tail stalk has double keels; tail fin large and crescentic with long symmetrical lobes; two anal fins II,12 or 13–6; flat, movable pectoral fins. First anal fin of blue marlin is pointed whereas anal fin of white marlin is rounded. Coloration: dorsally brilliant cobalt blue; flanks silver with bright bands of light blue; tail and first dorsal fin with blue patches. After death the vivid body coloration fades. Lateral line indistinct. Scales long, thin, and embedded.
Size: Up to 2,000 lb (910 kg). The largest fish are females.
Distribution: Worldwide in warm to cool

temperate seas, ranging from offshore to midocean.
General: Not as heavily built as the black marlin; tail fin is noticeably larger than that of other species. As a sport fish it is aggressive, courageous, and a spectacular leaper. An important longline commercial species and an excellent table fish with firm, white flesh.

574 SAILFISH (ATLANTIC AND PACIFIC) S

Istiophorus platypterus
Other common names: Bayonetfish, spindle beak.

Features: Long, narrow, lightly built body tapering evenly towards tail; laterally compressed. Upper jaw is prolonged into a circular needle-like bill or beak, and is longer than the bill of spearfishes; lower jaw elongate. Characterized by a long, high first dorsal fin XXXII to XXXV which forms a 'sail' when fully raised; second dorsal 7 to 11 very small; tail stalk has double keels; tail fin is very deeply forked with long, pointed symmetrical lobes; two small anal fins 11 to 13–6 to 7; free-moving, marlin-like pectoral fins; retractable, long pelvic fins. Coloration: dorsally deep, dark blue or bluish purple; flanks and belly with yellowish-grey hues, sometimes with bluish-grey vertical bars composed of vivid blue patches or spots; open sail is slaty or dark blue, with the membrane showing a scattering of black spots. Lateral line is well defined along median line of flanks.
Size: Not generally larger than 7–8 ft (2–2 1/2 m) 200–240 lb (90–110 kg).
Distribution: Worldwide, but there is still some doubt whether there is only one species of sailfish or several closely related races.
General: The I.G.F.A. list both an Atlantic and a Pacific sailfish for record purposes, but this appears to have no biological foundation. It is also claimed that a subspecies occurs in Australian waters, i.e. one with a smaller eye and fin development. Like the marlin, the sailfish is one of the fastest of all sea fishes, and speeds up to 60 knots (110 kph) have been quoted, although more conservative authors consider that 20–30 knots (37–55 kph) may be more representative.

Food consists of flying fish, needlefish, anchovies, squid, and octopus. Young sailfish feed exclusively on plankton and have a head which measures one third of the total length of the body. When only 2 in (5 cm) long, the characteristic dorsal fin develops into a sail, much like that of the adult fish.

The function of the sail-like dorsal fin is not clearly understood, but may serve in maneuvering. The sailfish is a renowned sport fish and is capable of spectacular aerial acrobatics.

However, it tires quickly and is generally considered only a light-tackle species. Some of the flesh reaches the commercial markets smoked. In one year over 2,500 were captured off the Florida coasts near Palm Beach.

Many sailfish in recent years have been tagged after capture and subsequently released so that their migration patterns may be studied. To encourage sailfish conserva-

tion, many U.S. fishing clubs have inaugurated a system of awarding points.

575 MEDITERRANEAN SPEARFISH S

Tetrapturus belone
Other common names: Spearfish, shortbill spearfish, Atlantic shortbill spearfish, shortnose spearfish.

Features: Superficially resembling a hybrid cross between a marlin and a sailfish and belonging to the family, *Istiophoridae*. Has an elongate body with fine lancet-like scales in the skin. The body structure is more slim than other billfish species. The dorsal is high and continuous with a small but distinctly separate hind portion. There are two anal fins, two keels on each side of the peduncle. The upper jaw is produced into a rounded but fairly short spear that is almost cylindrical, rough on the sides and below, and less than a hand-space long. The pectorals are fairly short and the ventral fins contain three rays and are moderately well developed. Grooves in the skin accommodate the first dorsal and anal. Lateral line distinct. Rasp-like teeth in jaws and long, sharp teeth on broad area on the roof of the mouth. Spear approximately six inches in length from front to thé eye. Dorsal, 35 to 40; second dorsal, 7; first anal, 11 to 12; second anal, 7 according to one authority. The fish is everywhere rare and elusive. Coloration: Greyish above and lighter below though some fish are reported as dark blue to black or even green above fading through a grey to silvery white on the underside. The fins are dark. The tail is lunar shaped, deeply forked.
Size: Reported at 120 in (300 cm); 110 lb (50 kg) but more commonly less than half these dimensions.
Distribution: Variously reported from the Japan Current area off Formosa, the Mediterranean and the western Atlantic off Florida and Puerto Rico, though there is likely a confusion of species.
General: A commercial fishery of some importance is reported off Sicily in the Mediterranean. All spearfish will take an offshore anglers' trolled baits on occasion; while rare, they are eagerly sought by some ocean anglers.

576 SHORTBILL SPEARFISH S

Tetrapturus augustirostris
Other common names: Spearfish, Pacific shortbill spearfish, shortnose spearfish.

Features: The dorsal fin is very close to being an equal height through its entire length. The body shape is long and slender; more similar to a sailfish than the stockier marlin. Scales and pelvic fins are present; the spear is not much longer than the lower jaw. The lateral line is clearly apparent; the jaws possess rasp-like teeth and a broad area of long, sharp teeth is present on the roof of the mouth. Upper jaw is slender and short. The first dorsal, according to descriptions from Formosa, is well developed with a low anterior lobe, the central portion higher, the three most anterior rays are spines, the following eight or nine are clearly soft-rayed with branched tips, and the remaining posterior ones are again spines. The

125

pectoral fins are comparatively short; ventrals fins have three rays and are moderately well developed. Developed grooves in the skin where the first dorsal and anal may be folded. Coloration: A bright bluish green on the back and the upper sides with bluish green stripes from the back toward the belly; remainder of the body silvery. Dorsal fin in brilliant dark blue to black with dark spots; pelvic fins black; other fins a dark greenish hue. The eye is a grey-blue with a dark pupil rimmed with a yellowish tinge. The caudal forked; dorsal fin lobe rounded rather than sickle-shaped or pointed.

Size: Believed to reach in excess of 72 in (180 cm) and 44–110 lb (20–50 kg).
Distribution: Rare, but widespread in many areas of the tropical and sub-tropical Atlantic and Pacific oceans as well as in some numbers off Formosa in the Japan Current. Reported off Puerto Rico and the Florida coast of the United States, and in the Mediterranean.
General: Little to nothing is known of the life history of this billfish though flesh is certainly edible and has attained some importance in the Mediterranean area.

577 LONGBILL SPEARFISH S
Tetrapturus pfluegeri

Features: Head, body, and fins very similar to those of *T. belone.* It is best distinguished from this species by the higher numbers of fin rays, first part of dorsal fin 45–53 against 40–46, first anal fin 12–16 against 11–12; further by the longer pectoral fins and by the anus being placed more anteriorly. The tail fin is broadly forked; two longitudinal keels on each side of the tail stalk. The second dorsal and anal fins are short. Coloration: back and upper sides dark greyish, lower sides and belly silvery; no darker spots, but the young may have some darker bands.
Size: Maximum 6 1/2 ft (2 m), 65 lb (30 kg); generally only up to 5 ft (150 cm) 22–45 lb (10–20 kg).
Distribution: A pelagic, migratory fish from the open seas of the Northwest Atlantic between New Jersey and Venezuela, also in the Mexican Gulf.
General: The species is nowhere abundant. It is hardly of importance to the commercial fisheries, but is highly esteemed as a game fish.

578 SWORDFISH S
Xiphius gladius
Other common names: Broadbill swordfish, broadbill.

Features: Deep, stout body, very moderately compressed. Forehead slightly concave; large mouth; upper jaw is greatly prolonged into a flat sword that is wider than it is deep; lower jaw is slightly elongate. Two dorsal fins III,15 to 30–4 set wide apart, first is rigid and fleshy and not retractable with a profile higher than it is long; large keels either side of tail stalk; tail fin very broad and crescentic; two anals 9 to 11–3 to 5; pectoral fin scythe-shaped; no pelvic fins. Coloration: dorsally dark metallic-purple or bronze; flanks dusky, paling to dull white on belly; fins dark with a silvery sheen. The sword is black above

and paler on the underside. Rudimentary scales in young fish. *Note:* Very young fish have only single dorsal and anal fins.
Size: Up to 20 ft (6 m) and over 1,500 lb (780 kg); but average 6–10 ft (2–3 m), 100–300 lb (45–135 kg).
Distribution: Worldwide, with preference for temperate seas.
General: Usually a solitary fish, but occasionally seen in pairs and more rarely in groups. Its speed through the water is comparable to that of other billfishes, and in a similar fashion to other billfishes the sword is used both as a defensive and hunting weapon. Primarily a deep-feeder preferring bottom-dwelling food.

Spawning occurs in the open sea, and the eggs hatch in 2 1/2 days; young begin by feeding on fish larvae. The physiology of swordfish and other billfishes is different from that of other fishes. The gills have comparatively large surfaces in order to absorb oxygen at a high rate; this in turn maintains a very vigorous blood circulation, which appears to be a necessary factor in the very active sea life that a billfish leads.

Among many sport fishermen the swordfish is a coveted trophy, difficult to find, difficult to hook, with tremendous fighting ability. The swordfish is also an important commercial species. Its flesh is light-coloured with a unique rich flavour. The majority of commercial fish are taken by harpooning or by longline.

579 BUTTERFISH S
Peprilus triacanthus
Other common names: Dollarfish, skipjack.

Features: The small, deep body is strongly compressed sidewise and has a single long dorsal with soft rays except for a few substantial spines at the forward end. The anal fin is of equal shape and size, no pelvic fins. The tail is deeply forked. The nose is blunt and the mouth small. An extremity of the pelvic bone protrudes through the body skin, looking like a small thorn, but is difficult to see and sometimes can be found only by feel. Body depth is about one-half of body length. Dorsal fin, II–III, and about 45. It starts close behind the pectoral fin axils and tapers first sharply, then at a more gradual angle toward the tail. Anal fin, III, very short spines at front, nearly embedded in skin with first spine pointing forward. Dorsal and anal fins terminate almost at the tail. Pectoral fins are long and pointed. The slender caudal peduncle has no lateral keels. Body scales are small, semitransparent, and easily rubbed off. A row of distinct mucous pores under the forward portion of the dorsal fin. Coloration: Pewter or dull silver-blue above, pale silver on the sides, many irregular dark spots on body that fade on death.
Size: Up to 12 in (30 cm), 1.1 lb (1/2 kg), but most fish are smaller.
Distribution: Western Atlantic from Cape Hatteras to Nova Scotia and Newfoundland; southward at times to northern Florida in deep water.
General: A schooling fish with high commercial value and considered a delicacy on the table. When inshore, prefers sandy and rocky bottom to mud. Not actively sought by anglers, but may take a very small bait.

29 PLAICE, FLOUNDERS, SOLES, TURBOTS

580 WINTER FLOUNDER S, B
Pseudopleuronectes americanus
Other common names: Blackback, sole, flounder, Georges Bank flounder, carrelet.

Features: Oblong body, laterally compressed. Eyes on right side, but reversals not uncommon; small mouth. Dorsal fin 60 to 76 (beginning very far forward opposite eye); tail fin large and rounded; anal fin 44 to 58. Coloration: variable and very dependent on bottom habitat, frequently muddy, red brown to almost black, occasionally spotted or mottled; blind side white, but bluish near edges, very rarely blind side is dark coloured or bears dark spots.
Size: Average up to 18 in (45 cm), maximum 25 in (65 cm), 8 lb (3 1/2 kg).
Distribution: Western Atlantic, from Labrador south to Cape Hatteras.
General: Found among bottoms ranging from soft mud to hard sand 6–120 ft (2–36 m), occasionally down to 300 ft (90 m). Tolerant to a wide range of temperatures, but is most abundant in waters ranging 53–60°F (12–16°C). Excellent food fish.

581 SUMMER FLOUNDER S
Paralichthys dentatus
Other common names: Flounder, fluke.

Features: Oblong body, laterally compressed. Eye on left side; lower jaw projects beyond upper; large mouth. Dorsal fin 85 to 94 (beginning in front of right eye and extending to tail stalk); tail fin rounded; anal fin 60 to 73. Coloration: eye-side, variable, shades of brown or grey, but may range through blue, green, or black, usually with a scattering of 10 to 14 eye-like spots; blind side whitish. Lateral line arches over pectoral fin. Small scales that extend over head.
Size: Up to 37 in (95 cm), 26 lb (11 3/4 kg).
Distribution: Western Atlantic, from Maine to South Carolina.
General: Inhabits moderate depths, 60–480 ft (18–145 m) over sandy or muddy bottoms. Spawning occurs in spring. During the summer many enter inshore shallow waters. At this time it is found in estuaries, canals, creeks, near piers and bridges, and becomes a popular light-tackle sport fish. Food is mainly crustaceans, worms, squid, and small fish. Locally it forms an important commercial species and is an excellent table fish.

A related but smaller species, the southern flounder (*P. lethostigmus*), overlaps the range of the summer flounder in South Carolina and extends its distribution southward to the Gulf of Mexico. Another related species, the Gulf flounder (*P. albiguttus*), is a small abundant fish which is more plentiful in the Gulf of Mexico than along the Atlantic coasts (see also Index).

582 YELLOWTAIL FLOUNDER S
Limanda ferruginea
Other common names: Flatfish, dab, mud dab, rusty dab, yellowtail, rusty flounder, snowshoe flounder.

Features: Flatfish that lies on its right side, with a long single fin on each edge of the body, thus one dorsal and one anal. Well-developed ventral fins, also pectorals, with the lateral line arched behind the gill opening. Small-mouthed with a fairly pointed snout, concave dorsal outline. It is a comparatively wide fish, about one half as broad as it is long, with a fairly narrow head. The eyes are set so close together that their rounded orbits almost touch each other. Scales are rough on the eyed side, smooth on the blind side. Dorsal fin, 76 to 85; anal, 56 to 63. Coloration: brownish to a olive with a red hue, and large, irregular, red or rusty spots on the eyed side; whitish on the blind side. Caudal and dorsal/anal margins are yellowish. The yellow tail is a field characteristic. Caudal peduncle is also yellowish.
Size: Maximum of 36 in (90 cm), 6.6 lb (3 kg), but most are smaller.
Distribution: Atlantic coast of North America from about Labrador to New York and Virginia, most common in the northern sector.
General: Important commercially, edible, moves around considerably during migratory runs. Trawled on sand or mixtures of sand and a mud bottom. Locally favoured by sport fishermen.

583 DAB S
Limanda limanda

Features: Oval body, very compressed. Dorsal fin 65 to 81; tail fin moderately rounded; anal fin 50 to 64. Coloration: eye-side, yellowish brown, often with reddish-yellow blotches and spots; blind side white. Lateral line strongly arched over orange-tinted pectoral fin, then follows median line. Eye-side is very rough at touch.
Size: Average up to 8 in (20 cm), maximum 16 in (40 cm), 4 1/2 lb (2 kg).
Distribution: Northeast Atlantic, from White Sea and Iceland south to Spain, including English Channel, North Sea, and Baltic.
General: The smallest and one of the most common of the European inshore flatfishes which inhabits a sand or sandy-muddy bottom. It feeds mainly on crustaceans but also on mollusks and small fish. Immature fish may be found in depths often less than 3 ft (1 m). A typical lightweight sport fish frequently taken off beaches, in harbours, near jetties, and over shallow inshore grounds. An excellent table fish, if eaten very fresh, and of some local commercial importance.

584 PLAICE S
Pleuronectes platessa

Features: Elongate-oblong body and much compressed. Both eyes on right side. Dorsal fin 65 to 79, tail fin rounded; anal fin 48 to 59. Coloration: eye-side, brown or greyish brown with characteristic red brown or orange spots also extending over fins; left (blind side) white, occasionally with dark blotches. Lateral line begins between eyes and then arches over the pectoral fin back to the body median line. Small, smooth scales.

Size: Average up to 24 in (60 cm), maximum sometimes up to 36 in (90 cm), 13 1/4 lb (6 kg).

Distribution: North Atlantic, from White Sea and Iceland south to Spain and bordering seas; Mediterranean.

General: An abundant bottom flatfish found in relatively deep water over sand, gravel, or mud. After spawning, when the larvae are hatched, they take on the appearance of a normal fish, but gradually the left eye moves round to join the one on the right side, and the blind side then faces the sea bottom. Food consists of shellfish, worms, and squid. The highly adapted throat teeth act as blunt crushers to break up the large molluscs before they are swallowed. Plaice is an important commercial species and a highly prized sport fish, and is particularly sought after as a best quality table fish.

585 LEMON SOLE S
Microstomus kitt
Other common names: Smear dab, lemon dab.

Features: This rather elongate flatfish has an almost oval body with upper and lower contours evenly rounded. Small head, small mouth, and short caudal stalk. The long dorsal fin starts over the eye, and is highest posteriorly. The hind margin of the tail fin is only little convex. The fish is characterized by the lacking of the strong, short spine in front of the anal fin. The lateral line is only weakly elevated over the pectoral fin. The scales are small, and the skin appears as smooth. Coloration: Upper surface red brown to reddish, slightly marbled with dark or green. Lower surface white.

Size: Normally 10–11 in (25–30 cm), but can reach 1 1/2 ft (45 cm).

Distribution: East Atlantic from Iceland and the White Sea to Bay of Biscay; North Sea, Irish Sea, Skagerak and eastern Kattegat.

General: Lives in moderately deep water 15–80 fathoms (30–150 m). An excellent food fish.

586 WITCH S
Glyptocephalus cynoglossus
Other common name: Pole dab.

Features: This flatfish is comparatively elongated with a very thin body. Small head but large mouth. Large eyes. The lateral line is almost straight. No spine before the anal fin. The rather large scales are thin, weak, and loose-fitting. Tail fin strongly convex, almost pointed at its middle. Coloration: upper (right) surface greyish to reddish or brownish, the lower white to light grey.

Size: The common length is 10–12 in (25–30 cm), but older individuals may reach 1 1/2 ft (45 cm).

Distribution: Both sides of the North Atlantic, in west from Greenland to off New York, in east from northern Norway to Spain.

General: The witch belongs to the deeper water 60–350 fathoms (100–600 m) and the soft bottom, where it feeds mainly on worms and mussels. It is of only little importance to the commercial fisheries.

587 LONG ROUGH DAB S
Hippoglossoides platessoides

Features: Thin and elongate body; large head with large mouth and eyes. The anterior part of the lateral line is only little upwards curved. Convex tail fin almost pointed at the middle. The scales are large and rough, both on the upper and lower surfaces. Coloration: The upper (right) surface is brownish with a lilac sheen and a few indistinct, darker patches, the lower surface is whitish.

Size: Mostly 10–12 in (25–30 cm), but can attain 1 1/4–1 3/4 ft (40–55 cm) with a weight of 1 1/2 pound (700 g).

Distribution: Both sides of the North Atlantic, from southern Greenland to Nova Scotia and from Iceland and Novaya Zemlya to the English Channel; North Sea, Skagerak, Kattegat, Belts and western Baltic.

General: Lives in moderately deep water 6–200 fathoms (15–400 m) on the soft bottom. It is often caught in trawls, but has hardly any market value.

588 COMMON SOLE S
Solea solea
Other common name: Dover sole.

Features: Oval, elongate, and compressed body. Eyes on right side of head; snout rounded; mouth small. Long dorsal fin 75 to 93 (beginning above snout); tail fin small and rounded; long anal fin 59 to 79. Coloration: variable and depends on the sea-bottom pattern, but generally brownish or greyish brown on eye-side with large, dark irregular blotches; blind side whitish; pectoral fin on eye-side has a black spot at the tip; dorsal and anal fins have white edges. Lateral line scale count 140 to 165.

Size: Up to 2 ft 2 in (65 cm), but smaller maximum in its Mediterranean distribution.

Distribution: Eastern North Atlantic, including the western Baltic, southern North Sea, English Channel; Mediterranean.

General: A shallow-water flatfish found to depths c. 600 ft (180 m) either over or partly buried in sand or mud. During the winter months it migrates to deeper offshore waters. Feeding takes place at night, and food consists of other small bottom-living species such as molluscs, starfish, and small fish. After hatching, the young fish live in midwater regions, swimming in the vertical or "normal" fish position until they reach a length of c. 1/2 in (15 mm), then they descend to the bottom region and swim in the horizontal or typical flatfish mode for the rest of their lives. Common sole is an extremely valuable commercial species and a table fish of the very highest quality. It is frequently caught by coastal anglers.

589 BUTTER SOLE S
Isopsetta isolepis

Features: Elliptical body, much compressed, moderately deep. Head strongly compressed; profile above the eye a little depressed; eye rather large; comparatively large mouth. Dorsal fin 88; anal fin 65. Coloration: brownish, mottled and blotched with darker markings. Lateral line scale count 88. Lateral line has a slight arch in front.

Size: Average up to c. 15 in (38 cm), 4 1/2 lb (2 kg).

Distribution: Eastern Pacific, range Puget Sound to Point Conception.

General: A small flounder common off the coast of California; found in rather deep water.

590 DOVER SOLE S
Microstomus pacificus
Other common names: Sole, right-eye flounder, deep water sole.

Features: Small mouth and large eyes, which are on the righthand side of the body. Lateral line is straight, unbranched. Gill opening is small. Body is slender and covered with tiny scales and heavy slime. Mouth contains teeth only on the blind side. Tail border straight or slightly wavy. The dorsal and anal fins run completely around the body edge with a small break ahead of the tail and just behind the head, where the dorsal extends forward further than the anal fin. Small pectoral fins. Coloration: Light to dark uniform brown on right (upper) side, occasionally with indistinct blotches. Darker fins and white underneath.

Size: Up to 30 in (75 cm) and 11 lb (5 kg).

Distribution: Eastern Pacific coast from southern California to Alaska.

General: Prefers deep water where it feeds on worms and other invertebrates. Firm, delicate flesh with delicious flavour makes it a valuable commercial catch, and one sought by many anglers.

591 FLOUNDER (EUROPEAN) S, B
Platichthys flesus

Features: Body elongate and very compressed. Dorsal fin 52 to 67; tail fin square-cut; anal fin 35 to 46. Coloration: eye side, greenish to brownish grey with mottled, often very indistinct, light yellowish or brownish spots; blind side white, occasionally with darker markings. Lateral line arches over pectoral fin and then follows median line. Small, smooth scales, and small, hard, bony warts along base of dorsal and anal fins and on either side of lateral line.

Size: Average 12–16 in (30–40 cm), maximum up to 20 in (50 cm), 5 1/2 lb (2 1/2 kg).

Distribution: Eastern Atlantic, from White Sea to Spain, North Sea, most of Baltic; Mediterranean.

General: The flounder is a flatfish which often swims at various levels above the bottom and is highly tolerant and adaptable to differences in salinity, so that it may even be encountered in the freshwater reaches of estuaries. For this reason it thrives particularly well in the Baltic regions and around river mouths throughout its distribution where it is often found in depths less than 3 ft (1 m) over sandy or muddy bottoms.

Flounder spawn in offshore waters 100–180 ft (30–55 m), and all river fish will migrate to the sea in February–May. Like other flatfish, such as the plaice (which see) the eye in the immature fish slowly moves round to the right. However, reverse flounders, with eyes on the left side (opposite side) are frequent.

The flounder is an excellent sport and table fish and valuable commercially.

592 STARRY FLOUNDER S (B)
Platichthys stellatus
Other common names: English sole, rough jacket.

Features: Both eyes on the same side of the head (left or right). The body is more or less covered by rough, platelike and bony scales. Eyes and mouth rather small. The long dorsal and anal fins are highest a little behind the middle of the body; the tail fin is slightly convex. Coloration: The eye-side is dark-brown to black with still darker patches and many minute dark spots; the blind side is whitish; the dorsal, anal and caudal fins are orange with large black patches.

Size: Usual length c. 20–30 in (50–75 cm); it can reach a weight of 20 lb (9 kg), but most individuals caught are much smaller.

Distribution: Northern and even arctic regions of both sides of the Pacific, south to southern California and to the Amur River.

General: The starry flounder lives in coastal waters, from where it may enter the estuaries of larger rivers. Some commercial importance. Sport fishermen catch it often with hook and line.

593 HOGCHOKER S, B, F
Trinectes maculatus
Other common names: American sole, little sole, sole, rough-scaled flounder.

Features: Right-handed and small-mouthed; no pectoral fin on either side which is the most distinctive field characteristic. Right-hand ventral fin is continuous with the anal fin; long fins are highest toward their rear ends; left-hand dorsal fin originates at the very tip of the nose; small eyes set flat instead of in prominent orbits. Gape of the mouth is shorter and much more crooked on the blind side than on the eyed with the upper jaw projecting beyond the lower. Evenly oval in outline without a definite caudal peduncle. Caudal fin is definitely rounded rather than forked. Scales are very rough on both sides. Skin is slimy with mucus. Dorsal fin, 50 to 56; anal, 36 to 42. Coloration: Dusky or a slaty olive ranging to a dark brown on the eyed side; blind side is dirty white and usually marked with dark round spots. Eyed side is barred transversely with seven or eight indistinct darker stripes, a dark longitudinal stripe along the lateral line and sometimes with a pale mottling. All the fins are over the general body tint variously dark clouded.

Size: About 8 in (20 cm) at maximum.
Distribution: Atlantic and Gulf coast, North America from Massachusetts Bay to the Atlantic coast of Panama in Central America. Abundant in Chesapeake Bay and southward.
General: Delicious eating, but generally not fished because of small size.

594 BRILL S, B
Scophthalmus rhombus

Features: Oval body, very compressed, and much like the turbot. Eyes on left side of body; large mouth. Dorsal fin 73 to 83 (the first rays are free of membrane and branched); tail fin rounded; anal fin 56 to 62. Coloration: eye-side, variable, ranging from sandy to grey brown and dark brown, with small irregular spots which extend over tail fin; blind side white with occasional dark blotches. Lateral line arches over pectoral fin and then follows median line. Smooth scales and no skin tubercles.
Size: Maximum up to 28 in (70 cm).
Distribution: Eastern Atlantic, from Norway south to Spain and into Mediterranean, including North Sea, English Channel, western Baltic.
General: Found in salt water to 200 ft (60 m) over sandy, gravel, or muddy bottoms. The older fish favour deeper water. Often found frequenting deep estuaries, and they occasionally enter brackish waters. A voracious feeder, mainly on other young fish. Spawning occurs March–August. Not of importance as a commercial species, but an excellent table fish.

595 DIAMOND TURBOT S
Hypsopsetta guttulata
Other common name: Diamond flounder.

Features: Body very deep, rather angulate near middle of dorsal area and belly; tail stalk deeper than long; tail as long as head. Eyes separated by a flattish raised area; head without spines or tubercles; no teeth on right side of either jaw. Dorsal fin 68; anal fin 50. Coloration: brown with numerous pale bluish blotches in life which disappear after death; blind side white with a strong tinge of yellow along head profile; fins plain but occasionally with black specks. Lateral line scale count 95.
Size: Up to 18 in (45 cm).
Distribution: Eastern Pacific, ranging coast of California southward, Cape Mendocino to Magdalena Bay.
General: One of the most abundant flatfishes in the shore waters of California. A food fish of fair-to-moderate quality.

596 TURBOT S
Scophthalmus maximus

Features: Body between ovalate and diamond-shaped; very compressed. Eyes positioned on left side of head; large, curved mouth. The dorsal fin is long and extends from the eye to the tail stalk 57 to 71; tail fin rounded; anal fin 43 to 56. Coloration: variable and dependent on colour and pattern of sea bed habitats; varies from grey brown to chocolate brown, with reddish, yellowish, or greenish spots; dark

mottling or speckling on dorsal, anal, and tail fins; right side (bottom or blind side) usually white with occasional dark blotches. The lateral line is arched above pectoral fin, and then follows the median line. No scales. Scattered over the body are a number of blunt, bony tubercles which occur more frequently on eyed side.
Size: Average 16–24 in (40–60 cm), maximum up to *c.* 40 in (100 cm).
Distribution: Mediterranean; Atlantic; English Channel; North Sea; Irish Sea, and Baltic.
General: One of the largest of the European flatfishes, the turbot is a first class bottom marine sport fish which is found over sand and muddy ground in shallow water. It offers strong resistance when hooked, and is an excellent table fish.

597 PACIFIC HALIBUT S
Hippoglossus stenolepis
Other common names: Butt, northern halibut.

Features: The shape of body and fins is as in the Atlantic halibut. Large mouth, both eyes on the right side. The lateral line has a distinct arch over the pectoral fin. The dorsal fin begins just over the eye and continues almost to the tail fin; the tail fin is slightly concave. Coloration: The upper side (the eye-side) is almost uniformly dark brown with a few small, lighter spots; the lower side is white.
Size: Maximum *c.* 9 ft (3 m) with a weight of 400–500 lb (180–225 kg).
Distribution: Northeastern Pacific from San Francisco and northwards into the Bering Sea.
General: This halibut lives in depths right from 20–1600 fathoms (50–4000 m), feeding mainly on fish (cod, herring), squids, and crabs. It is of great importance to the fisheries from northern California to Alaska. It has been badly overfished, and heavy international regulations have been introduced to protect the stocks. Many scientists consider the Pacific and Atlantic halibuts to be one and the same species.

598 ATLANTIC HALIBUT S
Hippoglossus hippoglossus

Features: Moderately elongate, thick body. Normally the eyes are positioned on right side of head, but reverse (left side) fish are not uncommon. Dorsal fin 92 to 107, beginning above eye and extending to tail stalk; tail fin concave or square-cut; anal fin 69 to 84 preceded by a spinelike bone (covered by skin in older fish). Coloration: variable, upper surface green or olive brown to very dark brown; blind side white, but some fish suffused with reddish tint ("cherrybellies"). Lateral line is arched over pectoral fin and then follows median line.
Size: Average up to 100 in (250 cm), maximum occasionally 145 in (370 cm); 120 in (300 cm) fish may weigh 650 lb (290 kg). Rod-caught sport fish range 10–50 lb (4 1/2–22 1/2 kg).
Distribution: North Atlantic; in west, from west coast of Greenland (Disko Bay) south to Virginia; in east, from Spitsbergen, Iceland, and White Sea south to northern Spain, including English Channel and North Sea. Confined to waters with tem-

peratures above 35°F (2°C).
General: The largest north Atlantic flatfish. The Atlantic halibut is usually found in deep water 250–5,000 ft (75–1,500 m), occasionally in shallower water, particularly in its North Sea range. It is a highly predatory fish, which often moves into midwater to feed. Adult fish feed almost exclusively on other fish. It is very important commercially, taken by trawling and longline methods, and among flatfishes halibut have the highest landed commercial value. As a sport fish taken by boat-fishing in deep water, it has attracted increasing attention in recent years and puts up an outstandingly powerful fight when hooked. A table fish of the very highest quality.

599 CALIFORNIA HALIBUT S
Paralichthys californicus
Other common names: Monterey, bastard halibut.

Features: Oblong body. Large mouth, each jaw with a single row of slender teeth; eyes may be on either side of the head. Dorsal fin very long and begins in front of eye; tail fin characteristically double; anal fin very long. Coloration: dorsally usually brown; belly whitish; occasionally fish may be brown on both upper and lower surfaces (ambicoloured) or more rarely white on both upper and lower surfaces (albinistic). Lateral line is strongly arched above the pectoral fin. Scales are very small.
Size: Average up to 36 in (90 cm), 50 lb (22 1/2 kg); large fish (all females) up to *c.* 65 in (165 cm), 72 lb (33 kg).
Distribution: Eastern Pacific coasts, ranging Baja California to Oregon.
General: The largest, commonest, and most abundant of the flatfishes within its range along the west Pacific coast. It is found on sandy bottoms in water usually shallower than *c.* 120 ft (35 m), but may be found deeper than 300 ft (90 m).

Food consists of anchovy, queenfish, and other small fishes. When the anchovy are present in large schools, the California halibut is often seen to leap clear of the water when pursuing them. In turn the halibut is preyed upon by sharks, rays, bottlenose dolphins, and in particular by sea lions which play havoc with trammel nets when poaching halibut from them.

As a sport fish they are usually taken by drifting or trolling. Popular as a table fish.

600 GREENLAND HALIBUT S
Reinhardtius hippoglossoides
Other common names: Kalleraglik.

Features: Body and fins as in the common halibut, but the left eye is on the mid-line of the head. Coloration: The eye-side and also the blind side is – what is characteristic for the species – dark greyish or a little brown.
Size: Length up to 3 1/4 ft (1 m), weight 8–14 pounds (4–6 kg).
Distribution: The northernmost North Atlantic Davis Strait and Baffin Bay.
General: Lives mostly in depths of 300–800 fathoms (500–1500 m). The species is important to the local fisheries.

601 NORTHERN PUFFER S, sometimes B
Sphaeroides maculatus
Other common names: Puffer, swelltoad, blower, swellbelly, swellfish, toadfish, bellowsfish, balloonfish, globefish.

Features: One dorsal fin, soft-rayed, the spiny dorsal being obsolete. No ventral fins. Gill openings reduced to short slits; teeth fused into cutting plates; no scales. Able to inflate its body by ballooning the belly with air or water, deflating at will. Eyes set very high and horizontally oval in outline. No scales but skin is rough because of close-set prickles. No spiny dorsal fin. Soft dorsal fin, 8, rhomboid in outline, set far back close to the caudal peduncle, about twice as high as long. Anal fin 7, similar in size and shape to dorsal and originates on a line close behind it. Caudal fin weakly rounded, moderate size, with angular corners. Pectorals are fan-shaped, situated close behind gill openings. Coloration: Ashy, dusky, or dark green to olive-green above, the sides orange or greenish yellow, crossbarred with six to eight rather indefinite blotches or dark bands, belly dirty white.
Size: Reported at 14 in (35 cm) maximum. Average fish about half that length. Under 1.1 lb (0.5 kg) at maximum size.
Distribution: Atlantic coast of the United States from Cape Ann to St. Johns River and Biscayne Bay, Florida.
General: Edible and becoming commercially valuable in local areas as demand for the meat spreads. Will bite on an angler's baits, popular locally as panfish.

602 TRUNKFISH S
Lactophrys tricornis

Features: As in the other trunkfish species, the body, when transversely viewed, seems to be encased in a triangular boxy carapace, formed by large, bony plates firmly jointed together. The edges of this carapace are rather sharp, one edge runs dorsally, the two others latero-ventrally; a broad, low ridge is present on each side of the dorsal edge. The belly is almost flat. Above each eye is a stout spine; the mouth is small, but with very strong teeth. All fins are small, the ventrals are missing. Coloration: upper sides brown to yellow or greenish with irregular blue patches; white belly; the head has several smaller blue spots.

Size: About 18 in (45 cm).

Distribution: Tropical part of western Atlantic from the Carolinas to Brazil; only rare north of Chesapeake Bay.

General: Its home is the stony and rocky bottom, especially the coral reefs. The fish is poisonous.

603 QUEEN TRIGGERFISH S
Balistes vetula

Other common names: Bastard turbot, queen turbot, old-wife.

Features: Medium-sized, diamond-shaped body, laterally compressed. Eye set well back in head; snout angular; small mouth with large, pointed teeth; large fleshy lips. Dorsal fins III–29 to 31 (first soft rays characteristically long and filamentous); tail fin large with outermost rays extended and filamentous; anal fin 26 to 28. Coloration: striking and very variable, dorsally greenish or bluish grey; lower head and abdomen orange yellow; characteristically cheeks have two broad curved bands of blue followed by narrower bands above; a broad blue bar across tail stalk and blue submarginal bands on middle fins. Leathery skin and prominent scales.

Size: Average up to 15 in (38 cm).

Distribution: Western Atlantic, Massachusetts south to West Indies and Brazil; eastern Atlantic, from Azores to Ascension Island. Many related worldwide forms (see Index).

General: A schooling fish usually found around reefs and seaweed-covered grounds. The name triggerfish stems from the unusual mechanism controlling the dorsal spine movements: the first dorsal spine can be released only by manipulating the second spine and cannot be depressed by external force. The erect spine is used as a device to wedge the fish firmly in rocky crevices away from the attention of predators.

604 OCEAN SUNFISH S
Mola mola

Other common name: Headfish.

Features: Rectangular and oval body, laterally compressed with the general appearance suggestive of the head of a fish cut off behind the dorsal fin. Blunt snout; small mouth; a single fused beaklike tooth in each jaw. Tall dorsal fin 16 to 20, tail fin extremely narrow, much like a fold of skin and scalloped into a number of rounded lobes; anal fin 14 to 18. Coloration: highly variable, but dorsally often dark grey; flanks greyish brown with silvery reflections; belly dusky to dirty white. Juveniles show dark spots on hind parts. Lateral line absent. No scales. The skin is thick and leathery and it may be smooth or rough.

Size: Up to 11 ft (340 cm), 1,000 lb (450 kg).

Distribution: Worldwide in tropical and temperate seas.

General: An unusual species of fish belonging to the family Molidae, which resides in midwater and bottom regions, although specimens are sometimes seen floating on the surface. In some areas they are fre-

quently seen close inshore. After hatching, the juveniles appear like normal fishes with a well-developed tail fin but with large spiny conical projections on the body. At a later stage these projections and the tail disappear. Food consists of jellyfish, crustaceans, mollusks, brittle stars, and squid. No sport or commercial value.

605 TRUNCATED SUNFISH S
Ranzania truncata

Other common name: Oblong sunfish.

Features: In many respects similar to the ocean sunfish, but the body is elongate (height only 1/4 to 1/3 of length), and the head, eyes, and pectoral fins are larger. Dorsal and anal fins are placed far back on the body, and the tail fin is a stout, straight ridge across the fish from the ends of the dorsal and anal fins. Coloration: back dark brown, sides and belly greyish; the sides have large, brown spots, on the gill cover are vertical light bands; fins brown or grey.

Size: 2–3 ft (60–90 cm).

Distribution: Tropical and warm-temperate seas; in the East Atlantic north to the British Isles, also in the Mediterranean.

General: A pelagic fish with pelagic eggs and larvae; the larvae have large spines on the body.

606 OCEAN SURGEONFISH S
Acanthurus bahianus

Features: High, almost oval body. Large head with small mouth. Like the other surgeonfishes it has on each side of the tail stalk a sharp "knife" which normally is withdrawn into a furrow, but can be raised and used as a defensive weapon. The dorsal fin is long, starting a little behind the eye and reaching right to the tail stalk; also the anal fin is long. The pectoral and ventral fins are large. The caudal fin is forked with pointed lobes. Coloration: violet to reddish almost all over; the front and throat bluish; also the hind margin of the tail fin and the margins of the ventral and anal fins are blue. The eye is red.

Size: About 1 1/2–1 3/4 ft (40–50 cm).

Distribution: Tropical part of the western Atlantic.

General: The habitat of the surgeonfish is coral reefs where it feeds mainly on plants.

607 OYSTER TOADFISH S
Opsanus tau

Features: This small fish has a very large head with small eyes and big mouth; above the eyes are a few small spines; small barbels on the lower jaw. Two dorsal fins, the first very small with only 2–3 short, poisonous spines, the second is very long; convex tail fin; long anal fin; broad pectoral fins, long pointed ventral fins placed much forward under the gill cover. Coloration: all over brown to yellow brown with darker patches.

Size: About 4–8 in (10–20 cm).

Distribution: West Atlantic, along the coasts of USA.

General: Lives in shallow water, mostly on a bottom with stones and vegetation.

608 RIVER CARPSUCKER F, sometimes B
Carpoides cyprinus

Other common names: Quillback carpsucker, broad mullet, white carp, silver carp, carp, American carp, carp sucker, quillback, mullet, bréme, white buffalo.

Features: Deep-bodied, laterally compressed, a highly arched back and a large head. Thick lips in a small and sucker-like mouth. Caudal peduncle is short, deep and laterally compressed; scales are large. High dorsal fin with a long base and in which the first few rays are very elongated, providing the fin with a pointed appearance. The remaining rays are short. Pointed dorsal fin and absence of barbels around the mouth distinguish the quillback from the carp. Coloration: green or an olive brown or light olive above, shading to silvery on the sides and a hite belly. Tail is deeply forked. No spines in the fins; mouth is toothless. Thirty three to forty one lateral line scales.

Size: May reach 24 in (60 cm), 4.4 lb (2 kg) at maximum.

Distribution: Missouri, Mississippi and Ohio River systems; streams around Chesapeake Bay; common in the Chesapeake and Potomac but rare in the Delaware–mostly in large rivers but also in the Great Lakes. Known in Canada in the St. Lawrence and Ottawa rivers, Lake Erie and Lake of the Woods.

General: Coarse fish of a small size with only slight commercial importance, sometimes found in the market as "carp". Taken occasionally but usually not deliberately by anglers. Edible, but often muddy in taste.

609 LUMPFISH S
Cyclopterus lumpus

Other common names: Cock and hen paddle, sea owl, paddle, licorne de mer, lumpsucker, lump, sea hen, hen-fish.

Features: Short, thick, high-arched body with a bony sucking disc on the chest with very much reduced ventral fins at its center; skin set with tubercles. Body about twice as long as it is deep, head short and rounded, mouth wide, lips thick, eyes relatively small. The head and body are covered with distinct and bony denticles, with four rows of much larger bony plates, one along the raised mid-line of the back, dividing into two just before the dorsal fin; one row from above the eye to the tail fin. One row running backwards from behind the pectoral fin; one marking the line of transition between the sides and the belly in the near ventral section. Each of these ridges is marked by a line of large pointed tubercles, and the entire skin between the ridges is thickly studded with small knobs. Teeth are small, gill openings moderate. First dorsal, only on small specimens, VI to VIII; second dorsal I, 9 to 11; anal I, 9 to 11. Caudal is broad based and slightly convex or square tipped, pectorals large and rounded so they almost meet on the throat. Ventrals altered into six pairs of fleshy knobs which form sucking disc just behind the throat. Coloration: variable, grey to slate grey, bluish grey, olive, brown, yellow green, chocolate, kelp brown or slaty blue on upper portions. Lighter beneath.

Size: Maximum 24 in (60 cm); 22 lb (10 kg)

but mostly half these measurements.

Distribution: Rocky shores of both coasts of the North Atlantic, south to Cape Cod and France. White Sea, northern Norway and Iceland to the Bay of Biscay and occasionally to Portugal; also in the Baltic.

General: Not commonly eaten though sometimes used for a food fish in Europe, mostly smoked. Flesh of the males most palatable, but no real commercial or sport fishing value.

610 COMMON OCTOPUS S
Octopus vulgaris

Features: The name octopus means eight feet, and the animal characteristically consists of eight arms (4 pairs) joined at their bases with the front pair shorter than the others. Each arm has 2 rows of suckers (each without a strengthening of horny rings seen in the suckers of squid). The body has no trace of an internal shell and is short and rounded instead of streamlined. The upper body surface sometimes has wartlike bumps. Coloration: greyish yellowish and brown with green spots, but capable of changing colour very rapidly.

Size: Including arms, up to 40 in (100 cm), but average usually 8 to 24 in (20 to 60 cm), 11 lb (5 kg).

Distribution: Mediterranean; Atlantic, but only seldom in the North Sea area. Several related forms with similar appearance occur in the same areas.

General: The common octopus is a bottom dweller found among rocks in shallow water where it constructs a hide or den. When swimming, it usually moves backward with the arms trailing and gains its propulsion by forcing water through a siphon-type organ. All octopuses are masters of colour change and camouflage. They can adapt very quickly to their backgrounds making them difficult to see. Changes also involve skin texture and posture; the arms may be tucked underneath or curled back over the body to serve as a protection. When attacked, it can discharge a cloud of ink to confuse its pursuer. Although, in the warmer seas, large octopuses may be dangerous to man, the smaller species are harmless, and any encounter by a swimmer with the grip of a tentacle will be accidental.

Food consists of fish and crustaceans which are trapped by the arms and then transferred to the grip of the parrotlike, horny beak. At the same time a poison is released which paralyses the prey. The common octopus is highly edible, and much esteemed in Latin and Southeast Asian countries. Octopus flesh also represents a first choice sport-fish bait in many areas.

129

INDEX TO COMMON NAMES

The numbers refer to illustrations and descriptions.

71 Common Sawfish *Pristis pectinatus*
199 Common Shiner *Notropis cornutus*
54 Common Skate *Raja batis*
588 Common Sole *Solea solea*
48 Common Sting Ray *Trygon pastinaca*
339 Coney *Epinephelus fulvus*
96 Conger Eel *Conger oceanicus*
497 Coral Fish *Abudefduf sordidus*
531 Corkwing *Crenilabrus melops*
469 Corvina *Cynoscion reticulatus*
370 Couch's Sea Bream *Pagrus pagrus*
47 Cownose Ray *Rhinoptera bonasus*
401 Crevalle Jack *Caranx hippos*
189 Crucian Carp *Carassius carassius*
440 Cubera Snapper *Lutjanus cyanopterus*
57 Cuckoo Ray *Raja naevus*
530 Cuckoo Wrasse *Labrus mixtus*
521 Cunner *Tautogolabrus adspersus*
126 Cutthroat Trout *Salmo clarki*

583 Dab *Limanda limanda*
177 Dace *Leuciscus leuciscus*
41 Darkie Charlie *Dalatias licha*
271 Deal-Fish *Trachypterus arcticus*
394 Dentex *Dentex dentex*
595 Diamond Turbot *Hypsopsetta guttulata*
442 Dog Snapper *Lutjanus jocu*
566 Dogtooth Tuna *Gymnosarda nuda*
132 Dolly Varden *Salvelinus malma spectabilis*
429 Dolphin *Coryphaena hippurus*
416 Dorade *Gnathanodon speciosus*
178 Dorado *Salminus maxillosus*
590 Dover Sole *Microstomus pacificus*
305 Dusky Flathead *Platycephalus fuscus*
314 Dusky Perch *Epinephelus guaza*
11 Dusky Shark *Carcharhinus obscurus*

46 Eagle Ray *Myliobatis aquila*
348 Eastern Pike-Perch *Stizostedion volgense*
98 Eel American *Anguilla rostrata*
98 Eel European *Anguilla anguilla*
212 Electric Eel *Electrophorus electricus*
51 Electric Ray *Torpedo nobiliana*
342 Estuary Perch *Percalates colonorum*
516 European Barracuda *Sphyraena sphyraena*
155 European Grayling *Thymallus thymallus*
158 European Pike; Northern Pike *Esox lucius*

207 Fathead Minnow *Pimephales promelas*
275 Fifteen-Spined Stickleback *Spinachia spinachia*
240 Five-Beard Rockling *Gaidropsaurus mustela*
166 Flathead Catfish *Pylodictus olivaris*
257 Flat Needlefish *Strongylura exilis*
82 Florida Gar *Lepisosteus platyrhynchus*
591 Flounder (European) *Platichthys flesus*
239 Four-Beard Rockling *Gaidropsaurus cimbrius*
281 Four-Horned Sculpin *Myoxocephalus quadricornis*
453 French Grunt *Haemulon flavolineatum*
473 Freshwater Drum *Aplodinotus grunniens*
550 Frigate Mackerel *Auxis thazard*
6 Frilled Shark *Chlamydoselachus anguineus*

168 Gaff-Topsail Catfish *Felichthys marinus*
324 Gag *Mycteroperca microlepis*
192 Galjoen *Dichistius capensis*
252 Garfish (Garpike) *Belone belone*
498 Garibaldi *Hypsypops rubicundus*
482 Geelbek *Atractoscion aequidens*
402 Giant Trevally *Caranx sexfasciatus*
392 Gilthead *Sparus auratus*
109 Gizzard Shad *Dorosoma cepedianum*
503 Golden Grey Mullet *Mugil auratus*
340 Golden Perch *Plectroplites ambiguus*
457 Golden Spotted Sweetlips *Plectorhynchus pictus*
123 Golden Trout *Salmo aguabonita*
88 Goldeye *Hiodon alosoides*
204 Goldfish *Carassius auratus*
532 Goldsinny *Ctenolabrus rupestris*
186 Goliath *Hydrocion goliath*
183 Grass Carp *Ctenopharyngodon idella*
160 Grass Pickerel *Esox americanus vermiculatus*
378 Grass Porgy *Calamus arctifrons*
512 Great Barracuda *Sphyraena barracuda*
237 Greater Forkbeard *Phycis blennioides*
528 Greater Sandeel *Hypteroplus lanceolatus*
130 Greater Silver Smelt *Argentina silus*
538 Greater Weever *Trachinus draco*
24 Great Hammerhead *Sphyrna mokarran*
220 Greenland Cod *Gadus ogac*
600 Greenland Halibut *Reinhardtius hippoglossoides*
42 Greenland Shark *Somniosus microcephalus*
97 Green Moray *Gymnothorax funebris*
78 Green Sturgeon *Acipenser acutirostris*
295 Grey Gurnard *Eutrigla gurnardus*
506 Grey Mullet *Mugil cephalus*
33 Grey Nurse Shark *Odontaspis taurus*
438 Grey Snapper *Lutjanus griseus*
13 Grey Whaler Shark *Carcharhinus menisorra*
514 Guaguanche *Sphyraena guachancho*
191 Gudgeon *Gobio gobio*

232 Haddock *Melanogrammus aeglefinus*
3 Hagfish *Myxine glutinosa*
229 Hake *Merluccius merluccius*
250 Halfbeak *Hyporamphus unifasciatus*
338 Hapuka *Polyprion oxygeneious*
341 Harlequin Bass *Serranus tigrinus*
116 Herring *Clupea harengus*
101 Hickory Shad *Alosa mediocris*
593 Hogchoker *Trinectes maculatus*
520 Hogfish *Lachnolaimus maximus*
299 Hook Sculpin *Artediellus uncinatus*
390 Hottentot *Pachymetopon blochi*
253 Houndfish *Tylosurus crocodilus*
146 Houting *Coregonus oxyrhynchus*
122 Huchen *Salmo hucho*
142 Humpback Salmon *Oncorhynchus gorbuscha*

195 Ide *Leuiscus idus*
156 Inconnu *Stenodus leucichthys*
131 Iwana *Salvelinus pluvius*

376 Japanese Bream *Acanthopagrus latus*
460 Javelin Fish *Pomadasys hasta*
329 Jewfish *Epinephelus itajara*
386 John Brown *Gymnocrotaphus curvidens*
268 John Dory *Zeus faber*
377 Jolthead Porgy *Calamus bajonado*

478 Kabeljou *Sciaena hololepidota*
450 Kahawai; Australian Salmon *Arripis trutta*
565 Kawakawa *Euthynnus affinis*
284 Kelp Greenling *Hexagrammos decagrammus*
484 Kelp Perch *Brachyistius frenatus*
291 Kelp Rockfish *Sebastes atrovirens*
407 King Amberjack *Seriola grandis*
541 Kingfish *Scomberomorus cavalla*
403 King Trevally *Caranx speciosus*

92 Ladyfish *Elops saurus*
202 Lake Chub *Couesius plumbeus*
75 Lake Sturgeon *Acipenser fulvescens*
128 Lake Trout *Salmo trutta lacustris*
148 Lake Whitefish *Coregonus clupeaformis*
1 Lampern *Lampetra fluviatilis*
127 Landlocked Salmon *Salmo salar sebago*
441 Lane Snapper *Lutjanus synagris*
144 Large Bottom Whitefish *Coregonus pidschian*
358 Largemouth Black Bass *Micropterus salmoides*
38 Large-Spotted Dogfish *Scyliorhinus stellaris*
89 Leach *Mormyrops deliciosus*
181 Leather Carp *Cyprinus carpio*
428 Leerfish *Hypacanthus amius*
17 Lemon Shark *Negaprion brevirostris*
585 Lemon Sole *Microstomus kitt*
19 Leopard Shark *Triakis semifasciata*
523 Lesser Catfish *Anarhichas minor*
287 Lesser Redfish *Sebastes viviparus*
125 Lesser Silver Smelt *Argentina sphyraena*
39 Lesser-Spotted Dogfish *Scyliorhinus caniculus*
537 Lesser Weever *Trachinus vipera*
242 Lingcod *Ophiodon elongatus*
234 Ling (European) *Molva molva*
139 Little Redfish *Oncorhynchus kennerlyi*
309 Little Snook *Centropomus parallelus*
563 Little Tunny *Euthynnus alletteratus*
577 Longbill Spearfish *Tetrapturus pfluegeri*
205 Longnose Dace *Rhinichthys cataractae*
52 Long-Nose Skate *Raja oxyrinchus*
587 Long Rough Dab *Hippoglossoides platessoides*
280 Longspined Bullhead *Taurulus bubalis*
437 Lookdown *Selene vomer*
491 Luderick *Girella tricuspidata*
609 Lumpfish *Cyclopterus lumpus*
344 Lunar-Tailed Rock Cod *Variola louti*

418 Ma-Aji *Trachurus japonicus*
93 Machete *Elops affinis*
542 Mackerel *Scomber scombrus*
319 Mahata *Epinephelus septemfasciatus*
444 Mahogany Snapper *Lutjanus mahogani*
196 Mahseer *Barbus tor*
27 Mako Shark *Isurus oxyrhynchus*
50 Marbled Electric Ray *Torpedo marmorata*
328 Marbled Grouper *Dermatolepis inermis*
458 Margate *Haemulon album*
476 Meagre *Argyrosomus regium*
233 Mediterranean Ling *Molva elongata*
575 Mediterranean Spearfish *Tetrapturus belone*
100 Menhaden, Atlantic *Brevoortia tyrannus*
225 Merluza *Merluccius gayi*

162 Milkfish *Chanos chanos*
194 Minnow *Phoxinus phoxinus*
182 Mirror Carp *Cyprinus carpio*
501 Moki *Latridopsis ciliaris*
72 Monkfish *Squatina squatina*
545 Monterey Spanish Mackerel *Scomberomorus concolor*
86 Mooneye *Hiodon tergisus*
432 Moonfish *Mene maculata*
95 Moray Eel *Muraena helena*
477 Mulloway *Sciaena antarctica*
263 Mummichog *Fundulus heteroclitus*
343 Murray Cod *Maccullochella peeli*
161 Muskellunge *Esox masquinongy*
445 Mutton Snapper *Lutjanus analis*

313 Nassau Grouper *Epinephelus striatus*
495 Natal Tilapia *Tilapia mossambica*
310 Nile Perch *Lates niloticus*
273 Nine-Spined Stickleback *Pungitius pungitius*
99 Northern Anchovy *Engraulis mordax*
480 Northern Kingfish *Menticirrhus saxatilis*
601 Northern Puffer *Sphaeroides maculatus*
293 Northern Searobin *Prionotus carolinus*
515 Northern Sennet *Sphyraena borealis*
193 Northern Squawfish *Ptychocheilus oregonensis*
286 Norway Haddock *Sebastes marinus*
219 Norway Pout *Boreogadus esmarkii*
32 Nurse Shark *Ginglymostoma cirratum*

272 Oarfish *Regalecus glesne*
241 Ocean Pout *Macrozoarces americanus*
604 Ocean Sunfish *Mola mola*
606 Ocean Surgeonfish *Acanthurus bahianus*
398 Ocean Whitefish *Caulolatilus princeps*
278 Oni Kajika *Ceratocottus diceraus*
270 Opah *Lampris guttatus*
487 Opaleye *Girella nigricans*
470 Orangemouth Corvina *Cynoscion xanthulus*
124 Ouananiche *Salmo salar ouananiche*
94 Ox-Eye Tarpon *Megalops cyprinoides*
607 Oyster Toadfish *Opsanus tau*

413 Pacific Amberjack *Seriola colburni*
511 Pacific Barracuda *Sphyraena argentea*
218 Pacific Cod *Gadus macrocephalus*
346 Pacific Flagtail *Kuhlia taeniura*
224 Pacific Hake *Merluccius productus*
597 Pacific Halibut *Hippoglossus stenolepis*
419 Pacific Jack Mackerel *Trachurus symmetricus*
424 Pacific Pomfret *Brama japonica*
373 Pacific Porgy *Calamus brachysomus*
110 Pacific Sardine *Sardinops sagax*
259 Pacific Saury *Cololabis saira*
79 Paddlefish *Polyodon spatula*
67 Painted Ray *Raja microcellata*
427 Palometa *Trachinotus goodei*
389 Pandora *Pagellus erythrinus*
176 Parahyba *Barachyplatystoma filamentosa*
496 Peacock Bass *Cichla ocellaris*
117 Pearlside *Maurolicus mulleri*
351 Perch (European) *Perca fluviatilis*
493 Pescada *Plagioscion squamosissimum*
510 Pick-Handle Barracuda *Sphyraena jello*
114 Pilchard Sardine *Sardina pilchardus*
422 Pilot Fish *Naucrates ductor*

481 Pinfish *Lagodon rhomboides*
298 Pingel's Scorpion *Triglops pingeli*
184 Piranha *Serrasalmus nattereri*
85 Pirarucu *Arapaima gigas*
584 Plaice *Pleuronectes platessa*
569 Plain Bonito *Orcynopsis unicolor*
282 Pogge *Agonus cataphractus*
221 Polar Cod *Boreogadus saida*
228 Pollack (European) *Pollachius pollachius*
430 Pompano Dolphin *Coryphaena equisetis*
153 Pond Smelt *Hypomesus olidus*
216 Poor Cod *Gadus minutus*
28 Porbeagle Shark *Lamna nasus*
459 Porkfish *Anisotremis virginicus*
245 Pouting *Gadus luscus*
145 Powan *Coregonus lavaretus*
363 Pumpkinseed *Lepomis gibbosus*
279 Pygmy Sculpin *Taurulus lilljeborgi*

486 Queen Angelfish *Holacanthus ciliaris*
411 Queenfish *Chorinemus lysan*
316 Queensland Grouper *Epinephelus lanceolatus*
603 Queen Triggerfish *Balistes vetula*

73 Rabbitfish *Chimaera monstrosa*
420 Rainbow Runner *Elagatis bipinnulatus*
118 Rainbow Trout *Salmo gairdneri*
535 Rainbow Wrasse *Coris julis*
73A Ratfish *Hydrolagus colliei*
366 Redbreast Sunfish *Lepomis auritus*
471 Red Drum *Sciaenops ocellatus*
447 Red Emperor *Lutjanus sebae*
360 Redeye Bass *Micropterus coosae*
258 Redfin Needlefish *Strongylura notata*
159 Redfin Pickerel *Esox americanus americanus*
315 Red Grouper *Epinephelus morio*
296 Red Gurnard *Aspitrigla cuculus*
231 Red Hake *Urophycis chuss*
323 Red Hind *Epinephelus guttatus*
371 Red Porgy *Pagrus sedecim*
384 Red Sea Bream *Pagellus bogaraveo*
443 Red Snapper *Lutjanus campechanus*
304 Red-Spotted Flathead *Platycephalus coeruleopunctatus*
393 Red Steenbras *Dentex rupestris*
436 Remora *Remora remora*
608 River Carpsucker *Carpoides cyprinus*
198 Roach *Rutilus rutilus*
367 Rock Bass *Ambloplites rupestris*
325 Rock Cod *Epinephelus tauvinus*
533 Rock Cook *Centrolabrus exoletus*
345 Rock Flagtail *Kuhlia rupestris*
326 Rock Hind *Epinephelus adscensionis*
518 Rock Wrasse *Halichoeres semicinctus*
431 Roosterfish *Nematistius pectoralis*
150 Round Whitefish *Prosopium cylindraceum*
203 Rudd *Scardinius erythrophthalmus*
355 Ruffe *Gymnocephalus cernua*

369 Sacramento Perch *Archoplites interruptus*
574 Sailfish *Istiophorus platypterus*
461 Sailor's Choice *Haemulon parra*
9 Sandbar Shark *Carcharhinus milberti*
527 Sandeel *Ammodytes marinus*
302 Sand Flathead *Platycephalus arenarius*
524 Sand Lance *Ammodytes tobianus*
65 Sandy Ray *Raja circularis*

66 Sandy Skate *Raja fyllae*
247 Sargassumfish *Histrio histrio*
353 Sauger *Stizostedion canadense*
260 Saury Pike *Scomberesox saurus*
417 Scad *Trachurus trachurus*
534 Scale-Rayed Wrasse *Acantholabrus palloni*
318 Scamp *Mycteroperca phenax*
446 Schoolmaster *Lutjanus apodus*
278 Sculpin *Cottus scorpius*
372 Scup *Stenotomus chrysops*
336 Sea Bass *Centropristis striatus*
169 Sea Catfish *Arius felis*
276 Seahorse *Hippocampus ramulosus*
2 Sea Lamprey *Petromyzon marinus*
121 Sea Trout *Salmo trutta trutta*
499 Sergeant Major *Abudefduf saxatilis*
5 Seven-Gilled Shark *Heptranchias perlo*
56 Shagreen Ray *Raja fullonica*
63 Sharpnose Skate *Raja lintea*
380 Sheepshead *Archosargus probatocephalus*
576 Shortbill Spearfish *Tetrapturus augustirostris*
70 Shovelnose Guitarfish *Rhinobatus productus*
546 Sierra Mackerel *Scomberomorus sierra*
10 Silky Shark *Carcharhinus falciformis*
200 Silver Bream *Blicca bjoerkna*
230 Silver Hake *Merluccius bilinearis*
474 Silver Sea Trout *Cynoscion nothus*
243 Silvery Pout *Gadiculus thori*
4 Six-Gilled Shark *Hexanchus griseus*
105 Skipjack Herring *Alosa chrysochloris*
558 Skipjack Tuna *Euthynnus pelamis*
564 Slender Tuna *Allothunnus fallai*
359 Smallmouth (Black) Bass *Micropterus dolomieui*
152 Smelt *Osmerus eperlanus*
16 Smooth Dogfish *Mustelus canis*
23 Smooth Hound *Mustelus mustelus*
526 Smooth Sandeel *Gymnammodytes semisquamatus*
553 Snake Mackerel *Gempylus serpens*
391 Snapper (Australian) *Chrysophrys auratus*
555 Snoek *Thyrsites atun*
306 Snook *Centropomus undecimalis*
141 Sockeye Salmon *Oncorhynchus nerka*
266 Soldierfish *Holocentrus spiniferus*
22 Soupfin Shark *Galeorhinus zyopterus*
375 Southern Bream *Acanthopagrus australis*
456 Spanish Grunt *Haemulon macrostomum*
547 Spanish Mackerel *Scomberomorus maculatus*
112 Spanish Sardine *Sardinella anchovia*
12 Spinner Shark *Carcharhinus maculipinnis*
36 Spiny Dogfish *Squalus acanthias*
475 Spot *Leiostomus xanthurus*
463 Spotfin Croaker *Roncador stearnsi*
356 Spotted Bass *Micropterus punctulatus*
45 Spotted Eagle Ray *Aetobatus narinari*
81 Spotted Gar *Lepisosteus oculatus*
549 Spotted Mackerel *Scomberomorus niphonius*
68 Spotted Ray *Raja montagui*
467 Spotted Weakfish *Cynoscion nebulosus*
397 Spotted Whiting *Sillaginodes punctatus*
115 Sprat *Sprattus sprattus*
592 Starry Flounder *Platichthys stellatus*
119 Steelhead Trout *Salmo gairdneri*
167 Stonecat *Noturus flavus*
509 Striped Barracuda *Sphyraena obtusata*
332 Striped Bass *Morone saxatilis*
567 Striped Bonito *Sarda orientalis*
262 Striped Killifish *Fundulus majalis*

571 Striped Marlin *Tetrapturus audax*
301 Striped Searobin *Prionotus evolans*
502 Striped Trumpeter *Latris lineata*
223 Suketodara *Theragra chalcogramma*
581 Summer Flounder *Paralichthys dentatus*
357 Suwannee Bass *Micropterus notius*
488 Sweep *Scorpis aequipinnis*
578 Swordfish *Xiphias gladius*

244 Tadpole-Fish *Raniceps raninus*
179 Tambaquy *Colossoma bidens*
548 Tanguigue *Scomberomorus commersoni*
500 Tarakihi *Nemadactylus macropterus*
91 Tarpon *Megalops atlanticus*
308 Tarpon Snook *Centropomus pectinatus*
382 Tarwhine *Rhabdosargus sarba*
519 Tautog *Tautoga onitis*
208 Tench *Tinca tinca*
507 Thick-Lipped Mullet *Mugil chelo*
505 Thin-Lipped Mullet *Liza ramada*
58 Thornback Ray *Raja clavata*
55 Thorny Skate *Raja radiata*
108 Threadfin Shad *Dorosoma petenense*
238 Three-Beard Rockling *Gaidropsaurus tricirratus*
300 Three-Horned Sculpin *Gymnacanthus tricuspis*
274 Three-Spined Stickleback *Gasterosteus aculeatus*
34 Thresher Shark *Alopias vulpinus*
174 Tigerfish *Hydrocyon lineatus*
303 Tiger Flathead *Neoplatycephalus macrodon*
317 Tiger Grouper *Mycteroperca tigris*
14 Tiger Shark *Galeocerdo cuvieri*
494 Tilapia *Tilapia nilotica*
395 Tilefish *Lopholatilus chamaeleonticeps*
255 Timuco *Strongylura timuco*
217 Tomcod *Microgadus proximus*
452 Tomtate *Haemulon aurolineatum*
21 Tope *Galeorhinus galeus*
468 Totuava *Cynoscion macdonaldi*
410 Trevally *Usacaranx georgianus*
449 Tripletail *Lobotes surinamensis*
374 Tropical Black Bream *Acanthopagrus berda*
605 Truncated Sunfish *Ranzania truncata*
602 Trunkfish *Lactophrys tricornis*
596 Turbot *Scophthalmus maximus*
236 Tusk *Brosme brosme*
106 Twaite Shad *Alosa fallax*
297 Two-Horned Sculpin *Icelus bicornis*

64 Undulate Ray *Raja undulata*

37 Velvet Belly *Etmopterus spinax*
143 Vendace *Coregonus albula*

552 Wahoo *Acanthocybium solanderi*
172 Walking Catfish *Clarias batrachus*
352 Walleye *Stizostedion vitreum*
364 Warmouth Bass *Lepomis gulosus*
312 Warsaw Grouper *Epinephelus nigritis*
465 Weakfish *Cynoscion regalis*
173 Wels *Silurus glanis*
31 Whale Shark *Rhincodon typus*
331 White Bass *Morone chrysops*

381 White Biskop *Sparodon durbanensis*
170 White Catfish *Ictalurus catus*
365 White Crappie *Pomoxis annularis*
462 White Grunt *Haemulon plumieri*
570 White Marlin *Tetrapturus albidus*
504 White Mullet *Mugil curema*
333 White Perch *Morone americana*
466 White Sea Bass *Cynoscion nobilis*
492 White Seaperch *Phanerodon furcatus*
29 White Shark *Carcharodon carcharias*
62 White Skate *Raja alba*
388 White Steenbras *Pagellus lithognathus*
76 White Sturgeon *Acipenser transmontanus*
209 White Sucker *Catostomus commersoni*
20 White-Tipped Shark *Carcharhinus longimanus*
226 Whiting *Merlangius merlangus*
133 Windermere Char *Salvelinus willoughbyi*
580 Winter Flounder *Pseudopleuronectes americanus*
586 Witch *Glyptocephalus cynoglossus*
522 Wolffish *Anarhichas lupus*
111 Wolf Herring *Chirocentrus dorab*
337 Wreckfish *Polyprion americanus*

140 Yamame *Oncorhynchus masou*
334 Yellow Bass *Morone mississippiensis*
362 Yellow Belly *Lepomis megalotis*
171 Yellow Bullhead *Ictalurus natalis*
383 Yellowfin Bream *Mylio australis*
322 Yellowfin Grouper *Mycteroperca venenosus*
556 Yellowfin Tuna *Thunnus albacares*
294 Yellow Gurnard *Trigla lucerna*
404 Yellow Jack *Caranx bartholomaei*
321 Yellowmouth Grouper *Mycteroperca interstitialis*
350 Yellow Perch *Perca flavescens*
415 Yellowtail *Seriola lalandi*
582 Yellowtail Flounder *Limanda ferruginea*
448 Yellowtail Snapper *Ocyurus chrysurus*

206 Zaehrte *Vimba vimba*
349 Zander *Stizostedion lucioperca*
292 Zebrafish *Pterois volitans*

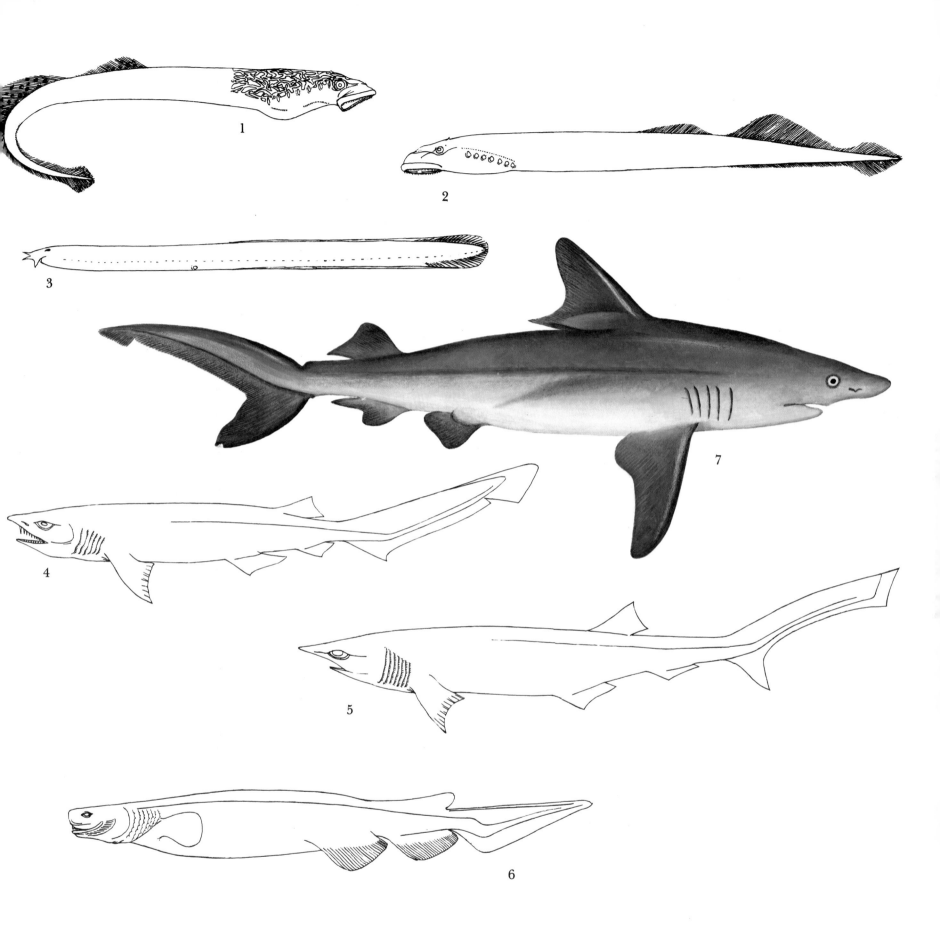

1 LAMPERN
Lampetra fluviatilis
Max ln 20 in (50 cm)

2 SEA LAMPREY
Petromyzon marinus
Max ln 36 in (90 cm)

3 HAGFISH
Myxine glutinosa
Max ln 36 in (90 cm)

4 SIX-GILLED SHARK
Hexanchus griseus
Max ln 26 ft (8 m)

5 SEVEN-GILLED SHARK
Heptranchias perlo
Max ln 10 ft (3 m)

6 FRILLED SHARK
Chlamydoselachus anguineus
Max ln 6 ft (2 m)

7 BLACKTIPPED SHARK
Carcharhinus limbatus
Max ln 6 ft (1.80 m)
Max wt 70 lb (32 kg)

8 BULL SHARK
Carcharhinus leucas
Max ln 10 ft (3 m)
Max wt 440 lb (200 kg)

9 SANDBAR SHARK
Carcharhinus milberti
Max ln 7 ft (2.10 m)
Max wt 130 lb (60 kg)

10 SILKY SHARK
Carcharhinus falciformis
Max ln 10 ft (3 m)
Max wt 440 lb (200 kg)

11 DUSKY SHARK
Carcharhinus obscurus
Max ln 11 ft 8 in (3.50 m)
Max wt 400 lb (180 kg)

12 SPINNER SHARK
Carcharhinus maculipinnis
Max ln 8 ft (2.40 m)
Max wt 330 lb (150 kg)

13 GREY WHALER SHA
Carcharhinus menisorra
Max ln 7 ft (2.10 m)

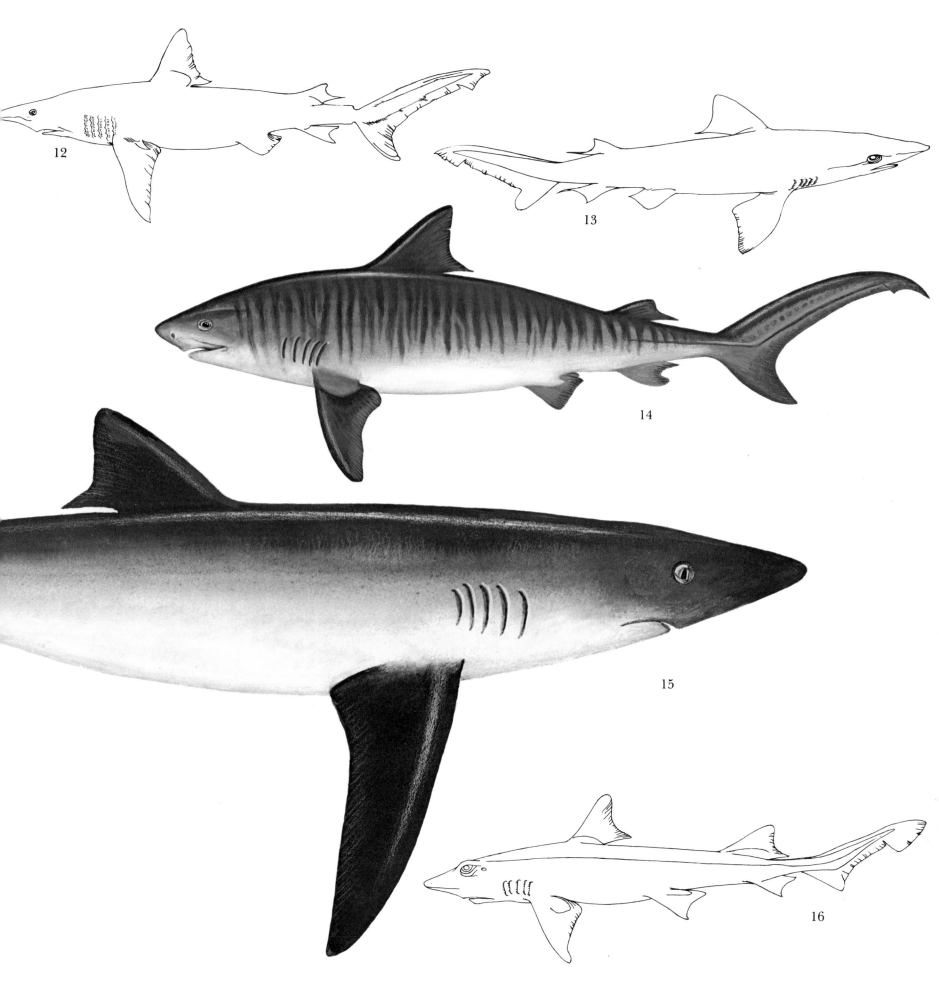

14 TIGER SHARK
Galeocerdo cuvieri
Max ln 18 ft (6 m)
Max wt 2,500 lb (1,100 kg)

15 BLUE SHARK
Prionace glauca
Max ln 13 ft (4 m)
Max wt 400 lb (180 kg)

16 SMOOTH DOGFISH
Mustelus canis
Max ln 5¼ ft (1.60 m)

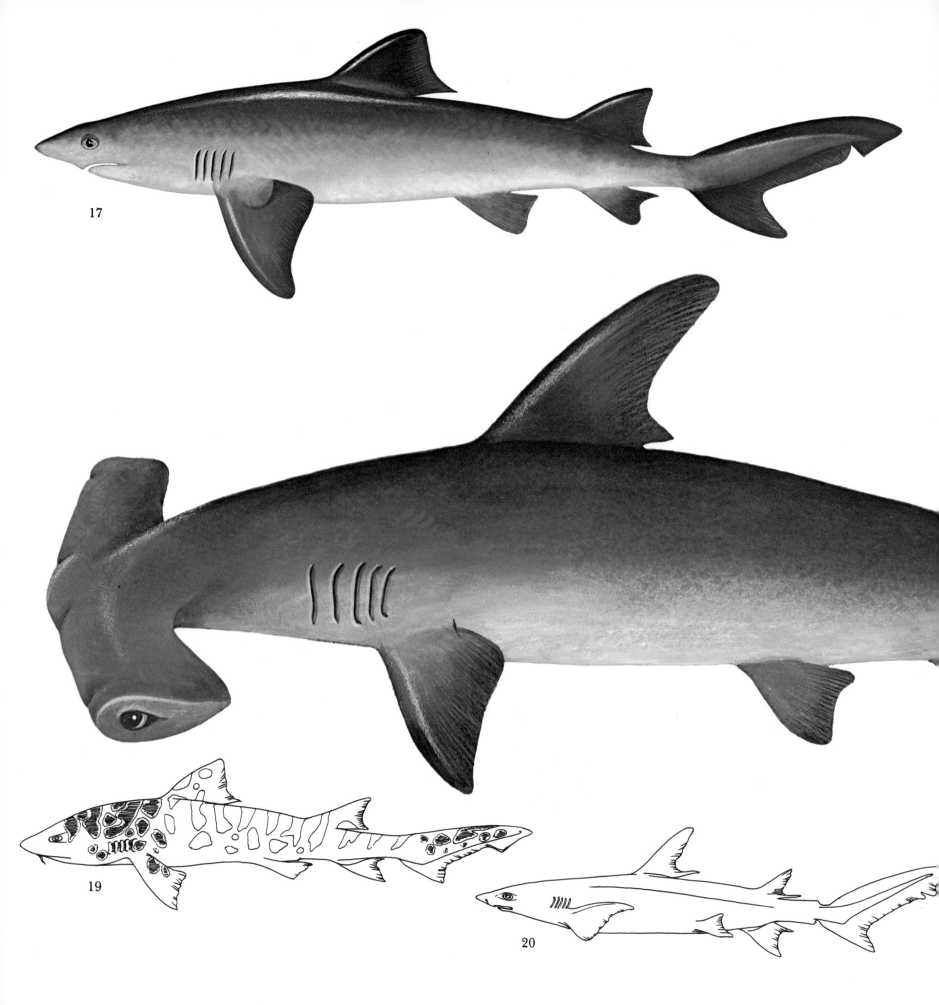

17 **LEMON SHARK**
Negaprion brevirostris
Max ln 11 ft (3.30 m)
Max wt 330 lb (150 kg)

19 **LEOPARD SHARK**
Triakis semifasciata
Max ln 5 ft (1.50 m)
Max wt 65 lb (30 kg)

20 **WHITE-TIPPED SHARK**
Carcharhinus longimanus
Max ln 13 ft (3.90 m)
Max wt 660 lb (300 kg)

21 **TOPE**
Galeorhinus galeus
Max ln 6 ft 8 in (2 m)

22 **SOUPFIN SHARK**
Galeorhinus zyopterus
Max ln 7 ft (2.10 m)
Max wt 110 lb (50 kg)

23 **SMOOTH HOUND**
Mustelus mustelus
Max ln 6 ft (1.80 m)

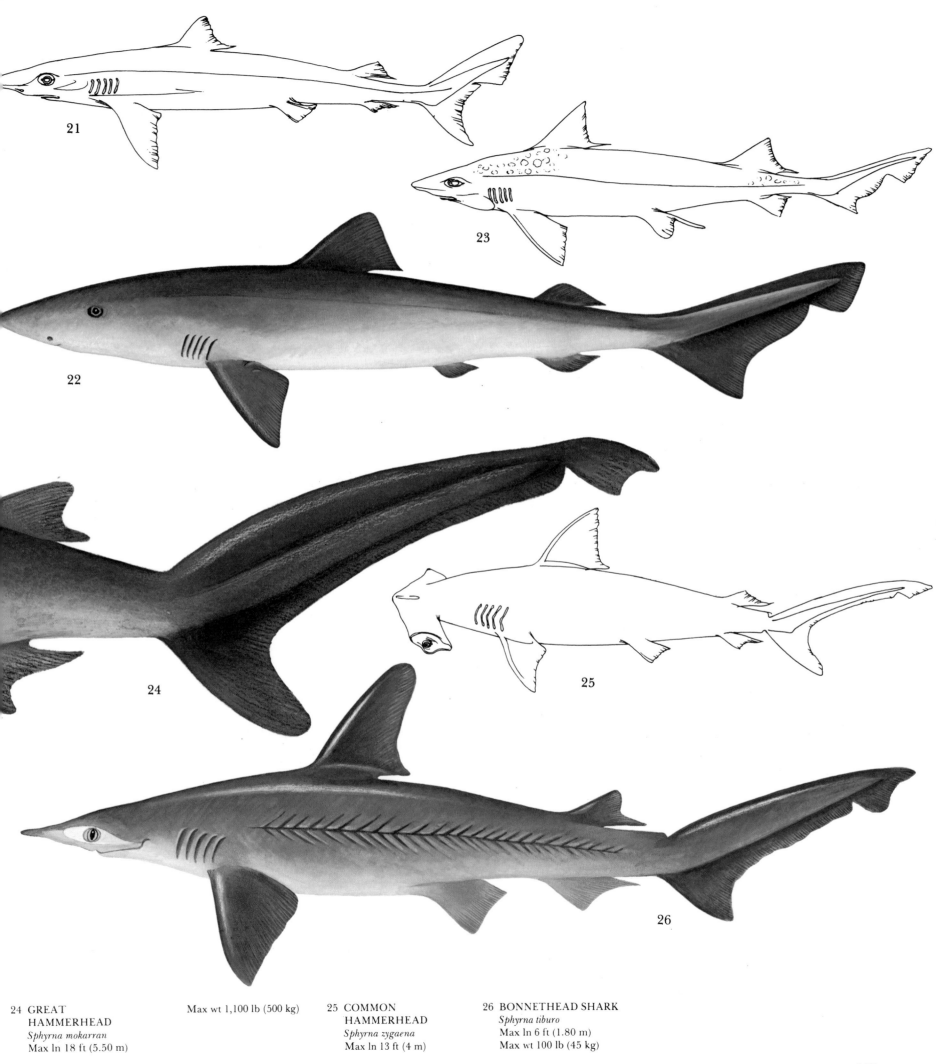

24 GREAT
HAMMERHEAD
Sphyrna mokarran
Max ln 18 ft (5.50 m)

Max wt 1,100 lb (500 kg)

25 COMMON
HAMMERHEAD
Sphyrna zygaena
Max ln 13 ft (4 m)

26 BONNETHEAD SHARK
Sphyrna tiburo
Max ln 6 ft (1.80 m)
Max wt 100 lb (45 kg)

27 **MAKO SHARK**
Isurus oxyrhynchus
Max ln 12 ft 2 in (3.6 m)
Max wt 1,061 lb (482 kg)

28 **PORBEAGLE SHARK**
Lamna nasus
Max ln 8 ft (2.40 m)
Max wt 465 lb (210 kg)

29 **WHITE SHARK**
Carcharodon carcharias
Max ln 40 ft (12 m)
Max wt 9,500 lb (4,300 kg)

28

30 **BASKING SHARK**
Cetorhinus maximus
Max ln 50 ft (15 m)

31 **WHALE SHARK**
Rhincodon typus
Max ln 60 ft (18 m)

32 **NURSE SHARK**
Ginglymostoma cirratum
Max ln 8½ ft (2.55 m)
Max wt 375 lb (170 kg)

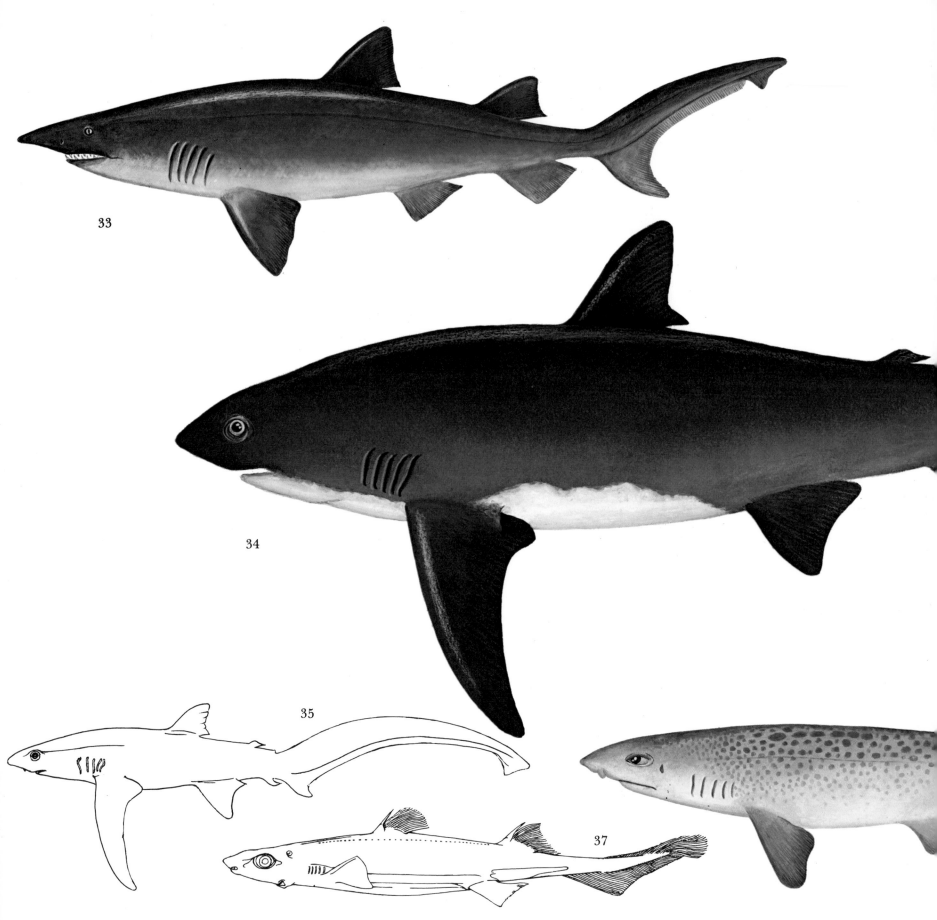

33 GREY NURSE SHARK
Odontaspis taurus
Max ln 10 ft (3 m)

34 THRESHER SHARK
Alopias vulpinus
Max ln 20 ft (6 m)
Max wt 1,000 lb (450 kg)

35 BIGEYE THRESHER SHARK
Alopias superciliosus
Max ln 18 ft (5.40 m)
Max wt 880 lb (400 kg)

36 SPINY DOGFISH
Squalus acanthias
Max ln 4 ft (1.20 m)
Max wt 30 lb (14 kg)

37 VELVET BELLY
Etmopterus spinax
Max ln 20 in (50 cm)

38 LARGE-SPOTTED DOGFISH
Scyliorhinus stellaris
Max ln 5 ft (1.50 m)
Max wt 21 lb (9.5 kg)

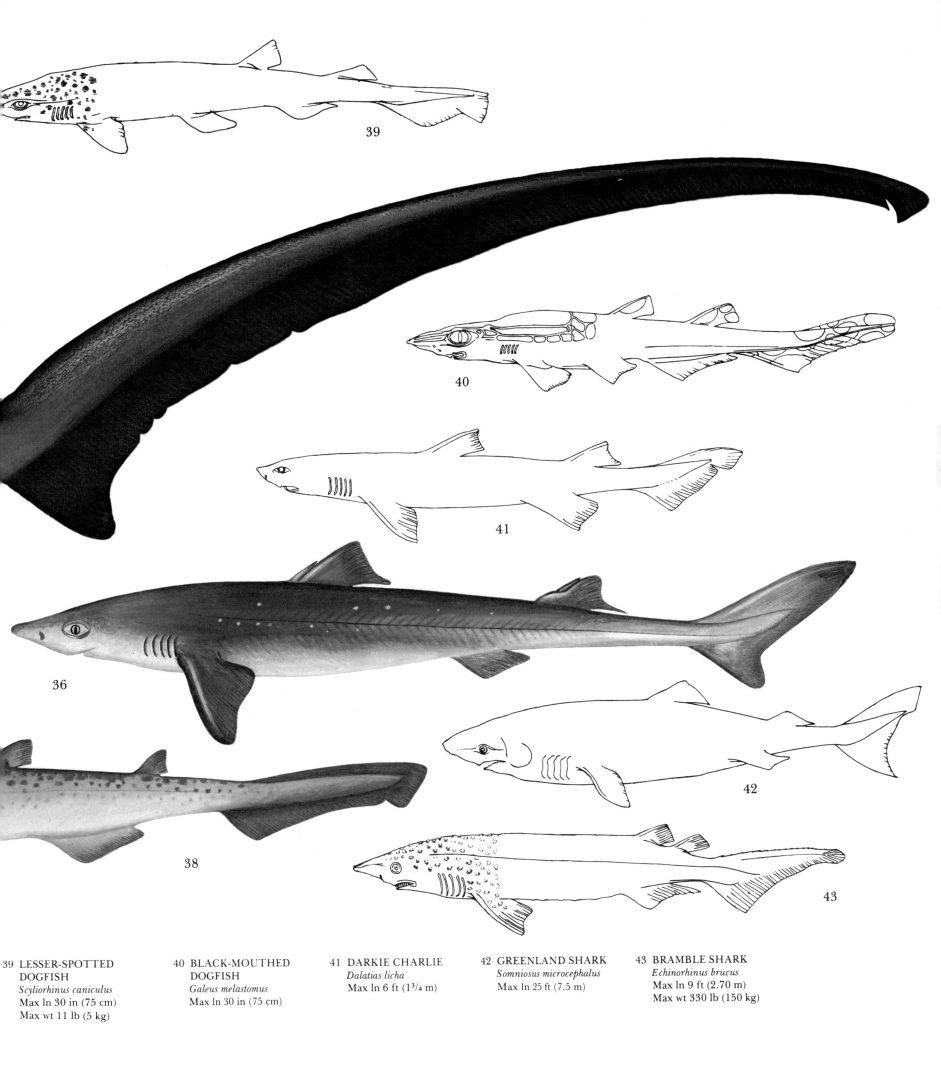

39 LESSER-SPOTTED DOGFISH
Scyliorhinus caniculus
Max ln 30 in (75 cm)
Max wt 11 lb (5 kg)

40 BLACK-MOUTHED DOGFISH
Galeus melastomus
Max ln 30 in (75 cm)

41 DARKIE CHARLIE
Dalatias licha
Max ln 6 ft (1¾ m)

42 GREENLAND SHARK
Somniosus microcephalus
Max ln 25 ft (7.5 m)

43 BRAMBLE SHARK
Echinorhinus brucus
Max ln 9 ft (2.70 m)
Max wt 330 lb (150 kg)

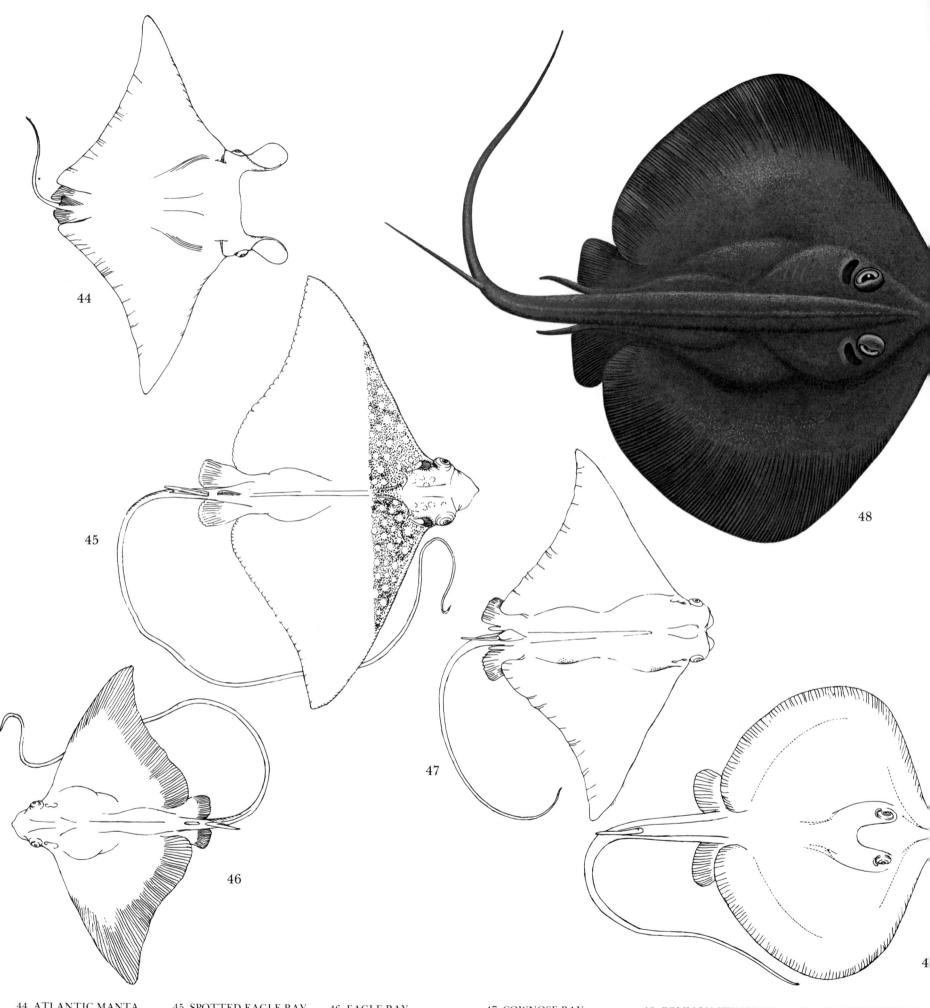

44 ATLANTIC MANTA
Manta birostris
Max ln 14 ft (4.20 m)
Max wt 2,200 lb (1,000 kg)

45 SPOTTED EAGLE RAY
Aetobatus narinari
Max ln 10 ft (3 m)
Max wt 650 lb (300 kg)

46 EAGLE RAY
Myliobatis aquila
Max ln 6.5 ft (2 m)
Max wt 500 lb (225 kg)

47 COWNOSE RAY
Rhinoptera bonasus
Max ln 7 ft 1 in (2.16 m)
Max wt 110 lb (50 kg)

48 COMMON STINGRAY
Trygon pastinaca
Max ln 8 ft (2.50 m)

49 ATLANTIC STINGRAY
Dasyatis sabina

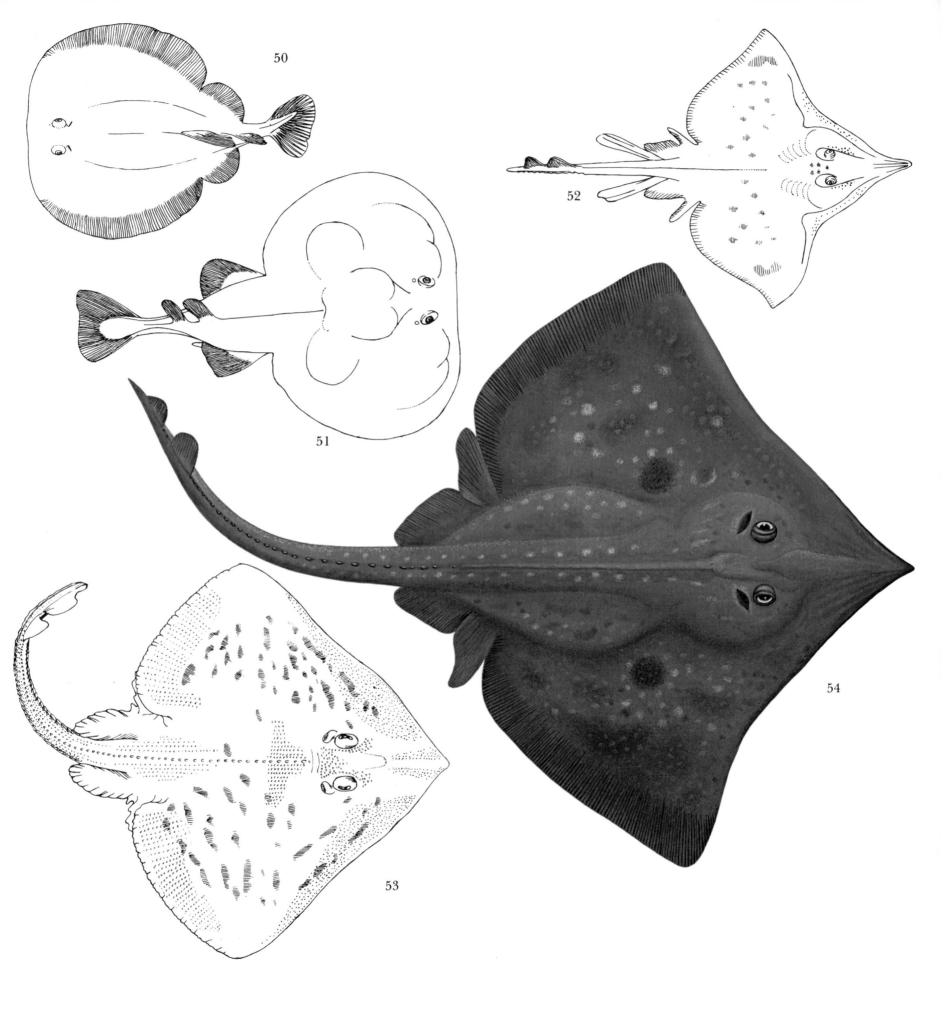

50 MARBLED ELECTRIC
RAY
Torpedo marmorata
Max ln 5 ft (1.5 m)

Max wt 70 lb (30 kg)

51 ELECTRIC RAY
Torpedo nobiliana
Max ln 6 ft (1.80 m)
Max wt 110 lb (50 kg)

52 LONG-NOSE SKATE
Raja oxyrinchus
Max ln 5 ft (1.5 m)

53 CLEARNOSE SKATE
Raja eglanteria
Max ln 24 in (60 cm)

54 COMMON SKATE
Raja batis
Max ln 8 ft (2.40 m)

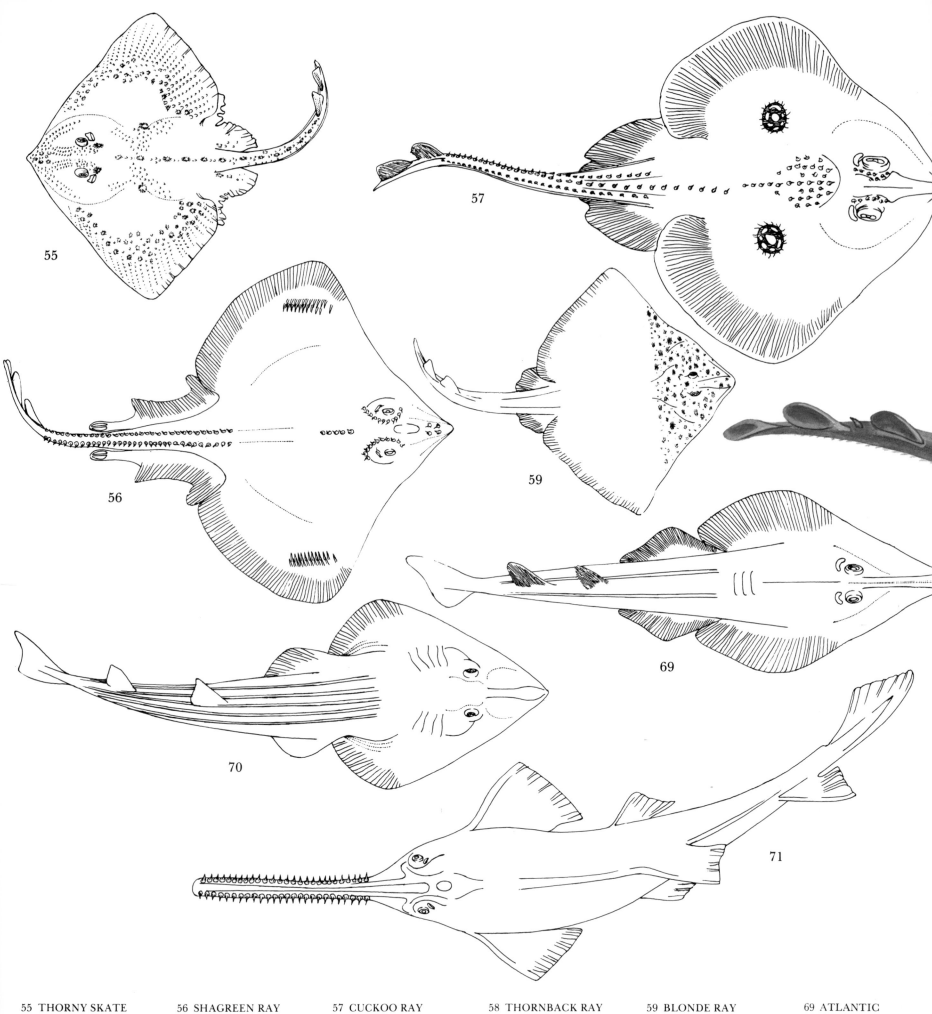

55 THORNY SKATE
Raja radiata
Max ln 3 ft 4 in (1 m)

56 SHAGREEN RAY
Raja fullonica
Max ln 3 ft 7 in (1.10 m)

57 CUCKOO RAY
Raja naevus
Max ln 2½ ft (75 cm)

58 THORNBACK RAY
Raja clavata
Max ln 32 in (80 cm)
Max wt 40 lb (18 kg)

59 BLONDE RAY
Raja brachyura
Max ln 3½ ft (1.10 m)

69 ATLANTIC GUITARFISH
Rhinobatus lentiginosus
Max ln 3–4 ft (1–1.5 m)

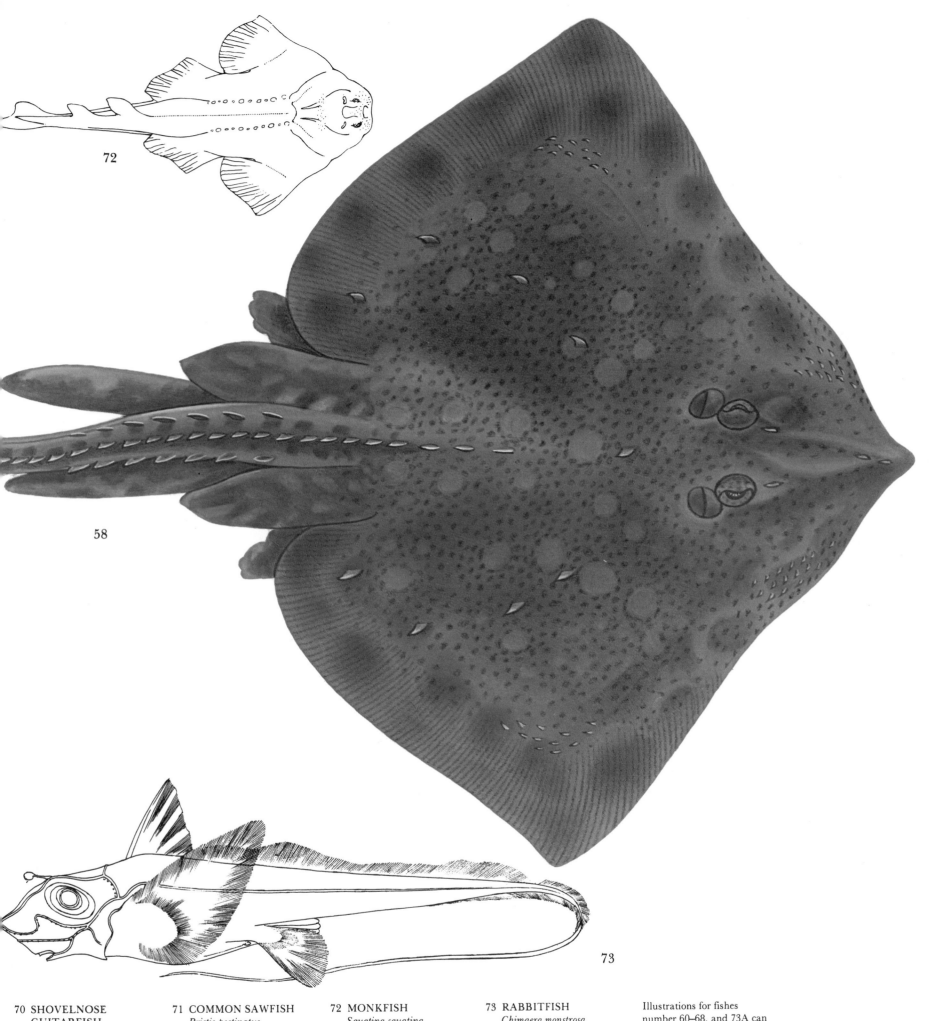

70 SHOVELNOSE
GUITARFISH
Rhinobatus productus

71 COMMON SAWFISH
Pristis pectinatus
Max ln 18 ft (5.50 m)
Max wt 5,000 lb (2,275 kg)

72 MONKFISH
Squatina squatina
Max ln 6 ft 8 in (2 m)
Max wt 88 lb (40 kg)

73 RABBITFISH
Chimaera monstrosa
Max ln 4 ft (1.2 m)

Illustrations for fishes
number 60–68, and 73A can
be found on page 65.

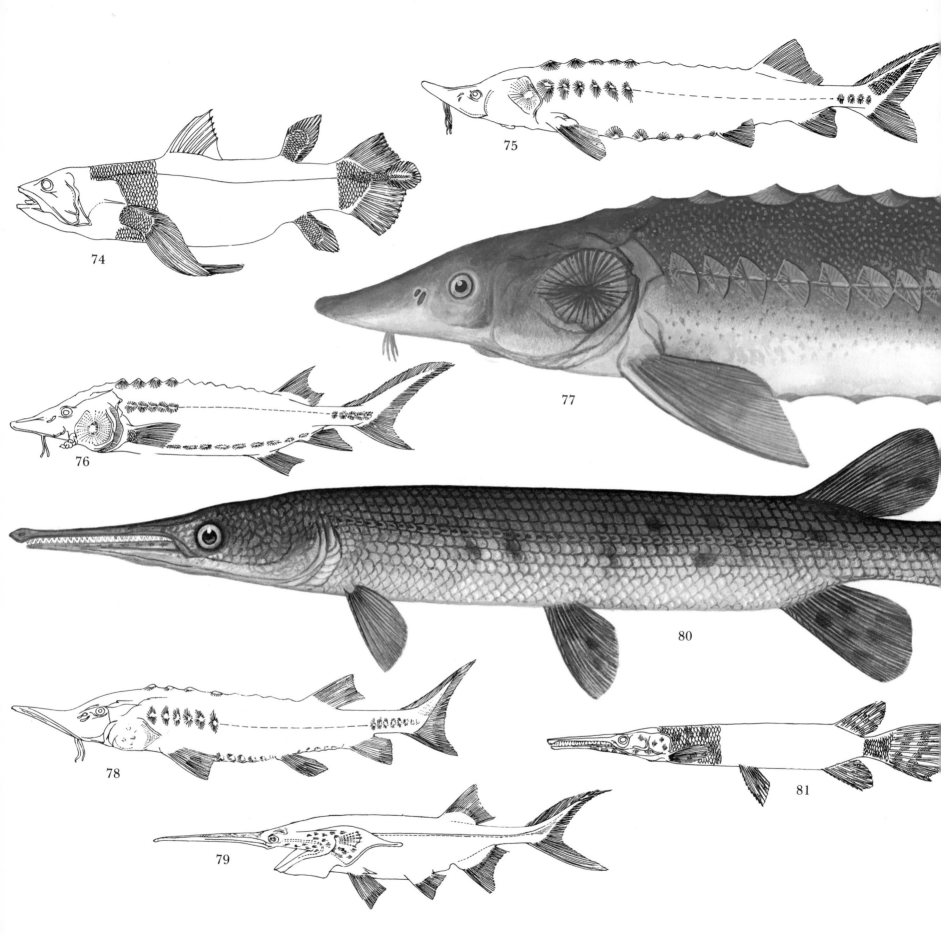

74 COELACANTH
Latimeria chalumnae
Max ln 5 ft (1.50 m)
Max wt 172 lb (78 kg)

75 LAKE STURGEON
Acipenser fulvescens
Max wt 100 lb (45 kg)

76 WHITE STURGEON
Acipenser transmontanus
Max ln 12 ft (3.70 m)
Max wt 1.000 lb (450 kg)

77 COMMON ATLANTIC
STURGEON
Acipenser sturio
Max ln 20 ft (6 m)

Max wt 880 lb (400 kg)

78 GREEN STURGEON
Acipenser acutirostris
Max ln 7 ft (2.10 m)
Max wt 350 lb (160 kg)

85 PIRARUCU
Arapaima gigas
Max ln 19 ft (6 m)
Max wt 450 lb (200 kg)

86 MOONEYE
Hiodon tergisus
Max ln 15 in (38 cm)
Max wt 4.4 lb (2 kg)

87 BELLIE
Heterotus niloticus
Max ln 30 in (75 cm)

88 GOLDEYE
Hiodon alosoides
Max ln 15 in (38 cm)

89 LEACH
Mormyrops deliciosus
Max ln 5 ft (1.50 m)
Max wt 40 lb (18 kg)

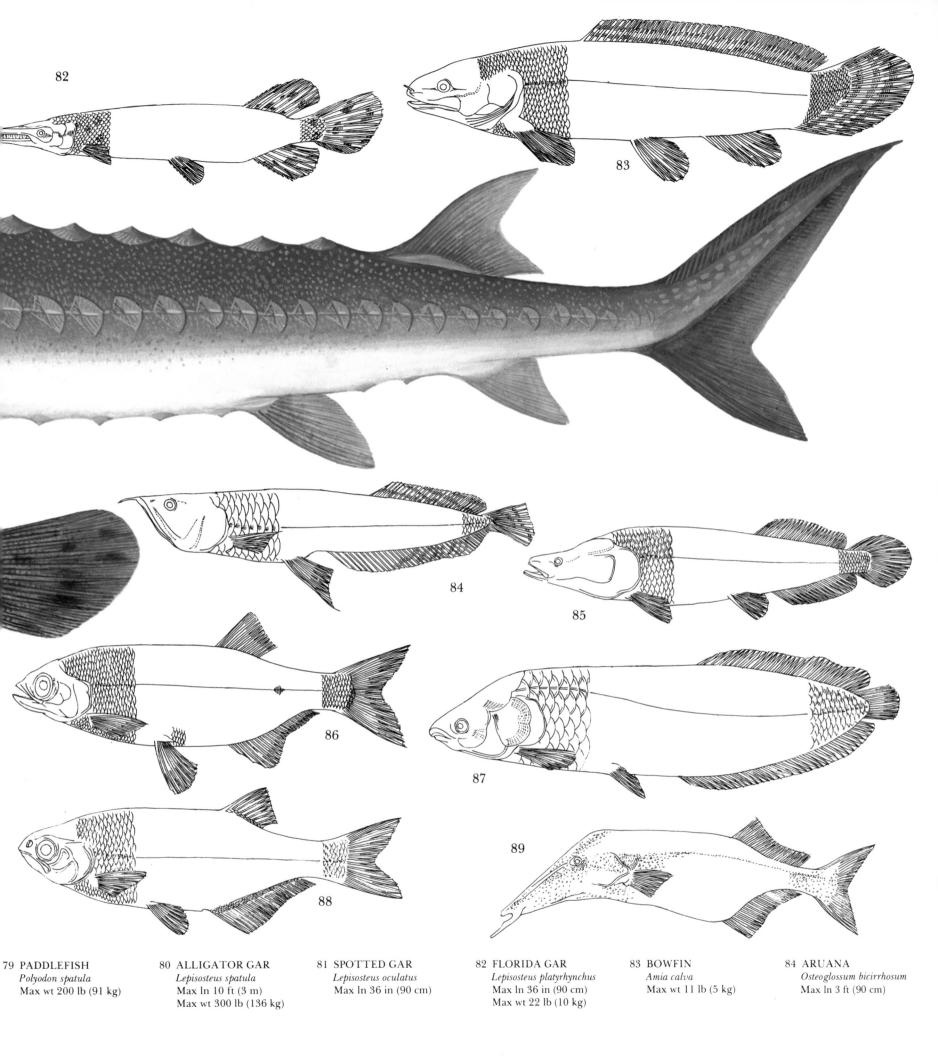

79 PADDLEFISH
Polyodon spatula
Max wt 200 lb (91 kg)

80 ALLIGATOR GAR
Lepisosteus spatula
Max ln 10 ft (3 m)
Max wt 300 lb (136 kg)

81 SPOTTED GAR
Lepisosteus oculatus
Max ln 36 in (90 cm)

82 FLORIDA GAR
Lepisosteus platyrhynchus
Max ln 36 in (90 cm)
Max wt 22 lb (10 kg)

83 BOWFIN
Amia calva
Max wt 11 lb (5 kg)

84 ARUANA
Osteoglossum bicirrhosum
Max ln 3 ft (90 cm)

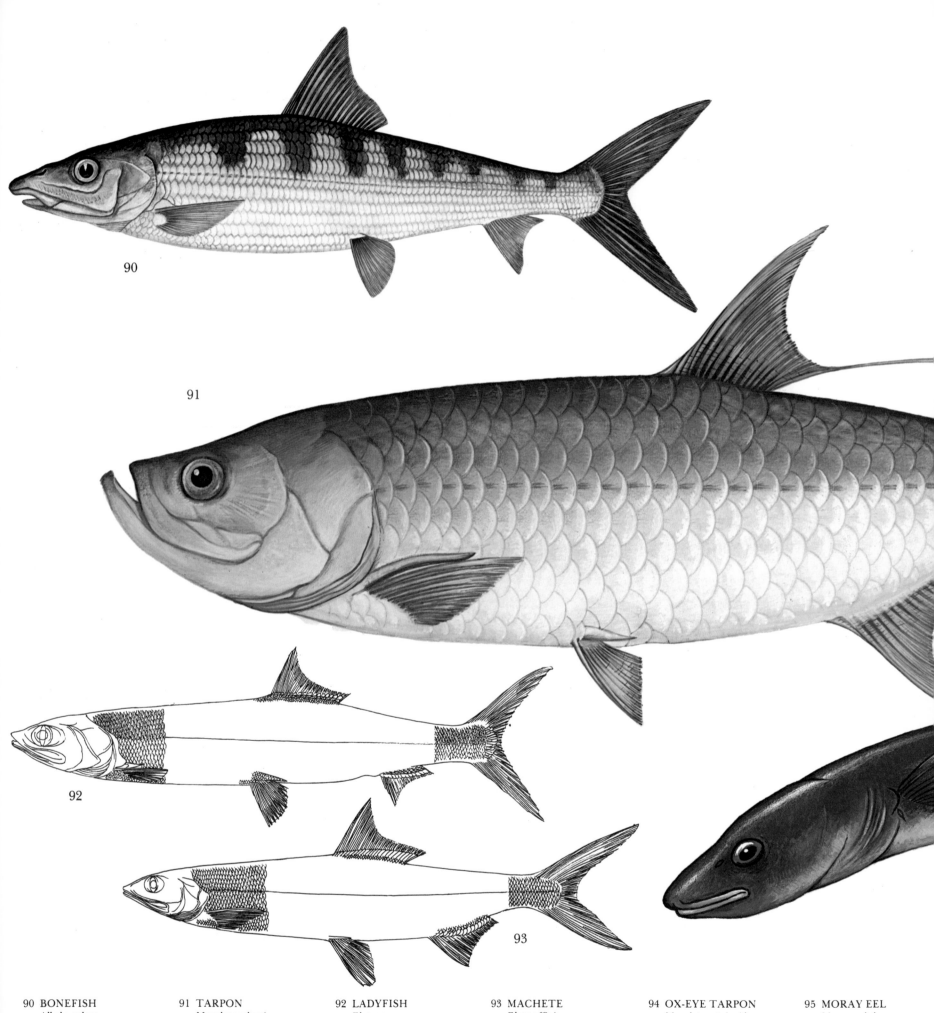

90 BONEFISH
Albula vulpes
Max ln 40 in (1 m)
Max wt 17 lb (7½ kg)

91 TARPON
Megalops atlanticus
Max ln 8 ft 4 in (2.50 m)

92 LADYFISH
Elops saurus
Max ln 3 ft (1 m)
Max wt 15 lb (7 kg)

93 MACHETE
Elops affinis
Max ln 36 in (90 cm)

94 OX-EYE TARPON
Megalops cyprinoides
Max ln 1½ ft (45 cm)

95 MORAY EEL
Muraena helena
Max ln 5 ft (1.5 m)
Max wt 26½ lb (12 kg)

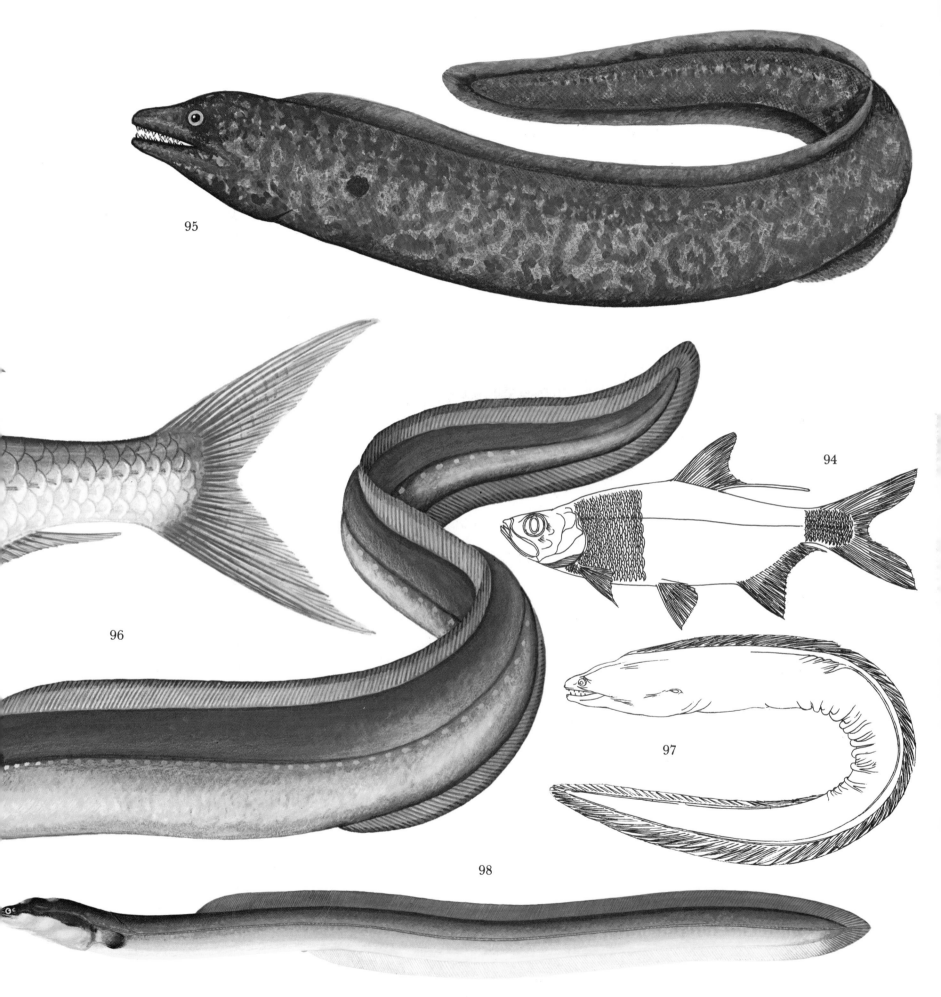

96 CONGER EEL
Conger oceanicus
Max ln 9 ft (2.7 m)

97 GREEN MORAY
Gymnothorax funebris
Max ln 6 ft (1.80 m)

98 EEL
Anguilla anguilla –
– anguilla rostrata
Max ln 3 ft 3 in (1 m)

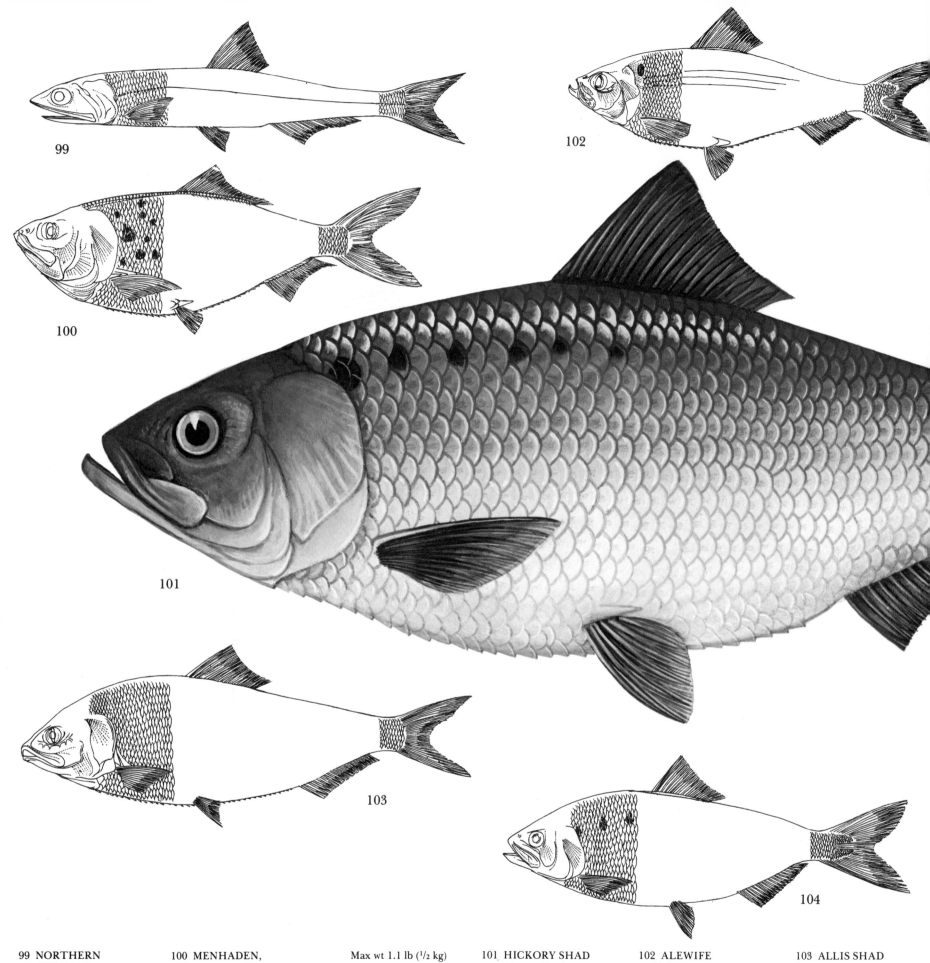

99 NORTHERN
ANCHOVY
Engraulis mordax
Max ln 10 in (25 cm)

100 MENHADEN,
ATLANTIC
Brevoortia tyrannus
Max ln 20 in (50 cm)

Max wt 1.1 lb (½ kg)

101 HICKORY SHAD
Alosa mediocris
Max wt 3 lb (1½ kg)

102 ALEWIFE
Alosa pseudoharengus
Max ln 14 in (36 cm)

103 ALLIS SHAD
Alosa alosa
Max ln 24 in (60 cm)
Max wt 8 lb (3½ kg)

110 PACIFIC SARDINE
Sardinops sagax
Max ln 12 in (30 cm)

111 WOLF HERRING
Chirocentrus dorab
Max ln 12 ft (3.5 m)
Max wt 220 lb (100 kg)

112 SPANISH SARDINE
Sardinella anchovia
Max ln 6½ in (16 cm)

Illustrations for fishes
number 113, 114, 115, 116,
and 117 can be found on page
72.

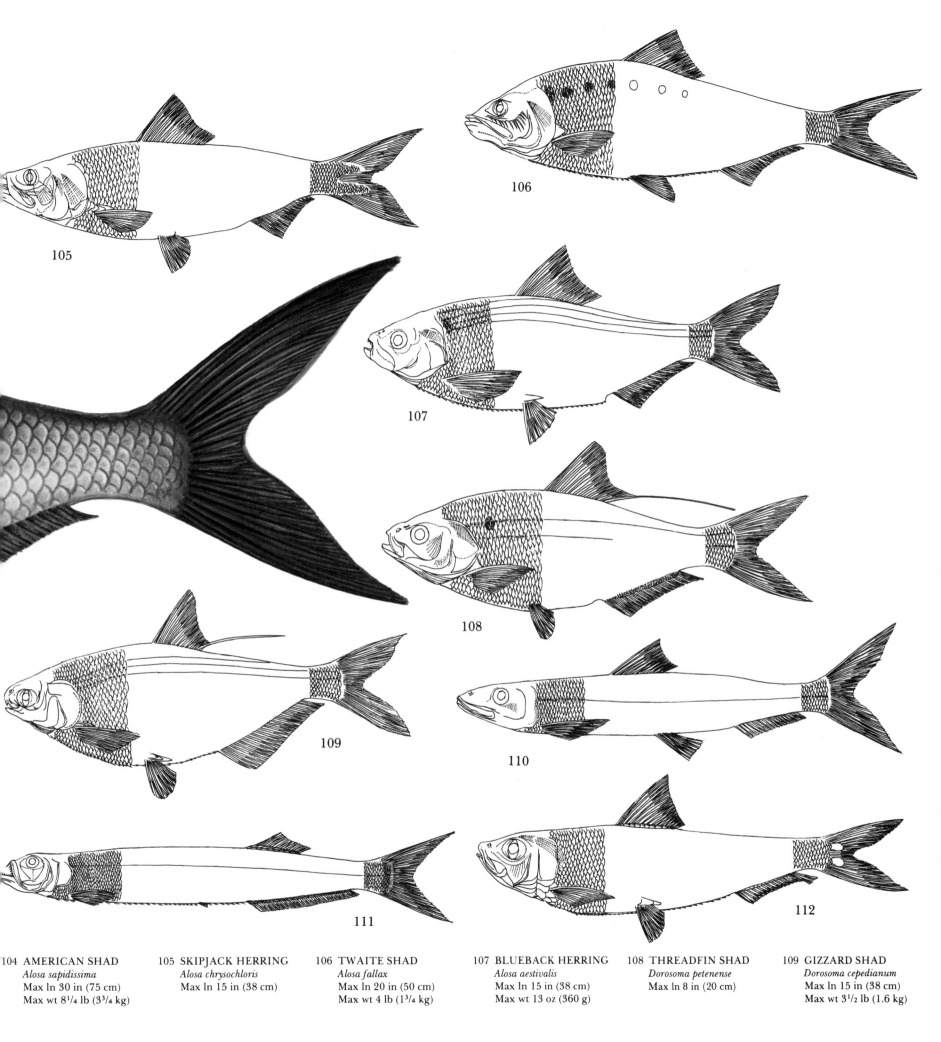

104 AMERICAN SHAD
Alosa sapidissima
Max ln 30 in (75 cm)
Max wt 8¼ lb (3¾ kg)

105 SKIPJACK HERRING
Alosa chrysochloris
Max ln 15 in (38 cm)

106 TWAITE SHAD
Alosa fallax
Max ln 20 in (50 cm)
Max wt 4 lb (1¾ kg)

107 BLUEBACK HERRING
Alosa aestivalis
Max ln 15 in (38 cm)
Max wt 13 oz (360 g)

108 THREADFIN SHAD
Dorosoma petenense
Max ln 8 in (20 cm)

109 GIZZARD SHAD
Dorosoma cepedianum
Max ln 15 in (38 cm)
Max wt 3½ lb (1.6 kg)

118

120A

120

120B

118 RAINBOW TROUT
Salmo gairdneri
Max ln 30 in (75 cm)
Max wt 20 lb (9 kg)

119 STEELHEAD TROUT
Salmo gairdneri
Max ln 28 in (70 cm)
Max wt 15 lb (7 kg)

120 BROWN TROUT
Salmo trutta fario
Max ln 45 in (1.10 m)
Max wt 40 lb (19 kg)

120A YOUNG BROWN
TROUT
showing parr marks

120B LOCH LEVEN
TROUT
*The best variety of the
Brown Trout for
"transplanting".*

152

119

121A

121

120D

120C

122

122 A

120C BROWN TROUT
from acid moorland

120D BROWN TROUT
from forest river

121 SEA TROUT (sea run)
Salmo trutta trutta
Max ln 4 ft 7 in (1.4 m)
Max wt 110 lb (50 kg)

121A SEA TROUT
Spawning colours

122 HUCHEN
Salmo hucho
Max ln 60 in (1.50 m)
Max wt 110 lb (50 kg)

122A YOUNG HUCHEN
showing parr marks

123 **GOLDEN TROUT**
Salmo aguabonita
Max ln 28 in (70 cm)
Max wt 11 lb (5 kg)

124 **OUANANICHE**
Salmo salar ouananiche

126 **CUTTHROAT TROUT**
Salmo clarki
Max wt 12 lb (5½ kg)

127 **LANDLOCKED
SALMON**
Salmo salar sebago

128 **LAKE TROUT**
Salmo trutta lacustris
Max wt 100 lb (45 kg)

129 **ATLANTIC SALMON**
Salmo salar
Max ln 5 ft (1.50 m)
Max wt 80 lb (36 kg)

129A **ATLANTIC SALMON**
Parr

129B **ATLANTIC SALMON**
spawning colours (male)

129C **LAKE TROUT**
Salvelinus namaycush
Max wt 100 lb (45 kg)

131 IWANA
Salvelinus pl vius
Max ln 1¹/₂ ft (45 cm)

132 DOLLY VARDEN
Salvelinus malma spectabilis
Max ln 3 ft 4 in (1 m)
Max wt 30 lb (14 kg)

134 ARCTIC CHAR
Salvelinus alpinus
Max ln 30 in (75 cm)
Max wt 22 lb (10 kg)

134A ARCTIC CHAR
spawning colours

135 BROOK TROUT
Salvelinus fontinalis (male)
Max ln 18 in (45 cm)
Max wt 10 lb (4 kg)

135A BROOK TROUT
(female)

135A

135 B

135B SPLAKE WENDIGO
Salvelinus namaycush ♀
Salvelinus fontinalis ♂

136 **CHINOOK SALMON**
Oncorhynchus tschawytscha
Max wt 108 lb (49 kg)

137 **COHO SALMON**
Oncorhynchus kisutch
Max ln 36 in (90 cm)
Max wt 30 lb (13½ kg)

138 **CHUM SALMON**
Oncorhynchus keta
Max ln 36 in (90 cm)
Max wt 30 lb (13½ kg)

139 **LITTLE REDFISH**
Oncorhynchus kennerlyi
Max ln 8 in (20 cm)

140 **YAMAME**
Oncorhynchus masou
Max ln 2 ft (60 cm)

141 **SOCKEYE SALMON**
Oncorhynchus nerka
Max wt 15 lb (7 kg)

142 **HUMPBACK SALMON**
Oncorhynchus gorbuscha
Max ln 24 in (60 cm)
Max wt 11 lb (5 kg)

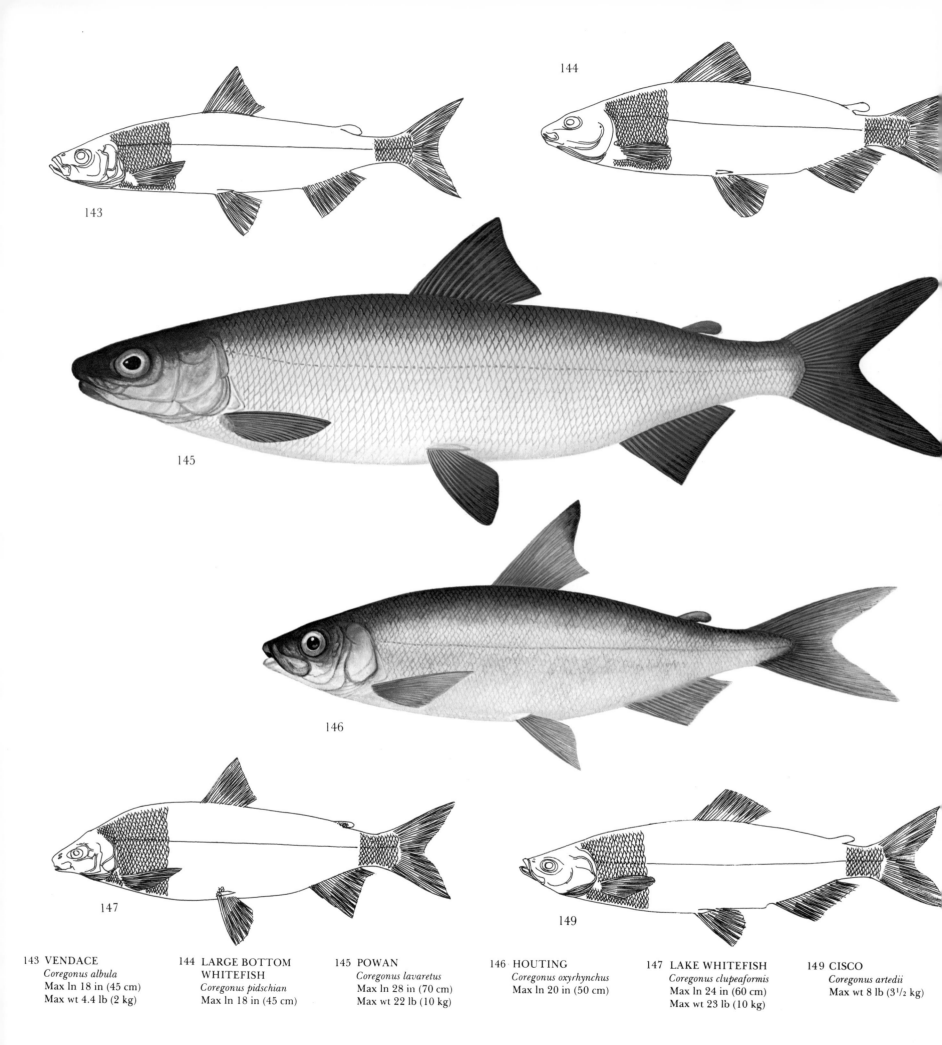

143 **VENDACE**
Coregonus albula
Max ln 18 in (45 cm)
Max wt 4.4 lb (2 kg)

144 **LARGE BOTTOM WHITEFISH**
Coregonus pidschian
Max ln 18 in (45 cm)

145 **POWAN**
Coregonus lavaretus
Max ln 28 in (70 cm)
Max wt 22 lb (10 kg)

146 **HOUTING**
Coregonus oxyrhynchus
Max ln 20 in (50 cm)

147 **LAKE WHITEFISH**
Coregonus clupeaformis
Max ln 24 in (60 cm)
Max wt 23 lb (10 kg)

149 **CISCO**
Coregonus artedii
Max wt 8 lb (3½ kg)

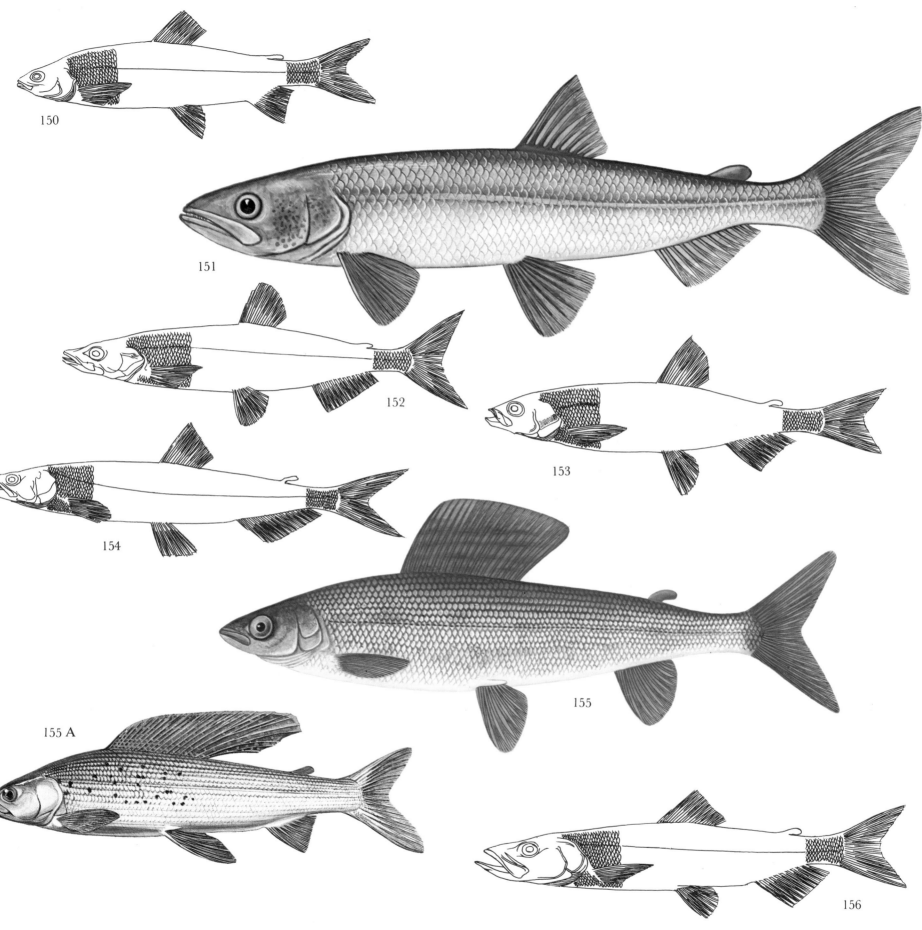

50 ROUND WHITEFISH
Prosopium cylindraceum
Max wt 3 lb (1½ kg)

151 AMERICAN SMELT
Osmerus mordax
Max ln 10 in (25 cm)
Max wt 1 lb (½ kg)

152 SMELT
Osmerus eperlanus
Max ln 12 in (30 cm)

153 POND SMELT
Hypomesus olidus
Max ln 1¼ ft (40 cm)

154 CANDLEFISH
Thaleichthys pacificus
Max ln 12 in (30 cm)
Max wt 10 oz (¼ kg)

155 EUROPEAN
GRAYLING
Thymallus thymallus
Max ln 24 in (60 cm)

155 A ARCTIC GRAYLING
Thymallus arcticus
Max ln 18 in (45 cm)

156 INCONNU
Stenodus leucichthys
Max wt 55 lb (25 kg)

157

158

159

157 CHAIN PICKEREL
Esox niger
Max wt 10 lb (4¹/₂ kg)

158 EUROPEAN PIKE
NORTHERN PIKE;
Esox lucius
Max ln 5 ft (1.50 m)
Max wt 80 lb (35 kg)

159 REDFIN PICKEREL
*Esox americanus
americanus*
Max ln 15 in (38 cm)

160 GRASS PICKEREL
*Esox americanus
vermiculatus*
Max ln 12 in (30 cm)

161 MUSKELLUNGE
Esox masquinongy
Max ln 5 ft (1.50 m)
Max wt 62 lb (28 kg)

170 WHITE CATFISH
Ictalurus catus
Max ln 24 in (60 cm)

171 YELLOW BULLHEAD
Ictalurus natalis
Max ln 16 in (40 cm)
Max wt 5 lb (2¼ kg)

172 WALKING CATFISH
Clarias batrachus
Max ln 1¼ ft (40 cm)

173 WELS
Silurus glanis
Max ln 10 ft (3 m)
Max wt 660 lb (300 kg)

174 **TIGERFISH**
Hydrocyon lineatus
Max ln 40 in (1 m)
Max wt 80 lb (36 kg)

175 **ASP**
Aspius aspius
Max wt 40 lb (18 kg)

177 **DACE**
Leuciscus leuciscus
Max ln 12 in (30 cm)

180 **CARP**
Cyprinus carpio
Max ln 3 ft 4 in (1 m)
Max wt 65 lb (30 kg)

181 **LEATHER CARP**
Cyprinus carpio

182 **MIRROR CARP**
Cyprinus carpio

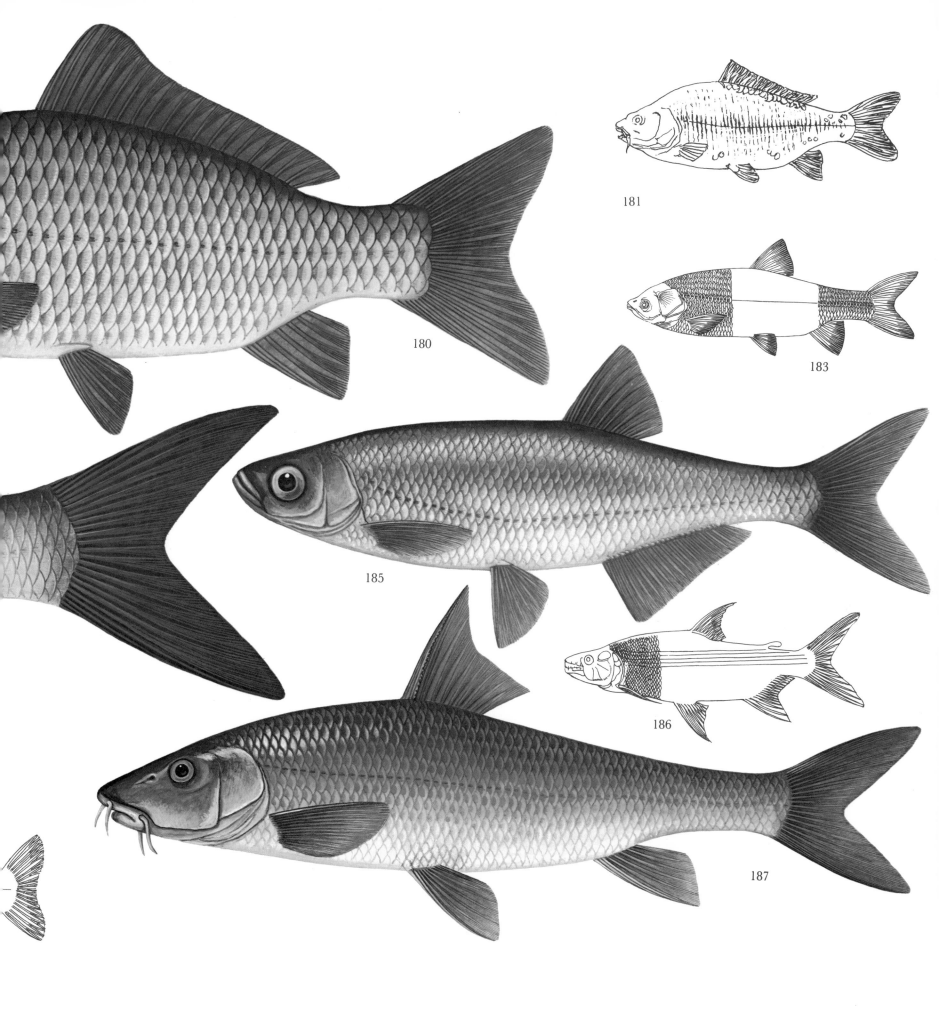

183 GRASS CARP
Ctenopharyngodon idella

184 PIRANHA
Serrasalmus nattereri
Max ln 12 in (30 cm)

185 BLEAK
Alburnus alburnus
Max ln 8 in (20 cm)
Max wt 2 oz (40 g)

186 GOLIATH
Hydrocion goliath
Max ln 4 ft (1.25 m)
Max wt 155 lb (70 kg)

187 BARBEL
Barbus barbus
Max ln 40 in (1 m)
Max wt 20 lb (9 kg)

188 CHUB
Leuciscus cephalus
Max ln 24 in (60 cm)
Max wt 9 lb (4 kg)

189 CRUCIAN CARP
Carassius carassius
Max ln 18 in (45 cm)
Max wt 7¾ lb (3.5 kg)

190 COMMON BREAM
Abramis brama
Max wt 20 lb (9 kg)

191 GUDGEON
Gobio gobio
Max ln 8 in (20 cm)

192 GALJOEN
Dichistius capensis
Max wt 16 lb (7¼ kg)

193 NORTHERN
SQUAWFISH
Ptychocheilus oregonen
Max ln 4 ft (1.20 m)

194 MINNOW
Phoxinus phoxinus
Max ln 4¾ in (12 cm)
Max wt ¹/₁₀ lb (50 g)

195 IDE
Leuciscus idus
Max wt 20 lb (9 kg)

196 MAHSEER
Barbus tor
Max ln 5 ft 10 in (1.75 m)
Max wt 155 lb (70 kg)

197 CLANWILLIAM
OLIFANT'S RIVER
YELLOWFISH
Barbus capensis

Max ln 30 in (75 cm)
Max wt 22 lb (10 kg)

198 ROACH
Rutilus rutilus
Max ln 20 in (50 cm)

199 COMMON SHINER
Notropis cornutus
Max ln 10 in (25 cm)
Max wt 1/2 lb (1/4 kg)

200 SILVER BREAM
Blicca bjoerkna
Max wt 4 1/2 lb (2 kg)

201 BIGMOUTH SHINER
Notropis dorsalis

02 LAKE CHUB
Couesius plumbeus
Max ln 6 in (15 cm)

203 RUDD
Scardinius
erythrophthalmus
Max ln 18 in (45 cm)
Max wt 4¹/₂ lb (2 kg)

204 GOLDFISH
Carassius auratus
Max ln 12 in (30 cm)
Max wt 2.2 lb (1 kg)

205 LONGNOSE DACE
Rhinichtys cataractae
Max ln 5 in (12,5 cm)

206 ZAEHRTE
Vimba vimba
Max ln 20 in (50 cm)
Max wt 2 lb (1 kg)

207 FATHEAD MINNOW
Pimephales promelas
Max ln 3 in (7¹/₂ cm)

208 TENCH
Tinca tinca
Max ln 28 in (70 cm)
Max wt 18 lb (8 kg)

209 WHITE SUCKER
Catostomus commersoni
Max ln 20 in (50 cm)
Max wt 6.6 lb (3 kg)

210 BIGMOUTH
BUFFALO
Ictiobus cyprinellus
Max ln 24 in (60 cm)
Max wt 22 lb (10 kg)

211 BITTERLING
Rhodeus amarus
Max ln 2¹/₂ in (6 cm)

171

213 ANGLERFISH
Lophius piscatorius
Max ln 6¹/₂ ft (2 m)

214 COD (ATLANTIC)
Gadus morhua
Max wt 200 lb (90 kg)

215 ATLANTIC TOMCOD
Microgadus tomcod
Max ln 15 in (38 cm)
Max wt 2¹/₄ lb (1 kg)

216 POOR COD
Gadus minutus
Max ln 10 in (25 cm)

217 TOMCOD
Microgadus proximus
Max ln 14 in (35 cm)

218 PACIFIC COD
Gadus macrocephalus
Max ln 2¹/₂ ft (75 cm)
Max wt 60 lb (25 kg)

216

218

219

221

222

223

225

226

219 NORWAY POUT
Boreogadus esmarkii
Max ln 10 in (25 cm)

221 POLAR COD
Boreogadus saida
Max ln 18 in (45 cm)

222 BLUE WHITING
Micromesistius poutassou
Max ln 20 in (50 cm)

223 SUKETODARA
Theragra chalcogramma
Max ln 24 in (60 cm)

225 MERLUZA
Merluccius gayi
Max ln 25 in (60 cm)

226 WHITING
Merlangius merlangus
Max ln 28 in (70 cm)

227

229

228

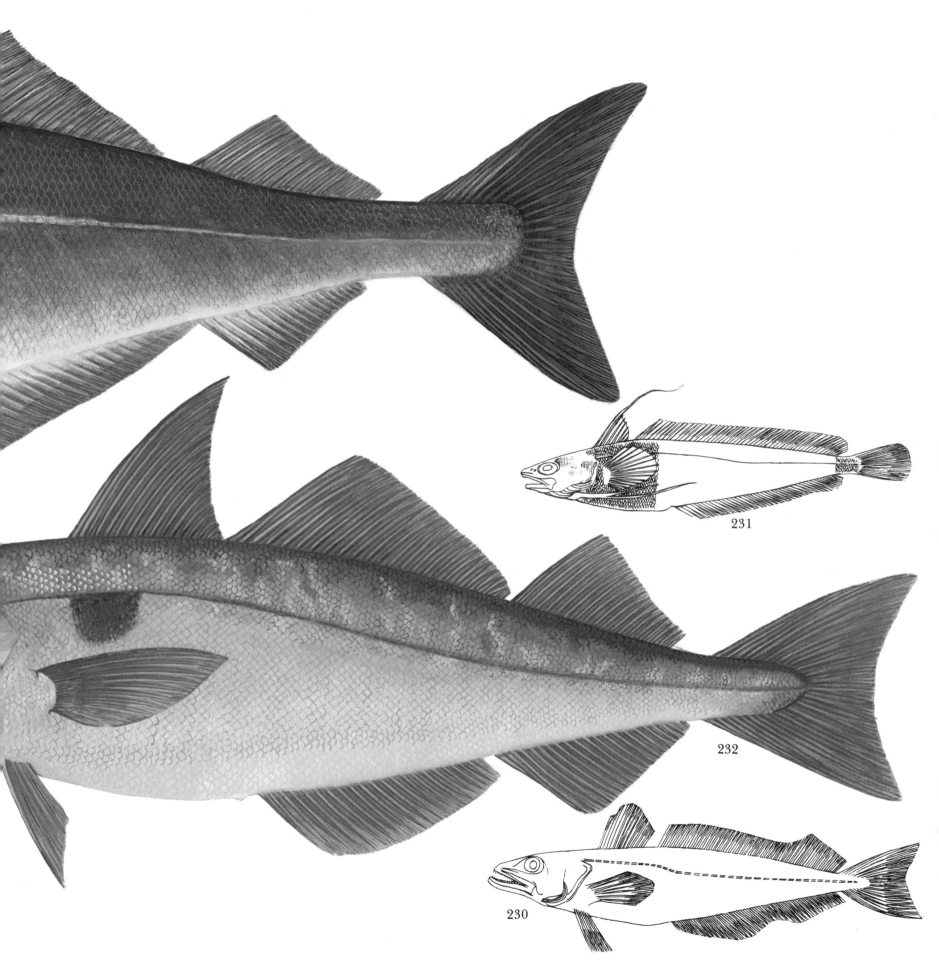

227 COALFISH
(POLLOCK)
Pollachius virens
Max ln 4 ft (1.20 m)

228 POLLACK
(EUROPEAN)
Pollachius pollachius
Max ln 4 ft (1.20 m)

229 HAKE
Merluccius merluccius
Max ln 4 ft 1 in (1.25 m)

230 SILVER HAKE
Merluccius bilinearis
Max ln 30 in (75 cm)
Max wt 5 lb (2¼ kg)

231 RED HAKE
Urophycis chuss
Max ln 30 in (75 cm)
Max wt 6.6 lb (3 kg)

232 HADDOCK
Melanogrammus aeglefinus
Max ln 3 ft 4 in (1 m)

233 MEDITERRANEAN
LING (SPANISH LING)
Molva elongata
Max ln 36 in (90 cm)

234 LING (EUROPEAN)
Molva molva
Max ln 7 ft 4 in (2.20 m)

235 BLUE LING
Molva byrkelange
Max ln 5½ ft (1.50 m)

242 LINGCOD
Ophiodon elongatus
Max ln 5 ft (1.50 m)
Max wt 70 lb (32 kg)

236 TUSK
Brosme brosme
Max ln 3 ft 4 in (1 m)
Max wt 27 lb (12 kg)

243 SILVERY POUT
Gadiculus thori
Max ln 6 in (16 cm)

237 GREATER
FORKBEARD
Phycis blennioides
Max ln 3½ ft (1.10 m)

244 TADPOLE-FISH
Raniceps raninus
Max ln 12 in (30 cm)

238 THREE-BEARD
ROCKLING
Gaidropsaurus tricirratus
Max ln 2 ft (60 cm)

245 POUTING
Gadus luscus
Max ln 18 in (45 cm)

239 FOUR-BEARD
ROCKLING
Gaidropsaurus cimbrius
Max ln 1½ ft (45 cm)

246 BURBOT
Lota lota
Max ln 3 ft 4 in (1 m)
Max wt 65 lb (30 kg)

240 FIVE-BEARD
ROCKLING
Gaidropsaurus mustela
Max ln 11 in (28 cm)

247 SARGASSUMFISH
Histrio histrio
Max ln 6 in (16 cm)

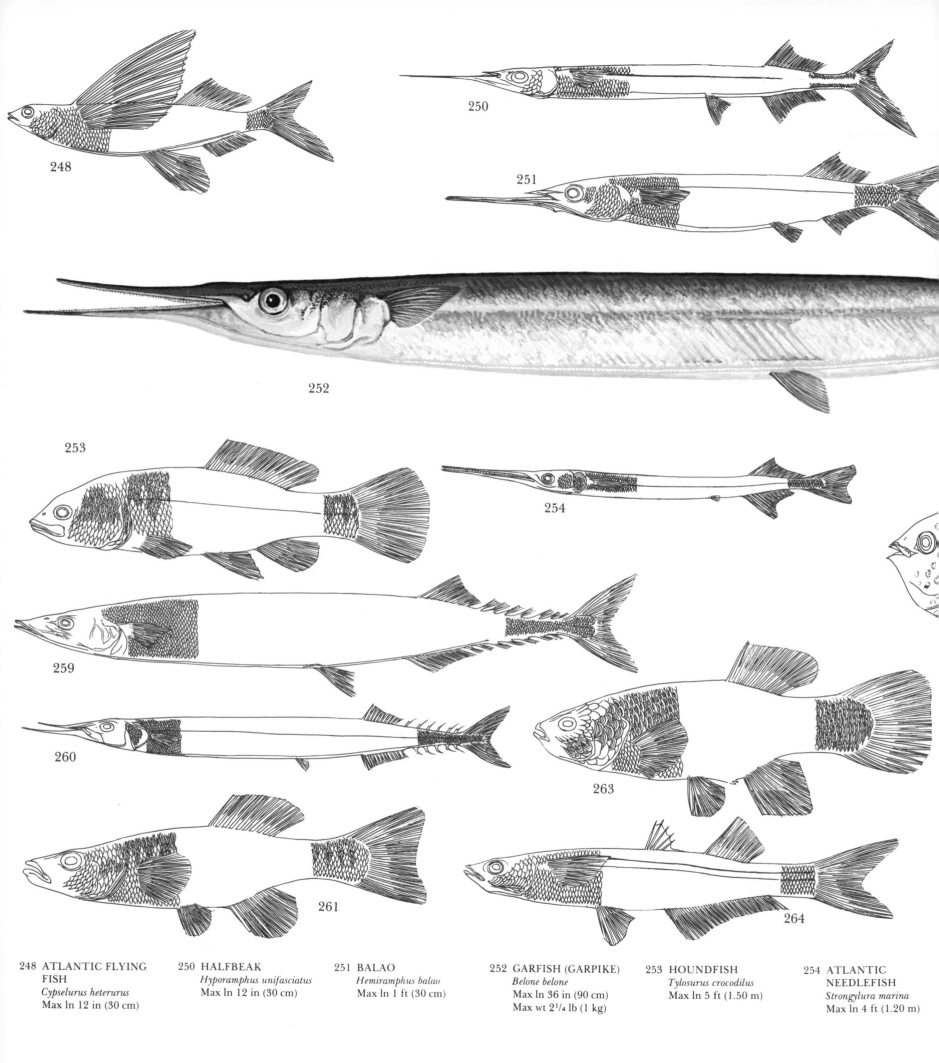

248 ATLANTIC FLYING FISH
Cypselurus heterurus
Max ln 12 in (30 cm)

250 HALFBEAK
Hyporamphus unifasciatus
Max ln 12 in (30 cm)

251 BALAO
Hemiramphus balao
Max ln 1 ft (30 cm)

252 GARFISH (GARPIKE)
Belone belone
Max ln 36 in (90 cm)
Max wt 2¹/₄ lb (1 kg)

253 HOUNDFISH
Tylosurus crocodilus
Max ln 5 ft (1.50 m)

254 ATLANTIC NEEDLEFISH
Strongylura marina
Max ln 4 ft (1.20 m)

178

Illustrations for fishes number 255, 256, 257, 258 and 262 can be found on page 90; 271, 274 and 275 on page 92.

259 PACIFIC SAURY
Cololabis saira
Max ln 18 in (45 cm)
Max wt 1½ lb (¾ kg)

266 SOLDIERFISH
Holocentrus spiniferus
Max ln 1¼ ft (38 cm)

260 SAURY PIKE
Scomberesox saurus
Max ln 20 in (50 cm)
Max wt 11 lb (5 kg)

268 JOHN DORY
Zeus faber
Max ln 24 in (60 cm)

261 BANDED KILLIFISH
Fundulus diaphanus
Max ln 5 in (12.5 cm)

270 OPAH
Lampris guttatus
Max ln 7 ft (2 m)
Max wt 230 lb (105 kg)

263 MUMMICHOG
Fundulus heteroclitus
Max ln 6 in (15 cm)

272 OARFISH
Regalecus glesne
Max ln 40 ft (12 m)

264 ATLANTC
SILVERSIDE
Menidia menidia
Max ln 5 in (12½ cm)

273 NINE-SPINED
STICKLEBACK
Pungitius pungitius
Max ln 3 in (7.5 cm)

265 CALIFORNIA
GRUNION
Leuresthes tenuis
Max ln 7 in 17.5 cm)

276 SEAHORSE
Hippocampus ramulosus
Max ln 6 in (15 cm)

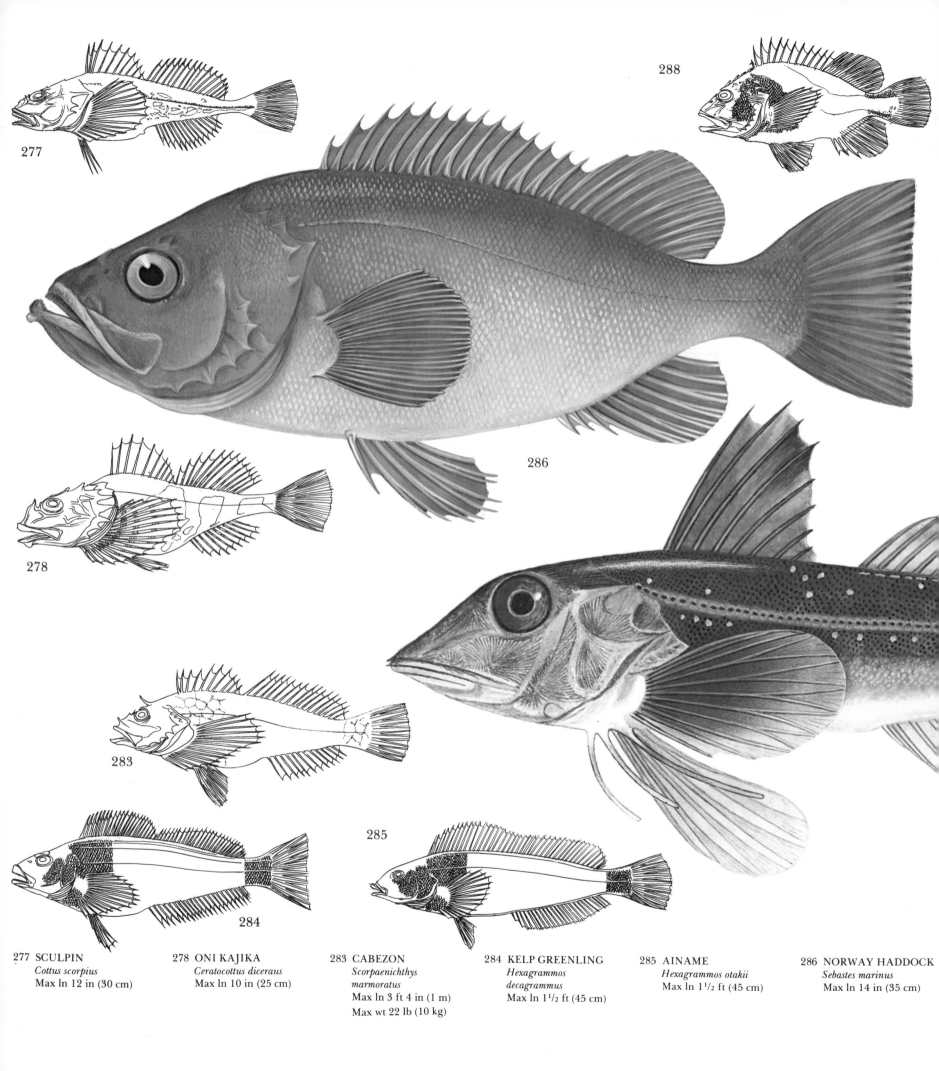

277 SCULPIN
Cottus scorpius
Max ln 12 in (30 cm)

278 ONI KAJIKA
Ceratocottus diceraus
Max ln 10 in (25 cm)

283 CABEZON
Scorpaenichthys marmoratus
Max ln 3 ft 4 in (1 m)
Max wt 22 lb (10 kg)

284 KELP GREENLING
Hexagrammos decagrammus
Max ln 1¹/₂ ft (45 cm)

285 AINAME
Hexagrammos otakii
Max ln 1¹/₂ ft (45 cm)

286 NORWAY HADDOCK
Sebastes marinus
Max ln 14 in (35 cm)

288 CHINA ROCKFISH
Sebastodes nebulosus
Max ln 12 in (30 cm)

289 BOCACCIO
Sebastes paucipinnis
Max ln 36 in (90 cm)
Max wt 22 lb (10 kg)

290 BLACK ROCKFISH
Sebastodes melanops
Max ln 24 in (60 cm)
Max wt 6½ lb (3 kg)

292 ZEBRAFISH
Pterois volitans
Max ln 12 in (30 cm)

293 NORTHERN
SEAROBIN
Prionotus carolinus
Max ln 14 in (36 cm)

294 YELLOW GUNNARD
Trigla lucerna
Max ln 30 in (75 cm)

295 GREY GURNARD
Eutrigla gurnardus
Max ln 18 in (45 cm)

296 RED GURNARD
Aspitrigla cuculus
Max ln 18 in (45 cm)

301 STRIPED SEAROBIN
Prionotus evolans
Max ln 18 in (45 cm)

302 SAND FLATHEAD
Platycephalus arenarius
Max ln 12 in (30 cm)

305 DUSKY FLATHEAD
Platycephalus fuscus
Max ln 3 ft 4 in (1 m)
Max wt 32 lb (14½ kg)

Illustrations for fishes 279,
280, 281, and 282, can be
found on page 92; 287,
297–300 on page 95.

181

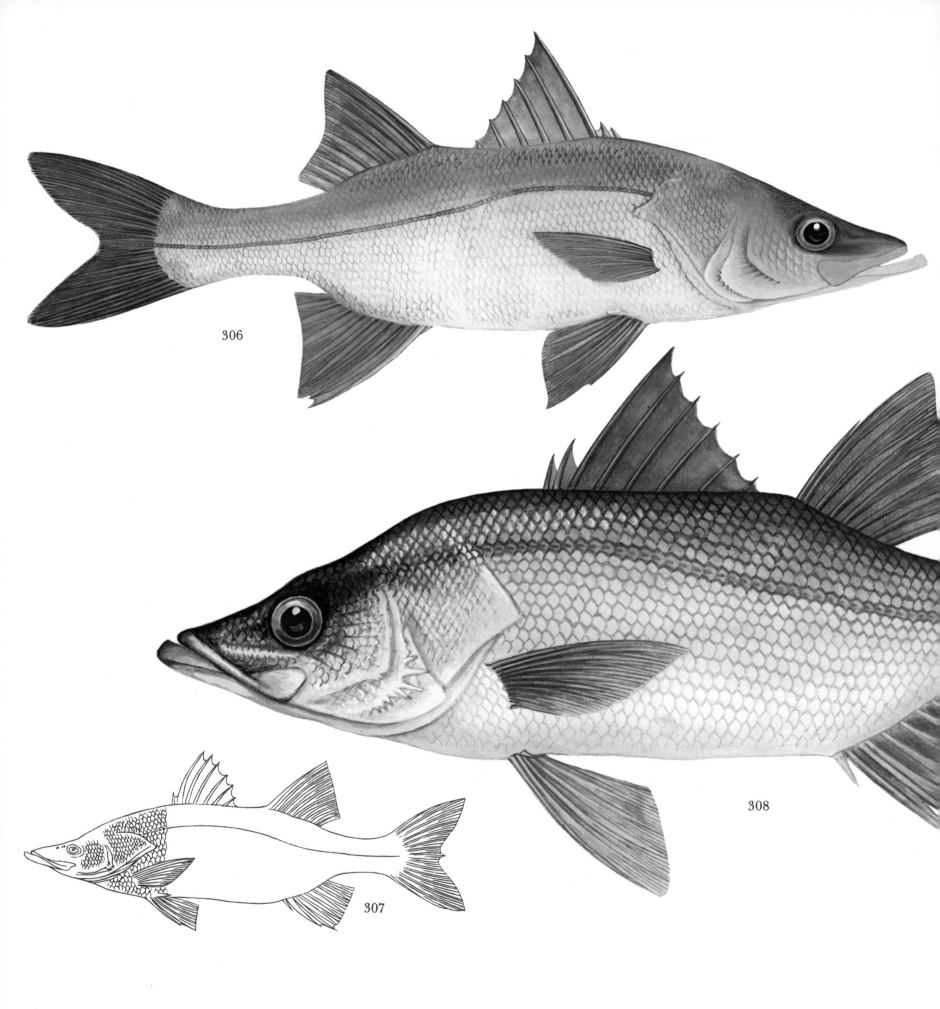

306 SNOOK
Centropomus undecimalis
Max ln 4ft 2 in (1.25 m)
Max wt 50 lb (22½ kg)

307 BLACK SNOOK
Centropomus nigrescens
Max ln 36 in (90 cm)
Max wt 22 lb (10 kg)

308 TARPON SNOOK
Centropomus pectinatus
Max ln 12 in (30 cm)
Max wt 1 lb (½ kg)

309 LITTLE SNOOK
Centropomus parallellus
Max ln 24 in (60 cm)

310 NILE PERCH
Lates niloticus
Max ln 6 ft (1.80 m)
Max wt 300 lb (140 kg)

311 BARRAMUNDI
Lates calcarifer
Max ln 6 ft (1.80 m)
Max wt 600 lb (270 kg)

312 WARSAW GROUPER
Epinephelus nigritus
Max ln 6 ft 8 in (2 m)
Max wt 400 lb (180 kg)

184

313 NASSAU GROUPER
Epinephelus striatus
Max ln 4 ft (1.20 m)
Max wt 55 lb (25 kg)

314 DUSKY PERCH
Epinephelus guaza
Max ln 4 ft 7 in (1.40 m)
Max wt 80 lb (36 kg)

315 RED GROUPER
Epinephelus morio
Max ln 36 in (90 cm)
Max wt 50 lb(23 kg)

316 QUEENSLAND
GROUPER
Epinephelus lanceolatus
Max ln 12 ft (3.7 m)
Max wt 800 lb (360 kg)

317 TIGER GROUPER
Mycteroperca tigris
Max ln 30 in (75 cm)
Max wt 50 lb (22 kg)

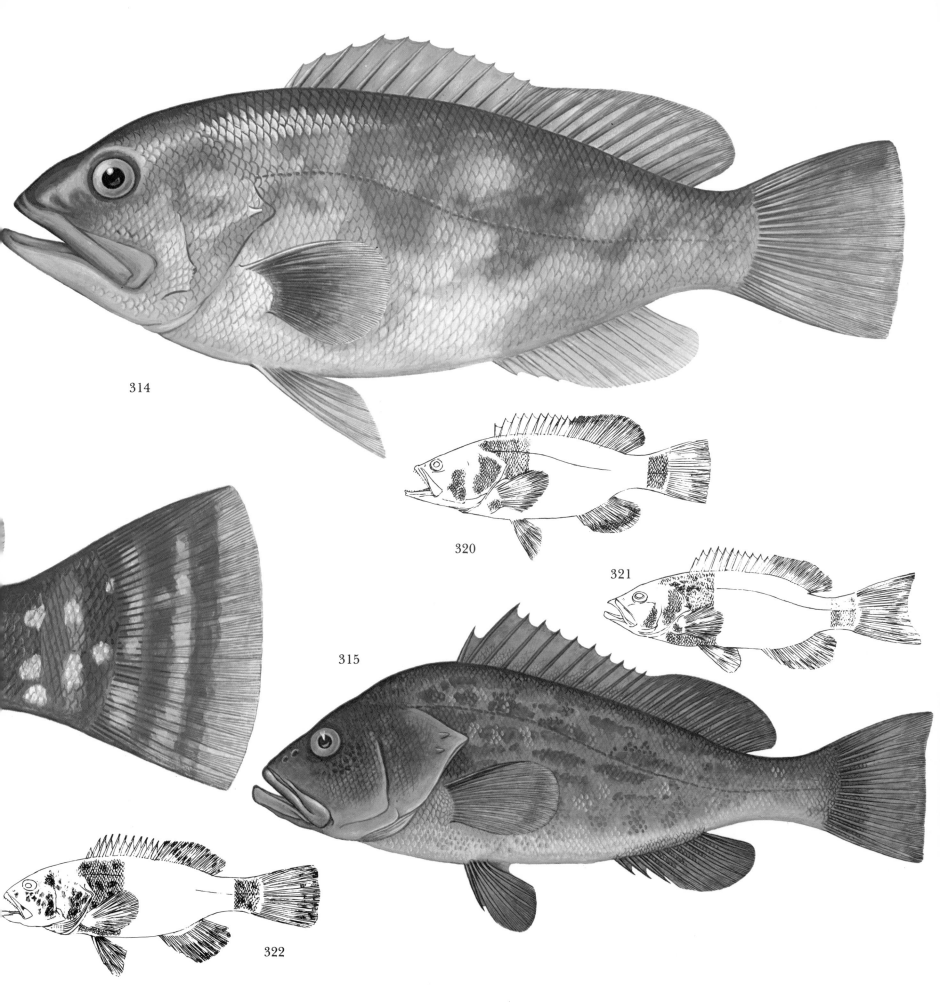

314

315

320

321

322

318 SCAMP
Mycteroperca phenax
Max ln 2 ft (60 cm)

319 MAHATA
Epinephelus septemfasciatus
Max ln 2 ft (60 cm)

320 BLACK GROUPER
Mycteroperca bonaci
Max ln 3 ft (90 cm)
Max wt 45 lb (20 kg)

321 YELLOWMOUTH
GROUPER
Mycteroperca interstitialis
Max wt 6¾ lb (3 kg)

322 YELLOWFIN
GROUPER
Mycteroperca venenosus
Max wt 15 lb (7 kg)

185

323 RED HIND
Epinephelus guttatus
Max ln 24 in (60 cm)

324 GAG
Mycteroperca microlepis
Max ln 3 ft (90 cm)

325 ROCK COD
Epinephelus tauvinus
Max ln 7 ft 1 in (2.15 m)
Max wt 500 lb (225 kg)

326 ROCK HIND
Epinephelus adscensionis
Max ln 24 in (60 cm)
Max wt 10 lb (4½ kg)

327 CABRILLA
Paralabrax clathratus
Max ln 20 in (50 cm)
Max wt 11 lb (5 kg)

328 MARBLED GROUPER
Dermatolepis inermis
Max ln 1 ft (30 cm)

329 JEWFISH
    Epinephelus itajara
    Max ln 8 ft (2.40 m)
    Max wt 700 lb (315 kg)

330 CALIFORNIA BLACK
    SEA BASS
    Stereolepis gigas
    Max ln 7 ft (2 m)

331 **WHITE BASS**
Morone chrysops
Max wt 3 lb (1½ kg)

332 **STRIPED BASS**
Morone saxatilis
Max ln 72 in (1.8 m)
Max wt 125 lb (56 kg)

333 **WHITE PERCH**
Morone americana
Max ln 20 in (50 cm)
Max wt 4¾ lb (2¼ kg)

334 **YELLOW BASS**
Morone mississippiensis
Max ln 12 in (30 cm)
Max wt 2.2 lb (1 kg)

335 **BASS(EUROPEAN)**
Morone labrax
Max ln 3ft 4 in (1 m)

336 **SEA BASS**
Centropristis striatus
Max ln 1 ft 6 in (45 cm)
Max wt 8 lb (3.5 kg)

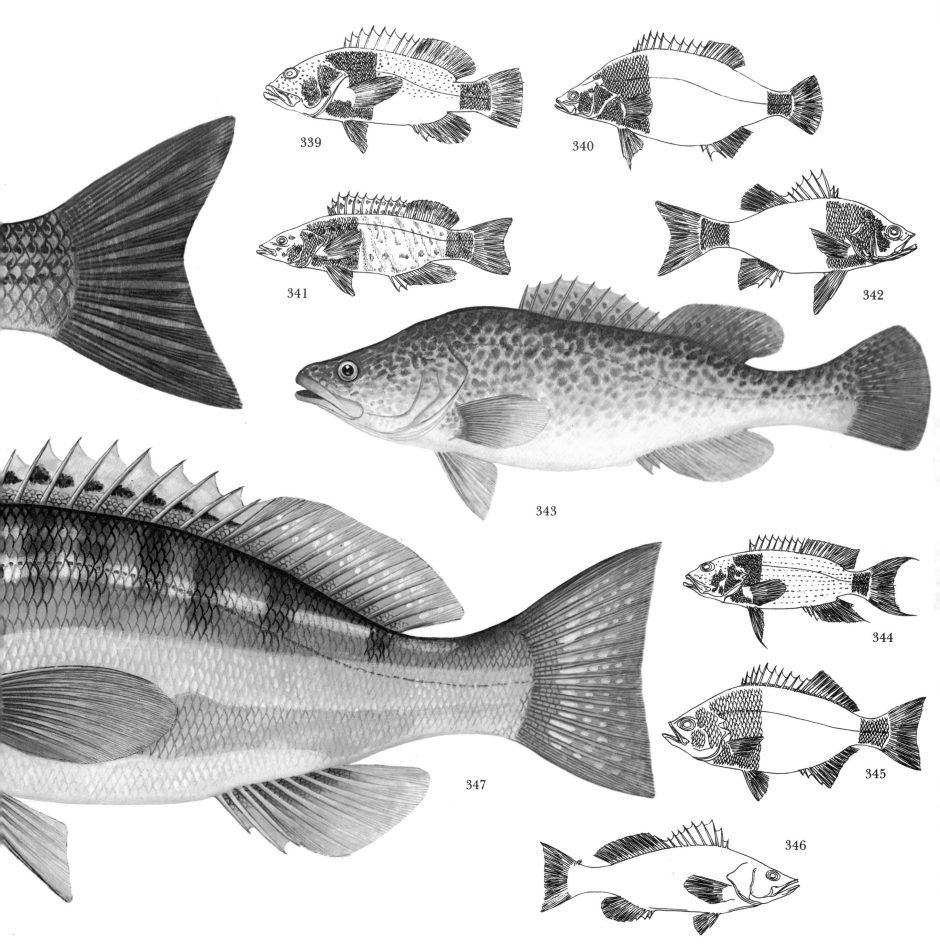

337 WRECKFISH
Polyprion americanus
Max ln 6 ft 8 in (2 m)
Max wt 220 lb (100 kg)

339 CONEY
Epinephelus fulvus
Max ln 16 in (40 cm)
Max wt 3¹/₃ lb (1¹/₂ kg)

340 GOLDEN PERCH
Plectroplites ambiguus
Max ln 30 in (75 cm)
Max wt 60 lb (27 kg)

344 LUNAR-TAILED
ROCK COD
Variola louti
Max ln 30 in (75 cm)

341 HARLEQUIN BASS
Serranus tigrinus
Max ln 4 in (10 cm)

345 ROCK FLAGTAIL
Kuhlia rupestris
Max ln 18 in (45 cm)
Max wt 3 lb (1.3 kg)

342 ESTUARY PERCH
Percalates colonorum
Max ln 24 in (60 cm)
Max wt 11 lb (5 kg)

346 PACIFIC FLAGTAIL
Kuhlia taeniura
Max ln 8 in (20 cm)

343 MURRAY COD
Maccullochella peeli
Max ln 6 ft (1.80 cm)
Max wt 200 lb (90 kg)

347 COMBER
Serranus cabrilla
Max ln 16 in (40 cm)

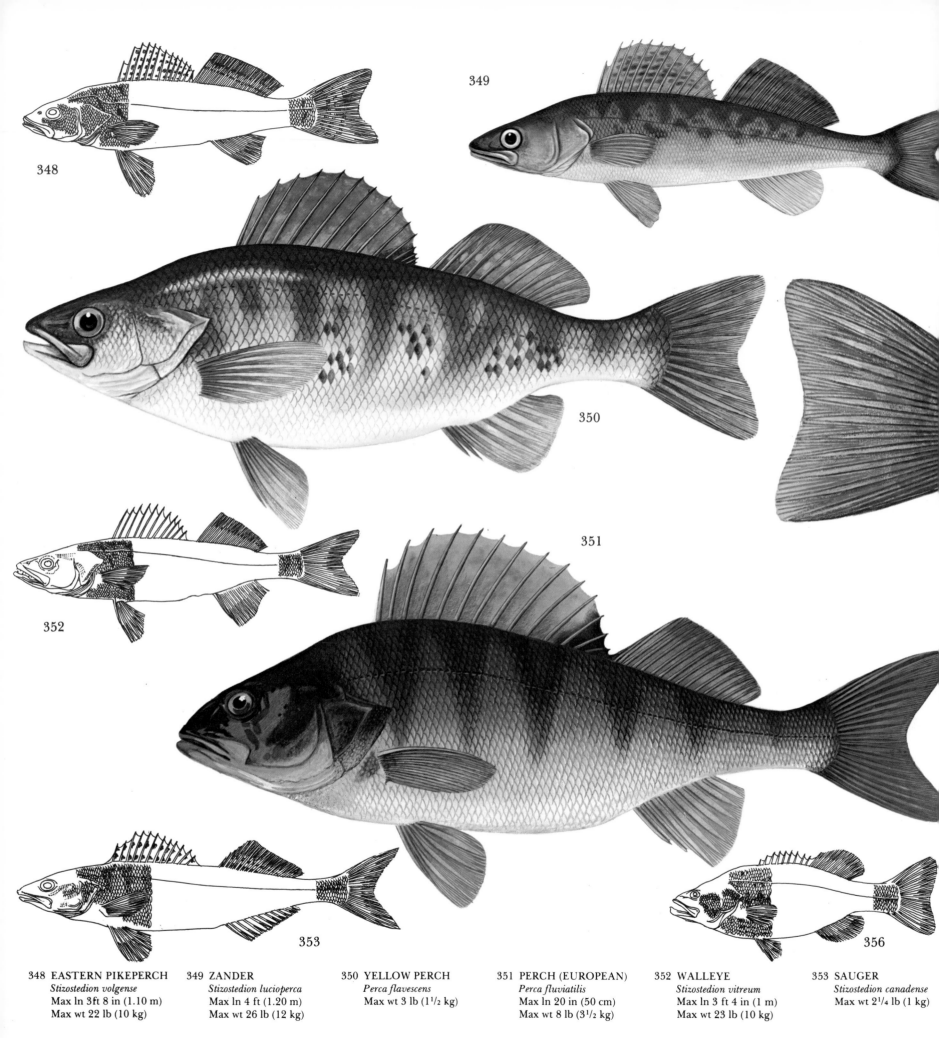

348 **EASTERN PIKEPERCH**
Stizostedion volgense
Max ln 3ft 8 in (1.10 m)
Max wt 22 lb (10 kg)

349 **ZANDER**
Stizostedion lucioperca
Max ln 4 ft (1.20 m)
Max wt 26 lb (12 kg)

350 **YELLOW PERCH**
Perca flavescens
Max wt 3 lb (1½ kg)

351 **PERCH (EUROPEAN)**
Perca fluviatilis
Max ln 20 in (50 cm)
Max wt 8 lb (3½ kg)

352 **WALLEYE**
Stizostedion vitreum
Max ln 3 ft 4 in (1 m)
Max wt 23 lb (10 kg)

353 **SAUGER**
Stizostedion canadense
Max wt 2¼ lb (1 kg)

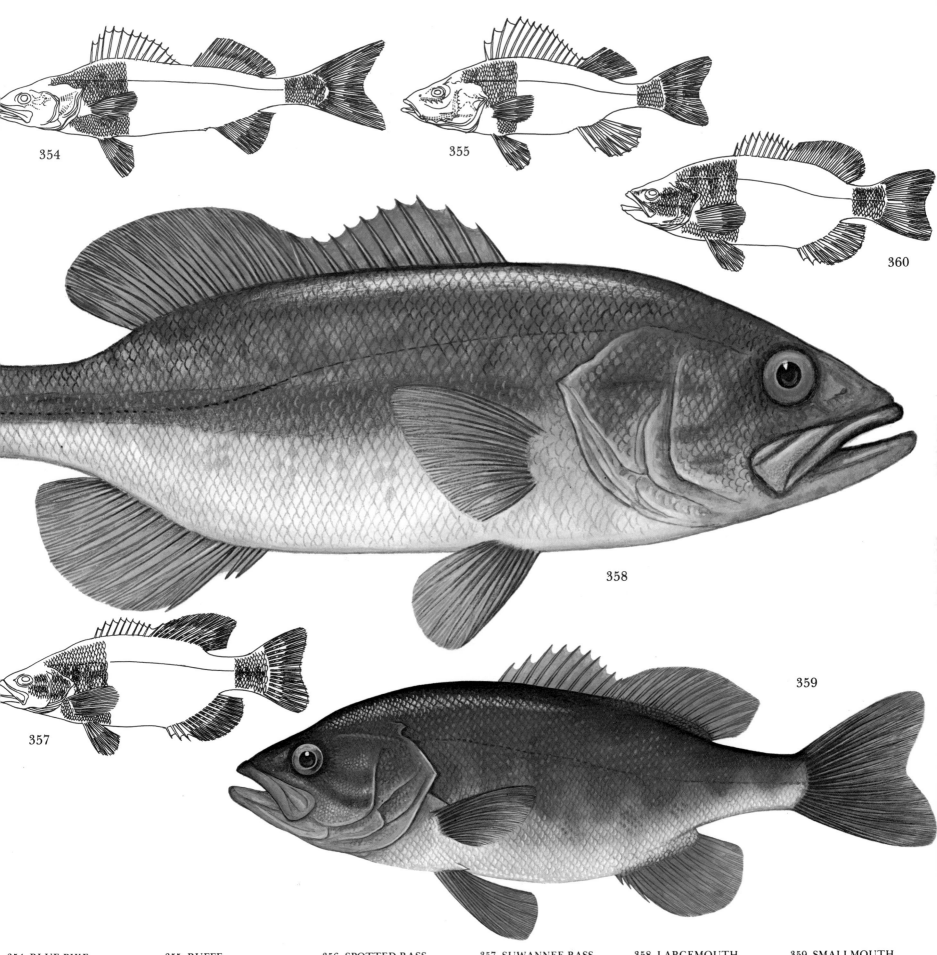

354 BLUE PIKE
Stizostedion vitreum glaucum
Max ln 13 in (33 cm)
Max wt 1 lb (½ kg)

355 RUFFE
Gymnocephalus cernua
Max ln 10 in (25 cm)
Max wt 14 oz (400 g)

356 SPOTTED BASS
Micropterus punctulatus
Max ln 15 in (37.5 cm)
Max wt 2.2 lb (1 kg)

357 SUWANNEE BASS
Micropterus notius
Max ln 15 in (35 cm)

358 LARGEMOUTH
BLACK BASS
Micropterus salmoides
Max ln 28 in (70 cm)
Max wt 22 lb (10 kg)

359 SMALLMOUTH
(BLACK) BASS
Micropterus dolomieui
Max wt 10 lb (4½ kg)

360 REDEYE BASS
Micropterus coosae
Max ln 18 in (45 cm)
Max wt 4½ lb (2 kg)

191

361   **BLUEGILL**
Lepomis macrochirus
Max ln 14 in (35 cm)
Max wt 1½ lb (¾ kg)

362   **YELLOW BELLY**

Max ln 8 in (20 cm)

363   **PUMPKINSEED**
Lepomis gibbosus
Max ln 9 in (23 cm)
Max wt ½ lb (¼ kg)

364   **WARMOUTH BASS**
Lepomis gulosus
Max ln 12 in (30 cm)
Max wt 2.2 lb (1 kg)

365   **WHITE CRAPPIE**
Pomoxis annularis
Max ln 12 in (30 cm)
Max wt 1 lb (½ kg)

366   **REDBREAST SUNFISH**
Lepomis auritus
Max ln 7 in (18 cm)
Max wt 1 lb (½ kg)

367 ROCK BASS
Ambloplites rupestris
Max ln 12 in (30 cm)
Max wt 2¹/₄ lb (1 kg)

368 BLACK CRAPPIE
Pomoxis nigromaculatus
Max ln 14 in (36 cm)
Max wt 2 lb (1 kg)

369 SACRAMENTO
PERCH
Archoplites interruptus
Max ln 24 in (60 cm)
Max wt 4 lb (1³/₄ kg)

370 COUCH'S SEA BREAM
Pagrus pagrus
Max ln 30 in (75 cm)

371 RED PORGY
Pagrus sedecim
Max ln 20 in (50 cm)
Max wt 4¹/₂ lb (2 kg)

372 SCUP
Stenotomus chrysops
Max ln 18 in(45 cm)
Max wt 4 lb (1³/₄ kg)

374 TROPICAL BLACK
BREAM
Acanthopagrus berda
Max ln 30 in (75 cm)
Max wt 15 lb (7 kg)

375 SOUTHERN BREAM
Acanthopagrus australis
Max ln 22 in (55 cm)
Max wt 7 lb (3¹/₄ kg)

376 JAPANESE BREAM
Acanthopagrus latus
Max ln 18 in (45 cm)

377 JOLTHEAD PORGY
Calamus bajonado
Max ln 24 in (60 cm)
Max wt 14 lb (6¹/₄ kg)

378 GRASS PORGY
Calamus arctifrons
Max ln 2 ft (60 cm)

379 BLACK BISKOP
Cymatoceps nasutus
Max wt 120 lb (54½ kg)

380 SHEEPSHEAD
Archosargus
probatocephalus
Max ln 30 in (75 cm)

381 WHITE BISKOP
Sparodon durbanensis
Max ln 3ft 4 in (1 m)
Max wt 70 lb (32 kg)

382 TARWHINE
·Rhabdosargus sarba
Max ln 20 in (50 cm)
Max wt 5½ lb (2½ kg)

383 YELLOWFIN BREAM
Mylio australis
Max ln 22 in (55 cm)
Max wt 7 lb (3¼ kg)

384 RED SEA BREAM
Pagellus bogaraveo
Max ln 20 in (50 cm)

391 SNAPPER
(AUSTRALIAN)
Chrysophrys auratus
Max ln 4 ft (1.20 m)
Max wt 40 lb (18 kg)

392 GILTHEAD
Sparus auratus
Max ln 28 in (70 cm)

385 BLACK BREAM
Spondyliosoma cantharus
Max ln 20 in (50 cm)

386 JOHN BROWN
Gymnocrotaphus curvidens
Max ln 14 in (35 cm)

387 BLUE HOTTENTOT
Pachymetopon grande
Max ln 24 in (60 cm)
Max wt 15 lb (7 kg)

388 WHITE STEENBRAS
Pagellus lithognathus
Max ln 6 ft (1.80 m)
Max wt 30 lb (14 kg)

389 PANDORA
Pagellus erythrinus
Max ln 24 in (60 cm)

390 HOTTENTOT
Pachymetopon blochi
Max ln 18 in (45 cm)
Max wt 9 lb (4 kg)

393 RED STEENBRAS
Dentex rupestris
Max ln 6 ft (1.80 m)
Max wt 154 lb (70 kg)

394 DENTEX
Dentex dentex
Max ln 3 ft 4 in (1 m)

395 TILEFISH
*Lopholatilus
chamaeleonticeps*
Max ln 3 ft 6 in (1.05 m)
Max wt 55 lb (25 kg)

396 AUSTRALIAN
WHITING
Sillago ciliata
Max ln 18 in (45 cm)
Max wt 2¼ lb (1 kg)

397 SPOTTED WHITING
Sillaginodes punctatus
Max ln 27 in (70 cm)
Max wt 4½ lb (2 kg)

398 OCEAN WHITEFISH
Caulolatilus princeps
Max ln 3 ft 4 in (1 m)

399 ATLANTIC
   HORSE-EYE JACK
   Caranx latus
   Max ln 30 in (75 cm)
   Max wt 8½ lb (3¾ kg)
196

400 BLUE RUNNER
   Caranx crysos
   Max ln 20 in (50 cm)
   Max wt 4 lb (1¾ kg)

401 CREVALLIE JACK
   Caranx hippos
   Max ln 2½ ft (75 cm)
   Max wt 20 lb (9 kg)

402 GIANT TREVALLY
   Caranx sexfasciatus
   Max wt 110 lb (50 kg)

403 KING TREVALLY
   Caranx speciosus
   Max ln 3 ft 4 in (1 m)

404 YELLOW JACK
   Caranx bartholomaei
   Max ln 30 in (75 cm)
   Max wt 15½ lb (7 kg)

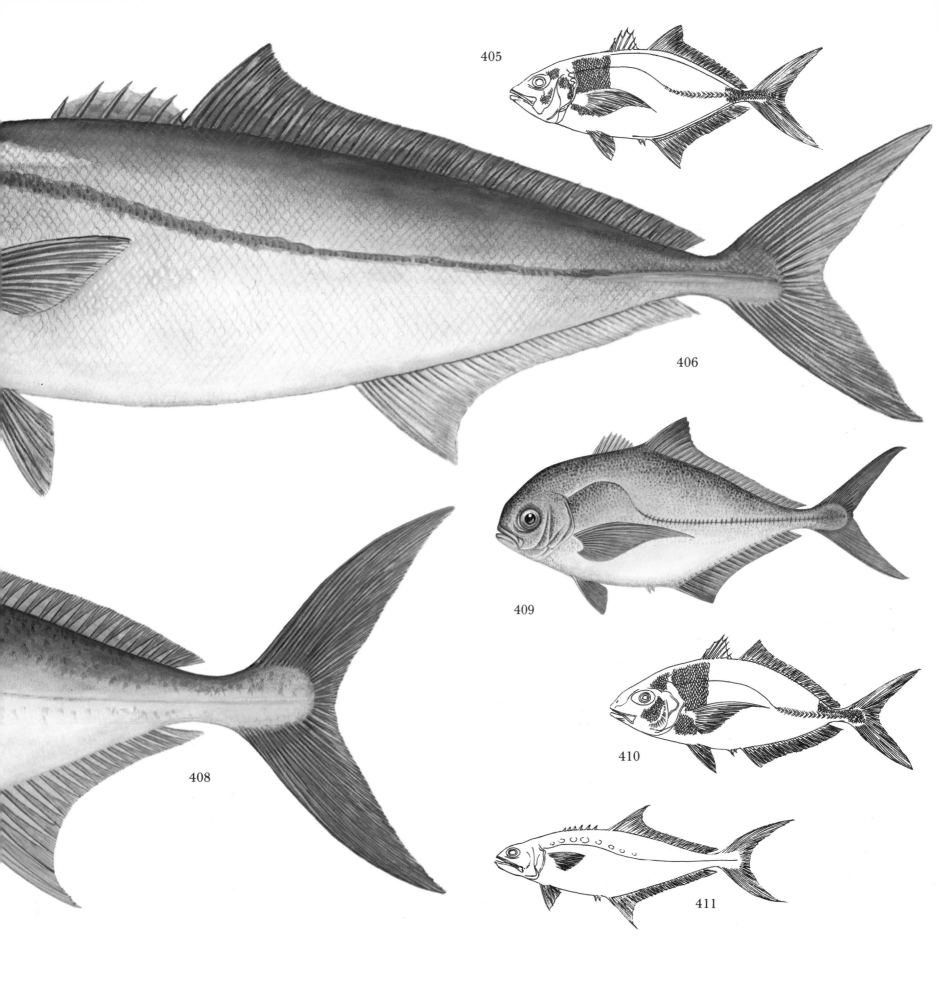

405 **BAR JACK**
Caranx ruber
Max ln 24 in (60 cm)
Max wt 15 lb (7 kg)

406 **AMBERJACK**
Seriola dumerili
Max wt 150 lb (68 kg)

408 **ALMACO JACK**
Seriola rivoliana
Max ln 4 ft (1.20 m)
Max wt 50 (22½ kg)

409 **BLUNTNOSE JACK**
(ATLANTIC)
Hemicaranx amblyrhynchus
Max ln 24 in (60 cm)

410 **TREVALLY**
Usacaranx georgianus
Max ln 36 in (90 cm)
Max wt 11 lb (5 kg)

411 **QUEENFISH**
Chorinemus lysan
Max ln 20 in (50 cm)

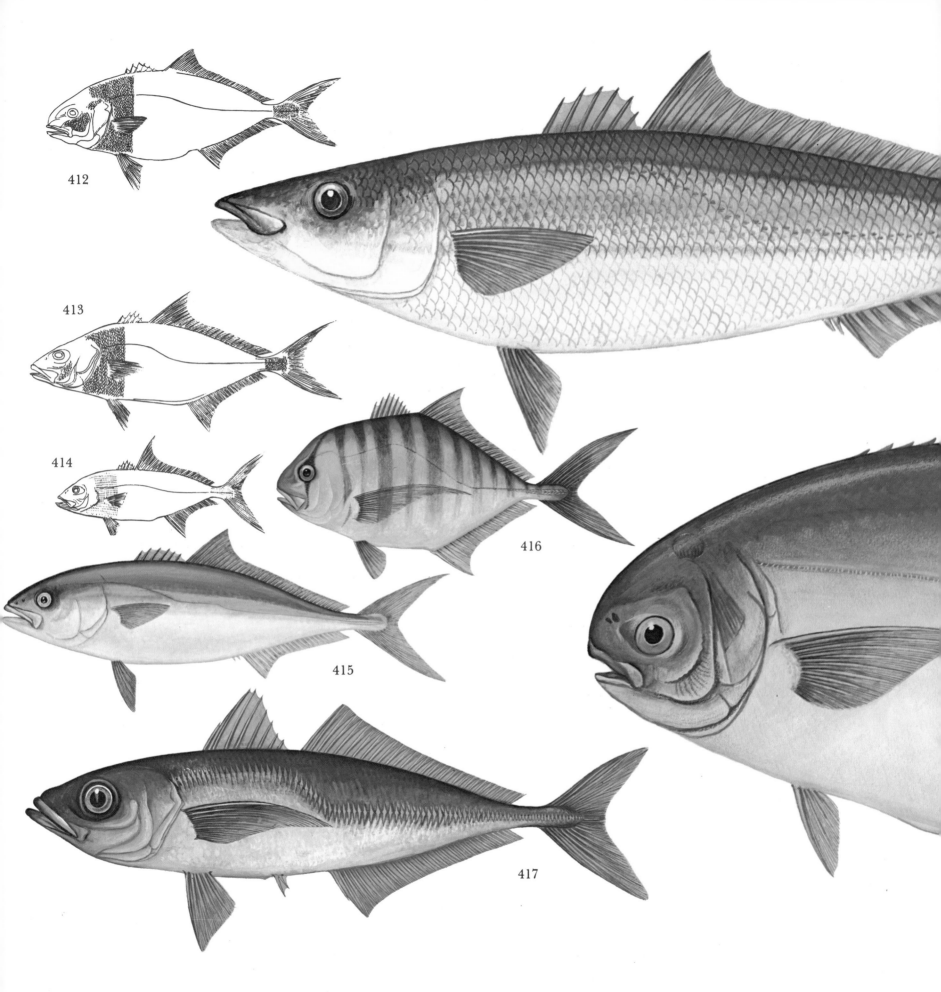

412 **BANDED
RUDDERFISH**
Seriola zonata
Max ln 24 in (60 cm)
Max wt 9 lb (4 kg)

198

413 **PACIFIC AMBERJACK**
Seriola colburni
Max wt 110 lb (50 kg)

414 **BURI**
Seriola quinqueradiata
Max ln 3 ft (1 m)

415 **YELLOWTAIL**
Seriola lalandi
Max wt 150 lb (68 kg)

416 **DORADE**
Gnathanodon speciosus
Max ln 3 ft 4 in (1 m)
Max wt 35 lb (16 kg)

417 **SCAD**
Trachurus trachurus
Max ln 20 in (50 cm)

418 MA-AJI
Trachurus japonicus
Max ln 2 ft (60 cm)

419 PACIFIC JACK
MACKEREL
Trachurus symmetricus
Max ln 2 ft (60 cm)

420 RAINBOW RUNNER
Elagatis bipinnulatus
Max ln 5 ft 10 in (1.80 m)
Max wt 30 lb (13½ kg)

421 AFRICAN POMPANO
Alectis crinitus
Max ln 36 in (90 cm)
Max wt 33 lb (15 kg)

422 PILOT FISH
Naucrates ductor
Max ln 24 in (60 cm)

423 COMMON POMPANO
Trachinotus carolinus
Max ln 18 in (45 cm)
Max wt 8 lb (3½ kg)

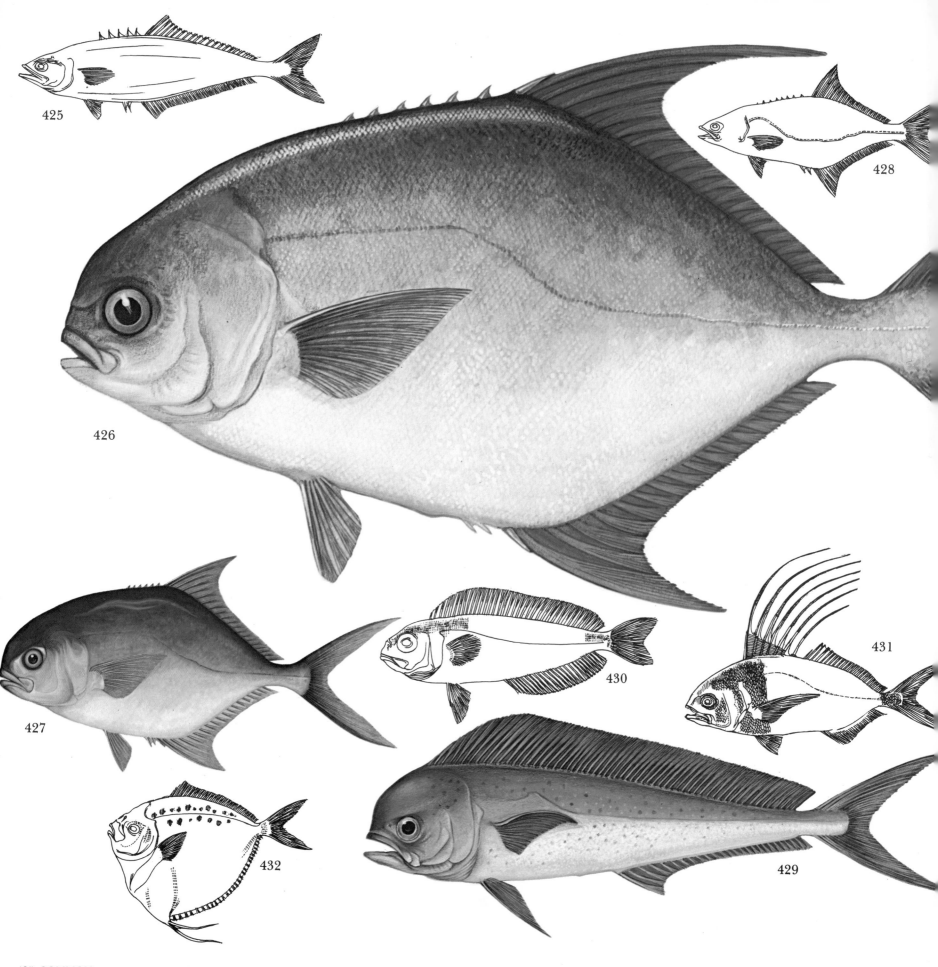

425 COMMON
   LEATHERJACKET
   Oligoplites saurus
   Max ln 12 in (30 cm)

426 ATLANTIC PERMIT
   Trachinotus falcatus
   Max ln 3 ft 4 in (1 m)
   Max wt 50 lb (22.5 kg)

427 PALOMETA
   Trachinotus goodei
   Max ln 20 in (50 cm)
   Max wt 3½ lb (1½ kg)

428 LEERFISH
   Hypacanthus amius
   Max ln 6 ft (1.80 m)
   Max wt 150 lb (70 kg)

429 DOLPHIN
   Coryphaena hippurus
   Max ln 6 ft (1.80 m)
   Max wt 70 lb (32 kg)

430 POMPANO DOLPHIN
   Coryphaena equisetis
   Max wt 6.6 lb (3 kg)

431 ROOSTERFISH
Nematistius pectoralis
Max ln 4 ft (1.20 m)
Max wt 75 lb (34 kg)

432 MOONFISH
Mene maculata
Max ln 12 in (30 cm)

433 ATLANTIC BUMPER
Chloroscombrus chrysurus
Max ln 8 in (20 cm)

434 BLUEFISH
Pomatomus saltatrix
Max ln 4 ft (1.20 m)
Max wt 31 lb (14 kg)

435 COBIA
Rachycentron canadum
Max wt 150 lb (70 kg)

436 REMORA
Remora remora
Max ln 18 in (45 cm)

437 LOOKDOWN
Selene vomer
Max ln 12 in (30 cm)

438

439

440

442

441

438 GREY SNAPPER
Lutjanus griseus
Max ln 36 in (90 cm)
Max wt 18 lb (8 kg)
202

439 BLACKFIN SNAPPER
Lutjanus buccanella
Max ln 12 in (30 cm)
Max wt 2.2 lb (1 kg)

440 CUBERA SNAPPER
Lutjanus cyanopterus
Max ln 4 ft (1.20 m)
Max wt 100 lb (45 kg)

441 LANE SNAPPER
Lutjanus synagris
Max wt 4¹/₂ lb (2 kg)

442 DOG SNAPPER
Lutjanus jocu
Max wt 25 lb (11 kg)

443 RED SNAPPER
Lutjanus campechanus
Max ln 3 ft (90 cm)
Max wt 35 lb (16 kg)

443 MAHOGANY SNAPPER
Lutjanus mahogani
Max ln 15 in (38 cm)

445 MUTTON SNAPPER
Lutjanus analis
Max ln 30 in (75 cm)
Max wt 25 lb (11¼ kg)

446 SCHOOLMASTER
Lutjanus apodus
Max wt 8 lb (3½ kg)

447 RED EMPEROR
Lutjanus sebae
Max wt 44 lb (20 kg)

448 YELLOWTAIL SNAPPER
Ocyurus chrysurus
Max ln 24 in (60 cm)
Max wt 6½ lb (3 kg)

449 TRIPLETAIL
Lobotes surinamensis
Max ln 3 ft 4 in (1 m)
Max wt 26½ lb (12 kg)

450 KAHAWAI;
AUSTRALIAN
SALMON
Arripis trutta
Max ln 36 in (90 cm)
Max wt 21 lb (9½ kg)

451 BLUESTRIPED
GRUNT
Haemulon sciurus
Max ln 18 in (45 cm)
Max wt 2¼ lb (1 kg)

452 TOMTATE
Haemulon aurolineatum
Max ln 10 in (25 cm)

453 FRENCH GRUNT
Haemulon flavolineatum
Max ln 12 in (30 cm)

454 CAESAR GRUNT
Haemulon carbonarium
Max ln 14 in (35 cm)

5 BROWN SWEETLIPS
Plectorhynchus nigrus
Max ln 24 in (60 cm)
Max wt 12 lb (5½ kg)

456 SPANISH GRUNT
Haemulon macrostomum
Max ln 18 in (45 cm)

457 GOLDEN SPOTTED
SWEETLIPS
Plectorhynchus pictus
Max ln 26 in (65 cm)

458 MARGATE
Haemulon album
Max ln 30 in (75 cm)

459 PORKFISH
Anisotremuss virginicus
Max ln 14 in (35 cm)

461 SAILOR'S CHOICE
Haemulon parra
Max ln 10 in (25 cm)

460 JAVELIN FISH
Pomadasys hasta
Max ln 24 in (60 cm)

462 WHITE GRUNT
Haemulon plumieri
Max ln 18 in (45 cm)
Max wt 4 lb (1¾ kg)

463 SPOTFIN CROAKER
Roncador stearnsi
Max ln 36 in (90 cm)
Max wt 12 lb (5½ kg)

464 ATLANTIC CROAKER
Micropogon undulatus
Max ln 15 in (38 cm)
Max wt 4 lb (1¾ kg)

465 WEAKFISH
Cynoscion regalis
Max ln 37 in (93 cm)
Max wt 20 lb (9 kg)

466 WHITE SEA BASS
Cynoscion nobilis
Max ln 5 ft 6 in (1.65 m)

467 SPOTTED WEAKFISH
Cynoscion nebulosus
Max ln 36 in (90 cm)
Max wt 16 lb (7¼ kg)

468 TOTUAVA
Cynoscion macdonaldi
Max wt 200 lb (90 kg)

469 CORVINA
Cynoscion reticulatus
Max ln 36 in (90 cm)

470 ORANGEMOUTH CORVINA
Cynoscion xanthulus
Max ln 6 ft (1.80 m)
Max wt 125 lb (56 kg)

471 RED DRUM
Sciaenops ocellatus
Max wt 80 lb (36 kg)

472 BLACK DRUM
Pogonias cromus
Max wt 150 lb (68 kg)

473 FRESHWATER DRUM
Aplodinotus grunniens
Max wt 24 lb (11 kg)

474 SILVER SEA TROUT
Cynoscion nothus
Max wt 3 lb (1½ kg)

475 **SPOT**
Leiostomus xanthurus
Max ln 10 in (25 cm)
Max wt 1.1 lb (½ kg)

476 **MEAGRE**
Argyrosomus regium
Max ln 6 ft 8 in (2 m)

477 **MULLOWAY**
Sciaena antarctica
Max ln 6 ft (1.80 m)
Max wt 125 lb (56 kg)

478 **KABELJOU**
Sciaena hololepidota
Max ln 6 ft (1.80 m)
Max wt 150 lb (70 kg)

479 **CALIFORNIA
CORBINA**
Menticirrhus undulatus
Max ln 20 in (50 cm)
Max wt 7 lb (3 kg)

480 **NORTHERN
KINGFISH**
Menticirrhus saxatilis
Max ln 12 in (30 cm)

496 PEACOCK BASS
Cichla ocellaris
Max ln 32 in (80 cm)
Max wt 20 lb (9 kg)

497 CORAL FISH
Abudefduf sordidus
Max ln 8 in (20 cm)

498 GARIBALDI
Hypsypops rubicundus
Max ln 14 in (35 cm)

499 SERGEANT MAJOR
Abudefduf saxatilis
Max ln 6 in (15 cm)

500 TARAKIHI
Nemadactylus macropterus
Max ln 3 ft 4 in (1 m)
Max wt 20 lb (9 kg)

502 STRIPED
TRUMPETER
Latris lineata
Max ln 4 ft (1.20 m)

509 STRIPED
BARRACUDA
Sphyraena obtusata
Max ln 16 in (40 cm)
Max wt 25 lb (12 kg)

510 PICK-HANDLE
BARRACUDA
Sphyraena jello
Max ln 6¹/₂ ft (2 m)

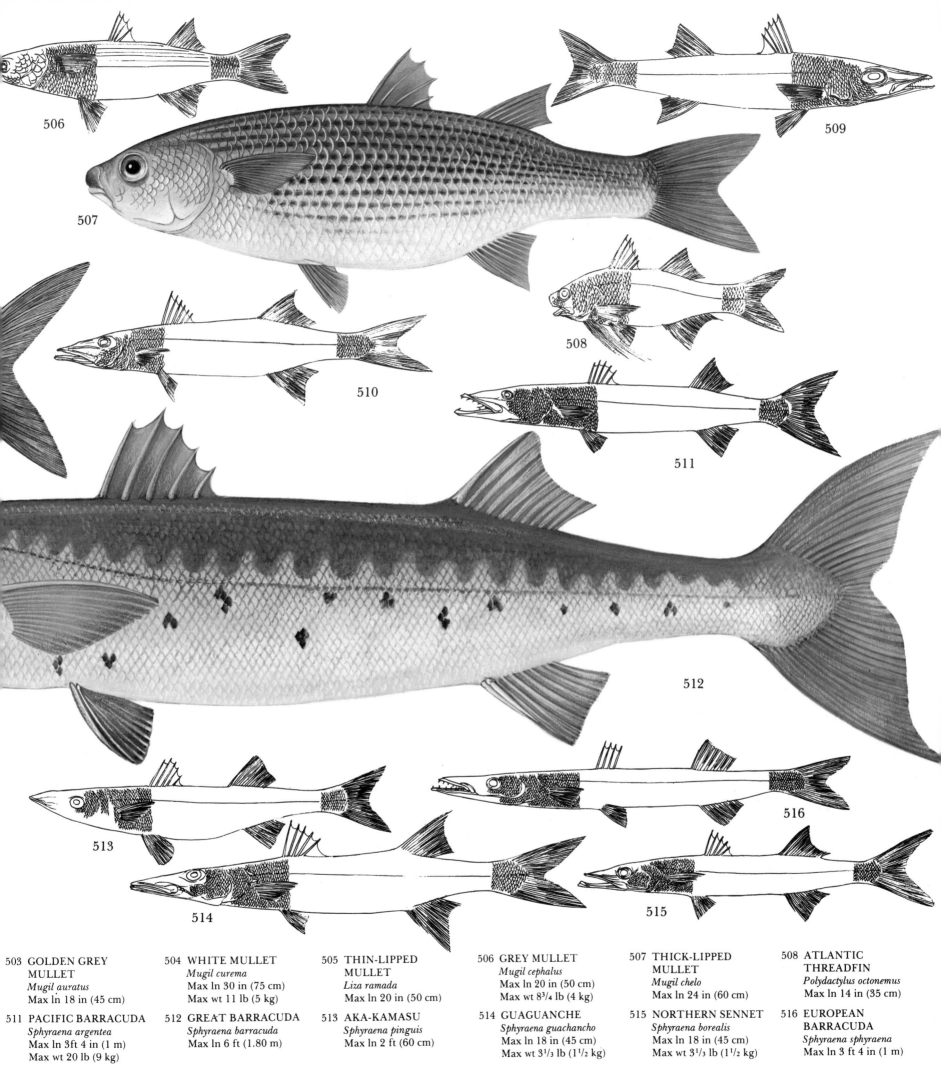

503 GOLDEN GREY
MULLET
Mugil auratus
Max ln 18 in (45 cm)

504 WHITE MULLET
Mugil curema
Max ln 30 in (75 cm)
Max wt 11 lb (5 kg)

505 THIN-LIPPED
MULLET
Liza ramada
Max ln 20 in (50 cm)

506 GREY MULLET
Mugil cephalus
Max ln 20 in (50 cm)
Max wt 8³/₄ lb (4 kg)

507 THICK-LIPPED
MULLET
Mugil chelo
Max ln 24 in (60 cm)

508 ATLANTIC
THREADFIN
Polydactylus octonemus
Max ln 14 in (35 cm)

511 PACIFIC BARRACUDA
Sphyraena argentea
Max ln 3ft 4 in (1 m)
Max wt 20 lb (9 kg)

512 GREAT BARRACUDA
Sphyraena barracuda
Max ln 6 ft (1.80 m)

513 AKA-KAMASU
Sphyraena pinguis
Max ln 2 ft (60 cm)

514 GUAGUANCHE
Sphyraena guachancho
Max ln 18 in (45 cm)
Max wt 3¹/₃ lb (1¹/₂ kg)

515 NORTHERN SENNET
Sphyraena borealis
Max ln 18 in (45 cm)
Max wt 3¹/₃ lb (1¹/₂ kg)

516 EUROPEAN
BARRACUDA
Sphyraena sphyraena
Max ln 3 ft 4 in (1 m)

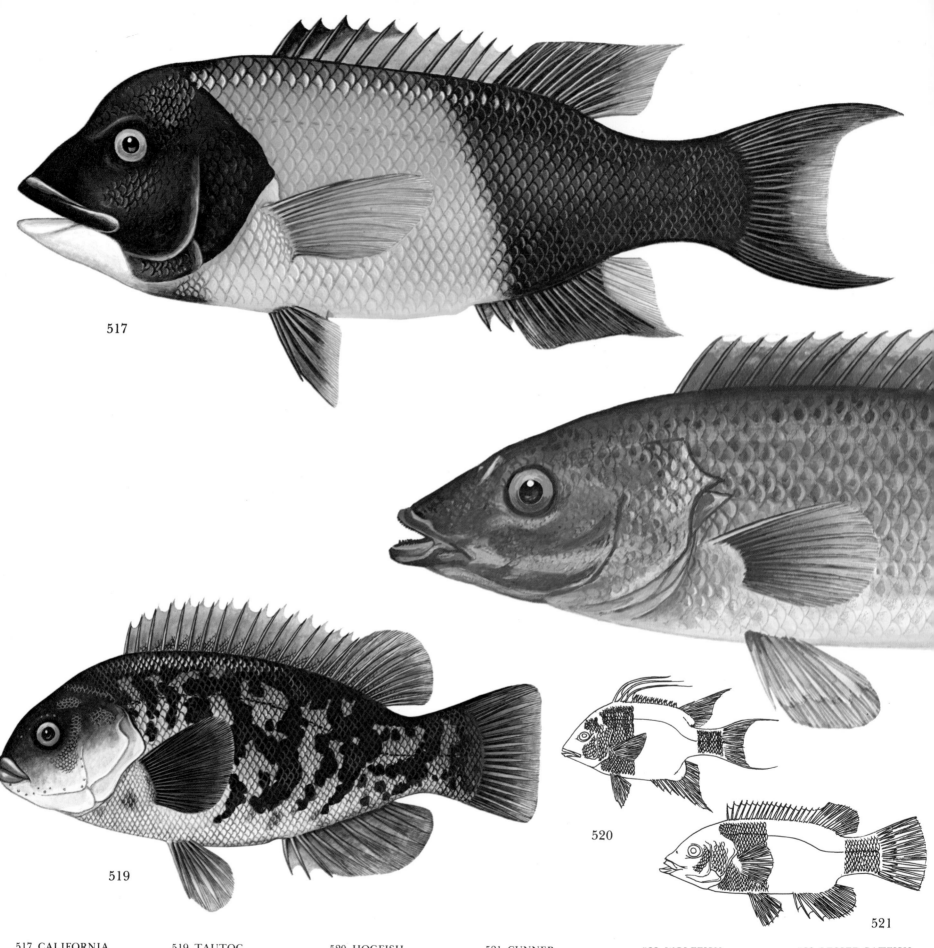

517

520

519

521

517 CALIFORNIA
SHEEPHEAD
Pimelometopon pulchrum
Max wt 20 lb (9 kg)

519 TAUTOG
Tautoga onitis
Max ln 3 ft (90 cm)
Max wt 22 lb (10 kg)

520 HOGFISH
Lachnolaimus maximus
Max ln 30 in (75 cm)
Max wt 44 lb (20 kg)

521 CUNNER
Tautogolabrus adspersus
Max ln 17 in (43 cm)
Max wt 3¼ lb (1½ kg)

522 WOLFFISH
Anarhichas lupus
Max ln 5 ft (1.50 m)
Max wt 40 lb (18 kg)

523 LESSER CATFISH
Anarhichas minor
Max ln 5 ft in (1.50 m)
Max wt 17 lb (8 kg)

524 **SAND LANCE**
Ammodytes tobianus
Max ln 8 in (20 cm)

525 **AMERICAN SAND LANCE**
Ammodytes americanus
Max ln 7 in (17½ cm)

529 **BALLAN WRASSE**
Labrus bergylta
Max wt 13 lb (6 kg)

530 **CUCKOO WRASSE**
Labrus mixtus
Max ln 14 in (35 cm)

531 **CORKWING**
Crenilabrus melops
Max ln 8 in (20 cm)

535 **RAINBOW WRASSE**
Coris julis
Max ln 12 in (30 cm)

536 **BLUE TANG**
Acanthurus coeruleus
Max ln 12 in (30 cm)
Max wt 2¼ lb (1 kg)

537 **LESSER WEEVER**
Trachinus vipera
Max ln 6 in (15 cm)

538 **GREATER WEEVER**
Trachinus draco
Max ln 16 in (40 cm)
Max wt 2¼ lb (1 kg)

539 **BLUE PARROTFISH**
Scarus coeruleus
Max ln 36 in (90 cm)
Max wt 22 lb (10 kg)

Illustrations for fishes number 526, 527, 528, 532, 533, and 534 can be found on page 121.

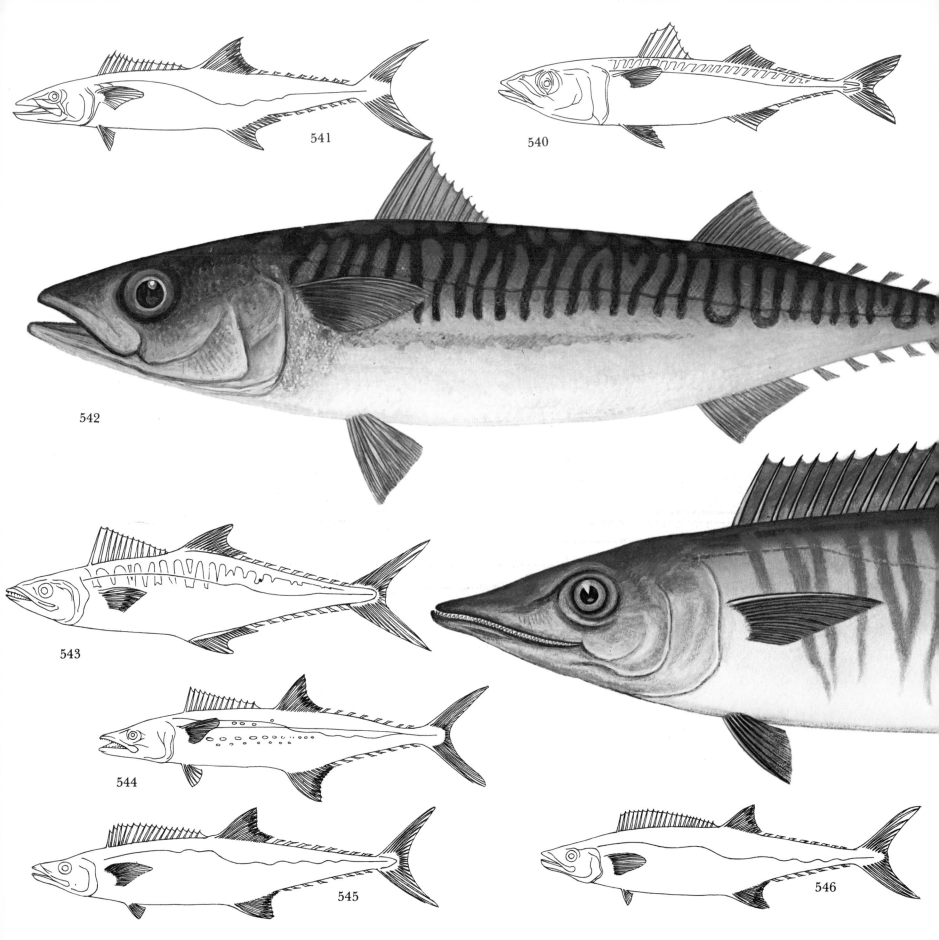

540 CHUB MACKEREL
Scomber japonicus
Max ln 24 in (60 cm)

541 KINGFISH
Scomberomorus cavalla
Max wt 150 lb (70 kg)

542 MACKEREL
Scomber scombrus
Max ln 22 in (55 cm)
Max wt 4½ lb (2 kg)

543 BROAD-BARRED
MACKEREL
*Scomberomorus
semifasciatus*
Max ln 6 ft (1.80 m)
Max wt 100 lb (45 kg)

544 CERO MACKEREL
Scomberomorus regalis
Max ln 36 in (90 cm)
Max wt 22 lb (10 kg)

545 MONTEREY SPANISH
MACKEREL
Scomberomorus concolor
Max ln 7 ft (2 m)
Max wt 60 lb (30 kg)

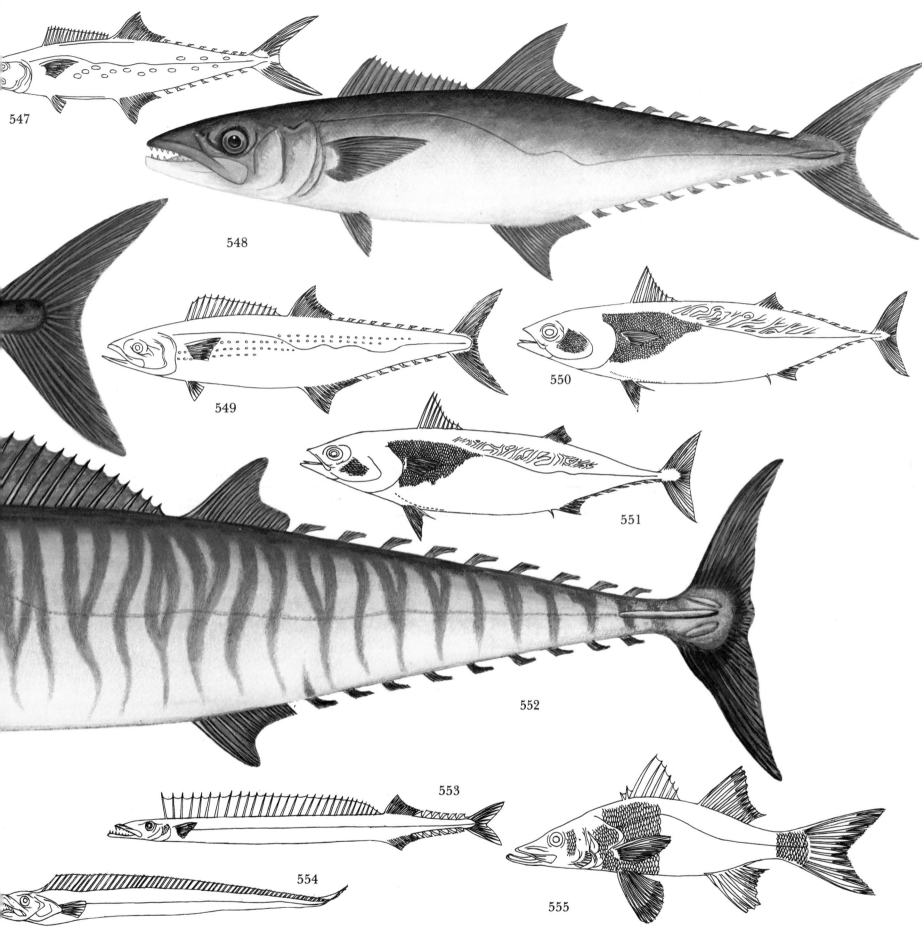

46 SIERRA MACKEREL
Scomberomorus sierra
Max ln 3 ft (1 m)

547 SPANISH MACKEREL
Scomberomorus maculatus
Max ln 36 in (90 cm)
Max wt 11 lb (5 kg)

548 TANGUIGUE
Scomberomorus commersoni
Max ln 6 ft (1.80 m)

549 SPOTTED MACKEREL
Scomberomorus niphonius
Max ln 3 ft (1 m)

550 FRIGATE MACKEREL
Auxis thazard
Max ln 30 in (75 cm)
Max wt 6 lb (2^3/$_4$ kg)

551 BULLET MACKEREL
Auxis rochei
Max ln 24 in (60 cm)
Max wt 11 lb (5 kg)

552 WAHOO
Acanthocybium solanderi
Max wt 160 lb (72 kg)

553 SNAKE MACKEREL
Gempylus serpens
Max ln 20 in (50 cm)

554 ATLANTIC CUTLASSFISH
Trichiurus lepturus
Max ln 4 ft (1.20 m)
Max wt 4^1/$_2$ lb (2 kg)

555 SNOEK
Thyrsites atun
Max ln 4^1/$_2$ ft (1.35 m)
Max wt 11 lb (5 kg)

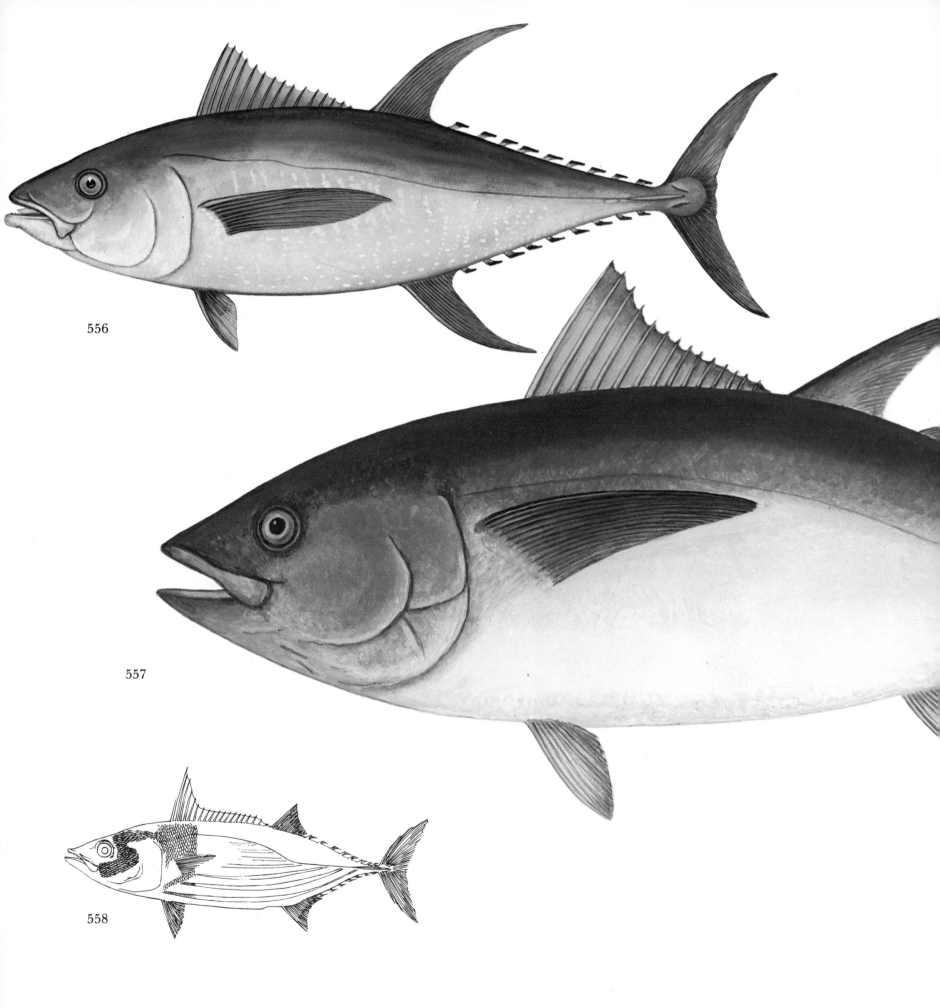

556

557

558

556 YELLOWFIN TUNA
Thunnus albacares
Max ln 9 ft (2.75 m)
Max wt 400 lb (180 kg)

557 BLUEFIN TUNA
Thunnus thynnus
Max ln 10 ft (3 m)
Max wt 1,500 lb (680 kg)

558 SKIPJACK TUNA
Euthynnus pelamis
Max ln 3 ft 4 in (1 m)
Max wt 50 lb (22½ kg)

559 BIGEYE TUNA
Thunnus obesus
Max ln 7 ft 9 in (2.35 m)
Max wt 435 lb (200 kg)

561 ALBACORE
Thunnus alalunga
Max ln 4 ft 2 in (1.25 m)
Max wt 72 lb (32 kg)

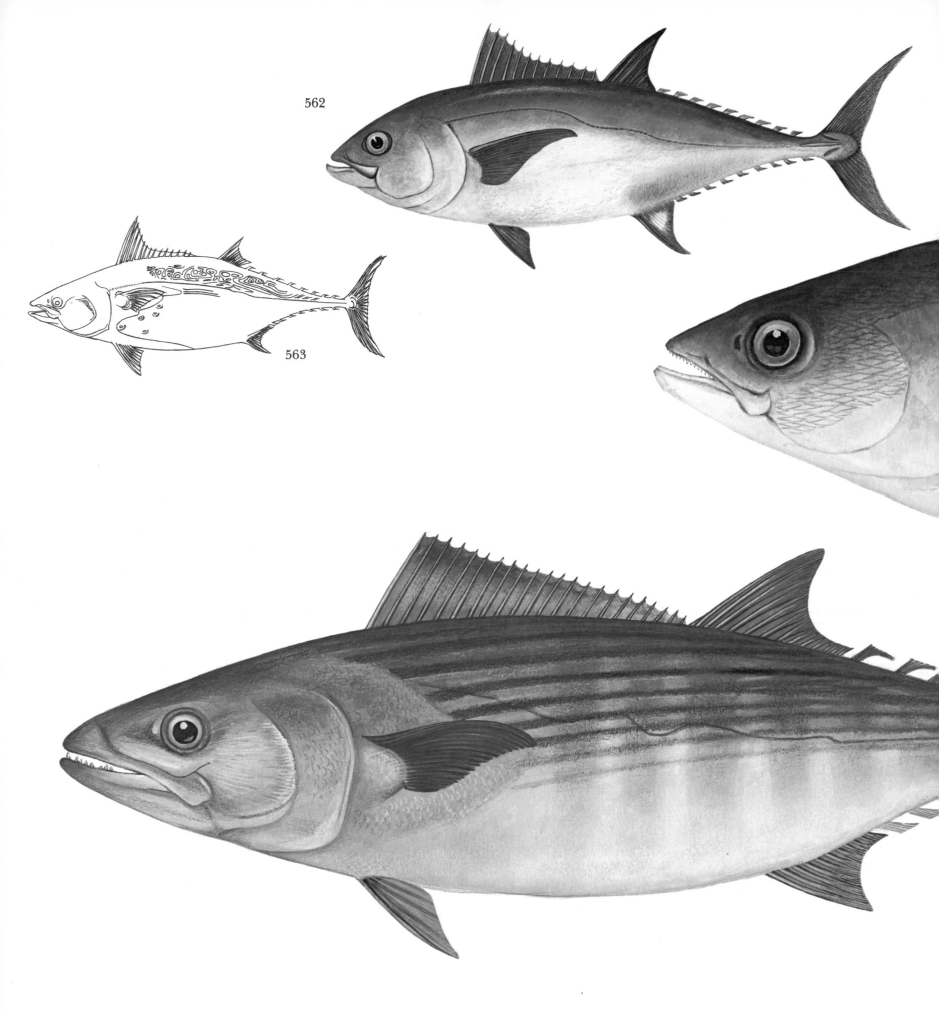

562 BLACKFIN TUNA
Thunnus atlanticus
Max ln 30 in (75 cm)
Max wt 24 lb (11 kg)

563 LITTLE TUNNY
Euthynnus alletteratus
Max ln 30 in (75 cm)

565 KAWAKAWA
Euthynnus affinis
Max ln 3 ft (1 m)
Max wt 22 lb (10 kg)

566 DOGTOOTH TUNA
Gymnosarda nuda
Max ln 6 ft (1.80 m)
Max wt 155 lb (70 kg)

567 STRIPED BONITO
Sarda orientalis
Max ln 2³/₄ ft (80 cm)
Max wt 6¹/₂ lb (3 kg)

568 ATLANTIC BONITO
Sarda sarda
Max ln 36 in (90 cm)

569 PLAIN BONITO
Orcynopsis unicolor
Max ln 3¹/₂ ft (1 m)

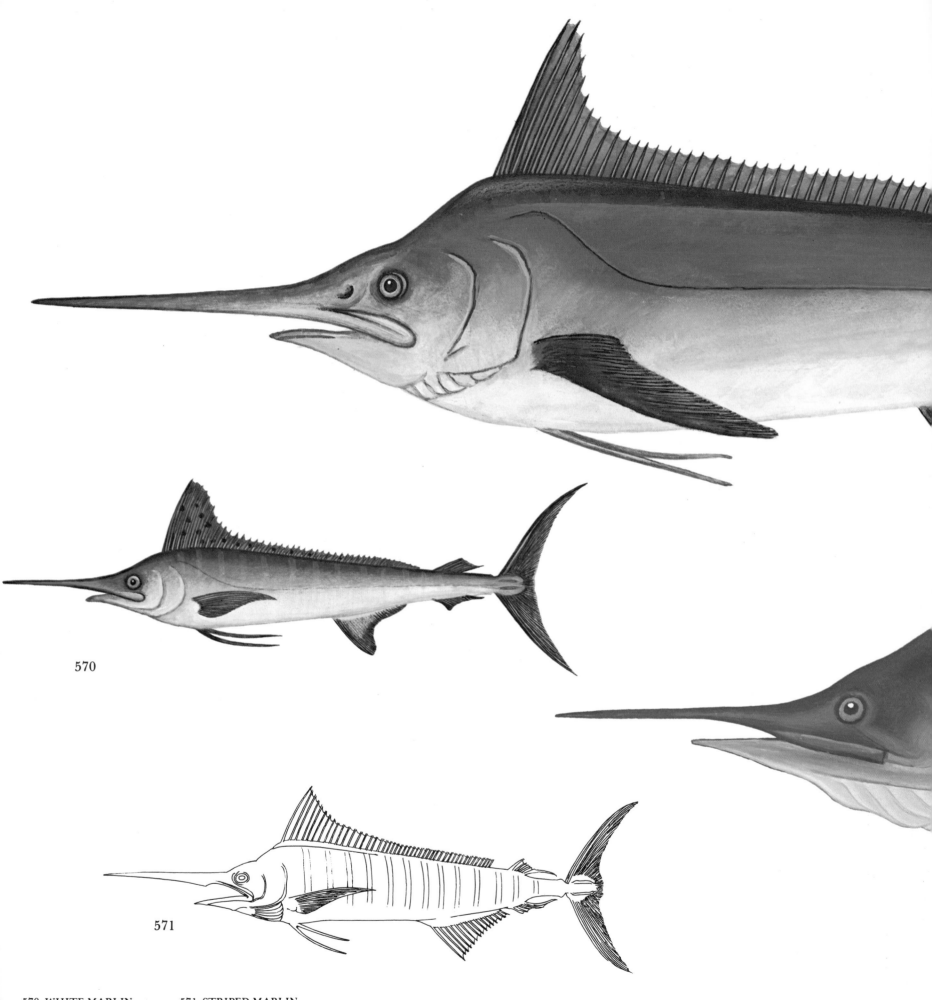

570

571

570 WHITE MARLIN
Tetrapturus albidus
Max ln 9 ft (2.75 m)
Max wt 160 lb (73 kg)

571 STRIPED MARLIN
Tetrapturus audax
Max ln 14 ft (4 m)
Max wt 800 lb (365 kg)

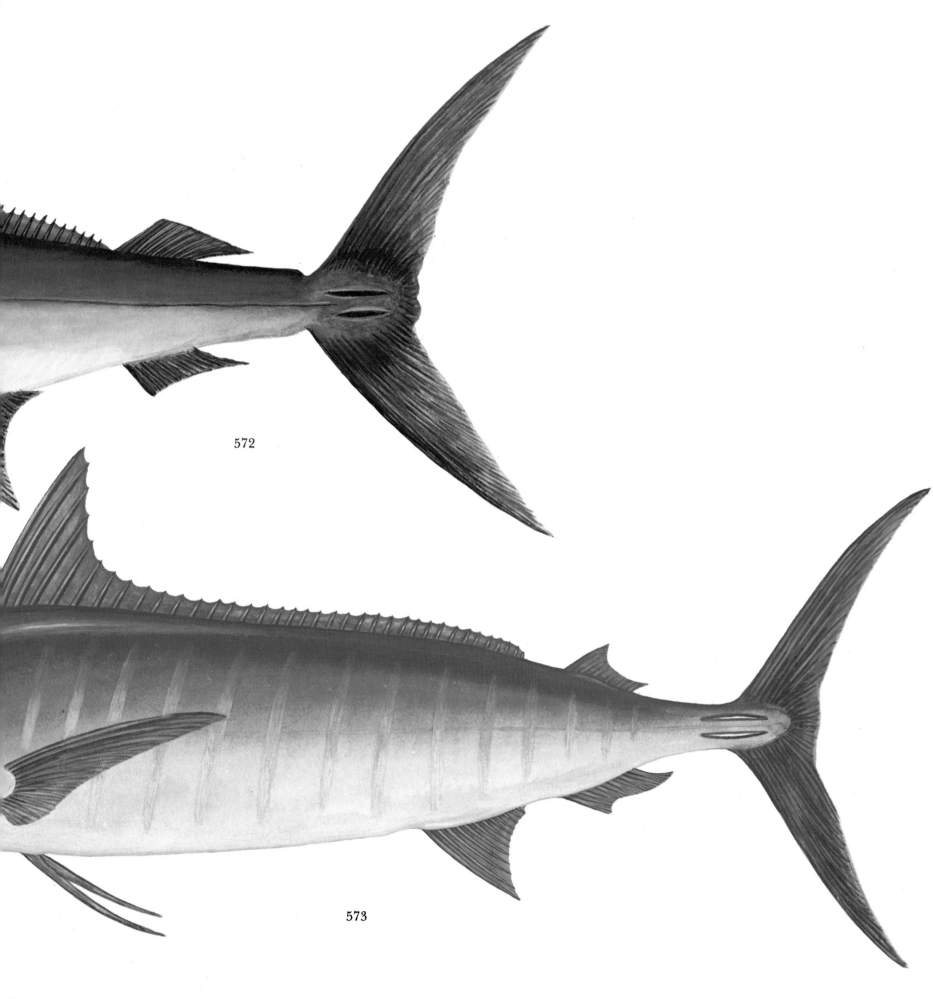

572 **BLACK MARLIN**
Makaira indica
Max wt 2,500 lb (1,125 kg)

573 **BLUE MARLIN**
Makaira nigricans
Max wt 2,000 lb (910 kg)

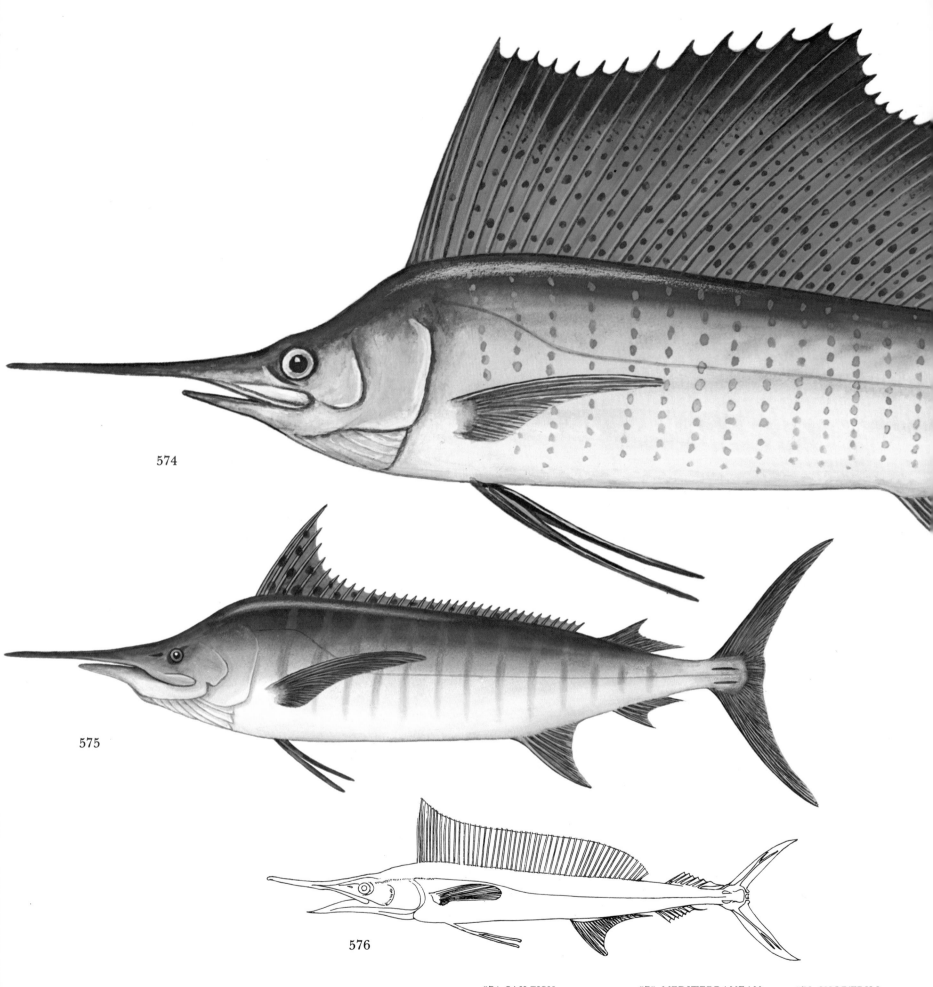

574 SAILFISH
Istiophorus platypterus
Max ln 8 ft (2.50 m)
Max wt 240 lb (110 kg)

575 MEDITERRANEAN SPEARFISH
Tetrapturus belone
Max ln 10 ft (3 m)
Max wt 110 lb (50 kg)

576 SHORTBILL SPEARFISH
Tetrapturus augustirostris
Max ln 6 ft (1.80 m)
Max wt 110 lb (50 kg)

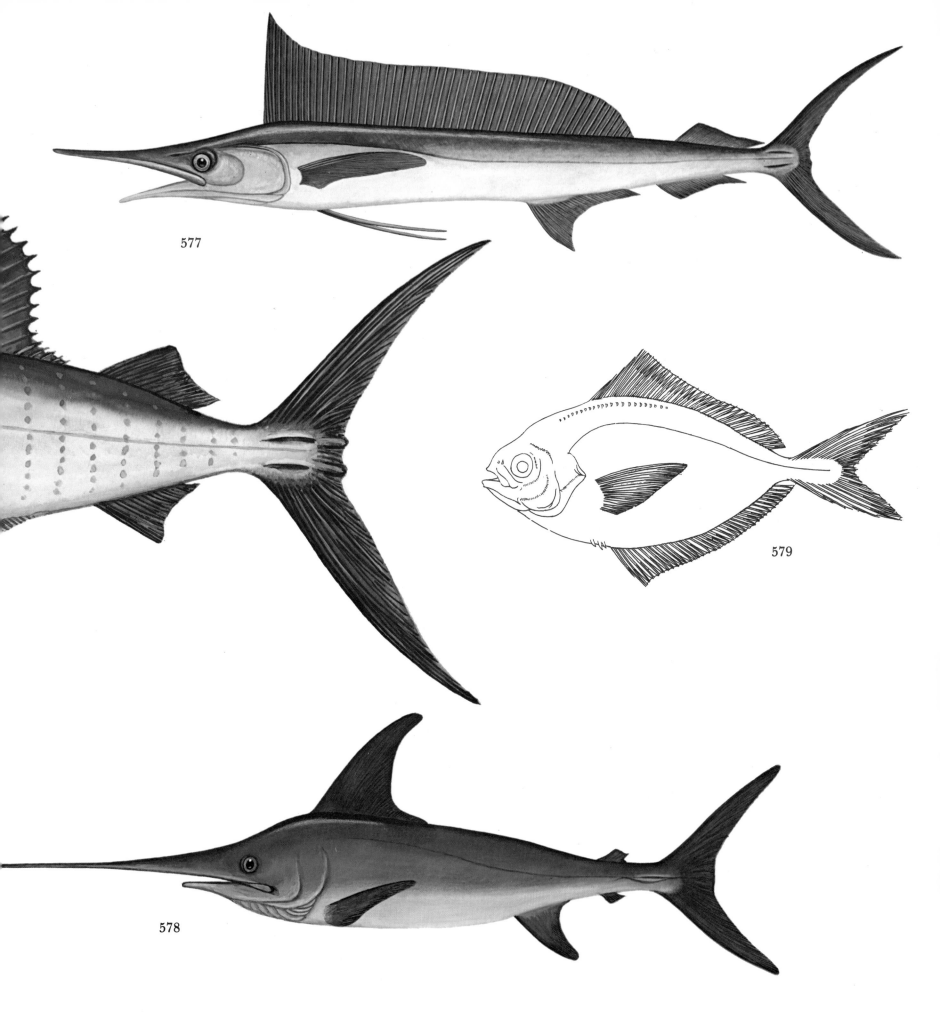

577 LONGBILL
SPEARFISH
Tetrapturus pfluegeri
Max ln 6¹/₂ ft (2 m)
Max wt 65 lb (30 kg)

578 SWORDFISH
Xiphias gladius
Max ln 20 ft (6 m)
Max wt 1,500 lb (680 kg)

579 BUTTERFISH
Peprilus thriacanthus
Max ln 12 in (30 cm)
Max wt 1.1 lb (¹/₂ kg)

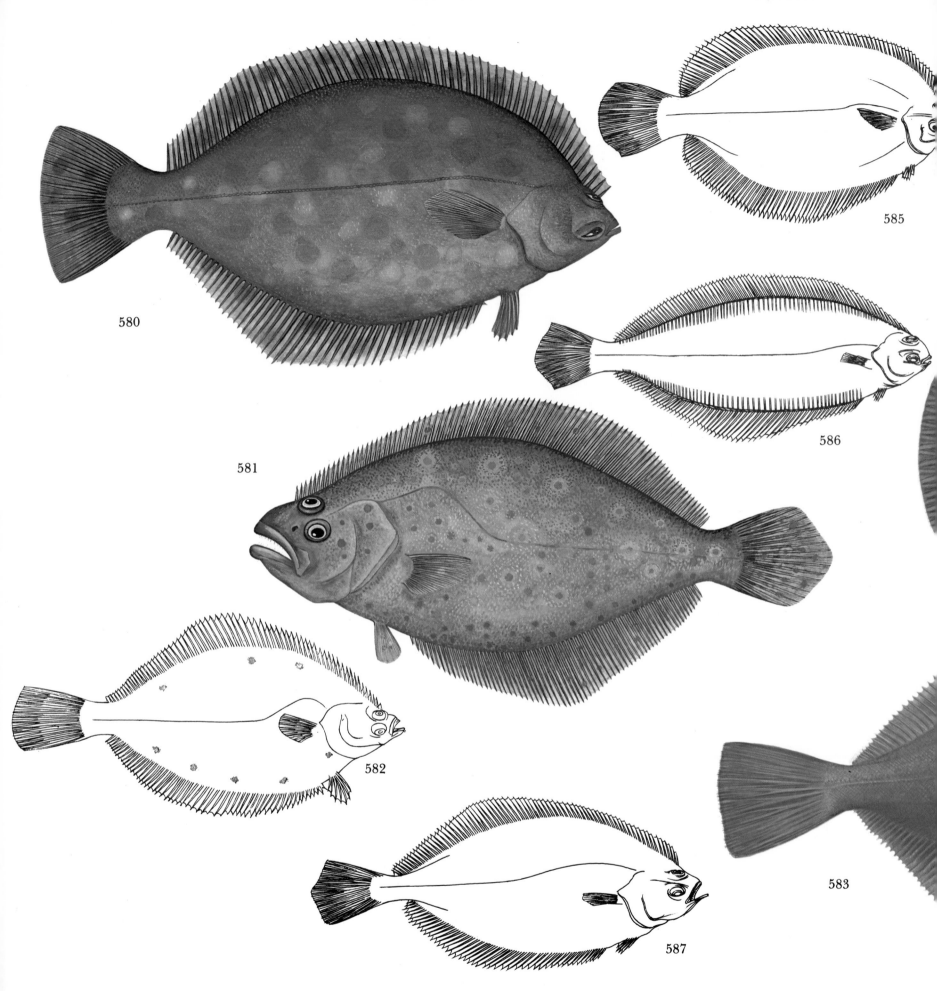

580 **WINTER FLOUNDER**
*Pseudopleuronectes
americanus*
Max ln 25 in (65 cm)
Max wt 8 lb (3¹/₂ kg)
224

581 **SUMMER FLOUNDER**
Paralichthys dentatus
Max ln 37 in (95 cm)

582 **YELLOWTAIL
FLOUNDER**
Limanda ferruginea
Max ln 36 in (90 cm)
Max wt 6.6 lb (3 kg)

583 **DAB**
Limanda limanda
Max ln 16 in (40 cm)
Max wt 4¹/₂ lb (2 kg)

584 **PLAICE**
Pleuronectes platessa
Max ln 36 in (90 cm)
Max wt 13¹/₄ lb (6 kg)

585 **LEMON SOLE**
Microstomus kitt
Max ln 1¹/₂ ft (45 cm)

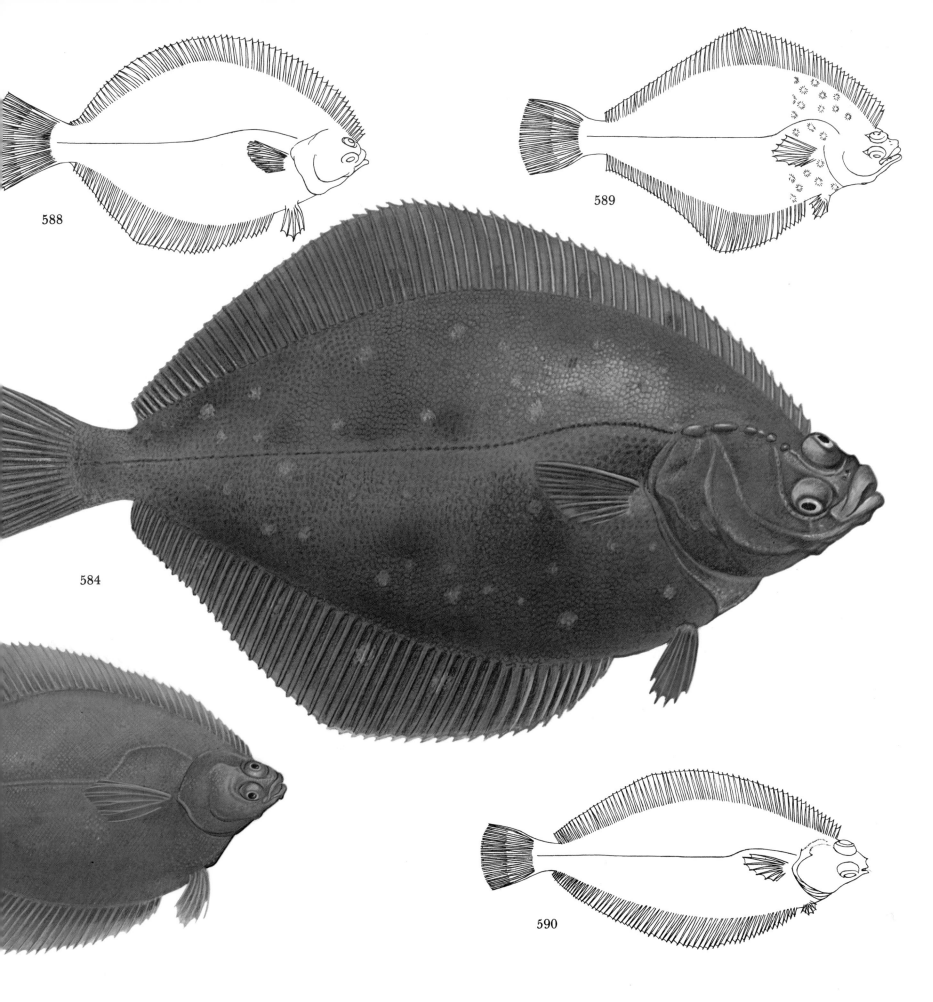

588

589

584

590

586 WITCH
Glyptocephalus cynoglossus
Max ln 1½ ft (45 cm)

587 LONG ROUGH DAB
Hippoglossoides platessoides
Max ln 1¾ ft (55 cm)
Max wt 1½ lb (0.7 kg)

588 COMMON SOLE
Solea solea
Max ln 26 in (65 cm)

589 BUTTER SOLE
Isopsetta isolepis
Max ln 15 in (38 cm)
Max wt 4½ lb (2 kg)

590 DOVER SOLE
Microstomus pacificus
Max ln 30 in (75 cm)
Max wt 11 lb (5 kg)

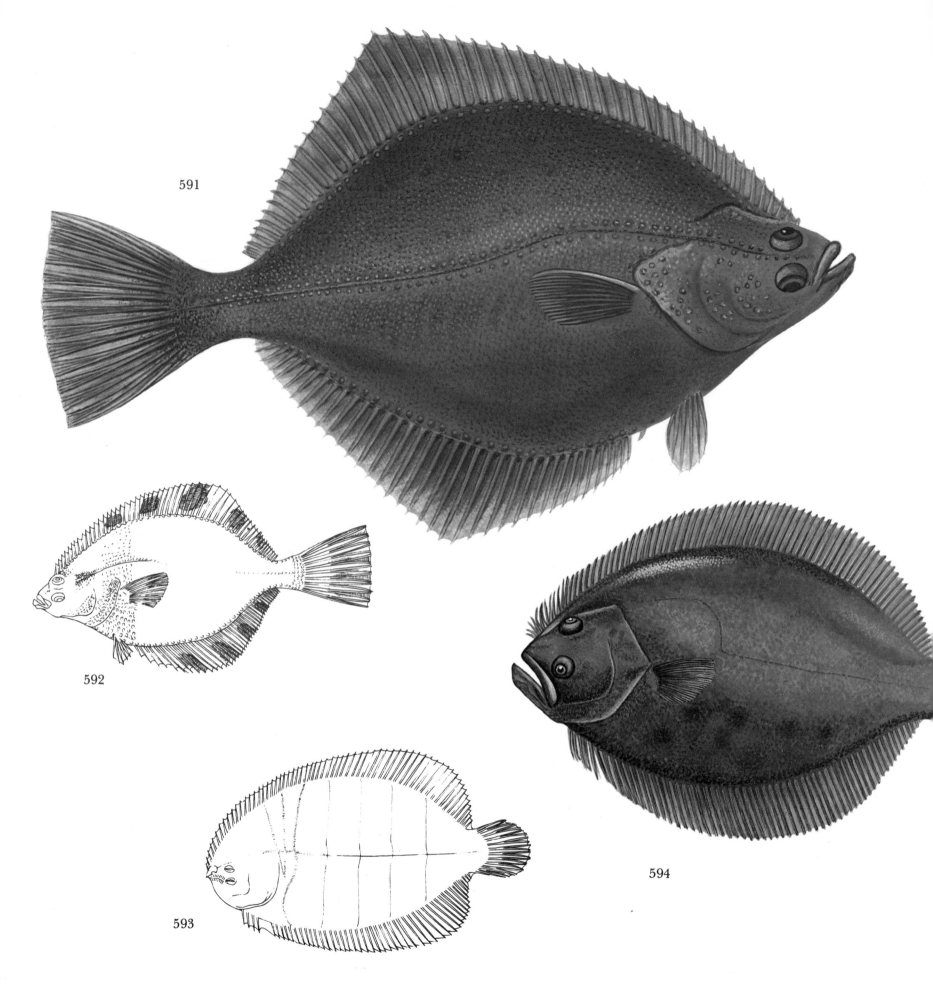

591 FLOUNDER
(EUROPEAN)
Platichthys flesus
Max ln 20 in (50 cm)
Max wt 5½ lb (2.5 kg)

592 STARRY FLOUNDER
Platichthys stellatus
Max ln 30 in (75 cm)
Max wt 20 lb (9 kg)

593 HOGCHOKER
Trinectes maculatus
Max ln 8 in (20 cm)

594 BRILL
Scophthalmus rhombus
Max ln 28 in (70 cm)

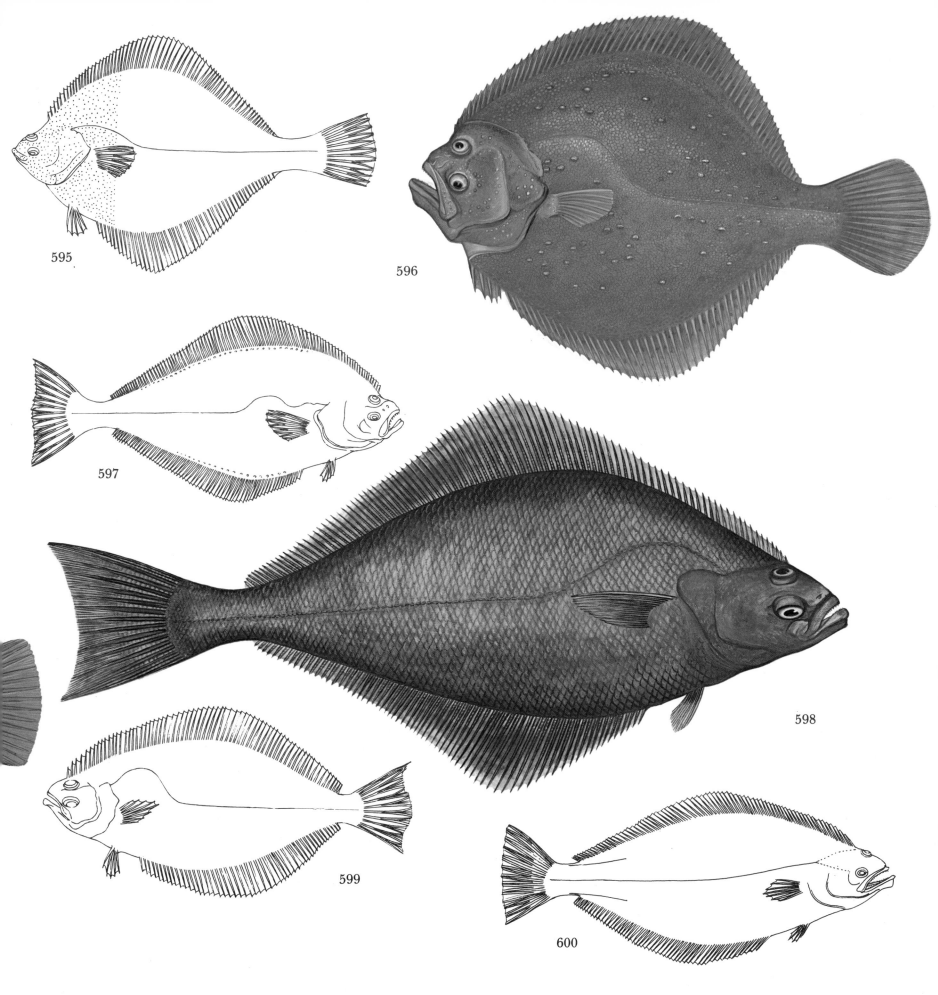

595 **DIAMOND TURBOT**
Hypsopsetta guttulata
Max ln 18 in (45 cm)

596 **TURBOT**
Scophthalmus maximus
Max ln 3 ft 4 in (1 m)

597 **PACIFIC HALIBUT**
Hippoglossus stenolepis
Max ln 9 ft (3 m)
Max wt 500 lb (225 kg)

598 **ATLANTIC HALIBUT**
Hippoglossus hippoglossus
Max ln 12 ft 1 in (3.70 m)

599 **CALIFORNIA
HALIBUT**
Paralichthys californicus
Max ln 5 ft 5 in (1.65 m)
Max wt 72 lb (33 kg)

600 **GREENLAND
HALIBUT**
*Reinhardtius
hippoglossoides*
Max wt 20 lb (9 kg)

601 **NORTHERN PUFFER**
Sphaeroides maculatus
Max ln 14 in (35 cm)
Max wt 1.1 lb (½ kg)

602 **TRUNKFISH**
Lactophrys tricornis
Max ln 18 in (45 cm)

603 **QUEEN
TRIGGERFISH**
Balistes vetula
Max ln 15 in (38 cm)

604 **OCEAN SUNFISH**
Mola mola
Max ln 11 ft (3.40 m)
Max wt 1,000 lb (450 kg)

605 **TRUNCATED
SUNFISH**
Ranzania truncata
Max ln 3 ft (90 cm)

606 **OCEAN
SURGEONFISH**
Acanthurus bahianus
Max ln 1¾ ft (50 cm)

608 **RIVER CARPSUCKER**
Carpoides cyprinus
Max ln 24 in (60 cm)
Max wt 4.4 lb (2 kg)

610 **COMMON OCTOPUS**
Octopus vulgaris
Max ln 3 ft 4 in (1 m)

For thousands of years, fishermen have pondered the mysteries of why fish bite, and why they frequently don't. Market fishermen, of course, are interested primarily in catching fish to sell, but the sport fisherman has a different goal. To him the important part of fishing is the challenge to his understanding and skill.

The idea of increasing the challenge by giving worthy game a chance to escape, thereby lengthening the odds, is as old as the sport of angling. The Chinese writer Chiang, who appreciated outdoor sports, explained his preference for straight rather than barbed iron hooks in these words: "Only volunteers would suffer themselves to be caught thus, since it gave all who wished a chance to escape."

There is a special excitement in watching a wild, free fish rise to a fly or lure that one has created and presented in artful imitation of the natural bait. The angler covets the trout as a lover courts a shy maiden.

Like the maiden, the fish often exercises an element of choice over the outcome, an element that is only imperfectly governed by the angler. One does not know the full depths of frustration until he has tried for an hour to entice a wild brook trout to rise to a dry fly. But when the fish's reserve is finally broken and it rises from its lair behind a protective boulder, then rolls on its side to slurp in the delicate fly, one is seized by an ecstacy of expectation that is almost sexual in its intensity.

Modern angling methods take advantage of much research into the behavior of fish, but they also reflect a universal demand for the element of challenge. On fresh water there is considerable variation on what constitutes tackle and methods of an approved type. What is "legitimate" in one area is not necessarily "legitimate" in another. But agreement on tackle rules and angling methods is very widespread. Conscientious anglers have no difficulty in complying with special requirements in a new area.

On salt water, the influence of the International Game Fish Association, with headquarters in Fort Lauderdale, Florida, U.S.A., has made it possible for an angler to go anywhere in the world and fish with tackle and under rules of behavior that are universally understood and respected.

The fishing methods described in this book may not arouse the full enthusiasm of all fishermen everywhere. But in the regions where they were developed, they are the standard methods for catching game fish with sporting tackle. Some of the techniques are very old. Others are quite new. They were selected to increase the reader's ability to meet greater fishing challenges through the growth of his understanding and personal skill.

ATLANTIC SALMON

Salmon fishing with rod and line in the estuaries of rivers is a chancy business and the angler would be best advised to defer conclusions with the salmon until they have reached good holding water, usually higher upstream. There can be no firm guide to what defines a good holding pool. So much depends on the time of year, temperature of the water, height of river, and other variables.

During the early months of the season when water temperatures are low, salmon tend to move slowly, content in most cases to stay in the deeper pools near the estuary. While in these lower reaches they may indeed be fished for, but it is not until they have gained the middle reaches, with a further possible fall in temperature, that they may be caught in greater quantities. Fresh-run salmon are always much better takers.

As the days lengthen the waters warm a little so the fish run faster, and by late spring or early summer the lower beats of the river may be devoid of fish. Any fresh fish that enter at this time most certainly run up into the higher reaches. With water temperatures well into the 50°F range (+10°C), the fish will take a small fly near the surface. On North American east coast rivers they will even take the dry fly, but such tactics have never brought more than passing success in the waters of Great Britain and Norway. Icelandic salmon are said to follow the North American pattern.

With the passing of spring, most salmon rivers have a good distribution of fish throughout their middle and upper reaches. As the sun's power increases the rivers shrink, confining the fish to the deeper sections of their chosen pools. By now the fish have become stale. They lose their pristine silveriness and turn a coppery red colour, losing some of their girth and muscle. They also are less inclined to take the angler's lure or fly, and fishing for them under a sunny sky is a doubtful pastime. Early morning and late evening are better. If they show no interest in fly or spinner, then the prawn, shrimp, or worm are always aces up the sleeve.

With the passing of summer, the autumn rains again fill the rivers and, although the earlier spring fish are now too red and wasted to be worth fishing for, there is usually a further run of fresh autumn fish to swell the stocks already in the river. The autumn run salmon is no mean fighter. Having the benefit of summer feeding in the sea, he is a worthy prize.

Tactics to hook the elusive salmon vary with the seasons. The standard legitimate methods include fly spinning, prawning, shrimping, and worming. Most anglers regard the fly as the most sporting means, but spinning undoubtedly takes the lion's share of the catch and is a favoured method for the early months of the season.

SPINNING

There is much more to spinning for salmon than merely throwing the bait across the river and winding it back. During the early months the bait or lure must be made to fish as slowly as possible. The lure is best cast across the stream and allowed to swing toward the angler's bank before the retrieve is commenced. If the weight of the bait has been carefully selected to suit the prevailing current and depth of water, it should fish slowly near the river bottom. Most novice salmon spinners pick too light a bait and then add extra lead, whereupon they have to wind too fast to present the bait to the fish at exactly the right speed and depth.

Tackle for such fishing depends to a large extent on preference. Most favoured are the fixed spool (spinning) reel, and the multiplier (bait casting) reel. During the early season on heavy waters, the multiplier (or star drag reel as it is called in North America) will throw a big spinning spoon or bait a long distance. Once the weight of the bait or lure falls below 5/8 oz (18 g), however, the fixed spool spinning outfit is decidedly more versatile. Spinning rods tend to be two-handed for all but the lightest outfits and normally are some 8 ft (240 cm) to 9½ ft (285 cm) in length.

During summer months in low waters, upstream spinning can often be quite rewarding. Here a small bait is cast upstream and is retrieved as quickly as possible, and will often induce a take when all other methods fail. Normally, however, as soon as the waters warm over 48°F (9°C), fishing the floating fly line is more profitable.

FISHING THE FLOATING FLY LINE

The late A. H. E. Wood, of Cairnton on the Scottish river Dee, is credited with discovery of fishing a small, lightly dressed fly on the floating line. In the older days a floating line was "greased" to make it float. Modern floating lines do not require greasing to float. The leader must be of a type that will sink, permitting the fly to drift only a few inches below the surface of the water. The thrill of the take is as exciting as dry fly trout fishing, for invariably a head and tail rise is seen before the heavy pull is felt.

It is vitally important that no attempt to strike be made when the rise is seen. Many anglers keep a coil of line in hand in order to give the fish slack line at the moment of the take. Others prefer to let the fish pull line off the reel before raising the rod tip to set the hook. If the current is fast it is often necessary to mend the line upstream to slow the drift of the fly. Conversely, in very low water it may help to throw a downstream mend into the line to make the fly move across the current at a quicker pace. *Only experience will indicate the best tactics.*

SHRIMP FISHING

If the fly and spinning baits fail to produce fish, one of the most killing baits is a small natural shrimp fished with light spinning tackle. A shrimp is mounted on a small triangle without any trace of curl in the body, head to the bottom. The shrimp is cast out over the pool and, after it has sunk to the required depth, is slowly retrieved with a sink-and-draw motion. Sometimes the fish merely play with the bait. At other times they take it as though it were the last meal of their lives, which well it may be. Another highly effective method of fishing the shrimp entails dropping it under a small float so it may be drifted over a known salmon lie. The take is often hardly noticeable, with just a slight dipping of the float.

PRAWN FISHING

For some strange reason salmon react completely differently to a prawn. Sometimes they will take it even more savagely than the shrimp. At other times the prawn may frighten the salmon out of the pool. Again the sink-and-draw technique is very effective, as is a prawn on spinning tackle allowed to drift downstream with slow, jerky movements. If there is any evidence, however, that the prawn is scaring the salmon, its use should be stopped immediately. The use of prawns is restricted on many waters, but where it is legal its use on a warm summer day can produce salmon when other methods fail.

WORM FISHING

Fishing the worm for salmon is regarded by most sportsmen as the poorest way of taking fish. Yet, surprisingly, considerable angling skill is required. Normally the bait-holder hook is baited with two or three large worms threaded well up onto the hook shank. The amount of lead to be put on depends entirely upon the depth of water and the strength of the current. It is essential to have the worms bouncing along the bottom.

There will be many times when the bait gets hung up on a rock, and to be really effective a great deal of local river knowledge is essential. When the bite is first detected only cautious giving of line should be attempted. The salmon may play with the bait for five minutes or more. Strike only when the fish is making off with it firmly in its mouth.

PLAYING THE SALMON

Many hooked salmon are lost in the play stage through careless handling. In the first few seconds following hooking, you may wade or walk to the nearest vantage point to play the fish. You should aim to stay downstream of the fish if possible so he fights not only your tackle, but also the river current. If he gets downstream of you, he can lean on the tackle to help him swim against the current. Don't be in too great a hurry to hustle him out of the deep, fast water. This part of the river will take most of the steam out of him.

Many fish are lost through overanxiousness, and the time spent keeping a steady strain on the fish while he fights the current is well spent. A minute a pound (or roughly two minutes per kilogram) is a rough guide to the time it should take you to land your salmon. If you are going to gaff him, wait until he is lying quietly on his side before striking the gaff home. If, on the other hand, there is a shelving sand or gravel beach handy, you may draw him onto his side, lay your rod down, and pick him out by the tail.

FISHING FOR TROUT

Trout fall into two classes, wild fish and stock fish. The wild fish live their lives from birth in the fresh waters they inhabit. Stock trout are reared in hatcheries and are introduced to angling waters at any stage of their growth in accordance with the requirements of fishery managers. The major difference is that wild trout are far more wary and selective than stock trout in taking both natural food and the angler's bait or lure.

Angling for trout falls into four general types: bait, spinner, sunken wet fly, and drifted floating dry fly. Fishing for trout with bait or spinner requires much the same methods as when this equipment is used in fishing for coarse fish, except that in clear water wild trout show greater timidity. The suitability of bait fishing or spinning is either that the angler prefers one method or the other, or that the available trout have grown to considerable weight and have lost interest in insects.

The techniques of bait fishing and spinning for trout are similar to those for other fish, but the angler must learn the reaction of every type of trout before assuming that a method good for one is equally effective, without modifications, for another. The three most suitable types of water for trout fishing are: spate rivers, chalk rivers, and still waters. The term "rivers" should be regarded as covering flowing waters of wide dimensions and also narrow flowing waters commonly called streams.

The spate river rises and falls in level with the downflow of rainwater from the hills of the river's watershed. The downflow carries a varying measure of sediment, with very heavy sediment content during and after rains. The effect is clouding water until the downflow turns the river to thick brown; then, as the downflow diminishes, the thick coloration gradually fades away until the river runs clear.

The effect on angling is twofold. During the major coloration of the river, the angler is invisible to the trout. As the river rises and falls, the trout usually shows increased inclination to feed as the result of extra vitality induced by the higher oxygen content of the water and the expectation of flood-brought food.

Chalk streams are rather few in number compared with spate rivers. They are the outflow of underground reservoirs of water in the chalk or limestone strata of the earth. The water level of these rivers does not vary a great deal and rarely shows appreciable coloration. The taking inclination of trout, in these consistently clear waters, is more dependent on the presence of natural food than is the case in spate rivers. The water clarity presents the angler with a greater and more consistent problem of self-concealment.

In all flowing waters the trout either remains in a settled condition or, on occasion, cruises back and forth within a few yards of its settled location from time to time. Its only far wanderings in the river come with the urge to spawn during the winter. This behaviour is in complete contrast to trout behaviour in still waters, the lakes and reservoirs, in which all trout are inconsistent wanderers about the entire water area.

The methods of fishing for trout in all three groups of water vary considerably with the type of water. The fundamental requirement in attempting to catch trout is to present the bait, spinner, or fly in such a way that it does not alarm the fish. Presentation of bait requires a sling-cast with light weight, so

Love of fishing begins in childhood. Behold the boy, armed with cane pole, kite string, and worm-laden hook.
No angler in fancy waders, carrying expensive tackle, finds more joy in fishing than the boy.
But, as he grows older, the boy's increasing love of fishing is no longer satisfied with the simple implements and methods of childhood. He discovers that bigger and better fish await those who have sophisticated tackle and greater knowledge of how to outwit elusive fishes. When he first starts fishing, the boy subscribes to the theory that it should be possible to catch almost any kind of fish with just a pole, line, and worm-laden hook. But experience soon teaches him that many fish are selective and timid, not so easily fooled. Every

fisherman begins as an innocent. But as his experience deepens, the angler's goal turns from the mere gathering of meat to the answering of greater challenges that once existed only in his dreams.

The methods shown and the lessons suggested here are designed to inspire fishermen with a desire to strive for perfection in methods they already know, and to experiment with new methods that may increase the chances of success with reluctant fish found under difficult conditions. No fisherman is ever satisfied with his equipment or the state of his understanding.
Eternally he seeks to know the unknowable. Perfection is the goal, just a step ahead, promising rewards that are won, not bought.

The boy begins his fishing life as an improvisor, creating tackle out of cast-off odds and ends. His native cunning may help him to outfish the occasional 'swell' who appears with polished rod and reel, resplendent in expensive outdoor clothing. But the boy is a realist and his ambition is to own and use a rod as fine as the rich man's rod, and a reel of equal quality. In pursuing his goal the boy is not wasting the substance of his lifespan. Fishing teaches him patience and love of nature. He does not have to set records to be successful. Success is measured by the peace in his heart.

the bait drops into the water and follows the current in such a way that it appears as natural food to the trout.

The spinner requires the same accuracy of casting as bait, but the spinner is worked across the water instead of being allowed to drift. It must be borne in mind that bait reacts on the trout's senses of sight, taste, and smell; whereas the spinner reacts only on sight and the sense of water vibration.

Fishing the sunken wet fly downstream, dragging it across the current, has basic similarity to spinning as a method of impact on trout reaction. The spinner plays on trout reaction to small fish, while the small wet fly in wide use on rivers plays on trout reaction to the larval subsurface forms of natural insects. Against this, the larger wet flies, often called nymphs, are designed to cause precisely the same trout reaction as that caused by the spinner. But these creations are much lighter than the spinner and require the use of entirely different tackle and casting method for their presentation.

The three foregoing methods of catching trout require far lower casting ability in the angler than presentation of the floating, drifting, dry fly.

Use of the floating fly for trout did not come into general practice until late in the last century. When it came, its attraction as a method developed very fast. This does not mean that the effectiveness of the dry fly was not known much earlier. The Macedonian *hippouros* fly of the second century A. D., may well have been designed to float.

In 1846 G. P. R. Pulman wrote this glowing comment, "If the wet and heavy fly be exchanged for a dry and light one, and passed in artist-like style over the feeding fish, it will, partly for the simple circumstance of its buoyancy, be taken in nine cases out of ten, as quickly as the living insect itself."

Since then anglers have discovered that if the design of the fly does not create the same, or at least similar, trout reaction as that which has been developed by the natural insects of the moment, the trout will often (but not always) ignore the floating object. It was this trout selectiveness and the problem of designing and using artificial flies to overcome it, that caused the rapid increase in popularity of dry fly fish in the chalk rivers of the south of England, and in the mountain streams of North America.

A number of anglers and angling writers have attempted to translate the play of dry fly fishing on trout reaction into a more cultured activity than any other form of fishing. Its complexities provide them with theories galore, which they have no compunction in twisting into supporting evidence for their translation. As the years have moved on, however, the majority of anglers have tended to ignore the assertions of the "purists," as they have been termed. Every form of angling is, in the end, a high test of the reflective ability and practical skill of the angler. The basic objective of all angling is to provide man with an attractive diversion.

A reasonable assessment of angling for trout, thanks mainly to fishing the dry fly, is that their range of feeding, selectiveness, and timidity provides a broader challenge than the less complicated reactions of other fish. It is the quality of this never-ending challenge that brings the angler back to the waters, often frustrated, but always hopeful.

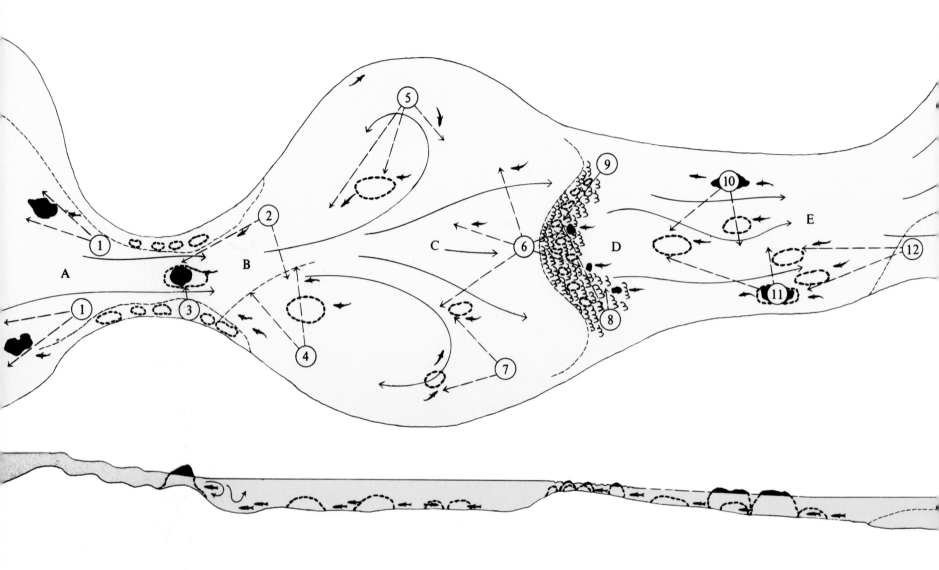

LEARNING TO "READ" A TROUT STREAM

To an experienced angler a trout stream is like an open book. Each portion of the stream is a chapter, and each potential fish position a page.

In this presentation the pages of the trout stream book have been compressed into a sort of continuous synopsis. A few streams may be more complicated, many are much simpler. The secret of reading trout streams successfully lies in careful observation and interpretation of what one sees.

Trout in a swift stream live on a precarious energy budget. They select stations, or "lays" as anglers call their resting places, where they are out of the main force of the current, yet close to aquatic or terrestrial food that may drift by. Anglers learn to spot these favored locations and choose positions for casting that work to their advantage.

Eddies behind rocks are prime trout locations, as are overhanging banks that afford a bit of shelter from the eyes of predators ashore.

A MOUTH OF A FAST RUN LEADING OUT OF A POOL

1 Two identical good casting positions on either side of head of the run. Angler hooking a large fish in the current may have to run downstream to save line.

B UPPER END OF A POOL BELOW A FAST RUN

2 Good position on far bank for casting upstream to large rock and for working the lower part of run.

3 A clever angler with good tackle may take fish from behind the midstream rock.

4 Good position for working fish in the shelter of near bank and the submerged rock below the run.

C DEEP, QUIET POOL

5 Angler works the back current and the submerged rocks.

6 Excellent position for working lower end of pool above a wide rocky riffle. Reached by wading.

7 From this position the angler works the sheltered near bank and the submerged rocks, taking good advantage of the countercurrent.

D WIDE RIFFLE ACROSS MAIN CHANNEL OF STREAM

8 Strangely, a riffle is often a very good trout location. The fish lie behind the stones and rocks, waiting for insects and baitfish. The riffle can be fished from position 6 if the angler is adept at downstream work.

9 This is a companion location to 8 and is sometimes chosen by a left-handed angler. Right-handed angler would fish better at position 8. Facing upstream, he casts with offshore arm.

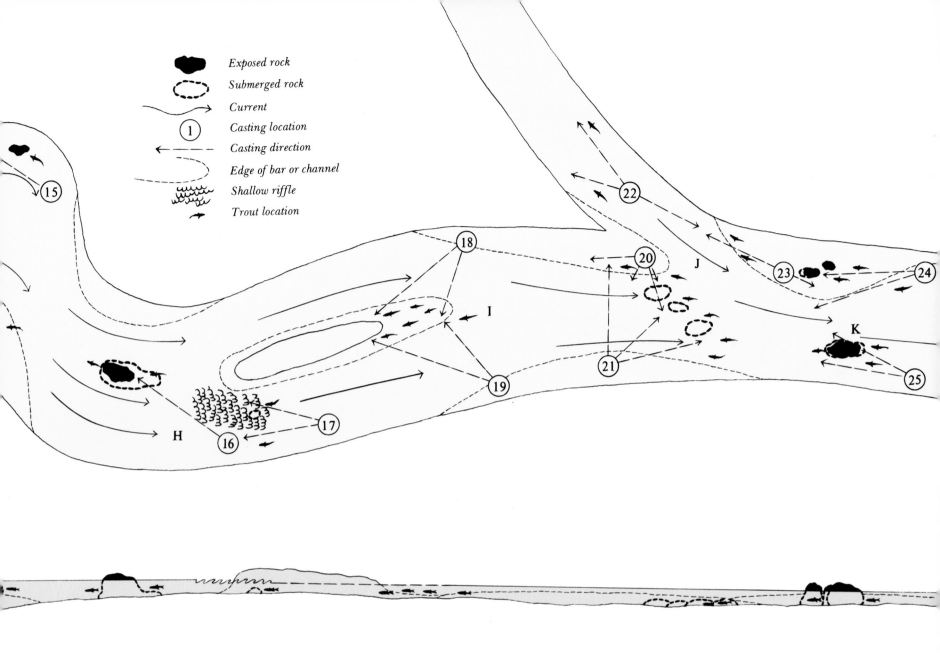

Exposed rock
Submerged rock
Current
Casting location
Casting direction
Edge of bar or channel
Shallow riffle
Trout location

E LARGE ROCKS IN DEEP WATER WITH CURRENT

10–11 Position on top of rocks is ideal for working rocky area in midstream. Wet flies and nymphs are good for such deepwater work.

12 Position on upstream side of shallow bar lets angler cast to rocks at 11.

F SHALLOW BAR WITH BIG EXPOSED ROCKS OFFSHORE

13 Wading the bar may spook the fish, so an inshore position is best for casting to the large rocks that may harbor fish farther offshore.

G DEEP BEND WITH FAST CURRENT, LARGE ROCKS, AND UNDERCUT BANKS

This is a prime trout location, if one can get in position to fish.

14 Upstream position is favored by right-handed anglers who require the casting arm to be offshore so as to place flies under the overhanging bank without hooking the brush.

15 Left-handed angler is better off at a downstream position for the same reason. Either dry or wet flies will work here, depending on season.

H MIDSTREAM LOCATION WITH LARGE ROCK UPSTREAM AND RIFFLE OFF UPPER END OF SMALL ISLAND

16 Good position for long casts to the midstream rock. The fly makes a long, slow drift to head of the riffle which can be fished from this location.

17 Lower part of riffle and bank of island are worked from here.

I EDDY BEHIND ISLAND IS A PRIME TROUT AREA

18 Left-handed angler works island eddy best from the far bank of the river.

19 Right-handed angler casts best here.

J JUNCTION OF TWO STREAMS IS ANOTHER TOP TROUT LOCATION

20 Most advantageous position is at end of shallow bar.

21 Strategic location for working rocks off the junction bar.

22 Midstream position in smaller stream is good for upstream or downstream casting.

23 Position at upper end of bar on far bank permits angler to work current edge above rocky area downstream.

K CHANNELS

Between bar on far bank, large rock off the near bank. Fish can be expected to rest in deep, quiet water, but are always alert to pick up food that comes drifting by.

24 Position near bank, downstream of bar, lets angler work the rocks on the bar.

25 Position downstream of large rock, close to near bank, lets a right-handed angler work both the large rock and the deep water between the rock and the near bank. Wet flies are best here.

ternal organs undergo a biological change. Reproductive organs swell to ripeness while the digestive tract becomes inoperative. Once they leave the sea, salmon stop feeding.

But this does not stop many salmon from reacting in the old food-pursuit pattern when an angler presents the proper fly or lure. Living on stored fat, the fish move upstream in loose groups, resting in quiet pools between the exhausting rapids and dangerous falls. Salmon of the Pacific coast die after spawning and bears and other wildlife reap a harvest of the spent fish before death finally claims them. Atlantic salmon, on the other hand, frequently are able to return to the sea after spawning. In the fresh water Great Lakes of North America, Pacific salmon have been introduced. They mature in the deep lakes and ascend tributary rivers in the fall in an attempt to find suitable spawning bottom to reproduce their species. Many are taken by fisheries workers, stripped of eggs and milt, assuring fertile eggs for the hatcheries.

Here are several important but common definitions and names that are applied to salmon in various stages of their growth, using the Atlantic salmon as an example.

THE MIRACLE OF A SALMON RIVER

To nonfishermen, a river is merely a way of draining rainwater to the sea, but to fishermen a river is a complete living environment, a self-renewing resource with many complex life cycles hidden from most eyes. To the salmon, a river is the ultimate life goal. Born in a river, the salmon when young goes to the sea to attain full growth and maturity. In the fullness of time it returns to the river of its birth, guided by chemical memory, where it carries out the final supreme act of its life–reproduction.

Nature has provided safeguards that rivers shall not be stripped of their natural foods by voracious salmon returning to fresh water to spawn. As the fish enter their native rivers, their in-

A

Juveniles less than six inches long, still marked with the dark trout bars of youth, are called parr.

Parr become smolts when they lose the characteristic parr markings and start moving toward the sea. Some smolts may take as long as four years to reach the sea.

Young salmon returning to fresh water after their first winter at sea are known as grilse, and are usually three to five years old.

True salmon are mature individuals that have spent at least two winters at sea. Oddly, large parr often spread milt in company with mature breeding salmon.

The salmon's streambed nest is called a redd and is dug by the female with powerful beats of her tail.

A *The angler pictured has cast for hours over salmon resting in the deep pool. Suddenly a salmon takes his fly and leaps into the air as it feels the hook. The other salmon ignore the fight, gaining strength for the struggle up the rapids of the river. One by one they leave the pool, swimming and leaping up the cascade, seeking the gravel spawning beds.*

B *The spawning beds of fine gravel lie in shallow headwaters. Facing the current, the female scoops a deep nest, or redd, with her tail. Her activity attracts males, who may fight for possession of the female. The one that wins joins her when the redd is ready to receive the eggs.*

C *The female arches her body, extruding a stream of eggs into the cup-shaped redd. Slightly heavier than water, the eggs cover the bottom. Meanwhile, the male extrudes sperm-laden milt into the water. Eggs and milt mix in the current. The act of fertilization is complete in moments.*

D *When the bottom of the redd is covered with fertile eggs, the female starts a new redd upstream. Gravel from the new redd fills the first one, protecting the eggs until the fry hatch in the spring. Eggs get oxygen from water permeating the gravel. Silt or mud can smother the eggs.*

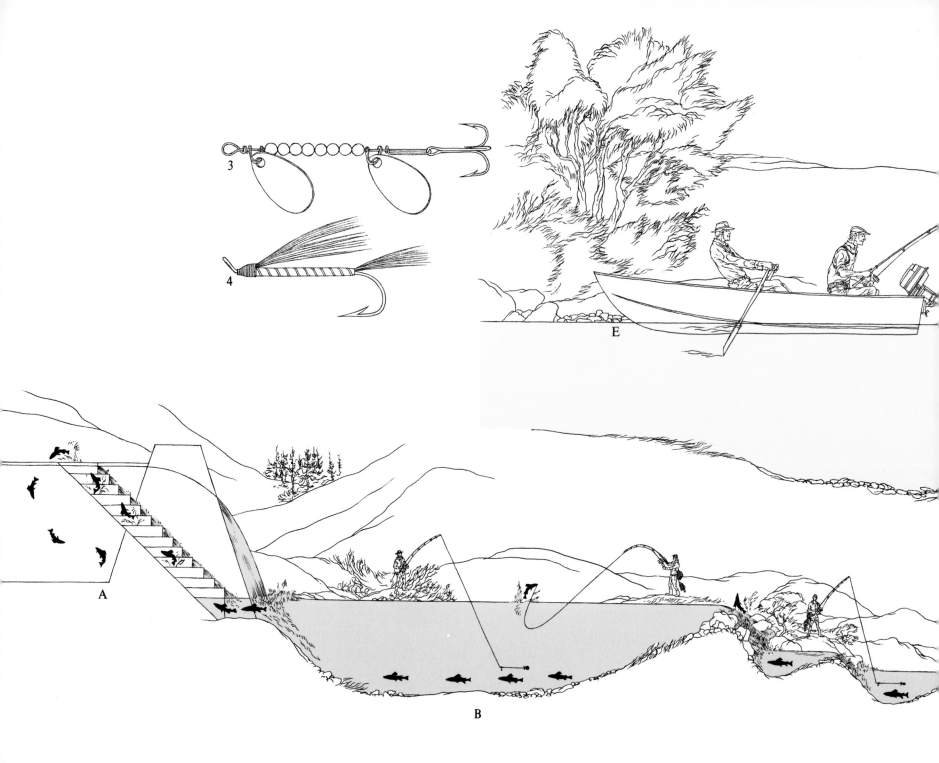

STEELHEAD TROUT OF THE PACIFIC NORTHWEST

In the northwestern states of the U.S.A. and the western provinces of Canada, the rainbow trout becomes a sea-run fish with many of the characteristics of salmon. These include river spawning, refusal of migrating mature fish to feed in the normal manner, and migration of juvenile fish to the sea after a few months of early development. The rivers are swift, cold, and turbulent, which makes for rugged fishing. The best season is usually winter when mature fish are bound upstream from the sea to gravel spawning beds in the headwaters. Spinning tackle is popular, but a specialized type of heavy-duty fly-casting tackle is also used.

A FISH LADDERS

There are many hydroelectric power dams on the rivers and fish ladders have been built around most of these to provide migrating trout and salmon with a means of getting around the dams. The steelhead leap from water-step to water-step, guided by their instinct to fight upstream against the prevailing current. Hatcheries maintained by the various state, provincial, and federal governments supplement natural reproduction with fingerlings raised from eggs collected by fisheries biologists.

B TYPICAL RESTING POOL

Swimming upstream is an exhausting business, and tired steelhead like to rest in quiet pools before undertaking a strenuous swim up a fish ladder or extensive rapids of the river. Steelhead usually stay quite deep and it is necessary to fish with weighted lures or baits carried to the bottom by sinkers. Even though the fish are not feeding in the true sense, they will often pause to hit a lure or bait that is attractive and artfully presented.

C FISHING THE RAPIDS

In fast, shallow rivers anglers usually fish from the riverbanks, casting upstream so their baits or lures will drift down with the current to fish resting in pools or behind rocks that break the current. When a sinker is used, it is fastened to the line with a device that drops the sinker if it lodges in the bottom.

D FISHING FROM BOATS

Boat fishing is done in portions of the rivers where it is safe. Two men work together, alternately rowing and fishing. Outboard motors are used to bring the boats to fishable water, but oars are

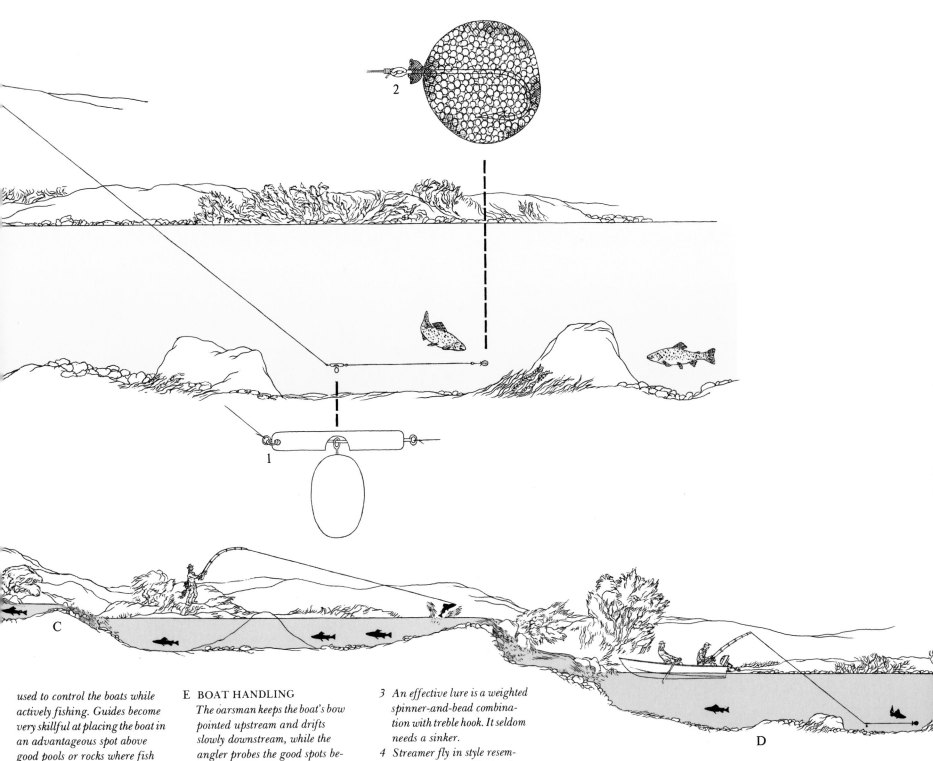

used to control the boats while actively fishing. Guides become very skillful at placing the boat in an advantageous spot above good pools or rocks where fish can be found.

The steelhead is a very strong, courageous fish with great jumping ability and capable of long-sustained runs. It is also an excellent table fish which helps to account for its great popularity within its home waters and wherever it has been introduced in Europe, Asia, and the Southern Hemisphere.

E BOAT HANDLING

The oarsman keeps the boat's bow pointed upstream and drifts slowly downstream, while the angler probes the good spots below them with his lures or bait.

1 A sinker-release device carries the bait or lure deep and drops off if it snags bottom or when a fish takes the hook.
2 A popular bait is a cluster of salmon or trout eggs sewn in a bag of stocking-silk. The hook is 6– 2.
3 An effective lure is a weighted spinner-and-bead combination with treble hook. It seldom needs a sinker.
4 Streamer fly in style resembling baitfish is effective for fly-casting.

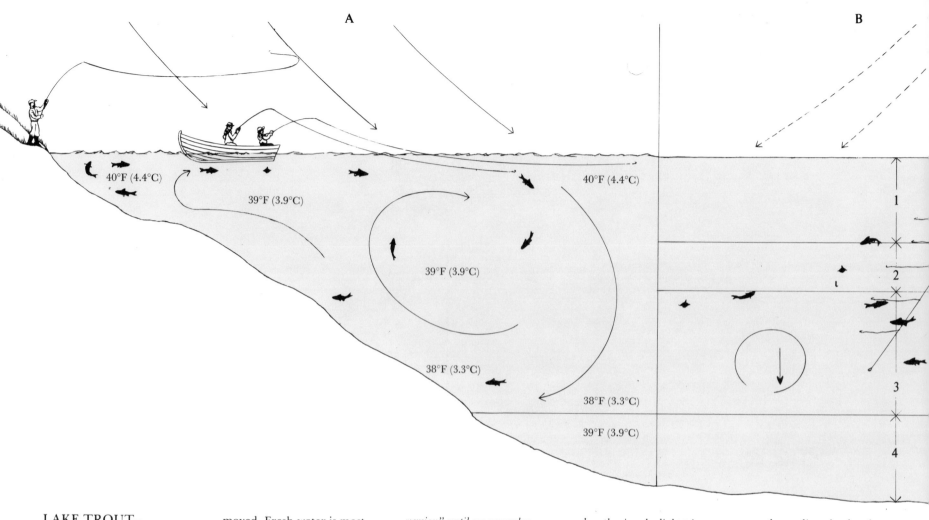

A

B

40°F (4.4°C)

39°F (3.9°C)

39°F (3.9°C)

38°F (3.3°C)

40°F (4.4°C)

38°F (3.3°C)

39°F (3.9°C)

1

2

3

4

LAKE TROUT–
SEASONAL PATTERN

Lakes of the temperate zones of the Northern and Southern Hemispheres undergo a complex seasonal shift of temperatures during the annual weather cycle, and the fish that live in the lakes respond to these changes by altering their behavior to suit the environment. Lake trout are perfect fish for observing these reactions to seasonal variations in popular fishing lakes. Other predatory species such as bass and pike react in essentially the same manner.

The cold-water lakes in which lake trout occur are usually fairly deep. For several months of the year in winter they are ice-covered. Ice forms a barrier between lake water and the atmosphere and ice-covered lakes go into what might almost be called a state of hibernation when the water-moving action of winds and the warming action of direct sunlight is re-

moved. Fresh water is most dense at 39° F (3.9°C), not 32° (0°), which is water's freezing point. This means that during winter the densest water in the lake gravitates to the bottom where it stays unless affected by internal lake currents. This is 39° (3°) water, 7° (3.9°C) removed from the freezing point. Freezing water is found up under the ice. Ice, of course, is less dense than water, therefore floats on the surface. This is one of the true miracles of nature for if ice were more dense than water, ice would sink to the bottom, preventing the circulation of water in our lakes and oceans.

A SPRING SITUATION AT TIME OF ICE-OUT

The first dramatic change in the lake's environment takes place at the time of ice-out in spring. By now the water has achieved a nearly homogenous temperature gradient from 32° F (0° C) just under the ice to 39° (3.9°) in the deepest spots. This may look like a "temperature in-

version" until we remember that 39° (3.9°) water is actually more dense than 32° (0°) water. Now comes the time when the ice disappears, melted by warm winds and sunlight.

Because the vertical temperature structure of the lake has little variation, the water is easily moved by the strong, warm winds of spring. The wind pushes surface water toward the downwind shore, at the same time warming it. This caused displacement of warm surface water toward the bottom at the downwind shore and upwelling of deep, cold water at the upwind shore. The lake's water, in a sense, "turns over."
Oxygen-depleted deep water is brought to the surface where its oxygen content is recharged by contact with the atmosphere.
The fish in the lake, naturally, are part of its living ecosystem and go through a similar dramatic change in behavior with the "turning over" of the lake's water. Increasing warmth and

lengthening daylight trigger the biological clocks in their nervous systems. They come out of a winter-induced state of low metabolism and go on feeding orgies, invading the shallows and nearshore areas where they are sought by knowing anglers.

B STABILIZED SUMMER SITUATION

The mixed-up wonderful fishing of spring lasts only a relatively short time. By midsummer the lake has stabilized into an entirely different temperature pattern. Because warm water is lighter than cold water, it rises to the surface. Cold water sinks into the deep holes of the lake. If the lake is deep enough and does not have strong internal currents generated by inflowing or outflowing rivers, there may develop a very deep layer of maximum-density water at or close to the magic 39° F (3.9°C) mark. When summer winds generate surface currents, the down-welling warm surface water slides over the deeper cold water and a distinct boundary area, called a

thermocline, develops between the cold, stable, deep water and the warmer, more mobile water of the wind- and sun-affected surface region.
The vertical temperature column in the illustration above shows the rather broad temperature range from a surface temperature of 72°F (22°C) to a deepest and coldest temperature of 39°. Water colder than 39° F (3.9°C) cannot exist in a lake in summer. There is no ice at the surface to generate a 32° (0°) layer, and if springwater of less than 39° F (3.9°C) enters the lake bottom via springs or an underground stream, the colder springwater, being less dense than the surrounding 39° (3.9°) water, will rise through the deep 39° (3.9°) layer until it finds still warmer water above that has a density equal to that of the very cold springwater. Transfer of heat will soon bring the springwater to the 39° (3.9°) level, at which time it will join the 39° (3.9°) bottom layer. The strata of the

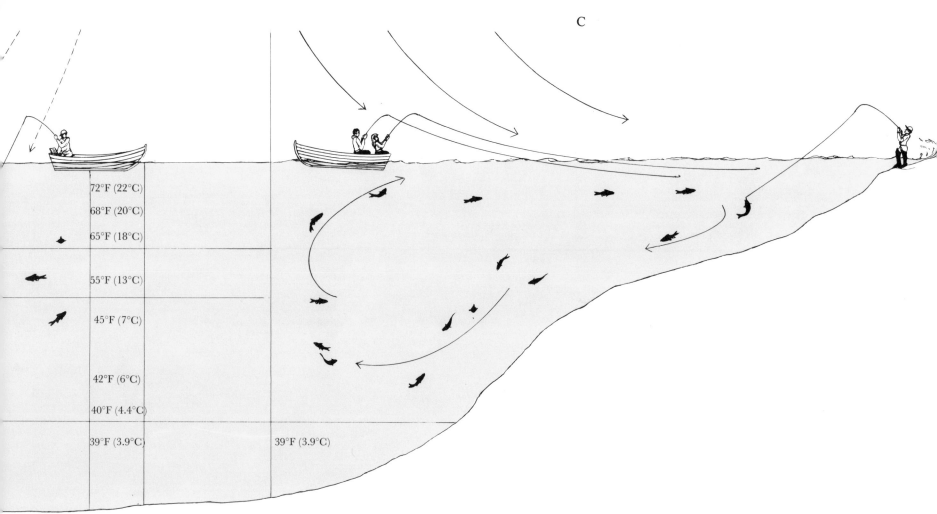

72°F (22°C)

68°F (20°C)

65°F (18°C)

55°F (13°C)

45°F (7°C)

42°F (6°C)

40°F (4.4°C)

39°F (3.9°C)   39°F (3.9°C)

C

lake, dividing it vertically into different layers or temperature zones, have specific names given to them by scientists.

THE EPILIMNION

1 In the illustration above, the epilimnion is Layer "A," the band of warm surface water ranging in temperature from around 72° F (22° C) at the surface to 65°–55° (18°–12°) at the upper portion of the temperature-mixing zone. The epilimnion is warm, well-oxygenated water that is attractive to warmwater fishes. In summer it may be too warm to suit coldwater species such as lake trout. These may rise into the warm water to feed at times, but usually spend their time in the colder strata lower down.

THE THERMOCLINE

2 The mixing zone or thermocline between the warm upper water and the cold water down deep usually shows rapid changes of temperatures

as depth increases. Because cold, deep lake waters seldom come in contact with the atmosphere during summer, they become deoxygenated and less attractive to many species of fish. Lake trout, for example, like cold water, but must have oxygen, so they will frequent the thermocline where temperature, oxygen content, and the presence of forage fish create a "comfort zone" that the lake trout prefer during summer.

THE HYPOLIMNION

3 The region of cold water under the thermocline is known as the hypolimnion. Its temperature range is usually rather narrow, dropping from about 45° (7°) just under the thermocline to a minimum of 39° (3.9°). Oxygen content may be so low as to be nonsupportive of normal fish life, although this is generally rare.

THE 39° F (3.9° C) SINGLE-TEMPERATURE STRATUM

4 This deepest layer of water is

usually considered to be part of the hypolimnion, and not all lakes will have it, especially if they are shallow. But in very deep lakes with quiet water the 39° (3.9°) layer may be very deep indeed, because it is the densest fresh water that can exist in nature. So-called "heavy water" is a rare chemical isotope of ordinary water that has no direct relationship to the seasonal pattern of natural fishing lakes.

C FALL FISHING SITUATION

In autumn, as weather gets colder and winds increase, another "turnover" of the lake water takes place. The chilly fall winds soon cool the surface waters of the lake to the point that, before freezing occurs, a general mixing happens when the overall water temperature approaches the critical 39° F (3.9°C) mark. Once again the fish go through a major behavioral shift. Their familiar thermocline of the summer has been destroyed and for a brief time the whole lake is a "comfort zone."

D FISHING THE THERMOCLINE

During summer, when the majority of anglers are on the water, the successful fishermen usually are those who take lake trout and related species by fishing the thermocline. There are two ways to do this:

1 Locate the thermocline by using a depth-selective type of fishing gear. The multilevel, multilure trolling or drifting arrangement shown in the center illustration is such a piece of tackle. Five, six, or more branch lines with baits or lures are fished at different levels until a pattern of fish strikes starts to appear. Once the depth of the fish has been established, single-lure tackle can be used provided it is fished at the required level.

2 Locate the thermocline by means of a temperature-sensitive device. This may be an electric depth-temperature probe that gives instant temperature

read-out, or it may be a weighted bottle containing a small thermometer arranged in such a way that the bottle cork is removed by a yank on the line at a selected depth, obtaining a water temperature sample from that depth. This is also called the "Armstrong" method because it requires much line-pulling.

Once the thermocline is located in depth, the angler fishes at that depth with live or natural dead bait, or by one of several deep-trolling methods.

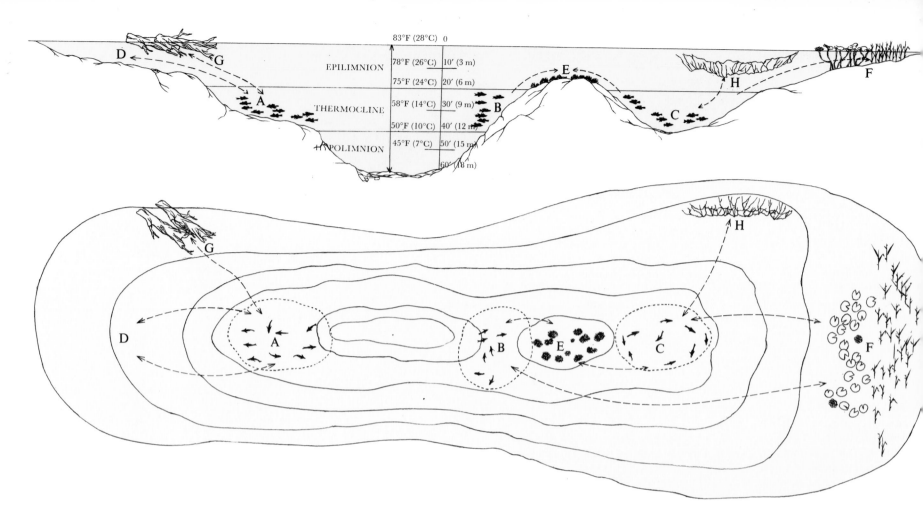

STRUCTURE OF A TYPICAL BASS LAKE

The largemouth bass (*Micropterus salmoides*) is typical of a number of species of lake-dwelling freshwater fish that are most active during the warmer months of the year and exhibit definite behaviour habits governed by the thermal structure of the lake. These fish are generally considered to be warm-water fish in that their "comfort zone" lies between 62° F (16° C) and 75° F (23° C), with an optimum preference of 68° F (20° C).

The lake illustrated has a definite thermocline, or temperature-mixing area, located between the warm surface water and the cold water down deep. There is little interchange of water through the thermocline during summer, so the surface water is usually well oxygenated and the cold, deep water often lacks enough oxygen to support some types of fish.

Locations A, B, and C in the lake are resting areas with water temperature at or close to the optimum for the species involved. Locations D, E, F, G, and H are inshore feeding spots with geographical or biological features that attract the bass.

G Submerged trees at shoreline.

D Wide flat shoal with sharp slope offshore.

E Rocky top of submerged hill in midlake.

H Face of submerged rocky cliff.

F Lily pads and reed bed in shallow water.

Dashed arrows show the most probable routes of fish moving from deep resting areas to the various shallow-water feeding grounds. Food they seek includes small baitfish, fry of their own and other species, insects, nymphs and larvae of aquatic insects, frogs, and even small land animals such as shrews and mice. The latter sometimes fall into the water from overhanging shrubs. Morning and evening twilight are traditionally good fishing hours, but fishing is often best late at night, when most anglers have sought their beds.

EPILIMNION

The epilimnion is the sun-warmed upper portion of the lake. It has good oxygen content because of constant contact with the atmosphere. Warm water is less dense than cold, therefore rises. In spring and fall, fish may inhabit the entire epilimnion if the water temperature is at or near the range of their comfort zone.

THERMOCLINE

The mixing zone between warm upper water and the cold water down deep is called the thermocline. The temperature gradient is usually fairly steep and the oxygen content is less than that of the surface water, but more than that of deep water. Bait and game fish find their comfort zones in or close to the lake's thermocline layer.

HYPOLIMNION

Being dense, cold water sinks, seeking its own density level. Fresh water is most dense at 39° F (3.9°C). With no currents to cause mixing, the coldest water in a lake will be at bottom, 39°F (3.9° C). Water of the hypolimnion, as this deep, cold layer is called, has little or no contact with air and usually has not enough oxygen for fish comfort.

SHELF RESTING AREA

A *This is an ideal bass resting area with a gently sloping shelf extending through the thermocline, giving the fish considerable latitude of movement to follow variations of temperature. Fish resting here feed at feeding stations D and G.*

SLOPE RESTING AREA

B *Steep slope at B has less resting area than A, but may hold larger fish.*

POCKET RESTING AREA

C *This area could hold a sizable body of fish, having three good feeding stations nearby. Fish at C may visit B, and vice versa. Fish from both areas will feed at E, a submerged hilltop, and a few fish from B may visit F and H.*

SHELF FEEDING AREA

D *A shallow shelf like this supports small baitfish, worms, insect nymphs and larvae; it is* a prime feeding ground for small to medium fish.

REEF FEEDING AREA

E *"Reef", actually a submerged hilltop, is good only when a school of baitfish or body of insect nymphs is present.*

WEEDBED FEEDING AREA

F *A bed of lily pads is always a prime bass-holding feature. Lily pads grow in water of 3–10 ft (1–3 m) depth. The reed bed inshore is a good bass feeding area and two such areas close together constitute a very favourable spot for twilight, night, or cloudy day summer lake fishing.*

SUBMERGED TIMBER

G *Excellent feeding and resting area for a few very large fish which may stay in the shadow of submerged limbs and tree trunks during daylight hours.*

SUBMERGED CLIFF

H *A rocky cliff that is partially or totally submerged will draw both small and large fish and often hold them during the day.*

PIKE AND MUSKEL-LUNGE–HABITAT

Of the several species of pikes, the northern pike, (*Esox lucius*) is probably the best known and most actively pursued by anglers. Range of the northern pike is circumpolar in northern Europe, Asia, and North America throughout central Canada and the northern U.S.A. All of the pikes, including the muskellunge, are considered to be solitary predators with a distinct sense of territoriality except during the spring breeding season when large gatherings of both sexes come together at the most favoured breeding areas.

Largest of the pikes, the muskellunge (*Esox masquinongy*) is primarily a North American fish ranging throughout the lake regions of Canada and the northern United States. Because of its desirability as game it has been introduced in many bodies of water outside its natural range. The musky, as it is popularly called, is thought to have evolved from a saltwater species that entered the Mississippi valley from the sea and eventually became isolated in northern lakes and rivers during the retreat of glaciers. Fossil species have been found in Europe where related species now live.

Both pike and muskellunge prey heavily on smaller fish including juveniles of their own kind. They prefer the upper strata of a lake or deep river, frequently lying in wait in the shelter of a reed bed, under lily pads, or beneath the roots and branches of a wind-fallen tree at the edge of the shore. From such hiding places they pounce forth on unsuspecting smaller fish passing by. The majority of large pike and muskies are caught at depths of 3.3–20 ft (1–6 m).

Small pike and muskies are often caught at greater depths where they go to find the small baitfish on which they feed and also to escape the attention of adult members of their own families. The rate of growth of the pikes is rapid under good conditions, with small fish such as yellow perch, suckers, sunfish, ciscos, sticklebacks, crappies, whitefish, walleyes, shiners, and others included in the diet. Mature pike and muskies also take such nonfish bait as ducklings, mice, frogs, crayfish, young muskrats, leeches, and some of the larger insect nymphs and larvae.

The map and sketches at right illustrate a typical pike and muskellunge lake of the north-temperate country. The dashed line x–x in the main sketch shows the location of the cross-section of the lake demonstrated in the lower sketch. Pike and muskellunge usually stay above the thermocline in a lake in summer, but may be found at much greater depths under ice in winter when the lake's temperature structure has changed to the winter configuration with maximum temperature 39° F (3.9° C) at the bottom of the lake.

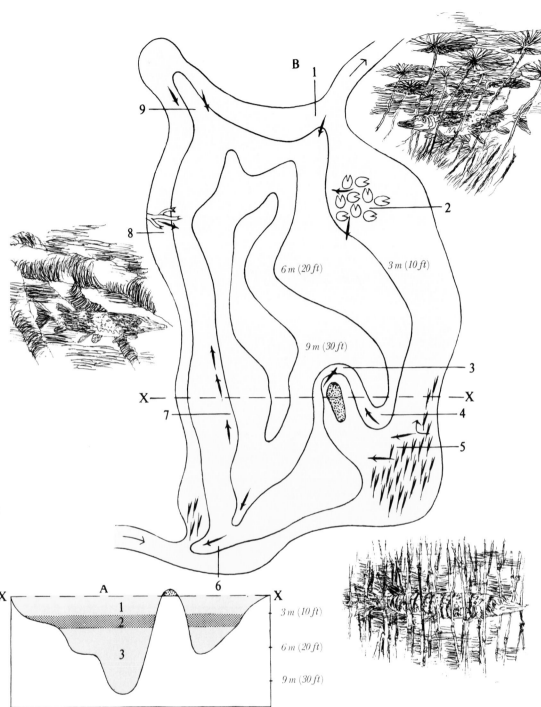

A KEY TO THE CROSS-SECTION SKETCH IS AS FOLLOWS:

1 *Epilimnion: upper layer of water warmed by contact with air and summer sun.*

2 *Thermocline: mixing zone between warmer upper layer and colder water down deep.*

3 *Hypolimnion: cold water with low oxygen content.*

B KEY FISHING LOCATIONS

1 *Mouth of stream that drains the lake.*

2 *Under lily pads on a shelf extending from shore into deep water.*

3 *Off tip of island where there is deep water just beyond.*

4 *In pocket formed by tongue of deep water extending into a shallow area.*

5 *Edge of reed bed.*

6 *At edge of grass bed bordering a deep channel into which water flows from a stream feeding lake.*

7 *Along edge of a deep shelf parallel to the shore where thermocline lies at or just over the shelf.*

8 *Under tree partially submerged at shore.*

9 *In deep, narrow cove between two shores.*

Topographical maps of good fishing lakes are often available and are a great help in learning to "read" the lake's fish-holding features. Other aids to locating the fish are:
Portable sounder.
Depth-temperature probe.
Indications of baitfish by sight or by bird action.

MATCH FISHING

Match fishing has long defied accurate analysis. What is the motivation behind the regimented activity of tens of thousands of dedicated British anglers every weekend of the fishing season? Some of the attempts to explain it have been at best uncharitable and at worst downright mischievous. Why should these people choose to spend their leisure hours in a fishing situation which has been imposed upon them by a draw for places, rather than pick themselves waterside places of generally far greater potential?

By and large match anglers are a friendly lot. They don't thrive on seclusion, they don't hide themselves away and they are happy to talk about what they do and why they do it.

They like to put money on their chances of winning. The average match angler invests anything from 50p to as much as £10 a week on his prospects, which, some say, distorts angling's image and even ruins the pleasures it can give.

But the real *raison d'être* for match fishing is not, one suspects, the money involved. Perhaps it has something to do with the special challenge presented by this branch of the sport. To keep fishing at peak interest, to provide the tuning which makes it imperative that he catches as many fish as possible, a match angler needs another ingredient – in short he needs competition.

There may be other and deeper reasons for some anglers if not for all; possibly the chance to win some form of accolade at weekends when such opportunity is denied by a boring job during the week. And there is, undeniably, the fact that match fishing offers the opportunity of winning money.

Let's put this into perspective, however. There are few rich rewards. A top return for a season would be around £4,000. On average only a score of anglers win £1,000 in any one year – and none is able to top £1,000 year after year.

Cash prizes are getting bigger, though. The sponsorship of major contests is bringing outside money into fishing though there are still no professionals. No-one makes a living at it and most are delighted if, in the course of a season, they are able to pay for their fishing out of their winnings.

Cost and time commitment are both very high in relation to the cash return and it would certainly be true to say that everyone could, in fact, earn very much more money if he gave those extra hours and all that commitment to working overtime at his ordinary job.

The best the match fisherman can expect is the chance to earn a living from fishing in some other way and it is far from coincidental that many of the top match anglers are connected with the tackle trade.

Among the better-known English international anglers, Ivan Marks, Clive Smith, Percy Anderson and Billy Lane are all involved with their own tackle shops. Kevin Ashurst is a maggot breeder. Regular high-level performance in competitions can provide publicity for a successful career in the trade itself.

Match anglers are not averse to making sly digs at their specimen-hunting counterparts. One suggestion is that a specimen hunter (that is, an angler who concentrates on capturing 'specimen' fish) uses time in the way that a match angler uses skill. But that does perhaps underline the match angler's philosophy.

Protracted fishing sessions are totally foreign to match anglers. They rarely sit down for more than five hours at a stretch. They have to speed the pace rather than lay siege to their quarry, so they adopt the quite simple policy of going for the best possible weight of fish that can be landed in the time allowed. The size of individual fish is not irrelevant but the match angler bases his tactics on size allied to numbers. He may not be able to land one 10 lb (4·5 kg) bream or even five 2 lb (0·9 kg) bream but the water could perhaps give him the chance of 40 bream averaging 4 oz (100 g) apiece.

One of Britain's most noted match fishermen, Ivan Marks, sets himself a target weight in every contest he fishes. The state of the river, the air temperature, past form for the venue, the calibre of competing anglers; all help to dictate exactly what that target weight will be.

If, for example, Ivan were fishing the Great Ouse Championship on the Relief Channel in East Anglia, he would most likely say he would need 40 lb (17 kg) to win. There's only one way to get 40 lb of fish from that water and that's by going all out for bream, big bream. And since they average 3 lb (1·25 kg) each, Ivan knows he needs 13 or 14 big fish to give himself a winning chance.

That sort of logic reveals the problems. Ivan will need 15 bites or more in five hours – a bite every 20 minutes. This immediately suggests there is plenty of time – which there is. There's no need to rush. A gentle but decisive approach is more likely to succeed.

The experienced match angler's knowledge allows him to select the species most likely to give him a winning weight, but his swim may not hold any of those fish on that day. They could be a mile or even just 50 yards away. He has to back his hunches—and, in truth, many swims can never be expected to produce match-winning weights.

This is where knowledge of past form becomes useful. It may be a trifle dispiriting to know all the swims in a river well, simply because the angler then becomes aware that he has been allocated a poor swim and his chances are minimal; but at least he can revise his tactics so that he fishes for a section rather than an overall win.

Policies can change as a match progresses. Let's assume Ivan decided to go for bleak and reckoned he needed 14 lb (6 kg) to win. If at half time he has caught only 3 lb (1·25 kg) of bleak, he knows there's no chance of 11 lb (4·75 kg) in the remaining time. So he is obliged to change tactics – unless sport is slow all along the match line and he has set his target too high.

But if other anglers are catching fish and it seems his 14 lb target was accurate, then he has to change to fishing for bigger fish: roach, bream or chub – and he may have to try for all three to keep his hopes alive until the last hour.

The matchman's tackle and tactics have come in for as much sweeping criticism from other anglers as has his obsession with aggregate weight rather than specimen fish. For the match angler's tackle is often very different from that used to catch big fish.

What is known as the Sheffield style of fishing – fine and far off – is being adopted more and more. It has been made necessary because most of the waters on which matches are arranged are very hard-fished and, as a result, the fish have become wary and suspicious. The match angler will fish as fine as he dares, depending on the quarry he has chosen to pursue. He will choose the lightest possible rod, from 11 to 14 feet (3·5-4·5 m) in length, both to facilitate striking and to ease the strain of holding the rod all the time (the serious match angler rarely places it in a rest).

Whereas a specimen-fish angler will say that since he is hoping to catch a 6 lb (2·5 kg) bream on a lobworm he needs a size 6 hook, the match angler believes that fish are scared by too much iron and prefers to fish a much smaller bait and hook. Ivan Marks, for example, is convinced that the best hook for roach and bream fishing in the Fenland drains is a size 20. His big catches from the Great Ouse Relief Channel, including a river championship record weight of 62 lb 8 oz (about 27 kg), are usually made on a size 20 hook. Small hook, plenty of bites, big hook few bites—that's Ivan's logic.

Most match fishing is carried out in the middle of the day, when the sun is at its brightest, when the light is clearest, when fish are least hungry (most of them having eaten at first light) and when there is more disturbance both on the bank and on the water itself as the result of other activity. In short, it's the most difficult time of the day for catching fish in summer. Winter is another matter altogether.

If an angler fishes at first light, when bream, for example, are having their major meal of the day, then bigger baits and heavier hooks can be used.

The basic fact, though, is that the size of the hook the match angler uses is related to the size of the bait – not the size of the fish he hopes to catch: single or even double maggots, one or two casters, a single redworm, they can all be adequately contained on a size 20 hook. That, of course, is not intended as hard-and-fast advice for beginners, but it is the very first link in a chain of balanced tackle which allows a match angler to fish very light.

It is quite customary for a match angler fishing a size 20 hook to use a hook length of 1 lb (0·4 kg) breaking strain, a reel line of 1½ lb to 2 lb (0·6-0·8 kg) breaking strain and a rod which can apply a maximum load of a very few ounces. If this seems fragile in the extreme, remember that big roach and bream can be landed on it with ease, although the situation becomes complicated if the water is weedy or otherwise snag-ridden. Even so, first principles apply and the primary object is to get the bait into the fish's mouth.

Multiple worms, bread, wasp grubs, cheese, luncheon meat; these are all big or at least relatively big baits which are more usually fished on bigger hooks, but even here the match angler is never afraid to reduce the size of his hook to mini-proportions if he feels this gives him a better chance of making contact.

By and large the average angler is not over-fussy about his bait. He will pop into his local tackle shop and buy himself a pint or so of whatever maggots he fancies for the weekend's fishing. Match anglers are far more demanding, even to the extent of breeding their own maggots, having their own wormeries in the garden and undertaking special cleansing and colouring processes, all calculated to get their bait to peak efficiency.

The gosser, a creamy-white, extra soft and thin-skinned maggot, is reckoned the best of all for bream and some other types of fishing. Match anglers have perfected methods by which these can be bred in a closely-knit community of semi-detached houses and with, they claim, the neighbours being unable to detect the slight odour. Whether or not that is the complete truth only those neighbours can ever confirm, and the less they know about it the better!

Maggots are riddled and then washed in lukewarm water on being brought home from the tackle shop. They are stained various colours but are preferably colour-fed while in the growing stage. Their food is dyed and they unwittingly become redskins, yellow-skins, or whatever is fancied. All very complicated and demanding in time but there is no substitute for adequate preparation.

One thing you will notice during a competition is the precise way in which the serious match fisherman lays out his tackle. He brings to this matter the kind of thought which the work study specialist applies to the industrial environment. Every item must be readily available – the rod, of course, the landing and keep nets, the bait and groundbait (frequently hurled into the right place in the swim by means of a catapult). Barbless hooks are often used so that fish can be easily detached, often shaken straight into the keep net. Any

Match fishing is at its peak during the summer months, when the fish are likely to be feeding most freely. Every water, virtually each length of river or canal, is filled by such anglers at the weekend. The more popular rivers like the Severn and the Welland are match-fished on successive days.

Anglers do not, of course, have the exclusive use of the rivers. Boat traffic is developing as a major problem and match anglers have, in effect, been driven off the Norfolk Broads during the summer months.

There are perhaps 20,000 coarse fishing clubs in England and Wales, with 75 per cent of them fishing a regular series of fixtures throughout the season. Many contests are low-level, small-entry affairs involving a score or so of competitors, but many of these small clubs are in turn affiliated to associations. These associations have their own fixtures in which the entry may run into hundreds, even into thousands.

The overall organisation for match anglers is the National Federation of Anglers, with its own permanent secretariat and headquarters at Derby. It claims a membership of 460,000 and organises most of the premier events in match angling.

The NFA organises three National Championships every summer, each for 80 teams of 12 anglers operating in divisions and with promotion and relegation, as in the Football League. In addition it operates what is known as the East Anglian Cup, named after its tackle trade sponsors. This is the angling equivalent of the FA Cup, with teams of 12 drawn together in a sudden-death knock-out contest. And there is the Embassy Challenge, a contest for individuals rather than clubs, progressing to a grand finale which in recent years has been held in Denmark.

In addition, the NFA enters a team in World Championships and, although England has yet to win the team honours, it is continuing to run close and has already provided two individual world champions in Billy Lane, of Coventry, and Robin Harris, of Peterborough.

It is, therefore, easy to see that there is a ladder of progression along which the novice can travel with the ultimate possibility of becoming an international or even a world champion.

Match fishing becomes much more demanding in winter. During difficult conditions an individual often has a far better chance of a worthwhile catch, but such is the appeal of competitive fishing that a nationwide system of Winter Leagues has been set up by the weekly newspaper *Angling Times*.

There are some 30 leagues, each involving from 8 to 15 teams, fishing five- or six-match series. Close on 8,000 match anglers compete, often in the worst of weather when it is difficult if not impossible to catch fish. Yet their enthusiasm never flags.

The competitive scene is very much a part of angling today and whatever criticism may be made, it cannot be denied that success at this branch of angling calls for a high degree of skill. The match fisherman who is consistently among the prizewinners is he who knows how to make the most of his opportunities.

The modern match fisherman and his tackle:
1 Large fine-mesh keepnet
2 Extra-wide rod rest
3 Micromesh landing net, pan-type
4 Sunshield
5 Nail clippers for easy and accurate line trimming
6 Forceps for removing hooks
7 Bait assortment tray
8 Extra rod
9 Large rod holdall
10 Continental-style fishing 'basket' and seat
11 Tackle box
12 Groundbait mixing bowl
13 Hand towel

COARSE FISHING

Whoever invented the term "coarse" to describe the fishing for most freshwater species was being less than fair both to fish and fishermen. There is certainly nothing coarse about a fine roach in the peak of condition, the beautiful bold-biting perch or the silvery dace, which can tweak at a bait and be off before the angler has time to flex his muscles to strike. Nor can anyone deride the sport to be provided by the predatory pike, the powerful barbel and chub or the cunning carp.

And when you realise that the term, strictly speaking, also embraces one fish of the salmon species, none other than 'the lady of the stream', the grayling, the absurdity of the description is quite plain. Why the grayling should be deemed a coarse fish merely

because its spawning period coincides with that of other coarse fish is always causing raised eyebrows. In fact, most angling writers ignore the classification and treat the grayling as a companion to the trout, which it so often is.

Nor could anything be more misleading than to describe as "coarse" the techniques used to take these fish. With the remarkable growth in the number of anglers which has taken place since the war, most of the lakes, ponds, canals and slow-flowing rivers of Europe which harbour these fish are so hard-pressed that to take good fish in numbers with any regularity calls for a high degree of skill coupled with a willingness to take pains and to employ the finest of techniques. Every angler knows that fish become educated after a while, especially when they are caught and returned to the water, as is the practice in Britain, where it is believed that stocks would soon be entirely destroyed if all those

caught were killed. The fact that coarse fish are not widely eaten in Britain is another reason for returning them.

Coarse fish thus provide a challenge which should not be under-estimated. As in other branches of the sport, success comes only to the angler prepared to study the characteristics of his quarry, to familiarise himself with catching techniques found by long experience to be most successful and with the range of equipment available. Having done this, he must then be prepared to apply himself with all the diligence and patience he can muster to achieve success – there are no short cuts.

Because each species is distinctive and calls for a special approach, each of the principal fish will now be considered in turn. . . .

BARBEL

This strong, powerful fish is much sought after for its splendid sporting qualities. Unfortunately, it is found only in relatively few European rivers. The most noted barbel fishery in Britain is the Royalty on the Hampshire Avon near Christchurch, where the fish run very large indeed – fish of 10 lb (4·5 kg) and upwards have been taken there. Other good barbel waters are the Thames, its famous tributary the Kennet, the Severn and a number of streams in Yorkshire.

Weir pools and mill-races are good places to find barbel early in the season; later on they tend to move downstream and populate fast-flowing stretches with a clean, gravel bottom.

A strong rod, 12 or 13 feet long, with a line of at least 6 lb (2·5 kg) breaking strain and hooks suited to take the large baits required are recommended, though tackle should be adapted to the location and conditions. Legering in the current with sausage meat, lobworms, cheese or maggots is probably the best method, but don't put your rod in a rest; the take of a big barbel can be quite spectacular.

Groundbait with worms in balls of clay, but make sure you cast well upstream of your swim to ensure the groundbait is not carried downstream. A 'swim feeder' is useful for this purpose.

Try a running leger consisting of a stop shot about eighteen inches from the hook above which is positioned a swivel and a short length of monofilament containing as many swan shot as are needed to hold the bottom. This form of legering is excellent for many other fish, too.

BREAM

Nobody can pretend that bream are strong fighters, or even that they are particularly difficult to catch,

once located. The attraction here lies largely in quantity, because if the fish are there, and feeding, the angler can expect to take them in large numbers provided he keeps them in the swim with careful groundbaiting and does nothing to scare them away.

Bream like the deep, slow-moving and even turbid waters and are fairly catholic in their tastes. Knobs of breadpaste, pieces of crust or the tail of a lobworm, as well as the ubiquitous maggots, are all good baits. A rod of average size, line of ³/4 lb (0·3 kg) breaking strain and hooks from 8 to 16 can be used.

A typical bream bite is the float lying flat on the surface; this is

caused by the fish standing on its nose and lifting the bait and weights. But the strike should not be made until the float begins to move away.

CARP

Here is a quarry to tax the ingenuity of any fisherman. Immensely suspicious, easily disturbed, unpredictable and difficult to interest in any bait, carp have in recent years attracted the attention of internationally famous British anglers like Richard Walker, whose 44 lb (19 kg) fish from Redmire Pool, Herefordshire, captured the British record.

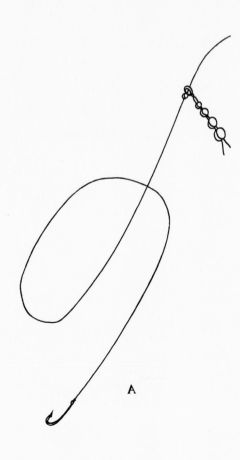

A *Running leger:*
   The number of shot on the link can be varied as required.

Catching carp is a specialist operation, to which much time, thought and careful preparation must be devoted. Extensive preliminary groundbaiting is required, followed by a silent assault at dawn or dusk, or during the night. Dick Walker's record fish was taken on a cold, black night with threatening rain.

A powerful rod, line of 7 to 10 lb (3-4·5 kg) breaking strain or more and bait the size of a golf ball on a large hook size 3 or 4 should be employed. The bait must cover the hook completely and the use of a fixed-spool reel with the bale arm off to allow the fish a free and unfettered run is desirable —if the carp should feel the slightest check it is liable to drop the bait at once. No weight is used, as the weight of the bait is enough to allow it to rest on the bottom. For night fishing the rod is usually placed in two rests, taking care to ensure free play for the line. Many carp fishermen use electric bite alarms for night fishing.

For daytime fishing a float is undesirable as it scares the fish. As an alternative to legering, carp can frequently be taken on floating crust. This is cast to a suitable place among the lily pads or close to the bank in the carp's cruising area.

Carp are mostly found in stillwaters, though they also thrive in slow-flowing rivers.

CHUB

Described by Izaak Walton as the "fearfullest of fishes" because of its cautious nature, the chub is, however, by no means so hard to catch as the carp.

Make a quiet quest for chub in weir pools on the edge of the fast water, holes in the bank, beneath trees and anywhere, in fact, where the water is fairly deep and there is plenty of cover. Having located your quarry, approach as quietly as possible and try floating a piece of cheese on an unweighted line down the swim, or if fish have been seen rising, a piece of floating breadcrust, a natural Daddy-longlegs or a beetle-type artificial.

A large chub will give excellent sport, especially on the fairly fine tackle required to interest the fish. Legering with bread, cheese, lobworms or maggots are excellent ways of taking them, but long-trotting with float is also successful, especially on the Hampshire Avon, where fish of more than 4 lb (1·75 kg) in weight are frequently taken.

DACE

Often found to occupy the same swims as roach, dace are caught by very similar baits and methods. The main differences between them are that dace are more silvery and streamlined, and run smaller. They also call for even quicker reactions from the angler; frequently the float shoots down and up before he has had time even to think of striking.

PERCH

The perch is beloved of schoolboys because of his readiness to swallow a worm or maggot, in which operation he will often pull the float under and hook himself.

Small perch can be taken by the score with a float-fished bait positioned about midwater in likely spots, but the bigger fish demand a more studied approach. A minnow hooked through the lip or back or a large lobworm will frequently take them – though it must be added that perch of more than 3 lb are rare.

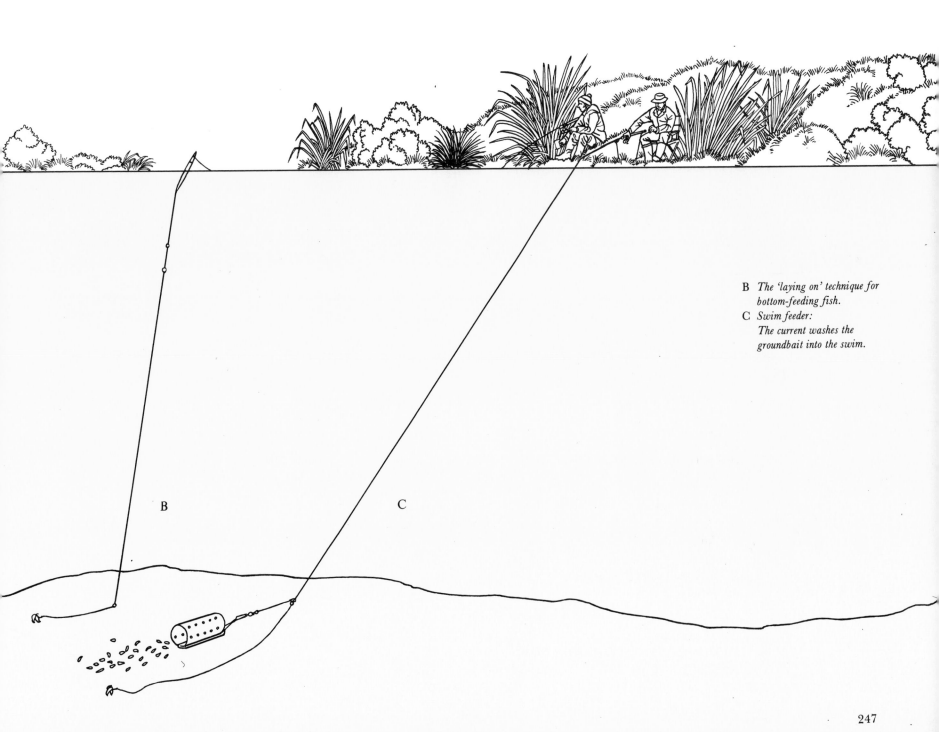

B The 'laying on' technique for bottom-feeding fish.
C Swim feeder:
The current washes the groundbait into the swim.

247

Perch are partial to situations where small tributary streams or pipes emerge, and around jetties and moored boats. They prefer quiet, fairly deep water and are to be found in streams, canals and lakes.

ROACH

The coarse fisherman's most familiar quarry – found in lakes, ponds, canals, rivers and streams in most lowland areas in Europe. The anglers you see lining the banks of the Thames, Seine or Rhine will almost invariably be fishing for them.

The fish can be taken with a variety of baits. Breadpaste or crust, maggots, worms, boiled wheat and cheese are among the

caught by legering in rivers and streams, as well as in canals and ponds, but again careful groundbaiting is necessary.

Roach do not run large – a three-pounder is a fish of a lifetime – but they can fight exceptionally well when in the peak of condition. Nevertheless the lightest possible tackle and the smallest hooks should be used.

Provided he remembers that RUDD feed mainly in the surface area, the angler will find that in most respects he can fish for them as he would for roach.

E *Floats for different purposes:*
1 *Trotting.*
2 *Antenna for heavy water.*
3 *Float for shallow water.*
4 *General-purpose float.*

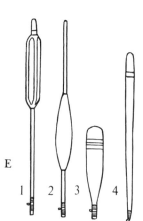

E

1 2 3 4

PIKE FISHING METHODS

The principle of 'big bait for big fish' applies to all members of the pike family. These fishes are true predators, feeding almost exclusively on smaller fish, amphibians, and even birds and small land animals when the opportunity presents itself. Live bait is always a good bet, with roach and dace high on the preferred list. Also favoured are bleak, gudgeon and small perch. Live bait is usually fished in an area where the pike may be found along a shelf or rise, or not far from shore cover. Patience is the

rule, plus a long drop-back after the strike to give the big fish a chance to swallow the bait.

Pike feed almost entirely by day. One type of artificial lure that has won favour in recent years is the so-called 'bottom-bumping' plug. This heavy plug has negative buoyancy and sinks to the bottom unless kept in motion on the line. It is cast out, allowed to sink to the bottom, then retrieved in a series of swimming hops toward the boat until it can be lifted straight up from the bottom. The tail end of the plug is usually buoyant so it will float

best, but hempseed – prepared by boiling the seed until the white roots show – has proved so deadly on some waters that its use has even been banned. Roach will also sometimes take an artificial fly most readily, as well as the natural insect.

As with all fish, the angler must be prepared to adapt his methods to the type of water he is fishing – legering is best on stillwaters, for instance, and what is known as 'long-trotting' is the method found most successful on clear, fast-flowing streams like the Hampshire Avon. This entails the use of a large quill float preferably coloured orange so that it can be seen from a long way off, shotted so that no more than an inch or so appears above the surface and positioned to permit the bait to trip along the bottom. The float is allowed to travel downstream for a considerable distance before being retrieved. Bites are usually decisive and the strike must be made instantly.

Many of the bigger roach are

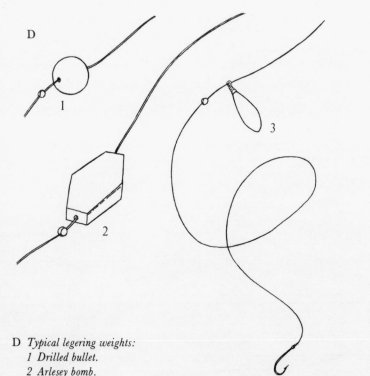

D

1

2

3

D *Typical legering weights:*
1 *Drilled bullet.*
2 *Arlesey bomb.*
3 *Coffin.*

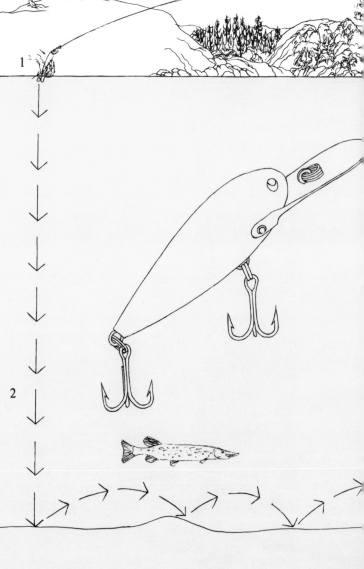

1

2

tail-up at the bottom, thus preventing the hooks from fouling the bottom. This kind of 'bottom bumping' is best done on fairly clear sand or mud bottom where there are no weeds or old tree debris to foul the lure. It is very effective where the angler can work the plug up an underwater slope from deeper into shallower water, especially if the slope coincides with the presence of a thermocline. Trolling with plugs or natural baits is the third important method for taking these large, powerful fish. Trolling or casting tackle should be top quality with line of at least 10 lb (5 kg) class. A heavier monofilament or light wire leader is used to prevent the fish's teeth from cutting off the lure or bait. The plug or bait is trolled at fair speed past the places where these big fish may be lying in wait. The angler strikes hard at the first indication of a pickup to set the hooks, and then applies maximum reel drag tension to try to keep the strong fish out of the weeds, roots, stumps, rocks and other obstacles where it may cut or break the line. When the fish is finally exhausted it is gaffed with a stout gaff or taken in a large, deep hoop net.

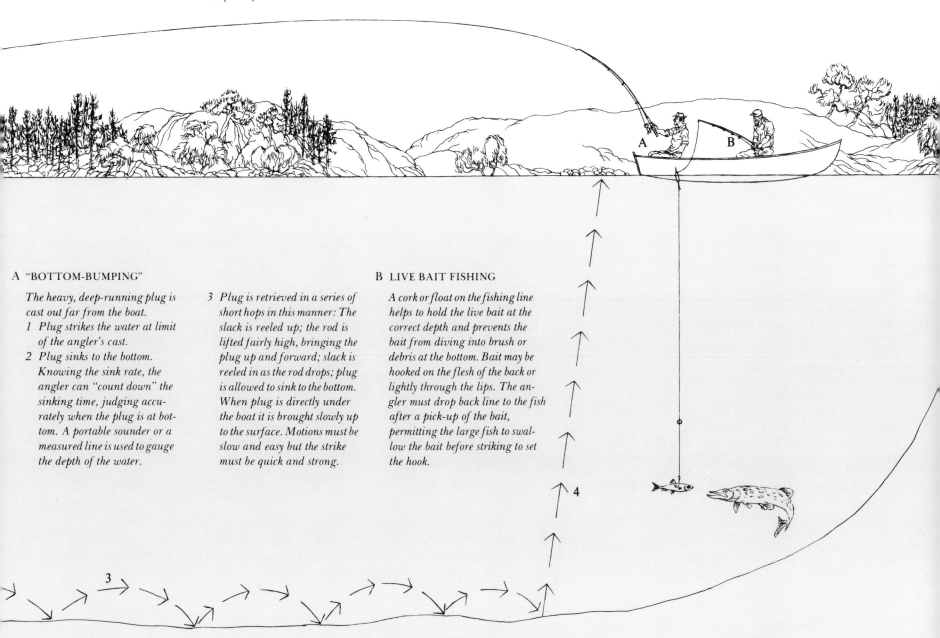

A "BOTTOM-BUMPING"

The heavy, deep-running plug is cast out far from the boat.
1. *Plug strikes the water at limit of the angler's cast.*
2. *Plug sinks to the bottom. Knowing the sink rate, the angler can "count down" the sinking time, judging accurately when the plug is at bottom. A portable sounder or a measured line is used to gauge the depth of the water.*

3. *Plug is retrieved in a series of short hops in this manner: The slack is reeled up; the rod is lifted fairly high, bringing the plug up and forward; slack is reeled in as the rod drops; plug is allowed to sink to the bottom. When plug is directly under the boat it is brought slowly up to the surface. Motions must be slow and easy but the strike must be quick and strong.*

B LIVE BAIT FISHING

A cork or float on the fishing line helps to hold the live bait at the correct depth and prevents the bait from diving into brush or debris at the bottom. Bait may be hooked on the flesh of the back or lightly through the lips. The angler must drop back line to the fish after a pick-up of the bait, permitting the large fish to swallow the bait before striking to set the hook.

FISHING A THERMOCLINE

When a thermocline is established in a lake during summer weather conditions, bass and other lake-dwelling species retire to the comfort zone of temperature they prefer, and they usually find this somewhere in the thermocline layer of the lake's deeper water. Anglers have two different methods for locating the deep, resting fish electronically. Both are demonstrated in Sketch A. One requires the use of an electric depth-temperature probe to determine the depth of the thermocline and the fish's presumed comfort zone. The other is the electronic sounder.

The depth-temperature probe can be used independently of the sounder, and

then retrieves it by bouncing it slowly up the slope of the rise, fishing through the area where the thermocline touches the slope. He has found the rise by using his electronic depth sounder and a topographical map of the lake.

The angler in Sketch C is live bait fishing for bass that are resting in a cool depression filled with water of thermocline temperature which he has located with a depth-temperature probe. Lacking a probe, one can obtain water temperatures at predetermined depths by using this method:

1 Obtain a widemouthed pickle jar of about 1-pt (1/2-liter) capacity. Ballast the jar with sinkers so it will sink with the cork inserted.
2 Screw a strong eye-screw into the cork and tie a loose piece of strong twine between eye-screw and the bottle's neck.

A USING SOUNDER AND TEMPERATURE PROBE

1 Smaller probe shows temperature in dial of handheld unit, thermistor probe is lowered on a coaxial depth-marked cable.
2 Reel-type temperature probe measures length of cable and shows temperature on meter. To use probes, boat must be motionless.
3 Transducer of sounder clamps to boat's side in use, shows depth of bottom and fish.

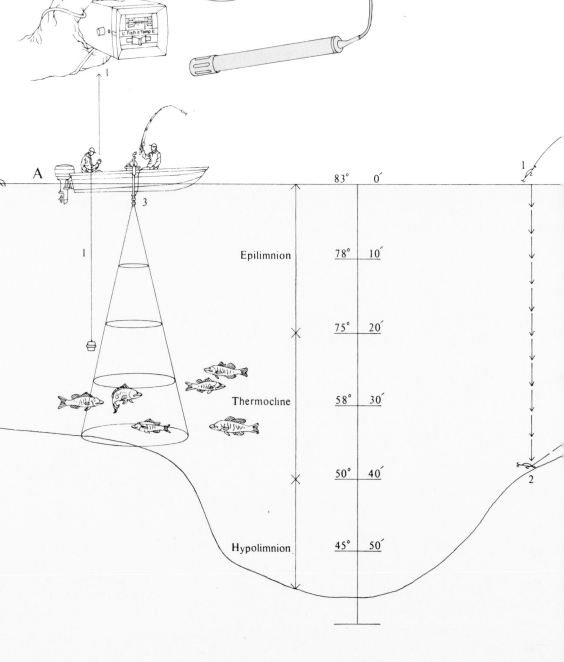

the sounder does not require a depth temperature probe to be used successfully to locate fish. But both together give the angler a great advantage over the fisherman who has only one or the other of the two aids to fish location. The anglers in the boat at A, for example, have located a wide, fairly shallow shelf with the sounder and suspect that they see the flashes indicating fish on their machine's dial. Testing the temperature of the water with the temperature probe indicates the presence of a comfort zone of about 68° F (20° C) over the shelf, suggesting that the fish present are probably bass.

In Sketch B, an angler has located a submerged rise and is fishing one slope of the rise with a bottom-scraping lure called a spoonplug. He casts the lure out and lets it sink,

3 Measure and mark a strong hand line in feet or meters, depending on the measurement used.
4 Place a small thermometer in the jar, insert cork.
5 Tie measured hand line to eye-screw of cork. Lower the bottle to any desired depth, then obtain a water sample from that depth by yanking the line, pulling the cork, admitting water into the jar.
6 Read temperature, repeat at different depths.

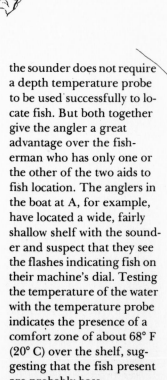

	83°	0'
Epilimnion	78°	10'
	75°	20'
Thermocline	58°	30'
	50°	40'
Hypolimnion	45°	50'

C LIVE BAIT FISHING

Live bait fishing is very effective when fish are found resting in the thermocline comfort zone. Popular natural baits include:

1 *Shiner hooked through the back.*
2 *Shiner hooked through the lips.*
3 *Shiner hooked through the tail.*
4 *Single nightcrawler (large earthworm) hooked through ring.*
5 *Bundle of small worms threaded onto a bait-holder hook.*
6 *Grasshopper hooked under carapace.*
7 *Dragonfly larva or nymph hooked through the back.*
8 *Frog hooked through hind leg.*
9 *Fresh water crayfish hooked through tail.*
10 *Japanese beetle grub threaded on hook.*

Live fish should be kept in a live bait container, as should nymphs and crayfish. Pack worms in rich, damp earth. Keep frogs, hoppers, grubs in cool, ventilated boxes.

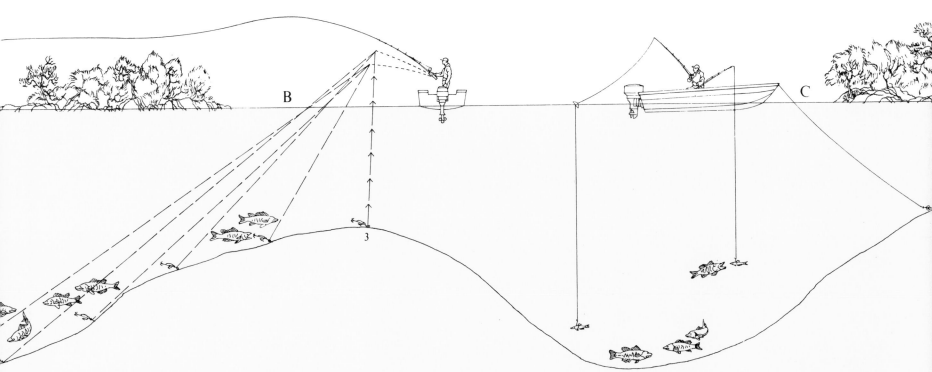

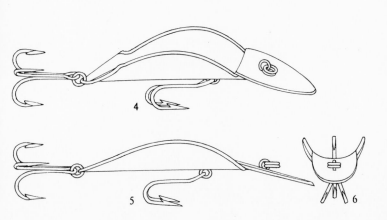

B FISHING A SPOONPLUG

1 *The spoonplug is cast out from the boat so it will sink into the deep water well down the slope of the rise. Boat holds position on top of the rise.*
2 *Spoonplug is hopped up the slope stirring up mud, making noise, attracting the fish. Hopping is caused by rod action.*
3 *Fish usually strike near top of the rise, otherwise spoonplug is hauled in here. Spoonplug has a molded plastic body, metal lip. Pair of double hooks is* attached to underside, gang hook to the tail.
4 *Perspective view.*
5 *Side view.*
6 *Head-on view. The spoonplug's secret is the way it digs and roots into the bottom, making noise and boils of loose mud that are quite attractive to bass and other lake fish. The angler must be quick to strike hard at any sign of a hit from a fish. Once a thermocline is established in a lake, its depth and gradient of temperature will stay fairly constant from* day to day unless there is a major change in weather. Strong winds cause the warm surface waters to move toward the downwind shore, depressing the thermocline near that shore. Upwelling of cold water under the windward shore may raise or move the thermocline away from that shore changing the habits of the fish.

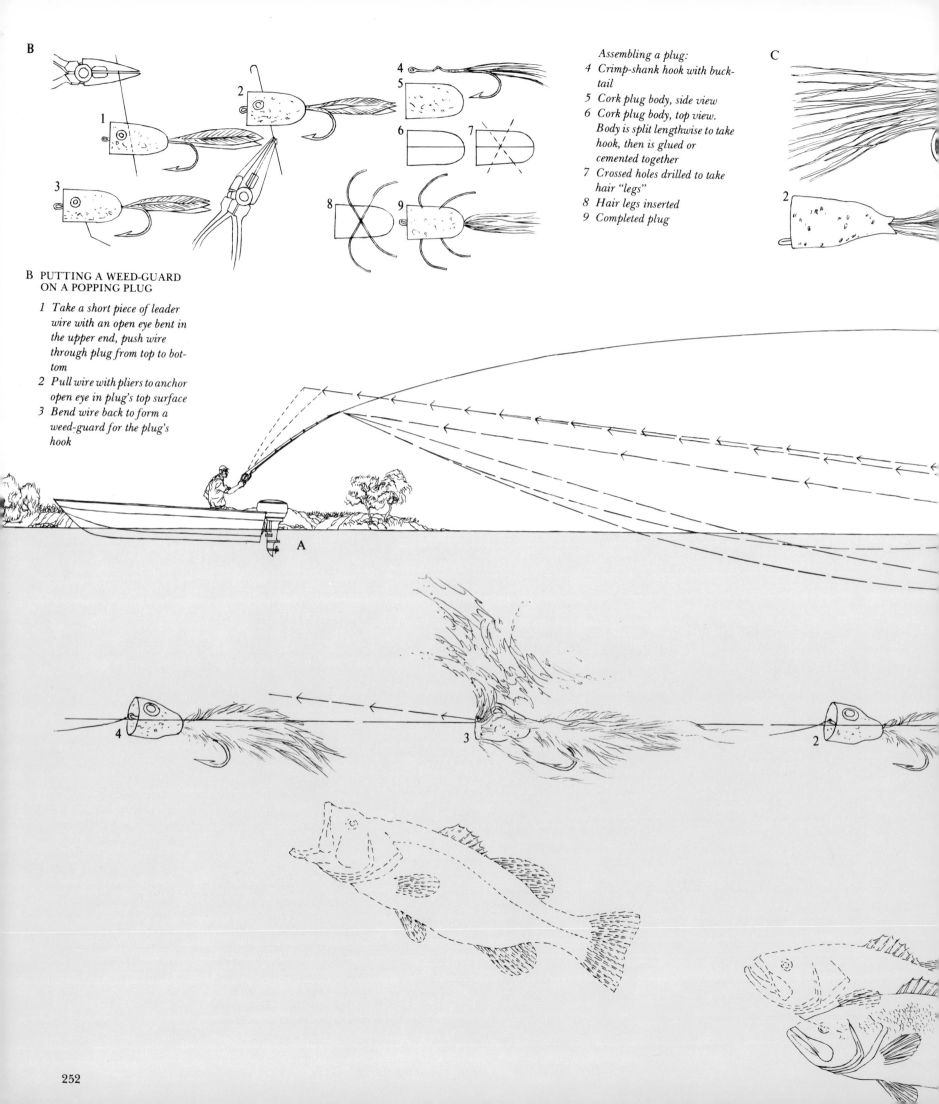

B

Assembling a plug:

4 Crimp-shank hook with buck-tail

5 Cork plug body, side view

6 Cork plug body, top view. Body is split lengthwise to take hook, then is glued or cemented together

7 Crossed holes drilled to take hair "legs"

8 Hair legs inserted

9 Completed plug

C

B PUTTING A WEED-GUARD ON A POPPING PLUG

1 Take a short piece of leader wire with an open eye bent in the upper end, push wire through plug from top to bottom

2 Pull wire with pliers to anchor open eye in plug's top surface

3 Bend wire back to form a weed-guard for the plug's hook

A

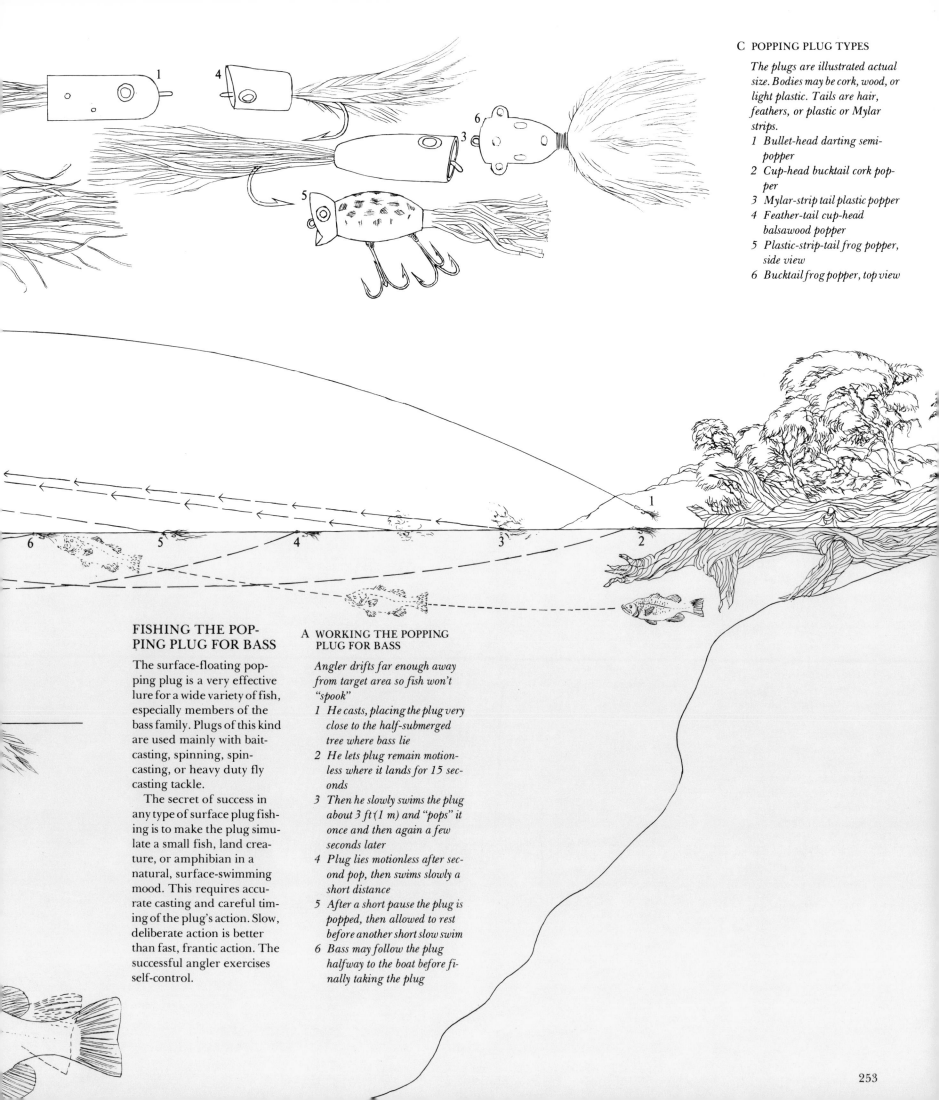

The plugs are illustrated actual size. Bodies may be cork, wood, or light plastic. Tails are hair, feathers, or plastic or Mylar strips.

1 *Bullet-head darting semi-popper*
2 *Cup-head bucktail cork popper*
3 *Mylar-strip tail plastic popper*
4 *Feather-tail cup-head balsawood popper*
5 *Plastic-strip-tail frog popper, side view*
6 *Bucktail frog popper, top view*

FISHING THE POPPING PLUG FOR BASS

The surface-floating popping plug is a very effective lure for a wide variety of fish, especially members of the bass family. Plugs of this kind are used mainly with baitcasting, spinning, spincasting, or heavy duty fly casting tackle.

The secret of success in any type of surface plug fishing is to make the plug simulate a small fish, land creature, or amphibian in a natural, surface-swimming mood. This requires accurate casting and careful timing of the plug's action. Slow, deliberate action is better than fast, frantic action. The successful angler exercises self-control.

A WORKING THE POPPING PLUG FOR BASS

Angler drifts far enough away from target area so fish won't "spook"

1 *He casts, placing the plug very close to the half-submerged tree where bass lie*
2 *He lets plug remain motionless where it lands for 15 seconds*
3 *Then he slowly swims the plug about 3 ft (1 m) and "pops" it once and then again a few seconds later*
4 *Plug lies motionless after second pop, then swims slowly a short distance*
5 *After a short pause the plug is popped, then allowed to rest before another short slow swim*
6 *Bass may follow the plug halfway to the boat before finally taking the plug*

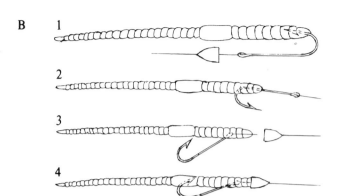

B

1

2

3

4

B RIGGING THE WORM

1 Slip a small lead or plastic nose cap on the line before tying on the hook. Push the hook point into nose of the worm, letting it penetrate until worm nose is at bend of the hook.

2 Bring hook point out through body of worm.

3 Push shank of hook completely through until just the hook eye is buried in the body of the worm.

4 Bury the hook point in the body of the worm, preferably in the ring. This makes the hook "weedless" and easier to fish in dirty water.

C 1

2

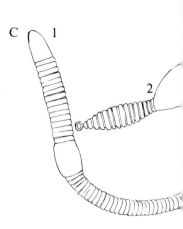

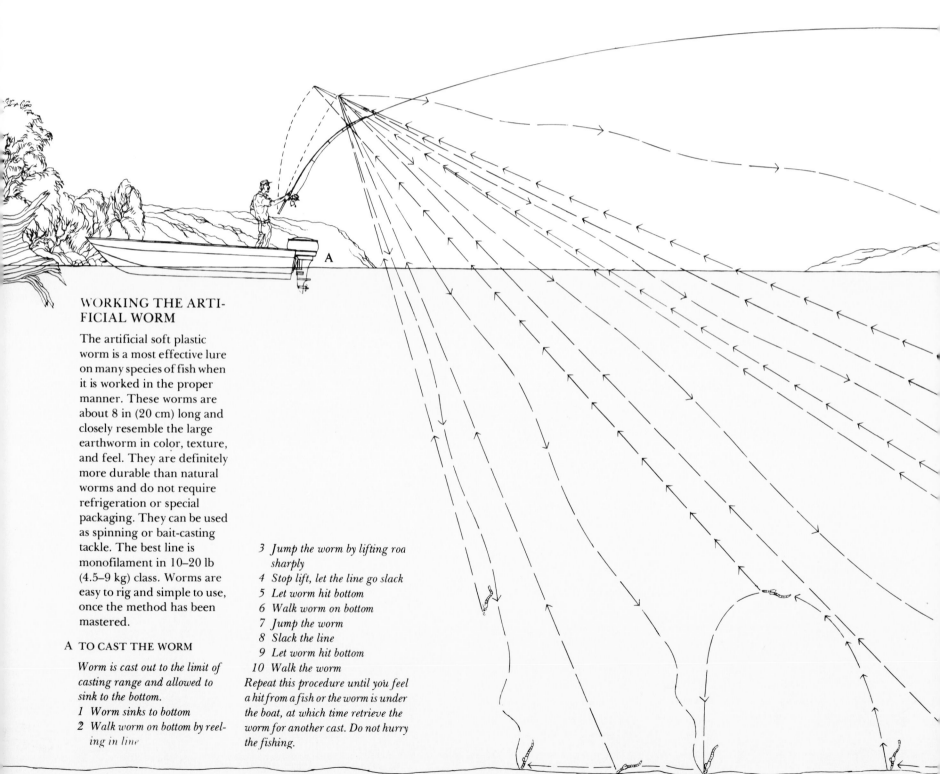

WORKING THE ARTI-FICIAL WORM

The artificial soft plastic worm is a most effective lure on many species of fish when it is worked in the proper manner. These worms are about 8 in (20 cm) long and closely resemble the large earthworm in color, texture, and feel. They are definitely more durable than natural worms and do not require refrigeration or special packaging. They can be used as spinning or bait-casting tackle. The best line is monofilament in 10–20 lb (4.5–9 kg) class. Worms are easy to rig and simple to use, once the method has been mastered.

A TO CAST THE WORM

Worm is cast out to the limit of casting range and allowed to sink to the bottom.

1 *Worm sinks to bottom*
2 *Walk worm on bottom by reeling in line*

3 *Jump the worm by lifting roa sharply*
4 *Stop lift, let the line go slack*
5 *Let worm hit bottom*
6 *Walk worm on bottom*
7 *Jump the worm*
8 *Slack the line*
9 *Let worm hit bottom*
10 *Walk the worm*

Repeat this procedure until you feel a hit from a fish or the worm is under the boat, at which time retrieve the worm for another cast. Do not hurry the fishing.

A

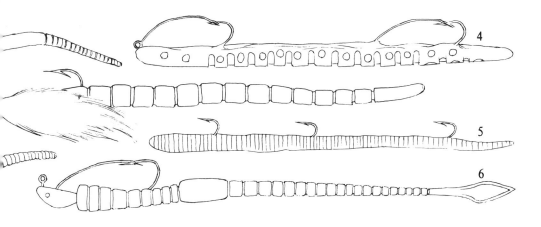

Practical tips for fishing with artificial or natural worms. Remember that fish like slow-moving worms.
Try to make the worm move in a natural way in the water.
Worms like weeds and grass cover, so fish weedless hooks or bury the hook point in the worm's body.
When you feel a bite, wait only 3–4 seconds before striking to set the hook.

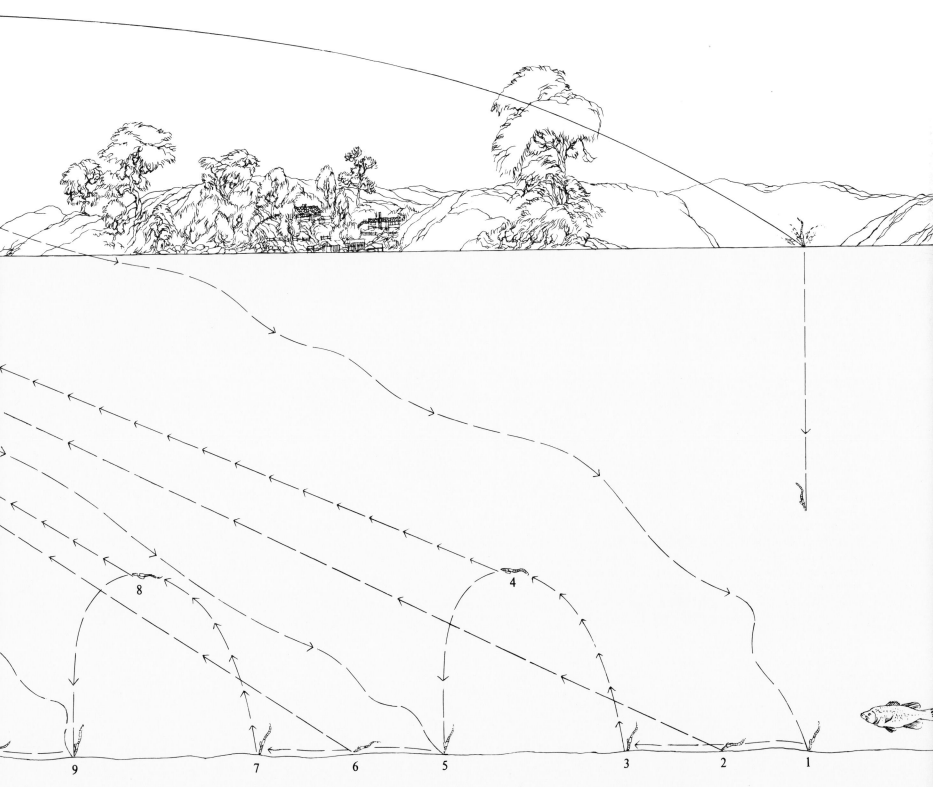

RESERVOIR TROUT FISHING

Never in the history of angling in Britain has there been such a transformation of the trout-fishing scene as has been witnessed in recent times.

At one period the outlook for the fly fisherman looked bleak indeed. The growth in population and the continued expansion of towns and development in the countryside had resulted in many rivers becoming polluted and many others overfished. Those which still provided good sport were either inaccessible or so expensive to fish as to put them beyond the reach of all but a privileged few.

What has dramatically changed the situation has been the creation of hundreds of new reservoirs and other man-made lakes, and their stocking with brown and rainbow trout, mostly the latter.

In the past relatively few reservoirs were stocked with trout and only one or two – like Blagdon Lake in Somerset and Lake Vyrnwy in Wales – had become notable trout fisheries. The potential was not appreciated until Chew Valley, some ten miles from Bristol, and Grafham Water, in Cambridgeshire, came on the scene in the late 1950s and 1960s respectively.

The opportunity provided by these lakes to catch trout of unheard-of sizes – weighing 6 lb (2·5 kg) and over – at relatively cheap rates appealed enormously to British anglers and there was a remarkable response. Hundreds of coarse fishermen decided to try casting a fly for the first time. More and more reservoirs were created – about 75 were opened between 1945 and 1973 alone – and it became almost axiomatic that they be stocked with trout. Fisheries were also made from existing reservoirs and one result of this was that trout fishing became available in the heart of London, to the delight of the capital's sorely deprived fly fishermen.

Over the same period scores of private commercial lake fisheries came into being – so many, in fact, that it could even be suggested that in some parts of the country supply was running ahead of demand. Some of these waters, like Avington and Two Lakes in Hampshire, have become noted big-trout fisheries, producing many fish of well over 10 lb (4·5 kg), but charges for fishing on these commercial lakes tend to be a good deal higher than those on the reservoirs.

Although there has been some slowing down in the creation of commercial fisheries, the construction of new reservoirs has continued, as indeed it must to meet the continuing demand for clean water. A high point in this process, and a historic day for the angling community in Britain, was the opening in 1977 of the giant 3,100-acre reservoir near Empingham in the county of Leicestershire. Known as Rutland Water, this lake is as large as Lake Windermere and the biggest trout reservoir in Europe.

It was conceived from the outset as a trout fishery, fashioned and landscaped to resemble a natural lake as much as possible, and the facilities are excellent although, at the time of writing, still incomplete. It has convincingly set the seal, as it were, on the development of reservoir fishing in Britain. There are some 20 miles of bank fishing.

To fish big waters of this kind, special techniques have been evolved, especially for casting from the bank. It has been found that during the course of a season the trout tend to move farther out, possibly to escape the attentions of hundreds of anglers lining the banks. The long caster thus has an advantage. At first fishermen tried to get the extra distance by using long and rather heavy rods but they found continual casting with these very tiring. More recently, lighter hollow-glass and carbon-fibre rods have come into prominence. These generally stand up better to continual casting than the old cane rods and are less exhausting to use.

They are frequently employed with "shooting heads"; that is, some ten yards of fly line, to the rear end of which is attached 100 yards or so of monofilament of 20/25 lb (8·5/11 kg) breaking strain. When the join is extended by false casting to beyond the top ring, distances of 35–40 yards can be achieved – though striking fish at such distances can be difficult.

Anglers are still experimenting with such techniques – with longer shooting heads, for instance. There have also been several developments with sinking lines – slow, medium and fast – lines in which only the tip is made to sink and so on.

Then there are those who believe in using longer leaders than the conventional length of slightly under nine feet. Brian Clarke, author of *The Pursuit of Stillwater Trout* – advocates a leader of up to 40 feet for casting to deep trout. This in turn means that a special casting technique has to be devised.

At first most reservoir fishermen used large, gaudy lures or 'flashers' to attract the trout – by no stretch of the imagination could these be termed 'flies' – but recently there has been a growing emphasis on the imitation of natural insects and their delicate presentation. The relatively crude casting-out and stripping-in practice is still most widely employed, however, and is often the most effective method early in the season.

Traditional boat-fishing methods employed on Scottish lochs have also undergone some modification by reservoir anglers. One often sees long casts being made from boats using shooting heads and sometimes special rudder-control devices are used – where permitted.

The whole situation is a very flexible one, in which processes are constantly being looked at afresh with the needs of the reservoir angler in mind. Reservoir fishing has clearly become not only a very important branch of the sport in Britain, attracting thousands of anglers a week – who eagerly study the regular returns from their favourite reservoirs – but it has given birth to a whole range of specialised methods which in some respects can be adapted for use elsewhere, thus increasing the general body of angling knowledge.

1 *The Richard Walker adaptation of a Nail Knot for attaching nylon to a shooting head, which is used to provide casting weight beyond the rod tip.*

2 *A situation frequently met on reservoirs – the back cast must be raised to clear a high bank or dam wall behind the angler.*

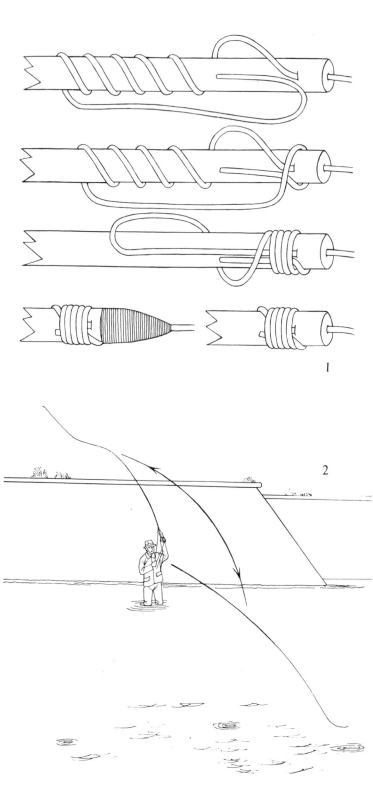

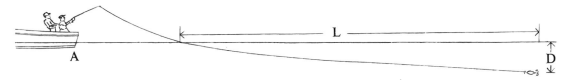

TROLLING SYSTEMS FOR SALT AND FRESH WATER

The early Polynesians, with their fast sailing canoes, were probably the first trolling fishermen. Since those early days many systems for catching fish by trolling have been perfected. Illustrated on the following pages are some of the more important modern trolling methods.

DEEP TROLLING WITH WIRE LINE

Where it is legal throughout the world, deep trolling with wire line has proved to be an extremely efficient method for taking game fish at depths that cannot be fished by normal surface trolling methods. The wire line can be considered to be a greatly elongated sinker that takes the place of an ordinary sinker-and-line trolling combination. Wire trolling line has several distinct advantages over the line-and-sinker combination:

1 Wire line has less surface friction than natural or synthetic fiber soft line and therefore generates less friction drag while moving through the water. Friction drag in trolling tends to prevent a line from sinking below the surface.

2 There is very little stretch in wire. This works advantageously in two ways: (a) the great "sensitivity" of wire line permits the angler to feel each touch and vibration traveling up from the lure: (b) when fishing with lures that require rod action, there is no stretch of line between the angler's rod and the lure to dampen the rod action applied.

3 It takes much less weight of wire line to gain the desired trolling depth. There is less strain on the angler and his tackle.

4 Finally, when a fish is hooked, there is no heavy, bulky weight hanging in one big lump between the rod and the fish. The wire line is just another length of fishing line and the angler fights the fish in the normal manner without the apparent effect of a heavy sinker on his line.

Contrary to some opinion, the types of wire line used by game fishermen are not superstrength material. For instance, on the North American Great Lakes and along the U.S. east and west coasts, one of the most popular types of wire line is soft-drawn Monel wire in diameters of from .020"–.024" (.5–.6 mm) This wire has a normal breaking strain of 36–45 lb (16–20 kg), which is consistent with the breaking strain of the linen or synthetic lines regularly used in the same areas.

In use, wire trolling line is spooled onto the reel on top of a portion of soft-line backing of appropriate breaking test. The breaking test of the backing should be equal to the breaking test of the wire. It is a big advantage to spool on only enough wire to take the lure to the desired depth at normal trolling speed. Depth is regulated by line length and trolling speed with a 1-oz. lure weight and 3–4 knot speed taken as standard.

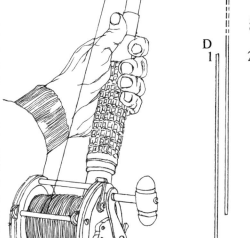

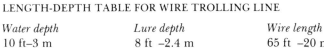

LENGTH-DEPTH TABLE FOR WIRE TROLLING LINE

Water depth	Lure depth	Wire length
10 ft–3 m	8 ft –2.4 m	65 ft –20 m
20 ft–6 m	16 ft–5. m	135 ft–40 m
30 ft–9 m	24 ft–7.5 m	200 ft–60 m
40 ft–12 m	35 ft–10.5 m	280 ft–85 m
50 ft–15 m	45 ft–13.5 m	350 ft–107 m

Table above is for deep trolling with soft-drawn solid Monel wire of .020"–.024" (.5–.6 mm) at 3–4 knots.

SALT AND FRESH WATER FISH THAT RESPOND TO DEEP TROLLING

Species	Depth range
Big-eye tuna	50–100 ft – 15–30 m
Black bass	16–60 ft – 5–18 m
Bluefish	10–50 ft – 3–15 m
Groupers	20–60 ft – 6–18 m
Kingfish	30–60 ft – 9–18 m
Lake trout	20–100 ft – 6–30 m
Mackerel (Boston)	10–30 ft – 3–9 m
Pike	10–40 ft – 3–12 m
Pollock-Cod	10–60 ft – 3–18 m
Salmon	20–100 ft – 6–30 m
School tuna	20–60 ft – 6–18 m
Striped bass	10–50 ft – 3–15 m
Wahoo	20–60 ft – 6–18 m

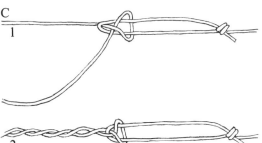

WIRE-PLUS-TROLLING SINKER DEPTH RATIOS
(100 ft, 30 m 4 knots)

Plain Monel or lead-core wire = 8/1 length/depth ratio
Wire plus 4 oz (.11 kg) lead = 5/1 length/depth ratio
Wire plus 8 oz (.23 kg) lead = 3/1 length/depth ratio
Wire plus 12 oz (.34 kg) lead = 2/1 length/depth ratio

A LENGTH-DEPTH RATIO

At the normal trolling speed of 3–4 knots and with lures weighing not over 1–oz, solid wire line achieves a length-depth ratio of about 8/1. This means that for a line length (L), the depth (D) will be L/8. Thus, a wire line 100 ft (32 m) long will put the lure down to a depth of 12.5 ft (4 m). Trolling depth can be controlled by raising or lowering speed, or by lengthening or shortening the line.

B WIRE LINE TACKLE

Almost any star or lever drag game fishing reel with a fairly wide spool will work with wire line. A measured length of wire is spliced on top of suitable soft-line backing that fills the reel spool approximately two-thirds full. The backing should match the wire in breaking strain. Thus, wire testing 45 lb (20 kg) should have IGFA 50 lb (22 1/2 kg) test soft line as backing. A connector is fastened to the outer end of the wire line.

C TO SPLICE WIRE TO THE BACKING

Tie first a loop in the backing (right), then tie the wire to the loop with a Becket Bend (1). Finish Becket Bend in the wire with a number of twists and finishing turns (2).

D TO SPLICE WIRE TO WIRE

"Marry" the two wire ends together with firm twists, (1,2) then finish off the ends of wire with closely spaced finishing turns at both ends of splice.

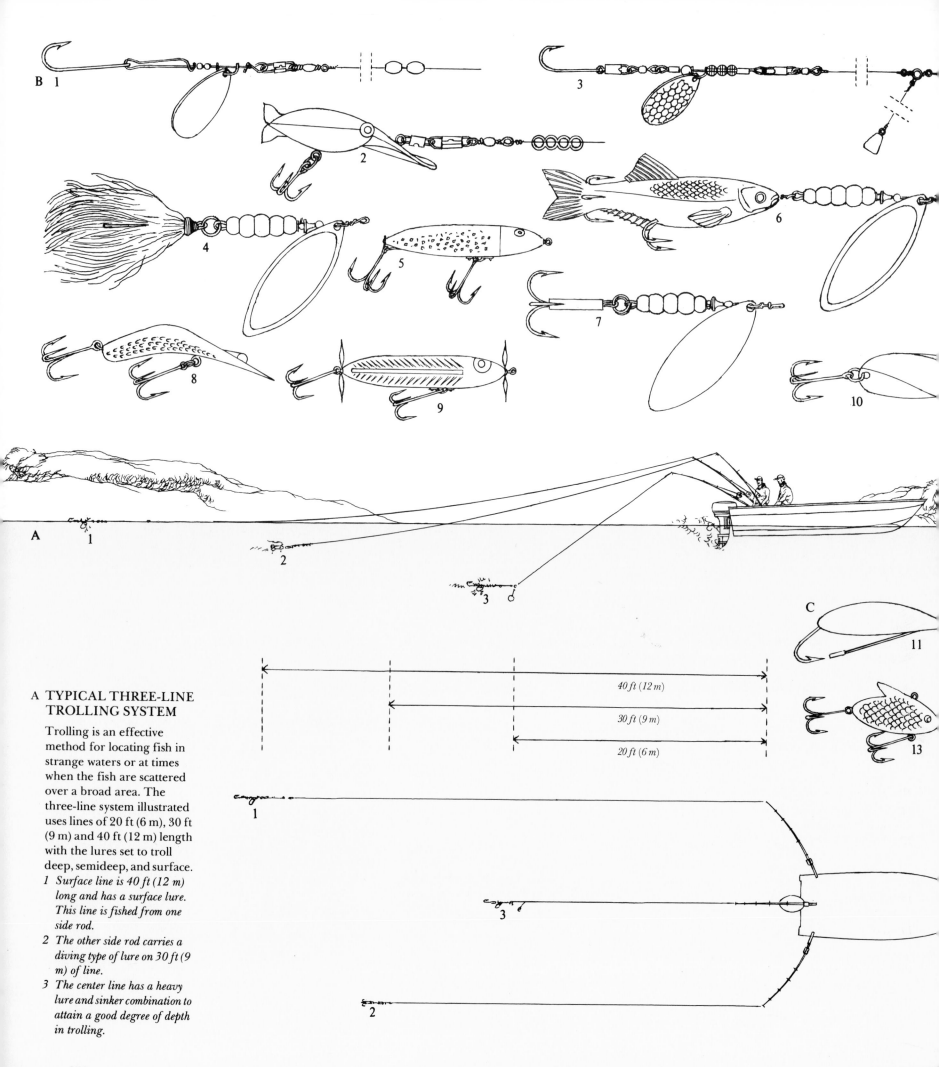

B 1

3

2

4

5

6

7

8

9

10

C

11

13

A

1

2

3

40 ft (12 m)

30 ft (9 m)

20 ft (6 m)

1

3

2

A TYPICAL THREE-LINE TROLLING SYSTEM

Trolling is an effective method for locating fish in strange waters or at times when the fish are scattered over a broad area. The three-line system illustrated uses lines of 20 ft (6 m), 30 ft (9 m) and 40 ft (12 m) length with the lures set to troll deep, semideep, and surface.

1 Surface line is 40 ft (12 m) long and has a surface lure. This line is fished from one side rod.

2 The other side rod carries a diving type of lure on 30 ft (9 m) of line.

3 The center line has a heavy lure and sinker combination to attain a good degree of depth in trolling.

B REPRESENTATIVE LURES FOR BASS TROLLING

1 *Worm or bait rig with spinner (surface)*
2 *Floating-diving plug, floats at rest, dives when trolled*
3 *Worm or bait rig with spinner and auxiliary sinker on branch line*
4 *Spinner with beads and bucktail treble hook*
5 *Surface-running night glow (luminescent) plug*
6 *Spinner with beads and artificial bait*
7 *Spinner with beads and fluorescent hook shank sheath*
8 *Flatfish diving lure*
9 *Double-propellor plastic surface plug with internal mirror*
10 *Dardevle spoon*

D TROLLING OFF A POINT OF LAND

A point of land often has a ridge of rocks extending offshore on the bottom. This ridge or reef is a prime place for bass and other fish to congregate during the usual feeding periods. One method of trolling such a location is to move along lines of the same depth. For example, a boat would start at point 1 in Sketch D and, with sounder running, follow the 5-ft (1 1/2-m) curve around the point. Then it would follow the 10-ft (3-m) curve back to the starting side. The third pass follows the 15-ft (4 1/2-m) curve.

E TROLLING OVER AN OFFSHORE REEF

The same system is used to test by trolling a shallow reef surrounded by deeper water. The boat starts at point 1 in Sketch E and moves over the shallowest part of the reef staying in a depth of, say 5 ft (1 1/2 m). Then the boat traces an elliptical course around the reef, following the 10-ft (3-m) curve. The next circle is on the 15-ft (4 1/2-m) line, and so on until the boat reaches spot 2. Following a definite line or curve of equal depths permits the boat to troll over new water on each pass and assures that the maximum fishable area will be covered. When fish are found by getting strikes on the lures, the boat trolls in water of the same depth in which the fish were found, or stops and anchors or drifts while casting or bait fishing.

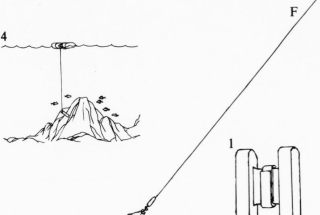

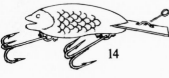

C MORE TROLLING LURES

11 *Johnson silver spoon with weedless hook guard*
12 *Lead-head bucktail jig with weed guard, often used for casting and jigging as well as trolling*
13 *Deep-running plastic sonic lure*
14 *Reverse sonic diving plug*

USING A MARKER FLOAT TO MARK A PRODUCTIVE FISHING SPOT

Frequently, in trolling, the boat will find fish at a previously untried spot, a location that may be difficult to find on a return trip. One way to mark such a spot as soon as a strike has been had is to carry a small marking buoy and drop it overboard where a strike has been had.

1 *This marker float is made of two pieces of balsa or other light wood joined by a smaller piece of wood.*
2 *Enough line is wound around the center piece to reach bottom in any depth to be fished. A sinker acts as the anchor. When dropped over, the line unwinds as the sinker falls to bottom.*
3 *Marker remains at the spot where the strike was had.*
4 *Using the marker buoy as a center, the boat fishes around it and establishes the value of the location in terms of fish. Marker is retrieved when no longer needed.*

THREE POPULAR DEEP-TROLLING SYSTEMS

Three trolling systems that work well in deep water on inland lakes and the ocean are:

The multiple-depth, multi-lure system employing a fixed weight and any number of trolling lures.

The fish-planer or paravane system.

The expendable-weight drop-sinker system.

Wire fishing line is not used in any part of the tackle in these systems.

Deep-trolling can be done from small rowing boats, but is more effective when a motor is used to drive the boat. Power provides better speed control and ability to work upwind or up-current.

The systems shown here do not require elaborate tackle. Depth of lures is easily controlled by varying the boat speed or the line length. Lures can be spoons, jigs, plugs, artificial baits, eels, or rigged natural baits.

A MULTIDEPTH SYSTEM, NAMES OF PARTS

1 Lightweight surface type trolling lure.
2 Plastic or painted metal spoon.
3 Darting type diving plastic lure.
4 Nickel, copper, or chrome-plated spoon.
5 Wooden or plastic diving plug.
6 Fixed sinker 1–2 lb (.5–1 kg).
7 Details of how branch lines are attached to main fishing line.

B DETAILS OF PLANER OR PARAVANE

1 The planer is a metal or plastic device with a heavy wire towing yoke to which the line is attached by means of a swivel. In the trolling mode, forward motion forces the planer to go deep, carrying with it the line and lure.
2 When a fish strikes, the added line-drag "trips" the planer into the nondiving position, putting less tension on the fishing tackle while planer and fish are being hauled in.

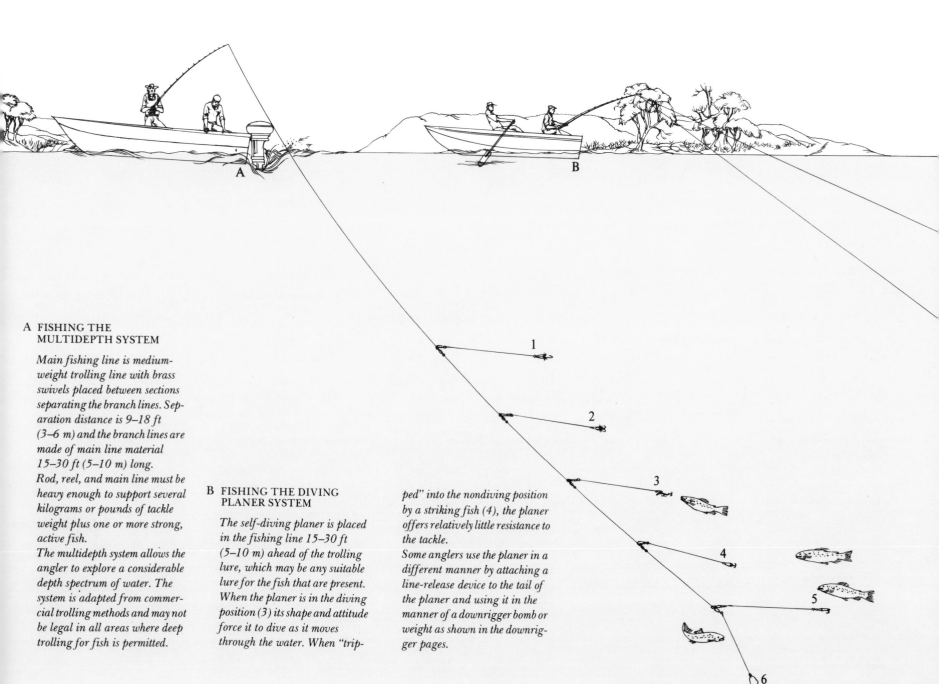

A FISHING THE MULTIDEPTH SYSTEM

Main fishing line is medium-weight trolling line with brass swivels placed between sections separating the branch lines. Separation distance is 9–18 ft (3–6 m) and the branch lines are made of main line material 15–30 ft (5–10 m) long. Rod, reel, and main line must be heavy enough to support several kilograms or pounds of tackle weight plus one or more strong, active fish.

The multidepth system allows the angler to explore a considerable depth spectrum of water. The system is adapted from commercial trolling methods and may not be legal in all areas where deep trolling for fish is permitted.

B FISHING THE DIVING PLANER SYSTEM

The self-diving planer is placed in the fishing line 15–30 ft (5–10 m) ahead of the trolling lure, which may be any suitable lure for the fish that are present. When the planer is in the diving position (3) its shape and attitude force it to dive as it moves through the water. When "trip-ped" into the nondiving position by a striking fish (4), the planer offers relatively little resistance to the tackle.

Some anglers use the planer in a different manner by attaching a line-release device to the tail of the planer and using it in the manner of a downrigger bomb or weight as shown in the downrigger pages.

260

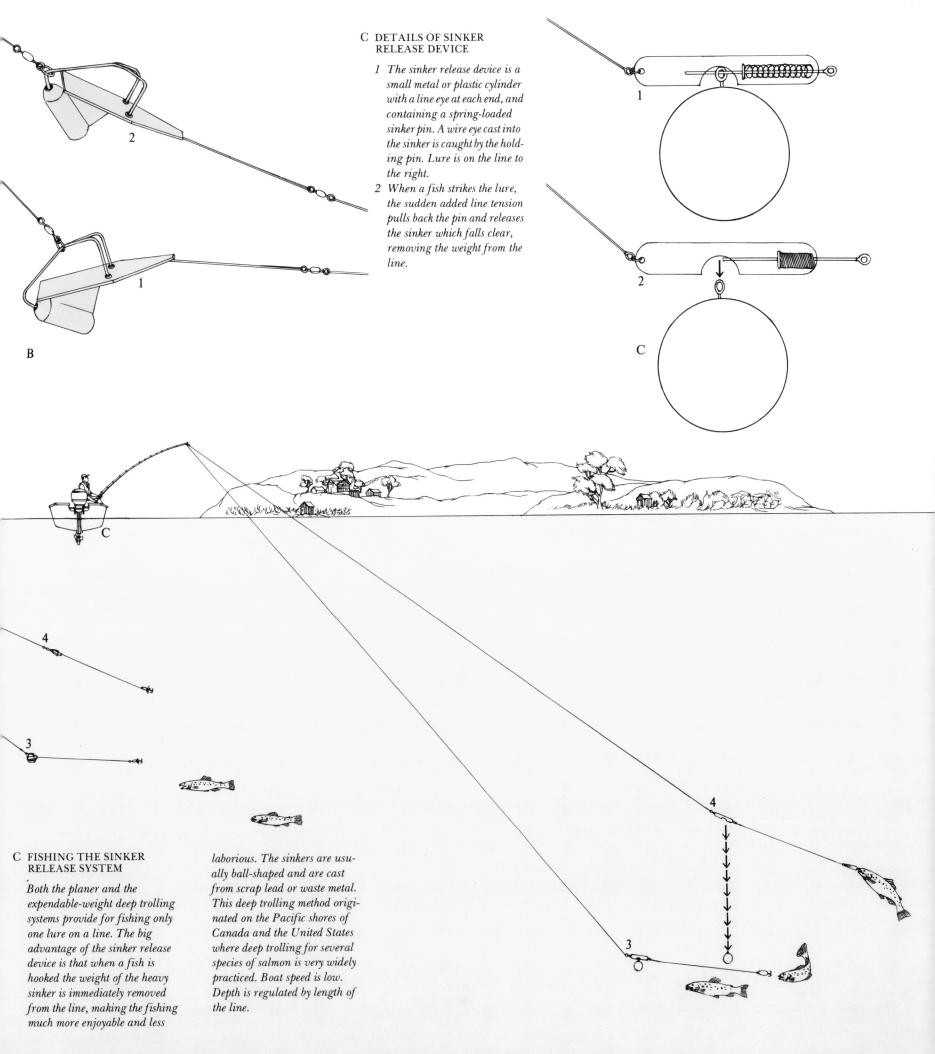

C DETAILS OF SINKER RELEASE DEVICE

1 *The sinker release device is a small metal or plastic cylinder with a line eye at each end, and containing a spring-loaded sinker pin. A wire eye cast into the sinker is caught by the holding pin. Lure is on the line to the right.*

2 *When a fish strikes the lure, the sudden added line tension pulls back the pin and releases the sinker which falls clear, removing the weight from the line.*

B

C

C FISHING THE SINKER RELEASE SYSTEM

Both the planer and the expendable-weight deep trolling systems provide for fishing only one lure on a line. The big advantage of the sinker release device is that when a fish is hooked the weight of the heavy sinker is immediately removed from the line, making the fishing much more enjoyable and less laborious. The sinkers are usually ball-shaped and are cast from scrap lead or waste metal. This deep trolling method originated on the Pacific shores of Canada and the United States where deep trolling for several species of salmon is very widely practiced. Boat speed is low. Depth is regulated by length of the line.

DEEP-TROLLING WITH THE DOWNRIGGER

The downrigger is an underwater outrigger that carries a fishing line to any desired depth. Trolling depth is achieved by a heavy weight that is lowered over the side or stern of the boat on the end of a stainless steel or Monel wire line. This wire line is stored on a separate special hand reel that usually has some sort of line-measuring or revolution-counting device to show exactly how much line is out at any given time.

The weight is equipped with an outrigger type of line release. This may be a spring-loaded jaw device or a twin-roller device of the type illustrated. The line is placed between the rollers of the release device after the lure has been streamed 15–30 ft (5–10 m) behind the boat. Then both the heavy downrigger weight and the fishing line are lowered at the same time to the desired trolling depth. This depth may be a few feet or meters above the bottom, or it may be at the location of a thermocline in much deeper water.

When a fish strikes at the lure, the fishing line is pulled from between the jaws or rollers of the line release device and the fisherman plays the fish unencumbered by weight on the line itself. Meanwhile, one

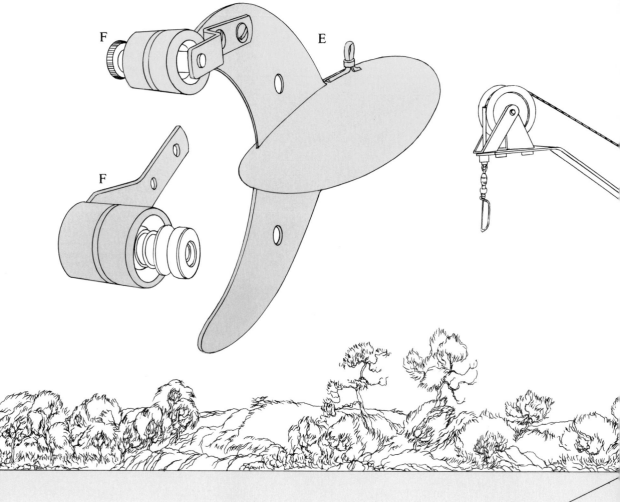

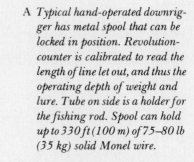

of the other anglers in the boat hauls up the weight, drops back another lure, clips the line into the downrigger release device, and lowers the fresh lure and line down to the working depth. In this manner it is possible to get lures down rapidly to a considerable depth while fish are in a striking mood.

Fishing with downriggers requires constant knowledge of the depth of water under the boat. Therefore the boat is usually equipped with either a permanent or portable electronic sounding machine. The sounder serves three primary purposes:

a It indicates the water depth and character of bottom.

b It indicates fish under the boat.

c It indicates rocks and other obstructions that might damage the downrigger equipment if they were not detected in time.

The boat illustrated, for example, has just hooked a fish from the downrigger and a second line has been put out. Meanwhile, one angler, watching the sounder, observes that the boat is moving over a large rock. He will quickly reel in some of the downrigger line, lifting the weight above the rock. He can actually "see" the downrigger weight on the dial of his sounder.

Downriggers are now available with electric motor drive to raise or lower the weights, and with extension rods so as many as four downriggers, two astern and two over the sides, may be fished from one boat. They work well in fresh or salt water and to depths of more than 165 ft (50 m) at trolling speeds of under 4 knots. The downrigger weight is usually made of cast iron and weighs 11–15 lb (5–7 kg). The wire tests 75–80 lb (35 kg).

A *Typical hand-operated downrigger has metal spool that can be locked in position. Revolution-counter is calibrated to read the length of line let out, and thus the operating depth of weight and lure. Tube on side is a holder for the fishing rod. Spool can hold up to 330 ft (100 m) of 75–80 lb (35 kg) solid Monel wire.*

B *Fishing rod is kept in a rod holder until a fish has taken lure. Almost any type of tackle will suffice but the best is star drag trolling tackle of a calibre matching the fish available.*
The fishing line can be quite light, for no weight is placed upon it.

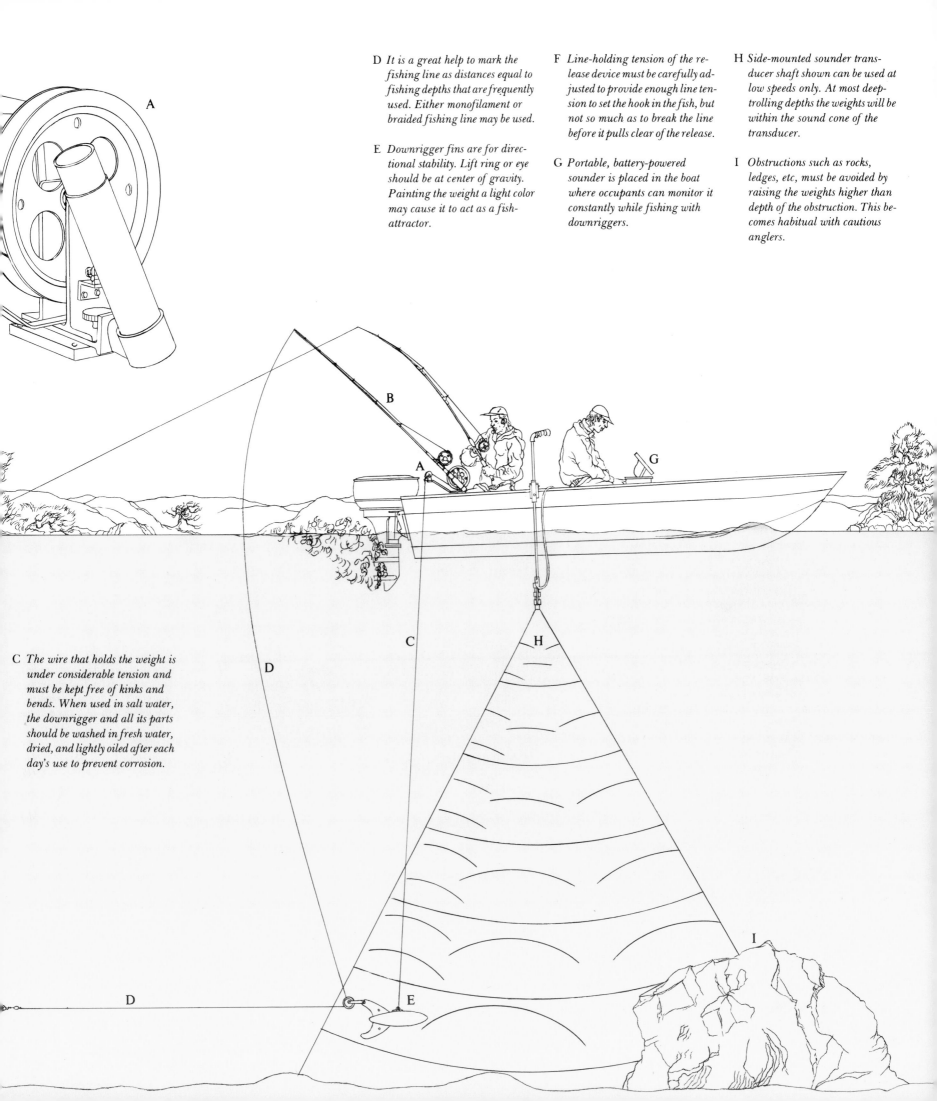

A

D It is a great help to mark the fishing line as distances equal to fishing depths that are frequently used. Either monofilament or braided fishing line may be used.

E Downrigger fins are for directional stability. Lift ring or eye should be at center of gravity. Painting the weight a light color may cause it to act as a fish-attractor.

F Line-holding tension of the release device must be carefully adjusted to provide enough line tension to set the hook in the fish, but not so much as to break the line before it pulls clear of the release.

G Portable, battery-powered sounder is placed in the boat where occupants can monitor it constantly while fishing with downriggers.

H Side-mounted sounder transducer shaft shown can be used at low speeds only. At most deep-trolling depths the weights will be within the sound cone of the transducer.

I Obstructions such as rocks, ledges, etc, must be avoided by raising the weights higher than depth of the obstruction. This becomes habitual with cautious anglers.

B

A

G

C

D

H

C The wire that holds the weight is under considerable tension and must be kept free of kinks and bends. When used in salt water, the downrigger and all its parts should be washed in fresh water, dried, and lightly oiled after each day's use to prevent corrosion.

D

E

I

RIVER DRIFT FISHING

Whether it is practiced in Canada, South America, Africa, Europe, or the American heartland, river drift fishing is a relaxing, easy way to take an angler's holiday. The ingredients are a small group of congenial companions, commodious, comfortable boats, camping equipment, fishing tackle, and time for unhurried exploration of the fish populations of a quiet river. Anglers coming from a distance usually employ a guide who provides the boats and makes camp at the overnight camping locations. Some anglers prefer to bring their own outboard-powered boats by truck or trailer.

One type of riverboat widely used in the U.S.A. for river drift fishing is the so-called "John-boat," a flat-bottomed, scow-nosed wooden or metal vessel that is a direct descendent of hand-propelled riverboats used by early explorers probing the vast Mississippi River basin where rivers were often the only avenues of transportation. In Africa and South and Central America, variations of the dugout canoe are still used on rivers, although the outboard motor has largely replaced oars and paddles for motive power.

The object of the journey, of course, is to combine the pleasures of camping and fishing with a leisurely passage down a quiet, beautiful river. Campers often carry only staple foods, depending on the fish they catch for a good part of their food intake. Fishing methods combine bait fishing with artificial lures, depending on the types of fish present. Many anglers bring along quantities of ice in insulated ice chests and pack their dressed fish in ice to be taken home and eaten by their families or preserved by freezing.

In the United States, river drift fishing has been elevated to a fine art in the Current River and Black River region of Arkansas (map below). Guides provide complete service including boats, tents, food, and transportation back to the point of origin of the trip. The river systems are unique in that they provide both warm-water and cold-water species. In some rivers the overflow from flood-control dams brings warm surface water to the river below. In others, the overflow is taken from the cold, deep waters of the impoundment behind the dam. This makes for an interesting mixture of fishing styles, cold-water trout being available in some streams and warm-water bass in others, a condition seldom found in other river fishing areas.

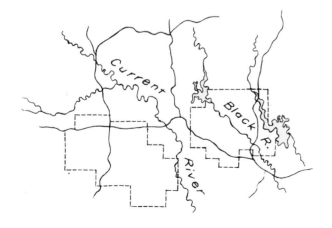

A Largemouth bass: a warm-water species responding to live or dead natural bait and artificial top-water or deep-diving lures on almost any tackle.

B Smallmouth bass: a cool-water species much like the largemouth in habits, but more northerly in its distribution in the north American rivers.

C Catfish: an extremely popular warm-water family of related species; responds to bait fishing and may reach a weight of 100 lb (45 kg).

D Crappie: a warm-water fish primarily of ponds and lakes, but also found in deep quiet rivers; will take natural bait or small artificials.

E Trout: brown, brook, and rainbow trout are present where cold-water draw-down from dams provides proper habitat; bait or fly-fishing tackle.

F Walleye: a lover of temperate rivers with deep, slow currents, the walleye is prime table fare; responds to live bait, lures, any normal tackle.

BIG GAME IN FRESH WATER

Many people think that big game fishing is limited to deep sea angling, but there are several freshwater species that, by virtue of their size and fighting ability, qualify as big game. The family of sturgeons, for example (Sketch B), has several closely related species distributed throughout the world's temperate rivers, some specimens of which have been recorded as weighing more than 2,200 lb (1,000 kg). In eastern Europe and Asia the sturgeon is primarily a commercial food fish, but in western Europe and in North America it is fished for frequently by anglers using natural bait or snag hooks. The sturgeon's fight is slow and ponderous although the fish is able to jump.

The Nile perch (*Lates noliticus*) often grows to more than 175 lb (80 kg) and has provided both food and sport to African anglers far back into the dawn of recorded history. The fish will take natural bait or large artificial lures. The tackle must be quite strong. The fishing is done from boats in the larger rivers and lakes of the Nile valley and headwaters, and also from shore. The flesh is excellent on the table.

A freshwater big game speciality of the lower Mississippi basin in the United States is the ugly-looking and potentially dangerous alligator gar (*Lepisosteus spatula*). Largest of the true gars, this powerful fish often exceeds 220 lb (100 kg) in weight. Its jaws, head, and teeth resemble its saurian namesake, the alligator. The example illustrated (Sketch A) is a mature specimen weighing about 200 lb (90 kg) from the White River in Arkansas. Heavy saltwater tackle is used and bait of old meat or fish. These large gars are edible, but have no economic importance.

The subcontinent of India supports two outstanding examples of freshwater big game. One is the mahseer (*Barbus tor*). A large fish often weighing more than 110 lb (50 kg), it resembles the tarpon in general shape and size of scales although it is a member of the ubiquitous carp family. The mahseer will take natural bait or large metal spoons or wooden plugs. The second Indian freshwater big game fish is the goonch (*Bagarius bagarius*), an outsized member of the catfish family that sometimes reaches well over 220 lb (100 kg) in weight. It is described as being sluggish but powerful, with a liking for old meat.

Most spectacular of freshwater big game is the well-known tarpon (*Megalops atlanticus*), a fish more often associated with saltwater fishing. Sometimes reaching a weight approaching 280–290 lb (130 kg), the tarpon is found in great numbers in perfectly pure fresh water in Mexico and Central America. In Honduras and Costa Rica, a number of fishing camps have built successful businesses around light tackle fishing for tarpon in coastal rivers. Tarpon respond to live or dead natural baits and a wide variety of artificial lures. Because they have relatively little commercial food value, but are very important as fishing tourist attractions, many governments now encourage or require the release of tarpon after they have been brought to boat.

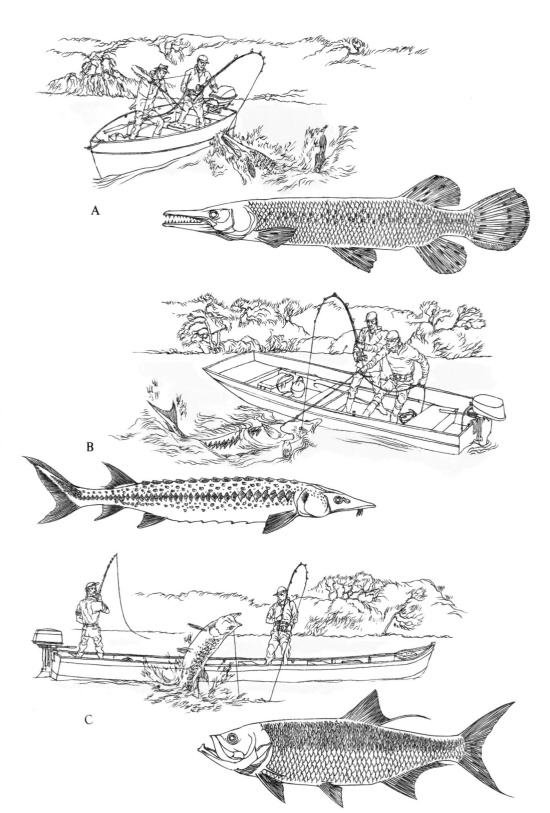

A ALLIGATOR GAR

Habitat: rivers of the lower Mississippi basin, U.S.A.
Tackle: 50-lb (23-kg) line class saltwater rod, reel, and line.
Bait: fish, meat, or chicken cleanings.
Method: drifting or anchored, or from the shore.
Season: spring to autumn.
Best location: White River, Arkansas.

B STURGEON

Habitat: rivers of temperate Europe, Asia, North America.
Tackle: any strong saltwater type up to 50-lb (23-kg) line class.
Bait: fish or fowl offal, meat, some types of vegetables.
Methods: bait fishing or "snagging."
Season: depends on local conditions.
Best location: Snake River, Idaho.

C TARPON

Habitat: coastal rivers and lagoons, Central America.
Tackle: quality fly rod, spinning, or bait-casting tackle.
Bait: live bait or artificial lures.
Methods: casting or live bait fishing, preferably from boat.
Season: late winter to early summer.
Best location: Costa Rica, Honduras.

SALT WATER FISHING

Two factors make salt water angling quite different from its fresh water counterpart. One is the great diversity of size and character of the fish found in the sea. The other is the fact that most ocean fish are governed by the ebb and flood of the tides as well as daily and seasonal fluctuations of sunlight, temperature and weather. The ocean angler must learn to time his fishing to coincide with favorable phases of the tides, otherwise he may find himself fishing for fish that refuse to bite or that have moved to a more favorable locality.

Learning to fish the phases of the tides to best advantage is largely a matter of education and experience. Education includes knowing how the tides affect local fish and being able to predict favorable hours to fish. Experience is acquired over a period of time and serves to temper one's knowledge and judgment. Fish, like people, frequently change their minds and a response to tidal conditions that holds true one week may not hold true a week later. This penchant of the fish to alter their habits introduces an element of chance into the fishing, a gamble that confirmed saltwater anglers find enjoyable and stimulating.

The variety of fish that many salt water anglers find available can present problems. What do you do when you are equipped for bonefish, which seldom exceed 11 lb (5 kg) in weight, and suddenly you are confronted by a tarpon 20 times as heavy? If you relish long odds and a real challenge you try to hook the tarpon and then hope for the best.

The great diversity of fish in salt water makes it possible for anglers of equally diverse character and aspirations to enjoy the kinds of fishing they like best. The big game angler, for instance, often goes to sea with a selection of tackle that will enable him to handle anything from a small bonito to a half-ton marlin. The casual family angler, on the other hand, is quite content to sit with his wife and children in a small boat, catching mackerel and flatfish for supper.

The surf fisherman is usually an action-oriented man or woman whose sense of achievement is fulfilled by taking fish under difficult conditions and by the exercise of superior personal fishing skill. The surf angler is often something of a mystic and a philosopher. The late American fishing writer Van Campen Heilner, in his delightful book *Salt Water Fishing*, expressed the striped bass angler's credo this way:

"Ten-pounders, twenty-pounders, forty-pounders, what difference does it make? The roar of Old Ocean, the cries of the gulls, the clean salt smell of seaweed, and the surging rush of a striper on light tackle; those are the things that count. Those are the things that linger when the season's over and the fish have departed. Those are the things one sees in the dying embers of a fire as a blizzard whines past the frosty windows of your room. Those are the memories one carries to the grave."

Gregarious party-boat fishermen look at fishing from still another viewpoint. Fun-loving and competitive, they crowd onto large boats by the dozen and the score, wagering among themselves as to who shall catch the largest "eatable" fish. The trip may be for a full day or, as is frequently the case at the southern California port of San Diego, for as much as a week at a time. Each angler keeps all the food fish he can catch and takes them home to eat or store in the family freezer.

Party-boat fishing is big business around the world. In the United States, for example, at least 5,000 boats up to 100 gross tons are registered in this trade. They are said to carry around 15,000,000 passenger-days of fishing traffic a year, producing at least 300,000,000 lb (nearly 150,000 metric tons) of edible fish annually.

In recent years a new class of saltwater anglers has come into being. This group views fishing as a means of learning more about the lives of fish and their relationship to the marine environment. These anglers catch fish not as trophies or for the table, but to tag and release alive so the fish may be recaptured

again some day at a distant location, thereby yielding valuable information on migration routes, growth, sexual maturity, and population densities.

Science-oriented anglers usually do not begrudge other fishermen their fun and games nor the fish they take home for food, but they decry the overfishing, industrial pollution, and other factors that are reducing some fish stocks to the vanishing point and damaging marine habitats beyond the point of natural self-recovery.

Modern power boats, fishing tackle, aids to navigation and fish location, and fishing techniques have opened this activity to great numbers of people. The result has been the development of a new class of anglers different from any that has lived before.

These new anglers are avid for greater understanding of the relationship of fish to their environment and to humans, but as their understanding grows they also learn restraint. In the history of angling over the years, this has not always been the case. A growing number of salt water anglers regard the acquisition of personal skills to be as desirable as catching quantities of fish. Ocean fishing is a self-renewing challenge. As each hurdle is overcome a fresh challenge presents itself. One's knowledge is never complete. When one thinks he has learned everything, the fish conspire to prick his balloon of self-esteem. In the end, after many such purifying experiences, one finds himself wiser and happier.

SURF FISHING

Surf fishing is a sport of individualists, rugged men and women who delight in wind, rain, sun, waves, and bad weather if the elements bring them the fish they seek. Students of fish and the sea, they govern their lives not by the clocks of civilization, but by the pulsing tide-clock of the moon and sun. They are proud of their knowledge, skill, and endurance. In the United States surf fishermen probably number one million souls, plus perhaps 500,000 specialized cars and light trucks that they lovingly call "beach buggies." Originally, beach buggies were old

momentarily through a curling wave. Among these fishermen the striped bass is top favorite. Surf fishermen work the Atlantic coast from the Canadian border to Florida and around the Gulf of Mexico from the Florida Keys to Brownsville, Texas. On the Pacific coast they are active from Canada to Baja California. Besides stripers, bluefish, sea trout (weakfish), channel bass, black drum, flounders, pompano, surf perch, and rock bass, many other species are popular. Even those inland seas of fresh water, the Great Lakes, are starting to feel the impact of lures cast from shore. Here coho and chinook

vehicles that had been equipped with oversize tires for running on soft sand. Now very often they are modern Jeeps and other 4-wheel-drive cars, station wagons, or light trucks equipped with camper bodies for seaside living. Rod holders on the front bumpers hold fishing rods rigged for instant use. Many beach buggies have CB (Citizens Band) radio for exchanging information. Some tow outboard-powered boats on trailers and launch the boats into the ocean directly from the beach.

During slow periods between tides they retire to open-air camps among the sand dunes back from the open beach. But always two or three scouts patrol the surf, eyes and ears attuned for signs of fish action. This may be a school of bait fish splashing, gulls diving, or perhaps the glint of a silver-sided striped bass glimpsed

salmon, black bass, trout, and panfish are the quarry. Wherever they are found, surf fishermen stand out from the great mass of everyday pleasure anglers. Like the cowboys of the Old West, they are a breed of men apart.

The anglers in the foreground have just brought in a striped bass of about 45 lb (20 kg). They are fishing in a secluded cove of the New England coast. Their 11-foot spinning rods give them an effective casting range of more than 165 ft (50 m). Some tournament casters have scored almost 500 ft (150 m).

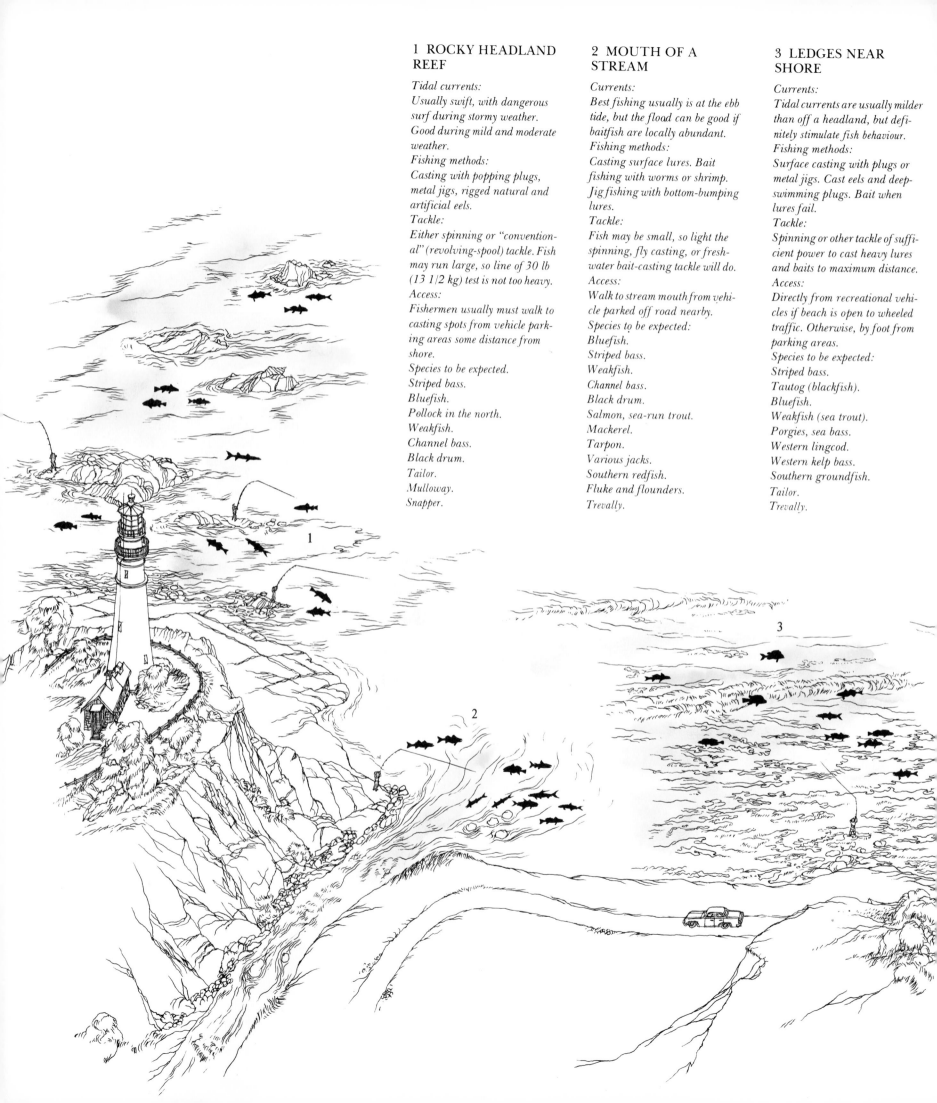

1 ROCKY HEADLAND REEF

Tidal currents:
Usually swift, with dangerous surf during stormy weather. Good during mild and moderate weather.
Fishing methods:
Casting with popping plugs, metal jigs, rigged natural and artificial eels.
Tackle:
Either spinning or "conventional" (revolving-spool) tackle. Fish may run large, so line of 30 lb (13 1/2 kg) test is not too heavy.
Access:
Fishermen usually must walk to casting spots from vehicle parking areas some distance from shore.
Species to be expected.
Striped bass.
Bluefish.
Pollock in the north.
Weakfish.
Channel bass.
Black drum.
Tailor.
Mulloway.
Snapper.

2 MOUTH OF A STREAM

Currents:
Best fishing usually is at the ebb tide, but the flood can be good if baitfish are locally abundant.
Fishing methods:
Casting surface lures. Bait fishing with worms or shrimp. Jig fishing with bottom-bumping lures.
Tackle:
Fish may be small, so light the spinning, fly casting, or fresh-water bait-casting tackle will do.
Access:
Walk to stream mouth from vehicle parked off road nearby.
Species to be expected:
Bluefish.
Striped bass.
Weakfish.
Channel bass.
Black drum.
Salmon, sea-run trout.
Mackerel.
Tarpon.
Various jacks.
Southern redfish.
Fluke and flounders.
Trevally.

3 LEDGES NEAR SHORE

Currents:
Tidal currents are usually milder than off a headland, but definitely stimulate fish behaviour.
Fishing methods:
Surface casting with plugs or metal jigs. Cast eels and deep-swimming plugs. Bait when lures fail.
Tackle:
Spinning or other tackle of sufficient power to cast heavy lures and baits to maximum distance.
Access:
Directly from recreational vehicles if beach is open to wheeled traffic. Otherwise, by foot from parking areas.
Species to be expected:
Striped bass.
Tautog (blackfish).
Bluefish.
Weakfish (sea trout).
Porgies, sea bass.
Western lingcod.
Western kelp bass.
Southern groundfish.
Tailor.
Trevally.

4 CHANNEL INSIDE BAR

Currents:
Usually run parallel to shore, but undertow may create a suction current that runs offshore. Fish here show less dependence on currents to trigger feeding.
Fishing methods:
Casting surface or deep-running plugs and metal jigs, bait fishing with clams, crabs, squid, etc.
Tackle:
Light, medium, or heavy tackle of any normal casting type, depending on local surf and weather.
Access:
Directly from beach buggies if beach is open to traffic. Otherwise, by foot.
Species to be expected:
All those mentioned previously, plus:
Pompano, palometa.
Western surf perch.
Cobia in south.
Cod in the north.
Various flatfish.
Tailor.
Mulloway.
Bream.

5 JETTY OR BREAKWATER

Currents:
Tidal currents may be swift and water rough, especially when ebb tide flows out against inshore-coming swells. Best fishing just before and after high and low water slacks.
Fishing methods:
Surface and deep casting with plugs, eels, metal jigs.
Tackle:
Strongest spinning or "conventional" tackle with line of at least 20, often 30 lb test.
Access:
By foot from shore parking areas. Some caution is needed on slippery rocks.
Species to be expected:
Striped bass.
Bluefish.
Tarpon in south.
Salmon in the west.
Weakfish (sea trout).
Fluke, tautog.
Bream.
Tarpon.
Trevally.
Luderick.

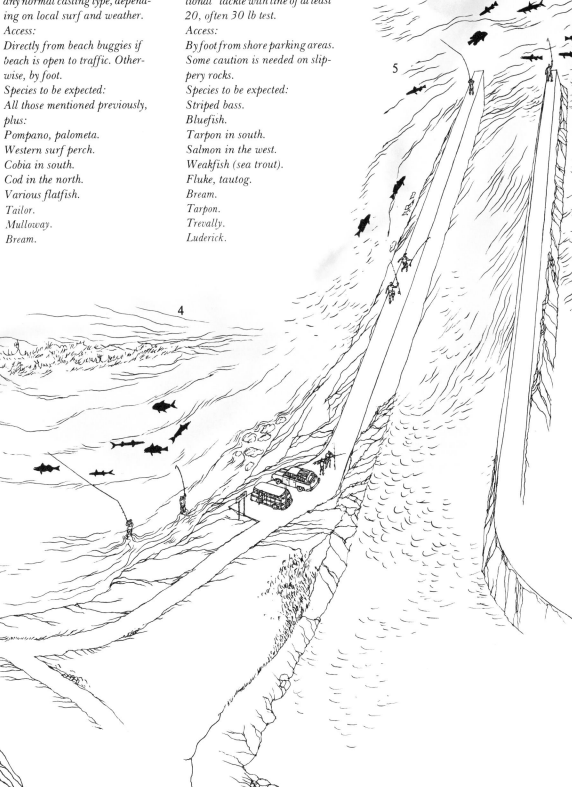

TYPICAL SURF FISHING SITUATIONS

Surf fishermen fishing the ocean shores find themselves in a multitude of situations, but these can be boiled down to five major types.

1 Reef off a rocky headland, with tidal flow.

2 Mouth of a stream, where a flowing current brings small baitfish into the ocean.

3 Ledges, rocks, and mussel beds near shore.

4 A deep channel or slough between the beach and an outer bar built up by wave action on beach sand.

5 Outer extremity of a rock jetty, especially where a tidal current moves out from an inner bay.

All ocean fish are regulated by the ebb and flow of tidal currents. In some areas the fish may strike best on the flood tide. In other regions the ebb may be best. Some species switch their preference from ebb to flood, or vice versa, without advance warning to the fishermen. This is part of the enjoyment of fishing–learning how to utilize local tidal information to predict when to go fishing with a good chance of success.

Knowledgeable surf fishermen plan a whole season's activities in advance. They know, for example, that springtime brings flounders and striped bass, summer sees the arrival of bluefish, autumn is often best for big stripers and salmon. They plan their trips to take advantage of good tidal conditions, predictable through the universally available Tide Tables. Local knowledge also plays a large part in making last-minute decisions regarding specific places to fish.

When he arrives at the shore, the surf fisherman finds many natural aids ready to help him locate fish.

1 Gulls, terns, and other seabirds often flock over schools of small bait that have been driven to the surface by larger game fish beneath.

2 Most shore-loving game fish love rough water, and a moderate to slightly heavy surf often provides better fishing than calm water for men and women who are rugged enough to withstand the cold, wet, and discomfort of what landlubbers call "indoor weather."

3 Game fish feeding down deep on smaller fish sometimes reveal their presence by the oil slick that their voracious feeding creates on the surface.

4 The activities of other fishermen are often a good sign of fishing action. All surf anglers carry binoculars and many are radio-equipped to exchange information–or to eavesdrop on their buddies.

Fishing the ocean surf requires a high degree of personal skill. It appeals most highly to men and women who are at home in the natural elements and who find their greatest satisfaction when they are able to outwit and capture wary game fish under conditions that would discourage less self-reliant fishermen. But while the feeling of competition is high among them, they willingly go out of their way to help and encourage beginners who show real spirit.

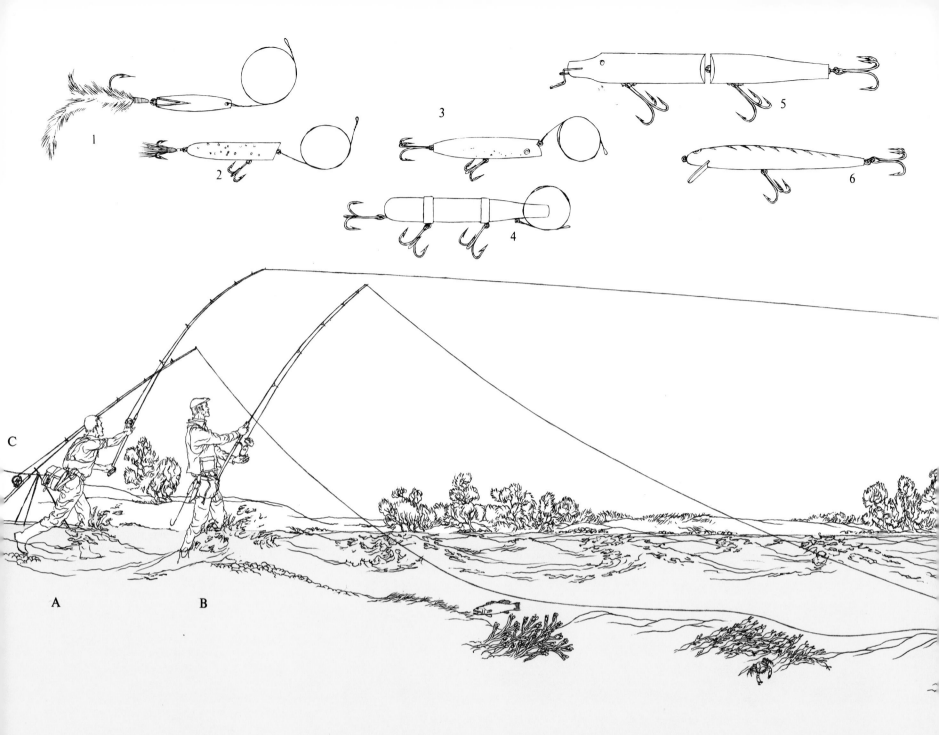

Part of the pleasure of surf casting is the realization that you are never quite sure what kind of fish may strike your lure or bait. Here two casters are using three types of surf casting tackle.

A *Man at left has completed a cast with a popping plug that he will retrieve with rapid rod action to make the plug splash along the surface of the water. This kind of surface action is very attractive to predatory game fishes which rise and take the plug within sight of the surf caster.*

B *Not all fishes will take the surface-action plug, so the angler to the right is using a deep-running type of lure. Deep-running plug or lure (see examples above) is retrieved with a slower, more steady type of reeling motion and occasional slow rod action. Speed of the retrieve is adjusted so the plug or lure will not hit the bottom, picking up weed or dirt on the hooks. At the slightest touch from a fish the anglers must strike back strongly with the rod to set the hooks.*

C *Natural bait is often quite effective in surf fishing. One of the anglers has cast out a baited set*

of hooks, which lie in a slight depression of the bottom caused by the surf undertow. Good baits are clam, mussel, worms, squid. The so-called fish finder hook rig, illustrated in other pages of the book, is very effective in surf fishing with baited hooks. Here the fishing line is passed through the eye of the lead sinker before the hooks are attached. Thus the hooks can drift with the current.

Successful surf casting calls for adequate tackle and also knowledge of local conditions that are attractive to the fish. Anglers judge the

state of the tide before planning a fishing trip so favorable tidal conditions may prevail. Rising or falling tide may be best, depending on the local habits of the fish. Periods of slack tide usually are less productive. A moderate surf is usually best, with the wind blowing offshore or parallel to the shore. Period after a storm is good as the swells subside and the water clears.

Surf casters recognize many natural signs that reveal the presence of fish. Fish that break the surface after bait

are easy to spot. At other times the presence of smaller fish may suggest that large fish will soon find the bait and action will result. Gulls and other sea birds diving into the water are a sure sign of bait fish and probable fishing action. Predatory fish sometimes feed near bottom, but oil released from the bait on which they feed floats to the surface where it forms a shiny, fragrant, oily slick.

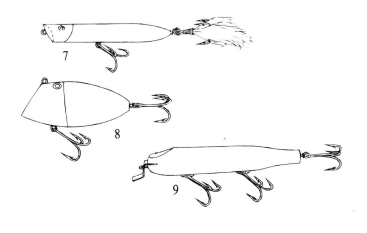

While natural bait is used frequently by surf casters, most fishermen prefer to fish with artificial lures. A fisherman's skill is often revealed by the way he "works" the lure with the rod, making it appear alive in the water.

Here is a selection of salt water surf casting lures that have proven their worth on both Atlantic and Pacific ocean shores.

1 Eastern keel jig is moulded of lead or tin. Good for windy weather or when long casts are necessary.

2 Atom Striper-Strike, a light plastic topwater popper with good action for many species of fish.

3 Gibbs Darter, a plug that floats with side-to-side action on a slow retrieve.

4 The famous Reverse Atom is retrieved tailfirst and is a deadly striper lure in the Northeast.

5 Creek Chub Jointed Pikie was originally designed for large pike. Stripers and bluefish love it.

6 The Rapala plug is a floater, but dives deeply on retrieve because of its large metal nose lip.

7 Striper-Swiper is a small popper surface with negative float.

8 Salty Bogie sinks and vibrates when it is retrieved slowly, attracting game fish in very deep water.

9 Creek Chub Pikie is excellent for large striped bass, works equally well when cast or trolled.

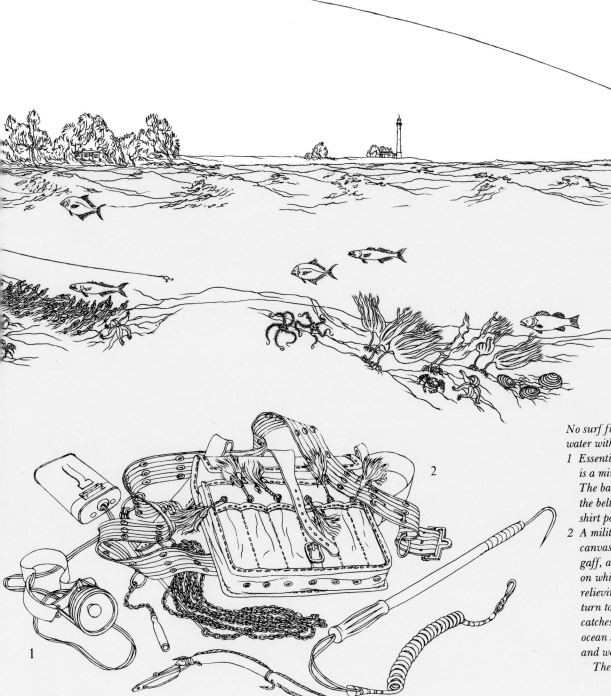

No surf fisherman goes to the water without proper equipment.

1 Essential for fishing at night is a miner's electric lamp. The battery case is clipped to the belt or carried in an inner shirt pocket.

2 A military web belt supports a canvas lure pouch, the hand gaff, and a long brass chain on which he strings his fish, relieving him of having to return to the beach each time he catches one. Men who fish the ocean surf hate inefficiency and wasted motion.

The lure pouch also contains spare line, hooks, leader material, and perhaps a rigged eel or two.

The point of the gaff fits like a knife blade into a rubber or leather tube-sheath, ready for instant use. The gaff safety line is threaded through a number of small corks so it will float if it falls into the water. Hip boots or chest-high waterproof waders make up the surf angler's wardrobe. A waterproof parka windbreaker is belted on over all.

273

SALT WATER FLY FISHING

Perhaps the fast-growing segment of salt water sport fishing is that of fly fishing on the ocean. Many erstwhile fresh water anglers are finding out that taking their fly tackle to salt water is one way of breaking into light tackle ocean fishing without the bother of investing in or having to learn how to use other forms of tackle. At the same time, a great many salt water anglers are discovering the superior challenge that fishing with fly tackle offers. With the fly rod the emphasis is on the quality of the fishing, not the massiveness of the catch.

But salt water game fish, in general, are large, strong fish where fly tackle is concerned. Success usually depends on selecting tackle that will make the long, accurate casts frequently necessary, and stand up to the powerful, punishing runs the fish produce before they can be brought to net or gaff. Tackle must be equal to or heavier than what is often called "good salmon tackle." This means that fly lines in the U.S. weight-8 class are considered light, and lines, with rods to cast them, frequently are found in the weight 10, 11, or 12 category.

Salt water fly fishermen

Six popular salt water flies
1 Marabou Fly
2 Lefty's Deceiver
3 Caterpillar Wet Fly
4 Honey Blonde Streamer
5 Keel Hook Fly
6 Pink Shrimp Fly

1 Sailfish
2 Striped bass
3 Bluefish
4 Barracuda
5 Permit
6 Bonefish
7 White marlin
8 Weakfish
9 Bonito
10 Tarpon
11 Salmon
12 Sharks

are no less record-conscious than their fresh water counterparts. In the United States, where a number of ocean fly rod clubs and associations are active, the Salt Water Fly Rodders of America, Inc., have standardized records of fish taken in salt water with fly tackle. The criterion of tackle class is the breaking strain of the tippet used in the leader, or trace. Fish records are classified under various tippet breaking strains up to 15 lb. (6.8 kg), the heaviest recognized.

Just as in fresh water, salt water fly fishermen have developed a large stable of fly and streamer patterns that simulate typical salt water baits. The late great American sportsman Joseph Brooks, for example, is credited with originating the popular and very effective "Blonde" family of salt water bucktail flies and streamers.

Florida, with its vast, protected shallow water flats, reefs, and thousands of miles of beaches, is prime salt water fly fishing country. So are the islands of the Bahamas, the West Indies, and many other similar tropical aquatic settings. In North America, fly fishing anglers are active wherever the revered striped bass, the pugnacious bluefish, the weakfish or sea trout, or other desirable species are found. The fly rod has made purists of many former salt water meat fishermen.

PIER FISHING

Fishing from piers, bridges, and similar structures is a popular pastime around the world. In some regions, notably the U.S.A., long piers jut out into deep water along lake and ocean shores, expressly built and operated for the benefit of recreational fishermen. Elsewhere, anglers make do with any pier, bulkhead, or jetty that may be handy to fish.

A The old-fashioned hand line. Simplest and least expensive form of tackle. A sinker, pair of hooks, worms, clams, or mussels for bait, and you are in business for fish ranging from eels to small inshore food species.

B The fish-finder rig. The line is passed through the eye of the sinker before the hook is attached. Thus, the hook and bait are free to drift with the current and are more attractive to the fish.

C The chum can is a perforated container filled with ground fish, clam or mussel shells, or fish heads and bones. It is dropped to the bottom on a hand line to attract fish to the area by virtue of its enticing taste and smell.

D A long-handled gaff is used to lift a heavy fish from the water to the level of the pier. Large hoop nets on ropes or extension poles are also used to secure fish too heavy for lifting with the fishing line and hooks.

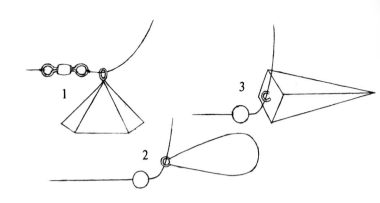

Three methods of making the popular fish-finder rig.
1 Swivel and sand sinker
2 Split shot and bank sinker

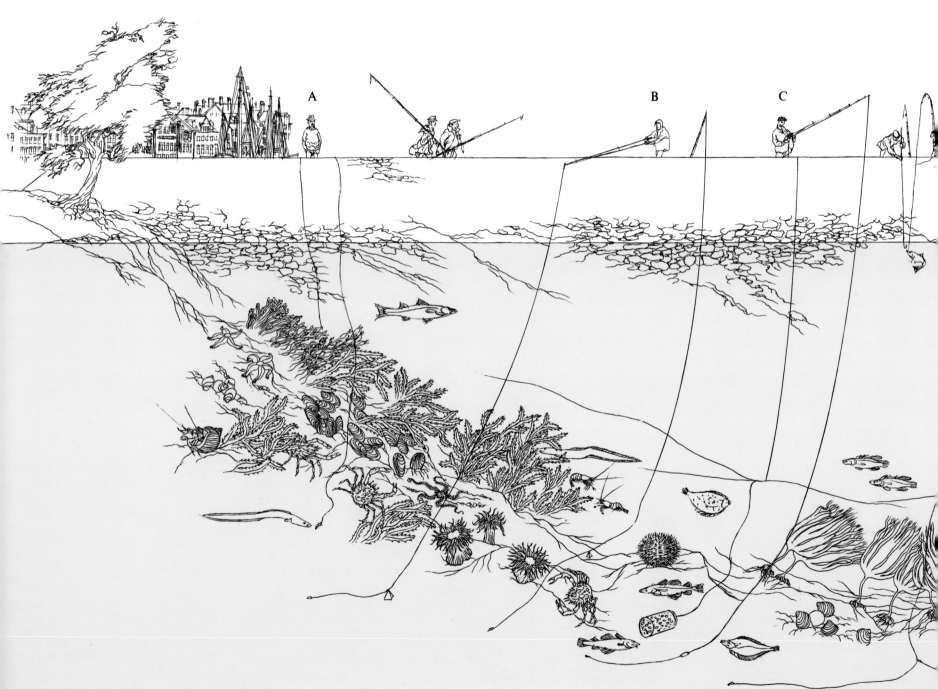

276

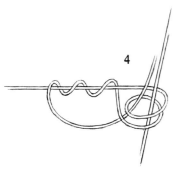

3 Split shot and pyramid sinker
4 How to attach the looped end
   of the hook snell to dropper
   loop of line

E *In using the fish finder rig, the sinker and hooks are dropped to the bottom and the line is allowed to pay out slowly, letting the bait drift away with the current. This gives the baited hooks a natural kind of movement.*

F *The high-low hook rig is another popular one. A hook is tied on just above the sinker to attract bottom-dwelling fish. The second hook is placed 1–2 yards (or meters) above the first for free-swimming fish.*

G *Jigging in deeper water is a proven method for larger fish. The metal jig is cast out, allowed to drop to the bottom, and is retrieved with a quick, intermittant jigging action of the rod to imitate a small fish.*

H *Other metal and composition jigs are cast far out and retrieved with steady reeling action. This works well with predatory species like pollock, mackerel, bluefish. Spinning or revolving-spool tackle may be used.*

I *Float fishing is effective for some species, using one or several baited hooks. Adjustment of depth can be controlled by using the float arrangement at right, which permits rapid change of hook depth without altering the tackle.*

J *Crab trap made of metal mesh on a wooden or metal frame is popular in areas where blue-claw and other edible, free-swimming crabs abound. It can be suspended from a stout pole and is baited with pieces of dead fish.*

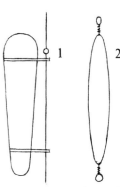

Split shot (1) is attached to the line at the upper limit of desired float travel. Sinker (2) can be a cigar model or lead strip wound around line.

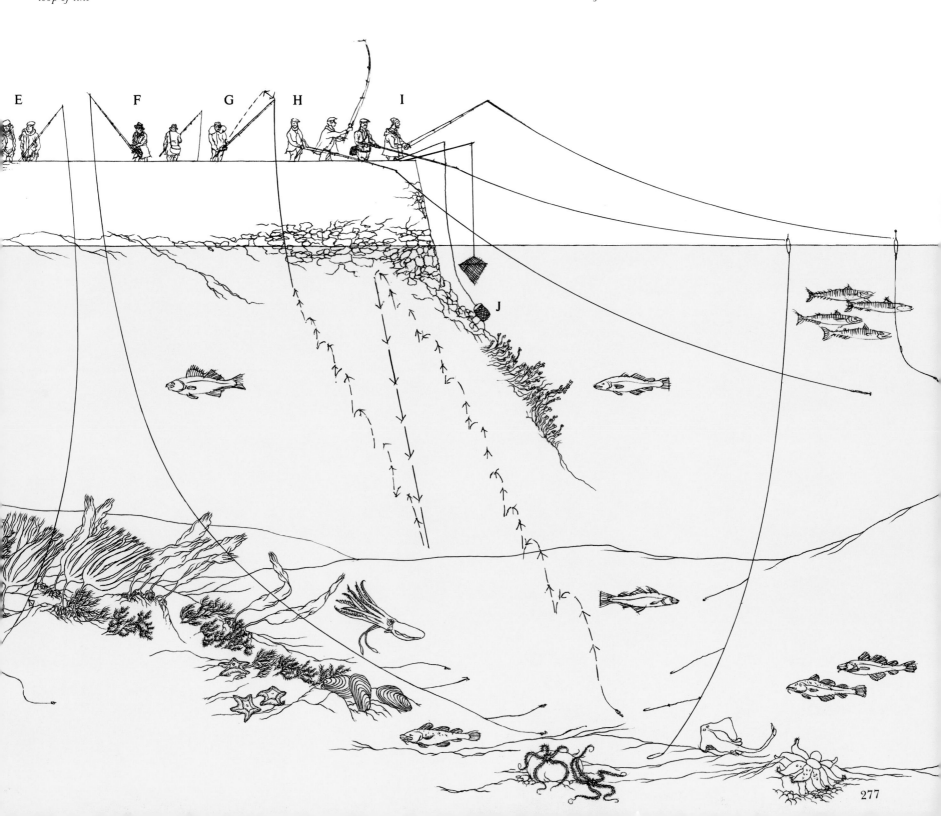

FISHING FROM ROCKY SHORES

The term "surf casting" usually conjures up a mental image of fishing from a sandy beach. But ocean surfs beat also upon rocky shores where fishing is often excellent, but where special conditions prevail that require precautions and equipment not normally found else-where. At Rooikrantz, South Africa, for example, tuna often are abundant in the deep water that comes right in to the rocky shoreline, and powerful tackle is required to hook and hold these fish. The ability to hold powerful fish is more important than the ability to cast a lure or bait a great distance. Along the coasts of New England, for a differ-ent example, the waters next to rocky shores are frequently shallow, calling for casting tackle with maximum distance ability.

The recent advent of large-capacity, very strong spinning reels capable of handling monofilament line up to 45 lb. (20 kg) test has given the rocky shore fisherman long range casting tackle that is also quite pow-erful in terms of holding large fish such as trophy striped bass, mature salmon, cod, pollack, small to medium tuna, and even good-sized sharks. In some areas, notably the U.S. West Coast, there is a definite trend toward using large capacity single-action casting reels of the type made popular by the surf and shore anglers of Australia and South Africa.

Rods average from 10–13 ft (3–4 m) long and are carefully selected by their users to match the class of line and weight of lures or baits to be used. Fiberglass is now the predominant rod-building material although split bamboo and cane rods are still being used in some regions. Lures include popping, swimming, darting, and diving plugs, metal casting

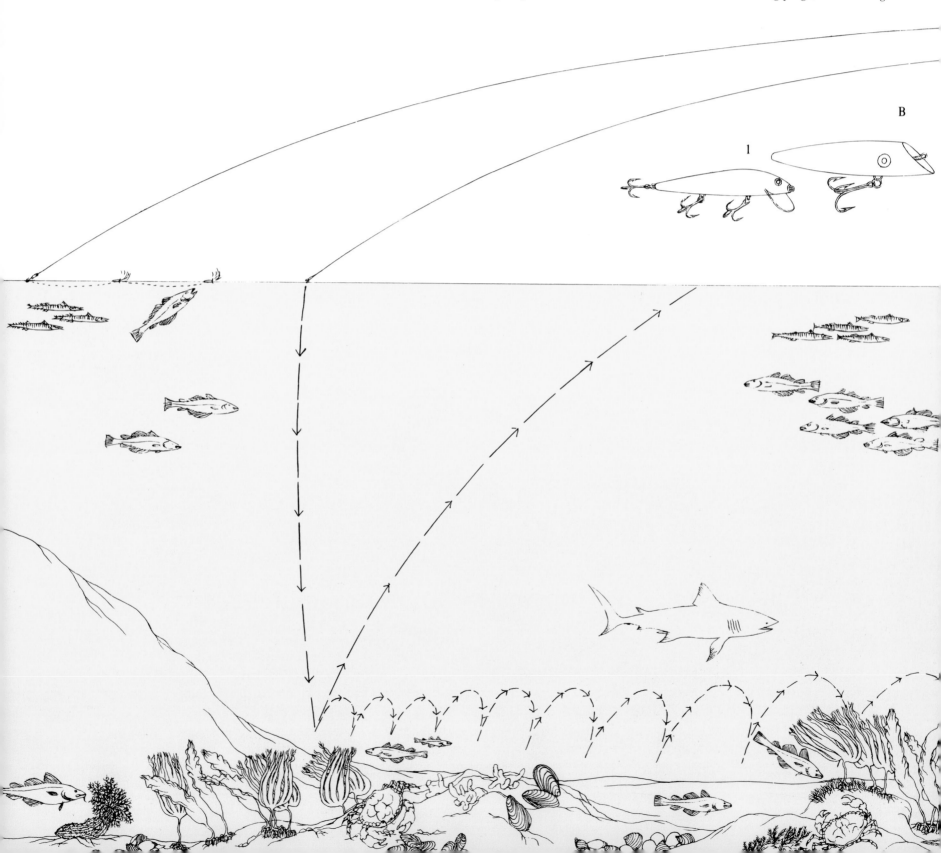

lures, and various types of bait rigs.

Sand beach surf casters usually wear boots or waders, but rock hounds prefer shoes with spiked soles for a firm grip on slippery rocks. How to get heavy fish up out of the water and onto the rocks is often a problem. One popular solution is the extra-long gaff hook, frequently made by fastening a gaff hook to a full-length surf casting rod shaft. A belt socket to take the lower end of the rod butt is standard equipment and some anglers also wear a light shoulder harness to relieve the arms of the rather extreme tension caused by the long rod.

Rock fishing is practiced wherever good fishing water occurs along a rocky shore. In Scandinavia, for example, cod and related cold water species are the targets. Along North American shores, striped bass, bluefish, cod and pollack, rock bass, and many other surface and deep-swimming species attract the attention of anglers. Rocky shore fishermen are inclined to regard themselves as a brotherhood apart from other anglers, more individualistic and rugged than run-of-the-mill fishermen. But the equipment they use and the methods they employ stem directly from the standard tackle and methods employed by ordinary anglers elsewhere. The differences are not of kind, but of degree, which should be encouraging news to anglers with a yen to penetrate the mysteries of the sport.

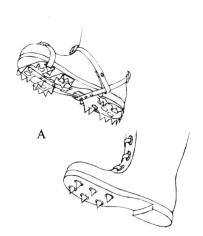

A

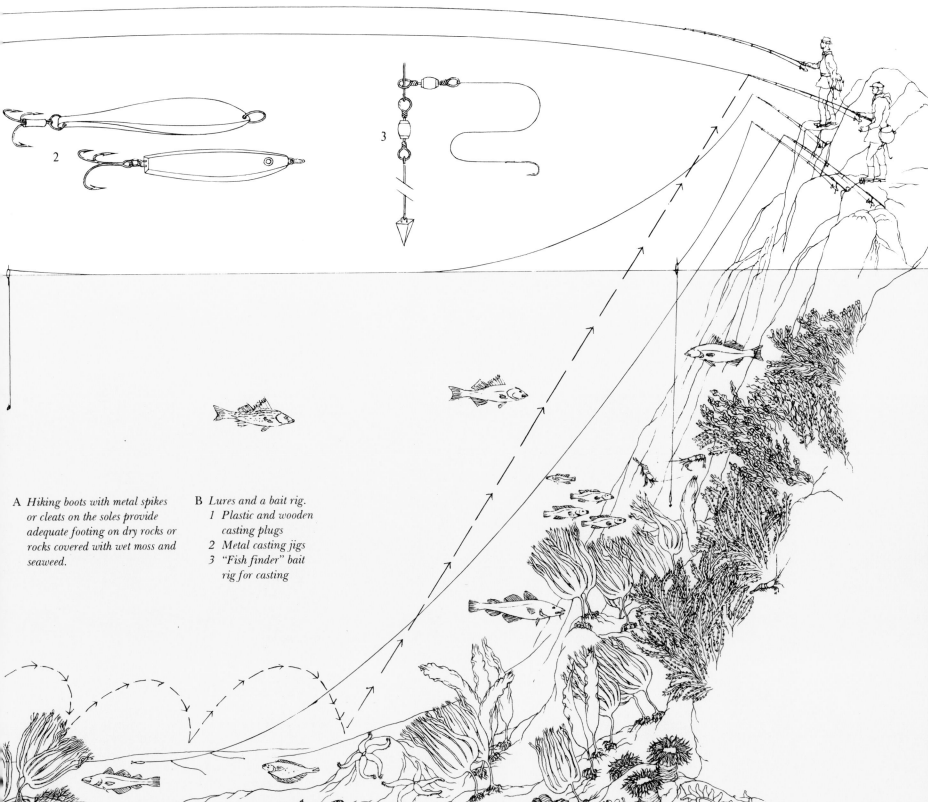

A *Hiking boots with metal spikes or cleats on the soles provide adequate footing on dry rocks or rocks covered with wet moss and seaweed.*

B *Lures and a bait rig.*
  1 *Plastic and wooden casting plugs*
  2 *Metal casting jigs*
  3 *"Fish finder" bait rig for casting*

RIGS FOR SALT WATER PANFISHING

Salt water panfishing is essentially hook-and-sinker fishing and the simplest rigs work best.

E Single-hook rig for shallow water has a pyramidal sinker of 2–5 oz weight, one snelled hook 1/0 to 4/0 in size. Three-way swivel is used to connect line to hook and sinker.

F Two-hook rig for use in shallow water has 2–6 oz bank sinker, and a matched pair of hooks arranged one over the other.

The two-hook rig is sometimes called the high-low rig and is very effective in deep water for fish feeding on and off the bottom. Bank sinkers up to 16 or 20 oz are used.

G High-low rig has two three-way swivels. Hooks are 40"–60" (100–150 cm) apart. Hooks are usually of 5/0 to 8/0 size and are snelled with tarline or monofil. Bottom hook receives clam bait for cod while the top hook is baited with squid for pollock. Line for deep water fishing should be at least 30-lb test.

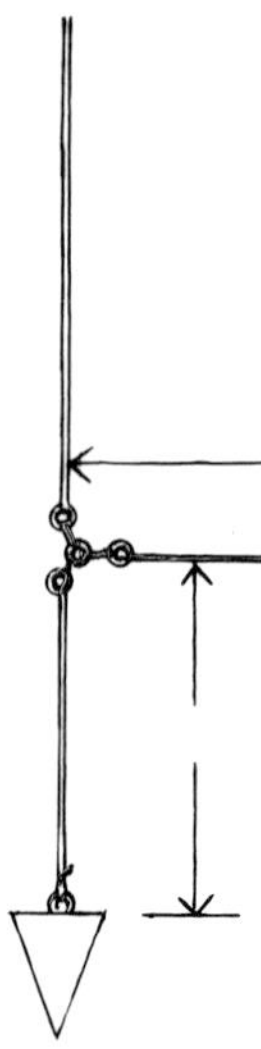

E

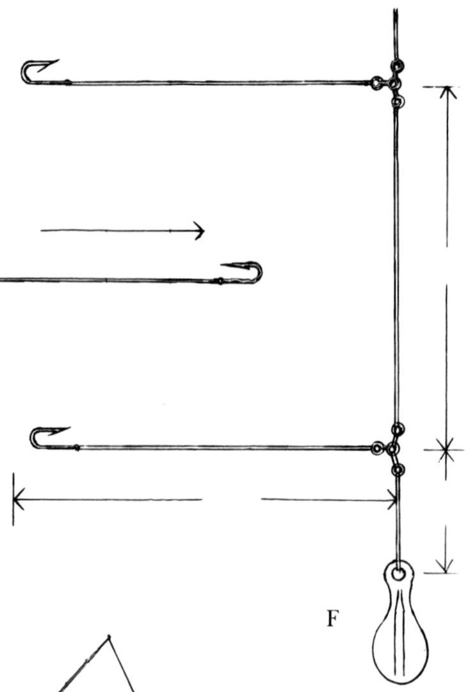

F

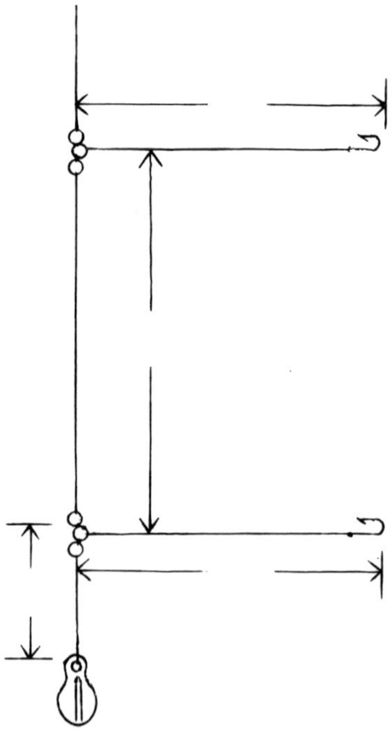

G

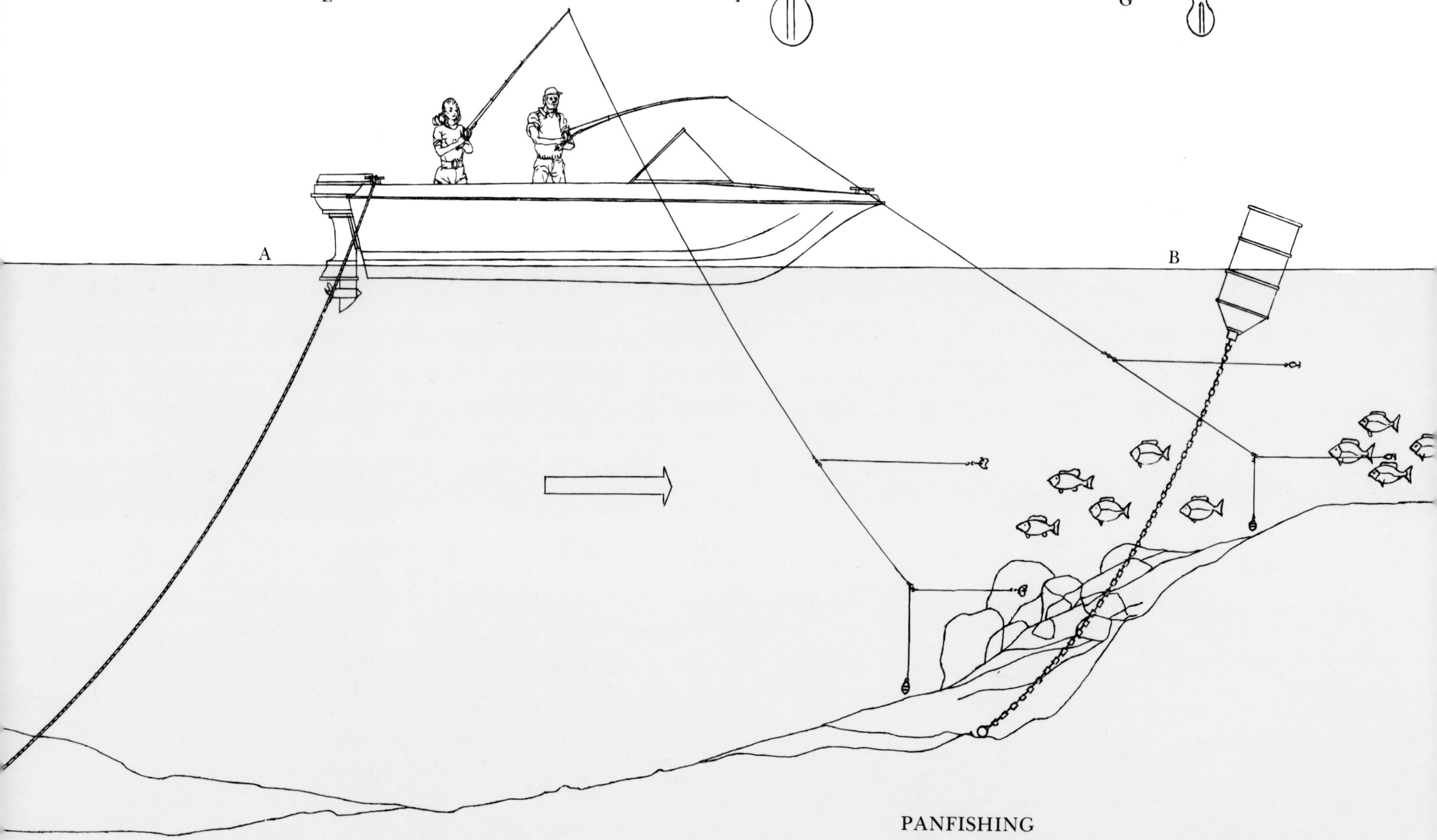

A

B

PANFISHING

Here is a typical case of coastal shallow water panfishing. Tidal current (broad arrows) flows from left to right over an obstruction marked by a buoy. Three kinds of fishing are possible: from an anchored boat, from a drifting boat, and from a pier.

A Anglers in the boat at anchor let their baited lines drift down-tide to where fish are known to gather around the rocky obstruction. Their baits consist of clams, mussels, and worms, good for fish that prefer non-moving baits.

280

FOUR VARIATIONS OF THE BASIC BOTTOM-FISHING RIG

H *Floater rig has a small block of cork on the hook snell to lift the bait above the bottom.*

I *The "fish-finder" or slider rig has the line passed through a drilled sinker placed above the hook swivel. This permits the line to render freely with the tide.*

J *Short-coupled rig is often used for flatfish, has the sinker attached directly to the fishing line.*

K *Mackerel rig has a number of hooks or jigs placed above a suitable sinker.*

THREE SPECIALIZED RIGS FOR OCEAN PANFISHING

L *The dropper bait rig has one, two, or more hooks tied into the main hook snell, dropper-fashion, and is often used with small live or dead minnows for bait.*

M *The spreader rig for flounders has a wire spreader arranged to carry a hook at each end and a sinker at the centre. The line is attached at the spreader's centre.*

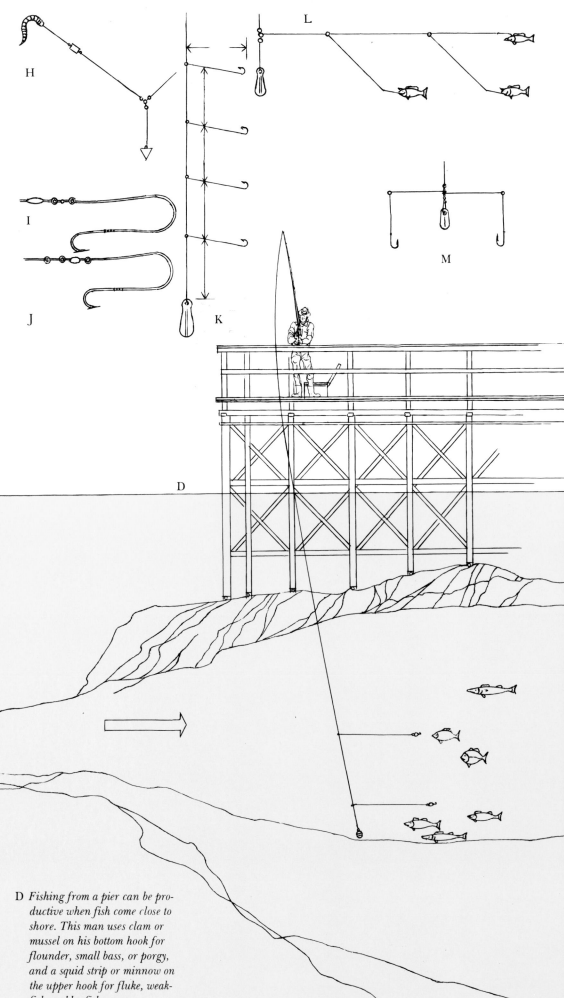

B *State of the tidal current is shown by the displacement of the buoy by the current. Fish bite best during the run of the tide, least when the tide is at high or low water slack. Tide tables help predict when to go out fishing.*

C *Man in the drifting boat uses a single hook rig arranged for fluke. His bait is a squid strip or small minnow, bait that is attractive to fish that like motion in their food. He runs back up-tide when he drifts out of the productive area.*

D *Fishing from a pier can be productive when fish come close to shore. This man uses clam or mussel on his bottom hook for flounder, small bass, or porgy, and a squid strip or minnow on the upper hook for fluke, weak-fish, or bluefish.*

281

PARTY BOAT AND WRECK FISHING

The class of recreational fishing boats known as party boats performs a very important function wherever these boats are found. They are the boats that cater to the general fishing public, anglers with a strong desire to get out onto the water and fish for sport or for food for the table, yet who cannot or do not wish to own boats of their own specifically for fishing. In operation, party boats charge a flat fee per passenger up to the limit of passengers imposed by law. Some large American party boats, for example, are licensed to carry upward of 100 passengers at a time. Such a large group automatically limits the type of fishing to drifting or bottom fishing where all on board can fish at the same time.

Passengers are encouraged to bring their own rods and reels, although adequate tackle usually is available for rent on board the boats. Bait is usually supplied, but passengers bring their own food and beverages or purchase these from the boat's galley. Most party boat and wreck fishing operators adhere to schedules that are pre arranged to take advantage of various types of good fishing as they develop during the season. The catch is iced or frozen in warm weather so as to be in prime condition for home consumption or freezer storage for future use.

Far from being haphazard, party boat and offshore wreck fishing takes advantage of modern electronic aids to navigation, communication, and fish finding. Many good wrecks, for instance, lie far from shore, completely out of sight of visual aids to navigation. They are located first by such electronic navigation means as Decca or Loran, and then pin pointed by the use of sensitive sonar equipment. The most productive fishing captains are often understandably secretive about the locations of their best wrecks and visit them only when other vessels are not around to prevent depletion by over-fishing. As a rule, however, captains cooperate with each other on the exchange of safety, weather, and fishing information.

Tackle for party boat fishing usually consists of a short, stiff-action boat rod carrying a star drag multiplier reel with a capacity of 200–300 yards or meters of 20–30 lb (9–14 kg) test line. Lead sinkers of various weights are used depending on the depth of water and strength of tidal currents. Baits include sea worms, clams, herring, squid, conch, anchovies, and similar items. Metal jigs are sometimes used. The boat's crew always helps the passengers to rig the tackle to the best advantage.

While party boat fishing in most areas is a single day operation, in a few regions the boats make trips of up to a week or 10 days duration. The long range party boats of Southern California, for example, make scheduled excursions to distant banks and islands off the Mexican coast, accommodating up to 50 passengers a trip. Their catches often measure 2 or 3 tons in weight. However it is accomplished, party boat fishing around the world is a popular way to combine the sport and pleasure of deep sea fishing with the gathering of excellent sea food.

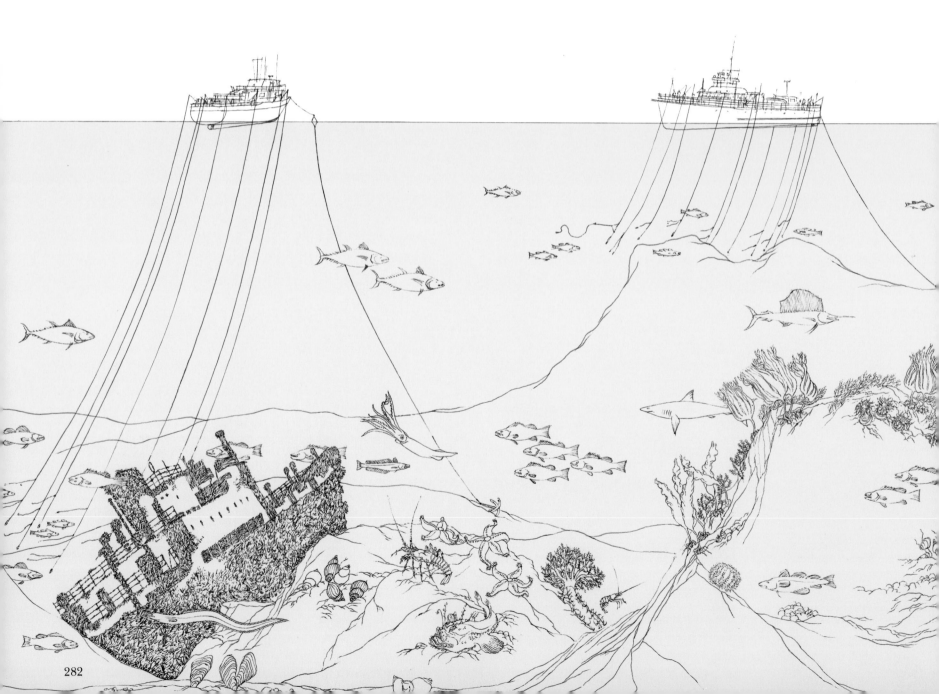

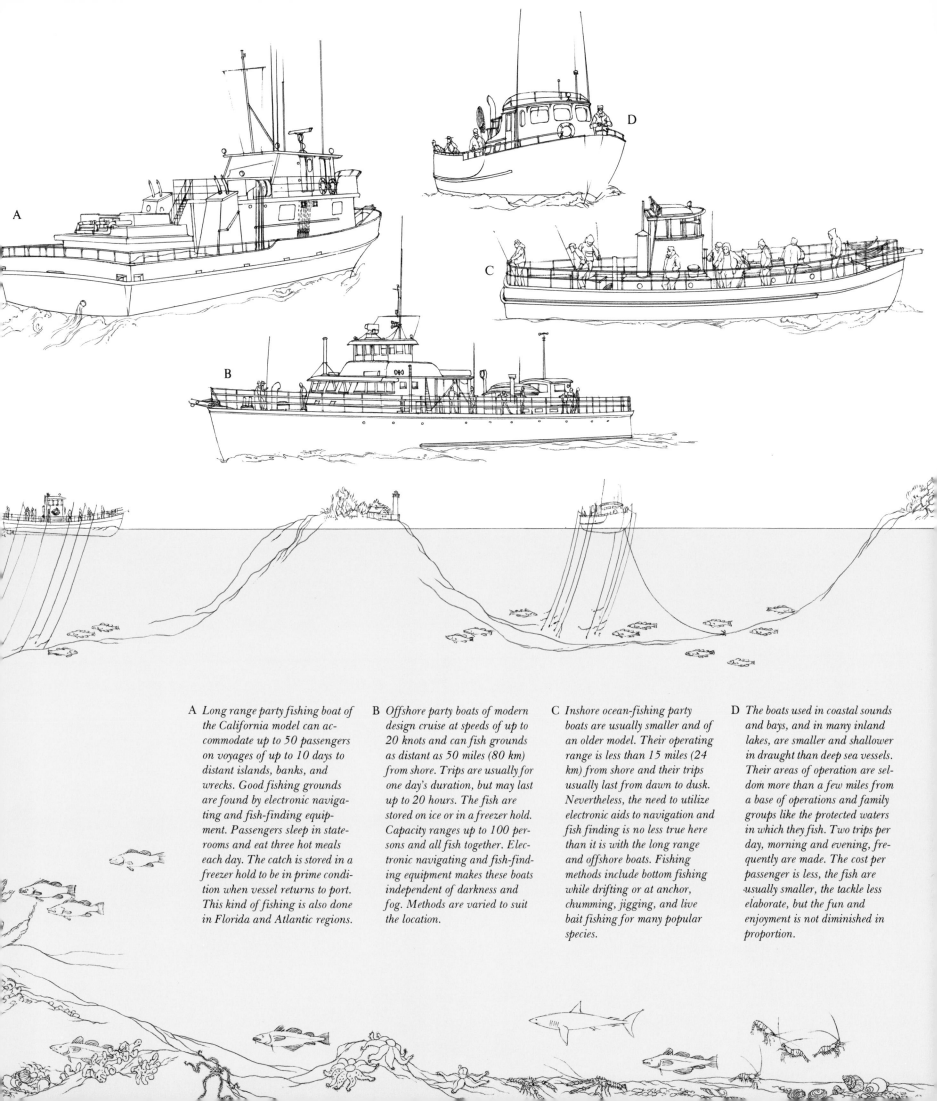

A Long range party fishing boat of the California model can accommodate up to 50 passengers on voyages of up to 10 days to distant islands, banks, and wrecks. Good fishing grounds are found by electronic navigating and fish-finding equipment. Passengers sleep in staterooms and eat three hot meals each day. The catch is stored in a freezer hold to be in prime condition when vessel returns to port. This kind of fishing is also done in Florida and Atlantic regions.

B Offshore party boats of modern design cruise at speeds of up to 20 knots and can fish grounds as distant as 50 miles (80 km) from shore. Trips are usually for one day's duration, but may last up to 20 hours. The fish are stored on ice or in a freezer hold. Capacity ranges up to 100 persons and all fish together. Electronic navigating and fish-finding equipment makes these boats independent of darkness and fog. Methods are varied to suit the location.

C Inshore ocean-fishing party boats are usually smaller and of an older model. Their operating range is less than 15 miles (24 km) from shore and their trips usually last from dawn to dusk. Nevertheless, the need to utilize electronic aids to navigation and fish finding is no less true here than it is with the long range and offshore boats. Fishing methods include bottom fishing while drifting or at anchor, chumming, jigging, and live bait fishing for many popular species.

D The boats used in coastal sounds and bays, and in many inland lakes, are smaller and shallower in draught than deep sea vessels. Their areas of operation are seldom more than a few miles from a base of operations and family groups like the protected waters in which they fish. Two trips per day, morning and evening, frequently are made. The cost per passenger is less, the fish are usually smaller, the tackle less elaborate, but the fun and enjoyment is not diminished in proportion.

CHUMMING FOR TUNA AND SHARKS

Chumming is one of the oldest methods for attracting fish. The primary idea is to lure the fish close to the boat by exciting their senses of taste and smell without satisfying their growing hunger. This is done by doling overboard a steady stream of ground fish meal, diluted with seawater. Sometimes sand is mixed with the fish meal to carry it deep quickly and to add the glint of the sand particles to the visual attractiveness of the chum mixture.

Sharks respond greedily to chumming and often become so bold as to take bits of fish held out to them on the end of a stick. When the piece of fish contains a fish-hook attached to a line, then the shark falls victim to the passion of its hunger. Tuna also rise to a chum line, but usually for a different reason. Chumming attracts many mackerel, a favorite food of tuna. A school of mackerel under the boat, brought there by the chumming, will quickly attract tuna if tuna are about. Fresh-caught live baits of mackerel cause tuna to abandon caution. Mackerel not used for bait, incidentally, never go to waste. They are taken home to make a tasty supper.

ANCHORING

A light anchor is used and a flag buoy is made fast to the anchor line just ahead of the boat's bow. This is so the anchor and line will not be lost when the anchor line is let go at the strike of a big tuna or large shark, enabling the boat to fight the fish without the encumbrance of the anchor and line.

TACKLE

The best combination of fishing tackle is:

Two or more heavy tuna outfits with reels of 12/0 size containing 80 or 130 lb (36 or 58 kg) test line.

Two or more medium shark outfits, reels of 6/0 size with 50 lb (22 1/2 kg) line.

Two or more light spinning or bottom fishing rigs to catch mackerel for live bait.

OTHER EQUIPMENT

Besides tackle, one will also need:
Several cans of chum, preferably preground.

Bait-cutting board and sharp knives.

Flying gaff and tail ropes for controlling sharks and big tuna.

Shoulder harness and fishing belts with rod butt sockets.

Fighting chair if the boat is large enough.

Both sharks and tuna prefer inshore ocean areas where groundfish abound, so such an area is a good place to chum. Local fishermen are often helpful and may give valuable clues on the whereabouts of tuna or sharks. Avoid areas full of lobster traps or other obstacles. Do not anchor in busy water traffic channels.

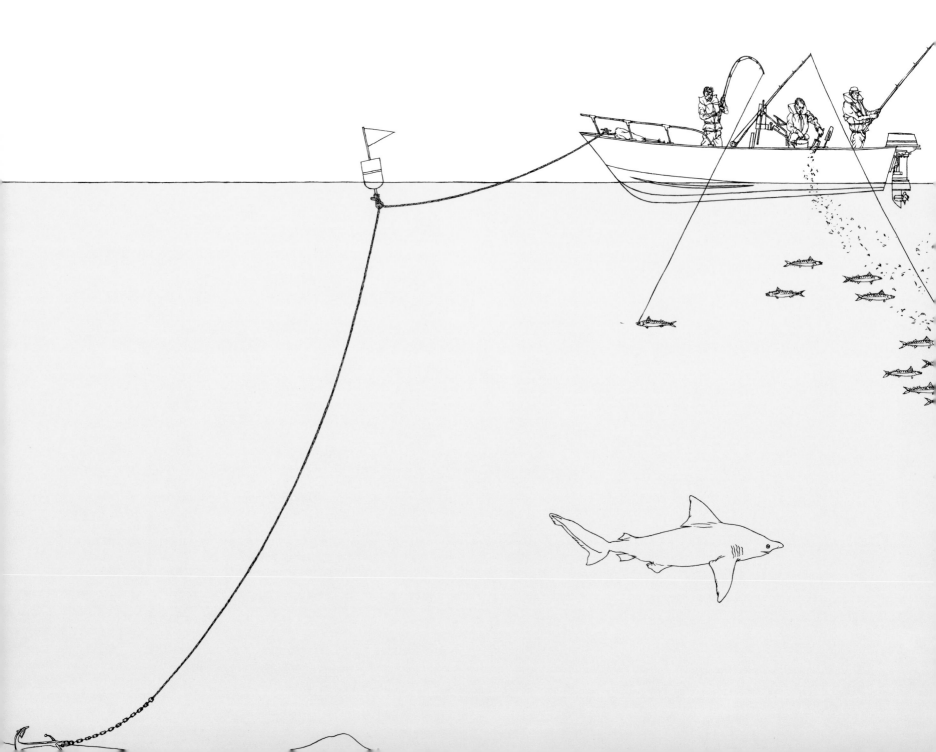

METHODS

Chumming is a continuous task unless a small fish or shark is hooked. Even then chumming continues if the fish is small enough for the boat to remain anchored. In the illustration below, one man chums while another in the bow catches mackerel to use as bait. The third tends the two big game rods. The men change jobs frequently.

A school of mackerel is under the boat. The men have seen at least one shark on the surface and they suspect there may be tuna down deep. The rod amidships is set in a rod holder with the reel drag set at minimum ten-sion and the clicker engaged. If a fish takes the bait the clicker will keep the reel spool from overrun-ning, which would cause a back-lash on the spool. The man in the stern has just rebaited his hook with a freshly caught live mack-erel and is dropping his line back to place the bait 50–60 ft (15–18 m) behind the boat. He has placed a split cork on the line about 30 ft (9 m) up from the hook. The cork will hold the bait at a fairly even depth. Separat-ing the baits prevents tangles when the fish strike.

PRECAUTIONS

Chumming for tuna and sharks is frequently done from boats as small as the one illustrated, although fishing from boats this small is not recommended to an-glers of little experience. These fishermen wear flotation jackets and each man carries a sharp sheath knife at his belt to cut a fishing line in an emergency.

Tuna are very powerful and even a 50-pounder can pull a man off his feet if the reel drag has too much tension. Sharks are extremely tenacious of life and "dead" sharks often come back to life without warning. Three strong men can "swamp" a 500 lb (225 kg) tuna into a small boat, but all sharks should be towed back to port with a rope around the tail.

OCEAN GAME FISH SEARCH TACTICS

In the old days, those who fished on the ocean were dependent on their eyes for detecting fish. Nowadays, eyes are still important, but science and improved fishing tactics have combined to give fishermen more and better opportunities to locate deep-water game fish. For example, several boats may work an ocean area together, exchanging information by radio and using their electronic sounders to probe the depths for signs of fish or the bait that fish feed on. "Fishermen's luck" now combines with science to give fishermen a new sense of purpose and security on the ocean.

A SOUNDING MACHINES

The electronic sounder reports the depth of water under the boat, but also displays schools of baitfish or large individual fish that come within the sounder's cone of high-frequency pulses.
Sounders include:
Neon-flasher models.
Paper recorders.
Flasher-recorders.
Digital readouts.
Directional sonars.
For practical fishing, flashers are best for small boats and shallow water. Recorders work better in deep water.

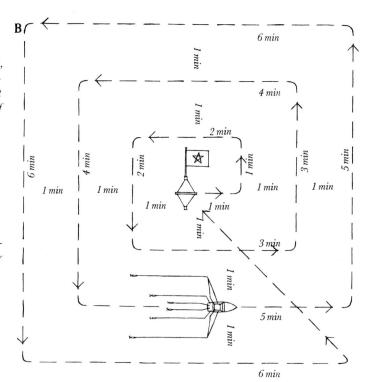

B EXPANDING SPIRAL SEARCH PATTERN

Adapted from a naval search technique, the expanding spiral search pattern is a method for relocating a big fish or a school of fish in foggy weather. The boat drops a flag buoy at the spot of last contact with the fish, then starts running at fast trolling speed (8 knots) one minute East one minute North, two minutes West, and so on, developing a box spiral search pattern. It will take exactly 48 minutes to complete the spiral and then about 4 1/2 more minutes to return to the flag's position.

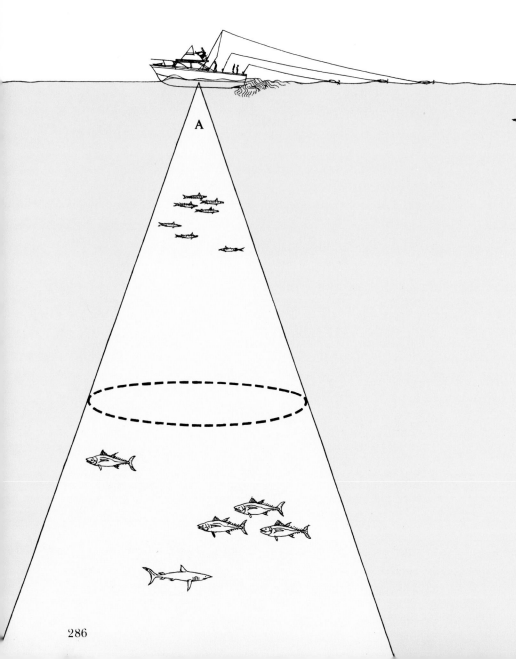

C BIRDS AND BAIT

Feeding seabirds are usually a sure sign of baitfish and larger game fish in the water. Herring gulls prefer large bait. Terns mark bluefish, mackerel, and striped bass. Gannets are a sure sign of mackerel. Shearwaters gather over tuna, as do fulmars, frigate birds, and petrels. Diving pelicans in tropical waters betray mullet. Ocean fishermen become expert bird-watchers.

D LEAPING FISH

Fish often reveal their unexpected presence by jumping out of the water. Tuna jump in the pursuit of prey, as do marlin, sailfish, and some sharks. Swordfish often leap, apparently for the fun of it. The striper seldom jumps, but often breaks the surface when after bait. When a boat approaches a breaking school, it circles the perimeter of the school so as not to "spook" the fish or the bait they are after.

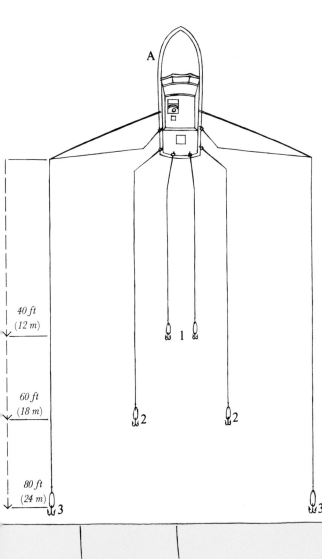

HOW BOAT SOUND AFFECTS TUNA

A fishing boat moving under power generates a rich and powerful sound field that some fish, especially tuna, find attractive. Lures and baits trolled through water also generate a variety of sounds that game fish identify as coming from something worth chasing and eating. A smart captain trolls his lures and baits in a pattern like the one in the sketch to the immediate left.

A TROLLING PATTERN

1 Two lures on light lines are set out to a distance of not more than 40 ft (12 m) for school tuna.

2 Two more are set out 60 ft (18 m) from corners of the stern for tuna.

3 Two marlin baits are streamed from the outriggers on heavy tackle. Lures troll in the boat's wake, but the outrigger baits troll outside the wake in clear, undisturbed water.

B SOUND EFFECTS FOR GAME FISH

The boat's sound field travels through water at nearly five times the speed of sound in air. Tuna hear it and rise to investigate this strange intrusion into their world. The boiling water of the wake attracts them. Quickly they spot the lures and baits in the wake, flashing and darting like small live fish. Competitive among themselves, they grab the lures, filling the lines within seconds.

TACKLE

The two inner stern rods carry 4/0 reels loaded with 30 lb (13 1/2 kg) test monofilament fishing line.

The two corner rods carry 6/0 reels and 50 lb (22 1/2 kg) test Dacron or monofilament line. The two outrigger rods carry either 9/0 reels filled with 80 lb (36 kg) test Dacron line, or 12/0 reels loaded with 130 lb (58 1/2 kg) test Dacron line. All rods are held in rod holders.

40 ft
(12 m)

60 ft
(18 m)

80 ft
(24 m)

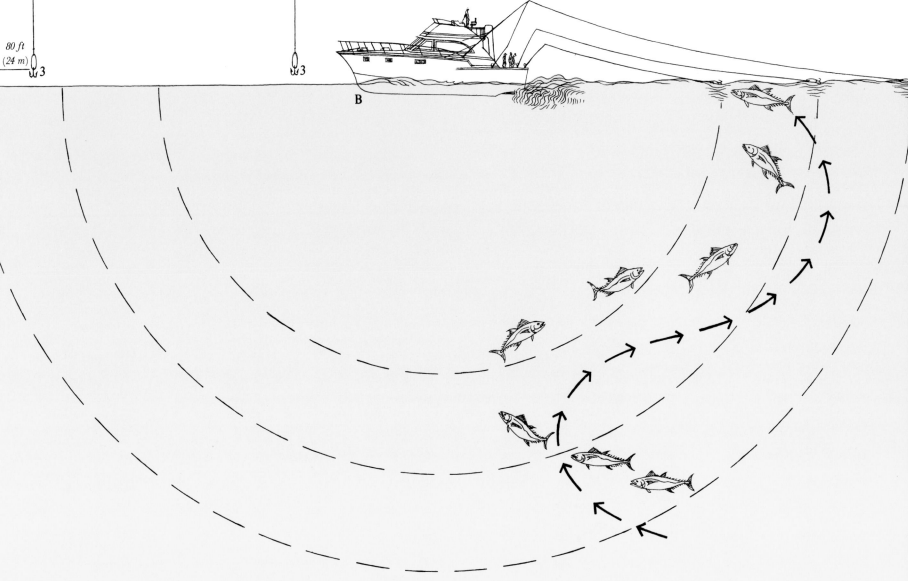

*A kite can be used to carry a
fishing bait downwind any
practical distance. Line is wound
onto a common handline reel
which is mounted on a shaff or
shaft that can be fastened to the
boat's gunwale or side.*
A *End view of reel, kite line, and
the mounting shaft.*
B *Side view of reel, 10 in (25 cm)
dia.*

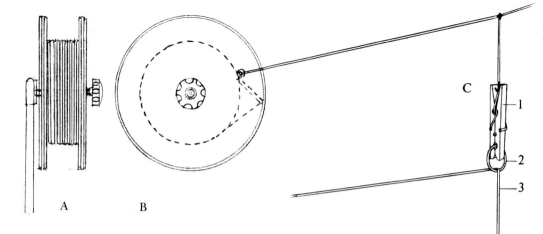

A   B

C *Line-release clip on dropper line.
Sudden tension of a strike on
fishing line pulls ring and line
from clip.*
1 *Release clip can be clothesline
clip.*
2 *Line-holding ring.*
3 *Fishing line.*

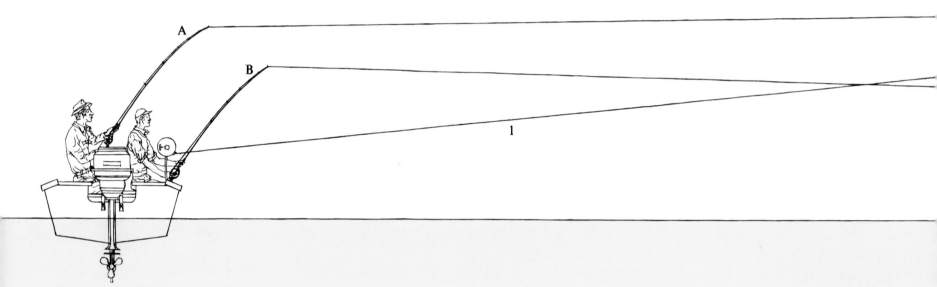

KITE FISHING WITH
LIVE BAIT

Historians claim that fishing
kites were used many years
ago by the Fiji Islanders.
Their kites were made of
plaited palm fronds covered
with the thin, cured
membranes of swim-
bladders of various fish. The
line was sennit made from
braided coconut fibre. Modern fishing kites came into
use early in this century
when sport fishermen at
Catalina Island, California,
tried them as a means of taking baits far out from the
boat to entice wary game fish.

KITE FISHING FROM BOAT
In the central sketch two men
in a boat are fishing live baits
from one fishing kite.
1 *This is the kite line which is
stored on the round hand-reel
attached to a shaft clamped to
a seat of the boat. The line is
usually heavy Dacron or
monofilament in the 60–80 lb
(27–36 kg) class. Their fishing rods (A, B) may be of any
type suitable for live bait fishing.*
2 *The fishing kite, which does
not have to be hauled in if only
one of the two baits is taken by
fish.*
3 *Fishing line extending down
from the release clip. This line
and bait is fished by Fisherman B.*
4 *Fishing line extending down
from second release clip. Line
and bait fished by Fisherman
A.*
5 *Release clip and release ring
for B.*

6 *Release clip and release ring
for A.*
*One advantage of using the
release ring is this: the line is
passed through the plastic or
metal ring before the bait is
hooked onto the hook. Thus,
when the ring is clipped into the
release clip, the line is free to
render through the ring. If a
shark or other unwanted fish
threatens the bait, the angler can
haul the bait up into the air
momentarily, merely by reeling in
line. Or, if he wants to allow the
bait more swimming room and
deeper action, he can permit the
bait to swim deeper by paying out
line through the release ring.
When a fish takes the live bait,
the sudden increase of line tension pulls the line clear of the
release clip. The slack line, falling through the air, gives the
fish exactly the right amount of
drop-back.*
*Drop-back is a term used to
describe giving a fish completely
free line so it can eat or swallow a*

*bait without hinderence of line
tension. The fact that the line
and leader are held up in the air
by the kite, making them virtually
invisible to the fish, is said by
many expert anglers to increase
the percentage of strikes from
otherwise wary game fish.*
*Experienced kite fishermen
usually own two or even three
sizes and weights of kites. Very
light winds call for kites up to 40
in (1 m) in side dimensions. A
kite of 20 in (.5 m) side dimensions is about right for winds of
8–15 m.p.h. (12.8–25 km/h.). A
small storm kite of 12–15 in
(30–38 cm) side dimensions is
used in stronger winds of 20–30
m.p.h. (32–48 km/h). In calm
weather, or when the wind is very
light, the boat can assist in keeping the kite aloft by trolling
slowly upwind or across-wind.
Thus, the kite is often used as a
sort of extension outrigger, especially when one has to get baits to
boat-shy tuna or billfish.*

KITE FISHING FROM
SHORE

Kite fishing is often done
from shore when there is an
offshore wind. In this instance, the fisherman uses a
spare fishing rod and its line
to fly the kite. The spare rod
is thrust into a sand-spike
driven into the earth on
shore.
1 *The sand-spike is a hollow
tube about 18 in (45 cm) long
with a sharp spike at the lower
end.*
2 *Driven into earth until the
flange is touching ground, the
sand-spike forms a stable rod
holder.*
3 *Fisherman ashore is able to
send bait out to any desired
distance, adjusting length of
the lines.*
4 *Dropper line and its release-
clip are tied to kite line 40–50
ft (15 m) below the kite.*

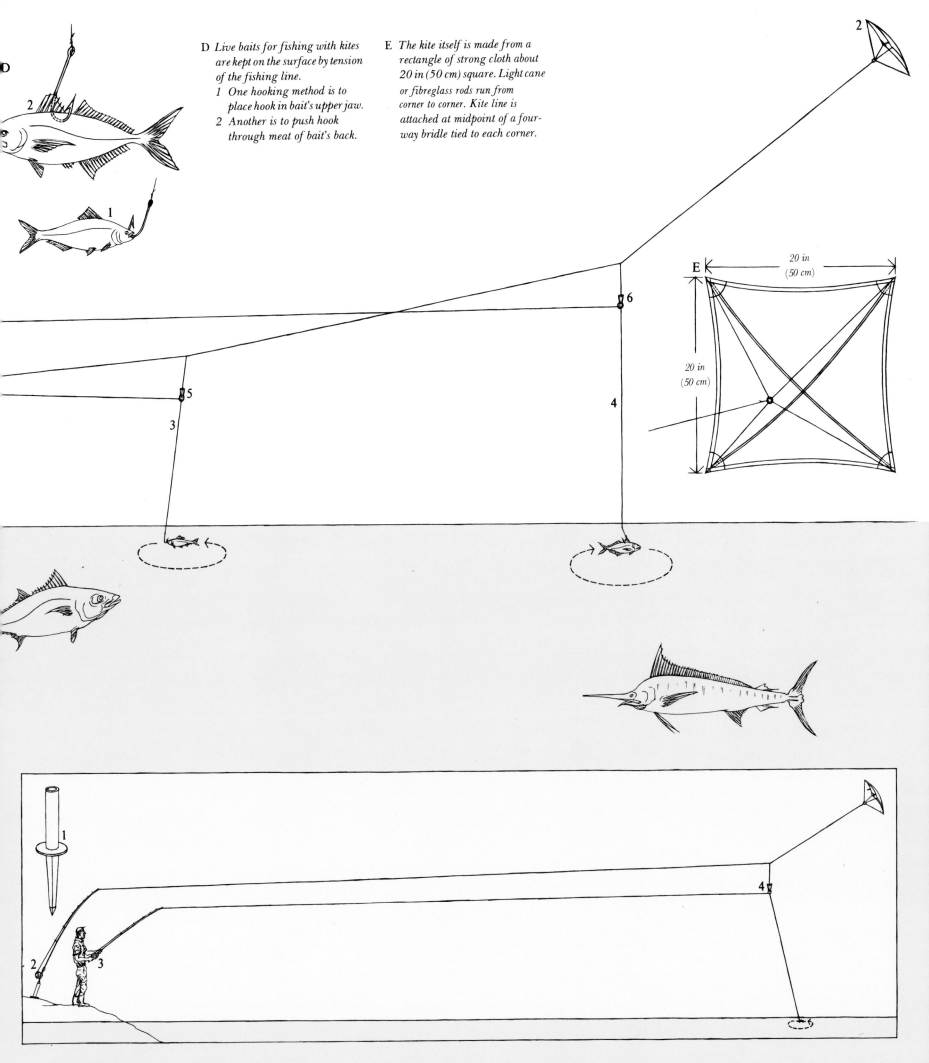

D Live baits for fishing with kites are kept on the surface by tension of the fishing line.
1 One hooking method is to place hook in bait's upper jaw.
2 Another is to push hook through meat of bait's back.

E The kite itself is made from a rectangle of strong cloth about 20 in (50 cm) square. Light cane or fibreglass rods run from corner to corner. Kite line is attached at midpoint of a four-way bridle tied to each corner.

20 in (50 cm)

20 in (50 cm)

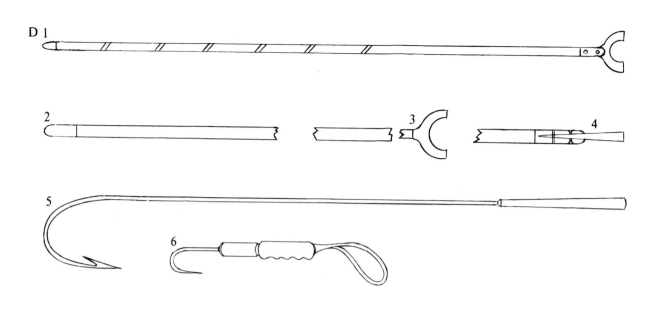

D 1 *The push-pole is 16 ft (5 m) long, made of aluminium tubing or fiberglass.*

2 *One end is plugged firmly with wood.*

3 *The other carries a wooden crotch which is pressed against the soft bottom when the boat is poled.*

4 *Edgeview of crotch.*

5 *For taking large fish a gaff with a shaft up to 8 ft (2.4 m) is often used.*

6 *If a large fish is to be released, a small hand gaff is used. The hand gaff hook is thrust into the lip of the fish so the fish may be lifted and the hook removed.*

AMPHIBIOUS FISHING—FLORIDA STYLE

In Florida, especially on the extensive flats of Florida Bay and the Keys, a specialized kind of amphibious fishing has developed. The primary targets are tarpon, bonefish, and permit, a jack that may exceed 50 lb (20.5 kg). The fish are located by sight-hunting. One man poles the boat quietly over the shallow flats while the other stands prepared to cast to any fish that comes in range. A special type of boat has been developed, the ultimate in amphibious fishing boat design.

The favorite types of tackle used in South Florida for amphibious fishing are:

Spinning tackle, in line-test classes from medium-light to medium-heavy.

Salt water fly rod equipment in AFTMA line-weight classes 6 (for bonefish) to 10 for tarpon and permit on the flats.

Bait-casting tackle such as used inland for large black bass, pike, muskellunge.

Spinning tackle is most popular, bait-casting equipment finds favor with anglers from fresh water areas, and fly tackle is recognized as offering the greatest sporting challenge.

THE ACTION

A *Fishing guide stands on boat's forward semi-raised deck and poles craft backward over shallow water of the flats. Angler has tackle ready to cast to fish that show within range.*

B *Angler casts toward target spot (X) just ahead of tarpon. The guide drives sharp end of the push-pole into the bottom to hold the boat in a favorable position.*

C *Boat is tied to the push-pole while the angler fights hooked fish and the guide prepares to gaff the tarpon when it comes to the boat's side.*

290

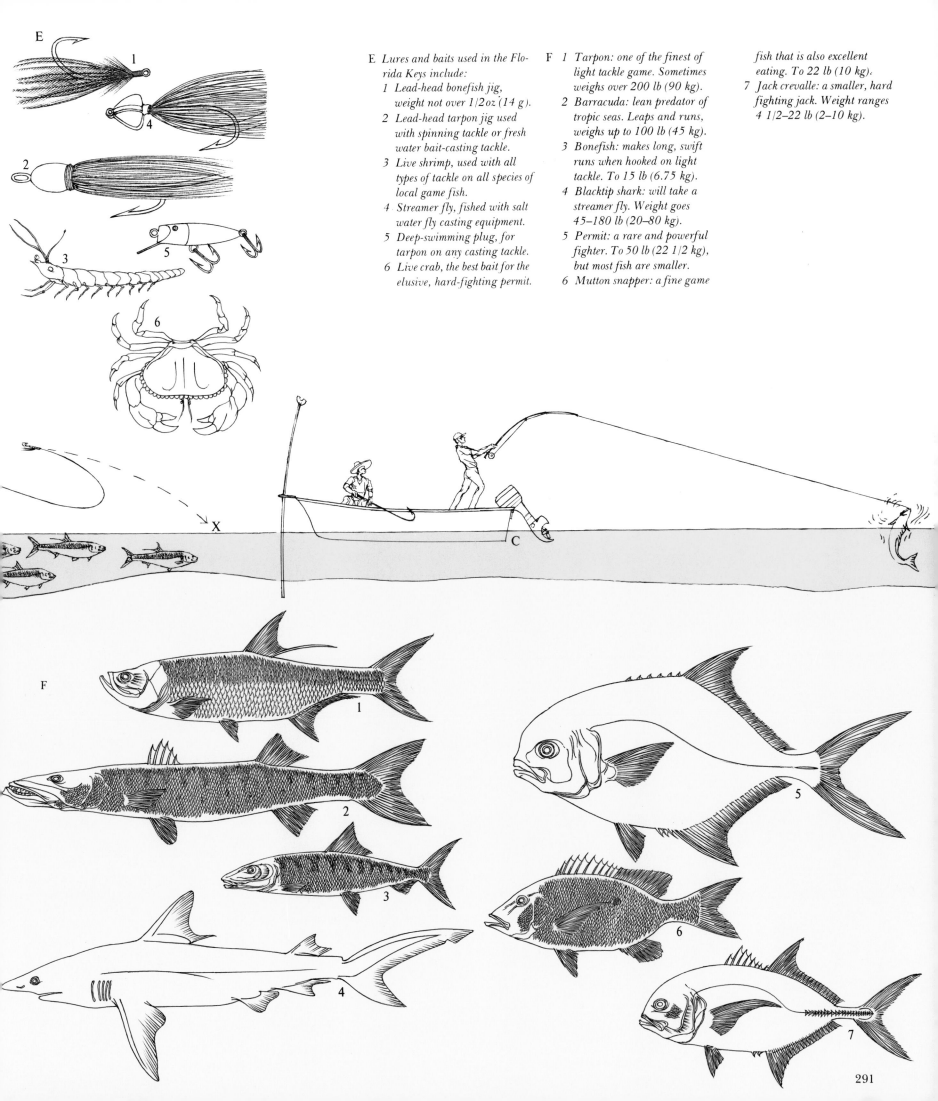

E *Lures and baits used in the Florida Keys include:*

1 *Lead-head bonefish jig, weight not over 1/2oz (14 g).*

2 *Lead-head tarpon jig used with spinning tackle or fresh water bait-casting tackle.*

3 *Live shrimp, used with all types of tackle on all species of local game fish.*

4 *Streamer fly, fished with salt water fly casting equipment.*

5 *Deep-swimming plug, for tarpon on any casting tackle.*

6 *Live crab, the best bait for the elusive, hard-fighting permit.*

F 1 *Tarpon: one of the finest of light tackle game. Sometimes weighs over 200 lb (90 kg).*

2 *Barracuda: lean predator of tropic seas. Leaps and runs, weighs up to 100 lb (45 kg).*

3 *Bonefish: makes long, swift runs when hooked on light tackle. To 15 lb (6.75 kg).*

4 *Blacktip shark: will take a streamer fly. Weight goes 45–180 lb (20–80 kg).*

5 *Permit: a rare and powerful fighter. To 50 lb (22 1/2 kg), but most fish are smaller.*

6 *Mutton snapper: a fine game fish that is also excellent eating. To 22 lb (10 kg).*

7 *Jack crevalle: a smaller, hard fighting jack. Weight ranges 4 1/2–22 lb (2–10 kg).*

291

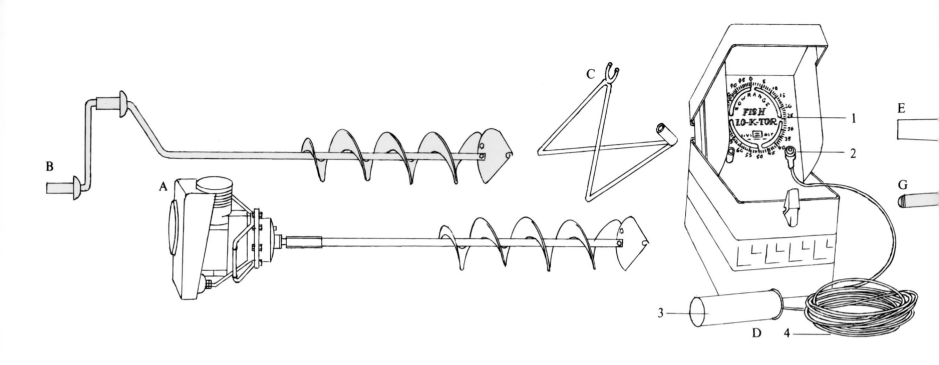

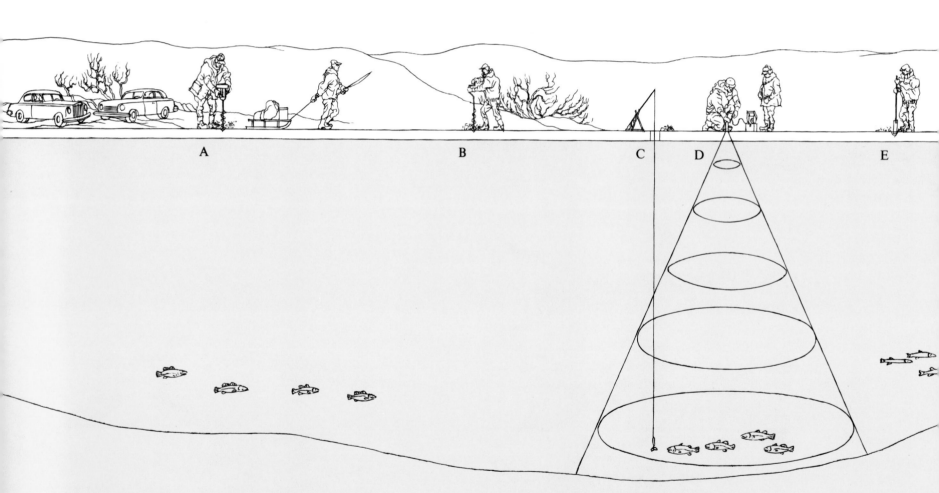

WINTER ICE FISHING

Fishing through the ice in winter for panfish, bass, pike, and other species is great sport. Many new devices make ice fishing more fun and less of an ordeal. Even so, anglers should never venture onto ice before testing it.

A *Power-driven ice auger drills round hole in thick ice in moments, the power coming from a small outboard-type motor mounted on top of the drill shaft. One power drill can make holes for dozens of ice fishermen in an hour or two.*

B *The hand auger costs less, is lighter to transport, and is faster at making a hole in ice than the ice spud or chisel.*

C *Tripod metal rod holder is light and stable, holds any conventional fishing rod in the normal fishing position.*

D *Portable sounding machine is a new ice fishing tool. With it the angler can locate good fishing bottom, bait, and fish.*

1 *Depth indicator dial.*
2 *Coaxial cable plug.*
3 *Transducer.*
4 *Transducer cable. In use, the sounder's transducer can be hung through the fishing hole or put into a smaller hole in the*

ice containing anti-freeze liquid.

E *The ice spud is a heavy steel chisel with a long wooden handle. It is used to chop holes in ice or to enlarge holes.*

F *Two types of shanties or small fishing huts are shown. They are insulated, heated by stoves, and*

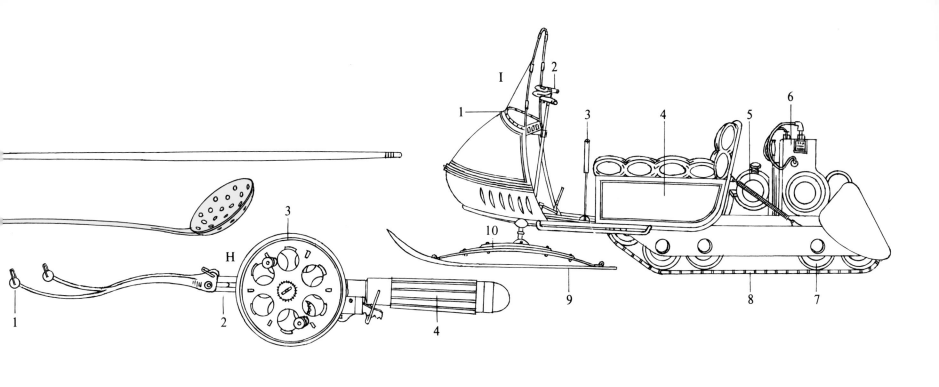

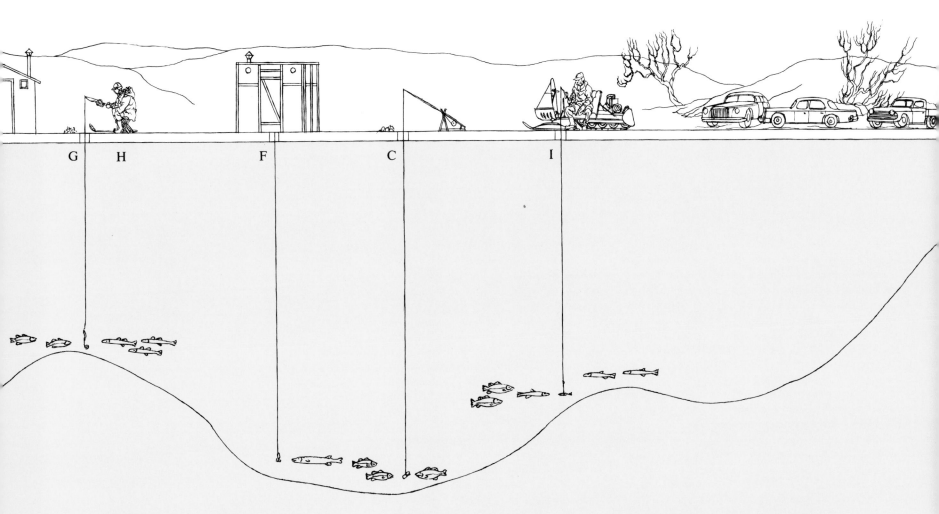

have a hole in the floor for fishing.

G Slush strainer. This valuable tool is for straining slush and ice chips from the fishing hole.

H Ice-jigging rod. This double-shafted model fishes two jig lines at the same time. Small lures are kept in constant motion, attracting fish that soon bite.

1 Twin jigging shafts.
2 Take-down lock.
3 Line spool.
4 Removable handle.

Many anglers use natural bait while others like artificial lures. Bait works best with lines that are left untended. Lures require con-stant jigging rod action. In some regions, great numbers of ice shanties form what look like small towns of houses out on the ice.

I The motorized snowmobile has revolutionized ice fishing as well as many other winter sports. Here is a light, fast, rugged off-the-road vehicle that makes it possible for ice anglers to visit remote lakes not accessible by other means of transportation. Machine has 1 power tread, 2 steering skis.

1 Cowl and windscreen.
2 Steering handle.
3 Clutch lever.

4 Storage under seat.
5 Fuel tank.
6 Air-cooled motor.
7 Drive wheel.
8 Endless drive tread.
9 Steering skis.
10 Steering ski spring.

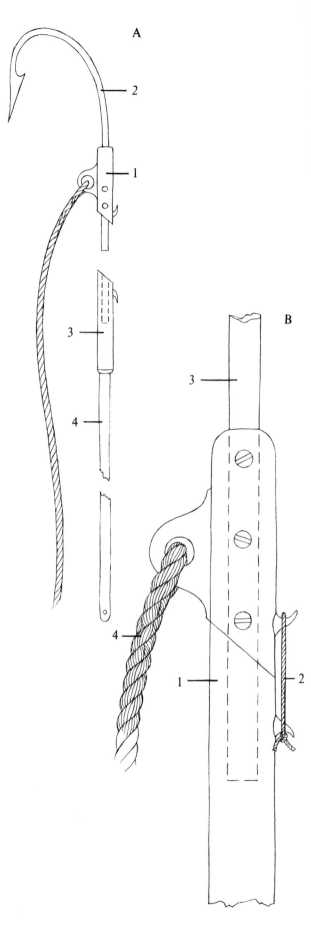

FIGHTING A BIG FISH

Many nonfishermen do not realize that when an angler fights a very large game fish he uses the fighting chair and a fishing harness, as well as the rod and reel, as vital aids to the fishing. A fighting chair differs from an ordinary fishing chair in that the former has an adjustable footrest and a removable back while the latter usually does not. The footrest enables the angler to use his legs in direct opposition to the powerful pull of the line and the fish. The chair is mounted on a very strong swivel mount and can be turned in a full circle. In operation, another angler usually stands behind the fisherman and keeps the chair constantly pointed toward the fish.

The fishing harness (Sketch C) is a specialized sort of vest that the angler wears across his lower back. Strong canvas or leather straps, securely anchored to the harness body, terminate in metal snap-hooks that in turn may be quickly locked into metal lift rings attached to the upper portion of the reel frame. With the straps properly adjusted and the rod butt in the gimbal of the fighting chair, the angler is able to take the weight of the rod and the fish with his body, leaving both hands free to manipulate the reel.

The undercarriage of the chair seat is equipped with metal legs, from which the footrest bars are suspended. Notches in the bars engage a strong retaining pin on each side. By sliding the footrest backward or forward, it can be adjusted to suit the leg-

length of any fisherman. There is also a swivel clamp which operates a friction brake around the chair-mount pipe. This can be used to dampen swiveling action, or even lock the chair in one position if needed.

The flying gaff is a very large gaff hook with a long, detachable handle. A 30 ft (10 m) length of rope is spliced into an eye in the gaff head sleeve. The hook shaft is keyed to slip into the handle sleeve in a nonslip fit. In this position the gaff head and the handle are secured by means of one turn of light line.

A large fish like the marlin is gaffed in the following manner:

1) The angler fights the fish and brings it in until one of the crew can take the wire or heavy monofilament leader in his gloved hands.

2) The crewman then pulls the fish closer with the leader, bringing it within reach of a second crewman who is ready with the flying gaff.

3) The gaffer pulls the gaff hook firmly into the body of the fish, pulling mainly on the safety rope, using the handle as a guide. This prevents premature separation of the gaff head from the handle.

4) As soon as the fish is gaffed the gaffer pulls strongly on the handle, breaking the tie string. He then hauls in the detached gaff handle and takes the weight of the fish on the safety rope.

A *The flying gaff*
   1 Gaff head sleeve
   2 Gaff head
   3 Gaff handle sleeve
   4 Gaff handle

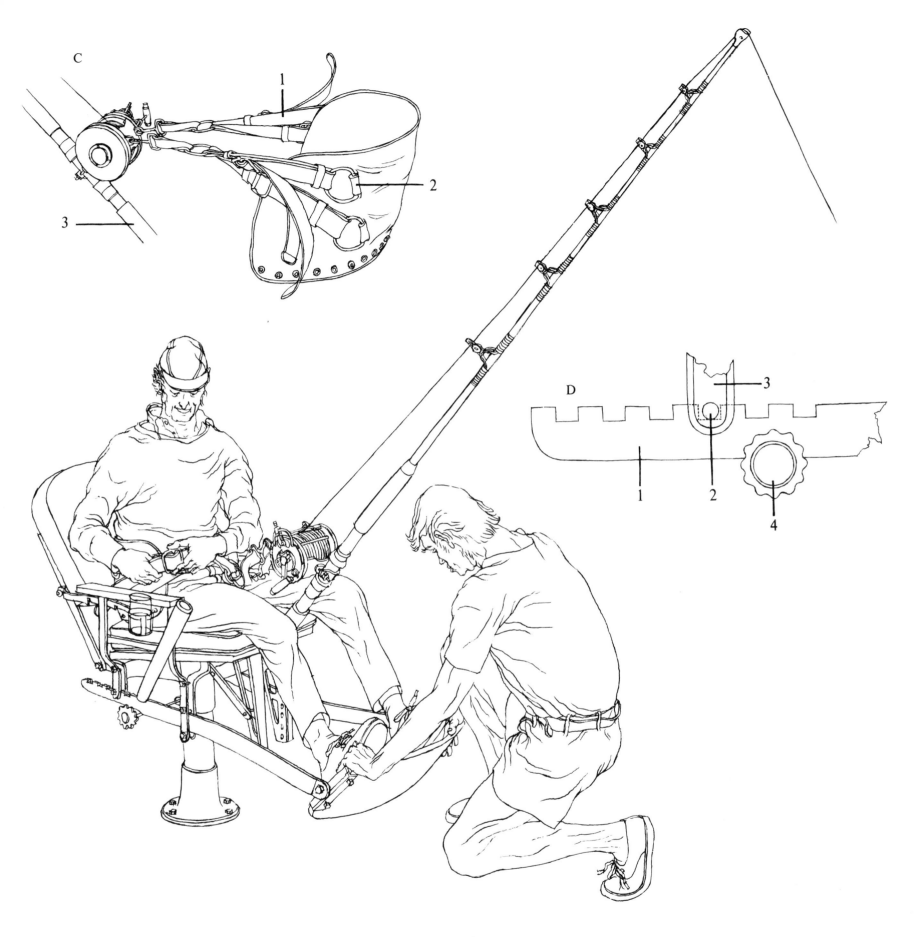

B *Gaff sleeve details*
  1 *Gaff head in the secured position*
  2 *Securing line*
  3 *Gaff head shaft*
  4 *Gaff safety rope*

C *The fishing harness*
  1 *Adjustable straps*
  2 *Strap anchors*
  3 *Rod butt shaft*

D *Chair control details*
  1 *Footrest bar*
  2 *Retaining pin*
  3 *Chair bottom leg*
  4 *Chair pivot clamp*

295

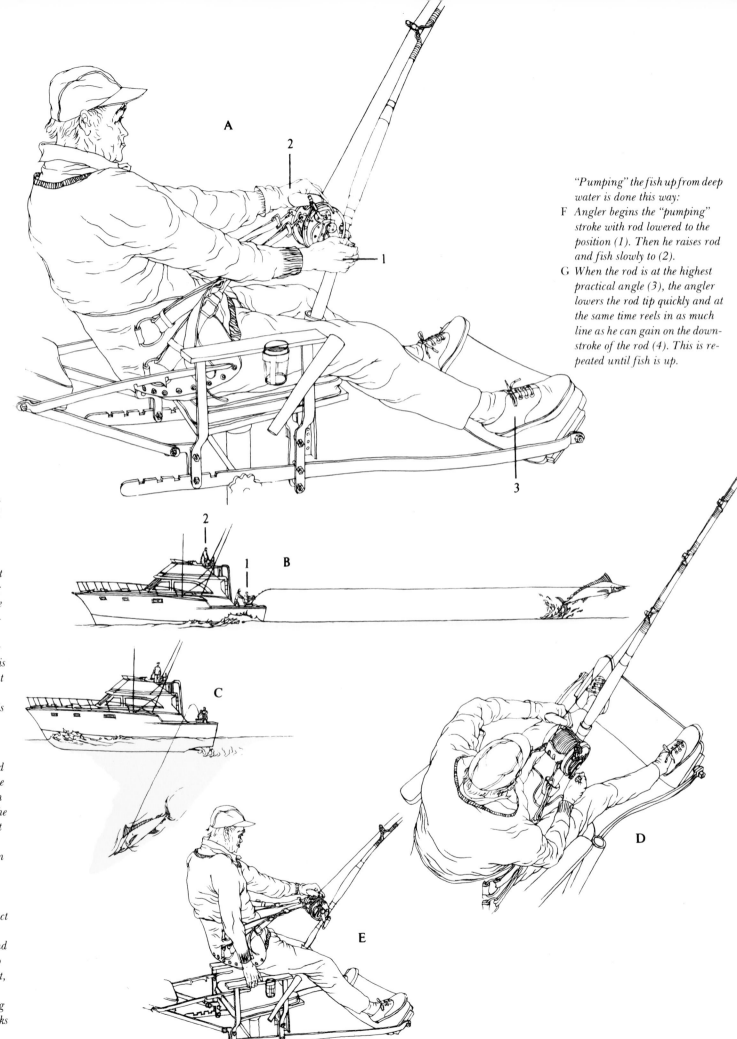

"Pumping" the fish up from deep water is done this way:

F Angler begins the "pumping" stroke with rod lowered to the position (1). Then he raises rod and fish slowly to (2).

G When the rod is at the highest practical angle (3), the angler lowers the rod tip quickly and at the same time reels in as much line as he can gain on the downstroke of the rod (4). This is repeated until fish is up.

FIGHTING A BIG FISH

A When a fish strikes, the angler takes the weight of the fish with the harness. Right hand (1) is on reel winding handle. Left hand (2) is held ready to guide line. Feet (3) are braced against footrest.

B The fish leaps away from the boat while the angler in the fighting chair (1) is pointed directly at the fish by one of the crew. The captain (2) directs the action from his vantage point on the bridge and may back the boat if there is danger that the reel may run out of line. Teamwork among the angler, crew, and the captain is important to the success of the fishing venture.

C Should the fish make a swift change of course and run ahead of the boat, the boat must pursue in such a manner as not to run over the line. Crewman keeps the fighting chair aimed directly at the fish.

D When the angler is able to gain line he winds the reel handle rapidly with the right hand, guiding the line onto the spool with his left hand. Gloves protect his hands.

E If the fish should decide to sound deep, the angler does not try to prevent this, but sits back to rest, holding the weight of the fish with the harness and regaining strength while the big fish works at peak power.

296

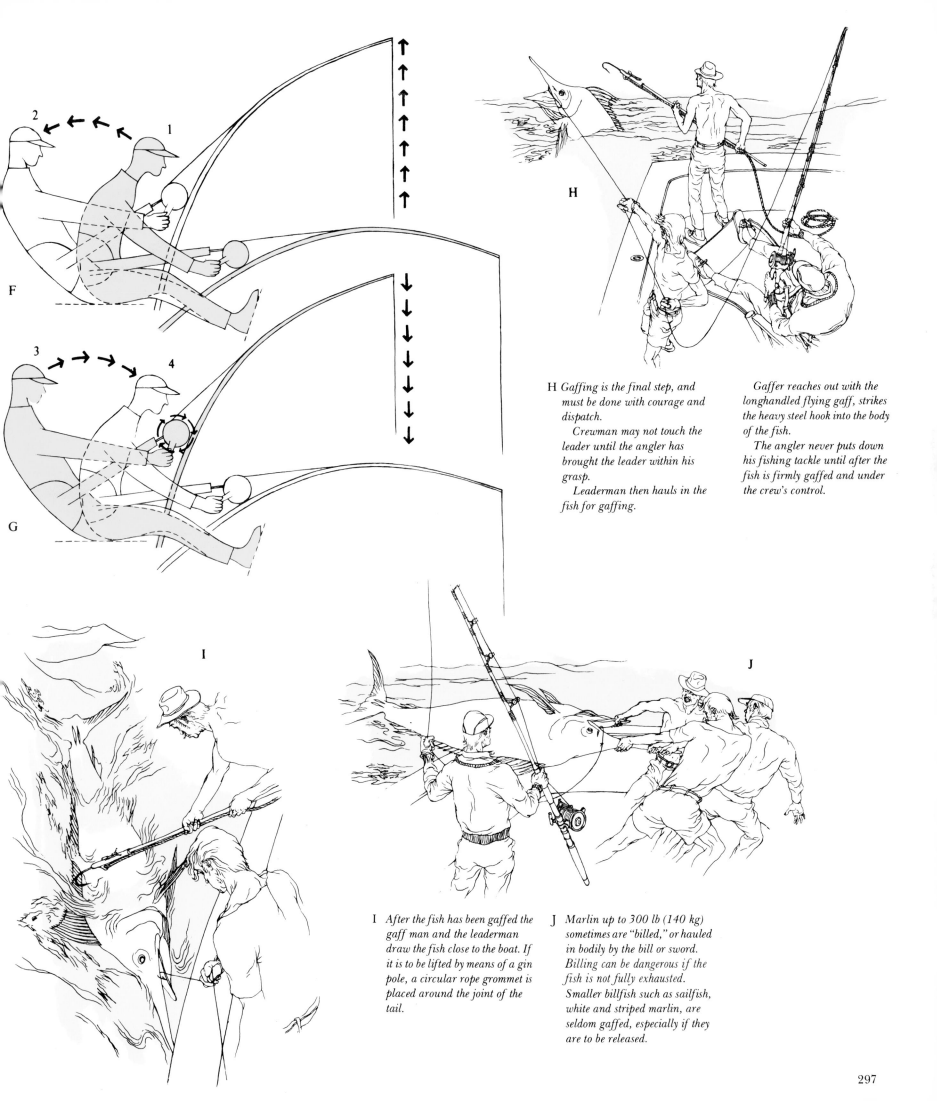

F

G

H *Gaffing is the final step, and must be done with courage and dispatch.*

Crewman may not touch the leader until the angler has brought the leader within his grasp.

Leaderman then hauls in the fish for gaffing.

Gaffer reaches out with the longhandled flying gaff, strikes the heavy steel hook into the body of the fish.

The angler never puts down his fishing tackle until after the fish is firmly gaffed and under the crew's control.

I *After the fish has been gaffed the gaff man and the leaderman draw the fish close to the boat. If it is to be lifted by means of a gin pole, a circular rope grommet is placed around the joint of the tail.*

J *Marlin up to 300 lb (140 kg) sometimes are "billed," or hauled in bodily by the bill or sword. Billing can be dangerous if the fish is not fully exhausted. Smaller billfish such as sailfish, white and striped marlin, are seldom gaffed, especially if they are to be released.*

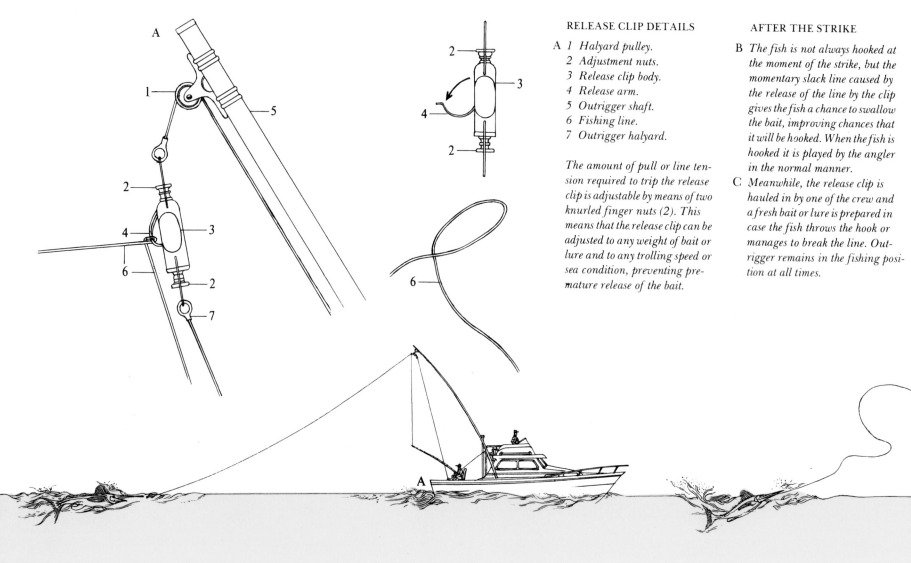

RELEASE CLIP DETAILS

A 1 *Halyard pulley.*
  2 *Adjustment nuts.*
  3 *Release clip body.*
  4 *Release arm.*
  5 *Outrigger shaft.*
  6 *Fishing line.*
  7 *Outrigger halyard.*

The amount of pull or line tension required to trip the release clip is adjustable by means of two knurled finger nuts (2). This means that the release clip can be adjusted to any weight of bait or lure and to any trolling speed or sea condition, preventing premature release of the bait.

AFTER THE STRIKE

B *The fish is not always hooked at the moment of the strike, but the momentary slack line caused by the release of the line by the clip gives the fish a chance to swallow the bait, improving chances that it will be hooked. When the fish is hooked it is played by the angler in the normal manner.*

C *Meanwhile, the release clip is hauled in by one of the crew and a fresh bait or lure is prepared in case the fish throws the hook or manages to break the line. Outrigger remains in the fishing position at all times.*

HOW OUTRIGGERS WORK

Fishing outriggers are long poles of wood, fiberglass, bamboo, or light metal that are extended at an angle of about 45° from vertical from the sides of the sport fishing boat. Their purpose is to give lift and separation to trolling lines, and to provide a means of presenting a trolling bait or lure to a game fish with a longer line than can be managed directly from the boat's cockpit. This reduces nervousness on the part of the fish.

In operation, a bait or trolling lure is let out about 60ft (20m) aft of the boat on rod and reel fishing line. The fishing line is then looped around the metal release hook or arm of the outrigger's release clip. Clip and line are then hauled out to the tip of the outrigger. The bait then skips on the surface of the water behind the boat outside the boat's wake. When a fish strikes at the bait, the sudden increase of line tension pulls the release arm down, letting the fishing line fall to the water.

VIEWED FROM ABOVE

D *The outriggers look like this when in use. Length of fishing line depends on boat speed, size and type of trolling bait, condition of the sea.*
Outriggers rake aft so release clips, when hauled out, are abreast of the stern. Outrigger rods are placed in fighting chair rod holders while trolling.

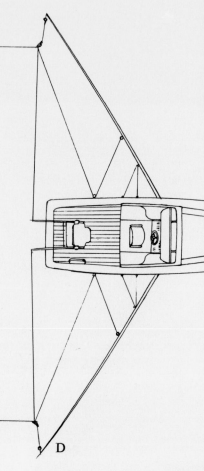

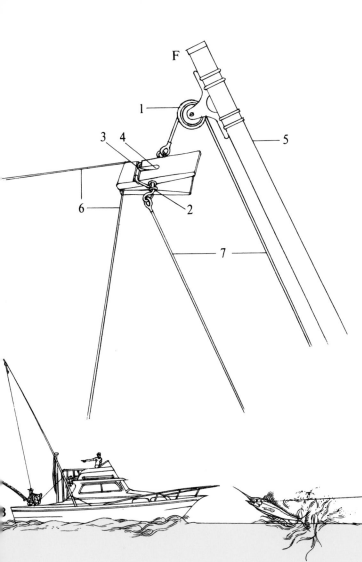

SPRING-JAW RELEASE

F 1 Halyard pulley.
   2 Tension spring.
   3 Wood release jaw.
   4 Tension adjustment.
   5 Outrigger shaft.
   6 Fishing line.
   7 Outrigger halyard.

The spring-jaw release is similar in action to the metal arm release shown in (A), except that the fishing line is held between two wooden or plastic jaws that are pressed together by an adjustable spring.

One advantage of the metal jaw release (A) is that if the fishing line is passed behind the metal jaw without looping the line, it will render freely through the release clip if one wishes to drop back or shorten up the line in fishing. With the spring-jaw release clip (F), the clip must be hauled back to the boat and the line released if the line length is to be altered while fishing.

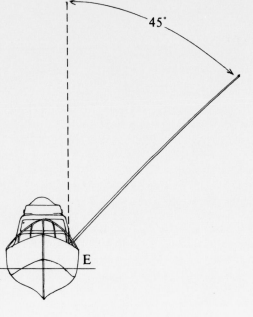

OUTRIGGER ANGLE

E *Outrigger angle of elevation is about 45° when lowered to fishing position. Poles stand upright and are clamped in position when not used for fishing.*

Trolling speed for outrigger fishing may vary from 2 to 6 knots depending on the bait, the fish, and weather. Generally speaking, big tuna and large billfish, with the exception of swordfish, like a fast trolling speed of 4–6 knots. Swordfish and small billfish require a slower bait speed of 2–5 knots.

Modern outrigger poles are made of bamboo, fiberglass, or metal tubing such as aluminum. Nylon parachute cord is excellent for outrigger halyards. Poles must be fastened in the fishing position with struts to keep them from flopping in rough weather, or when large fish strike.

OUTRIGGER BAITS FOR OCEAN GAME FISH

1 Squid: swordfish, tuna, marlin, sharks.
2 Mullet: sailfish, marlin, tuna, wahoo, swordfish.
3 Balao: small marlin, sailfish, tuna, wahoo.
4 Bonito: blue and black marlin, tuna, sharks.
5 Black eel: white marlin, tuna.
6 Konahead: Pacific blue marlin, ahi (yellowfin tuna).
7 Plastic lures: Most game fish that take the natural kind.

USING OUTRIGGERS TO BAIT A BILLFISH

Fishing outriggers are used to give separation and lift to bait lines while trolling. The bait is first dropped back about 80 ft (25 m) behind the boat, then the fishing line is clipped into a special quick-release device attached to the halyard of the outrigger. The release "clip" is then hauled to the outer end of the outrigger, the line being carried out with it.

When a fish strikes the trolled bait, increased tension on the line is enough to pull the line out of the release clip and the angler fights the fish unencumbered by the outrigger. Maneuvering the boat to place the bait in a good position, and to give the angler help with a difficult fish, is the responsibility of the boat's captain or professional guide.

C *The fish chases the skipping bait while the boat continues at its normal trolling speed. At position (3) the fish has finally caught the tantalizing bait and is in the act of pulling the fishing line down from the outrigger clip. Angler holds his rod in readiness to strike the instant he feels the fish's weight on line. Captain puts boat into slow turn to right.*

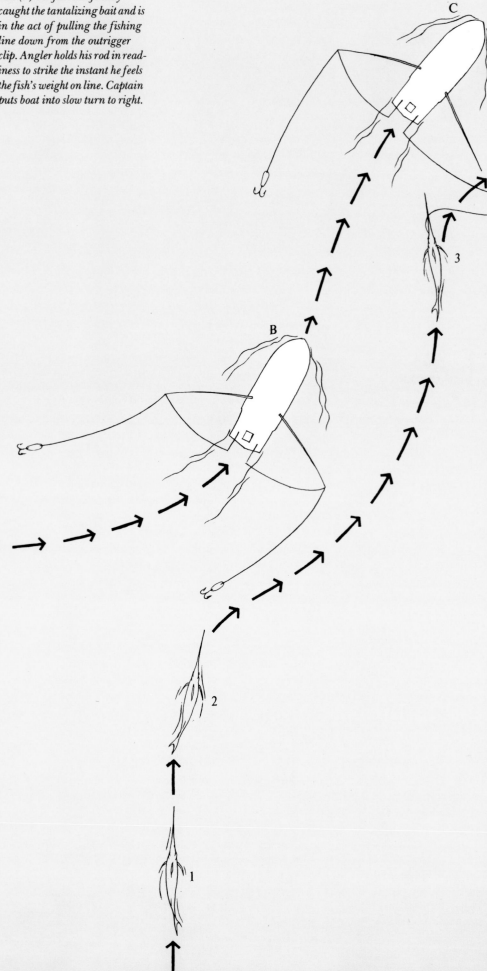

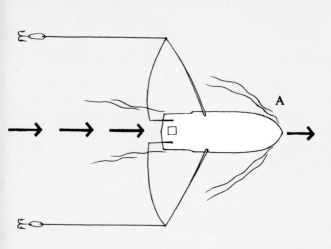

A *The boat is trolling at 5–6 knots from left to right, a bait line working from each outrigger, when the captain on the elevated flying bridge sees a billfish at position (1). The fish is swimming from right to left as seen from the boat. Captain decides to intercept the fish and present to it the starboard outrigger bait. Fish's speed is not over 1 1/2–2 knots.*

B *As the boat comes abreast of the fish, the captain starts a turn to the left. Fish now is at location (2). The boat is now starting to move away from the fish, but the starboard outrigger bait, held by the outrigger well wide of the wake, passes a few feet in front of the fish, skipping actively on the water surface. The billfish sees the bait, moves to pursue.*

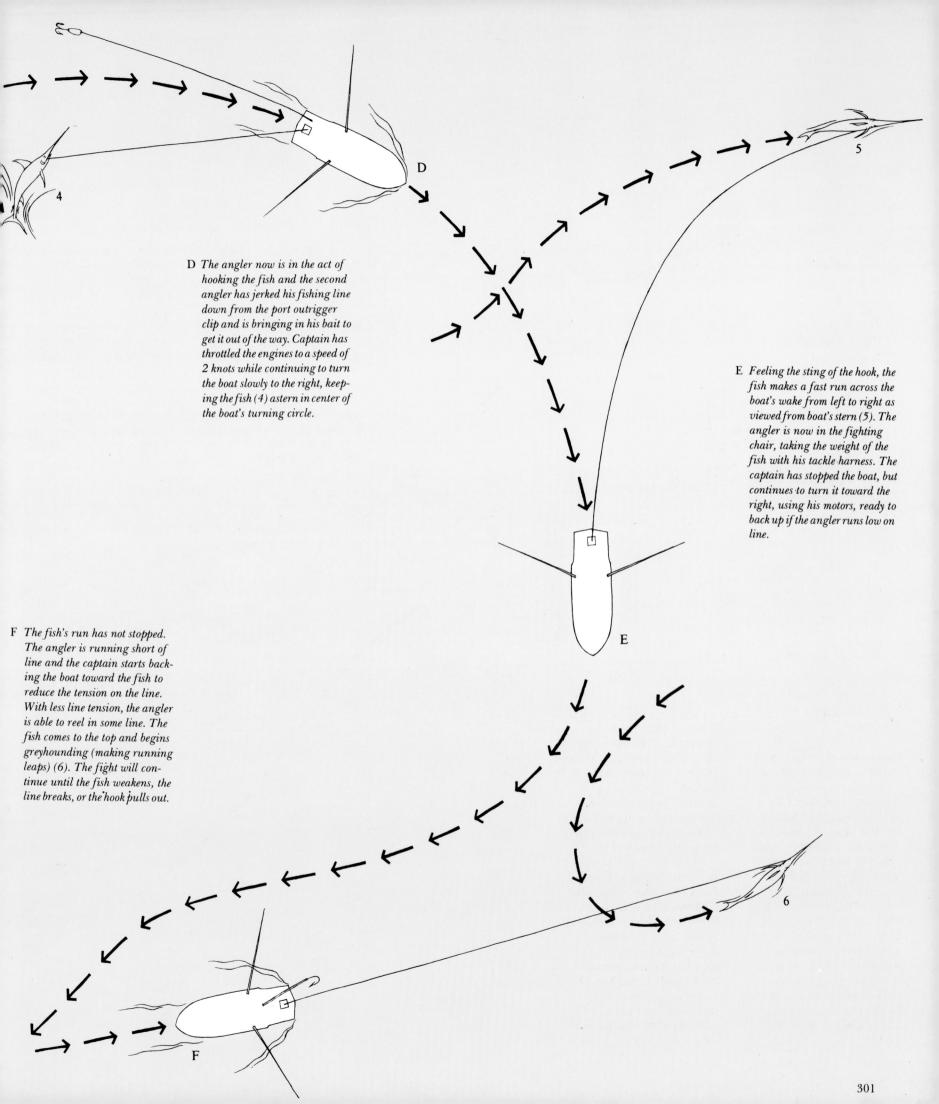

D The angler now is in the act of hooking the fish and the second angler has jerked his fishing line down from the port outrigger clip and is bringing in his bait to get it out of the way. Captain has throttled the engines to a speed of 2 knots while continuing to turn the boat slowly to the right, keeping the fish (4) astern in center of the boat's turning circle.

E Feeling the sting of the hook, the fish makes a fast run across the boat's wake from left to right as viewed from boat's stern (5). The angler is now in the fighting chair, taking the weight of the fish with his tackle harness. The captain has stopped the boat, but continues to turn it toward the right, using his motors, ready to back up if the angler runs low on line.

F The fish's run has not stopped. The angler is running short of line and the captain starts backing the boat toward the fish to reduce the tension on the line. With less line tension, the angler is able to reel in some line. The fish comes to the top and begins greyhounding (making running leaps) (6). The fight will continue until the fish weakens, the line breaks, or the hook pulls out.

301

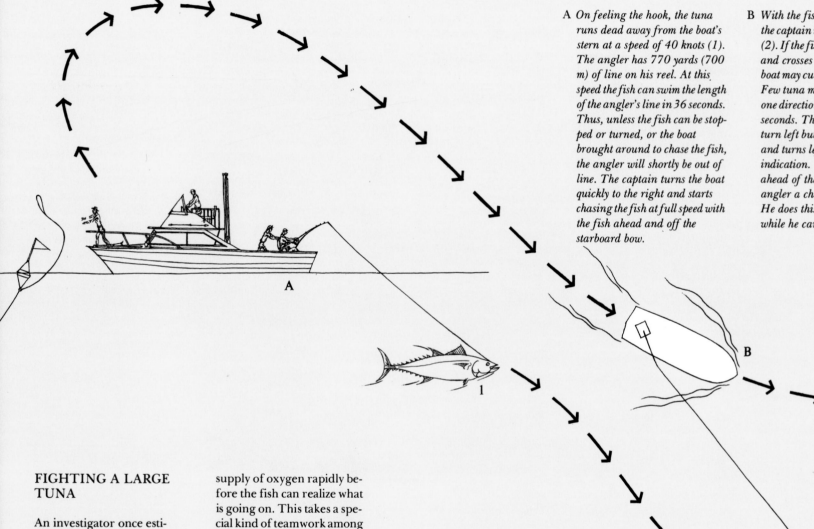

A

1

B

2

A *On feeling the hook, the tuna runs dead away from the boat's stern at a speed of 40 knots (1). The angler has 770 yards (700 m) of line on his reel. At this speed the fish can swim the length of the angler's line in 36 seconds. Thus, unless the fish can be stopped or turned, or the boat brought around to chase the fish, the angler will shortly be out of line. The captain turns the boat quickly to the right and starts chasing the fish at full speed with the fish ahead and off the starboard bow.*

B *With the fish ahead of the boat, the captain is in a dangerous spot (2). If the fish suddenly turns left and crosses the boat's bow, the boat may cut its own fishing line. Few tuna maintain a fast run in one direction for more than a few seconds. The fish does decide to turn left but the captain is ready and turns left himself at the first indication. This puts the boat ahead of the fish and gives the angler a chance to regain line. He does this by reeling rapidly while he can.*

FIGHTING A LARGE TUNA

An investigator once estimated that a 600 lb (280 kg) bluefin tuna has at least 90 hp that it can expend for a few moments after being hooked, power in excess of that needed to swim at between 40 and 50 knots. Certainly, on a dead pull a big tuna can break any fishing line now used by sportsmen. How is it then that men in boats are frequently able to take these very powerful fish in less than 15 minutes?

The answer is that the fishermen use the boat much as a cowboy uses his horse to herd and drive the hooked tuna, forcing it to burn up its supply of oxygen rapidly before the fish can realize what is going on. This takes a special kind of teamwork among angler, captain, and boat. If the tactics fail and the fish gets its "second wind," the fight may go on for hours and the fisherman may give up before the fish.

Here, a sport fishing boat has been chumming for tuna and a fish has just taken one of the baits. The captain goes to the flying bridge control station, starts the motors, and waits for one of the crew to go forward and throw off the buoyed anchor line. The angler-captain-boat team cannot fight the tuna advantageously with the boat tethered to the anchor line.

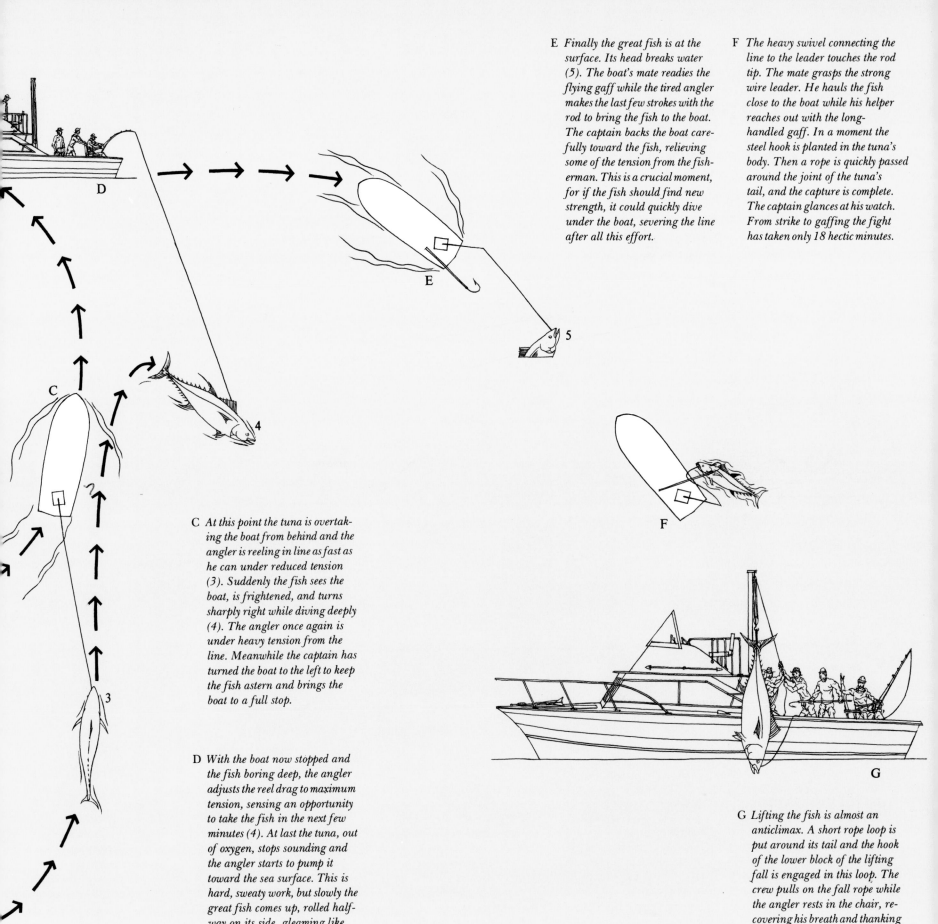

E Finally the great fish is at the surface. Its head breaks water (5). The boat's mate readies the flying gaff while the tired angler makes the last few strokes with the rod to bring the fish to the boat. The captain backs the boat carefully toward the fish, relieving some of the tension from the fisherman. This is a crucial moment, for if the fish should find new strength, it could quickly dive under the boat, severing the line after all this effort.

F The heavy swivel connecting the line to the leader touches the rod tip. The mate grasps the strong wire leader. He hauls the fish close to the boat while his helper reaches out with the long-handled gaff. In a moment the steel hook is planted in the tuna's body. Then a rope is quickly passed around the joint of the tuna's tail, and the capture is complete. The captain glances at his watch. From strike to gaffing the fight has taken only 18 hectic minutes.

C At this point the tuna is overtaking the boat from behind and the angler is reeling in line as fast as he can under reduced tension (3). Suddenly the fish sees the boat, is frightened, and turns sharply right while diving deeply (4). The angler once again is under heavy tension from the line. Meanwhile the captain has turned the boat to the left to keep the fish astern and brings the boat to a full stop.

D With the boat now stopped and the fish boring deep, the angler adjusts the reel drag to maximum tension, sensing an opportunity to take the fish in the next few minutes (4). At last the tuna, out of oxygen, stops sounding and the angler starts to pump it toward the sea surface. This is hard, sweaty work, but slowly the great fish comes up, rolled halfway on its side, gleaming like silver in the water.

G Lifting the fish is almost an anticlimax. A short rope loop is put around its tail and the hook of the lower block of the lifting fall is engaged in this loop. The crew pulls on the fall rope while the angler rests in the chair, recovering his breath and thanking his stars that this was an "easy" fish.

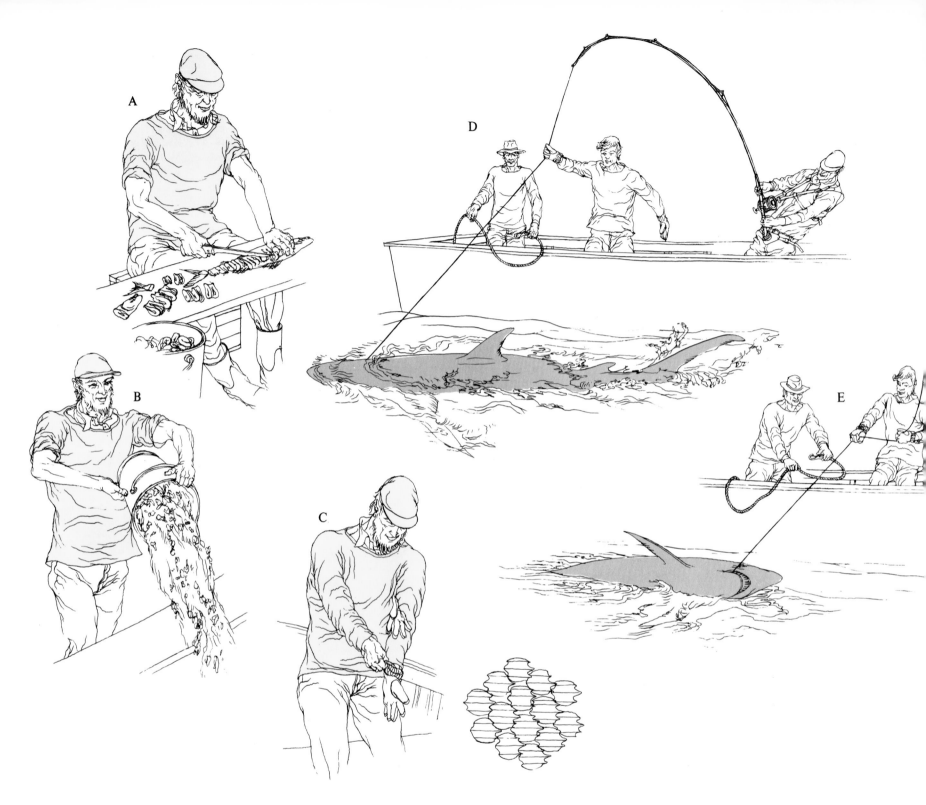

HANDLING SHARKS WITH SAFETY

Sharks, even those of the "nonmaneater" species, have dental equipment capable of inflicting serious harm to fishermen. But the teeth of sharks are not their only weapons. All sharks have tiny "skin teeth," properly called denticles, that give their skin a rasping, sandpaper quality when rubbed from tail toward head. In fact, sharkskin was used in olden times as a

substitute for sandpaper by carpenters and cabinet-makers.

A shark's tail is also a dangerous weapon. It can inflict a bad blow if the shark is able to get its tail out of the water beside the boat. But sharks can be taken with relative safety, even without a flying gaff, if the anglers employ a strong tail rope in the manner shown here.

A *One duty of shark fishing is cutting up the bait and chum.*

B *Finely cut chum is doled over-*

board to attract sharks close to the boat before they are hooked.

C *Before attempting to handle a shark that has been hooked and brought to the boat, anglers put on stout canvas gloves to protect their hands from rough sharkskin.*

D. *Tail roping a live shark is usually a three-man job. The angler plays the beast and brings it to the boat. The leaderman grasps the cable or wire leader and hauls the shark in close. The angler never lets go of the rod until the shark is safely tail roped and immobile.*

E *When the shark is close enough, the rope-man passes the end of his tail rope around the leader and makes a loop large enough to slip back over the shark's head and body.*

F *This may take some careful work with a small hand gaff. The gaff is used only to get the rope loop over the shark's fins. It is not stuck into the shark. To do so might anger the shark into dangerous thrashing beside the boat before the roping job is done. The shark tail rope is made up from 30 ft (10 m) of 1/2 inch*

(12 mm) manila or nylon rope. The bitter end is given a standard seaman's rope-end whipping. The working end is provided with a pair of sister hooks (1) or a self-mousing single hook (2). Some shark anglers make tail ropes from flexible bronze tiller cable.

No attempt should be made to tail rope any shark until the beast has been thoroughly whipped by rod and reel and is quiet in the water. The tail rope is frequently used after a shark has been secured with a flying gaff, as is

illustrated elsewhere in the book. A shark that resists roping should be worked by rod until it is exhausted.

G When the tail rope has been brought to the joint of the shark's tail, the loop is drawn tight and the shark's tail is firmly tied to the boat's side. The fishing leader may now be cut with pliers close to the shark's head, or disconnected from the fishing line and made up into a coil.

One final warning! Never take even a small shark into the boat unless its tail has been firmly roped. Large sharks should be towed into port and no attempt made to take them on board until they are completely dead. All sharks are extremely hardy and "dead" sharks may revive when least expected.

H FISHING FOR SHARKS FROM SHORE

In many areas, sharks can be fished for from shore. In Durban, South Africa, for example, fishermen use the harbor's stone breakwaters for shark fishing, with success.

Tackle for sharks:
Rod–heavy Tonkin cane or fiberglass.

Line–50 or 80 lb (22 1/2 kg or 36 kg) test, Dacron or mono.

Hook–double extrastrong, 10/0 to 16/0.

Leader–cable-laid or heavy single wire.

Gaffs–long-handle heavy-duty fixed or flying gaffs.

Tail rope–1/2-inch manila or Nylon.

Bait for sharks:
Fish-bonito, bass, grouper, cod, tuna.

Meat-beef, horse, chicken, etc.

Chum-beef blood, fowl blood, ground fish meal, slaughterhouse trimmings.

Lines and leaders:
Sharks hooked from shore rarely make long runs, but they can exert a strong pull on the line, so heavy line and a stout rod are needed. For very large sharks make up leaders of solid or cable wire testing at least 250 lb (112 kg) breaking strain.

Getting the bait out:
Use a rowboat if one is handy. Otherwise, drift the bait out with a cork, balloon, or other float on the line to keep the bait off bottom. Let the shark eat the bait slowly before you strike him hard.

Landing the shark:
Helpers should wear gloves. Have them haul the shark into shallow water, using the wire leader, then gaff him and hold him while one man puts a stout rope around his tail.

IDENTIFYING GAME SHARKS

While many species of sharks are fished for all over the world, only six species are considered to be truly game by virtue of the quality of their fight when hooked.

The International Game Fish Association (IGFA) recognizes these species as true game sharks:
Porbeagle shark
(*Lamna nasus*)
Thresher shark
(*Alopias vulpinus*)
Blue shark
(*Prionace glauca*)
Tiger shark
(*Galeocerdo cuvieri*)
Mako shark
(*Isurus oxyrhynchus*)
White shark
(*Carcharodon carcharias*)
Hammerhead Shark
(*Sphyrna zygaena*)

A PORBEAGLE SHARK

Dark bluish grey above changing to white below. Body is well streamlined, stocky and muscular in build. Nose comes to a definite point.

Range: a cold water shark of the North Atlantic. Found in coastal waters, but more abundant in deeper water of 40 to 70 fathoms (80 to 140 m).

Fast swimmer preying on mackerel, herring, etc. Leaps when hooked. Caudal peduncle is flattened laterally with two side keels. Dagger-shaped teeth have small cusps at sides of roots. Mako teeth have no cusps.

B THRESHER SHARK

Easily identified by its very long upper tail lobe which is as long as the body.

Range: temperate and sub-tropical regions. Surface-swimmer that feeds on mackerel and other swift fish. Uses tail to group fish before feeding.

Caution advised when gaffing. This shark can inflict dangerous blows with its tail.

Enormously long tail makes it impossible to confuse this shark with others in the same waters. The rare Bigeye thresher has much larger eye.

C BLUE SHARK

Easily distinguished by its bright blue colour, long pectoral fins, tips of which shade to white. Slim body is white below.

Range: Abundant in tropical, temperate seas. Migrates north during summer months. Found both inshore and in deep water.

An aggressive shark that travels in loose packs, easily aroused to a feeding frenzy by chumming.

Small ridges but no side keels on tail. Teeth have saw edges, curve back toward hinges of the jaw. Blue skin colour does not fade at death.

D TIGER SHARK

Body is greyish brown, darker above than below with "tiger" markings on back, fins, and tail. Markings may fade with maturity.

Range: Worldwide in subtropical and tropical seas, most frequently near large land masses.

A very large, sluggish shark with a penchant for garbage, but also a reputation for being dangerous to swimmers.

Only large sharks with light-and-dark "tiger" markings on dorsal surfaces. The teeth are heavily saw-edged, indented on outer edges.

E MAKO SHARK

Resembles, but is slimmer than the porbeagle. Very fast and game on sporting tackle. Frequently jumps when hooked. Nose is pointed.

Range: worldwide in warm-temperate and tropical seas.

A powerful, aggressive shark, said to be the only natural enemy of swordfish and the large marlins. Edible flesh resembles swordfish. Feeds on fast-moving surface bait fish.

Tail joint flattened like porbeagle and swordfish, single keel on each side. Teeth are dagger-like, smooth-edged, have no side cusps.

F WHITE SHARK

Grey brown to black above, dirty white below. Largest of the game sharks, the true "maneater."

Range: Worldwide in warm-temperate and tropical seas.

Feeds often on large prey. Is found inshore and offshore. Specimens taken by rod and reel are often immature or juveniles. Size makes it dangerous to gaff. Side keels on tail like swordfish and mako. Teeth are saw-edged, symetrical, do not indent or curve toward outer corners of the jaw.

G HAMMERHEAD SHARK

The unusual, broad hammershaped head is positive identification. Medium greyish brown on back shading to dull white on belly. Long and slim.

Range: worldwide in warm and tropical waters, both offshore and fairly close to land. Wide-ranging in loose packs or schools.

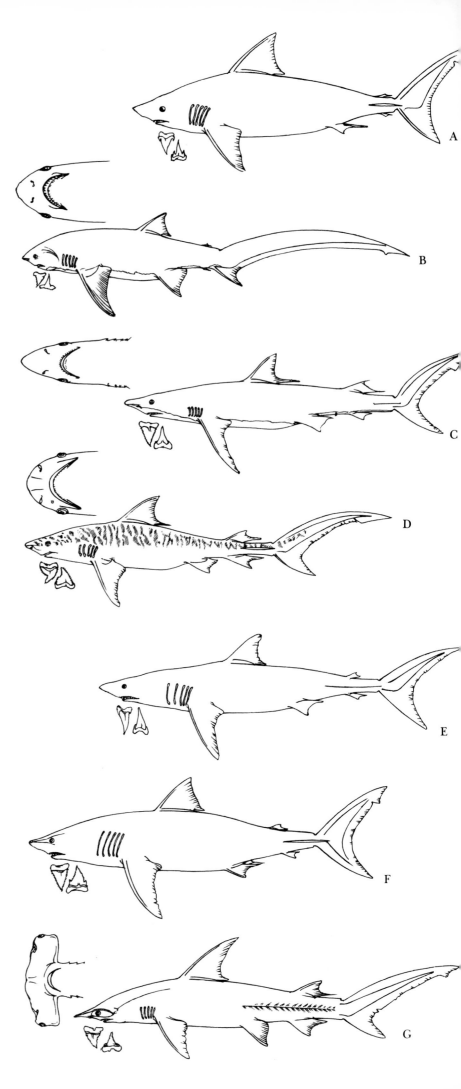

First let your rod be light and gentle.
I take the best to be two pieces.

IZAAK WALTON

The modern angler who has difficulty making a choice of suitable fishing tackle in a well-equipped tackle shop has little conception of the amount of work that fishermen once had to expend to make the tackle they needed for catching fish. The best tackle has always been relatively expensive, and ordinary fishermen very often had to make their own equipment or not fish at all. Skill in making rods, reels, lines and hooks was closely guarded by a handful of artisans and frequently an angler had to make do with a single rod and reel.

Such a single rod and reel were rather unsuitable for many forms of angling, naturally, but anglers of an earlier era literally did not know what they were missing. In recent years, however, wide diversification in types and styles of fishing tackle has developed. Each such type or style is the answer to a specific set of angling problems. Engineering has made it possible to analyze the requirements of combinations of rods, reels, lines and hooks, with the result that a bewildering number of such combinations are now offered.

But the knowledgable angler does not allow this great diversity of modern tackle to confuse him too deeply. He knows that there are only a few families of rods and reels and that modern tackle is designed to offer considerable versatility of use and action within fairly broad limits. For example,

spinning tackle is universally popular with both beginners and experts. Originally designed for casting light lures and baits, spinning tackle is used by a great many anglers for trolling, bottom fishing, jigging, and other noncasting uses.

The modern angler can select one rod and reel combination that will perform acceptably in almost any fishing situation he may encounter, or he can select more specialized types of tackle that will perform superlatively in selected types of fishing.

No single chapter in a book can possibly deal with all the variations of fishing tackle now in use throughout the world. In this book the emphasis is on families of tackle that have proven superior in modern sport fishing. There are many variations within families, and a few of the most important variations are illustrated and explained. Some of the tackle described may appear slightly old-fashioned to ultramodern anglers. Other items of tackle may look space-age to more conservative fishermen.

Readers of this book are reminded that we live in an age of transition and development. Modern tackle is definitely lighter and easier to use than older equipment. The purpose of tackle is to catch fish, and anything that enhances the fun and enjoyment of fishing, while preserving the essential challenge of the fishing, is worthwhile.

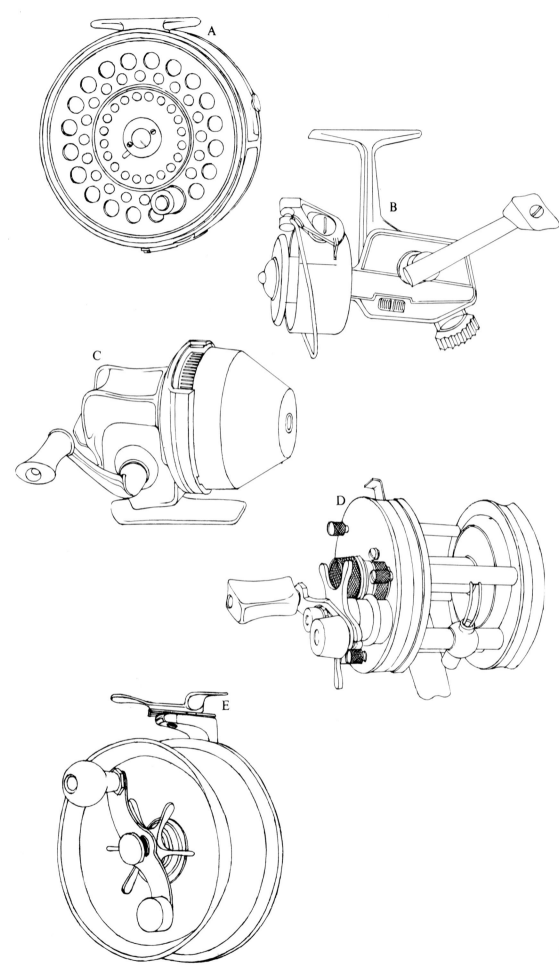

REELS

The main purpose of a reel is to hold the fishing line and to contain the multiplier gears and slip clutch or drag of the drive train. Reels have been specially designed for every angling activity and range from small single-action models used for panfish to large winchlike models for big game fishing. Although the types of reels are the same in the United States and Great Britain, there are important differences in nomenclature.

U. S. Single action reel
G. B. Revolving drum reel

U. S. Fly reel
G. B. Fly reel

U. S. Spinning reel
G. B. Fixed spool reel

U. S. Spinning casting reel
G. B. Closed face, fixed spool reel

U. S. Bait-casting reel
G. B. Multiplier reel

U. S. Casting reel
G. B. Multiplier reel

U. S. Surf-casting reel
G. B. Multiplier reel

A FLY REEL

The standard fly reel for trout is a single-action model from 3 in to 3 1/2 in in diameter, with a ratchet check. Fly reels for salmon and other heavy, powerful fish are similar in style with greater line capacity. Some have multiplier gears and/or an adjustable brake or drag.

B SPINNING REEL

Originally designed for casting light baits, these reels now are used extensively for still fishing and trolling. There are scores of models ranging from the very lightest to large models designed to handle lines up to 40 lb (18 kg) breaking test.

C SPIN-CASTING REEL

This is a fixed-spool reel with the mechanism enclosed. The line emerges from a small hole in the "nose" of the casing. Re-

lease of the line is by means of a thumb trigger. These reels work best with casting rods with offset handles designed for bait-casting reels.

D BAIT-CASTING REEL

Equipped with multiplier gears, star drag, and usually some sort of level-wind mechanism. Many models have an anti-backlash feature for casting. Larger models without the level-wind feature are used in surf casting. These are smaller members of the family that includes big game reels.

E SINGLE-ACTION REEL

This simplest type of reel has the handle directly connected to the spool or drum with no increase gears. Large models capable of spooling 60–80 lb (27–36 kg) test line are used by surf casters in South Africa, the American West Coast and Australia. Smaller models are still used in many areas for deep-sea bottom fishing.

The reels illustrated here demonstrate the various types mentioned. There are dozens and sometimes scores of models available within any particular type. Each model is made for a specific range of fishing situations.

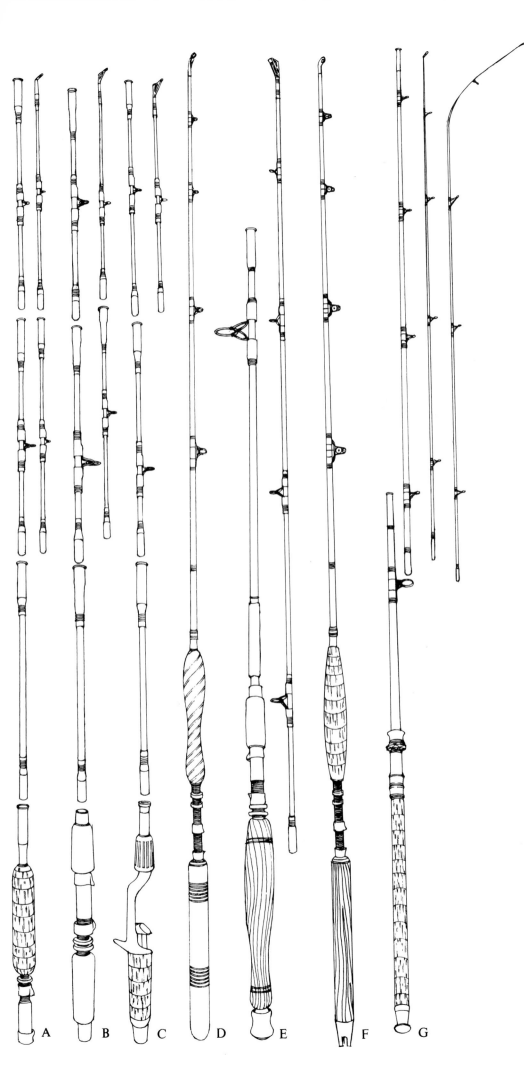

TYPES OF RODS

A fishing rod is a tapered length of wood, bamboo, fiberglass, or tubular metal equipped with ring or roller guides to carry the line, and with a reel seat at the butt end to accept the reel.

In the past, wood and bamboo were the primary rod-building materials and while some bamboo and a few wooden rods are still being built, modern rod construction makes large use of fiberglass and even artificially produced graphite fibers. A few tubular metal rods have been built, but fiberglass has largely supplanted metal in rod construction. While there are literally thousands of different rod models to choose from, the primary types are these:

A FLY RODS

(*Fiberglass, bamboo, graphite fiber*).

Ranging from about 6 ft to more than 10 ft long (1.8–3 m) the fly rod is specifically designed to cast the fly line as a linear weight or sinker, rather than a weighted lure. Most popular modern material is fiberglass, but split bamboo is still used in quality construction and graphite fiber is increasing in use.

B SPINNING RODS

(*Fiberglass, split bamboo, graphite fiber*).

Spinning tackle is probably the single most popular type now sold. The spinning reel is mounted under the rod shaft, and the first ring guide is quite large to minimize line friction in casting. Lengths vary from under 6 ft (1.8 m) for one-handed light spinning rods to more than 14 ft (4.25 m) for surf-spinning equipment. Average length for a two-handed rod built to handle 12–18 lb (5.5–8.2 kg) test line is 6 1/2–8 ft (2–2.4 m).

C BAIT-CASTING RODS

(*Fiberglass, tubular metal, graphite*).

These specialized rods are designed for accurate casting of small, light baits and lures while using either the spin-casting (closed-face fixed spool) reel or the bait-casting reel. The offset handle and reel seat help to maintain casting accuracy. Lengths average 5 1/2–7 1/2 ft (1.7–2.3 m).

D BOTTOM-FISHING RODS

(*Fiberglass, split bamboo, metal*).

These are relatively short, fairly stout rods in the 5–6 1/2 ft (1.5–2 m) length range, designed for stand-up fishing from boats or piers for such bottom species as cod, flatfish, sea bass, coalfish, congers, and the like. Line test ability ranges from about 20 lb (9 kg) to 50–60 lb 22.7–27.2 kg). Shafts are relatively stiff for lifting heavy fish rather than for casting ability.

E SURF RODS

(*Fiberglass, split bamboo, graphite fiber*).

Used with either spinning or multiplier casting reels, these very long rods range in length from 8–14 ft (3.6–6.4 m). The butt end is longer than in any other type, to provide casting leverage. Surf rods are designed to handle lines of 15–40 lb (6.8–18 kg) test. Distances of 300–400 ft (90–120 m) are often achieved in casting.

F TROLLING RODS

(*Fiberglass, laminated wood, split bamboo*).

Trolling rods are refinements of the popular bottom-fishing type of rod, usually equipped with roller rather than ring guides and tip-top. Butt is hardwood or aluminum, and is usually equipped with a cleft gimbal nock to fit into the crossbar of a fishing chair gimbal fitting. Line test range of various models spans the gamut from ultralight 6 lb (2.7 kg) to heavy-duty 130 lb (59 kg) line.

G MATCH RODS

(*Split bamboo, cane, fiberglass*).

This very long, specialized type of rod is used in match fishing in Great Britain and on the Continent, a type of competition that calls for a very long shaft of up to 20 ft (9 m) with a stiff lower section and flexible outer tip. Used primarily on small fish of under 2 lb (1 kg) weight, from a position on the bank or shore, or while wading.

FISHING LINES

Along with the club, the spear, the knife, and the use of fire, the fishing line is one of the truly basic inventions of prehistoric man. Here is a tool that vastly extends the human reach, enabling the fisherman to cast his baits far out into the water and then retrieve the hooked fish. Very early fishing lines were made of whatever natural fibers happened to be handy: thin strips of hide or gut, plaited or braided strands of bark or plant-stem fiber, horsehair, human hair, and finally flax, cotton, and other cultivated fibers.

Modern fishing line came into existence near the end of the nineteenth century with the development of standardized lines of pure linen. Linen line reigned supreme until shortly after World War II when synthetic fiber lines displaced natural fiber materials. Modern sport and commercial fishing lines are of three general types: braided synthetic fiber lines; nylon monofilament lines; and single or multistrand metal lines for special fishing purposes.

Braided synthetic lines are made primarily from Dacron or nylon fibers and are used for trolling, casting, and still fishing. Single strand monofilament lines are made almost exclusively of nylon and are used for trolling, casting, still fishing, and also for the manufacture of traces or leaders to go between the line and the hook. Metal lines are almost universally used for deep trolling or still fishing in very deep water.

Because linen line is still used in some regions, and because there is a distinct relationship between the thread count of linen line and its rated breaking strain, Table 1 is arranged to show a number of standard thread-counts of linen lines, their rated breaking strain, and the equivalent breaking test of modern Dacron braided line. Dacron lines in Table 1 follow the internationally accepted standard rating system of the International Game Fish Association.

Table 2 gives the relationship of diameter to breaking test for standard nylon monofilament lines. Some types of monfilament are stronger and some are weaker than those indicated in Table 2, depending on chemical composition of the line and the way it is stretched and heat tempered during manufacture. Because hollow Dacron lines collapse flat under tension, they cannot be table-rated in a visual diameter-strength display.

Table 3 gives the relationship of diameter to breaking test for solid metal fishing lines made from soft-drawn Monel wire. Braided wire lines and lead core lines are difficult to rate on a diameter-strength basis in table form, but all modern fishing lines, be they synthetic or wire, carry manufacturer's breaking test ratings that are usually accurate to ± 5 percent.

Because fly lines for casting weightless flies are a special case, they are treated elsewhere in the book. Fly lines are now made primarily of synthetic materials, although a few pure silk lines are still made to special order by specialty manufacturers.

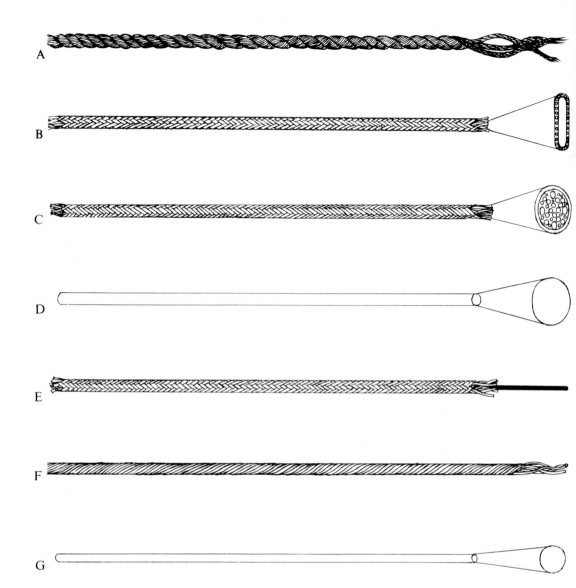

A

B

C

D

E

F

G

A LINEN FISHING LINE
1 Linen line is twisted like miniature rope from three separate strands, has the least elastic stretch of any of the soft fiber lines, from 4 to 6 percent of total line length.
2 Strands are twisted as in making rope.
3 Each strand is spun from an equal number of linen threads. Thread count is used as a measure of the line's rated size.

B HOLLOW BRAIDED DACRON LINE
1 Hollow braided Dacron line has walls formed of many interwoven fibers. Line has a flat cross section when no filler is used. Most Dacron for fishing is hollow.
2 Hollow center of line does not support the thin braided walls which form a flattened tube of fabric with an elastic stretch factor of 10–12 percent of total line length.

C FILLED BRAIDED DACRON LINE
1 Braided outer Dacron sheath surrounds a core of straight fibers.
2 Filler fibers give bulk and shape to the line, add to its strength. The line remains fairly round in cross section. Sometimes used for fishing, but usually for other purposes. Elastic stretch factor varies from 6 to 12 percent.

D MONOFILAMENT LINE
1 Made from nylon, this line is extruded in a single continuous fiber of any desired thickness. Tensile strength is same as that of mild steel.
2 The stretch, stiffness, tensile strength, and other factors are set by the chemical ingredients and the degree of heat tempering and stretching during manufacture. The elastic stretch factor varies from 20 to 30 percent of total length.

E LEAD CORE LINE
1 Braided outer sheath of Dacron fibers gives strength to the inner core of soft lead.
2 Core of soft lead wire is designed to carry the line down deep without additional sinkers.
Elastic stretch factor is zero, but lead core line will elongate 20–25 percent before breaking. Once elongated by heavy strain, it does not draw to its original length, having no inherent elasticity.

F BRAIDED WIRE LINE
A number of strands of soft copper, stainless steel, or Monel wire are braided or twisted into a flexible metal line for trolling or still-fishing in very deep water. Zero elastic stretch factor, but may elongate 10 to 15 percent before breaking.

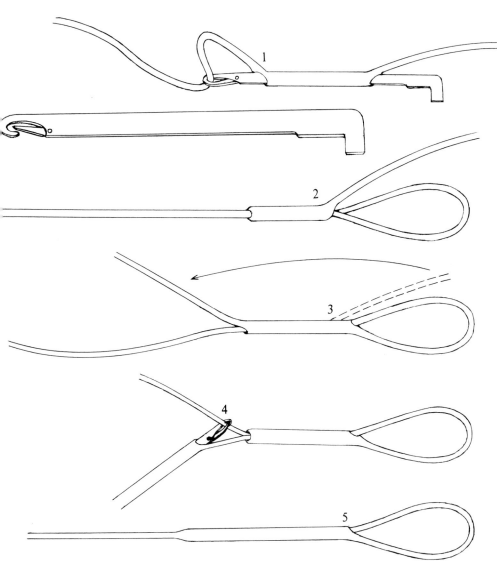

TABLE 1

Comparative strengths of representative linen fishing lines and equivalent Dacron lines from IGFA line classes.

Linen line	Breaking test		IGFA Dacron lines	
thread count	*Pounds*	*Kilograms*	*Pounds*	*Kilograms*
			6	2.7
3 threads	9	4.1	12	5.5
6 threads	18	8.2	20	9.1
9 threads	27	12.3	30	13.6
15 threads	45	20.5	50	22.7
24 threads	72	32.7	80	36.4
39 threads	117	53.2	130	59.1

TABLE 2

Diameter and breaking strain of solid soft-drawn Monel wire fishing line.

Wire diameter		Breaking strain	
Inch	*mm*	*Pounds*	*Kilograms*
.015″	.381	18	8.2
.018″	.4572	25	11.4
.021″	.5334	35	15.9
.024″	.6096	45	20.5
.027″	.6858	57	26
.030″	.762	70	31.8

TABLE 3

Diameter and breaking strain of nylon monofilament line.

Line diameter		Breaking strain	
Inch	*mm*	*Pounds*	*kilogram*
.004″	.1016	1.2	.55
.006″	.1524	2.7	1.2
.008″	.2023	4.8	2.2
.010″	.254	7.5	3.4
.012″	.3048	10.8	4.9
.014″	.3556	14.7	6.7
.016″	.4064	19	8.6
.018″	.4572	24.2	11
.020″	.508	30	13.6
.022″	.5588	36	16.4
.024″	.6096	43.1	19.6
.026″	.6604	50.6	23
.028″	.7112	58.6	26.6
.030″	.762	67.3	30.6
.032″	.8128	76.5	34.7
.034″	.8636	86.5	39.3
.036″	.9144	97	44
.038″	.9652	109	49.5
.040″	1.016	120	54.5
.042″	1.0668	132	60
.044″	1.1176	145	66
.046″	1.1684	158	72
.048″	1.2192	173	78.6
.050″	1.27	187	85
.052″	1.3208	200	91
.058″	1.4732	250	113.6
.063″	1.6	300	136.4
.072″	1.8288	400	182
.084″	2.1336	500	227.3

SOLID WIRE LINE

Monel wire has greater fatigue resistance than copper. Wire line can be regarded as a linear sinker when used for deep trolling. Elastic stretch factor is zero with 10–15 percent elongation before breaking.

SPLICING A LOOP INTO DACRON LINE

To splice an end loop into a Dacron fishing line, use the special splicing tool illustrated for pulling the tucks of the line through the line's hollow interior.

1 *Main part of the line is to the left, end is to the right. Insert the splicer into the line about 12 in (30 cm) from the end of the line, pointed toward the left. Run the length of the splicer toward the main part of the line. Push the tip of the splicer out of the line and pick up the main part of the line in the tool's hook. Make the loop extending above the tool's hook. Make the loop extending above the tool end equal to the size of the loop desired.*

2 *Pull the splicer and line back through the line creating a loop under the loose end.*

3 *Skin the loose end of the line back on the main part until* the end points away from the loop just formed. Now adjust the loop for its exact desired length.

4 *Insert the splicer into the line about 2 in (5 cm) below the loop with the tip pointed toward the loop. Pick up the loose end with the splicer and pull it back through the hollow part of the main line.*

5 *If the tip of the end of the line protrudes out of the line, trim it off with a sharp blade so the end will be buried inside the main part of the line. Finished splice is knotless and self-gripping.*

LINES, LEADERS AND TACKLE FOR FRESH WATER FLY FISHING

For a number of years, the best fly lines were made of braided silk which was oiled or greased if the angler wished the line to float. Then braided nylon lines came into popularity as silk became scarce and synthetics more available. Now, ultra-modern fly lines are made of plastic-coated braided nylon, or even of single filament nylon with tapers molded into the line. These new lines are marvels of uniformity and conform closely to the new AFTMA (U.S.) weight standards.

Originally, a fly line was the same diameter throughout its length, but anglers soon discovered that if the line were tapered from a thicker section near the middle to a thinner section near the end, a better tranformation of casting power was achieved. A single-tapered line is tapered only on one end while a double-tapered line is tapered on both ends. Modern double tapered lines average about 30 yards (27 m) for trout lines to 40 yards (36 m) for salmon lines.

On salt water, a special weight-forward or rocket taper line is often used. This line has a relatively short forward taper with weight concentration in the forward, casting portion of the line to achieve distance and carry the larger, air-resistant flies of salt water fishing. Lines for dry fly fishing are treated with a special "flotant" preparation and are purposely made light in weight. Lines for wet fly fishing are heavier per unit of cross section area, and often are treated with a wetting agent to aid in sinking the line.

The weight of the line should suit the rod (and vice versa, naturally). For many years tapered lines were classified by a three-letter system in which the first and last letters indicated the diameter of the ends and the centre letter the diameter of the middle, which was thicker. The table below gives the diameter rating system in thousandths of an inch and in millimeters.

A = .060″ = 1.53 mm	F = .035″ = 0.89 mm
B = .055″ = 1.40 mm	G = .030″ = 0.76 mm
C = .050″ = 1.27 mm	H = .025″ = 0.64 mm
D = .045″ = 1.14 mm	I = .020″ = 0.51 mm
E = .040″ = 1.02 mm	

Thus, a line rated GAF would have one end with a tip diameter of .030″ (0.76 mm), a middle diamter of .060″ (1.53 mm), and the other end with a diameter of .035″ (0.89 mm). The three-letter rating system now has largely been superceded by the A.F.T.M.A. method described on this page.

Other letters are used to identify special qualities of a fly line: F = floating; S = sinking; DT = double taper; L = level line (no taper); WF = weight-forward taper. A weight-forward, floating line of Weight 8, for example, would be indicated as WF-8-F.

UNDERSTANDING LINES AND LEADERS

Whether one calls it a "leader", as do the Americans, or a "trace" in the British and European manner, the connecting link between the fly line and the fly itself is most important to successful casting. The line is bulky and the fly is usually extremely small and light.

The leader or trace acts as a sort of lineal power transformer between the bulky fly line and the almost weightless fly. This linear transformer action is accomplished by placing a *tapered* leader or trace between the fly line and the fly.

Some manufacturers now provide tapered monofilament leaders in various lengths and weights, but the more traditional method is to tie together short sections of monofilament material with a gradual step-down of diameter. A 10 ft (3 m) leader, for example, may be made of as many as five sections of monofilament ranging from 30–40 lb (14–18 kg) test down to as little as 1 lb (.5 kg) test, measuring only .004 in (0,1 mm) in diameter. The most popular knot for tying up tapered leaders is the Blood Knot. The thickest part of the leader is tied to the end of the line with the Nail Knot or a similar line-leader knot.

The portion of the leader that carries the fly is known as the "tippet", and is crucial to proper fly performance. Lighter tippets get more strikes, but are also weaker. Fly fishing tippets in the most commonly used sizes are rated in so-called "X-ratings." A table on this page gives the nominal diameter, breaking strength, and recommended hook size for tippets from OX down to the ultra fine 7X size. Another table suggests the proper combinations of length and diameter for built-up leaders for a variety of types of fresh and salt water fly fishing.

A.F.T.M.A. FLY LINE WEIGHTS

A few years ago the American Fishing Tackle Manufacturer's Association (A.F.T.M.A.) adopted a standard fly line grading system in which lines are rated from Weight 1 to Weight 12, depending on the actual weight of the first 30 ft (9 m) of the line. An accompanying table gives the weight factor for each of the 12 A.F.T.M.A. line classes in terms of classic English and metric weight values. The A.F.T.M.A. fly line grading system is now recognized in many parts of the world.

No.	Wt. (grains)	Wt. (grams)	Tolerance
1	60	3,9	± 6 gr (0.39 g)
2	80	5,2	± 6 gr (0.39 g)
3	100	6.5	± 6 gr (0.39 g)
4	120	7.8	± 6 gr (0.39 g)
5	140	9.1	± 8 gr (0.52 g)
6	160	10.4	± 8 gr (0.52 g)
7	185	12.0	± 8 gr (0.52 g)
8	210	13.6	± 8 gr (0.52 g)
9	240	15.6	± 10 gr (0.65 g)
10	280	18.1	± 10 gr (0.65 g)
11	330	21.4	± 12 gr (0.78 g)
12	380	24.6	± 14 gr (0.91 g)

FOUR COMMON TAPERED LEADERS

There are hundreds of combinations for making up tapered fly casting leaders, but the four examples described below will suffice to take an angler through almost any kind of fishing situation.

Full-taper trout-salmon leader, 9 ft (270 cm):
1st section = 18 in (45 cm), .021″ (.525 mm) mono.
2nd section = 18 in (45 cm), .019″ (.475 mm) mono.
3rd section = 18 in (45 cm),

4th section = 18 in (45 cm), .016″ (.400 mm) mono.
5th section = 7 in (17½cm), .014″ (.350 mm) mono.
6th section = 6 in (15 cm), .012″ (.300 mm) mono.
7th section = 5 in (12½cm), .010″ (.250 mm) mono.
tippet = 18 in (45 mm), .009–.006″ (.225–.150 mm).

"Simplicity" all-purpose leader, 9 ft (270 cm):
1st section = 42 in (105 cm) .019″ (.475 mm) mono.
2nd section = 42 in (105 cm) .017″ (.425 mm) mono.
3rd section = 24 in (60 cm), .014″ (.350 mm) mono.

Fresh water bass-bugging leader, 7½ ft (225 cm):
1st section = 26 in (65 cm) .020″ (.500 mm) mono.
2nd section = 24 in (60 cm), .018″ (.450 mm) mono.
3rd section = 22 in (27½cm).016″ (.400 mm) mono.
4th section = 18 in (45 cm), .014″ (.350 mm) mono.

9 ft (2.7 m) general purpose fly leader.
1 42 in × .018″ dia. (107 cm × .48 mm dia.)
2 34 in × .016″ dia. (86 cm × .57 mm dia.)
3 12 in × .013″ dia. (30 cm × .46 mm dia.)
4 20 in × .010″ dia. (51 cm × .25 mm dia.)

9 ft (2.7 m) medium heavy fly leader.
1 30 in × .018″ dia. (76 cm × .46 mm dia.)
2 30 in × .016″ dia. (76 cm × .41 mm dia.)
3 24 in × .014″ dia. (61 cm × .36 mm dia.)
4 12 in × .011″ dia. (30 cm × .28 mm dia.)
5 12 in × .021″ dia. (30 cm × .53 mm dia.)

FLY-LEADER TIPPET X-RATINGS

X	Diameter	Strength	Hook size
0X	.011″ (.275 mm)	8.4 lb (3.8 kg)	No 1/0–No 2
1X	.010″ (.250 mm)	6.8 lb (3.1 kg)	No 4–No 8
2X	.009″ (.225 mm)	5.3 lb (2.4 kg)	No 6–No 10
3X	.008″ (.200 mm)	4.0 lb (1.8 kg)	No 10–No 14
4X	.007″ (.175 mm)	3.2 lb (1.5 kg)	No 12–No 16
5X	.006″ (.150 mm)	2.5 lb (1.1 kg)	No 14–No 18
6X	.005″ (.125 mm)	1.7 lb (0.8 kg)	No 16–No 22
7X	.004″ (.100 mm)	1.0 lb (0.5 kg)	No 18–No 24

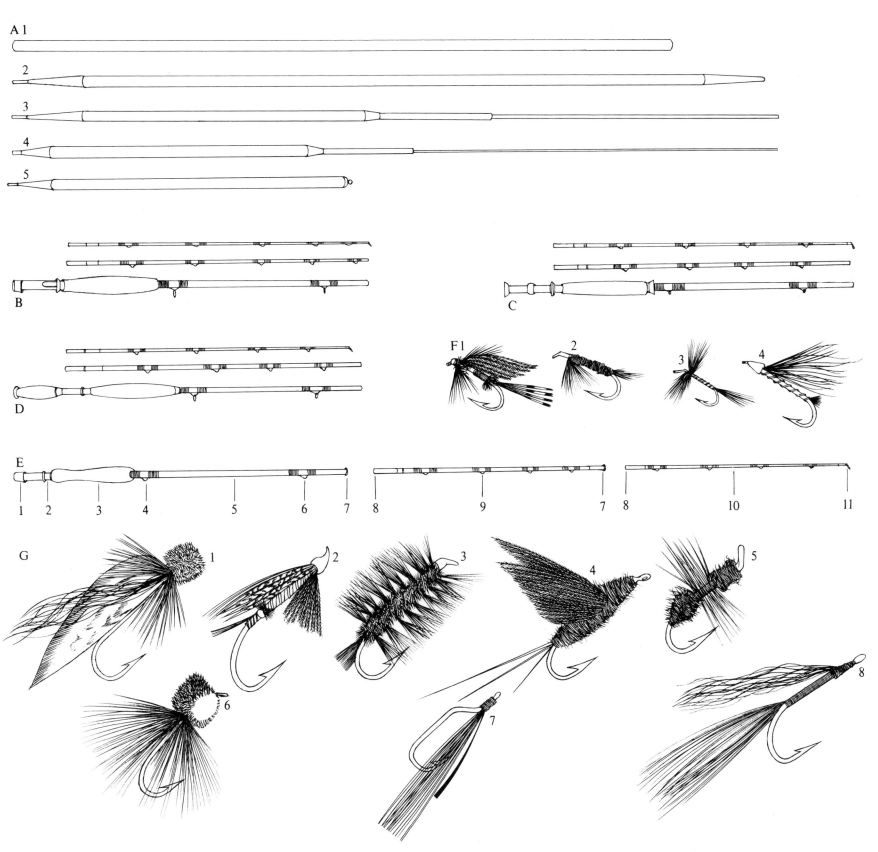

A Modern fly lines are grouped
   into 5 classes.
   1 Level line (same diameter
      overall).
   2 Double taper (taper at each
      end).
   3 Weight-forward (more weight
      at head end).
   4 Salt water taper (very heavy
      head).
   5 Shooting-head (all weighted
      head).

B Ultra light fly rod for midge
   and gnat fly fishing with very
   light lines.
C One-handed, sectional fly rod
   for trout, panfish, small bass,
   other small game.
D Medium-duty, onehanded rod
   with butt extension for larger
   game fish.

E Two-handed heavy-duty fly rod,
   primarily used in European
   waters for salmon.
   1 Reel seat
   2 Lock ring
   3 Grip
   4 Hook keeper
   5 Butt section
   6 Snake guide
   7 Female ferrule
   8 Male ferrule
   9 Mid-section

10 Tip section
11 Tip-top guide
F Four commonly used classes of
   flies.
   1 Wet fly (the popular Royal
      Coachman)
   2 Nymph (the effective Beaver
      Nymph)
   3 Dry fly (the floating Ginger
      Quill)
   4 Streamer fly (the Black Nosed
      Dace)

G Special types of flies.
   1 Muddler Minnow (wet)
   2 Dusty Miller (salmon)
   3 Wooly Worm (wet)
   4 Fanwing (dry)
   5 Ant (terrestrial)
   6 Bubble Pup (bass)
   7 Stawberry Blonde (tarpon)
   8 Keel Hook Fly (striped bass)

313

TACKLE FOR SALT WATER FLY FISHING

Most fresh water fly casters are familiar with the modern forward-taper fly line in which weight is concentrated in the forward half of the line, making the line easier to cast and permitting longer casts. Salt water anglers have taken the weight-forward idea a step further. The result is a heavily forward-weighted line that concentrates even more weight in the forward section of the line. This is commonly called the "salt water taper." Compare a standard forward-taper fly line (B2) with the newer salt water taper line represented in (B1). Another fresh water innovation, the forward-taper line with a sinking tip (B3), has found popularity with salt water anglers. The sinking tip is also combined with the salt water taper line, creating a line, the forward portion of which is a linear sinker when considered from the viewpoint of the fly rod.

Because of the need for large-capacity, strongly built reels with smooth-acting, powerful drags, salt water fly reels are quite different from the great mass of fresh water fly reels. In most fresh water fishing, the reel is hardly more than a convenient device for storing the line and its backing. Seldom is the reel called on to carry the weight of a large, powerful fish. But in fresh water it is impossible to handle many species of fish without a reel equipped with a drag mechanism capable of putting tension on the fishing line up to the breaking point of the tippet, one that will not burn up or fail in action. Some heavy duty salt water fly reels are single-acting. Others are multiplying reels with gear ratios of from 1.5–1 to as much as 3–1. Choice of reel type depends on the feelings of the angler.

Rods to handle these large fly reels and their heavy lines are almost universally built of fiberglass, although

there is an ultra-modern trend toward experimentation with space-age carbon filament material. Interestingly, these powerful rods are actually much shorter and lighter than the great two-handed rods once used by salmon fishermen. Few modern salt water fly rods are over 9¾ ft (3 m) long. One concession to comfort when heavy fish are being fought is the short extension-butt below the reel seat. The extension butt (removable in some rods) is pressed against the angler's stomach and permits him to wind the reel with greater efficiency.

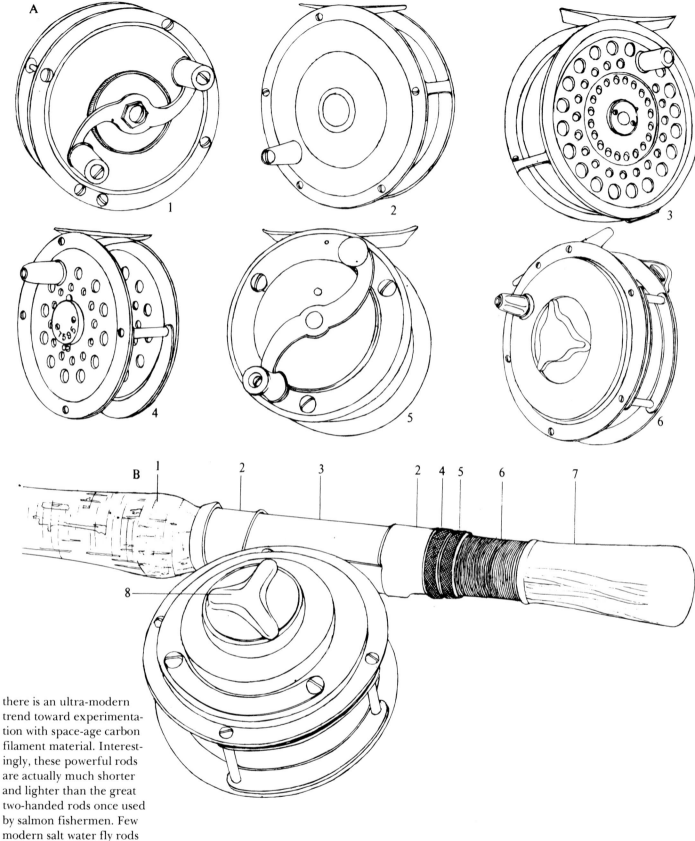

A Six popular types of salt water fly reels that are used also in salmon fishing.
1 Seamaster (2 sizes)
2 Fin-Nor (2 sizes)
3 Scientific Anglers
4 Shakespeare (2 sizes)
5 Bogdan (multiplier)
6 Pflueger Supreme

B Parts of a mounted salt water fly reel and seat
1 Cork foregrip
2 Retainer bands
3 Reel seat body
4 Retainer ring
5 Lock ring
6 Seat threads
7 Extension butt
8 Reel drag knob

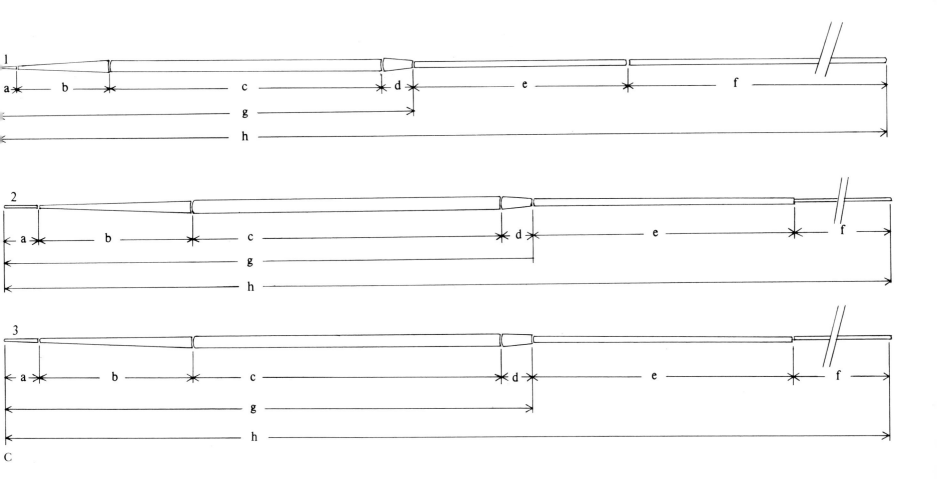

C

FLY TACKLE FOR SALT WATER GAME FISH

C 1 *Salt water taper fly line.*
   (SWT)
   a 1 ft (30 cm)
   b 6 ft (180 cm)
   c 17 1/2 ft (5.3 m)
   d 1 1/2 ft (45 cm)
   e 14 ft (4.25 m)
   f 50 ft (15 m)
   g 26 ft (7.9 m)
   h 90 ft (27.4 m)

2 *Weight-forward fly line*
   (WF)
   a 2 ft (60 cm)
   b 10 ft (3 m)
   c 20 ft (6 m)
   d 2 ft (60 cm)
   e 17 ft (5.2 m)
   f 39 ft (11.8 m)
   g 34 ft (10.3 m)
   h 90 ft (27.4 m)

´3 *W.F. sinking tip fly line.*
   (WFS)
   a 2 ft (60 cm)
   b 10 ft (3 m)
   c 20 ft (6 m)
   d 2 ft (60 cm)
   e 17 ft (5.2 m)
   f 39 ft (11.8 m)
   g 34 ft (10.3 m)
   h 90 ft (27.4 m)

Sailfish
Rod   – 9–9 1/2 ft (2.7–2.9 m) medium action, magnum.
Reel – Single-action, large capacity, good drag.
Line – SWT-12 with 300 yd (270 m) Dacron backing.

Striped bass
Rod   – 8 ft (240 cm) slow action, salmon quality.
Reel – Single action, medium capacity, good drag.
Line – WFS-8-9 with 200 yd (180 m) Dacron backing.

Bluefish
Rod   – 7 1/2 ft (225 cm) medium action, trout quality.
Reel – Single-action, medium capacity, good drag.
Line – WFS-7-8 with 200 yd (180 m) Dacron backing.

Barracuda
Rod   – 8 ft (240 cm) medium action, salmon quality.
Reel – Single-action, medium capacity, good drag.
Line – SWT-7-8-9, 200 yd (180 m) Dacron backing.

Permit
Rod   – 8 ft (240 cm) fast action, salmon quality.
Reel – Single-action, medium capacity, good drag.
Line – SWT-8, 200 yd (180 m) Dacron backing.

Bonefish
Rod   – 7 ft (210 cm) fast action, trout quality.
Reel – Multiplier, medium capacity, good drag.
Line – WFS-6-7, 200 yd (180 m) Dacron backing.

White marlin
Rod   – 9–9 1/2 ft (2.7–2.9 m) medium action, magnum.
Reel – Single-action, large capacity, good drag.
Line – SWT-12 with 300 yd (270 m) Dacron backing.

Weakfish
Rod   – 6 1/2–7 ft (195–210 cm) slow action, trout.
Reel – Single-action, trout capacity, click drag.
Line – WFS-6-7, 100 yd (90 m) Dacron backing.

Bonito
Rod   – 8 ft (240 cm) fast action, salmon quality.
Reel – Multiplier, medium capacity, good drag.
Line – SWT-8 with 200 yd (180 m) Dacron backing.

Tarpon
Rod   – 9 ft (270 cm) medium action, magnum.
Reel – Single-action, large capacity, good drag.
Line – WSF-10-11-12 with 300 yd (270 m) backing.

Salmon
Rod   – 8 ft (240 cm) medium action, salmon quality.
Reel – Single-action, large capacity, good drag.
Line – WF-8-9 with 250 yd (225 m) Dacron backing.

Sharks
Rod   – 9 ft (270 cm) medium action, magnum.
Reel – Single-action, large capacity, good drag.
Line – WFS-10-11-12 with 300 yd (270 m) backing.

315

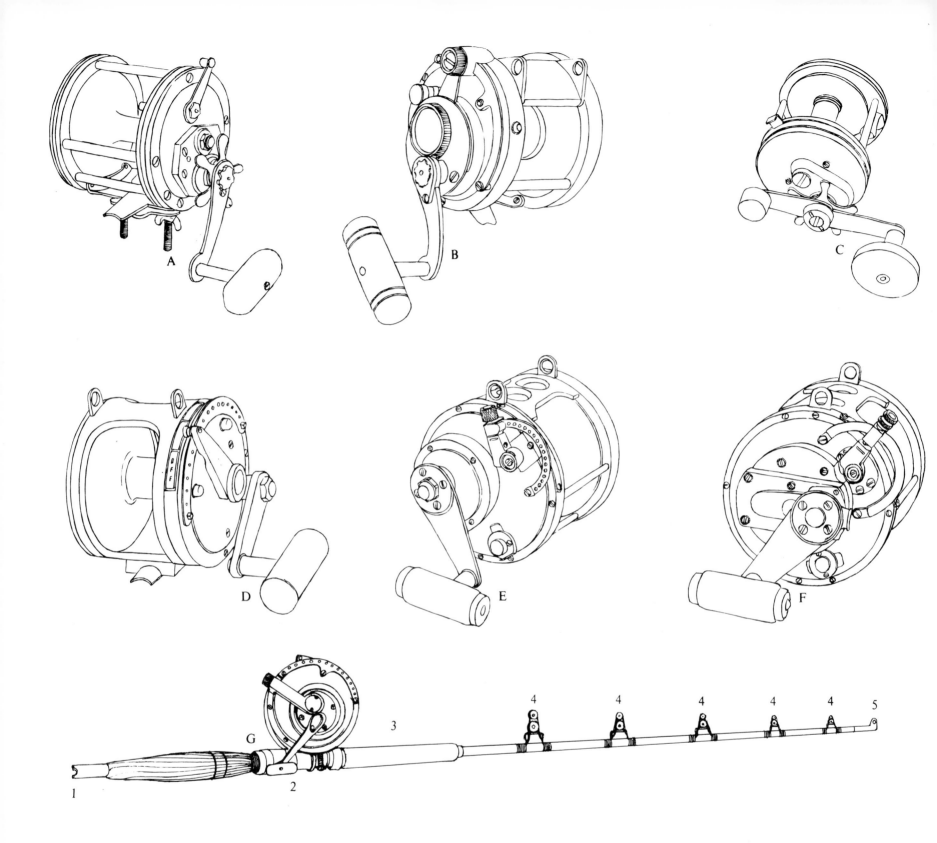

A *Penn "Senator" star-drag big game reel, available in size ratings from 2/0 to 16/0. Metal-plastic.*
B *Penn "International" lever-drag big game reel, size ratings from 2/0 to 12/0. Anodized metal.*
C *Garcia star-drag small game* reel, one of a number of number of small-to-medium reels. Metal-plastic.
D *Fin-Nor "Golden Regal" lever-drag reel, sizes up to about 4/0. Small to medium game. Metal-plastic.*
E–F *Fin-Nor lever-drag big game reels, sizes 4/0 to 12/0, special* order to 16/0. Anodized metal.
G *Typical modern big game fishing rod and reel.*
  1 Gimbal fitting at lower end of rod butt.
  2 Reel seat fitted to upper end of rod butt.
  3 Foregrip on fiberglass rod shaft.
  4 Roller line guides mounted on shaft.
  5 Roller tip-top line guide.
H *Details of one type of roller line guide. Frame is attached to rod shaft with silk wrappings.*
I *The foot of the fishing reel slips under collars of the reel seat. Threaded rings of the reel seat* take up the slack and place reel foot under strong compression. As a precaution, a safety lock plate is fastened to the reel foot under the reel seat tube by means of long screws straddling the tube.
J *The mounted reel becomes an integral part of the rod-and-reel combination. Modern rods can*

316

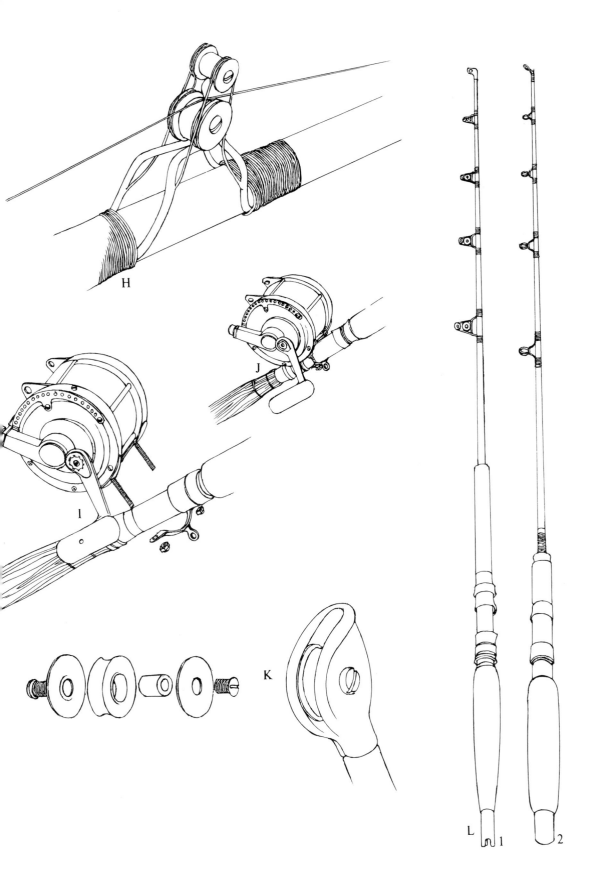

"CONVENTIONAL" SALT WATER FISHING TACKLE

Fishing tackle of the revolving-spool type is often called "conventional" tackle to give it a name distinct from spinning tackle. Revolving-spool tackle came into popularity long before spinning tackle, and for some unknown reason it never achieved a special class name equal in descriptive power to the self-descriptive term "spinning tackle." Hence the cumbersome, but almost universally-used name of "conventional" tackle.

Two drag-clutch systems are used, the star-drag system and the lever-drag system.

Star-drag system:

The clutch, or "drag," is actuated by a star wheel mounted on the main reel handle drive shaft, under the reel handle (Fig. A). Screwing the star wheel away from the reel case reduces drag or clutch tension, causing the clutch to slip at lower line tension. The clutch washers are usually a combination of metal (brass) and fiber or leather, and are "loaded" by means of a flat compression spring. They are contained in a special drum that is also part of the main power drive train, or gears. Lubrication is via special grease fittings and the drive and spool shafts revolve in bronze bearings. The spool is usually turned from a single casting or forging. Frame and internal parts are plastic and non-corrosive metal. Exterior metal parts are chrome-plated if non-aluminum, or anodized if made from salt-resistant aluminum alloy.

Lever-drag system:

The lever-drag system works generally similarly to the star-drag system in that both achieve clutch-action between the drive train and the line spool by means of the adjustable slip-clutch, or drag. The lever-drag clutch is actuated by means of a special lever mounted independently of the main handle drive shaft (Fig. B). One great advantage of the lever-drag system is that the drag adjustment device does not revolve with the handle, as does the star-drag star wheel. This means that the drag lever can be returned to a definite spot along its arc of throw, and at that spot the drag line tension will always be the same. Lever-drag reels usually have much more friction area in the clutch than do star-drag reels, and dissipate the heat of friction more quickly. Construction is usually all-metal, leaning heavily to salt-resistant, anodized aluminium. Clutch plates are alternately metal (stainless steel) and brake-lining-coated metal. Both types are rated as to line capacity by the "O" system, described elsewhere.

Salt water rods now are largely manufactured of fiberglass with roller line guides and tip-tops. They are engineered to work best with lines of standard breaking strain, usually the IGFA line-class system. Some quality rods for light tackle feature ring guides, but roller guides are considered best for trolling.

accept a wide variety of reel sizes and shapes, but each rod has an optimum reel size that it handles best.

K A roller tip-top, like roller guides, contains a stainless steel line roller that greatly reduces line friction. Bushings, spacer discs, and screws are bronze. Rollers should be washed with fresh water after use, are lubricated with light oil.

L Typical salt water game fish trolling rods.
1 Heavy-duty big game models universally have roller guides and tip-tops. Butts are ash or similar light hardwood, some- times aluminum.
2 Light tackle rods sometimes have ring guides.

HOOKS

Hooks have been an essential part of sport fishing equipment from the very earliest times. Almost any sort of line will do, with or without a rod, but an efficient hook was and still is the single most important part of the angler's tackle. Hooks are made for every sort of commercial and sport fishing. In the latter division they range in size from tiny No. 24 hooks for delicate match and fly casting to huge meat hooks for sharks.

In earlier days, hooks were named for their distinctive style by using the name of their inventors or the region of their origin. These names have survived until today. Hooks were also given numbers to designate their relative sizes, and the numbering systems of one region often did not relate to those of another. Confusion existed for a long time, naturally, but common sense and common interest prevailed in the end and the system of hook sizes that we use now finally emerged.

For example, a No. 6 hook manufactured in England, is very close in size to one made in Norway or the United States. There may be differences, but they are slight. This means that a fisherman can wander from Iceland to New Zealand and ask for a hook of a certain name and size and rest assured that the hook that will be offered to him will correspond almost exactly to what he needs to complete the rigging of his tackle.

Hooks for use in fresh water are usually finished "bright" (polished but unplated) and then given a coat of lacquer. Hooks for use in salt water are usually plated with tin, cadmium, zinc, or even gold alloy. In each style of hook and each size there is a standard wire diameter that is "normal" for that style and size of hook. The same style and size of hook can also be manufactured in models with wire of lesser or greater diameter than normal. Thus, thinner hooks will be designated "thin" or "light" while wider hooks will be designated "double strong", "triple strong", or whatever the case may be.

The design of a fishhook is not left to chance. Each hook style has evolved over the years to accomplish a particular quality of hooking action or combination of such qualities. Hooks for trolling, for example, are almost always made with no offset to the point of the hook. Hooks for flatfish, on the other hand, are usually made with the point "kirbied" or "reversed". Increasing interest is being shown in barbless hooks, most often created by simply removing the barb. The advantages are mainly twofold – fish can be more easily removed (hence the attraction for match fishermen) and they are not so badly injured as with a barb which tears the flesh.

Many anglers, especially beginners, fish with hooks too large for the fish they are after. Very often, changing to hooks of smaller size will make the difference between feeding the fish a lot of free bait and hooking them almost at will. Another "secret" of successful fishing is to keep hooks needle-sharp. A small, fine-toothed file or a fine-grit oilstone is perfect for putting a very sharp point on a hook. The point should be honed after each use. Finally, remove every trace of bait from hooks and wash them in fresh water before drying them, oiling them lightly, and returning them to the tackle box.

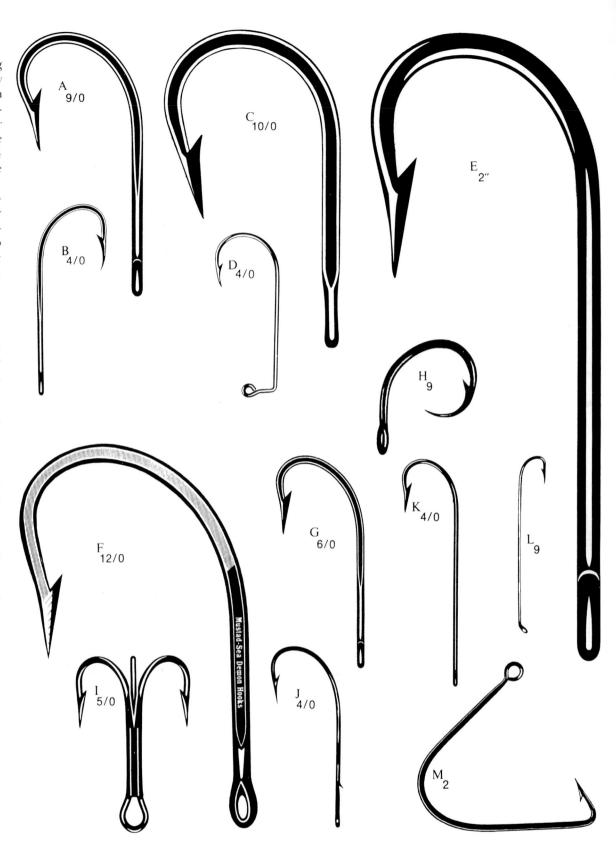

A *Filed Point Mustad Tarpon Hook: sizes 12/0–20*
B *Mustad Beak Hook: sizes 9/0–6, 8, 10, 12*
C *Mustad Giant Tuna Hook: sizes 16/0–3/0*
D *Mustad Aberdeen Hook: sizes 4/0–10*
E *Mustad Shark Hook: sizes 6"–1"*

F *Knife Edge Point Mustad Sea Demon Hook: sizes 16/0–1/0*
G *Mustad O'Shaughnessy Hook: sizes 14/0–4*
H *Mustad Tuna Circle Hook: sizes 3–9*
I *Superior Mustad Treble Hook: sizes 10/0–20*

J *Mustad Sproat Hook: sizes 6/0–3/0*
K *Superior Mustad Carlisle Hook: sizes 10/0–20.*
L *Mustad Hollow Point Flounder Hook: sizes 2–10*
M *Mustad Pike Hook: sizes 1/0–12*

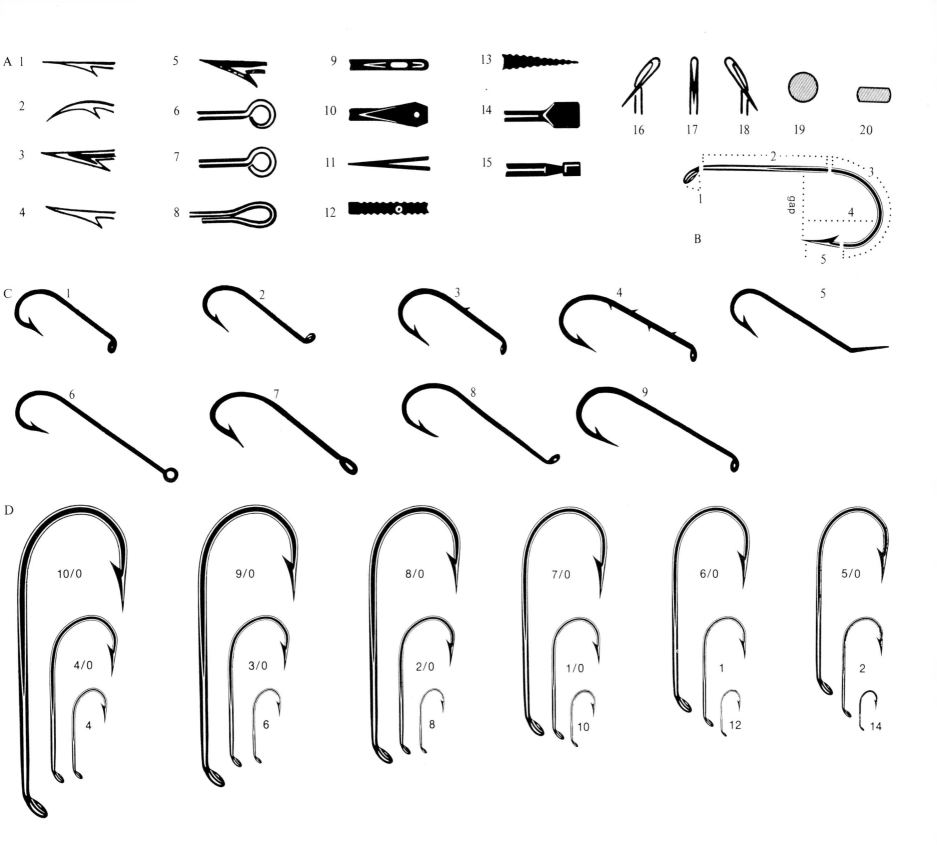

HOOK TERMINOLOGY

A POINTS, EYES, SHARKS
1 Hollow point
2 Curved-in point
3 Superior point
4 Dublin point
5 Knife-edge point
6 Tapered eye
7 Ball eye
8 Looped eye
9 Needle eye
10 Hole-in-flat eye
11 Tapered shank
12 Marked shank
13 Marked tapered shank
14 Flatted shank
15 Knobbed shank
16 Kirbied point
17 Straight point
18 Reversed point
19 Regular section
20 Forged section

B PARTS OF A HOOK
1 Eye
2 Shank
3 Bend
4 Throat
5 Point
6 Gap

**C VARIOUS CONFIGURA-
TIONS**
1 Turned down ball eye
2 Turned up ball eye
3 Sliced shank
4 Four slices in shank
5 Tipped shank bent back
6 Ringed hook
7 Eyed hook
8 Turned up tapered eye
9 Turned down tapered eye

D Hook sizes ranging from
14 (very small) to 10/0
(medium-large) are
typical of similar
sizes in most styles
and models of hooks.
(Adapted with permission
from a chart prepared by
O. Mustad & Son, Oslo,
Norway.)

GENERAL EQUIPMENT

It would require a catalogue the size of this book to list all the various types of general equipment now available. But here are samples of the more important pieces of equipment now in use on fresh and salt water.

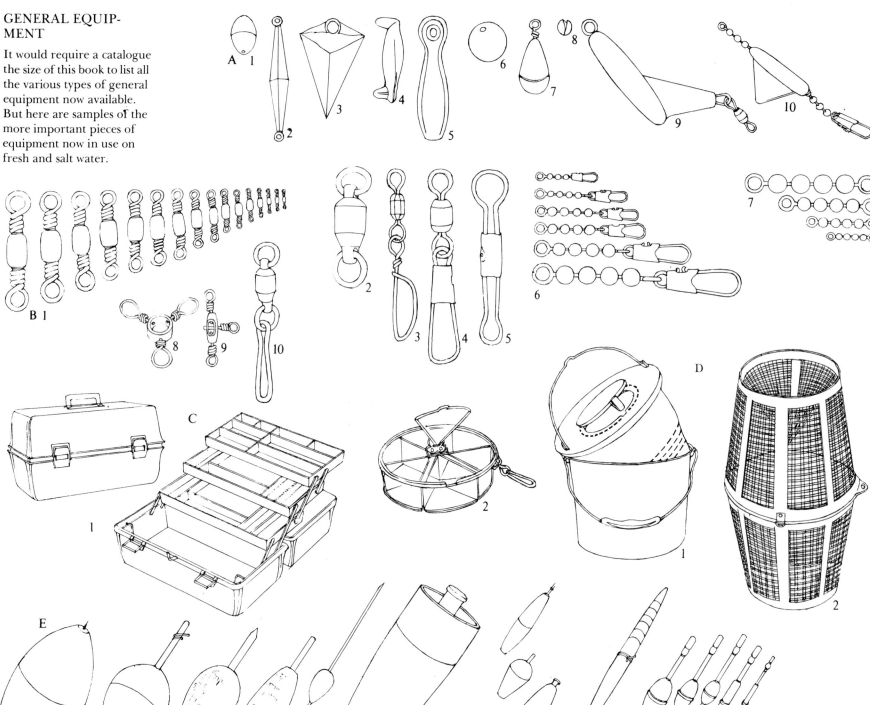

A SINKERS	B SWIVELS	C TACKLE BOXES	4 Barrel (natural)	G FISHING GAFFS
1 Egg	1 Barrel (assorted)	1 General purpose	5 Stick-up	1 Flying gaff
2 Diamond	2 Big game ball bearing	2 6-section fly box	6 Popping	2 Heavy boat gaff
3 Pyramid	3 Coastlock snap		7 Perch (3 types)	3 Surf gaff
4 Clinch	4 Common snap	D BAIT CARRIERS	8 Hollow quill	4 Spinning gaff
5 Bank	5 Connector	1 Minnow bucket	9 Panfish (5 types)	5 Pike gaff
6 Ball	6 Bead chain snaps	2 Minnow trap		
7 Dipsey	7 Bead chain swivels		F Prepared hand line	H Rod travel caddy
8 Split-shot	8 3-way ring swivel	E FISHING FLOATS		
9 Drail (trolling)	9 3-way barrel swivel	1 Casting		
10 Keel (trolling)	10 Link snap swivel	2 Egg (bicolor)		
		3 Egg (natural)		

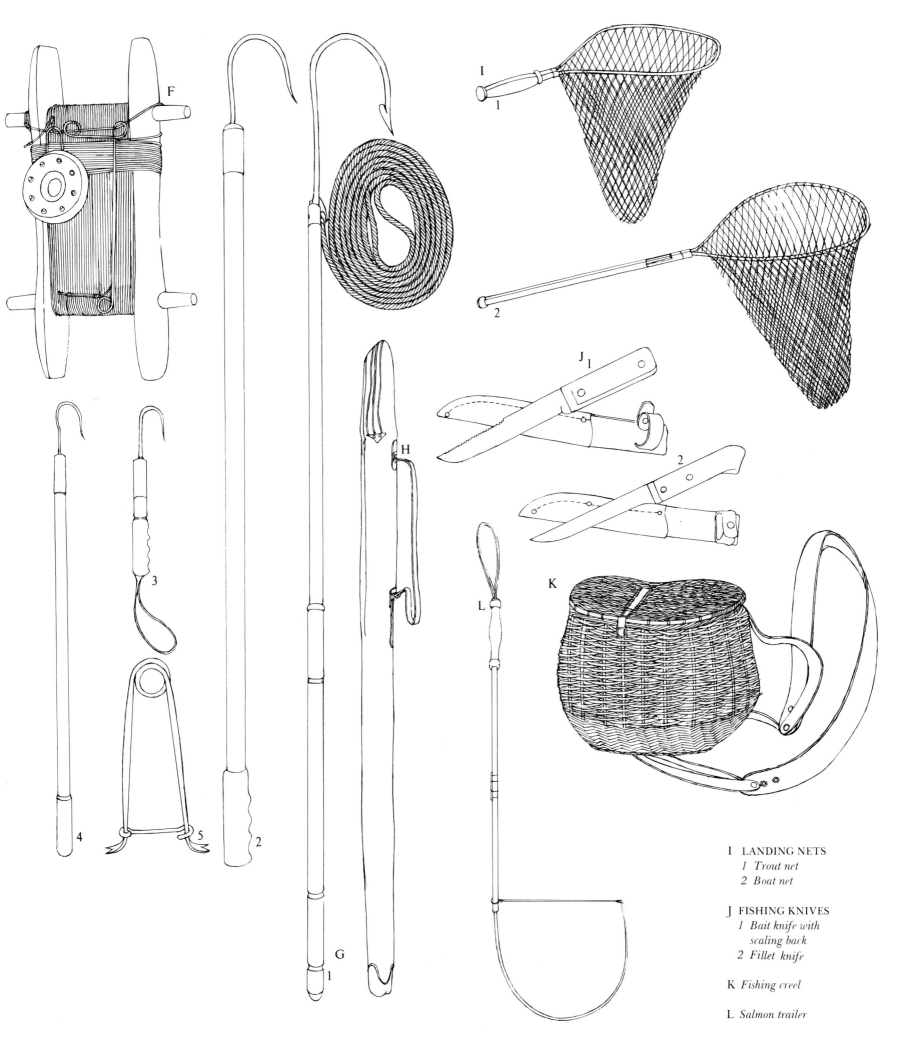

F

G

H

I
1
2

J 1
2

K

L

I LANDING NETS
 1 Trout net
 2 Boat net

J FISHING KNIVES
 *1 Bait knife with
  scaling back*
 2 Fillet knife

K *Fishing creel*

L *Salmon trailer*

GATHERING AND USING FRESH-WATER NATURAL BAITS

Artificial lures are excellent for catching many types of fish, but there always comes a time when artificials fail to work, or one does not have the proper lure in one's tackle box. This is when knowledge of live natural baits can make the difference between a mere outing and a memorable fishing trip. Freshwater natural baits fall into several categories:

Small fish–minnows, mummichogs, shiners, etc.
Amphibians–frogs, salamanders, newts.
Land insects–grasshoppers, grubs, caterpillars, beetles, dragonflies, moths, mayflies.
Aquatic insects–nymphs, hellgramites.
Crustáceans–crayfish, freshwater shrimps.
Worms–earthworms, nightcrawlers, centipedes.
Molluscs–snails, mussels, clams.

One of the secrets of success with natural baits is to use bait that matches the preference of the fish at the location and time of season. During the spring and early summer, for example, it is useless to try to entice trout with adult land insects while a hatch of mayflies is taking place. Likewise, later in the season, terrestrial insects often form the major part of fish's diet and therefore are important bait.

Aquatic life such as nymphs, amphibians, small fish, crayfish, and molluscs make up the greater part of the diet of most fish and are usually excellent bait. Small bait fish can be gathered with a minnow seine. Nymphs are easily collected with a circular wire mesh strainer-net. Each stream or lake is a living community of creatures and the observant angler quickly learns how to hold the net or strainer downstream of the rocks and brush piles that harbor the baits.

Each bait requires a particular method of applying the hook and presenting the bait to the fish. Worms, for example, should be allowed to drift quietly downstream as if freshly fallen into the water. A frog should be hooked lightly in the flesh of the hind leg to permit it to swim in a lifelike manner. Nymphs and larvae are fished in situations where the angler knows the fish are taking this bait. Keep baitfish and crayfish in a ventilated bait bucket with water. Worms prefer rich, damp soil or moss. Land insects often require a cool, dry, ventilated box or container. Handle the bait as little as possible to avoid damage.

1 The fine-mesh minnow seine is usually drawn between two persons working the bait toward the shore in shallow water.

2 Circular wire-mesh net or strainer can be used by one man, is especially good for collecting small larvae, nymphs, etc.

3 Put the captured bait immediately into proper containers and refrain from handling it more than needed to prevent injury.

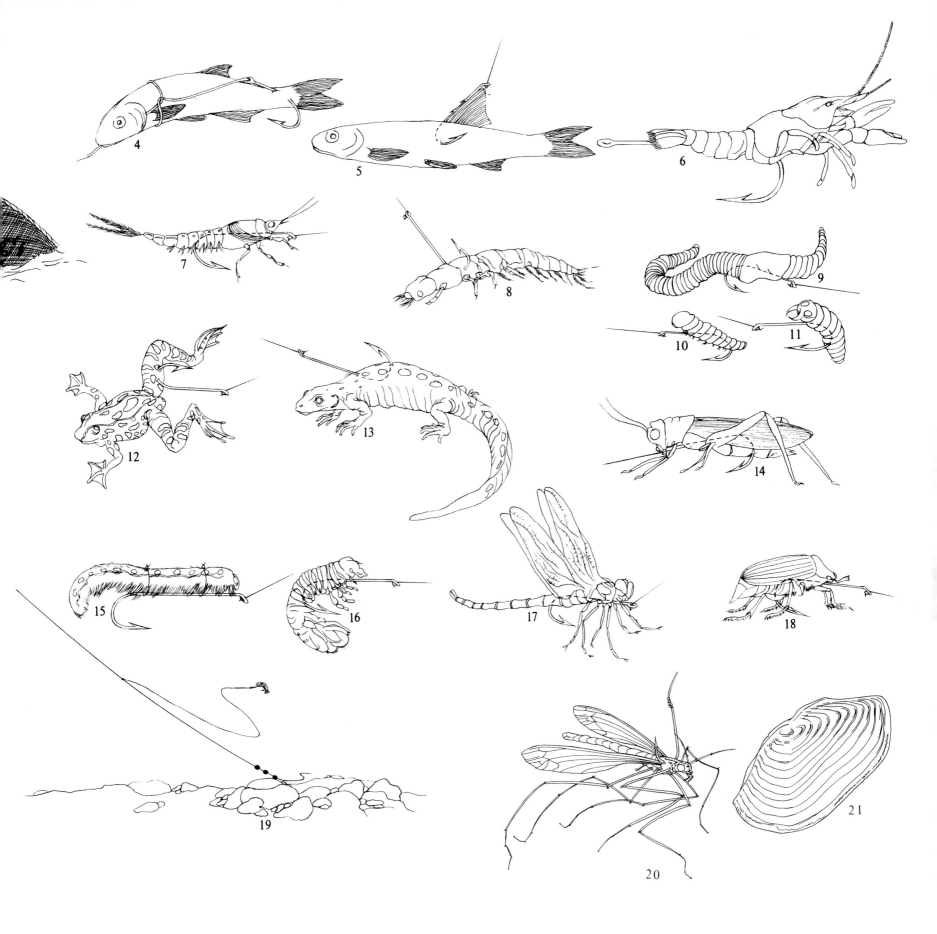

4 Bridle rig for dead minnow bait

5 Hook live minnow in the back flesh

6 Put hook through tail of crayfish

7 Mayfly nymph

8 Hellgramite or dragonfly larva

9 Nightcrawler hooked through egg ring

10 Beetle grub

11 Japanese beetle grub

12 Frog should be hooked in hind leg

13 Salamander is hooked in skin of back

14 Grasshopper

15 Caterpillar should be tied lightly to hook with fine thread

16 Freshwater shrimp

17 Dragonfly

18 Terrestrial beetle

19 A popular type of bait rig uses small split shot for depth so the bait drifts naturally downstream with the current.

20 Daddy-longlegs (crane fly)

21 Freshwater mussel

NATURAL BAITS FOR OCEAN GAME FISH

There are many types of natural baits for ocean game fish, but these seven baits will catch fish anywhere and are easily made aboard the boat before fishing.

Balao–sailfish, marlin
Mullet–marlin, tuna
Catalina–large marlin
Pork rind–small game
Tuna belly–sharks
Black eel–white marlin
Squid–swordfish, tuna

A BALAO BAIT

1 Using 4/0 to 6/0 hook and 7 wire, make up leader and hook as shown, with 1/2-in (1 cm) wire end standing away from the leader wire. Position hook and leader to the fish.
2 Start point of hook into body via gill.
3 Bend bait around the hook. Aim hook point to emerge from body as in Fig. A.
4 Push short end of wire up through jaws pinning them together.
5 Break off the "bill" at point of the jaw.
6 Position the leader splice along center line of lower jaw.
7 Using thin wire, bind jaws and leader in a smooth, continuous circular wrapping.

B MULLET BAIT

Rig mullet with 5/0 to 8/0 hook, depending on bait size. A barrel sinker secured to head and leader under lower jaw makes mullet sink and swim in a lifelike manner without skipping on the surface.

C CATALINA BAIT

For very large marlin and tuna, a whole small tuna or bonito is prepared with a 12/0 to 16/0 hook on heavy wire sewed to the top of the bait's head as shown. Entrails are removed and belly is sewed.

D BLACK EEL BAIT

Black eels 12–16 in (30–40 cm) long are good baits for white marlin and large school tuna. The 5/0 to 7/0 hook is attached to a wire or monofilament leader of 110–165 lb (50–75 kg) breaking strain.

E TUNA BELLY BAIT

A thin slice of belly skin from a tuna makes an excellent strip bait for sharks, tuna, and small billfish. The hook may be 5/0 to 8/0 in size, depending on the size of the bait, and is sewed in place.

F PORK RIND STRIP BAIT

This very effective small game fish bait is cut from a strip of prepared pork rind. The 4/0 to 6/0 hook is sewed to the bait with thread. Leader may be light wire or medium to heavy monofilament material.

G SQUID BAIT

One of the best baits in any sea, for almost any game fish, is a fresh squid 8–16 in (20–40 cm) long. One or two hooks may be used. In the single-hook bait, a fairly large hook is sewed inside the body.

In the two-hook bait, illustrated, two medium-sized hooks are used, one in the body and one in the bait's head. The leader may be wire or monofilament heavy enough for the type and size of fish that may be encountered.

H TOOLS FOR RIGGING BAITS

1 Thread or twine must be light but strong. Shoemaker's thread is excellent. Old light fishing line is often used for bait rigging.
2 Parallel-jaw pliers are the best for making wire leaders.
3 Large darning needle makes a good needle for sewing baits.
4 Backbone remover is a hollow metal tube with sharp teeth cut into one end.
5 Bait knife should be sharp with a thin, flexible blade.

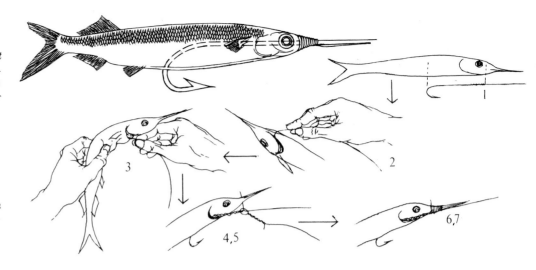

A

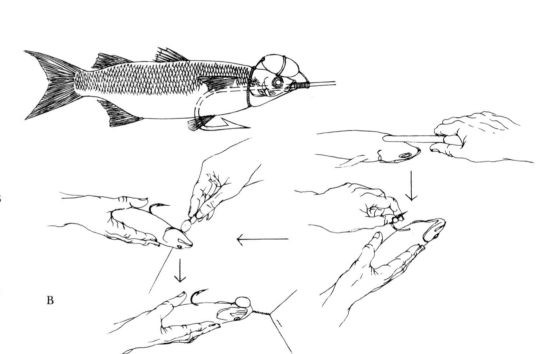

B

C

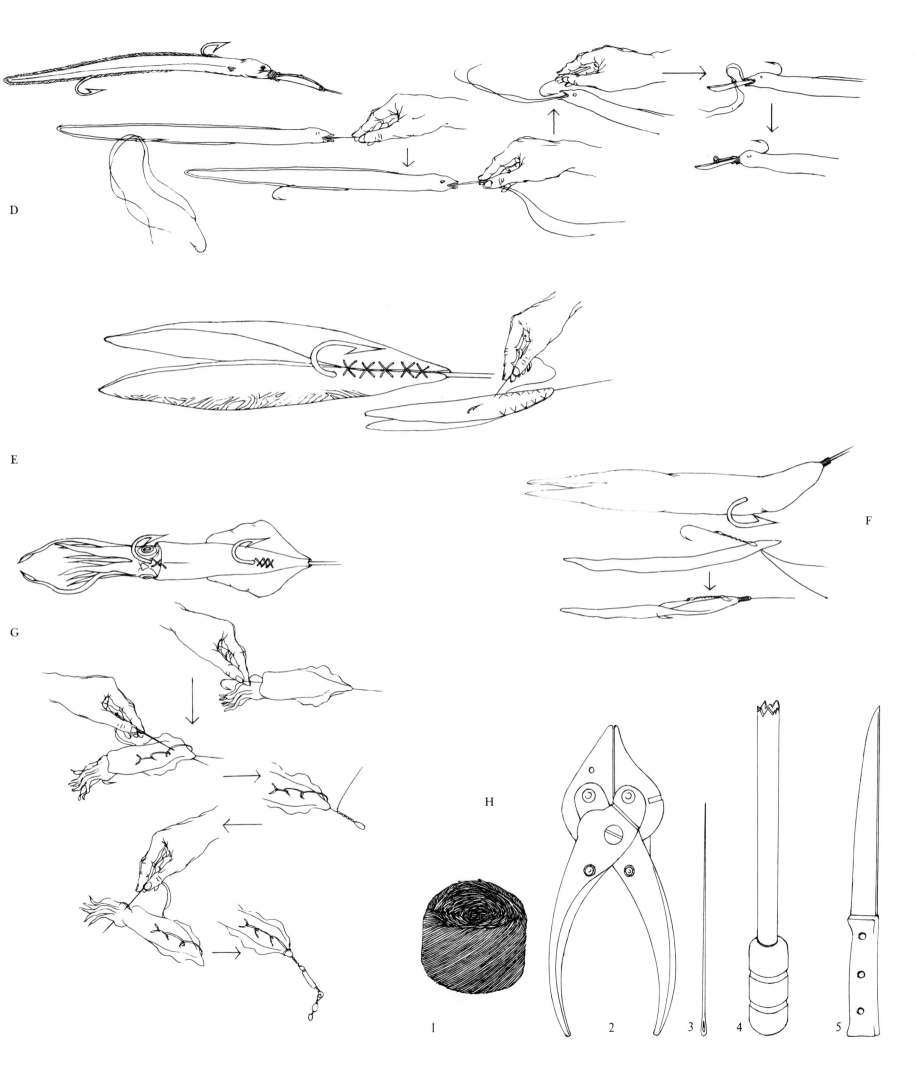

D

E

F

G

H

1   2   3   4   5

SALTWATER ARTIFICIAL LURES FOR TROLLING

Traditionally, natural baits have been considered the most effective baits on ocean game fishing, but in recent years the advent of extremely realistic baits of man-made origin have added new dimensions to game fishing on the ocean. Generally speaking, artificial saltwater game fish lures can be divided into two major classes:

1 Lures that simulate natural baits.
2 Lures that do not simulate natural baits, but have intrinsic action and attractiveness that fish find irresistible.

Lures that simulate natural baits are usually made of soft but durable plastic and closely follow the form and texture of the original living baitfish. For example, the artificial squid (A) feels remarkably like a squid to the touch and, when trolled at the end of a fishing line, has squidlike action. Taste does not seem to be much of a problem as long as the bait does not have a taste that is actually repulsive to the game fish involved. Most pelagic game fish feed by sight, having been attracted to the bait either by vision or by the vibrations given off by the bait in its passage through the water.

As with all other trolling lures, artificial saltwater bait-simulating lures have definite trolling speeds and types of rod action at which they work best. For instance, the artificial ballyhoo (balao) (B) is most attractive to sailfish, small marlin, and various members of the tuna family when trolled from an outrigger at the normal ballyhoo trolling speed of 4–6 knots. On the other hand, the teaser-type plastic-headed Konahead lure (J) resembles no known natural baitfish and is most effective on large marlin and yellowfin tuna when trolled either from outriggers or directly from the fishing rod at the relatively high trolling speed of 8–9 knots.

Many artificial saltwater lures have built-in action and do not require the angler to impart rod action to make the lure work at top efficiency. The Creek Chub Pikie plug (K), and the jointed Rapala Diver (O), both have pronounced side-to-side dodging action caused by their body shape and the forward metal lip, They should be trolled without jigging rod action. But leadhead small game jigs such as the feathered jig with pork rind strip (F), the Kramer Parrot-head (M), the Upperman bucktail (L), and the No-Alibi bullethead (N), all catch more fish when quick jigging rod action is applied by the angler. The artificial eel (C), the Hopkins spoon (G), the Dardevle spoon (H), and the surgical tubing eel or snake (E) sometimes work best with no rod action, but also may be very effective if a slow, sweeping type of rod action is applied.

Getting the most out of artificial saltwater lures is mainly a matter of intelligent experimentation. The best of these lures are as good as natural baits and they give fishermen many practical advantages.

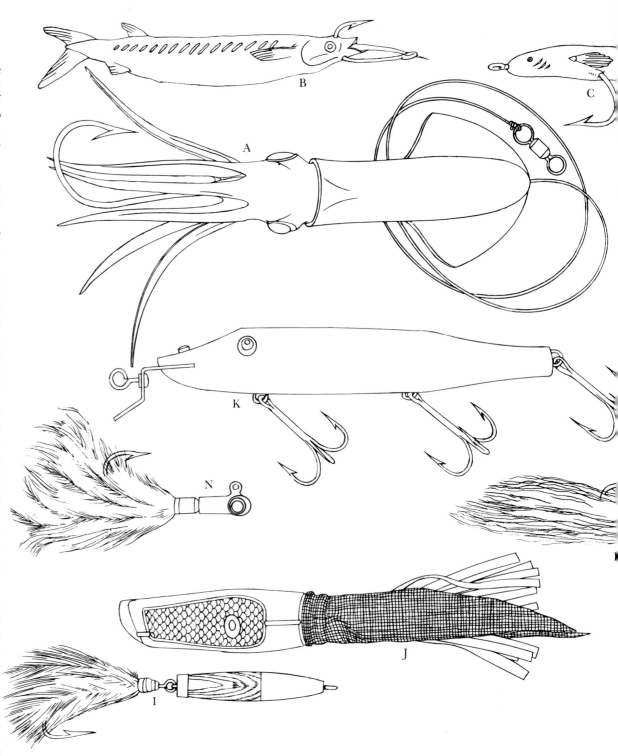

PLASTIC BAIT SIMULATORS

A Squid, 8–12 in (20–30 cm): white marlin, swordfish, tuna.
B Ballyhoo, 12 in (20 cm): sailfish, small marlin, school tuna.
C Eel, 8–20 in (20–50 cm): striped bass, white marlin, tuna.
D Mullet, 12–16 in (30–40 cm): all billfish, wahoo, most tunas.
E Surgical tubing eel, 8–20 in (20–50 cm): striped bass.

RIGGING BAIT SIMULATORS

Hooks:
Should be from 4/0 to 12/0 size, depending on size of lure and the target fish.
Leaders:
Monofilament, rating 3–5 times line test. Solid wire, testing 3–5 times line test. Wire cable for very heavy-duty fishing.
Connectors:
Full-swivel (R & S) 8 times line test.

LEADHEAD TROLLING JIGS

F Common feathered jig, 2–5 in (5–13 cm): striped bass, channel bass, bluefish, weakfish, school tuna.
L Upperman bucktail, 2–5 in (5–13 cm): same species.
M Kramer Parrot-head, 4 in (10 cm): all game species up to 60 lb (27 kg).
N No-Alibi Bullethead. 2–5 in (5–13 cm): all inshore game species.

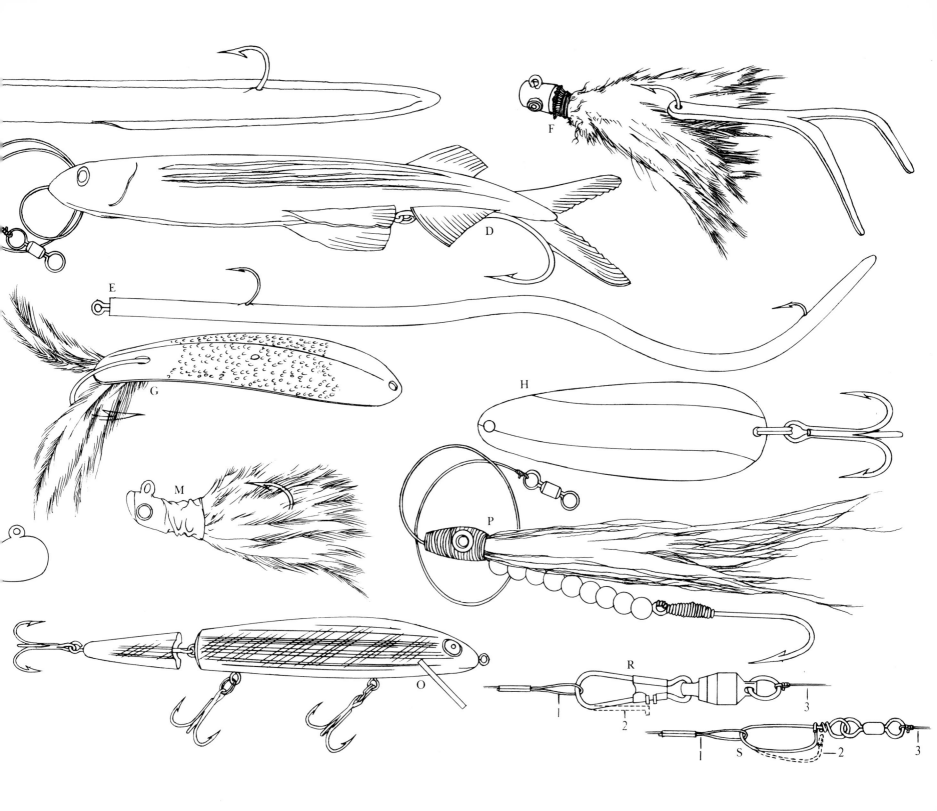

RIGGING TROLLING JIGS

Hooks:
Hooks are cast into the lead heads, run 2/0 to 8/0 size.
Leaders:
Monofilament or wire rating 3–5 times the break test of line.
Connectors:
Nonswivel or full swivel, at least 5 times line test.
Trolling tails:
Pork rind strips do improve catch rate.

SPOONS AND PLUGS

G *Hopkins spoon, 8 in (20 cm): bluefish, striped bass, salmon, most inshore species.*
H *Eppinger Dardevle, 3–6 in (7 1/2–15 cm): all inshore species.*
K *Creek Chub Pikie plug, 9–12 in (23–30 cm): striped bass, larger inshore species.*
O *Jointed Rapala plug, 8–12 in (20–30 cm): inshore species taken by deep trolling.*

RIGGING SPOONS & PLUGS

Hooks:
Most spoons and plugs come with single or treble hooks in sizes of 2/0 to 6/0.
Leaders:
Light wire for fish with sharp teeth, otherwise monofil.
Connectors:
Full-swivel models testing at least 5 times line test.
Trolling sinkers:
2–12 oz as needed.

SPECIAL TROLLING LURES

I *Leadhead cedar jig, 4–7 in (10–18 cm): 6/0 to 8/0 hook, used surface trolling for school tuna, bonito.*
J *Konahead lure, 10–16 in (25–40 cm): tuna, large marlin, wahoo, other large game. Used on heavy tackle, 1 or 2 12/0 hooks.*
P *Salmon-trolling fly, 4–7 in (10–18 cm): all species of salmon in salt water.*

LINE-LEADER CONNECTORS

R *Ball-bearing model, heavy-duty fishing.*
1 Leader eye.
2 Connector detail.
3 Fishing line. A low-line-twist. type for lures that spin.
S *Common snap swivel.*
1 Leader eye.
2 Connector detail.
3 Fishing line.
This popular model is often used without the swivel barrel for non-spinning lures.

TABULATED OCEAN GAME FISH BAITS

Live bait is one of the oldest and most successful attractants for ocean game fish. In some situations the use of live bait is the only method that gives the angler a reasonable chance of success with the fish. Over the years, definite ways of rigging and presenting live baits have been developed. While one might assume that all live baits are pretty much alike in appearance and action, there are actually many subtle variations of bait action and attractiveness that must be understood before one can use live bait with the greatest effectiveness.

The table and illustrations on this page give the basic differences between the various types of live bait that are commonly used in salt water. Some baits are ideal for use with very light tackle. Others can be used with the heaviest tackle for very large fish. Baits are usually kept alive in a special tank or well in the boat. A liberal supply of circulating seawater is necessary to provide the baits with oxygen. Injured or dead baits should be removed from the tank. Baits must be protected from extremes of heat and cold.

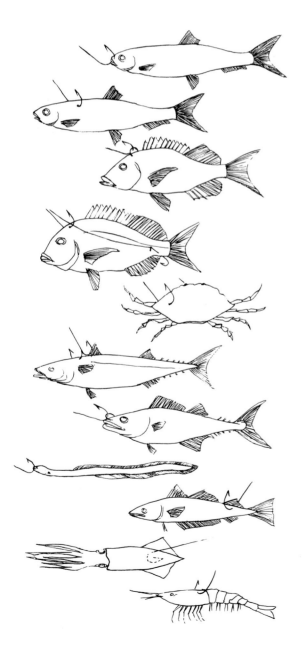

Bait Species	Game Fish	Fishing Method and How Rigged
Anchovy Sardine	Yellowtail Yellowfin tuna Bluefin tuna Bonito Albacore Wahoo	*Tackle:* 6–30 lb (2,7–13,6 kg) test line, 4 to 2/0 single hook. *Method:* Casting to surface fish, or deep-fishing from drifting or anchored boats. Bait is usually hooked through upper lip or under arch-bone behind gill cover. Hook is tied to line without a leader. *Areas:* California, western Mexico, Bermuda.
Herring Menhaden	Striped bass Bluefish Mako shark Bluefin tuna	*Tackle:* 20–50 lb (9–22,7 kg) test line, 3/0 to 8/0 single hook. *Method:* Fished free-swimming or with cork float from drifting or anchored boats or from shore. Bait is hooked through flesh of back. Hook is tied to the line, or to a short monofilament or wire leader. *Areas:* U.S. Atlantic coast, Maine to Florida.
Jack Pinfish Mullet	Tarpon Wahoo Barracuda Grouper Amberjack Snook	*Tackle:* 12–50 lb (5,4–22,7 kg) test line, 1/0 to 8/0 single hook, depending on size of game fish being sought. *Method:* Fished free-swimming from anchored or drifting boats, or from shore. Bait is back-hooked, or hook is placed in a loop of strong line passed through the back flesh of the live bait, as shown. *Areas:* Florida, Bahamas, Gulf of Mexico, all tropics.
Porgy Grunt	Amberjack Striped bass Grouper Black drum Channel bass	*Tackle:* 30–50 lb (13,6–22,7 kg) test line, 5/0 to 8/0 single hooks. *Method:* Fished deep from drifting or anchored boats. Bait is often rigged with two single hooks, one in the head and one in the tail. Leaders are 6–8 stainless steel wire and are separated from the fishing line by a suitable snap swivel. *Areas:* All temperate and sub-tropical waters.
Crab Shrimp	Permit Tarpon Channel bass Black drum Tautog	*Tackle:* 6–30 lb (2,7–13,6 kg) test line, 2 to 2/0 single hook. *Method:* Bait is cast to fish that have been located visually, or fished deep from anchored or drifting boats. Crab's large claws are broken off. Hook is tied to line or to monofilament or wire leader. *Areas:* All U.S. coastal waters.
Mackerel Whiting Red hake	Swordfish Striped bass Bluefish Marlin Bluefin tuna Shark	*Tackle:* 20–30 lb (9–13,6 kg) test line for smaller game, up to 130-lb. line for big game. 2/0 to 4/0 treble hook. *Method:* Fished free-swimming or with cork on the line from drifting or anchored boats. Hook is tied to line for small game (except bluefish), wire leader used for bluefish and big game. *Areas:* All temperate Atlantic and Pacific areas.
Runner Bonito	Sailfish Marlin Tuna Shark	*Tackle:* 20–50 lb (9–22,7 kg) test line for sailfish, white marlin; 80–130 lb. test line for big game. *Method:* Fished free-swimming or from a kite from drifting or slow-trolling boats. 6/0 to 12/0 single hook, rigged on wire or monofilament trolling leader. *Areas:* Most Atlantic and Pacific big game areas.
Eel	Striped bass Bluefish	*Tackle:* 20–50 lb (9–22,7 kg) test line, 1/0 to 5/0 single hook. *Method:* Fished free-swimming or with cork on line from drifting or anchored boats, or from shore. Hook is tied to the line for striped bass. A light wire leader is required when fishing for bluefish. *Areas:* Atlantic coast from Cape Cod to New Jersey.
Squid	Albacore Yellowtail Yellowfin tuna Bluefin tuna Bonito Wahoo	*Tackle:* 20–50 lb (19–22,7 kg.) test line, 2 to 3/0 single hook. *Method:* Bait is hooked through the tail and cast to surface – showing fish from drifting or anchored boats while chumming with other live bait. Hook is tied directly to the fishing line, no leader. *Areas:* California, western Mexico, Bermuda.

CASTING AND CASTING TECHNIQUE

Who hath not seen Scarus rise,
Decoyed and killed by fraudful
flies?

MARCUS VALERIUS MARTIALIS

The great appeal of fly casting to modern anglers is that here is a technique of fishing that puts emphasis on personal fishing skill, yet is relatively easy to master with the equipment and teaching techniques now available. It once was that a few neophyte anglers came directly into fly casting and, after a lengthy and sometimes difficult apprenticeship, became skilled at this challenging sport and remained fly-fishing purists for the rest of their lives. Now this most ancient of fishing arts involving the rod and reel is undergoing a great expansion of popularity. Anglers who have gained their experience in other forms of fishing are flocking to fly casting because of its challenge and the satisfactions that come with the mastery of handling the tackle.

It is quite important to understand the very close relationship between the fly rod and its line. In older days, very long rods were used because length of rod was considered to be a factor in achieving distance in casting. But as anglers and tackle makers began to understand the engineering principles involved in casting a linear sinker (the fly line) rather than a lumped-weight sinker (as in weighted-lure casting), they began to develop rods that work best with lines of a specific weight, and lines whose weight matches specific types and actions of rods. This was a fairly lengthy process in time, but it led up to the present situation in which an angler may go into a tackle shop and purchase one single rod that will work fairly well in a variety of fishing situations, or specific rods that will work extremely well in specific fishing conditions. In each case the rod is usually marked with the weight of line that it will accept for best results, and the angler is spared much experimenting with rods and lines to arrive at a combination that is best.

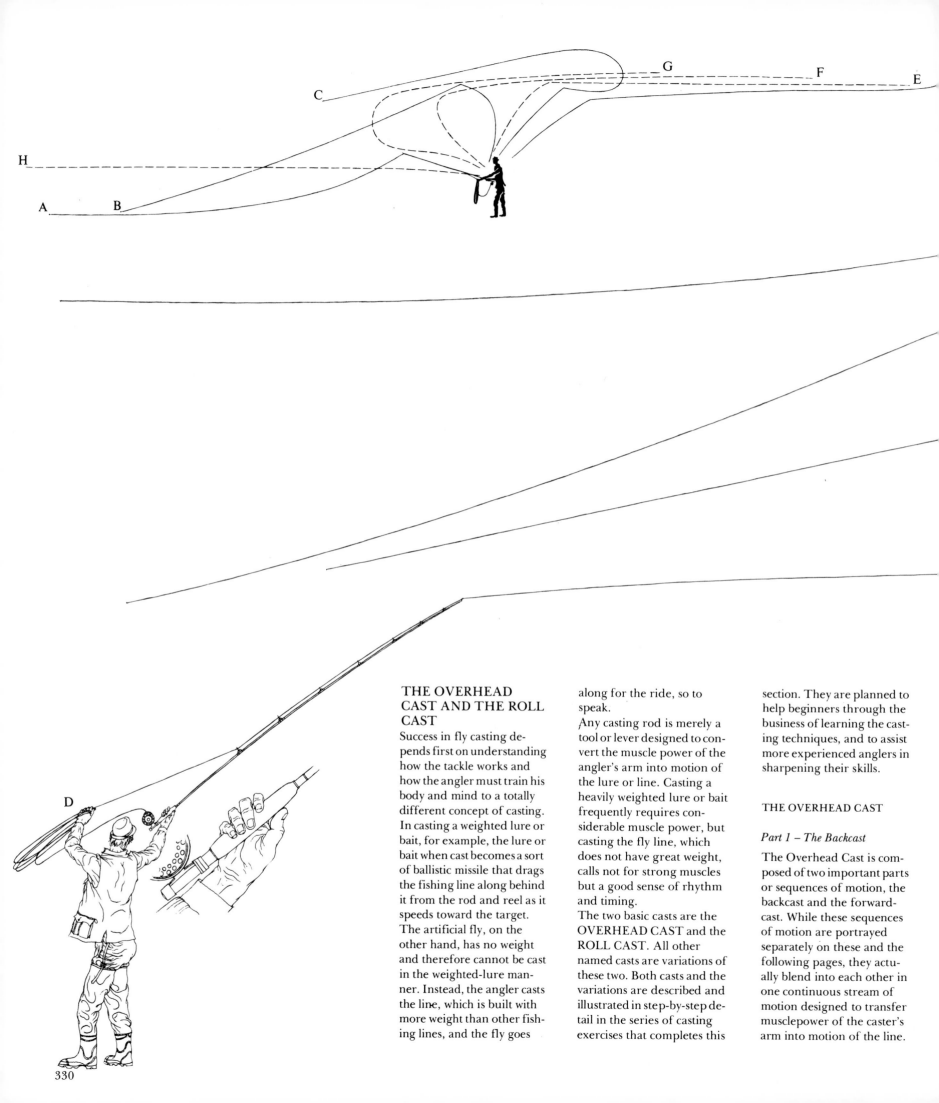

A B C D E F G H

THE OVERHEAD CAST AND THE ROLL CAST

Success in fly casting depends first on understanding how the tackle works and how the angler must train his body and mind to a totally different concept of casting. In casting a weighted lure or bait, for example, the lure or bait when cast becomes a sort of ballistic missile that drags the fishing line along behind it from the rod and reel as it speeds toward the target. The artificial fly, on the other hand, has no weight and therefore cannot be cast in the weighted-lure manner. Instead, the angler casts the line, which is built with more weight than other fishing lines, and the fly goes along for the ride, so to speak.

Any casting rod is merely a tool or lever designed to convert the muscle power of the angler's arm into motion of the lure or line. Casting a heavily weighted lure or bait frequently requires considerable muscle power, but casting the fly line, which does not have great weight, calls not for strong muscles but a good sense of rhythm and timing.

The two basic casts are the OVERHEAD CAST and the ROLL CAST. All other named casts are variations of these two. Both casts and the variations are described and illustrated in step-by-step detail in the series of casting exercises that completes this section. They are planned to help beginners through the business of learning the casting techniques, and to assist more experienced anglers in sharpening their skills.

THE OVERHEAD CAST

Part 1 – The Backcast

The Overhead Cast is composed of two important parts or sequences of motion, the backcast and the forward-cast. While these sequences of motion are portrayed separately on these and the following pages, they actually blend into each other in one continuous stream of motion designed to transfer musclepower of the caster's arm into motion of the line.

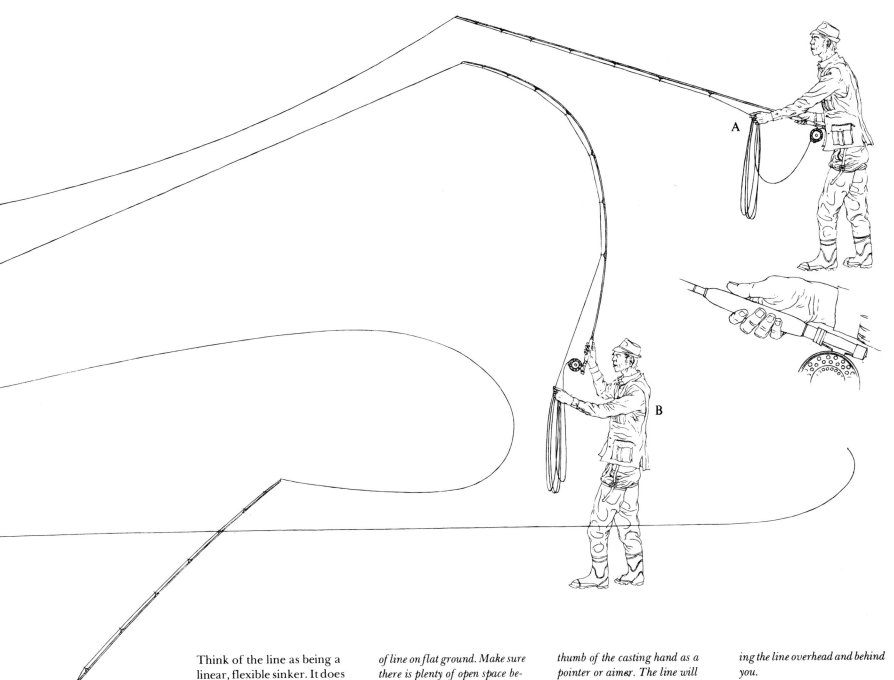

Think of the line as being a linear, flexible sinker. It does not weigh much when compared with conventional sinkers, but to the delicate fly-casting rod it "looks like" a sinker. If you were to try to cast the line with a perfectly stiff rod, it would be impossible. This is because there would be no timed transfer of power between the rod and the line. The line cannot start moving instantaneously. It must accelerate gradually from a motionless to a moving state. The flexibility of the casting rod provides this gradual acceleration, acting as a spring to store power.

A *In executing the back-cast portion of the overhead cast, start by stripping out 25–30 ft (8–10 m)* of line on flat ground. Make sure there is plenty of open space behind you to accommodate the line that will be cast behind you in completing the backcast. The best position of the feet is with the left foot slightly forward and parallel to the direction of the cast. The right foot is placed slightly back with the toes pointed outward, to the right, at any comfortable angle up to 45° from the line of the cast. This makes it easier to pivot the body and watch the progress of the line in the backcast.

Grasp the fishing line with the left hand between the reel and the first rod guide, allowing a small amount of free line to hang loose, as indicated. The best way to hold the rod is with the thumb extended along the top of the grip, as shown. In casting, use the thumb of the casting hand as a pointer or aimer. The line will follow the lead of the thumb. Some casters stand perfectly erect while casting. Others move the body slightly. Do what is natural for yourself.

B *The secret of good fly casting lies in proper timing of the backcast and forward cast. Start the backcast with a quickly increasing upward motion of the rod from the extended to the overhead position. Do not attempt to jerk the line into the air. Rather, let the weight of the line "load" or put bend into the rod during the brief moment of upward motion.*

C *Then, when you stop the rod's motion at about the 1 o'clock position, the power stored in the bent or "loaded" rod shaft will be transferred into line motion, send-* ing the line overhead and behind you.

D *You must pause after completing the back-cast motion to give the line time to reach its fully extended position behind you. Timing comes with practice, but even the best casters often turn the body and look back over the casting shoulder to watch the line as it unrolls behind the caster's position. The left or noncasting hand holds the line between the reel and the first rod guide and exercises a degree of control over line speed. Later in this section its part in "shooting" the line for distance will be shown.*

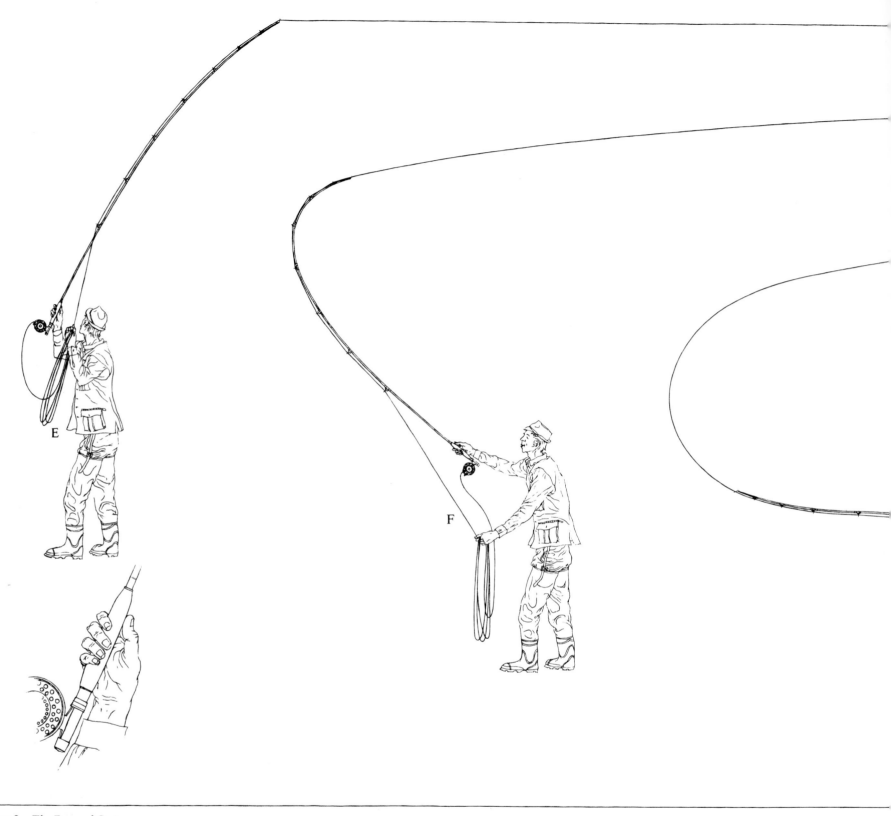

Part 2 – The Forward Cast

In the forward cast, the rod is "loaded" in the same manner as in the backcast. Power is applied with the arm, not with the body. Some instructors insist that the wrist be held stiff. Others allow the caster to use wrist motion in making the forward cast. Both methods work well provided the flow of power from rod to arm is smooth.

E *As the line is extended to the rear, thrust the casting arm forward and at the same time start moving the rod shaft in a forward hammer-stroke manner. Remember that a smooth flow of power is more important than any sudden application of force. Position of the hand remains unchanged.*

F *Full power of the arm is applied swiftly but smoothly as soon as the weight of the line is felt. Work to achieve a satisfactory "feel" to the casting motion. The rod will take only so much "loading," and trying to force more power into the cast will only overload the rod, causing the cast to be poor and sloppy.*

G *At the instant of maximum rod loading you can impart more speed to the line by hauling down with the left hand against the pull of the line. The rod unloads power to the line very rapidly. The follow-through requires that you terminate the power stroke smoothly without bringing it to a sudden stop at end of the cast.*

H *As the line unrolls, release the line held by the left hand. The extra amount of slack line will "shoot" out through the guides, adding somewhat to the distance of the cast. Keep the rod tip above the horizontal position. The rod shaft should not vibrate up and down when the power stroke has been completed.*

Sometimes it is an advantage to be able to "shoot" additional line toward a distant target. The extra shooting line, up to 20 ft (6 m), may be held in coils between the reel and the rod. The extra line is "shot" or released exactly as illustrated at sketch H. The forward inertia of the line is enough to carry it forward.

1 The mouth carry. The loops or coils of shooting line may be held in the mouth and released at the end of the cast. This carry is popular when standing in water deeper than normal.

2 A "shooting basket" is a popular device for holding the extra shooting line.

3 Some anglers prefer to coil the line on the ground or deck of the fishing boat.
   When the cast is made the line uncoils and shoots freely through the rod guides. It must be coiled so as to shoot without any kinks or knots.

4 Some anglers hang the coils of shooting line from a buckle of the wading boot, or a holder taped to the boot's side.

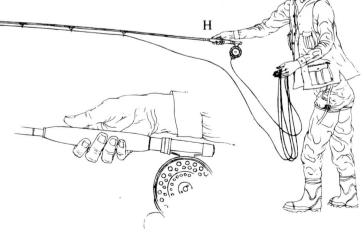

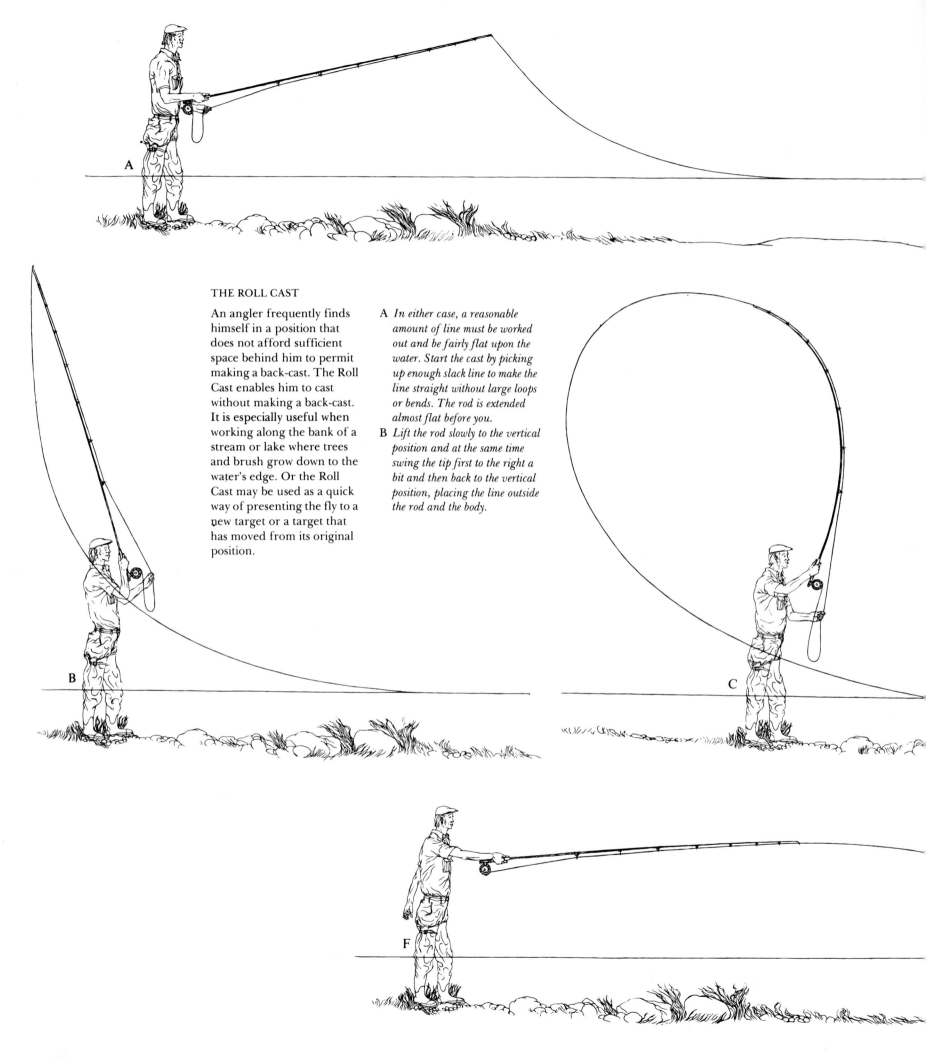

THE ROLL CAST

An angler frequently finds himself in a position that does not afford sufficient space behind him to permit making a back-cast. The Roll Cast enables him to cast without making a back-cast. It is especially useful when working along the bank of a stream or lake where trees and brush grow down to the water's edge. Or the Roll Cast may be used as a quick way of presenting the fly to a new target or a target that has moved from its original position.

A *In either case, a reasonable amount of line must be worked out and be fairly flat upon the water. Start the cast by picking up enough slack line to make the line straight without large loops or bends. The rod is extended almost flat before you.*

B *Lift the rod slowly to the vertical position and at the same time swing the tip first to the right a bit and then back to the vertical position, placing the line outside the rod and the body.*

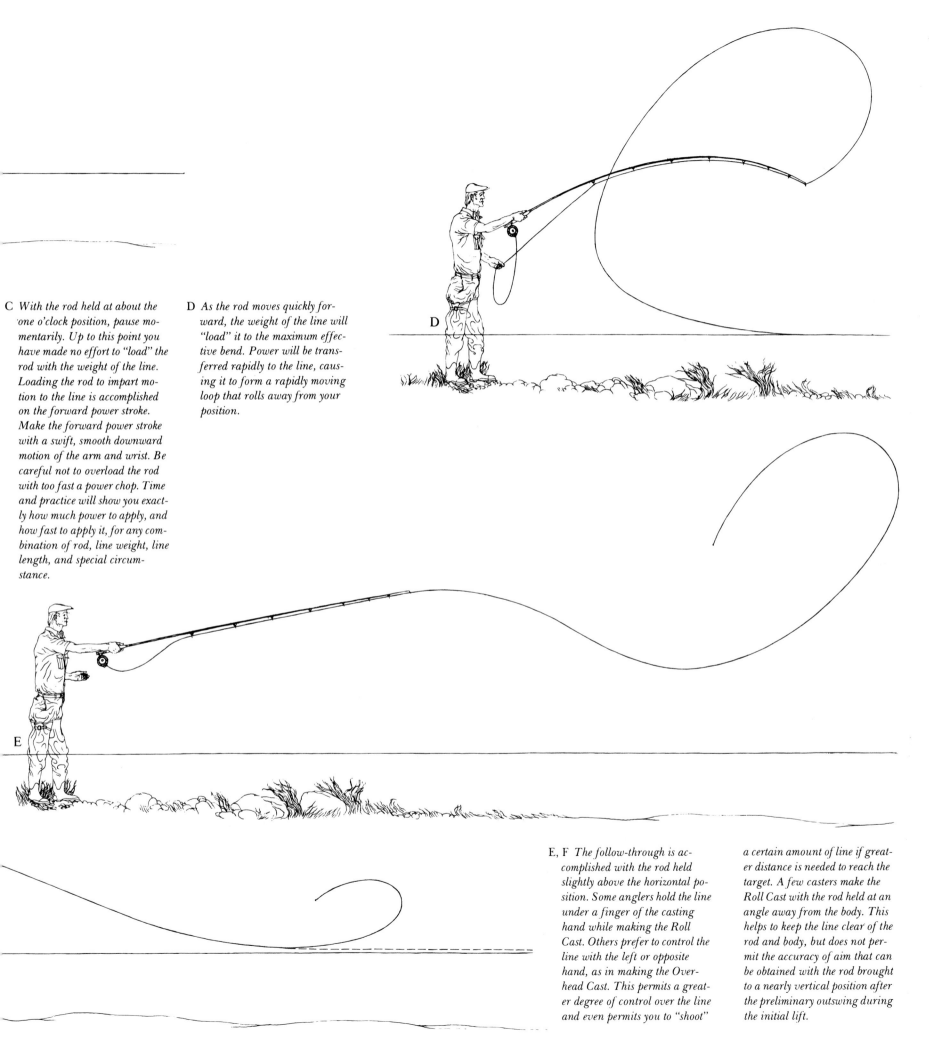

C *With the rod held at about the one o'clock position, pause momentarily. Up to this point you have made no effort to "load" the rod with the weight of the line. Loading the rod to impart motion to the line is accomplished on the forward power stroke. Make the forward power stroke with a swift, smooth downward motion of the arm and wrist. Be careful not to overload the rod with too fast a power chop. Time and practice will show you exactly how much power to apply, and how fast to apply it, for any combination of rod, line weight, line length, and special circumstance.*

D *As the rod moves quickly forward, the weight of the line will "load" it to the maximum effective bend. Power will be transferred rapidly to the line, causing it to form a rapidly moving loop that rolls away from your position.*

E, F *The follow-through is accomplished with the rod held slightly above the horizontal position. Some anglers hold the line under a finger of the casting hand while making the Roll Cast. Others prefer to control the line with the left or opposite hand, as in making the Overhead Cast. This permits a greater degree of control over the line and even permits you to "shoot"* *a certain amount of line if greater distance is needed to reach the target. A few casters make the Roll Cast with the rod held at an angle away from the body. This helps to keep the line clear of the rod and body, but does not permit the accuracy of aim that can be obtained with the rod brought to a nearly vertical position after the preliminary outswing during the initial lift.*

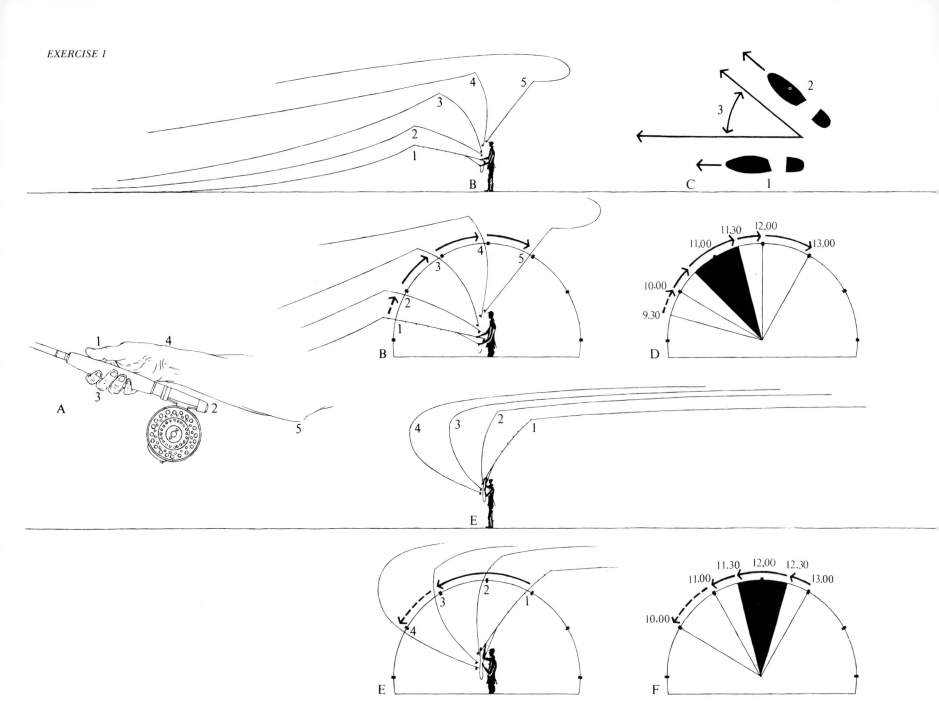

EXERCISE 1

THE OVERHEAD CAST

The only real secret of making good overhead casts is to learn how to apply the power stroke in each phase of the cast with perfect timing between the backcast and the forward cast.

REVIEWING THE GRIP

A 1 *Thumb over shaft.*
  2 *Rod shaft parallel to caster's forearm.*
  3 *Fingers firm but not tense in their grip.*
  4 *Wrist firm but not inflexible.*
  5 *Pivoting motion comes from the elbow.*

THE BACKCAST

B 1 *With line extended, hold rod at 9:30 and start an easy lift.*
  2 *At 10:00 start power stroke, letting the weight of the line bend or "load" the line smoothly.*
  3 *Apply maximum power from 10:30 to 11:30.*
  4 *Power stroke ends at 12:00. Start "drift" to stopped position 5.*

PROPER FOOT POSITION

C 1 *Left foot parallel to line of aim.*
  2 *Right foot slightly behind, toed out.*
  3 *Toe-out angle 35°–40°.*

BACKCAST DIAGRAM

D 1 *Rod at 9:30, ready to start backcast.*
  2 *After an easy lift, power stroke begins at 10:00 position.*
  3 *Power increases and reaches maximum at 11:00 position, with shaft heavily loaded.*
  4 *Power stroke tapers off from 11:30 to 12:00 position as the rod "unloads," transferring power to the line in the form of motion.*
  5 *Rod is allowed to "drift" from 12:00 to 13:00 as line flies overhead to the rear.*

THE FORWARD CAST

E 1 *After a momentary pause to allow the line to extend fully backward, the forward cast starts at 13:00 with a combined forward thrust and arm hammer-stroke.*
  2 *Maximum power starts at 12:30, reaches a peak at 12:00, and declines at 11:30.*
  3 *At 11:00 power stroke is ended and the rod "drifts" to 10:00.*
  4 *Rod stops at 10:00 as line extends to the target. Remember that the two periods of peak power are very brief and must be achieved smoothly to avoid overloading the rod and spoiling the cast.*

FORWARD CAST DIAGRAM

F 1 *Rod shaft starts to load between 13:00 and 12:30 as weight of line is felt.*
  2 *Peak loading of rod is at 12:00.*
  3 *Power stroke ends at 11:00. Continuing it beyond this point adds no power to the line and throws cast-spoiling vibrations down the line.*
  4 *Rod comes to rest at 10:00 position as the line flies to the target.*

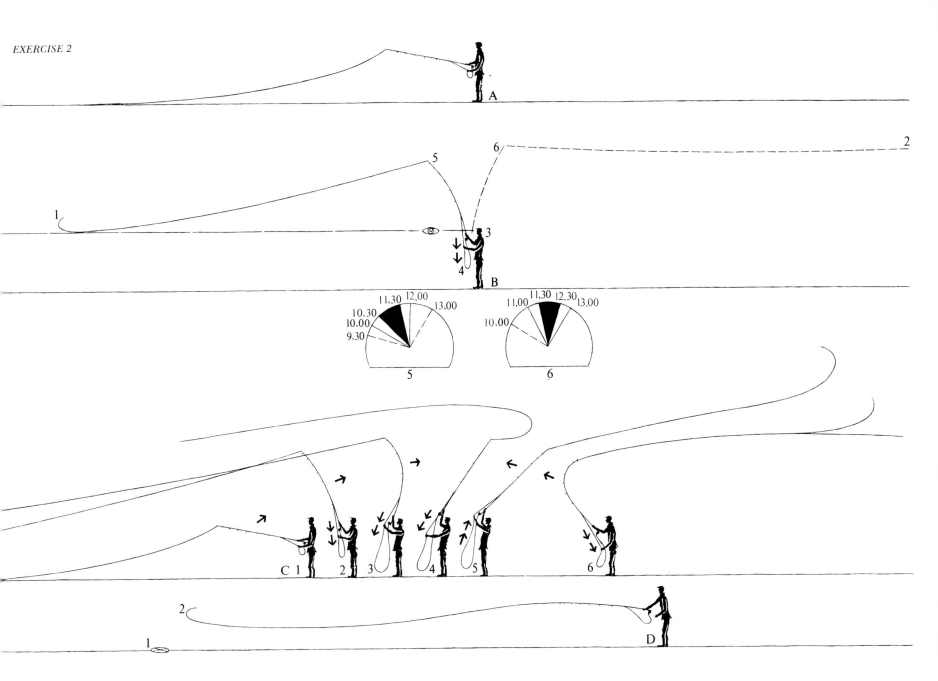

EXERCISE 2

FALSE CASTING

Nonfishermen sometimes laugh at a fly caster who indulges in false casting, calling it "fanning the air." Actually, false casting serves a very definite purpose. It allows the caster to work out his line and measure the length of the line with respect to the distance to the target. It also helps him to dry a fly that has become watersoaked. All good casters practice false casting. It sharpens their skill and improves timing.

THE PROPER STANCE

A *The body should be erect with weight equally distributed on the feet. The foot position shown in Exercise 1 is good for most occasions, but some anglers prefer to keep both feet parallel and pointed toward the target. Exaggerated body motions serve no purpose. The body must remain well balanced and relaxed. Power is applied to the rod with the casting arm only. Body twists during the power stroke sequence only serve to spoil the cast, but you may turn to watch the backcast.*

CONTROLLING THE LINE

B *1 Try to maintain the forward cast at eye level. Do not let it touch the surface.*

2 Keep backcast high by correct timing.

3 Body erect, turn only to watch backcast.

4 Left hand controls the fishing line.

5 Strive to achieve a power stroke with the peak of power between 10:30 and 11:30 for the backcast.

6 The forward power stroke peak comes between the 12:30 and 11:30 positions with smooth transition of arm and rod velocity.

THE OVERHEAD CAST IN SLOW MOTION

C *1 Start pickup, left hand controls line.*

2 Begin power stroke, lifting the rod with force while left hand pulls down on line.

3 Maximum power is not quite, but almost, a strong jerk.

4 Bring the rod to a gradual halt at 13:00 to dampen vibrations in the rod and line.

5 Pause at 13:00 and watch the line as it extends behind you. Strive for perfect timing. Left hand rises to head height to control the line.

6 Pull down with left hand on the line as the arm delivers the forward power stroke. This increases line speed and control.

CAST TO A TARGET

D *1 Select a target in normal casting range and mentally score yourself on accuracy.*

2 Control the length of the line as well as its side-to-side motion. Drop line to the water or ground only when you know a perfect cast has been accomplished. Strive for control before attempting speed and distance.

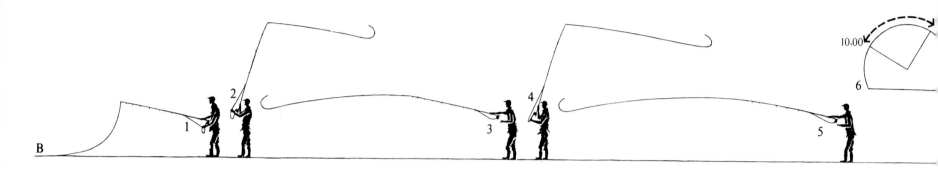

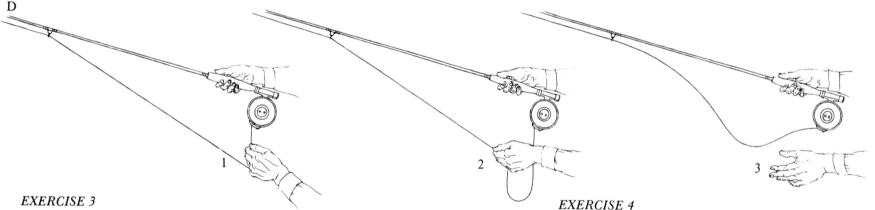

EXERCISE 3

WORKING OUT LINE

When fishing, an angler seldom can walk out line for casting, the way he does when he is preparing to do some practice casting. The line must be worked out by stripping line from the reel and shooting the extra line while false casting until the line is long enough.

A *Start with 10 ft (3 m) of line plus the leader off the rod.*

SINGLE-ACTION METHOD

B *1 Start as for a cast.*
  2 At end of backcast, hold extra line.
  3 At end of forward cast, shoot the line.
  4 Strip line from reel while backcasting.
  5 Shoot stripped line on the forward cast.
  6 The power diagram.

DOUBLE-ACTION METHOD

C *1 Strip line while starting backcast.*
  2 Shoot line at the end of the backcast.
  3 Strip line while making forward cast.
  4 Shoot line at end of the forward cast.
  5 Strip line while making backcast.
  6 Shoot line at end of backcast, continue until enough line has been worked out.

STRIPPING THE LINE

D *1 Draw extra line down from the reel with the left hand while making the start of a power stroke.*
  2 Hold extra line for the remainder of the power stroke.
  3 Release and shoot the extra line at the end of either cast. You gain as much line length as there is extra line to shoot. Some anglers work out line by coiling the needed amount in the left hand, then shooting it a few coils at a time until the proper length has been achieved.

EXERCISE 4

TO CHANGE THE DIRECTION OF A CAST

Frequently an angler may wish to change the direction of a cast while he is in the act of casting or false casting. This can be done by turning the body in the direction of the new target at the proper moment during the cast. The proper moment is when the backcast is extended fully behind the caster, giving him the opportunity to shift the cast angle toward the new target.

CHANGE OF DIRECTION

1 Angler standing at Y is casting along the line X-X. He sees fish at target Z. He starts backcast from forward X to rear X.
2 When backcast to rear X is extended, angler pivots body to right and aims the forward cast at target Z.
3 If the cast does not appear to be accurate to hit Z, the angler false casts until he has the new angle and distance under control. A large change of direction may require two or more changes of body angle before the line can be brought to the new target. Most anglers should be able to change cast-

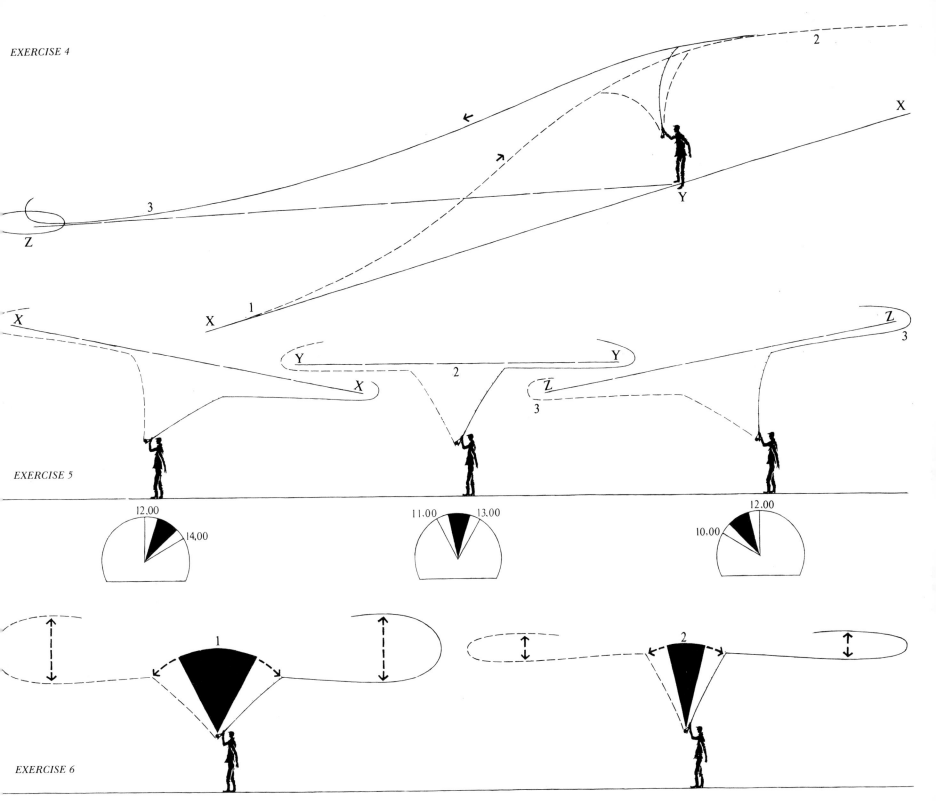

ing angle by 20° in one shift. Larger changes should be broken up into steps of false casts with an angle shift of 15° per false cast. Good casters can change direction through a full 360° circle.

EXERCISE 5

LOW AND HIGH BACK AND FORWARD CASTS

Proper line control requires that you know how to make low or high back and forward casts. Cast elevation control is often needed to clear obstacles such as grass, bushes, or rocks.

CAST ELEVATION

1 *High forward cast (on cast axis X-X) is achieved by holding the power stroke between positions 14:00 and 12:00 on the forward cast.*

2 *Normal cast power stroke falls between 13:00 and 11:00 on cast axis Y-Y.*

3 *Low forward, high backcast (axis Z-Z) requires shift of the power stroke forward to the sector between 12:00 and 10:00 on the power diagram.*

EXERCISE 6

DEEP AND SHALLOW LINE LOOPS

A large loop in the line during the cast causes excessive air resistance and spoils distance and accuracy. Good anglers strive to achieve small casting loops through careful control of the power stroke during both the backcast and the forward cast.

KEEPING LOOPS SMALL

1 *Large, air-resistant loop is caused by a wide, slow, sloppy power stroke.*

2 *Keep your loops small by applying power in a relatively short arc. Concentrate on a smooth transition of rod speed between initial lift, power stroke, and slowdown at the end of the back or forward cast.*

EXERCISE 7

THE ROLL CAST

The roll cast enables you to fish the tight spots where there isn't space for the overhead cast. It also is good for repeated casts to a moving target nearby. Practice the roll cast carefully with special attention to form and accuracy.

A *The cast starts with line extended to a maximum distance of 30 ft (10 m). Take in . slack line before starting the cast. For best line control, hold the line in the left hand as in the overhead cast.*

B *Swing the rod up to the 12:30 position with a slow, easy motion. Let the line fall down from the rod tip in a long, deep bend.*

C *Start the power stroke at 12:30 and apply full power to the rod from 12:00 to 10:30. Then let the rod "drift" to the 10:00 position. The line will form a moving loop following the arc of the rod.*

D *Follow through by holding the rod at 10:00. The moving line loop should roll away from you in a smooth, easy flow toward the target.*

E *With proper control, the entire line will be free of the water at midroll. At this moment the left*

hand can release the line and extra line can be "shot" toward the target.

F *Always cast toward a definite target. You must seek to achieve complete control over each phase of the cast. Learn how to make longer or shorter casts and to change the direction of the cast to left or right as a fish (the target) may move.*

EXERCISE 8

WORKING OUT LINE IN THE ROLL CAST

Working out line in the roll cast can be done only when the line is fully airborne in the forward cast. Because there is no backcast, there is no way that line can be worked out except during the brief instant when the line is in the air, moving away from the angler.

WORKING OUT LINE

A *To extend the cast from X to Y, strip out enough line (1) to reach the target. Hold coils of extra line*

in the left hand while casting.

B *Execute the roll cast with enough power to lift the line from the water during the forward roll. At the moment when the line is airborne, release enough extra line (2) from the left hand to drop the fly on the new target.*

C *Done properly, the line and leader will unroll smoothly and effortlessly in a loop of decreasing size as it rolls to the target. Under ideal conditions the last bit of energy in the line (3) is expended as the fly touches the water like a tired insect.*

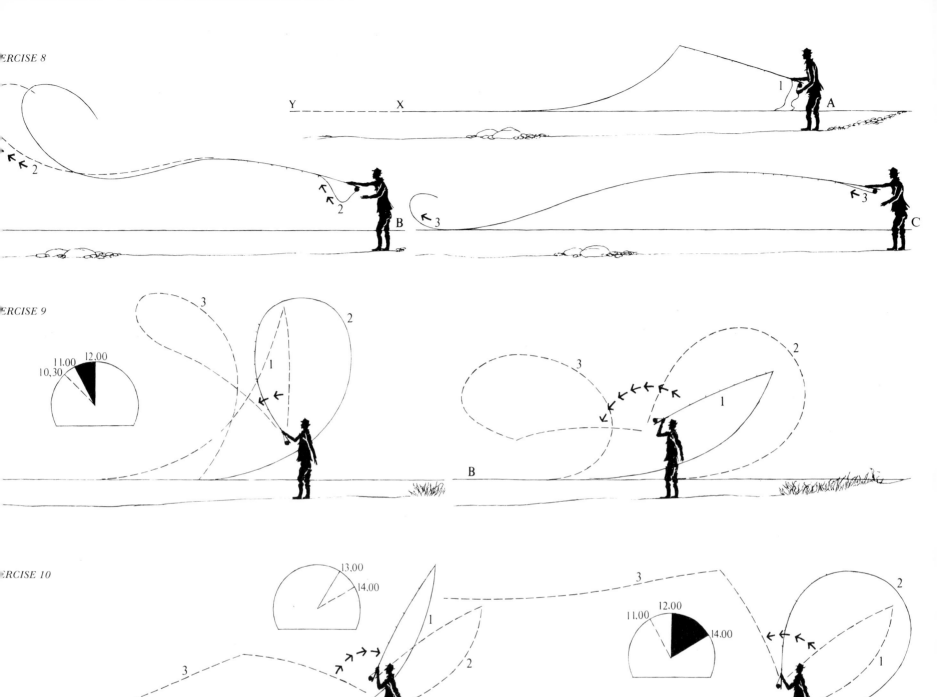

EXERCISE 8

EXERCISE 9

EXERCISE 10

EXERCISE 9

DEEP AND SHALLOW ROLL CAST LOOPS

In the roll cast, as in the overhead cast, a deep loop is more air resistant than a tight, shallow loop. A high, shallow loop lifts the line from the water, permitting one to shoot line for distance.

HIGH, SHALLOW LOOP

Drive the rod from 12:00 to 11:00 and drift to 10:30.
1 *High, tight bend.*
2 *Fast lift of line.*
3 *High, tight loop forms, lifting line quickly from water.*

LOW, DEEP LOOP

B *The low, deep loop is sometimes preferred for short casts.*
1 *Swing rod far back.*
2 *Low, slack bend.*
3 *Power stroke is slow, relatively long. The line rolls forward without lifting from the water. Remember that variations of any cast are based on a standard set of physical motions.*

EXERCISE 10

TIPPING THE ARC

(Using the roll cast as a pick-up for the overhead cast.) Frequently, after the angler has stripped in line on the retrieve following an overhead cast, he finds it to his advantage to use a roll cast for picking up the line and getting it into the air before making a fresh overhead cast to the target.

ROLL CAST PICKUP

A 1 *Slow, easy rod lift to position 13:00, then drift rod to about 14:00.*
2 *Loose line bend.*
3 *No slack in line.*

TIPPING OUT

B 1 *Start forward cast from position 14:00.*
2 *Loop forms small and low with fast, hard power stroke.*
3 *Stop power stroke at 12:00, drift to 11:00. When line is extended, start working out the line by false overhead casting before making the final cast.*

TIPS ON PRACTICE CASTING

1 *Don't force the cast. Remain relaxed and at ease. Remember that you cast with the arm, not the entire body.*
2 *Let an expert angler observe your casts. He can suggest ways in which you can improve your timing, distance, accuracy, and form.*
3 *Practice regularly, and in off-season.*

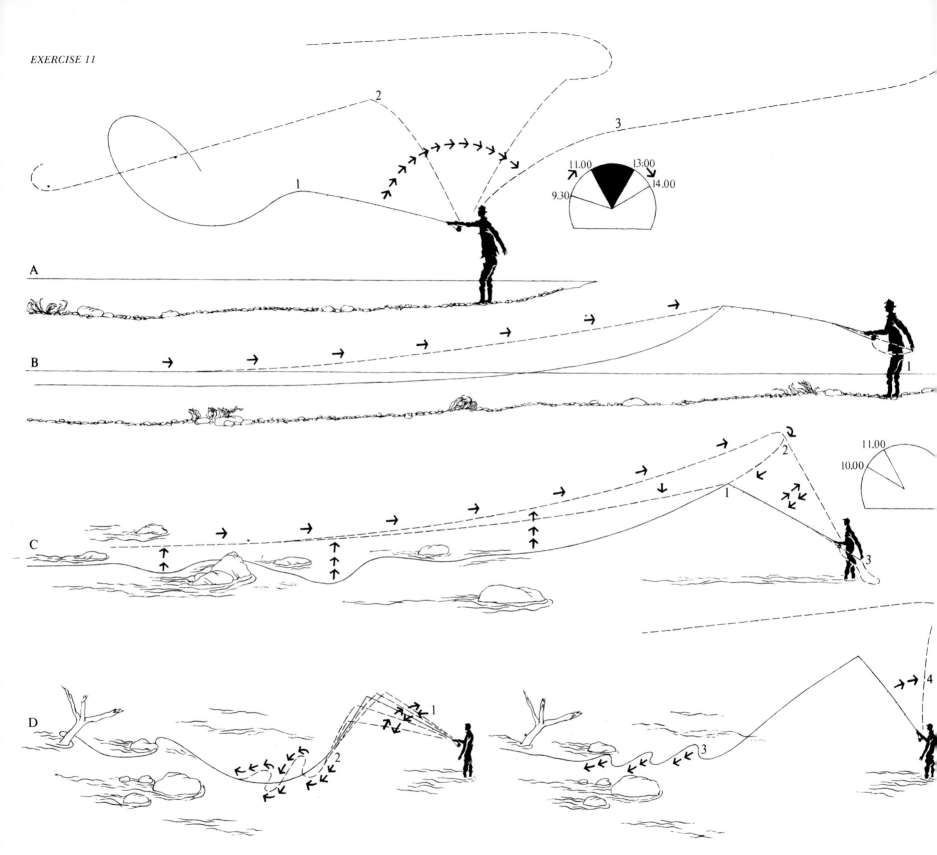

EXERCISE 11

THE PICKUP

FROM A ROLL CAST

A *This pickup is used when one wishes to cast to fish beyond the normal roll cast distance.*
1 *Execute roll cast.*
2 *Pickup 9:30 to 11:00 with moderate lift.*
3 *Power backcast 11:00 to 13:00 and drift rod to stop at 14:00. Then execute forward cast, shooting line.*

THE LEFT-HAND PULL

B 1 *Pull back on line with left hand before starting pickup to straighten line and bring it to surface of the water.*

THE SNAP PICKUP

C *For taking much slack or many bends out of a line before making an overhead cast.*
1 *With rod low, grasp line near stripping guide with left hand.*
2 *Pick up line with rod from 10:00 to 11:00 without pulling with left hand.*
3 *Pull with left hand as rod returns to low position. Take fresh grip on line just under the stripping guide, letting the slack fall at feet. Now execute regular pickup and cast.*

THE SNAKE PICKUP

D *Letting the current straighten the line for a pickup when casting downstream.*
1 *As line settles to the water at the end of the downstream cast, wave the rod left-to-right and throw bends into the line before it starts its downstream drift.*
2 *Current will carry fly and line in a natural drift (3) as bends of line all straighten out.*
4 *Execute snap pickup and overhead cast.*

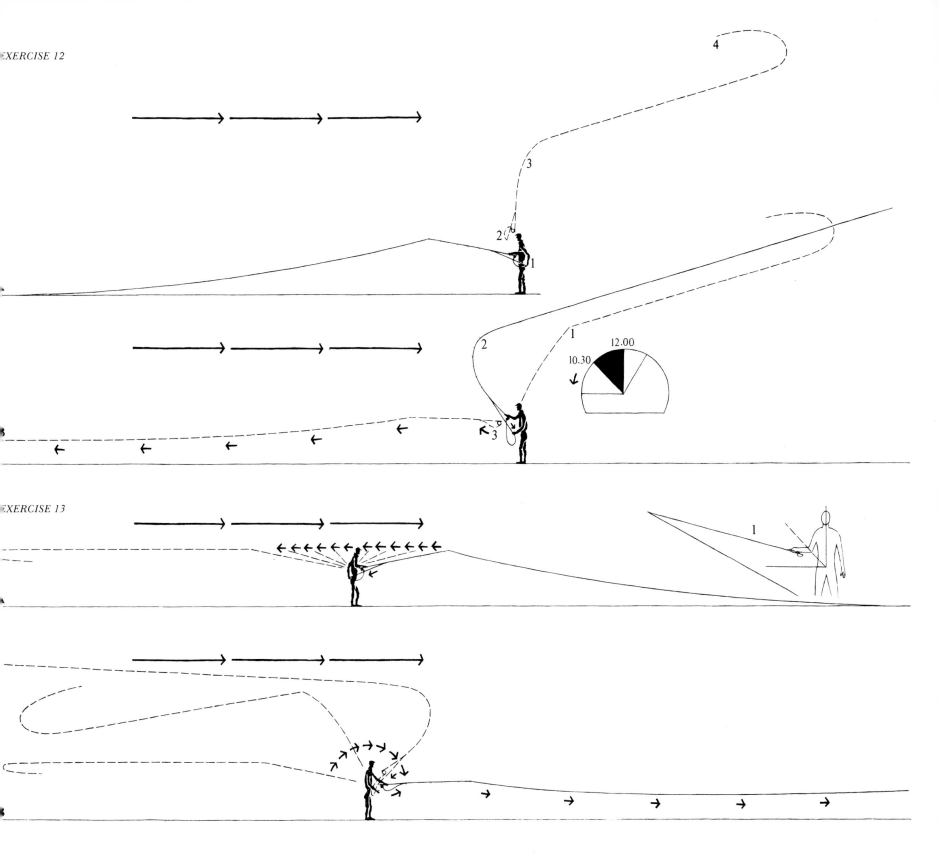

EXERCISE 12

CASTING IN HEAD-WINDS

HEAD-WIND BACKCAST

A 1 Left-hand pull.
  2 Raise left hand to head level on the backcast.
  3 High backcast.
  4 Keep the line loop small and tight.

THE FORWARD CAST

B 1 Start forward cast a moment before line is fully extended.
  2 Quick, powerful drive from 12:00 to 10:30. Haul down hard with left hand on line at peak of power stroke.
  3 Terminate cast low, shoot reserve line from left hand.

EXERCISE 13

CASTING IN TAIL WINDS

In casting into a headwind, the problem is to keep the forward cast from collapsing before the fly reaches the target. In tail wind casting, the backcast must not collapse.

SIDEARM PIVOT CAST

A 1 By keeping the rod below 45° elevation and casting to the side rather than overhead, effect of wind is minimized.
  2 Make backcast into wind by sidearm cast.
  3 Pivot body to face the wind at end of the backcast.

BACKCAST DOWNWIND

B 1 Before line can collapse, start a backcast downwind.
  2 Line-haul with left hand at power peak and pivot body downwind at end of power stroke.
  3 Finish cast low and shoot reserve line at end of cast.

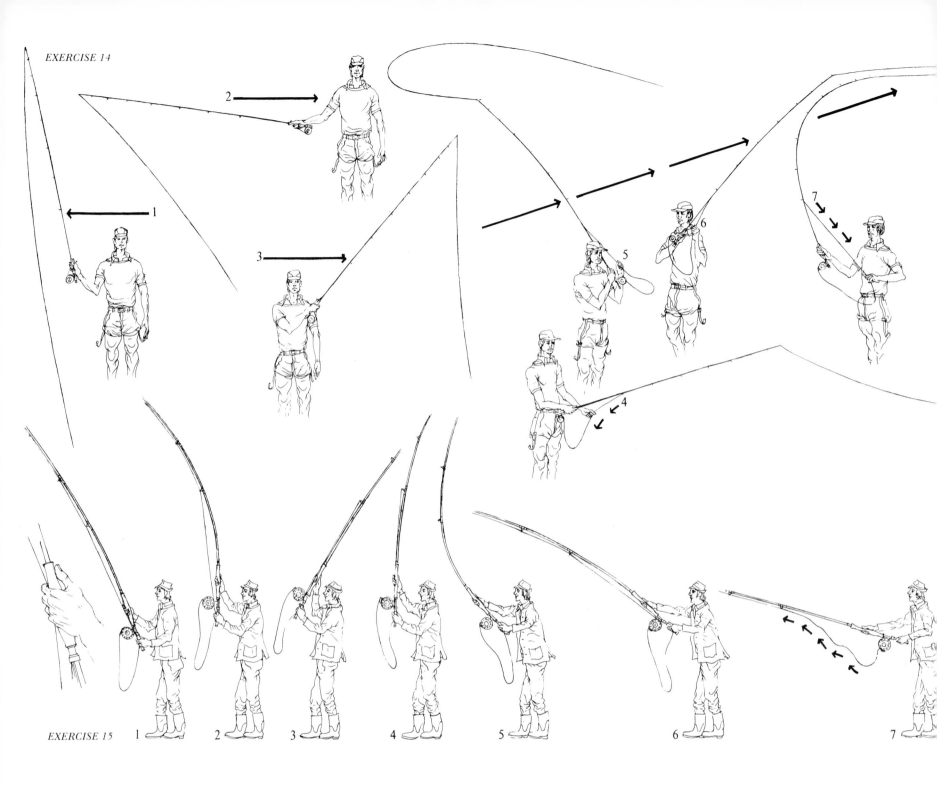

EXERCISE 14

CASTING IN CROSS-WINDS

The main problem of casting in a crosswind is that on the pickup and backcast, the line may strike the rod or body thus spoiling the cast.

WIND LEFT TO RIGHT

1 A normal pickup will cause the line to blow to the right, away from caster's body.

WIND RIGHT TO LEFT

2 If the wind velocity is low, you may be able to pick up the line successfully by swinging the rod far to the right on the pickup.

CROSS-CHEST PICKUP

3 With a stronger wind, the cross-chest type of pickup will place the line downwind of the caster's body. To overcome wind drift during the forward cast, turn the body into the wind before casting.

4 Line haul with left hand to straighten the line.

5 Pick up and swing the rod across chest so it comes back over the left shoulder.

6 Before starting the forward cast, turn body into the wind to deliver a change of direction cast.

7 Hand haul line while making forward cast slightly upwind of the target to offset the wind drift.

EXERCISE 15

THE TWO-HANDED FLY CAST

With very long salmon rods and some saltwater fly rods, a two-handed cast is necessary. The timing is the same as that of the one-handed cast, but the position of the left hand is different.

1 Line haul with left hand to take up slack and grasp lower grip with the left hand, which also holds the line from the rod.

2 Pick up, both hands.

3 Pause for the line to fly back.

4 Forward cast, using both hands.

5 Power stroke.

6 Follow-through.

7 Shoot the reserve line at the proper moment at end of the follow-through. Line is shot by releasing grip of left hand on the line, retaining grip on the rod.

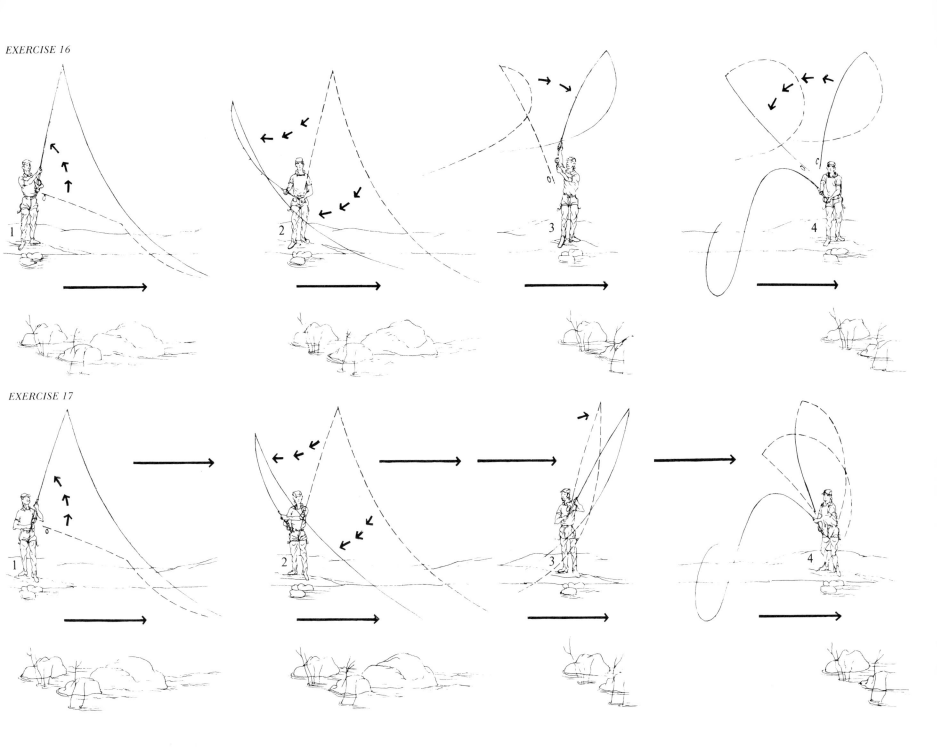

EXERCISE 16

1

2

3

4

EXERCISE 17

1

2

3

4

EXERCISE 16

THE SPEY CAST

This is a variation of the roll cast that is useful in overcoming the drift of a stream's current when casting across the current. The roll cast, as mentioned before, is used where there are obstructions behind the caster that prevent him from using the overhead cast and its long backcast. The current here drifts across the angler from his right to left.

1 *Elevate the rod in a normal roll cast manner.*
2 *At the peak of rod elevation, swing the rod tip to about a 45° angle to the right.*
3 *Now swing the rod back preparatory to making a roll cast. Turn body to right.*
4 *Make the roll cast with rod tip swung wide of the body, casting up-current.*

EXERCISE 17

THE DOUBLE SPEY CAST

This cast is designed to overcome the effects of both current and wind crossing the area of casting from the same direction. The problem here is that the wind may carry the line into the caster's rod or body when he tries to execute the final roll cast. The double spey cast is a combination of the spey cast just described and the cross-chest cast described in Exercise 15. It should not be attempted until both of the other casts have been mastered. It is described here as done with two hands, but can be done one-handed.

1 *Pick up by elevating the rod as for the spey cast.*
2 *At top of elevation swing rod to right to draw more line up-current.*
3 *As you start to swing the rod back to make a roll cast, swing the rod tip across your chest so the line will be able to roll on your left or downwind side. At the peak of the backswing, turn your body to face upwind.*
4 *Make a strong roll cast, keeping the loop as low and tight as possible to avoid wind drift of line.*

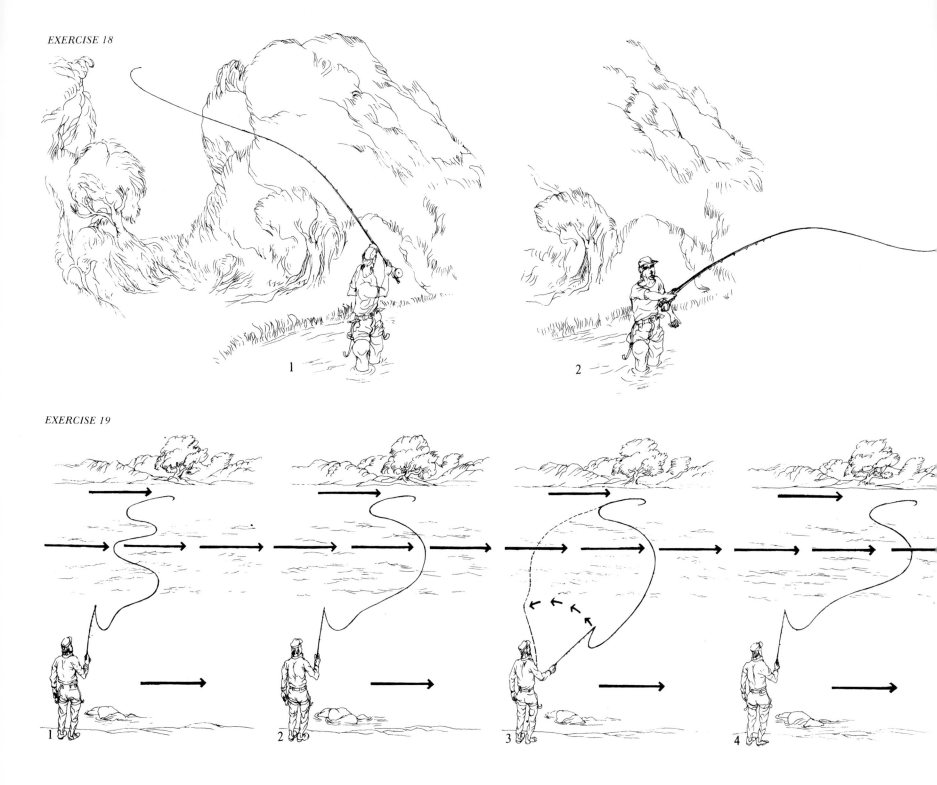

EXERCISE 18

CASTING TO A WINDOW

Once in a while a hole or "window" may appear in a wall of brush or trees along a stream bank. If you can direct your backcast to this window, you may be able to use the overhead cast rather than a roll cast to reach targets that would be out of reach of a roll cast on that stream.

1 *This usually calls for a high backcast with careful control of angle and height. Practice first with no fly on the line to avoid snagging the trees and brush.*

2 *The forward cast is made in the normal manner, but do not cast out more line than you can handle on the carefully controlled backcast to the window.*

EXERCISE 19

MENDING THE LINE

Sometimes you have to cast across a current to place the fly in a good drift in the quiet water beyond. The cast should be made with snake bends in the line, and the current may quickly pull the bends downstream, spoiling the drift of the fly. You can prolong the fly's drift if you "mend" the line by throwing an upstream loop into it as shown.

1 *Line position after casting with snake loops across current.*

2 *Current has carried midsection of line downstream and will soon spoil the drift of the fly.*

3 *Lift and throw the near section of the line upstream with a high left-handed lift and sweep of the rod.*

4 *After a short time the current will once again sweep the line downstream. This time it will be necessary to recast the line.*

It is seldom possible to "mend" the line more than once in a cast.

EXERCISE HINTS

1 *Exercise regularly.*
2 *But not when tired.*
3 *Keep a record.*
4 *Score your progress.*
5 *Strive for timing, accuracy, style.*
6 *Let an expert angler watch you perform at regular intervals.*

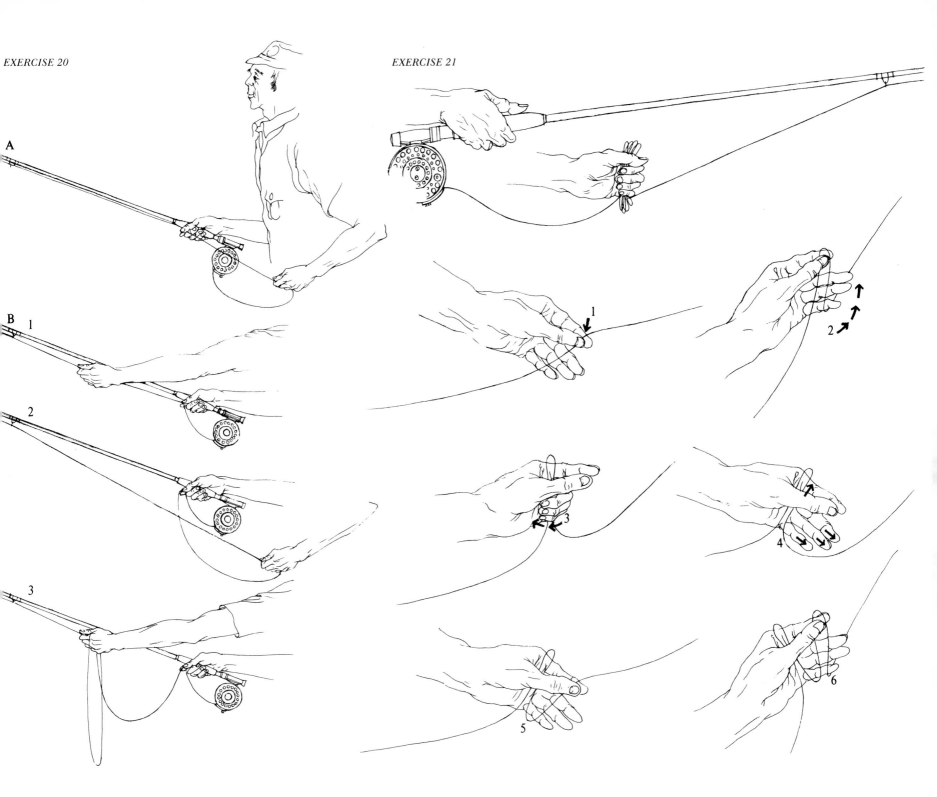

A

B 1

2

3

1

2

3

4

5

6

EXERCISE 20

THE STRIP
RETRIEVE

To retrieve line by the
stripping-in method, hold
the rod with the casting hand
so thumb and forefinger
touch, holding the line between thumb and forefinger.

A *Strip in line with the left hand
while keeping light tension on the
line with the casting hand.*

B *1, 2 For a longer, faster strip-
in, grasp the line ahead of the
casting hand, laying the line be-*

*tween the thumb and fore-
finger as it is stripped in.*

*3 Coil excess line on the ground,
or hold the line in coils with
the left hand.*

EXERCISE 21

THE FIGURE 8
RETRIEVE

A Many anglers prefer to store
retrieved line in the left hand
by balling the line in a continuous figure eight motion.
This is slower than the strip
retrieve, but does not require
that the rod hand hold the
line.

B *1 Hold the line between thumb
and forefinger of the left hand
as illustrated, with the other
three fingers held straight.*

*2 Move left hand up and for-
ward, gathering line under
the free fingers. Bring loop
into palm of hand.*

*3 Withdraw forefinger, pick up
another loop of line to the
palm.*

*4 Holding loop under thumb,
extend fingers.*

*5 Pick up fresh loop of line with
fingers.*

*6 Continue until enough line
has been picked up.*

BAIT-CASTING – AN AMERICAN SPECIALTY

Bait-casting has been described as the technique of casting an artificial lure or bait with a revolving-spool reel. Actually, this definition requires a bit of qualification. The true bait-casting reel and rod are specialized developments. Bait-casting, as the practicing angler defines it, means using this special tackle to cast artificial lures or baits to specific types of fish, notable the black basses, northern pike, and the like. The technique of bait-casting was primarily an American development of the nineteenth century, but the effectiveness of the equipment on both fresh and salt water small to medium game fish has caused anglers in many parts of the world to take up this specialized form of casting.

The modern baitcasting rod is a fairly short, fiberglass shaft that comes in at least four weight classes.

Class	Lure weight (max.)	Line test	
Extra light	3/8 oz. (10.7 gr)	4–8 lb	(1.8–3.6 kg)
Light	1/2 oz. (14.3 gr)	6–12 lb	(2.7–5.4 kg)
Medium	3/4 oz. (21.5 gr)	10–20 lb	(4.5–9 kg)
Heavy	1 1/4 oz. (36 gr)	18–25 lb	(8.2–11.4 kg)

Suitable rods vary from 5½ to 6½ ft (1.7–2 m), but a 6 ft (1.8 m) shaft is most popular. As in fly casting, the casting motion is largely controlled by the forearm, bending from the elbow, with only slight wrist bending. But the motion and "feel" of the cast is quite different from that of the fly rod. Bait-casting was originally developed to permit the angler to place a relatively small bait or lure with precise control of accuracy and distance. A typical situation would be to cast an artificial frog on top of a lily pad 33 feet (10 m) from the caster, then pull the frog off the lily pad with the line and "swim" it through the water in a realistic manner. The "medium" class of bait-casting rod is by far the most popular.

The modern bait-casting reel is a direct development of the first multiplying-gear reels perfected by Kentucky jewelers as early as 1810. Present-day reels have the star drag and a free-spool device, and many are equipped with a level-wind feature. Quite a few now have an anti-backlash device built into the reel. This greatly assists the beginning angler in learning how to control his casts without getting a bird's nest of loose line in his reel. The great appeal of bait-casting tackle is its versatility. A good outfit can be used for casting, trolling, live bait or bottom fishing, and will perform very well in any of these situations.

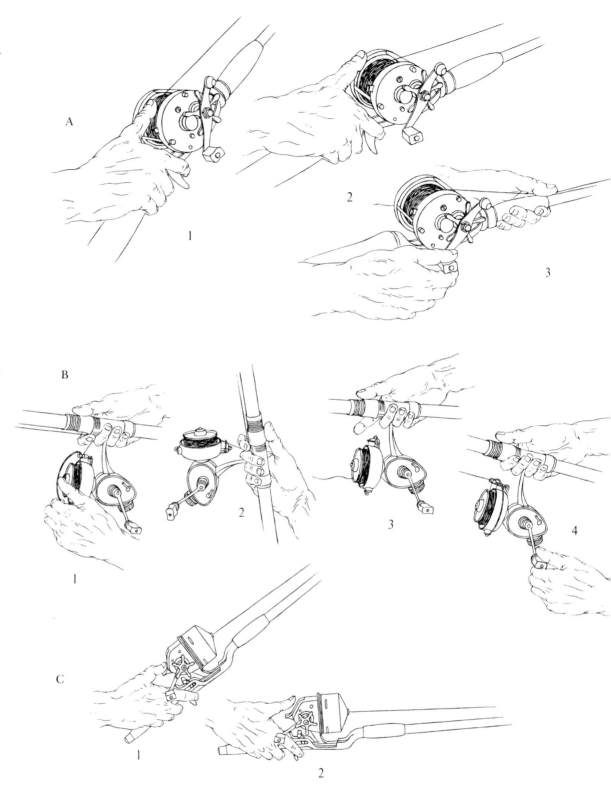

A BAIT-CASTING REEL

1 Put thumb on spool to prevent it from turning faster than line goes out.
2 Lift thumb when no more line goes out.
3 Add thum pressure when line is retrieved for tight, smooth spooling.

SPINNING AND SPIN-CASTING REELS

Fixed-spool reels are divided into two classes, the open- faced type (B) known as spinning reels, and the closed-face type (C) known as spin-casting reels.

B The spinning reel is mounted under the rod and the line, while casting, is controlled by the forefinger.

1 Forefinger picks up line, disengage bail.
2 Forefinger holds line during back-cast.
3 Forefinger releases line in fore-cast.
4 Rotating handle makes bail pick up line.

C 1 Thumb lever releases line during the cast.
2 Lifting thumb stops line from paying out.

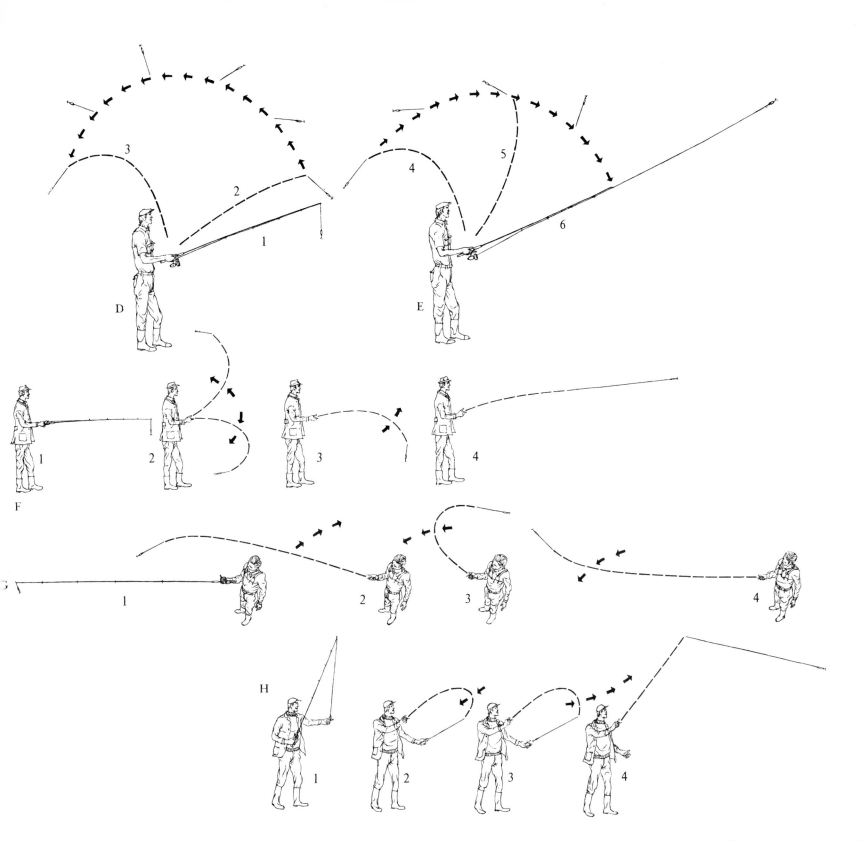

D MAKING THE BACK-CAST

Lure hangs down 1 ft (30 cm) from tiptop of rod.
1. *Starting position, thumb on spool. (Line over forefinger if spinning reel is used.)*
2. *Rod shaft is lifted smoothly and swiftly.*
3. *Rod is stopped at this point. Weight of lure bends the shaft.*

E MAKING THE POWER CAST

4. *Forward motion of rod begins at this point with no pause between end of back cast and start of power cast.*
5. *Thumb is taken off spool at this point. (Forefinger releases line if spinning reel is used.)*
6. *Thumb touches spool for distance control.*

F THE UNDERHAND CAST

This cast is useful for casting under overhanging limbs or brush.
1. *Start with rod flat.*
2. *Whip rod tip up, but keep rod shaft flat. Whip rod tip down, "loading" rod while shaft is held flat.*
3. *Release line and lure as tip starts to whip up after "loading."*
4. *Follow-through.*

G THE SIDE CAST

1. *Starting position, hold rod horizontaly pointing at target.*
2. *Move rod slightly to the right.*
3. *Forward motion begins at this point. Add wrist emphasis to increase power.*
4. *Follow-through.*

H THE SLINGSHOT CAST

The slingshot cast is a good cast to use where one cannot do the overhead cast.
1. *Drop lure halfway down rod, grasp lure in left hand.*
2. *Bend rod by pulling back on lure while taking careful aim.*
3. *Release lure, then the line. Lure will shoot toward target.*
4. *Follow-through.*

349

DISTANCE CASTING WITH THE SURF ROD

It is the ambition of every surf caster to be able to cast "a country mile." Whether one uses the "conventional" reel with revolving spool or a spinning reel, the unit of rod and reel is used to impart motion to the weighted lure. The lure in turn pulls the line out from the reel as it flies through space.

With a revolving spool reel the angler holds the thumb of his reel hand against the spool until the power stroke has been completed, at which moment the

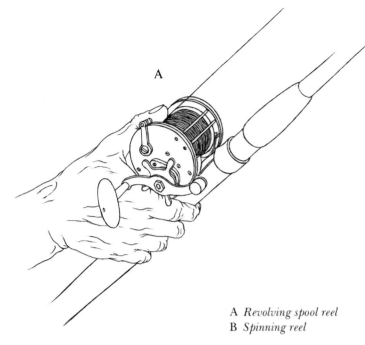

A

thumb is lifted from the reel permitting the lure and the line to fly through space toward the target. Light thumb pressure on the spool thereafter is necessary to prevent an over-run of the spool resulting in a backlash or tangle of line on the rotating reel spool.

Spinning reel spool does not revolve. With the pickup bail open, the fisherman holds the line with forefinger of the reel hand, letting it go at the end of the power stroke, allowing the lure to fly toward the target area. Motion is smoothly continuous with body weight flowing from right leg to left.

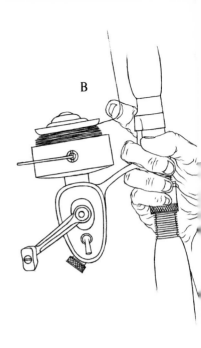

B

A *Revolving spool reel*
B *Spinning reel*

1   2   3   4

Before starting the distance cast, angler pauses momentarily, weight on both feet, adjusts the "drop" of the lure to between 4 and 5 feet (about 1.35 m). The angler illustrated is using a fiberglass rod 10 1/2 feet long (3.2 m), and a "conventional" (revolving spool) reel with a capacity of 250 yards (225 m) of 36-lb. (16.3 kg) test line. Braided Dacron line is best with reels of revolving spool type. Monofilament line is favored for spinning reels. For distance casting, lure weight of 3 1/2 to 4 1/2 ounces works best.

2 Standing with target directly to his left, 90° left of the way he is facing, angler extends rod full-arm to his right, in the opposite direction of the target. Caster's body weight is on the right foot. He fixes his eyes on the lure and watches its path as he starts to cast. Distance casting of this kind is usually done where the beach is unobstructed with smooth, firm footing. It is effective when one has to cast into a strong wind, or to fish showing beyond the normal range of less specialized casting tackle.

3 Starting the cast, the angler begins to shift his weight from left to right and at the same time pivots his body toward the left. He also lifts his right hand to the position shown before his face while bringing the left hand to the left. As he does this, he drives the rod strongly to the left, butt-first as he would a spear. This causes the lure to trail out behind the rod and the line, putting it into the proper position for the remainder of the power stroke. Action is unhurried, with a smooth power delivery.

4 The caster has now turned completely to the left, facing the target for the first time. He starts the power stroke when he thrusts forward with the right hand while pulling back equally hard with the left. Tha casting rod is a lever, the fulcrum is the fisherman's right hand. Acceleration of the lure now is rapid with maximum stress on the rod, the line, and the angler. Most surf casting rods are built of fiberglass, a material that takes heavy abuse, keeping strength, flexibility, good appearance, and reliable performance.

5 The caster's weight is now almost fully on his left leg as he continues to apply power to the rod with the strong push-pull of his arms. As the lure passes over his head it is at maximum speed and starts to overtake the tip of the rod. When the rod shaft is 45° beyond the vertical, angler releases his thumb or forefinger from the reel's spool or line and the lure begins free flight in the direction of target. Learning the precise moment when the lure must be released is a function of practice and more practice.

6 The follow-through is important. The eye of the caster remains on the lure in flight and his thumb touches the revolving spool or the uncurling line ever so lightly in an effort to control the lure's trajectory. While course of the lure cannot be swung right or left once it is in flight, range can be controlled to a considerable degree. Becoming an expert at distance casting is a combination of steady practice and adequate instruction. The best distance casters are not always the best fishermen, but they have a big advantage.

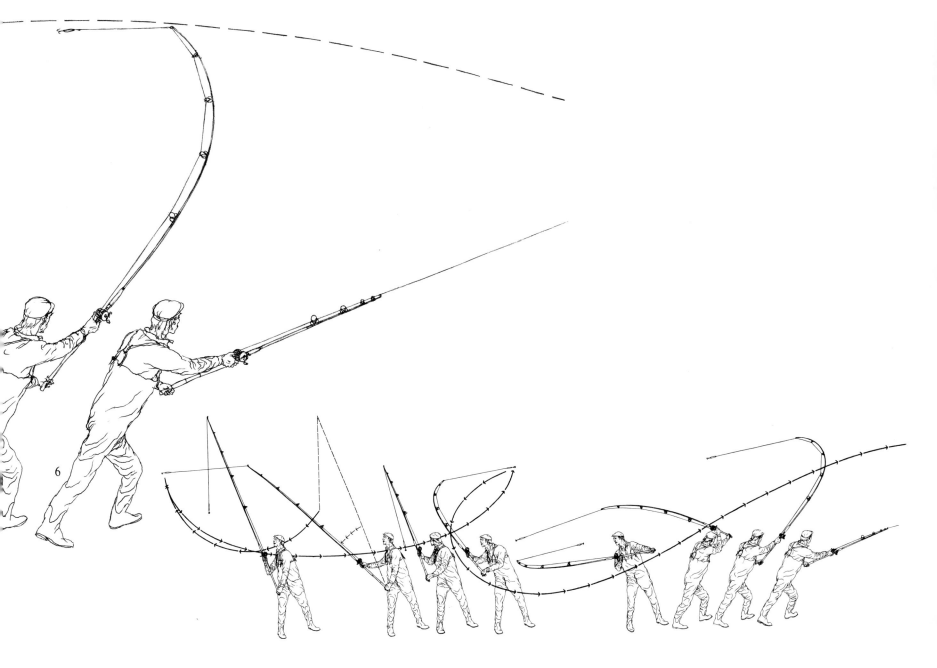

HOW TO SOLVE YOUR CASTING PROBLEMS

Problem: The rod "collapses" when you try to make a distance cast.

Solution: Don't try to force the cast. Relax and cast more slowly, relying on style and form rather than brute strength to put the line out. Don't try to cast or false-cast with more line out than you can comfortably handle. Learn to shoot reserve line for distance. Finally, shift to one weight lighter line if the line appears to overpower the rod when you reach out for distance.

Problem: The line "collapses" in a heap in front of you when you cast, especially when casting into a breeze.

Solution: You may be trying to cast too long a line. Reduce the length of line you try to cast. Improve the timing of your transition from backcast to forward cast. Learn how to achieve maximum loading of the rod in the forward cast while keeping the line loops tight and low. In windy weather, shift to one weight heavier line.

Problem: A new or strange rod does not give you the casting range and accuracy you normally expect.

Solution: Select a lighter or heavier line that gives a better match to the rod's inherent action.

Problem: A floating line refuses to float.

Solution: Clean the line and dress it with a good floating line dressing compound.

Problem: The leader or trace becomes curly in storage.

Solution: Stretch out the leader and restore its limpness by rubbing it briskly within a fold of soft sheet rubber held between thumb and forefinger.

Problem: You miss hooking too many fish.

Solution: Sharpen your hooks with a fine oilstone.

Problem: Fish swim out of range before you can complete the false casts to lengthen your line to the required distance.

Solution: Learn to "shoot" extra line by the doublehaul or any other method so you can extend your line without having to resort to several false casts.

Problem: The line strikes the water or ground behind you during the backcast.

Solution: Improve your timing of the transition between backcast and forward cast. Don't let your rod dip excessively beyond the one o'clock position when you pause on the backcast. Watch the line by turning your body. Start the forward cast a fraction of a second sooner, but not so soon as to "crack" the line like a whip. Have an expert observe and correct your casting difficulties.

Problem: You have trouble casting and controlling large, air-resistant streamers and poppers.

Solution: Shift to a combination of line (usually weight-forward) and tapered leader better suited to handling air-resistant lures. Slow down your casting rhythm and learn to use power without losing good form and style.

Problem: Your dry fly "drags" too much in a current.

Solution: Learn how to make the snake cast which puts loose bends of line on the water when accomplished. The bends will straighten out with the current, giving your fly a little more driftless floating time. Learn how to mend the line to prolong a good fly drift.

Problem: You have difficulty changing casting angle to follow moving fish with your casts.

Solution: Practice the various forms of change-of-direction casts to correct this deficiency.

Problem: Other anglers hook fish almost under your feet.

Solution: Pay more attention to the water close by. Alternate long casts with short casts. Learn how to cast accurately to fish with only the leader or trace clear of the rod tip.

Problem: Rolling or "bulging" trout refuse dry flies in low, clear water.

Solution: Shift to the smallest flies and the lightest, longest leaders and tippets you have. Fish with great caution to avoid noise and disturbance.

Problem: You cannot raise fish in high, fast, dirty water.

Solution: Shift to sinking line and leader, and a highly visible, attractor type of wet fly or nymph.

Problem: You cannot cast well at night, when fishing is often the best.

Solution: Begin practicing casting in darkness by starting your practice just before evening twilight and extending it into the period of darkness. Try to develop your "feel" for the tackle. Perfect a style of casting that is simple, does not get you into trouble with snarled lines and other problems. Remember that plenty of practice is needed to train your hands, arms, and muscles to feed back information to your brain when your eyes are largely useless in darkness. Equip yourself with a good caster's night-light, but use it only sparingly. Develop your night vision. You'll be surprised at how much you can see on a dark night, once your eyes are adjusted to the darkness.

RULES FOR SUCCESSFUL FLY CASTING

Take your time. Don't try to force the cast. Remember that it is skill rather than brute strength that counts. Seek to develop accuracy and control. Casting distance will take care of itself.

Do your practice casting with no fly on the line, and have an expert analyze your style.

Approach a stream or lakeside with caution. Avoid unnecessary commotion when entering the water.

Don't crowd other anglers on the water. Practice good fishing sportsmanship.

Learn to select flies that match the natural conditions of food available to the fish.

When trout or other fish are wary, switch to smaller flies and a lighter tippet.

Do not fish one spot continuously if it fails to produce fish. Move on, but plan to return under different light and weather conditions. A change of light, weather, or time of day overcomes the natural shyness of the fish.

If you plan to release the fish, use barbless hooks to reduce the chance of causing them injury.

Select and use tackle proper for the fishing.

Match rod, line, and leader for casting efficiency.

Study the waters where you fish. Learn where the fish lie and how to present your flies to them.

Fish dry flies upstream when possible to let the floating fly drift downstream in a natural manner.

Fish wet flies, nymphs, and streamers across the current or downstream so their underwater action will resemble that of natural live bait.

Fish fly rod, plugs, and surface poppers slowly and deliberately, especially when after bass.

Develop your sense of feel via the rod and line so you can detect the lightest touch of a fish.

Don't fish or practice casting when you are tired or in a nonfishing frame of mind.

Keep records of your fishing activities.

Observe fishing laws and regulations.

Join a fishing club or association with an active program of conservation and restoration of waters.

Do not be ashamed to eat what you catch, but kill only those fish you intend to eat and release the rest. Encourage good fishing manners in others by setting a good personal example.

FLY TYING AND OTHER HOBBIES

To look for hobbies within the great hobby of fishing is like looking for pearls while eating oysters. Yet, at least three pearls of hobbies are practiced by fishermen, hobbies that yield rewards more tangible than a pile of fish bones after a sea food dinner. Fly tying is one of the oldest of hobbies, and it is more than a mere hobby because flies are essential to the art of fly fishing.

Learning to tie flies for fishing is a three-fold art. First, you must know the names and uses of all of the various kinds of feathers, fibers, furs, and other materials used in the tying of fishing flies. Next, you must develope skill in using the tools of the trade and master the basic steps in creating a fly that will ttract and catch fish. Finally, you must learn how to discover from the stomach contents of the fish themselves what natural flies the fish are taking and reproduce imitations of the naturals that the fish will accept in their environment.

Fly fishermen who tie their own flies enjoy double satisfaction. They know the joy of creating something beautiful and useful with their own hands, and they have the added pleasure of catching fish with flies and lures of their own personal design and creation. Fly tying now is easily learned and beginners often progress quickly from tying the traditional patterns to modifying old patterns and creating new ones to answer problems created by fish in their local waters.

A different kind of hobby is that of taxidermy, the art of preserving the fish itself for future observation and appreciation. There are a number of ways to preserve fish for display, several of which are described in the following pages. Like fly tying, taxidermy often progresses from the amateur status to that of the professional.

A third hobby based on fish and fishing is the creation of Japanese fish prints. This is a true decorative art form, yet one that is easily mastered by relatively inexperienced people. Oddly enough quite a few individuals have become interested in the sport of fishing by entering the sport through the back door, so to speak, of fish printing. Japanese fish printing differs from taxidermy in one important aspect. While the taxidermist strives to make a life-like reproduction of the original fish, the fish printer works to create the illusion of a fish without resorting to physical preservation of the body or skin of the subject. But despite their differences, all three hobbies develop one's powers of creative ability.

353

TYPES OF FLIES

Beginners at angling and non-anglers invariably are mystified by the great number and variety of artificial flies. Each recognized pattern has its own special name which may commemorate the fly's inventor, a friend of the inventor, or some whimsical place, thing, or event of the inventor's fishing experience. Witness a few of the more fanciful names. Royal Coachman. Woolly Worm. Zulu. Professor. Artful Dodger. Queen of the Waters. Irresistable. Ratfaced MacDougal.

While there are hundreds of named flies, there is only a handful of distinct fly families. These can be described by just six family names. Within each family there may be many variants, but the purpose and design of variants within each family remains the same. For the purpose of this discussion, the families are:

Dry flies (trout): Dry flies are probably the most highly refined of all flies. They are tiny bits of steel and fluff designed to float delicately on the surface film of water where they simulate recently hatched aquatic flies, drying their virgin wings before taking initial flight. They also are designed to resemble egg-laying females dipping to the water to deposit eggs, and spent adults at the final stage of their brief lifespan.

Wet flies (trout): Wet flies designed primarily for trout are tied to resemble adult natural flies that have fallen into the water and are drifting beneath the surface film, or the larvae and nymphs of aquatic insects that live beneath the surface. They are heavier than dry flies, although not always larger. They include many flies that resemble terrestrial insects that frequently fall into water and are consumed by trout in the natural state.

Special wet flies (trout and other game): This family includes a number of larger wet flies that are not in the true streamer category. Included are shrimp models, worm flies, grasshopper flies, and flies that resemble no creature normally found in nature, but which have proven attractive power.

Salmon flies: While salmon will sometimes take the dry fly, most salmon flies are tied with hair or feather wings to make them resemble small bait or forage fish on which salmon normally feed. They are large, frequently gaudy, and visually attractive.

Bass flies (fresh water): In North America especially, fresh water bass respond enthusiastically to large surface-floating flies made to resemble frogs, mice, baby ducks, and other creatures that make a commotion at the surface when swimming.

Salt water flies: Salt water fly fishing is growing rapidly in popularity and several subfamilies of flies have been developed specifically for salt water species of game fish. These flies include streamers types, surface poppers, and weighted flies for deep fishing. They are the largest of all flies and very often the easiest for a beginner to tie.

The flies presented here have been selected to represent the six major families of flies just mentioned, and for their proven effectiveness in attracting a wide variety of fresh and salt water game fish.

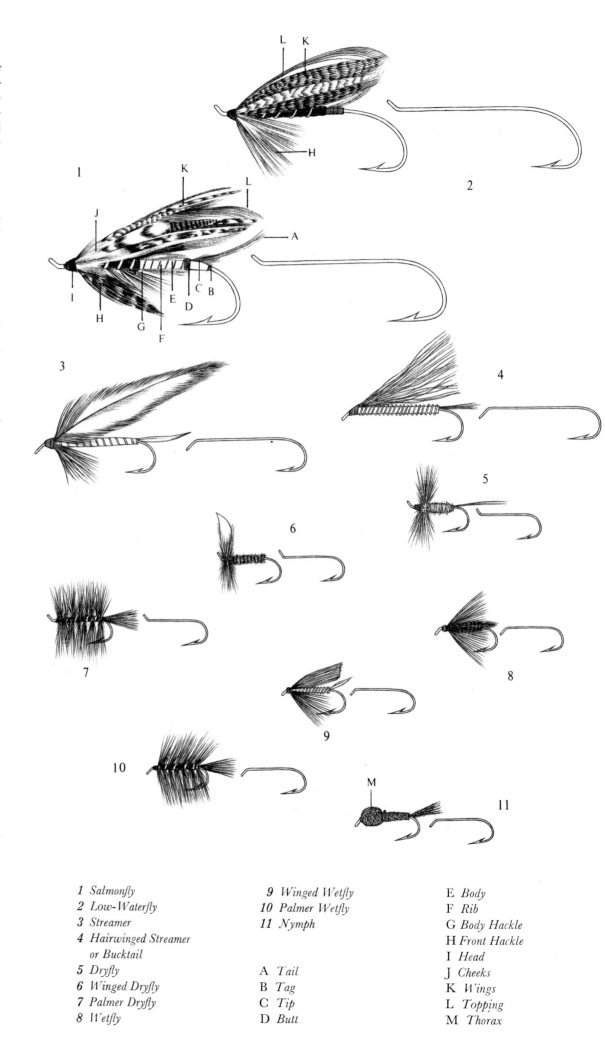

1 Salmonfly	9 Winged Wetfly	E Body
2 Low-Waterfly	10 Palmer Wetfly	F Rib
3 Streamer	11 Nymph	G Body Hackle
4 Hairwinged Streamer		H Front Hackle
or Bucktail		I Head
5 Dryfly	A Tail	J Cheeks
6 Winged Dryfly	B Tag	K Wings
7 Palmer Dryfly	C Tip	L Topping
8 Wetfly	D Butt	M Thorax

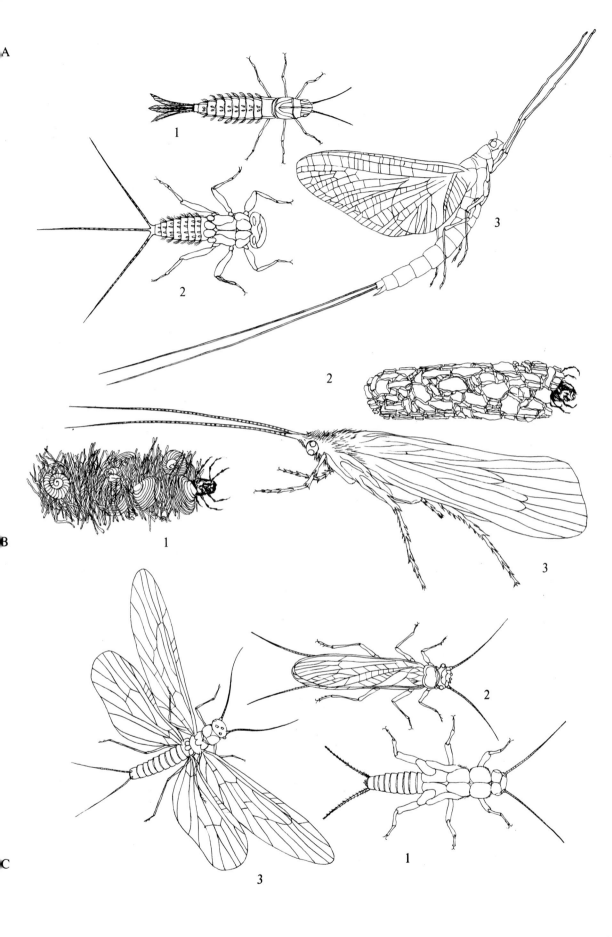

ENTOMOLOGY

By inspecting the natural foods one finds in stomachs of freshly caught fish, one can quickly discover the types of flies and insects the fish are taking. Much has been written about the need to "match the hatch" where flies are concerned. Understanding the major families of flies and aquatic insects helps greatly in making a wise choice of artificial fly to present to the fish in stream or lake. The succession will vary from stream to stream and common names will vary from region to region, but the principal groups will be the same everywhere.

Ephemeroptera: mayflies and up-wing flies.
Trichoptera: sedge flies and caddis flies.
Plecoptera: stoneflies.
Diptera: black gnats and black flies.

All are closely related to fresh water. Eggs are laid by the adult females in or on the water where they sink to the bottom and eventually hatch into larvae that, after several moults, finally seek the surface and emerge as winged adults.

The larvae of *Ephemeroptera* in their final stages are called nymphs and are important food for fish. The fly that emerges from the nymphal case is called a subimago or dun. After some days of maturing, the duns undergo a final moult and mating takes place. The females drop the ripe eggs into the water where they eventually develop into larvae and nymphs, repeating the reproductive cycle.

The larvae of *Trichoptera,* the caddis flies, are notable for encasing themselves in protective sheaths of bits of wood, grains of sand, and other small debris. They pupate inside the self-made "houses" and finally emerge from the water to shed the pupal skin and take up a relatively short existance as a winged insect. The eggs are eventually laid in water to repeat the age-old life cycle.

Stoneflies, *Plecoptera*, are of the greatest importance for fly fisherman on fast streams with gravel bottom. The nymphs resemble those of the mayflies, but bear two tails. They crawl ashore for the final moult to the mature fly. Stoneflies have two pairs of wings and, at rest, keep the wings flat on the body, whereas caddis flies at rest keep the wings flat to the sides and mayflies carry theirs erect.

Black gnats, "no-see-'ums," and black flies are members of the group known as *Simulidae,* part of the larger group of *Diptera* or two-winged flies. In spite of their small size they are important food for fish in running streams. Mature females bite humans and animals to obtain the blood they apparently need to form the eggs they eventually lay in or close to fast running water.

The knowledgeble fly fisherman trains himself to recognize the various aquatic insects and their larvae that inhabit the waters where he fishes, and thus is better able to "match the hatch" with artificials. He also learns when the various important hatches of insects may be expected to take place, and where, so as to be present for the excellent fishing that usually takes place at these favorable times.

A MAYFLIES
1 *Nymph*
2 *Nymph*
3 *Imago or adult*

B CADDIS FLIES
1 *Nymph*
2 *Nymph*
3 *Caddis fly*

C STONEFLIES
1 *Nymph*
2 *Stonefly at rest*
3 *Stonefly in flight*

TOOLS FOR FLY TYING

Good tools are important for success in any handcraft, especially in fly tying. The first and most important tool is a good fly vise to hold the hook firmly while the fly is being dressed. For turning various materials around the hook shank, hackle pliers are essential. Medium size is the best to start with. In many instances they act as a "third hand." A pair of tweezers with fine points is needed for grasping small hooks and tiny bits of feather. To part materials and to pick out dubbing on fur bodies, one must have a dubbing needle. This is easily made by mounting a darning needle in a small wooden handle. The dubbing needle is also handy for lacquering the fly head and removing lacquer from the hook eye.

Small scissors of surgical quality are essential for cutting fine materials. Many tyers keep handy a second set of older scissors for cutting rough material. To slice materials close to the hook shank, a razor blade is frequently used, but a sharp art or hobby knife is better. A thread bobbin holder is another important tool. It helps to maintain proper tension on the thread and does away with the need to cut lengths of thread to suit the work. All flies are finished with the so-called whip finish knot. This can be made with the fingers, but a whip finishing tool is a big help, especially on smaller flies.

Finally, one needs a comfortable table to which the vise can be clamped, and good lighting. Tools and the various tying materials should be stored in a small-parts chest. Many tyers find that a pair of close work 2× or 3× magnifying eyeglasses help to relieve eyestrain. Tools and materials should be kept in the fly tying kit box or chest when not in use.

MATERIALS

Only the very best quality hooks should be used. Hooks are discussed elsewhere in the book, but special attention to standard fly models is in order. As a rule, a hook with a turned-up eye (eye turned away from the hook point) is best for dry flies and a turned-down eye (eye turned toward the hook point) is best for wet flies, but occasionally this rule is not observed. The two most popular older hook bends are the Round Bend and the Limerick Bend (see section on hooks for illustrations). In recent years, especially in the United States, the Eagle Claw hook style has become popular. If the tip of the hook point is turned outward to the right when holding the point up and the eye toward you, this is called a "snecked" point. The reverse is a "reversed" point.

The thread used for tying the fly should be a good grade of silk designed for this work, and should be waxed before use. Several special types of thread are used to achieve special effects.

Gossamer: An extremely fine silk used for the smallest and lightest of flies.

Marabou floss: Two-stranded silk that is easily separated. Holds color well.

Stout floss: Heavier than marabou, used on many salmon flies and other larger models.

Cellulite floss body silk: A special rayon silk that is

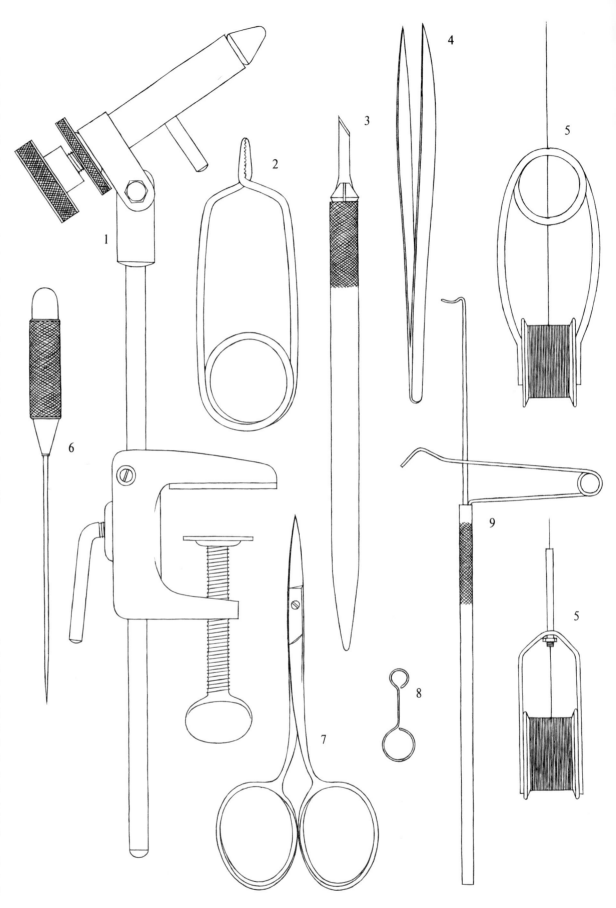

TOOLS FOR FLY
TYING

1 Fly vise
2 Hackle pliers
3 Hobby knife
4 Tweezers

5 Bobbin in holder
6 Dubbing needle
7 Surgical scissors
8 Hackle guard
9 Whip finisher

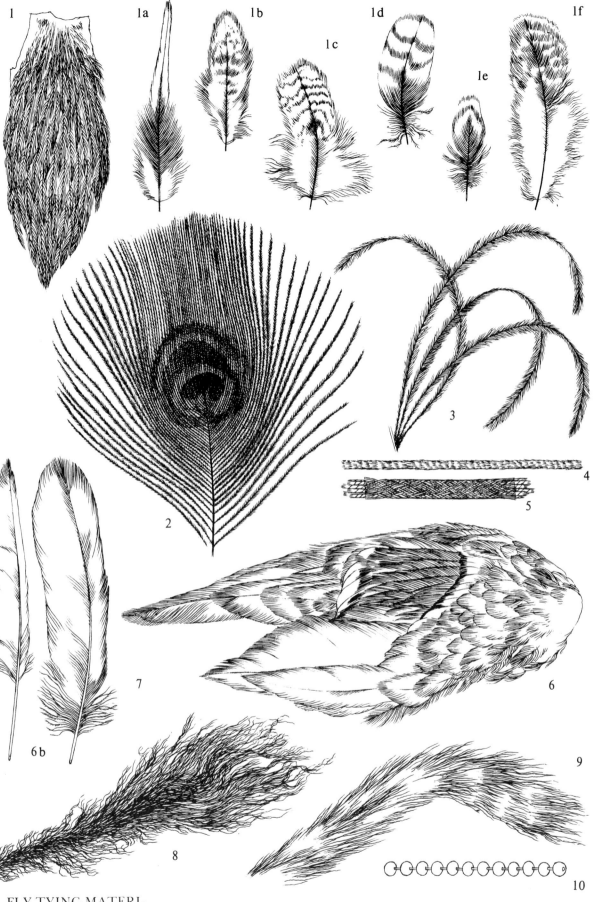

transparent when lacquered, allowing underlying colors to shine through for special effects.

Chenille: A fuzzy silk suitable for nymph bodies, streamers, and various wet fly types.

Fluorescent thread: Specially treated fibers that glow under ultraviolet light, increasing visibility of flies in daytime in clouded water. Available in thin floss, wool yarn, chenille.

Wool yarn: Frequently used to build up a rough-looking body in wet or dry flies.

Tinsels: Thin metalic ribbons or threads in various colors, designed to impart flash and glitter to fly bodies. Synthetic plastic "Mylar" tinsel is now widely used, especially in the United States.

Wire: Gold and silver wires are often used to give a special effect on fly bodies. Thin lead wire is occasionally used to add weight to wet flies that are designed to be fished very deep.

Body and wings of a fly are built up of a variety of types of feather, thread, wool, and similar materials, each pattern according to a carefully worked out routine or sequence of application, which is dealt with later in this section. Important materials follow.

Hackle: The most essential part of the tier's collection. Hackles represent the legs and wings of the fly, and in dry flies constitute the portion that keeps the fly afloat on the surface film. Obtained primarily from domestic fowl body feathers, but also include feathers from partridge, swan, pheasant, grouse, duck, goose, jay, guinea fowl, and snipe.

Body material: Usually a form of fur that is glued to thread, then wrapped onto the hook shank to form the body. Includes seal and hare fur, hare's ear, ram's wool, mohair, mole fur, rabbit fur.

Herls: Herl refers to strands obtained from whole feathers, lengths of quill split away from the main quill with very short side fibers or "flue" adhering to the strip of quill. From the following birds: swan, ostrich, heron, turkey, goose, magpie tail, cock pheasant, peacock.

Material for wings: Most salmon and trout fly wings are made from tail and wing feathers of such birds as mallard duck, blackbird, grouse, jay, various owls, partridge, jungle fowl, peacock, etc. Wings are also sometimes tied with bucktail or polar bear hair.

Other materials that are needed include solid wax for waxing the thread, clear varnish for the final finishing coat, lacquer for building up heads and solid bodies, bead chain for making eyes, an assortment of various sizes and models of hooks for the styles of flies that are to be tied. Fly tying materials can be purchased at many sporting goods stores and complete tying kits are offered by a number of manufacturers. Kits include complete instructions on how to use the various tools and how to tie examples of popular styles of flies.

In fly tying, as in any other handcraft, the key to success is patience and attention to details. It serves no purpose to rush the work. But beginners should remember that every expert was once a beginner, and the fish themselves don't really care whether a fly was tied by a professional or an amateur.

FLY TYING MATERIALS

1	Cock neck
1a	Cock hackle
1b	Hen hackle
1c	Partridge hackle
1d	Woodcock hackle
1e	Snipe hackle
1f	Grouse hackle
2	Peacock eye
3	Ostrich herls
4	Chenille yarn
5	Mylar piping
6	Mallard duck wing
6b	Mallard feather
7	Goose feather
8	Calf tail
9	Squirrel tail
10	Ball chain for eyes

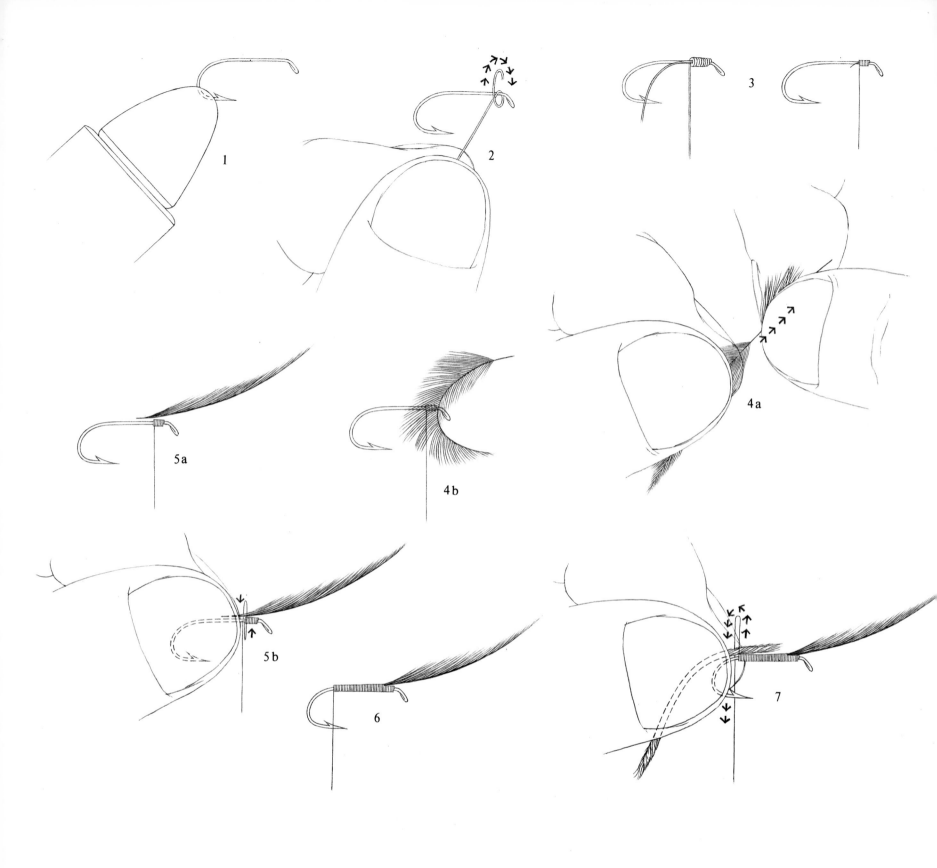

RED TAG WET FLY

A simple pattern, easy for beginners.

Materials.
Hook size: 10–12 wet.
Winding silk: Black.
Body: Peacock herl.
Tail: Bright red wool.
Hackle: Red or brown cock hackles of a length equal to the distance between the eye and the point of the hook.

1 Fix hook in the vise.
2 Wax the silk and tie. Wind it back 4 turns to fasten it securely.
3 Wind 5 more turns, cut off the short end. Maintain even tension. Place each turn close to the one before.

4 Prepare hackle. Use thumb nail to pull off the lower fuzzy fibers which are not stiff. Match length of fibers to those in 4b.
5 Lay hackle on the hook as illustrated, with the shiney side down. Fasten it with 4 turns of silk. Cut away the excess feather root.

6 Wind the silk downward tightly, each turn against the foregoing to a point above the barb of the hook.
7 Fasten a bit of red wool yarn for the tail using the same method as for the hackle.

358

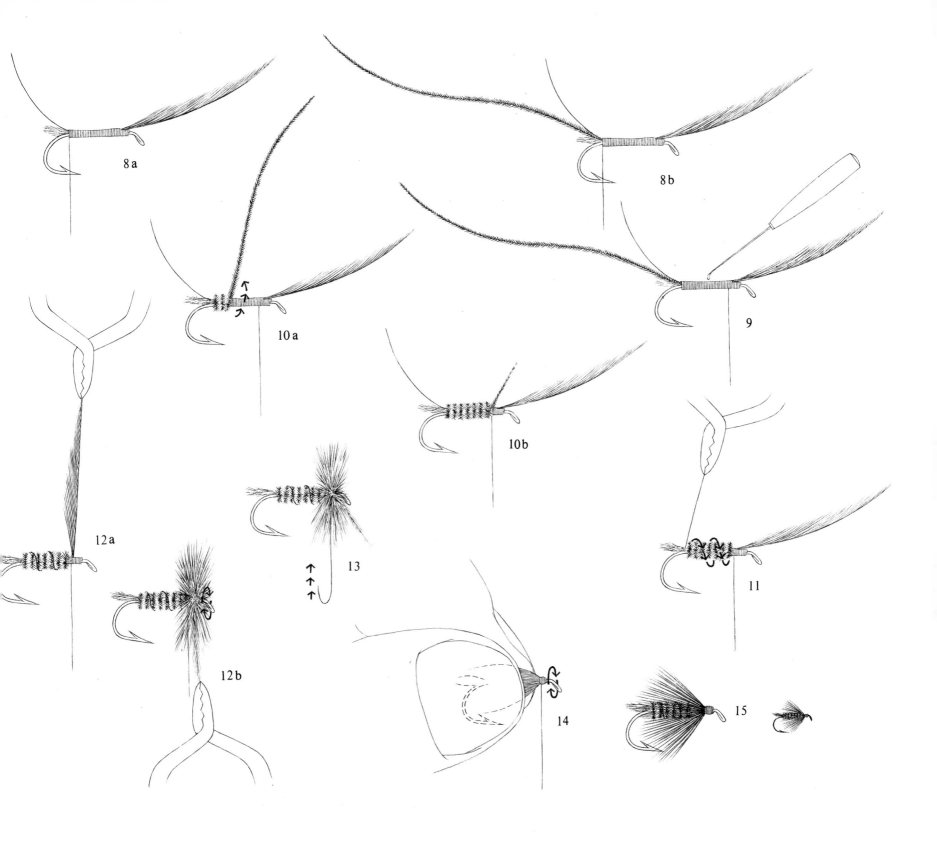

8   Then fasten 2 peacock herls and a bit of green winding silk.

9   Wind the black silk forward tightly until just under the hackle, then lacquer this winding.

10 Wind the peacock herls, one at a time, tightly up to the hackle to form a tight, downy body. Tie them down with the silk; cut away the excess.

11 Wind the green silk sparsely over the peacock herls without deforming the body. Tie it down.

12 Fasten hackle pliers in the tip of the hackle. Wind hackle 5 turns about the hook.

13 Wind silk carefully through the hackle without depressing the hair. Then tie down the tip of the hackle and cut off the excess.

14 On this and most wet flies the hackle should lean backward. This is done by pulling the fibers back with the fingertips and winding a few turns of silk above the hackle. Be careful not to make it lean too much.

15 Now, with the silk, make a rounded, tapered head. Finish off with a whip finish and lacquer the head and the knot.

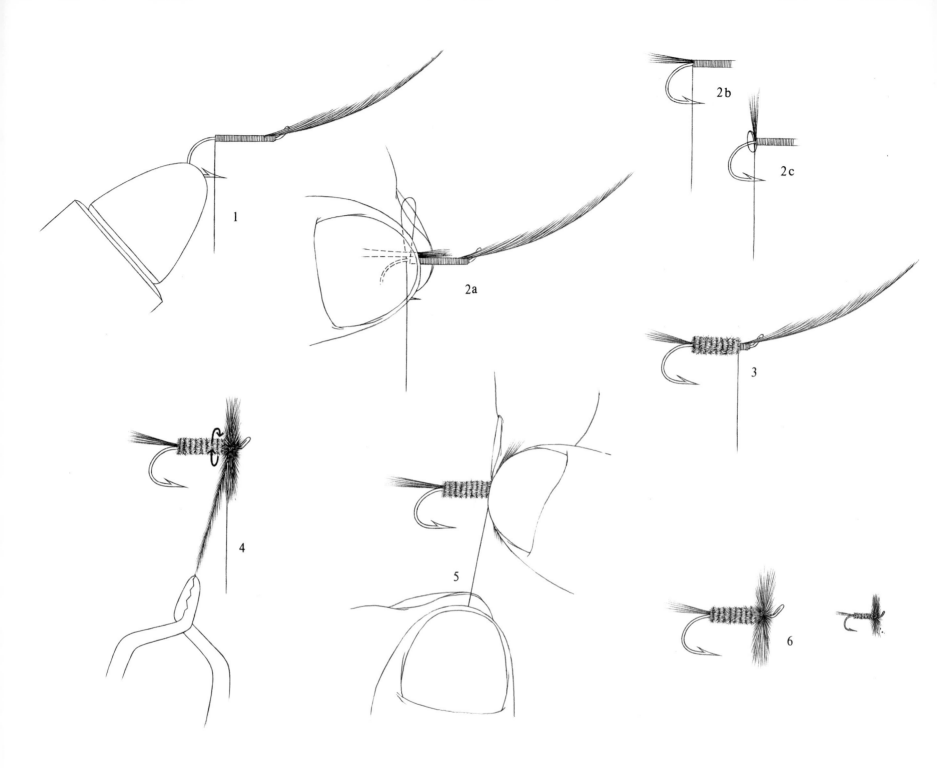

RED TAG DRY FLY

Material for this is the same as for the wet fly, with these exceptions: the hackle should be shorter and of better quality; instead of wool use red hackle fiber for the tail to increase buoyancy. Hook size: 8–12 dry.

1–3 This fly is tied in the same way as the wet, but the tail consists of hackle fibers. Pull off 16 to 20 fibers from a hackle, lay them on top of the hook and fasten with silk. It is often good to spread the fibers out horizontally by putting a turn of silk behind the fibers.

4 Hackles of a dry fly should be short and stand out straight. Take extra care to remove fuzzy fibers from the hackles. Sometimes two hackles are needed to obtain the desired density. Wind hackles around the hook until the right density has been obtained. Then wind the silk carefully through the hackle without depressing any of the fibers. Tie down the tips of the hackle with a few turns of the winding silk. Round off with a whip finish and lacquer.

5 If the hackle doesn't stand up straight enough, it can be picked up with a few turns of silk before and behind the hackle. Strive for a light, trim look.

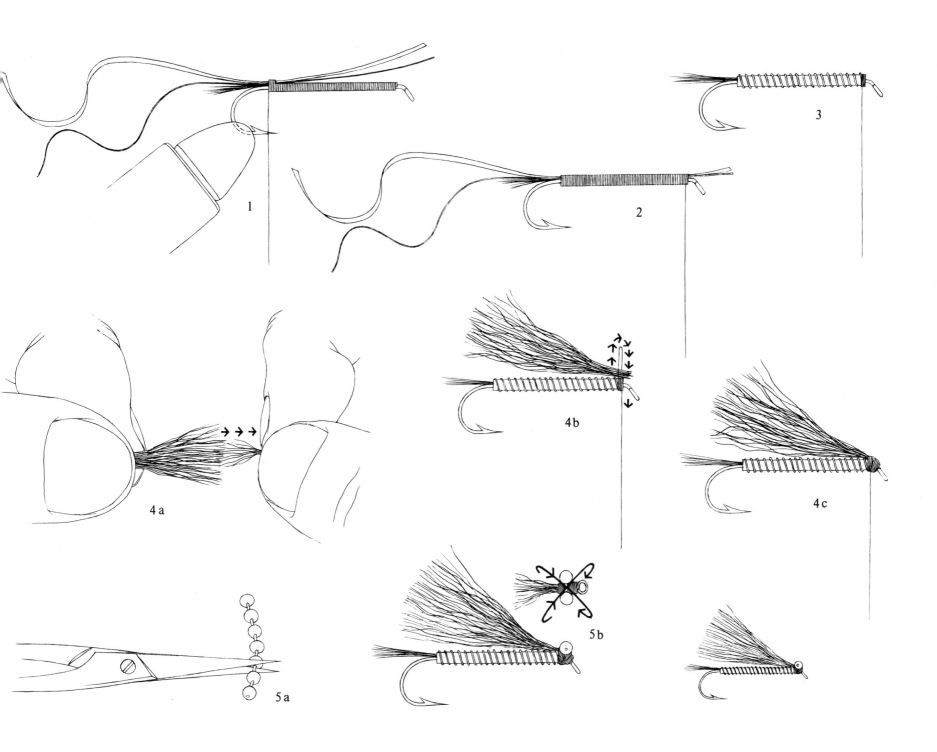

GOLD DOLL

This is a streamer built to imitate small fish.

Material.
Hook size: 6–8 streamer.
Tail: Orange-red hackle.
Body: Flat gold tinsel, and oval gold tinsel.
Wings: Black cow or squirrel tail hair.
Eyes: Bead chain.

1 Begin as with earlier flies, fixing the silk by the hook eye and winding back to above the barb. Fasten in a bit of red orange hackle for the tail. Clip off the forward stubs, then fasten a bit of flat gold tinsel and a bit of oval gold tinsel.

2 Don't cut off the forward stubs of the tinsel. Lay them along the shaft and cover with windings to make a firm body base.

3 Wind the flat gold tinsel forward, the turns meeting but not overlapping. Make the body as even as possible. Tie off the tinsel. Wind the oval tinsel sparsely in the opposite direction. Tie it off and cut off the tinsel stubs.

4 Pinch or cut off some cow or squirrel hair. Lay the hair on top of the hook (4b). Tie it hard with the silk so it cannot fall out. Cut the hair so none shows above the knot. Wind on a head (4c).

5 Cut off 2 beads of chain (5a). Lay it on the top of the head and wind silk in a cross over the link between the beads. Continue until eyes are firmly in place. Shape head with silk; whip finish and coat with lacquer (5b).

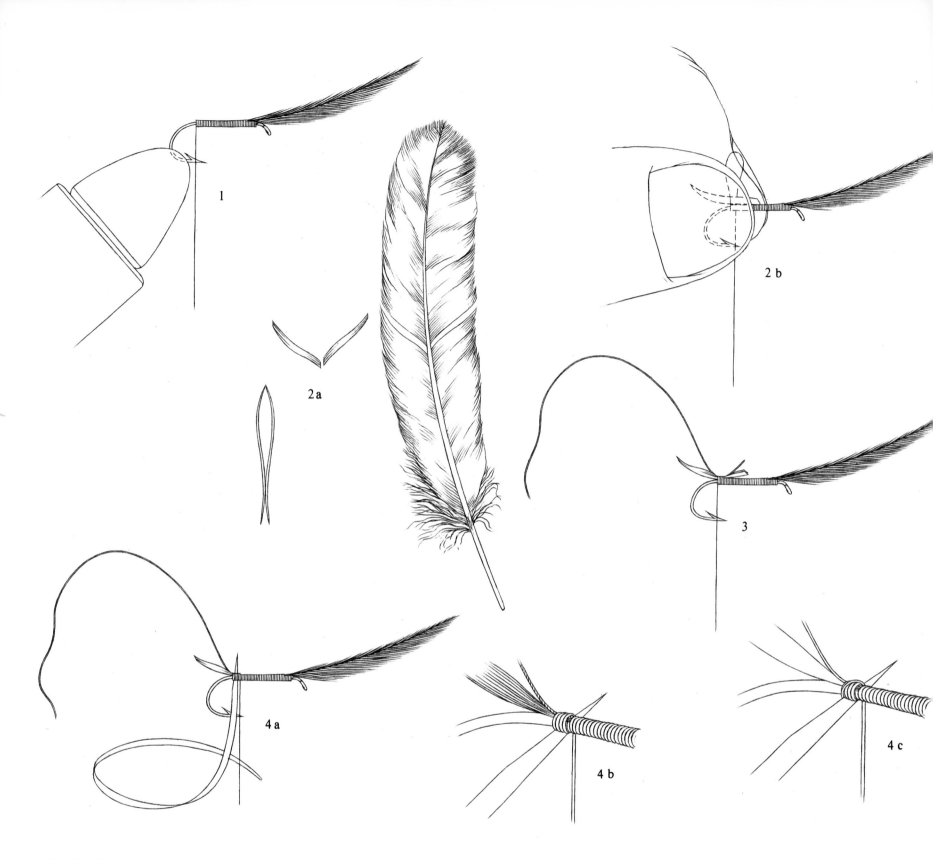

BUTCHER

Another popular wet fly.

Material.
Hook size: 10–12 wet.
Tail: Red ibis or substitute.
Hackle: Black cock.
Body: Flat silver tinsel with oval silver tinsel.
Wings: 2 sections from a blue-black mallard wing feather.

1–2 This fly is tied like the others until you get to the tail. This should be red ibis, but as this is impossible to get, we substitute red-dyed goose feather. Cut a little section from both sides of the feather (2a). Put the sections together with concave sides touching. On a good fly they fit together so well they look like one piece.

The best way to fasten them is to hold them between thumb and forefinger. Place them on edge above the hook. Insert 2 loops of silk between the fingers and pull carefully. Then tie with harder windings (2b).

3 Tie on a bit of oval silver tinsel about 2 in (5 cm) long and cut off the stub above the knot.

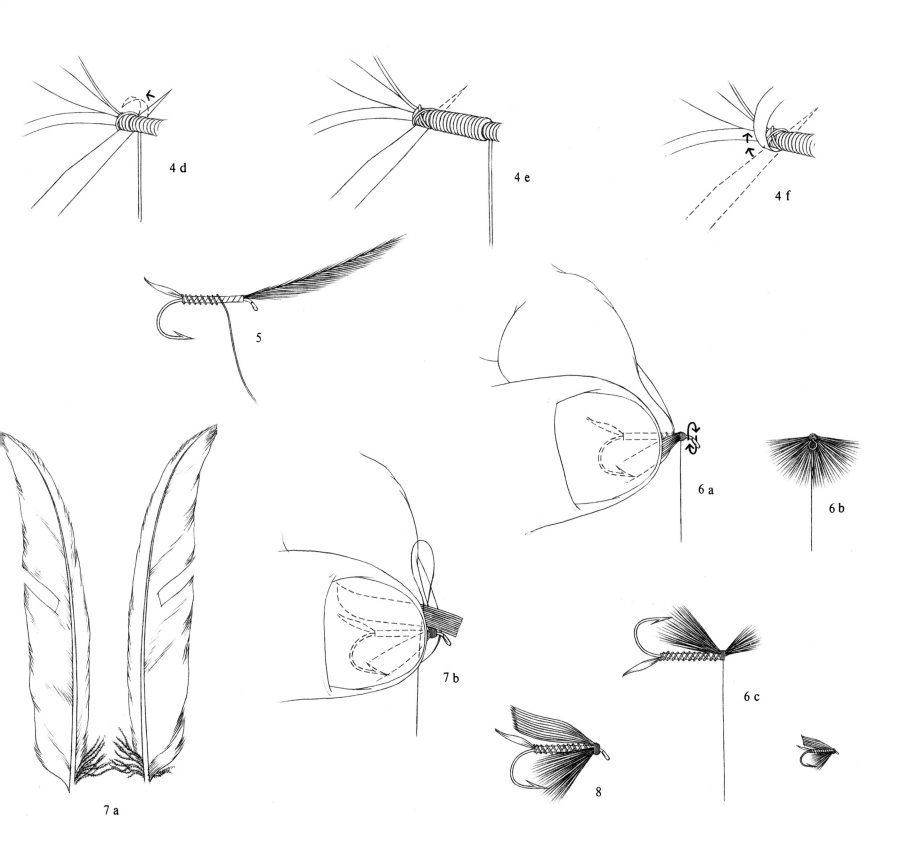

4 d

4 e

4 f

5

6 a

6 b

6 c

7 a

7 b

8

4 (a–f) When winding on the flat tinsel, be careful not to cut the silk or make the lower body too bulky. Note how this is done in the illustrations.

5 When the tinsel has been wound tightly up to the hackle and fastened, wind the oval tinsel sparsely so it covers the seams of the flat tinsel, then fasten at the hackle.

6 (a–c) The hackle is bound the same way as on the Red Tag Wet Fly except that the fibers are drawn down on both sides and fastened so all hackle is underneath (6b). Another way to do this is to pull loose a bunch of hackle fibers and fasten these under the hook. (See fiber tail, Red Tag Dry Fly, 6c).

7 For the wings, cut out one section from each of two feathers from opposite wings of a male mallard and place them carefully together as with the tail. Place them above the hook and tie in as in (7b). This may be hard to do, so take time and learn how to get the wings balanced.

8 Wind a few extra turns so the wings remain stable. Cut off the rest of the wings above the knot and cover the stubs with a few turns of silk. Tie off with a whip finish and lacquer. This is a more complicated fly and if you are not satisfied, try again – harder!

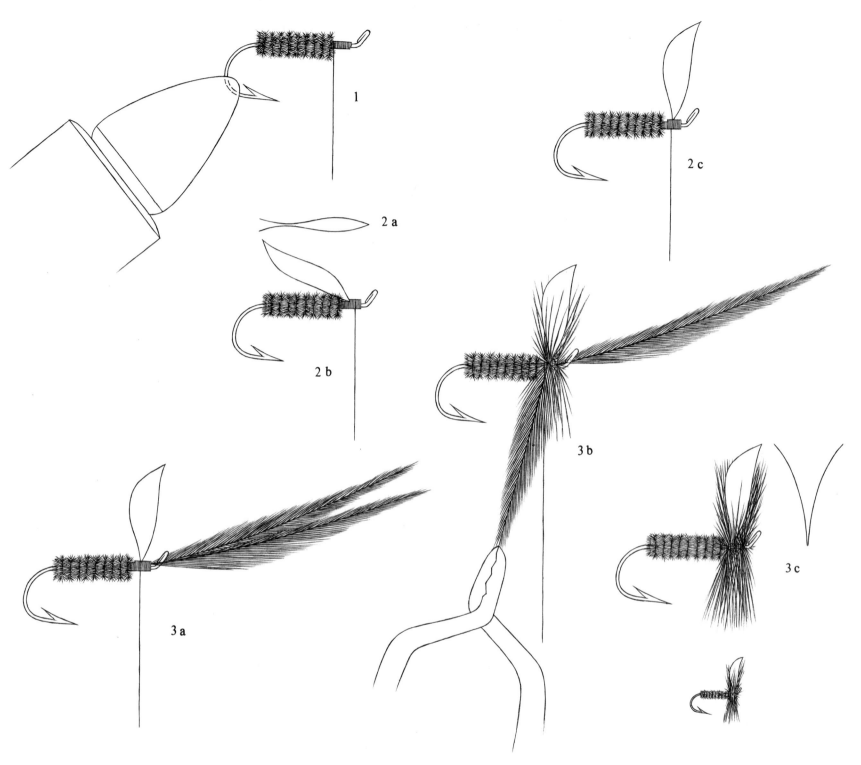

1

2 a

2 c

2 b

3 b

3 a

3 c

COACHMAN

Winged dry fly.

Material.
Hook size: 10–12 dry.
Body: Copper-coloured peacock herl.
Hackle: Red brown cock hackle.
Wings: Two sections of wild duck wing feather.

1 This winding resembles earlier examples but here the wings are upright. Begin by tying a herl body as on a Red Tag.

2 Cut out 2 corresponding sections from 2 white wing feathers. There are many ways to fasten the wings. Some fly tyers fix the wings pointed forward, others point them backward. Here we use the latter method. Fit the two sections together so the tops point outward and away from each other (2a). Fasten them on the hook the same way as on the Butcher (2b). Lift them up with a few turns of silk behind the roots of the wings (2c).

3 Fasten 2 cock hackles (3a) and wind in front of and behind the wings (3b). Even here there are different ways to do this. Some tyers fasten the stubs of the hackles in front of the wings, others behind. In either case the fly is finished with a whip finish at the eye of the hook and the usual lacquer.

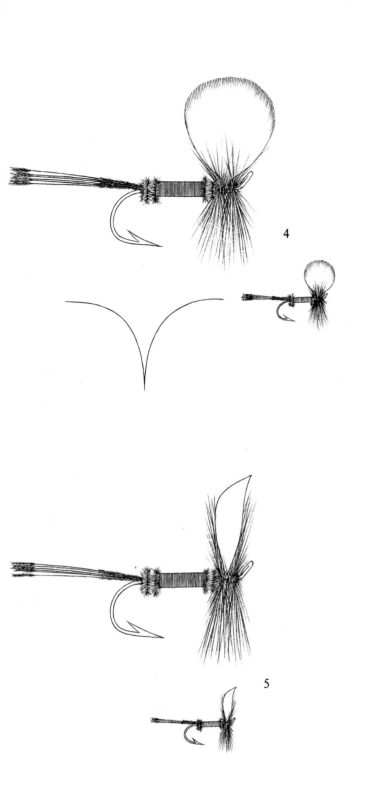

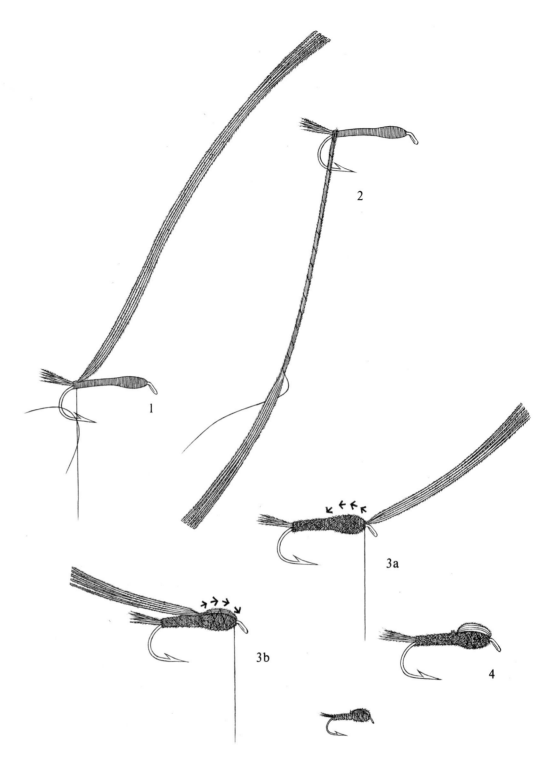

FRANK SAWYER'S PHEASANT TAIL NYMPH

4 **ROYAL COACHMAN FANWING** – tied with the middle body made of red floss silk and with breast feathers of wild duck as wings. Wings are "fanned" in position. The tail ribs are tips of golden pheasant.

5 **ROYAL COACHMAN** – is tied the same as the Royal Coachman Fanwing, but with the smaller wings of the Coachman pattern. The Coachman pattern is an old and honored one and is tied in a number of variations, some dry and some wet.

Material.
Hook size: 10–16 dry or wet.
Wire: .004"–.006" pure copper (.1–.15 mm).
Tail: Pheasant cock tail feathers.

1 *The copper wire is used to tie this fly to give it weight. Begin winding wire as if it were winding silk. Wind tightly to a point 1/3 of the hook length. Wind forward again to the eye and then down again to a point just above the barb. With a few turns of wire attach some fibers of pheasant tail so 1/5 in (5 mm) sticks out to form a short tail.*

2 *Wind the wire around the fibers to form one strand and wind this forward to the eye.*

3 *Bend the pheasant tail fibers back over the thorax bulge, fasten with a few turns of wire. Bend them forward again and fasten once more. Bend them back one last time and fasten with halfhitches of wire.*

4 *The finished fly.*

WOOLLY WORM

This fly is tied in many different color combinations, but materials are the same for all models.

Material.
Hook size: 6–10 wet or streamer.
Winding silk: Black.
Tail: Bit of red wool.
Body: Olive green chenille.
Hackle: Grizzly cock.
Rib: Oval silver tinsel.

1 *Begin as on the earlier flies. Fasten the silk at the eye of the hook and wind back to a point just above the barb. Attach there a bit of red wool for a tail.*
2 *Pull off the fuzzy fibers at the bottom of a grizzly cock hackle and pull it through your fingers so the fibers point in all directions.*

3 *Fasten the feather with the shiny side to the hook. Pull off the fluff from the end of the chenille and fasten it with the silk. Attach a piece of oval silver tinsel.*
4 *Wind the chenille in tight turns forward to form a fuzzy but even spoollike body. Tie it down with silk. Wind the tinsel sparsely and tie it down hard. Cut away everything above the knot.*

5 *Wind the hackle forward, not too tightly, to the head and tie it down.*
6 *Round it off with a whip finish and apply lacquer. Woolly Worm is a good fly for hot summer days.*

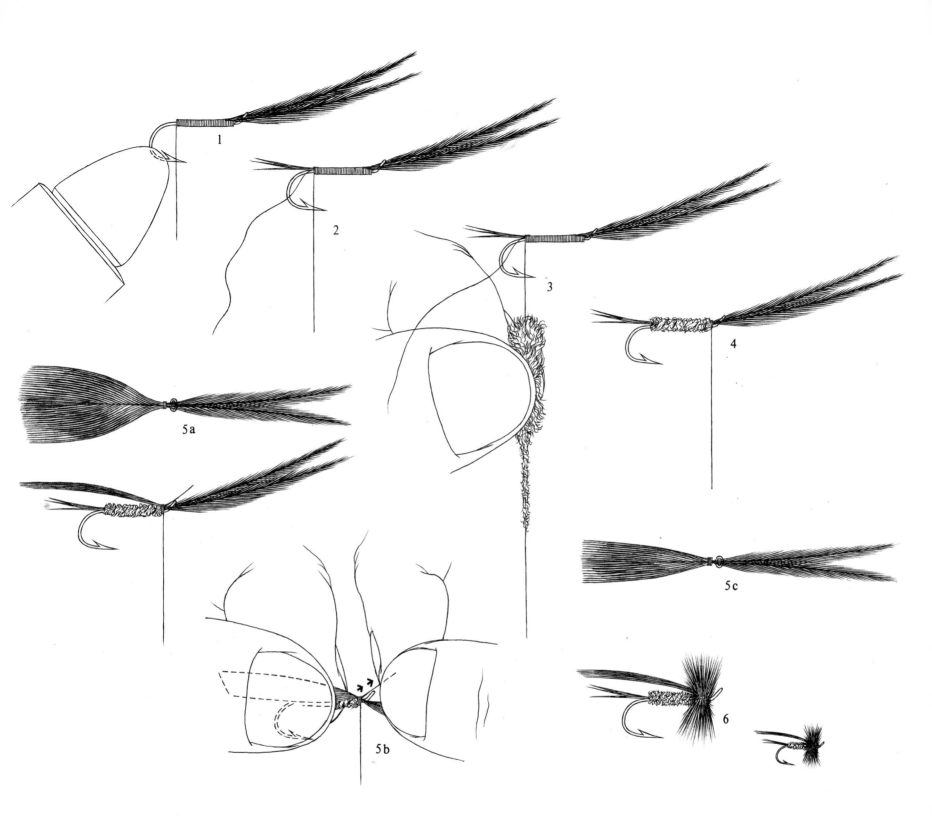

EUROPA 12

Dry fly of the sedge type.

Material.
Hook size: 12 dry.
Winding silk and rib: Yellow.
Body: Hare wool.
Tail: 3 fibers from a hen pheasant tail feather.
Wings: Breast feathers from a wild duck hen.
Hackle: 2 brown cock hackles.

1 Fasten the silk at the eye and attach the two brown cock hackles pointed forward. Wind the silk back to a point above the barb.

2 Fasten 3 fibers from a hen pheasant tail feather with a bit of tying silk. Make the fibers stick out to imitate tail feelers.

3 Wax the silk well. Cut out a good pinch of hare wool and roll it around the silk with finger tips so it looks like wool yarn. This is dubbing.

4 Wind the dubbing forward to the hackle. Wind the loose bit of silk over the dubbing sparsely as ribbing.

5 Take a breast feather from a wild duck hen and pull off the lower fuzz. Lay the feather with its concave side to the hook and fasten with 2 loose turns of the silk (5a). Hold it in the fingers (5b) and pull the root end so the feather is pressed together by the turns of the silk (5c).

6 Wind the hackle as on earlier dry flies. End with whip finish and lacquer.

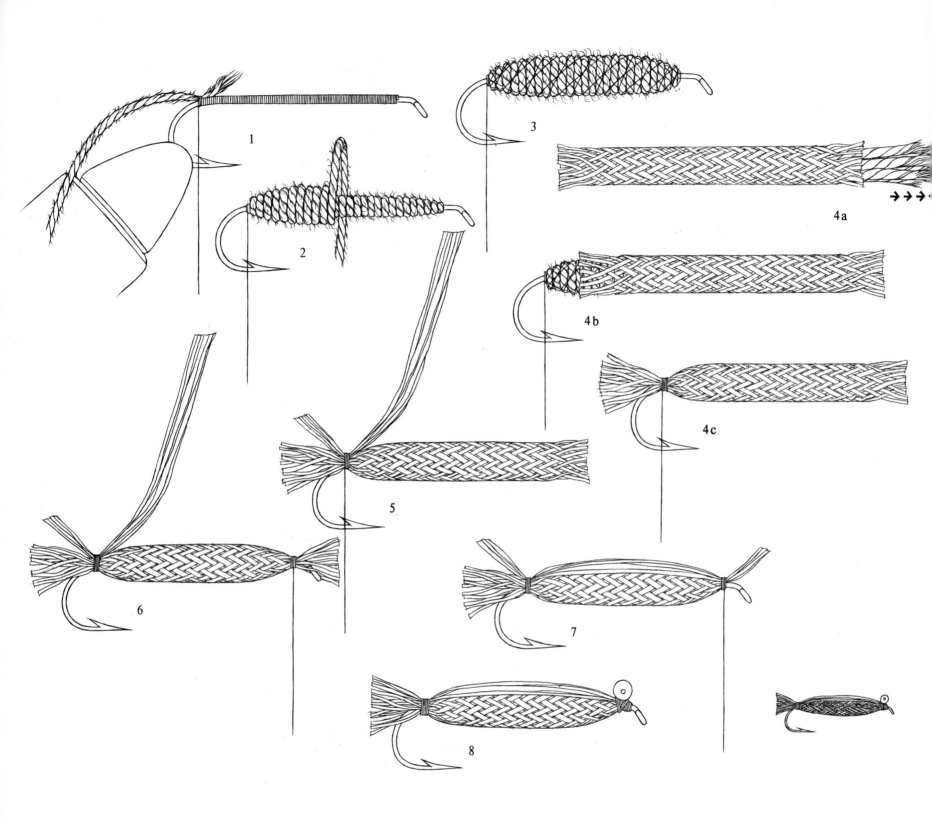

TOBIS

A fly intended to imitate small fish. Colors may be varied to suit conditions.

Material.
Hook size: 4–10 streamer.
Winding silk: Blue.
Inner body: Yarn.
Body: Mylar tubing.
Eyes: Bead chain.
Weight: Lead wire can be added under the yarn.
Back: Blue plastic raffia.

1 *Fastern the silk 1/8 in (3 mm) from the eye and wind back tightly to a point above barb. Attach there a piece of yarn 1 in (2.5 cm) long.*
2 *Wind the yarn to make an even, spool-shaped body.*
3 *Tie down the yarn and cut away the excess. Take a few turn of silk over the yarn to stabilize it on the hook.*

4 *Cut a piece of Mylar tubing about 3/4 in (2 cm) longer than the body of the fly. Take out the stuffing and insert the fly body into the tube (4a–4c).*
5 *Fasten a piece of raffia as shown. Tie off the silk with a whip finish, cut off the excess, lacquer the knot.*

6 *Tie down the forward end of the tube with silk and cut off any part of the tube above the knot.*
7 *Bend the plastic raffia forward as a back and tie it down with silk. Cut off the excess.*
8 *Attach 1 section of bead chain for eyes. Make a whip finish and lacquer. Trim the tail as shown.*

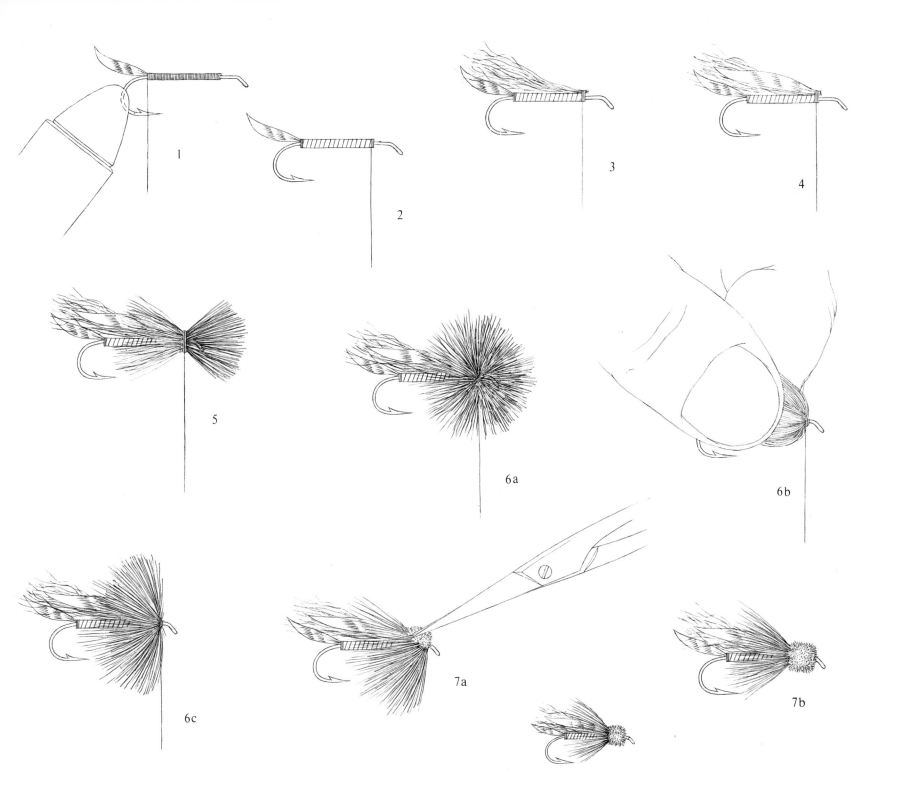

MUDDLER MINNOW

An excellent bait fish imitation.

Material.
Hook: 1–12 streamer.
Winding silk: Black.
Tail: Section of brown turkey wing feather.
Body: Flat gold tinsel.
Wings: Bit of grey brown squirrel fur and on each side a section of spotted turkey wing feather.
Head: Deer fur.

1 *Fasten silk a bit down from the eye to give room for wings and head. Wind silk evenly back to point above the barb. Fasten there left and right sections of turkey feather as on the Butcher Fly.*
2 *Attach a bit of flat gold tinsel and wind first the silk and then the tinsel forward to form a nice even body.*

3 *Fasten a bit of gray brown squirrel hair, wind hard to make it secure.*
4 *Attach a section of brown speckled turkey feather on each side of the squirrel hair.*
5 *Cut a rather large tuft of deer hair and lay it on the hook with the tips away from the eye. Make 2 loose turns of silk above the wings and pull carefully while rolling the*

hair with the fingers so it is spread evenly around the hook shank.
6 *Pull the silk tight so the hairs stand up (6a) and lift the forward hairs with a few turns of silk (6b–6c). End with whip finish and lacquer.*
7 *With sharp scissors trim the hair to a ball, but leave a small collar at the back as a hackle.*

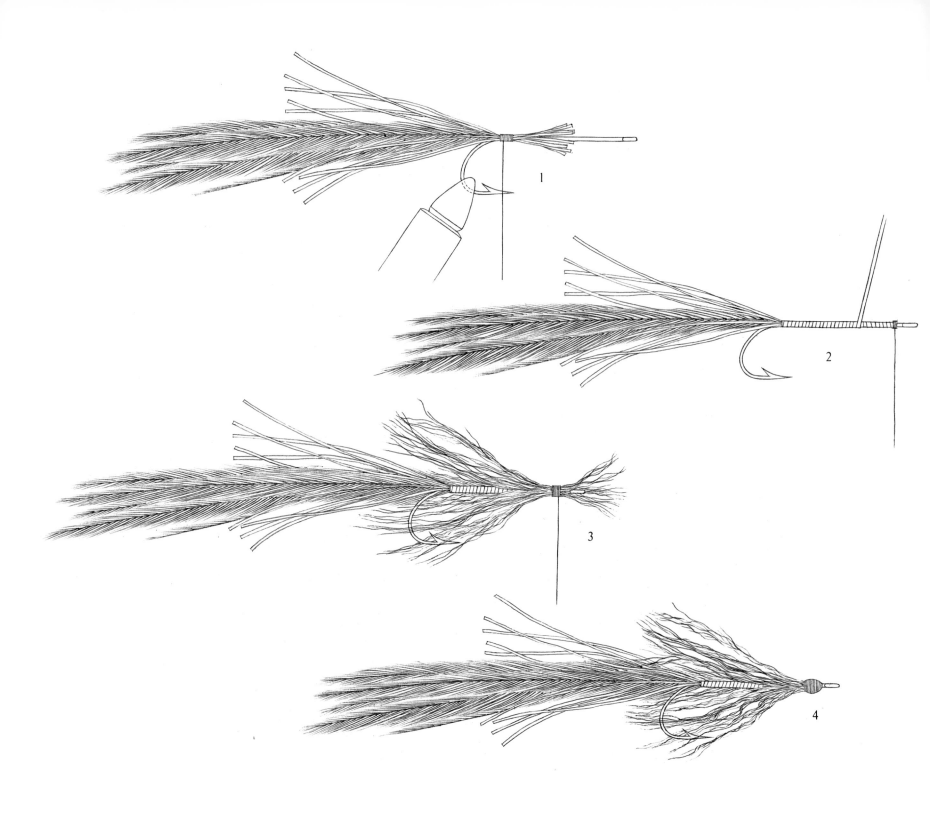

LEFTY'S DECEIVER

This salt water fly is used for many different kinds of salt water fish. It is usually tied all white or white with a red collar.

Material.
Hook size: 2 to 3/0 forged.
Tail: 6–8 cock hackles and 10 strands of Mylar.
Body: Silver Mylar.
Collar: Bucktail, calf, or polar bear hair.

1 *Tie in first 6–8 cock hackles and then the 10 Mylar strands. Try to lay these around the hackles.*

2 *Wind the silk forward to the eye and fasten there a strand of silver Mylar. Wind the Mylar back to the tail and then forward again to the eye. Fasten it with the silk.*

3 *Cut some hair and fasten it to the hook, not as wings but as a collar laid evenly around the hook. Make the winding secure.*

4 *End with a whip finish and lacquer.*

BUBBLE PUP BASS FLY

A surface-action fly for fresh water bass.

Material.
Hook: 4–1 streamer.
Tail: Black cock hackle.
Body: Yellow deer hair.

1 Begin by tying two black cock hackles to the middle of the hook. Lacquer the knot for security.
2 Cut a pinch of deer hair (see Muddler Minnow). Lay it with the tips pointed back and the middle over the knot. Distribute the hair evenly around the shank and pull turns of silk around the hair so the hairs stand up (2a). Lift the forward hair with a few turns of silk (2b). Be careful to zigzag the silk through the hair so it doesn't get pressed down.
3 Tie in a new pinch of hair, shorter this time, ahead of the first bunch. A large hook may require many such pinches.
4 Tie in a new pinch of hair on top of the last, but don't distribute it. Leave it bunched on top. Make a whip finish and apply lacquer.
5 With sharp scissors, trim the fly to the shape illustrated.

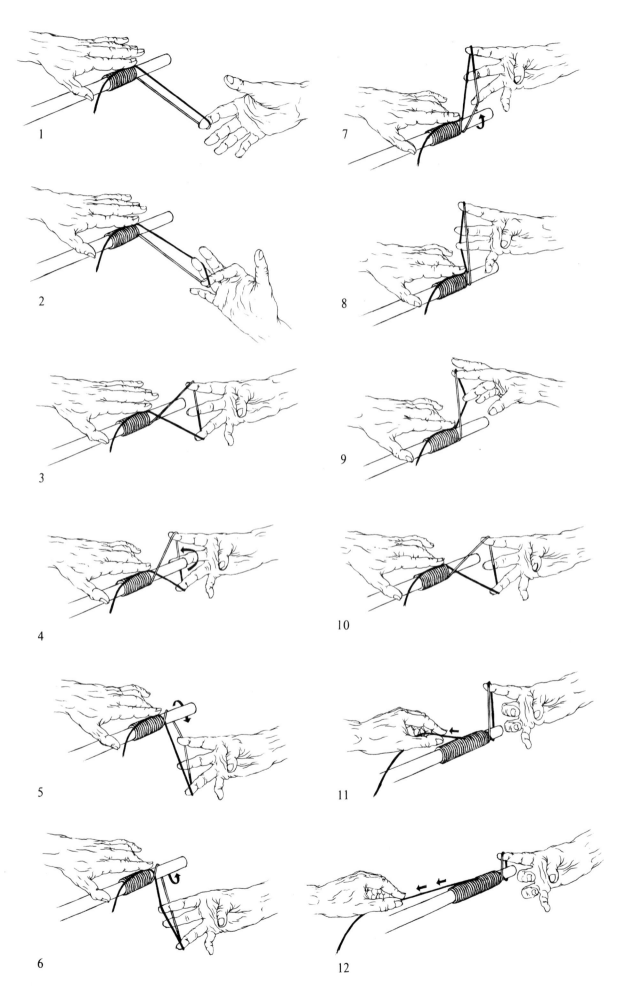

1

2

3

4

5

6

7

8

9

10

11

12

TIPS FOR GOOD RESULTS IN FLY TYING

1 Always wash your hands before starting to tie flies. Certain materials such as floss silk are easily discolored by perspiration and the natural oils of human skin.

2 Begin by trying simple flies on large hooks. Take your time and do not rush the work. Learn how to hold and use the various tools. Learn how the different types of materials react to handling and to being bound to the hook shank.

3 In starting, wind the shank of the hook with waxed winding silk before any material is tied to the hook. This provides a waxy substratum to which hair and feather materials will adhere, making the placement and winding of the materials much easier.

4 In planning your winding, remember to leave room on the hook shank for the head and the finishing knot. Some tiers diagram a new fly on paper 3 to 5 times natural size before attempting to tie the fly.

5 When making dubbing, take just a few strands of hair at a time. This avoids creating lumpy dubbing that is hard to control and gives the fly an unnatural look when it is finished.

6 When attaching hair wings, always make sure the knot is hard and tight. Apply a little lacquer to the knot before continuing with the tying so it won't slip.

7 On flies like the Tobis, it is a good idea to apply a few drops of lacquer to the yarn body before inserting it into the Mylar tube. This increases the fly body's solidity appreciably.

8 Check all new material for vermin and keep only clean material. Otherwise, the entire collection may be spoiled. Unsure materials can be deep-frozen for a few weeks. This usually destroys vermin eggs and most mold spores.

9 Don't be afraid to experiment. There are thousands of patterns and variations of patterns, and new patterns are emerging constantly. One of the great joys of fly tying is to develop one's own personal patterns that catch fish as successfully as the popular patterns available everywhere.

10 The final test of a good fly tier is to be able to reproduce, in the field, flies that will match the hatch of a local stream. Trout and other fish are often extremely selective. The ability to diagnose the feeding problem and then create a fly on the spot that will take fish under these circumstances is perhaps the most satisfying of all.

THE WHIP FINISH

While it is possible to make the whip finish with a mechanical tool, many anglers prefer to tie the knot as illustrated to the left. Practice with heavy line on a stick, then diminish the size of line and stick until you can tie the whip finish on tiny flies.

FISH TAXIDERMY

How many times have you said, "If I ever catch a trophy fish I'm going to have it mounted to hang on the wall of my room!"

Fish taxidermy – mounting fish for display – is not difficult and is a pleasurable way of preserving one's finest fish for future enjoyment.

The ancient Egyptians embalmed fish as well as humans, and sometimes placed embalmed fish in the burial vaults containing the remains of deceased important persons. Both sugar and honey were used as preservatives back in the days of Aristotle, and this method was not rediscovered until early in the present century.

Basically, one's task in preparing a fish for mounting is to remove and preserve the head and skin, and to make a suitable body mold over which the preserved skin can be drawn and fastened. Fins, artificial eyes, and proper skin coloring are added in the final steps. The end result is a "fish" that very closely resembles the original in nature. If you catch a fish that you want to preserve by the taxidermy method, start by taking pictures in color of the fish while it is still alive, or as soon after capture as possible. Fish colors fade on death, and you need a permanent record.

Make notes also on the exact position and attitude of the fins, the depth and amount of distension of the stomach, and any other physical points that appear to be important. Also make a careful outline of the contours of the fish on paper in the position in which the fish is to be mounted. Common practice is to mount the fish with the left side exposed. Therefore, incisions into the fish's body should be made through opposite or right side.

Transport the fish home wrapped in soft, wet cloths. Don't bind it with string. The string will mark the skin. The entire fish may be frozen soon after capture if work on the taxidermy cannot start soon. Lay the fish on its right side, or the side that will be attached to the mounting board. Be very careful not to brush scales from the display side.

The mucus on the fish's skin should be washed off. Do this by placing the fish in a solution of 30–40 % alcohol, or in lukewarm alum water (1 tsp alum in 2 liters or quarts of water). Acetone, diluted with 20 % of water by volume, can also be used. Coagulated mucus can be scraped off with a blunt knife. Rinse with running cold water after cleaning the skin.

Flaying or skinning the fish requires care. Make the incision along the lateral line of the right side, or the side that will go on the mounting board, using a scalpel, sharp scissors, or sharp filet knife. Loosen the skin carefully from the body using the fingers and knife blade. Be careful not to damage the layer of silvery pigment just under the outer skin. Free the fin bases with a knife or cut the fins free of the muscle tissue with sharp scissors. Cut the spinal column at the tail fin and the base of the skull.

When the skin has been removed, carefully cut away all traces of fat and flesh. Remove the gills and the eyes. Cut away the neck and head muscles and remove the brain via the hole in the neck. After removing the eye, the cheek muscles can be removed through the eye opening. Take out also the tongue and all head tissue, leaving only the skull and jawbones. Through the entire skinning procedure, keep skin and fins moist and supple.

Rinse the skin carefully in pure water. Defatten a fatty skin by soaking for a while in gasoline or tetrachloride, observing safety precautions, naturally. Rub the inside of the skin with salt and let it lie overnight. Rinse before mounting. Brush a 10 % solution of Formalin inside the skin, around the gills, and over fin bases and into the skull, before mounting.

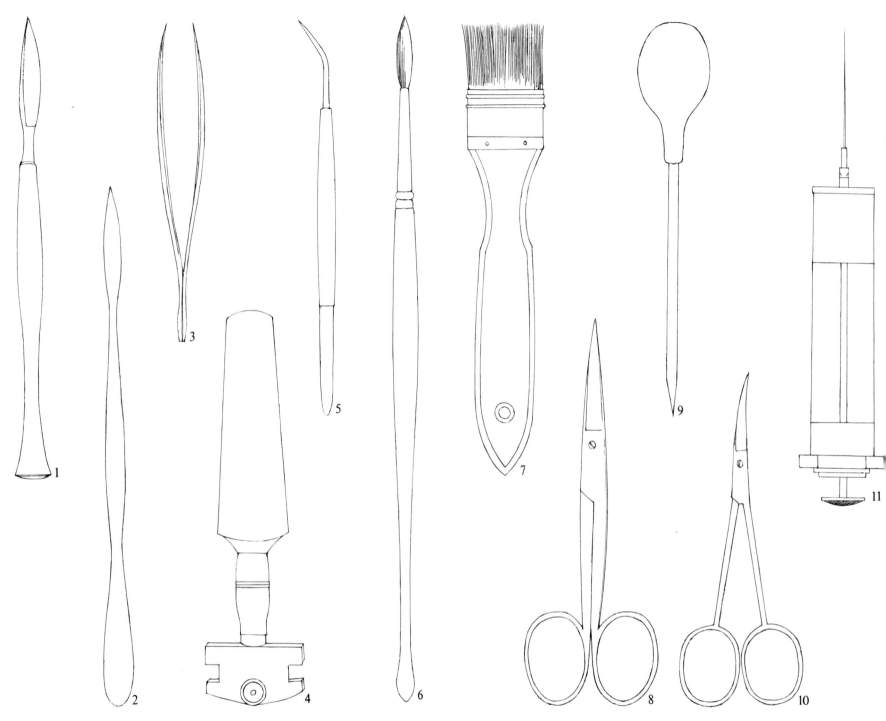

The tools and materials for home taxidermy of fishes are quite simple and can be obtained from most local art, hardware, and surgical supply stores. If a scalpel is hard to locate, use a similar knife from an art carving kit. A fisherman's fillet knife is a big help. The syringe may be a medical item, but if you can't locate one, the pipette with its rubber bulb will work as a syringe as well as a tool for sucking up excess liquids. You'll need pieces of wood for mounting and a heavy U-shaped piece of stainless steel or aluminium wire, or light rod. Papier-mâché is easy to make from shredded paper, water, and glue. The sawdust mentioned should be quite fine and dry. Fine sand is used in wet and dry forms in different stages of taxidermy.

BASIC TOOLS:

1 Scalpel or art knife
2 Fillet knife
3 Straight tweezers
4 Glass cutter
5 Offset tweezers
6 Camel's hair brush
7 Small bristle brush
8 Straight scissors
9 Pipette
10 Cuticle scissors
11 Syringe

OTHER MATERIALS:

Set of hand drills
Small funnel
Air-spray gun
Stainless steel wire
Wood-wool (excelsior)
Pieces of wood
Styrofoam or peat
Thread and twine
Sawdust, sifted
Fine sand
Soft rags
Tinfoil strips
Sheet cardboard
Paper clips, pins
Cotton wool
Assorted needles
Wood or metal box
Old newspapers
Camera and film

Large glass jar
Glass or plastic bowls
Oval glass plate
Cork
Portable oven
Celluloid strips
Sandpaper (assorted)
Galvanized nails
Sponge
Alcohol
Alum
Salt
Acetone
Formic acid
Formalin
Gasoline
Tetrachloride
Acetic acid
Vegetable oil
Varnish (copal)

Shellack
Zapon lacquer
Granulated sugar
Distilled water
Benzol
Soap
Paraffin
Silicone rubber
Polyester resin
Pearl essence
Oil base paints
Plaster
Resin
Joiner's glue
Modeling clay
Cotton gauze
Glass fiber fabric
Talcum
Floor wax

PREPARING TO SKIN OR FLAY A FISH

1 Photograph the fish in color, make notes and sketches of the important details like size and color of eyes, attitude of fins, fullness of the fish's body.

2 Wrap the fish in wet cloths, but do not bind tightly. Fish may be frozen if it cannot be worked on immediately. Treat with great care.

3 Remove mucus from the fish's body by bathing the fish in 30–40 % solution of alcohol, or in alum water. Rub from the head toward the tail without scraping off body scales. Keep skin and fins moist at all times.

4 With sharp fillet knife, make incision on the mounting side, cutting along the lateral line. The cut should extend from head to tail.

5 Start working the skin away from the body, using fingers if possible. If not, use a scalpel or art carving knife very carefully.

6 Take care not to damage the layer of skin that contains the silvery pigment. Do not pull or bend the skin so sharply as to stretch it or rub off scales. Try to keep the muscle mass of the body intact, especially if you intend to use it for making a body cast of plaster.

7 Sever the spine at the skull and at the beginning of the tail.

8 When skin has been stripped from the body, carefully cut away muscle tissue from the fin bases, the head, and other parts. Remove brain, gills, head flesh as previously directed. Moisten skin and fins frequently with a little salt water.

9 Rinse the skin in fresh water. If it is from an oily or fatty fish, remove any fat and oil by soaking the skin and head for a few hours in gasoline or carbon tetrachloride.

10 Thoroughly rub the inside of the skin with salt and let it lie covered with salt overnight. Rinse well with running water before brushing the inside of the skin with Formalin.

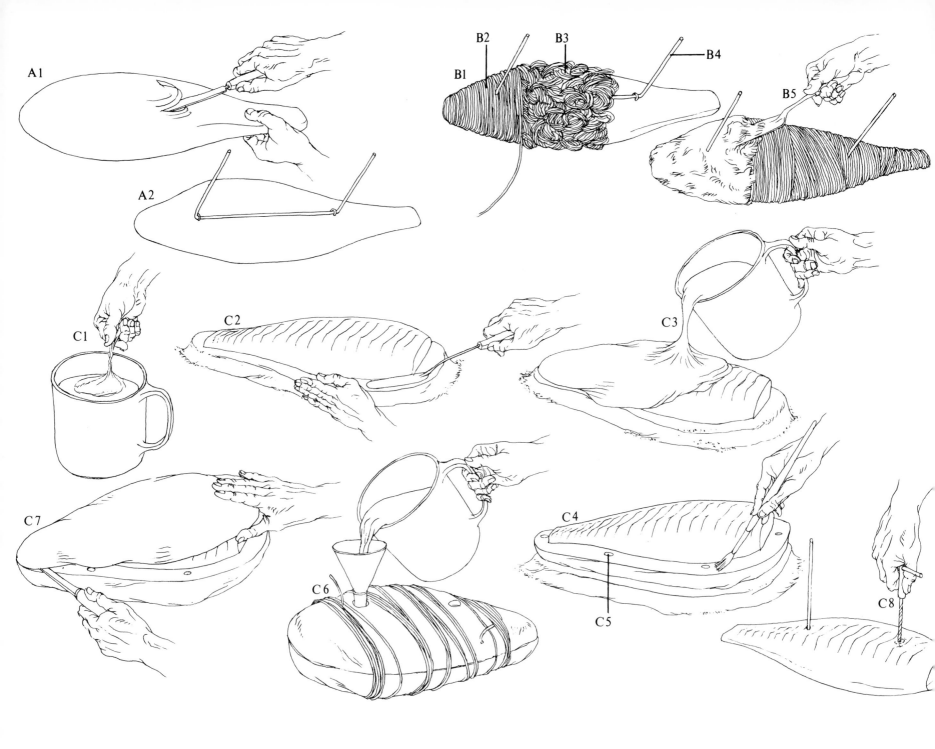

MAKING A CARVED BODY FORM

A 1 A block of foam plastic (Styrofoam), balsawood, or similar material is shaped to the size and outline of the fish's body.

2 A U-shaped yoke of heavy wire or light metal rod is fastened to the body form on the back or mounting side. The yoke, in turn, will be made fast to the mounting board when the mount is completed.

BUILT-UP BODY FORM

B 1 Cut a core of stiff cardboard or thin wood to the exact outline of the fish.

2 Wrap the core with twine or cord.

3 Put a padding of wood-wool or glass fiber wool under the twine wrapping.

4 The metal rod mount yoke is attached before wrapping.

5 Bring body form to full size with an application of papier-mâché smeared on.

MAKING A PLASTER BODY CAST

C 1 Mix a supply of plaster of Paris.

2 Place the body of the fish with the display side down in moist sand. Shape the sand so exactly that the other half projects above the sand. Brush the exposed side with oil.

3 Cover the exposed side with plaster to a thickness of 1 in. (25 mm), with good overlap at the edges of the half-mold.

4 When the plaster is hard, turn the half-mold leaving the fish within it.

5 Cut several holes or depressions in the edge of the first half-mold, into which the second half-mold will key when cast. Shellac the edges of the first half-mold until shiny, then oil the mold edges and the remaining side of the fish. Prepare a fresh batch of plaster.

6 Pour the other half.

7 When hard, separate the halves, remove the fish body, clean both half-molds. Shellac thoroughly inside after cutting two plaster pouring holes in one half. Tie halves together and pour in thin run of plaster, shaking the mold to settle the plaster and expel trapped air.

8 When body is hard remove it and cement on two mounting rods.

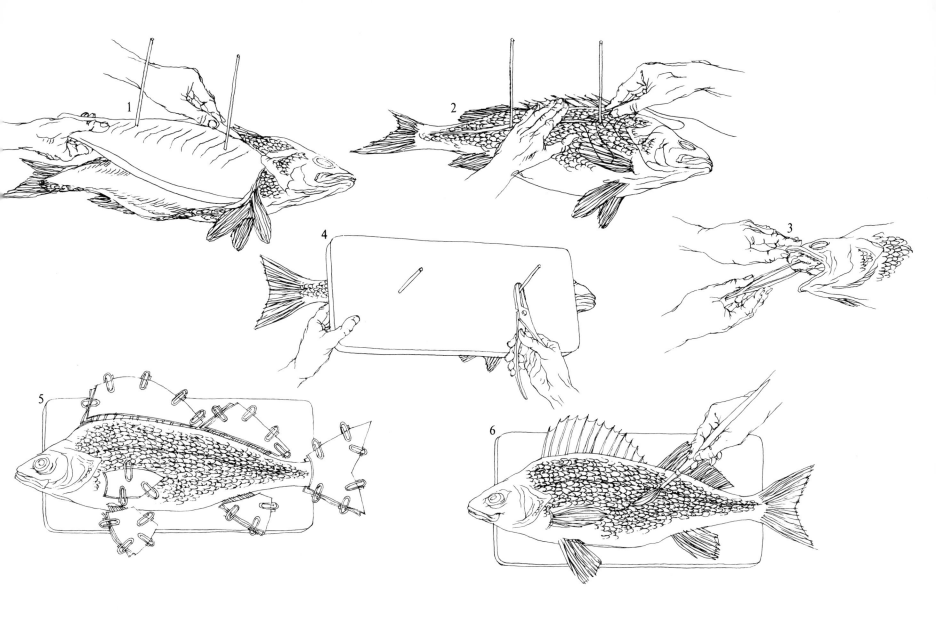

MOUNTING THE FISH ON ITS BOARD

(The same system is used for the body form types just described).

1 Carefully place the body form inside the cured fish skin with the mounting bracket or yoke in position. If the body form is made of papier-mâché, the fin bases must be put into the not-yet-dry mass and the fish molded to its final form as the skin is drawn onto the form.

2 With the skin drawn and fitted over the body form, the skin is sewed together. It pays to plan ahead so the mount bracket or rods will coincide with the cut in the side skin of the fish.

3 The head is formed, cheeks and other cavities are built up with modeling clay or papier-mâché. Glass or other prepared eyes are cemented into their sockets. Every effort should be made to achieve a clean, natural look.

4 Drill two holes in the mounting board to receive the rods or wires of the mount bracket or yoke. Some taxidermists bend the rods behind the board but others thread the rods and cut them off after the nuts have been drawn down tight. The fins are held in position with pieces of paper and clips. The fish is then left to dry completely, which may take several weeks.

5 If any fin has been torn or damaged it may be repaired after the fish is dry by reinforcing the fin web with tissue paper, gauze, and glue. Now fill the eye rims with melted wax and flow wax into any depressions around the fin bases, jaws, or other parts. Finally, a thin coat of shellac prepares the surface of the mounted fish for its finishing coat of paint and color.

6 Any fish that is gold or silver under its color should be first primed with pearl essence applied by brush or air spray.

Then another layer of shellac should be applied. Use oil paints for a lifelike effect that closely matches the original life colors, finishing with a thin coat of varnish.

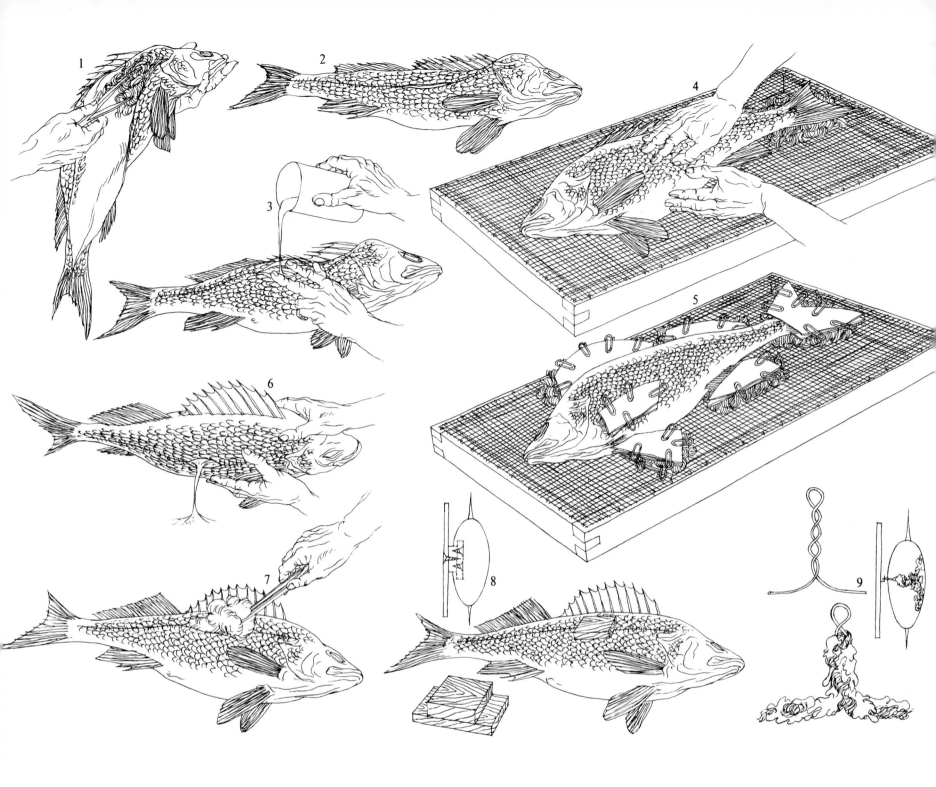

FISH DRIED WITH SAND

A disadvantage of the "stuffing" method of fish mounting is that the fish skin easily cracks. Furthermore, the skin may "perspire" while drying out, with problems of mildew. It's wise to check a drying fish frequently and wipe off any moisture. Drying the fish skin with sand, after it has been properly cured and shaped, is another good mounting method. First, skin the fish as before.

1 Stuff a handful of slightly moist wood wool up into the head of the fish. This keeps the sand from flowing out of the mouth.

2 Sew up the cut in the backside of the fish leaving a slit about 2 in (5 cm) long.

3 Pour fine, dry sand in through this hole until the fish body is properly filled. When body is full and naturally shaped, sew the slit closed.

4 Place the sand-filled fish seam-side down on a metal mesh like an old window screen. Put moist wood wool under head and tail. Shape the fish into its final position.

5 The fins, which have been kept moist, are stretched in pieces of cardboard with paper clips and are held in place by wood wool under them. The fish is now placed in a well-ventilated place to dry. Drying make take several weeks. Wipe off any mildew with alcohol.

6 When the skin is dry, cut a hole in the backside and pour out the sand. Shellac the inside via the hole.

7 The skin can be stuffed with wood or cotton wool or filled with plaster, in which case a U-shaped mounting bracket can be cast into the back when the plaster is poured into the fish body.

8 A varnished wood piece like that shown can be cast into the back. The mounting board is fastened to the body piece with wood screws.

9 If no stuffing is used, or if stuffing is very light, a bent steel wire can be fastened inside the fish with cotton and glue, or plaster. Stuff the head, put in the eyes, and do the final painting as described before.

CASTING WITH PLASTER MOLD, WHOLE OR HALF

1 After the fish has been photographed and the mucus washed off, inject a 10% solution of Formalin into the belly to hold shape.

2 Cut off the fins at the base, stretch in cardboard with pins. Then place in 80% alcohol solution to soak. Resoak in full strength alcohol. Fix in xylenol and coat with copal varnish.

3 If desired, castings of the stretched fins can be made in fine plaster or plastic.

4 To do a half-cast of a fish, cardboard cutouts the same size as the fins are glued to the backside of the fins. Breast fins are folded close to the body.

5 Shellac the inside of a suitable box and pour in enough soft plaster to "float" the fish to half its body depth.

6 Oil the display side of the fish, then press it into the plaster to exactly half of its body thickness. Let this plaster harden. Then remove the fish, fill any cavities in the body mold. Brush mold with shellac and leave in the box.

7 Oil interior of box and mold, then pour in fresh plaster. If a plaster backing is desired, plaster to fill the box 1 in (2½ cm) is added.

8 Before the plaster hardens, press into it a varnished wooden mounting block.

9 When the plaster is hard, upset the box over crumpled paper and remove the final casting, which may be shellacked after the fins have been glued on, and then painted.

10 To make a hollow resin casting, first make two half molds as described before, but do not cut in the pouring holes.
Shellac insides, then apply parting agent (resin insulation). Coat interior of each mold with resin to build up a layer.

11 When each hollow half is cured, apply some resin mixture to the edges of each mold, insert piece of thin lath for strength.

12 Tie the two halves together and let cure. Glue the preserved fins to the body, put in eyes, and paint to duplicate live fish.

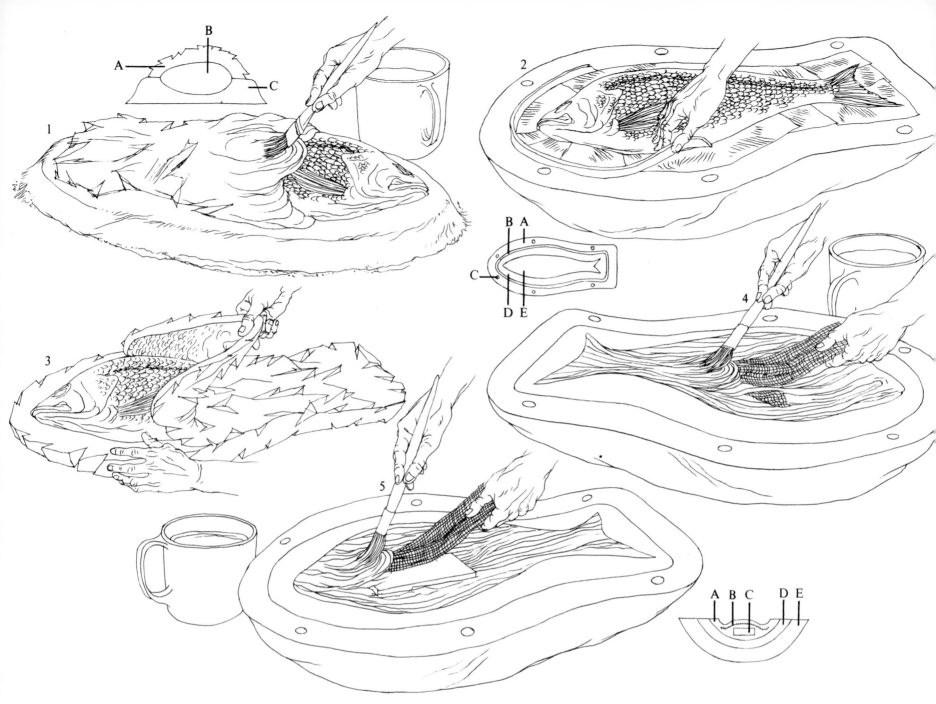

CASTING WITH PARAFFIN OR SILICONE MOLDS

First, photograph the fish, clean the mucus, inject Formalin into the belly, cut off and mount the fins in cardboard.

1 Place the fish in moist sand as before, cover the free side with melted paraffin or silicone rubber to a thickness of 2 in (5 cm).
   A Paraffin or silicone
   B Fish body
   C Moist sand
   When wax or silicone is firm, add a coat of plaster over all.

2 When plaster is set, cut mold-key holes in edge of plaster after removing mold from the sand. Before casting the second half,

insulate the first half. With a warm knife, fasten tinfoil strips to the exposed paraffin edge and oil the tinfoil. Coat exposed silicone with soapy water or floor wax. Next, on the border between the plaster and the paraffin or silicone, place a strip of clay to prevent the wax or silicone of the other half from overflowing the plaster coat. See the small sketch 2.
   Legend:
   A Plaster coat
   B Clay strips
   C Mold-key holes
   D Paraffin or silicone
   E The fish body
   The other half of the fish is covered with wax or silicone as before. The clay strips are removed, the paraffin or silicone edges are insulated, and the other half of

the plaster coat is applied. When set, the molds are separated and the fish removed. If silicone was used, the plaster should be taken off first and then the silicone coat. The two coats are then put back together. If paraffin is used, this will remain in the outer plaster coat throughout. Wipe the molds inside.
   Paraffin mold:
   Drill two holes in one mold half. Tie molds tightly together. Pour in a little thin plaster. Turn and twist the mold so plaster coats all of the interior. When this has set, pour in more and repeat the turning. Continue until the mold is full. Remove plaster.

3 Soften paraffin in warm water and strip from the casting.

4 Silicone mold: the fish is cast in polyester resin, taking care

to follow the mixing instructions. Mix a small quantity of plastic mass and catalyst with white pigment added. Paint on layers of resin, adding strips of glass fiber cloth for strength, forming a hollow final casting.

5 While the first layer of resin is still soft, cast a wooden mounting block into the backside half.
   A Resin
   B Glass fiber fabric
   C Wood mounting block
   D Silicone mold
   E Plaster coat
   When both halves are cured, apply resin to the edges of the two fish halves and bind the halves together until the two halves have joined together.
   After the mold has been opened

and the casting removed, trim it to cut away excess resin. Put in artificial eyes, and cement on the prepared fins before applying the final coats of paint.

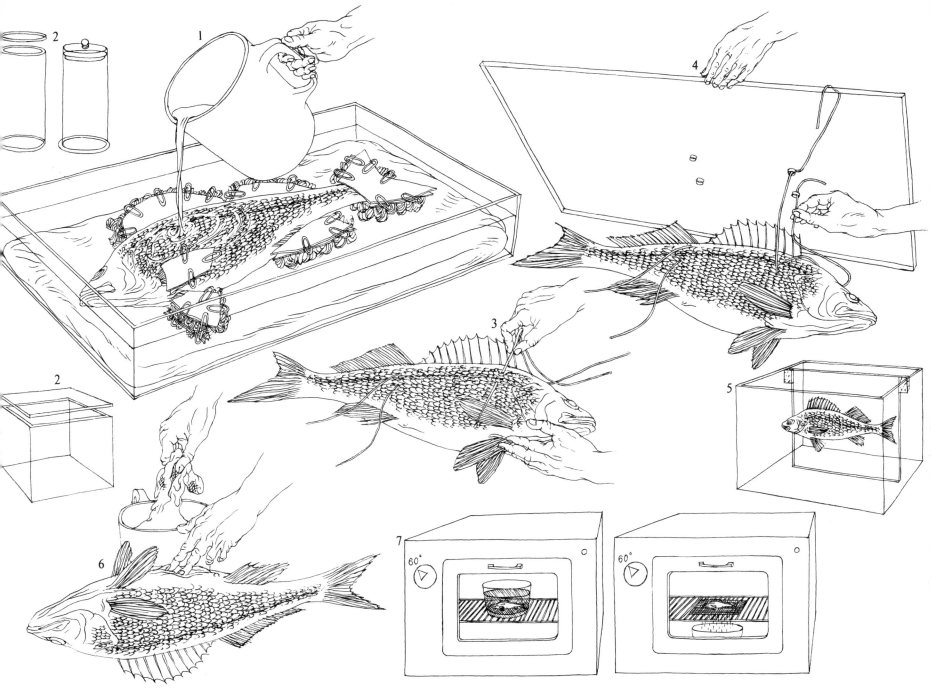

WET PRESERVATION

Wet preservation is best suited to small fish. The disadvantage is that colors are not so well retained: poorest in spirits, a little better in Formalin, best of all in a sugar solution.

First, remove mucus and inject a 4–10 % Formalin solution via the mouth and anal opening. Bend and massage the fish to distribute the liquid.

1 Place fish in plastic tray with fins held in place by cardboard, clips, and wood wool soaked in the fixing solution. Pour fixing solution over fish to cover it. Let stand for about a week or until fully fixed. Then the fin supports are re-moved and the fish is transferred to the glass container that will hold it permanently in a bath of fixing solution.

FIXING SOLUTIONS
Alcohol, 70–80 %
Formalin, 4 %
Formol-alcohol; one part 40 % Formalin, 9 parts 80 % alcohol.

SUGAR SOLUTION
The fish is first fixed in 4 % Formalin for two days, then rinsed and put in sugar solution of 8 oz sugar to 1 qt of water (250 grams/1 liter).

GLYCERINE SOLUTION
1 part 96 % alcohol,
1 part glycerine,
2^1/ 2 parts distilled water.

MOUNTING A FISH ON PRESERVATION GLASS

2 *Any kind of glass jar will do to hold a wet preserved fish, but a square fish tank or similar vessel is best. A glass sheet is used to mount the fish. This is cut a touch smaller than the inside dimensions of the container.*
3 *A strong thread is sewn through the back of the fish.*
4 *Holes are drilled at the proper spots in the glass sheet to receive the thread, which ties the fish to the glass sheet.*
5 *The sheet is held in place by cork pieces wedged on both sides.*
If the fish's belly shrinks, shape may be restored by injecting

Formalin solution. Let the tank stand open three days before adding the cover.

PARAFFIN REPLACE-MENT METHOD

Paraffin is used to replace the tissue liquids of the fish. Clean fish as before and inject Formalin into stomach.

6 *Remove viscera via a small cut and fill body with gauze soaked in plaster. Replace eyes with artificial eyes. Dehydration is done by soaking the fish in successively stronger solutions of alcohol for 24 hours for each solution.*
50 % alcohol
70 % alcohol
80 % alcohol
90 % alcohol

96 % alcohol
Pure alcohol
Soak fish in solution of 50 % alcohol, 50 % benzol for 96 hours. Repeat with pure benzol for 96 hours.
7 *Place fish in mixture of equal parts of benzol and paraffin, heated to about 140° F (60° C) for 12–24 hours. Repeat with pure melted paraffin Finally, place fish on a metal rack in the heater to melt away excess paraffin. Shellac and paint.*

CASTING IN SOLID PLASTIC

A fish cast in a solid block of clear plastic is spectacular and long-lasting, provided the necessary precautions are observed. Blocks should be cast in layers of 1 in (2½ cm) each. Clear polyester is used. The fish must be dry and contain no air bubbles. A fish prepared by the paraffin method is good.

1 Construct a mold box of wood, cardboard, glass, or plexiglass. Make sure the box is level before casting.
2 Casting is done in 3 steps. First, pour in a layer of plastic 1 in (2½ cm) thick. Cover box to keep out dust which would mar the finished casting.

A The first layer. Let this set until it is jellylike.
3 The fish is first soaked in acetone and allowed to dry. When completely dry, press the fish very gently into the jelly-like first layer of plastic. Pour in the middle layer or layers of plastic, no layer thicker than the first. Make sure no bubbles form in the liquid plastic. If any form, suck them up out of the plastic with a hand vacuum pipette syringe. Immediately clean the syringe with plastic solvent.
4 Fill the mold box to the desired level by pouring in fresh layers of plastic, no layer more than 1 in (2½ cm) thick.

A First or bed layer
B Second or body layer
C Third or final layer

For large fish, use as many layers as needed. After the plastic block has solidified for a few hours, bake it in oven for 1 hour at 160° F (70°C) to complete the curing. Then turn off the oven and let the block cool slowly in the oven. Remove block from box and let stand for 2 weeks to harden. Wash the block with acetone, then polish with sandpaper and a good polishing compound.
5 For a high-quality surface finish, each viewing surface can be glass-polished in the following manner:

Coat a glass plate with parting-agent (nonstick insulation) and spread a thin layer of plastic on it.

Moisten the sanded block with acetone and press the glass sheet onto the surface.

Cure in oven at 120°–140° F (50°–60°C).

Repeat on the other viewing surfaces. The glass sheet comes off after each curing, leaving a perfectly smooth surface that can be polished with a buffing wheel and polishing compound.

MOUNTING A FISH HEAD

First, photograph the fish, clean the mucus.

6 Cut skin of neck away from body before you remove the head.
7 Nail head as shown to temporary mount board. Remove eyes, prop the mouth open. Fix head by soaking in 8–10% Formalin for 10 days. Rinse, hang up to dry. When fully dry, head is removed from board, the skin edges are cut evenly, and the head is remounted on a new prepared mount board. Install artificial eyes, fill any holes with wax or clay, and then shellac and paint the head to resemble the living fish.

GYOTAKU – JAPANESE FISH PRINTS

Gyotaku is the art of making Japanese fish prints. It reproduces the size, form, and features of the fish exactly as they are in nature, and is accomplished by pressing a smooth sheet of paper or fabric against the prepared surface of the fish. As an art form, it has been practiced in China and Japan for many years. The expression *gyotaku* is a phonetic translation of an old Chinese word that is now part of the Japanese language. The first part, *gyo-*, stands for fish. The second part, *-taku*, means stone rubbing. *Gyotaku*, consequently, means "to produce an impression by rubbing".

In April, 1955, the Association of *Gyotaku* (*Gyotaku-no-kai*) was formed in Japan. Somewhat later that year the Fish Prints Friends or Association of *Gyotaku* was founded in the United States. Through these associations the correct procedures and technical methods for making Japanese fish prints were established and became widely known.

The method has been widely used in Japan and other countries to make permanent records of the appearance of various species of fish. In recent years it has been accorded enthusiastic reception as a decorative and interpretive art form. It has shown great possibilities when it comes to expressions of composition, form, texture, color, and the use of materials. Expositions featuring *gyotaku* have received excellent reviews in press and on radio.

Originally used merely to record impressions of fishes for future identification, *gyotaku* lends itself to the decoration of many household and similar objects. Through the "transplanting method," for example, an impression can be transferred to such articles as lampshades, book covers, etc. The materials – paper, ink, colors, tampos, brushes, etc., – must be of high quality. Results also depend on practice and experimentation, as in any other artistic venture.

Paper: Fish contain much water, so the paper must be water resistant and tough. What is known as Japanese rice paper comes nearest in quality and type, and is generally available. Various sheer fabrics can also be used.

Color: Beginners should start with *sumi*, a special charcoal ink also known as Chinese ink. Water colors, oils, pastels, and even acrylics can be used.

Brushes: A variety will be needed; hard brushes for oils, soft brushes for water colors, pointed ones for details, and broad ones for extended areas.

Tampos: These are unspun cotton pledges or swabs, wooden sticks tipped with cotton, and small sponges wrapped in nylon, cotton, or linen cloth.

Other minor articles: Thin toweling or other sheer, absorbent cloth, single-edge razor blade or art knife, scissors, tweezers, needles, thumbtacks, alcohol, hydrogen peroxide, formalin, a good-sized worktable, assorted dishes, flat pieces of wood, sheet cardboard.

The best way to start is to obtain a supply of the most essential materials, a few small fish, and go to work. *Gyotaku* is not expensive, is wide open for experimentation, and affords great satisfaction as one's skill improves with experience.

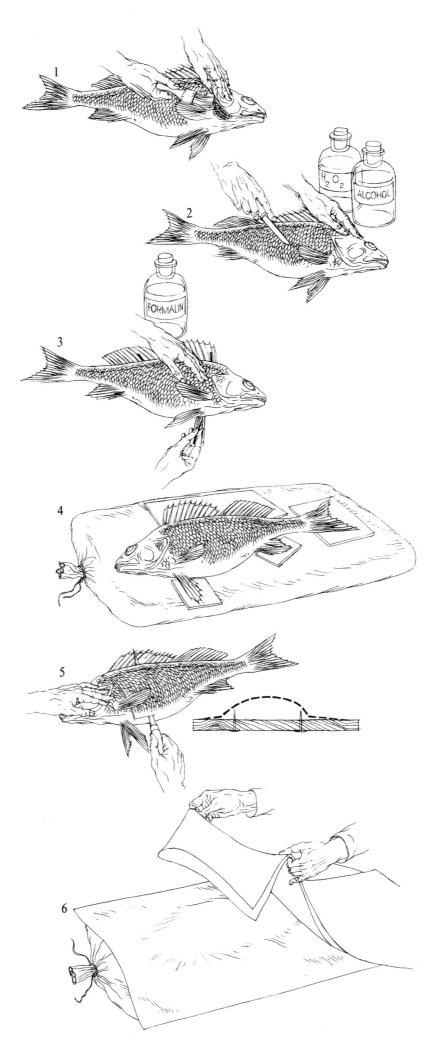

1 Wash the fish thoroughly with detergent or, if needed, alcohol to remove all traces of skin mucous, blood, and body oil. Rinse with fresh water until all detergent has been removed.

2 In warm weather, if there is any risk of the fish spoiling, the viscera should be removed. Blood is removed with alcohol. Blood stains on paper can be bleached with hydrogen peroxide (H_2O_2).

3 The fins of dead fish tend to fold down. A pin or small nail is thrust into the muscular base of one of the foremost spines. The spine thus erected will pull the remaining spines along. Then formalin or alcohol should be applied.

4 A bag filled with wet sand is used to hold the fish firmly during printing. Thin pieces of wood or cardboard can be placed beneath the fins to hold them steady and well spread.

5 Another popular way to fix the fish is to split the fish into halves and put the upper half on a wooden board where it is fastened with pins or small nails.

THE INDIRECT METHOD

6 In the indirect method, a sheet of thin rice paper is applied to the surface of the fish, and on top of that a thin damp towel which is removed when the paper is sufficiently moist.

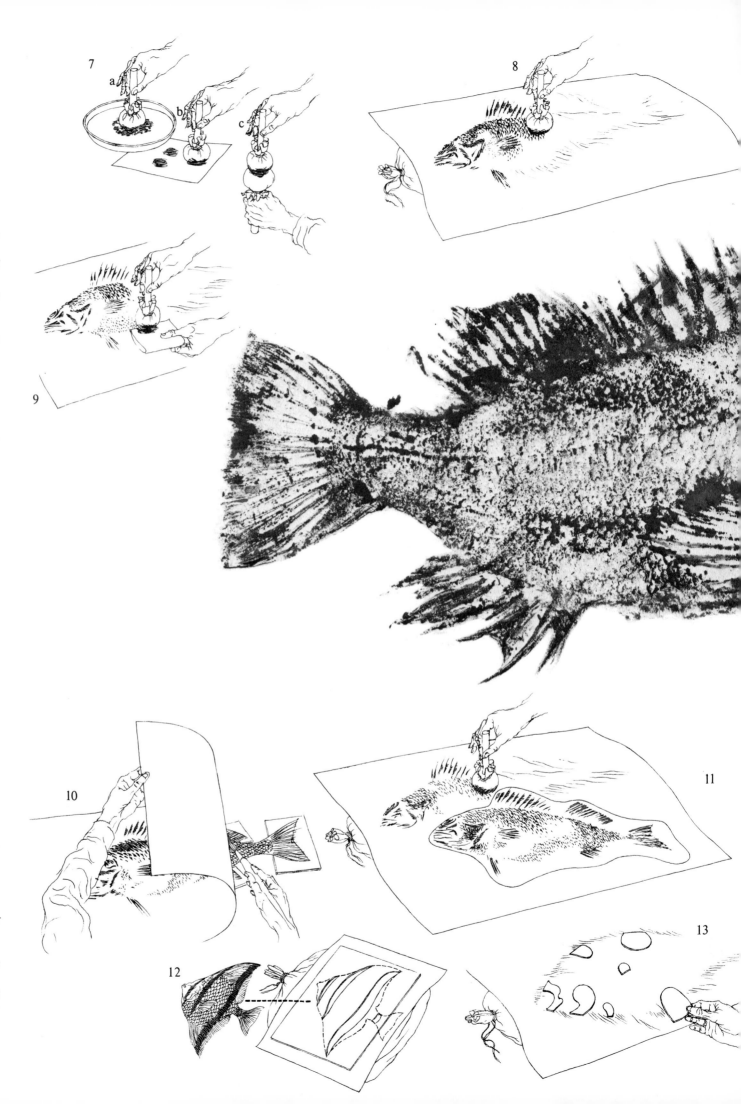

7 Paint or Chinese ink is spread on a plate and a tampo is dipped into it. The amount of paint or ink absorbed by the tampo is tested by touching it to a piece of paper. A large tampo can be used as a stamp pad.

8 Touch the paper very lightly with the tampo, using a stroking motion. Use smaller tampo to bring out details.

9 To keep the color from overflowing, place a strip of paper along the outline of the fish body on top of the print paper.

10 To remove the rice paper from the fish, first gently moisten the back of the fins with a wet brush. After a while moisture will spread from underneath and the paper will easily let go from the fish body.

11 For a print to achieve the impression of two fish swimming side by side, make a print in the normal way. Then make an extra print and cut it out with scissors. Place the second print partly on top of the first. The final printing procedure is then followed.

12 In case the fish has dark spots or stripes, a firm but not too thick paper with appropriate cutouts should be used as a stencil. Place this on top of the fish. The cutouts are then filled with paint or ink with a brush or a tampo.

13 If the fish has white or light colored spots, identical pieces of paper should be cut out and put over such spots so they show when the rice paper is removed.

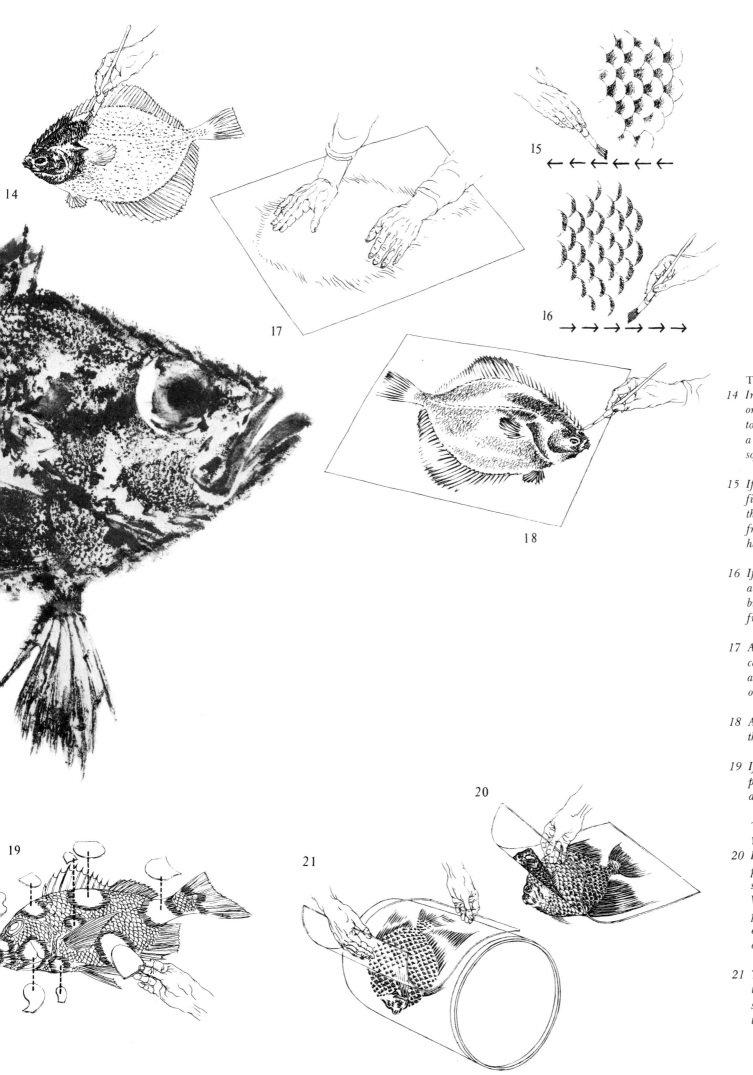

THE DIRECT METHOD

14 *In the direct method, paint or ink is applied directly to the fish with a flat brush; a hard brush for oils or a soft brush for water colors.*

15 *If the concave part of the fins are to be accentuated, the brush should be moved from the tail toward the head.*

16 *If the convex part of the fins are to be accentuated, the brush should be applied from head toward the tail.*

17 *A piece of rice paper is now carefully placed on the fish and rubbed by the fingers all over the surface of the fish.*

18 *Accentuate details with a thin brush.*

19 *If the fish has light spots, proceed in the same manner as described in sketch 13.*

THE TRANSPLANTING METHOD

20 *In the Tensho-ho or transplanting method, oil is smeared on top of the fish. With some sort of transparent material, nylon, polyethylene, etc., an imprint can be made.*

21 *The imprint can now be transferred to other objects such as lampshades, leather, books, etc.*

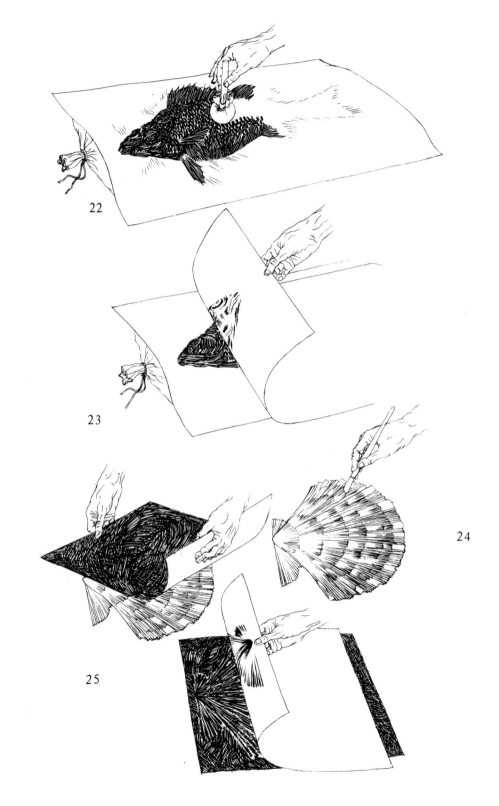

22 In the "quick method," a sheet of thin paper is pressed against the surface of the fish. Ink, paint, or water color is then applied with a tampo or brush as in the direct method.

23 A rice paper is pressed against the first paper and then is treated as in the direct method.

24 In making prints of hard surfaces such as sea horses, shells, etc., a layer of glue is first applied.

25 A carbon paper is now pressed upon the surface with the carbon side out. A thin paper is pressed against the carbon paper and the impression is created by rubbing with a hard object such as the bowl of a spoon.

*The oceans are the last
frontier still open to most
modern men for individual
exploration. Present day boats,
motors, and fishing and navigation
equipment have put this mysterious,
exciting frontier within reach
of almost all who have a yen to
discover for themselves the true
identity of the sea and its denizens.*

FRANK T. MOSS
in Successful Ocean
Game Fishing

To the fisherman, a boat is as necessary a tool as the rod, reel, hook or line. Boats have been used by fishermen for thousands of years, yet it is only in the last half-century that specialized types have been developed expressly for use in sportfishing on fresh water and salt.

Take, for example, the so-called high-speed "dory" – an outboard-powered craft with an unsinkable foam-filled triple-V hull providing speeds ranging from 20 to 40 knots, depending on the hull size and engine rating. The great advantages of these craft are their stability, speed, buoyancy, manoeuvrability and shallow draft; while, in addition, the interior layout of the hull leaves plenty of space for the fishermen and their gear.

Constructed of fibreglass, these modern dories are available in a wide range of sizes from modest tiller-steered 11-footers (3.3 m) to sea-going centre-console models of over 21 ft (6.5 m).

Smaller boats in the 11 to 13 ft range (3.3–4.0 m) are ideally suited for the inshore and estuary angler who needs a speedy craft to keep in touch with fast-moving bass shoals. They can be trailed easily behind a car.

There will, however, be many occasions when local conditions demand the use of a boat with a more traditional type of displacement hull. For example, fishermen wishing to launch a boat off an open beach must look for a beamy craft with a high, upswept prow which will ride easily over the incoming breakers.

Of special interest are those traditional craft, like the Yorkshire coble and the "lute-sterned" boats of Kent and Sussex, both of which were specially designed for beach launching and have proved their worth over the centuries. Nowadays, many of these traditional craft are being produced with modern maintenance-free fibreglass hulls – thus combining the best of both worlds.

At the other end of the scale, of course, there are the large offshore sportfishing craft – many of them privately owned; while others, run by professional skippers, take out parties of sea anglers on charter trips. Many top-ranking charter boat skippers tend to specialize in some particular aspect of deep-sea angling, such as shark fishing, wreck fishing for giant conger and ling, or "reefing" for pollack, cod and – in some favoured areas – big bass.

Equipment, also, has become highly specialized. Modern electronic echo-sounders and navigation equipment has taken the guesswork out of mark location and fish detection, and vastly improved radio communication means extra safety on the water. On the larger deep-sea craft such refinements as fighting chairs enable fish weighing many hundreds of pounds to be played out with maximum efficiency and minimum discomfort.

BOATS FOR SHELTERED WATERS

A This utility punt is square-
ended with a scow bow and
flat bottom. Built in sizes of
13–20 ft (4–6 m), it can be
propelled by oars or outboard
motor. Construction is of
wood or fiberglass. It is easily
built in "solid" timber or
marine-plywood by the home
handyman.

B A medium-sized inflatable
dinghy can open up all sorts
of opportunities for the tour-
ing sportfisherman. It can be
carried ready-inflated on a car
roof rack (B1), or stowed
deflated in the boot and
inflated within minutes upon
arrival at the fishing water
(B2). Propulsion is by oars or
small outboard motor.
There's little risk of a good-
quality inflatable being punc-
tured by small fish hooks, but it
is advisable to use a landing net
– NOT a sharp-pointed gaff!

C Almost any beamy rowing or
outboard-powered dinghy in
the 10–14 ft (3–4.3 m) range
can be used for freshwater
and estuary fishing. Available
mainly in fiberglass or
marine-ply, many of the
smaller models are light
enough to load on a car
roof-rack.

AMPHIBIOUS FISHING: BOAT TYPES

Boats of 16 ft (5 m) and lesser
lengths which are carried by
trailer or car roof- rack are
usually built of fiberglass,
although many marine-ply
models are popular.
Round-bilge models are easier
to launch from an open beach
than hulls with V-bottoms.
Emergency flotation is
provided by buoyancy blocks
of expanded polystyrene foam
placed under the thwarts, or
foamed into place.

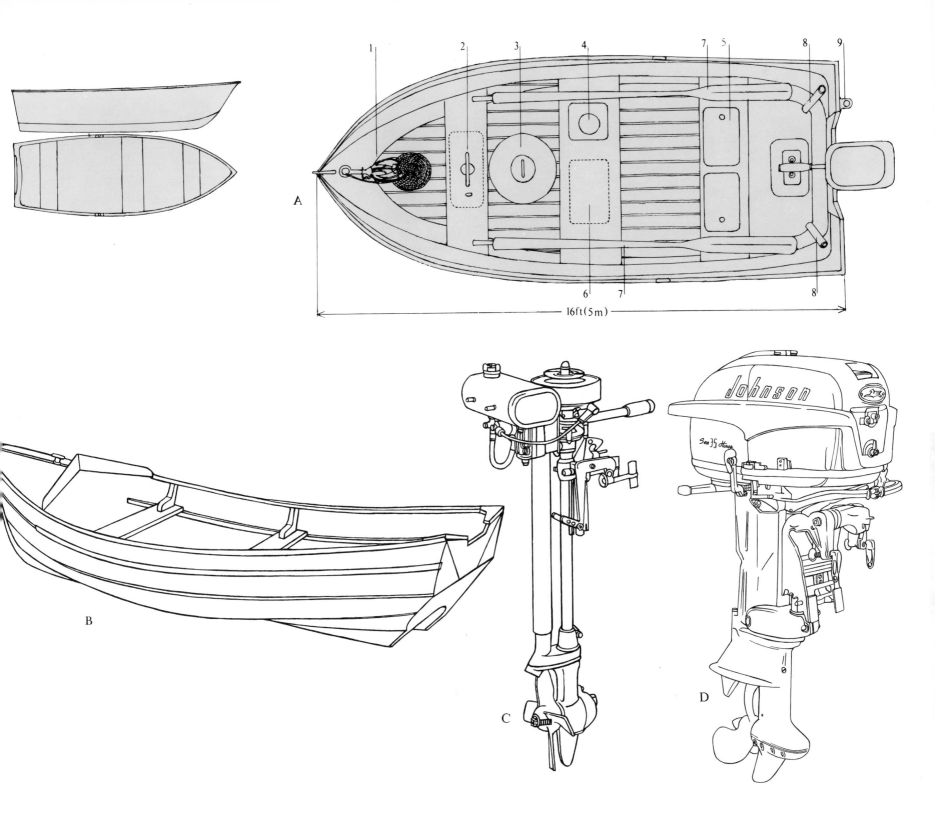

A A fishing dinghy can be as basic and simple as you like, provided it is seaworthy and properly equipped with anchor, rope, oars, rowlocks, bailing can and other essential items of safety equipment. Alternatively, it can incorporate all sorts of refinements to make your fishing trips more interesting and successful. The round-bilge dinghy shown here contains the following items:

1 Folding anchor and anchor line.
2 Spare fuel tank under the forward thwart.
3 Circular live-bait tank made from a plastic waste can.
4 "Lunch box" portable echo-sounder.
5 Complete tackle box.
6 Fish box or storage locker built into the after seat.
7 Pair of oars.
8 Trolling rod holders.
9 Sounder transducer.

B Yorkshire "Pebble" trailable fishing boat. Constructed of heavy duty fibreglass along the traditional lines of the Yorkshire "coble". Note the upswept prow and raked stern – two features which make it an extremely good boat for launching from an open beach. Available in 14 ft (4.3 m) and 16 ft (4.9 m) versions.

OUTBOARD MOTORS
When choosing an outboard motor, the majority of dinghy anglers look for reliability, low running costs and easy maintenance. An outboard used for sea or estuary fishing should have a good saltwater-proof specification. There are two main types:
C The slow-revving, strictly utilitarian sort, with all working parts readily accessible and with no unnecessary gadgets. Starting

is usually by means of a thin piece of rope wound around the flywheel pulley. This type of motor is sturdy, comparatively light to carry and reasonably priced.
D Faster revving models fitted with a streamlined cowling and usually with separate fuel tank. The smaller models usually have manual recoil starting; larger and more powerful motors are equipped with electric starting.

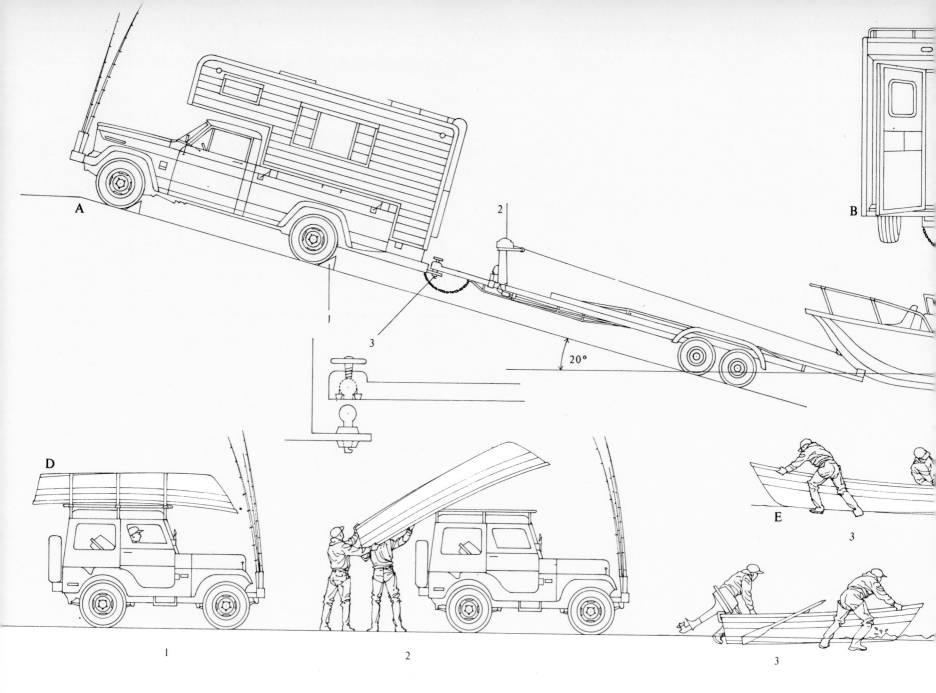

AMPHIBIOUS FISHING

Attach a boat trailer to the rear end of a motorised caravan and you have one of the most mobile rigs a fisherman could dream up for wandering with the fish wherever they happen to migrate. The boat pictured here is a typical 16-footer (5 m) such as is used the world over for amphibious fishing in both salt and fresh water. The secret of success in this kind of fishing is to have versatile equipment that catches fish wherever you go.

Amphibious fishing appeals to the man who yearns to fish far from the noisy crowd.

A motorised caravan, Jeep, or family car provides land mobility. On the water the boat carries the fisherman beyond the farthest casting range of shore-bound anglers. Many owners of small fishing boats once were surf casters. The fish they catch often repay operating costs. The adventures they and their families experience constitute a bonus beyond price.

THE TOW VEHICLE

Whether the tow vehicle is a 4-wheel-drive Landrover, a light truck, or just the family car, certain requirements must be fulfilled:

Adequate trailer hitch properly attached to tow vehicle frame.

Brakes in top shape.

Legal trailer light connections.

Hydraulic jack for lifting the vehicle and a complete repair kit.

THE BOAT TRAILER

Small boat trailers are constructed of welded steel. Tyres usually are smaller than on a car. Boat's keel and bilges engage rollers on the trailer frame. Bilge rollers can be adjusted to shape of the boat. Hull is tied down with heavy canvas straps. A geared hand winch on a raised stanchion forward aids in retrieving the boat from the water. Weight capacity of the trailer should be 50 per cent more than boat's weight. Trailers used around salt water require care to prevent corrosion of wheels, springs, lights, other vital parts.

HANDLING TRAILER AND CARTOP BOATS

Getting small fishing boats off their trailers or cartop carriers and into the water is not difficult, but requires some care and planning. Heavy boats that cannot be slid by hand over a sandy beach must be launched where there is a hard-top launching ramp.

A *Most such ramps are made with a pitch angle of not over 20°. Even so, the driver should block the tow vehicle's rear wheels (1) before letting go the trailer winch cable (2) The towing hitch (3) does not have to be disconnected for launching from a ramp.*

B *The sketch illustrates the degree of turning that can be achieved with a good trailer rig.*

C *This sketch is a closeup of trailer tongue and winch unit. The winch (1) may be electric or*

hand-powered. Cable (2) is stored on an internal brake-equipped drum. Boat's bow is brought up close to winch head before the boat is tied down for trailing. The safety chains shown are required by law in some countries to hold trailer to tow vehicle if the ball-hitch fails.

LAUNCHING SMALL BOATS IN THE SURF

1 13-ft (4-m) boat is carried on a Jeep in an inverted position on heavy ladder racks. It is easily lifted down by two fishermen. Fishing rods, rigged for action, are in PVC tubing holders on the front bumper, ready for action when fish are located.

2 Preparing for launch, the anglers lift the boat down from the cartop carrier, place it on the beach, and load it with fishing equipment, tackle, oars, anchor and line, and personal gear. Outboard motor is attached to the stern and spare fuel tank placed in the boat under a thwart.

3 Before loading, the boat is hauled close to the water's edge. When all is ready, the boat is slid to the water. Sometimes wooden or inflated rubber or canvas rollers are used to facilitate hauling. A 13-ft fibreglass boat, fully-equipped for two anglers, will weigh over 300 lb (140 kg) without passengers.

4 As soon as the boat is waterborne the oarsman gets in and unships the oars. He starts rowing while his companion, who will operate the motor, continues to push the boat off as long as he can. The oarsman rows directly away from the beach, keeping the boat's bow pointed into the incoming waves.

5 The water is getting deeper under the boat and the motorman jumps in after giving the boat a last, hard push. As soon as he can, the motorman lowers the outboard motor into operating position. If the lower unit bumps the bottom, he must raise it again to save the propeller from damage on stones or rocks.

6 When the water is deep enough to use power, the motorman starts the outboard. The oarsman can now relax, but he keeps his oars ready to resume rowing if the motor should suddenly stop functioning. Speed is kept quite low until the boat is through the breaking waves close to shore and in deep water.

RETURNING TO SHORE THROUGH A SURF

E 1 Coming in through a breaking surf, the motorman slows the boat to trolling speed while taking the seas directly on the stern. He waits for a succession of larger waves to go by and watches to sea for a lesser wave to ride in to the beach.

2 When the right wave comes, the operator speeds the boat just enough to maintain position on the front slope of the wave. Riding the wave like a surfboard, the boat speeds directly to the beach. This takes nerve and skill, but in the hands of a practical surf-rider it is less dangerous than it may appear.

3 The ride ends when the boat slides up onto the sandy beach. Frequently the men can step ashore dryshod. Quickly they leap out and drag the boat up above reach of the largest waves. In some areas surf fishermen do beach safety patrol work during nonfishing hours and over big holiday weekends.

SMALL SPORT-FISHING BOATS

Here is a group of small sportfishing boats such as are found in many British and European fishing areas. The larger outboard and stern-drive models often fish many miles at sea. Smaller models are at home in inshore waters.

A Popular fibreglass dinghy. 12–16 ft (3.7–4.9 m) in length. Cartop or trailer carrier.
B Unsinkable dory with fast-planing "triple-vee" hull. 11–17 ft (3.4–5.2 m). Note the beamy, flat standing space inside the boat.
1 Typical inboard layout of a 17 ft (5.2 m) dory with steering wheel and centre console.

Smaller models intended for inshore fishing can be obtained with tiller steering.
2 Cross-section of fibreglass dory hull showing the foam buoyancy system.
C Outboard-powered Sussex "Cob". 16½ ft (5 m). The seats incorporate built-in buoyancy tanks. Note the sharply raked 'lute' stern, which helps to

prevent pooping by a following sea when landing on an exposed beach.
1 Profile of the Sussex Cob with optional detachable cuddy fitted to provide protection from weather and flying spray.
2 This alternative ketch-rigged version of the Sussex Cob would be ideal for the inshore sport-fisherman who also enjoys sailing

– and its consequent saving in fuel costs! The sailing version can, of course, be powered also by an outboard motor.
D Small centre-console boat 17-19 ft (5·2-5·8 m) has trolling seat aft, casting deck forward of console.
1 Sounder on console.
2 Tackle under seat.
3 Cutaway profile:

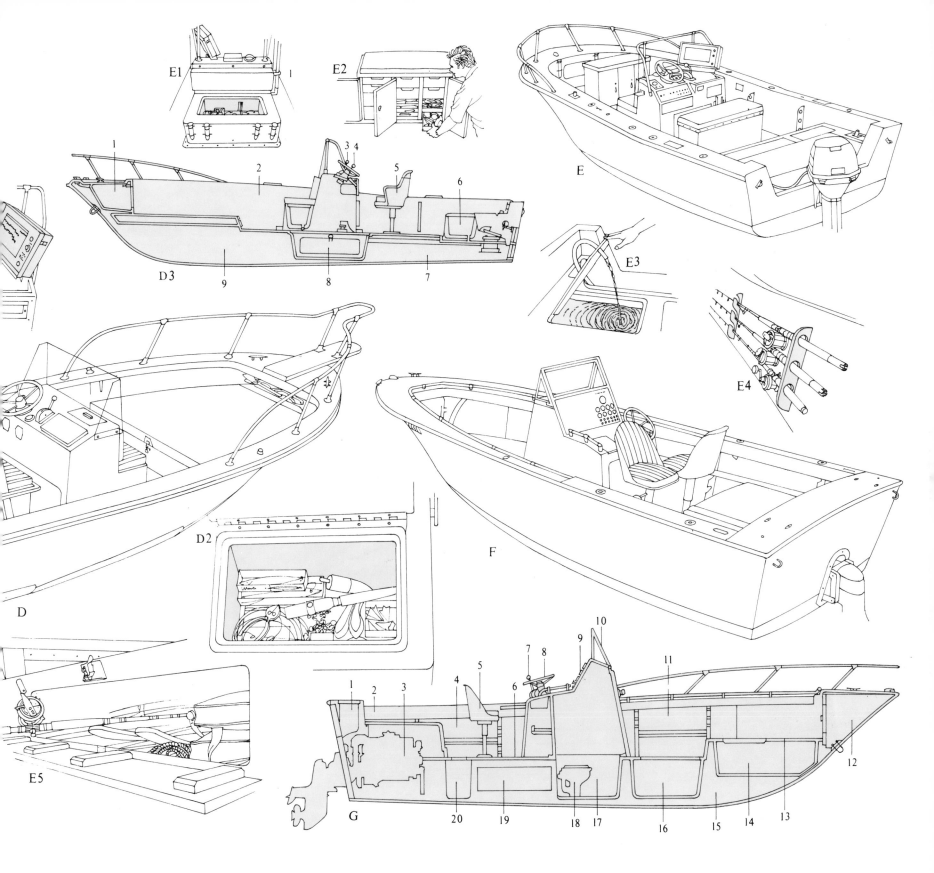

1 Anchorline locker.
2 Cockpit side.
3 Steering wheel.
4 Motor controls.
5 Operator's seat.
6 Fish box or well.
7 Underdeck storage.
8 Built-in fuel tank.
9 Underdeck storage.
Variation of layout of boat at
"D". This boat has a large tackle

locker on its forward deck.
1 Rod holders mounted on
  forward seat.
2 Tackle locker doors protect
  contents.
3 Pump supplies water to live
  bait tank.
4 Rods are stowed in cockpit
  side racks.
5 Rod locker can be built into
  cockpit side, as shown.

F This 26 ft (8 m) fisherman features sterndrive power. Engine
  may be either gasoline or diesel,
  developing up to 250 hp. One
  unique feature is a marine toilet
  or "head" located within the
  centre console.
G Inboard profile of the stern-
  drive boat.
  1 Bait wells P & S.
  2 Padded cockpit side.

3 Sterndrive motor.
4 Cockpit side locker.
5 Operator's seat.
6 Cockpit deck.
7 Motor controls.
8 Steering wheel.
9 Instrument panel.
10 Windshield.
11 Side rod locker.
12 Anchorline locker.
13 Forward deck.

14 Underdeck locker.
15 Flotation foam.
16 Underdeck storage.
17 Water tanks P & S.
18 Marine toilet (WC).
19. Built-in fuel tanks.
20 Underdeck fish well.

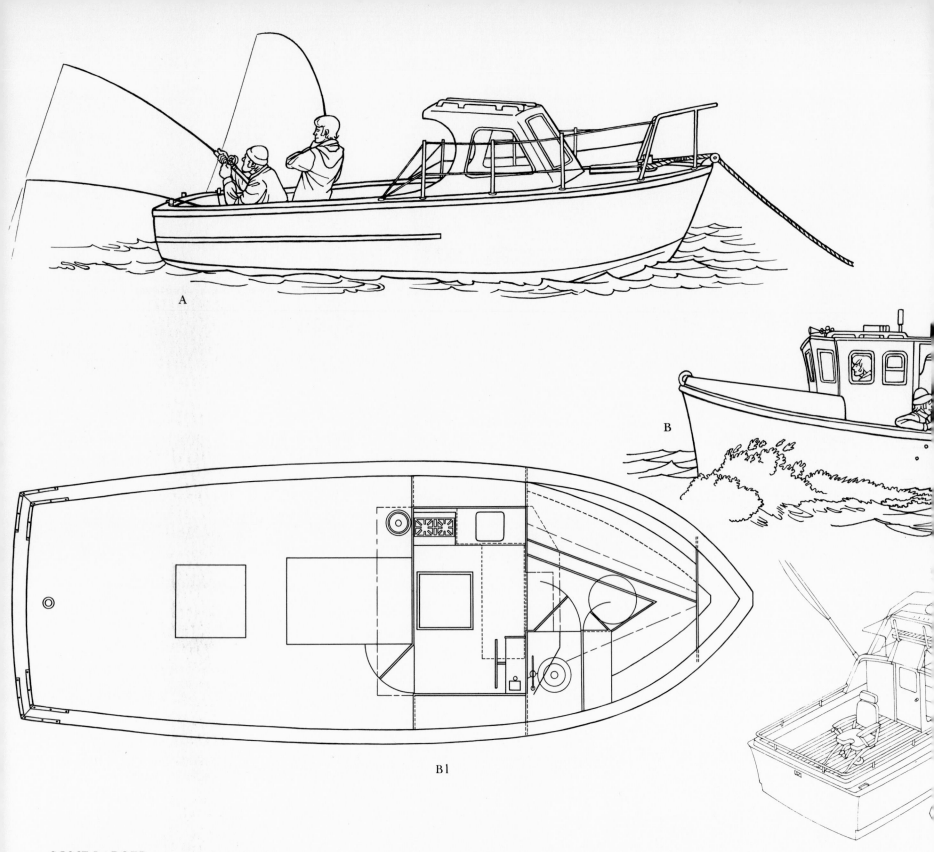

A

B

B1

SOME LARGER SPORTFISHING CRAFT

The boats depicted here are all fairly typical of their type. They range from medium-sized "day fishermen" suitable for private ownership to large offshore charter craft equipped with sleeping accommodation, and capable of undertaking prolonged fishing/cruising trips.

A PEARSON 26

A 26 ft (7.9 m) day fisherman with a fibreglass heavy duty round bilge displacement hull, specially designed and reinforced to take the ground in exposed drying harbours. Equipped with moulded fibreglass open wheelhouse, foredeck with hatch, side deck/coamings, and short aft deck with hatch. The open cockpit allows plenty of uncluttered space

for fishermen and their tackle. One interesting feature of this boat is that it can either be purchased complete, or as a basic hull with pre-moulded wheelhouse, decks, etc., for home completion. The hull is designed to take a wide range of power units.

B CYGNUS MARINE G.M. 26

Designed by Gary Mitchell, this 26 ft (7.9 m) boat is based on the

traditional Cornish timber fishing boats which have proved themselves over hundreds of years. The laminated G.R.P. hull is of the heavy displacement type, featuring a deep forefoot for plenty of grip, long straight keel section and full round bilges. One important advantage of the deep hull design is that, in most cases, the engine can disappear below the deck, thus obviating the need for a raised

engine hatch. The G.M. range of fishing boats are also available in the following alternative sizes: 21 ft (6.4 m); 32 ft (9.8 m) and 36 ft (11.0 m).

1 Interior layout of an alternative version of the G.M. 26, designed for the special needs of Scandinavian commercial fishermen, who often live on their boats for weeks at a time. More thought has therefore been put into

accommodation and "home
comforts" – which in turn is likely
to appeal to sportfishermen
planning to live aboard during
prolonged fishing/cruising trips.

C CONCORDE 27 FT (8.2 M)
*This American-style fast fishing
cruiser has a fibreglass hull and a
maximum speed in excess of 30
knots. It has accommodation for
4–6.*

D 33 FT (10 M)
FALMOUTH FAST
FISHERMAN
*Primarily designed to meet the
demands of modern offshore
sportfishing, especially by
professional charter skippers, this
boat is built on a fibreglass
semi-displacement hull giving a
cruising speed of about 17 knots.
Thus distant deep-sea fishing
marks can be reached without*

*losing too much valuable fishing
time through travelling. For
offshore wreck fishing the boat's
equipment includes Decca
navigation equipment, radar,
graph-type echo sounder, etc.*

E LARGE DEEP-SEA
PARTY BOAT
*A wide variety of craft are used to
take out large parties of
sportfishermen. Many are*

*primarily commercial fishing
vessels which change over to
rod-and-line charter work during
the holiday season, or at weekends.
Others are purpose-built, and
include a licensed bar among their
attractions. Normally they
specialise in deep-sea bottom
fishing, and cater mainly for large
sea angling clubs.*

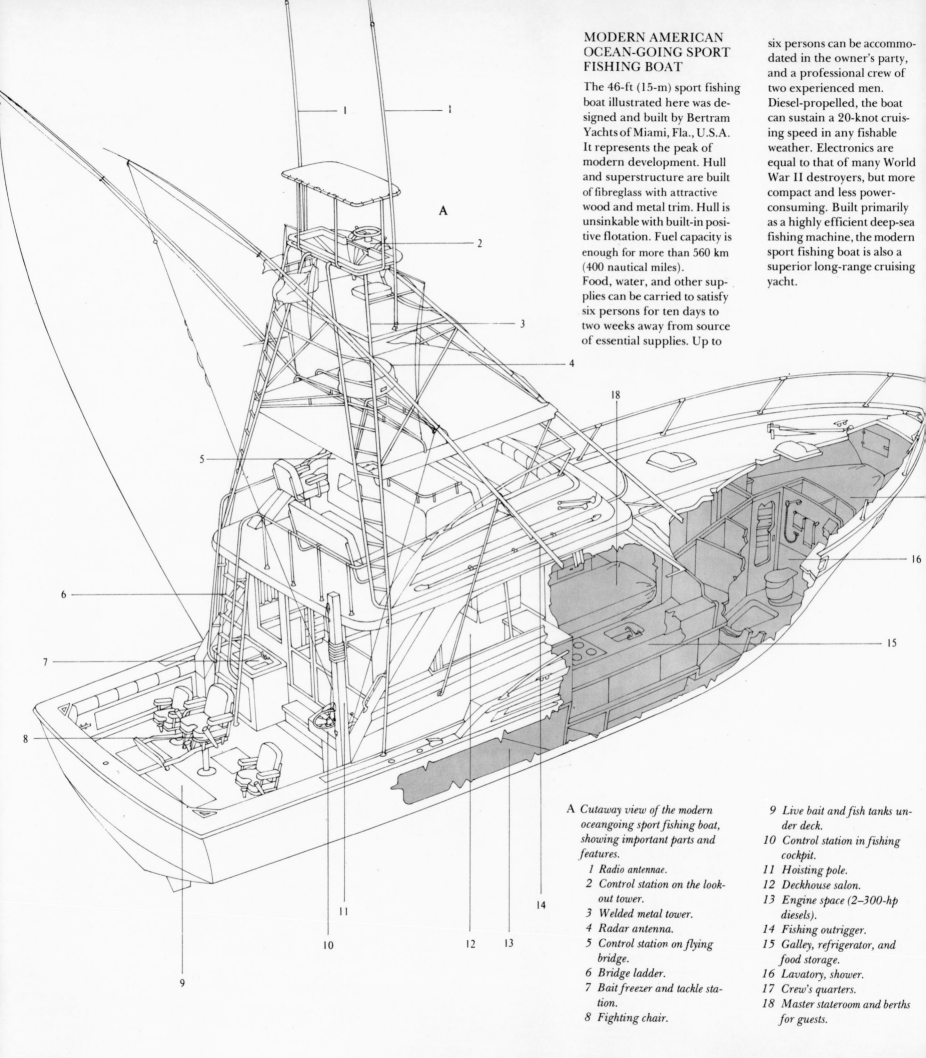

MODERN AMERICAN OCEAN-GOING SPORT FISHING BOAT

The 46-ft (15-m) sport fishing boat illustrated here was designed and built by Bertram Yachts of Miami, Fla., U.S.A. It represents the peak of modern development. Hull and superstructure are built of fibreglass with attractive wood and metal trim. Hull is unsinkable with built-in positive flotation. Fuel capacity is enough for more than 560 km (400 nautical miles). Food, water, and other supplies can be carried to satisfy six persons for ten days to two weeks away from source of essential supplies. Up to six persons can be accommodated in the owner's party, and a professional crew of two experienced men. Diesel-propelled, the boat can sustain a 20-knot cruising speed in any fishable weather. Electronics are equal to that of many World War II destroyers, but more compact and less power-consuming. Built primarily as a highly efficient deep-sea fishing machine, the modern sport fishing boat is also a superior long-range cruising yacht.

A Cutaway view of the modern oceangoing sport fishing boat, showing important parts and features.

1 Radio antennae.
2 Control station on the look-out tower.
3 Welded metal tower.
4 Radar antenna.
5 Control station on flying bridge.
6 Bridge ladder.
7 Bait freezer and tackle station.
8 Fighting chair.
9 Live bait and fish tanks under deck.
10 Control station in fishing cockpit.
11 Hoisting pole.
12 Deckhouse salon.
13 Engine space (2–300-hp diesels).
14 Fishing outrigger.
15 Galley, refrigerator, and food storage.
16 Lavatory, shower.
17 Crew's quarters.
18 Master stateroom and berths for guests.

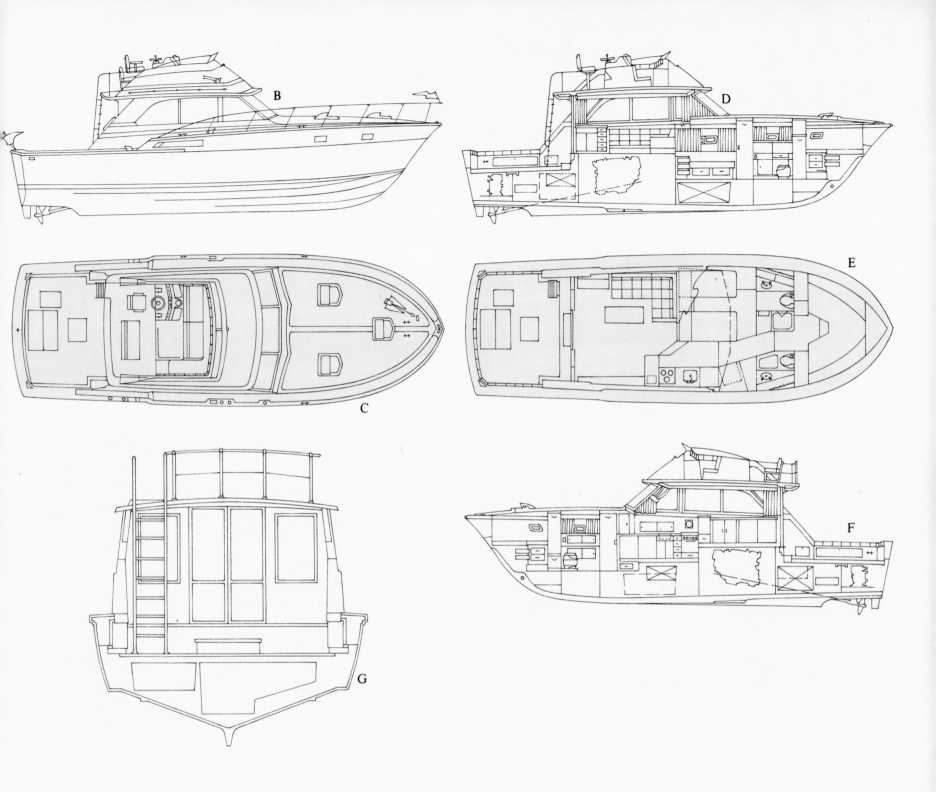

B OUTBOARD PROFILE

Outwardly, the boat is fairly conventional in design. The deep-V hull is designed to run fast in rough water without pounding. All windows and ports are shatterproof safety glass. Directional stability without an external keel is provided by the keel effect of the hull. Despite the boat's size she is highly maneuverable at fishing speeds.

C OUTBOARD PLAN VIEW

Seen from above, the boat has an excellent beam-length ratio with great static and dynamic stability. The flying bridge controls are placed well aft to give the captain clear vision into the fishing cockpit, essential for teamwork between angler and crew. A minimum of exposed wood and metal trim expedites easy maintenance.

D INBOARD PROFILE

The interior has been designed to utilize every bit of available space without giving the feeling of being crowded. Air-conditioning can be installed for tropical climates. This, the electric galley stove, and all other electric units are powered by a 7–10 kw diesel generator. An evaporator distills extra fresh water.

E INBOARD PLAN VIEW

The deckhouse salon occupies the space over the engine room. Amidship is a master stateroom and galley. Lavatory and storage space separate owner's and guests' quarters from crew's quarters forward. Tackle is stowed in special boxes or lockers built into the sides and overhead of the deckhouse salon, readily available.

F INBOARD PROFILE

Safety features include automatic bilge pumps, fire extinguishers, and fire-detecting units.

G HULL CROSS-SECTION

The deep-V hull carries its V-sections back to the stern, providing a soft, non-pounding ride in rough water, and excellent steering stability in following seas, qualities that are essential to good fishing boat operation.

VISUAL NAVIGATION
FOR FISHERMEN

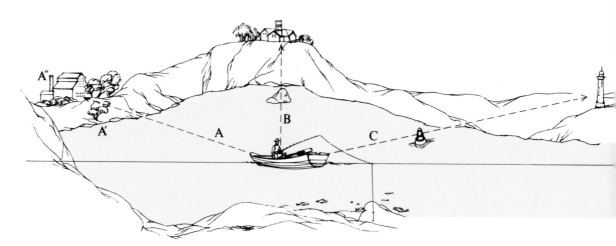

It is popular among non-fishermen to equate success in fishing with "luck". But experienced fishermen know that while luck or good fortune does play an important part in fishing success, the ability to come back to a newly found superior fishing spot is even more important. Out on the water where there are no visible landmarks, how can one return to exactly the same spot where he caught good fish before?

The simplest form of position location is visual and depends on using two or more "marks" on the nearby shore. Basically, a mark is a line drawn through two prominent, separated objects on shore that are visible from the fishing spot, the line being projected through the visible objects to the observer's location. In the accompanying illustration, mark lines A, B, and C all happen to cross at the fisherman's location.

Mark line A is observed by looking toward shore at a compass azimuth of 300° and seeing a tall tree (A'), that stands on the shore, lined up with a factory smoke stack (A'') further back from the shore.

Mark line B is observed by looking north (000°) to the shore where a large dark rock on the beach lies exactly under the tower of a residence some distance beyond. Range line C is observed by looking roughly north-east (055°) and seeing a bell buoy on the water directly in line with a lighthouse farther back on the land. These marks are imaginary of course, but they show what to look for on the shore to establish marks that can be recorded in a notebook and used in the future to return to the good fishing location.

While a compass in the boat is a great help in establishing the direction of marks, it is not necessary for getting onto a fishing spot by use of marks alone. But a compass is part of every experienced fisherman's essential equipment. Knowing the speed of his boat and the approximate running time required to reach the fishing location from shore or the harbour, the fisherman can place his boat quite close to the desired location before pinpointing his location by using marks.

The ultimate check for positive identification of the fishing spot is to take the depth of water with an electronic sounder or other means. The sounder will often also reveal the type of bottom and presence of fish. Marks require clear weather and a good eye for picking out objects ashore that create a visual mark line when observed. Drawing a picture of the mark in a notebook preserves a record of its appearance.

SELECTING MARKS

Choose objects on shore that have good separation between them when in line. A long base-line is more accurate than a short base-line.

USE BINOCULARS

A good pair of marine binoculars will help you see that marks might not be visible to the unaided eye. Keep binoculars protected from water.

WHAT ABOUT FOG?

Obviously, you can't see marks through fog, but if you can see just one mark, and run off on that mark, you may find your fishing spot by stopping to fish as you move down the visible mark. Have a small marker buoy ready to drop overboard when you feel you are close to the desired location.

WHAT ABOUT COMPASSES?

Boat's compass should be mounted where it can be used for taking bearings. In a small boat, a portable prismatic compass is a good substitute.

USING CHARTS

Nautical charts of coastal areas often give clues to good marks or objects that may provide bearings. Record the exact position of mark objects on your chart and draw mark lines on the chart to your favourite fishing spots. Marks are generally more accurate than bearings from a hand-held compass.

ANCHORING

Always anchor upwind and up-current of the best fishing spot. Plan on using three times the depth of water as an effective anchor line length.

USING MARKS
WHILE TROLLING

Here a long shoal runs from B to A at an angle to the shore. It is an excellent location for catching game fish by trolling.

1 *Tidal current in this instance flows in the direction of arrow at position 1.*
2 *Prevailing wind blows obliquely across tide as shown by arrow at position 2.*

This creates a broad tide rip or area of choppy water along the offshore edge of the shoal. A channel-marker navigation buoy lies inshore of the shoal as illustrated.

Trolling boats normally troll into a current, so the boats fishing the shoal start at the downtide end of the shoal (B), trolling slowly uptide to the upper end at Location A.

While there is a tide rip just offshore of the BA shoal axis line, the boats have no difficulty staying within the best shoal trolling area, but when there is no rip, staying within the best trolling area may

be troublesome. Therefore, when boats arrive at A, they watch for the range A-A', which forms when the buoy comes under a house or other marker on the shore.

As soon as the mark between the buoy and A' is closed, boats turn left and go down-tide to point B to resume trolling. They recognize point B when the buoy is in line with a bluff and tree, or similar clearly observed mark, up the beach, forming B-B' range line. The down-tide run is usually made at fast trolling speed, but slower than normal full cruising speed.

This circular follow-the-leader type of trolling manoeuvre allows a number of boats to fish over a fairly small area without problems of right-of-way arising to spoil the fishing.

When there is no tidal current or wind to make a rip, boats run from B to A by compass. When the tide flows the other way, the ranges stay the same, but the direction of trolling is reversed.

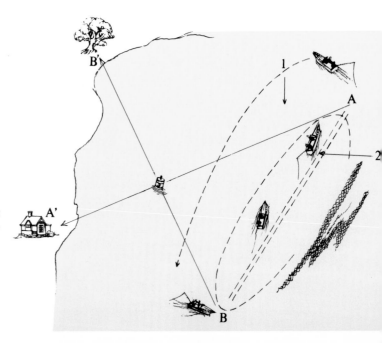

HIDDEN BENEATH THE SURFACE

If the water of this typical coastal cove were stripped away or made as transparent as air, here is what an observer might see from a high vantage point.

1 *Boat with sounder is passing over the submerged channel of an ancient stream. Hudson Canyon, off New York Harbour, is an example of such a hidden river channel on a grand scale. Bottom features of this type attract many species of fish and the electronic sounder is the only practical tool for locating them from the surface.*

2 *Relatively flat, featureless shelf of bottom on either side of the canyon usually harbours relatively few fish. Fish abhor a dead area as strongly as do humans. They are attracted to* areas of discontinuity, or "edges" as anglers sometimes call them, where strong bottom features break the monotony of the bare bottom plain.

3 *A rock pile, dropped by ancient ice from a pre-historic glacier, attracts bottom-dwelling fish such as cod, pollack, bass. Sea life grows on the rocks, providing food for the bottom-dwellers.*

4 *A submerged small hill or seamount is a prime location for many species of resident and wandering fish. Underwater features of this type can be located easily by marks on objects on shore, and by recording a profile of the hill or obstruction with a recording sounder.*

5 *Submerged bed of weed in shallow water that is exposed at low tide is liked by such fish as mullet, flounder, small bass. Weedy bottom gives a different indica-* tion on flasher dial or recorder graph than do bottoms composed of sand, mud, rocks, or gravel-and-shells.

6 *Shells and low rocks near the submerged channel may be a good spot for cod, flounder, bass. Clams in the bottom and mussels on rocks attract many fish.*

7 *A gullied underwater slope may attract some fish because it represents a change from the monotony of unbroken sand or mud bottom. Any submerged slope is worth a try.*

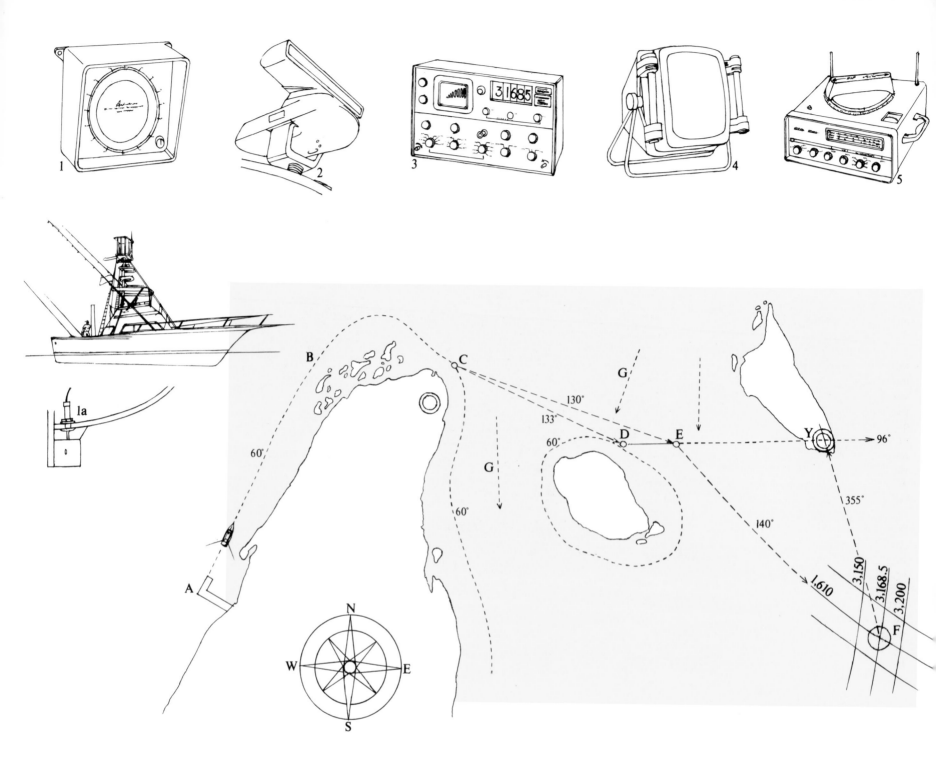

ELECTRONIC NAVIGATION FOR FISHING

Modern sport fishing boats use navigating methods that were the pride of naval vessels in World War II days. These include:
1 Electronic sounder
2 & 4 Radar
3 Loran positioning
5 Radio direction finder

Using combinations of these elements, let us follow the path of a sport fishing boat from its home port at Point A to a good fishing ground at Point F, in thick fog reducing visibility to zero.

Leaving A, the boat uses compass and its electronic sounder to run north-northeastward along the 60 ft depth curve skirting shore.

At B the boat uses both sounder and radar to stay on the 60 ft depth curve and avoid the dangerous rocks inshore. Radar provides what amounts to a "television picture" of objects and shorelines around the boat, including the buoy at location C. At C the boat takes course of 130° to pass inshore of the island at E.

But a tidal current (G) pushes the boat south of its course. At D off the island the captain sees the water shoal to the 60 ft depth and sees the island closer than it should be on the radar. His radio direction finder places the radio beacon at Y on a course of 96°. The radar confirms the buoy northeast of the island at location E to be on the same heading of 96°. The boat changes course to pick up the buoy at position E where it takes a new course of 140° headed toward the fishing grounds at F. Now the captain resorts to loran radio position finding to find point F. Loran obtains lines of position by comparing electrically the signals from pairs of stations. One pair of stations gives the captain the 1,650 line, along which he runs the boat, using his compass. Another pair of stations gives him the 3,000-series lines that cross the other lines on the map. The captain knows that when his loran tells him he is on the 3,168.5 line, he is at point F.

At F, as a final check, the captain takes a radio bearing of the beacon at Y. Bearing is 355°, exactly as it should be. A final check of position is provided by the sounder which indicates a depth equal to that shown on the chart for this position. This, in a simple way, is how fishermen use electronic navigation.

COMMUNICATIONS IN FISHING

In recent years, sport fishermen have learned how to use short- and long-range radio communication for exchanging vital fishing information, obtaining safety and weather reports, and for conducting the sometimes complex business of fishing far from an operating base. In order to know how radio serves fishermen at sea, one must understand the three major types of modern marine radio service. These are:

1 Short-range line-of-sight communication between vessels on the water and between vessels and shore. Short-range radio communication at sea is now largely confined to VHF/FM (very high frequency, frequency-modulated) signals in the 150–170 MHz radio band. VHF signals do not normally "bend" over the horizon as do some lower-frequency signals and they are not easily reflected or refracted by the ionosphere, as are some "skywave" signals. Therefore they were selected for short-range radio work to minimize interference with medium- and long-range radio communications. VHF/FM radio antennae must "see" each other in a direct line to permit adequate communication at these high frequencies. Effective working ranges are from a low of about 8 miles to a high of perhaps 50 or slightly more. Power of VHF units is usually not over 25 watts.

2 Medium-range communication beyond the horizon between ships at sea and ships and shore. This type of communication is usually carried out in the 2–3 MHz band in other bands up to 7 MHz. Amplitude-modulated (AM) signals have been standard in marine radio telephony for many years, but are now being replaced by the more efficient single-sideband (SSB) mode of radio communication. Power of modern AM and SSB medium-range units runs from 50 to 150 watts, range extends up to 300 miles.

3 Long-range radio, 300 to many thousands of miles. Here, "skywave" radio propagation, popularly called "skip", gives tremendous distance to radio signals. Multiple bounces of signals between earth and the ionosphere are common. Long-range radio units made for private and sport fishing use seldom exceed 150 watts input power. AM mode has been widely used, but SSB is rapidly displacing the older AM. Frequencies between 7 and 14 MHz are considered best for very long range radio communication.

The diagram to the right illustrates an exaggerated view of the earth's curvature together with a section of the ionosphere. This layer of rarefied gases high in the atmosphere reflects or refracts certain radio "skywave" signals, bending them earthward at distances far beyond the visible horizon. Ionosphere normally extends from about 30 to 70 miles above the earth's surface, and consists of several distinct "layers".

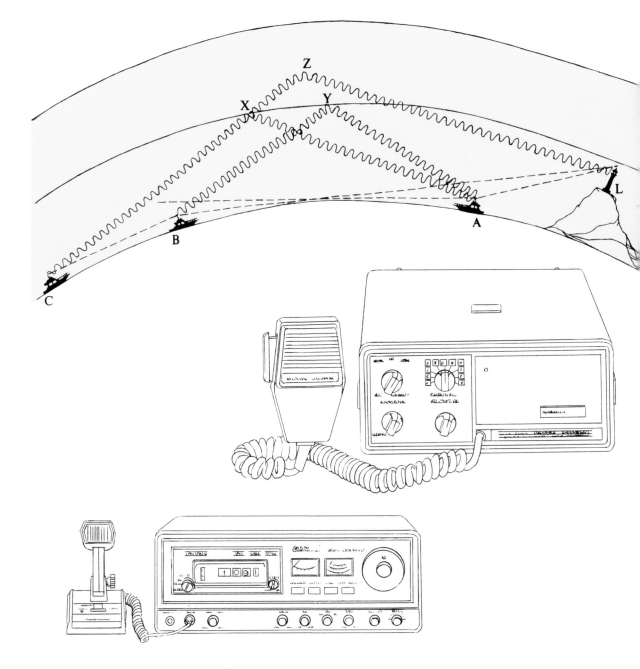

Boat C has VHF/FM, long-range, and medium-range radio equipment. C can communicate with:
   Boat B via direct radio path CB using short-range VHF/FM.
   Boat A via "skywave" radio path CXA using medium-range SSB.
   Lighthouse L via "skywave" path CZL using long-range SSB.
   Radio capability of Boat C is complete for all marine areas.

Boat B has VHF/FM and medium-range radio equipment. Boat B can communicate with:
   Boat C via direct radio path BC using short-range VHF/FM.
   Boat A via "skywave" radio path BYA using medium-range SSB.

   Lighthouse L using VHF/FM short-range radio because the antenna of L is high enough to "see" the antenna of Boat B in a direct line.

Boat A has VHF/FM and medium-range SSB; can communicate with:
   Lighthouse L via AL direct path using short-range VHF/FM.
   Boat C via "skywave" radio path AXC using medium-range SSB.
   Boat B via "skywave" radio path AYB using medium-range SSB.
   A cannot talk with B via VHF/FM because antenna of B is below the horizon.

Modern VHF/FM equipment is now largely solid-state (transistorized) and features relatively low power drain while in the "standby" or "receive" conditions.
   Medium and long-range SSB equipment is now also largely solid-state with crystal control of sending and receiving.

Exactly how do fishermen benefit from the use of marine radio?
   By exchanging water temperature, weather, catch information.
   By coordinating fish search efforts among fleets of boats.
   By cooperating with the Coast Guard in search and rescue operations.
   By transmitting important messages to stations ashore.

HOW ELECTRONIC SOUNDERS LOCATE FISH

In the days before electronics, depth of water was learned by lowering a weighted, marked line to the bottom and counting how many fathom markers were out when the deep-sea lead hit the bottom. Sometimes a sample of the bottom itself was brought up adhering to some grease or wax rubbed into a concave hollow in the bottom of the sounding lead. The lead-line method of sounding was accurate but slow, and required highly trained leadsmen when soundings were taken while the ship or vessel was underway.

Nowadays, finding the depth of water, the character of the bottom, and the presence of fish under the boat is vastly simplified. Instead of a weighted line, the modern electronic sounder projects a broad beam of high-frequency sound waves at the bottom and then receives, amplified, and displays the returning echo in such a way that the visual readout can be interpreted in terms of feet, metres, or fathoms of depth.

The basic sounder consists of two units, the electronic package that reproduces, detects, amplifies, and displays the sound pulse; and the transducer that converts electric pulses into sound waves in water, and reconverts the returning echoes into electric pulses. Electronic package and transducer are connected by coaxial cable. The depth of water may be displayed by marks on a slow-moving paper chart, by a flashing light rotating behind a calibrated dial, by meter, or by digital readout. Some sounders have both flashing or recording displays that can be selected by a switch.

Early electronic sounders generally used sound beams pulsing at the frequency of 50 kHz, but many modern instruments employ frequencies specially selected to resonate with and obtain strong echoes from various species of fish or types of bottom. Thus, by selecting an instrument that is selective toward the fish or bottom he wants to explore, a boat operator can greatly enhance his chances of locating what he is looking for. Knowing the kind of bottom that some fish prefer, the fisherman can seek that kind of bottom and find fish. Free-swimming fish or bait will often show on the sounder, telling the skipper when to stop the boat and at what depth to place his baits or lures.

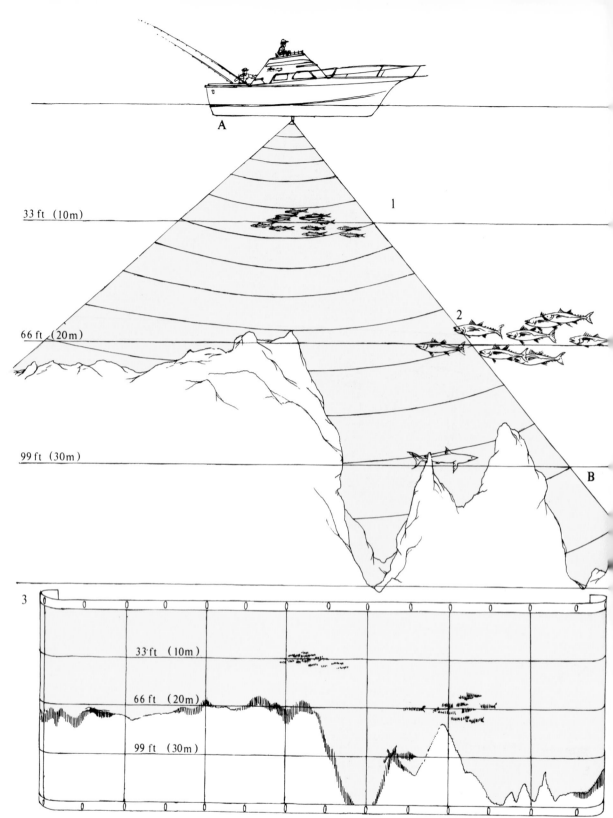

A Boat using sounder passes over fish and rough bottom. The recording sounder marks a profile of the bottom on the paper tape at the proper depth in scale. Fish are also marked at their depths.

1 A school of small fish swimming at 10 m depth leaves a trace of small marks on the paper tape at the corresponding depth.

2 Several larger fish at 20 m depth leave larger marks on the recorder tape. These marks appear at the 20 m depth line on the paper tape.

3 Profile of bottom is traced in a heavy band of marks at the proper depth in scale on the tape. Recorder provides a permanent depth record.

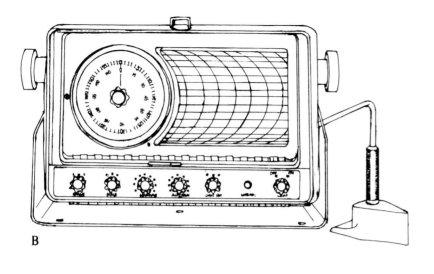

B

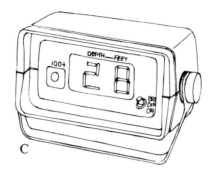

C

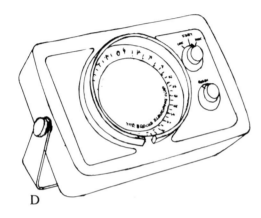

D

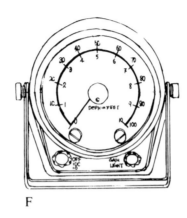

F

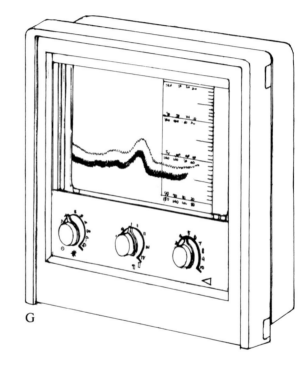

G

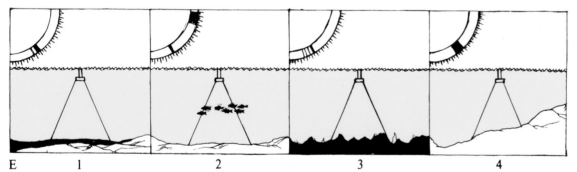

E   1   2   3   4

B Combination flasher-recorder operates in either mode. Max depth: 60 fath. 2-speed paper tape. Flasher and graph units can operate separately or at the same time. Power: 12 v.d.c.

Digital readout sounder has no parts that move. Max depth: 200 ft (60 m) with 100 ft (30 m) over-range potential. Day and night light intensity adjustment. Power: 12 v.d.c. at 0.4 amp.

D Flasher sounder with neon indicator bulb on a rotating arm. Max depth: 60 fath. A portable unit that operates on internal 9-v battery or 12–40 v.d.c. external power. Automatic voltage regulation.

E FOUR BASIC TYPES OF FLASHER DISPLAY

1 Thin layer of soft mud over hard bottom.
2 Hard bottom with fish at depth 18.
3 Irregular rock bottom giving multiple depth indications.
4 Sloping bottom.

F Meter sounder has 2 depth ranges, 0–10 ft and 0–100 ft (0–3.3 m and 0–33 m). Solid state electronics and low current drain. Shows depth only, has no way of indicating fish under the boat. Power: 12 v.d.c.

G Recording sounder with high resolution throughout range. Max depth: 180 fath. 70 kHz frequency of pulse for definition of fish and bait. Power: 12 v.d.c. or other voltages with external converter.

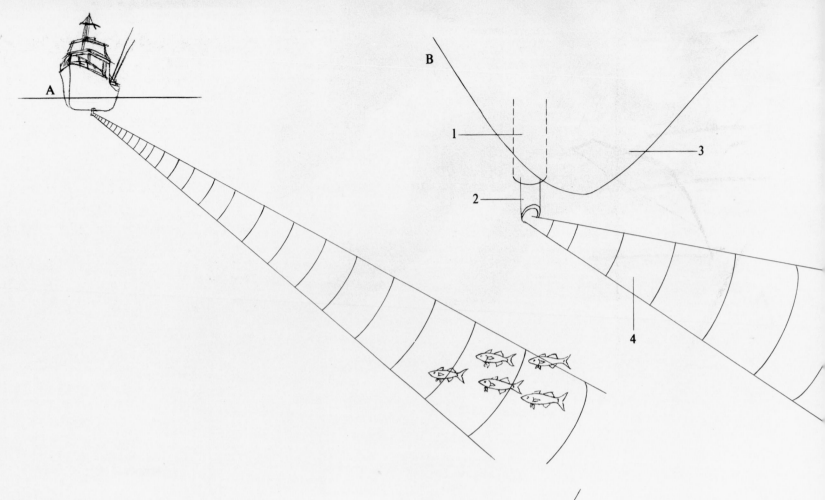

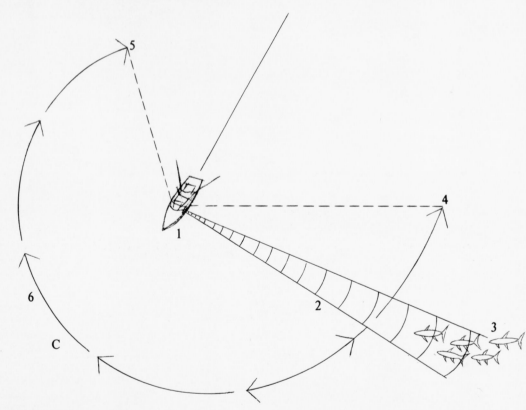

SIDE-LOOKING SONAR

Sonar was used as far back as World War II by surface ships and submarines to locate other submarines by means of an aimed beam of highfrequency sound pulses. In recent years sonar has been refined for use by commercial and sport fishing boats to locate schools of fish that are not directly under the vessel and therefore undetectable by ordinary sounders.

A THE SOUND BEAM

The beam of sound pulses is created and focused by the transducer located in a retractable tube that can be extended downward under the hull. The beam of sound can be aimed in desired vertical angle from vertical to horizontal, and can be swept from side to side. The frequency of the pulses of the sound beam may vary from 40 to 70 kHz (cycles per sec. × 1000).

B SOUND-HEAD DETAILS

1 Permanent mounting tube extends up into the hull through the skin of the bottom.
2 Transducer tube is extended or pulled back by electric or hydraulic power. "O" ring or packing keeps out the water.
3 Vessel's hull.
4 Sound beam is shaped to desired form by the transducer.

C LOCATING A SCHOOL

1 Boat proceeds on course, sweeping the sea around it with the sonar beam.
2 Beam sends back echo from any object it intercepts.
3 School of fish sends echoes back to the boat's sonar.
4–5 Maximum limits of sonar swing. Some models swing through a full 360° circle. Advanced models can stop the swing and "lock onto" any fish they locate.
6 Circle of range may vary from 300 yards (roughly 300 m) to nearly a mile, depending on power.

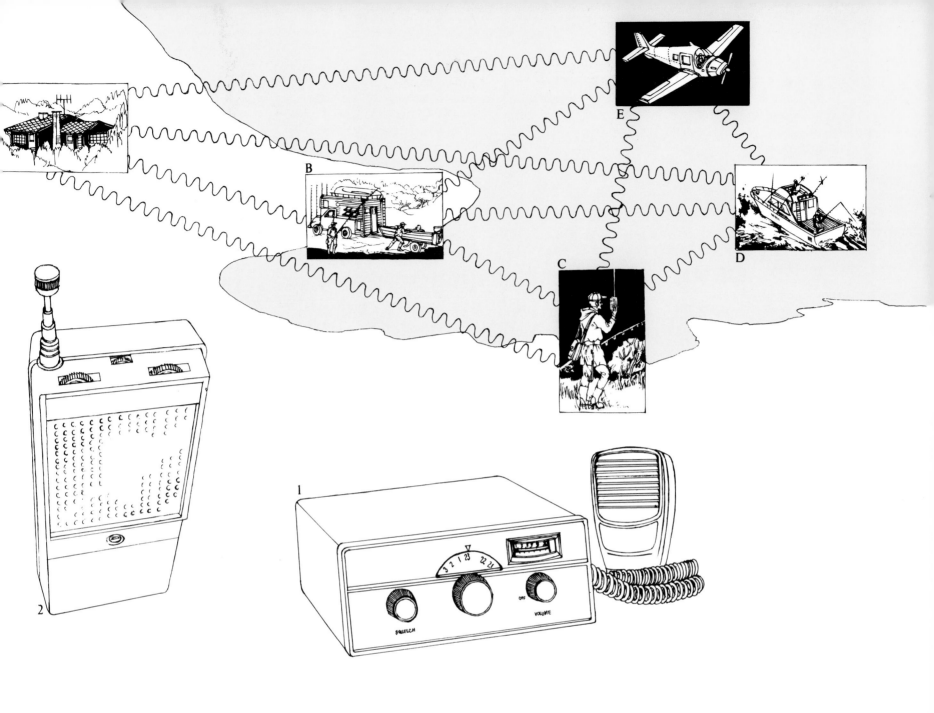

CITIZENS BAND–THE SPORTSMAN'S RADIO SERVICE

The so-called Citizens Band radio service, operating in the 27 MHz band, has become, by virtue of its flexible nature, a favorite of mobile sportsmen in many areas. Power is limited to 5 watts, units costs under $300.

1 A typical home base or mobile unit has both transmitter and receiver functions contained in a single box. There is instant band-switching for up to 23 phone channels.
2 Smaller walkie-talkie model is powered by batteries, can be carried anywhere on land or water.

A Base station at home or office is powered from house current, usually has a high-gain directional antenna for maximum range, exceeds 30 miles (48 km) under ideal conditions. CB personal-station license requires no test of technical radio aptitude, is easy to obtain.
B Mobile station in an auto or recreational vehicle is powered by the vehicle's batteries, usually has a "loaded" whip quarter-wave antenna. Operating range is 8–20 miles (13–32 km) under normal use. Land-mobile stations can talk to aircraft, boats, base stations, or anglers on foot.
C Fisherman on foot, using a portable walkie-talkie, can report back to home or to his boat or land mobile vehicle. Low power re-

stricts range to 2–3 miles (4 km) depending on efficiency of unit. Cost of hand-held portable units is from under $100 to around $250, depending on power.
D Many sport fishing boats use CB as an adjunct to VHF/FM for short-range radio communication between boats and with shore. One limitation is the fact that neither the Coast Guard nor commercial shore stations monitor CB frequencies to take distress or routine radio traffic. But many marinas that cater to the fishing trade maintain CB base stations, thus providing a measure of shore service.
E Where aircraft are used for spotting fish, CB provides a link between planes, boats, and stations at shore bases and boat marinas.

APPENDIX

INDEX TO SCIENTIFIC NAMES

The numbers refer to illustrations and descriptions

336 *Centropristis striatus* Sea Bass
278 *Ceratocottus diceraus* Oni Kajika
30 *Cetorhinus maximus* Basking Shark
490 *Chaetodipterus faber* Atlantic Spadefish
162 *Chanos chanos* Milkfish
73 *Chimaera monstrosa* Rabbitfish
111 *Chirocentrus dorab* Wolf Herring
6 *Chlamydoselachus anguineus* Frilled Shark
433 *Chloroscombrus chrysurus* Atlantic Bumper
411 *Chorinemus lysan* Queenfish
391 *Chrysophrys auratus* Snapper (Australian)
496 *Cichla ocellaris* Peacock Bass
489 *Cichla temensis* Butterfly Bass
172 *Clarias batrachus* Walking Catfish
116 *Clupea harengus* Herring
259 *Cololabis saira* Pacific Saury
179 *Colossoma bidens* Tambaquy
96 *Conger oceanicus* Conger Eel
143 *Coregonus albula* Vendace
149 *Coregonus artedii* Cisco
148 *Coregonus canadensis* Atlantic Whitefish
147 *Coregonus clupeaformis* Lake Whitefish
145 *Coregonus lavaretus* Powan
146 *Coregonus oxyrhynchus* Houting
144 *Coregonus pidschian* Large Bottom Whitefish
535 *Coris julis* Rainbow Wrasse
430 *Coryphaena equisetis* Pompano Dolphin
429 *Coryphaena hippurus* Dolphin
277 *Cottus scorpius* Sculpin
202 *Couesius plumbeus* Lake Chub
531 *Crenilabrus melops* Corkwing
532 *Ctenolabrus rupestris* Goldsinny
183 *Ctenopharyngodon idella* Grass Carp
609 *Cyclopterus lumpus* Lumpfish
379 *Cymatoceps nasutus* Black Biskop
468 *Cynoscion macdonaldi* Totuava
467 *Cynoscion nebulosus* Spotted Weakfish
466 *Cynoscion nobilis* White Sea Bass
474 *Cynoscion nothus* Silver Sea Trout
465 *Cynoscion regalis* Weakfish
469 *Cynoscion reticulatus* Corvina
470 *Cynoscion xanthulus* Orangemouth Corvina
180 *Cyprinus carpio* Carp
181 *Cyprinus carpio* Leather Carp
182 *Cyprinus carpio* Mirror Carp
249 *Cypselurus californicus* California Flying Fish
248 *Cypselurus heterurus* Atlantic Flying Fish

41 *Dalatias licha* Darkie Charlie
49 *Dasyatis sabina* Atlantic Sting Ray
394 *Dentex dentex* Dentex
393 *Dentex rupestris* Red Steenbras
328 *Dermatolepis inermis* Marbled Grouper
192 *Dichistius capensis* Galjoen
109 *Dorosoma cepedianum* Gizzard Shad
108 *Dorosoma petenense* Threadfin Shad

43 *Echinorhinus brucus* Bramble Shark
420 *Elagatis bipinnulatus* Rainbow Runner
212 *Electrophorus electricus* Electric Eel
93 *Elops affinis* Machete
92 *Elops saurus* Ladyfish
483 *Embiotoca jacksoni* Black Surfperch
113 *Engraulis encrasicholus* Anchovy
99 *Engraulis mordax* Northern Anchovy
326 *Epinephelus adscensionis* Rock Hind

339 *Epinephelus fulvus* Coney
314 *Epinephelus guaza* Dusky Perch
323 *Epinephelus guttatus* Red Hind
329 *Epinephelus itajara* Jewfish
316 *Epinephelus lanceolatus* Queensland Grouper
315 *Epinephelus morio* Red Grouper
312 *Epinephelus nigritis* Warsaw Grouper
319 *Epinephelus septemfasciatus* Mahata
313 *Epinephelus striatus* Nassau Grouper
325 *Epinephelus tauvinus* Rock Cod
159 *Esox americanus americanus* Redfin Pickerel
160 *Esox americanus vermiculatus* Grass Pickerel
158 *Esox lucius* European Pike; Northern Pike
161 *Esox masquinongy* Muskellunge
157 *Esox niger* Chain Pickerel
37 *Etmopterus spinax* Velvet Belly
18 *Eulamia ahena* Bronze Whaler Shark
565 *Euthynnus affinis* Kawakawa
563 *Euthynnus alletteratus* Little Tunny
560 *Euthynnus lineatus* Black Skipjack
558 *Euthynnus pelamis* Skipjack Tuna
295 *Eutrigla gurnardus* Grey Gurnard

168 *Felichthys marinus* Gaff-Topsail Catfish
261 *Fundulus diaphanus* Banded Killifish
263 *Fundulus heteroclitus* Mummichog
262 *Fundulus majalis* Striped Killifish

243 *Gadiculus thori* Silvery Pout
245 *Gadus luscus* Pouting
218 *Gadus macrocephalus* Pacific Cod
216 *Gadus minutus* Poor Cod
214 *Gadus morhua* Cod (Atlantic)
220 *Gadus ogac* Greenland Cod
239 *Gaidropsaurus cimbrius* Four-Beard Rockling
240 *Gaidropsaurus mustela* Five-Beard Rockling
238 *Gaidropsaurus tricirratus* Three-Beard Rockling
14 *Galeocerdo cuvieri* Tiger Shark
21 *Galeorhinus galeus* Tope
22 *Galeorhinus zyopterus* Soupfin Shark
40 *Galeus melastomus* Black-Mouthed Dogfish
274 *Gasterosteus aculeatus* Three-Spined Stickleback
553 *Gempylus serpens* Snake Mackerel
32 *Ginglymostoma cirratum* Nurse Shark
487 *Girella nigricans* Opaleye
491 *Girella tricuspidata* Luderick
586 *Glyptocephalus cynoglossus* Witch
416 *Gnathanodon speciosus* Dorade
191 *Gobio gobio* Gudgeon
300 *Gymnacanthus tricuspis* Three-Horned Sculpin
526 *Gymnammodytes semisquamatus* Smooth Sandeel
355 *Gymnocephalus cernua* Ruffe
386 *Gymnocrotaphus curvidens* John Brown
566 *Gymnosarda nuda* Dogtooth Tuna
97 *Gymnothorax funebris* Green Moray

458 *Haemulon album* Margate
452 *Haemulon aurolineatum* Tomtate
454 *Haemulon carbonarium* Caesar Grunt
453 *Haemulon flavolineatum* French Grunt
456 *Haemulon macrostomum* Spanish Grunt

461 *Haemulon parra* Sailor's Choice
462 *Haemulon plumieri* White Grunt
451 *Haemulon sciurus* Bluestriped Grunt
518 *Halichoeres semicinctus* Rock Wrasse
409 *Hemicaranx amblyrhynchus* Bluntnose Jack (Atlantic)
251 *Hemiramphus balao* Balao
5 *Heptranchias perlo* Seven-Gilled Shark
87 *Heterotus niloticus* Bellie
284 *Hexagrammos decagrammus* Kelp Greenling
285 *Hexagrammos otakii* Ainame
4 *Hexanchus griseus* Six-Gilled Shark
88 *Hiodon alosoides* Goldeye
86 *Hiodon tergisus* Mooneye
276 *Hippocampus ramulosus* Seahorse
587 *Hippoglossoides platessoides* Long Rough Dab
598 *Hippoglossus hippoglossus* Atlantic Halibut
597 *Hippoglossus stenolepis* Pacific Halibut
247 *Histrio histrio* Sargassumfish
486 *Holacanthus ciliaris* Queen Angelfish
266 *Holocentrus spiniferus* Soldierfish
186 *Hydrocion goliath* Goliath
174 *Hydrocyon lineatus* Tigerfish
73A *Hydrolagus colliei* Ratfish
428 *Hypacanthus amius* Leerfish
153 *Hypomesus olidus* Pond Smelt
250 *Hyporamphus unifasciatus* Halfbeak
595 *Hypsopsetta guttulata* Diamond Turbot
498 *Hypsypops rubicundus* Garibaldi
528 *Hypteroplus lanceolatus* Greater Sandeel

297 *Icelus bicornis* Two-Horned Sculpin
170 *Ictalurus catus* White Catfish
164 *Ictalurus furcatus* Blue Catfish
171 *Ictalurus natalis* Yellow Bullhead
165 *Ictalurus nebulosus* Brown Bullhead
163 *Ictalurus punctatus* Channel Catfish
210 *Ictiobus cyprinellus* Bigmouth Buffalo
589 *Isopsetta isolepis* Butter Sole
574 *Istiophorus platypterus* Sailfish
27 *Isurus oxyrhynchus* Mako Shark

345 *Kuhlia rupestris* Rock Flagtail
346 *Kuhlia taeniura* Pacific Flagtail
485 *Kyphosus sectatrix* Bermuda Chub

529 *Labrus bergylta* Ballan Wrasse
530 *Labrus mixtus* Cuckoo Wrasse
520 *Lachnolaimus maximus* Hogfish
602 *Lactophrys tricornis* Trunkfish
481 *Lagodon rhomboides* Pinfish
28 *Lamna nasus* Porbeagle Shark
1 *Lampetra fluviatilis* Lampern
270 *Lampris guttatus* Opah
311 *Lates calcarifer* Barramundi
310 *Lates niloticus* Nile Perch
74 *Latimeria chalumnae* Coelacanth
501 *Latridopsis ciliaris* Moki
502 *Latris lineata* Striped Trumpeter
475 *Leiostomus xanthurus* Spot
81 *Lepisosteus oculatus* Spotted Gar
82 *Lepisosteus platyrhynchus* Florida Gar
80 *Lepisosteus spatula* Alligator Gar
366 *Lepomis auritus* Redbreast Sunfish
363 *Lepomis gibbosus* Pumpkinseed
364 *Lepomis gulosus* Warmouth Bass
361 *Lepomis macrochirus* Bluegill
362 *Lepomis megalotis* Yellow Belly

188 *Leuciscus cephalus* Chub
195 *Leuciscus idus* Ide
177 *Leuciscus leuciscus* Dace
265 *Leuresthes tenuis* California Grunion
582 *Limanda ferruginea* Yellowtail Flounder
583 *Limanda limanda* Dab
505 *Liza ramada* Thin-Lipped Mullet
449 *Lobotes surinamensis* Tripletail
213 *Lophius piscatorius* Anglerfish
395 *Lopholatilus chamaeleonticeps* Tilefish
246 *Lota lota* Burbot
445 *Lutjanus analis* Mutton Snapper
446 *Lutjanus apodus* Schoolmaster
439 *Lutjanus buccanella* Blackfin Snapper
443 *Lutjanus campechanus* Red Snapper
440 *Lutjanus cyanopterus* Cubera Snapper
438 *Lutjanus griseus* Grey Snapper
442 *Lutjanus jocu* Dog Snapper
444 *Lutjanus mahogani* Mahogany Snapper
447 *Lutjanus sebae* Red Emperor
441 *Lutjanus synagris* Lane Snapper

343 *Maccullochella peeli* Murray Cod
241 *Macrozoarces americanus* Ocean Pout
572 *Makaira indica* Black Marlin
573 *Makaira nigricans* Blue Marlin
44 *Manta birostris* Atlantic Manta
117 *Maurolicus mulleri* Pearlside
91 *Megalops atlanticus* Tarpon
94 *Megalops cyprinoides* Ox-Eye Tarpon
232 *Melanogrammus aeglefinus* Haddock
432 *Mene maculata* Moonfish
264 *Menidia menidia* Atlantic Silverside
480 *Menticirrhus saxatilis* Northern Kingfish
479 *Menticirrhus undulatus* California Corbina
226 *Merlangius merlangus* Whiting
230 *Merluccius bilinearis* Silver Hake
225 *Merluccius gayi* Merluza
229 *Merluccius merluccius* Hake
224 *Merluccius productus* Pacific Hake
217 *Microgadus proximus* Tomcod
215 *Microgadus tomcod* Atlantic Tomcod
222 *Micromesistius poutassou* Blue Whiting
464 *Micropogon undulatus* Atlantic Croaker
360 *Micropterus coosae* Redeye Bass
359 *Micropterus dolomieui* Smallmouth (Black) Bass
357 *Micropterus notius* Suwannee Bass
356 *Micropterus punctulatus* Spotted Bass
358 *Micropterus salmoides* Largemouth Black Bass
585 *Microstomus kitt* Lemon Sole
590 *Microstomus pacificus* Dover Sole
604 *Mola mola* Ocean Sunfish
235 *Molva byrkelange* Blue Ling
233 *Molva elongata* Mediterranean Ling
234 *Molva molva* Ling (European)
89 *Mormyrops deliciosus* Leach
333 *Morone americana* White Perch
331 *Morone chrysops* White Bass
335 *Morone labrax* Bass (European)
334 *Morone mississippiensis* Yellow Bass
332 *Morone saxatilis* Striped Bass
503 *Mugil auratus* Golden Grey Mullet
506 *Mugil cephalus* Grey Mullet
507 *Mugil chelo* Thick-Lipped Mullet
504 *Mugil curema* White Mullet
95 *Muraena helena* Moray Eel
16 *Mustelus canis* Smooth Dogfish
22 *Mustelus mustelus* Smooth Hound
320 *Mycteroperca bonaci* Black Grouper
321 *Mycteroperca interstitialis* Yellowmouth Grouper

324 *Mycteroperca microlepis* Gag
318 *Mycteroperca phenax* Scamp
317 *Mycteroperca tigris* Tiger Grouper
322 *Mycteroperca venenosus* Yellowfin Grouper
383 *Mylio australis* Yellowfin Bream
46 *Myliobatis aquila* Eagle Ray
281 *Myoxocephalus quadricornis* Four-Horned Sculpin
3 *Myxine glutinosa* Hagfish

422 *Naucrates ductor* Pilot Fish
17 *Negaprion brevirostris* Lemon Shark
500 *Nemadactylus macropterus* Tarakihi
431 *Nematistius pectoralis* Roosterfish
303 *Neoplatycephalus macrodon* Tiger Flathead
199 *Notropis cornutus* Common Shiner
201 *Notropis dorsalis* Bigmouth Shiner
167 *Noturus flavus* Stonecat

610 *Octopus vulgaris* Common Octopus
448 *Ocyurus chrysurus* Yellowtail Snapper
33 *Odontaspis taurus* Grey Nurse Shark
425 *Oligoplites saurus* Common Leatherjacket
142 *Oncorhynchus gorbuscha* Humpback Salmon
139 *Oncorhynchus kennerlyi* Little Redfish
138 *Oncorhynchus keta* Chum Salmon
137 *Oncorhynchus kisutch* Coho Salmon
140 *Oncorhynchus masou* Yamame
141 *Oncorhynchus nerka* Sockeye Salmon
136 *Oncorhynchus tschawytscha* Chinook Salmon
242 *Ophiodon elongatus* Lingcod
607 *Opsanus tau* Oyster Toadfish
569 *Orcynopsis unicolor* Plain Bonito
152 *Osmerus eperlanus* Smelt
151 *Osmerus mordax* American Smelt
84 *Osteoglossum bicirrhosum* Aruana

390 *Pachymetopon blochi* Hottentot
387 *Pachymetopon grande* Blue Hottentot
384 *Pagellus bogaraveo* Red Sea Bream
389 *Pagellus erythrinus* Pandora
388 *Pagellus lithognathus* White Steenbras
370 *Pagrus pagrus* Couch's Sea Bream
371 *Pagrus sedecim* Red Porgy
327 *Paralabrax clathratus* Cabrilla
599 *Paralichthys californicus* California Halibut
581 *Paralichthys dentatus* Summer Flounder
579 *Peprilus thriacanthus* Butterfish
350 *Perca flavescens* Yellow Perch
351 *Perca fluviatilis* Perch (European)
342 *Percalates colonorum* Estuary Perch
2 *Petromyzon marinus* Sea Lamprey
492 *Phanerodon furcatus* White Seaperch
194 *Phoxinus phoxinus* Minnow
237 *Phycis blennioides* Greater Forkbeard
517 *Pimelometopon pulchrum* California Sheephead
207 *Pimephales promelas* Fathead Minnow
493 *Plagioscion squamosissimum* Pescada
591 *Platichthys flesus* Flounder (European)
592 *Platichthys stellatus* Starry Flounder
302 *Platycephalus arenarius* Sand Flathead
304 *Platycephalus coeruleopunctatus* Red-Spotted Flathead

305 *Platycephalus fuscus* Dusky Flathead
455 *Plectorhynchus nigrus* Brown Sweetlips
457 *Plectorhynchus pictus* Golden Spotted Sweetlips
340 *Plectroplites ambiguus* Golden Perch
584 *Pleuronectes platessa* Plaice
472 *Pogonias cromus* Black Drum
228 *Pollachius pollachius* Pollack (European)
227 *Pollachius virens* Coalfish (Pollock)
508 *Polydactylus octonemus* Atlantic Threadfin
79 *Polyodon spatula* Paddlefish
337 *Polyprion americanus* Wreckfish
338 *Polyprion oxygeneious* Hapuka
460 *Pomadasys hasta* Javelin Fish
434 *Pomatomus saltatrix* Bluefish
365 *Pomoxis annularis* White Crappie
368 *Pomoxis nigromaculatus* Black Crappie
15 *Prionace glauca* Blue Shark
293 *Prionotus carolinus* Northern Searobin
301 *Prionotus evolans* Striped Searobin
71 *Pristis pectinatus* Common Sawfish
150 *Prosopium cylindraceum* Round Whitefish
580 *Pseudopleuronectes americanus* Winter Flounder
292 *Pterois volitans* Zebrafish
193 *Ptychocheilus oregonensis* Northern Squawfish
273 *Pungitius pungitius* Nine-Spined Stickleback
166 *Pylodictus olivaris* Flathead Catfish

435 *Rachycentron canadum* Cobia
62 *Raja alba* White Skate
54 *Raja batis* Common Skate
59 *Raja brachyura* Blonde Ray
65 *Raja circularis* Sandy Ray
58 *Raja clavata* Thornback Ray
53 *Raja eglanteria* Clearnose Skate
56 *Raja fullonica* Shagreen Ray
66 *Raja fyllae* Sandy Skate
61 *Raja hyperborea* Arctic Skate
63 *Raja lintea* Sharpnose Skate
67 *Raja microcellata* Painted Ray
68 *Raja montagui* Spotted Ray
57 *Raja naevus* Cuckoo Ray
60 *Raja nidrosiensis* Black-Bellied Skate
52 *Raja oxyrinchus* Long-Nose Skate
55 *Raja radiata* Thorny Skate
64 *Raja undulata* Undulate Ray
244 *Raniceps raninus* Tadpole-Fish
605 *Ranzania truncata* Truncated Sunfish
272 *Regalecus glesne* Oarfish
600 *Reinhardtius hippoglossoides* Greenland Halibut
436 *Remora remora* Remora
382 *Rhabdosargus sarba* Tarwhine
31 *Rhincodon typus* Whale Shark
205 *Rhinichthys cataractae* Longnose Dace
69 *Rhinobatos lentiginosus* Atlantic Guitarfish
70 *Rhinobatus productus* Shovelnose Guitarfish
47 *Rhinoptera bonasus* Cownose Ray
211 *Rhodeus amarus* Bitterling
463 *Roncador stearnsi* Spotfin Croaker
198 *Rutilus rutilus* Roach

178 *Salminus maxillosus* Dorado
123 *Salmo aguabonita* Golden Trout
126 *Salmo clarki* Cutthroat Trout
119 *Salmo gairdneri* Steelhead Trout
118 *Salmo gairdneri* Rainbow Trout

122 *Salmo hucho* Huchen
129 *Salmo salar* Atlantic Salmon
124 *Salmo salar ouananiche* Ouananiche
127 *Salmo salar sebago* Landlocked Salmon
120 *Salmo trutta fario* Brown Trout
128 *Salmo trutta lacustris* Lake Trout
121 *Salmo trutta trutta* Sea Trout
134 *Salvelinus alpinus* Arctic Char
135 *Salvelinus fontinalis* Brook Trout
132 *Salvelinus malma spectabilis* Dolly Varden
131 *Salvelinus pluvius* Iwana
133 *Salvelinus willoughbyi* Windermere Char
567 *Sarda orientalis* Striped Bonito
568 *Sarda sarda* Atlantic Bonito
114 *Sardina pilchardus* Pilchard Sardine
112 *Sardinella anchovia* Spanish Sardine
110 *Sardinops sagax* Pacific Sardine
203 *Scardinius erythrophthalmus* Rudd
539 *Scarus coeruleus* Blue Parrotfish
477 *Sciaena antarctica* Mulloway
478 *Sciaena hololepidota* Kabeljou
471 *Sciaenops ocellatus* Red Drum
260 *Scomberesox saurus* Saury Pike
540 *Scomber japonicus* Chub Mackerel
542 *Scomber scombrus* Mackerel
541 *Scomberomorus cavalla* Kingfish
548 *Scomberomorus commersoni* Tanguigue
545 *Scomberomorus concolor* Monterey Spanish Mackerel
547 *Scomberomorus maculatus* Spanish Mackerel
549 *Scomberomorus niphonius* Spotted Mackerel
544 *Scomberomorus regalis* Cero Mackerel
543 *Scomberomorus semifasciatus* Broad-Barred Mackerel
546 *Scomberomorus sierra* Sierra Mackerel
596 *Scophthalmus maximus* Turbot
594 *Scophthalmus rhombus* Brill
283 *Scorpaenichthys marmoratus* Cabezon
488 *Scorpis aequipinnis* Sweep
39 *Scyliorhinus caniculus* Lesser-Spotted Dogfish
38 *Scyliorhinus stellaris* Large-Spotted Dogfish
291 *Sebastes atrovirens* Kelp Rockfish
286 *Sebastes marinus* Norway Haddock
289 *Sebastes paucipinnis* Bocaccio
287 *Sebastes viviparus* Lesser Redfish
290 *Sebastodes melanops* Black Rockfish
288 *Sebastodes nebulosus* China Rockfish
437 *Selene vomer* Lookdown
413 *Seriola colburni* Pacific Amberjack
406 *Seriola dumerili* Amberjack
407 *Seriola grandis* King Amberjack
415 *Seriola lalandi* Yellowtail
414 *Seriola quinqueradiata* Buri
408 *Seriola rivoliana* Almaco Jack
412 *Seriola zonata* Banded Rudderfish
347 *Serranus cabrilla* Comber .
341 *Serranus tigrinus* Harlequin Bass
184 *Serrasalmus nattereri* Piranha
397 *Sillaginodes punctatus* Spotted Whiting
396 *Sillago ciliata* Australian Whiting
173 *Silurus glanis* Wels
588 *Solea solea* Common Sole
42 *Somniosus microcephalus* Greenland Shark
381 *Sparodon durbanensis* White Biskop
392 *Sparus auratus* Gilthead
601 *Sphaeroides maculatus* Northern Puffer
511 *Sphyraena argentea* Pacific Barracuda
512 *Sphyraena barracuda* Great Barracuda
515 *Sphyraena borealis* Northern Sennet
514 *Sphyraena guachancho* Guaguanche
510 *Sphyraena jello* Pick-Handle Barracuda

509 *Sphyraena obtusata* Striped Barracuda
513 *Sphyraena pinguis* Aka-Kamasu
516 *Sphyraena sphyraena* European Barracuda
24 *Sphyrna mokarran* Great Hammerhead
26 *Sphyrna tiburo* Bonnethead Shark
25 *Sphyrna zygaena* Common Hammerhead
275 *Spinachia spinachia* Fifteen-Spined Stickleback
385 *Spondyliosoma cantharus* Black Bream
115 *Sprattus sprattus* Sprat
36 *Squalus acanthias* Spiny Dogfish
72 *Squatina squatina* Monkfish
156 *Stenodus leucichthys* Inconnu
372 *Stenotomus chrysops* Scup
330 *Stereolepis gigas* California Black Sea Bass
353 *Stizostedion canadense* Sauger
349 *Stizostedion lucioperca* Zander
352 *Stizostedion vitreum* Walleye
354 *Stizostedion vitreum glaucum* Blue Pike
348 *Stizostedion volgense* Eastern Pike-Perch
257 *Strongylura exilis* Flat Needlefish
254 *Strongylura marina* Atlantic Needlefish
258 *Strongylura notata* Redfin Needlefish
256 *Strongylura stolzmanni* Aguja
255 *Strongylura timuco* Timuco

280 *Taurulus bubalis* Longspined Bullhead
279 *Taurulus lilljeborgi* Pygmy Sculpin
519 *Tautoga onitis* Tautog
521 *Tautogolabrus adspersus* Cunner
570 *Tetrapturus albidus* White Marlin
571 *Tetrapturus audax* Striped Marlin
576 *Tetrapturus augustirostris* Shortbill Spearfish
575 *Tetrapturus belone* Mediterranean Spearfish
577 *Tetrapturus pfluegeri* Longbill Spearfish
154 *Thaleichthys pacificus* Candlefish
223 *Theragra chalcogramma* Suketodara
561 *Thunnus alalunga* Albacore
556 *Thunnus albacares* Yellowfin Tuna
562 *Thunnus atlanticus* Blackfin Tuna
559 *Thunnus obesus* Bigeye Tuna
557 *Thunnus thynnus* Bluefin Tuna
155A *Thymallus arcticus* Arctic Grayling
155 *Thymallus thymallus* European Grayling
555 *Thyrsites atun* Snoek
495 *Tilapia mossambica* Natal Tilapia
494 *Tilapia nilotica* Tilapia
208 *Tinca tinca* Tench
50 *Torpedo marmorata* Marbled Electric Ray
51 *Torpedo nobiliana* Electric Ray
423 *Trachinotus carolinus* Common Pompano
426 *Trachinotus falcatus* Atlantic Permit
427 *Trachinotus goodei* Palometa
538 *Trachinus draco* Greater Weever
537 *Trachinus vipera* Lesser Weever
418 *Trachurus japonicus* Ma-Aji
419 *Trachurus symmetricus* Pacific Jack Mackerel
417 *Trachurus trachurus* Scad
271 *Trachypterus arcticus* Deal-Fish
19 *Triakis semifasciata* Leopard Shark
554 *Trichiurus lepturus* Atlantic Cutlassfish
294 *Trigla lucerna* Yellow Gurnard
298 *Triglops pingeli* Pingel's Scorpion
593 *Trinectes maculatus* Hogchoker
48 *Trygon pastinaca* Common Sting Ray
253 *Tylosurus crocodilus* Houndfish

PLAYING THE METRIC NUMBERS GAME

As a result of a bill passed by the Congress in 1975, the United States is on the road to eventual conversion from the older English to the newer metric system of weights and measures. To ease the confusion of trying to convert from one to the other, the following tables and conversion formulas have been prepared. The table below converts knots into km/h (kilometers per hour) and vice versa for speeds from one to 60 knots.

KNOTS x 1.84 = km/h	Km/h x 0.545 = KNOTS
1 knot = 1.84 km/h	1 km/h = 0.545 knots
2 knots = 3.68 km/h	2 km/h = 1.09 knots
3 knots = 5.52 km/h	3 km/h = 1.635 knots
4 knots = 7.36 km/h	4 km/h = 2.18 knots
5 knots = 9.2 km/h	5 km/h = 2.725 knots
6 knots = 11.04 km/h	6 km/h = 3.27 knots
7 knots = 12.88 km/h	7 km/h = 3.815 knots
8 knots = 14.72 km/h	8 km/h = 4.36 knots
9 knots = 16.56 km/h	9 km/h = 4.9 knots
10 knots = 18.4 km/h	10 km/h = 5.54 knots
20 knots = 36.8 km/h	20 km/h = 10.9 knots
30 knots = 55.2 km/h	30 km/h = 16.35 knots
40 knots = 73.6 km/h	40 km/h = 21.8 knots
50 knots = 92.0 km/h	50 km/h = 27.25 knots
60 knots = 110.4 km/h	60 km/h = 32.7 knots

Knowing the conversion factor for speed conversion given in the conversion formulas at the head of each column, one can set up the conversion factor on the K key of a calculator and work out any desired variation. Conversion formulas for velocity work equally well for distance, converting nautical miles to kilometers and vice versa. Here are some more handy formulas.

1 kilometer = 0.621 statute mile, about ⅝ mile
1 kilometer = approx. 3279 feet

1 kilometer = 1093 yards
1 kilometer = 546 fathoms
1 meter = 39.4 inches
1 meter = 3.3 feet
1 meter = 0.547 fathom
1 centimeter = 0.394 inch
1 millimeter = 0.039 inch
1 liter = 1.06 quart
1 liter = 0.265 gallon
1 kilogram = 2.2 pounds
1 metric ton = 2204 pounds, or one long ton

Being able to convert metric values into English values is especially valuable when one is cruising in European waters. Bill Robinson, editor at *Yachting*, tells of his own confusion in learning to convert European wind velocity values of meters-per-second into English wind velocity values of miles-per-hour that had some meaning for him. He finally arrived at a quick conversion formula that helped a great deal, mps/2.2 = m.p.h.

A different problem is faced by those who have to convert Celsius (Centigrade) to Fahrenheit temperatures in order to understand how hot or cold it may be. Everybody knows that the Fahrenheit scale is based on a reading of 32° F at the freezing point of water and 212° F at the boiling point of water. This is a span of 180°. The Celsius scale, on the other hand, registers 0° C at the freezing point of water and 100° C at the boil-point of water. Therefore, 1° C = 1.8° F.

IF YOU KNOW	YOU CAN FIND	BY THIS FORMULA
° Fahrenheit	° Celsius	$\dfrac{°F - 32}{1.8} = °C$
° Celsius	° Fahrenheit	$°C(1.8) + 32 = °F$

One final European gambit merits special attention. This is the present tendency for European engine makers to list engine speed in terms of revolutions per second rather than revolutions per minute. What does "engine speed 50/sec" mean in terms that we understand? Very simple. Just multiply the "50/sec" by 60 to get revolutions per minute. Thus, 50/sec x 60 = 3000 rpm.

10/sec = 600 rpm	45/sec = 2700 rpm
15/sec = 900 rpm	50/sec = 3000 rpm
20/sec = 1200 rpm	55/sec = 3300 rpm
25/sec = 1500 rpm	60/sec = 3600 rpm
30/sec = 1800 rpm	65/sec = 3900 rpm
35/sec = 2100 rpm	70/sec = 4200 rpm
40/sec = 2400 rpm	75/sec = 4500 rpm

Table 1 and Table 2 are arranged in vertical columns under the headings indicating the meaning of the material in the columns. The symbols for metric values are correct by metric usage. Some of the English symbols were selected to save space and are explained in the tables. "English" is used to describe our present system because it originated in England centuries ago. England at present is nearly 100 percent metric.

The conversion formulas in Table 1 and Table 2 are designed with a maximum number of multiplications to work with the K-constant feature of most simple hand calculators. The example mm(.039) means millimeters x .039; in²/1552 means square inches divided by 1552.

TABLE 1
METRIC TO ENGLISH CONVERSIONS

Metric unit	Symbol	English unit	Conversion formula
LINEAR MEASURE			
Millimeter	mm	0.039 in	mm(.039) = in
Centimeter	cm	0.394 in	cm(.394) = in
Meter	m	39.4 in	m(39.4) = in
Meter	m	3.3 ft	m(3.3) = ft
Meter	m	1.094 yd	m(1.094) = yd
Meter	m	0.547 fath	m(.547) = fath
Kilometer	km	3279. ft	km(3279.) = ft
Kilometer	km	1093. yd	km(1093.) = yd
Kilometer	km	546. fath	km(546.) = fath
Kilometer	km	0.621 smi*	km(.621) = smi*
Kilometer	km	0.54 nmi*	km(.545) = nmi*

*smi = statute miles
*nmi = nautical miles

Metric unit	Symbol	English unit	Conversion formula
SQUARE MEASURE			
Square mm	mm²	0.0015 in²	mm²(.0015) = in²
Square cm	cm²	0.1552 in²	cm²(.1152) = in²
Square meter	m²	1152. in²	m²(1152.) = in²
Square meter	m²	10.76 ft²	m²(10.76) = ft²
Square meter	m²	1.3 yd²	m²(1.3) = yd²

Metric unit	Symbol	English unit	Conversion formula
CUBIC AND LIQUID MEASURE			
Cubic cm (cc)	cm³	0.06 in³	cm³(0.06) = in³
Cubic meter	m³	35.4 ft³	m³(35.4)' = ft³
Cubic meter	m³	1.31 yd³	m³(1.31) = yd³
Liter	1	1.06 qt	1(1.06) = qt
Liter	1	0.265 gal	1(.265) = gal

Metric unit	Symbol	English unit	Conversion formula
WEIGHT			
Gram	g	0.035 oz	g(.035) = oz
Kilogram	kg	2.2 lb	kg(2.2) = lb
Metric ton	t	2204. lb	t(2204.) = lb
Metric ton	t	0.907 ston*	t(.907) = ston*
Metric ton	t	1.0 lton*	t = long ton

*ston = short ton (2000 lb)
*lton = long ton (2200 lb)

Metric unit	Symbol	English unit	Conversion formula
SPEED			
Millimeter/sec	mm/sec	0.039 in/sec	mm/s(.039) = in/sec
Centimeter/sec	cm/sec	0.394 in/sec	cm/s(.394) = in/sec
Meter/sec	m/sec	39.4 in/sec	m/s(39.4) = in/sec
Meter/sec	m/sec	3.3 ft/sec	m/s(3.3) = ft/sec
Meter/min	m/min	3.3 ft/min	m/min(3.3) = ft/min
Meter/min	m/min	0.055 mph	m/min(.055) = mph
Kilometer/hour	km/h	0.621 mph	km/h(.621) = mph
Kilometer/hour	km/h	0.545 knots	km/h(.545) = knots

Metric unit	Symbol	English unit	Conversion formula
POWER			
Kilowatt	kw	0.746 hp	kw(.746) = hp

TABLE 2
ENGLISH TO METRIC CONVERSIONS

English unit	Symbol	Metric unit	Conversion formula
LINEAR MEASURE			
Inch (to mm)	in	25.4 mm	in(25.4) = mm
Inch (to cm)	in	2.54 cm	in(2.54) = cm
Inch (to m)	in	0.0254 m	in(.0254) = m
Foot (to m)	ft	0.305 m	ft(.305) = m
Yard (to m)	yd	0.914 m	yd(.914) = m
Fathom (to m)	fath	1.827 m	fath(1.827) = m
Foot (to km)	ft	0.0003 km	ft(.0003) = km
Yard (to km)	yd	0.0009 km	yd(.0009) = km
Fathom (to km)	fath	0.0018 km	fath(.0018) = km
Statute mile*	smi	1.61 km	smi(1.61) = km
Nautical mile*	nmi	1.825 km	nmi(1.825) = km

*Statute mile = 5280 ft   *Nautical mile = 6020 ft

English unit	Symbol	Metric unit	Conversion formula
SQUARE MEASURE			
Square inch	in²	645. mm²	in²(645.) = mm²
Square inch	in²	6.45 cm²	in²(6.45) = cm²
Square inch	in²	0.00064 m²	in²/1552. = m²
Square foot	ft²	0.093 m²	ft²/10.76 = m²
Square yard	yd²	0.77 m²	yd²(.77) = m²

English unit	Symbol	Metric unit	Conversion formula
CUBIC AND LIQUID MEASURE			
Cubic inch	in³	16.39 cm³	in³(16.39) = cm³
Cubic foot	ft³	0.028 m³	ft³(.028) = m³
Cubic yard	yd³	0.76 m³	yd³(.76) = m³
Quart/liter	qt/1	0.94 l	qt(.94) = l
Gallon/liter	gal/1	3.77 l	gal(3.77) = l

English unit	Symbol	Metric unit	Conversion formula
WEIGHT			
Ounce/gram	oz/g	28.57 g	oz(28.57) = g
Pound/kilogram	lb/kg	0.455 kg	lb(2.2) = kg
Pound/ton	lb/t	0.00045 t	lb(2204.) = t
Short ton*	ston	1.102 t	ston(1.102) = t
Long ton*	lton	1. t	Long ton = t

*Short ton = 2000 lb   *Long ton = 2200 lb

English unit	Symbol	Metric unit	Conversion formula
SPEED			
Inch/second	in/sec	25.4 mm/sec	in/sec(25.4) = mm/sec
Inch/second	in/sec	2.54 cm/sec	in/sec(2.54) = cm/sec
Inch/second	in/sec	0.025 m/sec	in/sec(.025) = m/sec
Foot/second	ft/sec	0.303 m/sec	ft/sec(.303) = m/sec
Foot/minute	ft/min	0.303 m/min	ft/min(.303) = m/min
Mile/hour	mph	26.67 m/min	mph(26.67) = m/min
Mile/hour	mph	1.61 km/h	mph(1.61) = km/h
Knot	knot	1.84 km/h	knot(1.84) = km/h

English unit	Symbol	Metric unit	Conversion formula
POWER			
Horsepower	hp	1.34 kw	hp(1.34) = kw

By Frank T. Moss

(Also published in *Yachting*)

NORTH AMERICAN SURF FISHING LOCATIONS

While individual fishermen will swear that there are literally thousands of different surf-fishing locations in North America, and in a sense they are correct, for the sake of this discussion we can divide the North American active surf-fishing territory into five major regions. This is mainly for geographic convenience, for there is a world of difference, for example, between the chilly, fog-bound coast of the Maritime Provinces of eastern Canada and the sun-drenched Florida Keys. Each area has its "special" species. Many have fish populations that overlap those of other nearby fishing areas. One thing can be said. From Puget Sound and Vancouver Island to the southern tip of Baja California, and from Texas around the Gulf of Mexico, around Florida, and up the Atlantic coast to Nova Scotia, it's difficult to find one beach or rocky headland that isn't at some time populated by anglers.

The Pacific Northwest is primarily salmon country and the shore angler who fishes for species other than salmon or sea-run trout is a rare bird. Swinging down from Puget Sound into the state of Washington, one finds rockfish and lingcod added to the salmon menu. It is in Oregon that one starts to discover signs of that great coastal fish, the striped bass. Here big stripers are taken in many of the coastal rivers, but once again the fishing outlook is generally salmon-oriented. Northern and central California is the stronghold of Pacific striped bass, with lesser species affording equally interesting fishing. In southern California surf-fishing is not what it was years ago. Overfishing and loss of prime bait species have taken heavy toll.

Baja California and western Mexico are a world apart. Those American anglers who have made the long, rough trip by car or truck-camper down the Baja trail have reported virtually virgin surf-fishing locations. But lack of access, even on foot, to some shores prevents exploration in depth. Here the roosterfish and totuava (a giant weakfish) test surf tackle to the limit.

The entire Gulf of Mexico shore from below Texas to western Florida is one vast soft-sand surf-fishing area. Many species are seasonal, and some are exotic, but the fishing season is year-long and access to good fishing beaches is seldom a real problem.

Florida is another region quite separate from the rest. This is the land of delightful light tackle fishing under generally benign skies. Swinging up the Atlantic coast, southern species carry north as far as Cape Hatteras. The region from North Carolina to southern New Jersey is a vast fish mixing pot. In the New York Bight and through southern New England the striped bass and bluefish share top surf honours. Stripers do extend well into Canadian waters and, if present trends in fishing are any guide, the striped bass may rival the Atlantic salmon soon in eastern Canada.

SURF-FISHING IN BRITAIN AND IRELAND

Several species can be taken from the surf at British and Irish locations. Most notable is the European bass, which is very highly prized as a sporting and table fish. It can be taken at many places along the south and south-west coasts of Britain and is even more widespread in Ireland – though the south-west is especially favoured. The bass is, however, a slow-growing fish and strict conservation measures have been introduced to preserve it.

U.S.–CANADIAN WEST COAST

1 Pacific Northwest
Chinook salmon
Silver salmon
Steelhead trout
2 Washington
Salmon
Rockfish
Lingcod
3 Oregon
Striped bass
Salmon
Rockfish
Lingcod
4 Northern California
Striped bass
Rockfish
Salmon
Lingcod
Surf perch
5 Central California
Striped bass
Rockfish
Surf perch
Flatfish
6 Southern California
Rockfish
Kelp bass
Flatfish
Cabezone
7 Western Mexico
Rockfish
Cabezone
8 Sea of Cortez
Totuava
Roosterfish

9 Cabo San Lucas
Roosterfish
Yellowtail

GULF OF MEXICO REGION

10 Northern Mexico
Sea trout (weakfish)
Flatfish
Tarpon
Snook
11 Southeast Texas
Sea trout
Flatfish
Tarpon
Snook
Redfish
12 Central Texas
Same as 11
13 Mississippi delta
Same as 11–12
14 Northwest Florida
Same as 11–13 plus,
Cobia
Barracuda
15 Southwest Florida
Same as 11–14 plus,
Pompano
Ladyfish

ATLANTIC COAST, FLORIDA KEYS TO CANADA

16 Florida Keys
Sea trout (weakfish)
Redfish

Tarpon
Snook
Cobia
Pompano
Flatfish
17 Central Florida
Sea trout
Redfish
Snook
Bluefish
Pompano
18 Georgia–South Carolina
Sea trout
Redfish
Bluefish
Black drum
Flatfish
19 Cape Hatteras area
Same as 18 plus
Striped bass
20 Chesapeake Bay area
Same as 18–19 plus
Croaker
Spot
Sea bass
21 Delmarva Peninsula
Same as 18–20
22 New York Bight
Striped bass
Bluefish
Weakfish
Flatfish
23 Southern New England
Striped bass
Bluefish
Tautog (blackfish)
Weakfish
24 Gulf of Maine
Striped bass
Pollock
Cod
25 Eastern Canada
Striped bass
Pollock
Cod

GREAT LAKES REGION (ALL SPECIES IN ALL AREAS.)

26 Lake Superior
27 Georgian Bay and Lake Huron
28 Lake Michigan
29 Lake Ontario
30 Lake Erie
Smallmouth bass
Coho salmon
Chinook salmon
Yellow perch
Sunfish (bream)
Walleye pike
Northern pike
Muskellunge
Lake trout
Brown trout
Brook trout
Rainbow trout

TABULATED OCEAN GAME FISHING DATA

Special legend
Under "Tackle," the tackle ratings are given in standard
"O" ratings and equal line-test values as follows:
 2/0 = 6–12 lb test line
 3/0 = 20 lb test line
 4/0 = 30 lb test line
 6/0 = 50 lb test line
 9/0 = 80 lb test line
12/0 = 130 lb test line

Name	Range	Best fishing method	Tackle	Bait
Albacore *Thunnus alalunga*	Worldwide in tropical, warm-temperate seas: best water temperature 56°–61° F (13°–16°C).	Trolling 4–7 mph (6,5–11 km/h): or live bait fishing with anchovies	Light – 3/0 Medium – 4/0 Heavy – 6/0	Trolling lures, strip baits, anchovies
Amberjack *Seriola dumerili*	Worldwide in tropical, warm-temperate seas: tolerates temperatures of 65°–80° F (18°–29°C).	Trolling 3–5 mph (4,8–8 km/h): or live bait fishing with any small live bait	Light – 3/0 Medium – 4/0 Heavy – 6/0	Trolling lures, strip baits, live baits
Barracuda *Sphyraena barracuda*	Worldwide in tropical seas, usually near land masses: prefers water of 68°–82° F (20°–28°C).	Trolling, kite fishing 2–4 mph (3,2–6,4 km/h): drift fishing with live bait	Light – 2/0 Medium – 3/0 Heavy – 4/0	Trolling lures, plugs, spoons, small live bait
Sea Bass *Centropristis striatus* (USA)	Temperate waters, Atlantic coast of USA: tolerates temperatures 42°–70° F (6°–21°C).	Anchored or drifting, bait fishing or jigging with small metal jigs	2/0 or 3/0 reel, 20 lb test line	Squid, clams, crabs, worms, mackerel jigs
California Black Sea Bass *Stereolepis gigas*	Tropical, subtropical areas near land masses, Pacific and Indian oceans 65°–78° F (18°–26°C).	Bait fishing with large live or dead natural baits from anchored or drifting boat	Light – 4/0 Medium – 6/0 Heavy – 9/0	Whole fish, fish slabs, live baits
Striped Bass *Morone saxatilis* (USA)	Temperate waters of east and west coasts of USA, inland lakes: prefers 56°–72° F (13°–23° C).	Surface or deep trolling, 2–5 mph (3,2–8 km/h): live bait fishing, casting	Light – 2/0 Medium – 3/0 Heavy – 4/0	Trolling lures, casting lures, live baits
White Sea Bass *Cynoscion nobilis*	Warm-temperate and tropical waters of eastern Pacific in coastal areas	Surface or deep trolling, casting, live bait fishing, jigging with metal jigs	Light – 2/0 Medium – 3/0 Heavy – 4/0	Trolling lures, casting lures, live baits
Blackfish (Tautog) *Tautoga onitis* (USA)	Temperate waters, western Atlantic, preferring waters of 42°–70° F (6°–21°C).	Bait fishing or jigging from anchored boat close to shore over rocky bottom	2/0 reel, 20 lb test line	Green crabs, fiddler crabs, worms, clams
Bluefish *Pomatomus saltatrix*	Sporadically worldwide in temperate to subtropical waters of 56°–75° F (13°–24°C).	Trolling, casting, jigging, chumming, bait fishing, from moving or anchored boats	Light – 2/0 Medium – 3/0 Heavy – 4/0	Trolling lures, casting lures, natural baits
Bonefish *Albula vulpes*	Tropical and subtropical coastal shallow flats: best temperatures 72°–84° F (22°–29° C).	Casting with shrimp or light lures, from boat or while wading on tidal flats	Spinning, fly, or bait casting, 6–15 lb line	Shrimp, special jigs, streamer flies
Cobia *Rachycentron canadum*	Worldwide in tropical and warm-temperate waters in temperatures of 68°–86° F (20°–30°C).	Trolling 3–5 mph (4,8–8 km/h) or live or dead bait fishing while anchored or drifting	Light – 2/0 Medium – 3/0 Heavy – 4/0	Trolling lures and baits, live pinfish

Cod *Gadus morhua*	Subarctic to cool temperate Atlantic waters: prefers temperatures 36°–58° F (2°–15° C)	Bait fishing or jigging from anchored or drifting boats, sometimes taken deep trolling	Light – 2/0 Medium – 3/0 Heavy – 4/0	Clam, squid, herring, metal jigs
Dolphin *Coryphaena hippurus*	Worldwide in tropical and warm-temperate seas, deep water: prefers 72°–88° F (22°–31°C).	Trolling 4–8 mph (6,4–12,8 km/h): bait fishing or casting to fish at surface	Light – 2/0 Medium – 3/0 Heavy – 6/0	Strip bait, balao, squid, yellow lures
Black Drum *Pogonias cromus* (USA)	North American Atlantic coast from northern Florida to New Jersey: 56°–75° F (13°–24°C).	Surface or deep trolling 3–4 mph (4,8–6,4 km/h): casting, bait fishing, boat or shore	Light – 2/0 Medium – 3/0 Heavy – 4/0	Trolling lures, metal jigs, cut fish bait
Red Drum *Sciaenops ocellatus* (USA)	Gulf of Mexico, Atlantic coast of USA from Mexico to New Jersey: 56°–84° F (13°–29°C).	Trolling 2–5 mph (3,2–8 km/h) and casting or bait fishing from boats or shore	Light – 2/0 Medium – 3/0 Heavy – 4/0	Trolling lures, shrimp, squid, casting lures
Flounder *Paralichthys sp.*	Worldwide in temperate and warmer waters, preferring temperatures of 65°–80° F (18°–27°C).	Bait fishing with strip bait or small live baits from drifting or anchored boats	Light – 2/0 Medium – 3/0 Heavy – 4/0	Squid, killie, worms, clam, metal spoons
Jewfish *Epinephelus itajara*	Tropical and subtropical waters near land masses: temperatures of 72°–88° F (22°–31°C).	Bait fishing with live or dead baits on bottom from an anchored boat, or from shore	Light – 4/0 Medium – 6/0 Heavy – 9/0	Conch, meat, mackerel, cut fish bait
Kingfish *Scomberomorus cavalla*	Tropical and subtropical western north Atlantic: temperatures of 70°–88° F (21°–31°C).	Trolling 3–6 mph (4,8–9,6 km/h), surface or deep, or bait fishing while drifting	Light – 3/0 Medium – 4/0 Heavy – 6/0	Strip baits, trolling lures, small live bait
Black Marlin *Makaira indica*	Indo-Pacific tropical waters adjacent to large land masses prefers water 75°–85° F (24°–30°C).	Trolling with large whole fish baits from outriggers, 4–6 mph (6,4–9,6 km/h)	Light – 6/0 Medium – 9/0 Heavy – 12/0	Mackerel, bonito, flying fish
Atl. Blue Marlin *Makaira nigricans*	Tropical and warm-temperate Atlantic waters: preferred temperatures, 68°–88° F (20°–31°C).	Trolling with large whole fish baits from outriggers, 4–6 mph (6,4–9,6 km/h)	Light – 4/0 Medium – 9/0 Heavy – 12/0	Mullet, balao, mackerel, squid
Pac. Blue Marlin *Makaira nigricans*	Tropical and warm-temperate Pacific waters: preferred temperatures 70°–85° F (21°–29°C)	Trolling with whole fish bait or Konahead lures at speeds of 5–8 mph (8–12,8 km/h)	Light – 4/0 Medium – 9/0 Heavy – 12/0	Mackerel, mullet, konahead
Striped Marlin *Tetrapturus audax*	Tropical and warm-temperate Indo-Pacific waters: temperatures of 60°–85° F (16°–30°C).	Trolling 3–6 mph (4,8–9,6 km/h) with small to medium fish baits, trolling lures	Light – 2/0 Medium – 4/0 Heavy – 6/0	Balao, flying fish, squid, plastic lures
White Marlin *Tetrapturus albidus*	Western Atlantic tropical and warm-temperate waters: temperatures of 70°–85° F (21°–30°C).	Trolling 4–7 mph (6,4–11,2 km/h) with small fish baits, tuna-type trolling lures	Light – 2/0 Medium – 4/0 Heavy – 6/0	Balao, squid, mullet, eel, trolling lures
Permit *Trachinotus falcatus*	Tropical and subtropical coastal shallow flats: best temperatures 74°–84° F (23°–29°C).	Casting to fish sighted in shallow water: bait fishing over inshore wrecks	Light – 2/0 Medium – 3/0 (casting gear)	Crabs, shrimp, streamer flies, bonefish jigs

Pollock (Coalfish) *Pollachius virens*	Temperate to cold-temperate North Atlantic waters: best in temperatures 45°–65° F (7°–18°C).	Bait fishing or jigging from anchored boats, trolling at inshore reefs and rips	Light – 2/0 Medium – 3/0 Heavy – 4/0	Squid, herring, clams, metal or plastic lures
Rainbow Runner *Elagatis bipinnulatus*	Worldwide in tropical and warm-temperate waters: best in temperatures of 70°–85° F (21°–30°C).	Trolling 3–6 mph (4,8–9,6 km/h) with small baits, lures, or live bait fishing	Light – 2/0 Medium – 3/0 Heavy – 4/0	Strip baits, balao, squid, trolling lures
Roosterfish *Nematistius pectoralis*	Eastern Pacific coastal areas Mexico to Peru; prefers water of 68°–85° F (20°–30°C).	Trolling small lures, casting with lures, live bait fishing from boats or shore	Light – 2/0 Medium – 3/0 Heavy – 4/0	Small live baits, casting trolling lures
Atlantic Sailfish *Istiophorus platypterus*	Tropical and subtropical Atlantic waters near land masses: 72°–85° F (22°–30°C).	Trolling 3–5 mph (4,8–8 km/h), kite fishing with live bait, trolling with plastic lures	Light – 2/0 Medium – 3/0 Heavy – 4/0	Balao, mullet, live pinfish, trolling lures
Pacific Sailfish *Istiophorus platypterus*	Tropical and subtropical Pacific waters, Indian Ocean: prefers water of 72°–85° F (22°–30° C).	Trolling 3–5 mph (4,8–8 km/h), kite fishing with live bait, trolling with plastic lures	Light – 2/0 Medium – 3/0 Heavy – 4/0	Flying fish, mullet, small live baits
Spotted Weakfish *Cynoscion nebulosus*	Warm-temperate and tropical waters of North and Central America: best in 68°–85° F (20°–30° C).	Bait fishing with shrimp, casting or trolling with small artificial lures	Any light gear in 10 to 20 lb line test range	Shrimp, crabs, worms, small artificials
Blue Shark *Prionace glauca*	Worldwide in tropical and warm-temperate seas: prefers waters of 68°–85° F (20°–30°C).	Trolling 3–5 mph (4,8–8 km/h) or chumming with live or dead fish baits from drifting boat	Light – 4/0 Medium – 6/0 Heavy – 9/0	Herring, squid, mackerel, any cut fish
Mako Shark *Isurus oxyrynchus*	Worldwide in tropical and warm-temperate seas: prefers waters of 64°–80° F (18°–27° C)	Trolling 3–6 mph (4,0–9,6 km/h) or chumming live or dead bait from drifting boat	Light – 4/0 Medium – 6/0 Heavy – 9/0	Mackerel, squid, herring, tuna strip, mullet
White Shark *Carcharodon carcharias*	Worldwide in tropical and warm-temperate seas: prefers waters of 64°–84° F (18° – 29° C)	Trolling 2–4 mph (3,2–6,4 km/h) or bait fishing with large meat or fish chunks	Light – 6/0 Medium – 9/0 Heavy – 12/0	Dead fish or animal meat, trolling baits
Porbeagle Shark *Lamna nasus*	Cold waters of North Atlantic in temperate to arctic zones, temperatures of 40°–68° F (4°–20°C).	Bait fishing while chumming, or trolling 3–6 mph (4,8–9,6 km/h) with rigged fish baits	Light – 4/0 Medium – 6/0 Heavy – 9/0	Mackerel, squid, herring, cut fish bait
Thresher Shark *Alopias vulpinus*	Worldwide in warm to cool temperate waters: range of temperatures 60°–75° F (16°–24° C).	Trolling 3–5 mph (4,8–8 km/h) with small fish baits, or chumming with live baits	Light – 4/0 Medium – 6/0 Heavy – 9/0	Mackerel, herring, squid, cut fish bait
Tiger Shark *Galeocerdo cuvieri*	Worldwide in tropical and warm-temperate seas: prefers temperatures of 70°–85° F (21°–30°C).	Chumming or bait fishing with fish or animal flesh, occasionally taken trolling	Light – 6/0 Medium – 9/0 Heavy – 12/0	Any fish or animal flesh, rigged baits
Snook (Robalo) *Centropomus undecimalis*	Tropical and warm-temperate waters of Atlantic, Pacific, coastal: 72°–86° F (22°–30° C).	Trolling with artificial lures, bait fishing with shrimp, small live fish	Light – 2/0 Medium – 3/0 Heavy – 4/0	Shrimp, small bait fish, artificials

Swordfish *Xiphias gladius*	Worldwide in temperate seas, including Mediterranean: best temperatures, 54°–70° F (12°–21° C).	Trolling 3–5 mph (4,8–8 km/h) or bait fishing in deep water at edge of continental shelf	Light – 6/0 Medium – 9/0 Heavy – 12/0	Squid, mullet, herring, eel, live whiting
Tanguigue *Scomberomorus commersoni*	Tropical and warm-temperate waters of western Pacific: temperatures of 68°–84° F (20°–29° C).	Trolling 4–7 mph (6,4–11,2 km/h) or live bait fishing from drifting boat	Light – 3/0 Medium – 4/0 Heavy – 6/0	Mullet, balao, strip bait, artificials
Tarpon *Megalops atlanticus*	Tropical and subtropical western Atlantic coastal area: temperature, 70°–88° F (21°–31° C).	Casting, trolling, or live bait fishing from boats or shore; depending on area	Light – 2/0 Medium – 3/0 Heavy – 4/0	Shrimp, live small fish, artificials
Tuna, Yellowfin *Thunnus albacares*	Worldwide warm-temperate seas in deep water, preferring temperatures of 60°–80° F (16°–27° C).	Trolling 4–8 mph (6,4–12,8 km/h), or bait fishing with chum while drifting	Light – 4/0 Medium – 6/0 Heavy – 9/0	Balao, small strip baits, artificials
Tuna, Bigeye *Thunnus obesus*	Worldwide in warm-temperate waters, usually quite deep. temperatures of 60°–80° (16°–27°C).	Trolling 4–6 mph (6,4–9,6 km/h), or bait fishing deep from drifting boat	Light – 4/0 Medium – 6/0 Heavy – 9/0	Squid, mullet, small baits, artificials
Tuna, Blackfin *Thunnus atlanticus*	Tropical and warm-temperate western Atlantic: favors temperatures of 65°–82° F (18°–28°C).	Trolling 3–7 mph (4,8–11,2 km/h) with small artificial trolling lures and baits	Light – 2/0 Medium – 3/0 Heavy – 4/0	Trolling lures, feathers, jigs, shrimp lures
Tuna, Bluefin *Thunnus thynnus*	Tropical to cool-temperate seas, worldwide: favors temperatures of 56°–84° F (13°–29° C).	Trolling 3–7 mph (4,8–11,2 km/h), or chumming with live baits, sometimes kite fishing	Light – 4/0 Medium – 9/0 Heavy – 12/0	Herring, squid, mackerel, eel, whiting, mullet
Tuna, Skipjack *Euthynnus pelamis*	Tropical, warm-temperate seas, worldwide: prefers temperatures of 64°–82° F (18°–28°C).	Trolling 3–4 mph (4,8–11,2 km/h), occasionally taken by fishing with small live bait	Light – 2/0 Medium – 3/0 Heavy – 4/0	Feather lures, casting jigs, etc.
Wahoo *Acanthocybium solanderi*	Tropical to warm-temperate seas, worldwide; prefers temperatures of 70°–86° F (21°–30°C).	Trolling 7–8 mph (11,2–12,8 km/h), or surface or deep fishing with live bait	Light – 3/0 Medium – 4/0 Heavy – 6/0	Spoons, lures, mullet, balao, live pinfish
Yellowtail *Seriola lalandi*	Tropical and warm-temperate Pacific waters near land: temperatures of 70°–84° F (21°–29°C).	Live bait fishing, casting, trolling 3–5 mph (4,8–8 km/h) sometimes deep jigging	Light – 2/0 Medium – 3/0 Heavy – 4/0	Casting and trolling lures, anchovies
*Hammerhead Shark *Sphyrna zygaena*	Tropical and warm-temperate waters of Atlantic, Pacific, offshore: 72°–86° F (22°–30° C).	Trolling 3–5 mph (4,8–8 km/h) with whole or cut fish baits, chumming while drifting.	Light – 4/0 Medium – 6/0 Heavy – 9/0	Mackerel, herring, squid, cut fish bait

*Recently added to IGFA game fish list.

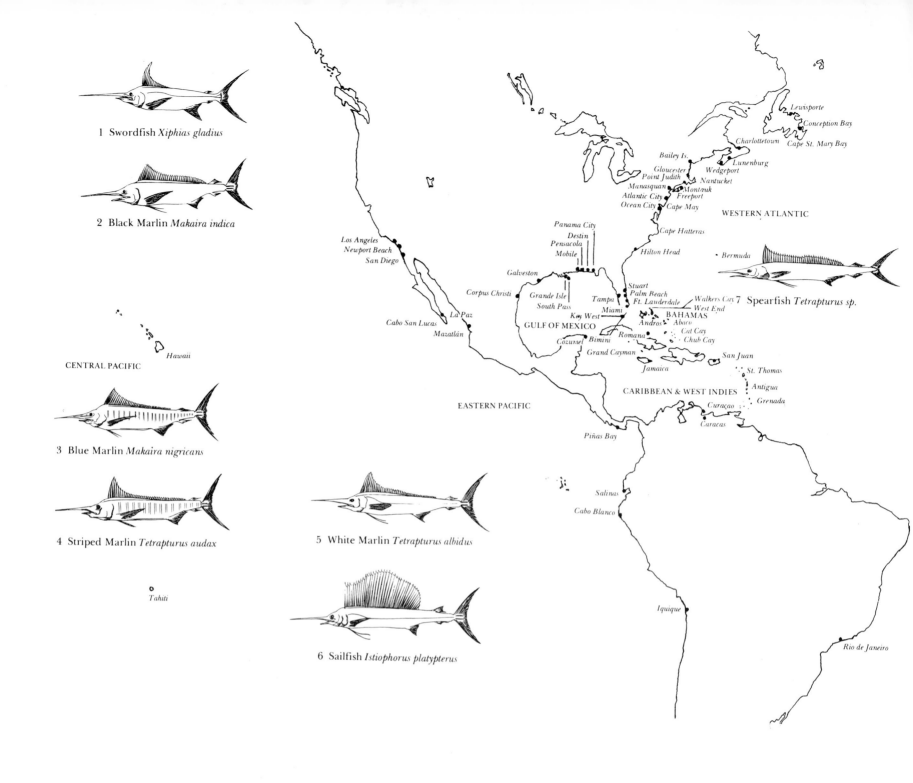

1 Swordfish *Xiphias gladius*

2 Black Marlin *Makaira indica*

CENTRAL PACIFIC

3 Blue Marlin *Makaira nigricans*

4 Striped Marlin *Tetrapturus audax*

5 White Marlin *Tetrapturus albidus*

6 Sailfish *Istiophorus platypterus*

7 Spearfish *Tetrapturus sp.*

WESTERN ATLANTIC

EASTERN PACIFIC

GULF OF MEXICO

CARIBBEAN & WEST INDIES

BAHAMAS

TEN WORLD-WIDE BIG GAME SPECIES

Big game at sea may be found at many places other than those shown here. But the ports and areas named are known to have fish in season and boats to pursue them. The wise angler seeks expert local knowledge on seasons, weather, boats, crews, costs, tackle, and transportation before starting out on a big game fishing venture.

CENTRAL PACIFIC
Hawaii 2, 3, 4, 7, 9, 10
Guam 2, 3, 4, 6, 9
Fiji 2, 3, 4, 9, 10
Tahiti 2, 3, 4, 9, 10
Samoa 2, 3, 4, 9, 10

EASTERN PACIFIC
Los Angeles, Cal. 1, 4, 9
Newport Beach, Cal. 1, 4, 9
San Diego, Cal. 1, 4, 9
Cabo San Lucas, Mex. 1, 2, 3, 4, 6, 9
Mazatlán, Mex. 2, 4, 6, 9
La Paz, Mex. 2, 4, 6, 9
Piñas Bay, Panama 2, 3, 4, 6

Salinas, Ecuador 2, 4, 6
Cabo Blanco, Peru 1, 2, 3, 4, 9, 10
Iquique, Peru 1, 2, 3, 4, 9, 10

GULF OF MEXICO
Corpus Christi, Tex. 3, 5, 6, 9
Galveston, Tex. 3, 5, 6, 9
South Pass, La. 3, 5, 6, 7, 8, 9, 10
Grande Isle, La. 3, 5, 6, 9
Mobile, Ala. 3, 5, 6, 9
Pensacola, Fla. 3, 5, 6, 9
Destin, Fla. 3, 5, 6, 9
Panama City, Fla. 3, 5, 6, 9
Tampa, Fla. 3, 5, 6, 9
Key West, Fla. 3, 5, 6, 9

CARIBBEAN & WEST INDIES
Cozumel, Mex. 3, 5, 6, 8, 9
Jamaica, W.I. 3, 5, 6, 7, 9
Caracas, Venezuela 3, 5, 6, 9
San Juan, P.R. 3, 5, 6, 9
Romana, D.R. 3, 5, 6, 9
St. Thomas, V.I. 3, 5, 6, 9, 10
Grand Cayman, W.I. 3, 5, 6, 9
Antigua, W.I. 3, 5, 6, 9
Grenada, W.I. 3, 5, 6, 9
Curaçao, N.A. 3, 5, 6, 9

BAHAMAS
Bimini 3, 5, 6, 8, 9, 10
Cat Cay 3, 5, 6, 8, 9, 10
West End 3, 5, 6, 8, 9, 10

Chub Cay 3, 5, 6, 8, 9, 10
Walkers Cay 3, 5, 6, 8, 9, 10
Abaco 3, 5, 6, 9, 10
Andros 3, 5, 6, 10

WESTERN ATLANTIC
Lewisporte, Newf. 8
Conception Bay, Newf. 8
Charlottetown, P.E.I. 8
Lunenburg, N.S. 1
Wedgeport, N.S. 8
Cape St. Mary Bay, N.S. 8
Bailey Is., Me. 8
Gloucester, Mass. 8, 10
Nantucket, Mass. 1, 5, 8, 10
Point Judith, R.I. 1, 5, 8, 10

9 Yellowfin Tuna *Thunnus albacares*

10 Mako Shark *Isurus oxyrhynchus*

in Tuna *Thunnus thynnus*

Montauk, N.Y. 1, 5, 8, 10
Freeport, N.Y. 1, 5, 8, 10
Manasquan, N.J. 1, 3, 5, 8, 10
Atlantic City, N.J. 3, 5, 8, 10
Cape May, N.J. 3, 5, 8, 10
Ocean City, Md. 3, 5, 8, 10
Cape Hatteras, N.C. 3, 5, 6, 9, 10
Hilton Head, N.C. 3, 5, 6, 9, 10
Stuart, Fla. 3, 5, 6, 7
Palm Beach, Fla. 3, 5, 6, 7, 9, 10
Ft. Lauderdale, Fla. 3, 5, 6, 7, 9, 10
Miami, Fla. 3, 5, 6, 7, 9, 10
Bermuda 3, 7, 9, 10
Rio de Janeiro, Brazil 3, 5, 9

EASTERN ATLANTIC
Azores 3, 5, 7, 9
Madeira 3, 5, 7, 9
Bergen, Norway 8
Isle of Wight, G.B. 10
Looe, Cornwall, G.B. 10
Kinsale, Ireland 8, 10
Lorient, Fr. 8, 10
Santander, Sp. 8, 10
Nazare, Port. 8, 10
Lisbon, Port. 8, 10

MEDITERRANEAN
Monte Carlo, Monaco 8, 9
Cannes, Fr. 8, 9
Messina, Sicily 1, 7, 9

Naples, Italy 1, 7, 9
Liguria, Italy 8, 9
Lipari, Is. 1, 5, 7, 9
Malta 1, 5, 7, 8, 9
Mallorca 1, 5, 7, 8, 9
Malaga, Sp. 7, 8, 9
Gibraltar 1, 5, 7, 8, 9

AFRICA
Cape Town, S.A. 1, 2, 3, 8, 9
Hermanus, S.A. 2, 3, 8, 9
Mossel Bay. S.A. 2, 3, 8, 9
Durban, S.A. 2, 3, 9, 10
Port Elizabeth, S.A. 2, 3, 8, 9
Mozambique 2, 3, 4, 6, 9
Shimoni, Kenya 2, 3, 4, 6, 9

Monrovia, Liberia 3, 5, 6, 8, 9

INDIAN OCEAN
Mauritius 2, 3, 6, 9
Seychelles, Is. 2, 3, 6, 9
Madagascar 2, 3, 6, 9

AUSTRALIA
Cairns 1, 2, 6, 9
Brisbane 1, 2, 3, 4, 6, 9, 10
Melbourne 8
Sydney 1, 2, 3, 4, 8, 9, 10
Perth 2, 3, 4, 8, 9, 10
Hobart 1, 4, 8, 10

NEW ZEALAND
Bay of Islands and other bases
North Island 1, 2, 3, 4, 8, 9, 10
South Island 1, 3, 8, 9, 10

WESTERN PACIFIC
Philippine Is. 2, 3, 4, 6, 7, 9
Indonesia 2, 3, 4, 6, 7, 9
Taiwan 2, 3, 4, 8, 9
Japan 3, 8, 9, 10

BIBLIOGRAPHY

Andersson, K.A.
Fiskar och Fiske i Norden. Bokförlaget Natur och Kultur, Stockholm, Sweden (1942).

Arber, A.
Water Plants. Cambridge University Press (1920).

Arnow, B.
Fishing for Everyone. Hawthorn Books, New York (1970).

Bagenal, T.B.
The Observer's Book of Freshwater Fishes. Frederick Warne & Co. Ltd., London (1941).

Barder, R.C.R.
Spinning for Pike. Arco (1970).

Barnhart, Percy S.
Marine Fishes of Southern California. University of California Press, Berkeley, California (1936).

Bates, Joseph D. Jr.
Streamer Fly Tying and Fishing. The Stackpole Company, Harrisburg, Pennsylvania (1950).

Bay, Kenneth E. and Kessler, Hermann
Salt Water Flies. J.B. Lippincott Company, New York (1972).

Berg, Lev S.
Classification of Fishes, Both Recent and Fossil. J.W. Edwards, Ann Arbor, Michigan (1947).

Bertin, Léon
Eels, a Biological Study. Philosophical Library, New York (1957).

Bigelow, Henry B. and Schroeder, W.C.
Fishes of the Western North Atlantic. Sears Foundation for Marine Research, Yale University, New Haven, Connecticut (1958–1953).

Boyer, Paul
La Pêche Sportive en Eau Douce. Editions Denoël, Paris (1973).

Brooks, Joe
Complete Guide to Fishing Across North America. Outdoor Life Harper & Row, New York (1966).

Brown, Margaret E.
The Physiology of Fishes. Academic Press, Inc., New York (1957).

Caine, Lou S.
North American Fresh Water Sport Fish, Description and Habits, Fishing Tackle and Methods. A.S. Barnes & Co., New York (1949).

Calman, W.T.
Life of Crustacea. Methuen (1911).

Carr, Donald E.
Death of the Sweet Waters. Berkley Publishing Corporation, New York (1971).

Clegg, John
Freshwater Life. Frederick Warne & Co. Ltd., London (1974).

Clemens, W.A., and Wiley, G.V.
Fishes of the Pacific Coast of Canada. Bulletin of the Fisheries Research Board of Canada (1961).

Cook, Fannye A.
Freshwater Fishes in Mississippi. Mississippi Game and Fish Commission, Jackson, Mississippi (1959).

Curry-Lindahl, K.
Fiskarna i färg. Almqvist och Wiksell, Stockholm, Sweden (1957).

Cust, George, and Cox, Graham
Tropical Aquarium Fishes Freshwater and Marine. The Hamlyn Publishing Group Limited, London (1972).

Dalrymple, Byron
Sportsman's Guide to Game Fish. Popular Science Publishing Company, Inc., New York (1968).

Dymond, John R.
The Game Fishes of Canada. Canadian Pacific Railway Co., Montreal, Canada (1928).

Falkus, Hugh
Sea-Trout Fishing a Guide to Success. H.F. & G. Witherby Ltd., London (1962).

Fichter, George S. and Francis, Phil
A Guide to Fresh and Salt-Water Fishing. Golden Press, Inc., New York.

Flick, Art
Master Fly-Tying Guide. Crown Publishers, Inc., New York (1972).

Frank, S.
The Pictoral Encyclopedia of Fishes. The Hamlyn Publishing Group Limited, London (1971).

Gammon, Clive
Sea Fishing. The Hamlyn Publishing Group Limited, London (1969).

Garnett, W.J.
Freshwater Microscopy. Constable & Co. Ltd. (1953).

Gilbert, Perry W.
Sharks and Survival. D.C. Heath Co., Boston, Massachusetts (1963).

Goode, George B., and Bean, T.H.
Oceanic Ichtyology. Washington, D.C. (1895).

Gordon, Sid
How to Fish from Top to Bottom. Telegraph Press, Harrisburg, Pennsylvania (1957).

Green, J.
A Biology of Crustacea. Witherby, London (1961).

Greenwood, P.H., and Norman, J.R.
A History of Fishes. Ernest Benn (1963).

Grote, W., Vogt, C., and Hofer, B.
Die Süsswasserfische von Mittel-Europa. Werner & Winter, Frankfurt, Germany (1909).

Guttfield, Frank
In Search of Big Fish. E.M. Art and Publishing (1964).

Günther, Albert C.L.G.
An Introduction to the Study of Fishes. Adam & Charles Black, London (1880).

Hall, C.B.
The Culture of Fish in Ponds. H.M. Stationery Office. (Ministry of Agriculture and Fisheries Bulletin No. 12.) (1936).

Harbour, D.
Super Freshwater Fishing Systems. Stackpole Books, Harrisburg, Pennsylvania (1971).

Herald, Earl S.
Living Fishes of the World. Doubleday and Co., Inc., Garden City, New York (1961).

Hiyama, Yoshio
Marine Fishes of the Pacific Coast of Mexico. Nissan Fisheries Institute and Co., Ltd., Tokyo (1937).
Gyotaku Fish Print. University of Tokyo Press (1964).
Gyotaku an Art of Fish Print. Kodandha (1972).

Housby, Trevor
Shore Fishing. Pan Books Ltd., London (1974).
Boat Fishing. Pan Books Ltd., London (1973).
Art of Sea Angling. Evans (1966).

Hvass, Hans
Fishes of the World. Methuen & Co. Ltd., London (1965).

Hynes, H.B.N.
The Biology of Polluted Waters. Liverpool University Press (1960).
The Ecology of Running Water. The University of Toronto Press, Toronto (1972).

Jensen, Albert C.
The Cod. Thomas Y. Crowell Company, New York (1972).

Jordan, David S.
A Guide to the Study of Fishes. Holt, Rinehart and Winston, Inc., New York (1905).

Jordan, David S., and Evermann, Barton W.
The Fishes of North and Middle America. Bulletin United States National Museum, Washington D.C. (1896–1900).

Judd, S.
Inshore Fishing. Fishing News (1971).

Kaplan, Moise N.
Big Game Angler's Paradise,

Department of Agriculture, State of Florida (1937).

Koller, Larry
The Treasury of Angling. Golden Press, Inc., New York (1963).

Kyle, Harry M.
The Biology of Fishes. The Macmillan Co., New York (1926).

Lagler, Karl F., Bardach, John E., and Miller, Robert R.
Ichtyology. John Wiley & Sons, Inc., New York (1962).

La Monte, Francesca
North American Game Fishes. Doubleday & Company, Inc., Garden City, New York (1945).
Marine Game Fishes of the World. Doubleday & Co., Inc., Garden City, New York (1952).

Lanham, Url
The Fishes. Colombia University Press, New York (1962).

Le Danois, Edouard
Fishes of the World. George G. Harrap & Co., London (1957).

Leiser, Eric
Fly-Tying Materials. Crown Publishers Inc., New York (1973).

Macan, T.T.
Freshwater Ecology. John Wiley & Sons, Inc., New York (1963).
A Key to the Nymphs of British Ephemeroptera. Freshwater Biological Association. Scientific Publication No. 20. (1970).

Mansfield, Kenneth
Coarse Fishing. Pan Books Ltd., London (1973).

Marshall, N.B.
The Life of Fishes. Weidenfeld & Nicolson (1965).

Marston, Norman A.
Encyclopedia of Angling. The Hamlyn Publishing Group Limited, London (1963).

McClane, A.J.
McClane's Standard Fishing Encyclopedia and International Angling Guide. Holt, Rinehart and Winston, New York (1965).

Meek, Alexander
The Migrations of Fish. Edward Arnold, London (1916). (1916).

Miall, L.C.
The Natural History of Aquatic Insects. Macmillan (1902).

Migdalski, Edward
Angler's Guide to the Salt Water Game

Fishes. The Ronald Press Company, New York (1958).

Migel, Michael J.
The Stream Conservation Handbook. Crown Publishers, Inc., New York (1974).

Mosley, M.E.
Insect Life and the Management of a Trout Fishery. Routledge (1936).

Moss, Frank T.
Successful Ocean Game Fishing. International Marine Publishing Company, Camden, Maine (1971).
Successful Striped Bass Fishing. International Marine Publishing Company, Camden, Maine (1974).

Muus, B.J. and Dahlstrøm, P.
Europas Ferskvandsfisk. Copenhagen (1967).

Needham, Paul R.
Trout Streams. Winchester Press, New York (1971).

Norman, J.R., and Fraser, F.C.
Giant Fishes, Whales and Dolphins. W.W. Norton & Company, Inc. Publishers, New York (1938).

Organisation for Economic Co-operation and Development
Multilingual Dictionary of Fish and Fish Products. Fishing News (Books) Ltd., London (1968).

Orton, D.A.
Where to Fish. Harmsworth Press Ltd., London (1975–76).

Otis, Maurice
Guide to Stream Improvement. New York State Conservation Department, Division of Conservation Education.

Ovington, R.
Introduction to Bait Fishing. Stackpole Books, Harrisburg, Pennsylvania (1971).

Parsons, P. Allen
Complete Book of Fresh Water Fishing. Outdoor Life, New York (1963).

Perlmutter, Alfred
Guide to Marine Fishes. New York University Press, New York (1961).

Pincher, Chapman
A Study of Fish. Duell, Sloan & Pearce, Inc., New York (1948).

Plaskett, F.J.W.
Microscopic Fresh Water Life. Chapman & Hall. (1926).

Randall, John E.
Caribbean Reef Fishes. T.F.H. Publications, Inc. Ltd., The British Crown Colony of Hong Kong (1968).

Schindler, O.
Guide to Freshwater Fishes. Thames & Hudson, (1957).

Seely, H.G.
The Fresh-Water Fishes of Europe. Cassell & Co., Ltd., London (1886).

Sosin, Mark, and Dance, Bill
Practical Black Bass Fishing. Crown Publishers, Inc., New York (1974).

Stokes, A.C.
Aquatic Microscopy. John Wiley & Sons (1918).

Sturgis, William Bayard
Fly-Tying. Charles Scribner's Sons, New York (1940).

Swisher, Doug, and Richards, Carl
Selective Trout. Crown Publishers Inc., New York (1971).

Veniard, John
Reservoir and Lake Flies, Fly Dressings and Fishing Techniques. A. & C. Black Limited, London (1970).

Veniard, John, and Downs, Donald
Fly-Tying Problems and Their Answers. A. & C. Black Limited, London (1970).

Vevers, Gwynne
Fishes in Colour, Marine and Freshwater. H.F. & G. Witherby Ltd., London (1963).

Walford, Lionel A.
Marine Game Fishes of the Pacific Coast from Alaska to the Equator. University of California Press, Berkeley, California (1937).

Walker, Richard
Still-Water Angling. MacGibbon and Kee (1960).

Wallis, H.F.
Stillwater Trout Fisheries. Ernest Benn Ltd., London (1976).

Waterman, C.F.
Modern Fresh and Saltwater Flyfishing. Winchester Press, New York (1972).

Wells, Laurence.
The Observer's Book of Sea Fishes. Frederick Warne & Co. Ltd. London.

Wheeler, Alwyne
The Fishes of the British Isles and North-West Europe. Macmillan and Co. Ltd. London (1969).

Willock, Colin
A.B.C. of Fishing, a Complete Guide to Angling for Coarse, Sea and Game Fish. Deutsch (1969).

Unsinger, Robert L.
The Life of Rivers and Streams. McGraw-Hill Book Company, New York (1967).